GROLIER
ENCYCLOPEDIA
OF KNOWLEDGE

Grolier Incorporated
Danbury, Connecticut

ISBN 0-7172-5300-7 (complete set)
ISBN 0-7172-5301-5 (volume 1)

Printed and manufactured in the United States of America.

This publication is an abridged version of the *Academic American Encyclopedia.*

1 0 9 8 7 6 5 4 3

Preface

The *Grolier Encyclopedia of Knowledge* is a 20-volume, alphabetically arranged, general encyclopedia specially created for use at home. Clearly written and richly illustrated, the encyclopedia provides a comprehensive, up-to-date, easy-to-use reference resource for every member of the family—students from the elementary level through college, and inquisitive adults. More than 50 staff employees, 2,000 subject authorities, and hundreds of other advisors, editors, designers, illustrators, photographers, and cartographers have created the 6.5 million words, 22,000 articles, and 13,000 illustrations that make up the *Grolier Encyclopedia of Knowledge*. They have organized, described, and interpreted the world's knowledge in a manner that is useful, accessible, and exciting to the at-home reader.

A good modern reference work should be broad in scope, accurate in detail, current, objective, easy to use, and pictorially illuminating. These goals have guided the preparation of this encyclopedia. The *Grolier Encyclopedia of Knowledge* will provide quick access to definitive factual information, whether for researching a school paper, understanding current events, or answering that dinner-table trivia question. Even without a specific subject in mind, exploring its pages is sure to enlighten, to entertain, and to inspire the imagination.

Comprehensiveness

The *Grolier Encyclopedia of Knowledge* provides basic information for the nonspecialist reader, coverage of all significant aspects of a subject, and presentation of important events and ideas in a historical or cultural context.

The encyclopedia contains broad coverage of contemporary events, popular culture, international affairs, and current technology. There is enough information to take the reader beyond what he or she already knows; dictionary-type entries are avoided. Articles include not only the most interesting or controversial, but all relevant aspects of a topic. Thus the article SLAVERY does not confine itself to that variety practiced in the United States during the 18th and 19th centuries. No subject is excluded on grounds of political or religious belief, social or legal disapproval, or moral prejudice. Unpopular—even notorious—figures and ideas are impartially and systematically discussed. While recognizing a need to be topical, our editors are aware that much contemporary interest is transient, and they have tried to achieve a balance between the timely and the timeless.

The content of the *Grolier Encyclopedia of Knowledge* is global in scope, providing wide-ranging coverage of countries, peoples, cultures, history, physical geography, and wildlife. General survey articles are written and illustrated from a cross-cultural perspective; the entries DANCE, EDUCATION, and RELIGION, for example, grant appropriate recognition to the diversity of practice and experience throughout the world. At the same time, a sympathetic awareness of non-Western cultures and alternate life-styles need not interfere with a fuller explanation of the traditions and perspectives of the audience's dominant culture. Thus the history, geography, and cultural traditions of the United States find a prominent place in the encyclopedia.

The list of entries in the *Grolier Encyclopedia of Knowledge* has been designed to reflect the curriculum of American schools and colleges; virtually any subject covered in school and college textbooks can be found in this work as either a main subject entry or an index entry. Thus SCIENCE FICTION and AFRICAN-AMERICAN LITERATURE are included not simply because they are artifacts of the times, but because they are currently studied in secondary-school and university programs. Beyond such curriculum-oriented material, the encyclopedia devotes ample space to a myriad of topics of contemporary, nonacademic interest—AUTOMOBILE, ROCK MUSIC, and VIDEO, to name a few.

Currency

A current encyclopedia must have more than up-to-date information on populations, planetary probes, Nobel laureates, and the latest speculations about the origins of the universe. It should also include biographies in the performing arts and popular culture, as well as in the more academic fields. Thus the *Grolier Encyclopedia of Knowledge* includes articles on Woody ALLEN, Luciano PAVAROTTI, and Wayne GRETZKY. Scientific theory and social phenomena are introduced in biographical entries on, for example, the theoretical physicist Stephen HAWKING and the anthropologist Claude LÉVI-STRAUSS.

All population statistics in these volumes represent recent census figures or official estimates. The maps and city plans are accurate and up-to-date, reflecting current urbanization, new highways and airports, and so on. Articles, tables, and charts were updated at the last possible moment in the editorial process to reflect the most recent prize winners, sports champions, book and movie titles, and death dates.

Authority

The authority of a reference work is evident in the credentials of the people responsible for creating it and, within the articles themselves, in an explanatory style that both retains the subtlety and explains the essence of a given subject. More than 90 percent of the entries in the *Grolier Encyclopedia of Knowledge* have been written by outside scholars and authorities from all over the world. These 2,000 authorities, listed in the Contributors section beginning on page 8 of this volume, were selected to write for this encyclopedia on the basis of their knowledge and expertise in a particular subject area.

Most of our editors have advanced degrees, and some are published scholars in their own right. Most also have experience on one or more of the major general or specialized encyclopedias published in North America or Europe. A large team of research editors—all specialists in their field—verified every fact, inference, and conclusion against primary and other authoritative sources. After this quality-control effort, edited copy had to clear several layers of senior editorial review before it was prepared for publication. Every article in the *Grolier Encyclopedia of Knowledge* has been subjected to multiple review to assure objectivity and accuracy.

Objectivity

If an encyclopedia is to be reliable, the facts and inferences must be accurate and reflect current scholarship. Scholars may differ among themselves, however, even on questions that do not involve social policy. The aim of the *Grolier Encyclopedia of Knowledge* is to reflect such differences and to consider alternate theories or opposing points of view—on, for example, such subjects as ABORTION, CAPITAL PUNISHMENT, and CENSORSHIP. Because balanced, objective treatment of such topics should neither reflect the opinion of the author nor ignore the fact of controversy, the article must seek to incorporate multiple perspectives and to tell who supports what position and why.

A concerted effort has been made to produce an encyclopedia free of sexist language and attitudes, although that task is especially difficult in certain articles in philosophy and religion, where writers before the 20th century commonly used "man" in both a generic and a literal sense.

Ease of Use

The *Grolier Encyclopedia of Knowledge* has been designed, written, and illustrated for easy use. It is organized in a way that allows the reader to find what he or she is looking for quickly and simply, with the material presented in clear, easy-to-understand words and pictures.

Entries are arranged alphabetically rather than topically, and cross-references abound; that is, if the entry is not where the reader looks first, there is generally a "see" reference that indicates where the subject is covered. The *Grolier Encyclopedia of Knowledge* is a short-entry reference work—more than half the articles are less than 500 words long. Many of the longer articles are subdivided by smaller bold-face topic headings, such as "Land and Resources," "People," and "Economic Activity" in country articles.

The text of the articles has been carefully edited to be readable; foreign words, abbreviations, and specialized jargon have been avoided. Technical terms generally are defined in the sentence in which they are used, and readers are referred to other entries for additional information. Even in the most technical articles, no special preparation in higher mathematics is necessary; where the use of some algebra or geometry is of interest to advanced readers, the concepts contained in the article are explained in plain English as well.

Both metric and standard measurement systems are used, with meters and kilograms preceding feet and pounds; where appropriate, Celsius and Fahrenheit temperatures, as well as Kelvin, are used. Nomenclature in the life sciences includes both the Latin and common names, although most subjects are alphabetized by their common name.

Design
Article headings are set in bold type, with a solid black bar above for ease in picking out a particular article on the page. A contemporary, sans-serif typeface (Trade Gothic) was selected for the main text because of its legibility and clean, open appearance. Captions are set in the italic form to achieve a clear distinction from the main article text.

Guide words at the top of each page enable users to turn quickly to the desired page and entry. Page numbers are also prominently displayed in the upper left and right corners of each page-spread for rapid access.

Alphabetical Arrangement
The encyclopedia is arranged alphabetically throughout. A "word-by-word" system, the same one used in the telephone book or library card catalog, is followed. Entries beginning with a short word appear before entries with the same short word forming the first letters of a longer word. Thus, NEW YORK is placed before NEWFOUNDLAND, and RADIO FREE EUROPE precedes RADIOACTIVITY.

Pronunciation and Alternate Names
Article headings that contain foreign or other unfamiliar words or names include pronunciation guides much like the ones used by *Time* Magazine—thus, the heading Mikhail GORBACHEV carries the following pronunciation guide: [gahr-bah-chawf'].

For Chinese names and terms, the new Chinese transliteration system, Pinyin, is employed; the traditional Wade-Giles spelling is provided in parentheses in the heading—for example, BEIJING (Peking) or MAO ZEDONG (Mao Tse-tung).

Cross-References
There are three kinds of cross-references in the *Grolier Encyclopedia of Knowledge*. A reader who looks first for CIRCADIAN RHYTHM is told to "see BIOLOGICAL CLOCK." Thus, even if one does not know for certain where the information is to be found, the encyclopedia will guide the reader to the proper place with a minimum of hunting and guessing.

The second type of cross-reference is internal within the text of an article, and appears in small capital letters. In the article GENESIS, BOOK OF, such names and phrases as CREATION ACCOUNTS, ABRAHAM, ISAAC, JACOB, and NOAH appear in small capitals, indicating that there are separate articles by those titles in which additional information about the Book of Genesis can be found.

The third type of cross-reference appears at the end of many articles. The article ALLOSAURUS concludes with the note "See also: FOSSIL RECORD; GEOLOGIC TIME." This tells the reader that relevant background information can be found under those headings.

Fact Boxes, Tables, and Charts

For readers seeking quick answers to common questions about countries, states, continents, Canadian provinces, and U.S. presidents, the *Grolier Encyclopedia of Knowledge* provides hundreds of illustrated fact boxes titled "At a Glance." Other detailed data—from sports records to chemical elements to computer technology—are presented in hundreds of tables, charts, graphs, and glossaries.

Illustrations and Maps

Approximately 13,000 photographs, maps, and other illustrations, occupying about one-third of the available space, appear in the *Grolier Encyclopedia of Knowledge*. A substantial amount of the information contained in this encyclopedia is found in these illustrations and their captions—information that supports, explains, and expands facts and concepts discussed in the text. For example, more than 50 illustrations accompany the BIRD article, detailing anatomy, physiology, the dynamics of wing action in flight, the structure of different types of feathers, and nest construction. In addition, nearly 200 separate species are illustrated elsewhere in the encyclopedia.

In many cases, artwork rather than photographs is used because of the greater detail and clarity possible in a drawing. Exploded views, cutaway drawings, and other sophisticated renderings provide a new look and help explain processes in time and space.

The 1,000 maps contained in this encyclopedia, created by the cartographic experts of Rand McNally, Donnelley Cartographic, and Lothar Roth Associates, are based on the latest research and cover all continents and countries of the world; all U.S. states and Canadian provinces; major world cities, mountain ranges, and rivers; and important historic regions and military battles. In addition, specially created locator maps help place countries and states in a global or regional context.

Index

A 90,000-entry index, in volume 20, provides quick, helpful, practical, unambiguous guidance to the information contained in the encyclopedia. The index entries distinguish among identical headings by providing additional information—for example, BACON, FRANCIS (painter) and BACON, FRANCIS (philosopher). Each entry includes the volume number and page number of the corresponding article, as well as textual references elsewhere in the encyclopedia and the location of illustrations and maps. Complete information on how to use the index is found on pages 130–132 of volume 20.

Staff

Contributors

TOIVE AARTOLAHTI
Professor of Geography, University of Helsinki, Helsinki, Finland.

HOWARD ABADINSKY
Associate Director and Associate Professor, Program in Criminal Justice, Saint Xavier College, Chicago.

R.L. ABRAHAMSON
Instructor, Rutgers Preparatory School, Somerset, N.J.

PETER ABRAMOFF
Chairman and Wehr Distinguished Professor of Biology, Marquette University, Milwaukee, Wis.

MARIA ISABEL ABREU
Chairman of Department and Professor of Portuguese, Georgetown University, Washington, D.C.

HAZARD ADAMS
Professor of English, University of Washington, Seattle, Wash.

NICHOLAS ADAMS
Chairman, Department of Fine Arts, Lehigh University, Bethlehem, Pa.

WILLIAM W. ADAMS
Professor of Mathematics, University of Maryland, College Park.

PHILIP J. ADLER
Professor of History, East Carolina University, Greenville, N.C.

ALAN R. ADOLPH, M.D.
Head, Neurosciences Laboratory, Eye Research Institute, Retina Foundation, Boston.

JAMES ADSHEAD
Public Affairs Department Manager, DuPont Company, Wilmington, Del.

CHARLES AFFRON
Professor of French, New York University, New York City.

JAAKKO A. AHOKAS
Professor (Acting), Department of Romance Languages, University of Jyvaskyla, Jyvaskyla, Finland.

E. JOHN AINSWORTH
Manager, Bevalac Radiobiology-Radiotherapy Program, Division of Biological and Medical Research, Lawrence-Berkeley Laboratory, Berkeley, Calif.

ERNEST T. AJAX, M.D.
Chief of Neurology Service, Salt Lake City Veterans Administration Hospital, and Professor of Neurology, University of Utah College of Medicine, Salt Lake City.

S.-I. AKASOFU
Professor of Geophysics, Geophysical Institute, University of Alaska, Fairbanks.

JAIME ALAZRAKI
Professor of Romance Languages, Harvard University, Cambridge, Mass.

JOHN ALCOCK
Professor of Zoology, Arizona State University, Tempe.

MADELEINE ALCOVER
Associate Professor of French, Rice University, Houston, Tex.

JAMES W. ALEXANDER
Chairman, Department of Medieval Studies, University of Georgia, Athens.

ROBERT J. ALEXANDER
Professor of Economics, Rutgers University, New Brunswick, N.J.

THERON ALEXANDER
Professor of Human Development, Temple University, Philadelphia.

MARGARET ALEXIOU
Senior Lecturer in Byzantine and Modern Greek, University of Birmingham, Birmingham, England.

MAJOR JOHN I. ALGER
Assistant Professor of History, United States Military Academy, West Point, N.Y.

THEODORE H. ALLEGRI, SR.
Professional Engineer and Consultant, McLean, Va.

JOHN L. ALLEN
Chairman, Department of Geography, University of Connecticut, Storrs.

P. W. ALLEN
Malaysian Rubber Producers' Research Association, Hertford, England.

LAWRENCE H. ALLER
Professor of Astronomy, University of California, Los Angeles.

EILEEN JORGE ALLMAN
Assistant Professor of English, Herbert H. Lehman College, Bronx, N.Y.

DAVID N. ALLOWAY
Professor of Sociology, Montclair State College, Upper Montclair, N.J.

WILLARD ALLPHIN, P.E., F.I.E.S.
Former Sales Engineer, GTE Sylvania.

ARTHUR B. ALPHIN
Assistant Professor, Department of History, United States Military Academy, West Point, N.Y.

PHILIP G. ALTBACH
Professor of Higher Education, State University of New York, Buffalo.

CRAIG AMERIGIAN
Geologist, Amoco Minerals Co., Chicago.

HARRY AMMON
Chairman, Department of History, Southern Illinois University, Carbondale.

EDWARD F. ANDERSON
Professor of Biology, Whitman College, Walla Walla, Wash.

JAMES M. ANDERSON
Professor of Linguistics, University of Calgary, Calgary, Alberta.

LAWRENCE C. ANDERSON
Professor of Geography, Mankato State University, Mankato, Minn.

MILTON W. ANDERSON, M.D.
Emeritus Professor of Medicine, Mayo Medical School, Rochester, Minn.

ROBERT T. ANDERSON
Professor of Anthropology, Mills College, Oakland, Calif.

STEVEN C. ANDERSON
Associate Professor of Biology and Environmental Sciences, University of the Pacific, Stockton, Calif.

WILLIAM S. ANDERSON
Professor of Classics, University of California, Berkeley.

JOHANA GAST ANDERTON
Managing Editor, Athena Publishing Co., North Kansas City, Mo.

CHARLES F. ANDRAIN
Professor of Political Science, California State University, San Diego.

KLAUS ANDRES
Research Physicist, Bell Telephone Laboratories, Murray Hill, N.J.

WARREN ANDREW, M.D.
Professor of Anatomy, Indiana University, School of Medicine, Indianapolis.

F. T. ANDREWS
Professional Engineer, F. T. Andrews, Inc., Fullerton, Calif.

DONALD L. ANGLIN
Automotive and Technical Writer.

HEINZ L. ANSBACHER
Professor Emeritus of Psychology, University of Vermont, Burlington.

MARY C. ANSBRO
Assistant Public Affairs Director, The Soap and Detergent Association, New York City.

RICHARD A. ANTHES
Professor of Meteorology, Pennsylvania State University, University Park.

JAMES ANTHONY
Professor of Musicology, University of Arizona, Tucson.

JUDITH APPLEGATE
Assistant Curator, Museum of Fine Arts, Boston.

MILO DON APPLEMAN, F.R.S.M., F.R.S.A.
Professor of Bacteriology, Emeritus, University of Southern California, Los Angeles.

GARY ARLEN
Editor/Publisher, Arlen Communications, Inc., Bethesda, Md.

ROY ARMES
Senior Lecturer in Film, Television Studies, Middlesex Polytechnic, London.

JOHN B. ARMSTRONG, M.D.
Neurologist, Montreal Children's Hospital, Montreal.

DALE H. ARNER
Head of the Department of Wildlife and Fisheries, Mississippi State University, Mississippi State.

ROBERT D. ARNER
Professor of English, University of Cincinnati, Cincinnati, Ohio.

ROBERT F. ARNOVE
Associate Professor, School of Education, Indiana University, Bloomington.

ARNOLD ARONSON
Assistant Professor, University of Virginia, Charlottesville.

AVNER ASH
Ritt Assistant Professor of Mathematics, Columbia University, New York City.

NEIL ASHBY
Professor of Physics and Astrophysics, University of Colorado, Boulder.

HARRY ASHER
Former Lecturer, Birmingham University, Birmingham, England

MAURICE ASHLEY
Former Editor of *The Listener.*

FRANK ASKIN
Professor of Law, Rutgers Law School, Newark, N.J.

BRIAN ASTLE
Fellow, Digital Systems Research, RCA Laboratories/David Sarnoff Research Center, Princeton, N.J.

R. J. C. ATKINSON
Professor of Archaeology, University College, Cardiff, Wales.

GEORGE E. ATWOOD
Associate Professor of Psychology, Rutgers University, New Brunswick, N.J.

STAN AUGARTEN
Author of *Bit by Bit: An Illustrated History of Computers.*

JOHN HENRY AURAN
Senior Editor, *Skiing* Magazine, New York City.

ROBERT AUSTERLITZ
Professor of Linguistics and Uralic Studies, Columbia University, New York City.

WILLIAM S. BABCOCK
Associate Professor of Church History, Perkins School of Theology, Southern Methodist University, Dallas, Tex.

BERNARD S. BACHRACH
Professor of History, University of Minnesota, Minneapolis.

WALTER M. BACON, JR.
Associate Professor of Political Science, University of Nebraska, Omaha.

LAWRENCE BADASH
Associate Professor of History of Science, University of California, Santa Barbara.

ALAN BADDELEY
MRC Applied Psychology Unit, Cambridge, England.

E. BADIAN
Professor of History, Harvard University, Cambridge, Mass.

GALAL A. BADR
Associate Professorial Lecturer of Sociology, George Washington University, Washington, D.C.

CHARLES F. BAES, JR.
Senior Research Scientist, Oak Ridge National Laboratory, Oak Ridge, Tenn.

HOWARD G. BAETZHOLD
Professor of English, Butler University, Indianapolis, Ind.

CAROLYNN BAILEY
Director of Music, Trinity Episcopal Church, Fredericksburg, Va.

ROGER BAILEY
Director of Choral Music, Mary Washington College, Fredericksburg, Va.

JAY W. BAIRD
Professor of History, Miami University, Oxford, Ohio.

ROBERT M. BAIRD
Professor of Philosophy, Baylor University, Waco, Tex.

CARL JAY BAJEMA
Professor of Biology, College of Arts and Sciences, Grand Valley State Colleges, Allendale, Mich.

CARLOS BAKER
Woodrow Wilson Professor of Literature, Emeritus, Princeton University, Princeton, N.J.

HENRY BAKER
Senior Paintbox Artist/Digital Editor, Charlex, Inc., New York City.

JAMES R. BAKER
Associate Professor of Entomology, North Carolina State University, Raleigh.

JOHN F. BAKER
Editor in Chief, *Publishers Weekly,* New York City.

STUART E. BAKER
Assistant Professor, School of Theater, Florida State University, Tallahassee.

V. K. BALAKRISHNAN
Associate Professor of Mathematics, University of Maine, Orono.

DAVID A. BALDWIN
John Sloan Dickey Third Century Professor, Department of Government, Dartmouth College, Hanover, N.H.

MICHAEL J. BALICK
Director and Philecology Curator of Economic Botany, The Institute of Economic Botany, New York Botanical Garden, New York City.

TERENCE BALL
Professor of Political Science, University of Minnesota, Minneapolis.

KENNETH J. BALLARD, PHARM. D.
Assistant Clinical Professor of Pharmacy, University of Southern California School of Pharmacy, Los Angeles.

LOUIS WAYNE BALLARD
Composer and Former Program Director, Music, Central Office of Education BIA, Department of Interior.

AURORA GARCIA BALLESTEROS
Profesora Adjunta Geografia, Universidad Complutense, Madrid.

DONALD E. BALLOU
President, Spaulding and Slye Construction Co. Inc., Burlington, Mass.

BERNARD J. BAMBERGER, D.D.
Rabbi Emeritus, Temple Shaaray Tefila, New York City.

H.-G. BANDI
Professor of Prehistory and Paleontology, University of Berne, Berne, Switzerland.

AARON BAR-ADON
Professor of Linguistics, University of Texas, Austin.

DAVID P. BARASH
Professor of Psychology, University of Washington, Seattle.

JACK BARBASH
Professor, Economics and Industrial Relations, University of Wisconsin, Madison.

THOMAS K. BARBER, D.D.S., M.S.
Chairman, Division of Preventive Dental Sciences and Section on Pediatric Dentistry, School of Dentistry, University of California, Los Angeles.

KARL K. BARBIR
Associate Professor of History, Siena College, Loudonville, N.Y.

EUNICE B. BARDELL
Professor Emeritus, Health Science, University of Wisconsin, Milwaukee.

JONAS A. BARISH
Professor of English, University of California, Berkeley.

COL. ARTHUR JAMES BARKER, RETIRED
Military Historian and Former Infantry Weapons Instructor, Royal Military College of Science, Swindon, England.

BARBARA MACKIN BARKER
Instructor of Dance, University of Texas, Austin.

JOHN W. BARKER
Professor of History, University of Wisconsin, Madison.

LT. COL. WAYNE G. BARKER, RETIRED
U.S. Army Signal Corps, Author and Editor.

HAROLD M. BARROW
Professor of Physical Education, Wake Forest University, Winston-Salem, N.C.

GIULIA BARTRUM
Researcher for the Menil Foundation in the British Museum, London.

DAVID G. BASILE
Professor of Geography, University of North Carolina, Chapel Hill.

JOHN V. BASMAJIAN, M.D., F.A.C.A.,F.R.C.P. (C)
Director of Rehabilitation Programs, Chedoke Hospitals, and Professor of Medicine, McMaster University School of Medicine, Hamilton, Ontario,

GEORGE F. BASS
Distinguished Professor of Anthropology, Texas A&M University; Archaeological Director, Institute of Nautical Archaeology, Texas A&M University, College Station.

PAUL MERRITT BASSETT
Professor of History of Christianity, Nazarene Theological Seminary, Kansas City, Mo.

ALAN BATES
Editor, *ABC Travel Guides.*

W. SCOTT BAUMAN
Professor of Business Administration, The Colgate Darden Graduate School of Business Administration, University of Virginia, Charlottesville.

NANCY CURRY BAVOR
Curatorial Assistant, Edward Clark Streeter Collection of Weights and Measures, Yale Medical Library, New Haven, Conn.

CRAIG BAXTER
Professor of Politics and History, Juniata College, Huntingdon, Pa.

TANIA BAYARD
Art Historian.

STEPHEN BAYLEY
Lecturer in the History and Theory of Art, University of Kent, Kent, England.

FORREST E. BECK
Director of Technical Services, The Parker Pen Company, Janesville, Wis.

HENRY JAY BECKER
Principal Research Scientist, Center for Social Organization of Schools, Johns Hopkins University, Baltimore, Md.

JOSEPH F. BECKER
Professor of Biology, Montclair State College, Montclair, N.J.

ROBERT P. BECKINSALE
Fellow, University College, Oxford, England.

KARL BECKSON
Professor of English, Brooklyn College, City University of New York, Brooklyn, N.Y.

HUGO ADAM BEDAU
Austin B. Fletcher Professor of Philosophy, Tufts University, Medford, Mass.

RICHARD R. BEEMAN
Associate Professor of History, University of Pennsylvania, Philadelphia.

ALFRED F. L. BEESTON
Professor of Arabic, University of Oxford, Oxford, England.

THOMAS O. BEIDELMAN
Professor of Anthropology, New York University, New York City.

HUGO BEKKER
Professor of German, Ohio State University, Columbus.

JOHN D. BELL
Professor of History, University of Maryland, Baltimore.

THOMAS L. BELL
Associate Professor of Geography, University of Tennessee, Knoxville.

WAYNE H. BELL
Assistant Professor of Biology, Middlebury College, Middlebury, Vt.

KENNETH BENDINER
Assistant Professor of Art, Wellesley College, Wellesley, Mass.

MICHAEL LES BENEDICT
Associate Professor of History, Ohio State University, Columbus.

DWIGHT G. BENNETT, D.V.M.
Professor of Equine Medicine, College of Veterinary Medicine, Colorado State University, Ft. Collins.

GEOFFREY R. BENNETT
Captain, Royal Navy (ret.).

WM. R. BENNETT, JR., D.SC.
C. B. Sawyer Professor of Engineering and Applied Science and Professor of Physics, Yale University, New Haven, Conn.

HENRY A. BENT
Professor of Chemistry, North Carolina State University, Raleigh.

MARTIN J. BERAN
Member of the Firm of Blum, Kaplan, Friedman, Silberman and Beran, New York City.

W. A. BERESFORD
Professor of Anatomy, School of Medicine, West Virginia University, Morgantown.

DAVID M. BERGERON
Professor of English, University of Kansas, Lawrence.

J. L. BERGGREN
Professor of Mathematics, Simon Fraser University, Burnaby, British Columbia.

THOMAS G. BERGIN
Professor of Romance Languages, Yale University, New Haven, Conn.

BERNARD BERGONZI
Professor of English and Comparative Literature, University of Warwick, Coventry, England.

LAURENCE BERGREEN
Former Assistant to the President, The Museum of Broadcasting. Author of *Look Now, Pay Later: The Rise of Network Broadcasting.*

KARL ERIK BERGSTEN
Professor of Physical Geography, University of Lund, Lund, Sweden.

R. N. BERKI
Senior Lecturer of Politics, University of Hull, Hull, England.

BARBARA BERKMAN
Professor and Director, Social Work in Health Care Program, Massachusetts General Hospital Institute of Health Professions.

EDWARD A. BERLIN
Author of *Ragtime: A Musical and Cultural History.*

BRUCE BERMAN
Teaching Assistant in Films, Columbia University, New York City.

GRETA BERMAN
Assistant Professor of Art History, State University of New York, Stony Brook.

ALBERT BERMEL
Professor of Theatre, Herbert H. Lehman College, Graduate Center of the City University of New York, New York City.

RONALD M. BERNDT
Foundation Professor of Anthropology, University of Western Australia, Nedlands, Western Australia.

DAVID K. BERNINGHAUSEN
Professor, Library School, University of Minnesota, Minneapolis.

CHARLES A. BERRY, M.D.
President, National Foundation for Prevention of Disease, Houston, Tex.

WILLIAM B. N. BERRY
Professor of Paleontology and Director of Museum of Paleontology, University of California, Berkeley.

NIKO BESNIER
Department of Anthropology, Yale University, New Haven, Conn.

ALAN C. G. BEST
Associate Professor of Geography, Boston University, Boston.

JOEL BEST
Associate Professor of Sociology, California State University, Fresno.

JANE COLVILLE BETTS
Assistant Professor of English, University of Wisconsin, Eau Claire.

CHARLES ROWAN BEYE
Professor of Classics, Boston University, Boston.

JACQUELYN L. BEYER
Professor of Geography and Environmental Studies, University of Colorado, Colorado Springs.

ROBERT T. BEYER
Professor of Physics, Brown University, Providence, R.I.

SABYASACHI BHATTACHARYA
James Franck Fellow, James Franck Institute, University of Chicago, Chicago.

ROBERT STEVEN BIANCHI
Associate Curator, Department of Egyptian and Classical Art, The Brooklyn Museum, Brooklyn, N.Y.

MARTIN A. BIERBAUM
Assistant Professor of Urban Studies, Rutgers University, New Brunswick, N.J.

JULIAN BIGELOW
Institute for Advanced Study, Princeton, N.J.

WILLEM A. BIJLEFELD
Professor of Islamic Studies, The Hartford Seminary Foundation, Hartford, Conn.

GEORGE ATHAN BILLIAS
Professor of American History, Clark University, Worcester, Mass.

ROGER E. BILSTEIN
Professor of History, University of Houston at Clear Lake City, Houston, Tex.

THOMAS BIRACREE
Author of *The Complete Book of Thoroughbred Horse Racing.*

STEPHEN S. BIRDSALL
Professor of Geography, University of North Carolina, Chapel Hill.

DONALD BIRN
Assistant Professor of History, State University of New York, Albany.

ALAN C. BIRNHOLZ
Associate Professor of Art History, State University of New York, Buffalo.

ADRIANA SCALAMANDRÉ BITTER
Executive Vice-President, Scalamandré, Inc., Long Island City, N.Y.

RICHARD BJORNSON
Associate Professor of Comparative Studies, Ohio State University, Columbus.

ROBERT F. BLACK
Professor of Geology and Geophysics, University of Connecticut, Storrs.

COIT D. BLACKER
Associate Professor, School of International Relations, University of Southern California, Los Angeles.

R. JOHN BLACKLEY
Director, Schola Antiqua, New York City.

JOHN T. BLACKMORE
Visiting Scholar, History of Philosophy of Science Department, Cambridge University, Cambridge, England.

WILFORD A. BLADEN
Associate Professor of Geography, University of Kentucky, Lexington.

PETER BLAKE
Chairman, Boston Architectural Center, Boston.

J. W. BLAKER
Professor of Physics, Vassar College, Poughkeepsie, N.Y.

JOSEPH L. BLAU
Professor Emeritus in Religion, Columbia University, New York City.

JOHN P. BLEWETT
Senior Physicist, Brookhaven National Laboratory, Upton, N.Y.

CHARLES W. BODEMER
Professor and Chairman, Department of Biomedical History, School of Medicine, University of Washington, Seattle.

PAUL BOHANNAN
Professor of Anthropology, University of California, Santa Barbara.

ALBERT BOIME
Professor of Art History, University of California, Los Angeles.

DANIEL P. BOLGER
Captain, U.S. Army, United States Military Academy, West Point, N.Y.

LARISSA BONFANTE
Associate Professor of Classics, New York University, New York City.

JOHN LAWRENCE BOOJAMRA
St. Vladimir's Seminary, Tuckahoe, N.Y.

JEAN BOORSCH
Professor of French, Emeritus, Yale University, New Haven, Conn.

JAMES A. BOOTH
Senior Research Engineer, Monsanto Research Corp.

JOHN E. BOOTY
Professor of Church History, Episcopal Divinity School, Cambridge, Mass.

RICHARD J. BORD
Associate Professor of Sociology, Pennsylvania State University, University Park.

JACQUES BORDAZ
Associate Professor of Anthropology, University of Pennsylvania, Philadelphia.

LOUISE ALPERS BORDAZ
Assistant Professor of Art History and Archaeology, Columbia University, New York City.

MORTON BORDEN
Professor of History, University of California, Santa Barbara.

ROBERT F. BORKENSTEIN
Professor of Forensic Studies, Indiana University, Bloomington.

DONALD J. BORROR
Emeritus Professor of Entomology, Ohio State University, Columbus.

MERLE L. BORROWMAN
Professor of Education, University of California, Berkeley.

BURIS R. BOSHELL, M.D.
Ruth Lawson Hanson Professor of Medicine, University of Alabama, Birmingham.

THOMAS BOSWELL
Assistant Professor of Geography, University of Miami, Miami, Fla.

ISSA J. BOULLATA
Professor of Islamic Studies, McGill University, Montreal.

CEDRIC G. BOULTER
Professor of Classics, University of Cincinnati, Cincinnati, Ohio.

FRANK C. BOURNE
Kennedy Professor of Latin, Emeritus, Princeton University, Princeton, N.J.

HENRY WARNER BOWDEN
Associate Professor of Religion, Douglass College, Rutgers University, New Brunswick, N.J.

MARY ELLEN BOWDEN
Assistant Dean and Lecturer in History, Goucher College, Towson, Md.

BARBARA C. BOWEN
Professor of French, University of Illinois, Urbana.

CALVIN M. BOWER
Professor of Music, University of North Carolina, Chapel Hill.

FREDSON BOWERS
Emeritus Linden Kent Professor of English, University of Virginia, Charlottesville.

LARRY W. BOWMAN
Professor, Department of Political Science, University of Connecticut, Storrs.

THADIS W. BOX
Dean of College of Natural Resources and Professor of Range Management, Utah State University, Logan.

PAUL S. BOYER
Assistant Professor of Geology, Fairleigh Dickinson University, Madison, N.J.

PHILIP S. BRACHMAN
Director, Epidemiology Program Office, Center for Disease Control, Atlanta, Ga.

IAN BRADLEY
Superintendent, Research and Development, Vickers-Armstrong Ltd., Wiltshire, England.

ALAN E. BRANCH
Shipping Consultant to British Government, London.

CHARLES M. BRAND
Professor of History, Bryn Mawr College, Bryn Mawr, Pa.

HERBERT BRAND
Chairman, Transportation Institute, Washington, D.C.

JAMES R. BRANDON
Professor, Asian Theatre, University of Hawaii, Honolulu.

E. N. BRANDT
Director, Business Communications, Dow Chemical Company, Midland, Mich.

JAMES BRASHLER
Dean, Ecumenical Institute, St. Mary's Seminary and University, Baltimore, Md.

WARWICK BRAY
Professor of Archaeology, Institute of Archaeology, London University, London.

WALTRAUD A. R. BRINKMANN
Professor of Geography, University of Wisconsin, Madison.

WESLEY E. BRITTIN
Professor of Physics and Astrophysics, University of Colorado, Boulder.

MICHAEL BROADBENT
Wine Auctions Director, Christie's, London.

KING BROADRICK-ALLEN
Professor-Director of Honors, University of Illinois, Urbana.

J. J. BRODY
Professor of Art and Anthropology, University of New Mexico, and Director of Maxwell Museum of Anthropology, Albuquerque.

SELWYN A. BROITMAN
Professor of Microbiology and Nutritional Sciences, Boston University School of Medicine, Boston.

BETH ARCHER BROMBERT
Lecturer of Romance Languages, Princeton University, Princeton, N.J.

COLETTE R. BROOKS
Yale University School of Drama, New Haven, Conn.

DAVID S. BROSE
Curator of Archaeology and Professor of Anthropology, Cleveland Museum of Natural History, Case Western Reserve University, Cleveland, Ohio.

KENNETH N. BROSTROM
Assistant Professor of Russian, Wayne State University, Detroit.

C. J. BROWN
Professor of Animal Science, University of Arkansas, Fayetteville.

DAVID ALAN BROWN
Curator of Italian Paintings, National Gallery of Art, Washington, D.C.

JOSEPH E. BROWN
Professor, School of Printing Management and Sciences, Rochester Institute of Technology, Rochester, N.Y.

MALCOLM HAMRICK BROWN
Professor of Music, Indiana University, Bloomington.

RICHARD P. BROWN
Professor of Theater, University of California, Riverside.

ROBERT HAROLD BROWN
Professor of Geography, University of Wyoming, Laramie.

ROGER BROWN
John Lindsley Professor of Psychology, Harvard University, Cambridge, Mass.

RONALD F. BROWN
Professor Emeritus of Chemistry, University of Southern California, Laguna Hills.

CLYDE E. BROWNING
Professor of Geography, University of North Carolina, Chapel Hill.

STANLEY L. BRUE
Professor of Economics, Pacific Lutheran University, Tacoma, Wash.

ROBERT S. BRUMBAUGH
Professor of Philosophy, Yale University, New Haven, Conn.

DIETER BRUNNSCHWEILER
Professor of Geography, Michigan State University, East Lansing.

MICHAEL H. BRUNO
Consultant.

RUTH V. BUCKLEY
Principal Lecturer in Electrical Engineering, Leeds Polytechnic School of Electrical Engineering, Leeds, England.

THOMAS R. BUCKMAN
President, The Foundation Center, New York City.

DAVID N. BUCKNER
Major, U.S. Marine Corps.

OSCAR BÜDEL
Professor of Italian, University of Michigan, Ann Arbor.

ROBERT BUDNY
Professor of Physics, Plasma Physics Laboratory, Princeton, N.J.

HOWARD A. BUECHNER, M.D., F.A.C.P.
Professor of Medicine, Louisiana State University School of Medicine, New Orleans.

GEORGE BUELOW
Professor of Musicology, Indiana University, Bloomington.

GLENN S. BULMER
Associate Professor of Microbiology and Immunology, University of Oklahoma School of Medicine, Oklahoma City.

C. VICTOR BUNDERSON
President, Learning Design Laboratories, Wicat Inc., Orem, Utah.

JOHN G. BUNKER
Maritime writer; author of *Harbor Haven: An Illustrated History of the Port of New York.*

EDMUNDS V. BUNKSE
Assistant Professor of Geography, University of Delaware, Newark.

AMBY BURFOOT
East Coast Editor, *Runner's World* Magazine.

FREDRIC D. BURG, M.D.
Professor of Pediatrics, University of Pennsylvania, Philadelphia.

MARCUS B. BURKE
Lecturer, The New School, New York City.

MARIAN BURLEIGH-MOTLEY
Lecturer, Metropolitan Museum of Art, New York City.

THOMAS BUSER
Associate Professor, Allen R. Hite Art Institute, University of Louisville, Louisville.

JOHN H. BUSHNELL
Professor of Environmental, Population, and Organismic Biology, University of Colorado, Boulder.

EDOUARD BUSTIN
Professor of Political Science and Research Associate, African Studies Center, Boston University, Boston.

FRANCELIA BUTLER
Professor of English, University of Connecticut, Storrs.

PATRICK H. BUTLER III
Director, Institute of Museums, History and Secondary Education, North Texas State University, Denton.

RICHARD BUTWELL
Former President and Professor of Political Science, California State University, Dominguez Hills.

MARYLOU BUYSE, M.D.
Assistant Professor of Pediatrics, Tufts University School of Medicine, Boston.

ROBERT BYCK, M.D.
Professor of Psychiatry and Pharmacology, Yale University School of Medicine, New Haven, Conn.

RICHARD D. CADLE
Scientist, National Center for Atmospheric Research, Boulder, Colo.

JOHN CADY
Professor of History, Ohio University, Athens.

ARNO CAHN
Director of Development, Household Products, Lever Brothers Company, Edgewater, N.J.

RONALD CALINGER
Associate Professor of History, Rensselaer Polytechnic Institute, Troy, N.Y.

ROBERT G. CALKINS
Chairman and Associate Professor, Department of History of Art, Cornell University, Ithaca, N.Y.

JAMES T. CALLOW
Professor of English, University of Detroit, Detroit.

A. G. W. CAMERON
Professor of Astronomy, Harvard University, Cambridge, Mass.

ROBERT CAMMAROTA
Musicologist, New York City.

JONATHAN A. CAMPBELL
Curator of Amphibians and Reptiles, University of Texas, Arlington.

CHAS. CANTALUPO
Professor of English, Rutgers University, New Brunswick, N.J.

PHILIP V. CANNISTRARO
Professor of History, Florida State University, Tallahassee.

LOUIS J. CANTORI
Professor of Political Science, University of Maryland, Baltimore.

LEON CANTRELL
Chairman, School of Humanities, Griffith University, Queensland, Australia.

NICHOLAS CAPALDI
Professor of Philosophy, Queens College, Flushing, N.Y.

ROBERTA CAPLAN
Mental Health Section, University of Rochester, Rochester, N.Y.

ROBERT T. CARGO
Professor of Romance Languages, University of Alabama, University.

RICHARD L. CARLIN
Professor of Chemistry, University of Illinois, Chicago Circle.

ROBERT F. CARLINE
Fishery Biologist, U.S. Fish and Wildlife Service, Columbus, Ohio.

ERIC G. CARLSON
Associate Professor of Art History, State University of New York, Purchase.

F. PAUL CARLSON
Vice-President, Oregon Graduate Center, Beaverton.

FRANCIS J. CARMODY
Professor of French, Emeritus, University of California, Berkeley.

PETER CARSTENS
Professor of Anthropology, University of Toronto, Toronto.

DORWIN CARTWRIGHT
Professor of Psychology, University of Michigan, Ann Arbor.

ERIC J. CASSELL, M.D., F.A.C.P.
Clinical Professor, Department of Public Health, Cornell Medical Center, New York City.

DAVID CAST
Associate Professor of Art History, Yale University, New Haven, Conn.

BARBARA CAVALIERE
Art Critic, *Arts Magazine.*

ALFRED A. CAVE
Dean, College of Arts and Sciences, University of Toledo, Toledo, Ohio.

MARY ANN CAWS
Professor of Romance Languages and Comparative Literature, Graduate Center of the City University of New York, New York City.

FRED A. CAZEL, JR.
Professor of History, University of Connecticut, Storrs.

ALPHONSE CERZA
Lawyer, Formerly of John Marshall Law School, Chicago.

JOHN CHADWICK
Reader in Greek Language, Downing College, University of Cambridge, Cambridge, England.

ROBERT A. CHADWICK
Professor of Geology, Montana State University, Bozeman.

C. K. CHAI
Senior Staff Scientist, The Jackson Laboratory, Bar Harbor, Maine.

H. D. CHAMBLISS, JR.
Vice-President of Public Affairs, Aluminum Association, Inc., Washington, D.C.

T. C. CHAMPION
Lecturer in Archaeology, University of Southampton, Southampton, England.

JAMES CHAN
Visiting Professor of Geography, Boston University, Boston.

STANLEY A. CHANGNON, JR.
Chairman, Atmospheric Sciences Section, Illinois State Water Survey, and Professor of Atmospheric Sciences, University of Illinois, Urbana.

CORNELIA POST CHANNING, M.D.
Professor of Physiology, University of Maryland School of Medicine, Baltimore.

C. RICHARD CHAPMAN
Associate Professor of Anesthesiology, University of Washington School of Medicine, Seattle.

LOREN J. CHAPMAN
Professor of Psychology, University of Wisconsin, Madison.

MILES L. CHAPPELL
Chairman and Associate Professor of Fine Arts, College of William and Mary, Williamsburg, Va.

MAURICE CHARNEY
Distinguished Professor of English, Rutgers University, New Brunswick, N.J.

JOSEPH V. CHARYK
President, Communications Satellite Corp., Washington, D.C.

CLINTON I. CHASE
Department of Education, Indiana University, Bloomington.

GILBERT CHASE
Visiting Professor of American Studies, History, and Music, University of Texas, Austin.

HAROLD W. CHASE
Professor of History, University of Minnesota, Minneapolis.

WILLIAM A. CHECK
Medical and Scientific Communications, Incorporated, Atlanta, Ga.

DONALD CHENEY
Professor of English, University of Massachusetts, Amherst.

ERIC S. CHENEY
Associate Professor of Geology, University of Washington, Seattle.

DAVID A. CHIRIBOGA
Assistant Professor in Residence, University of California, San Francisco.

ROBERT F. CHIRICO
Art Historian, Institute of Fine Arts, New York City.

HONG-YEE CHIU
Goddard Space Flight Center, Greenbelt, Md.

CAROL T. CHRIST
Associate Professor of English, University of California, Berkeley.

J. R. CHRISTIANSON
Professor of History, Luther College, Decorah, Iowa.

CHU-YUAN CHENG
Department of Economics, Chairman, Asian Studies Committee, Ball State University, Muncie, Ind.

CHUEN-YAN DAVID LAI
Associate Professor of Geography, University of Victoria, Victoria, British Columbia.

ANNA M. CIENCIALA
Professor of History, University of Kansas, Lawrence.

CHARLES E. CLARK
Professor of History, University of New Hampshire, Durham.

E. L. CLARK
Consultant, Formerly the Acting Assistant Director for Gasification Development, U.S.Department of Energy.

GEORGE A. CLARK, JR.
Associate Professor of Biology, University of Connecticut, Storrs.

JOHN J. CLARK
Director of M.B.A. Program in Finance, Drexel University, Philadelphia.

N. BROOKS CLARK
Reporter, *Sports Illustrated.*

ROBERT JUDSON CLARK
Associate Professor, Department of Art and Archaeology, Princeton University, Princeton, N.J.

MARY H. CLENCH
Associate Curator of Birds, Carnegie Museum of Natural History, Pittsburgh, Pa.

CHRISTIAN CLERK
Researcher, Department of Anthropology, University College, London.

JAMES A. CLIFTON
Professor of Anthropology, University of Wisconsin, Green Bay.

ROBERT S. CLINE
Professor of Insurance, University of North Carolina, Greensboro.

JEROME W. CLINTON
Assistant Professor of Near Eastern Studies, Princeton University, Princeton, N.J.

LAWRENCE M. CLOPPER
Associate Professor of English, Indiana University, Bloomington.

STANLEY W. CLOUD
White House Correspondent, *Time* Magazine.

J. L. CLOUDSLEY-THOMPSON, D.SC.
Birkbeck College, University of London, London.

NICHOLAS H. CLULEE
Associate Professor of History, Frostburg State College, Frostburg, Md.

HAROLD CLURMAN
Former Adjunct Professor of Theatre, Hunter College, New York City, and Theatre Critic, *The Nation*

GEORGE W. COATS
Professor of Old Testament, Lexington Theological Seminary, Lexington, Ky.

ROBERT COCKBURN
Chairman, Department of English, University of New Brunswick, Fredericton, New Brunswick.

JONATHAN COHEN
Professor of Orthopedic Surgery, Tufts Medical School, Medford, Mass.

PHILIP K. COHEN
Author of *The Moral Vision of Oscar Wilde.*

JOHN COLARUSSO
Professor of Linguistics, McMaster University, Hamilton, Ontario.

RALPH M. COLEMAN
Professor of Engineering Design Graphics, University of Texas, El Paso.

MARJORIE COLLINS
Assistant Professor of English and Linguistics, Mary Washington College, Fredericksburg, Va.

ROBERT L. COLLISON
Professor Emeritus, Library and Information Science, University of California, Los Angeles.

JOEL COLTON
Director for Humanities, The Rockefeller Foundation, New York City.

STEELE COMMAGER
Professor of Greek and Latin, Columbia University, New York City.

THOMAS J. CONCANNON
Project Manager, Gilbert/Commonwealth Engineers & Consultants, Reading, Pa.

PHILIP CONDAX
Director, Technology Collections, International Museum of Photography at George Eastman House, Rochester, N.Y.

CARL W. CONDIT
Professor of History, Art History, and Urban Affairs, Northwestern University, Evanston, Ill.

SEYMOUR V. CONNOR
Professor of History, Texas Tech University, Lubbock.

DOUGLAS M. CONSIDINE
Engineer.

NICHOLAS D. CONSTAN, JR.
Lecturer, Department of Legal Studies, Wharton School, University of Pennsylvania, Philadelphia.

JAMES A. CONSTANTIN
David Ross Boyd Professor of Business Administration, University of Oklahoma, Norman.

JON R. CONTE
Assistant Professor, School of Social Service Administration, University of Chicago.

DONALD J. COOK
Chairman, Department of Chemistry, DePauw University, Greencastle, Ind.

J. PATRICK COONEY
Lecturer and Curatorial Assistant, The Frick Collection, New York City.

MARTIN COOPER
Former Music Editor, *London Daily Telegram.*

RITA V. COPELMAN
Publicity Director, Tanners' Council of America, New York City.

EDWARD P. J. CORBETT
Professor of English, Ohio State University, Columbus.

MARY B. CORCORAN
Professor of German, Vassar College, Poughkeepsie, N.Y.

DENNIS D. CORDELL
Assistant Professor of History, Southern Methodist University, Dallas, Tex.

LINDA CORDELL
Irvine Curator, California Academy of Sciences, San Francisco.

CARL F. CORI
Visiting Professor of Biochemistry, Harvard Medical School, Boston.

MALCOLM CORMACK
Curator of Paintings, Yale Center for British Art, New Haven, Conn.

JEAN DWYER CORMICK
Assistant Professor of English, Rutgers College, New Brunswick, N.J.

JEFFREY M. CORNELIUS
Associate Dean and Associate Professor of Music, Temple University College of Music, Philadelphia.

CHARLES H. COTTER
Department of Maritime Studies, University of Wales Institute of Science and Technology, Cardiff, Wales.

WILLIAM R. COTTON
Associate Professor of Atmospheric Science, Colorado State University, Fort Collins.

ARNOLD COURT
Professor of Climatology, California State University, Northridge.

GERALD COUZENS
Author of *A Baseball Album.*

ALEXANDER COWIE
Emeritus Professor of Mechanical Engineering, Illinois Institute of Technology, Chicago.

JOEL CRACRAFT
Associate Professor of Anatomy, University of Illinois, Chicago.

GEORGE B. CRAIG, JR.
Clark Professor of Biology, Vector Biology Laboratory, University of Notre Dame, Notre Dame, Ind.

ROBERT I. CRANE
Ford-Maxwell Professor of South Asian History, Syracuse University, Syracuse, N.Y.

SAM CRAVER
Professor of Education, Virginia Commonwealth University, Richmond.

JOHN STEPHENS CRAWFORD
Associate Professor of Art History, University of Delaware, Newark.

DON M. CREGIER
Professor of History, University of Prince Edward Island, Charlottetown.

FREDERICK CREWS
Professor of English, University of California, Berkeley.

HOWARD J. CRITCHFIELD
Professor of Geography, Western Washington University, Bellingham.

MELVIN CROAN
Professor of Political Science, University of Wisconsin, Madison.

LESTER G. CROCKER
Kenan Professor of French, University of Virginia, Charlottesville.

LAWRENCE J. CROCKETT
Professor, Department of Biology, City College, City University of New York, New York City.

RALPH D. CROSS
Associate Professor of Geography and Area Development, University of Southern Mississippi, Hattiesburg.

F. JOE CROSSWHITE
Professor of Mathematics Education, Ohio State University, Columbus.

WILLIAM H. CROUSE
Consulting Editor, Automotive Books, McGraw-Hill Book Company, Naples, Fla.

JOHN CRUICKSHANK
Professor of French, University of Sussex, Brighton, England.

PRESSLEY L. CRUMMY
Emeritus Professor of Anatomy, Kirksville College of Osteopathic Medicine, Kirksville, Mo.

J. A. CUDDON
Author of *A Dictionary of Literary Terms.*

JACK CUMBEE
Associate Professor of Philosophy, Tuskegee Institute, Tuskegee Institute, Ala.

W. WILSON CUMMER III
Associate Professor of Architecture, School of Architecture, Cornell University, Ithaca, N.Y.

WILLIAM K. CUMMINGS
Project Specialist, Ford Foundation, New York City.

AGNES CUNNINGHAM, S.S.C.M.
Associate Professor of Patristic Theology and Early Christianity, Saint Mary of the Lake Seminary, Mundelein, Ill.

RICK CUNNINGHAM
Administrative Assistant, Office of the Baseball Commissioner, New York City.

NANCY A. CURTIN
Professor of Physiology, University College, University of London, London.

MORTON CURTIS
W. L. Moody, Jr., Professor of Mathematics, Rice University, Houston, Tex.

WILLIAM W. CURTIS
Associate Professor of Marketing, University of Nebraska, Lincoln.

H. C. CURTISS, JR.
Professor of Aerospace and Mechanical Sciences, Princeton University, Princeton, N.J.

NICHOLAS CUSHNER
Adjunct Professor of History, State University of New York, Buffalo.

FRANK A. D'ACCONE
Professor of Music, University of California, Los Angeles.

MAGDALENA DABROWSKI
Curatorial Assistant, Museum of Modern Art, New York City.

MITCHELL DAHOOD
Professor of Ugaritic Language and Literature, Pontifical Biblical Institute, Rome.

D. MARTIN DAKIN
Honorary Member of the Sherlock Holmes Society, London.

ROBERT T. DALAND
Professor of Political Science, University of North Carolina, Chapel Hill.

LYA R. DAMS
Prehistoric Archaeologist.

J. M. ANTHONY DANBY
Professor of Mathematics and Physics, North Carolina State University, Raleigh.

GLYN DANIEL
Disney Professor of Archaeology, University of Cambridge, Cambridge, England.

LAWRENCE DANSON
Associate Professor of English, Princeton University, Princeton, N.J.

MICHAEL R. DARBY
Professor of Economics, University of California at Los Angeles.

ALAN P. DARR
Assistant Curator, European Art Department, Detroit Institute of Arts, Detroit.

GAUTAM DASGUPTA
Publisher and Editor, *Performing Arts Journal.*

JOSEPH WARREN DAUBEN
Associate Professor of History, Herbert H. Lehman College, City University of New York, New York City.

ABRAHAM A. DAVIDSON
Professor of Art History, Tyler School of Art, Temple University, Ambler, Pa.

JULIAN M. DAVIDSON
Associate Professor of Physiology, Stanford University, Stanford, Calif.

HYWEL DAVIES, M.D., F.R.C.P., F.A.C.P.
Abdulla Fouad Hospital, Dammam, Saudi Arabia.

REVEREND CYPRIAN DAVIS, O.S.B.
Associate Professor of Church History, Saint Meinrad School of Theology, Saint Meinrad, Ind.

DEWITT DAVIS, JR.
Assistant Professor of Geography, Ohio State University, Colombus.

EDWARD W. DAVIS, JR.
Associate Professor of Computer Science, North Carolina State University, Raleigh.

J. G. DAVIS, O.B.E.
Dr. J. G. Davis and Partners, Reading, Berkshire, England

KEITH F. DAVIS
International Museum of Photography at George Eastman House, Rochester, N.Y.

ROBERT MURRAY DAVIS
Professor of English, University of Oklahoma, Norman.

STANLEY N. DAVIS
Professor of Hydrology and Water Resources, University of Arizona, Tucson.

BENJAMIN M. DAWSON
Research Scientist, Massachusetts Institute of Technology, Cambridge.

BUCK DAWSON
Executive Director of the International Swimming Hall of Fame, Fort Lauderdale.

DOUGLAS DAY
Chairman, Department of Geography, Saint Mary's University, Halifax, Nova Scotia.

R. J. De CRISTOFORO
Author of *The Hand Tool Book* and *Carpentry Handbook.*

PETER DEHLINGER
Professor of Geophysics, University of Connecticut, Storrs.

JUAN M. del AGUILA
Associate Professor of Political Science, Emory University, Atlanta, Ga.

SCOTT DeLANCEY
Associate Professor of Linguistics, University of Oregon, Eugene.

ROBERT J. DELATOUR, JR.
Geologist, Environmental Assessment Council, Inc., New Brunswick, N.J.

CHARLES F. DELZELL
Professor of History, Vanderbilt University, Nashville, Tenn.

ROBERT DeMARIA, JR.
Assistant Professor of English, Vassar College, Poughkeepsie, N.Y.

JOHN G. DENNIS
Professor of Geology, California State University, Long Beach.

PAUL E. DESAUTELS
Curator, Division of Mineralogy, National Museum of Natural History, Smithsonian Institution, Washington, D.C.

C. D. DESHPANDE
National Fellow, Jawaharlal Nehru University, New Delhi, India.

ANDRÉE DÉSILETS
Professor of History, University of Sherbrooke, Sherbrooke, Quebec.

ROBERT W. DESMOND
Professor Emeritus of History, University of California, Berkeley.

DONALD S. DETWILER
Professor of History, Southern Illinois University, Carbondale.

DANIEL DEUDNEY
Worldwatch Institute, Washington, D.C.

JOSEPH A. DeVITO
Professor of Communication Arts and Sciences, Queens College of The City University of New York, New York City.

SAMUEL DEVONS
Professor of Physics, Columbia University and Director of Barnard-Columbia History of Physics Laboratory, New York City.

TON DeVOS
Professor of Political Science, Trinity University, San Antonio, Tex.

ROBERT E. DEWAR
Assistant Professor of Anthropology, University of Connecticut, Storrs.

ROBERT S. DEWERS
Professor of Forest Science, Texas A&M University, College Station.

SEYMOUR DIAMOND, M.D.
Director, Diamond Headache Clinic, Ltd., and Adjunct Professor of Pharmacology, Chicago Medical School, Chicago.

JOSE LUIS DIAZ, M.D.
Psychopharmacology Research, Instituto de Investigacions Biomedicas, Universidad de Mexico, Unam, Mexico.

ROBERT H. DICK
Supervisory Tea Examiner, U.S. Food and Drug Administration, Brooklyn, N.Y.

STEVEN J. DICK
U.S. Naval Observatory, Washington, D.C.

DAVID DICKASON
Professor of Geography, Western Michigan University, Kalamazoo.

SAMUEL N. DICKEN
Emeritus Professor of Geography, University of Oregon, Eugene.

DENIS DICKINSON
Former Head of Department of Biotechnology, Institute for Industrial Research and Standards, Dublin.

PAUL DICKSON
Independent Writer.

R. S. DIETZ
Professor of Geology, Arizona State University, Tempe.

DAVID DILKS
Chairman, School of History, Leeds University, Leeds, England.

FRANCIS P. DINNEEN
Professor of Linguistics, Georgetown University, Washington, D.C.

JANE VanZANDT DINGMAN
Lecturer in Zoology, University of New Hampshire, Durham.

S. LAWRENCE DINGMAN
Associate Professor of Water Resources, Institute of Natural and Environmental Resources, University of New Hampshire, Durham.

ANASTASIA N. DINSMOOR
American School of Classical Studies, Athens.

JOSEPH R. DiPALMA, M.D.
Professor of Pharmacology, Vice-President and Dean, Hahnemann Medical College, Philadelphia.

MARK DITTRICK
Writer and Craftsman.

J. MICHAEL S. DIXON, M.D., F.R.C.P. (C)
Professor of Bacteriology and Director of Provincial Laboratory, University of Alberta, Edmonton.

JAN E. DIZARD
Professor of Sociology, Amherst College, Amherst, Mass.

FREDERICK J. DOCKSTADER
Indian Art Consultant, Former Director, Museum of the American Indian.

DONALD O. DOEHRING
Associate Professor of Earth Resources, Colorado State University, Fort Collins.

DIRAN KAVORK DOHANIAN
Professor of Fine Arts, University of Rochester, Rochester, N.Y.

RALPH DOLGOFF
Assistant Dean, School of Social Work, Adelphi University, Garden City, N.Y.

MICHAEL W. DOLS
Associate Professor of History, California State University, Hayward.

DONALD J. DONALDSON
Associate Professor of Anatomy, University of Tennessee Center for the HealthSciences, Memphis.

DAVE DOOLING
Science Writer for *Huntsville Times,*
Huntsville, Ala.

JESSE S. DOOLITTLE
Professor Emeritus of Mechanical and
Aerospace Engineering, North Carolina State
University, Raleigh.

ROBERT H. DOREMUS
New York State Professor of Glass and
Ceramics, Rensselaer Polytechnic Institute,
Troy, N.Y.

RICHARD M. DORSON
Distinguished Professor of History and Folklore,
Indiana University, Bloomington.

RICHARD G. DOTY
Associate Curator of Modern Coins, American
Numismatic Society, New York City.

RICHARD L. DOTY
Director, Smell and Taste Center, Hospital of
the University of Pennsylvania, Philadelphia.

JACK D. DOUGLAS
Professor of Sociology, University of California,
San Diego.

HERNDON G. DOWLING
Professor of Biology, New York University,
New York City.

ERIC DOWTY
Assistant Professor, Department of Geological
and Geophysical Sciences, Princeton
University, Princeton, N.J.

JOHN P. DOYLE
Professor of Philosophy, St. Louis University,
St. Louis, Mo.

ROBERT M. DOYLE
Coordinator, Media and Educational Programs,
Visual Studies Workshop, Rochester, N.Y.

MILORAD M. DRACHKOVITCH
Senior Fellow and Archivist, Hoover Institution
on War, Revolution, and Peace, Stanford
University, Stanford, Calif.

FRANK D. DRAKE
Director, National Astronomy and Ionosphere
Center, Cornell University, Ithaca, N.Y.

STILLMAN DRAKE
Former Professor, University of Toronto,
Toronto.

CECELIA HODGES DREWRY
Assistant Dean of the College, and
Department of English,
Princeton University, Princeton, N.J.

HENRY N. DREWRY
Lecturer, Professor in History, Princeton
University, Princeton, N.J.

PHILIP DRUCKER
Professor Emeritus of Anthropology, University
of Kentucky, Lexington.

R. N. DRUMMOND
Professor of Geography, McGill University,
Montreal.

ALASDAIR DRYSDALE
Associate Professor, University of New
Hampshire, Durham.

ROY DUBISCH
Professor of Mathematics, University of
Washington, Seattle.

ALDEN W. DUDLEY, JR., M.D.
Director, Neuropathology Training Program,
University of Southern Alabama, Mobile.

JOSEPH W. DUFFY
Dean, School of Technology, Central
Connecticut State College, New Britain.

NORMAN V. DUFFY
Professor of Chemistry, Kent State University,
Kent, Ohio.

J. R. DUHART
Senior Economist, Lloyds Bank International,
London.

WILLIAM J. DUIKER
Professor of East Asian History, Pennsylvania
State University, University Park.

CHARLES S. DUNBAR, F.C.I.T.
Transport Consultant.

CHARLES T. DUNCAN
Professor of Journalism, University of Oregon,
Eugene.

THOMAS W. DUNFEE
Associate Professor of Legal Studies, The
Wharton School, University of Pennsylvania,
Philadelphia.

MARVIN D. DUNNETTE
Professor of Psychology, University of
Minnesota, Minneapolis.

COL. T. N. DUPUY
President and Executive Director, Historical
Evaluation and Research Organization, Dunn
Loring, Va.

G. H. DURY
Professor of Geography and Geology Emeritus,
University of Wisconsin, Madison, Wis.

ASHOK K. DUTT
Professor of Geography and of Urban Studies,
University of Akron, Akron, Ohio.

ARNDT J. DUVALL III, M.D.
Professor of Otolaryngology, University of
Minnesota, Minneapolis.

MARTIN DWORKIN
Professor of Microbiology, University of
Minnesota, Minneapolis.

JOHN M. DYCKMAN
Clinical Psychologist, Kaiser Foundation
Hospital, Vallejo, Calif.

JAMES S. DYER
Associate Professor, School of Management,
University of California, Los Angeles.

MARY LEE DYER
Former Office Manager and Head Bookkeeper,
U.S. Building Packages and Restaurant
Construction Services.

JOHN W. EADIE
Professor of History, University of Michigan,
Ann Arbor.

VALERIE A. EARLE
Professor of Government, Georgetown
University, Washington, D.C.

SIR ERIC EASTWOOD, C.B.E., F.R.S.
Former Director of Research, General Electric
Co. Limited.

JONATHAN EBERHART
Space Sciences Editor, *Science News.*

JOHN EDWIN EBINGER
Professor of Botany, Eastern Illinois University,
Charleston.

KENNETH EBLE
Professor of English, University of Utah, Salt
Lake City.

JOHN A. EDDY
Senior Scientist, High Altitude Observatory,
National Center for Atmospheric Research,
Boulder, Colo.

I. E. S. EDWARDS
Former Keeper of Egyptian Antiquities, British
Museum, London.

MARY JANE EDWARDS
Associate Professor of English, Carleton
University, Ottawa.

W. FARRELL EDWARDS
Professor of Physics, Utah State University,
Logan.

DANIEL B. EISENBERG
Professor of Spanish, Florida State University,
Tallahassee.

SALAH EL-SHAKHS
Professor and Director, School of Urban and
Regional Policy, Rutgers University, New
Brunswick, N.J.

STEPHEN ELLEN
Geologist, U.S. Geological Survey, Menlo
Park, Calif.

DANIEL S. ELLIOT
Research Assistant, University of Michigan,
Ann Arbor.

JAMES E. ELLIS
Scientific Director, Colorado State University,
Fort Collins.

KEITH ELLIS
Professor of Spanish, University of Toronto,
Toronto.

ROBERT S. ELLWOOD, JR.
Bishop James W. Bashford Professor of
Oriental Studies, University of Southern
California, Los Angeles.

BETTY ELZEA
Formerly at Victoria and Albert Museum,
London.

ROWLAND ELZEA
Curator, Delaware Art Museum, Wilmington.

MELVIN EMBER
Professor of Anthropology, Hunter College of
the City University of New York, New York City.

R. L. EMERSON
Professor of History, University of Western
Ontario, London.

ALAN R. EMERY
Associate Curator, Royal Ontario Museum,
Toronto.

MICHAEL EMERY
Professor of Journalism, California State
University, Northridge.

SAMUEL T. EMORY
Professor of Geography, Mary Washington
College, Fredricksburg, Va.

A. G. ENGELHARDT
Staff Member, Los Alamos Scientific
Laboratory, University of California, Los
Alamos, N.Mex., and Adjunct Professor of
Electrical Engineering, Texas Tech University,
Lubbock.

ALFRED GARVIN ENGSTROM
Alumni Distinguished Professor of French,
Emeritus, University of North Carolina,
Chapel Hill.

CHRIS W. ESKRIDGE
Assistant Professor, Department of Criminal
Justice, University of Nebraska, Lincoln.

MARTIN ESSLIN
Professor of Drama, Stanford University,
Stanford, Calif.

DAVID S. EVANS
Professor of Astronomy, University of Texas,
Austin.

WILLIAM L. EVANS
Professor of Zoology, University of Arkansas,
Fayetteville.

DAVID EWEN
Musicologist-Author.

DAVID N. EWERT
Assistant Professor of Biology, Central
Michigan University, Mount Pleasant.

PHYLLIS MARIE EWY
Department of History, Brandeis University, Waltham, Mass.

DOUGLAS EZELL
Associate Professor of New Testament, Southwestern Baptist Theological Seminary, Fort Worth, Tex.

BRIAN M. FAGAN
Professor of Anthropology, University of California, Santa Barbara.

MICHAEL A. FAHEY, S.J.
Professor of Theology, Concordia University, Montreal, Quebec.

MICHAEL C. FAIRLEY
Information Services Advisor, Paper and Paper Products Industry Training Board.

STANLEY L. FALK
Chief Historian, U.S. Air Force Office of Air Force History, Washington, D.C.

JACQUELINE V. FALKENHEIM
Assistant Professor of the History of Art, Cornell University, Ithaca, N.Y.

ANN FARKAS
Professor, New School of Liberal Arts, Brooklyn College, City University of New York, New York City.

EDWARD L. FARMER
Associate Professor of History, University of Minnesota, Minneapolis.

LOUIS C. FARON
Professor of Anthropology, State University of New York, Stony Brook.

DAVID M. L. FARR
Professor of History, Carleton University, Ottawa.

STEPHEN E. FAUER
Terrestrial/Wetlands Ecologist, Environmental Assessment Council, Inc., New Brunswick, N.J.

GUNTER FAURE
Professor of Geology, Ohio State University, Columbus.

SYLVIA F. FAVA
Professor of Sociology and Director, Urban Studies Program, Brooklyn College, City University of New York, New York City.

FELIX FAVORITE
National Marine Fisheries Service, Seattle, Wash.

LAUREL E. FAY
Assistant Professor of Music, Ohio State University, Columbus.

JOE R. FEAGIN
Professor of Sociology, University of Texas, Austin.

OLIN S. FEARING
Professor of Biology, Trinity University, San Antonio, Tex.

GERALD FEINBERG
Professor of Physics, Columbia University, New York City.

MORDECHAI FEINGOLD
Professor of History, Boston University, Boston.

S. NORMAN FEINGOLD
National Director, B'nai B'rith Career and Counseling Services, Bethesda, Md.

JOHN F. FELDHUSEN
Professor of Education, Purdue University, Lafayette, Ind.

LEONARD FELDMAN
Leonard Feldman Electronic Laboratories, Great Neck, N.Y.; Senior Editor, *Audio Magazine;* Technical Editor, *Video Review.*

JOHN H. FENTON
Commonwealth Professor of Political Science, University of Massachusetts, Amherst.

M. BROCK FENTON
Associate Professor of Biology, Carleton University, Ottawa.

JOHN C. FENTRESS
Professor of Psychology, Dalhousie University, Halifax, Nova Scotia.

EDWARD A. FERNALD
Professor of Geography and Director, Florida Resources and Environmental Analysis Center, Florida State University, Tallahassee.

RAFAEL A. FERNANDEZ
Curator of Prints and Drawings, Sterling and Francine Clark Art Institute, Williamstown, Mass.

ROBERT A. FERNEA
Professor of Anthropology and Middle Eastern Studies, University of Texas, Austin.

W. CONARD FERNELIUS
Adjunct Professor of Chemistry, Kent State University, Kent, Ohio.

ROBERT H. FERRELL
Distinguished Professor of History, Indiana University, Bloomington.

ANNE FERRY
Professor of English, Boston College, Chestnut Hill, Mass.

G. WALLIS FIELD
Professor of Germanic Languages and Literature, University of Toronto, Toronto.

KATE FIELDEN
Corpus Christi College, Oxford, England.

ZIRKA ZAREMBA FILIPCZAK
Associate Professor of Art History, Williams College, Williamstown, Mass.

EDWARD R. FINCH, JR.
Finch and Schaefler, New York City.

ULRICH FINKE
Senior Lecturer in Art History, University of Manchester, Manchester, England.

K. THOMAS FINLEY
Professor of Chemistry, State University College, Brockport, N.Y.

BERNARD S. FINN
Curator, National Museum of History and Technology, Smithsonian Institution, Washington, D.C.

CARL D. FINSTAD
Associate Professor of Biology, University of Wisconsin, River Falls.

ALFRED G. FISCHER
Professor of Geology, Princeton University, Princeton, N.J.

SCOTT K. FISCHER

JAMES S. FISHER
Associate Professor of Geography, University of Georgia, Athens.

ROBERT C. FITE
Professor and Director, Environmental Extension Project, Oklahoma State University, Stillwater.

GERALD FITZGERALD
Professor of Classical Studies, Monash University, Victoria, Australia.

JOAN FITZPATRICK
Research Scientist, Denver Research Institute, University of Denver, Denver, Colo.

JOSEPH P. FITZPATRICK
Professor of Sociology, Fordham University, Bronx, N.Y.

KJETIL A. FLATIN
Assistant Professor of Scandinavian Languages, University of Washington, Seattle.

WOLFGANG B. FLEISCHMANN
Dean, School of Humanities, Montclair State College, Upper Montclair, N.J.

BARBARA FLICKER
Associate Director, USC Paralegal Program, and Adjunct Assistant Professor of Paralegal Studies, University of Southern California Law Center, Los Angeles.

HOWARD H. FLIERL
Professor of Geography, State University of New York, Albany.

STEVE FLINK
World Tennis magazine.

ROY K. FLINT
Professor of History, United States Military Academy, West Point, N.Y.

MARILYN R. FLOWERS
Assistant Professor of Economics, University of Oklahoma, Norman.

VIRGINIA FLOYD
Professor of English, Bryant College, Smithfield, R.I.

PHILIP FLYNN
Associate Professor of English, University of Delaware, Newark.

DONALD E. FOARD
Biologist, Comparative Animal Research Laboratory, University of Tennessee, Oak Ridge.

C. L. FOILES
Professor of Physics, Michigan State University, East Lansing.

BLISS FORBUSH III
Assistant Professor of Physiology, Yale University School of Medicine, New Haven, Conn.

BARBARA BRENNAN FORD
Instructor, Connecticut College, New London.

C. C. FORD
Lecturer in Developmental Biology, University of Sussex, Sussex, England.

RICHARD FORD

CHARLES W. FORNARA
Professor of Classics and History, Brown University, Providence, R.I.

FRED FORTRESS
Director, Textile and Apparel Research, Philadelphia College of Textiles and Science, Philadelphia.

EDWARD W. FOSS
Professor of Agricultural Engineering, Cornell University, Ithaca, N.Y.

BRIAN L. FOSTER
Associate Professor of Anthropology, State University of New York, Binghamton.

PETER V. FOUKAL
Lecturer in Astronomy, Harvard University, Cambridge, Mass.

EDWARD B. FOWLER
University of California, Berkeley, Calif.

GARY L. FOWLER
Professor of Geography, University of Illinois, Urbana.

GRANT R. FOWLES
Professor of Physics, University of Utah, Salt Lake City.

ELIZABETH FOX-GENOVESE
Director, Institute of Women's Studies, Emory University, Atlanta, Ga.

MARCUS FRANDA
Associate American Universities Field Staff, New Delhi, India.

JERRY F. FRANKLIN
College of Forest Resources, University of Washington, Seattle.

F. W. FRANZ
President, Watch Tower Bible and Tract Society of Pennsylvania, Brooklyn, N.Y.

HUGO F. FRANZEN
Professor of Chemistry, Iowa State University, Ames.

DEREK FRASER
Reader in History, University of Bradford, Bradford, England.

DOUGLAS FRASER
Professor of Art History and Archaeology, Columbia University, New York City.

MICHAEL FREDE
Professor of Philosophy, Princeton University, Princeton, N.J.

AARON D. FREEDMAN, M.D.
Professor of Medicine, Sophie Davis School of Biomedical Education, City College, City University of New York, New York City.

RICHARD B. FREEMAN, M.D.
Associate Professor of Medicine, University of Rochester School of Medicine, Rochester, N.Y.

THOMAS WALTER FREEMAN
Emeritus Professor of Geography, University of Manchester, Manchester, England.

WARREN FRENCH
Professor of English, Indiana University, Indianapolis.

HERBERT FREY
Research Associate, Geophysics Branch, Goddard Space Flight Center, University of Maryland, Greenbelt.

H. M. FRIED
Professor of Physics, Brown University, Providence, R.I.

MAURICE FRIEDBERG
Professor of Russian Literature, and Head, Department of Slavic Languages and Literatures, University of Illinois, Urbana-Champaign.

ROBERT L. FRIEDLY
Executive Director, Office of Communication, Christian Church (Disciples of Christ), Indianapolis, Ind.

GERALD M. FRIEDMAN
Professor of Geology, Rensselaer Polytechnic Institute, Troy, N.Y.

MELVIN J. FRIEDMAN
Professor of Comparative Literature and English, University of Wisconsin, Milwaukee.

NORMAN FRIEDMAN
Professor Emeritus of English, Queens College, City University of New York.

SAUL S. FRIEDMAN
Associate Professor of History, Youngstown State University, Youngstown, Ohio.

MARILYN SIBLEY FRIES
Assistant Professor of Germanic Languages and Literatures, Yale University, New Haven, Conn.

H. HOWARD FRISINGER II
Professor of Mathematics, Colorado State University, Fort Collins.

HAROLD C. FRITTS
Professor of Dendrochronology, University of Arizona, Tucson.

STEVEN H. FRITTS
Bell Museum of Natural History, University of Minnesota, Minneapolis.

KARLFRIED FROEHLICH
Professor of Church History, Princeton Theological Seminary, Princeton, N.J.

J. WILLIAM FROST
Director, Friends Historical Library, Swarthmore College, Swarthmore, Pa.

WILLIAM G. FRY
Department of Science, Luton College, Luton, England.

RICHARD NELSON FRYE
Aga Khan Professor of Iranian, Harvard University, Cambridge, Mass.

LAWRENCE H. FUCHS
Meyer and Walter Jaffee Professor, American Civilization and Politics, Brandeis University, Waltham, Mass.

ARMAND J. FULCO
Professor of Biological Chemistry, University of California School of Medicine, Los Angeles.

REGINALD H. FULLER
Professor, Protestant Episcopal Seminary in Virginia, Alexandria.

J. Z. FULLMER
Professor of History, Ohio State University, Columbus.

ROBIN FULTON
Førstelektor Rogaland Distriktshøgskole Stavanger, Norway.

BJARNE FURHAUGE
Lecturer, Emdrupborg College of Education, Copenhagen.

JOHN FURSE
The Open University, Milton Keynes, Buckinghamshire, England.

LILIAN R. FURST
Marcel Bataillon Professor of Comparative Literature, University of North Carolina, Chapel Hill.

CHRISTOPHER GABEL
U.S. Army Command and General Staff College, Leavenworth, Kans.

RALPH W. GABLE
Associate Professor of Chemistry, Davidson College, Davidson, N.C.

WARREN J. GADPAILLE, M.D.
Assistant Clinical Professor, University of Colorado Medical Center, Denver.

ALAN M. GAINES
Program Director for Geochemistry, National Science Foundation, Washington, D.C.

PETER GALASSI
Curator, Department of Photography, The Museum of Modern Art, New York City.

ROBERT L. GALE
Professor of American Literature, University of Pittsburgh, Pittsburgh, Pa.

GILBERT J. GALL
Assistant Professor, Department of Labor Studies and Industrial Relations, Pennsylvania State University, University Park.

ARTHUR W. GALSTON
Eaton Professor of Botany, Yale University, New Haven, Conn.

JAMES F. GAMMILL, JR.
Harvard Business School, Boston.

LEWIS H. GANN
Senior Fellow, Hoover Institution, Stanford University, Stanford, Calif.

MARGARET GANZ
Professor of English, Brooklyn College, City University of New York, New York City.

PAUL GARDNER
Author of *The Simplest Game: The Intelligent American's Guide to the World of Soccer.*

WAYLAND D. GARDNER
Professor of Economics, Western Michigan University, Kalamazoo.

SOL L. GARFIELD
Professor of Psychology, Washington University, St. Louis, Mo.

H. B. GARLAND
Emeritus Professor of German, University of Exeter, Exeter, England.

C. WILLIAM GARNER
Associate Professor of Urban Education, Rutgers University, New Brunswick, N.J.

H. F. GARNER
Professor of Geology, Rutgers University, Newark, N.J.

RONALD G. GARST
Assistant Professor of Geography, University of Maryland, College Park.

ROY H. GARSTANG
Professor of Astrophysics, University of Colorado, Boulder.

KENNETH W. GATLAND, F.R.A.S., F.B.I.S.
Past President, The British Interplanetary Society.

WILLIAM GAUNT
Special Correspondent on Art to *The Times*, London.

ADDISON GAYLE
Professor of English, Bernard Baruch College, City University of New York, New York City.

LT. COL. ROBERT GAYRE OF GAYRE AND NIGG
Baron of Lochoreshyre, Editor, *Armorial Who is Who.*

ADELHEID M. GEALT
Curator, Indiana University Art Museum, Bloomington.

IGNACE J. GELB
Frank P. Hixon Distinguished Service Professor of Assyriology, The Oriental Institute, University of Chicago, Chicago.

ALBERT GELPI
Coe Professor of American Literature, Stanford University, Stanford, Calif.

FRANK GEORGE
Professor, Brunel University, Uxbridge, Middlesex, England.

JAMES M. GERHARDT
Associate Professor of Political Science, Southern Methodist University, Dallas, Tex.

LARRY R. GERLACH
Professor of History, University of Utah, Salt Lake City.

DANIEL GEROULD
Professor of Theatre and Comparative Literature, Graduate Center, City University of New York, New York City.

MARVIN E. GETTLEMAN
Professor of History, Polytechnic Institute of New York, New York City.

DIANE Y. GHIRARDO
Assistant Professor of Architectural History and Theory, University of Southern California, Los Angeles.

J. WHITFIELD GIBBONS
Research Ecologist, Savannah River Ecology Laboratory, Aiken, S.C.

JAMES LOWELL GIBBS, JR.
Professor of Anthropology, Stanford University, Stanford, Calif.

WALTER B. GIBSON
Author, *The Complete Illustrated Book of Close-Up Magic, Mastering Magic.*

FRANCES CARNEY GIES
Coauthor of *The Ingenious Yankees.*

JOSEPH C. GIES
Editor of Publications, Association of Governing Boards of Universities and Colleges, Washington, D.C.

LARRY A. GIESMANN
Associate Professor of Botany, Northern Kentucky University, Highland Heights.

RAY W. GIFFORD, JR., M.D.
Senior Vice Chairman, Division of Medicine, The Cleveland Clinic Foundation, Cleveland, Ohio.

PERRY W. AND CLAIRE K. GILBERT
Directors, Mote Marine Laboratory, Sarasota, Fla.

REX L. GILBREATH
Associate Professor of Animal Sciences, Cook College, New Brunswick, N.J.

LANGDON GILKEY
Shailer Mathews Professor of Theology, The Divinity School, University of Chicago, Chicago.

RICHARD T. GILL
Former Lecturer in Economics, Harvard University, Cambridge, Mass.

B. von HALLER GILMER
Professor of Psychology, Virginia Polytechnic Institute and State University, Blacksburg.

MICHAEL E. GILPIN
Associate Professor of Biology, University of California, San Diego.

SOL GITTLEMAN
Professor of German, Tufts University, Medford, Mass.

S. F. GLASSMAN
Professor of Biological Sciences, University of Illinois, Chicago.

MARTIN IRA GLASSNER
Assistant Professor of Geography, Southern Connecticut State College.

NAHUM N. GLATZER
Professor of Religion and of Judaica, Boston University, Boston.

WILLIAM GLOVER
Former Theater Critic, The Associated Press.

W. EARL GODFREY
Curator Emeritus of Ornithology, National Museums of Canada, Ottawa.

W. L. GODSHALK
Professor of English, University of Cincinnati, Cincinnati, Ohio.

ALVIN GOLDFARB
Assistant Professor of Theatre, Illinois State University, Normal.

LAWRENCE GOLDHIRSCH
Attorney, Speiser & Krause, New York City.

FREDERICK GOLDIN
Professor, City College and the Graduate School, City University of New York, New York City.

DAVID T. GOLDMAN
Associate Director, Long Range Planning, National Measurement Laboratory, National Bureau of Standards, Washington, D.C.

RALPH M. GOLDMAN
Professor of Political Science, San Francisco State University, San Francisco.

WILLIAM GOLDSMITH, M.D.
Assistant Clinical Professor of Psychiatry, University of California, and Staff Psychiatrist, Brentwood Veterans Administration Hospital, Los Angeles.

MALCOLM GOLDSTEIN
Professor of English, Queens College and the Graduate School, City University of New York, Flushing.

JAMES A. GOLDSTON
Attorney, Human Rights Watch, New York City.

RICHARD P. GOLDTHWAIT
Professor Emeritus of Polar Studies, Ohio State University, Columbus.

JERRY P. GOLLUB
Professor of Physics, Haverford College, Haverford, Pa.

DANNY GONSALVES
Assistant Professor of Geography, Southern Connecticut State College, New Haven.

ROBERTO GONZÁLEZ-ECHEVARRÍA
Associate Professor of Spanish and Portuguese, Yale University, New Haven, Conn.

ERICH GOODE
Professor of Sociology, State University of New York, Stony Brook.

ALVIN S. GOODMAN
Professor, Department of Civil and Environmental Engineering, Polytechnical Institute of New York, Brooklyn.

WILLIAM GOODMAN
Professor Emeritus of Political Science, Southern Illinois University, Edwardsville.

NORMA L. GOODRICH
Professor of French and Comparative Literature, Claremont Colleges, Claremont, Calif.

ALDEN RAND GORDON
Assistant Professor of Fine Arts, Trinity College, Hartford, Conn.

DAVID S. GORDON
Emory University, School of Medicine, Atlanta, Georgia.

JOHN L. GORDON, JR.
Professor of History, University of Richmond, Richmond, Va.

MEL GORDON
Assistant Professor of Drama, New York University, New York City.

PEARL GORDON
Researcher, Museum of Modern Art, New York City.

GEORGE GORIN
Professor of Chemistry, Oklahoma State University, Stillwater.

CHARLES W. GORODETZKY, M.D.
Adjunct Associate Professor of Pharmacology, University of Kentucky College of Medicine, Lexington.

DONALD GOTTERBARN
Assistant Professor of Philosophy, Albright College, Reading, Pa.

NORMAN K. GOTTWALD
Professor of Old Testament and of Biblical Theology and Ethics, Graduate Theological Union, Berkeley, Calif.

WILLIAM H. GOTWALD, JR.
Professor of Biology, Utica College of Syracuse University, Utica, N.Y.

LEWIS L. GOULD
Professor of History, University of Texas, Austin.

PHILIP GOULD
Professor of Art History, Sarah Lawrence College, Bronxville, N.Y.

ANTHONY J. GOW
Research Geologist, U.S. Army Cold Regions, Research and Engineering Laboratory, Hanover, N.H.

OLEG GRABAR
Professor of Fine Arts, Harvard University, Cambridge, Mass.

NELSON H. H. GRABURN
Professor of Anthropology, University of California, Berkeley.

PATRICK GRANFIELD
Professor of Systematic Theology, The Catholic University of America, Washington, D.C.

RAYMOND E. C. GRAUNKE
Former Editor and Publisher, *Soundings.*

DONALD J. GRAY
Professor of English, Indiana University, Bloomington.

ELIZABETH A. GRAY
Assistant Professor of Celtic Languages and Literatures, Harvard University, Cambridge, Mass.

ALFRED de GRAZIA
Research Professor of Social Theory in Government, New York University, New York City.

ERIKA GREEN
Senior Scientist, Hoffmann-La Roche, Inc., Nutley, N.J.

MICHAEL E. GREEN
Associate Professor of Chemistry, City University of New York, New York City.

TAMARA M. GREEN
Assistant Professor of Classics, Hunter College, City University of New York, New York City.

WILLIAM M. GREEN, M.D.
Department of Radiology, Medical Center at Princeton, Princeton, N.J.

FRED GREENBAUM
Professor of History, Queensborough Community College, City University of New York, New York City.

BERNARD GREENBERG
Professor of Biological Sciences, University of Illinois, Chicago.

RICHARD GREENBERG
Senior Scientist, Planetary Science Institute, Tucson, Ariz.

DAVID H. GREENE
Professor of English, New York University, New York City.

LEE SEIFERT GREENE
Distinguished Professor Emeritus, University of Tennessee, Knoxville.

CHARLOTTE GREENSPAN
Mellon Post-Doctoral Teaching Fellow in the Humanities, Cornell University, Ithaca, N.Y.

EDWARD T. GREENSTEIN, D.V.M.
University Veterinarian, Rutgers University, New Brunswick, N.J.

ROY O. GREEP
Professor of Anatomy Emeritus, Harvard Medical School, Boston.

EAMON GRENNAN
Assistant Professor, Department of English, Vassar College, Poughkeepsie, N.Y.

JOHN A. C. GREPPIN
Director, Program in Linguistics, Cleveland State University, Cleveland, Ohio.

ROBERT R. GRIFFETH
Assistant Professor of History, University of Washington, Seattle.

DANA GRIFFIN III
Associate Professor of Botany, University of Florida, Gainesville, Fla.

JAMES B. GRIFFIN
Senior Research Scientist, Museum of Anthropology, University of Michigan, Ann Arbor.

MARGERY B. GRIFFITH
Director, The Playing Card Museum, Cincinnati, Ohio.

WILLIAM S. GRIFFITH
Professor and Chairman, Department of Adult Education, University of British Columbia, Vancouver.

A. R. G. GRIFFITHS
Senior Lecturer, Flinders University of South Australia, South Australia.

JOHN F. GRIFFITHS
Professor and Texas State Climatologist, Texas A&M University, College Station.

WILLIAM G. GRIGSBY
Professor of City and Regional Planning, University of Pennsylvania, Philadelphia.

E. R. GRILLY
Staff Member, Los Alamos Scientific Laboratory, University of California, Los Alamos, N.Mex.

ROBERT E. GRINDER
Professor of Educational Psychology, College of Education, Arizona State University, Tempe.

MERILEE S. GRINDLE
Research Associate, Harvard Institute for International Development, Harvard University, Cambridge, Mass.

LARRY R. GRISHAM
Physicist, Princeton University, Plasma Physics Laboratory, Princeton, N.J.

E. E. GRISSELL
Research Entomologist, Systematic Entomology Laboratory, Washington, D.C.

DANIEL P. GRISWOLD, JR.
Associate Director, Chemotherapy Research, Southern Research Institute, Birmingham, Ala.

CHARLES F. GRITZNER
Associate Professor of Geography, University of Houston, Houston, Tex.

LAWRENCE GROSSMAN
Associate Professor of Geochemistry, University of Chicago, Chicago.

DAVID I. GROSSVOGEL
Goldwin Smith Professor of Comparative Literature and Romance Studies, Cornell University, Ithaca, N.Y.

PAUL A. GROVES
Associate Professor of Geography, University of Maryland, College Park.

JOHN H. GROWDON, M.D.
Program Director, Massachusetts Alzheimer's Disease Research Center, Boston.

JOHN F. GUILMARTIN, JR.
Former Associate Professor of History, U.S.Air Force Academy, USAF Academy, Colo.

HARVEY L. GUNDERSON
Associate Director, State Museum, and Professor of Zoology, University of Nebraska, Lincoln.

SAMUEL C. GUNDY
Assistant Professor of Biology, Kutztown State College, Kutztown, Pa.

BILL GUNSTON
Assistant Compiler, *Jane's All the World's Aircraft* (annual), and European Editor, *Aircraft.*

PETE A. Y. GUNTER
Professor of Philosophy, North Texas State University, Denton.

MARIA TERESA GUTIÉRREZ DE MACGREGOR
Doctora en Geografía, Instituto de Geografía, Universidad Nacional Autónoma México, Ciudad Universitaria, Villa Obregón.

FRANÇOIS HAAS
Assistant Professor, Department of Physiology, New York University Medical Center, New York City.

JEFFREY K. HADDEN
Professor of Sociology, University of Virginia, Charlottesville.

ELBERT H. HADLEY
Professor of Chemistry, Southern Illinois University, Carbondale.

KENNETH J. HAGAN
Associate Professor of History, U.S. Naval Academy, Annapolis, Md.

H. G. HAILE
Professor of German, University of Illinois, Urbana.

FRANKLYN S. HAIMAN
Professor of Communication Studies, Northwestern University, Evanston, Ill.

JAY L. HALIO
Professor of English, University of Delaware, Newark.

CHARLES V. HALL
Professor of Horticulture, Iowa State University, Ames.

JOHN WHITLING HALL
Professor of Geography and Chairman, Department of Social Sciences, Louisiana State University, Shreveport.

ROBERT B. HALL
Professor of History and Geography, University of Rochester, Rochester, N.Y.

ANTHONY HALLAM
Professor of Geological Sciences, University of Birmingham, Birmingham, England.

RICHARD P. HALLION
Associate Professor, University of Maryland, College Park.

LESLIE HALLIWELL
Film Buyer, ITV Network of Great Britain, and Author, *The Filmgoers Companion, Halliwell's Filmguide.*

JOHN HALPERIN
Professor of English, University of Southern California, University Park, Los Angeles.

ARTHUR M. HALPERN
Associate Professor of Chemistry, Northeastern University, Boston.

RICHARD S. HALSEY
Dean, School of Information Science and Policy, The University at Albany, State University of New York, and Former Chairman, Reference and Subscription Books Reviews Committee, American Library Association.

ROY HALVERSON
Associate Professor of Journalism, University of Oregon, Eugene.

MARGARET A. HAMBURG, M.D.
Special Assistant to the Director, National Institute of Allergy and Infectious Diseases, National Institute of Health, Bethesda, Md.

ALONZO L. HAMBY
Professor of History, Ohio University, Athens.

JERROLD F. HAMES
Editor, *Canadian Churchman.*

HEIDI B. HAMMEL
National Research Council Resident Research Associate, Jet Propulsion Laboratory, Pasadena, Calif.

STEPHEN HANDEL
Professor of Psychology, University of Tennessee, Knoxville.

TED L. HANES
Professor of Biology, California State University, Fullerton.

CHAD HANSEN
Professor of Philosophy, University of Vermont, Burlington.

KENT F. HANSEN
Professor of Nuclear Engineering, Massachusetts Institute of Technology, Cambridge.

JOHN W. HARBAUGH
Professor of Geology, Stanford University, Stanford, Calif.

WILLIAM H. HARBOLD
Professor of Political Science, Whitman College, Walla Walla, Wash.

D. W. HARDING
Professor of Archaeology, University of Edinburgh, Edinburgh.

ROBERT D. HARE
Professor of Psychology, University of British Columbia, Vancouver.

MAURICE HARMON
Lecturer in Anglo-Irish Literature, University College, Dublin.

ROBERT A. HARPER
Professor and Chairman, Department of Geography, University of Maryland, College Park.

DALE HARRIS
Professor of Literature, Sarah Lawrence College, Bronxville, N.Y.; College Professor of the Arts, Trinity College, Hartford, Conn.; Adjunct Professor of Art History, Cooper Union for the Advancement of Science and Art, New York City; and Visiting Professor of Dance History, School of the Arts, New York City

DUDLEY ARTHUR HARRIS
Author of *Hydroponics: Growing without Soil.*

EDWARD GRANT HARRIS
Professor of Physics and Astronomy, University of Tennessee, Knoxville.

JESSICA HARRIS
Associate Professor of Library and Information Science, St. John's University, Jamaica, N.Y.

R. BAINE HARRIS
Eminent Professor of Philosophy, Old Dominion University, Norfolk, Va.

THOMAS L. HARRISON
Brearley School, New York City.

DONN V. HART
Professor of Anthropology and Director, Center for Southeast Asian Studies, Northern Illinois University, De Kalb.

JAMES A. HART
Associate Professor of English, University of British Columbia, Vancouver.

ROY HARTENSTEIN
Professor of Zoology, State University College of Environmental Science and Forestry, Syracuse, N.Y.

THOMAS B. HARTMANN
Professor of Journalism and Urban Communications, Rutgers University, New Brunswick, N.J.

JOSEPH H. HARTSHORN
Professor of Geology and Geography, University of Massachusetts, Amherst.

TRUMAN HARTSHORN
Associate Professor of Geography, Georgia State University, Atlanta.

DONALD J. HARVEY
Professor of History, Hunter College, City University of New York, New York City.

VAN A. HARVEY
Professor of Religious Studies, Stanford University, Stanford, Calif.

ROBERT E. HASKELL
Chair, Department of Social and Behavioral Sciences, University of New England, Biddeford, Maine.

DAYTON HASKIN, S.J.
Assistant Professor of English, Boston College, Chestnut Hill, Mass.

WARREN W. HASSLER, JR.
Professor of American History, Pennsylvania State University, University Park.

ROBERT D. HATCHER, JR.
Professor of Geology, Florida State University, Tallahassee.

PAUL G. HATTERSLEY, M.D.
Professor of Internal Medicine and Pathology, School of Medicine, University of California, Davis.

JOSEPH P. HAUGHTON
Professor of Geography, University of Dublin, Dublin.

WILLIAM B. HAUSER
Assistant Professor of History, University of Rochester, Rochester, N.Y.

CHARLES H. HAWS
Director of the Institute of Scottish Studies, Old Dominion University, Norfolk, Va.

FRANK C. HAWTHORNE
Professor of Earth Sciences, University of Manitoba, Winnipeg.

JOHN HAY
Assistant Professor of Fine Arts, Harvard University, Cambridge, Mass.

EDWIN V. HAYDEN
Christian Minister, Former Editor of the *Christian Standard.*

WILLIAM HAYS
Associate Professor of Organ, Westminster Choir College, Princeton, N.J.

DANIEL R. HEADRICK
Associate Professor of Social Sciences, Roosevelt University, Chicago.

J. R. HEALY
Professor of Geography, Hilo College, University of Hawaii, Hilo.

THOMAS K. HEARN, JR.
Professor of Philosophy and Dean, School of Humanities, University of Alabama, Birmingham.

MELVIN E. HECHT
Professor of Geography, University of Arizona, Tucson.

FRED HEILIZER
Associate Professor of Psychology, De Paul University, Chicago.

JUDITH HEILIZER
Clinical Psychologist, Private Practice.

MICHAEL HENRY HEIM
Assistant Professor of Slavic Languages, University of California, Los Angeles.

PETER HELLER
Professor of German and Comparative Literature, State University of New York, Buffalo.

HAL HELLMAN
Author of *Communications in the World of the Future.*

JONATHAN E. HELMREICH
Dean of Instruction and Professor of History, Allegheny College, Meadville, Pa.

PAUL C. HELMREICH
Professor of History, Wheaton College, Norton, Mass.

RANDEL HELMS
Assistant Professor of English, Arizona State University, Tempe.

JANICE A. HENDERSON
Visiting Member, Institute for Advanced Study, Princeton, N.J.

JEFFREY HENDERSON
Associate Professor of Greek and Latin, University of Michigan, Ann Arbor.

JOHN S. HENDERSON
Assistant Professor of Anthropology, Cornell University, Ithaca, N.Y.

RAY HENKEL
Professor of Geography, University of Arizona, Tempe.

PAUL HENKIND, M.D.
Chairman, Department of Ophthalmology, Albert Einstein College of Medicine, Bronx, N.Y.

JOHN BELL HENNEMAN
Professor of History, University of Iowa, Iowa City.

ROBERT J. HENNING, M.D.
Assistant Professor of Medicine, University of Southern California, Los Angeles.

WILLIAM R. HENNING
Department of Dairy and Animal Science, Pennsylvania State University, University Park.

J. DAVID HENRY
Biological Consultant, Henry and Associates Co., Waskesiu, Saskatchewan.

CHRISTOPH HERING
Professor of German and Comparative Literature, University of Maryland, College Park.

MARY ANN HERMAN
Co-Director of Folk Dance House and Folk Dance Consultant for Dance Division of Performing Arts Library, New York City.

ROBERT HERMAN
Associate Professor of Zoology, Rutgers University, New Brunswick, N.J.

EDWIN L. HERR
Professor and Head, Division of Counseling and Educational Psychology, Pennsylvania State University, University Park.

JAMES W. HERRICK
Adjunct Professor of Anthropology, State University of New York College of Technology, Utica-Rome.

ROBERT O. HERRMANN
Professor of Agricultural Economics, Pennsylvania State University, University Park.

CHARLES A. HERUBIN
Associate Professor, Hudson Valley Community College, Troy, N.Y.

BRUCE HERZBERG
Rutgers University, New Brunswick, N.J.

ROBERT HETZRON
Professor of Hebrew, University of California, Santa Barbara.

KATHRYN HIESINGER
Curator of Decorative Arts after 1700, Philadelphia Museum of Art, Philadelphia.

ULRICH HIESINGER
Art Historian.

ANNA HIETANEN
Geologist, U.S. Geological Survey, Menlo Park, Calif.

DON HIGGINBOTHAM
Professor of History, University of North Carolina, Chapel Hill.

ROBERT A. HIGHAM
Consultant, Euro-Data Analysts, Ashtead, Surrey, United Kingdom.

CHRISTOPHER R. HILL
Director, Centre for Southern African Studies, University of York, Heslington, York, England.

JOHN WALTER HILL
Associate Professor of Music, University of Illinois, Urbana.

RICHARD LESLIE HILLS
Director, North Western Museum of Science and Industry, Manchester, England.

RONALD HINGLEY
Department of Russian, Oxford University, Oxford, England.

WILLIAM M. HINKLE
Professor Emeritus of Art History, Columbia University, New York City.

JERRY HIRSCH
Professor of Psychology and of Ecology, Ethology, and Evolution, University of Illinois, Champaign-Urbana.

RICHARD F. HIRSH
Humanities Center, University of Florida, Gainesville.

DAVID W. HIRST
Senior Research Historian and Associate Editor, *The Papers of Woodrow Wilson,* Princeton University, Princeton, N.J.

HOMER W. HISER
Director, Remote Sensing Laboratory, University of Miami, Coral Gables, Fla.

WILBERT M. HITE
Consultant, Trucking Industry.

RICHARD F. HIXSON
Professor of Journalism and Urban Communications, Livingston College, Rutgers University, New Brunswick, N.J.

FRED HOBSON
Associate Professor of English, University of Alabama, University.

JULIAN HOCHBERG
Professor of Psychology, Columbia University, New York City.

PAUL W. HODGE
Professor of Astronomy, University of Washington, Seattle.

C. WALTER HODGES
Theatre Historian and Designer, Lewes, Sussex, England.

GEORGE W. HOFFMAN
Professor of Geography, University of Texas, Austin.

MICHAEL J. HOFFMAN
Professor of English, University of California, Davis.

PAUL HOFFMAN
Department of Philosophy, Harvard University, Cambridge, Mass.

PERSHING B. HOFSLUND
Professor of Zoology, University of Minnesota, Duluth.

EDWARD PATRICK HOGAN
Associate Dean of Arts and Sciences, and Head, Department of Geography, South Dakota State University, Brookings.

ROBERT HOGAN
Professor of English, University of Delaware, Newark.

WILLIAM T. HOGAN, S.J.
Professor of Economics and Director, Industrial Economics Research Institute, Fordham University, Bronx, N.Y.

ARTHUR R. HOGUE
Professor Emeritus of History, Indiana University, Bloomington.

CAROL J. ROWLAND HOGUE
Chief, Pregnancy Epidemiology Branch, Division of Reproductive Health, Centers for Disease Control, Atlanta, Ga.

RANDALL G. HOLCOMBE
Professor of Economics, Auburn University, Auburn University, Ala.

LEO E. HOLLISTER, M.D.
Professor of Medicine, Psychiatry, and Pharmacology, Stanford University School of Medicine, Palo Alto, Calif.

W. EUGENE HOLLON
Ohio Regents Professor of History, University of Toledo, Toledo, Ohio.

FREDERIC B. M. HOLLYDAY
Professor of History, Duke University, Durham, N.C.

GEORGE HOLMES
St. Catherine's College, Oxford, England.

JACK D. L. HOLMES
Director, Louisiana Collection Series of Books and Documents on Colonial Louisiana.

R. F. HOLMES
Deputy Registrar, University of Cambridge, Cambridge, England.

JAMES R. HOLTON
Professor of Atmospheric Sciences, University of Washington, Seattle.

SINCLAIR HOOD
Former Director of the British School of Archaeology at Athens.

WILLIAM HOOD
Assistant Professor of Art, Oberlin College, Oberlin, Ohio.

MARJORIE L. HOOVER
Emeritus Professor of German and Russian, Oberlin College, Oberlin, Ohio.

WILLIAM G. HOPKINS
Associate Professor of Plant Sciences, University of Western Ontario, London.

PETER C. HOPPE
Staff Scientist, Jackson Laboratory, Bar Harbor, Maine.

DAVID J. HORN
Associate Professor of Entomology, Ohio State University, Columbus.

MICHAEL H. HORN
Professor of Biology, California State University, Fullerton.

RODERICK H. HORNING
Manager, Environmental Affairs, Dyes and Chemicals Division, Crompton & Knowles Corp., Reading, Pa.

FRANKLIN E. HOROWITZ
Associate, American Language Program, Columbia University, New York City.

REGINALD HORSMAN
Distinguished Professor of History, University of Wisconsin, Milwaukee.

DONALD D. HORWARD
Professor of History, Florida State University, Tallahassee.

FRAN P. HOSKEN
Publisher and Editor, *Women's International Network News.*

J. R. HOUCK
Associate Professor of Astronomy, Cornell University, Ithaca, N.Y.

JOHN G. HOUGHTON
Associate Professor of Geography, University of Nevada, Reno.

DAVID A. HOUNSHELL
Assistant Professor of History, Harvey Mudd College, Claremont, Calif.

CHARLES HOWARD
Professor of Chemistry, University of Texas, San Antonio.

WAYNE HOWARD
Former Assistant Professor of Music, Kent State University, Kent, Ohio.

THE VERY REVEREND WILBUR K. HOWARD
The United Church of Canada, Ottawa.

JEFFERY W. HOWE
Assistant Professor of Fine Arts, Boston College, Chestnut Hill, Mass.

ALMONTE HOWELL
Research Professor of Musicology, University of Georgia, Athens.

JOHN HOWELL
Contributing Editor, *Performing Arts Journal.*

ROBERT J. HUCKSHORN
Professor of Political Science, Florida Atlantic University, Boca Raton.

ROBERT V. HUDSON
Associate Professor of Journalism, Michigan State University, East Lansing.

FRANKLIN E. HUFFMAN
Associate Professor of Linguistics and Asian Studies, Cornell University, Ithaca, N.Y.

GEORGE J. HUFFMAN
Acting Maryland State Climatologist, University of Maryland, College Park.

CHARLES C. HUGHES
Professor of Anthropology, and Family and Community Medicine, University of Utah, Salt Lake City.

JEROME HULL, JR.
Professor and Extension Horticulturalist, Michigan State University, East Lansing.

CHAS. B. HUNT
Geologist, Formerly with the U.S.Geological Survey.

EDWARD E. HUNT, JR.
Professor of Anthropology and Health Education, Pennsylvania State University, University Park.

CORNELIUS S. HURLBUT, JR.
Professor Emeritus of Mineralogy, Harvard University, Cambridge, Mass.

FARLEY K. HUTCHINS
Professor of Music, University of Akron, Akron, Ohio.

RUSSELL J. HUTNIK
Professor of Forest Ecology, Pennsylvania State University, University Park.

RAY HYMAN
Professor of Psychology, University of Oregon, Eugene.

ERNEST C. HYNDS
Associate Professor of Journalism and Mass Communication, University of Georgia, Athens.

DAVID W. ICENOGLE
Department of Geography, Auburn University, Auburn, Ala.

CLARENCE P. IDYLL
Chief, Division of International Fisheries Development and Services, National Marine Fisheries Service, National Oceanic and Atmospheric Administration, U.S. Department of Commerce.

GEORG G. IGGERS
Professor of History, State University of New York, Buffalo.

AARON J. IHDE
Professor of Chemistry, Integrated Liberal Studies and History of Science, University of Wisconsin, Madison.

J. ROWLAND ILLICK
Professor of Geography, Middlebury College, Middlebury, Vt.

RITA J. IMMERMAN
Assistant Professor of Political Science, William Paterson College of New Jersey, Wayne, N.J.

CYNTHIA E. IRVINE
Research Astronomer, Monterey Institute for Research in Astronomy, Monterey, Calif.

DAVID IRWIN
Chairman, Department of History of Art, University of Aberdeen, Old Aberdeen, Scotland.

JOHN B. IRWIN
Former Associate Professor, Kean College of New Jersey, Union, N.J.

MARK A. ISAACS
Landscape Architect, U.S. Department of Housing and Urban Development, Washington, D.C.

REGINALD R. ISAACS
Charles Dyer Norton Professor of Regional Planning, Emeritus, Harvard University, Cambridge, Mass.

DONALD W. IVEY
Professor of Music, University of Kentucky, Lexington.

DONALD JACKSON
Professor Emeritus of History, University of Virginia, Charlottesville.

DAVID MICHAEL JACOBS
Assistant Professor of History, Temple University, Philadelphia.

JAY JACOBS
Food Historian.

DANIEL JACOBSON
Professor of Geography and Education, Adjunct Professor of Anthropology, Michigan State University, East Lansing.

MARTIN JACOBSON
Supervisory Research Chemist, U.S. Department of Agriculture, Beltsville, Md.

IRMA B. JAFFE
Professor of Art History, Fordham University, Bronx, N.Y.

HAROLD L. JAMES
Former Research Geologist, U.S.Geological Survey.

JULES JANICK
Professor of Horticulture, Purdue University, West Lafayette, Ind.

RAYMOND JARVI
Associate Professor of Swedish, North Park College, Chicago.

GRAHAM H. JEFFRIES, M.D.
Professor of Medicine, Pennsylvania State University, University Park.

JOSEPH R. JEHL, JR.
Assistant Director, Hubbs-Sea World Research Institute, San Diego, Calif.

BURGESS H. JENNINGS
Emeritus Professor of Mechanical Engineering, Northwestern University, Evanston, Ill.

R. BRUCE JENNINGS
Assistant Professor of Political Science, Stockton State College, Pomona, N.J.

H. JAMES JENSEN
Professor of English, Indiana University, Bloomington.

WAYBURN S. JETER
Professor and Head, Department of Microbiology, University of Arizona, Tucson.

ROBERT JEWETT
Professor of New Testament Interpretation, Garrett-Evangelica Theological Seminary, Evanston, Ill.

J. MICHAEL JOBANEK
So-Cal Safety Associates, Reston, Va.

ERWIN V. JOHANNINGMEIER
Professor, Historical Foundations of Education, University of South Florida, Tampa.

DONALD C. JOHANSON
Curator of Physical Anthropology, Cleveland Museum of Natural History, Cleveland, Ohio.

T. S. K. JOHANSSON
Professor of Biology, Queens College, City University of New York, Flushing.

BERNARD JOHN
Professor, Department of Population Biology, Australian National University, Canberra.

B. EDGAR JOHNSON
General Secretary, Church of the Nazarene, Kansas City, Mo.

CURTIS D. JOHNSON
Associate Professor, College of Technology, University of Houston, Houston, Tex.

DONALD JOHNSON
Director, Asian Studies, New York University, New York City.

DOUGLAS JOHNSON
Associate Professor of Music, University of Virginia, Charlottesville.

EARL JOHNSON, JR.
Professor of Law, University of Southern California Law Center, Los Angeles.

GARY E. JOHNSON
Associate Professor of Geography, University of North Dakota, Grand Forks.

J. THEODORE JOHNSON, JR.
Professor of French, University of Kansas, Lawrence.

LEONARD R. JOHNSON
Professor of Physiology, University of Texas Medical School, Houston.

RICHARD A. JOHNSON
Professor of English, Mount Holyoke College, South Hadley, Mass.

RONALD D. JOHNSON
Senior Organic Chemist, Eli Lilly and Company, Indianapolis, Ind.

SHERMAN E. JOHNSON
Dean and Professor of New Testament, Emeritus, The Church Divinity School of the Pacific, Berkeley, Calif.

TIMOTHY R. B. JOHNSON, M.D.
Director, Maternal/Fetal Medicine, Johns Hopkins University Hospital, Baltimore, Md.

DONALD H. JOHNSTON
Associate Professor, Graduate School of Journalism, Columbia University, New York City.

PATRICIA A. JOHNSTON
Professor, Department of Classical and Oriental Studies, Brandeis University, Waltham, Mass.

S. PAUL JOHNSTON
Former Director, National Air and Space Museum, Smithsonian Institution, Washington, D.C.

CLIFFORD JOLLY
Professor of Anthropology, New York University, New York City.

DAVID O. JONES, D.V.M.
Professor, Department of Veterinary Preventive Medicine, Ohio State University, Columbus.

LESLIE JONES
Associate Professor of Art History, Trenton State College, Trenton, N.J.

LYLE V. JONES
Vice-Chancellor and Dean of the Graduate School, University of North Carolina, Chapel Hill.

RICHARD C. JONES
Assistant Professor of Geography, University of Texas, San Antonio.

TOM B. JONES
Regents' Professor, Emeritus, University of Minnesota, Minneapolis.

ALAN V. JOPLING
Professor of Geography, University of Toronto, Toronto.

JOHN E. JORDAN
Professor of English, University of California, Berkeley.

TOM JORDAN
Assistant Publisher, *Track & Field News.*

AAGE JØRGENSEN
Adjunkt, Cand. art., Langkær Gymnasium, Mundelstrup, Denmark.

ROBERT A. JOYCE, M.D.
Assistant Professor of Medicine, University of Pittsburgh School of Medicine, Pittsburgh, Pa.

ROBERT W. JUGENHEIMER
Professor of Plant Genetics and Director of Overseas Projects, Emeritus, University of Illinois, Urbana.

SIDNEY R. JUMPER
Professor and Head, Department of Geography, University of Tennessee, Knoxville.

JACOB KABAKOFF
Professor of Hebrew, Lehman College, City University of New York, Bronx.

ADRIENNE L. KAEPPLER
Anthropologist, Bishop Museum, Honolulu, Hawaii.

ALAN L. KAGAN
Associate Professor of Ethnomusicology, University of Minnesota, Minneapolis.

M. P. KAHL
Author of *Wonders of the Stork World.*

PAUL S. KAISER
National Commander, The Salvation Army National Headquarters, New York City.

JESSE G. KALIN
Associate Professor of Philosophy, Vassar College, Poughkeepsie, N.Y.

HAROLD KALTER, M.D.
Professor of Research Pediatrics, College of Medicine, University of Cincinnati, Cincinnati, Ohio.

JONATHAN KAMIN
President and Editor in Chief, Bay Arts Press Service, Oakland, Calif.

MICHAEL KANDEL
Freelance Writer.

JOHN F. KANE
Special Librarian, ALCOA, Alcoa Center, Pa.

WILLIAM B. KANNEL, M.D., M.P.H., F.A.C.P., F.A.C.C.
Director, Framingham Heart Study, N.H.L.B.I., U.S. National Institutes of Health, Framingham, Mass.

BERNARD KAPLAN
Professor of Psychology and Director, Graduate Training Program in Developmental Psychology, Clark University, Worcester, Mass.

MARSHALL H. KAPLAN
Professor of Aerospace Engineering, Pennsylvania State University, University Park.

RONALD A. KAPON
President, Profit Plus Marketing and Merchandising Company, New York City.

STUART A. KARABENICK
Professor of Psychology, Eastern Michigan University, Ypsilanti.

YEHUDA KARMON
Professor of Geography, Hebrew University, Jerusalem, Israel.

NELSON M. KASFIR
Professor of Government, Dartmouth College, Hanover, N.H.

JACK J. KASULIS
Assistant Professor of Business Administration, University of Oklahoma, Norman.

JUDITH A. KATES
Assistant Professor of English and Comparative Literature, Harvard University, Cambridge, Mass.

MICHAEL KATZ
New York Times Sportswriter.

GEORGE B. KAUFFMAN
Professor of Chemistry, California State University, Fresno.

BRUCE E. KAUFMAN
W. T. Beebe Institute of Personnel and Employment Relations, Georgia State University, Atlanta.

BRUCE F. KAWIN
Professor of English and Film Studies, University of Colorado, Boulder.

PAUL A. KAY
Assistant Professor of Geography, University of Utah, Salt Lake City.

JANET KEAR
Assistant Director, Wildfowl Trust, and Curator, Martin Mere, Lancashire, England.

HOWARD CLARK KEE
William Goodwin Aurelio Professor of Biblical Studies, Boston University, Boston.

JOHN KEEGAN
Professor, Royal Military Academy, Sandhurst, England.

ROGER M. KEESING
Professor of Anthropology, Australian National University, Canberra.

NOELLE L. KEHRBERG
Assistant Professor, Foods, Nutrition, and Dietetics, Western Carolina University, Cullowhee, N.C.

FRANK S. KELLAND
Department of Physics/Geoscience, Montclair State College, Upper Montclair, N.J.

MARYLIN C. KELLAND
Department of Economics, Geography, and Management Science, Kean College of New Jersey, Union.

PHILIP C. KELLER
Professor of Chemistry, University of Arizona, Tucson.

ANDREW J. KELLY
Development Director, Circle in the Square, New York City.

LAWRENCE C. KELLY
Professor of History, North Texas State University, Denton.

NORA HICKSON KELLY
Senior Author of *The Royal Canadian Mounted Police: A Century of History.*

JOHN G. KELTON
Assistant Professor, McMaster Medical Centre, Hamilton, Ontario.

FREDERICK G. KEMPIN, JR.
Professor of Legal Studies, The Wharton School, University of Pennsylvania, Philadelphia.

WALTER KENDRICK
Professor of English, Fordham University, New York City.

GEORGE KENNEDY
Paddison Professor of Classics, University of North Carolina, Chapel Hill.

JOHN S. KENNEDY
Professor Emeritus, Imperial College, University of London, London.

RICHARD S. KENNEDY
Professor of English, Temple University, Philadelphia.

HUGH KENNER
Professor of English, Johns Hopkins University, Baltimore, Md.

J. ALISTAIR KERR
Senior Lecturer in Chemistry, The University, Birmingham, England.

K. AUSTIN KERR
Associate Professor of History, Ohio State University, Columbus.

NORMAN S. KERR
Professor of Genetics and Cell Biology, University of Minnesota, Minneapolis.

WILLIAM KESSEN
Eugene Higgins Professor of Psychology and Professor of Pediatrics, Yale University, New Haven, Conn.

RALPH KETCHAM
Professor of American Studies, Syracuse University, Syracuse, N.Y.

WILLIAM C. KETCHUM, JR.
Author, Lecturer, and Teacher, New School for Social Research, Hunter College, New York City.

JULIA KEYDEL
Art Historian and Filmmaker.

NATHAN KEYFITZ
Professor of Sociology and Demography, Harvard University, Cambridge, Mass.

LOUIS KIBLER
Associate Professor of Italian, Wayne State University, Detroit.

ROBERT KIELY
Loker Professor of English and American Literature, Harvard University, Cambridge.

MICHAEL D. KILIAN
Columnist, *Chicago Tribune.*

KENNETH W. KILMER
Executive Project Director, Environmental Assessment Council Inc., New Brunswick, N.J.

ROBERT KIMBROUGH
Professor of English, University of Wisconsin, Madison.

WAYNE R. KIME
Professor, Fairmont State College, Fairmont, W.Va.

PETER J. KING
Associate Professor of History, Carleton University, Ottawa, Ontario.

KEITH KINGBAY
Cycling Activities Manager, Schwinn Bicycle Company, Chicago.

DOUGLAS KINNARD
Professor of Political Science, University of Vermont, Burlington.

E. T. KIRBY
Professor of Theatre, University of Maryland, Baltimore.

F. E. KIRBY
Professor of Music, Lake Forest College, Lake Forest, Ill.

MAX C. KIRKEBERG
Assistant Professor of Geography, San Francisco State University, San Francisco.

EDITH W. KIRSCH
Research Assistant, Institute for Advanced Study, Princeton, N.J.

W. CHANDLER KIRWIN
Professor of Art History, Amherst College, Amherst, Mass.

JOSEPH M. KITAGAWA
Dean of the Divinity School and Professor of History of Religions, University of Chicago, Chicago.

MICHAEL KITSON
Readers in the History of Art, Courtauld Institute of Art, University of London, London.

GARY KLEE
Assistant Professor of Environmental Studies, San Jose State University, San Jose, Calif.

DONALD W. KLEIN
Professor of Political Science, Tufts University, Medford, Mass.

HELEN ALTMAN KLEIN
Associate Professor of Psychology, Wright State University, Dayton, Ohio.

MARCUS KLEIN
Professor of English, State University of New York, Buffalo.

MILTON KLEIN
Electric Power Research Institute, Palo Alto, Calif.

ART KLEINER
Writer for Computer Science Journals.

CHRISTOPHER KLEINHENZ
Associate Professor of Italian, University of Wisconsin, Madison.

E. D. KLEMKE
Professor of Philosophy, Iowa State University, Ames.

JEROME KLINKOWITZ
Professor of English, University of Northern Iowa, Cedar Falls.

ALEXANDER B. KLOTS
Research Associate in Entomology, American Museum of Natural History and Professor of Biology, Emeritus, City College of New York, New York City.

BETTINA L. KNAPP
Professor of Romance Languages and Comparative Literatures, Hunter College and the Graduate Center, City University of New York, New York City.

LAURANCE A. KNECHT
Professor of Chemistry, Marietta College, Marietta, Ohio.

ROBERT J. KNIGHT, JR.
Research Horticulturist, U.S. Department of Agriculture, Miami, Fla.

RODERIC KNIGHT
Assistant Professor of Ethnomusicology, Oberlin College Conservatory of Music, Oberlin, Ohio.

VIRGINIA CURTIN KNIGHT
Contributing Editor, *Current History.*

WILLIAM J. KNOX
Professor of Physics, University of California, Davis, Calif.

RONALD D. KNUTSON
Professor of Agricultural Economics, Texas A&M University, College Station, Tex.

A. ROBERT KOCH
Professor of Agricultural Economics, Cook College, Rutgers University, New Brunswick, N.J.

VIRGINIA R. KOEHLER
Professor of Education, University of Arizona, Tucson.

LOUIS W. KOENIG
Professor of Government, New York University, New York City.

H. G. KOENIGSBERGER
Professor of History, University of London.

GERHARD M. KOEPPEL
Associate Professor of Classical Archaeology, University of North Carolina, Chapel Hill, N.C.

NORETTA KOERTGE
Associate Professor, Department of History and Philosophy of Science, Indiana University, Bloomington, Ind.

BENJAMIN G. KOHL
Professor of History, Vassar College, Poughkeepsie, N.Y.

PHILIP L. KOHL
Professor of Anthropology, Wellesley College, Wellesley, Mass.

ALAN J. KOHN
Professor of Zoology, University of Washington, Seattle.

WALTER B. KOLESNIK
Professor of Education, University of Detroit, Detroit.

WILLEM J. KOLFF, M.D.
Distinguished Professor of Medicine and Surgery, University of Utah, Salt Lake City.

PAUL D. KOMAR
Professor of Oceanography, Oregon State University, Corvallis.

RAMUNAS KONDRATAS
Medical Sciences Division, National Museum of American History, Smithsonian Institution, Washington, D.C.

VICTOR A. KONRAD
Assistant Professor of Geography and Canadian Studies, University of Maine, Orono.

ZDENĚK KOPAL
Professor of Astronomy, University of Manchester, Manchester, England, and Naval Research Laboratory, Washington, D.C.

SHELDON J. KOPPERL
Associate Professor, Grand Valley State Colleges, Allendale, Mich.

JACOB KORG
Professor of English, University of Washington, Seattle.

DAVID H. KORNHAUSER
Professor of Geography, University of Hawaii at Manoa, Honolulu.

L. A. KOSMAN
Professor of Philosophy, Haverford College, Haverford, Pa.

STEPHEN A. KOWALEWSKI
Assistant Professor of Anthropology, University of Georgia, Athens.

ALLAN KOZINN
Music Critic, *New York Times.*

ENNO E. KRAEHE
William W. Corcoran Professor of History, University of Virginia, Charlottesville.

JON KRAUS
Professor of Political Science, State University of New York, Fredonia.

KONRAD B. KRAUSKOPF
Professor of Geochemistry, Emeritus, Stanford University, Stanford, Calif.

JAN F. KREIDER
Director, Joint Center for Energy Management, University of Colorado, Boulder.

EDWARD V. KRICK
Associate Professor of Engineering Science, Lafayette College, Easton, Pa.

M. KRISTIANSEN
P. W. Horn Professor of Electrical Engineering, Texas Tech University, Lubbock.

JAMES KRITZECK
University of Toronto, Toronto.

SAM KUCZUN
Professor, School of Journalism, University of Colorado, Boulder.

ALBERT E. KUDRLE
Director of Public Relations, American Hotel and Motel Association, New York City.

ROBERT G. KULLER
Associate Professor of Mathematics, Northern Illinois University, De Kalb.

BERNHARD KUMMEL
Professor of Geology, Harvard University, Cambridge, Mass.

ARMAND KURIS
Assistant Professor of Biology, University of California, Santa Barbara.

DIANA KURZ
Artist and Former Faculty Member, State University of New York at Stony Brook, Stony Brook.

PATRICIA KUTZNER
Executive Director, World Hunger Education Service, Washington, D.C.

MATTI KUUSI
Professor, Emeritus, University of Helsinki, Helsinki, Finland.

MORT La BRECQUE
Science Writer.

BRUCE La ROSE
Assistant Professor of Geography and Cartography, Pace University, New York City.

DAVID LACHENBRUCH
Editorial Director, *TV Digest.*

DAVID LADD
Former U.S. Register of Copyrights, Washington, D.C.

TAIVO LAEVASTU
National Marine Fisheries Service, Seattle, Wash.

ANGUS LAIDLAW
Writer on Automotive Technology.

LLOYD LAING
Senior Lecturer in Medieval Archaeology, Liverpool University, Liverpool.

KEVIN LAMB
Sports Writer, *Chicago Sun-Times.*

C. C. LAMBERG-KARLOVSKY
Professor of Anthropology and Director of the Peabody Museum, Harvard University, Cambridge, Mass.

ROBERT L. LAMBORN
Executive Director, Council for American Private Education, Washington, D.C.

STEVEN L. LAMY
Associate Professor, School of International Relations, University of Southern California, Los Angeles.

ROBERT GERAN LANDEN
Dean of the College of Liberal Arts and Professor of History, University of Tennessee, Knoxville.

H. C. ROBBINS LANDON
John Bird Professor of Music, University College, Cardiff, Wales.

LARRY N. LANDRUM
Associate Professor of English, Michigan State University, East Lansing.

FERNAND LANDRY
Professor of Physical Education, Université Laval, Québec.

RONALD W. LANGACKER
Professor of Linguistics, University of California, San Diego.

PAUL LANGFORD
Fellow and Tutor in Modern History, Lincoln College, Oxford, England.

WANN LANGSTON, JR.
Professor of Geology and Research Scientist, Texas Memorial Museum, University of Texas, Austin.

STEPHEN LARSON
Astronomer, Lunar and Planetary Laboratory, University of Arizona, Tucson.

MICHAEL C. LATHAM
Professor of International Nutrition, Cornell University, Ithaca, N.Y.

ABRAHIM LAVI
Professor of Engineering, Carnegie-Mellon University, Pittsburgh, Pa.

ROBERT LAWRENCE
Former Artistic Director and Conductor, Friends of French Opera, and Associate Professor of Vocal Studies, Temple University, Philadelphia.

MERLIN P. LAWSON
Associate Professor of Climatology, University of Nebraska, Lincoln.

DONALD L. LAYTON
Professor of History, Indiana State University, Terre Haute.

THOMAS LEABHART
Editor, *Mime Journal* and *Mime, Mask, and Marionette.*

DOUGLAS EDWARD LEACH
Professor of History, Vanderbilt University, Nashville, Tenn.

PETER B. LEAVENS
Associate Professor of Geology, University of Delaware, Newark.

ALAN L. LEBOWITZ
Associate Professor of English, Tufts University, Medford, Mass.

CHARLES F. LECK
New Jersey State Ornithologist, Rutgers University, New Brunswick, N.J.

MICHAEL T. LEDBETTER
Assistant Professor, Department of Geology, University of Georgia, Athens.

JOSEPH LeDOUX
Postdoctoral Research Fellow, National Institute of Health, New York Hospital-Cornell University Medical Center, New York City.

LESLIE W. LEE
Administrative Director, Laboratories, Orlando Regional Medical Center, Orlando, Fla.

MARC LEEPSON
Contributing Editor, *American Politics Magazine.*

GERALD S. LEFEVER, M.D.
Assistant Professor of Anesthesia, University of Pennsylvania School of Medicine, Philadelphia.

WINFRED P. LEHMANN
Ashbel Smith Professor, Linguistics and Germanic Languages, University of Texas, Austin.

STANFORD E. LEHMBERG
Professor of History, University of Minnesota, Minneapolis.

HENRY M. LEICESTER
Emeritus Professor of Biochemistry, University of the Pacific, Stockton, Calif.

THOMAS R. LEINBACH
Associate Professor of Geography, University of Kentucky, Lexington.

HARRIET LEMBECK
Director, Wine/Beverage Program, Forest Hills, N.Y.

REUEL LEMMONS
Editor, *Firm Foundation.*

ROBERT E. LEMON
Department of Biology, McGill University, Montreal.

MARGUERITE R. LERNER, M.D.
Professor of Dermatology, Yale University School of Medicine, New Haven, Conn.

MICHAEL LERNER
Professor of Dermatology, Yale University School of Medicine, New Haven, Conn.

LAURENT LeSAGE
Professor of Romance Languages, Emeritus, Pennsylvania State University, University Park.

DANIEL R. LESNICK
Assistant Professor of History, Hiram College, Hiram, Ohio.

STEPHEN V. LETCHER
Professor of Physics, University of Rhode Island, Kingston.

ROSA MARIA LETTS
Panel Lecturer, Victoria & Albert Museum, London.

A. LEO LEVIN
Director, The Federal Judicial Center, and Professor of Law, University of Pennsylvania, Philadelphia.

GEORGE L. LEVINE
Professor of English, Livingston College, Rutgers University, New Brunswick, N.J.

HERBERT M. LEVINE
Professor of Political Science, University of Southwestern Louisiana, Lafayette.

LOUIS LEVINE
Professor of Biology, City College, City University of New York, New York City.

SANFORD LEVINSON
Professor of Law, University of Texas Law School, Austin.

SAR A. LEVITAN
Research Professor of Economics and Director, Center for Social Policy Studies, George Washington University, Washington, D.C.

MILTON E. LEWINE
Professor of Art History, Columbia University, New York City.

DAVID LEVERING LEWIS
Professor of History, University of the District of Columbia, Washington, D.C.

GEORGE K. LEWIS
Professor of Geography, Boston University, Boston.

JULIAN H. LEWIS
Department of Biology as Applied to Medicine, Middlesex Hospital Medical School, London.

PETER M. H. LEWIS
Aviation Author, Illustrator, and Photographer.

RICHARD S. LEWIS
Freelance Science Writer.

RONALD L. LEWIS
Assistant Professor of Black American Studies, University of Delaware, Newark.

T. G. LEWIS
Professor of Computer Science, Oregon State University, Corvallis.

JAY LEYDA
Gottesman Professor of Cinema Studies, New York University, New York City.

VIOLA G. LEWIS
Instructor in Medical Psychology, The Johns Hopkins University School of Medicine and Hospital, Baltimore, Md.

ILSE LICHTENSTADTER
Department of Near Eastern Languages and Civilizations, Emerita, Harvard University, Cambridge, Mass.

CHARLES T. LICHY
Field Research & Development Specialist, Dow Chemical, USA.

DAVID LIDMAN
Former News Editor and stamp news columnist, *New York Times.*

DAVID S. LIFSON
Professor, Monmouth College, West Long Branch, N.J.

ERIC LINCOLN
Author of *Backyard Games.*

JOHN R. LINDBECK
Professor of Industrial Education, Western Michigan University, Kalamazoo.

JERZY LINDERSKI
Professor of History, University of Oregon, Eugene.

BERNTH LINDFORS
Professor of African and English Literature, University of Texas, Austin.

ROBERT LINDSAY
Brownell-Jarvis Professor of Natural Philosophy and Physics, Trinity College, Hartford, Conn.

M. E. LINES
AT&T Bell Laboratories, Murray Hill, N.J.

HOWARD A. LINK
Curator of Asian Art and Keeper of the Ukiyo-e Center, Honolulu Academy of Arts, Honolulu.

HAROLD A. LINSTONE
University Professor, Portland State University, Portland, Oreg.

STEPHEN J. LIPPARD
Professor of Chemistry, Columbia University, New York City.

SOL LIPTZIN
Professor Emeritus, City University of New York, New York City.

HOWARD LISS
Free-lance Sports Writer.

RAYMOND LISTER
Fellow of Wolfson College, University of Cambridge, and President, Royal Society of Miniature Painters, Sculptors, and Gravers and Chairman of the Board of Governors, Federation of British Artists, Cambridge, England.

MONROE H. LITTLE
Assistant Professor of History, Massachusetts Institute of Technology, Cambridge, Mass.

RICHARD STARK LITTLE
Associate Professor of Geography, West Virginia University, Morgantown.

C. SCOTT LITTLETON
Associate Professor of Anthropology, and Chairman, Department of Sociology and Anthropology, Occidental College, Los Angeles.

JOHN LLOYD
Assistant Professor of Special Education, University of Virginia, Charlottesville.

PHOEBE LLOYD
Graduate Center of the City University of New York, New York City.

JOHN LOBELL
Associate Professor of Architecture, Pratt Institute, Brooklyn, N.Y.

ROBERT J. LOESCHER
Professor and Chairperson, Department of Art History and Criticism, The School of the Art Institute of Chicago.

RICHARD F. LOGAN
Professor of Geography, University of California, Los Angeles.

TOM LOGSDON
Aerospace Engineer, Rockwell International, Satellite Systems Division, Seal Beach, Calif.

FRED E. LOHRER
Librarian, Archbold Biological Station, Lake Placid, Fla.

ANTHONY J. LOMANDO, JR.
Queens College of CUNY, Flushing, and Lamont-Doherty Geological Observatory, Palisades, N.Y.

GLENN LONEY
Professor of Theatre, Graduate Center of the City University of New York, New York City.

CHARLES H. LONG
William Rand Kenan, Jr., Professor of History of Religions, University of North Carolina, Chapel Hill, and Professor of History of Religions, Duke University, Durham, N.C.

ROBERT LONG
Audio-Video Editor, *High Fidelity* magazine.

D. B. LONGMORE, F.R.C.S.
Consultant Physiologist, National Heart Hospital, London.

R. M. LONGYEAR
Professor of Music, University of Kentucky, Lexington.

O. A. LORENZ
Professor of Vegetable Crops, University of California, Davis.

D. J. LOVELL
Professor and Consultant.

MARGARETTA M. LOVELL
Acting Instructor, Department of History of Art, Yale University, New Haven, Conn.

JAMES S. LOVETT
Professor and Associate Head of the Department of Biological Sciences, Purdue University, West Lafayette, Ind.

JOHN LOWRY
Deputy Keeper, Indian Department, Victoria & Albert Museum, London.

STEVEN LUBAR
Department of History, University of Chicago, Chicago.

JOHN C. LUCCHESI
Professor of Zoology and Genetics, University of North Carolina, Chapel Hill.

GEORG LUCK
Professor of Classics, The Johns Hopkins University, Baltimore, Md.

WILLIAM A. LUNK
Exhibit Curator and Associate Director, Exhibit Museum, University of Michigan, Ann Arbor.

GERARDO LUZURIAGA
Associate Professor of Spanish, University of California, Los Angeles.

WILLIAM G. LYCAN
Professor of Philosophy, University of North Carolina, Chapel Hill.

JAMES G. LYDON
Professor of History, Duquesne University, Pittsburgh, Pa.

DOROTHY SIEGERT LYLE
Director of Consumer Relations, International Fabricare Institute, Silver Spring, Md.

DONALD F. LYNCH
Professor of Geography, College of Arts and Sciences, University of Alaska, Fairbanks.

JOHN E. LYNCH
Chairman, Department of Canon Law, Catholic University of America, Washington, D.C.

JOHN MAASS
Information Officer, City of Philadelphia, Philadelphia.

PATRICK D. McANANY
Associate Professor of Criminal Justice, University of Illinois, Chicago.

RICHARD P. McBRIEN
Chairman, Theology Department, University of Notre Dame, Notre Dame, Ind.

JAMES C. McCANN
African Studies Center, Boston University, Boston, Mass.

JEANNE McRAE McCARTHY
Professor of Special Education, University of Arizona, Tucson.

WILLIAM McCARTHY
Associate Professor of English, Iowa State University, Ames.

STEPHEN P. McCARY
Director of Psychological Services, Almeda Clinic, Houston, Tex.

WILLIAM J. McCAULEY
Professor of Biology, University of Arizona, Tucson.

J. FORBES McCLELLAN
Associate Professor of Zoology, Colorado State University, Ft. Collins.

JAMES E. McCLELLAN III
Assistant Professor of the History of Science, Stevens Institute of Technology, Hoboken, N.J.

CAMPBELL R. McCONNELL
Professor of Economics, University of Nebraska, Lincoln.

JON P. McCONNELL
Professor, Washington State University, Pullman.

VIRGINIA F. McCONNELL
Associate Professor, Emeritus, Tulane University, New Orleans, La.

ARTHUR O. McCOUBREY
Associate Director for Measurement Services, National Measurement Laboratory, National Bureau of Standards, Washington, D.C.

JAMES M. McCULLOUGH
Formerly Senior Specialist in Science and Technology, Science Policy Research Division, Congressional Research Service, Library of Congress, Washington, D.C.

GAIL McCUTCHEON
Assistant Professor, School of Education, University of Virginia, Charlottesville.

W. A. McCUTCHEON
Director, Ulster Museum, Belfast, Northern Ireland.

ETTA MacDONALD, M.D.
Associate Professor of Microbiology, University of Texas Medical Branch, Galveston.

FORREST McDONALD
Professor of History, University of Alabama, University.

JOHN E. MacDONALD
Foreign Service Officer (ret.).

GERALD W. McFARLAND
Professor of History, University of Massachusetts, Amherst.

JAMES M. McGLATHERY
Associate Professor of German, University of Illinois, Urbana.

ALICE McGRATH
Consultant, lecturer of self-defense and co-author of *Self-Defense & Assault Prevention for Girls & Women.*

JOHN C. McGREGOR
Professor Emeritus of Anthropology, University of Illinois, Urbana.

WILLIAM J. McGUIRE
Professor of Psychology, Yale University, New Haven, Conn.

THOMAS L. McHANEY
Associate Professor of English, Georgia State University, Atlanta.

RALPH McINERNY
Michael P. Grace Professor of Medieval Studies, and Director, The Medieval Institute, University of Notre Dame, Notre Dame, Ind.

MICHAEL McINTYRE
Professor of Geography, San Jose State University, San Jose, Calif.

F. EUGENE McJUNKIN
Engineer, Environmental Sciences Corp., Chapel Hill, N.C.

GUY W. McKEE
Professor of Agronomy, Pennsylvania State University, University Park.

G. CALVIN MACKENZIE
Assistant Professor of Government, Colby College, Waterville, Maine.

ROSS MACKENZIE
Former Professor of Church History, Union Theological Seminary in Virginia, Richmond.

TOM L. McKNIGHT
Professor of Geography, University of California, Los Angeles.

PETER MACKRIDGE
Lecturer in Modern Greek Language and Literature, University of London, King's College, London.

CHARLES A. McLAUGHLIN
Director of Education and General Curator, Zoological Society of San Diego (San Diego Zoo), San Diego, Calif.

CHARLES MACLEAN
Author of *The Wolf Children.*

DAVID S. McLELLAN
Professor of Political Science, Miami University, Oxford, Ohio.

J. T. McMULLAN
Energy Study Group, New University of Ulster, Coleraine, Northern Ireland.

RICHARD M. McMURRY
Professor of History, Valdosta State College, Valdosta, Ga.

JOHN MACQUARRIE
Lady Margaret Professor of Divinity, University of Oxford, Oxford, England.

EDMUND J. McTERNAN
Professor of Health Sciences and Dean, School of Allied Health Professions, State University of New York, Stony Brook.

JEFFREY McVEY
Department of Chemistry, Princeton University, Princeton, N.J.

EUGENE W. McWHORTER
Engineering Consultant and Writer.

MARGARET McWILLIAMS
Professor, California State University, Los Angeles.

NANCY R. McWILLIAMS
Coadjutant Professor of Psychology, Livingston College, Rutgers University, New Brunswick, N.J.

CHARLES MAECHLING, JR.
Senior Fellow, Carnegie Endowment for International Peace, Washington, D.C.

LOIS N. MAGNER
History Department, Purdue University, West Lafayette, Ind.

MARCIA E. MAGUIRE
Former Professor of Persian, University of Pennsylvania, Philadelphia.

VICTOR H. MAIR
Assistant Professor, University of Pennsylvania, Philadelphia.

MARIA MAKELA
School of the Art Institute of Chicago.

ELLA A. MALIN
Contributing Editor, *The Burns Mantle Theater Yearbook: Best Plays.*

V. STANDISH MALLORY
Professor of Geological Science, University of Washington, Seattle.

WILLIAM P. MALM
Professor of Music, University of Michigan, Ann Arbor.

R. E. MALMSTROM
Assistant Professor, University of Wisconsin, Milwaukee.

JOSEPH L. MALONE
Professor of Linguistics, Barnard College and Columbia University, New York City.

WILLIAM S. MALTBY
Associate Professor, University of Missouri, St. Louis.

LEONARD MALTIN
Member of the Faculty, New School for Social Research, New York City.

BARRY N. MALZBERG
Writer and Critic, Author of *The Engine of the Night: Science Fiction in the Eighties.*

FRANK MANCHEL
Associate Dean, College of Arts and Sciences, University of Vermont, Burlington.

LEWIS MANDELL
Professor of Finance, University of Connecticut, Storrs.

OSCAR MANDEL
Professor, Division of Humanities and Social Sciences, California Institute of Technology, Pasadena.

MICHAEL MANDELBAUM
Research and Editorial Director, The Lehrman Institute, New York City.

JOHN MANDEVILLE
Assistant to the President, American Kennel Club, New York City.

PAUL A. MANKIN
Professor, Department of French and Italian, University of Massachusetts, Amherst.

ALAN MANN
Associate Professor of Anthropology, University of Pennsylvania, Philadelphia.

WILLIAM E. MANN
Professor of Philosophy, University of Vermont, Burlington.

ROBERT S. MANTHY
Professor of Forestry, Michigan State University, East Lansing.

ROGER MANVELL
Visiting Professor of Film, Boston University, Boston.

NINA L. MARABLE
Assistant Professor, Human Nutrition and Foods, Virginia Polytechnic Institute and State University, Blacksburg.

GEORGE E. MARCUS
Professor and Chairman, Department of Anthropology, Rice University, Houston, Tex.

PAUL MARETH
Consultant, AT&T Bell Laboratories, Business Planning, Product Requirements, and Customer Communications Groups in the Interactive Information Systems Department.

ROBERT MARKLEY
Lecturer in English, Vassar College, Poughkeepsie, N.Y.

WILLIAM MARKOWITZ
Adjunct Professor of Physics, Nova University, Dania, Fla.

JONATHAN MARKS
Director of Publications, American Conservatory Theater, San Francisco, Calif.

THERESA MAROUSEK
Managing Editor, American College of Hospital Administrators, Chicago.

BONNIE MARRANCA
Editor, *Performing Arts Journal*.

MICHAEL T. MARSDEN
Associate Professor, Department of Popular Culture, Bowling Green State University, Bowling Green, Ohio.

ROBERT L. MARSHALL
Professor of Music, University of Chicago, Chicago.

ROBERT T. MARSHALL
Professor of Food Science & Nutrition, University of Missouri, Columbia.

ALVIN R. MARTIN
Assistant Professor, University of Texas, San Antonio.

JAY MARTIN
Leo S. Bing Professor of Literature, University of Southern California, Los Angeles.

WILLIAM H. MARTIN
Director, Division of Natural Areas, Eastern Kentucky University, Richmond.

ANDREW MARTINDALE
Professor of Visual Arts, University of East Anglia, Norwich, England.

MARTIN E. MARTY
F. M. Cone Distinguished Service Professor, University of Chicago Divinity School, Chicago.

JOHN D. MARTZ
Professor of Political Science, Pennsylvania State University, University Park.

JAMES M. MASON
Assistant Professor of Pathology, University of Tennessee Center for the HealthSciences, Memphis.

GERALD MAST
Professor of English, University of Chicago, Chicago.

JOHN R. MATHER
Professor, University of Delaware, Newark.

THOMAS G. MATHEWS
Research Professor, University of Puerto Rico, Rio Piedras.

SUSAN MATISOFF
Associate Professor of Japanese, Stanford University, Stanford, Calif.

MYRON MATLAW
Professor of English, Queens College, City University of New York, Flushing.

RALPH E. MATLAW
Professor of Russian and Comparative Literature, University of Chicago, Chicago.

J. H. MATTHEWS
Professor of French, Syracuse University, Syracuse, N.Y.

WILLIAM H. MATTHEWS III
Regent's Professor of Geology, Lamar University, Beaumont, Tex.

THOMAS P. MATTINGLY, M.D.
Department of Ophthalmology, University of Florida, Gainesville.

SAMUEL A. MATZ
Vice-President, Research and Development and Regulatory Affairs, Ovaltine Products, Inc., Villa Park, Ill.

HUNTINGTON MAVOR, M.D.
Associate Professor of Neurology, University of Utah College of Medicine, Salt Lake City.

O. ORLAND MAXFIELD
Professor and Chairperson, Department of Geography, University of Arkansas, Fayetteville.

CHARLES E. MAY
Professor of English, California State University, Long Beach.

GEORGES MAY
Sterling Professor of French, Yale University, New Haven, Conn.

JOHN GUINN MAY
Department of History and Office for History of Science and Technology, University of California, Berkeley.

THOMAS MAYER
Professor of Economics, University of California at Davis, Davis.

THOMAS C. MAYER
Professor of Biology, Rider College, Lawrenceville, N.J.

DONALD N. MAYNARD
Professor of Plant Science, University of Massachusetts, Amherst.

LAURENCE W. MAZZENO, JR.
Retired Supervisory Chemist, Southern Regional Research Center, Agricultural Research Service, U.S. Department of Agriculture.

CHRISTOPHER MEAD
Department of Art History, University of Pennsylvania, Philadelphia.

GORDON P. MEANS
Department of Political Science, McMaster University, Hamilton, Ontario, Canada.

JOHN A. MEARS
Associate Professor of History, Southern Methodist University, Dallas, Tex.

BEATRICE MEDICINE
Anthropologist, University of Wisconsin, Madison.

RUSTEM S. MEDORA
Professor of Pharmacy, University of Montana, Missoula.

HAROLD A. MEEKS
Associate Professor of Geography, University of Vermont, Burlington.

H. MEIJER
Information and Documentation Centre for the Geography of the Netherlands, Utrecht.

R. P. MEIJER
Professor of Dutch Languages and Literature, University of London, London.

JEFFREY L. MEIKLE
Assistant Professor, American Studies and Art History Department, University of Texas at Austin.

GEOFFREY W. MELLORS
Senior Technology Associate, Battery Products Division, Union Carbide Corporation, Parma, Ohio.

BARBARA MELOSH
Curator, Medical Sciences Division, National Museum of American History, Smithsonian Institution, Washington, D.C.

WILLIAM H. MENKE
National Science Foundation Fellow, Lamont Doherty Geological Observatory of Columbia University, Palisades, N.Y.

M. MEO
Department of History, University of California, Berkeley, Calif.

PAUL MERCHANT
Lecturer, Department of English and Comparative Literature, University of Warwick, Coventry, Warwickshire, England.

JOHN C. MERRILL
Professor of Journalism, Emeritus, University of Missouri, Columbia.

RICHARD H. MERRITT
Professor of Horticulture and Dean of Instruction, Cook College, Rutgers University, New Brunswick, N.J.

BRUCE E. MESERVE
Professor of Mathematics, University of Vermont, Burlington.

LISA M. MESSINGER
Curatorial Assistant, Museum of Modern Art, New York City.

DAVID F. METTRICK
Professor and Chairman, Department of Zoology, University of Toronto, Toronto.

S. METZGER
Assistant Vice-President and Chief Scientist, Communications Satellite Corporation, Washington, D.C.

JOHN MEYENDORFF
Professor of Church History and Patristics, St. Vladimir's Orthodox Theological Seminary, and Professor of History, Fordham University, New York City.

ALBERT L. MICHAELS
Associate Professor of History and Director, Council of International Studies, State University of New York, Buffalo.

JOHN T. MICKEL
Curator of Ferns, New York Botanical Garden, Bronx.

PAOLO MIGLIORINI
Professor of Economic Geography, University of Rome, Rome.

DAVID H. MILES
Associate Professor of German, University of Virginia, Charlottesville.

EDWIN A. MILES
Professor of History, University of Houston, Houston, Tex.

ANNE MILLBROOKE
Fellow, Smithsonian Institution, Washington, D.C.

ARTHUR H. MILLER
Director, Institute for Social Research, Center for Political Studies, University of Michigan, Ann Arbor.

DAVID HARRY MILLER
Associate Professor of History, University of Oklahoma, Norman.

DAVID L. MILLER
Feature Editor, *Modern Photography* magazine.

DAVID W. MILLER
Professor of History, Carnegie-Mellon University, Pittsburgh, Pa.

DOUGLAS T. MILLER
Professor of History, Michigan State University, East Lansing.

E. WILLARD MILLER
Associate Dean for Resident Instruction and
Professor of Geography, Pennsylvania State
University, University Park.

EDWIN HAVILAND MILLER
Professor of English, New York University,
New York City.

ELEANOR M. MILLER
Department of Sociology, University of
Wisconsin, Milwaukee.

FORRESTT A. MILLER
Professor of History, Vanderbilt University,
Nashville, Tenn.

HENRY KNIGHT MILLER
Professor of English, Princeton University,
Princeton, N.J.

MARY ELLEN MILLER
Professor, History of Art, Yale University,
New Haven, Conn.

PHOEBE OTTENBERG MILLER
Associate Professor of Comparative Sociology,
University of Puget Sound, Tacoma, Wash.

RICHARD GORDON MILLER
Foresta Institute for Ocean and Mountain
Studies, Carson City, Nev.

ROBERT H. MILLER
Professor of Agronomy, Ohio State University,
Columbus.

ROBERT P. MILLER
Professor of English, Queens College, City
University of New York, Flushing.

ROY ANDREW MILLER
Professor of Asian Languages and Literature,
University of Washington, Seattle.

RICHARD L. MILLETT
Department of Historical Studies, Southern
Illinois University, Edwardsville.

ALARIC MILLINGTON
Lecturer in Mathematics Education, Chelsea
College, University of London, London.

LORUS J. MILNE
Professor of Zoology, University of New
Hampshire, Durham.

MARGERY MILNE
Author and Lecturer, University of New
Hampshire, Durham.

EDWARD J. MILOWICKI
Associate Professor of English, Mills College,
Oakland, Calif.

KIMBALL A. MILTON
Adjunct Assistant Professor of Physics,
University of California, Los Angeles.

FORREST M. MIMS III
Science Writer.

ELLIS D. MINER
Jet Propulsion Laboratory, California Institute
of Technology, Pasadena.

NORMAN MINERS
Political Science Department, University of
Hong Kong.

ELI C. MINKOFF
Associate Professor of Biology, Bates College,
Lewiston, Maine.

CHARLES I. MINOTT
Associate Professor of the History of Art,
University of Pennsylvania, Philadelphia.

RICHARD MINSKY
Founder, Center for Book Arts, New York City.

LEIGH W. MINTZ
Dean of Undergraduate Studies and Professor
of Earth Sciences, California State University,
Hayward.

NANCY MINUGH
Teaching Fellow in Anthropology, University of
Pennsylvania, Philadelphia.

WILLIAM MISHLER
Associate Professor of Scandinavian, University
of Minnesota, Minneapolis.

LEONEL L. MITCHELL
Professor of Liturgies, Seabury-Western
Theological Seminary, Evanston, Ill.

PETER MITCHELL
Recording and Product Design Engineer,
author of articles on audio and video
technology.

CHARLES S. MOFFETT
Associate Curator, European Paintings,
Metropolitan Museum of Art, New York City.

RABINDRA N. MOHAPATRA
Professor of Physics, University of Maryland,
College Park.

CHARLES MOLESWORTH
Professor, Queens College, City University of
New York, Flushing.

JOHN MONEY
Professor of Medical Psychology and Associate
Professor of Pediatrics, The Johns Hopkins
University School of Medicine and Hospital,
Baltimore, Md.

KAREN MONSON
Author and former music critic, *Chicago Daily
News.*

ASHLEY MONTAGU
Former Chairman, Department of Anthropology,
Rutgers University, New Brunswick, N.J.

E. WILLIAM MONTER
Professor of History, Northwestern University,
Evanston, Ill.

DAVID S. MOORE
Professor of Statistics, Purdue University, West
Lafayette, Ind.

HARRY T. MOORE
Research Professor in English, Southern Illinois
University, Carterville.

J. N. MOORE
Professor of Horticulture, University of
Arkansas, Fayetteville.

J. T. MOORE
Professor of Philosophy, Phillips University,
Enid, Okla.

KATHRYN M. MOORE
Professor, Department of Education
Administration, Michigan State University,
East Lansing.

A. LLOYD MOOTE
Professor of History, University of Southern
California, Los Angeles.

MARTA MORELLO-FROSCH
Professor of Latin American Literature,
University of California, Santa Cruz.

LOIS MORAN
Editor, *American Craft.*

LAWRENCE P. MORIN
Assistant Professor of Psychology, Dartmouth
College, Hanover, N.H.

J. H. MORLEY
Director, Royal Pavilion, Art Gallery and
Museums, Brighton, East Sussex, England.

HAROLD J. MOROWITZ
Professor of Biophysics and Biochemistry,
Yale University, New Haven, Conn.

CRAIG MORRIS
Associate Curator, American Museum of
Natural History, New York City.

JOHN W. MORRIS
Professor Emeritus of Geography, University of
Oklahoma, Norman.

ROGER B. MORRISON
Former Research Geologist, U.S. Geological
Survey, and Adjunct Professor, Department of
Geosciences, University of Arizona, Tucson.

THOMAS E. MORRISSEY
Associate Professor of History, State University
College, Fredonia, N.Y.

LESTER R. MORSS
Associate Professor of Chemistry, Rutgers
University, New Brunswick, N.J.

DONALD E. MORTON
Associate Professor of English, Syracuse
University, Syracuse, N.Y.

PHILLIP W. MORTON
Manager, Information Department, Alcoa
Technical Center, ALCOA, Alcoa Center, Pa.

JACOB E. MOSIER
Professor of Veterinary Medicine, Kansas State
University, Manhattan.

VICTOR L. MOTE
Associate Professor of Geography, University of
Houston, Houston, Tex.

ALLEN MOTTERSHEAD
Professor, Physical Science Department,
Cypress College, Cypress, Calif.

BENJAMIN MOULTON
Chairman and Professor, Department of
Geography and Geology, Indiana State
University, Terre Haute.

TIMOTHY L. MOUNTS
Supervisory Research Chemist, Oilseeds Crops
Laboratory, Northern Regional Research
Center, U.S. Department of Agriculture,
Peoria, Ill.

K. E. MOYER
Professor of Psychology, Carnegie-Mellon
University, Pittsburgh, Pa.

CARL R. MUELLER
Associate Professor of Theater Arts, University
of California, Los Angeles.

WILLARD F. MUELLER
Vilas Research Professor, University of
Wisconsin, Madison.

EDWARD J. MULLEN
Professor of Spanish, University of Missouri,
Columbia.

FRANKLIN MULLINAX, M.D.
Professor of Medicine, Medical College of
Virginia, Richmond.

DELMAR C. MULTHAUF
Professor of Geography and Chairman of the
Geography and Geology Department, University
of Wisconsin, Stevens Point.

ALICIA H. MUNNELL
Assistant Vice-President and Economist,
Federal Reserve Bank of Boston, Boston.

PAMELA MUNRO
Associate Professor of Linguistics, University of
California, Los Angeles.

HUGO MUNSTERBERG
Professor Emeritus, New York State University
College at New Paltz.

RHOADS MURPHEY
Professor of Geography, University of Michigan,
Ann Arbor.

JOHN F. MURPHY
Professor of History and Government, U.S.
Coast Guard Academy, New London, Conn.

HAYDN H. MURRAY
Professor of Geology, Indiana University, Bloomington.

RAYMOND L. MURRAY
Professor Emeritus, Department of Nuclear Engineering, North Carolina State University, Raleigh.

JAY C. MUSSER
Owner and General Manager, Jay C. Musser Consulting Chemist, Mount Joy, Pa.

THOMAS A. MUTCH
Associate Administrator, NASA, Washington, D.C.

RODNEY G. MYATT
Assistant Professor of Biology, San Jose State University, San Jose, Calif.

JOEL MYERSON
Professor of English, University of South Carolina, Columbia.

JACK NACHBAR
Associate Professor of Popular Culture, Bowling Green State University, Bowling Green, Ohio.

HARRY S. NACHMAN
Consulting Engineer, H. S. Nachman & Associates, Inc., Chicago.

PAUL S. NADLER
Professor of Business Administration, Rutgers University, New Brunswick, N.J.

RONALD D. NADLER
Developmental Biologist, Yerkes Regional Primate Research Center, Emory University, Atlanta, Ga.

TAKESI NAGATA
Professor, and Director, National Institute of Polar Research, Tokyo.

ANDREW C. NAHM
Professor of History, Western Michigan University, Kalamazoo.

PAUL NASH
Professor and Chairman, Department of Humanistic and Behavioral Studies, Boston University, Boston.

SYDNEY NATHANS
Associate Professor of History, Duke University, Durham, N.C.

MILDRED NAVARETTA
Lecturer, Moorpark College, Moorpark, Calif.

PHILLIP CHIVIGES NAYLOR
Assistant Professor of History, Merrimack College, North Andover, Mass.

JOHN E. NEELY
Professor of Machine Technology, Lane Community College, Eugene, Oreg.

MARK E. NEELY, JR.
Director, Louis A. Warren Lincoln Library and Museum, Fort Wayne, Ind.

LAWRENCE NEES
Assistant Professor of Art History, University of Delaware, Newark.

BRUCE C. NEHRLING
Assistant Professor of Naval Architecture, United States Naval Academy, Annapolis, Md.

J. MEDEDITH NEIL
Arts Writer.

ULRIC NEISSER
Professor of Psychology, Cornell University, Ithaca, N.Y.

JAMES D. NELSON
Professor of Church History, United Theological Seminary, Dayton, Ohio.

MARION JOHN NELSON
Professor of Art History, University of Minnesota, Minneapolis.

ROY PAUL NELSON
Professor of Journalism, University of Oregon, Eugene.

JOHN T. NETTERVILLE
Chairman, Department of Chemistry, David Lipscomb College, Nashville, Tenn.

BRUNO NETTL
Professor of Music and Anthropology, University of Illinois, Urbana.

ROBERT M. NEUMAN
Instructor, School of Art and Art History, University of Iowa, Iowa City.

STEPHANIE G. NEUMAN
Senior Research Scholar, Research Institute on International Change, and Director of Comparative Defense Studies Program, Columbia University, New York City.

ALVIN L. NEUMANN
Professor of Animal Science, Emeritus, University of Illinois, Urbana.

RICHARD MORGAN NEUMANN
Research Scientist, Polymer Science Institute, University of Massachusetts, Amherst.

JACOB NEUSNER
Professor of Religious Studies, The Ungerleider Distinguished Scholar of Judaic Studies, Brown University, Providence, R.I.

ADAM NEVILLE
Principal and Vice-Chancellor, University of Dundee, Dundee, Scotland.

RAY L. NEWBURN, JR.
Member of the Technical Staff, Jet Propulsion Laboratory, California Institute of Technology, Pasadena.

RICHARD S. NEWELL
Professor of History and Asian Studies, University of Northern Iowa, Cedar Falls.

DIKA NEWLIN
Professor of Music, Virginia Commonwealth University, Richmond.

BARBARA NEWMAN
Critic, *Dancemagazine* and *Classical Music Weekly*.

LAWRENCE W. NEWMAN
Assistant Professor, Ohio Wesleyan University, Delaware.

WILLIAM S. NEWMAN
Alumni Distinguished Professor Emeritus of Music, University of North Carolina, Chapel Hill.

BROTHER G. NICHOLAS
Professor of Biology, La Salle College, Philadelphia.

ROBERT L. NICHOLS
Professor Emeritus, Tufts University, Medford, Mass.

NORMAN L. NICHOLSON
Professor of Geography, University of Western Ontario, London.

MALCOLM F. NICOL
Professor of Physical Chemistry, University of California, Los Angeles.

WILLIAM A. NIERING
Professor of Botany, Connecticut College, New London.

DONALD L. NIEWYK
Associate Professor of History, Southern Methodist University, Dallas, Tex.

ELENA O. NIGHTINGALE, M.D.
Carnegie Corporation of New York, Washington, D.C.

DANIEL NOIN
Professor, University of Paris, Paris.

KENNETH P. NOLAN
Attorney, Speiser & Krause, P.C., New York City.

JAMES WM. NOLL
Department of Education Policy and Administration, University of Maryland, College Park.

MARK A. NOLL
Associate Professor of History, Wheaton College, Wheaton, Ill.

R. ÅKE NORBERG
Department of Zoology, University of Göteborg, Göteborg, Sweden.

AUGUSTUS RICHARD NORTON
Associate Professor of Comparative Politics, U.S. Military Academy, West Point, N.Y.

THOMAS E. NORTON
Senior Vice-President, Sotheby Parke Bernet, Inc., New York City.

FREDERICK A. NORWOOD
Professor of History of Christianity, Garrett-Evangelical Theological Seminary, Evanston, Ill.

ROBERT NOVAK
Research Associate, Vector Biology Laboratory, University of Notre Dame, Notre Dame, Ind.

MARTHA CRAVEN NUSSBAUM
Assistant Professor of Philosophy and the Classics, Harvard University, Cambridge, Mass.

MERLE C. NUTT
Professor Emeritus of Engineering Sciences, Arizona State University, Tempe.

JAMES NYBAKKEN
Professor of Biological Sciences, Moss Landing Marine Laboratories, Moss Landing, Calif.

WILLIAM H. NYCE
Associate Professor of Chemistry, University of New Haven, West Haven, Conn.

FRANCIS OAKLEY
President, Williams College, Williamstown, Mass.

ALCESTIS R. OBERG
Author of *Spacefarers of the '80's and '90's*, and, with James E. Oberg, *Pioneering Space* (1986).

JAMES E. OBERG
Author of *Red Star in Orbit* (1981) and *Mission to Mars* (1984).

JOHN J. OBERLE
Chief Chemist, Benjamin Moore & Co., Newark, N.J.

HAROLD A. OBERMAN, M.D.
Professor of Pathology and Head, Section of Clinical Pathology, University of Michigan Medical School, Ann Arbor.

JOSEPH F. O'CALLAGHAN
Professor of History, Fordham University, New York City.

DAVID O'CONNOR
Associate Professor of Egyptology, Associate Curator, Egyptian Section, The University Museum, University of Pennsylvania, Philadelphia.

J. DEAN O'DONNELL, JR.
Associate Professor, Virginia Polytechnic Institute and State University, Blacksburg.

DANIEL OFFER, M.D.
Chairman, Department of Psychiatry, Michael Reese Hospital and Medical Center, Chicago.

JOHN PETER OLESON
Associate Professor, University of Victoria, Victoria, British Columbia.

L. JAY OLIVA
Vice-President for Academic Affairs and Professor of History, New York University, New York City.

CHADWICK OLIVER
Professor of Silviculture, College of Forest Resources, University of Washington, Seattle.

FRANK J. OLIVER
Former Editor, *Electro-Technology* Magazine.

WILL OLIVER
President, Feed-A-Form, Inc., Westwood, Mass.

BERTELL OLLMAN
Professor, Department of Politics, New York University, New York City.

JAMES L. OLSEN
Head, Division of Pharmaceutics, University of North Carolina, Chapel Hill.

LINDA OLSHEIM
Assistant Director, College and Community Relations, Fashion Institute of Technology, New York City.

JOHN W. O'MALLEY
Professor, Weston School of Theology, Cambridge, Mass.

ELLIOTT I. ORGANICK
Professor of Computer Science, University of Utah, Salt Lake City.

LOUIS L. ORLIN
Professor of Ancient Near Eastern History and Literature, University of Michigan, Ann Arbor.

MARTIN ORNE, M.D.
Professor of Psychiatry, Yale University, New Haven, Conn.

NORMAN J. ORNSTEIN
Associate Professor, Department of Politics, Catholic University of America, Washington, D.C.

ROBERT T. ORR
Senior Scientist, California Academy of Sciences, San Francisco.

JAMES M. ORTEGA
Professor and Head, Department of Mathematics, North Carolina State University, Raleigh.

STUART OSKAMP
Professor of Psychology, Claremont Graduate School, Claremont, Calif.

DONALD E. OSTERBROCK
Director and Professor of Astronomy, Lick Observatory, University of California, Santa Cruz.

R. C. OSTLE
Lecturer in Arabic, School of Oriental and African Studies, University of London, London.

JOHN H. OSTROM
Professor of Geology, Yale University, New Haven, Conn.

DONALD K. OURECKY
Associate Professor, Department of Pomology and Viticulture, New York State Experiment Station, Geneva.

ROGER C. OWEN
Professor of Anthropology, Queens College, City University of New York, Flushing.

SUSAN S. OWICKI
Assistant Professor of Electrical Engineering, Stanford University, Stanford, Calif.

DAVID W. OXTOBY
Assistant Professor of Chemistry, University of Chicago, Chicago.

HOWARD OZMON
Professor of Education, Virginia Commonwealth University, Richmond.

SERGIO PACIFICI
Professor of Romance Languages and Comparative Literature, Queens College and Graduate Center, City University of New York, Flushing.

DON. N. PAGE
Assistant Professor, Department of Physics, Pennsylvania State University, University Park.

ELLIS BATTEN PAGE
Professor of Educational Psychology and Research, Duke University, Durham, N.C.

THORNTON PAGE
Research Astrophysicist, NASA Johnson Space Center, Houston, Tex.

LISA L. PAINE
Assistant Professor, Gynecology and Obstetrics, Johns Hopkins University Medical School, Baltimore, Md.

ANGELA JUNG PALANDRI
Professor of Chinese, University of Oregon, Eugene.

DAVID PANKOW
Professor, School of Printing Curator, Melbert B. Cary, Jr., Graphic Arts Collection, Rochester Institute of Technology, Rochester, N.Y.

NICHOLAS C. PANO
Professor of History, Western Illinois University, Macomb.

S. VICTOR PAPACOSMA
Associate Professor of History, Kent State University, Kent, Ohio.

ROBERT J. PARADOWSKI
Assistant Professor of History of Science and Chemistry, Eisenhower College, Seneca Falls, N.Y.

GEORGE PARK
Professor of Anthropology, Memorial University of Newfoundland, Saint John's.

DONN B. PARKER
Senior Management Consultant, SRI International, Menlo Park, Calif.

FRANKLIN PARKER
Distinguished Visiting Professor of Education, Western Carolina University, Cullowhee, N.C.

ROBERT L. PARKER
Professor of Music, University of Miami, Coral Gables, Fla.

SANDY PARKER
Publisher, *Sandy Parker Reports*, and Associate Editor, *Fur Chic* Magazine.

RUSSELL J. PARKINSON
Historian, History and Museums Divisions Headquarters, U.S. Marine Corps, Washington, D.C.

CHARLES PARSONS
Professor of Philosophy, Columbia University, New York City.

MELINDA B. PARSONS
Lecturer, History of Art, Freshman Honors Program, University of Delaware, Newark.

T. R. PARSONS
Professor, Institute of Oceanography, University of British Columbia, Vancouver.

WILLIAM T. PARSONS
Director, Pennsylvania Dutch Studies, and Editor, *Pennsylvania Folklife*, Ursinus College, Collegeville, Pa.

J. FRANCIS PASCHAL
Professor of Law, Duke University, Durham, N.C.

ROBERT PATCH
Instructor in Social Sciences, University of Texas, Dallas.

JAMES T. PATTERSON
Professor of History, Brown University, Providence, R.I.

SAMUEL C. PATTERSON
Professor of Political Science, University of Iowa, Iowa City.

PHIL PATTON
Arts Writer for *Artforum, Art in America, Portfolio*, and other magazines.

W. J. PATTON
Consulting Engineer, author of *Plastics Technology.*

WENDELL K. PATTON
Professor of Zoology, Ohio Wesleyan University, Delaware.

ERICH ROBERT PAUL
Assistant Professor of the History of Science, Dickinson College, Carlisle, Pa.

K. B. PAUL
Assistant Professor, Lincoln University, Jefferson City, Mo.

MATTHEW D. PAUL, M.D.
Attending Staff, Danbury Hospital, Danbury, Conn.; Instructor in Ophthalmology, Columbia-Presbyterian Medical Center, New York City.

ROBERT A. PAUL
Associate Professor, Graduate Institute of the Liberal Arts, Emory University, Atlanta, Ga.

FRANK M. PAULSEN
Professor of English, Kuwait University, Kuwait.

JOHN PAWLIKOWSKI
Professor of Social Ethics, Catholic Theological Union, Chicago.

DAVID L. PAWSON
Curator of Echinoderms, Smithsonian Institution, Washington, D.C.

MAUNG HLA PE
Professor of Physics, Manhattan College, Riverdale, N.Y.

LEONARD A. PEARLMAN
Professor of Music, Director of Orchestras, University of Arizona, Tucson.

NEAL J. PEARSON
Associate Professor of Political Science, Texas Tech University, Lubbock.

WILLIAM S. PECHTER
Author, *Twenty-four Times a Second* and *Movies Plus One.*

MICHAEL J. PELCZAR, JR.
President, Council of Graduate Schools in the United States, Washington, D.C.

SIMON PEPPER
Lecturer in Architecture, University of Liverpool, Liverpool.

DON PERETZ
Professor of Political Science, State University of New York, Binghamton.

ALFRED PERLMUTTER
Professor of Biology, New York University, New York City.

LAURENCE PERRINE
Frensley Professor of English, Southern
Methodist University, Dallas, Tex.

LAWRENCE A. PERVIN
Professor of Psychology, Rutgers University,
New Brunswick, N.J.

JEFFREY L. PETERS, M.D.
Associate Research Professor of Bioengineering
and Assistant Research Professor of Surgery,
University of Utah, Salt Lake City.

IVARS PETERSON
Mathematics and Physics Editor,
Science News.

JOHN MILO PETERSON
Professor of Mathematics, Brigham Young
University, Provo, Utah.

MARTIN SEVERIN PETERSON
Former General Physical Scientist, U.S. Army,
Natick Research and Development Command,
Natick, Mass.

THEODORE PETERSON
Dean, College of Communications, University
of Illinois, Urbana.

PETER L. PETRAKIS
Editor-in-Chief, Life Sciences Editorial Service,
Silver Spring, Md.

TERRY F. PETTIJOHN
Assistant Professor of Psychology, Ohio State
University, Marion.

DAVID E. PETZAL
Managing Editor, *Field & Stream* Magazine.

R. L. PEURIFOY
Author and Consulting Engineer, and former
Professor of Construction Engineering,
Oklahoma State University, Stillwater.

TROY L. PÉWÉ
Professor and Director, Museum of Geology,
Arizona State University, Tempe.

CARL J. PFEIFFER
Division of Veterinary Biology and Clinical
Studies, College of Veterinary Medicine,
Virginia Polytechnic Institute, Blacksburg.

ALLAN R. PHILLIPS
Guest Research Associate, Autonomous
University of Nuevo León, Nuevo León, Mexico.

JANE PHILPOTT
Professor of Botany, Duke University,
Durham, N.C.

MARTIN PIOKER
Professor of Music, Rutgers University, New
Brunswick, N.J.

CALDER M. PICKETT
Professor of Journalism, University of Kansas,
Lawrence.

ROGER A. PIELKE
Department of Atmospheric Science, Colorado
State University, Fort Collins.

ROBERT J. PIERCE
Dance Critic, *Soho Weekly News.*

JOHN F. PILE
Professor of Design, Pratt Institute,
Brooklyn, N.Y.

EDMUND L. PINCOFFS
Professor of Philosophy, University of
Texas, Austin.

DAVID H. PINKNEY
Professor of History, University of
Washington, Seattle.

ROY PINNEY
Former Professor of Journalism, University of
Alaska, Fairbanks.

JOHN F. PIPER, JR.
Associate Professor of History, Lycoming
College, Williamsport, Pa.

LARRY L. PIPPIN
Professor of Political Science, Elbert Covell
College, University of the Pacific,
Forest Grove, Oreg.

HANNA FENICHEL PITKIN
Professor of Political Science, University of
California, Berkeley.

HARVEY PITKIN
Professor of Anthropology, Columbia
University, New York City.

HENRY PITOT, M.D.
Professor of Oncology and Pathology, McArdle
Laboratory for Cancer Research, University of
Wisconsin, Madison.

DAVID J. PITTMAN
Professor and Chairman, Department of
Sociology, Washington University,
Saint Louis, Mo.

ROBERT PLONSEY
Professor and Chairman, Department of
Biomedical Engineering, Case Western Reserve
University, Cleveland, Ohio.

HENRY A. PLOTKIN
Department of Community Affairs,
State of New Jersey.

RITA M. PLOTNICKI
Lecturer, Hunter College, New York City.

E. M. PLUNKETT
Art Historian.

ROBERT PLUTCHIK
Professor of Psychiatry, Albert Einstein College
of Medicine, Bronx, N.Y.

RICHARD POLENBERG
Professor of American History, Cornell
University, Ithaca, N.Y.

ELIZABETH POLLOCK
Former Assistant for Photography, Department
of Prints, Drawings and Photographs,
Philadelphia Museum of Art, Philadelphia.

MARTIN A. POMERANTZ
Director, Bartol Research Foundation of The
Franklin Institute, University of Delaware,
Newark.

GERALD M. POMPER
Chairman and Professor, Department of
Political Science, Rutgers University,
New Brunswick, N.J.

RICHARD H. POPKIN
Professor of Philosophy, Washington
University, Saint Louis, Mo.

JOHN H. PORTER
Author.

DONALD POSNER
Professor of Fine Arts, New York University,
New York City.

STEPHEN E. POSTEN
Project Manager, Environmental Assessment
Council, Inc., New Brunswick, N.J.

KARL H. POTTER
Professor of Philosophy, University of
Washington, Seattle.

LEON B. POULLADA
Professor of Political Science,
Northern Arizona University.

NORMAN J. G. POUNDS
Professor of Geography and History, Indiana
University, Bloomington.

EVAN POWELL
Director, Chestnut Mountain Research Center,
Taylors, S.C. Author of *The Complete Guide to
Home Appliances.*

JAMES M. POWELL
Professor of History, Syracuse University,
Syracuse, N.Y.

ROBERT A. POWERS
Director of Technology, Battery Products
Division, Union Carbide Corporation,
Cleveland, Ohio.

IVAN L. PRESTON
Professor, School of Journalism and Mass
Communication, University of Wisconsin,
Madison.

RICHARD A. PRETO-RODAS
Director, Language Department, University of
South Florida, Tampa.

RONALD T. PRETTY
Editor, *Jane's Weapon Systems.*

KARL H. PRIBRAM
Professor of Neuroscience, Stanford University,
Stanford, Calif.

STEVEN D. PRICE
Editorial Director, *The Whole Horse Catalog,*
New York City.

RICHARD K. PRIEDE
Assistant Professor of English, Virginia
Commonwealth University, Richmond.

WILLIAM H. PRITCHARD
Editorial Board, *Hudson Review,* and Professor
of English, Amherst College, Amherst, Mass.

**ROLAND I. PRITIKIN, M.D., F.A.C.S., F.I.C.S.,
F.R.S.H., F.A.C.N.M.**
Member of the Faculty, Rockford School of
Medicine, University of Illinois
Ophthalmology Section, Rockford, and
Consultant in Ophthalmology, U.S.
Army Health Services Command.

CARROLL PURSELL
Professor of History, University of California,
Santa Barbara.

ELIZABETH PUTZ
Instructor, California State University,
Northridge.

LEWIS PYENSON
Professeur Agrégé, Institut d'histoire et
desociopolitique des sciences, Université
deMontréal, Montreal.

PETER QUENNELL, C.B.E.
Author of *Byron: The Years of Fame, Byronin
Italy, Alexander Pope: The Education of
Genius,* and other works.

QUENTIN W. QUEREAU
Assistant Professor of Music, Case Western
Reserve University, Cleveland, Ohio.

DENNIS E. QUILLEN
Assistant Professor of Geography, Eastern
Kentucky University, Richmond.

PAUL J. QUIRK
Institute of Government and Public Affairs,
University of Illinois, Chicago.

SUZANNE RABITZ
Research Scientist, Exxon Corporation,
Linden, N.J.

RAMASWAMI RADHAKRISHNAN
Associate Professor of Linguistics, The
University of Calgary, Calgary, Alberta.

EUGENE RADWIN
Research Associate, Huron Institute,
Cambridge, Mass.

JOHN B. RAE
Professor of the History of Technology,
Emeritus, Harvey Mudd College,
Claremont, Calif.

MARC RAEFF
Bakhmeteff Professor of Russian Studies,
Columbus University, New York City.

KRISTJAN I. RAGNARSSON, M.D.
Institute of Rehabilitation Medicine, New York
University Medical Center, New York City.

ROBERT J. RAIKOW
Associate Professor of Biological Sciences,
University of Pittsburgh, Pittsburgh, Pa.

O. BERTRAND RAMSAY
Professor of Chemistry, East Michigan
University, Ypsilanti.

HARRY RAND
Chairman, Department of 20th Century
Painting & Sculpture, Smithsonian Institution,
Washington, D.C.

JOHN RANDOLPH
Assistant Professor, Environmental and Urban
Systems, Virginia Polytechnic Institute and
State University, Blacksburg.

JOAN A. RANGE
Associate Professor of Theology, Saint Louis
University, Saint Louis, Mo.

REV. CHARLES W. RANSON
Former Professor of Theology and Ecumenics,
Hartford Seminary Foundation, Hartford, Conn.

CARTER RATCLIFF
Contributing Editor, *Art in America* and
Instructor, School of Visual Arts,
New York City.

HUGH M. RAUP
Charles Bullard Professor of Forestry, Emeritus,
Harvard University, Cambridge.

STEPHEN L. RAWLINS
Research Leader, Physics and Engineering,
U.S. Salinity Laboratory, Riverside, Calif.

PHILIP RAWSON
Curator, Gulbenkian Museum of Oriental Art,
University of Durham, England.

D. MICHAEL RAY
Professor of Geography, Carlton University,
Ottawa, Ontario.

REGINALD LEE REAGAN
Major, U.S. Army (ret.), Biologist and
Virologist, Laboratory of Toxicology, National
Cancer Institute, National Institute of Health,
Bethesda, Md.

GILBERT REANEY
Professor of Music, University of California, Los
Angeles.

MELVIN L. REED, M.D., F.A.C.P.
Associate Director (Education), Comprehensive
Cancer Center of Metropolitan Detroit, and
Associate Professor of Oncology, Wayne State
University School of Medicine, Detroit.

ROBERT REEDER
Associate Professor of Mining Engineering,
Colorado School of Mines, Golden.

ROBERT REGAN
Professor of English, University of
Pennsylvania, Philadelphia.

JOHN B. REHDER
Associate Professor of Geography, University of
Tennessee, Knoxville.

LYNN P. REHM
Professor of Psychology, University of Houston,
Houston, Tex.

JOHN J. REICH
Associate Professor of the Classics, Florida
State University, Tallahassee.

ABIGAIL REIFSNYDER
Writer.

MICHAEL F. REIN, M.D.
Assistant Professor of Medicine, University of
Virginia School of Medicine, Charlottesville.

STEPHEN CHARLES REINGOLD
Research Fellow in Biology, Princeton
University, Princeton, N.J.

JOHN F. REINHARD
Professor of Pharmacology Emeritus,
Massachusetts College of Pharmacy and Allied
Health Sciences, Boston.

JONATHAN REISKIND
Associate Professor of Zoology, University of
Florida, Gainesville.

W. MICHAEL REISMAN
Professor of Law, Yale Law School,
New Haven, Conn.

JOSEPH A. REITER
Assistant Professor of Modern Languages,
Phillips Exeter Academy, Exeter, N.H.

MOSTAFA REJAI
Professor of Political Science, Miami
University, Oxford, Ohio.

FRANKLIN V. RENO
Consultant on Physical Problems.

NICHOLAS RENOUF
Assistant Curator, Yale University Collection of
Musical Instruments, New Haven, Conn.

RICHARD REPHANN
Director, Yale Collection of Musical
Instruments and Associate Professor of
Organology, Yale University, New Haven, Conn.

WALTER REUTHER
Professor of Horticulture, University of
California, Riverside.

EDWARD RICCO
Dance Critic and Writer.

PETER R. RICH
Department of Biochemistry, University of
Cambridge, Cambridge, England.

MARY JO RICHARDSON
Research Assistant, Woods Hole
Oceanographic Institution, Woods Hole, Mass.

JOHN J. RICHETTI
Professor of English, Rutgers University,
New Brunswick, N.J.

TIMOTHY J. RICKARD
Professor of Geography, Central Connecticut
State College, New Britain.

DAVID F. RICKS
Professor of Psychology, University of
Cincinnati, Cincinnati, Ohio.

HERBERT RIEHL
Professor Emeritus, Colorado State University,
Boulder.

RODERICK R. RIEWE
Associate Professor of Biology and Zoology,
University of Manitoba, Winnipeg.

IDA KATHERINE RIGBY
Assistant Professor of Art History, San Diego
State University, San Diego, Calif.

WILLIAM H. RIKER
Wilson Professor of Political Science,
University of Rochester, Rochester, N.Y.

PATRICK RILEY
Professor of Political Science, University of
Wisconsin, Madison.

INGRID RIMA
Professor of Economics, Temple University,
Philadelphia.

BERNARD RIMLAND
Director, Institute for Child Behavior Research,
San Diego, Calif.

JOHN S. RINEHART
Adjoint Professor of Mechanical Engineering,
University of Colorado, Boulder.

ARTHUR J. RIOPELLE
Boyd Professor of Psychology, Louisiana State
University, Baton Rouge.

WALTER W. RISTOW
Formerly Chief, Geography and Map Division,
Library of Congress.

S. A. A. RIZVI
Dept. of Asian Civilizations, Australian National
University, Canberra.

ROBERT A. RIZZA
Assistant Professor of Medicine, Mayo Medical
School, Mayo Foundation, Rochester, Minn.

DAVID C. ROBERTS
Assistant Professor of Chemistry, Rutgers,
The State University of New Jersey,
New Brunswick.

J. J. M. ROBERTS
Associate Professor of Near Eastern Studies,
University of Toronto, Toronto, Ontario.

DONALD ROBERTSON
Professor, History of Art, Newcomb College,
Tulane University, New Orleans, La.

KENNETH C. ROBERTSON
Recording Engineer, CBS/Columbia Records,
New York City.

KENNETH R. ROBERTSON
Curator of the Herbarium, Illinois Natural
History Survey, Urbana.

MARTHA BARTON ROBERTSON
Library Assistant, Latin American Library,
Tulane University, New Orleans, La.

MICHAEL ROBERTSON
Associate Critic, *Dancemagazine.*

FRANKLIN W. ROBINSON
Associate Professor of Art, Williams College,
Williamstown, Mass.

JAMES K. ROBINSON
Professor of English, University of Cincinnati,
Cincinnati, Ohio.

J. LEWIS ROBINSON
Professor of Geography, University of British
Columbia, Vancouver.

JAMES W. ROBINSON
Dean, School of Business, Shippensburg State
College, Shippensburg, Pa.

WILLIAM C. ROBISON
Geographer, former U.S. Army Engineer,
Topographic Laboratories, Fort Belvoir, Va.

HOWARD D. RODEE
Associate Professor in Art History, University of
New Mexico, Albuquerque.

DELMER D. ROGERS
Head, Theory Composition, University of Texas,
Austin.

LT. COL. LANE ROGERS, U.S.M.C.
Assistant Chief Historian, History and
Museums Division, Headquarters, U.S. Marine
Corps, Washington, D.C.

SUSAN D. ROGERS
Drug Information Specialist, Emory University
Hospital, Atlanta, Ga.

JOSEPH A. ROIZEN
President, Telegen, Palo Alto, Calif.

ELDRED ROLFE
Associate Professor of Geography, University of Maine, Farmington.

ROBERT C. ROMANS
Associate Professor of Biology, Bowling Green State University, Bowling Green, Ohio.

WILLIAM D. ROMEY
Professor of Geology, St. Lawrence University, Canton, N.Y.

WILLIAM S. ROMOSER
Professor of Zoology, Ohio University, Athens.

PETER A. RONA
Senior Research Geophysicist, Atlantic Oceanographic and Meteorological Laboratories, Miami, Fla.

GERALD C. ROPER
Professor of Chemistry, Dickinson College, Carlisle, Pa.

STEPHEN C. ROPP
Associate Professor of Government, New Mexico State University, Las Cruces.

M. RICHARD ROSE
President, Alfred University, Alfred, N.Y.

PETER I. ROSE
Sophia Smith Professor of Sociology and Anthropology, Smith College, Northampton, Mass.

ELLIOT A. ROSEN
Professor of History, Rutgers University, Newark, N.J.

LINDA J. ROSEN
Research Scientist, New York State Drug Abuse Commission, New York City.

PETER D. ROSENBERG
Primary Examiner, U.S. Patent & Trademark Office, Washington, D.C.

WILLIAM G. ROSENBERG
Professor of History, University of Michigan, Ann Arbor.

DONALD ROSENTHAL
Curator of Collections, Memorial Art Gallery, University of Rochester, Rochester, N.Y.

ERICH ROSENTHAL
Professor of Sociology, Queens College, City University of New York, Flushing.

JANE ROSENTHAL
Professor, Department of Art History and Archaeology, Columbia University, New York City.

SANDRA B. ROSENTHAL
Professor of Philosophy, Loyola University, New Orleans, La.

PETER J. ROSENWALD
Dance Critic, *Wall Street Journal.*

MARK W. ROSKILL
Professor, History of Modern Art, University of Massachusetts, Amherst.

CHARLES A. ROSS
Professor of Geology, Western Washington University, Bellingham.

JACK E. ROSSMANN
Professor of Psychology, Macalester College, St. Paul, Minn.

ROBERT I. ROTBERG
Academic Vice President for Arts, Sciences and Technology, Tufts University, Medford, Mass.

ANN MACY ROTH
Museum of Fine Arts, Boston.

LELAND M. ROTH
Associate Professor of Art History, University of Oregon, Eugene.

HERBERT H. ROWEN
Professor of History, Rutgers University, New Brunswick, N.J.

A. L. ROWSE
Fellow of the British Academy.

R. R. ROY
Professor of Physics, Arizona State University, Tempe.

MELVIN L. RUBIN, M.D.
Professor of Ophthalmology, University of Florida College of Medicine, Gainesville.

ROBERT L. RUBINSTEIN
Senior Research Anthropologist, Philadelphia Geriatric Center, Philadelphia.

DARNELL RUCKER
Professor of Philosophy, Skidmore College, Saratoga Springs, N.Y.

DONALD L. RUCKNAGEL, M.D.
Professor of Human Genetics, University of Michigan Medical School, Ann Arbor.

RICHARD RUGGLES
Professor of Economics, Yale University, New Haven, Conn.

GEORGE R. RUMNEY
Professor of Geography, University of Connecticut, Storrs.

RICHARD H. RUNSER, M.D.
Department of Clinical Pharmacology, Hoffmann-La Roche, Inc., Nutley, N.J.

ROBERT C. RUNYARD
Technical Writer, Kawasaki Motors Corp., Santa Ana, Calif.

HELEN ROSS RUSSELL
Environmental Education Consultant and Author.

JOHN D. RYDER
Former Professor of Electrical Engineering, Michigan State University, East Lansing.

MENDEL SACHS
Professor of Physics and Astronomy, State University of New York, Buffalo.

RICHARD SAFERSTEIN
Chief Forensic Chemist, New Jersey State Police, Forensic Science Bureau, West Trenton.

EDWARD SAGARIN
Professor of Sociology, City College, City University of New York, New York City.

ARTHUR SAINER
Author of *The Radical Theatre Notebook.*

PETER P. SAKALOWSKY
Associate Professor of Geography, Southern Connecticut State College, New Haven.

ANTHONY J. SALDARINI
Associate Professor of Biblical Studies, Boston College, Chestnut Hill, Mass.

ROGER SALE
Professor of English, University of Washington, Seattle.

HENRY F. SALERNO
Professor of English, State University College, Fredonia, N.Y.

FRANK B. SALISBURY
Professor of Plant Physiology, Utah State University, Logan.

NEIL E. SALISBURY
Professor of Geography, University of Oklahoma, Norman.

J. H. M. SALMON
Goodhart Professor of History, Bryn Mawr College, Bryn Mawr, Pa.

P. B. SALMON
Professor of German, University of Edinburgh, Edinburgh, Scotland.

D. K. SALUNKHE
Professor, Department of Nutrition and Food Sciences, Utah State University, Logan.

DAVID SAMMONS
Assistant Professor of Crop Breeding, Department of Agronomy, University of Maryland, College Park.

WILLIAM F. SANDFORD
Associate Editor, *The Daily Register,* Shrewsbury, N.J.

RICHARD A. SANTER
Professor of Geography, Ferris State College, Big Rapids, Mich.

SOL SAPORTA
Professor of Linguistics, University of Washington, Seattle.

LEON SATKOWSKI
Assistant Professor of Architecture, Syracuse University, Syracuse, N.Y.

A. H. SAXON
Editor, The Shoe String Press, Inc., Hamden, Conn.

NIKOLA B. SCHAHGALDIAN
The Rand Corporation, Santa Monica, Calif.

DOUGLAS P. SCALARD
Major, U.S. Army, Department of History, United States Military Academy, West Point, N.Y.

EDWARD L. SCHAPSMEIER
Professor of History, Illinois State University, Normal.

ELAINE J. SCHECHTER
Department of Anthropology, Columbia University, New York City.

CARL H. SCHEELE
Curator, Division of Community Life, Smithsonian Institution, Washington, D.C.

KARL E. SCHEIBE
Professor of Psychology, Wesleyan University, Middletown, Conn.

MARC N. SCHEINMAN
Assistant Professor of Political Science, Douglass College, Rutgers University, New Brunswick, N.J.

HILBERT SCHENCK
Professor of Mechanical Engineering, University of Rhode Island, Kingston.

JOSEPH SCHERER
Formerly, Professor of Finance, Hofstra University; Economist, Federal Reserve Bank of New York, New York City.

LAWRENCE H. SCHIFFMAN
Associate Professor of Hebrew and Judaic Studies, New York University, New York City.

ALLAN W. SCHINDLER
Associate Professor of Composition, Eastman School of Music, Rochester, N.Y.

JAMES T. SCHLEIFER
Professor of History, College of New Rochelle, New Rochelle, N.Y.

ARTHUR SCHLISSEL
Associate Professor of Mathematics, John Jay College of Criminal Justice, City University of New York, New York City.

RAYMOND H. SCHMANDT
Professor of History, St. Joseph's College, Philadelphia.

FRED SCHNAUE
Director of Public Relations, American Association of Fund-Raising Counsel, New York City.

LAWRENCE J. SCHNEIDERMAN, M.D.
Professor, Department of Community/Family Medicine, University of California Medical School, San Diego.

GARY D. SCHNELL
Associate Professor of Zoology, Curator of Birds, University of Oklahoma, Norman.

C. H. SCHOLZ
Professor of Geology, Columbia University, New York City.

JAMES MORTON SCHOPF
Geologist (ret.), U.S. Geological Survey, Ohio State University, Columbus.

B. CHARLOTTE SCHREIBER
Professor of Geology, Queens College, City University of New York, Flushing, and Lamont-Doherty Geological Observatory, Palisades, N.Y.

CAROL SCHREIBER
Writer for School of the Art Institute of Chicago.

JOANNE SCHREIBER
Columnist, United Media Services, New York City.

ALLAN M. SCHRIER
Professor of Psychology, Brown University, Providence, R.I.

WALTER A. SCHROEDER
Instructor of Geography, University of Missouri, Columbia.

A. F. SCHUCH
Staff Member (ret.), Los Alamos Scientific Laboratory, University of California, Los Alamos, N.Mex.

JEROME L. SCHULLMAN
Professor of Microbiology, Mount Sinai School of Medicine, New York City.

RICHARD EVANS SCHULTES
Paul C. Mangelsdorf Professor of Natural Science and Director, Botanical Museum, Harvard University, Cambridge, Mass.

MAX F. SCHULZ
Professor of English, University of Southern California, Los Angeles.

ERNEST L. SCHUSKY
Professor of Anthropology, Southern Illinois University, Edwardsville.

JOHN A. SCHUSTER
University Assistant Lecturer in History of Science, University of Cambridge, and Director of Studies in History and Philosophy of Science, St. John's College, Cambridge, England.

PETER SCHWAB
Associate Professor of Political Science, State University of New York, Purchase.

BERNARD SCHWARTZ
Edwin D. Webb Professor of Law, New York University School of Law, New York City.

KESSEL SCHWARTZ
Professor of Foreign Languages, University of Miami, Coral Gables, Fla.

MARVIN D. SCHWARTZ
Art Historian.

DAVID J. SCHWENDEMANN
Chief Taxidermist, American Museum of Natural History, New York City.

JOAN M. SCOBEY
Author of *Rugs and Wallhangings*.

DAVID W. SCOTT
Planning Consultant, National Gallery of Art, Washington, D.C.

JAMES W. SCOTT
Chairman, Department of Geography and Regional Planning, and Director, Center for Pacific Northwest Studies, Western Washington University, Bellingham.

JOHN F. SCOTT
Professor of Art History, Rice University, Houston, Tex.

PETER SCOTT
Editor, *The Times Higher Education Supplement*, London.

CAPT. W. F. SEARLE, JR.
U.S. Navy (ret.) and Visiting Professor, Massachusetts Institute of Technology, Cambridge.

MARY ANNE SEDNEY
Associate Professor of Psychology, Providence College, Providence, R.I.

RAYMOND J. SEEGER
National Science Foundation, Retired.

CHARLES SEGAL
Professor of Classics, Brown University, Providence, R.I.

HAROLD B. SEGEL
Professor of Slavic Literatures, Columbia University, New York City.

MITCHELL A. SELIGSON
Assistant Professor of Political Science, University of Arizona, Tucson.

MOSTAFA A. SELIM, M.D.
Department of Obstetrics and Gynecology, Cleveland Metropolitan Hospital, Cleveland, Ohio.

LAWRENCE SENELICK
Associate Professor of Drama, Tufts University, Medford, Mass.

EVERETT E. SENTMAN
President, Sentman Publishing Enterprises, Lake Forest, Ill.

S. PRAKASH SETHI
Professor, Department of Management, Baruch College, City University of New York.

GARY S. SETTLES
Mechanical Engineering Department, The Pennsylvania State University, College Park.

DAVID SEVERN
Technical Information Manager, Amstar Corporation, New York, N.Y.

MARTIN SEYMOUR-SMITH
Formerly Visiting Professor of English, University of Wisconsin, Madison.

THEODORE SHABAD
Editor, *Soviet Geography* Magazine, New York City.

EDGAR F. SHANNON, JR.
Professor of English, University of Virginia, Charlottesville.

LLOYD S. SHAPLEY
Senior Mathematician, Rand Corporation.

DON SHARP
Associate Editor, *Motorboat* Magazine, Boston, Mass.

MITCHELL R. SHARPE
Historian, Alabama Space and Rocket Center, Huntsville, Ala.

MARSHALL S. SHATZ
Professor of History, University of Massachusetts, Boston.

PETER SHAW
Associate Professor, State University of New York, Stony Brook.

STANFORD J. SHAW
Professor of Turkish and Near Eastern History, University of California, Los Angeles.

THURSTAN SHAW
Professor of Archaeology, Cambridge University, Cambridge, England.

RONALD C. SHECK
Associate Professor of Geography, New Mexico State University, Las Cruces.

J. A. SHELLENBERGER
Distinguished Professor of Grain Science and Industries, Kansas State University, Manhattan.

LILLIAN OVERLAND SHEPS
Botanical Consultant, Scientific Engineering Systems, Inc., Reno, Nev.

ROBERT E. SHERIFF
Senior Vice-President, Seiscom Delta Inc., Houston, Tex.

S. SAMUEL SHERMIS
Professor, School of Education, Purdue University, West Lafayette, Ind.

NORMAN SHERRY
Professor of English Literature, University of Lancaster, Lancaster, England.

IRA M. SHESKIN
Assistant Professor of Geography, University of Miami, Miami, Fla.

JAMES H. SHIDELER
Professor of History Emeritus, University of California, Davis.

JOHN A. SHIMER
Professor of Geology (ret.), Brooklyn College, Brooklyn, N.Y.

SIR HUBERT SHIRLEY-SMITH, C.B.E.
Past President, Institution of Civil Engineers, Consultant to W. V. Zinn and Associates, Kent, England.

GERALD SHKLAR, D.D.S.
Charles A. Brackett, Professor of Oral Pathology, Harvard School of Dental Medicine, Cambridge, Mass.

B. M. SHMAVONIAN
Professor and Chief of Medical Psychology and Psychophysiology, Temple University Medical School, Philadelphia.

ROBERT SHOGAN
National Political Correspondent, *Los Angeles Times*.

DIANA SHOLTZ
Faculty, Massachusetts School of Professional Psychology, Newton.

A. H. SHORT
Senior Lecturer of Physiology and Pharmacology, University of Nottingham Medical School, Nottingham, England.

JAMES R. SHORTRIDGE
Associate Professor of Geography, University of Kansas, Lawrence.

WILLIAM R. SIEBENSCHUH
Assistant Professor of English, Case Western Reserve University, Cleveland, Ohio.

LEWIS H. SIEGELBAUM
Professor of History, Michigan State University,
East Lansing.

JOAN C. SIEGFRIED
Associate Professor of Art History, Skidmore
College, Saratoga Springs, N.Y.

JAY A. SIGLER
Professor of Political Science, Rutgers
University, New Brunswick, N.J.

ROBERT H. SILLIMAN
Associate Professor of History, Emory
University, Atlanta, Ga.

BURR A. SILVER
Professor of Geology and Geophysics,
University of Oklahoma, Norman.

GEORGE A. SILVER, M.D.
Emeritus Professor of Public Health, Yale
University School of Medicine,
New Haven, Conn.

LARRY A. SILVER
Assistant Professor of Art History, University of
California, Berkeley.

PHILIP W. SILVER
Professor of Spanish, Columbia University,
New York City.

JEAN SILVERMAN
Archaeological Institute of America, New York
Society, New York City.

VIRGINIA B. SILVERSTEIN
Translator and Author.

DENNIS SIMANAITIS
Engineering Editor, *Road and Track*, Newport
Beach, Calif.

N. W. SIMMONDS
Professor, School of Agriculture, Edinburgh
University, Edinburgh, Scotland.

EDWIN H. SIMMONS
Brigadier General, U.S. Marine Corps (ret.),
Director of Marine Corps History and Museums.

HAROLD J. SIMON, M.D.
Professor of Community Medicine and
Associate Dean, School of Medicine, University
of California, San Diego.

ANDREW SINCLAIR
Author of *Jack: A Biography of Jack London.*

MARCUS G. SINGER
Professor of Philosophy, University of
Wisconsin, Madison.

DONALD B. SINIFF
Professor of Ecology and Behavioral Biology,
University of Minnesota, Minneapolis.

GUY SIRCELLO
Professor of Philosophy, University of
California, Irvine.

HARVARD SITKOFF
Professor of History, University of New
Hampshire, Durham.

MARGARET W. SKINNER
Washington University School of Medicine,
St. Louis, Mo.

BARRY F. SKOFF
Clinical Director, Medical Education Evaluation
Center, North Shore Children's Hospital,
Salem, Mass.

ROBERT C. SLATER
Professor and Director, Department of Mortuary
Science, University of Minnesota, Minneapolis.

ELIZABETH M. SLAYTER
Former Assistant Professor of Biology and
Biochemistry, Brandeis University,
Waltham, Mass.

BERNICE SLOTE
Professor of English, University of Nebraska,
Lincoln.

DONALD SMALLEY
Professor Emeritus, University of Illinois,
Urbana-Champaign, Urbana.

LARRY SMARR
Associate Professor of Astronomy, University of
Illinois, Champaign-Urbana.

GEORGE M. SMERK
Professor of Transportation, School of
Business, Indiana University, Bloomington.

ALLEN R. SMITH
Assistant Professor of Geography, Central
Connecticut State College, New Britain.

CHARLES D. SMITH
Professor of History, San Diego State
University, San Diego, Calif.

CHARLES E. SMITH
Professor of Mechanical Engineering, Oregon
State University, Corvallis.

C. RAY SMITH
Architecture Critic, Historian, and Author,
*Supermannerism: New Attitudes in Post-
Modern Architecture.*

DAVID S. SMITH
Assistant Professor of Anesthesia, University of
Pennsylvania School of Medicine, Philadelphia.

ELWYN A. SMITH
Pastor, Garden Crest United Presbyterian
Church, Saint Petersburg, Fla.

J. D. SMITH
Professor of Genetics, Plant Sciences
Department, Texas A&M University,
College Station.

JOE K. SMITH
Associate Professor of Mathematics, Northern
Kentucky University, Highland Heights.

P. M. SMITH
Lecturer in Botany, University of Edinburgh,
Edinburgh, Scotland.

RICHARD K. SMITH
Aero Historian.

ROBERT SMITH
Associate Professor of Entomology, University
of Arizona, Tucson.

ROGER S. U. SMITH
Assistant Professor of Geology, University of
Houston, Houston, Tex.

RONALD C. SMITH
Southern Alberta Institute of Technology,
Calgary.

THOMAS M. SMITH
Professor of the History of Science, University
of Oklahoma, Norman.

WARREN THOMAS SMITH
Professor of Church History, The
Interdenominational Theological Center,
Atlanta, Ga.

WHITNEY SMITH
Executive Director, Flag Research Center,
Winchester, Mass.

HOWARD E. SMITHER
Professor of Music, Director of Graduate
Studies in Music, University of North Carolina
at Chapel Hill, Chapel Hill.

JAMES N. SNADEN
Department of Geography, Central Connecticut
State College, New Britain.

JOHAN P. SNAPPER
Queen Beatrix Professor of German and Dutch,
University of California, Berkeley.

IAN N. SNEDDON
Professor, University of Glasgow,
Glasgow, Scotland.

DANIEL C. SNELL
Associate Professor of History, University of
Oklahoma, Norman.

LOUIS L. SNYDER
Professor of History, City College, City
University of New York, New York City.

DOROTHY D. SOGN, M.D.
National Institutes of Health.

R. S. SOHAL
Associate Professor of Biology, Southern
Methodist University, Dallas, Tex.

THOMAS W. SOKOLOWSKI
The Institute of Fine Arts, Rome.

RALPH S. SOLECKI
Professor of Anthropology, Columbia
University, New York City.

BRUCE B. SOLNICK
Associate Professor of History, State University
of New York, Albany.

ROBERT C. SOLOMON
Professor of Philosophy, University of Texas,
Austin.

LAWRENCE M. SOMMERS
Professor of Geography, Michigan State
University, East Lansing.

WALDO SOMMERS
Professor Emeritus of Public Administration,
George Washington University,
Washington, D.C.

MARIAN SOTSKY
Reading Specialist, Enlarged City School
District of Middletown, N.Y.

DONALD SOUTHGATE
Reader in Modern Political and Constitutional
History, University of Dundee, Dundee,
Scotland.

BRIAN SOUTHWORTH
Head of Publications Group, European
Organization for Nuclear Research.

SUZANNE SPAIN
Assistant for Planning and Institutional
Research, Bryn Mawr College, Bryn Mawr, Pa.,
and Assistant Professor, Temple University,
Philadelphia.

ROBERT D. SPARKS, M.D.
Program Director, W. K. Kellogg Foundation,
Battle Creek, Mich.

EUGENE SPAZIANI
Professor of Zoology, University of Iowa,
Iowa City.

STUART M. SPEISER
Attorney, Speiser, Krause and Madole,
New York City.

NORMAN SPERLING
Assistant Editor, *Sky & Telescope* Magazine.

KERANO J. SPERRY
Department of Communications, American
College of Radiology, Reston, Va.

LEWIS W. SPITZ
William R. Kenan Professor of History,
Stanford University, Stanford, Calif.

BERNARD SPODEK
Professor of Early Childhood Education,
University of Illinois, Urbana-Champaign,
Urbana.

BRIAN SPOONER
Associate Professor of Anthropology, University
of Pennsylvania, Philadelphia.

FRANK G. SPREADBURY
Senior Member, The Institute of Electrical and Electronic Engineers, and Associate of the London College of Music, Paddington College, London.

SUSAN JAY SPUNGIN
National Consultant in Education, American Foundation for the Blind, New York City.

STEPHEN H. SPURR
Professor of Public Affairs, University of Texas, Austin.

JOHN F. STACKS
Correspondent, *Time* Magazine.

RALPH W. STACY
Research Scientist, U.S. Environmental Protection Agency.

WILLIAM J. STADELMAN
Professor of Animal Sciences, Purdue University, West Lafayette, Ind.

HILARY STANDING
School of African and Asian Studies, University of Sussex, Sussex, England.

GORDON J. STANG
Editor, *Tuesday* Magazine.

GEORGE F. G. STANLEY
Emeritus Professor of Canadian Studies, Mount Allison University, Sackville, New Brunswick.

THEODORE H. STANLEY, M.D.
Professor of Anesthesiology, Surgery, University of Utah Medical Center, Salt Lake City.

P. RICHARD STANLEY-BAKER
Assistant Professor of Art History, University of Victoria, Victoria, British Columbia.

C. WOODRUFF STARKWEATHER
Associate Professor of Speech, Temple University, Philadelphia.

ORESTES N. STAVROUDIS
Professor, Optical Science Center, University of Arizona, Tucson.

JOHN MONTAGUE STEADMAN
Professor of Law, Georgetown University, Washington, D.C.

ROBERT J. STEAMER
Vice Chancellor for Academic Affairs and Provost, University of Massachusetts, Boston.

COLIN STEELE
Deputy University Librarian, Australian National University, Canberra.

MERLE C. STEELMAN III
Instructor In Psychology, University of Tennessee, Knoxville.

WILLIAM C. STEERE
President Emeritus, New York Botanical Garden, Bronx.

J. EDWARD DE STEIGUER
U.S. Forest Service, Research Triangle Park, N.C.

HARRY L. STEIN, M.D.
Director, Department of Radiology, North Shore University Hospital-Cornell University Medical College, Manhasset, N.Y.

CARLENE E. STEPHENS
Museum Specialist, National Museum of History and Technology, Smithsonian Institution, Washington, D.C.

ROBERT M. STERN
Professor of Economics and Public Policy, University of Michigan, Ann Arbor.

DENIS W. STEVENS
President & Artistic Director, Accademia Monteverdiana Inc., Santa Barbara, Calif.

DAVID B. STEWART
Chief, Branch of Experimental Geochemistry and Mineralogy, U.S. Geological Survey.

JAMES BREWER STEWART
Professor of History, Macalester College, Saint Paul, Minn.

KENNETH M. STEWART
Professor of Anthropology, Arizona State University, Tempe.

PHYLLIS L. STEWART
Chairperson, Department of Sociology, George Washington University, Washington, D.C.

R. L. STIRRAT
School of African and Asian Studies, University of Sussex, Sussex, England.

NOEL STOCK
Professor of English, University of Toledo, Toledo, Ohio.

ROBERT P. STOCKWELL
Professor of Linguistics, University of California, Los Angeles.

ELLWYN R. STODDARD
Professor of Sociology and Anthropology, University of Texas, El Paso.

JOHN G. STOESSINGER
Professor of Political Science, Hunter College, City University of New York, New York City.

ROBERT D. STOLOROW
Associate Professor of Psychology, Yeshiva University, New York City.

JOYCE HILL STONER
Paintings Conservator, Winterthur Museum, Winterthur, Del.

WILLIAM B. STOREY
Professor Emeritus of Horticulture, University of California, Riverside.

JOHN F. STOVER
Emeritus Professor of History, Purdue University, Lafayette, Ind.

KAJ A. STRAND
Former Scientific Director, U.S. Naval Observatory, Washington, D.C.

LANCE STRATE
Professor of Communications, Fordham University, Bronx, N.Y.

HERBERT L. STRAUSS
Professor of Chemistry, University of California, Berkeley.

MICHAEL STRAUSS
Sportswriter, *New York Times*.

ARVAL L. STREADBECK
Professor of German, University of Utah, Salt Lake City.

ROBERT E. STREET
Professor of Aeronautics and Astronautics, University of Washington, Seattle.

ALAN M. STRIZAK
Medical Director, STAAR Institute, Fountain Valley Regional Hospital and Medical Center, Fountain Valley, Calif.

JOHN S. STRONG
Lecturer in History of Religions, University of Chicago, Chicago.

STERLING STUCKEY
Professor of History, Northwestern University, Evanston, Ill.

JEFFREY L. STURCHIO
Lecturer in History and Sociology of Science, University of Pennsylvania, Philadelphia.

CHARLES H. STYER
Department of Botany, University of Maryland, College Park.

LELI SUDLER
Assistant to the Chairman, Boston Architectural Center, Boston.

ALAN SUGARMAN
Assistant Professor of Psychiatry, Yale University, New Haven, Conn.

EDWARD J. SULLIVAN
Instructor of Art History, New York University, New York City.

JOSEPH H. SUMMERS
Professor of English, University of Rochester, Rochester, N.Y.

W. F. SUMMERS
Professor, Memorial University of Newfoundland, St. John's.

ERIC J. SUNDQUIST
Assistant Professor of English, The Johns Hopkins University, Baltimore, Md.

RONALD GRIGOR SUNY
Alex Manoogian Professor of Modern Armenian History, University of Michigan, Ann Arbor.

CHARLES SÜSSKIND
Professor of Engineering, University of California, Berkeley.

HERBERT L. SUSSMAN
Associate Professor of English, Northeastern University, Boston.

GEORGE P. SUTTON
Deputy Program Leader, University of California, Livermore.

MYRON AND ANN SUTTON
Authors of *Forests of the World* and *Wild Shores*.

B. SUTTON-SMITH
Professor of Education and of Folklore, University of Pennsylvania, Graduate School of Education, Philadelphia.

ROBERT SWANSON
Senior Scientist, Kodak Research Labs, San Diego, Calif.

CLIFFORD E. SWARTZ
Professor of Physics, State University of New York, Stony Brook.

CAMM C. SWIFT
Associate Curator of Fishes, Natural History Museum of Los Angeles County, Los Angeles.

THOMAS L. SWIHART
Professor of Astronomy, University of Arizona, Tucson.

RICHARD SWITZER
Dean of Humanities, California State College, San Bernardino.

M. J. SYDENHAM
Professor of History, Carleton University, Ottawa.

CURT SYLVESTER
Sports Writer, *Detroit Free Press*.

R. D. SYLVESTER
Professor of Russian, Colgate University, Hamilton, N.Y.

EDWARD TABORSKY
Professor of Government, University of Texas, Austin.

TIMOTHY TACKETT
Assistant Professor, Marquette University, Milwaukee, Wis.

LEE M. TALBOT
Fellow, World Resources Institute and Environment and Policy Institute, Washington, D.C.

JOHN L. TANCOCK
Vice-President, Sotheby Parke-Bernet, New York City.

E. J. TAPP
Associate Professor, University of New England, New South Wales, Australia.

RAYMOND TARAS
Hoover Institution, Stanford University, Stanford, Calif.

DAVID TATHAM
Professor of Fine Arts, Syracuse University, Syracuse, N.Y.

VALÉNTIN TATRANSKY
Art Critic and Historian.

IAN TATTERSALL
Associate Curator, American Museum of Natural History, New York City.

M. J. TAUSSIG
Principal Scientific Officer, Arc Institute of Animal Physiology, Cambridge, England.

MARGARET C. TAVOLGA
Professor Emeritus of Biology, Fairleigh Dickinson University, Teaneck, N.J., and Research Associate, Department of Animal Behavior, American Museum of Natural History, New York City.

WILLIAM N. TAVOLGA
Senior Research Associate, Mote Marine Laboratory, Sarasota, Fla., and Professor Emeritus of Biology and Psychology, City University of New York, New York City.

SANDRA C. TAYLOR
Professor of History, University of Utah, Salt Lake City.

RUTH TEETER
Associate Professor, Center for Youth Development and Research, University of Minnesota, Saint Paul.

BRUCE TEGNER
Author of *Bruce Tegner's Complete Book of Self-Defense, . . . Karate, and . . . Judo.*

STANLEY A. TEMPLE
Beers-Bascow Professor of Conservation, Department of Wildlife Ecology, University of Wisconsin, Madison.

WERNER H. TERJUNG
Professor, University of California, Los Angeles.

VINCENT TERRACE
Author of *Complete Encyclopedia of Television Programs.*

VICTOR TERRAS
Professor of Slavic Languages, Brown University, Providence, R.I.

ALBERT TEZLA
Professor of English, University of Minnesota, Duluth.

MICHAEL L. THALLER
Associate Professor of Geography, Carroll College, Waukesha, Wis.

H. S. THAYER
Professor of Philosophy, City College, City University of New York, New York City.

ERNST T. THEIMER
Consultant, International Flavors and Fragrances, Inc.

KENNETH F. THIBODEAU
Archivist, National Archives.

JOHN W. THIERET
Professor of Botany, Northern Kentucky University, Highland Heights.

ALAN G. THOMAS
Antiquarian Bookseller, London.

HARFORD THOMAS
Journalist, Formerly Deputy Editor, *The Guardian,* London.

VALERIE THOMAS
Research Associate, Center for Energy and Environmental Studies, Princeton University, Princeton, N.J.

F. J. THORPE
Chief, History Division, National Museum of Man, National Museums of Canada.

LASZLO TIKOS
Professor of Russian Language and Literature, University of Massachusetts, Amherst.

LOUISA SHEN TING
Lecturer in Art, State University of New York, Stony Brook.

OSWALD TIPPO
Commonwealth Professor of Botany, University of Massachusetts, Amherst.

CALDWELL TITCOMB
Professor of Music, Brandeis University, Waltham, Mass.

TOBI TOBIAS
Associate Editor, *Dancemagazine.*

RICHARD J. TOBIN
Department of Political Science, State University of New York, Buffalo.

JANET M. TODD
Associate Professor of English, Douglass College, Rutgers University, New Brunswick, N.J.

NEIL B. TODD
Adjunct Professor of Biology, Boston University, Boston.

MAJ. GEN. GEORGE E. TOMLINSON
Former Chief Engineer, Federal Power Commission.

MARTIN TORODASH
Professor of History, Fairleigh Dickinson University, Teaneck, N.J.

DAVID W. TOWLE
Associate Professor of Biology, University of Richmond, Richmond, Va.

TERRENCE J. TOY
Assistant Professor of Geography, University of Denver, Denver, Colo.

CARL J. TRACIE
Associate Professor of Geography, University of Saskatchewan, Saskatoon.

STANLEY W. TRIMBLE
Assistant Professor of Geography, University of California, Los Angeles.

CHARLES L. TROWBRIDGE
Senior Vice-President and Chief Actuary, Bankers Life Company, Des Moines, Iowa.

CHRISTOPHER G. TRUMP
Assistant Dean, Columbia University Graduate School of Journalism, New York City.

JONATHAN N. TUBB
Research Assistant, British Museum, London.

ARTHUR O. TUCKER
Research Associate, Delaware State College, Dover.

DAVID TUDOR
Veterinarian, Cranbury, N.J.

ELEANOR TUFTS
Professor of Art History, Southern Methodist University, Dallas, Tex.

JEAN MACINTOSH TURFA
Former Visiting Assistant Professor of Classical Studies, Loyola University of Chicago, Chicago.

LYNN TURGEON
Professor of Economics, Hofstra University, Hempstead, N.Y.

JOHN TURKEVICH
Eugene Higgins Professor Emeritus of Chemistry, Princeton University, Princeton, N.J.

MARTIN TURNELL
Fellow of the Royal Society of Literature, London.

ARTHUR CAMPBELL TURNER
Professor of Political Science, University of California, Riverside, Calif.

EUGENE F. TUTT
Eugene F. Tutt and Associates, Architects.

AMOS TVERSKY
Professor of Psychology, Stanford University, Stanford, Calif.

DAVID TWEEDIE
Associate Professor and Chairman of the Department of Education, Gallaudet College, Washington, D.C.

DOROTHY TWOHIG
Associate Editor, *The Papers of George Washington,* University of Virginia, Charlottesville.

LOUISE B. TYRER, M.D.
Vice-President for Medical Affairs, Planned Parenthood Federation of America, New York City.

JOHN TYTELL
Professor of English, Queens College, City University of New York, Flushing.

CRAIG D. UCHIDA
Assistant Professor, Institute of Criminal Justice and Criminology, University of Maryland, College Park.

NATALIE W. UHL
Senior Research Associate, L. H. Bailey Hortorium, Cornell University, Ithaca, N.Y.

RICHARD ULACK
Associate Professor of Geography, University of Kentucky, Lexington.

RICHARD H. ULLMAN
Professor of International Affairs, Princeton University, Princeton, N.J.

S. SIDNEY ULMER
Alumni Professor, University of Kentucky, Lexington.

HOMER ULRICH
Professor Emeritus, University of Maryland, College Park.

SANFORD J. UNGAR
Managing Editor, *Foreign Policy.*

PAUL E. UTGOFF
Computer and Information Science Department, University of Massachusetts, Amherst.

ROBERT M. UTLEY
Deputy Executive Director, Advisory Council on Historic Preservation.

PETER UTZ
Media Director, County College of Morris, Randolph, N.J.

GODFREY UZOIGWE
Professor and Head of Department of History, University of Calabar, Calabar, Nigeria.

ALBERT VALDMAN
Professor of French, Italian, and Linguistics, Indiana University, Bloomington.

ELIZABETH KRIDL VALKENIER
Senior Fellow, Russian Institute, Columbia University, New York City.

PIERRE L. van den BERGHE
Professor of Sociology and Anthropology, University of Washington, Seattle.

WILLEM van der BIJL
Associate Professor of Meteorology, Naval Postgraduate School, Monterey, Calif.

FRANK E. VANDIVER
Provost, Vice-President, and Harrison Masterson, Jr., Professor of History, Rice University, Houston, Tex.

PIETER van ROYEN
Chairman, Department of Botany, B. P. Bishop Museum, Honolulu.

LAWRENCE H. Van VLACK
Professor of Materials Engineering, University of Michigan, Ann Arbor.

ANN LORENZ Van ZANTEN
Architectural Historian.

AGNES HUSZAR VARDY
Associate Professor, Robert Morris College, Pittsburgh, Pa.

S. B. VARDY
Professor of East European History, Duquesne University, Pittsburgh, Pa.

V. STANLEY VARDYS
Professor of Political Science, University of Oklahoma, Norman.

DAVID VAUGHAN
Archivist, Cunningham Dance Foundation, Contributing Editor, *Ballet Review*, and Associate Critic, *Dancemagazine*.

DAME JANET VAUGHAN, M.D., F.R.C.P.
Bone Research Laboratory, Nuffield Orthopaedic Hospital, Oxford, England.

TERRY A. VAUGHAN
Professor of Zoology, Northern Arizona University, Flagstaff.

MILOS VELIMIROVÍC
Professor of Music, University of Virginia, Charlottesville.

CHARLES VERLINDEN
Professor Emeritus, State University of Ghent, Royal Belgian Academy, Brussels.

PHILIP E. VERNON
Professor of Educational Psychology, University of Calgary, Calgary, Alberta.

LAURENCE VEYSEY
Professor of History, University of California, Santa Cruz.

WALTER N. VICKERY
Professor of Russian Literature, University of North Carolina, Chapel Hill.

FRANÇOIS C. D. VIGIER
Professor of City Planning and Urban Design, Harvard University, Cambridge, Mass.

GENNARO F. VITO
Professor, School of Justice Administration, University of Louisville, Louisville, Ky.

GRIZEL C. VINES
Art Historian.

MARK S. VOGEL, O.D.
Clinical Instructor, State College of Optometry, State University of New York, Stony Brook.

PHILIP E. VOGEL
Chairman, and Professor, Department of Geography, University of Nebraska, Omaha.

FRED W. VOGET
Professor of Anthropology, Southern Illinois University, Edwardsville.

IVAN VOLGYES
Professor of Political Science, University of Nebraska, Lincoln.

JOHN O. VOLL
Associate Professor in History, University of New Hampshire, Durham.

E. PETER VOLPE
Professor, School of Medicine, Mercer University, Macon, Ga.

STEPHANIE VON BUCHAU
Performing Arts Editor, *San Francisco Magazine*.

EDWARD WAGENKNECHT
Professor of English, Emeritus, Boston University, Boston.

CHARLES WAGLEY
Graduate Research Professor of Anthropology, Emeritus, University of Florida, Gainesville.

LINDA W. WAGNER
Professor of English, Michigan State University, East Lansing.

THOMAS K. WAGNER
Business Publications Advisor, Former Editor, *Builder* Magazine.

REV. DR. WALTER D. WAGONER
Senior Minister, Asylum Hill Congregational Church, Hartford, Conn.

P. B. WAITE
Professor of History, Dalhousie University, Halifax, Nova Scotia.

ROBERT STARR WAITE
Assistant Professor, Division of Continuing Education, University of Utah, and Assistant Professor of Geography, Brigham Young University, Salt Lake City.

MARVALEE H. WAKE
Associate Professor of Zoology and Biology, University of California, Berkeley.

HERBERT J. WALBERG
Research Professor of Education, University of Illinois, Chicago.

ALAN M. WALD
Assistant Professor of English, University of Michigan, Ann Arbor.

BENJAMIN WALKER
Society of Authors, London.

ELAINE F. WALKER
Associate Professor of Psychology and Psychiatry, Emory University, Atlanta, Ga.

H. J. WALKER
Boyd Professor of Geography, Louisiana State University, Baton Rouge.

IAN G. WALKER
Professor of Biochemistry, University of Western Ontario, London, Ontario.

GEORGE J. WALLACE
Professor Emeritus of Zoology, Michigan State University, East Lansing.

L. WALSCHOT
Conservator, Geological Institute, University of Ghent, Ghent, Belgium.

J. JACKSON WALTER
President, National Trust for Historic Preservation, Washington, D.C.

BARBARA ANN WALTON
Assistant Professor of Biology, University of Tennessee, Chattanooga.

WILLIAM S.-Y. WANG
Professor of Linguistics, University of California, Berkeley.

HAROLD R. WANLESS
Assistant Professor of Marine Geology and Geophysics, Rosenstiel School of Marineand Atmospheric Science, University of Miami, Miami, Fla.

ALLEN MASON WARD
Professor of History, University of Connecticut, Storrs.

JOHN F. WARD
Professor of Physics, University of Michigan, Ann Arbor.

ROBERT A. WARNER
Professor of Music, University of Michigan, Ann Arbor.

DONALD I. WARREN
Professor of Sociology, Oakland University, Rochester, Mich.

DONALD R. WARREN
Professor and Chairman, College of Education University of Maryland, College Park.

EDWARD WASIOLEK
Avalon Distinguished Service Professor of Slavic and Comparative Literature, University of Chicago, Chicago.

JACK WASSERMAN
Wasserman, Orlow, Ginsberg, and Rubin, Washington, D.C.

ALAN WATSON
Professor of Civil Law, University of Pennsylvania, Philadelphia.

DON A. WATSON
Architect.

GEOFFREY S. WATSON
Professor of Statistics, Princeton University, Princeton, N.J.

RONALD G. WATT
Assistant Librarian and Archivist, Church of Jesus Christ of Latter-day Saints, Salt Lake City, Utah.

ROBERT J. WEAVER
Professor of Viticulture, University of California, Davis.

S. DAVID WEBB
Curator of Fossil Vertebrates and Professor of Zoology, Florida State Museum, University of Florida, Gainesville.

MARJORIE K. WEBSTER
Curator, Antique Instrument Collection, Adler Planetarium, Chicago.

PETER J. WEBSTER
Senior Research Scientist, Commonwealth Scientific and Industrial Research Organisation, Aspendale, Victoria, Australia.

RODERICK S. WEBSTER
Curator, Antique Instrument Collection, Adler Planetarium, Chicago.

WILLIAM C. WEES
Associate Professor of English, McGill University, Montreal.

LILLY WEI
Art Instructor, Kingsborough Community College, City University of New York, New York City.

DAVID L. WEIDE
Assistant Professor of Geography and Geology, University of Nevada, Las Vegas.

JON WEIL
Research Geneticist, University of California, San Francisco.

MAX H. WEIL, M.D.
Chairman, Division of Critical Care Medicine, and Director, Institute of Critical Care Medicine, University of Southern California, Los Angeles.

HERBERT WEINER, M.D.
Professor of Psychiatry and Biobehavioral Sciences, University of California, Los Angeles.

ROBERT S. WEINER
Lecturer in Geography, University of Connecticut, Storrs.

J. DONALD WEINRAUCH
Associate Professor of Business, Tennessee Technological University, Cookeville.

THOMAS R. WEIR
Professor Emeritus, University of Manitoba, Winnipeg.

JOSEPH S. WEISBERG
Professor and Chairman, Geoscience Department, Jersey City State College, Jersey City, N.J.

REV. JAMES A. WEISHEIPL
Professor of the History of Medieval Science, Pontifical Institute of Mediaeval Studies, and Professor of Medieval Studies, University of Toronto, Toronto.

RICHARD J. WEISS
Physicist, Materials Research Center, Watertown, Mass.

KENNETH F. WELCH
Lecturer in English and General Studies (ret.), Oxford College of Further Education, Oxford, England.

WAYNE W. WELCH
Professor of Educational Psychology, University of Minnesota, Minneapolis.

RENÉ WELLEK
Sterling Professor Emeritus of Comparative Literature, Yale University, New Haven, Conn.

JOHN M. WELLER, M.D.
Professor of Internal Medicine, University of Michigan, Ann Arbor.

WILLIAM E. WELMERS
Professor of Linguistics and African Languages, University of California, Los Angeles.

GENE WELTFISH
Professor and Graduate Fellow in Anthropology, New School for Social Research, New York City.

MANFRED W. WENNER
Department of Political Science, Northern Illinois University, DeKalb.

RICHARD P. WERBNER
Senior Lecturer in Social Anthropology, University of Manchester, Manchester, England.

WILLIAM E. WERNER, JR.
Professor of Biology, Blackburn College, Carlinville, Ill.

MICHAEL WERTHEIMER
Professor of Psychology, University of Colorado, Boulder.

ROBERT F. WESSER
Professor of History, State University of New York, Albany.

MORGAN WESSON
Curator, Film and Technology Collections, International Museum of Photography at George Eastman House, Rochester, N.Y.

BRUCE WEST
Columnist and Author, *The Globe and Mail*, Toronto.

ELLIOTT WEST
Associate Professor of History, University of Texas, Arlington.

DAVID WESTBY
Associate Professor of Sociology, Pennsylvania State University, University Park.

B. E. J. WHEELER
Reader In Plant Pathology, Imperial College Field Station, Silwood Park, Sunninghill, Berks, England.

ARTHUR K. WHEELOCK, JR.
Curator of Dutch and Flemish Painting, National Gallery of Art, Washington, D.C.

LUCY A. WHITE
Secretary-Treasurer, American Mobilehome Association, Lakewood, Colo.

THOMAS TAYLOR WHITE, M.D.
Clinical Professor of Surgery, University of Washington School of Medicine, Seattle.

JOHN R. WHITING
Former publisher of *Motor Boat and Sailing* magazine.

ROBERT M. WHITING
Research Associate, The Oriental Institute, University of Chicago, Chicago.

JAMES A. WHITNEY
Associate Professor of Geology, University of Georgia, Athens.

RONALD WIEDENHOEFT
Associate Professor, Graduate School of Architecture, University of Utah, Salt Lake City.

ELWYN A. WIENANDT
Associate Dean, School of Music, Baylor University, Waco, Tex.

DONALD N. WILBER
Author, *Iran, Past and Present.*

E. O. WILEY
Assistant Curator of Fishes, Museum of Natural History, University of Kansas, Lawrence.

HUBERT G. H. WILHELM
Professor of Geography, Ohio University, Athens.

JAMES J. WILHELM
Professor of Comparative Literature, Rutgers University, New Brunswick, N.J.

RICHARD WILKIE
Professor of Geology and Geography, University of Massachusetts, Amherst.

B. R. WILKINSON
Senior Lecturer, Department of Wool Science, Lincoln College, Canterbury, New Zealand.

ROBERT WILKINSON-LATHAM
British Military Historian.

CLIFFORD M. WILL
Assistant Professor of Physics, Stanford University, Stanford, Calif.

DAVID R. WILLIAMS, JR.
Chairman of the Board, Resource Sciences Corporation, Tulsa, Okla.

GEORGE HUNTSTON WILLIAMS
Professor of Church History, Harvard University Divinity School, Cambridge, Mass.

MICHAEL WILLIAMS
Associate Professor of Philosophy, University of Maryland, College Park.

STEPHEN E. WILLIAMS
Professor of Biology, Lebanon Valley College, Annville, Pa.

HAROLD F. WILLIAMSON
Professor Emeritus of Economics, Northwestern University, Evanston, Ill.

STEPHEN S. WILLOUGHBY
Professor of Mathematics and Mathematics Education, New York University, New York City.

CATHERINE W. WILSON
Visiting Lecturer, Barnard College, New York City.

CHARLES L. WILSON
Adjunct Professor, Ohio State University and Ohio Agriculture Research and Development Center, Wooster.

DAVID L. WILSON
Associate Professor of Physiology and Biophysics, University of Miami School of Medicine, Miami, Fla.

MARION R. WILSON
Decorative Arts Expert.

ROBERT E. WILSON
Associate Professor of Oceanography, Marine Sciences Research Center, State University of New York, Stony Brook.

JUDITH WILT
Professor of English, Boston College, Chestnut Hill, Mass.

CALVIN H. WILVERT
Assistant Professor of Geography, California Polytechnic State University, San Luis Obispo.

JOHN J. WINBERRY
Associate Professor of Geography, University of South Carolina, Columbia.

BRIAN F. WINDLEY
Lecturer in Geology, University of Leicester, Leicester, England.

ISABEL B. WINGATE
Professor Emeritus of Retail Management, New York University, New York City.

R. H. WINNICK
Co-author of *Robert Frost: The Later Years, 1938—1963.*

DAVID WISTOW
Lecturer and Art Historian, Art Gallery of Ontario, Toronto.

WILLIAM WITHINGTON
Associate Professor of Geology and Geography, University of Kentucky, Lexington.

NANCY L. WITYAK
Department of Sociology, George Washington University, Washington, D.C.

RICHARD WOJCIK
Assistant Professor, Barnard College, Columbia University, New York City.

SHARON L. WOLCHIK
Director, Russian and East European Studies, George Washington University, Washington, D.C.

ERNEST S. WOLF, M.D.
Training and Supervising Analyst, Chicago Institute for Psychoanalysis, Chicago.

MURRAY WOLFSON
Professor of Economics, Oregon State University, Corvallis.

HARRY WOLLMAN, M.D.
Robert Dunning Dripps Professor and
Chairman, Department of Anesthesia, and
Professor of Pharmacology, University of
Pennsylvania, Philadelphia.

EDWARD A WOLPERT, M.D.
Director, Clinical Services, Psychosomatic and
Psychiatric Institute, Michael Reese Hospital
and Medical Center, Chicago.

ROLAND E. WOLSELEY
Professor Emeritus of Journalism, Syracuse
University, Syracuse, N.Y.

ROBERT E. WOLVERTON
Vice-President for Academic Affairs and
Professor of Classics, Mississippi State
University, Mississippi State.

WILLIAM C. WONDERS
Professor of Geography, University of Alberta,
Edmonton.

GEORGE WOODCOCK
Former Editor, *Canadian Literature.*

CHARLES PLATTEN WOODHOUSE
Life-Fellow of the Royal Society of Arts.

ALBERT S. WOODHULL
Associate Professor of Computer Studies and
Biology, Hampshire College, Amherst, Mass.

ROSS WOODMAN
Professor of English, University of Western
Ontario, Canada.

PAUL B. WOODRUFF
Associate Professor of Philosophy, University of
Texas, Austin.

THOMAS E. WREN
Associate Professor of Philosophy, Loyola
University of Chicago, Chicago.

CONRAD WRIGHT
Professor of American Church History, Harvard
University, Cambridge, Mass.

DAVID WRIGHT
Music Journalist.

DAVID E. WRIGHT
Associate Professor, Lyman Briggs College,
Michigan State University, East Lansing.

MARION I. WRIGHT
Professor of Geography, Rhode Island College,
Providence, R.I.

DENNIS HUME WRONG
Professor of Sociology, New York University,
New York City.

WILLIAM F. WYATT, JR.
Professor of Classics, Brown University,
Providence, R.I.

DONALD WYMAN
Horticulturist, Emeritus, Arnold Arboretum,
Harvard University, Cambridge, Mass.

LEON YACHER
Assistant Professor of Geography, Southern
Connecticut State College, New Haven.

SEIICHI YASUMURA
Research Associate, Medical Department,
Brookhaven National Laboratory, Upton, N.Y.;
Associate Professor of Physiology, Downstate
Medical Center, State University of New York.

DAVID YERKES
Assistant Professor of English, Columbia
University, New York City.

T. LESLIE YOUD
Research Civil Engineer, U.S.Geological
Survey.

BRUCE A. YOUNG
Professor of Animal Physiology, University of
Alberta, Edmonton.

DONALD YOUNG
Author, *American Roulette: The History and
Dilemma of the Vice Presidency.*

DAVID C. YU
Professor of History of Religions, Colorado
Women's College, Denver.

HUGO ZAHND
Professor Emeritus of Chemistry, Brooklyn
College, City University of New York,
Brooklyn, N.Y.

DAVID J. ZAHNISER
Assistant Professor of Therapeutic Radiology,
Tufts—New England Medical Center, Boston.

ROBERT L. ZANGRANDO
Associate Professor of History, University of
Akron, Akron, Ohio.

CARL A. ZAPFFE
Professional Engineer, CAZ Lab,
Baltimore, Md.

OSCAR ZEICHNER
Professor Emeritus of History, City College, City
University of New York, New York City.

DAVID M. ZESMER
Professor of English, Illinois Institute of
Technology, Chicago.

HERMAN E. ZIEGER
Professor of Chemistry, City University of New
York, New York City.

EDWARD ZIGLER
Sterling Professor of Psychology, Yale
University; Head, Psychology Section, Yale
Child Study Center, New Haven, Conn.

THOMAS W. ZIMMERER
Professor of Industrial Management, Clemson
University, Clemson, S.C.

LORETTA E. ZIMMERMAN
Associate Professor of History, University of
Portland, Portland, Oreg.

GEORGE E. ZINSMEISTER
Associate Professor, Mechanical Engineering
Department, University of Massachusetts,
Amherst.

JACK ZIPES
Professor of German and Comparative
Literature, University of Wisconsin, Milwaukee.

VIRPI ZUCK
Assistant Professor of Scandinavian Studies,
University of Oregon, Eugene.

MARK J. ZUCKER
Assistant Professor of Art History, University of
Wisconsin, Milwaukee.

RICHARD L. ZUSI
Curator of Research, National Museum of
Natural History, Smithsonian Institution,
Washington, D.C.

GROLIER

ENCYCLOPEDIA
OF KNOWLEDGE

𝒜	A	A	A	A	A	A	∀	✦	⋉
GERMAN-GOTHIC	RUSSIAN-CYRILLIC	CLASSICAL LATIN	EARLY LATIN	ETRUSCAN	CLASSICAL GREEK	EARLY GREEK	EARLY ARAMAIC	EARLY HEBREW	PHOENICIAN

e English alphabet and of
from the ancient Semitic
f the letter and its position
t are from the Latin alpha-
he Greek by way of the

lpha. Its name, form, and
ong with the rest of the al-
yctom—probably Phoeni-
Semitic writing systems,
ere, it does not represent
similar to the glottal stop
etween the vocal chords)
nunciation of initial vow-

mber of vowel sounds, as
d *soda,* and occurs in a
essive vowels with a sin-
augh, steady, bear, bea-
The double *a* does not
is found in some words
en from languages that

nch: Aix-la-Chapelle) is
in the state of North
elgium and the Nether-
239,170 (1987 est.).
nt engineering school
and is a rail center of a
has important iron and
uce textiles, glass, and
operated since Roman

rthern capital and the
he German kings from
) were crowned there.
ity until occupied by
to Prussia by an act of
pied by the Allies after
avily damaged during
athedral, which Char-
tains his tomb, was
ale in Ravenna, Italy.

Aalborg   see ÅLBORG

Aalto, Alvar [ahl'-toh, ahl'-vahr]   Hugo Alvar Henrik Aalto, b. Finland, Feb. 3, 1898, d. May 11, 1976, one of the major architects of the 20th century, significantly influenced the development of MODERN ARCHITECTURE, humanizing the technocratic tenets of the BAUHAUS and other exponents of the INTERNATIONAL STYLE.

Aalto graduated from the Helsinki Polytechnic School in 1921. Within a decade he was the acknowledged mas

The civic center (1950–52) in Säynätsalo, Finland, was designed by Alvar Aalto. The red-brick buildings are grouped around a raised courtyard. Numbers indicate council chamber (1); library (2); municipal offices (3); main staircase (4); garden steps (5); shops (6); main entrance (7); and pool (8).

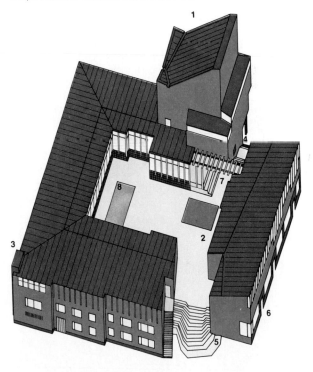

ter of Finnish architecture, establishing his distinctive style with two commissions: the Viipuri Library (1927–35; destroyed 1943), famous for the undulating acoustic wood ceiling in its lecture hall, and the Turun Sanomat newspaper building (1927–30), with its radically innovative tapered concrete columns in the pressroom. Aalto's functionalist cantilevered design for the tuberculosis sanatorium in Paimio (1929–33) brought him international fame.

With his first wife, the architect Aino Marsio, Aalto founded (1935) the Artek firm to produce their designs for household furnishings, many of them in molded and laminated wood. The informal elegance of Aalto's interiors can be seen in the Villa Mairea (1938–39), a country home he designed for his industrialist patrons Harry and Mairea Gullichsen. Aalto's Finnish pavilions for the Paris Exposition of 1937 and the New York World's Fair of 1939 added to his international stature, as did the serpentine Baker House dormitory (1947) at the Massachusetts Institute of Technology in Cambridge, Mass., where Aalto was a visiting professor for six years.

After World War II Aalto supervised the urban planning and rebuilding of much of Finland. His civic center for the island village of Säynätsalo (1950–52) incorporated traditional Finnish materials with modern design and integrated the cluster of buildings into their site. It epitomizes Aalto's style. The buildings of his later years are more austere, but even the monumental white marble Finlandia House (1967–75), the cultural center of Helsinki, retains a human scale, and an acoustically perfect concert hall.

aardvark   The aardvark (or ant bear), *Orycteropus afer*, is the only species in the mammal family Orycteropodidae, order Tubulidentata. Its name is derived from the Afrikaans for "earth pig," and this slow, massive animal

The aardvark claws soil from a termite mound and uses its long, sticky tongue to capture termites scattering from the mound. Some Africans keep aardvarks claws as good luck charms.

somewhat resembles a pig. It is brown to yellowish, about 150 cm (5 ft) long, with a 60-cm-long (2-ft) tail, and weighs 45 to 77 kg (100 to 170 lb). It has a narrow head and a long snout. Its ears are large and rabbitlike, and hearing is acute. The short, stout legs, partially webbed feet, and long claws are well suited for burrowing its large sleeping dens and for tearing apart mounds of the ants and termites on which it feeds with its long, sticky tongue.

Aardvarks are found throughout sub-Saharan Africa, usually in open country. They are shy, nocturnal creatures. The female bears one or two young in October or November. Aardvarks live about ten years in captivity.

Aare River [ah'-ruh]   The Aare River is the longest (295 km/183 mi) river in Switzerland and drains an area of 17,780 km^2 (6,865 mi^2). Rising in the Bernese Alps, it passes by Meiringen, through the Aare Gorge, into Lake Thun, past Bern, and joins the Rhine River at the village of Koblenz.

Aarhus   see ÅRHUS

Aaron   Brother of MOSES, Aaron was Moses' spokesman before Pharaoh and was his assistant during the Exodus from Egypt. Even though Aaron was involved in constructing the GOLDEN CALF that the Israelites worshiped while Moses was on Mount Sinai, he and his sons were appointed priests, with Aaron as high priest. He was also designated head of the LEVITES, ministers of lower rank, and his authority was miraculously confirmed by a flowering staff (Exod. 28–29, 32; Num. 8, 17–18). Aaron died before his people reached Canaan.

Aaron, Henry   Henry Louis "Hank" Aaron, b. Mobile, Ala., Feb. 5, 1934, is American baseball's all-time champion home-run hitter. Aaron entered the record

Henry Aaron unleashes the swing that launched the most home runs (755) in the history of American major-league baseball. Aaron, an outfielder, spent most of his 23-year career with the Braves of the National League. He was elected to the Hall of Fame in 1982.

books on Apr. 8, 1974, by breaking Babe Ruth's record of 714, and he went on to hit a total of 755 homers before completing his 23-year major-league career.

Aaron began playing professionally for all-black teams in Mobile and Indianapolis, Ind., but he signed with the National League's Milwaukee Braves organization at age 18. He reached the major leagues when he was only 20 and quickly established himself as one of the game's finest players. He played for the Braves almost exclusively, first in Milwaukee (1954–65), then in Atlanta (1966–74). He ended his career with the American League's Milwaukee Brewers (1975–76). Along with a lifetime batting average of .305, Aaron had 2,297 runs batted in (1st all-time), 6,856 total bases (1st), 12,364 at bats (2d), 3,771 hits (3d), 3,298 games played (3d), and 624 doubles (8th). Aaron was the NL's Most Valuable Player in 1957, and the right fielder won 3 Gold Glove awards for his fielding prowess. He led the NL in home runs, runs batted in, and slugging average 4 times each, and in batting average twice (1956: .328; 1959: .355).

abacus [ab'-uh-kuhs]   An abacus is an instrument that helps a person make arithmetic calculations. In its best-known form, as the Chinese *suan pan*, it is composed of beads strung on parallel wires in a rectangular frame. In ancient times, however, the abacus was composed of a row of grooves in sand into which pebbles were placed. Later, the use of a slate or board (in Greek, *abax*) made it a portable device; the pebbles were systematically arranged along parallel lines.

The value assigned to each pebble (or bead, shell, or stick) is determined by its position: one pebble on a particular line has the value of 1; two together have the value of 2. A pebble on the next line, however, might have the value of 10, and a pebble on the third line would have the value of 100. Therefore, three properly placed pebbles—two with values of 1 and one with the value of 10—could signify 12, and the addition of a fourth pebble with the value of 100 could signify 112, using a place-value notational system of multiples of 10.

Thus the abacus works on the principle of place-value notation: the location of the bead determines its value.

In a Chinese abacus, a bead's location determines its numerical value. Calculations are made by changing the positions of the beads.

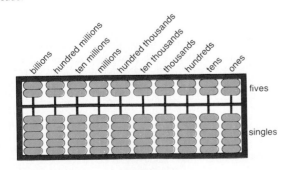

An abacus is used simply as a memory aid by a person making mental calculations. In contrast, ADDING MACHINES, electronic calculators, and computers are used to make physical calculations.

Abadan [ah-bah-dahn']   Abadan (1982 est. pop., 294,068) is a city on Abadan Island in the Shatt al-Arab, at the head of the Persian Gulf in Khuzestan province, Iran. About 402 km (250 mi) southwest of Isfahan, it is the terminus of pipelines from Iranian oil fields and has one of the world's largest oil-refinery complexes.

Settled as early as 1047, Abadan remained small until oil was discovered there in 1908 and the first refineries were constructed the next year. Abadan's refining facilities, the largest in the world until 1951, processed more than 18 million metric tons (20 million U.S. tons) of crude oil a year before the IRAN-IRAQ WAR erupted in 1980. Both Abadan's refinery and its port installations at Ma'shur and Kharg Island were repeatedly attacked and severely damaged during that war.

abalone [ab-uh-lohn'-ee]   Abalone is the common name applied to any marine gastropod in the MOLLUSK genus *Haliotis*. It is also sometimes applied to other gastropods. Unlike the many gastropods that have highly coiled shells, abalones have a broad, flattened, asymmetrical shell, the shape of which resembles the human ear—hence another common name, ear shell, or sea-ear. This shape minimizes water resistance in the abalones' intertidal habitats.

The animals respire and discharge wastes through a row of holes on one side of the shell; old holes fill up and new ones appear as the animals age. Abalones are primitive gastropods along with other members of the order Archaeogastropoda, such as the LIMPET. They are commercially valuable for their large, edible foot and for the mother-of-pearl that lines their shells, which is used to make articles such as buttons.

Abbado, Claudio [ah-bah'-doh]   The conductor Claudio Abbado, b. Milan, June 26, 1933, comes from a musical family. His father, Michelangelo, was vice-principal of the Milan Conservatory where Claudio and his elder brother, Marcello, studied. He began his career as a pianist, and he studied composition with Bruno Bettinelli and conducting with Hans Swarowsky in Vienna. In 1971 he became permanent conductor of the Vienna Philharmonic, the orchestra of the Vienna State Opera, whose music director he became in 1986. From 1969 to 1986 he was conductor and then music director of La Scala Opera House in Milan. During his tenure he extended La Scala's season and presented Alban Berg's *Wozzeck* in the original German, a considerable innovation for Milan. He also has had long-term associations with the London Symphony Orchestra, the Chicago Symphony, and the European Community Youth Orchestra. In 1989 he was named music director of the Berlin Philharmonic.

Abbas I, Shah of Persia [ah-bahs'] Abbas I, b. Jan. 27, 1571, d. Jan. 19, 1629, shah of Persia (1588–1629), expanded Persia's boundaries to the Indus in the east and to the Tigris in the west. He created a standing army, the first in Persia, and in 1598 launched an attack on the Uzbeks in the east, defeating them near Herat (now in Afghanistan).

From 1602, Abbas campaigned against the Ottoman Turks, capturing Tabriz, Erivan, Shirvan, Baghdad, and Mosul. He also restored internal order, promoted trade and the arts, and made his new capital at Isfahan one of the most beautiful cities in the world. A member of the Safavid dynasty, Abbas I is regarded as one of the greatest Persian rulers.

Abbasids [ah-bas'-ids] The Abbasids were the dynasty of caliphs who ruled the Islamic empire from 750 until the Mongol conquest of the Middle East in 1258. The dynasty takes its name from its ancestor al-Abbas, the uncle of the Prophet Muhammad. In 750 the Abbasids defeated the Umayyads and transferred the capital of the caliphate from Damascus to Baghdad, thereby shifting the empire's center from Syria to Iraq.

The regime reasserted the theocratic concept of the caliphate and continuity with orthodox Islam as the basis of unity and authority in the empire. The Abbasid "revolution" also made Islam and the fruits of power accessible to non-Arabs. A strong Persian influence persisted in the government and culture of the Abbasids, and Hellenistic ideas led to the rapid growth of intellectual life.

The Abbasid period may be divided into two parts. In the period from 750 to 945 the authority of the caliphs gradually declined, while the Turkish military leaders gained increasing influence. The dynasty's power peaked in the reign (786–809) of Harun al-Rashid. In the later period, from 945 to 1258, the caliphs generally held no more than nominal suzerainty; real power, even in Baghdad, passed to dynasties of secular sovereigns.

Abbe, Ernst [ahb'-uh] The German physicist Ernst Abbe, b. Jan. 23, 1840, d. Jan. 14, 1905, was the principal scientific figure behind the Carl Zeiss Optics Company, which he took over after the death of Zeiss in 1888. His innumerable contributions to optics, such as the Abbe refractometer and apochromatic lens, led directly to modern phase-contrast microscopy and the ELECTRON MICROSCOPE.

Abbevillian see Paleolithic Period

abbey In the Roman Catholic and Anglican churches an abbey is a monastery, usually belonging to the Benedictine or Cistercian order, governed by an abbot (for communities of men) or an abbess (for communities of women). An abbey is normally an independent institution. Subordinate or less important monasteries are called priories. In Britain the term *abbey* is also used for such churches as Westminster Abbey or such country houses as Woburn Abbey, which formerly belonged to monastic institutions.

Abbey Theatre Ireland's Abbey Theatre opened its doors in December 1904 and quickly became, along with André Antoine's Théâtre Libre and Konstantin Stanislavsky's Moscow Art Theatre, one of the seminal producers of modern drama. The Abbey's first directors were W. B. Yeats, Lady Gregory, and J. M. Synge. These writers, along with Padraic Colum and George Fitzmaurice, discovered a new subject in the Irish peasant. The riots over Synge's *Playboy of the Western World* (1907) drew attention to the theater as a major exponent of poetic folk drama. Later playwrights, such as Lennox Robinson, Saint John Ervine, and T. C. Murray turned the theater toward realism. However, in Sean O'Casey's city plays an urban realism was wedded to a kind of earthy poetry, even though Abbey audiences again rioted at *The Plough and the Stars* (1926). Later Abbey Theatre playwrights of world importance have been Brendan Behan, Brian Friel, and Paul Vincent Carroll. Over the years, dozens of Abbey actors, including Sara Allgood, Barry Fitzgerald, Cyril Cusack and his daughters, and Siobhan McKenna, have made their mark on the stages of London and New York, and in films as well.

Abbot, Francis Ellingwood Francis Ellingwood Abbot, b. Boston, Nov. 6, 1836, d. Oct. 23, 1903, was a philosopher and theologian who sought to reconstruct theology in accord with scientific method. As a spokesman for "free religion," he asserted that Christianity, understood as based on the lordship of Christ, is no longer tenable. He rejected all dogma and reliance on Scriptures or creeds, teaching that truth is open to every individual.

Abbot graduated from Harvard University and the Meadville Theological School. He served Unitarian churches in Dover, N.H., and Toledo, Ohio, but left the ministry in 1868 to write and teach. Abbot's theological position was stated in *Scientific Theism* (1885) and *The Way Out of Agnosticism* (1890). He committed suicide at his wife's grave.

Abbott, Berenice The American photographer Berenice Abbott, b. Springfield, Ohio, July 17, 1898, d. Dec. 10, 1991, began her career as assistant to the surrealist artist Man Ray. In the 1930s her series of documentary photographs of New York City received wide acclaim. Abbott also rediscovered and brought to public attention the work of the early 20th-century French photographer Eugène Atget. Her books include *Changing New York* (1939; repr. as *New York in the 30's,* 1973), *Greenwich Village Today and Yesterday* (1949), *Photographs* (1970), and *The World of Atget* (1980).

Abbott, Bud see Abbott and Costello

Abbott, George   An American playwright, director, and producer, George Abbott, b. Forestville, N.Y., June 25, 1887, is famous for such farces as *Three Men on a Horse* (1935) and for his fast-paced direction of musical plays, such as *On Your Toes* (1936; 1954; 1983). Among the musicals he coauthored and directed were *The Pajama Game* (1954; film, 1957), *Damn Yankees* (1955; film, 1958), and *Fiorello!* (1959; Pulitzer Prize, 1960). His autobiography, *Mister Abbott*, was published in 1963.

Abbott, Grace   The social worker Grace Abbott, b. Grand Island, Nebr., Nov. 17, 1878, d. June 19, 1939, whose special interests included immigrant and child labor problems, was a pioneer in public welfare administration. In 1908 she joined Jane ADDAMS at Hull House, where she worked with immigrant slum dwellers of Chicago. In 1917 she published *The Immigrant and the Community,* a book instrumental in arousing concern for the problems of recent immigrants from Europe.

Abbott later joined the U.S. Children's Bureau in Washington, D.C., where she helped draft the first Child Labor Act and served (1921–34) as director. She often lectured at the University of Chicago, where her sister Edith (1876–1957) was dean (1924–42) of the School of Social Service Administration.

Abbott, Sir John Joseph Caldwell   Sir John Abbott, b. St. Andrews, Lower Canada (now Quebec), Mar. 12, 1821, d. Oct. 30, 1893, was prime minister of Canada from 1891 to 1892. A lawyer, he was elected to the Legislative Assembly as a Conservative in 1857. He served there, and later in the Canadian House of Commons, until 1874. Abbott sat in the House again from 1880 to 1887, when he was appointed to the Canadian Senate. He was chosen prime minister on Sir John Macdonald's death in 1891, but poor health forced his resignation after 18 months.

Abbott, Lyman   Lyman Abbott, b. Roxbury, Mass., Dec. 18, 1835, d. Oct. 22, 1922, was an American Congregational minister and editor who popularized liberal theology through his sermons and lectures. In 1876 he joined Henry Ward Beecher (see BEECHER family) in editing the *Christian Union* (called *Outlook* after 1893); he succeeded Beecher in 1888 as pastor of the Plymouth Congregational Church in Brooklyn. His evolutionary interpretation of doctrine and society was stated forcibly in his many writings, which included *The Evolution of Christianity* (1892) and *Christianity and Social Problems* (1896).

Abbott and Costello   William A. "Bud" Abbott, b. Asbury Park, N.J., Oct. 2, 1895, d. Apr. 24, 1974, and Lou Costello (real name, Louis Francis Cristillo), b. Paterson, N.J., Mar. 6, 1908, d. Mar. 3, 1959, rose from the ranks of burlesque to become one of America's most popular comedy teams. Abbott portrayed a fast-talking con man and Costello a baby-faced patsy. Together they were famous for such rapid-fire dialogue routines as "Who's on First?" Critics called their material old hat, but Abbott and Costello's expert delivery made the oldest jokes seem fresh. They appeared in many films, including *Buck Privates* (1941) and *Hold That Ghost* (1941). Their television show was aired from 1952 to 1954.

abbreviation   An abbreviation is a shortened form of a word or phrase that is used to save space in written form. Certain types of abbreviations, such as some acronyms, may also facilitate memory and are spoken, if easily pronounced, as well as written. (An example is UNESCO, United Nations Educational, Scientific, and Cultural Organization.) Abbreviations date back to ancient times, but their proliferation has been greatest in the 20th century. This is because of the vast increase in information, especially in science and technology, and the ever-burgeoning number of agencies and organizations.

ABC   SEE RADIO AND TELEVISION BROADCASTING

Abd al-Hamid II, Sultan of the Ottoman Empire   [ahb-dul-hah-meed']   Abd al-Hamid II, b. Sept. 21, 1842, d. Feb. 10, 1918, the last major Ottoman sultan (1876–1909), modernized the Ottoman Empire and defended it against foreign attacks and national revolts. Initially he enacted a liberal constitution and frustrated foreign intervention at the Constantinople Conference (1876), turning partial authority over to an elected parliament. Defeats in the Russo-Turkish War of 1877–78 and the parliament's failure to rule efficiently caused him to dissolve it and rule autocratically. The remainder of his reign was disturbed by national revolts in Macedonia and eastern Anatolia as well as by foreign occupation of Cyprus, Tunisia, Egypt, Bosnia and Hercegovina, and East Rumelia.

Abd al-Hamid II stabilized Ottoman administration and finance but drove most intellectuals into exile. The exiled YOUNG TURKS and their Macedonian-army allies finally forced him to restore (1908) the constitution and parliament, but an abortive conservative counterrevolution (Apr. 13, 1909) led to his overthrow and exile.

Abd al-Rahman I, Emir of Córdoba   [ahb-dul-rah-mahn']   Abd al-Rahman I, b. 731, d. Sept. 30, 788, emir of Córdoba (756–88), created an independent Muslim kingdom in Spain. After the overthrow of his family, the UMAYYADS, who had ruled the Islamic world as successors to Muhammad, he fled to Spain. There he defeated the governor and established his own kingdom. Although faced with numerous rebellions, he maintained his throne and founded a dynasty that lasted until 1031. By beginning the construction of the great mosque of

Córdoba, Abd al-Rahman laid the basis for the future greatness of the city.

Abdul-Jabbar, Kareem [ab-dul'-juh-bar']   Kareem Abdul-Jabbar, b. Ferdinand Lewis Alcindor, Jr., in New York City, Apr. 16, 1947, blended height, coordination, and skills to become the "perfect big man" in basketball. Jabbar, 7 ft 2 in (2 m 18 cm) tall, led his New York City high school team, Power Memorial Academy, to 71 consecutive victories. At the University of California, Los Angeles, his team won 3 NCAA titles (1967–69); he was an All-American all 3 years and College Player of the Year twice. As a professional for the Milwaukee Bucks (1969–75) and the Los Angeles Lakers (1975–89) of the National Basketball Association, he accumulated a record 38,387 points (24.6 per game) and 17,440 rebounds (11.2 per game). Jabbar was voted the NBA's Most Valuable Player a record 6 times, and his teams won 6 NBA titles (1971, 1980, 1982, 1985, 1987, 1988).

Basketball star Kareem Abdul-Jabbar executes the most famous weapon in his offensive arsenal, the "skyhook." Perhaps the most astonishing aspect of Jabbar's professional career—in addition to many all-time records—was its longevity (1969–89). A superbly conditioned athlete, the center did not retire until the age of 42. The former Lew Alcindor, in devotion to Islam, changed his name in 1971.

Abdul Rahman, Tunku [ahb-dul rah-mahn']   Tunku Abdul Rahman, b. Feb. 8, 1903, d. Dec. 6, 1990, was the first prime minister of independent Malaya (1957–63) and then (1963–70) of the successor state of Malaysia. After early schooling in Malaya and Thailand, Abdul Rahman attended Cambridge University and studied law at London's Inner Temple. A founder of the United Malays National Organization (1946), he was chief architect of its alliance with the Malayan Chinese Association (1952) and the Malayan Indian Congress (1954) to form what became the ruling Alliance party. Abdul Rahman is credited with founding (1961) the Association of Southeast Asia, consisting of Malaya, Thailand, and the Philip-

pines, to resist the claims of SUKARNO of Indonesia; later it became (1967) ASEAN, including Indonesia and Singapore. He was also the key figure in the formation (1963) of the Federation of Malaysia. Domestically, he tried to accommodate the Chinese and Indian minorities. Agitation against this policy led to suspension of the constitution in 1969 and to Abdul Rahman's resignation in 1970.

Abdullah [ahb-dul'-ah]   Abdullah (Abd Allah ibn al-Husayn), b. 1882, d. July 20, 1951, was the first ruler of the Hashemite Kingdom of Jordan. A leading Arab nationalist, he occupied Transjordan in 1921 and became its ruler under the British mandate. After independence in 1946 he was crowned king. Abdullah accepted the partition of Palestine and the creation of Israel, but he took part in the 1948 ARAB-ISRAELI WAR, occupying the West Bank of the Jordan River and incorporating a large Palestinian population into Jordan. He was assassinated by a Palestinian nationalist.

Abe Kobo [ah'-bay koh'-boh]   Abe Kobo, b. Mar. 7, 1924, is a leading experimental Japanese prose writer and dramatist. His best-known works, such as *The Woman in the Dunes* (1962; Eng. trans., 1964; film, 1964), explore in a surrealistic fashion the emptiness and nightmare of urban life.

Influenced by Western avant-garde literature, Abe's novels and short stories have few of the lyrical qualities typical of Japanese literature. His work is often compared with that of Franz KAFKA. His narratives are sparse, elliptical, and normally unresolved. Abe's other works of fiction include *Red Cocoon* (1950; Eng. trans., 1966), *Kabe* (The Wall, 1951), *S. Karuma shi no hanzai* (Mr. S. Karuma's Crime, 1951), *Inter Ice Age Four* (1959; Eng. trans., 1970, repr. 1981), and *The Box Man* (1973; Eng. trans., 1974). One of his most widely performed plays is *Friends* (1967; Eng. trans., 1969).

Abel   According to Genesis 4, Abel was the second son of Adam and Eve. A shepherd, he was murdered by his brother CAIN out of envy. His innocence is praised in Matthew 23:35.

Abel, I. W.   Iorwith Wilbur Abel, b. Magnolia, Ohio, Aug. 11, 1908, d. Aug. 10, 1987, was president of the UNITED STEELWORKERS OF AMERICA from 1965 to 1977. He began working in a steel mill at the age of 17 and 11 years later he became an organizer for the union. Abel was known for his lack of pretension and for his tolerance of dissent.

Abelard, Peter [ab'-uh-lahrd]   Peter Abelard, b. c.1079, d. Apr. 21, 1142, a French philosopher and theologian, was an early exponent of SCHOLASTICISM. After

Peter Abelard, shown here in a 19th-century engraving, was the most famous of the early scholastics. A brilliant thinker and teacher, he is also known for his tragic love affair with Héloïse. In addition to his theological and philosophical works, Abelard wrote the autobiographical Historia calamitatum mearum *(History of My Adversities).*

studying in Paris under WILLIAM OF CHAMPEAUX and Roscellin, he soon became a recognized teacher himself. His brilliant academic career was cut short in 1118–19, however, by the consequences of his love affair with Héloïse (c.1098–1164), the young niece of Canon Fulbert of Notre-Dame. Castrated by order of Fulbert and publicly disgraced, Abelard became a Benedictine monk. He continued to devote his vast energies to theological studies and writing, but Saint BERNARD OF CLAIRVAUX, doubting the orthodoxy of Abelard's teaching on the Trinity, instigated the burning of one of his books on the subject at the Council of Soissons (1121).

In 1125, Abelard established a convent called the Paraclete near Troyes; Héloïse became prioress and a famous teacher there. Meanwhile Abelard was unexpectedly elected (1126) abbot of the notoriously immoral monks of Saint-Gildas-de-Rhuis in Brittany. His efforts to reform the monastery ended with his having to flee for his life. Returning to Paris, Abelard resumed his teaching, numbering among his pupils John of Salisbury. At the Council of Sens (1140), however, Saint Bernard again succeeded in having Abelard condemned for heresy. This condemnation was soon confirmed by the pope.

Already a broken man in his sixties, Abelard decided to travel on foot to Rome to appeal his case. He got only as far as Cluny, whose abbot, Peter the Venerable, effected a reconciliation between Abelard and Bernard. Abelard spent the rest of his life at Cluny, dying at the nearby priory of Saint-Marcel-sur-Saône.

In the philosophical controversy over UNIVERSALS, Abelard rejected both the extreme realism of William of Champeaux and the crude nominalism of Roscellin. While denying that universals are real things, he asserted that they are more than mere words since they express factors common to individual, real things; thus universals are the basis for logical predication. Abelard's moderate realism in philosophy, his development of the dialectical

method of argument, his familiarity with the Bible and many of the Church Fathers, and his intellectual brilliance—rather than any systematic presentation of Christian theology aided by reason—make him one of the important, although much neglected, pioneers of scholasticism.

___

Abell, George O. [ay'-buhl]   American astronomer George Ogden Abell, b. Los Angeles, Mar. 1, 1927, d. Oct. 7, 1983, is best known for his work on clusters of galaxies but was also a noted lecturer and author. He published a catalog of 2,712 clusters in 1958 and was preparing a catalog of southern clusters at the time of his death. Studies of these clusters have helped define the problem of missing mass in the universe that confronts COSMOLOGY today. Abell also determined the relative numbers of galaxies with various absolute magnitudes.

___

Aberdeen (city in Scotland)   Aberdeen (1987 est. pop., 213,228) is the major port and commercial center of northeastern Scotland. Located on the North Sea, it is the center of the Scottish fishing industry and the supply port for the Orkney and Shetland islands. The discovery and development of North Sea oil deposits have brought added growth and prosperity to Aberdeen.

Old Aberdeen developed around the Cathedral of Saint Machar (1424) and King's College (1495), on the Don River. New Aberdeen grew around the superior port on the Dee and around Marischal College (1593). The two colleges combined in 1860 to form the University of Aberdeen, and Old and New Aberdeen merged in 1891. Aberdeen's buildings are distinctive for their use of locally quarried granite.

___

Aberdeen, George Hamilton-Gordon, 4th Earl of   Lord Aberdeen, b. Jan. 28, 1784, d. Dec. 14, 1860, was prime minister of Britain (1852–55) through most of the CRIMEAN WAR. Earlier in his long political career he served twice as foreign secretary (1828–30, 1841–46), and his successes included the settling of two boundary disputes with the United States by the Webster-Ashburton and Oregon treaties (1842, 1846). As prime minister of a coalition government, Aberdeen allowed a diplomatic drift that led to Britain's entry (1854) into the Crimean War. He was blamed for poor management of the war and was forced to resign.

___

Aberdeen, University of   The University of Aberdeen (enrollment: 7,246; library: about 1,000,000 volumes) was formed by the merger in 1860 of King's College (1495) and Marischal College (1593). Located in Aberdeen, Scotland, it is a coeducational institution and has faculties of arts and social sciences, science, divinity, law, engineering, and medicine. All grant undergraduate and graduate degrees. Associated colleges include the North of Scotland College of Agriculture.

Aberhart, William [ay'-bur-hahrt] The Canadian political leader William Aberhart, b. near Seaforth, Ontario, Dec. 30, 1878, d. May 23, 1943, was the premier of the first Social Credit government (1935–43) in Alberta. A high school principal and radio evangelist, he adopted Social Credit ideas, calling for a redistribution of wealth, in the early 1930s and won a large following in western Canada. In 1935, Aberhart and his SOCIAL CREDIT PARTY swept to victory in the Alberta provincial elections. His reforms were opposed by the federal government, and many were declared unconstitutional by the courts. Aberhart remained in office, becoming increasingly conservative, until his death.

Abernathy, Ralph David Ralph David Abernathy, b. Linden, Ala., Mar. 11, 1926, d. Apr. 17, 1990, was a Baptist minister in Atlanta (1961–90) and black civil rights leader. Ordained in 1948, he accepted a pastoral post in Montgomery, Ala., in 1951. In 1955 he and the Rev. Martin Luther KING, Jr., organized the Montgomery bus boycott to protest discrimination. Two years later they founded the Southern Christian Leadership Conference (SCLC). White terrorists dynamited Abernathy's home and church in retaliation. After King's assassination in 1968, Abernathy served as president of the SCLC until 1977. His autobiography, *And the Walls Came Tumbling Down*, was published in 1989.

aberration, optical An aberration, in OPTICS, is some property of a LENS or a curved MIRROR that impairs its ability to form a perfect image. Several types exist, including chromatic aberration and the geometric types, called spherical aberration, coma, astigmatism, distortion, and curvature of field.

Chromatic aberration produces a colored fringe around an image when white light is involved. A lens's focal length depends on the curvature of the lens surfaces and on the INDEX OF REFRACTION of its material. The colored fringe occurs because the refractive index of any transparent substance varies with the wavelength (color) of the light—a phenomenon called DISPERSION.

Spherical aberration results from the geometry of the REFRACTION and REFLECTION of light rays. It limits the ability of a converging lens or mirror to bring parallel rays into perfect focus, because the focal length for rays focused by the central part of the lens differs from that for rays focused by the outer parts.

Coma is named for the cometlike appearance of the image of a point source of light formed by a simple lens when the source is located off the lens's central axis. The effect results from the fact that the optical focus of rays passing through the lens center is a point, but for those passing through the outer parts it is a circle. Similar geometric reasons account for astigmatism, in which an image is blurred; distortion, in which imaged lines bend either inward (pincushion effect) or outward (barrel effect);

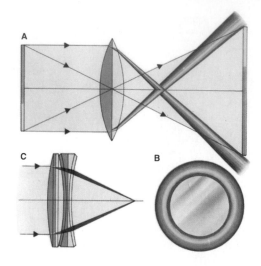

Chromatic aberration occurs because various wavelengths of light are refracted at different angles (A), resulting in a colored fringe surrounding the image (B). Combining concave and convex lenses (C) of different types of glass will correct this defect.

and curvature of field, in which the lens forms an image focused on a spherical rather than a flat plane.

Aberrations are reduced by varying the curvature of a lens or mirror surface. In most optical systems, two or more lenses of appropriately different dispersive qualities and curvatures are combined so as to cancel out each other's aberrational effects.

Aberystwyth [ab-ur-ist'-with] Aberystwyth (1981 pop., 8,666) is a municipal borough on Cardigan Bay in the county of Dyfed, Wales. The town grew around a 13th-century Norman castle that was later destroyed. With the establishment of the University College of Wales (1872) and the National Library of Wales (1907), it became a center of Welsh culture.

Abidjan [ah-bi-jahn'] Abidjan (1984 est. pop., 1,850,000), the largest city, former capital, and chief port of Ivory Coast, is located on the Ébrié Lagoon, Gulf of Guinea, on the coast of West Africa. Settled in 1898, Abidjan became a railroad terminus in 1904. It remained a small town until 1950, when the completion of the Vridi Canal opened the lagoon to the sea and made Abidjan an ocean port. Abidjan processes and exports coffee, cacao, timber, manganese, and fruit. In 1983 the capital was formally transferred to Yamoussoukro, the birthplace of Félix HOUPHOUËT-BOIGNY, although the legislature still meets in Abidjan.

The city is divided into several types of quarters: the commercial and administrative centers, such as the Plateau; the traditional residential and industrial centers of

Adjamé and Treichville, a suburb on the island of Petit-Bassam; and the modern residential section of Cocody. The climate is humid, and at the outskirts of the city is a tropical rain forest, the Banco National Park. Abidjan has a university (1964), a museum, and one of the world's largest cathedrals.

Abilene (Kansas) [ab'-uh-leen]

Abilene (1990 pop., 6,242), on the Smoky Hill River in east central Kansas, is an agricultural distribution center and the seat of Dickinson County. During the years 1867–71, Abilene was an important railhead, at the end of the CHISHOLM TRAIL. Wild Bill HICKOK was Abilene's marshal in the 1870s. Places of interest include Dwight D. Eisenhower's boyhood home and the Eisenhower Museum and Library.

Abilene (Texas)

Abilene (1990 pop., 106,654) is the marketing, shipping, and financial center of west central Texas and the seat of Taylor County. A rapidly growing city with varied industries, it has nevertheless retained its original frontier character. It was founded as a shipping point when the railroad arrived in 1881, and the town was named for Abilene, Kans. Livestock is still a major product of the region served by the city, but agriculture is now supplemented by related industries. Abilene is the site of Hardin-Simmons University, two colleges, and Dyess Air Force Base, a Strategic Air Command unit.

ABM   see ANTIBALLISTIC MISSILE

Abnaki [ab-nah'-kee]

A major group of Algonquian-speaking Indian tribes living along the river valleys of Maine, the Abnaki confederacy was important in American colonial history. The collective name for this confederacy, used by both French and English, means "people of the eastern lands." It included the PASSAMAQUODDY, PENOBSCOT, Sokoki, Malecite, and Etchimin tribes, sedentary, horticultural peoples who also depended upon hunting and fishing for subsistence.

Threatened by the northward expansion of the English seaboard colonies and aggressive raids of the Five Nations Iroquois, the Abnaki had become firm allies of New France by the middle of the 17th century. In the 1670s, weakened by constant wars, they began to abandon their homeland in Maine. Most migrated northward to Quebec and New Brunswick. In 1681 a group of Sokoki formed part of the sieur de La Salle's support party during his exploration of the Lake Michigan area, and they settled there. Other groups of Penobscot, Passamaquoddy, and Malecite remained in Maine after making peace with the English.

In 1972 descendants of the Abnaki brought a suit against the state of Maine for the illegal surrender of their lands in the 1790s. The 1980 settlement awarded the Indians about $81 million in federal funds.

abnormal psychology   see PSYCHOPATHOLOGY

abolitionists

In U.S. history, the abolitionists were reformers who sought to end the institution of black SLAVERY. In the late 18th and early 19th centuries, groups of abolitionists in Britain and France protested slavery in their nations' colonies and exposed the horrors of the African slave trade. In the United States, abolitionists first achieved prominence during the American Revolution. The opponents of slaveholding included some illustrious Founding Fathers. Certain that slavery violated the ideals of the Declaration of Independence, Benjamin FRANKLIN, Alexander HAMILTON, John JAY, Thomas PAINE, and Benjamin RUSH joined their antislavery efforts with those of the Quakers (Society of FRIENDS) and other religiously inspired Northerners.

By 1804 emancipation on a gradual basis had been enacted by every Northern state legislature. Partly as a result of abolitionists' pressure, measures were also taken on the national level to end U.S. participation in the African slave trade (1808) and to prohibit slavery's expansion in certain Western territories (the MISSOURI COMPROMISE, 1820). Some abolitionists formed the AMERICAN COLONIZATION SOCIETY, which sought to resettle freed slaves in Africa. During this era, however, abolitionist efforts proved ineffective in the Southern states, where slaveholding was deeply entrenched. From 1790 to 1830 the advocates of abolition in the South, led by Benjamin LUNDY, spoke mildly and favored gradual emancipation. A disruptive and radical abolitionism, however, had emerged by the early 1830s. Groups of New Englanders had begun branding slavery as a horrible sin and demanding "immediate, complete, and uncompensated emancipation" everywhere in the nation.

These abolitionists constituted one of the most controversial movements in American history. Its leadership included famous blacks and women as well as white males and was typified by editors such as the fiery Willi-

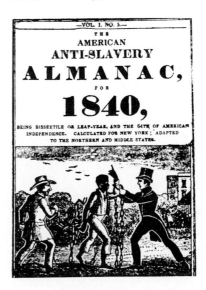

Abolitionists agitated against slavery with publications such as this almanac, whose cover shows a Northerner freeing a black slave from an angry Southern plantation owner.

am Lloyd GARRISON, orators such as Frederick DOUGLASS, Angelina GRIMKE, Wendell PHILLIPS, and Theodore WELD, and many other philanthropists, black agitators, and feminists. From the first, their aim was to transform the conscience of each white American, Northerner and Southerner, by preaching against the sin of slavery. They believed that through such agitation it was possible to convince slaveholders to show repentance by releasing their slaves. Abolitionists also called upon each white citizen to cast aside prejudice against blacks and to join the crusade against slavery. In December 1833 the abolitionists formed the American Anti-Slavery Society, hoping to mount a national campaign, and by 1835 they had established networks of state and local societies. As they founded abolitionist newspapers (for example, Garrison's *The Liberator*), held rallies, and distributed emancipationist tracts, these reformers also worked to improve conditions for Northern blacks by protesting segregation, founding schools and libraries, and protecting slaves who had escaped from the South. They also petitioned state legislatures and the U.S. Congress to act against slavery.

By the early 1840s, however, widespread and often violent opposition to the abolitionists' efforts had caused members of the movement to disagree profoundly about strategies and tactics. In 1840 some of the moderates formed the LIBERTY PARTY, which ran James BIRNEY as its presidential candidate in 1840 and 1844. These advocates of direct political action later supported the FREE-SOIL PARTY and ultimately the REPUBLICAN PARTY.

After the passage of the new FUGITIVE SLAVE LAW in 1850, many abolitionists involved themselves in the UNDERGROUND RAILROAD, by which slaves escaped to the North. That law also provoked Harriet Beecher STOWE to write the abolitionist classic UNCLE TOM'S CABIN (1852). Passage of the KANSAS-NEBRASKA ACT (1854), with its provision that the settlers in these territories decide whether there should be slavery, caused a migration of people dedicated to the antislavery cause. They clashed with proslavery settlers, and a local civil war developed. One such antislavery settler was John BROWN, whose extremism led him to murder five proslavery settlers in Kansas and subsequently (1859) to seize HARPERS FERRY.

During the Civil War many abolitionists pushed Abraham Lincoln to issue the EMANCIPATION PROCLAMATION (1863). After the war they lobbied for constitutional amendments and civil rights laws to protect the newly emancipated slaves. Others raised funds to support black education programs in the South and served there as teachers, ministers, and political reformers. Abolition ended with the passage in 1865 of the 13th Amendment, abolishing slavery.

abominable snowman   The abominable snowman, or yeti, is a giant creature believed by Himalayan tribesmen to roam the mountains at night searching for victims. It is described as having an upright stance, a covering of black to reddish hair, and the appearance of a bear, ape, or human. The yeti legend first became known out-side the area in 1921, when English explorers found tracks in the snow resembling huge human footprints. Several scientific expeditions failed to find any other evidence of the yeti's existence. Similar creatures are believed to have been sighted elsewhere—such as the Sasquatch, or Bigfoot, of U.S. Pacific Northwest forestland.

Aborigines, Australian [ab-uh-rij'-uh-neez]   The Australian Aborigines established themselves throughout Australia, including Tasmania, long before Europeans discovered it. By about 40,000 years ago small groups had arrived by sea, probably traveling from Southeast Asia to the north coast of Australia. Aborigines are dark skinned, with numerous regional variations in anatomical features and hair color. They were once considered a separate racial group, but blood group genetic studies have provided little definitive information about their racial composition. Before the first European settlement of Australia, the Aborigines numbered about 300,000. Their present population is estimated at about 125,000–130,000; about 45,000–50,000 are of homogeneous ancestry, and 70,000–80,000 are mixed Aboriginal and European.

Traditional Aboriginal Culture

About 500 different tribal groups existed, each occupying a particular stretch of country and speaking a different language or dialect. Among the best-known Aboriginal groups are the Aranda (Arunta), Bidjandjadjara (Pitjantjatjara), Gurindji, Gunwinggu, Kamilaroi, Murngin, Tiwi, Wailbri (Walbiri), Wurora, and Yir-yoront.

As seminomadic HUNTER-GATHERERS, the Aboriginal groups inhabited their own territories, but they joined with adjacent groups for certain purposes, among them religious gatherings and trade. They did not have permanent settlements but made small camps near watering places, building windbreaks and huts.

Because the Aborigines needed to be mobile, they had few everyday belongings. Men carried spears, spear-throwers, and various kinds of BOOMERANGS; women, their digging sticks, dishes, and bags or baskets. They usually went naked, but groups in cold southern areas made and wore fur cloaks. Aboriginal society had a well-developed trading economy: goods of various kinds (spears, ochres, implements, pendants) were exchanged and passed from one group to the next—the whole country was crisscrossed with trade routes.

Social Organization and Kinship. Religion and economics played an essential part in the two kinds of social units traditionally found throughout the continent. The first, a patrilineal local descent group, owned a specific area of land containing sacred sites of mythototemic significance; its adult male members were responsible for maintaining these sites and for conducting the associated rituals. The second kind of social unit, the mobile residential group, occupied and used available land in a given area. Every person was a member of a specific local

Yetibah Aborigines in Arnhem Land perform a ceremonial dance. Aborigines of unmixed descent, whose forebears were the original inhabitants of Australia, constitute less than 1% of the Australian population.

descent group but would join with others from the same and from other local descent groups for purposes of food collecting and other activities. The size of such residential groups varied according to the season.

All members of a tribe were linked through kinship, which was expressed in a complex system of genealogical and other types of classification. Every Aboriginal society had its own set of kin terms in its own particular kinship system, but all the societies had some elements in common. Kin terms indicated, among other things, marriage eligibility, responsibilities, and reasons for avoidance of particular individuals. Marriage rules varied, but generally a person had to marry someone who was related to him or her in a specified way. Marriage was seen as a union of individuals and kin groups.

Ritual and Art. In the traditional religious system of the Aborigines, human beings were believed to be a part of nature, intimately associated with other living things. This relationship underlined the concept sometimes called the Dreaming, of which totemism is one aspect. The Dreaming refers to the creative period when mythic spirits were believed to have shaped the land, establishing life. These beings were thought to live on eternally in spirit form and to have left tangible evidence of their presence in the shape of certain prominent land forms considered sacred. Religious ritual was pervasive in traditional Aboriginal life. Although presided over by males, it involved all members of the community. Some rituals, including elaborate funeral customs and initiation rites, served to renew the participants' ties with the Dreaming.

The Aborigines produced a wide range of ritual objects and emblems. Visual arts were highly developed, including fine bark and cave paintings, rock engravings, and sculptured posts and figures (see OCEANIA, ART OF). Song poetry ranged from the succinct verses of Central Australia and the Western Desert to the elaborate symbolic song cycles of northeastern Arnhem Land. Dance and the dramatic arts were also well developed.

Aboriginal Life after European Contact

With the arrival of Europeans in 1788, many Aboriginal societies were gradually destroyed. Clashes between Aborigines and Europeans were common. Large numbers of Aborigines were killed, others driven into the bush. Epidemics contributed to their dispersal and depopulation.

Maltreatment and violence gradually declined, but traditional sociocultural life became difficult to maintain. In some areas Aborigines of mixed European and Aboriginal ancestry replaced the traditional population. Over much of the southwestern, southeastern, and mideastern parts of the continent, traditional life ceased to exist; in the central and northern regions it continued in a modified form, especially in Arnhem Land and in the great Central Reserve. Today all Aborigines have had some contact with the Europeans. Those who live in the fringe settlements are rapidly incorporating Australian-European features into their culture.

All Aborigines are now Australian citizens and are no longer subject to restrictive legislation; they are eligible to vote and to receive Social Service benefits. In recent years they have been involved in political protest, particularly over land rights, housing and health, and political representation at all levels.

abortion   An abortion is the termination of a pregnancy before the fetus is viable, or capable of living outside the womb. An abortion may be spontaneous or induced. The latter is an act with ethical and legal ramifications.

Medical Aspects. Spontaneous abortion, or miscarriage, occurs when the embryo fails to develop, when there is complete or incomplete expulsion of the products of conception—the embryo or fetus, and placenta—or when the fetus dies prior to 20 weeks from the woman's last menstrual period (LMP). If fetal death occurs at 20 weeks or more after the LMP, it is termed a late fetal death or a stillbirth.

Perhaps as many as three-fourths of conceptions are spontaneously aborted. Most occur before the pregnancy can be confirmed, prior to 6 weeks after her LMP.

Induced abortion is a procedure intended to terminate a suspected or known pregnancy and to produce a nonviable fetus at any gestational age. Most induced abortions in the United States are performed in the first trimester—within 12 weeks of the LMP. The technique for virtually all first-trimester pregnancy terminations utilizes a procedure called vacuum aspiration or vacuum curettage. The cervix is dilated with a series of graduated, usually tapered dilators or with a type of dried seaweed, called laminaria, which expands as it absorbs moisture. After dilation, a hollow plastic tube with a hole near its end is inserted into the uterus. The embryo or fetus and placenta are drawn into the tube through vacuum pressure.

Second-trimester induced abortion involves a more complicated procedure. If the pregnancy has progressed to no more than 16 weeks since the LMP, the most common technique is dilation and evacuation, a method that is similar to vacuum aspiration. The next most common procedure, injection of fluid containing saline solution or hormones called prostaglandins into the amniotic sac, usually is postponed until after the 16th week in order to reduce the risk of injection outside the amniotic cavity.

In France during the 1980s an abortion-inducing drug called RU 486 was proving 85 percent effective during the first 6 weeks after LMP, especially when used with prostaglandins. By the end of the 1980s the drug remained licensed only in France, due to antiabortion pressures.

Legal Aspects. About half of the world's people live in countries where abortion is available on request, and another fourth live in areas where abortion is permitted to protect the woman's health. The most restrictive policies tend to be found in fundamentalist Islamic countries and countries of sub-Saharan Africa and Latin America.

In the United States legal induced abortion was generally unavailable until 1970, when a few states liberalized their abortion laws. In the cases ROE V. WADE and DOE V. BOLTON in 1973, however, the U.S. Supreme Court declared most restrictive abortion laws unconstitutional because they violate a woman's right of privacy. It left the decision to have a first-trimester abortion to the woman and her physician. States could pass regulations to ensure the safety of second-trimester abortions, and could prohibit third-trimester abortions. Since then, however, further restrictions have been legalized. In the 1989 case of *Webster* v. *Reproductive Services,* the Supreme Court upheld a Missouri law that prevented the performance of abortions by public employees or in taxpayer-supported facilities—a controversial decision that had reverberations in a number of states. In 1990 the Court ruled that states may require teenage girls to notify both parents before obtaining an abortion or else request a judicial hearing if they do not want to inform their parents of their decision.

The Hyde amendment passed by Congress in 1976 severely restricted federal funds for abortions, although many states continue to fund abortions for indigent women.

Impact of Legalization. In the 1960s, deaths from illegal abortions amounted to one-fifth of all deaths related to pregnancy and childbirth in the United States. After the 1973 decision, mortality and hospitalizations dropped dramatically, in part due to improved training and the use of safer techniques among abortion providers. Legalization also stimulated development of more convenient and lower-cost service. By the 1980s the majority of abortions were in freestanding clinics, and about one-half were outpatient procedures. About 27 per 1,000 U.S. women of childbearing age had induced abortions each year, a rate higher than in other industrialized Western nations but about half the worldwide rate.

Studies of long-term health consequences of abortion indicate that risks of spontaneous abortion, preterm delivery, and low birth weight for a second pregnancy following vacuum aspiration are no greater than risks for a first pregnancy. Furthermore, studies have been unable to link abortion with any latent long-term psychological problems.

Ethical Aspects. Opponents of legalized induced abortion, the "right-to-life" movement, believe that human life begins at conception and that abortion is the intentional killing of a human being and is thus morally wrong. In contrast, "pro-choice" proponents generally believe that human life begins when the fetus can survive outside the womb and that before then, since the fetus is not a separate human, it is morally acceptable to terminate the pregnancy. They argue that legal abortion is safer than illegal abortion and relieves the psychological and social problems associated with bearing an unwanted child.

Abraham　Abraham, originally called Abram, was Israel's first great patriarch. He probably lived in the late 3d or early 2d millennium BC, but the earliest source for information on his life is Genesis 11–25, written about 10 centuries later. He was born at Ur in Chaldea, where he married his half-sister SARAH. Under divine inspiration, he went to Haran in Mesopotamia. Later God commanded him to leave his home for a new land; in return God offered Abraham fame, land, and descendants, promising that he would become a blessing to all nations. Abraham obeyed and migrated to Canaan, where he lived as a nomadic chieftain. He soon became wealthy, but he still had no son. Because Sarah was advanced in years, she substituted her Egyptian slave HAGAR, who bore ISHMAEL, Abraham's first son. Later, in accord with a divine promise, Sarah gave birth to ISAAC. Abraham's faith was put to a severe test when God commanded that he sacrifice Isaac, his only son by Sarah. Abraham did not waver and he prepared for the sacrifice, but God spared the boy at the last moment, substituting a ram.

The Bible portrays Abraham as a man struggling to trust God's promises. By his faith Abraham became the father of the Israelite people and is still honored in three different religions. Jewish tradition stresses his monotheism. Christians see him as a model for the man of faith and recognize him as their spiritual ancestor. Muslims accept him as an ancestor of the Arabs through Ishmael. Numerous works of art are based on the story of the sacrifice of Isaac.

Abrahams, Peter　Peter Abrahams, who has used the pseudonym Peter Graham, was born in a township near Johannesburg on Nov. 19, 1919. He was the first black South African writer to gain worldwide recognition and to attract attention to the plight of blacks in that country. In an early novel, *Mine Boy* (1946), in his early short stories in *Dark Testament* (1942), and in his autobiographical novel, *Tell Freedom* (1954), he protests the treatment of blacks under apartheid. He has lived in England and Jamaica for more than 30 years, working as a journalist. Abrahams's later novels include *A Wreath for Udomo* (1956), set in West Africa, and *This Island Now* (1966), set in the Caribbean. Even in his writings set entirely outside Africa, however, Abrahams remains distinctly African in his outlook.

Abrams, Creighton As U.S. commander in the VIETNAM WAR from 1968 to 1972, Creighton Williams Abrams, b. Springfield, Mass., Sept. 15, 1914, d. Sept. 4, 1974, implemented the program of gradual U.S. withdrawal. A graduate (1936) of West Point, Abrams served in World War II and became army vice chief of staff in 1964. He was later army chief of staff (1972–74).

---

abrasive An abrasive is any powdered, granular, or solid substance used to wear off the surface of materials in order to alter their shape or to supply a finish. Common natural abrasives include garnet and emery, used for sandpaper; the quartz grains used in sandblasting stone and metals; and pumice, which is used as a scouring material in soaps and some dental pastes. The most important synthetic abrasives are silicon carbide, known by its trade name, CARBORUNDUM, which is used for grinding nonferrous metals and nonmetallic materials; aluminum oxide, a hard, steel-grinding abrasive; and metallic abrasives, such as iron and steel shot, steel wool, and metallic grit. Natural or synthetic diamonds, the hardest of all abrasives, are used in powdered form to grind or machine very hard materials, including solid diamonds.

Abrasives are glued or bonded onto grinding wheels or belts. They are also commonly used as a coating on cutting instruments and as a binder for cement. As a suspension in air, water, or oil, they can be projected against a surface that is to be ground.

See also: MACHINE TOOLS.

Abravanel, Isaac ben Judah [uh-brah'-vuh-nel] Isaac Abravanel (or Abrabanel), 1437–1508, was a Jewish biblical scholar, philosopher, and financier. Born in Lisbon, he served the rulers of Portugal (1471–83) and Castile (1484–92) until the Jews were expelled (1492) by Ferdinand and Isabella from Spain. He then served the government of Naples until the French conquered Naples (1495).

His biblical commentaries were unusual in introducing comparisons with the social situation of his own time. Abravanel was also one of the earliest Jewish commentators to refer to the contributions of Christian biblical scholars. His acceptance of the historical authenticity of the Bible led him to write a commentary criticizing MAIMONIDES' naturalistic view of prophecy. Abravanel also offered philosophic defenses of the expectation that the Jews would return to the Holy Land and the MESSIAH would rule the world.

Abravanel, Judah Judah Abravanel (or Abrabanel), 1460–1523, a Jewish physician and philosopher, wrote *Dialoghi d'Amore* (Dialogues of Love), one of the most widely circulated products of Renaissance NEOPLATONISM.

Born in Lisbon, the son of Isaac Abravanel, he fled to Spain in 1483 and then to Naples in 1492 after the expulsion of the Jews. His dialogues, composed by 1502, were first published posthumously in 1535. The central theme of the work is that love is the major creative force in the universe, and that love of God is the ultimate goal of the human soul. Thus a circle of love leads from God's creation in love to man's return to God through love. Abravanel was also a minor poet, but his dialogues had more influence on the poetry of his age than his verse.

Abruzzi [ah-broot'-see] A mountainous region of central Italy, Abruzzi has a population of 1,257,988 (1988 est.) and an area of 10,794 km^2 (4,168 mi^2). L'Aquila is the capital city of Abruzzi; its provinces include Chieti, L'Aquila, Pescara, and Teramo. The Adriatic Sea forms the region's eastern border. The average annual temperature is 13° C (55° F), and the rainfall averages 1,015 mm (40 in) in the Apennine Mountains. The Apennines cross the region in three northwest-southeast ranges, reaching a maximum altitude of 2,913 m (9,560 ft) in the Gran Sasso d'Italia group. Abruzzi's chief rivers are the Pescara, the Sangro, and the Tronto. The rugged terrain permits most agriculture of the subsistence variety. The chief crops are grapes, olives, sugar beets, and tobacco. Small amounts of foodstuffs, textiles, and clothing are produced.

Conquered by the Romans in the 4th century BC, Abruzzi later was held by the Lombards (6th–11th centuries), the Normans (12th–13th centuries), and the Kingdom of Naples (13th–19th centuries). The neighboring region of Molise was separated from Abruzzi in 1965.

Abruzzi, Luigi Amedeo, Duca degli [loo-ee'-jee ah-may-day'-oh] An Italian explorer, Abruzzi, b. Jan. 29, 1873, d. Mar. 18, 1933, was the son of Amadeus, king of Spain (1870–73), prince of Savoy-Aosta, and a cousin of Victor Emmanuel III, king of Italy. Abruzzi was the first to climb (1897) Mount St. Elias in Alaska and led (1899) a polar expedition that set a new record in the northern latitude reached. He later led mountain-climbing expeditions in the RUWENZORI range of East Africa (1906) and the HIMALAYAS (1909). In World War I, Abruzzi commanded an Italian fleet in the Adriatic Sea and afterward took part in the Italian colonization effort in East Africa.

Absalom, Absalom! In William FAULKNER's complex, difficult, and innovative novel *Absalom, Absalom!* (1936), racial pride and innocence of human needs and desires destroy the dynastic dreams of Thomas Sutpen. The novel is constructed as a reverie and debate on the meaning of the past, using multiple narrators, including Quentin Compson of *The Sound and the Fury* (1929), and varieties of the stream-of-consciousness technique to speculate on rather than reveal the Sutpen family's mysterious history of aggrandizement, miscegenation, abandonment, and murder. *Absalom, Absalom!*, perhaps

Faulkner's most demanding novel, is considered one of his greatest works.

ABSCAM The ABSCAM (a contraction of "Abdul Scam") investigation, conducted by the Federal Bureau of Investigation (FBI) in 1978–80, resulted in the conviction of seven members of the U.S. Congress and five other public officials for bribery, conspiracy, and related charges. As revealed early in 1980, FBI agents impersonating an Arab sheikh and his henchmen had offered bribes in return for preferential treatment in gaining entry into the United States, building casinos in Atlantic City, N.J., and other favors. Videotapes of their encounters showed public officials and their associates accepting bribes.

Sen. Harrison Williams and Reps. John Jenrette, Richard Kelly, Raymond Lederer, John Murphy, Michael Myers, and Frank Thompson were the members of Congress convicted. Critics of the FBI's methods in the ABSCAM case questioned whether ENTRAPMENT had taken place, but a Senate panel later concluded that civil rights had not been violated.

abscess An abscess results when bacteria—usually *Streptococcus*—spreading into tissue cause INFLAMMATION. A fibrous wall forms so that the infection is sealed off from other tissue, and pus—yellowish white fluid containing white blood cells, bacteria, and dead tissue—fills the center of the walled-in region. An abscess is painful when the inflamed area becomes congested, causing pressure on nearby nerve endings. In order to heal, an abscess must be drained and then treated with antibiotic drugs. Common skin abscesses are BOILS and carbuncles, and they can affect such areas as the middle ear (see EAR DISEASE) and the eye. An abscess of a tooth root can occur if dental decay is advanced (see TEETH), and tuberculosis begins with abscesses in the lungs.

absolute The word *absolute* is used by philosophers and by theologians to indicate ultimate reality conceived as an all-inclusive whole—everything that exists physically, mentally, and spiritually.

The phrase *the absolute* became prominent through the writings of the 18th- and 19th-century German idealists Johann Gottlieb FICHTE, Friedrich W. J. SCHELLING, and especially G. W. F. HEGEL. In Hegelian IDEALISM the absolute is interpreted as rational mind, known and analyzed only as it is manifested in human experience and history. The term is prominent in the writings of the English idealist F. H. BRADLEY and the American philosopher Josiah ROYCE.

absolute zero Absolute zero is the lowest theoretical TEMPERATURE, representing the complete absence of heat. At this temperature matter would possess zero ENTROPY and maximum molecular order, the volume of an ideal gas would vanish, and a thermodynamic heat engine would operate at 100 percent efficiency. Although absolute zero cannot actually be reached, approximations of less than $0.001°$ C above absolute zero have been created in the laboratory.

Absolute zero is the lowest point of an absolute temperature scale. Such a scale can be established by measuring the pressure of a trapped volume of gas as a function of its temperature in ordinary Celsius or Fahrenheit degrees. Most gases display a linear relationship between pressure and temperature under conditions not far from ambient; this experimental fact is known as Charles's law. Extrapolating this linear relationship to the point at which the gas pressure becomes zero defines the absolute zero of temperature. The extrapolation is necessary because all gases turn to liquid before absolute zero is reached. The absolute zero thus determined is $-273.15°$ C ($-459.67°$ F). This temperature is the zero point of the absolute Kelvin and Rankine temperature scales. One Celsius degree and one Kelvin are equal in magnitude, as are one Fahrenheit degree and one Rankine degree.

The fact that absolute zero is unattainable in any real process is known as the third law of THERMODYNAMICS. Formulated by Walther Nernst in 1906, this natural law states that no matter how cold an object becomes, it can be made still colder without quite reaching absolute zero.

See also: CRYOGENICS; SUPERCONDUCTIVITY; SUPERFLUIDITY

absolutism Absolutism is a political system that concentrates power in the hands of one person or a group of persons who have almost unlimited authority. History is replete with tyrants and dictators, but the notion of absolutism became prominent in Europe during the 16th, 17th, and 18th centuries when monarchs were struggling to wrest power from groups such as the church and the nobility and to create national states. The most famous absolutist was Louis XIV of France, who is said to have declared that he himself was the state: "L'état, c'est moi." Others were the Tudor and Stuart rulers of England and Frederick the Great of Prussia.

absorption In chemistry, absorption is the process by which energy or a material called the absorbate is taken up by some other material, called the absorbent, in such a way that the former is distributed throughout the latter. A commonplace example of absorption is the action of blotting paper, which is essentially a mat of cellulose fibers; liquids are readily taken up into the interstices between the fibers. In industry, absorption is often used to remove a noxious gas that could cause air pollution, such as the sulfur dioxide produced in the burning of coal. The absorption of light is widely used in quantitative chemical analysis. In biology, absorption refers to the taking up of substances by the blood or lymph.

Absorption is differentiated from adsorption, which is a surface phenomenon. This distinction can be made clearly when the absorbent is liquid. It often becomes blurred, however, in solid absorbents, which are criss-crossed with fine pores, so that taking up of the absorbate on the surface of the pores can result in its dispersion throughout the absorbent. In some instances the absorbent reacts chemically with the absorbate.

absorption, light   When light is incident on a material, some or all of it may be absorbed, reflected, transmitted, or scattered. Each effect is caused by the interaction of the light with the atoms and molecules of the material; the optical effect that predominates depends on the nature of the material and the wavelength of the incident light.

Light energy that is absorbed is transformed into internal ENERGY within the material. The most common transformation is to thermal energy, or heat, although changes to other forms, such as chemical energy (see PHOTOCHEMISTRY), are possible. Energy that is reradiated at the same wavelength is known as scattered light. FLUORESCENCE and PHOSPHORESCENCE are phenomena in which the incident radiation is reemitted at longer wavelengths.

All transparent substances absorb light to some extent; even through water light is diminished, as is obvious at ocean depths. The degree of light absorbance by a substance depends on the wavelength of the incident light. A colorless substance, such as air or quartz crystals, absorbs light uniformly throughout the range of visible wavelengths. Grass absorbs red light so that the reflected component is seen as green, the complementary COLOR of red.

Devices that measure light absorption are the colorimeter (usually used only for visible light) and the spectrophotometer (which is able to function at additional wavelengths, including ultraviolet light and infrared radiation). These instruments are common to most laboratories.

See also: SPECTROSCOPY.

abstract art   Abstract art is generally taken to mean painting and sculpture by artists for whom the manner and the means are the subject rather than the representation of any object. All art is abstract to some degree; that is, it is removed from the perceived elements of nature. The sculpture of archaic Greece, of Egypt, of primitive tribes, both ancient and modern, use simplified, often geometricized forms, and the frescoes of GIOTTO DI BONDONE thus honor the two-dimensionality of his medium. The term *abstract art*, however, is best used to signify a main line of development that only began in this century with the profound desire in MODERN ART to express the continuum of inner life in purely pictorial terms. Abstract art's beginnings can be traced to James McNeill WHISTLER's "art for art's sake" theories and to his *Arrangements, Symphonies,* and *Nocturnes*, closely related to the art of music, which, to many abstractionists, is the universal abstract language.

Wassily KANDINSKY, in 1910, made his first conscious-

Composition with Red, Yellow, and Blue *(1920) is by the Dutch artist Piet Mondrian. Mondrian restricted his abstract paintings to straight lines and right angles, using only three primary colors and gray, black, and white. (Private collection, Amsterdam.)*

ly abstract watercolor, a composition of swirling, interacting spots of color deeply related to his love of music, the basis of his aesthetic principle. During the same year, Kandinsky began to write *Concerning the Spiritual in Art*, expounding his metaphysically based ideas concerning inner reality. In 1911–12, the Czech artist Frantisek KUPKA painted what is often considered the first totally abstract canvas, *Fugue in Red and Blue* (National Gallery, Prague), whose rhythmic patterns of color were directly inspired by musical correspondences. Pure color as both form and subject was the central idea in the Orphism of Robert DELAUNAY and Francis PICABIA, which developed beginning in 1912.

Pure abstraction was, however, carried to its most extreme limits by the Russians, beginning in 1913, who extended the philosophical and geometric elements of CUBISM and developed an architecturally based abstraction completely removed from exterior realms. The most far-reaching experimentation in abstract art as the expression of the reality of the fourth dimension (inner reality) took form in the rayonism of Natalia Goncharova and Mikhail LARIONOV (begun by Larionov in Moscow in 1911–12); the CONSTRUCTIVISM of Naum GABO, Antoine PEVSNER and Vladimir TATLIN; the nonobjectivism of Aleksandr RODCHENKO; and the SUPREMATISM of Kasimir MALEVICH. The principles established by these artists have had wide significance in successive abstract art movements from the BAUHAUS during the 1920s and '30s to the structures of MINIMAL ART during the 1960s.

Chief among the other innovators of abstract art are Piet MONDRIAN and artists of the DE STIJL movement (such as Theo van DOESBURG and Bart van der Leck), developed in the Netherlands around 1917. In neoplasticism, Mon-

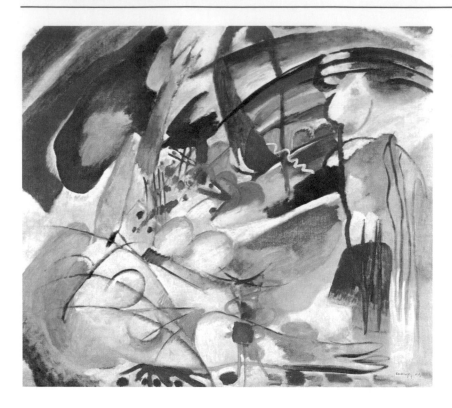

In Improvisation 33 *(1913) Wassily Kandinsky, one of the principal pioneers of abstract art, used the interaction of color, line, and form to express an inner reality or spirituality. (Stedelijk Museum, Amsterdam.)*

drian developed his ideas of pure plastic (formative) relationships as the basis for attaining the objective purity and universality of mathematics. In his philosophical reduction of form to the use of the three primary colors (red, yellow, and blue) and the right angle in horizontal-vertical position, Mondrian exerted great influence both on architecture and on painting, from the Bauhaus to the American Abstract Artists (founded in New York in 1936) to the American ABSTRACT EXPRESSIONISTS of the 1940s and '50s.

Abstract art, defined as the expression in pictorial terms of the universal structures and rhythms of inner reality, has continued as the central concern of numerous painters, sculptors, and architects to the present, all of whom have, to some degree, worked from the fundamental contributions of the pioneers in the field.

See also: ARCHITECTURE; ART; PAINTING; SCULPTURE.

abstract expressionism   Abstract expressionism is the collective name for the work of a heterogeneous group of New York artists who produced vivid, emotionally charged nonrepresentational paintings characterized by very bold uses of color and mass. The term *abstract expressionism* was used in 1929 by Alfred H. BARR, Jr., founder of the MUSEUM OF MODERN ART in New York, in reference to the early improvisations of Wassily KANDINSKY. In 1946, Robert Coates, art critic of the *New Yorker* magazine, employed it in relation to a group of paintings

done in New York. The term was popularized during a series of discussions that took place in 1952 at the "Club" on Eighth Street in New York City among a number of painters and sculptors; during the sessions, the artists themselves rejected it as an unsatisfactory indicator of their art. Although the term, along with others used to refer to the art that developed in New York during the 1940s—*action painting, the New York school,* and *American-type painting*—is in many ways misleading, it has remained the predominant one in discussion of this art. Abstract expressionism is not a unified artistic style; what the artists who promulgated it had in common was the search for a significant subject in an abstract format. They sought a format that could express their individual personalities and at the same time could lead to the expression, through the process of painting, of a universal, timeless content.

During the 1930s many of these artists had worked on the Federal Art Project under the Works Progress Administration. Some had come in contact with Hans HOFMANN, already an influential teacher of modernist theory in New York City. The majority had been exposed to various modernisms (such as CONSTRUCTIVISM, DADA, SURREALISM, and the work of Paul KLEE and Kandinsky) through gallery and museum shows, and most had grappled with CUBISM, specifically in the then overwhelming person of Pablo PICASSO. In 1937, John Graham's influential book *System and Dialectics of Art* was published, and his ideas on the prominence of the subconscious, based on the theories of

Sigmund FREUD and C. G. JUNG, were already becoming an important topic of conversation. Willem DE KOONING and Arshile GORKY, then close friends of Graham, were already showing a shift in style and direction. By the end of the 1930s, a few small groups of painters in New York City were expressing their dissatisfaction with the current,

prevalent trends of social realism and geometric abstraction (as exemplified by the group called American Abstract Artists). During the next few years many prominent European modernist artists such as Max ERNST, Fernand LÉGER, André MASSON, and Piet MONDRIAN emigrated to New York to escape the war in Europe. Their arrival reinforced the American artists, who were politically conscious of, as well as schooled in, modernist art theory, Freudian and Jungian psychology, existentialist philosophy, theories of symbolist poetry, and Oriental art and ideas. They also knew the work of Milton AVERY, Arthur DOVE, and the group shown by Alfred STIEGLITZ at his American Place Gallery, the most avant-garde artists of that period in the United States.

During the early 1940s, two important groups of artists were actively meeting and discussing an art that combined mastery of painterly values with psychologically intense content, and thus expressed universal human emotions appropriate to the tragic climate of World War II. In 1941–42 the American artists Robert MOTHERWELL and William Baziotes, along with the Chilean surrealist Roberto MATTA ECHAURREN, were discussing such ideas; they were soon joined by Jackson POLLOCK and Lee KRASNER. They based their work on surrealism's generative principle of "psychic automatism" but differed from the

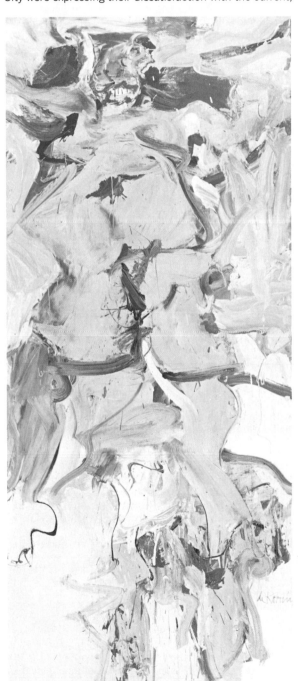

(Left) *Willem de Kooning's* Woman, Sag Harbor *(1964) reflects the energetic nature of the "gestural" wing of abstract expressionism. The painting is one of a series entitled* Women. *(Hirshhorn Museum and Sculpture Garden, Washington, D.C.)* (Below) *Mark Rothko's* Blue, Orange, Red *(1961) is an example of the "color-field" branch of abstract expressionism. In his paintings, Rothko uses the interaction of color relationships to convey such basic human emotions as joy and sorrow. (Private collection.)*

Europeans in their equal regard for the process of painting, for the plastic qualities of the painterly medium. At the same time, Adolph GOTTLIEB and Mark ROTHKO, soon joined by Barnett NEWMAN and Theodoros Stamos, were advocating the use of ancient mythology and primitivizing content in their similar efforts to forego current aesthetics. Separately and simultaneously, other artists such as Richard POUSETTE-DART, Ad REINHARDT, and Clyfford STILL were evolving their art of parallel ideas. By the mid-'40s these artists had discovered their unique painting approach, one that placed them at the forefront of abstract painting at midcentury. By the end of the decade, they were moving apart; interrelationships, although intense, were always tentative, largely because of the individualistic nature of their art.

The abstract expressionists are usually divided into two groups: the "gestural" wing includes Gorky, de Kooning, Hofmann, and Pollock; the "color-field" wing, Gottlieb, Newman, Rothko, and Stamos. Any such classification, however, is an oversimplification. Even though the abstract expressionists benefited mutually during their formative years of the 1940s, in the end they must be considered separately, as painters who always work toward the universal via the personal, striving to convey a timeless and deeply emotional human content through abstract form.

See also: ABSTRACT ART; ART; MODERN ART; PAINTING.

---

absurdism   Absurdism is an idea commonly associated with EXISTENTIALISM. Beginning in the 19th century, mainly through the influence of Søren KIERKEGAARD, religion was often described as absurd because it could not be justified on rational principles; rather, it was considered as based on what Kierkegaard called "a leap of faith." In their discussions of consciousness, Martin HEIDEGGER and Jean Paul SARTRE described the human consciousness as facing an apparently absurd world—absurd because it finds itself at the crossroads of Being and Nothingness, baffled by the meaninglessness of the human condition. Sartre's ideas of absurdity, anguish, and disgust are expressed in his plays and novels, especially in *Nausea* (1938; Eng. trans., 1949). A philosophical basis for the modern THEATER OF THE ABSURD has been established by other existentialists, such as Albert CAMUS, Karl JASPERS, and Gabriel MARCEL.

See also: ALIENATION.

Abu Bakr [ah'-boo bak'-ur]   Abu Bakr, b. *c*.573, d. Aug. 23, 634, father-in-law of the Prophet MUHAMMAD, was first caliph ("successor") after the Prophet's death in 632. An early convert and loyal follower of Muhammad, Abu Bakr led the Muslim community from 632 to 634, but his caliphate was contested by ALI, the Prophet's son-in-law. He also faced opposition from unruly tribes and led successful military campaigns across the Arabian peninsula into Syria and Palestine.

Abu Dhabi [ah'-boo dah'-bee]   Abu Dhabi (1980 pop., 242,975) is the capital of the Abu Dhabi sheikhdom on the southeast shore of the Persian Gulf and the capital of the United Arab Emirates. Its climate is arid, with an average annual rainfall of 60 mm (2.4 in). Income from oil production has transformed it from a fishing village in the 1960s into a high-rise city with an international airport and an artificial harbor.

Abu Madi, Iliya [ah'-boo mah'-dee, ee'lee-yah]   Abu Madi, 1889–1957, was a Lebanese poet and journalist who emigrated to the United States and collaborated with Kahlil Gibran. He published several collections, of which *The Brooks* (1927) and *The Thickets* (1940) are the most notable. Nostalgia for happiness, philosophical skepticism about the purpose of life, optimism, egalitarianism, and brotherly love among humans are his main themes.

Abu Nuwas [ah'-boo noo-wahs']   The Arabic poet Abu Nuwas, Father of the Forelocks, *c*.756–*c*.810, got this nickname from two locks of hair that reached to his shoulders. His real name was Hasan ibn Hani. Although he composed a variety of poems in traditional style, such as panegyrics, satires, hunting verses, and elegies—even religious poems—his fame rests on his wine (*khamr*) poetry called *Khamriyat* and on his love poems addressed to young boys.

Abu Simbel [ah'-boo sim'-bul]   Abu Simbel, or Ibsambul, located 282 km (175 mi) south of Aswan, Egypt, on the west bank of the Nile, is the site of two famous rock-hewn temples built during the reign of Ramses II (1304–1237 BC). Four colossal statues of Ramses, measuring about 20 m (65 ft) high, are carved on the facade of the larger temple. Four others, about 10 m (33 ft) high, together with two statues of his principal queen, Nefertari, embellish the facade of the smaller temple.

The inner walls of the larger temple bear painted reliefs of the king performing religious ceremonies and fighting against the Hittites and other foreign foes. At the far end, 55 m (180 ft) from the entrance, are statues of the gods Ptah, Amon-Re, Re-Harakhti, and the deified king, on which the direct rays of the Sun shine at sunrise twice annually, on Feb. 20 and Oct. 20. The smaller temple was dedicated to the goddess Hathor and the deified Nefertari.

The construction of the Aswan High Dam and the creation of Lake Nasser made it necessary to move the temples to high ground above the original site. The project was finished in 1968 at a cost of $40 million.

Abydos [uh-by'-duhs]   Abydos, approximately 521 km (324 mi) south of Cairo, is the Greek name for the ancient Egyptian city of Abdu. The shrine of its primeval local god, Khenti-amentiu, became the major sanctuary

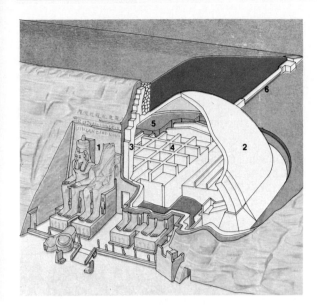

The Great Temple at Abu Simbel, Egypt, was built during the 13th century BC. Guarding its facade (1) are four seated colossi of Ramses II. Inside are two halls, eight adjoining chambers, a vestibule, three apartments, and a sanctuary consecrated to Ramses II and the pantheon of Egyptian gods. The temple was threatened in 1964 by the rising waters of Lake Nasser, an artificial lake created by the Aswan High Dam. A $40 million rescue operation required the disassembling and reconstruction of the temple at a higher elevation. Beneath an artificial mountain, an immense concrete dome (2) protects the temple from tons of rock that were piled up to simulate Abu Simbel's original setting. Stepped walls (3) behind the facade serve as reinforcement for the ancient colossi. A gridlike structure (4) supports the ceiling blocks (5) of the inner chamber, and a pipe at the rear (6) draws fresh air into the shrine.

The Abyssinian cat, a short-haired domestic breed, is believed to be related to the cats depicted in ancient Egyptian art.

dedicated to OSIRIS, whose head was traditionally believed to be buried there. Abydos was continuously occupied from the Predynastic to the Roman period. What may be the tombs of kings of the Archaic period were excavated by Sir Flinders PETRIE in the northwest sector of the site. Among the most impressive monuments are the temple of SETI I of the 19th (1320–1200 BC) dynasty, which contains perhaps the finest royal painted relief preserved from ancient Egypt, and the famous Gallery of the List of Kings, on the walls of which appears the chronological succession of most of the Egyptian rulers from Menes to Seti I. To the east of the temple lies the Osireion, also built by Seti I. It is a subterranean complex of chambers dedicated to the cult of Osiris and perhaps symbolizes the emergence of the world from the waters of chaos.

Abyssinia   see ETHIOPIA

Abyssinian cat   [ab-uh-sin'-ee-uhn]   The Abyssinian is a medium-sized cat with a triangular face, large pointed ears, lean body, and long tail. The almond-shaped eyes are hazel to orange, and the fine, short-haired coat ranges from light brown to silver. Each hair is ticked with darker brown, gray, or black. The tail and ears are darker toward the tip. The red Abyssinian is a recognized breed.

Despite its name, the Abyssinian probably originated in the upper Nile Valley and may be the closest living relative of the sacred cat of ancient Egypt. It differs from many cats in that it enjoys playing with water.

Abzug, Bella S.   [ab'-zuhg]   Bella Savitzky Abzug, b. New York City, July 24, 1920, represented New York's 19th and 20th districts in Congress from 1971 to 1976. A lawyer long active in liberal causes, particularly the civil rights and peace movements, Abzug became nationally prominent in the early 1970s as an articulate advocate of women's rights and as a leader of the House of Representatives' anti–Vietnam War group. In 1976, Abzug was unsuccessful in a bid for the U.S. Senate, and she was defeated in 1978 in an attempt to reenter Congress. Prominent in several women's political organizations, she was cochairwoman of the President's National Advisory Committee on Women from November 1977 to January 1979. Subsequently, she returned to the private practice of law in New York City. Abzug has written Bella! Ms. Abzug Goes to Washington (ed. by Mel Ziegler, 1972) and Gender Gap: Bella Abzug's Guide to Political Power for American Women (with Mim Kelber, 1984).

AC   see ALTERNATING CURRENT

acacia   [uh-kay'-shuh]   Acacia is the common name for plants of the genus Acacia of the legume family, Leguminosae. The genus contains many familiar and useful species. Acacias are known as wattles in Australia and as thorns in eastern Africa, and are sometimes sold by florists as mimosa in Europe and North America.

World climatic zones that have a long, dry winter and a short, wet summer often support a shrubby vegetation known as thorn scrub and savanna. Acacia trees constitute much of the vegetation in such climatic regimes. The

The catlaw acacia grows in Mexico and the southwestern United States. It is about 4.5 m (15 ft) tall, with yellow, cylindrical flowers and thin, twisted fruit pods.

trees are characterized by their umbrella shape, with basal branching of the stems; the foliage forms a flattened or curved crown. The flowers, usually yellow, grow in crowded, globose heads or cylindrical spikes. Spines are common, and the Central American bull-horn acacia, *A. cornigera,* hosts a pulp-eating ant that hollows out the plant's large spines in search of food and then lives in them. Acacias can tolerate long periods of drought and, because of the thorns, survive heavily grazed areas.

Acacias are used as ornamentals in tropical and subtropical gardens, as shade trees, and as indoor plants. Livestock are fed the leaves of some acacias; in Australia and parts of Africa the seeds or pods of other acacias are eaten by humans.

Australians use acacia wood for railroad ties, wheels, handles, and furniture. Some pods yield a substance used for washing silk and as a shampoo. Acacias are also sources of gums, tannin, and a dye called cutch.

academic art   see ACADEMIES OF ART

▬

academic freedom   Academic freedom refers to the freedom of scholars, usually at college and university levels, to teach, publish, and engage in research unhindered, regardless of their political and social beliefs or affiliations. Those protected by academic freedom, in turn, have the responsibility to conduct research honestly, to report their findings accurately, and to teach without bias. In democratic societies academic freedom is respected as a right but is nevertheless often challenged during critical periods. In totalitarian societies, where education is partly directed toward indoctrination, it is rejected.

In the United States the American Association of Uni-

versity Professors (AAUP) has generally been accepted as the leader in the movement toward academic freedom for professors. Its *1940 Statement of Principles on Academic Freedom and Tenure,* adopted jointly with the Association of American Colleges, is widely accepted as definitive.

Tenure, the practice of assuring professors of continued employment once they have passed successfully through a probationary period and provided they are not later found seriously deficient by a carefully specified procedure, is an important protection of academic freedom. Although academic freedom of untenured professors, and of students, is not formally protected, it is of equal concern in academic communities. Until the STUDENT MOVEMENTS of the 1960s, the United States lagged in recognizing student academic freedom.

The U.S. Supreme Court has given legal status to academic freedom claims as falling under the 1st Amendment in decisions such as *Sweezy* v. *New Hampshire* (1957) and *Perry* v. *Sinderman* (1972).

▬

Académie des Sciences [ah-kah-day-mee' day see-awns']   Founded in 1666 by Jean Baptiste Colbert and Louis XIV, the Académie des Sciences in Paris quickly became the national center for French science and for the French scientific establishment, as well as the model for similar institutions elsewhere. Until its reform in 1699, the academy numbered a dozen men who worked collectively and anonymously. Enlarged to 50 resident members in various classes and grades, from adjunct to funded pensioner, the academy then formally assumed bureaucratic control over French science and technology.

From 1699 the academy published its famous scientific series *Mémoires,* offered prizes for scientific research, and supported several important scientific expeditions. Buffon, Condorcet, Fontenelle, Laplace, and Lavoisier numbered among its more important members and officers. The academy was closed in 1793 during the French Revolution and reconstituted as part of the INSTITUT DE FRANCE in 1795. It served as an active center for scientific research and debate until the 1830s. Today it continues as the national academy and the premier scientific society in France.

▬

Académie Française [ah-kah-day-mee' frawn-sez']   The Académie Française (French Academy) is the most renowned and oldest of the five learned societies that make up the INSTITUT DE FRANCE. Established by Cardinal Richelieu, the Académie received its charter from Louis XIII in 1635. The founding members were to work "at the development, unification, and purification of the French language." The Académie still fulfills this mission in its revision of the *Dictionnaire.* Eight editions were published from 1694 to 1932, and work on the ninth continues. Words are illustrated with literary citations, and slang and colloquialisms are avoided.

Membership in the Académie today is largely honorary, with writers, professors, theologians, historians, and philosophers filling the 40 chairs to which they are elected for life. Candidates for the Académie file a formal application, and the new member delivers a discourse thanking the Académie and praising his or her predecessor.

Since 1914 the Académie has annually bestowed a literary prize on an author whose work is of "elevated inspiration and style." Laureates have included Georges Bernanos, François Mauriac, and Antoine de Saint-Exupéry. Landmarks in the society's long history occurred in 1971, when the Académie installed its first foreign member, Julian Green (an American novelist who wrote in French), and in 1981, when the first woman, Marguerite Yourcenar, took her seat.

Académie Royale de Danse   see BALLET

---

academies of art   Academies of art are generally both art schools and honorary bodies; they provide training for students and, through restricted membership, prestige for recognized professionals. Their aim is to preserve the Renaissance identification of artistic practice with the ideals of humanism and to perpetuate the craftsmanship that makes this association meaningful.

Until recent times, art academies epitomized the highest expression of art for an elite audience and for various government bodies, who relied on academy members to design and decorate royal houses and public monuments. Modernist ideals have done much to devalue and discredit the historical contribution of the academies; since 1900 academic art has for many people been associated with "official art," and the term *academic* is often used as a reproach for hackneyed work. It is worth noting that almost all artists revered in modern times, both by specialists and by the public, attended some form of art academy, and that academic art is now being reevaluated.

Most of the major academies of fine arts are still in existence. The first were founded in Italy: the Accademia del Disegno (Academy of Design) in Florence in 1563 under the sponsorship of Duke Cosimo I de'Medici (see MEDICI family); and the Accademia di San Luca (St. Luke was the patron saint of artists) in Rome in 1593. These were primarily associations of artists and patrons that attempted to challenge the powerful and restrictive GUILD system, in which artists were identified with artisans. In contrast to the practical, on-the-job training in the workshops of the guilds, the academies formulated a theoretical component they termed *disegno*—the drawing and design that underlaid all artistic activity and embraced the principles of PERSPECTIVE and ANATOMY. Since Renaissance humanism regarded the human being as the highest expression of the divine ideal, life drawing became the keystone of academic curricula.

The art schools of later academies were divided into two basic sections: one for the study of the antique (plaster casts of ancient Greek and Roman statues and reliefs) and an advanced section for study from live models. Teaching that art should ennoble nature, the academies claimed that nature itself was an insufficient model for "high" art and that the "ideal" works of the ancients

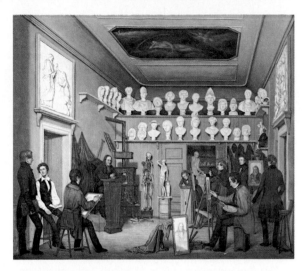

A portraiture class is the subject of Joachim Ferdinand Richardt's Painting Class at the Royal Academy of Fine Arts in Charlottenborg Palace *(1839). The academy was established in Copenhagen in 1754. (Thorvaldsen Museum, Copenhagen.)*

compensated for nature's imperfections and were therefore a necessary first step in preparation for work with a live model.

The most important academy of modern times was the Académie Royale de Peinture et de Sculpture, founded in 1648 in Paris to overcome restrictions pressed on court painters by the guild. Eventually, this organization was encompassed in the centralized planning of LOUIS XIV and his finance minister Jean Baptiste COLBERT, and was subject to their review. They had clear ideas about how art should be used (to glorify the king and embellish the royal residences), and consequently the Académie Royale systematized its pedagogical procedures. For the first time, problems of technique and composition were explicitly formulated, methods explained, and basic conventions defined. These procedures were handed down to later academies, most notably Madrid's Academia de San Fernando (1752), the Düsseldorf Akademie (1767), London's Royal Academy (1768), the Munich Akademie (1770), and New York's National Academy of Design (1825), founded by the painter-scientist Samuel F. B. MORSE.

Although academies originally obtained support from artists who sought improved social and professional status, they proliferated because the dominant classes saw in them an instrument for their own glorification. The hierarchy of modes instituted by the French Académie Royale reflected that influence, and it persisted through the 19th century in practice, if not in principle. Subjects for painting were carefully ranked: at the top were history painting and PORTRAITURE, and at the bottom STILL LIFE, LANDSCAPE, and GENRE PAINTING (scenes of everyday life). History painting comprised biblical motifs, events from ancient and contemporary history, especially scenes featuring the king or his ancestors, and allegorical and mythological representation.

During the French Revolution, the Académie Royale was suppressed, but it was reconstituted in 1795 as part of the Institut de France, with the honorary and pedagogical functions strictly separated. The art school, which eventually became the world-famous ÉCOLE DES BEAUX-ARTS (School of Fine Arts), offered advanced drawing instruction, architectural training, and a series of competitions culminating with the Prix de Rome—a special traveling fellowship enabling the gifted pupil to reside at the academy's branch in Rome. Other art academies were established in Rome, notably the American Academy in Rome, founded in 1894 as a school of architecture.

The Royal Academy in London became one of the best regulated in the world under the painter Sir Joshua REYNOLDS, its founder. GEORGE III provided it with "patronage, protection, and support," and he early made his influence felt in selecting as its second president the American expatriate artist Benjamin WEST.

Many American academies of art are both schools and bodies of professionals. The National Academy of Design in New York and the PENNSYLVANIA ACADEMY OF THE FINE ARTS, founded in 1805, were unique in admitting women much earlier than the European academies.

---

academy   An academy is an association dedicated to learning and the arts. It may be a learned society, a professional body, an institution for specialized instruction in a particular subject, or even a high school.

The original Academy, established by the Greek scholar Plato in 387 BC, appears on a mosaic unearthed at Pompeii. The school was named for its location in the grove of Akademe.

The original Academy was a school founded (387 BC) near Athens by PLATO to embody a new educational idea. Plato planned to have a single center for teaching and research that would bring together experts in all branches of learning and that would include younger scholars to give continuity to its work. Mathematics, astronomy, and legislation were three areas in which the Academy became distinguished. The school had a library, a residential building, and a garden. Tradition held that, long ago, the garden had been owned by Akademus, a local hero of the Trojan War. His former garden, or olive grove, was therefore called *akademia* before Plato established his Academy there. In addition to Plato, the mathematician Eudoxus of Cnidus was a senior member; younger academicians included Aristotle, Xenocrates, and Speusippus. The Academy continued as a center of learning until it was closed by the emperor Justinian in AD 529. It is the direct ancestor of all later Western colleges and universities.

Several academies of poets and artists thrived in France and Italy in the 13th and 14th centuries. The Accademia Platonica, founded in Florence during the 1440s, was the most famous of the Renaissance academies. It stressed the study of Plato's works, the purification of the Italian language, and the study of Dante.

The ACADÉMIE FRANÇAISE, chartered in 1635 and still operating today, was established to render the French language "pure, eloquent, and capable of treating the arts and sciences." Other academies, such as the British ROYAL SOCIETY, chartered in 1662, encouraged the growth of experimental science through discussion and occasional sponsorship of scientific projects. Academies of painting and sculpture became common in Europe in the 17th and 18th centuries.

In colonial America, "academies" were established in Pennsylvania, New Jersey, and the Southern states to educate the middle classes in useful skills as well as academic subjects. The word has regained its professional and artistic connotations in modern America without losing the technical overtones of the schools. Perhaps the best known of the professional institutions is the Academy of Motion Picture Arts and Sciences, which annually gives ACADEMY AWARDS to outstanding motion pictures, performers, and technicians.

Academy Awards   The Academy Awards are annual awards presented by the Academy of Motion Picture Arts and Sciences for achievement in various categories of filmmaking. Nominees are selected by their colleagues in the movie industry (for example, cinematographers nominate cinematographers and producers nominate producers), and the winners are chosen in secret ballot by a vote of the full academy membership. About two dozen awards are given for American films, of which the most famous are those for best performance by an actor and actress, best director, and best picture. At the awards ceremony, televised each spring, each winner is presented with a gold statuette, dubbed "Oscar" in 1931 by a subsequent executive director of the academy, Margaret Herrick, who thought it resembled her uncle of the same name.

The first Academy Awards were presented in 1929, with Paramount's *Wings* (1928) taking the coveted best-picture prize. M-G-M's 1959 epic *Ben-Hur*, with 11 awards, holds the record for the most prizes won by any single film. Actress Katharine Hepburn and director John Ford each hold 4, the most given to an individual.

Academy of Sciences of the USSR

The Academy of Sciences of the USSR oversees the natural and social sciences in the Soviet Union. Organized in 17 scientific, technical, and scholarly departments, including a department for the development of Siberia, the academy supervises more than 260 scientific institutions. Its membership comprises 260 academicians, 412 corresponding and 54 foreign members, and many affiliated scientists. It supervises and publishes numerous books and journals and is responsible to the Council of Ministers of the USSR. Founded in 1724 at the request of Peter I (the Great), it was given control of Soviet science and technology in 1917. In 1934 its headquarters moved from Leningrad to Moscow.

The Library of the Academy of Sciences, founded in 1714 by Peter I, is the oldest Russian science library. Located in Leningrad, it contains more than 17,500,000 items and numerous collections, including all materials published by the Academy. In 1988 the library suffered a devastating fire that destroyed more than 400,000 books and damaged many millions more.

Acadia

[uh-kay' dee-uh] Acadia (in French, Acadie) is a region of present-day Canada that was a province or colony of NEW FRANCE. Never clearly defined, the term always referred to at least part of today's Maritime Provinces of Canada (New Brunswick, Nova Scotia, and Prince Edward Island) and to part of Maine.

Throughout the 17th century and until 1713, the colony of Acadia included the mainland of Nova Scotia and some settlements on the Bay of Fundy shore of present-day New Brunswick. The population of the former centered in the settlement of Port Royal (now Annapolis Royal), first founded (1605) by the sieur de MONTS, and never exceeded 2,100 persons of European descent. Given very little economic support by France and finding itself a pawn in the colonial power struggle among France, Holland, and Britain, the colony was forced to become virtually self-sufficient. It lived off agriculture, fishing, and trade—the last often illicit in the eyes of France.

When the main part of Acadia was ceded to Britain as Nova Scotia in 1713, France retained the rest of the region and tended to refer to all of it, whether under British or French rule, by the traditional name. Some of the French-speaking Acadians moved to Cape Breton and Prince Edward Island, but most remained in Nova Scotia until they were harshly expelled in 1755 and again in 1758 because they would not swear allegiance to the British crown. Of those among them who survived the resulting severe hardship, many returned later to reestablish themselves in Acadia, or, more commonly, in north-

Acadia was a French colony that occupied parts of Canada's present-day Maritime Provinces. Modern place names appear in parentheses.

ern New Brunswick and in pockets of the other Maritimes. Other survivors settled in Louisiana, where their descendants—known as CAJUNS—still preserve a distinct culture. Still others returned to France.

Acadia National Park

SEE NATIONAL PARKS

acanthus (architecture)

SEE ARCHITECTURE

acanthus (plant)

[uh-kan'-thuhs] The acanthus family, Acanthaceae, contains about 250 genera of mainly

An acanthus adorns this Corinthian capital (right). The decoration, developed in ancient Greece, was patterned after the Mediterranean acanthus (left), or bear's-breech.

perennial, thistlelike shrubs native to warmer regions of the world. The name applies most commonly to about 12 species that make up the genus *Acanthus.* Their whitish rose to lilac flowers grow on spikes up to 46 cm (18 in) high, and the leaves are up to 60 cm (24 in) long. The spiny leaves of some species, such as varieties of the Mediterranean acanthus, *A. mollis,* have a hairy, attractive upper surface, and the shrubs are cultivated as border plants. Other genera are also popular, including species of *Ruellia* that are grown in the southern United States.

Acapulco   Acapulco (or in full: Acapulco de Juárez) is a seaport on the Pacific coast of Mexico in the state of Guerrero. It has a population of 301,902 (1980). Located on the bay of Acapulco 305 km (190 mi) south of Mexico City, it is a major resort area and a shipping point for cotton, coffee, and sugar.

Acapulco was founded (1550) by Spaniards, and until 1815 it was the center for trade with the Philippines and for the transshipment of goods across Mexico to Spain. Fort San Diego was built there in 1616 to protect Spanish shipping. Destroyed by an earthquake (1776) and later rebuilt, Fort San Diego was the site of a Mexican victory over the Spanish in 1821. The climate, atmosphere, deep-sea fishing, and beautiful beaches have made Acapulco an international vacation spot. Many visitors enjoy the cliff divers who leap from the 40-m (140-ft) promontory west of the bay.

acceleration   Acceleration is the rate of change of an object's velocity. The concepts of "speeding up" and "slowing down" actually imply positive and negative accelerations (negative acceleration is commonly called deceleration). For example, if the speed of an automobile traveling in a straight line increases from 15 to 25 m/sec (34 to 55 mph) in 10 seconds, then the auto's average acceleration is 1 m/sec per second (2.1 mph per second). The auto's speed increases every second by an amount equal to 1 m/sec.

Objects falling freely toward the ground experience a uniform acceleration of 9.8 m/sec^2 (32 ft/sec^2) due to gravity.

Types of acceleration other than the uniform linear acceleration described above include angular acceleration and (for an object traveling in a circle) centripetal acceleration.

See also: FREE FALL; LAWS OF MOTION.

accelerator, particle   A particle accelerator is a device for increasing the energy of electrically charged atomic particles. The particles may be electrons, protons, or charged atomic nuclei. The purpose of increasing the energy of charged particles is to make them useful in studies of nuclear and particle physics, by shooting them at atoms and studying the resulting products with DETECTORS. At very high energies, the charged particles can

break up the nuclei of other atoms and interact with other particles, producing transformations that make it possible to study the nature and behavior of the fundamental units of matter. Particle accelerators are also important tools in the effort to develop nuclear-fusion devices (see FUSION, NUCLEAR).

The energy of a charged particle is measured in electron volts, where one electron volt is the energy gained by an electron when it passes between electrodes having a potential difference of one volt. A charged particle can be accelerated only by the application of an electric field, which moves it toward the opposite charge. Beams of particles may be focused by magnets; the effectiveness of the magnets is further enhanced if they are superconducting (see SUPERCONDUCTIVITY). Early machines in nuclear physics used static, or direct, electric fields; but most modern machines, particularly those for the highest particle energies, use alternating fields. The latter are arranged so that particles are exposed to the field only when the field is in the accelerating direction. When the field is reversed and is in a decelerating direction, the particles are shielded from the field by various electrode configurations.

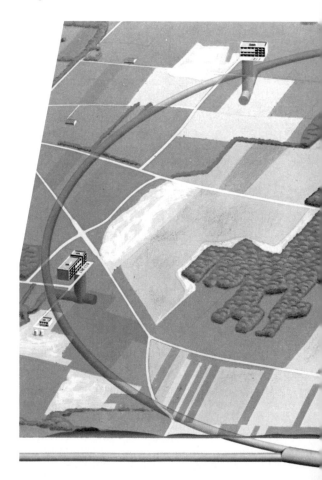

Direct-Voltage Accelerators

The first accelerator used in nuclear physics was the machine designed by Sir John Douglas COCKCROFT and E. T. S. Walton and built in 1932 at the Cavendish Laboratory in Cambridge, England. Its high-voltage TRANSFORMER accelerated protons to an energy of 700,000 electron volts (700 keV) to yield the first artificially produced nuclear disintegrations.

Van de Graaff Electrostatic Generator. During the early 1930s another type of direct-voltage generator was developed by R. J. Van de Graaff at Princeton University. In this machine a charge is carried on an insulating belt to a high-voltage terminal where the belt is discharged and the voltage builds up on the terminal. Eventually, if the process is not limited, an electric discharge similar to a lightning bolt will discharge the terminal. With care, voltages as high as 3 million volts can be achieved. Later it was shown that much higher voltages can be achieved if the machine is enclosed in a tank where a pressure of several atmospheres is maintained. The art of building electrostatic Van de Graaff generators continues to advance.

Betatron. Another type of direct-voltage accelerator is the BETATRON, a device in which a varying magnetic field generates the electric field that accelerates a beam of electrons, while the electrons are maintained in a circular orbit by a second magnetic field.

Accelerators Using Alternating Electric Fields

By using alternating electrical fields in the radio-frequency (rf) range for acceleration, it becomes possible to accelerate a particle in a number of steps while maintaining the electric fields at manageable levels, thus avoiding problems connected with electrical breakdown.

Linear Accelerator. The simplest rf accelerator is the linear accelerator, or linac. It has different forms, de-

Three underground loops are part of the accelerator facilities of the European Organization for Nuclear Research (CERN) near Geneva, Switzerland. The largest loop has a diameter of 2.2 km (1.4 mi). It can accelerate protons to 500 GeV (a GeV—1,000 million volts, or 1 gigavolt— is a measure of particle energy). The smallest loop is a 28-GeV proton synchrotron. The remaining loop is a particle storage, or colliding-beam, ring, where collision energies of 630 GeV can be attained.

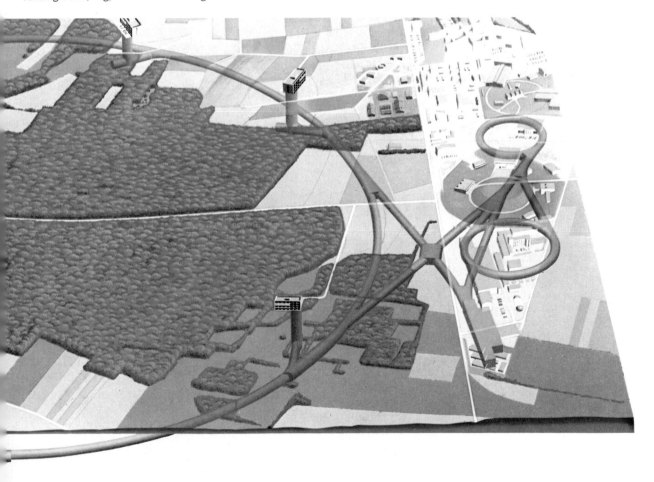

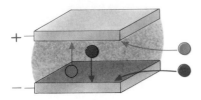

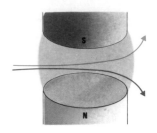

Two means of controlling the motion of a charged particle are an electric field (left) and a magnetic field (right). In an electric field a positive particle (red) is accelerated straight toward the negative electrode and a negative particle (blue) is accelerated toward the positive electrode. In a magnetic field, the moving particles curve toward the south magnetic pole (red) or the north magnetic pole (blue), depending on the charge.

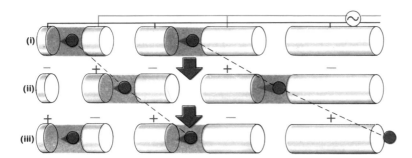

(Left) Linear accelerators use an oscillating electric field and a series of hollow "drift tubes" to accelerate charged particles to high speeds. As positive particles (red) move to the right between tubes, they are pushed by the positively charged tube on their left, and pulled by the negatively charged tube on their right. The electric field on the tubes is reversed only when the particles are within the tubes and shielded from any retarding force. Because the accelerated particles move faster with each alternation of the field (i, ii, iii), it is necessary to lengthen successive drift tubes.

pending on whether the purpose is to accelerate electrons or ions. For the ion version, ions are injected along the axis of a long tank, which is excited by a high-powered rf system. While the field is in the decelerating phase, the ions are shielded from it by drift tubes in the tank, which are pipes through which the beam passes.

The first linear accelerator, built in 1928 by Rolf Wideröe in Norway, was used solely to demonstrate the principle of rf acceleration. Shortly after the war, Luis Walter ALVAREZ built the first proton linear accelerator, in which protons reached an energy of 32 million electron volts (MeV). Since 1950 several proton and ion linear accelerators have been built, some as injectors for still larger machines and some for use in nuclear physics. The largest accelerator is the 800-MeV machine at the Los Alamos Scientific Laboratory in New Mexico. It is used as a meson factory, producing for study the particles of mass that are intermediate between the electron and the proton and that seem to give the force necessary for holding the atomic nucleus together.

The largest electron linac in existence began operation in 1966 at the Stanford Linear Accelerator Center (SLAC) in California. This machine, more than 3.2 km (2 mi) long, has been able to provide electrons with energies of more than 50,000 MeV; that is, 50 billion, or giga, electron volts (50 BeV or GeV). The addition to SLAC of colliding-beam facilities (discussed below) culminated in the late 1980s in the Stanford Linear Collider (SLC), which can provide collision energies of more than 100 GeV between a beam of electrons and a beam of positrons.

Cyclotron. Although the ion linear accelerator evolved slowly, a research report by Wideröe in 1928 was the inspiration for another machine that has proved important: the cyclotron. Ernest Lawrence of the University of California realized that an ion can be deflected in a circle by a magnetic field in such a way that it will return to a gap

where it can receive additional acceleration. The linac's drift tubes are replaced by half-pillboxes (called *dees* because they are shaped like the letter *D*), in which the ions are shielded during the deceleration phase of the rf field. With M. S. Livingston, Lawrence built a working cyclotron in 1931. During the 1930s and '40s larger and larger machines were built at the University of California and elsewhere, primarily for the purpose of accelerating protons and deuterons to energies that would reach into the hundreds of MeV. Frequency-modulated cyclotrons, also called synchrocyclotrons, were built to reach energies of more than 700 MeV.

Synchrotron. To achieve still higher energies, a new device known as the synchrotron was developed. In this machine particles travel on a roughly circular orbit of constant radius. The magnetic field that maintains the particles in orbit is increased as a radio-frequency field increases the energy of the particles.

Early synchrotrons were used to accelerate electrons, and a number have reached energies of several GeV, but the largest synchrotrons are designed to accelerate protons. The first proton synchrotron, BROOKHAVEN NATIONAL LABORATORY's Cosmotron, became operational in 1952 and was the first accelerator to produce energies above 1 GeV. The largest synchrotrons are the 500-GeV machine at the CERN Laboratory in Geneva, Switzerland (see EUROPEAN ORGANIZATION FOR NUCLEAR RESEARCH), and the 500-GeV machine at the FERMI NATIONAL ACCELERATOR LABORATORY (Fermilab) in Chicago. The use of superconducting magnets at Fermilab in 1983 raised that machine's potential to 1 TeV (1 trillion eV) and gained it the name of Tevatron (see SUPERCONDUCTIVITY).

Storage Rings. The most recent development in the field has been the storage ring, in which accelerated particle beams circulate in opposite directions for several hours, if necessary. Using an antiproton storage ring, Fermilab is achieving collision energies of nearly 1.8 TeV; at CERN, a similar system provides energies of more than 600 GeV. Both U.S. and European scientists are planning still larger accelerators. The proposed U.S. machine, the Superconducting Super Collider (SSC), would yield collision energies of 40 TeV and will require construction of an oval 87 km (54 mi) in circumference. In 1988, Ellis County, Tex., was chosen as the site for the SSC. First ground for the project was broken the following year.

CERN's large project, the Large Electron-Positron Collider (LEP), was completed in 1989. Starting energies for the LEP were in the 100-GeV range, but CERN scientists hope to double that capacity within a few years. Meanwhile, the Soviet Union is working to complete a 600-GeV proton accelerator at Protvino, south of Moscow. With the addition of superconducting magnets, the USSR hopes to boost this capacity to 3 TeV by the mid-1990s.

See also: DETECTOR, PARTICLE; FUNDAMENTAL PARTICLES.

accipiter   see HAWK

acclimatization   In biology, *acclimatization*, or *acclimation*, is a general term for the responses an organism exhibits as it adjusts to some long-term change or changes in its environment, or to being moved into a new environment. The term suggests climatic changes only, but acclimatization also includes the adjustment of wild plants to cultivation and of wild animals to captivity, as well as any other situations involving such essential changes in environmental conditions.

The degree to which a given organism is able to acclimatize has its bases in the genetics of the organism. For example, some plants prove highly successful when introduced into a new setting, whereas others may grow under the new conditions but still require human intervention to propagate. Acclimatization is considered reversible, and its results are not genetically encoded for passing on to a new generation. It thus differs from adaptation (see ADAPTIVE RADIATION), the evolutionary process by which entire populations of organisms change in their genetic makeup.

accordion   The accordion, a WIND INSTRUMENT, produces sound by means of reeds over which wind is forced by working a bellows. The instrument was invented (1821) in Germany by Friedrich Buschmann, who supplied it with right-hand buttons for producing treble pitches. Left-hand buttons for playing bass chords were added in 1829. Eventually, a keyboard supplanted the right-hand buttons, producing the piano accordion. A popular instrument, the accordion has only a limited place in the classical repertoire, although some modern composers have used the instrument in their works. The CONCERTINA is a type of miniature accordion.

(Right) The accordion uses air forced by bellows (center) through tuned reeds to produce its sound. The right hand plays the melody on the keyboard, while the left hand plays the harmony by pressing the buttons.

accounting   Accounting is the compilation of financial information for use in making economic decisions. BOOKKEEPING provides the basic accounting data, by systematically recording specified day-to-day financial information such as revenue from the sale of products or services; expenses of business operations such as the cost of merchandise sold; and overhead expenses such as rent, wages, and so forth.

Functions of Accounting

The various financial statements produced by accountants provide informational access to a firm's financial condition for three broad interest groups. First, they give the firm's management the information to evaluate financial performance over a previous period of time, and to make decisions regarding the future. Second, they inform the general public, and particularly the firm's stockholders or those interested in buying its stock, about the financial status of the firm over the previous quarter or year. Third, accountants provide reports for the tax and regulatory departments of the various levels of government. Accountants also perform many of these same functions for agencies of the government, nonprofit organizations, and other entities.

Financial Accounting. Large corporations maintain their own internal accounting departments; small firms may hire the services of an outside accountant. In either case, the accountant's principal duty is to gather the figures that relate to such financial matters as profits, losses, costs, tax liabilities, and other debts, and to present them to the firm's management in a form that is logical and readily understood.

For publicly traded companies—those which offer stocks and bonds for sale to the public—accountants also prepare regularly published reports of interest to many outside the organization: investors and potential investors, creditors, and the general public. At the end of the fiscal year, a summary, or annual report, is published, which must include the "opinion" of an outside reviewer as to its accuracy. The reviewer is an independent accountant called an auditor.

These reports represent, usually, the only communication a company has with stockholders and other outsiders. They are prepared in accordance with rules known as Generally Accepted Accounting Principles, which are established by professional organizations of accountants. A standard set of financial statements is always included in an annual report. The statements include the following items.

The *balance sheet* compares the firm's assets and liabilities. Assets include cash, accounts receivable (moneys owed to the company), the cash value of inventories, and the worth of property, plant, and equipment. Liabilities include company debts, "stockholders' equity," or the amount of stock held by investors, as well as the amount of "retained earnings," or assets that are invested back into the company rather than disbursed in the form of dividends to stockholders.

Although some balance-sheet items, like cash, are easily measured for reporting, the value of others, like plant and equipment, must be estimated. Plant and equipment are usually represented by figures that are reduced by a certain proportion each year. For example, a truck worth $X when it is purchased will be worth $X minus 15% the next year, and $X minus 30% the second year after purchase. The percentage of depreciation—the presumed worth of the truck over time—varies according to the depreciation method used, but almost every item of plant and equipment is subject to depreciation, which is listed by accountants as an expense. Inventory valuation is also subject to a variety of accounting methods, since many inventory items cannot be specifically costed. The grain in a grain elevator, for example, comes from different sources and may have been bought at several prices. An accountant must choose among several methods for valuing the grain; each will provide a slightly different value figure, as well as a different basis for figuring taxes.

The *statement of changes in financial position* shows the sources and applications of working capital, and indicates whether the company generated sufficient cash to fund operations, or whether borrowing was necessary.

The *income statement* shows the results of a company's operations over time, as well as for the current period. Income is the difference between revenues and expenses. Accountants usually report revenues at the time when they are earned (when a sale is made, not when cash for the sale is received), and expenses only when they are incurred, rather than when they are paid out. This practice—of relating current expense with current revenues earned—is called *accrual accounting* and is fundamental to almost all accounting systems. The simpler cash method, which records revenues when cash for sales is received and expenses when cash is disbursed, rarely presents a true financial-activity picture of an organization.

The *statement of retained earnings and stockholder's equity* demonstrates for investors what has happened with their ownership in the company, how earnings and new stock issuance have affected its worth, and what dividends were paid.

Each of these reports will contain figures for previous quarters and years, as well as for the current period, providing a way of comparing present and past company performance. Accompanying the statements will be a set of notes, presenting information about the particular accounting methods used, as well as explanations of the impact of important events within the previous year.

Managerial Accounting. The process of providing management with data to evaluate costs, practice budgetary planning, and review employee and executive performance is the basis of the work of the managerial, or cost, accountant. Cost accounting is primarily responsible for determining the cost of manufacturing a specific product or providing a particular service. This usually requires complex estimates of overhead costs, variable costs, and unit costs for services such as advertising or consulting. Costs may be monitored daily, in order to warn management when performance is off budget; with computerized bookkeeping, reports can be generated almost as soon as the data has been collected. Cost statements will also help management determine whether it might be more profitable to make or to buy a particular item; to invest in more machinery or other capital assets, or to make do with the old; to increase production by hiring more workers or by automating plant facilities; and so forth.

Working with each division of the firm, the accountant may also be responsible for creating a budget setting forth goals based on realistic estimates of what can be accomplished. Comparing actual performance with the planned-for goals is another function of budgetary planning and is useful in evaluating the performance of individual divisions and managers.

Tax Accounting. Tax and compliance reporting together make up another major accounting function. In the United States, tax accounting is a matter of legal compliance with the Internal Revenue Code and various state and local tax laws. The tax accountant must keep abreast of the numerous changes in tax law that apply to his or her organization. Many tax accountants are, therefore, also lawyers.

Companies must also report to the Securities and Exchange Commission (SEC), which, since 1934, has required its own form of compliance accounting from publicly traded corporations. In addition to the basic data included in the annual report, the SEC requires disclosure of ownership, management backgrounds, company operations, and other information useful to investors in deciding whether to buy into a company.

Auditing

Auditors are accountants who review financial statements, and their responsibility is to verify the accuracy of company reporting. Internal auditors—those who are hired by and work within the company itself—help identify accounting weaknesses and correct them before significant errors occur. They are often systems-oriented people who make flowcharts of accounting systems and evaluate these flowcharts to suggest improvements in division of labor, paper flow, cash control, or other accounting responsibilities. They usually work under the company's treasurer or controller, who can thus provide a check and balance on the accounting department.

Independent auditors are hired by a company's board of directors to review financial statements. The independent auditor issues an opinion whose wording is standardized so that readers can easily identify what it implies. The standard "clean opinion" reads as follows:

> In our opinion, the financial statements . . . present fairly the position of XYZ Corporation as of Dec. 31, 19XX, and the results of its operations and the changes in its financial position for the year then ended, in conformity with generally accepted accounting principles applied on a basis consistent with that of the preceding year.

Any other wording in an opinion probably indicates trouble. Independent auditors may qualify their opinion or even disclaim it if they find some reason that prevents them from completing an audit. Finally, and rarely, an opinion can state that the financial statements do not fairly represent the company's actual financial situation.

The notion of "materiality"—what kind of information is relevant and necessary, and what data can be omitted because it is "immaterial" to a reporting function—is central to the profession of accounting. To a bookkeeper, even a few cents "out of balance" constitutes a material misstatement that must be rectified. However, the accountant's reports contain rounded figures, and reflect judgments about what kinds of depreciation, expense accruals, and other data should be included. To the auditor, whose certification will be based on reports involving rounded thousands, or even millions, of dollars, a number may not be "materially" misstated if it can be proved to within 5%. Thus, at each reporting level, the accuracy required to present fairly the company's financial position changes.

Development of Accounting

Historians generally credit 14th-century Italian merchants with developing the practice of double-entry bookkeeping, which is the basis for modern-day accounting. The method was invented when investors sought a way of recording the financial aspects of ventures that might last for months, or even years (the commissioning of a merchant fleet, for example), and in which many investors had bought shares. The Italian system resembled its modern counterpart. The balance sheet had two sections: one listed assets and the effect of sales, purchases, and investments on assets; the other recorded shares and shareholders, along with other liabilities incurred. Thus, owners who had bought shares from the original shareholders, or had inherited them, could claim their proportion of the profits when and if the venture succeeded.

Modern accounting has developed in response to changes in the legal structure of companies, as well as to rising public demand for accurate financial reports, and to government regulations. Of the changes in the legal structures of businesses, the development of the corporation has probably had the greatest impact, because it allowed public scrutiny of accounting records. Under earli-er forms of ownership, the sole proprietorship and the partnership, public scrutiny was almost unheard of. The rise of the multinational corporation has also increased accounting responsibilities, for it requires foreign-currency translation, reporting under a variety of legal environments, and the adjustment of ownership and income reporting to achieve the least costly payments within many different systems of taxes, tariffs, and other government controls.

The Accounting Industry

Public accountants are those who are available to the public at large for such accounting functions as monthly bookkeeping and tax preparation. Most states do not regulate the qualifications or performance of public accountants.

The only accountants permitted to offer opinions about financial statements, however, are certified public accountants (CPAs), who have passed rigorous national examinations and must also fulfill the requirements of the state in which they practice—including several years of varied experience within the profession.

As auditors, CPAs are expected to maintain a relationship of strict independence and professionalism with the firms for whom they work (for example, they do not hold stock in their client companies), so that the independence of their opinions may not be questioned.

Most U.S. CPA firms are relatively small and represent individuals and privately held businesses for whom they prepare financial statements and act as advisors on tax matters. The largest accounting firms in the United States are known collectively as "The Big Six." They are immense organizations offering services that reach well beyond their principal function, the auditing of financial reports.

Accounting Standards

The Financial Accounting Standards Board (FASB) researches accounting issues and writes advisory statements that are generally accepted as accounting principles. (Other sources of principles include the rules of the SEC, the tax laws, and general practice.)

The auditing industry is largely responsible for disciplining itself to ensure the independence of its auditors; and where an auditor differs from management as to the appropriate reporting principles, the auditor will require adherence to generally accepted accounting principles. The American Institute of Certified Public Accountants (AICPA) has developed standards of performance for auditors designed both to ensure independence and to protect against liability for inadequate audit work. Large-scale financial scandals such as the savings and loan failures of the late 1980s (see SAVINGS INDUSTRY) have increased scrutiny of accounting firms—especially the Big Six.

——

Accra [uh-krah'] Accra, a manufacturing center, is the capital and largest city of Ghana. Situated on the coastal Accra Plains on the Gulf of Guinea, it has a population of 949,100 (1988 est.). The landscape is primarily flat, with the exception of some notable hills, including Legon, where the University of Ghana is located. The main streets of the city radiate from the center and are connected by Ring Road. The economy is based upon the busy port and the manufacturing of processed foods, timber and plywood, and clothing.

The site of modern Accra has been occupied for centuries by Ga villages. Between 1650 and 1680, European activity began with the construction of a castle and two fortified trading posts near the site of present-day Accra. The city of Accra traces its formation to 1877, when the capital of the British Gold Coast colony was transferred from Cape Coast to Osu, one of the Ga villages in the area. In 1898 the Accra Municipal Council was formed to carry out local government functions. Today Accra is a federal area separate from the regions of Ghana.

Acetabularia mediterranea, *a green algae, has a delicately shaped ridged disk attached to a slender stalk. This species, as well as* A. crenulata, *is used to study the role of a cell's nucleus during reproduction.*

accreditation of schools and colleges

Accreditation is the practice of certifying schools and universities to ensure that their educational programs and practices meet generally recognized standards. This procedure is usually performed by national governments, but in the United States, which has a long tradition of locally controlled education, it is done by six private regional organizations. These organizations were established between 1885 and 1924, as increases in public education and geographical mobility made it necessary for students, educators, parents, and universities to be able to judge schools with which they were personally unfamiliar. The six regional accreditation associations in the United States, in the order of their founding, are the New England Association of Colleges and Secondary Schools (1885), the Middle States Association of Colleges and Secondary Schools (1887), the North Central Association of Colleges and Secondary Schools (1895), the Southern Association of Colleges and Schools (1895), the Northwest Association of Secondary and Higher Schools (1917), and the Western Association of Schools and Colleges (1924). The Southern Association is the only accrediting body that accredits elementary as well as secondary schools and colleges. In the other regions, the state education department evaluates the performance of elementary schools. Evaluations take into account credentials of the teachers, the courses offered in the school, the amount of money spent on each student in the school, and physical facilities such as the number of library books and the laboratory facilities for science courses.

Acetabularia

[as'-uh-tab-yoo-lair'-ee-uh] *Acetabularia* is a genus of unicellular green ALGAE with a unique umbrellalike shape and a height of up to several centimeters (1–3 in). This curious organism, with its single cell differentiated into a long stalk, a cap, and a rootlike base that contains the cell nucleus, has played a key role in the history of biology. Some of the best evidence that hereditary information is transmitted by the cell nucleus comes from experiments with *Acetabularia* conducted by

the German embryologist Joachim Hämmerling in the 1930s. Hämmerling found that when he cut one of these algae in fragments, those fragments containing at least some nuclear material could develop into complete new, fertile algae, whereas those without nuclear material might also grow a while but remained sterile.

acetaldehyde   see ALDEHYDE

acetaminophen   see ANALGESIC

acetate   see ACETIC ACID; CELLULOSE; PLASTICS

acetic acid

[uh-see'-tik]   Acetic acid, CH_3COOH, is a weak organic acid and the sour constituent of VINEGAR. In industry, acetic acid is produced by the destructive distillation of wood and by the catalytic oxidation of acetaldehyde. The pure acid is called glacial acetic acid and is a corrosive, colorless liquid with a pungent smell. It solidifies at 16.63° C (61.93° F). Acetic acid reacts with alcohols to form acetates that are widely used as solvents. It reacts with cellulose to form cellulose acetate, which is the starting material for rayon and other artificial fibers and for photographic film.

acetone

[as'-uh-tohn]   Acetone, CH_3COCH_3, or 2-propanone, or dimethylketone, is a fragrant, colorless, and flammable liquid that boils at 56.2° C and solidifies at −34.8° C. Small amounts of acetone are present in blood and urine, but some diabetic patients show larger than normal concentrations. Diabetics evacuate this excess in urine (acetonuria) and through their lungs. In industry, acetone is an important solvent for cellulose nitrate and cellulose acetate and is also used in the production of explosives.

See also: RAYON.

acetylcholine   see NEUROTRANSMITTER

acetylene

[uh-set'-uh-leen]   Acetylene, or ethyne, C_2H_2, is a colorless and flammable gas. It sublimes at

−84° C at normal pressure. Most acetylene is manufactured by the reaction of water with calcium carbide: $CaC_2 + 2H_2O \rightarrow Ca(OH)_2 + C_2H_2$. This reaction also occurs in carbide lamps, where a steady gas flow is obtained from water dripping on a carbide tablet.

The structure of acetylene is $CH \equiv CH$. Because of its triple bond, acetylene easily undergoes addition reactions. Vinyl chloride is manufactured from acetylene by the addition of hydrogen chloride: $CH \equiv CH + HCl \rightarrow CH_2 = CHCl$. Similar additions with acetic acid, CH_3COOH, and with hydrogen cyanide, HCN, yield vinyl acetate, $CH_3COOCH = CH_2$, and acrylonitrile, $CH_2 = CHCN$. Both compounds are important in the production of artificial fibers and plastics. Acetylene gas is used in metal cutting and welding because of its high combustive temperature.

See also: ALKYNES.

Achad ha-Am [ah-kahd' hah-ahm'] Achad ha-Am, b. Aug. 18, 1856, d. Jan. 2, 1927, was a Jewish scholar and Zionist leader originally named Asher Ginzberg. He was born in the Ukraine and adopted the name Achad ha-Am (One of the People) with his first published article, *Lo Zeh ha-Derech* (This is Not the Way, 1889). In that article he disagreed with those advocating mass settlement in Palestine (see ZIONISM). Like others in the pacifist *Choveve Zion* movement, Achad ha-Am saw the need for a cultural and spiritual revival of Jews. However, he believed that what was needed was not "a state of Germans or Frenchmen of the Jewish race", but a cultural center where "the creative faculties of the nation" would imbue ghetto Jews with pride. After World War I, Achad ha-Am emigrated to Palestine, where he worked to create this cultural hub without impinging on the rights of the Arabs.

Achaea [uh-kee'-uh] Achaea was an area of ancient Greece in the northern Peloponnesus and southeastern Thessaly, settled by a people known since the 14th–13th centuries BC as the Achaeans. Probably of Mycenaean origin, the Achaeans by the 4th century BC had formed a confederation of small cities, the first of two Achaean leagues, as a defense against pirates. A more powerful second league, formed in 280 BC, liberated Sicyon (251 BC), and later CORINTH, from Macedonian domination. CLEOMENES III of Sparta warred with the confederacy (228 BC), which first allied itself with Rome and Macedonia and then in 146 BC opposed Rome in a battle at Corinth that resulted in the dissolution of the league. Modern Achaea (Akhaia), a Greek department, roughly corresponds to the Peloponnesian portion of the ancient region.

Achaemenids [uh-kee'-meh-nidz] The Achaemenids were Persian kings who ruled over a vast empire extending from the Aegean Sea to the Indus River from 549 to 330 BC. They were named after an eponymous ancestor, Achaemenes. This was the first world empire of antiquity, and many civil institutions first appeared under the Ach-

aemenids' rule. Universal law (the king's law), the postal system, coinage, and other institutions were used, and ZOROASTRIANISM became widespread in this period. The first Achaemenid ruler was CYRUS THE GREAT, but DARIUS I was the real architect of the empire; DARIUS III, its last monarch, was defeated and succeeded by Alexander the Great.

Achebe, Chinua [uh-chay'-bay, chin'-wah] The Nigerian Chinua Achebe, b. Nov. 16, 1930, is among the best known of contemporary African writers. His works, written in English, give a sharply realistic view of Ibo society from the late 1890s, when British missionaries first arrived, to present-day black Africa and its struggle to reintegrate its damaged society, the legacy of colonialism. Achebe's first novel, *Things Fall Apart* (1958), remains his most famous. Three other novels followed: *No Longer at Ease* (1960), *Arrow of God* (1964), and *A Man of the People* (1966). After more than two decades spent as a teacher, editor, diplomat, essayist, and short-story writer, Achebe returned to the novel and his major themes with *Anthills of the Savannah* (1988).

Achebe grew up in a small, traditional Ibo community, where his father taught in a mission school. He graduated (1953) from Ibadan University and worked for the Nigerian Broadcasting Company. During the Biafran secession (1967–70) he served Biafra as a diplomat. Subsequently, he taught at several universities in the United States and Nigeria.

Acheson, Dean [ach'-uh-suhn] Dean Gooderham Acheson, b. Middletown, Conn., Apr. 11, 1893, d. Oct. 12, 1971, was a U.S. secretary of state (1949–53) and a major architect of the nation's foreign policy after World

Dean Acheson, U.S. secretary of state under President Truman, helped establish the North Atlantic Treaty Organization (NATO) as part of the policy of containment of Communist expansion.

War II. Acheson graduated from Yale (1915) and Harvard Law School (1918) and was private secretary to U.S. Supreme Court Justice Louis D. Brandeis before joining (1921) a prominent Washington law firm. In 1933, President Franklin D. Roosevelt appointed him undersecretary of the treasury. Except for several brief periods with his law firm, Acheson worked for the State Department from 1941 to 1953.

Acheson helped formulate an active role for the United States in the postwar world, reversing earlier isolationist policies. As undersecretary of state to George C. Marshall, he helped to develop a policy of containment toward Communism and to secure aid for Greece and Turkey against Communist-backed insurgents in 1947. He also helped draft the MARSHALL PLAN to rebuild Western Europe.

Appointed secretary of state by President Harry S. Truman, Acheson continued the containment policy by supporting the formation of the NORTH ATLANTIC TREATY ORGANIZATION (NATO) in 1949. In Asia he attempted to distance the United States from the Chinese Nationalist regime on Taiwan while rejecting recognition of the Communist regime on the mainland. In 1950, Acheson used the Soviet boycott of the United Nations Security Council to secure UN support for U.S. intervention in the Korean War. The war also enabled Acheson to push for expansion of U.S. and NATO forces and for West German rearmament. By signing a peace treaty with Japan and supporting France in Indochina, Acheson extended containment to include East Asia.

While in office, Acheson received much criticism. Despite his strong anti-Communist stand, he was accused of having permitted the Communist victory on mainland China, and the military setbacks in Korea brought additional criticism. Sen. Joseph R. McCarthy even accused Acheson of harboring known Communists in the State Department. Acheson, however, remained in office until the end of Truman's administration and afterward continued to advise succeeding presidents.

Acheulean   see PALEOLITHIC PERIOD

Achilles [uh-kil'-eez]

In Greek mythology Achilles was the strongest, swiftest, and most competent of the Greek heroes who fought in the TROJAN WAR. He was the son of the nymph THETIS, who dipped him as an infant into the River Styx and thus made every part of his body invulnerable—except the heel by which she held him. Knowing that Achilles would die at Troy, Thetis hid him among the women of the court, but Odysseus found him and persuaded him to join the Greek army.

According to Homer's ILIAD, in the tenth year of the Trojan War, Achilles withdrew from the fighting after Agamemnon seized Briseis, his favorite slave girl. He sulked in his tent until the death of his close friend Patroclus stirred him to return to battle. The smith-god Hephaestus forged him a famous shield on which was depicted the whole range of the human condition. Thus equipped, he avenged Patroclus's death in a celebrated

Achilles, the great warrior of the Greek army that fought against Troy in Homer's Iliad, is shown in this vase painting after he had been slain. His body is carried by his comrade-in-arms Ajax.

duel with the great Trojan hero HECTOR. According to other traditions, Achilles died shortly after when wounded in his heel—his one vulnerable spot—by an arrow fired by Paris or Apollo.

acid rain

Acid rain is a common term for pollution caused when sulfur and nitrogen dioxides combine with atmospheric moisture to produce a rain, snow, or hail of sulfuric and nitric acids. Such pollution may also be suspended in a fog or deposited in dry form. Environmental damage from acid rain has been reported in northern Europe and North America. High levels of acid rain have also been detected in other areas of the world, such as above the tropical rain forests of Africa. Acid rain has destroyed plant and animal life in lakes, damaged forests and crops, endangered marine life in coastal waters, eroded structures, and contaminated drinking water.

Research has shown that although some of the damage attributed to acid rain is a result of natural causes, sulfur dioxide from oil and coal combustion and nitrogen oxides produced by automobile engines have greatly intensified the acid-rain problem. Winds can carry the pollutants thousands of kilometers away from their source. Canadian emissions contribute substantially to acid rain in the northeastern United States, for example, and much of the sulfur falling in eastern Canada is believed to originate in the United States. In 1986 the U.S. National Academy of Sciences acknowledged that acid rain from U.S. sources had become a serious problem in the eastern United States and Canada. Although the Canadian government has agreed to reduce sulfur dioxide emissions, the United States has not placed limitations on its sulfur emissions that may drift into Canada.

Scientists agree that acid rain is harmful, but reports concerning its severity conflict. A U.S. government report issued in September 1987 minimized the environmental damage caused by acid rain and concluded that the acid-rain problem is not increasing. A 1988 survey conducted by the Environmental Protection Agency, however, indicated that streams in the eastern United States were more acidic than was previously believed. In 1990 the National Acid Precipitation Assessment Program (NAPAP), created by Congress in 1980, issued a report on the results of its study. The report indicated that acidic waters also occur in the southern and midwestern United States, but downplayed acid-rain damage to forests.

Many scientists urge that measures to control acid rain begin immediately. The most direct action would be to cut off pollution at the source. Regulations require that new coal-burning plants must install expensive scrubbers in their smokestacks to remove most of the dioxides (see POLLUTION CONTROL). Other possible measures include burning low-sulfur oil or coal, or removing the sulfur from coal with a high sulfur content. Amendments have been proposed to the 1970 Clean Air Act that are designed to reduce sulfur and nitrogen emissions. The costs of such measures are considerable, however, and who should pay them continues to arouse controversy.

----

acids and bases   Acids and bases, and the SALTS produced by the reaction between acids and bases, are principal classifications of chemical substances. These categories were established long before their physical nature or the reasons for their characteristic properties were understood (see CHEMISTRY, HISTORY OF). Acids were recognized originally by their sour taste in water and because they could attack and dissolve some metals. The word *acid* is derived from the Latin *acetum,* "vinegar." Bases were substances that were usually soapy to the touch and that could react with acids in water to form salts.

Arrhenius Definition. In 1884, the Swedish chemist Svante ARRHENIUS realized that when acids, bases, and salts are dissolved in water they are separated (dissociated) either partially or completely into charged particles called IONS, that is, positively charged cations and negatively charged anions. Because solutions of ions are good electrical conductors, the substances that produce them are called electrolytes. Acids were considered electrolytes that produced the hydrogen ion (H^+), and bases as electrolytes that produced the hydroxide ion (OH^-).

Brønsted-Lowry Definition. The hydrogen ion–hydroxide ion definition of acids and bases was confined by its nature to solutions that contained water, not organic solvents. In 1923 the Danish chemist Johannes Brønsted and the English chemist Thomas Lowry independently proposed defining an acid as any species that could give up a proton, and a base as any species that could accept a proton. The term *species* includes ions and molecules,

and the proton denotes a hydrogen atom that has lost an electron (H^+). Although the definition of an acid was not greatly changed by this theory, that of a base became more general. Any acid, by definition, produces a (conjugate) base by loss of a proton. Thus, for the reaction $HCl + NH_3 \rightleftharpoons NH_4^+ + Cl^-$ the anion Cl^- is the conjugate base of the acid HCl. Because some acids can yield two or more protons by stepwise dissociation, certain species produced can act as both acids and bases; that is, they are amphoteric compounds. For example, phosphoric acid (H_3PO_4) produces three species, $H_2PO_4^-$, HPO_4^{2-}, and PO_4^{3-}, the first two of which are amphoteric.

Lewis Acids. In 1923 the American chemist Gilbert Lewis defined acids and bases in terms of electron rather than proton transfer. By his definition an acid can accept electrons from a base to form a chemical bond. The Lewis definition has proved useful, especially in describing systems that do not contain hydrogen. It has not been as widely accepted, however, as the Brønsted-Lowry definition. The term *Lewis acid* is generally reserved for reagents that function by accepting electrons from donor molecules without the participation of hydrogen or hydroxide ions.

Acid Strength. The strength of an acid in water is indicated by the extent of its DISSOCIATION. Dissociation is the separation of an acid, HA, into the hydrogen ion, H^+, and its conjugate base, A^-. Similarly, a base MOH can dissociate into the hydroxide ion, OH^-, and a metal ion, M^+. Strong acids and bases are highly dissociated in water; weak acids and bases may be dissociated to the extent of only a few percent, and often considerably less than 1 percent.

The strength of a solution of an acid or base is designated by its pH on a scale of 0 to 14. A pH of 7 is defined as neutral; solutions with a lower pH are acidic, and those with a higher pH are basic, or alkaline. The pH scale is related to the concentration of hydrogen ions in solution so that a tenfold increase or reduction in the hydrogen-ion concentration reduces or increases the pH of the solution by 1 pH unit (see INDICATOR).

Neutralization. Acids and bases can react with each other to produce a neutral salt solution. As an example, when sodium hydroxide (NaOH) and hydrochloric acid (HCl) are mixed, the hydrogen ions (H^+) and hydroxide ions (OH^-) react to form water (HOH, or H_2O), leaving only the sodium ions (Na^+) and chloride ions (Cl^-) in solution.

Inorganic Acids and Bases. Inorganic acids and bases are those made from such ELEMENTS as sulfur, phosphorus, and nitrogen. The inorganic acid sulfuric acid (H_2SO_4) is by far the largest single product of the chemical industry. It is used in the manufacture of fertilizer, the refining of petroleum, and the pickling of metals. Nitric acid (HNO_3) is used in the manufacture of explosives and dyestuffs. Of the bases, the hydroxides of sodium (NaOH) and potassium (KOH) are used in soap, and ammonia (NH_3) is used in fertilizer.

Organic Acids and Bases. The several classes of organic acids have characteristic acid groups that are attached to one or more hydrocarbon (R) groups. Thus CARBOXYLIC ACIDS have the general formula RCOOH, and sulfonic acids, the formula RSO_2OH. AMINES, R_nNH_{3n}, are an important class of organic bases. They form their conjugate acids by attaching an additional proton to the nitrogen atom.

See also: BUFFER; TITRATION.

acmeists [ak'-mee-ists] The acmeists were a group of Russian poets, including Anna AKHMATOVA and Osip MANDELSTAM, who were active between 1912 and 1922. Their concrete imagery and coherent expression were a reaction to the mystical vagueness of the Russian symbolists. Their name is derived from the Greek *acme*, "highest point," or "perfection."

acne [ak'-nee] Acne is a disorder of the sebaceous glands of the skin. Sebaceous glands secrete through pores and hair follicles—which are most abundant on the face and scalp—a fatty lubricant known as sebum. Acne occurs when the pores become clogged with sebum. Blackheads—external plugs formed of sebum and dead cells—may be invaded by bacteria, which cause pus-filled inflammations, or pimples. The overlying skin may become stretched to the point of rupture, resulting in lesions and, in prolonged severe cases, eventual scarring. Adolescents are most prone to acquiring a case of acne.

The exact cause of acne is not known but is believed to be related both to genetic predisposition and to the increased hormonal activity that occurs during puberty. Poor skin hygiene and lack of sunlight or exercise can often aggravate acne. In a reaction comparable to allergy, certain foods may increase irritation in susceptible persons.

A physician may evacuate the contents of blackheads and pimples under aseptic conditions, thus lessening the possibility of scarring. Astringent lotions are sometimes used to counteract the oiliness of the skin, and therapeutic creams are considered useful in releasing blackheads. Antibiotics, particularly tetracycline, are prescribed in more severe cases of acne to reduce infection from bacteria and prevent the appearance of new lesions. Long-term use of antibiotics, however, can result in bacterial resistance. The appearance of scarred skin may be improved by a surgical procedure called dermabrasion.

Two drugs related to vitamin A, tretinoin (brand name Retin-A) and isotretinoin (brand name Accutane), have been used in acne treatment. Tretinoin also shows promise as a treatment for smoothing out wrinkled, sun-aged skin, and isotretinoin might deter some forms of skin cancer. Isotretinoin has caused birth defects among pregnant users, however. Doctors are concerned that the two drugs might cause other harmful side effects.

Acoma [ak'-oh-maw] Acoma, a pueblo founded *c.*1100, is possibly the oldest continuously inhabited settlement in the United States. It is located 135 km (84 mi) west of Albuquerque, N.Mex., atop a sandstone mesa 109 m (357 ft) above the valley floor. Since prehistoric times, a PUEBLO Indian people who speak a Western Keresan language have lived there in three-storied stone and adobe homes, irrigating fields of maize, beans, and squash up to 19 km (12 mi) away. Acoman legend refers to ancestors who pushed their way up from the worlds below. Latiku, their mother-creator, established the religious and social order of matrilineal clans with animal and plant names. The male head of the Antelope clan, traditionally considered the father of the KACHINAS (spirits who bring rain for the crops), was also the religious and political head of the village. Although a majority of the Acoma people today are Catholic, a number of social and religious traditions are maintained.

Spaniards led by Francisco Vázquez de Coronado contacted the Acoma people in 1540; in 1599, Juan de Oñate brought about their conquest. They supported the Pueblo Revolt of 1680; only after intense fighting did they again submit to colonial rule in 1699. At the time of European contact, the Acoma population was probably about 3,000. In 1760, 1,052 villagers were reported; in the mid-1980s, more than 3,000.

Aconcagua [ah-kohn-kah'-gwah] Mount Aconcagua is a peak in the Andes Mountains in Argentina near the Chilean border. It is the highest peak in the Western Hemisphere, rising 6,960 m (22,834 ft) above sea level and a total of 12,954 m (42,500 ft) above the deep ocean trench off the nearby coast of Chile. The peak, first scaled in 1897 by Mattias Zurbriggen, a Swiss climber, is located in a region of frequent earthquakes.

aconite see MONKSHOOD

acorn worm see HEMICHORDATE

acoustics see SOUND AND ACOUSTICS

Acquired Immune Deficiency Syndrome see AIDS

Acre (Brazil) [ah'-kray] Acre is a state in western Brazil, bordered by Peru on the west and south and Bolivia on the east. It covers an area of 152,590 km^2 (58,915 mi^2) and has a population of 406,800 (1989 est.). The capital is Rio Branco. Located in the rain-forest zone, Acre is a major producer of rubber and brazil nuts, and coffee, rice, and sugar are grown. Acre was ceded to Bolivia by Brazil in 1867, but it was settled in the late 19th century by Brazilian rubber gatherers who declared Acre an independent nation in 1899. Acre was reannexed to Brazil as a territory in 1903, and it became a state in 1962.

Acre (Israel) [ahk'-ur] Acre (Hebrew: Akko) is a coastal city of Israel, on the Bay of Haifa, 19 km (12 mi) north of Haifa. It has a population of 38,700 (1980 est.). Although its once thriving port has filled with sand, its beaches are popular with vacationers. A fortified harbor and old crusader capital, Acre has been besieged repeatedly over the centuries by Romans, Arabs, Crusaders, Turks, and British. The Crusaders called it Saint Jean d'Acre. In 1922, Acre became part of the British mandate of Palestine, and in 1948, part of Israel. The ancient section of the city includes the Crypt of Saint John, dating from the 13th century, and old Arab inns. The Mosque of Jazzar Pasha and other elaborate buildings were constructed in the 18th century. The British citadel prison in Acre was the scene of fierce Jewish resistance fighting in 1948.

Acropolis

Acropolis [uh-krahp'-uh-lis] The term *acropolis* (Greek, "uppermost city") refers to the highest and most defensible part of an ancient Greek city. In classical Greece every important settlement had an acropolis, on which were placed temples, treasuries, and other important civic buildings (see GREEK ARCHITECTURE).

The best-known acropolis is that of Athens, upon which the ancient Greeks built one of the finest groups of temples in the ancient world. First settled in Neolithic times, by the Bronze Age (*c.*3000 BC) the plateau was occupied by houses and a royal palace. The buildings that survive date from an extensive building program initiated in the 5th century BC by PERICLES. The major monuments are the temple of Athena Parthenos (the Parthenon), 447–432 BC; the Propylaea (gateway), 437–432 BC; the temple of Athena Nike, 427–424 BC; and the temple of Erechtheus (the Erechtheum), 421–405 BC. Sizable portions of these structures are still standing. An extensive restoration project designed to protect them from industrial pollution began in the 1980s.

Parthenon. The largest building atop the Athenian Acropolis is the Parthenon, a temple dedicated to Athena Parthenos (Athena the Warrior Maiden). It is a Doric building, made entirely of white pentelic marble and surrounded by free-standing columns. It was designed by ICTINUS and Callicrates, with sculpture by PHIDIAS: a giant ivory and gold figure of Athena, a continuous frieze inside the colonnade depicting the Panathenaic procession, and metope panels depicting, among other scenes, the Battle

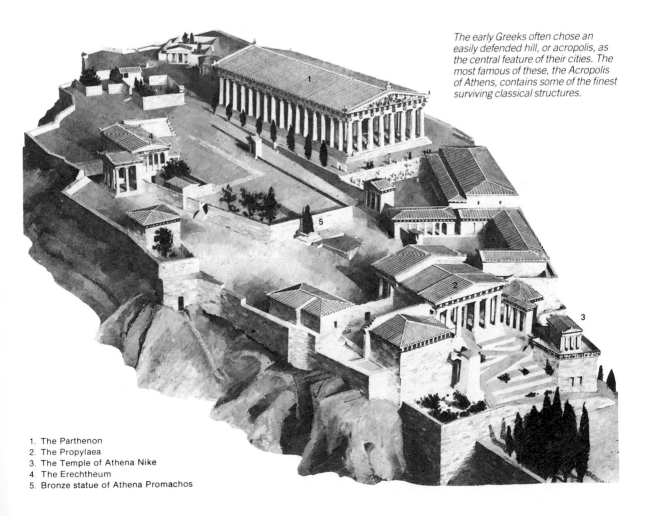

The early Greeks often chose an easily defended hill, or acropolis, as the central feature of their cities. The most famous of these, the Acropolis of Athens, contains some of the finest surviving classical structures.

1. The Parthenon
2. The Propylaea
3. The Temple of Athena Nike
4. The Erechtheum
5. Bronze statue of Athena Promachos

of the Lapiths and the Centaurs. The temple was unusual in that it had two rooms inside the colonnade. The smaller room, dedicated to the maiden goddess (parthenon), eventually lent its name to the whole building. The larger chamber housed the huge image of Athena by Phidias, which much later was removed by the Crusaders to Constantinople and there destroyed.

The Parthenon served in succession as a Byzantine church, a Roman Catholic church, a Turkish harem, and a Turkish powder magazine. On Sept. 16, 1687, a direct hit by Venetian artillery caused the powder in the Parthenon to explode, scattering debris across the Acropolis. The remaining sculpture rapidly began to disappear. A few pieces were taken to France by the duc de Choiseul, but most of it was sent to Britain in 1802–03 by the 7th earl of Elgin. In 1922–23 the Greek archaeologist Nicolas Balanos collected the remaining fragments of the temple and restored a number of columns and parts of the entablature that they carried.

Propylaea. The Propylaea, located at the west end of the hill, is the gateway into the Acropolis. Although never completed, the present structure was worked on from 437 BC to 432 BC by the architect Mnesicles. The inner and outer colonnades are Doric, recalling those of the Parthenon, although they are much more severe. Inside are more slender Ionic columns. Flanking the central gate-hall are two chambers. One was used as a *pinakotheke* ("painting gallery"); the other, although never completed, was probably intended to be a *glyptotheke* ("sculpture gallery").

Temple of Athena Nike. The diminutive temple of Athena Nike (Athena of Victory), which measures only 5.64 by 8.34 m (18.5 by 27 ft), stands southwest of the Propylaea, on a rebuilt Mycenaean fortification. The only wholly Ionic building on the Acropolis, it was designed by the architect Callicrates. The delicately styled Nike temple remained intact until 1686, when the Turks dismantled the building to use the blocks in fortifications. It was reassembled hastily in 1836 and then more carefully reerected by Balanos and A. K. Orlandos between 1935 and 1940.

Erechtheum. The temple of Erechtheus, or *Erechtheum*, was the last, the most complex, and the most richly embellished of the Periclean buildings. The unorthodox two-level plan adopted by the architect (perhaps Mnesicles) served to accommodate several sites long held sacred by the Athenians, including a sanctuary dedicated to Athena Polias (Athena Protectress of the City) and three smaller chambers dedicated to local gods and to Poseidon. The large north porch protected a stone believed to have been struck by Poseidon's trident.

The Erechtheum is best known for the porch on the south side, facing the Parthenon. Its roof is supported by six caryatids, columns in the form of female figures. The present caryatids are copies, the originals having been moved to the Acropolis Museum in order to preserve them.

—

acrostic [uh-kraws'-tik] An acrostic is formed when the words of a poem or other composition are so ordered that the first, last, or middle letters (sometimes syllables) of successive lines make a word or phrase when read verti-cally or diagonally. Acrostics are found in the Old Testament and were especially popular among the early Christians. One of history's better-known examples is a play on the name Jesus Christ. The initial Greek letters in the words making up the phrase "Jesus Christ, Son of God, Savior" spell out ΙΧΘΥΕ ("fish"), a symbol with which Jesus and his followers were associated. Acrostics were also a characteristic feature of Renaissance poetry.

acrylic   see PLASTICS

—

acrylonitrile   Acrylonitrile is a colorless, flammable, toxic liquid with a boiling point of 77° C. An organic molecule with formula $CH_2{=}CHCN$, acrylonitrile is slightly soluble in water and completely soluble in most organic solvents. Because acrylonitrile readily undergoes POLYMERIZATION, it is a valuable precursor to such common acrylic fibers as Orlon and Acrilan. It is also used in the making of surface coatings, adhesives, and beverage and food containers.

ACTH   see HORMONE, ANIMAL

—

acting   Acting is the practice of performing a role so that an audience may participate in the illusion that it is observing and reacting to a character rather than the actor. No simple definition can fully cover what the actor does to create this illusion, but most theorists agree that a strong link exists between acting and the imaginative structures created in childhood, in everyday social interaction, and in religious rituals.

Theories

Foremost among the 20th-century theorists of Western theatrical traditions who sought to create a practical system for disciplined creativity was Konstantin STANIS-LAVSKY, founder (1898) and director of the MOSCOW ART THEATER. Stanislavsky approached acting by dividing it into two parts: work on the self and work on the role. In the first area he stressed the need for freeing spontaneous impulses, for responding to imaginative stimuli, for concentrating attention, and for using personal experience. Work on the role stressed a full understanding of the world of the character within the play, and communicating that character by a system of physical actions.

Most modern theories of acting have taken Stanislavsky's work as their starting point, even if their major thrust is not the direct emotional involvement of the realistic theater. Bertolt BRECHT worked with the Berliner Ensemble to put the audience in a judicial frame of mind (see EPIC THEATER). Even Jerzy GROTOWSKI, director of the Polish Laboratory Theater, claims that his almost acrobatic performance mode is aimed at the revelation of inner truth.

Training

Professionally oriented actor training programs usually include script analysis and scene studies, ensemble techniques, improvisation, and sensory and imaginative awareness training, as well as the development of physical, voice, and speech skills. Fencing, dance, martial arts, and circus techniques are often taught, and some courses include specialized camera work.

History

Acting in a formal sense probably began in Greece in the 5th century BC, growing out of the celebration of religious festivals. The Greek THESPIS, standing apart from the chorus to deliver a separate solo text, is the first recorded actor. Later, Aeschylus added a second actor to his tragedies, making dialogue and play structure possible. Sophocles introduced a third actor to the cast, increasing complexity. Euripides gave drama greater potential by diminishing the use of the chorus.

Acting under the Romans grew increasingly bawdy. Performances were stopped by the Christian church in the 6th century; for several centuries actors were denied access to the rites of the church and were reduced to the status of jugglers and mountebanks. During the Middle Ages, simple plays based on the Bible and the lives of the saints were performed by members of trade guilds and by priests, but it was not until the Renaissance that acting became a profession once again. Versions of Greek and Roman plays were performed throughout Italy in elaborate theaters at the great courts of the princes. Troupes of actors meanwhile traveled around playing pieces that were essentially improvisations built on traditional characters and situations, developing a style called COMMEDIA DELL'ARTE.

In Elizabethan England, theatrical companies played in a simple style to audiences that represented a cross section of the community. Like many playwrights of his time, William SHAKESPEARE was himself an actor, taking such roles as the ghost in *Hamlet*. Prominent in his company were Will Kemp, who created many great comic roles, particularly Falstaff, and Richard BURBAGE, who first played most of the major tragic roles. Female roles were played by boys, since women were not allowed on the public stage until the Restoration.

In France, between 1658 and 1673, MOLIÈRE also combined the functions of actor and playwright. Building on the *commedia dell'arte* tradition, he founded an acting company that became the COMÉDIE FRANÇAISE, which continues today.

In the late 17th century, actors emerged as powerful figures, and a florid and artificial style of acting held the stage until David GARRICK appeared in 1741 and introduced simplified movement and gesture and a diction closer to everyday speech.

At about the same time, America's first significant acting company was established. Lewis Hallam opened his performance schedule in Williamsburg, Va., in 1752 and then toured from the Carolinas to New England. The 19th century was a golden age for actors in the United States. English stars, including Edmund Kean (see KEAN FAMILY), Fanny and Charles KEMBLE, and William Charles MACREADY, toured the nation. American stars such as Edwin FORREST and Edwin Booth had devoted followers. Joseph JEFFERSON, playing in *Rip Van Winkle*, was among the most popular comedy stars.

The stars' domination of the theater began to diminish when George II, duke of SAXE-MEININGEN, formed a company in Germany devoted to the notion that all members of the ensemble were of equal importance. Between 1874 and 1890 his troupe toured widely and greatly in-

(Below) *The comic role of the slave, as portrayed by this ceramic figure (2d century BC), was popular in Greek plays.*

(Above) *Molière (far left), a famous 17th-century French playwright and actor, introduces a farce by his theatrical company, the Comédie Française. Acting of this era was highly stylized because of lingering theories about classical Greek tragedy.*

Sir Henry Irving, the first British actor to achieve knighthood, appears in the title role of Hamlet in 1874. Like many actors before and since, Irving established his career by his interpretation of Shakespearean characters.

fluenced André Antoine, proponent of naturalism who founded the Théâtre Libre in Paris in 1887. Realistic ensemble acting came to dominate early 20th-century theater. In the United States, Stanislavsky's work was taken up by the GROUP THEATER, which included, among others, Lee Strasberg, a founder of the ACTORS STUDIO. Such teachers as Uta Hagen, Stella Adler, Herbert Berghof, and Sanford Meisner have contributed to the widespread use of Stanislavsky's system, which came to be called The Method. It inspired other groups that have grown in individualistic ways: Viola Spolin created a systematic approach to theater improvisation that can be seen in the

Sir Laurence Olivier, one of the greatest contemporary British actors, appears in the 1956 screen adaptation of Richard III.

work of The Second City Company and Paul Sills's Story Theater; American directors such as Joseph CHAIKIN, Richard SCHECHNER, and André Gregory have founded acting companies that perform in a style incorporating both the improvisational thrust of Spolin and the physical activity characteristic of Grotowski. Today, productions everywhere blend elements of realistic and nonrealistic acting styles to produce what they consider to be truthful human characters.

See also: MIME AND PANTOMIME; THEATER, HISTORY OF THE.

---

actinide series [ak'-tuh-nyd]   The actinide elements are the 14 chemical elements that follow actinium in Group IIIB of the PERIODIC TABLE. Because of some chemical similarities, actinium is usually included in the series. All of the actinides are radioactive. Most of them are not found in nature but are artificially produced in the laboratory.

Actinides Found in Nature. Two of the actinides have isotopes with such long half-lives that they have not completely decayed since the Earth was formed. One isotope of thorium, Th-232, has a half-life of 14 billion years. It is a principal constituent of some minerals, notably thorite and monazite. Three isotopes of uranium are found in nature. Their isotopic abundances and half-lives are U-234, 0.006%, 230,000 years; U-235, 0.72%, 696 million years; and U-238, 99.27%, 4.51 billion years.

The overall abundance of uranium in the Earth's crust is about 4 parts per million, and it is concentrated in many minerals, principally pitchblende, autunite, torbernite, and carnotite. Deposits of uranium minerals large enough to be profitably mined are found principally in Africa, Canada, the Soviet Union, and the southwestern United States.

Discovery of Actinide Series. Neils Bohr suggested in 1923 that actinium might begin a series of elements similar to the series of rare-earth elements, the LANTHANIDE SERIES. In 1944, Glenn Seaborg and coworkers hypothesized that the elements following uranium would indeed parallel the lanthanides. These predictions were correct, and many of the actinides are in fact chemically similar to the lanthanides. All of the heavier actinide elements, the TRANSURANIUM ELEMENTS, as well as some isotopes of the lighter actinides, have been synthesized since 1940.

Characteristics. All of the actinide elements are shiny, hard metals that tarnish in air and are so electropositive that they are difficult to reduce from their compounds. Many compounds of the actinide elements have been studied, often using only a few micrograms because of the elements' scarcity and intense radioactivity. Because U-235 and Pu-239 undergo nuclear fission when they absorb neutrons, they are used in nuclear reactors and in nuclear weapons.

---

actinium [ak-tin'-ee-uhm]   The chemical element actinium is a radioactive metal, the first member of the actinide series. Its symbol is Ac, its atomic number 89, and its atomic weight 227 (stablest isotope). Actinium was discovered in 1899 by French chemist Andre Debierne, who found it in pitchblende residues. Many isotopes are known, one of which, ^{227}Ac, has a half-life of 21.6 years and is present in natural uranium. The other isotopes have half-lives of 10 days to less than 5 seconds.

actinometer [ak-tih-nahm'-uh-tur]   An actinometer is an instrument for measuring the ability of ELECTROMAGNETIC RADIATION coming from the Sun or an artificial light source to produce chemical changes. Actinic rays range from the ultraviolet to infrared. Actinometers are primarily used in photography to measure light intensity; there they are called light meters or exposure meters. The first actinometer was devised in 1840 by French optician Jean Baptiste François Soleil. The modern form of actinometer is the photoelectric exposure meter. It typically uses a cadmium sulfide photoconductive cell, a type of PHOTOELECTRIC CELL that changes resistance and thus causes a change in the current produced by a miniature battery in response to changes in light intensity.

ACTION   ACTION is an independent U.S. government agency, established in 1971, which administers volunteer service programs within the United States. The underlying purpose of these programs is essentially to support self-help efforts to overcome poverty conditions. One well-known program is Volunteers in Service to America (VISTA), launched in 1964 as a domestic counterpart of the PEACE CORPS. VISTA volunteers spend a year living and working among the poor in urban or rural areas and receive a subsistence allowance and health insurance. Volunteers are usually recruited locally for community projects seeking to alleviate aspects of illiteracy, unemployment, hunger, and homelessness.

ACTION also oversees the Foster Grandparent Program, created in 1965; this activity offers men and women at least 60 years of age an opportunity to help children with special needs. Foster grandparents (who receive a small stipend) serve in schools, hospitals, and other institutions for handicapped, disturbed, disadvantaged, or neglected children. Participants in the Senior Companion Program usually serve older persons in their own homes. The Retired Senior Volunteer Program organizes projects that permit older persons to perform various services on a regular basis in their communities.

Action Française [ahk-see-ohn' frawn-sez']   The Action Française was a right-wing political movement in France active from 1899 to 1944. Founded by Charles Maurras (1868–1952), it espoused royalism, authoritarianism, nationalism, and anti-Semitism. Through its newspaper, *L'Action Française*, and its student groups, called Camelots du Roi, the movement attacked the country's democratic institutions. In 1926, Pope Pius XI banned Roman Catholic participation in the movement, and in 1936 it was officially dissolved by the French government for complicity in an attack on Léon Blum. Surviving clandestinely, the Action Française contributed to the ideology of the VICHY GOVERNMENT during World War II. It disintegrated in 1944, when France was liberated and Maurras was imprisoned for collaboration.

action painting   Action painting is a term first used by the American critic Harold Rosenberg in an article in 1952. He had the painting of Willem DE KOONING especially in mind, with the idea that a work was itself a permanent record of the action, or process, of painting. Soon the term was used more or less interchangeably with ABSTRACT EXPRESSIONISM, although usually linked with the "gestural" abstract expressionists, such as Jackson POLLOCK and Hans HOFMANN, as well as de Kooning.

Actium [ak'-tee-uhm]   Actium was an ancient town and sanctuary in western Greece, famous for the naval battle that occurred offshore in the Ionian Sea Sept. 2, 31 BC, in which the fleet of Octavian (later the Roman emperor AUGUSTUS) decisively defeated the forces of Mark ANTONY and CLEOPATRA to win control of the Roman world. To commemorate his victory, Augustus built the city of Nicopolis nearby.

active transport   Active transport is the process by which dissolved substances (solutes) are moved across biological membranes and accumulated against concentration gradients at the expense of metabolic energy. This process contrasts sharply with passive diffusion, whereby a dissolved substance becomes evenly distributed on both sides of a membrane that is permeable (allowing passage) to it. The membranes of cells and the special structures, or organelles, within them are impermeable to most water-soluble substances. The contents of cells and organelles are controlled by transport proteins embedded in the membranes and designed for the movement of particular solutes across them (see MEMBRANE CHEMISTRY). This movement occurs against concentration gradients, that is, in the direction of the greater existing concentration. Without this control system life would be impossible, because cells and their organelles would simply not contain the necessary materials for metabolism and other life activities. For example, specific concentrations of ions of certain chemical elements are essential to enzyme function, muscle contraction, protection of cells from osmotic swelling (see OSMOSIS), and the conduction of nerve impulses.

Primary active transport directly uses metabolic energy in the form of adenosine triphosphate, or ATP (see ATP), which contains a high-energy phosphate bond, to move small ions across membranes. The transport proteins are termed *ion pumps* or transport "ATPases." These include the sodium pump, which transports sodium ions (Na^+) outward and potassium ions (K^+) inward across animal cell membranes, and the calcium pump, which moves calcium ions (Ca^{2+}) back into the sarcoplasmic reticulum (an intracellular membrane system for calcium storage) following MUSCLE CONTRACTION.

Other small molecules, such as sugars and amino acids, are accumulated by secondary active transport, in which a transport protein couples the movement of two different solutes across a membrane. In such a case, an ionic concentration gradient established by primary active transport provides the energy for moving the second solute.

Although the detailed molecular mechanism is still a mystery, it is now known that transport proteins are too large to shuttle back and forth across the membrane in the manner of a ferry. Rather, they appear to operate as restricted pores, with a binding site accessible to one and then the other side of the membrane. Energy enters the cycle when the transport protein reacts with ATP. The high-energy phosphate bond of ATP breaks, and a phosphate group becomes bonded to the transport protein, causing a change in the shape of the protein that alters the position of the binding site.

Acton, John Emerich Edward Dalberg Acton, 1st Baron

The historian John Emerich Edward Dalberg Acton, b. Jan. 10, 1834, d. June 19, 1902, was one of the greatest spokesmen of English liberalism. He served in the House of Commons from 1859 to 1865 and was created 1st Baron Acton in 1869. Although he was a devoted member of the Roman Catholic church, Acton opposed such measures as the declaration on papal infallibility at the First Vatican Council.

Lord Acton espoused the rigorous methods of the new scientific school of history and set out to write the definitive history of liberty. He never completed this book, but he set forth his ideas in two lectures delivered in 1877—"The History of Freedom in Antiquity" and "The History of Freedom in Christianity." In 1895, Acton was named regius professor of modern history at Cambridge. In 1899 he also became the editor of the *Cambridge Modern History*, which under his direction became a model of careful scholarship.

It was Acton's contention that "Power tends to corrupt, and absolute power corrupts absolutely."

Actors' Equity Association

Actors' Equity Association, founded in 1913, is the union encompassing all professional performers who work in the legitimate theater in the United States. It affiliated with the American Federation of Labor in 1919 and is now part of the AFL-CIO. The union determines the minimum pay scales for Broadway and Off Broadway performers, provides for arbitration arising out of members' contracts, and regulates the importation of foreign actors and the use of nonunion performers. Any actor who has worked within Equity's jurisdiction or who has a bona fide offer from an Equity producer is qualified to join.

Actors Studio

The Actors Studio is an actors' workshop founded in New York City in 1947 by Cheryl Crawford, Elia Kazan, and Robert Lewis and joined in 1948 by Lee Strasberg, who was its artistic director until his death in 1982. The studio is known for its controversial "method" approach to acting, an adaptation of the acting system first developed by the Russian director Konstantin STANISLAVSKY. In such training the actor works by improvisation and emotional exercises.

During the 1950s the Actors Studio had a profound influence on American theater, training for the stage and screen such leading actors as Marlon Brando, Montgomery Clift, Julie Harris, Paul Newman, and Geraldine Page. Although its influence has declined, the studio still trains actors at its principal centers in New York City and Los Angeles. In 1957 the studio added a Playwrights Unit, in 1960 a Directors Unit, and in 1962 a Production Unit.

Acts of the Apostles

The Acts of the Apostles is the fifth book of the New Testament, written between AD 70 and 90 by the author of the Gospel according to LUKE. Acts is an account of the early preaching about Jesus Christ, the growth of the primitive Christian community, and the spread of the Christian message. It covers the period from the Ascension of Christ (chapter 1) and the Pentecost to the visit of Saint PAUL to Rome, where he was placed under house arrest.

The early chapters of Acts contain an idyllic portrait of the Jerusalem community praying together, practicing common ownership of property, and preaching. The author attributes the vitality and activity of Christianity to the Holy Spirit. The early sermons of PETER summarize the message as understood by the author of Acts. Three key ideas are that Christ fulfills the promises of the Old Testament, that salvation comes through him, and that the Christian community is the new chosen people.

After chapter 10, the emphasis shifts to the spread of Christianity to the Gentiles through the missionary work of Saint Paul. In contrast to earlier New Testament documents, the end of the world is not considered imminent but has receded into the vaguely distant future. The very composition of Acts focuses attention on the present and on spreading Christianity "to the ends of the earth" (1:8). Thus Acts is a fairly detailed account of early Christianity in its progress from Jerusalem to Rome.

actuary

[ak'-chuh-wair-ee] An actuary estimates risks in order to determine premiums for insurance companies. For example, an actuary may calculate the likelihood of fires causing losses for a particular group of property owners, basing the projection on their rate of fires in the past. The profession requires intensive training in mathematics, statistics, accounting, and insurance probabilities.

acupuncture

Acupuncture is a form of medical therapy that involves inserting thin, solid needles into selective sites on the surface of the body. It has been part of Chinese medicine since ancient times (see MEDICINE, TRADITIONAL). Acupuncture was long in use in immigrant Chi-

Therapy was aimed at restoring normal energy flow so that perfect equilibrium existed throughout the body.

The use of acupuncture for controlling surgical pain is a recent development in China, and it does not strictly reflect the ancient medical philosophy. Classical Chinese medicine concerned itself with restoring normal function as opposed to creating abnormal conditions, such as total pain reduction. To control surgical pain in contemporary China, needles are inserted into various parts of the body, and the patient is stimulated by electrical current delivered through the needles or by the more traditional manual twirling of the needles. Practitioners may also inject various solutions at these body sites or use ultrasonic probes instead of needles. After about 20 minutes of stimulation, the surgery can begin. If acupuncture treatment has been effective, the patient will be wide awake, alert, and aware of all the major surgical procedures but will experience little or no pain (see ANESTHETICS).

The mechanisms by which patients are able to tolerate surgery during acupunctural stimulation are still unknown. Some scientists speculate that large sensory fibers are activated, which inhibits transmission of impulses from the small fibers carrying the sensory input of pain. Other scientists speculate that naturally produced morphinelike substances—endorphins and enkephalins—may be released within the brain in response to acupuncture. When these substances bind to OPIATE RECEPTOR cells, a pain-inhibition system is activated. More research is needed before mechanisms of acupuncture pain-control can be specified, and almost certainly psychological factors will be shown to play a crucial role.

Acupuncture pain-control for surgery may well be more a scientific curiosity than a practical innovation in the West. It cannot compete with conventional anesthesia and nerveblock anesthesia because these procedures are safe, fast, and virtually 100 percent reliable. Acupuncture is time-consuming and significantly less reliable, although Chinese researchers assert that besides reducing pain, it also reduces the possibility of shock and infection. It holds some promise for treating such chronic-pain states as backache, headache, and abdominal pain. Acupuncture is highly effective in giving short-term relief to patients suffering from such pain, but it is less impressive in the long-term rate of cure.

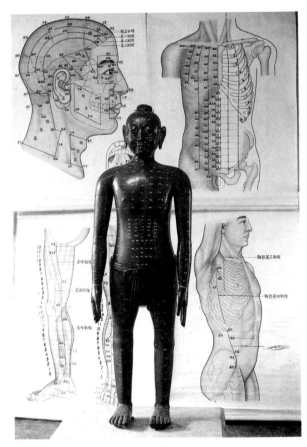

Diagrams and a model are used to study acupuncture meridian points. Needles inserted into specific meridian points supposedly affect energy flow and relieve pain in corresponding body organs.

nese communities, but Western interest in it did not become widespread until the 1970s, when physicians in the People's Republic of China demonstrated that it could be used to control surgical pain.

The early Chinese postulated a system of energy circulation that predated by many centuries current understanding of blood circulation and the nervous system. They thought that vital life energy flows through a series of pathways, or meridians, 12 of which were on each side of the body. Meridians were said to course through the deep tissues of the body, surfacing occasionally. The areas where the meridians touch the surface were considered useful treatment points for diseases, which were thought to be caused by imbalances in the energy flow. Inserting a needle into certain points could increase energy flow, and the needles also were used to drain away excessive pressure or to break down blocks or dams in energy flow. Meridians were variously related to the heart, the lungs, the colon, the gallbladder, the liver, and the other organs. The flow of energy in each meridian was read by taking the pulse associated with it at the wrist.

Ada Ada is a high-level COMPUTER LANGUAGE commissioned in the late 1970s by the U.S. Department of Defense and designed by a team at the French company CII-Honeywell Bull. It is named for Ada Lovelace (1815–52), Lord Byron's only legitimate daughter and a friend and commentator on the work of Charles BABBAGE, who anticipated many of the principles of the modern computer. Based on PASCAL, Ada was designed to reconcile the needs of machine efficiency and ease of use. Lack of adequate compiler software to handle Ada in the early 1980s belied initial, exaggerated claims for Ada's usefulness, but by 1990 the language was being adopted by aerospace and defense programs and, commercially, by European telecommunications firms.

Adam   According to the Bible, Adam was the first man. His name, which means "man" in Hebrew, is probably derived from the Hebrew word for "earth." The first three chapters of Genesis relate that God created Adam from dust, breathed life into him, and placed him in the Garden of EDEN, where he lived with his wife, EVE, until they ate the forbidden fruit from the tree of knowledge of good and evil (see ORIGINAL SIN). The biblical account is similar to Egyptian and Mesopotamian accounts, in which the first man was made from clay, infused with life by a divine being, and placed in a paradise of delight.

Adam, Adolphe   Adolphe Charles Adam, b. July 24, 1803, d. May 3, 1856, was a French composer who is today best known for his score to the ballet *Giselle* (1841). After overcoming parental opposition, he studied music at the Paris Conservatory. Adam composed music for 13 ballets and 20 comic operas, of which the most successful was *Le Postillon de Longjumeau* (1836).

Adam, Robert   Robert Adam, one of the major English architects of the second half of the 18th century, was a leader in international neoclassicism (see NEOCLASSICISM, art) and the creator of the Adam style in interior design.

Adam was born in Kirkcaldy, Scotland, on July 3, 1728. He was trained by his wealthy architect father, William Adam, and began his architectural career in Scotland with his oldest brother, John. During an extensive tour of Italy he was much inspired by the widespread renewed interest in antiquity and by personal acquaintances with such influential contemporaries as the French interior designer Charles Louis Clérisseau and the Italian artist and antiquarian Giovanni Battista PIRANESI. The presence in Italy of numerous well-traveled English noblemen (and potential clients) led Adam to establish himself in London on his return home early in 1758. By the early 1760s he had a great many commissions and had been appointed joint architect to the King's Works, along with Sir William Chambers, who was to be his principal rival for leadership in English architecture.

The publication of Adam's *Ruins of the Palace of the Emperor Diocletian at Spalatro in Dalmatia* (1764) firmly established his version of neoclassical style in England. The Adam style replaced the Burlingtonian Palladian style—derived from the much-published work of the Italian architect Andrea Palladio—which was heavier and closer to its Greek and Roman sources. Adam used the same elements but with far more freedom and imagination. His finest accomplishments were in the planning and decoration of interiors, always to the smallest details. Among his principal commissions were Syon House, Middlesex (*c*.1760–1769); Kedleston Hall, Derbyshire (*c*.1759–1771); Harewood House, Yorkshire (*c*.1758–1771); and Osterly Park, Middlesex (1761–80). His dining room for Lansdowne House in London (*c*.1760–1768; partially demolished) is in the Metropolitan Muse-

The Roman anteroom of Syon House, located in Middlesex, England, is an important example of Robert Adam's rich neoclassical decoration.

um of Art, New York City, and Home House (1775–77); is now the Courtauld Institute of Art.

Adam's public buildings include the Admiralty Screen, London (1759–60); the Register House, Edinburgh (*c*.1774–1792); and Edinburgh University (begun 1789–93). He was also responsible for a number of town-planning schemes, such as Portland Place (1776–*c*.1780) and Fitzroy Square (*c*.1790–1800) in London and Charlotte Square in Edinburgh (1791–1807). The Adelphi scheme (1768–72; destroyed), a group of sumptuous town houses on the River Thames, bankrupted Adam and may have been responsible for occasional lapses of quality in his output after 1775. During the last years of his life he received a number of commissions, many for large Gothic Revival castles, especially in Scotland. He died on Mar. 3, 1792, and is buried in Westminster Abbey.

Adam exerted an enormous influence, clearly seen in the work of such other English architects as George Dance, James Wyatt, and Sir John Soane, who in 1833 bought most of Adam's drawings, now in the Soane Museum, London.

Adam de la Halle   [duh lah ahl]   Adam de la Halle, known as Adam le Bossu (Adam the Hunchback), *c*.1250–*c*.1288, is regarded as the originator of French secular drama. Also a poet and musician, he wrote lyrics of courtly love, as well as two popular plays, *Le Jeu de la Feuillée* (The Play of the Greensward, 1276) and *Le Jeu de Robin et Marion* (*c*.1283).

Adams, Abigail Abigail Adams, b. Weymouth, Mass., Nov. 11, 1744, d. Oct. 28, 1818, was the wife of John Adams, the second president of the United States, and the mother of John Quincy Adams, sixth president. Originally named Abigail Smith, she was the daughter of a clergyman in Weymouth.

Educated at home by her grandmother, she displayed a lively intelligence and expressed her strong opinions in a straightforward manner. She is credited with having had a notable influence on the long and distinguished career of her husband, accompanying him on his diplomatic missions to Europe and advising him by letter when she remained in Massachusetts managing family affairs. As First Lady, she was a skillful political hostess, although she offended some by her strong Federalist views.

Abigail Adams was a prodigious letter writer, and many editions of her letters have been published. Her grandson Charles Francis Adams (1807–86) published the most nearly complete edition in 1841 and 1876.

Abigail Adams, wife of U.S. president John Adams, was one of history's most famous letter writers. A letter to her husband that Congress should "Remember the Ladies" was an early plea to the new American government to guarantee women's rights. (Courtesy National Gallery of Art, Washington, D.C. Gift of Mrs. Robert Homans, 1954.)

Adams, Ansel The American photographer Ansel Adams, b. San Francisco, Feb. 20, 1902, d. Apr. 22, 1984, became a recognized leader of modern PHOTOGRAPHY through his landscape photographs of the American West. Impressed by the work of Paul STRAND, Adams became a professional photographer in 1930. In 1932 he had his first solo show in a major museum, and with Imogen Cunningham, Edward Weston, and others, founded the influential Group f/64. In 1937, Adams moved to Yosemite, Calif., and after 1940 he photographed extensively in the national parks. Working exclusively in black and white, Adams used brilliant light to produce intense images. His sharply defined prints are in marked contrast with the evocative work of earlier pictorialists. His collections include *My Camera in Yosemite Valley* (1949); *Portfolio Two: The National Parks* (1950); *This Is the American Earth* (1960); *Ansel Adams, Images 1923–1974* (1975); and *The Portfolios of Ansel Adams* (1977).

Adams, Charles Francis Charles Francis Adams, b. Boston, Aug. 18, 1807, d. Nov. 21, 1886, was an American historian and diplomat. The son of President John Quincy Adams, he spent his early years managing the family property in Massachusetts, writing historical articles, and editing the letters of his grandmother Abigail Adams and writings of his grandfather John Adams. Holding antislavery views, he was the vice-presidential candidate of the Free-Soil party in 1848.

Elected to Congress in 1858 as a Republican, Adams was appointed minister to Great Britain in 1861. His major task was to prevent British recognition of the Confederate States. Personally well liked and an adroit and tactful diplomat, he was able to prevent a rupture in U.S.-British relations over the delicate TRENT AFFAIR. The success of his mission was a vital contribution to the Northern victory.

After his return to the United States in 1868, except for membership in the Alabama Claims Commission, Adams retired from public life. In 1874 he began publication, in 12 volumes, of his father's diary.

Adams, Charles Francis, Jr. Charles Francis Adams, Jr., b. Boston, May 27, 1835, d. Mar. 20, 1915, the son of Charles Francis Adams, was a railroad expert and writer of New England history. After publishing *Chapters of Erie* (1871), in which he exposed the stock manipulations of the directors of the Erie Railroad, he wrote *Richard Henry Dana: A Biography* (1890), *Massachusetts: Its Historians and History* (1893), and a biography (1900) of his father.

Adams, Henry Henry Brooks Adams, b. Boston, Feb. 16, 1838, d. Mar. 27, 1918, an American historian, was the son of Charles Francis Adams and the descendant of two presidents, but he gradually abandoned his family's involvement in politics to pursue the study of history. After completing his studies at Harvard, he traveled abroad as the secretary of his father, a diplomat. In 1870 he began teaching history at Harvard and became the editor of the *North American Review*, a reform journal that focused attention on corruption and advocated civil service reforms. From 1877 to 1879 he edited the papers and wrote a biography of Albert Gallatin. A decade later his research in this period of American history culminated in his 9-volume *History of the United States* (1889–91).

In the meantime, Adams's disillusionment with politics surfaced in a satirical novel, *Democracy*, which he published anonymously in 1880. In 1885 his wife's suicide drove him to search for new meaning in life and history. Adams recorded this spiritual odyssey in two important works that went far beyond the narrow political approach of his earlier work: in *Mont Saint Michel and Chartres* (1913) he expressed his admiration for the medieval church, and in his autobiography, *The Education of Henry Adams* (1918), he gave a moving account of one man's struggle to understand change.

AT A GLANCE

JOHN ADAMS
2nd President of the United States (1797–1801)

Nickname: "Atlas of Independence"

Born: Oct. 30, 1735, Braintree (now Quincy), Mass.

Education: Harvard College (graduated 1755)

Profession: Lawyer

Religious Affiliation: Unitarian

Marriage: Oct. 25, 1764, to Abigail Smith (1744–1818)

Children: Abigail Amelia Adams (1765–1813); John Quincy Adams (1767–1848); Susanna Adams (1768–70); Charles Adams (1770–1800); Thomas Boylston Adams (1772–1832)

Political Affiliation: Federalist

Writings: *The Life and Works of John Adams* (10 vols., 1856); *The Adams' Papers* (13 vols., 1961-77)

Died: July 4, 1826, Quincy, Mass.

Buried: First Unitarian Church, Quincy, Mass.

Vice President: Thomas Jefferson

John Adams

Adams, John   In three remarkable careers—as a foe of British oppression and champion of independence (1761–77), as an American diplomat in Europe (1778–88), and as the first vice-president (1789–97) and then the second president (1797–1801) of the United States—John Adams was a founder of the United States. Perhaps equally important, however, was the life of his mind and spirit; in a pungent diary, vivid letters, learned tracts, and patriotic speeches he revealed himself as a quintessential Puritan, patriarch of an illustrious family, tough-minded philosopher of the republic, sage, and sometimes a vain, stubborn, and vitriolic partisan.

John Adams was born in Braintree (now Quincy), Mass., on Oct. 30, 1735, in a small saltbox house still standing and open to visitors. His father, John Adams, a deacon and a fifth-generation Massachusetts farmer, and his mother, the former Suzanna Boylston, were, their son wrote, "both fond of reading"; so they resolved to give bookishly inclined John a good education. He became the first of his family to go to college when he entered Harvard in 1751. There, and in six further years of intensive reading while he taught school and studied law in Worcester and Boston, he mastered the technicalities of his profession and the literature and learning of his day. By 1762, when he began 14 years of increasingly successful legal practice, he was well informed, ambitious, and public spirited. His most notable good fortune, however, occurred in 1764 when he married Abigail Smith. John Adams's marriage of 54 years to this wise, learned, strong-willed, passionate, and patriotic woman began the brilliant phase of Adams family history that produced their son John Quincy, his son Charles Francis, his sons Henry and Brooks, and numerous other distinguished progeny.

In 1761, John Adams began to think and write and act against British measures that he believed infringed on colonial liberties and the right of Massachusetts and the other colonies to self-government. A pamphlet entitled *A Dissertation on the Canon and the Feudal Law* and town instructions denouncing the STAMP ACT (1765) marked him as a vigorous, patriotic penman, and, holding various local offices, he soon became a leader among Massachusetts radicals. Although he never wavered in his devotion to colonial rights and early committed himself to independence as an unwelcome last resort, Adams's innate conservatism made him determined in 1770 that the British soldiers accused of the BOSTON MASSACRE receive a fair hearing. He defended the soldiers at their trial. He also spoke out repeatedly against mob violence and other signs of social disintegration.

In 1774–76, Adams was a Massachusetts delegate to the CONTINENTAL CONGRESS in Philadelphia. His speeches and writings (especially a newspaper series signed "Novanglus" in 1775) articulating the colonial cause and his brilliant championing of American rights in Congress caused Thomas JEFFERSON to call him the "Colossus of Independence." Adams helped draft the DECLARATION OF INDEPENDENCE, secured its unanimous adoption in Congress, and wrote his wife on July 3, 1776, that "the most memorable Epoch in the History of America has begun."

After 18 months of toil in committee and on the floor of Congress managing the American Revolution, Adams crossed the Atlantic to be an American commissioner to France. The termination of this mission after less than a year in Paris allowed him to return home long enough to take a leading role in drafting the new Massachusetts constitution. He sailed again for Europe, accompanied by two of his sons, in November 1779 as a commissioner to seek peace with Britain. After quarrels in Paris with Benjamin FRANKLIN and French officials, he left for the Netherlands, where he secured Dutch recognition of American independence and a substantial loan as well. He returned to Paris in October 1782 to insist on American rights (especially to fish on the Grand Banks of Newfoundland) in the negotiations that led to Britain's recognition of the independence of the United States in the Treaty of Paris of Sept. 3, 1783.

For two more years Adams helped Franklin and Jefferson negotiate treaties of friendship and commerce with numerous foreign powers. Then, appointed the first American minister to Britain, Adams presented his credentials to George III in 1785, noting his pride in "having the distinguished honor to be the first [ex-colonial subject] to stand in your Majesty's royal presence in a diplomatic character." The king, aware of the poignancy of the occasion, returned Adams's compliments and hoped that the "language, religion, and blood" shared by the two nations would "have their natural and full effect," but the British ministry obstructed Adams's efforts to restore equitable commerce between the two nations.

When he returned to the United States in 1788, Adams was greeted by his countrymen as one of the heroes of independence and was promptly elected vice-president under the new Constitution. This post, regarded by Adams as "the most insignificant office that ever the invention of man contrived or his imagination conceived," left him time to work out his increasingly sober views of republican government. In Europe he had been impressed with both the unsuitability of self-government for masses of destitute, ignorant people, and the usefulness, in evoking patriotism and in maintaining order, of the pomp and ceremony of monarchy. He was thus appalled, but not surprised, at the riotous French Revolution and emphasized the need for dignity, ritual, and authority in a republic like the United States. He also supported the efforts of George WASHINGTON to give the presidency an almost regal quality and to extend executive power, and he

agreed with Alexander HAMILTON on most of the latter's fiscal plans. He never accepted, however, the "high" Federalist biases toward commercial growth and government by "the rich, the well-born, and the able."

Although his own presidency (1797–1801) was a troubled one, Adams made uniquely important contributions during his term as chief executive. He managed orderly transitions of power at both the beginning and the end of his administration, and he gave the government stability by continuing most of the practices established under Washington. The major crisis he faced, however, arose from strained relations with revolutionary France. When, in the so-called XYZ AFFAIR (1797–98), American peace commissioners returned from Paris with lurid stories of deceit and bribery, Adams called for an assertion of national pride, built up the armed forces, and even accepted the ALIEN AND SEDITION ACTS as emergency national security measures. With his opponents (led by Jefferson) charging oppression and some of his own FEDERALIST PARTY (led by Hamilton) urging war and conquest, Adams kept his nerve and, when the opportunity arose, dispatched another peace commission to France. This defused the crisis and led in 1800 to an agreement with France that ended the so-called Quasi-War. Nonetheless, deserted by Hamilton and other Federalists who disapproved of his independent course, and attacked by the Jeffersonian Republicans as a vain monarchist, Adams was forced out of office after one term.

When he and Abigail returned to Massachusetts, they moved into a comfortable but unpretentious house in Quincy (it is known today and open to visitors as the Adams National Historic Site) they had bought 12 years before. There, tending to his fields, visiting with neighbors, and enjoying his family, John Adams lived for 25 years as a sage and national patriarch. Of his numerous correspondences, the cherished 14-year (1812–26) one with Jefferson became a literary legacy to the nation. Although the debilitations of old age and the death of his beloved Abigail in 1818 troubled his last years, his mind remained sharp and his spirit buoyant until the end. Like Jefferson, he died on July 4, 1826, the 50th anniversary of the Declaration of Independence. Ninety years old at his death, Adams was revered by his countrymen not only as one of the founding fathers but also as a plain, honest man who personified the best of what the nation could hope of its citizens and leaders.

▬

Adams, John Couch   John Couch Adams, b. June 5, 1819, d. Jan. 21, 1892, was an English astronomer and mathematician who, at the age of 24, was the first person to predict the position of a planetary mass beyond Uranus. He subsequently became the subject of a famous priority dispute with the French astronomer Urbain Leverrier, whose later prediction was published before Adams's and led directly to the discovery of Neptune on Sept. 23, 1846. Adams was educated at Cambridge and became a fellow, tutor, and professor of astronomy and geometry before being named director of Cambridge Observatory in 1861.

AT A GLANCE

JOHN QUINCY ADAMS
6th President of the United States (1825—29)

Nickname: "Old Man Eloquent"

Born: July 11, 1767, Braintree (now Quincy), Mass.

Education: Harvard College (graduated 1787)

Profession: Lawyer

Religious Affiliation: Unitarian

Marriage: July 26, 1797, to Louisa Catherine Johnson (1775–1852)

Children: George Washington Adams (1801–29); John Adams (1803–34); Charles Francis Adams (1807–86); Louisa Catherine Adams (1811–12)

Political Affiliation: Federalist; Democratic-Republican; Whig

Writings: *Memoirs* (12 vols., 1874–7 7); *Writings of John Quincy Adams* (7 vols., 1913–17)

Died: Feb. 23, 1848, Washington, D.C.

Buried: First Unitarian Church, Quincy, Mass.

Vice President: John C. Calhoun

Adams, John Quincy   John Quincy Adams, the sixth president of the United States, was a child of American independence, the primary architect of the first century of the nation's foreign policy, and an implacable foe of slavery.

Adams was born in Braintree (now Quincy), Mass., on July 11, 1767, the first son of the brilliant, patriotic, and strong-willed Abigail Smith Adams and her husband, John Adams, then a little-known country lawyer. When John Quincy was seven years old, his father, who was in Philadelphia attending the First Continental Congress, wrote to his wife of her duty to "mould the minds and manners of our children. Let us teach them not only to do virtuously, but to excell. To excell they must be taught to be steady, active, and industrious." A year later, mother and son watched the smoke and heard the cannons of the Battle of Bunker Hill. The letter, and the close, frightening, but also exhilarating event, set the boy's life on its course.

John Quincy Adams began 70 years of public service when in 1778, at the age of 11, he acted as his father's secretary during a diplomatic mission to France. In 1780 he again went to Europe with his father, this time as an official secretary, and a year later he served as secretary and interpreter to Francis Dana on the first American mission to the Russian court at St. Petersburg. Returning to western Europe via Sweden, Denmark, and Germany in early 1783, Adams lived for the next two years in The Hague, London, and Paris, where he pursued his formal education. When he came back to America in 1785 to enter Harvard College, he knew five or six modern languages as well as Latin and Greek, had traveled throughout northern and western Europe, had been under the tutelage of his father for seven years, and had taken part in much of the diplomacy of the American Revolution.

Adams graduated from Harvard in 1787 and two years later finished his legal apprenticeship. Without enthusiasm he began to practice law in Boston in 1790. He was soon easily distracted into writing a notable series of newspaper articles attacking the ideas of Thomas Paine's *The Rights of Man*, and in 1794 he eagerly accepted President Washington's appointment of him as American minister to Holland. He subsequently served as minister to Prussia from 1797 to 1801. His letters to American officials contained by far the most perceptive and influential news about the crucial years of Napoleon's rise to dominance. During a mission to London in 1796–97 he married Louisa Catherine Johnson, the daughter of a Maryland merchant serving as U.S. consul in London. Their marriage produced three children and lasted until his death 51 years later.

Home again in 1801, Adams served briefly in the Massachusetts Senate and then in the U.S. Senate from 1803 to 1808. Although nominally in the FEDERALIST PARTY, he had no use for that party's increasingly regional posture and instead supported most of the policies of Thomas Jefferson's administration, including the EMBARGO ACT of 1807. His refusal to bow to heavy pressure from the Massachusetts legislature to repudiate that measure led to his resignation from the Senate—and, 150 years later, to his inclusion in John F. Kennedy's *Profiles in Courage.*

President James Madison then appointed Adams minister to Russia, and he sailed—this time with members of his own young family—for St. Petersburg, arriving just before ice closed the Baltic in December 1809. He lived there for four years and gained the confidence of Russian officials, who began negotiations leading to the end of the War of 1812. Adams traveled about northern Europe for 18 months pursuing these negotiations. As chief American commissioner, he signed the Treaty of Ghent on Christmas Eve, 1814. Madison promptly appointed him the first postwar American minister to Britain. Like his father before him and his son, Charles Francis Adams, after him, he stood proudly before the king of the former mother country as the representative of an independent nation.

As secretary of state during the administration (1817–25) of James MONROE, Adams took a leading role in all its deliberations and earned his standing as perhaps the most successful secretary of state in American history. He concluded negotiations he had begun in London to demilitarize the American border with Canada (1818), purchased Florida (1819), demarked a long southern boundary with Spanish Mexico that for the first time recognized American claims extending to the Pacific Ocean (1819), and set forth the principles of Anglo-American reconciliation and New World independence from the Old, known ever since as the MONROE DOCTRINE (1823).

Increasingly bitter political strife, however, puzzled and eventually infuriated Adams. He felt, justly, that he was entirely qualified—indeed that it was his due—to become president in 1825; yet he had only contempt for the selfish machinations and public circus apparently necessary for electoral success. His ambition triumphed, however. Although no candidate won a majority of the electoral vote in 1824, Adams accepted the support of Henry CLAY to secure his final selection—over Andrew JACKSON and William H. CRAWFORD—by the House of Representatives. Although inaugurated as a "minority president," he nonetheless submitted a broad, national program to an increasingly factional and sectionally oriented Congress and public. He called in 1825 for recognition of the new Latin American republics, support of canals and other internal improvements, establishment of a national university, support for scientific explorations, and in gen-

eral for Congress "to give efficacy to the means committed to us for the common good." Congress ignored these grand programs and instead increasingly responded to the rising tide of laissez-faire expansionism and frontier individualism that swept Adams out of and Andrew Jackson into the White House in 1829.

Retired permanently—he thought—to his books and to his farm, Adams nevertheless responded dutifully when his neighbors elected him to the House of Representatives in 1830 and kept him there for nine consecutive terms. There, as "Old Man Eloquent," again and again speaking his conscience and calling the nation to respond to its highest impulses, he lived out his last, perhaps most remarkable career. In his relentless, eventually successful opposition to the so-called GAG RULES, which stifled antislavery petitions, Adams dramatized for the nation the repressive character of slavery. When fatally stricken in the House in 1848, almost 70 years to the day after he had first sailed for Europe with his father, he had just voted against a resolution thanking the American generals of the Mexican War, a conflict he had opposed.

When Adams died on Feb. 23, 1848, he was not only the last surviving statesman of the American Revolution but also the first national leader to have dramatized the moral issue that precipitated the Civil War. He thus nearly encompassed in his public career the "four score and seven years" of which Abraham Lincoln was soon to speak; he had also defined the foreign and domestic purposes that in his view undergirded the nation that his father had helped to found and his son would help to preserve. Although he was at times rigid, demanding, self-righteous, and even quaint, John Quincy Adams possessed the personal integrity, devotion to principle, intellectual intensity, and strong will that have made his name and his family a national resource.

Adams, Maude   Maude Adams, b. Salt Lake City, Utah, Nov. 11, 1872, d. July 17, 1953, an American actress of both intellect and pixielike charm, is best remembered for her performance in the title role of Sir James M. Barrie's *Peter Pan* (1905–07). A successful child actress (she first appeared on stage at the age of nine months), she made her New York debut in 1888 and became famous playing threatened heroines of melodrama. Producer Charles Frohman made her a star, and Barrie wrote her most successful parts, in such plays as *The Little Minister* (1897–98), *Quality Street* (1902), and *What Every Woman Knows* (1908–09). After Frohman's death in 1915 her career declined, and she retired in 1918.

Adams, Samuel   Samuel Adams, b. Boston, Sept. 17, 1722, d. Oct. 2, 1803, was a major leader in the American Revolution. The son of a wealthy brewer, he inherited one-third of the family property but lost most of it through poor management. After attending Harvard, he became active in colonial politics and enjoyed a popular following through his activities in the Boston political

Samuel Adams, as a revolutionary spokesman and writer, profoundly swayed public opinion in favor of American independence. The artist, John Singleton Copley, portrayed Adams pointing to the Massachusetts Charter. (Courtesy Museum of Fine Arts, Boston. Deposited by the City of Boston.)

clubs, such as the Caucus Club, which was influential in nominating candidates for local office. He was an effective spokesman for the popular party opposed to the entrenched circle around the royal governor.

Adams organized the protest against the STAMP ACT (1765) and was a founder of the SONS OF LIBERTY. Undoubtedly the most influential member of the lower house of the Massachusetts legislature (1765–74), he drafted most of the major protest documents, including the Circular Letter (1768) against the TOWNSHEND ACTS. He also wrote frequently for the press in defense of colonial rights. Adams formed close ties with John HANCOCK, whose connections with the Boston merchants made him useful in the revolutionary cause. After 1770 he was the focal point in the creation of intercolonial committees of correspondence to sustain the spirit of resistance. He was a principal organizer of the BOSTON TEA PARTY (1773).

Because of the intemperate language of his essays for the press (Lt. Gov. Thomas Hutchinson called him the greatest "incendiary" in the empire) and his early advocacy of independence, Adams was regarded as a radical. At the First Continental Congress he worked closely with John Adams, his second cousin. Their influence was crucial in the rejection of the plan of union presented by Joseph GALLOWAY and in the adoption of a compulsory nonimportation agreement (in effect a boycott of British goods). Samuel Adams remained in Congress until 1781, participating in the drafting of the Articles of Confederation. After the Revolution his influence in Massachusetts was never as great, although he continued to be active in state politics, serving as lieutenant governor (1789–93) and as governor (1794–97). A more conservative figure in later years, he condemned the farmers' actions during SHAYS'S REBELLION and endorsed ratification of the federal Constitution.

Adamson, Robert see HILL, D. O., AND ADAMSON, ROBERT

Adana [ah-dah-nah'] Adana (1985 pop., 777,554) is the capital city of Adana province on the southern coast of Turkey. Located on the banks of the Seyhan River, 52 km (32 mi) north of the Mediterranean, it is Turkey's fourth largest city, and the center of the Turkish cotton industry. Possibly an ancient Hittite city, Adana was later a Roman military station. It became a Turkish city during the 16th century.

adaptation, biological see EVOLUTION

adaptive radiation Adaptive radiation is the EVOLUTION of a species into many diverse species, each adapted to a different habitat. Differentiation and complexity of the species are increased, with the resulting decrease in competition. As a result, the species is able to make use of all available niches in the habitat so that more populations flourish. Adaptive radiation occurs most rapidly when a species colonizes a new environment in which many ecological niches are unoccupied. The results are a population increase and multiple divergence. After a species radiates and diverges, dominant forms eventually prevail. When environmental conditions change, those forms of the species which cannot readapt may become extinct.

DARWIN'S FINCHES (see also DARWIN, CHARLES) are a classic example of adaptive radiation. All 14 species living on the Galápagos Islands are derived from a single species of finch—a ground-dwelling seedeater—that migrated to those islands. Because the ecological niches on the isolated islands were unoccupied, the finch differentiated into 14 diverse species. Some remained ground-dwelling seedeaters, and others lived on cacti or insects and dwelled in trees.

Addams, Charles The American cartoonist Charles Samuel Addams, b. Westfield, N.J., Jan. 7, 1912, d. Sept. 29, 1988, was an undisputed master of macabre humor in which humanoid monsters were shown in everyday situations. His cartoons began appearing in the *New Yorker* magazine in 1935. One depicted his favorite character, a haggard vamp, knocking at the door of an old crone and asking, "May I borrow a cup of cyanide?" His cartoons were published in several books, including *Drawn and Quartered* (1942), *My Crowd* (1970), and *Creature Comforts* (1981), and were the basis for a television series, "The Addams Family" (1964–66).

Addams, Jane Jane Laura Addams, b. Cedarville, Ill., Sept. 6, 1860, d. May 21, 1935, was an American social reformer, pacifist, and women's rights advocate. In 1889, influenced by British precedents, she founded Hull House, in Chicago, in which she and other social reformers lived and worked to improve conditions in the city's slums. Hull House became a model for many other settlement houses in the United States. Jane Addams

Jane Addams, an American social worker, was awarded the 1931 Nobel Peace Prize. She supported investigations that resulted in child labor reform, an 8-hour working day for women, and better housing. Hull House, the settlement house in Chicago that was the center of her work, furnished such services as day-care for working mothers.

became president of the Women's International League for Peace and Freedom in 1919. Together with Nicholas Murray Butler, she received the Nobel Peace Prize in 1931. Her books include *Democracy and Social Ethics* (1902) and *Twenty Years at Hull House* (1910).

addax [ad'-aks]   The addax, *Addax nasomaculatus*, is the single species of addax among many antelope species in the family Bovidae of the order Artiodactyla. It is found only in the Sahara, where it was once widespread. The plump, short-legged addax is more than 1.8 m (6 ft) long and about 1 m (39 in) tall at the shoulders, and it weighs up to 120 kg (265 lb). Both sexes have long horns that are ringed and screw-shaped. The coat is gray to white, with a black skullcap and facial markings. The broad hooves are an adaptation for travel on desert sands. Addaxes usually get water only from the plants they eat, but in captivity they drink large amounts. Unable to flee hunters speedily, the addax is an endangered species.

The addax, an endangered species of antelope, is hunted for its flesh and hide. Both male and female addaxes have curved, spiraled horns.

adder   An adder is any of several venomous snakes of the viper family, Viperidae. The name is also applied to several other kinds of snakes, some nonpoisonous. The species best known simply as "adder" is the common adder, or European viper, *Vipera berus*, found throughout Europe and northern Asia. Its stocky body—typical of vipers, which ambush and strike their prey and wait for them to die, rather than actively pursue them—reaches a length of about 60 cm (2 ft) and is usually brownish, with a black zigzag stripe down the back. The snake feeds on lizards and small mammals, and its bite is rarely fatal to humans. It is ovoviviparous; the eggs reach full development within the female and the young are born live or hatch immediately upon laying.

The common adder is a venomous snake of Europe and Asia. It feeds on rodents and birds and may hibernate during winter. The adder's venom is seldom fatal to human beings.

adder's-tongue   Adder's-tongue is any of about 25 species constituting the herb genus *Erythronium* of the lily family, Liliaceae. Other common names are dog's-tooth violet, fawn lily, and trout lily. The plants are 10–61 cm (4–24 in) high; their two broad leaves are richly mottled, and the graceful flowers may be a variety of colors, making them attractive plants for rock gardens. They are native to North America, with one species in Europe and Asia. Adder's-tongue fern is the common name for the fern genus *Ophioglossum*, which is widely dispersed in temperate and tropical regions.

addiction   see ALCOHOLISM; DRUG ABUSE; SMOKING

adding machine   The adding machine is a mechanical device that adds numbers. Knowledge of devices such as the abacus was used to design the earliest-known machine that itself added numbers by moving and shifting physical objects without requiring a human operator to know how to add. The physical objects were gear wheels and worm gears, meshed to form a train of gears. Described in a treatise by Hero of Alexandria that dates from the 2d century AD, this machine could add up the *stades* (kilometers or miles) that a carriage traveled. The principle of its operation, based on the rotation of the pegged, or single-tooth, wheel, is still found today in water meters, gas meters, and bicycle and automobile ODOMETERS.

In the 17th century the French mathematician Blaise Pascal converted the mechanical arrangement of the odometer into an adding machine that a clerk could operate. The mechanical principles of the adding machine were extended and incorporated in hand-cranked calculators during the 18th and 19th centuries and in electrically operated calculators during the 20th century. By the middle of the 20th century, the electronic circuitry of the COMPUTER began to replace the electromechanical adding operations of business office machines, and by the last quarter of the century microminiaturization of circuits made handheld CALCULATORS possible.

Addis Ababa [ad'-is ah'-buh-buh] Addis Ababa ("New Flower") is the capital of Ethiopia and has a population of 1,423,111 (1984 est.). It is located in the Entoto Mountains of Shewa province in the northwestern region of the African high plateau.

Addis Ababa was established in 1887 by Emperor Menelik II. The upper section of the city includes traditional living areas, shanty towns, the central market, and Addis Ababa University (1950). The newer and lower section contains government buildings, international offices, the Jubilee Palace, and other palaces of former emperors. The growth of the city has been sporadic and unplanned, however.

Addis Ababa serves as the headquarters for the ORGANIZATION OF AFRICAN UNITY (OAU) and the UN Economic Commission for Africa and is the site of numerous churches. Saint Michael's Church, consecrated in 1986, is one of the largest Christian churches in Africa. Many artists and craftspeople reside in the city. Addis Ababa's industrial establishments include cement factories, beer and tobacco plants, and textile mills.

Addison, Joseph Joseph Addison, b. May 1, 1672, d. June 17, 1719, an English poet and essayist, was co-author with Sir Richard STEELE of the great series of periodical essays *The Tatler* and *The Spectator*. He is ranked among the minor masters of English prose style and credited with raising the general cultural level of the English middle classes.

Political Career. Addison, educated at Oxford, had his first poem published in 1693 and achieved celebrity with *The Campaign* (1704), a poem commemorating the Battle of Blenheim. Later he wrote two series of essays, *The Whig Examiner* (1710) and *The Freeholder* (1715–16), in defense of his party. So closely was he identified with the Whigs that when he produced his only play, *Cato* (1713), a tragedy about the Roman patriot, it was taken as an allegory of contemporary politics.

These efforts proved effective: Addison was appointed undersecretary of state (1706), secretary to the lord lieutenant in Ireland (1709), and secretary to the Regency following the death of Queen Anne (1714). His highest office was secretary of state (1717–18), from which he retired with a generous pension. His personal conduct

Joseph Addison, an 18th-century English essayist, appears in this portrait by Michael Dahl. Addison's importance to English prose is summarized by Samuel Johnson, who claimed, "Whoever wishes to attain an English style, familiar but not coarse, and elegant but not ostentatious, must give up his days and nights to the volumes of Addison."

had always been sober; on his deathbed he is said to have summoned his stepson to his side so that he might see "in what peace a Christian can die."

Writings. Addison had been schoolboy friends with Steele, to whose *Tatler* (1709–11) he became chief contributor. In *The Spectator* (1711–12) their positions were reversed: of 555 essays, Addison wrote 274. Addison adopted Steele's purpose from *The Tatler*—"to enliven Morality with Wit, and to temper Wit with Morality"—and added a further purpose—to introduce his middle-class public to developments in philosophy and literature. Thus Addison helped popularize the philosophy of John Locke; he devoted a series of *Spectator* essays to criticism of John Milton's *Paradise Lost;* and he inculcated principles of good judgment in the arts.

He also continued from *The Tatler* the practice of inventing entertaining fictional characters, the most popular of which was Sir Roger de Coverley, a country gentleman of charming eccentricity, good sense, and kindness.

Addison's disease Addison's disease is caused by insufficient production of hormones by the cortex of the ADRENAL GLANDS, usually resulting from damage by tuberculosis or by fungal infections. The disease is named for Thomas Addison (1793–1860), the English physician who first described it in 1855. Symptoms are weakness, anemia, weight loss, gastrointestinal problems, low blood pressure, tanning of the skin, and sometimes nervousness and irritability. Although the disease was once nearly always fatal, patients treated with synthetic cortical hormones may now expect to recover completely.

addition   see ARITHMETIC

Ade, George [ayd] The journalist, humorist, and playwright George Ade, b. Kentland, Ind., Feb. 9, 1866,

d. May 16, 1944, mastered a midwestern idiom of homespun phrases and incongruous moralisms best illustrated in *Fables in Slang* (1899). His parables of naïveté and pomposity first appeared in his *Chicago Record* newspaper column. Ten of his plays appeared on Broadway, including *The County Chairman* (1903) and *The College Widow* (1904).

Adelaide

Adelaide is the capital city of South Australia and Australia's fifth largest city, with a population of 1,013,000 (1987 est.). More than 70% of all people in South Australia live in Adelaide. Located in the southeastern part of Australia, Adelaide was founded in 1836 and named for Queen Adelaide, consort of William IV. It is a planned and uncongested city, whose center is divided by the Torrens River into two areas, the northern, residential area and the southern, business area. A parkland belt runs along the river, and a green belt surrounds the central city.

Heavy industry—automobile plants, tire plants, steel works, chemical plants, oil refineries, and sugar refineries—is concentrated along the rail link between Adelaide and its port city, Port Adelaide. Dairy farming and apple orchards flourish in the fertile areas around the city.

Adelaide is the home of the University of Adelaide (1874) and the biennial Adelaide Festival of Arts. The South Australian Museum houses the world's largest collection of aboriginal artifacts. The Institute of Art and the Adelaide Museum are also located in the city.

Aden

[ay'-den or ah'-den] Aden (1984 est. pop., 318,000) was the capital of the People's Democratic Republic of Yemen until 1990, when the two Yemens merged and SANA became the political capital of the new Republic of Yemen. Located on the northwest shore of the Gulf of Aden, it is the country's principal port. Oil refining is the leading industry.

The city is made up of several separate areas. Crater, or the old city, is on a small peninsula and within the walls of an ancient volcano. The Crescent, or new city, includes the port and commercial area on the western peninsula. The oil refinery is on the mainland at Little Aden. The University of Aden was founded there in 1975.

Settled as early as the 3d century BC, Aden was a Roman trading port. It was captured by the Turks in 1538 and controlled by North Yemen until 1728. From 1839 to 1967 it was controlled by Great Britain. The port was important on the route from the Mediterranean to India via the Suez Canal.

Adenauer, Konrad

[ah'-duh-now-ur] Konrad Adenauer, b. Jan. 5, 1876, d. Apr. 19, 1967, was the first chancellor of the Federal Republic of Germany. The son of a court clerk in Cologne, he became a lawyer, entered politics, and was mayor of his native city from the last year of World War I until his expulsion by the National Socialists in 1933. He was a leader of the Catholic Center party; he also served (1920–33) as chairman of the Prussian upper house, the Council of State, during the WEIMAR REPUBLIC and twice was seriously considered for the chancellorship.

Relatively undisturbed during the THIRD REICH until, late in 1944, the Gestapo imprisoned him for two months, Adenauer was reinstated as mayor when U.S. forces took Cologne the in spring of 1945. He then became cofounder and leader of the postwar Christian Democratic Union, president of the assembly that drafted the constitution of the Federal Republic of Germany, and, in 1949, the republic's first chancellor. He retired from

Adelaide's Parliament House serves as the legislative center of South Australia. Important for its industry and manufacturing potential, Adelaide experienced rapid growth at the turn of the century after the discovery of iron ore deposits nearby.

Konrad Adenauer, as West German chancellor (1949–63), was a staunch foe of the Communist East German regime, which erected the Berlin Wall in 1961 to stem the flow of refugees to the West.

this office in 1963 at the age of 87, but he remained in the West German parliament until his death.

A stern patriarch and shrewd politician, Adenauer was deeply committed to the traditional values of Western Christendom that Adolf Hitler and many of his followers had repudiated. But he was no less opposed than Hitler to communism and therefore pursued throughout his long chancellorship a single-mindedly Western-oriented foreign policy, with the result that West Germany became not only a major economic and political power in Western Europe but also a pillar of NATO.

adenoids   see TONSILS

adenoma [ad-uh-noh'-muh]   An adenoma is a nonmalignant TUMOR of glandular tissue. It can occur in mucous glands of the gastrointestinal and respiratory tracts and in endocrine glands. Although adenomas are not likely to become malignant, they can cause medical problems. For example, adenoma in the stomach is associated with vague stomach pain, lack of stomach hydrochloric acid, and pernicious anemia. Bronchial adenoma is associated with the coughing up of blood and with repeated pulmonary infections. Adenoma in the endocrine glands can result in excessive secretion of endocrine hormones by these glands, which affects numerous body organs.

adhesion   In physics, adhesion is the attraction of two different substances, one of which is usually a liquid and the other a solid. Adhesion results from intermolecular forces between the substances and is distinct from cohe-

sion, which involves only intermolecular attractive forces within a single substance. The forces in both adhesion and cohesion are chiefly van der Waals forces. The competition of adhesive and cohesive forces results in CAPILLARITY, in which a liquid either rises or falls in a fine tube.

adhesive   An adhesive is a substance capable of holding two surfaces together in a strong, often permanent bond. Adhesives may be classified as natural or synthetic; or they may be classified by their reaction to heat (thermoplastic and thermosetting adhesives) or by their ability to stretch (elastomeric adhesives) or to remain rigid.

In the 20th century, natural adhesives—primarily organic and of animal or vegetable origin—have been replaced or modified by synthetics. Most synthetics are polymers—composed of huge molecules formed by the union of many simple molecules—and supply great strength and flexibility. Thermoplastic resin adhesives, such as vinyl resins and cellulose derivatives that can be softened by heating, are used for the manufacture of safety glass and for the bonding of wood, rubber, metal, and paper products. Some thermoplastics, such as the polyamides, ROSIN derivatives, polyethylene, and polyvinyl acetate, are used as hot-melt adhesives: they are applied in the molten state to form a rigid bond on cooling. Thermosetting adhesives, which include a large number of synthetic resins, are converted by heat or a catalyst into insoluble and infusible materials. Tough, strong EPOXY RESINS shrink little as they harden. Elastomeric adhesives include natural and synthetic rubber cements and are used for bonding flexible materials such as paper, textiles, and leather.

Medical researchers are investigating the use of adhesives, instead of sutures and staples, in delicate microsurgeries and other situations where tissue damage must be minimized. In Europe, surgeons are already using a natural adhesive made of blood-clotting agents, and a similar substance is being tried experimentally in the United States. Synthetic adhesives such as cyanoacrylates are also being used in eye surgeries, even though the substances are potentially damaging to tissues and have not yet been approved by the U.S. Food and Drug Administration.

adiabatic process [ad-ee-uh-bat'-ik]   Adiabatic compression and expansion are thermodynamic processes in which the pressure of a gas is increased or decreased without an exchange of heat energy with the surroundings. Any process that occurs without heat transfer is called an adiabatic process. (See HEAT AND HEAT TRANSFER.)

The adiabatic compression or expansion of a gas can occur if the gas is insulated from its surroundings or if the process takes place quickly enough to prevent any significant heat transfer. This is essentially the case in a number of important devices, including air compressors, rockets, and internal-combustion engines. The propagation of sound through the atmosphere also takes place due to a series of adiabatic compression and expansion waves.

An adiabatic expansion is usually accompanied by a decrease in the gas temperature. This can be observed in the case of a common aerosol can, which becomes cold after a quantity of gas has been released. The reason for the temperature drop is that the gas is released too quickly to absorb any significant heat energy from its surroundings. Thus, the work performed in expanding the released gas drains some of the internal energy of the gas still in the can, making it colder. Once the can itself becomes cold to the touch, however, the process is no longer adiabatic. In a similar fashion, adiabatic compression usually increases the temperature of a gas, because work is done on the system by the surroundings.

Adiabatic compression and expansion also occur in liquids and solids. Liquid and solid matter, however, compress and expand to a much smaller degree than matter in the gaseous state.

Adige River [ah-dee'-jay]   Located in northern Italy, the Adige River rises in Alpine lakes and runs 410 km (255 mi) past Bolzano and the Val Lagarina, near Verona, to enter the Adriatic Sea about 24 km (15 mi) south of Venice. It has a drainage area of 12,200 km^2 (4,710 mi^2). The Adige supplies hydroelectric power in the Alps and irrigates portions of the Veneto.

Adirondack Mountains   The Adirondack Mountains are a group of rounded, forested peaks in northeastern New York covering about 12,950 km^2 (5,000 mi^2). Forty-five summits exceed 1,200 m (4,000 ft) in height; the tallest is Mount Marcy (1,629 m/5,344 ft). Ancient Precambrian rocks (over 1 billion years old) underlie the mountains. Lake George, Lake Placid, and the Upper, Lower, and Middle Saranac lakes are among the many lakes created by glaciation. The Hudson River rises near the top of Mount Marcy. Other river systems draining the region are the Sacandaga, the Black, and the Oswegatchie.

Almost two-thirds of the region is included in the wilderness Adirondack State Park, created by the state, and it is a year-round recreation resort. Some iron ore deposits are mined. The Indians never settled permanently there, and the area remains sparsely populated. The name is derived from the Indian for "they of the Great Rocks."

Adivar, Halide Edib   see HALIDE EDIB ADIVAR

adjective   see PARTS OF SPEECH

Adler, Alfred   Alfred Adler, b. Feb. 7, 1870, d. May 28, 1937, was an Austrian physician and psychologist who created a socially oriented personality theory and system of psychotherapy called individual psychology. According to this theory, people are guided by values and goals of which they may be aware, not driven by unconscious instincts. Adler attended Sigmund FREUD's circle from 1902 to 1911, but rejected the label of disciple. He pioneered in preventive psychiatry by establishing more

than 30 child-guidance centers in Vienna and by countless speaking engagements. From 1926 until his death he lectured extensively in the United States, where he settled in 1935. Adler presented his system in *The Neurotic Constitution* (1912; Eng. trans., 1917), *Practice and Theory* (1920; Eng. trans., 1925), *Understanding Human Nature* (1927; Eng. trans., 1927), *Social Interest* (1933; Eng. trans., 1938), and other works.

In individual psychology, the person is seen as moving away from situations that make him or her feel inferior and toward goals of success and superiority. Adler accepted the phrase *inferiority complex* to denote extreme feelings of inadequacy. How one sees oneself and the world, one's goals, and one's manner of striving for these goals constitute one's *life-style*. It is manifested in all one does, including one's dreams and early recollections. An individual is part of larger systems: physical, social, and biological. These create the problems of work, friendship, and sexual love. Their solution requires development of the human capacity for *social interest*. All forms of maladjustment, failure in life, are striving for socially useless goals. In Adler's psychotherapy, patients' self-esteem is boosted, and they are made aware of mistakes in life-style so that they may correct them.

Adler, Felix   Felix Adler, b. Aug. 13, 1851, d. Apr. 24, 1933, was a German-born American educator and founder of the ETHICAL CULTURE movement. Adler founded (1876) the New York Society for Ethical Culture, which taught that an ethical reality existed independently of the existence of a personal God. The society was active in child welfare, medical care for the poor, slum improvement, labor relations, and city politics. Adler also pioneered in education, advocating progressive education, free kindergartens, and vocational training schools. He was professor of political and social ethics at Columbia. His books include *Creed and Deed: A Series of Discourses* (1877).

Adler, Jacob, Stella, and Luther   The Russian-born actor **Jacob P. Adler**, b. Jan. 1, 1855, d. Mar. 31, 1926, was one of the greatest dramatic actors of the Yiddish stage. While the YIDDISH THEATER was in its infancy, the 24-year-old Adler joined a professional troupe that toured Russia, presenting popular operettas. Although not a gifted singer, he excelled in romantic parts. Following the 1882 tsarist ban on Yiddish theater, Adler emigrated to London, and later he went to the United States. His first production there failed, but his second offering, *Soldier Moishele* (1890), was enthusiastically received. Overnight, he became the idol of the Yiddish stage, a position he held for the rest of his life. He played Shakespeare's Shylock (1893) in Yiddish with an English-speaking cast. He also adapted *Hamlet* and *King Lear* for the Yiddish theater and often directed the productions in which he appeared.

Adler (reverently referred to as the "Great Eagle") always starred in his own productions. He had commanding stage presence, enhanced by a fiery temperament, a striking physique, and a rich, sonorous voice. He was at his best when playing highly dramatic or tragic roles. Adler was also instrumental in introducing the plays of Jacob GORDIN, the most celebrated Yiddish playwright of his time.

Two of Adler's children distinguished themselves in the American theater. **Luther Adler**, b. May 4, 1903, d. Dec. 8, 1984, was a prominent character actor on stage and in movies. **Stella Adler**, b. Feb. 10, 1902, was one of the original members of the GROUP THEATER and later opened her own acting studio, establishing herself as one of the foremost American interpreters of the STANISLAVSKY acting method.

Adler, Mortimer J.   The American professor and editor Mortimer Jerome Adler, b. New York City, Dec. 28, 1902, is best known for conceiving large publishing ventures, including the 54-volume *Great Books of the Western World* (1952). Adler received his doctorate at Columbia University. For 22 years he taught philosophy of law at the University of Chicago, becoming associated with Robert M. Hutchins in revising the university's curriculum.

Adler became director of the Institute for Philosophical Research in 1952. For Encyclopaedia Britannica, Inc., he edited a 10-volume *Gateway to the Great Books* (with Hutchins) and a 20-volume *Annals of America*. He then served as director of planning of the *Britannica*'s 15th edition. Adler also wrote the best-selling *How to Read a Book* (1940), *Philosopher at Large: An Intellectual Autobiography* (1977), and *A Guidebook to Learning* (1986).

Adler, Renata   Renata Adler, b. Milan, Italy, Oct. 19, 1938, is an American writer known for her sharp, witty essays and inventive fiction. After studying at the Sorbonne and Harvard, Adler became a staff writer (1962) for the *New Yorker*. Her essays in *Toward a Radical Middle* (1970) covered a variety of political and cultural topics; her film reviews (1968–69) for the *New York Times* were collected in *A Year in the Dark* (1970). Her novels *Speedboat* (1976) and *Pitch Dark* (1983), artistically fragmented works, received mixed notices. *Reckless Disregard: Westmoreland v. CBS et al.; Sharon v. Time* (1986) is reportage.

admiralty   see MARITIME LAW

Admiralty Islands   The Admiralty Islands, in the Bismarck Archipelago, lie in the Pacific between the equator and New Guinea. They have a population of 27,000 (1984 est.). The daily mean temperature is 27° C (81° F); average annual rainfall is 2,030–2,540 mm (80–100 in). Manus Island makes up about three-fourths of their 2,070 km^2 (800 mi^2). Lorengau, the main port, is also the administrative center.

The Dutch mariner Willem Schouten sighted the is-

lands in 1616. Japan occupied Manus during World War II, after which the Admiralties became part of a UN trust territory administered by Australia (1946). They are now part of Papua New Guinea, which gained independence in 1975.

adobe [uh-doh'-bee]   Adobe is sun-dried brick made of clay mixed with vegetable matter. It is believed to be African in origin, the word being derived from the Arabic for "brick." Adobe dwellings are common in the southwestern United States and in Mexico, and the ruins of early pueblos reflect such construction.

An ideal building material for areas having little rainfall, adobe is made by kneading clay with a vegetable fiber such as straw, which acts as a binder and reduces shrinkage during the curing process. Water is added to make a stiff plastic compound that is forced by hand into a wooden mold. The brick is placed outside to bake in the hot sun for several weeks and then set with moist adobe as a cementing mortar. The finished building is also called an adobe. Inexpensive, fireproof, and an excellent insulating material, adobe is still used wherever the climate and the native clay are suitable.

adolescence   Adolescence is the developmental stage between childhood and adulthood, from age 12 or 13 through age 19 or 21. Although its beginning is often equated with the onset of puberty, adolescence is characterized by psychological and social stages as well as by biological changes (see YOUNG PEOPLE).

Adolescence can be prolonged, brief, or virtually nonexistent, depending on the type of culture in which it occurs. In technologically simple societies, for example, the transition from childhood to adulthood tends to be rapid and is marked by traditionally prescribed rites of PASSAGE. By contrast, in American and European society the transition has been steadily lengthening over the past 100 years, giving rise to an adolescent subculture and to a variety of problems and concerns specifically associated with this age group.

Physiological Change

Between the ages of 9 and 15, almost all young people undergo a rapid series of physiological changes, known as the adolescent growth spurt. Beginning in the pituitary gland, these hormonal changes include an acceleration in the body's growth rate; the development of pubic hair; the appearance of axillary, or armpit, hair about two years later; changes in the structure and functioning of the reproductive organs (see REPRODUCTIVE SYSTEM); the mammary glands in girls; and development of the sweat glands, which often leads to an outbreak of ACNE. In both sexes, these changes occur at different times in different cultures, generally later in northern climates.

Girls typically begin the growth spurt shortly after age 10, reach a peak at about age 12, and decelerate markedly by age 14. The enlargement of the breasts is usually the first external sign of impending puberty. Actual puberty is marked by the beginning of MENSTRUATION, or menarche. In the United States, 80 percent of all girls reach menarche between the ages of 11½ and 14½. The average age at which menstruation begins for American girls has been dropping about six months every decade; the average age a century ago was between 15 and 17.

Boys typically begin their rapid increase in growth at about 12½ years of age, reach a peak slightly after 14, and slow down sharply by age 16. This period is marked by the enlargement of the testes, scrotum, and penis; the development of the prostate gland; darkening of the scrotal skin; the growth of pubic hair and pigmented hair on the legs, arms, and chest; and the enlargement of the larynx, containing the vocal cords, which leads to a deepening of the voice following a transitional period in which the voice "cracks."

No diseases are unique to adolescence, other than problems directly related to the physical onset of puberty. Some conditions, however, tend to make their first appearance then, such as migraine (see HEADACHE), iron-deficiency ANEMIA, certain bone and thyroid problems, and various urinary tract infections. Mild acne is common. Girls may experience irregular menstruation or have painful periods, but these developments are usually self-correcting. Vision changes may become marked, and hearing impairment is sometimes observed (often in association with exposure to greatly amplified music). In addition, onset of certain congenital problems such as KLINEFELTER'S SYNDROME is most common during adolescent years.

Cognitive Development

Current views on the intellectual changes that take place during adolescence have been heavily influenced by the work of the Swiss psychologist Jean PIAGET, who sees the mental capability of adolescents as qualitatively and quantitatively superior to that of younger children. According to Piaget (see also DEVELOPMENTAL PSYCHOLOGY), the thinking capacity of young people increases in complexity as a function of age. Developmentalists find distinct differences between younger and older adolescents in ability to generalize, to handle abstract ideas, to infer appropriate connections between cause and effect, and to reason logically and consistently.

Whether these changes in cognitive ability should be attributed primarily to a new and invariant developmental stage, as Piaget suggests, or should be considered the result of accumulating knowledge and a greater awareness of and sensitivity to others, is a question on which psychologists continue to disagree.

Identity Formation

Psychologists also disagree about the causes and significance of the emotional and personality changes that occur during adolescence. Many Freudian psychologists believe that the overt sexual awakening of adolescents is an inevitable cause of emotional strain, sometimes leading to neurosis. Psychologists following other schools of thought place less emphasis on the specifically sexual aspects of adolescence, considering sex as only one of many adjustments young people must make in their search for a stable identity.

The effects of physical change, the development of sexual impulses, increased intellectual capacity, and social pressure to achieve independence all contribute to molding a new self-definition. If adolescents fail to meet the goals set for them by the important people in their lives, they usually feel obliged to reevaluate their motives, attitudes, or activities. The ensuing censure or approval to which they are subjected in this learning cycle help determine both their later commitment to responsible behavior and their sense of social competence throughout life.

The peer group also provides a standard by which individuals can measure themselves during the process of identity formation. Within the peer group, a young person can try out a variety of roles. The values and norms of the group permit adolescents to acquire a perspective on their own values and attitudes. A peer group can also help them to make the transition from reliance on the family to relative independence.

A prime source of identity for adolescents is the type of work chosen or envisioned. This can lead to an "identity crisis" before a specific career is finally chosen. Adolescent girls who marry early or make no plans beyond the prospect of marriage and children often experience a sense of identity diffusion, an incomplete sense of identity.

Parent-Adolescent Relations

The FAMILY has traditionally provided a set of values and the milieu where young people can observe and begin to learn adult ways of behavior. In modern industrial societies, however, the nuclear family has become relatively unstable, as divorce grows increasingly common and many children reach adolescence with only one parent. In addition, rapid social changes have weakened the continuity of life experience and values between the generations, and adolescents may often view their parents as having little capacity to guide them in their adjustment to the larger world. The conflict that sometimes results from differing parent-adolescent perceptions is called the "generation gap."

Other parental characteristics likely to influence adolescents include social class, the pattern of equality or dominance between mother and father, and the consistency with which parental control is exercised. Young people with parents whose guidance is firm, consistent, and rational tend to possess greater self-confidence than those whose parents are either overly permissive or authoritarian.

Adolescence in Modern Society

Adolescence is often looked upon as a period of stormy and stressful transition. Anthropologists have noted that in less developed cultures the adolescent years do not always exhibit such characteristics. In industrialized societies, however, adolescents are increasingly cut off from the activities of their elders, leaving most young people with education as their sole occupation. This has prolonged their adolescence. In advanced industrial societies such as the United States, the adolescent years have become marked by violence to an alarming degree; violence has replaced communicable diseases as the leading cause of juvenile death. Teenage SUICIDE has increased, and risk-taking behaviors of many sorts can be observed, including alcohol and DRUG ABUSE.

Adonis (mythology)   In Greek mythology, Adonis was a handsome young shepherd loved by APHRODITE. The infant Adonis was left by Aphrodite in the care of PERSEPHONE, the queen of the underworld, who also fell in love with him. After Adonis was killed by a wild boar, Zeus decided that for eternity he would spend springs and summers with Aphrodite and the rest of the year with Persephone. Adonis came to be revered as a dying-and-rising god. Athenians held Adonia, a yearly festival representing his death and resurrection, in midsummer. The anemone, the wild flower that each year blooms briefly and then dies, is said to have sprung from his blood.

adoption and foster care   Adoption is the legal proceeding whereby a court declares a person who is not a child's natural parent to be the child's legal parent and the relationship to be permanent. Adopted children have all the rights and duties of natural children. Foster care, on the other hand, is a temporary arrangement, usually made by a state or municipal child-welfare agency, that places a child from a broken, abusive, or poverty-stricken home in the care of a foster family until such time as the circumstances of the child's natural family can be corrected.

Adoptions are often arranged through public or private agencies who investigate both the child's parentage and the suitability of the adoptive family. Most U.S. states require the sealing of agency records to the adoptive family, the child, and the natural parents. Many adopted children have pressed for legislation to open these records, feeling that they have the right to know their "true" identities. In Great Britain a 1975 act gave adopted children over the age of 18 access to their birth records (some U.S. states also permit this). In the years immediately following the act's passage, only about 2 percent of British adoptees used it, but the number of children offered for adoption decreased by almost 50 percent.

In the past most babies put up for adoption were the children of unwed mothers. The wider use of contraceptives and the greater availability of abortion have dramatically reduced the number of available adoptees—especially white infants. In the face of the growing demand, foreign countries have become important sources for young adoptive children. Many U.S. babies are also adopted outside the usual agency channels, through black-market arrangements made between the natural mother and the prospective parents with the aid of a doctor or lawyer, often for a very high fee.

In 1980 the U.S. Congress passed legislation designed to encourage the adoption of children in foster care by providing foster families with maintenance payments and Medicaid when they adopt. (Under previous regulations, if the foster family adopted, maintenance payments were cut off.) By the late 1980s, with some 250,000 U.S. children in foster homes, agencies and state officials were striving to rehabilitate natural families and to provide stability in the foster-care system.

Adorno, Theodor W.   Theodor Wiesengrund Adorno, b. Sept. 11, 1903, d. Aug. 6, 1969, was a German sociologist, philosopher, and musicologist. He is perhaps best known as coauthor (with Else Frenkel-Brunswik and others) of *The Authoritarian Personality* (1950), a survey of Fascist mental attitudes. He also wrote *The Dialectic of Enlightenment* (1947; Eng. trans., 1972), with Max Horkheimer; *Philosophy of Modern Music* (1949; Eng. trans., 1971); studies of Hegel and Kierkegaard; and several other works. He spent the Nazi years in England and in the United States. Strongly influenced by Marx and Hegel, Adorno was an intellectual leader of West Germany's New Left movement in the 1960s.

adrenal gland [uh-dreen'-ul]   The adrenal glands are a pair of endocrine glands anatomically associated with the kidneys. Each consists of an inner portion, the medulla, and an outer portion, the cortex. Both parts secrete into the bloodstream HORMONES that regulate the functions of other organs and systems.

The adrenal medulla secretes only two hormones, ADRENALINE (or epinephrine) and noradrenaline (or norepinephrine), which have similar actions. The medulla is not essential to life and can be removed without causing much disturbance to body functioning, since its hormones are also secreted by portions of the nervous system. Adrenaline and noradrenaline regulate activity in the sympathetic nervous system, which controls automatic functions such as blood vessel constriction, heart rate, gastrointestinal movements, pupil dilation, and glucose METABOLISM. Thus, when secretion by the adrenal medulla is increased, blood vessels constrict, the heart accelerates, gastrointestinal movements diminish, and glucose is released into the bloodstream. These events occur in emergencies and are adaptations that help the individual survive.

The adrenal cortex secretes a variety of hormones called corticosteroid hormones. In contrast with the adrenal medulla, the cortex is essential to life. The steroid hormones secreted by the cortex regulate many important body functions, including salt and water metabolism; carbohydrate, fat, and protein metabolism; neuromuscular function; sexual function; resistance to infection and other stresses; and the action of other endocrine glands. Death after removal of the adrenal glands is the result of the loss of cortical hormones and is usually due to disturbances in water and salt metabolism or to circulatory lapse.

The most important corticosteroid hormone is 17-hydroxycorticosterone, since it regulates the greatest number of physiologic activities. It can be administered to maintain life in an animal that has had its adrenals removed or to a patient with Addison's disease, a disease of the ENDOCRINE SYSTEM in which hormone secretion by the cortex is impaired.

In some persons, the adrenal cortex may produce ex-

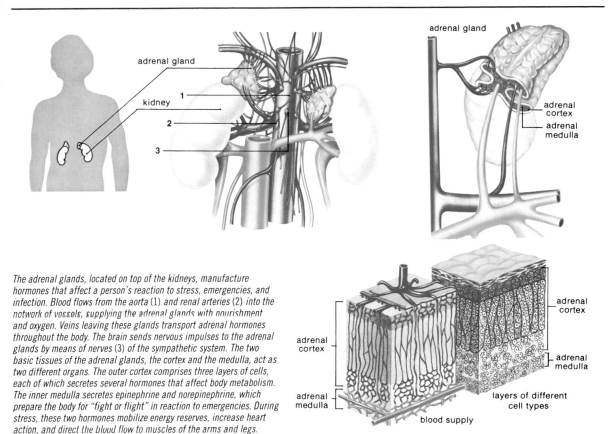

The adrenal glands, located on top of the kidneys, manufacture hormones that affect a person's reaction to stress, emergencies, and infection. Blood flows from the aorta (1) and renal arteries (2) into the network of vessels, supplying the adrenal glands with nourishment and oxygen. Veins leaving these glands transport adrenal hormones throughout the body. The brain sends nervous impulses to the adrenal glands by means of nerves (3) of the sympathetic system. The two basic tissues of the adrenal glands, the cortex and the medulla, act as two different organs. The outer cortex comprises three layers of cells, each of which secretes several hormones that affect body metabolism. The inner medulla secretes epinephrine and norepinephrine, which prepare the body for "fight or flight" in reaction to emergencies. During stress, these two hormones mobilize energy reserves, increase heart action, and direct the blood flow to muscles of the arms and legs.

cessive quantities of hormones, including those which regulate sexual function. This can cause precocious sexual development in very young male children or masculinization in women.

adrenaline [uh-dren'-uh-lin]   Adrenaline is another name for epinephrine, the HORMONE produced in the adrenal gland that is vital in enabling an individual to meet sudden dangers and emergencies. In states of alarm, adrenaline pours into the bloodstream, from which it affects other parts of the body. Carbohydrate reserves are mobilized; muscle strength is increased; pupils are dilated, letting in more light; and peripheral blood vessels contract, causing increased blood pressure. Adrenaline is synthesized for use as a drug to check the hemorrhaging of wounds, to relieve asthma, and to counteract the effects of hypoglycemia.

adrenocorticotropic   see HORMONE

Adrian I, Pope   Adrian I, b. c.720, d. Dec. 25, 795, was pope from 772 to 795. He allied the papacy with the Frankish king CHARLEMAGNE who, at Adrian's behest, deposed the Lombard king Desiderius and returned to Adri-

an papal territories that had been annexed by Desiderius. This alliance limited Adrian's independence, but his personal relations with Charlemagne were amicable. Adrian opposed ICONOCLASM and adoptionism, worked for uniformity in liturgy and canon law, and sponsored extensive building and fortification projects in Rome.

Adrian IV, Pope   Adrian IV, b. c.1115, d. Sept. 1, 1159, has been the only Englishman elected (Dec. 4, 1154) pope. His original name was Nicholas Breakspear. As pope, he was involved in the continuing reform of the papal financial administration and in the reclaiming of lands that had been usurped by the Italian nobility. Throughout his pontificate he was embroiled in serious difficulties with FREDERICK I of Germany concerning the conflicting claims of the German monarchy and the papacy to political and ecclesiastical overlordship in north and central Italy. He was once believed to have issued the bull Laudabiliter, giving Henry II of England the right to seize Ireland, but this document is now assumed to be a forgery.

Adrian VI, Pope   Adrian VI, b. Mar. 2, 1459, d. Sept. 14, 1523, was pope from 1522 to 1523. A Dutchman whose name was Adrian Florensz Dedal, he was the first pope to respond to the Protestant Reformation by attempting to reform the Roman Catholic church. After teaching theology at the University of Louvain, he succeeded LEO X. Adrian VI was the last non-Italian to be elected to the papacy before JOHN PAUL II.

Adrianople   see EDIRNE

—

Adriatic Sea
The Adriatic Sea is an arm of the Mediterranean Sea extending about 800 km (500 mi) northwest from the Strait of Otranto between Italy and the Balkan Peninsula. Its average width is 160 km (100 mi), and the average depth is 444 m (1,457 ft). In the Middle Ages the Adriatic served as the major shipping route between Europe and the Orient. Venice, located at its head, never regained commercial vitality after the fall of Constantinople in 1453 and the subsequent development of alternate sea routes around Africa.

The sea was named for the town of Adria, possibly an ancient Etruscan settlement and later a Roman port; now, because of siltage from the Po River, Adria is located 21 km (13 mi) inland. The Italian coast of the Adriatic is generally low and straight; much of it is sandy, with marshy northern headlands. The shores of Yugoslavia are steep and rocky, fretted with numerous islands and inlets.

Accessible to northern Europe and noted for its mild climate, the Adriatic coast, particularly Yugoslavia, has become popular with tourists.

adsorption   see ABSORPTION; CHROMATOGRAPHY

—

adult education
Adult education involves a variety of programs aimed at improving the skills, knowledge, or sensitivity of men and women after their formal schooling is completed. Public and private educational institutions, especially COMMUNITY AND JUNIOR COLLEGES, and religious and professional groups sponsor adult education, which includes elementary, secondary, and higher education programs as well as nondegree continuing education. Evening and weekend sessions make this form of education more convenient for many. Other forms of adult education include on-the-job training and self-education programs. Less formally, adult education is provided by libraries and museums and by television and radio.

Objectives. Adult education has traditionally been justified as serving a socially desirable purpose, and programs have frequently been funded on the premise that they would alleviate some major problem such as crime or unemployment. In Western countries, adult education is used to prepare women for jobs traditionally considered suitable only for men, to assist underprivileged segments of society, and to retrain workers for new industries. In Third World countries, adult education is an important part of modernization and industrialization, where goals cannot be met without increasing the literacy rate (see LITERACY AND ILLITERACY). Other campaigns are directed at preventing disease, raising agricultural production, and increasing the use of family planning.

In all countries, adult education is used to bring about a more equitable distribution of available opportunities. It has traditionally emphasized the practical rather than the academic, the applied rather than the theoretical, the acquisition of skills rather than knowledge of facts; but many adults take courses because they simply want to broaden their knowledge. Persons who are relatively secure economically and who have some postsecondary education show more interest in college credits, certificates, diplomas, and degrees.

Barriers to Adult Education. One obstacle to adult education is the misconception that adults do not learn as well as younger people—despite many studies by educators that demonstrate the contrary. The primary obstacle to full-time adult education for Americans, however, is cost. The second most important obstacle is lack of time. In the Western democracies, the most persistent problem facing adult education is the lack of participation by the least-educated groups. Illiterate adults do not perceive education as a means of improving their lives, so they generally do not enroll. If enrolled, they often do not attend the classes designed for them.

In the United States adult basic education (ABE) programs to improve basic reading, writing, and computation skills are designed to enable undereducated adults to function more effectively in the workplace, at home, and in the community. ABE was given impetus when economic opportunity legislation passed in the 1960s granted funds to the individual states for adult basic education programs.

In the mid-1980s more than 23 million people, or nearly 14 percent of the adult population, were enrolled in some form of adult education program in the United States. Of those enrolled, in over 40,000 courses, 65 percent were studying for job-related reasons.

adultery   Adultery is usually defined as voluntary sexual relations between a married person and someone other than his or her spouse. Most religions place strong taboos on adultery. Throughout history, social and religious sanctions against adultery have ranged from death by stoning to furnishing sufficient legal grounds for divorce, though men have usually been treated more leniently than women.

Advanced Placement Program   The Advanced Placement Program, established in 1955 by the College Entrance Examination Board, helps secondary schools offer college-level courses for advanced students. It sets, administers, and grades examinations and sends the grading documents to colleges, as well as providing consulting services to the schools. The program is administered by the Educational Testing Service in Princeton, N.J.

Advent   A Christian liturgical season, Advent is the period of preparation for both Christmas and the Second Coming of Christ. It extends over the four Sundays preceding Christmas. Festivities are discouraged, and the solemn character of the period is demonstrated by the use of purple vestments. Fasting was formerly prescribed. The first Sunday of Advent marks the beginning of the church year.

Adventists   Adventists are members of various Christian groups who believe that the SECOND COMING OF CHRIST is imminent. Their millennial hopes (see MILLENARIANISM) were aroused by the preaching of William MILLER (1782–1849). On the basis of a detailed examination of the Bible, especially the books of Daniel and Revelation, Miller predicted that Mar. 21, 1844, and later that Oct. 22, 1844, would be the day when Christ would return in glory and the Earth would be cleansed by fire, ushering in the millennium—a 1,000-year reign of righteousness and peace before the Last Judgment. When the time passed without event, many believers drifted away.

The faithful remnant of Millerites coalesced into several religious bodies, the most important of which are the Seventh-Day Adventists and the Advent Christian Church. Leaders of the former group had been influenced by Sabbatarian Baptists; thus, in that denomination, Saturday rather than Sunday is kept as the Sabbath. The most important early leader of the Seventh-Day Adventists was Ellen G. White (1827–1915). She was interested in health reform, and Seventh-Day Adventists continue to be noted for their medical missionaries, sanitoriums, and concern for sound health practices, as well as for their millennialism and Sabbatarianism.

adverb   see PARTS OF SPEECH

adversary procedure   Adversary procedure, in law, is the form of trial procedure used in England, the United States, and other COMMON LAW countries. The defense and prosecution both offer evidence, examine witnesses, and present their respective sides of the case as persuasively as possible. The judge or jury must then decide between the adversaries. In the inquisitorial procedure, used in countries with CIVIL LAW systems, the court—as well as the prosecution and defense—investigates the case before it. The court staff and the judge gather evidence and conduct interrogations, and the judge's decision of guilt or innocence is based on the investigation.

advertising   An advertisement is a message—printed in a newspaper or magazine, broadcast on radio or television, sent to individuals through the mails, or disseminated in some other fashion—that attempts to persuade readers or listeners to buy a particular product, favor a particular organization, or agree with a particular idea. It is paid for by the advertiser and may be prepared either by the advertiser or, more commonly, by a professional advertising agency.

National advertising, which promotes the products or the identity of a firm that markets nationwide, is the dominant form of advertising. Retail and other local business advertising is second in importance. Other types include trade advertising, which addresses retailers, asking them to stock and promote the advertised brand; industrial advertising, which sells goods from one producer to another; and professional advertising, from producers to professionals, such as doctors, who influence consumer purchases.

Supplementing the print and broadcast media of mass communication, direct mail is used by advertisers to mail advertisements to the persons appearing on lists of names that are chosen for particular characteristics, such as age or income.

The Advertising Industry. Essentially, the industry is a triad consisting of advertisers, the media, and the advertising agencies who create and place most national and many retail ads. About one-quarter of the total advertising outlay each year is spent by the 100 top national advertisers, including companies such as Procter and Gamble, General Motors, and Sears Roebuck. Much of the money spent by these firms is on national network and spot television. (Spot ads are those which appear on selected network stations and are used to target local markets.)

Despite the vast sums spent on national television advertising, however, the print media—newspapers, magazines, and direct mail—continue to earn over half of total advertising expenditures, with local newspapers gaining the largest share. Direct-response advertising is probably the fastest-growing segment of the industry, largely because computerized lists of names and addresses—which can be broken down by location, income, age, and so on—have allowed advertisers to pinpoint their potential customers.

The Advertising Agency. Agencies serve their clients with a variety of experts. The account executive acts as liaison between advertiser-client and agency, meeting with the client to determine objectives and budgets. The agency's copywriters and art directors take their assignments from the account executive, who brings their work back to the client for approval or modification. When decisions on content are completed, often after research studies to determine consumer response, the production department prepares the finished ads, with the aid of typographers, engravers, printers, and radio or television commercial production companies. The media department, in the meantime, has prepared a comprehensive media plan that will involve the purchase of space in a newspaper or magazine or time on radio or television.

Closely related MARKETING activities, such as PUBLIC RELATIONS and sales promotion, are handled by the agency, by other outside organizations, or by the advertiser. Advertising must be coordinated with these other activities and with the company's overall objectives.

The Advertising Media. A magazine, television program, or any other advertising medium is judged by an advertiser according to "exposure opportunity," the number of people who might see the ad, and "message opportunity," the way in which a particular medium allows the ad to communicate.

In considering exposure, advertisers speak of "reach"—the number of people who see the ad at least once—and "frequency"—the average number of times each person is reached. An ad's total impact is indicated by its number of gross impressions: reach × frequency. A further aspect of exposure is cost, usually stated as cost per thousand gross impressions (CPM). Another is target reach, the number of people within a specific audience who have seen the ad. Often advertisers want to reach only women, only teenagers, or Presbyterians, or residents of Chicago, and so on.

The media vary in these characteristics. Television provides high exposure and low CPM nationwide but is not efficient for specific targets. Newspapers have much lower absolute exposure, but they are excellent for geographic targeting. Radio is good for targeting to various geographic, age, and interest groups; its CPM is very low. Magazines provide less exposure nationally than television but are highly selective on audience interests. Direct-response advertising is not cheap but is the most selective of all, because the advertiser uses mailing lists containing only persons within the selected audience.

Because television supplies sound, pictures, and movement, it offers the most complete message opportunity; it cannot distribute coupons as can print, however. Television and radio messages disappear after running, but print can be saved for future reference. Radio, offering nothing but sound, is the most limited medium. Magazines can reproduce more attractively than newspapers, but newspapers are printed more often. Direct mail can offer lengthy messages but may be discarded without being examined.

Newspapers earn the highest proportion of total adver-

tising expenditures, 29% of the total (of which 85% comes from local advertisers). Television earns 21% (74% supplied by national advertisers); direct mail, 14%; magazines, 9%; and radio, 7%.

Advertising Goals. The most common advertising goal is to influence consumer choice of a particular brand. Marketing, or motivation, research can determine which types of consumers are most likely to buy the advertised product, and it can also test the features, benefits, images, or other appeals to which consumers might respond. The advertising will then associate the brand with those appeals.

Restraints on Advertising. The U.S. government and most states prohibit deceptive or unfair ads. The criterion is whether the consumer is harmed, not whether the ad is technically false. Some true claims may deceive by omitting important facts. For example, "This cat food contains more phosphorus" may be a true statement, but cats do not need phosphorus. On the other hand, some false claims may be unharmful because they are obviously false ("You'll feel like you're flying in a brandname auto!"). Violators are ordered to "Cease and desist" from running harmful ads. There are no fines or other criminal penalties for violations unless the advertiser persists beyond the order date.

U.S. advertisers are also controlled by their own self-regulatory body, the National Advertising Review Board, as well as by the media, which often refuse ads they consider unfit in their editorial or programming context. Public pressure and product boycotts have also been aimed at advertisers, not for the advertisements themselves, but rather for the programming they support. Some advertisers have withdrawn sponsorship of particular television programs under public pressure.

Economic Effects of Advertising. Critics claim that advertising costs consumers money; advertisers assert that it saves consumers money. Certainly, a low CPM makes

This Avis magazine advertisement set a trend in comparison advertising with its allusion to a larger, but less caring, competitor.

In a prize-winning series of television commercials, Brother Dominic praises the miraculous capacities of such Xerox products as the home computer. The cost of these sophisticated machines plummeted as manufacturers sold thousands to the mass market reached by television.

advertising more efficient than the personal selling it replaces and allows it to supply most efficiently the consumer information that can create a mass market, with its associated economies of scale.

Much of today's advertising, however, wastes money because competitors cancel out each other's efforts. If two companies producing similar soft drinks spend great sums to increase their market shares, with the result that neither gains, then that money has been spent with no benefit to either producers or consumers. Even when advertising reduces marketing costs, producers may refrain from passing the savings on to consumers and may actually raise prices when the artificial brand distinctions produced by advertising lead to consumer brand loyalty and a willingness to pay more.

The Social Impact of Advertising. Advertising has been accused of ruining everything from the environment (billboards blocking scenic views) to the English language ("Nobody doesn't like Sara Lee"). It has been charged with making people buy things they do not really need or want, often by invoking negative motivations such as guilt, anxiety, or fears of inferiority. It is said to encourage people to regard purchasing and consuming as the major activities of their lives and to create false images—depicting the average citizen, for instance, as young, attractive, wealthy, and leisured. There have been strong criticisms of the stereotypical images of women and minorities in many advertisements.

In defense, advertisers argue that consumers are well able to make up their own minds and will not buy things they do not want. The public, they claim, is very tolerant of mass persuasion and has generally not raised serious objections to advertising content.

Advertisers have sometimes created new social impacts by the heavy use of advocacy ads, which persuade the public not about products but about public issues over which companies wish to influence opinion. Mobil's

ad series in the late 1970s and early '80s, which presented its version of the role of the oil companies in the energy shortage, is a famous example. Critics say that such ads are unfairly one-sided; advertisers say that the mass media have been equally one-sided in failing to report company views.

Another important social impact stems from advertising's financial support of the mass media: it provides about two-thirds of print revenue and virtually all broadcast revenue. Media operators thus see the public not as their primary audience, but as bait for attracting advertisers; media content, by and large, is designed to attract those citizens whose spending power is greatest.

Advertising and Politics. Perhaps the most controversial of advertising's effects is in politics, where heavy media campaigns have been common since the 1952 presidential candidacy of Dwight D. Eisenhower. Unlike competing brands, political candidates are not usually similar, yet their campaign ads often hide important differences behind smokescreens of smiles and empty slogans. Although public pressures on occasion have resulted in the withdrawal of objectionable messages, political claims—even blatant lies—are not subject to regulation as are product claims.

Another source of complaint is that wealthy candidates can gain an unfair advantage and that third-party candidates cannot match the campaign funds available to nominees of the two major parties. Federal Elections Commission rules allow candidates to receive federal campaign funds in return for limiting private donations. Nevertheless, funding regulations permit sizable individual and group contributions to party committees and allow groups to mount their own advertising campaigns in support of candidates.

Of the three major types of political advertising—television, print, and direct mail—TV is by far the most costly and, in the judgment of most campaign experts, the most

(Left) *Posters, like these in London in 1835, remain an effective ad medium.* (Below) *"Uncle Sam" recruited Americans for service through two wars.*

effective. Heavy TV ad expenditures do not guarantee votes, however. Carefully targeted direct-mail campaigns—using computer-created mailing lists sorted by individual income, interests, education, and any of a thousand other politically significant qualities—have also produced positive results.

Ady, Endre

Ady, Endre [ah'-dee, en'-dreh]   Endre Ady, b. Nov. 22, 1877, d. Jan. 27, 1919, is considered the greatest Hungarian poet of the 20th century. His innovative poems, influenced by French symbolism, countered the earlier poetic tradition of János Arany and Sándor Petőfi.

Ady left the study of law for journalism. After he met Adele Brull, the "Leda" of his poems, he followed her to Paris. When he returned to Hungary, his unconventional beliefs and attacks on the aristocracy made him controversial. His break with poetic and social traditions came with *Uj versek* (New Poems, 1906) and continued in nine subsequent volumes. Beginning about 1909 he contributed poetry and prose to the journal *Nyugat* (West).

adz

adz [adz]   An adz, or adze, is a woodworking tool with a wide, thin, slightly curved blade placed at right angles to a long handle. A finishing tool, it is used to shape wood and give the wood surface a distinctive texture, ranging from uniformly rippled to flat and almost smooth. Various types of blade have been designed to meet the specific requirements of such operations as carpentry, shipbuilding, and wood carving. Most have removable heads so that they can be sharpened on a grindstone. Generally, the tool's application falls between that of the ax, which leaves a rough surface, and the plane, which leaves the smoothest surface of all.

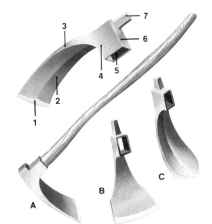

An adz tool comprises a cutting edge (1), blade (2), shoulder (3), head (4), eye (5), and poll (6), which may have a projecting pin (7). Different heads still presently in use include a carpenter's adz (A), a shipbuilder's adz (B), and a curved-blade adz (C), used to cut small hollows, as in making wooden bowls.

Æ   see RUSSELL, GEORGE

Aegean civilization

Aegean civilization [ee-jee'-uhn]   Aegean civilization is the name given to the highly developed BRONZE AGE culture in existence between 3000 and 1000 BC in the area that corresponds to modern Greece. The main geographical divisions of this area are the island of Crete, the Cycladic islands to the north, and the Greek mainland.

The first high civilization on European soil arose in Crete during the 3d millennium BC, triggered, perhaps, by the introduction of the working of copper and bronze by emigrants from Anatolia or Syria. Sir Arthur EVANS named the Cretan Bronze Age civilization Minoan, for MINOS, the legendary king of KNOSSOS, which was the chief Bronze Age center of the island. The Bronze Age of the Cyclades is known as Cycladic; and that of the Greek mainland as Helladic, from Hellas, the ancient name of Greece. The developmental sequences in these areas are divided into Early, Middle, and Late phases, based upon changes of fashion distinguishable chiefly in pottery styles. The term *Mycenaean*, after the site of MYCENAE on the mainland, is often used for the Late Bronze Age there, and sometimes for that of the whole Aegean.

The three main phases of the Aegean Bronze Age correspond roughly in time with the Old, Middle, and New Kingdoms in ancient Egypt. Approximate dates for the Aegean Bronze Age are based on connections with Egypt, supplemented by scientific methods of age determination.

Sources of Knowledge

Later Greeks were aware of a previous age when iron was unknown and weapons were of bronze, as described by Homer. Their legends preserved some names and vague traditions: massive defensive walls such as those at Mycenae and TIRYNS were thought to be the work of the giant CYCLOPS, but factual information about the Aegean Bronze Age has only come from excavations in the past hundred years.

In 1876, Heinrich SCHLIEMANN found unplundered royal shaft graves with spectacular gold treasures at Mycenae. Work there and at Tiryns and elsewhere in the PELOPONNESUS, the southernmost region of the mainland, revealed much about the Mycenaean civilization of the Late Bronze Age, with its palaces and impressive corbel-vaulted beehive tombs, or *tholoi*. In the 1890s the Cyclades were explored, and a complete Bronze Age town was cleared at Phylakopi on Melos.

From 1900 onward attention shifted to Crete, where Sir Arthur Evans exposed the great palace of Minos at Knossos, and a Minoan civilization was revealed, older than the Mycenaean and ancestral to it. In 1939 Carl Blegen discovered the well-preserved Mycenaean palace of Nestor at PYLOS. In recent years Nicolas Platon uncovered a Minoan palace at Zakros in eastern Crete, and Spyridon Marinatos identified a rich Minoan settlement buried under ash at Akrotiri on the volcanic island of THERA (Thira), also called Santorini.

Early Aegean Peoples

At the beginning of the 6th millennium BC or earlier, bands of people still using stone tools but with knowledge of agriculture reached the Aegean from Anatolia or farther east and settled in parts of the mainland and in Crete. Other emigrants from the east may have arrived at the beginning of the Bronze Age, about 3000 BC. Early Bronze Age settlements in the Aegean were usually small but situated in defensible positions and surrounded by strong walls, suggesting the existence of many tiny independent states ruled by chieftains inhabiting small palaces.

Names of centers like Knossos and Tiryns appear to be non–Indo-European and evidently date back to Early Bronze Age times or earlier. The early Aegean peoples may have spoken a common language, or related languages, akin to the earliest languages known in Anatolia. Throughout the Aegean area the same types of bronze tools and weapons were used, and similar fashions were followed in gold and silver jewelry. But considerable local differences existed, notably in pottery and in burial customs. Thus the remarkable beehive tombs were built in some parts of Crete to house the dead of a whole clan over many generations; smaller family vaults were more usual on the mainland. In the Cyclades, individual slab-lined cist-graves were prevalent.

Emergence of Minoan Civilization

From about 2500 BC Cretan civilization was marked by an extensive use of sealstones and the development of writing. Seal usage and perhaps even writing were also known in the Cyclades and on the mainland, notably at Lerna, but further progress there was inhibited by an influx of barbarous peoples from the east and north. These invaders may have spoken an Indo-European language, perhaps an early form of Greek.

Crete does not appear to have suffered invasion at this time. The Minoan civilization continued to develop, and great palaces were eventually built at PHAISTOS, Knossos, Mallia, and Zakros. The early palaces at Knossos and Phaistos were destroyed by fire about 1700 BC, perhaps in warfare between the Cretan states. But in the time of the second palaces, from about 1700 to 1450 BC, Minoan civilization reached its height in terms of artistic achievement, which may have been matched by political expansion. A Cretan colony was established well before 2000 BC at Kastri on the island of Kythera, between Crete and the Peloponnesus. After 1700 BC, Cretan settlers appeared alongside the native inhabitants on many other Cycladic islands, notably at Akrotiri on Thera, Phylakopi on Melos, and Hagia Irene (Ayia Iríni) on Kea.

The Cyclades and some parts of the mainland may by this time have become tributary to Crete, as suggested by legends about sons of Minos ruling the islands and by the legend of THESEUS and the tribute of youths imposed on Athens. The shaft graves at Mycenae, with their lavish funerary articles, also date from the 16th century BC. Many of the finest treasures found in the graves—magnificent swords, inlaid daggers, and gold signet rings engraved with scenes of warfare and hunting—may have been made by Cretan artists.

Emergence of Mycenaean Civilization

Modern dating techniques indicate that the settlements at Thera were buried by volcanic eruption c.1628 BC. Invaders—perhaps from Mycenae—overran Crete c.1450 BC and occupied the Cyclades. They built a palace on the

AEGEAN CIVILIZATION

▨	Areas under Minoan control c. 1700-1450 B.C.	☐	Areas under Mycenaen control c. 1450-1250 B.C.

The Aegean Bronze Age, which flourished from the 20th century BC until the 12th century BC, was dominated first by Minoans of the island of Crete and later by Mycenaeans of mainland Greece.

site of an earlier one at Phylakopi on Melos, and surrounded the town with defensive walls.

Mainland-style palaces like that at Phylakopi centered on a great hall with a large central hearth and an entrance porch, developed from the long house standard in the Middle Bronze Age on the mainland. This hall is called the *megaron* in Homer's *Odyssey,* in which comparable palaces are described. In front of its porch was a courtyard, with various rooms and offices clustered around it. In contrast to this, a Minoan palace was built around a spacious rectangular court, which was given a north-south orientation, perhaps for ritual reasons. The Mycenaean invaders of Crete destroyed the palaces at Phaistos, Mallia, and Zakros, but spared and adapted the one at Knossos. At Hagia Triada (Ayia Tríadha) near Phaistos, they appear to have constructed a palace of the mainland type on the ruins of a small Minoan one.

New burial customs and changes in pottery also reflect the presence of mainland conquerors on Crete. A different system of writing, called LINEAR B to distinguish it from the Linear A script used before the conquest, appeared at Knossos, where many clay tablets with inscriptions have been recovered. In 1952 the language of the tablets was deciphered by Michael Ventris as Greek. His decipherment, if accepted, implies that the Mycenaean conquerors of Crete spoke Greek and were ancestors of the non-Dorian Greeks of later times.

The Aegean, under Mycenaean domination from *c.*1450 BC onward, became the scene of a uniform civilization, although local differences can be distinguished, especially in the style of pottery decoration. Palaces at centers like Mycenae, Tiryns, Pylos, and Thebes on the mainland, or Knossos in Crete, indicate the existence of several relatively large independent states. Some of these states were probably absorbed by others before the end of the Bronze Age. The palace at Knossos in particular may have been destroyed for the last time in the 14th century BC.

In the 13th century BC, Mycenae, with the largest of the circular vaulted *tholoi* for royal burials (including the so-called Treasury of Atreus), may have been the capital

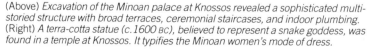

(Above) *Excavation of the Minoan palace at Knossos revealed a sophisticated multi-storied structure with broad terraces, ceremonial staircases, and indoor plumbing.* (Right) *A terra-cotta statue (c.1600 BC), believed to represent a snake goddess, was found in a temple at Knossos. It typifies the Minoan women's mode of dress.*

A death mask of beaten gold, found over the face of a mummified king in the royal tombs at Mycenae, dates from the 16th century BC. The mask portrays a man wearing a full beard and mustache, a Mycenaean fashion. (National Museum, Athens.)

lesser state. Mycenaeans were now in control of places on the western coast of Anatolia such as MILETUS, which Minoans had colonized before them.

Decline of Aegean Civilization

Warfare between the Mycenaean states may have led to the dissipation of wealth and military resources. In the years around 1200 BC the palaces on the mainland were destroyed and never rebuilt, although sites such as Mycenae and Tiryns, or Knossos in Crete, continued to be occupied in much-reduced fashion. Scholars have proposed several theories concerning the destruction of the palaces and the eventual disappearance of the Mycenaean civilization. In one view, the Mycenaeans were overwhelmed by the first wave of Greeks to invade from the north and settle in their lands; but this is incompatible with a belief that the language of the Linear B script is Greek. Other possible agents of destruction were the DORIANS, the last wave of Greeks to enter the Peloponnesus; but they seem to have come later. Alternatively, raiders such as the SEA PEOPLES, who attacked Egypt during this period, might, with concomitant drought and consequent famine, have created a vacuum that the Dorians afterward filled.

In the wake of the destructions, Mycenaean refugees from the Peloponneseus migrated to the Cyclades and to Crete, and even as far afield as Cyprus. Evidence indicates that at the same time barbarous peoples from beyond the northern frontiers of the Mycenaean world began to settle in the southern parts of Greece after about 1200 BC, introducing new burial customs and fashions in dress. These newcomers evidently mixed with remnants of the indigenous population and adopted some of the Mycenaean civilization, which continued in an adulterated form with many local variations until the end of the Bronze Age. Then,

of a miniature empire controlling most of the Aegean. *Ahhiyava*, which occurs in contemporary texts of the Hittite empire of Anatolia, appears to be the same word as *Achaioi*, Homer's name for the Greeks besieging Troy, and may refer to such a Mycenaean empire or to some

In this fresco (c.1500 BC) from the Palace at Knossos, a youth vaults over a bull in a dangerous sport that possibly had religious significance to Minoans. The vigorous, lively style characterizes Minoan art, which utilized bright colors and curving lines.

The Lion's Gate is the western entrance through a wall built about 1250 BC around Mycenae, a citadel that was a major center of Mycenaean culture. The entrance and wall are composed of massive stones fitted together without mortar. The two lions, which are now headless, stand 3 m (10 ft) tall.

about the middle of the 11th century BC, this hybrid evolved in some areas, notably ATTICA, into what is recognizably the ancestor of the civilization of classical Greece.

What brought about the downfall of the Mycenaean world is the most obscure and difficult question confronting scholars of the Aegean civilization. Much also remains to be learned about the beginnings of the Bronze Age in Crete and other parts of the Aegean. Meanwhile, excavations continue in Greek lands with spectacular results, notably at Akrotiri on Thera and at such long-established centers as Mycenae, Tiryns, and Knossos.

See also: GREECE, ANCIENT; MINOAN ART.

Aegean Sea [ee-jee'-uhn]   The Aegean Sea is a branch of the MEDITERRANEAN extending northward between Greece and Turkey. It covers an area of about 214,000 km² (82,625 mi²) and extends about 640 km (400 mi) from Crete northward to the coast of Thrace, and its width ranges from 195 to 400 km (120 to 250 mi).

The coast of the Aegean is mountainous, and only in Macedonia and Thrace in the north are there extensive coastal plains. The narrow waterway known as the DARDANELLES enters the Aegean from the northeast and carries the discharge from the Black Sea. It gives access through the Sea of Marmara and the Bosporus to Soviet and Danubian ports.

In the north the islands of Límnos and Imroz lie between the Khalkidhiki Peninsula in Greece and northwestern Turkey. To the south, the Sporades group, Psará, and Chios (Khíos), form another such island chain. From Attica and the island of EUBOEA (Évvoia), the CYCLADES (Kikládhes) stretch southeastward toward the promontories of southwest Anatolia. CRETE, RHODES, Kithera, and Karpathos stretch from southern Greece toward the Taurus Mountains of Turkey and partially block the southern entrance of the Aegean Sea. Recently, volcanoes have been active in the more southerly islands. The greatest depth, about 2,010 m (6,600 ft), is north of Crete.

A major feature of the Aegean is that no ship can be out of sight of land for long. In classical times, the sea was a link between the Greek cities that lay around it, fostering a cultural unity within the Aegean Basin that lasted with few interruptions from the 2d millennium BC until the Turkish conquest of Anatolia in the 11th century.

Aegina [ee-jy'-nuh]   Aegina (Greek: Aíyina), an island of Greece in the Saronic Gulf of the Aegean Sea, has an area of 83 km² (32 mi²) and a population of 11,127 (1981). The main seaport town, Aegina, is located on the northwestern coast, where olives, figs, nuts, and grapes are cultivated. Most of the rest of the island is rugged and unproductive. Tourism, sponge fishing, and ceramics aid the economy.

Named for the mythological nymph Aegina, the island has been settled since Late Neolithic times. There is evidence of Mycenaean occupation before about 1500 BC, followed by Dorian Greek conquest (c.1100 BC). During the Archaic Period, Aegina was noted for its powerful navy and merchant marine and was an important artistic center. Aeginetan coinage appeared in the 7th century, and the island flourished commercially until defeated by its rival, Athens, in the 5th century. Of several ancient towns and sanctuaries, the most important is the shrine of the goddess Aphaia.

aegirine   see PYROXENE

Ælfric [al'-frik or al'-fritch]   Ælfric, 955–1020, was one of the most prolific writers in Old English. A Benedictine monk, he was a respected scholar and educator. His *Homilies* and other works, including translations from Latin, were designed to give instruction in Christian doctrine. He also wrote biographies, a Latin grammar, and a series of dialogues in Latin called the *Colloquium*, which gives a vivid picture of Anglo-Saxon life and society.

Aeneas [i-nee'-uhs]   In the *Aeneid* of VERGIL, Aeneas was the Trojan hero whose descendants founded Rome. Son of the goddess Aphrodite and ANCHISES, a member of the Trojan royal family, Aeneas had fought heroically in the Trojan War and, at its end—during the Greek sacking of the city—fled with his small son and aged father. Leading a band of fugitives from the burning city, Aeneas set sail to found a new kingdom. Shipwrecked at Carthage, he fell in love with its queen, DIDO, but left her when the gods demanded that he press on to fulfill his destiny. The Roman epic the *Aeneid* describes the wanderings of the Trojans, who, after many adventures, reached the shores of Italy, establishing their kingdom only after years of bitter conflict with the indigenous Latins and Rutulians.

Aeneid [i-nee'-id]   VERGIL's epic masterpiece, the *Aeneid*, written from 26 to 19 BC, was to Augustan Rome what Homer's *Iliad* and *Odyssey* had been to the classical Greeks—an explanation of their origins and heroic past. The poem, in 12 books, treats of the founding of Roman civilization by the Trojan Aeneas. The *Aeneid* is cast in the heroic mold, with its characters and events modeled after those in Homer; Vergil thereby appears to be glorifying the ideals of Rome and its first emperor, Augustus. However, by a judicious use of symbol, image, and analogy, Vergil's critical emphasis falls on the cost in sacrifice and loss of humanity inherent in such ideals.

aerial sports Aviation has been a popular sport almost from the moment the airplane was invented. The Fédération Aéronautique Internationale (FAI), which oversees all international aerial competition and certifies all official aviation and space records, was founded in 1905, just two years after the WRIGHT brothers' famous first flight.

In its first full decade, aviation was considered nothing more than a sport, a pastime for daredevils. Its military possibilities were not fully realized until well into World War I, and commercial aviation did not begin to prosper until the 1930s.

Most of the early FAI-sanctioned competitions were for power-driven AIRCRAFT, but some competitions were held for ballooning and GLIDER flying (soaring). Since World War II, such pursuits as parachuting (skydiving), hang gliding, and model-airplane flying have been included as aerial sports. The FAI lists speed records for feats as obscure as a flight between Capetown, South Africa, and Auckland, New Zealand, via the South Pole at a speed of 860.09 km/h (534.43 mph) in a Pan American Airways 747 SP. It even considers the American-Soviet space race to have been a kind of aerial competition.

Powered Flight

The first official FAI-sanctioned air race, involving 38 primitive power-driven airplanes, was held at Reims, France, in 1909. Most of the entrants crashed before completing the contest. By the 1920s, competition for such air-racing trophies as the Bennett, Schneider, and Bendix cups was avidly followed and keenly waged as a matter of national honor. Speeds as high as 708 km/h (440 mph) were attained as early as 1933.

Since World War II, the fastest planes have been military aircraft costing millions of dollars, and therefore impractical for civilian use. Most of the planes used in continuing events, such as the U.S. National Air Races, are remodeled P-51 Mustangs and other World War II–era aircraft.

The first records for speed and for distance over a measured course—41.292 km/h (25 mph) and slightly more than 180 m (200 yd)—were certified by the FAI in 1906. More recent speed and altitude records—3,529.56 km/h (2,193.16 mph) by an American in 1976 and 37,650 m (123,524 ft) by a Russian in 1977—illustrate how far powered aviation has advanced.

Long-distance events such as the Powder Puff Derby in the United States for women, employing conventional pleasure aircraft and testing navigational skills and fuel economy, remain popular.

A glider, or sailplane, soars in silence after being launched by a powered aircraft. Competitive gliding is judged by distance, altitude, and duration of flight.

Precision aerobatics is another popular and spectacular powered-aircraft competition. Pilots must perform intricate maneuvers within specified altitude limits. An outgrowth of the barnstorming and dogfighting days, it has fostered the manufacture of an entirely new line of high-performance aircraft.

Competitions are organized for antique aircraft, such as the still numerous World War II–era Steerman biplane, and for experimental aircraft, including many bizarre designs powered by small automobile engines.

The holder of the most individual records for powered flight is Jacqueline Cochran, with more than 250 for speed, distance, altitude, and innovator flights.

Powerless Flight

Gliding, hang gliding, ballooning, and parachuting are aerial sports activities without benefit of motorized power.

Gliding. Gliding or soaring is considered the most beautiful of the aerial sports. It has enjoyed a phenomenal popularity in recent times. Towed aloft by powered aircraft (usually to about 600 m/2,000 ft) or launched by an automobile or winch tow, gliders fly by using air currents and updrafts in the atmosphere for lift. Their slender, fragile design and long wingspan permit them to travel as much as 12 meters forward for every meter they drop.

Although gliders were used by such aviation pioneers as the Wright brothers and their predecessor, Otto Lilienthal, in the late 1890s, the first FAI glider meet was not held until 1922. World soaring championships are now held every 2 years, for both open and standard classes.

Soaring's elite are the "diamond badge" pilots who must achieve a 4,000-m (13,125-ft) or more altitude gain, fly 500 km (310 mi) or more cross-country, and

(Left) *Hang gliding, a sport popularized in the 1970s, borrows designs and technology from the ancient pastime of kite flying. The pilot, who is suspended by a harness within a triangular frame, steers the hang glider by shifting his weight.* (Right) *Balloon racing, the oldest aerial sport, originated in 18th-century France.*

also fly 300 km (186 mi) or more to a specific goal to qualify for the honor. The long-distance record for a glider is 1,460 km (907 mi), achieved by Hans Grosse of West Germany on Apr. 25, 1972.

Hang Gliding. Hang gliding, in which fliers suspend themselves from what is little more than a rudimentary, kitelike wing and work the updrafts along cliffs and bluffs, was once considered only a dangerous novelty but is now accorded full .FAI status. World hang-gliding championships have been established, and a world-record distance of 153 km (95 mi) has been flown.

Ballooning. Ballooning, the oldest aerial sport, was inaugurated by the French MONTGOLFIER BROTHERS in 1783 with a hot-air balloon. Hydrogen, however, soon became the gas of choice because of its inherent buoyancy. BALLOON flights were common in the 1800s, with observation balloons used widely during the U.S. Civil War and World War I, after which safer, nonflammable helium rose to ascendancy.

Balloon competition includes cross-country races—for speed and distance—and hare-and-hound races—in which the "hare," with a head start, is chased by other balloons.

Even the most sophisticated balloon is at the mercy of the prevailing winds and can be steered only by seeking different winds at different altitudes. More than 15 attempts have been made to cross the Atlantic Ocean in a balloon since 1873, and some have been fatal. From 1978 to 1984, however, some major helium accomplishments occurred. In 1978 a three-man team (Ben Abruzzo, Maxie Anderson, and Larry Newman) from Albuquerque, N.Mex., crossed the Atlantic in the *Double Eagle II*. In 1980, Anderson made headlines again when he and his son, Kris, completed the first nonstop transcontinental flight in the *Kitty Hawk*. Early in 1981, Anderson and Don Ida failed

on an around-the-world attempt after only three days; they both died in a balloon crash in West Germany in 1983. Late in 1981, Abruzzo, Newman, Ron Clark, and Rocky Aoki became the first to cross the Pacific, in the *Double Eagle V*; Abruzzo died in an airplane crash in 1985. In 1984, Joe Kittinger achieved the first solo transatlantic flight, from Caribou, Maine, to Savona, Italy. In 1987, British entrepreneur Richard Branson and Swede Per Lindstrand achieved the first transatlantic hot-air balloon flight in a record 33 hours, from Sugarloaf Mountain in Maine to Northern Ireland.

Parachuting. Sport parachuting, or SKYDIVING, was not developed until the 1950s. The jumper falls several thousand feet at the rate of 193 km/h (120 mph) before opening the chute. Competitions are judged on style (maneuvers or group formations achieved during the free-fall) or accuracy (how close a jumper can land to a 15-cm/6-in disk on the ground).

See also: FLIGHT, HUMAN-POWERED.

Aerobee   Aerobee, one of the most successful SOUNDING ROCKETS developed in the United States, was designed in 1946 to explore the upper atmosphere. In its original form it weighed a little more than 453 kg (1,000 lb) and had an overall length of 5.73 m (18.8 ft). Following the first successful launching (1947), summit altitudes of more than 112 km (70 mi) were regularly achieved. A typical payload comprised a magnetometer, Geiger-Mueller counters, and a cosmic-ray telescope. Much-improved models have included Aerobee-Hi, Aerobee 200, and Aerobee 350. The Aerobee 350 can carry a 272-kg (600-lb) payload to a height of 325 km (202 mi).

aerodynamics Aerodynamics is the study of the flow of air and other gases and of the forces acting on bodies moving through the gases. It is a branch of fluid mechanics, in which the same principles are also applied to the study of liquids. Aerodynamics is mainly employed to study the flight of heavier-than-air craft and is so discussed here. It is also used to describe the motion of lighter-than-air craft, such as dirigibles and blimps, and to determine the aerodynamic forces acting on bridges, buildings, and other structures. WIND TUNNELS are basic tools of aerodynamic research.

Underlying aerodynamics and all other branches of theoretical mechanics are the laws of motion developed by Isaac NEWTON in the 17th century. These laws state the effects of forces acting on bodies in motion or at rest. Newton also developed the concept of fluid friction, or viscosity—the resistance of air or any other fluid to motion, whether its own or that of a body moving through it. A younger contemporary, Daniel BERNOULLI, applied Newton's laws of motion to the study of fluids in particular. He developed the principle that the velocity of a fluid is related to the pressure within it: the faster the fluid flow, the lower the pressure (see BERNOULLI'S LAW). These concepts formed the basis for future studies.

Airplane Flight. Such concepts were essential before humans could realize the ancient dream of being able to fly through the air. As early as the 16th century, Leonardo da Vinci had sketched devices resembling the modern helicopter, but without understanding the aerodynamic forces involved in flight, practical attempts were doomed to failure.

Four main forces act on an aircraft: thrust, gravity, and the aerodynamic forces of drag and lift. Thrust and drag work against each other, as do gravity and lift.

An aircraft moves forward because of the thrust supplied by its propellers or jet engines. Forward motion continues as long as the thrust forces are greater than the drag forces, which result from the viscosity of air. Aircraft are therefore designed to reduce as much as possible the drag forces acting on different parts of the craft.

To overcome the Earth's gravity and rise into the air, an aircraft must be acted on by a lift force. This is supplied mainly by the craft's wings. A wing or other surface designed to produce a desired effect when acted on by flowing air is called an airfoil. Bernoulli's law forms the basis for the theory of the lift exerted on an airfoil such as a wing. The cross section of a wing is designed so that the angle at which the wing meets the air causes the air to flow more rapidly past the upper surface of the wing than the lower surface. As a result, air pressure is lower above the wing than below it, resulting in lift.

Modern Aerodynamic Design. In making an aerodynamic analysis of an aircraft it is necessary to consider the component parts of the vehicle and calculate the airflow about each part separately. The results are combined to obtain the forces acting on the vehicle as a whole. Thus, the wing and tail are analyzed, and then the passage of air around the fuselage is included as a disturbance of the flow about the first two. In modern aerodynamic de-

The design of suspension bridges involves aerodynamics, as illustrated by the old Tacoma (Wash.) Narrows bridge. Opened to traffic in July 1940, it became famous for its violent motions even in light winds, leading to its final collapse on Nov. 7, 1940. The bridge's girder design had permitted fluttering motions like those seen in Venetian blind slats in a strong breeze.

sign, the availability of computers has made it possible to study the complete wing, body, and tail configuration.

Designers of high-speed aircraft must also take into account other aerodynamic concepts, such as the boundary layer. This is the layer of air nearest the skin of the craft where the effects of the turbulence caused by air resistance are exhibited most strongly. To minimize this turbulence, aircraft are designed to keep the stream of air flowing around the craft as undisturbed as possible—hence the term *streamlining.*

Supersonic Flight. Such considerations become especially important at very high speeds. High aircraft speeds are described in terms of Mach numbers, this number being the ratio of the speed of a given aircraft to the speed of sound in air of that density. When the two speeds are equal, the Mach number is 1. Speeds less than Mach 1 are called subsonic, those above Mach 1 are supersonic, and those above about Mach 5 are called hypersonic.

In the region of Mach 1 and above, special aerodynamic problems arise. At lower speeds, the air flowing around a craft can be considered an incompressible fluid, that is, a fluid whose density does not change. At high speeds, however, the density of the air increases sharply, as does its pressure and temperature. To offset this ef-

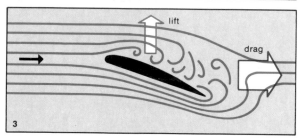

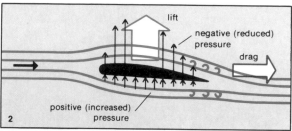

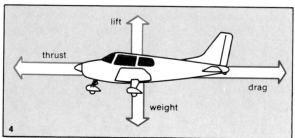

Turbulent airflow behind a vertical plate (1) results in high drag and no lift. A properly designed airfoil, or wing (2), generates lift by reducing air pressure above the wing. Decreased air friction and turbulence minimize drag. Increasing the angle at which the wing meets oncoming air increases lift to a point. Beyond a critical angle airflow becomes turbulent (3), increasing drag and decreasing lift. Four forces act on an aircraft in flight (4). Thrust, a forward-driving force, is opposed by air friction, or drag. Lift, an upward force, keeps the vehicle airborne. Weight, resulting from Earth's gravitational pull, must be overcome by the lift for flight to occur.

fect, supersonic aircraft fly at a considerably higher altitude than subsonic craft, to pass through thinner air. As the aircraft approaches the speed of sound, shock waves form on its body wherever the local Mach number exceeds 1. As the speed of the craft increases further, these shock waves produce a sonic boom.

The increase in speed from just below to just above the speed of sound is called the transonic speed range. Fighter pilots of World War II referred to it as "breaking the sound barrier" when, in flight, their craft entered this transonic region, developing shock waves that buffeted the craft. This buffeting was brought about by the unsteadiness of the shock waves at local spots on the wings in transonic flow. At supersonic speeds the shock waves become steady and remain firmly attached to the aircraft.

The swept-back wing was designed to delay the formation of shock waves on all aircraft made to fly at high subsonic speeds. For flying at higher, supersonic speeds, the sweepback is further increased to form a delta wing. Such a wing is seen on the Concorde, which flies at a Mach number of about 2. Only experimental craft have been designed to fly at still higher speeds, in the hypersonic region. For example, the SPACE SHUTTLE passes through this flight region as it reenters the Earth's atmosphere from orbit, slows down, and makes a conventional landing. Space vehicles that returned from outer space prior to the shuttle were not flown in but simply made a so-called ballistic landing (see BALLISTICS).

A characteristic feature of all supersonic flight, and a phenomenon even more characteristic of hypersonic flight, is the generation of intense heat. This is caused by friction between the vehicle and the atmosphere. To prevent returning spacecraft from burning up as meteors do when they enter the atmosphere, heat shields have been developed. These shields are insulated and coated with special material that melts and burns off at a carefully controlled rate.

Aerodynamic Testing. Aerodynamic testing is performed extensively, in conjunction with theoretical research, to provide a better understanding of aerodynamic problems. Most testing is done in wind tunnels; about 400 exist in the world, roughly half in the United States. Some wind tunnels are highly specialized; they can generate airflows of short duration or in an intermittent way, such as in large shock-tubes. Computer modeling is also used in conjunction with wind-tunnel testing, and such models are now available for transonic speeds.

aeronautics   see AERODYNAMICS; AEROSPACE INDUSTRY; AIRCRAFT

aerosol   An aerosol is a relatively stable suspension of liquid or solid particles in a gas, especially air. Smoke, fog, and mist are aerosols. Sometimes the term is applied to the particles alone.

Aerosols are ubiquitous in the Earth's ATMOSPHERE, which can properly be considered one huge aerosol, and these naturally occurring aerosol particles can have major effects on the Earth's CLIMATE. Aerosols can also be prepared by any of a large number of artificial methods; these usually involve either the dispersion of a liquid or powder or the condensation of a vapor. Aerosols in which the particles are nearly the same size (monodisperse) are often prepared for research purposes. The various properties of aerosols—particle concentrations, the rates of sedimentation and coagulation, light-scattering properties,

280 billion kg   1,250 billion kg

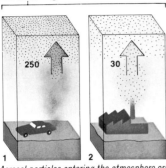

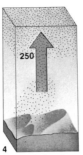

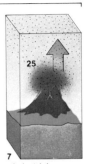

250   30   500   250   470   5   25

1   2   3   4   5   6   7

Aerosol particles entering the atmosphere originate mainly in natural sources, but an increasing proportion stems from industrial processes. Industrial sources include pollutants, such as nitrogen oxides, sulfur oxides, and hydrocarbons from automobile exhausts (1), as well as smoke from factories (2). Natural sources include salt spray from the ocean (3); windblown dust from arid areas, such as deserts (4); emanation of gaseous compounds, such as hydrocarbons, from plants and trees (5); smoke from forest fires (6); and emission from volcanoes (7). A large proportion of these particles begin as gases, which are converted to solids by chemical changes that occur in the atmosphere.

and the degree of penetration of the particles into the lungs—are often measured.

The term *aerosol* is now commonly used to refer to a metal or plastic container that dispenses a spray, foam, paste, or cream. The container is pressurized so that the contents are expelled through a nozzle when a valve is opened. A wide variety of products are packaged in this manner, among them deodorants, hair sprays, paints, and pesticides.

The propellants that furnish the pressurization may be either liquid or gaseous. In addition to forcing the contents from the chamber, they help to produce a spray or foam. Chlorofluorocarbons (CFCs) are efficient propellants, but their use for this purpose is damaging to the OZONE LAYER and is therefore being discontinued. In 1988 the Du Pont Company, the world's largest producer of CFCs, and the Dow Chemical Company pledged to phase out CFC production.

aerospace industry   The aerospace industry encompasses a worldwide complex of manufacturers who produce airplanes, helicopters, military aircraft, missiles, rockets, spacecraft, and satellites. These manufacturers employ a vast number of supplier firms who make a variety of products ranging from avionics and hydraulic systems to rubber gaskets and adhesives.

History. From its beginnings—from the Wright brothers' primitive wind tunnel—aerospace has depended on scientific research for the knowledge that could be translated into airborne and space-going machinery. The National Advisory Committee for Aeronautics (NACA; established 1915) began the first important programs in aeronautic research in the United States. Work done by NACA, and in the laboratories of aircraft manufacturers, culminated in the 1930s in a new generation of efficient and reliable metal airliners. The now classic DC-3, with its wing flaps, retractable gear, and controllable pitch propellers, set the standard for air travel for many years. On the eve of World War II, American manufacturers had already produced pressurized, four-engine airliners whose availability in the early postwar era lengthened the U.S. lead in the field of transport design.

World War II forced the urgent development of many technologies that would characterize the aerospace industry of the postwar years. Rocketry, for example, grew dramatically (see ROCKETS AND MISSILES), along with advanced electronic technologies, such as RADAR, a British invention, and jet-powered aircraft, which were first used during the war by both Great Britain and Germany (see JET PROPULSION). To mass-produce such highly complex air-

An aerosol can comprises a plunger cap (A) that is pressed to allow a high pressure mixture of liquefied gas and product (D) to flow through a plastic tube (E) and out of an exit orifice (C). A fine mist (B) of product results as the liquefied gas vaporizes at atmospheric pressure. The base (F) is domed at the bottom to withstand pressure.

A technician inserts a component into the shell of an Air-Launched Cruise Missile (ACLM) at the Boeing Space Center, near Seattle, Wash.

craft as the B-29, the United States developed systems for coordinating the work of thousands of independent contractors and suppliers. Moreover, these systems, which grew into the fields of SYSTEMS ENGINEERING and OPERATIONS RESEARCH, became essential for manufacturing the complex and interdependent products that would soon be required of the industry.

Research and development continued in the postwar era not only within NACA and in many aerospace firms but also in research facilities established by the military services. Universities also conducted research under contract. Entities such as the Jet Propulsion Laboratory of the California Institute of Technology were almost entirely government-funded.

In 1958, NACA became the NATIONAL AERONAUTICS AND SPACE ADMINISTRATION (NASA), underscoring the interrelated aspects of the growing aerospace field, which now included SPACE EXPLORATION vehicles and the development of long-range ballistic missiles (see also SPACE PROGRAMS, NATIONAL). New generations of civilian jet transports not only utilized advanced electronic instrumentation but also created new demands for navigational equipment and air-traffic control; new systems were evolved using advanced electronic techniques. Jet fighters and bombers, now flying at supersonic speeds, were equipped with increasingly sophisticated electronics, becoming integrated weapons systems.

The Industry Today. The space race and the cold war both created incentives for the United States and the USSR to promote their aerospace industries, and they continue to lead the world in engineering and manufacturing accomplishment, although Japan and several European nations possess equal technological skills in many areas.

Rocket-based space launches continue to be vital to the global industry. The United States, the USSR, Europe, China, and Japan have expanded their space programs. Private firms have begun to enter the space-launch business with such international, private-public projects as the joint Soviet-U.S. Space Commerce Corp. development of a new, commercial mobile launch vehicle based on the Soviet SS-20 medium-range missile. Both NASA and the Pentagon plan to hire commercial rockets for some government-sponsored space launches. (See also SPACE EXPLORATION, COMMERCIAL.)

With cold-war hostilities fading, those parts of the industry devoted to military aerospace began to shrink slowly in the 1980s, but industry analysts were confident that the loss would be compensated by a growth in the market for civilian aircraft, spurred by a projected rise in air traffic, by the need to replace aging aircraft, and by new regulations that call for modifications on existing aircraft to achieve lower noise levels.

Because of the immense costs of developing and producing aircraft, international risk-sharing agreements have become increasingly common in the modern aerospace industry.

The Role of Governments in Aerospace. Of the principal government agencies involved in U.S. aerospace activities, NASA plans, directs, and conducts nonmilitary research and development in the design, construction, and navigation of aircraft and spacecraft. NASA also has a special relationship with the Department of Defense in regard to space activities and aeronautical research that might apply to military aircraft. At its nine major installations, NASA engages in extensive research and development. Although production of NASA projects, such as the Space Shuttle, is accomplished by contractors across the country, management decisions are coordinated by NASA personnel at the lead center for each project.

Very similar arrangements are made by the Department of Defense and other government agencies. Defense, in addition to the acquisition of missiles and military aircraft, also funds a number of research-and-development projects for communications and surveillance satellites and for related technologies, including launch vehicles.

Scale models of future jet-plane designs are tested in wind tunnels under simulated flight conditions. Changes in design are made if the data obtained indicate problems.

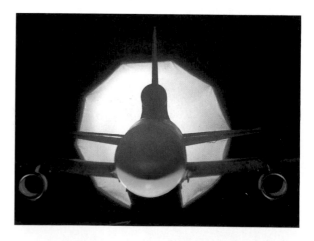

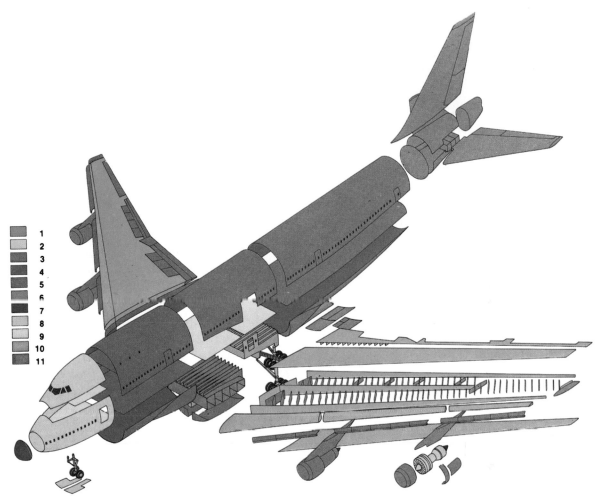

Final assembly of a Boeing 747 combines all components and systems. Each color represents a different manufacturer, showing how the workload is distributed to subcontractors throughout the industry. Manufacturers are Boeing, Everett division (1); Boeing, Wichita division (2); Ling-Temco-Vought, Aerocal and Aeronca (3); Norair and Fairchild-Hiller (4); Rohr Corporation (5); Rockwell International (6); Goodyear (7); Pratt and Whitney, General Electric, or Rolls Royce (8); Twin Industries (9); Cleveland Pneumatic (10); and Heath Technica (11).

Partly in an effort to compete with the United States in aerospace, the British, French, and Italians in the 1970s established nationalized industries (British Aerospace Corp., Aerospatiale, Aeritalia), which have assumed a primary role in aerospace development. Western Europe has also developed consortia, the largest of which, the EUROPEAN SPACE AGENCY (ESA), built the 3-stage Ariane launch vehicle.

The extensive aerospace industry in the USSR has separate ministries for astronautics and aeronautics. Aeronautics design work is carried out in a number of bureaus named for their founders (Ilyushin, Yakovlev, and so on). Manufacture takes place at plants run by a separate production ministry. In 1985 the Soviet Union also established a space-commercialization organization, Glavkosmos, to sell Soviet space services to foreign customers.

Research and Development. The evolution of most aerospace products relies heavily on applied research. In the case of an aircraft, designers use computers to generate mathematical models that are then used to simulate hundreds of different flight patterns. When a successful design has emerged from this process, extensive WIND–TUNNEL research, using scale models of the plane and its components, verifies the final configuration. A full–scale vehicle is then fabricated. Its wings, fuselage, landing gear, movable surfaces, and other assemblies are subjected to simulated flight loads and operational requirements. The findings of the simulated flights are incorporated into one or more operational aircraft, which undergo flight testing. For large airliners, testing may take several months. A complex military aircraft may require several years. When the aircraft finally enters production, the prime contractor assembles it from components and subsystems supplied by hundreds of subcontractors.

Specifications relating to the function of the aircraft also play a large role in its design. For a military fighter, designers must consider the types of targets to be attacked, desired speed, fuel capacity, and vehicle range, and its weaponry, which will differ in planes intended for high- or low-altitude combat. A low-level combat plane will generally carry heavier armor plate, more specialized weapon-control systems, and equipment to reduce the threat of ground-based heat-seeking missiles. The manufacturer of the craft must also consider the man-hours required to supply and maintain the vehicle, as well as the training required for maintenance crews.

Maintenance costs and training are also considerations in the design of civil aircraft, in addition to the other requirements peculiar to airline operations.

Aeschines [es'-kuh-neez]   Aeschines, c.390–c.322 BC, was a fine Athenian orator who is primarily known as the political enemy of DEMOSTHENES. Their point of contention was Athenian public policy with regard to PHILIP II of Macedonia. Although Aeschines initially favored resistance to Philip's expansionism, he came to advocate a negotiated peace. This was achieved in 346, after two diplomatic missions in which both Aeschines and Demosthenes participated. However, Demosthenes accused Aeschines first of accepting Macedonian bribes and then (343) of treason. Aeschines successfully defended himself against the latter charge in his speech *On the False Embassy*.

Perhaps encouraged by his victory, Aeschines attacked (336 BC) Demosthenes by accusing Demosthenes' friend Ctesiphon of illegally proposing a state honor for his friend. The case was not heard until 330. Demosthenes, speaking in Ctesiphon's defense, so successfully defended his own career that Aeschines lost the suit and was required to pay a fine. Discredited, he left Athens for Anatolia and apparently died there.

Aeschylus [es'-kuh-luhs]   Aeschylus, the Greek dramatist who wrote the earliest surviving Greek tragedies, was born about 525 BC at Eleusis in Attica and died in 456 BC at Gela, Sicily. The Persian Wars, in which he fought at Marathon (490) and Salamis (480), together with the consolidation of Athenian democracy and the spread of Athens's empire, strongly influenced his work. In his hands, early drama took on a high religious purpose, serving as a forum for resolving profound moral conflicts and expressing a grandeur of thought and language.

Aeschylus wrote between 80 and 90 plays. Of these, 7 tragedies are preserved intact, along with substantial fragments of a SATYR play and smaller bits of other works. He won 13 victories at the Greater Dionysia, the annual dramatic festival held in Athens.

Of Aeschylus's early life little is known. He began to submit plays in the opening decade of the 5th century and won his first victory in 484. Although associated with Athens, Aeschylus spent much of his life in Syracuse, which

he initially visited about 475. From at least 468 to 458 he was back in Athens but then returned to Sicily, allegedly dissatisfied with the Athenian public. Upon his death, the Geloans honored him with a splendid tomb and an epigram—possibly composed by the poet—commemorating his valor at Marathon but saying nothing of his many plays.

Contributions to the Development of Drama

Inheriting a primitive form of drama from THESPIS and others, Aeschylus added a second actor, reduced the role of the chorus, and gave greater prominence to dialogue. The anonymous *Life of Aeschylus* also credits him with introducing a third actor, but Aristotle assigned this innovation to Sophocles. Aeschylus, however, effectively utilized the third actor in the *Oresteia* and possibly in the *Prometheus*. He staged his own plays with striking visual effects: exotic robes, painted scenery, daring costumes and masks, high boots, and elaborate machinery to shock his audience.

In his earliest preserved play, the *Persians* (472 BC), Aeschylus exhibited remarkable sympathy for the defeated invaders: the audience sees Atossa, the Persian queen, experiencing the blow of her son's defeat, while Xerxes' initial pride in conquest degenerates into mere vengeful destructiveness toward his subjects' lives and property. *Seven against Thebes* (467 BC) is the last play of a trilogy about the destruction of the House of OEDIPUS. It focuses on the decision of Eteocles, the son of Oedipus and the ruler of Thebes, to meet his brother in battle, where each kills the other. The *Suppliant Women*, the

The painting on a Greek vase portrays Orestes in a scene from Aeschylus's Eumenides, *the final play of the* Oresteia *trilogy.*

first play in a trilogy, dramatizes the decision of the king of Argos to shelter the Danaids, 50 Egyptian women fleeing marriage to their cousins.

The ORESTEIA (458 BC)—comprising the *Agamemnon, Choephoroe,* and *Eumenides*—the only surviving trilogy from ancient times, dramatizes the curse on the House of Atreus from the time of AGAMEMNON's return and murder to Orestes' matricide and purification. Inspired by confidence in Athens's democratic institutions, Aeschylus here celebrated the evolution of justice from primitive blood vengeance to civic law. *Prometheus Bound* (c.460–456 BC), like the *Oresteia*, concerns divine justice and the cosmic order: Zeus punishes the Titan PROMETHEUS for giving fire to mortals. Because of its intellectual, sophistic vocabulary, however, some have doubted its Aeschylean origins.

Aeschylean Characteristics

Apart from the *Persians*, the surviving plays date from the last decade of Aeschylus's life and form parts of connected trilogies. His tragedies are generally more formal than those of Sophocles or Euripides, less concerned with character development, and more stylized in the use of ritual elements such as responsive prayer or chant. His heroes, rather than being three-dimensional individuals, are bearers of tragic conflicts often rooted in the acts of a past generation. His plots involve the rebellion of Titans, the downfall of aristocratic houses, and the capriciousness of the gods. The Aeschylean hero must make tragic choices between alternatives that both involve suffering. The hero's personal choice is the arena in which cosmic justice is worked out.

Aeschylus used bold metaphors, vivid images, flamboyantly poetic words, and magnificent geographical description. In Aristophanes' satire *The Frogs* (405 BC), Aeschylus defeats Euripides in a literary contest and embodies the original vitality of tragedy: its martial, public spirit, democratic energy, and nobility of language and ideas.

See also: GREEK LITERATURE, ANCIENT; TRAGEDY.

Aesop [ee'-sahp]   Aesop, a Greek folk hero who is supposed to have lived in the 6th century BC, acquired a great reputation as a teller of animal FABLES. According to one tradition, he was born in Thrace, lived for a while as a slave on the island of Samos, was freed and traveled widely, and was murdered while visiting Delphi.

Aristotle describes how Aesop defended a corrupt politician by telling the story of the fox and the hedgehog. A fox was troubled by fleas, and a hedgehog asked if he could help remove them. The fox replied: "No, these fleas are full and no longer suck much blood. If you take them away, new, hungry fleas will come." "So, gentlemen of the jury," Aesop supposedly said, "if you put my client to death, others will come along who are not rich and will rob you completely."

No evidence indicates that Aesop wrote down his fables or published them. Collections, authentic or imitative, were made as early as the 4th century BC. The two oldest surviving collections date from the 1st century AD,

An early engraving illustrates "The Fox and the Lion," a fable by Aesop. Like most of Aesop's tales, it reveals some aspect of human foibles through an amusing animal story.

written by Phaedrus in Latin and Babrius in Greek. Aesop's fables later inspired the verse satires of the 17th-century French writer Jean de LA FONTAINE. Because Aesop's fables are short, simply expressed, and entertaining to children, they have been used since classical times as texts in elementary schools.

---

aestheticism [es'-thet-ih-sizm]   Aestheticism was a literary and artistic movement that flourished in England and France toward the end of the 19th century. It was based on the theory that the intense perception of beauty is the highest good and is independent of social, political, or ethical considerations. For the so-called aesthete, life itself must be lived as a work of art.

The basic concept of aestheticism was derived from the writers and philosophers of German ROMANTICISM, particularly KANT. In France, Benjamin CONSTANT is believed to have coined the phrase *l'art pour l'art* ("art for art's sake") in 1804, and Théophile GAUTIER further articulated the concepts of aestheticism in the preface to his novel *Mademoiselle de Maupin* (1835). The works of the American writer Edgar Allan POE also influenced the French movement. The notion was central to the poetry of Charles BAUDELAIRE, particularly in his *Les Fleurs du mal* (*The Flowers of Evil*, 1857), and influenced the later writers and painters of French SYMBOLISM.

Aestheticism in England can be traced to the poetry of KEATS, the criticism of John RUSKIN and Walter PATER, and the paintings and poetry of such PRE-RAPHAELITES as Dante Gabriel ROSSETTI. Pater concluded in his *Studies in the History of the Renaissance* (1873) that in a world without God value lies in moments of intense sensation. He urged his readers "to burn always with this hard gemlike flame" and embrace "the love of art for art's sake." Pater's ideas particularly influenced Oscar WILDE and the poets of the Rhymers Club, founded by W. B. YEATS. Such painters as James McNeill WHISTLER rapidly moved away from representationalism and toward an abstract art of pure form and color. During the 1890s the elevated sentiments of aestheticism were gradually superseded by the more perverse and flamboyant style called DECADENCE.

aesthetics [es'-thet-iks]   Aesthetics is the branch of philosophy comprising the philosophy of beauty and the philosophy of art. The philosophy of beauty recognizes aesthetic phenomena outside of art, as in nature or in morality, science, or mathematics. However, there is much more to art than beauty, and art often has little to do with beauty. Since the 18th century, the focus of aestheticians' attention has shifted from beauty to art.

Philosophy of Art

Metaphysics of Art. Aestheticians ask two main questions about the metaphysics of art: (1) What kind of entity is a work of art? (2) What kind of knowledge, if any, does art yield? The first question arises because some works of art, such as sculptures, are much like physical objects, whereas others suggest that not all works of art can be physical objects. For example, what a painting represents often seems more relevant aesthetically than its physical dimensions. Some philosophers have concluded that works of art are mental entities like visions and dreams, which are also representational. Other philosophers, noticing that artists express some of their own attitudes, emotions, and personality traits in their art, have concluded that works of art belong in a category with nonverbal communications. A different line of thought also suggests that works of art are not like objects. A musical work can be composed, even if no one ever plays the score.

The question of whether art can provide knowledge of reality is as old as philosophy itself. PLATO argues in *The Republic* that art can represent only the appearances of reality. Many modern philosophers hold the counterposition, that art can yield insight into the real. Many critics claim that art offers a special intuitive knowledge of reality, a knowledge that science and philosophy cannot achieve.

Experience of Art. Modern discussions about how art is experienced have been dominated by 18th-century theories of the experience of beauty as distanced, disinterested, or contemplative. A few modern aestheticians, especially John DEWEY, have stressed the continuity between aesthetic experience and everyday experience and have claimed that art is psychologically integrating.

Judgments and Interpretations. The study of critics' judgments and interpretations of art tried to show what kind of reasoning is involved—whether evaluative conclusions can be deductively inferred from descriptions of the artwork, for example. A radical answer to this question is that such judgments are merely expressions of preference, neither true nor false. With respect to critical interpretations, as distinct from evaluations, a basic question is whether several incompatible but reasonable interpretations are possible.

Production of Art. Philosophical speculation about the production of art focuses on the role of genius in artistic production, the nature of creativity, and the difference between producing fine art and producing CRAFTS. Ancient and medieval philosophers did not distinguish between fine arts and crafts; the distinction emerged in Western culture after the RENAISSANCE.

Definition of Art. Attempts to define art generally aim at finding a set of characteristics applicable to all fine arts and distinguishing them from nonart. Aestheticians have not agreed upon a definition, and many believe that it is impossible in principle to define art.

Philosophy of Beauty

A comparable skepticism about the possibility of defining beauty arose in the 18th century, culminating in Immanuel KANT's *Critique of Judgment* (1790). Kant said that the judgment of beauty is subjective, contrary to the common assumption that "beauty" designated an objective feature of things. Most earlier theories had held that it was a relation, often called "harmony," between the parts of the whole. From the time of the Greeks, this relation was commonly thought to appear in cultural institutions and moral character, as well as in objects.

Whereas other theorists of beauty had thought that when beauty is perceived, one experiences pleasure, Kant said that people will judge a thing beautiful only if they take pleasure in experiencing it. Subjectivism was taken further by George SANTAYANA, who declared that beauty is the same as pleasure, except that it can be seen as "objectified" in things.

Æthelbert, King of Kent [ath'-uhl-burt]   Æthelbert, 552–616, king of Kent from 560, was the first Christian Anglo-Saxon ruler in England. He married Bertha, a Christian Frankish princess, and in 597 was converted by the missionary Saint Augustine of Canterbury. Æthelbert issued a code of laws (*c.*600) that is the oldest surviving document in Old English.

Æthelflæd [ath'-uhl-flad]   Æthelflæd, d. 918, daughter of King ALFRED of Wessex, ruled the semiautonomous Anglo-Saxon kingdom of Mercia, first with Æthelred, ealdorman of Mercia, whom she married *c.*880, and then on her own during the illness that preceded his death (911) and thereafter until her own death. Known as the Lady of the Mercians, she built fortresses and helped recover areas held by the Danes—victories that facilitated the ascendancy of her brother EDWARD THE ELDER. After her death, Edward incorporated English Mercia into Wessex.

Æthelred II, King of England (Æthelred the Unready) [ath'-uhl-red]   Æthelred II, 968–1016, king of England (978–1016), lost his kingdom to Danish conquerers. His nickname, "the Unready," is derived from the Old English *unrede*, meaning that he lacked advice. In 980 the Danes renewed their raids on England after a 25-year truce. Unable to mount effective resistance, Æthelred began payment (991) of the Danegeld, a form of tribute, to buy off the raiders. In 1013, however, the Danes under SWEYN overran the entire country, and Æthelred fled to Normandy. Although he returned in 1014, the Danish king CANUTE completed the Danish conquest of England in 1016, shortly after Æthelred's death.

Aetius, Flavius [ee'-shuhs, flay'-vee-uhs] Flavius Aetius, AD 396–454, was a Roman general who, winning favor with VALENTINIAN III, became virtual ruler of the western empire. He was first given command in Gaul. There, after the death (432) of the powerful rival general Boniface, he crushed (433) the rebels and destroyed the Burgundian kingdom. Allying his forces with the Visigoths in 451, Aetius defeated ATTILA and the Huns in the battle of Châlons. Aetius had been made consul three times, and his power threatened Valentinian, who had him assassinated.

Aetolia [ee-toh'-lee-uh] Aetolia was a district of ancient Greece lying north of the Gulf of Corinth, bordered on the east by Mount Oxya and on the west by the Achelous River. Most of the area was cut off from the sea by mountains, but the interior plains were agriculturally rich.

The Aetolian League, formed in the 4th century BC, seized DELPHI about 300 and became a major opponent of the Achaean League and Macedonia. The league allied with the Romans to defeat PHILIP V of Macedonia in 197 but later sided with ANTIOCHUS III against Rome, and with his downfall (189 BC) the Aetolians were forced to become subject allies of Rome.

Afars and Issas, Territory of the   see DJIBOUTI (country)

affenpinscher [ah'-fen-pin-shur] The affenpinscher is a toy dog that resembles the terriers. It has bushy eyebrows that hang down over large black eyes, a mustache, and a slightly protruding lower jaw that bears a hair-tuft. Its stiff, wiry coat is usually black but may have tan, gray, or red markings. The tail is usually docked. The affenpinscher stands about 25 cm (10 in) high at the shoulder and weighs up to 3.6 kg (8 lb). It was recognized as a separate species as long ago as the 17th century in Europe.

affirmative action Affirmative action is a formal effort to provide increased employment opportunities for women and ethnic minorities, to overcome past discrimination (see EQUAL OPPORTUNITY). Under the Equal Employment Opportunity Act of 1972, all state governments and institutions (including universities), and most federal contractors and local governments must initiate plans to increase the proportions of their female and minority employees.

Many affirmative action plans have been controversial. Those which establish racial quotas were declared unconstitutional by the Supreme Court in 1978 but upheld in the case of private businesses and unions in 1979. In 1984 and 1986 the justices ruled against upsetting seniority programs to favor minorities, but in 1986 they supported the limited use of racial preferences for minority groups to redress specific job discrimination. In 1987 the Court sanctioned quota remedies in promotions in agencies with a history of "egregious" racial bias. Rights advocates felt that several 1989 Court decisions undercut affirmative action.

Afghan hound The Afghan hound, a hunting dog and pet, originated in ancient Egypt but developed its present traits in mountainous Afghanistan. With wide-set, prominent hipbones, it can run easily over rocky and hilly terrain with powerful leaps and quick turns. A large and slender dog, the Afghan hound measures 61 to 71 cm (24 to 28 in) high at the shoulder and weighs 22 to 27 kg (50 to 60 lb). It is one of the few hounds that hunt by sight rather than scent. Long silky hair, which may be of any color, grows in a topknot on its head and also covers its body, legs, and long, drooping ears. The comparatively hairless tail is held in a high, tight curve.

The Afghan hound is a hunting dog that originated in ancient Egypt. It is admired for its regal stance and fluid, graceful movements.

Afghanistan The Democratic Republic of Afghanistan (DRA) is a country situated between the Indian subcontinent, Soviet Central Asia, and the Middle East. Although it has no access to the sea, its location was central to the wars, migrations, and trade that dominated inner Asia until early modern times. It is bordered by Pakistan on the east and south, the USSR on the north, Iran on the west, and China in the extreme northeast.

Land and Resources

Afghanistan is dominated by rugged mountains and arid plains. Its central and eastern regions are covered by high mountain ranges centering on the HINDU KUSH; many peaks in the extreme northeast reach more than 6,100 m (20,000 ft). Barren plains flank the mountain core to the north, west, and south. In the southwest the plains become deserts.

Afghanistan's dry, continental climate produces sharp

REPUBLIC OF AFGHANISTAN

Land: Area: 652,090 km^2 (251,773 mi^2). Capital and largest city: Kabul (1989 est. pop., 2,200,000).

People: Population (1990 est.): 15,862,293. Density: 24.3 persons per km^2 (63.0 per mi^2). Distribution (1988): 16% urban, 84% rural. Official languages: Pushtu, Dari (Persian). Major religion: Islam.

Government: Type: republic. Legislature: National Assembly. Political subdivisions: 31 provinces.

Economy: GNP (1989 est.): $3 billion; $200 per capita. Labor distribution (1987): agriculture—57%, commerce and services —13%; manufacturing—8%; construction—3%. Foreign trade (1988): imports—$996 million; exports—$512 million. Currency: 1 afghani=100 puls.

Education and Health: Literacy (1988): 12% of adult population. Universities (1988): 5. Hospital beds (1982): 6,875. Physicians (1982–83): 1,160. Life expectancy (1990): women—46; men—47. Infant mortality (1990): 154 per 1,000 live births.

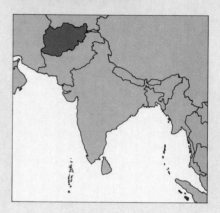

contrasts in temperatures by day, by season, and by elevation. Winters bring snow followed by early spring rains. Summers are hot and dry. Falls are moderate and also dry. Average annual rainfall is about 180 mm (7 in).

Afghanistan's major internal rivers rise in the central mountain core and flow outward generally in the four cardinal directions. Only the Kabul River, flowing east to join the Indus in Pakistan, reaches the sea. Thin soil and a harsh climate limit natural life to the sturdiest strains. Tree cover is concentrated in the east, where pine forests are common, and thin grasses briefly provide mountain grazing for nomadic herds in the spring and summer. Wildlife includes wolves, hyenas, foxes, leopards, gazelles, bears, and ibex.

Incompletely surveyed and only marginally exploited, Afghanistan's mineral resources offer considerable potential for development. There are major deposits of iron, chrome, copper, natural gas, and possibly of uranium and petroleum. Soft coal is available at numerous sites. Lapis lazuli continues to be taken from ancient mines in the northeast. There is considerable hydroelectric potential.

People

Afghan society is a composite of primary family, village, and tribal units scattered within a mosaic of ethnic, linguistic, and regional communities. Millennia of conquests and folk movements have left remnants of all the peoples who have roamed inner Asia.

The PATHAN (Pashtun) people form the dominant ethnic and linguistic community, accounting for just over half the population. Tribally organized, the Pathan are concentrated in the east and the south. As they gained control over the rest of the country in the 19th century, however, many of them settled in other areas too. The Dari- (Persian-) speaking Tadzhik (Tajik), the second largest community, are strongly identified with sedentary farming and town life, mostly in the fertile eastern valleys north and south of the Hindu Kush. Turkic peoples live in the northern plains as farmers and herders. The central mountains yield a meager living to the Hazaras, a Mongoloid people who mostly speak Persian. There are many smaller communities, the most important of which are the Nuristanis of the high mountains of the east and the BALUCH of the desert south.

Virtually all Afghans are Muslim, and four-fifths of them are Sunni. A few thousand Hindus and Sikhs live as traders in the cities.

Demography. Population data are imprecise and incomplete; there has never been a census. The pre-1980 population was at least 90% rural. Most farmers lived in settled villages in the best watered valleys where the major rivers intersect the plains. Various forms of nomadic herding were practiced by as much as 20% of the population. During the Soviet occupation (1979–89), some 5 million Afghans became international refugees, mostly in Pakistan and Iran. Large tracts of the best agricultural land were systematically depopulated, and perhaps 1 million Afghans were killed. The major cities were also swollen with internal refugees fleeing from the fighting in the countryside. The resettlement of the refugees, who began to return home in 1988, was complicated by continued civil war.

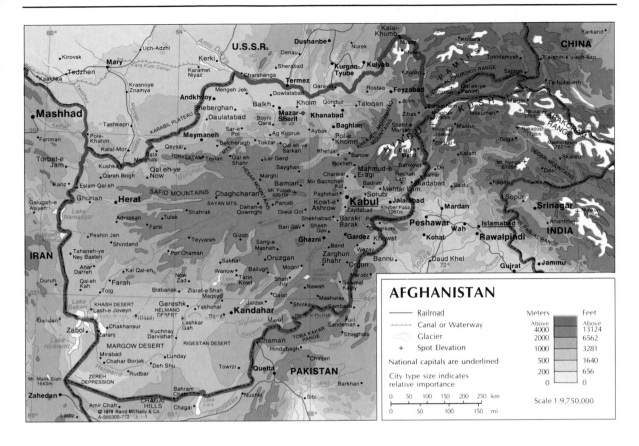

AFGHANISTAN

		Meters	Feet
—— Railroad			
┴┴┴┴ Canal or Waterway		Above 4000	Above 13124
Glacier		2000	6562
+ Spot Elevation		1000	3281
National capitals are underlined		500	1640
City type size indicates relative importance		200	656
		0	0

0 50 100 150 200 250 km
0   50   100   150 mi

Scale 1:9,750,000

© 1979 Rand McNally & Co.
A-560300-772 -1-1-1

Health.

Whereas such endemic diseases as malaria and cholera have been recently brought under control, effective medical care and public health services have been largely limited to the cities. The situation has been aggravated by warfare and the breakdown of central government control. The population is growing slowly, the high birthrate offset by very high infant and child mortality.

Education.

Great expansion in education was accomplished between 1950 and 1973. Despite this progress, made possible largely by assistance from many countries, 90% of the population remained illiterate. Since 1979, education, especially in the rural areas, has been devastated by war.

The Arts

Afghanistan has been a center of Persian, Indo-Greek, Buddhist, and Islamic cultures. Numerous archaeological sites of great potential significance await excavation. Among the architectural remains that have been excavated are the Buddhist monasteries at BAMIAN and Hadda, the Ghaznavid palace complexes at Ghazni, and the Greek city at ai-Khanum. Herat was a major center of Persian culture from the 11th to the 16th century, renowned especially for the exquisite miniature painting patronized by the Timurids in the late 15th century. Carpet making remains the primary folk art.

Economic Activity

Modern economic change began in Afghanistan early in the 20th century with superficial efforts to expand trade, begin manufacture, improve transportation, and generate greater government revenue. Substantial commercial progress came in the 1930s through the promotion of traditional fruit, fur, and carpet exports in return for manufactured imports, mostly from India. Substantial development was initiated in the 1950s, mostly through foreign aid from the United States and the USSR and, later, from Iran and the Persian Gulf states. After 1979 war destroyed most of the fruits of this development.

Agriculture.

Afghanistan's economy is essentially agrarian. Wheat, the primary food grain, is grown mostly as an irrigated winter crop; cotton is a major cash crop. Fruits, especially grapes and melons, are important seasonally. Skins, hides, and the fur of the karakul lamb are also exported. Agricultural output declined more than 50% between 1979 and 1988, however, and revival of the farming sector has been complicated by the destruction of irrigation canals and the presence of large numbers of unexploded land mines.

Industry and Transportation.

Industrial development remains rudimentary and is largely restricted to agricultural processing. All-weather paved roads connect all major cities, and a network of airports connects nearly all of the provinces. Parts of northern Afghanistan have been linked to the Soviet power grid. Substantial natural-gas exports to the USSR largely ended before the Soviet withdrawal for fear of sabotage.

History and Government

Afghanistan's crossroads position in Central Asia has subjected it to constant invasion and conquest throughout its long recorded history. The parade of conquerors in historic times includes Darius I of Persia in the 6th century BC; Alexander the Great in 328 BC; the Sakas (Scythians), Parthians, and the Buddhist Kushans in the 2d and 1st centuries BC; and the Hephthalites, or White Huns, in the 5th and 6th centuries AD. The Arabs introduced Islam in the 7th century, and the Turks under MAHMUD OF GHAZNI briefly made Afghanistan the center of Islamic power and civilization at the beginning of the 11th century. The Mongols invaded Afghanistan early in the 13th century, and TIMUR added it to his empire at the end of the 14th century. In the early 16th century, Timur's descendant BABUR, first of the MOGULS, founded an empire in India from his base at KABUL. During the 16th and 17th centuries some parts of the country owed allegiance to the Moguls, and others to the Safavids of Persia.

In 1747 the Pathan, having thrown off the Persian yoke, established a dynasty of their own under Ahmad Shah Sadozai, the leader of a tribal confederation. Pathan strength was consolidated by Dost Muhammad Khan (r. 1826–63), who founded a second dynasty early in the 19th century. Effective physical control over all of the country, however, was first achieved by Dost Muhammad's grandson, Abdur Rahman Khan (r. 1880–1901), whose diplomacy also prevented either the British or the Russian empires from gaining control of Afghanistan.

Frustrated by their failure to subdue the country in the Anglo-Afghan wars of 1839–42 and 1878–80, the British agreed to subsidize an Afghan ruler strong enough to serve as a buffer between the empires.

Abdur Rahman's grandson, Amanullah Shah (r. 1919–29), ended (1921) British involvement in Afghan affairs. He also initiated a series of ambitious efforts at social and political modernization, but tribal opposition forced him to flee the country. Zahir Shah ruled Afghanistan from 1933 to 1973. In 1964 he sponsored a serious attempt at liberal, Islamic constitutionalism including free elections and partial parliamentary democracy. When the experiment foundered, the king's cousin Mohammad Daud Khan seized power in a nearly bloodless coup and ruled as a republican president from 1973 to 1978. Zahir Shah went into exile in Europe.

Daud was killed in a Marxist coup in April 1978. This brought the semiclandestine People's Democratic party of Afghanistan (PDPA) to sudden power under Nur Mohammad Taraki. Its brutal methods and impractically radical reforms in education and land and family law fomented a popular backlash, especially in the rural areas. Despite growing Soviet support, the regime was increasingly threatened by general revolt, and its link with Moscow was weakened in September 1979 when Taraki was removed (and later killed) by his lieutenant, Hafizullah Amin.

The USSR intervened militarily in December 1979. Amin was executed and replaced by Babrak KARMAL, a long-time Marxist rival of Taraki and Amin. Karmal's government attempted to establish control over the country with the help of Soviet air and land forces and civilian advisors.

After the Soviet intervention, popular opposition became a national resistance movement active throughout

Pashtun herders shear karakul sheep in their summer camp in the Hindu Kush; the wool will be used to make felt and carpet thread. The nomadic life in Afghanistan is rapidly disappearing. Since 1979, many nomads have crossed the mountains into Pakistan and Iran.

the country. After several years of fighting, the poorly equipped *mujahadin* (Islamic warriors), aided by the United States and Pakistan, controlled most of the countryside. Najibullah, the former head of the Afghan secret police who had replaced Karmal as head of the ruling PDPA in 1986, all but abandoned the government's earlier revolutionary programs in an effort to gain moderate support. In November 1987 he convened a nationwide gathering of tribal leaders that approved a new constitution and elected Najibullah president. Elections were held in April 1988 for a two-chamber National Assembly to replace the PDPA Revolutionary Committee that had governed the country since 1978.

Accords signed in Geneva, Switzerland, in April 1988 set a timetable for the withdrawal of Soviet forces. Pakistan and Afghanistan agreed not to interfere in each other's affairs and to allow the return of millions of refugees. The USSR and the United States were to serve as guarantors of the accords, and a United Nations negotiator was given a mandate to help the Afghans form a broad-based government. Half of the Soviet forces were withdrawn by Aug. 15, 1988, and the remainder by Feb. 15, 1989. The politically divided *mujahadin*, who had not signed the accords, controlled the countryside but were unable to overthrow Najibullah, who ruled under a state of emergency from February 1989 to May 1990, when the constitution was amended to provide for multiple political parties. In June the PDPA was renamed the Homeland party. By early 1991 the United States and the USSR reportedly were close to agreement on ending outside arms supplies to the warring factions and on the form of a transitional government, pending internationally supervised elections.

AFL-CIO   see AMERICAN FEDERATION OF LABOR AND CONGRESS OF INDUSTRIAL ORGANIZATIONS

Afonso   see ALFONSO

Africa   Africa is the second largest continent after Asia. It is separated from Asia by the Suez Canal, the Gulf of Suez, and the Red Sea, and from Europe by the Straits of Gibraltar and Mediterranean Sea. It is bounded by the Atlantic Ocean on the west and the Indian Ocean on the east. Offshore islands considered part of Africa include, in the Indian Ocean, MADAGASCAR, MAURITIUS, RÉUNION, ZANZIBAR, PEMBA, the SEYCHELLES, and the COMOROS. In the North Atlantic Ocean are the CANARY ISLANDS, CAPE VERDE Islands, and MADEIRA ISLANDS; in the South Atlantic are ASCENSION ISLAND and SAINT HELENA; and in the Gulf of Guinea (see GUINEA, GULF OF) are Pagalu, BIOKO, and SÃO TOMÉ and PRÍNCIPE.

Africa is the second most populous continent after Asia. Its people—about 12% of the world's population—form a complex cultural mosaic of races, languages, religions, and forms of government. The earliest known protohuman fossils have been found in Africa, and the continent was the home of one of the world's oldest civilizations, that of ancient Egypt. South of the Sahara, a num-

ber of powerful African kingdoms flourished during the Middle Ages. A period of European colonization that reached its height in the early 20th century left modern Africa's 53 independent nations with arbitrarily defined boundaries, a diversity of political systems and problems, and economies dependent upon the industrial world.

Land and Resources

Africa has a number of outstanding natural features that have influenced its history and development. The northern coastal area is separated from the rest of the continent by the SAHARA, the largest desert in the world. The coastlines are remarkably straight with few large bays, estuaries, and protected indentations that can serve as harbors. Most major rivers have waterfalls and rapids close to the coast, which hindered colonial penetration and still limit navigation. In sub-Saharan Africa a narrow coastal plain, often swampy along the Gulf of Guinea, arid from Angola south to Cape Town, and swampy, forested, or arid northward along the east coast to the Red Sea, is backed by steep escarpments and mountain ranges that form the edge of the African high plateau.

Africa lacks a major mountain system like the Andes of South America or the Himalayas of Asia. Several small ranges, however, break the monotony of the flat to gently rolling plateaus that constitute the bulk of Africa. The ATLAS MOUNTAINS of northwest Africa extend from east to west across Tunisia, Algeria, and Morocco, reaching their highest elevation, 4,166 m (13,668 ft), at Mount Toubkal, Morocco. The DRAKENSBERG, rising above 3,000 m (10,000 ft), extends through eastern South Africa and Lesotho. The high plateau of Africa stretches from Ethiopia southwest to Angola and Namibia and includes the Ethiopian Massif, the East African Plateau, the RUWENZORI (Mountains of the Moon), the Munchinga Mountains of Zambia, and the Bihe of Angola. Rising above this plateau are Mount KILIMANJARO (5,895 m/19,340 ft), a semiactive volcano and Africa's highest peak, Mount Kenya (5,199 m/17,085 ft), and Mount Elgon (4,321 m/14,178 ft), also of volcanic origin. The Sahara is interrupted by the TIBESTI MASSIF and the Ahaggar and Air mountains. The Cameroon Mountains, a volcanic chain extending northeast through Cameroon, are the highest mountains in western Africa. The Futa Jallon of Guinea and Liberia contains the headwaters of the NIGER (Djouf) RIVER and the SENEGAL RIVER, West Africa's largest. Between these highland zones are a series of shallow sedimentary basins usually associated with rivers. They include the basins of the Niger, Chad, and Sudd rivers on the southern margins of the Sahara, the CONGO (Zaire) RIVER of central equatorial Africa, and the KALAHARI DESERT in southern Africa.

One of Africa's most distinct topographical features is the GREAT RIFT VALLEY. This is a giant trough that cuts into the high plateaus and extends from the Dead Sea in the Middle East southward to Mozambique and Swaziland, a distance of almost 6,900 km (4,300 mi). The northern section is filled by the Red Sea between Africa and Arabia. The central section cuts through Ethiopia and divides near Lake Rudolf, or Turkana (see RUDOLF, LAKE), into two

AFRICA

Area: 30,330,000 km² (11,710,500 mi²). 22% of the world's land area.

Population: 661,000,000 (1990 est.); 12% of the total world population. Density — 22 persons per km² (56 per mi²).

Coastline: 30,500 km (18,950 mi).

Elevation: highest—5,895 m (19,340 ft), at Mount Kilimanjaro; lowest—155 m (510 ft) below sea level, at Lake Assal.

Northernmost Point: Cape Ben Sekka, Tunisia, 77°46'N.

Southernmost Point: Cape Agulhas, South Africa, 34°52S.

Easternmost Point: Cape Hafun, Somalia, 51°26'E.

Westernmost Point: Cape Almadies, Senegal, 17°32'W.

Principal Rivers: Nile, Congo (Zaire), Niger, Zambezi, Orange, Volta.

Principal Mountain Ranges: Atlas, Ruwenzori, Drakensberg, Cameroon.

Principal Deserts: Sahara, Kalahari, Namib.

Political Divisions: 53 independent countries; Western Sahara (former Spanish Sahara), the status of which is in dispute; 2 Spanish exclaves; several island dependencies.

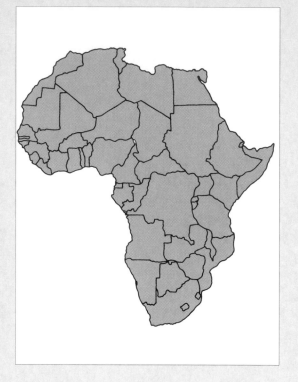

branches: the western rift arcs through Uganda to Lake NYASA (Lake Malawi) and is occupied by Lakes Albert (Mobuto Sese Seko), Edward, Kivu, and Tanganyika (see ALBERT, LAKE; EDWARD, LAKE; KIVU, LAKE; TANGANYIKA, LAKE); the eastern rift cuts through Kenya and Tanzania and joins the western rift near Lake Nyasa. In places the rift-valley walls rise more than 3,200 m (10,500 ft) above the flat and sometimes drowned valley floor.

Geology. Africa is a massive crystalline platform of ancient granites, schists, and gneisses, the oldest of which are more than 3.2 billion years old. They contain rich and varied minerals including copper, zinc, lead, gold, uranium, diamonds, and many rare metals. Present-day Africa was once part of the supercontinent known as Gondwanaland, which also included Australia, Antarctica, South America, Madagascar, and the Indian subcontinent. During the Late Jurassic and Early Cretaceous periods these land masses drifted apart, but compared with the other continents, Africa remained relatively stable. South America was separated from Africa about 80 million years ago. Arabia split off about 20 million years ago.

As Gondwanaland fractured and drifted, Africa acquired its scarp-dominated coastline, interior seas that occupied shallow depressions emptied, and rivers carved steep gorges and formed new courses. Volcanic outpourings

covered vast areas of east and southern Africa. As the Cretaceous Period came to an end, the sedimentary rocks of northwestern Africa were severely folded and uplifted in a series of orogenic phases to form the Atlas Mountains, which geologically are part of Europe's alpine system. Epicontinental seas extended across North Africa linking the present Mediterranean with the Gulf of Guinea, which in their wake left extensive deposits of limestone and sandstone. Gigantic meridian fractures occurred in the African shield producing the Great Rift Valley. As tensional forces wrenched the land apart, some land blocks sank while others rose and tilted, allowing volcanic materials to break the surface. Mount Kilimanjaro and Mount Cameroon were formed this way.

During Gondwana's last 100 million years of existence, southern Africa was covered by the Dwyka ice field, which scoured the crystalline surface and deposited tillites hundreds of meters thick. Following the glacial age, southern Africa became progressively drier, and a lengthy period of sedimentary accumulation began in the Kalahari and Karroo basins. These sediments in turn were covered by outpourings of basalt as much as 7,600 m (25,000 ft) thick.

Climate. The climates of Africa are predominantly tropical. Limited areas of subtropical and temperate cli-

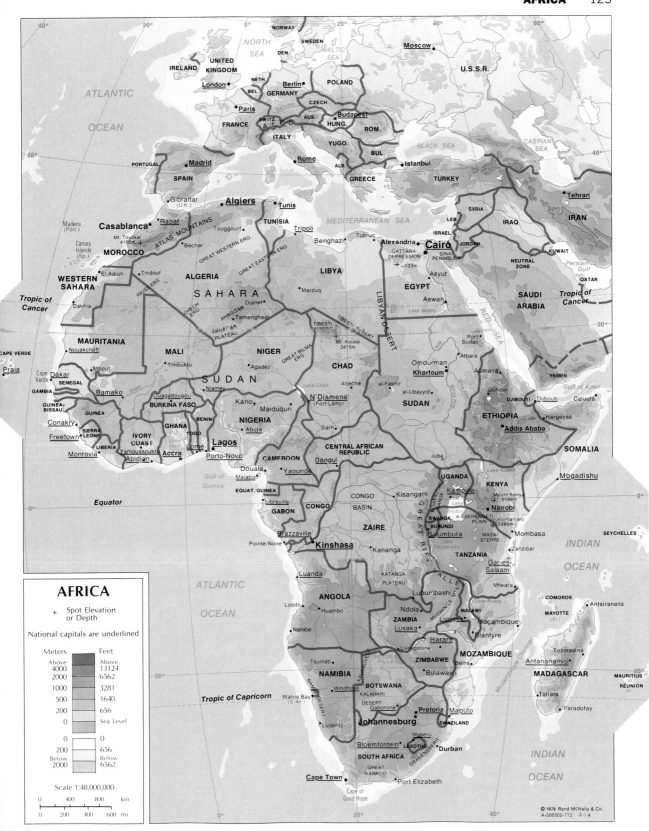

AFRICA

+ Spot Elevation
  or Depth

National capitals are underlined

Meters	Feet
Above 4000	Above 13124
2000	6562
1000	3281
500	1640
200	656
0	Sea Level
0	0
200	656
Below 2000	Below 6562

Scale 1:48,000,000

0   400   800 km
0   200   400   600 mi

© 1979 Rand McNally & Co.
A-580000-772 -3-1-4

A camel caravan winds its way across a stretch of the Sahara in southern Algeria. The world's largest desert, the Sahara dominates the topography of northern Africa. It spans the continent from the Atlantic Ocean to the Red Sea.

mates are found only at the northern and southern extremities and in the high altitudes of Ethiopia and East Africa. The cold ocean currents that parallel the western Sahara (Canaries Current) and Namibia (Benguela Current) modify the temperatures of the adjoining coastal lowlands. The absence of lengthy high mountains and other weather divides permits a free circulation of tropical air over the continent so that changes in climate occur very gradually. Rainfall is heaviest along the coast of the Gulf of Guinea, in the equatorial lowlands facing the Atlantic, in scattered mountain locations, and in eastern Madagascar. There the average annual rainfall exceeds 2,032 mm (80 in). Africa's wettest place is in western Cameroon (10,160 mm/400 in). Rainfall decreases poleward from the equator to the Sahara, Kalahari, and NAMIB deserts, regions that generally receive less than 150 mm (6 in) of rain in the average year. Rainfall rather than temperature is the most variable element of climate affecting distribution of soils, vegetation, and populations. There is increasing evidence that much of Africa is becoming progressively drier.

Six major climate types prevail and are arranged in a series of parallel zones ordered around the equator. The tropical wet climate is characterized by uniformly hot temperatures, a heavy and evenly distributed rainfall, and year-round high humidity. This climatic region is bounded by the tropical wet-dry, or savanna, climate, which is distinguished by its long dry season (coincidental with the period of low Sun) and by a short, wet summer. The savanna gives way to tropical steppes where rainfall is light and highly variable from year to year, and prolonged droughts are common. The steppes of West Africa are

called the SAHEL, literally the "border" of the desert.

The tropical deserts have the least rainfall and the greatest temperature range of any African climate. Diurnal temperature ranges may exceed 10°C (50°F). Africa's highest temperature (57.8°C/136°F) was recorded in the Libyan desert. Small areas of Mediterranean climate occupy coastal Morocco, Algeria, Tunisia, and South Africa's Cape of Good Hope region. A narrow zone of humid subtropical climate, similar to that of the southeastern United States, is located along South Africa's Natal coast.

Drainage. Africa's major rivers have cut deep gorges in their upper courses and through the coastal rimlands before emptying into the oceans. Waterfalls, rapids, and irregular flows due to seasonal variations in rainfall all make river navigation difficult. Only a small percentage of the continent's vast waterpower potential is used to generate electricity. The Congo River alone has 13% of the world's hydroelectric power potential.

The NILE, the world's longest river (6,650 km/4,132 mi), rises in Burundi and Uganda in equatorial east Africa. From Lake Victoria it flows north before entering the Mediterranean, where it has built a 25,000-km^2 (9,653-mi^2) delta. Its major tributary, the Blue Nile, rises in the headwaters of Lake Tana (see TANA, LAKE), Ethiopia, and joins the White Nile at Khartoum. The ASWAN HIGH DAM and Lake Nasser now regulate the flow of water downstream to the densely settled farmlands of lower Egypt. The Congo, Africa's second longest river (4,670 km/2,900 mi), drains an area larger than the Nile. Africa's third longest river, the Niger (4,185 km/2,600 mi), rises in the Futa Jallon of West Africa, flows northeast through the Djouf Basin of Mali, and then southeastward to Nigeria to form a delta on the Gulf of Guinea. The ZAMBEZI (about 2,650 km/1,650 mi) rises in south central Africa and flows east over the VICTORIA FALLS and through a narrow gorge between Zimbabwe and Zambia to the Indian Ocean in central Mozambique. The ORANGE RIVER (2,100 km/1,300 mi) rises in the Drakensberg and flows west through South Africa to the Atlantic.

Africa's largest and deepest lakes are found in East Africa, generally associated with the rift valley. They include, from north to south, Lakes Albert (Mobuto Sese Seko), Edward, Kivu, Tanganyika, and Nyasa in the western rift, and Lakes Rudolf (Turkana), Natron, and Eyasi in the eastern rift. Lake Tanganyika is the world's second deepest lake (1,436 m/4,710 ft). Between the two limbs of the rift valley lies Lake Victoria, Africa's largest (69,481 km^2/26,827 mi^2). Lake Chad (see CHAD, LAKE), between Nigeria and Chad, is extremely shallow, and its boundaries·vary greatly with rainfall.

(Right) A shaduf, an implement used by the ancient Egyptians, draws water from a well in the Algerian Sahara. This primitive device, which operates as a lever counterbalanced by a stone weight, is also used along the waterways of northern Africa for irrigation. (Below) The Kariba Dam restrains the fast-flowing Zambezi River downstream from Victoria Falls. The lake formed behind the dam (Kariba Lake) is one of the world's largest artificial bodies of water.

(Above) *The beauty of a waterfall is enhanced by lush vegetation on the banks of the Blue Nile in the highlands of western Ethiopia.* (Below) *Kilimanjaro, Africa's tallest mountain, rises to a height of 5,895 m (19,340 ft) above the grasslands, or savannas, of Kenya's Amboseli Park. The sub-Saharan savannas, which host a variety of wildlife, cover 40 percent of Africa's land area.*

The contrast between semiarid, mountainous northern Africa and wet, tropical central Africa is striking. The road to Marrakesh winds along the Tizi n'Test Pass (top) at 2,100 m (6,900 ft) in the High Atlas Mountains of Morocco. A rain forest (bottom) in equatorial Africa spreads a living canopy over the terrain.

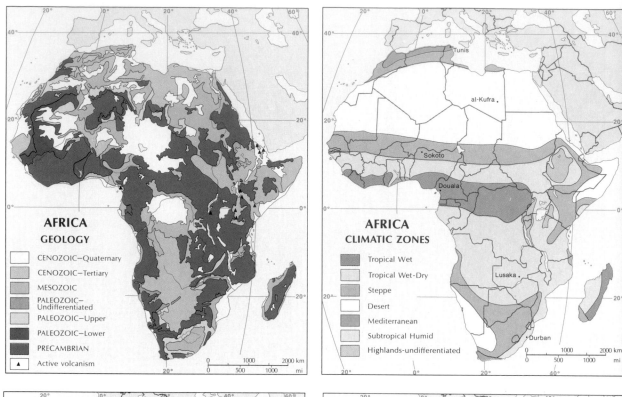

AFRICA
GEOLOGY

- CENOZOIC—Quaternary
- CENOZOIC—Tertiary
- MESOZOIC
- PALEOZOIC—Undifferentiated
- PALEOZOIC—Upper
- PALEOZOIC—Lower
- PRECAMBRIAN
- ▲ Active volcanism

0   1000   2000 km
0   500   1000 mi

AFRICA
CLIMATIC ZONES

Tunis
al-Kufra
Sokoto
Douala
Lusaka
Durban

- Tropical Wet
- Tropical Wet-Dry
- Steppe
- Desert
- Mediterranean
- Subtropical Humid
- Highlands-undifferentiated

0   1000   2000 km
0   500   1000 mi

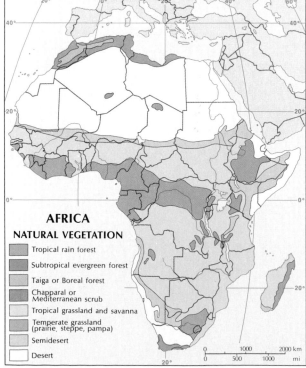

AFRICA
NATURAL VEGETATION

- Tropical rain forest
- Subtropical evergreen forest
- Taiga or Boreal forest
- Chapparal or Mediterranean scrub
- Tropical grassland and savanna
- Temperate grassland (prairie, steppe, pampa)
- Semidesert
- Desert

0   1000   2000 km
0   500   1000 mi

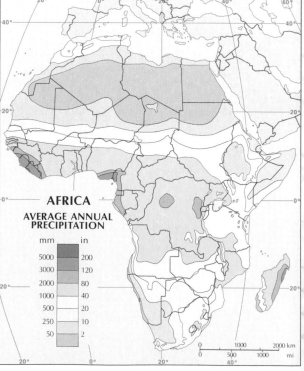

AFRICA
AVERAGE ANNUAL PRECIPITATION

mm	in
5000	200
3000	120
2000	80
1000	40
500	20
250	10
50	2

0   1000   2000 km
0   500   1000 mi

A young Masai tribesman from Kenya displays a colorful, feathered headdress. The egalitarian, nomadic Masai have proved extremely resistant to cultural changes.

Soils. Few areas of Africa possess fertile soils. In the humid tropics, lime, potash, phosphorus, and humus material are washed out of the soil's top layers while high temperatures accelerate bacterial activity. What remains is a soil high in iron and aluminum that forms a hardpan through which roots penetrate with difficulty and that facilitates runoff and the loss of surface water. In the dry regions the soils are thin, stony, high in calcium, and low in humus. The richest soils are associated with Africa's rivers. Among the richest, most extensive, and most productive alluvial soils are those along the Senegal, the central reaches of the Niger, and the lower Juba, those at the confluence of the White and Blue Niles in central Sudan, and those in the Nile delta. There, large-scale irrigation projects have been developed. Nonalluvial soils of good quality, often associated with volcanic materials, are found on the high veld of South Africa and in parts of Kenya and Cameroon. Inappropriate technology, such as the utilization of heavy farm machinery, and overuse have destroyed millions of hectares of marginal soil.

Vegetation. Africa has little natural vegetation that has not been modified by humans and their livestock. Overgrazing in the Sahel has destroyed the short grassland ecology and hastened desert encroachment. The forests and grasslands have been cut and burned to provide building materials, agricultural land, and pastures. The tropical forest of the west equatorial belt produces mahogany, teak, ebony, rubber, oil palm, and silk-cotton trees. Mangrove swamps clog many estuaries. North and south of the rain forests stretch the tropical grasslands or savannas with their characteristic acacia trees and baobabs. As rainfall decreases, the savannas give way to scrubby grasslands, thorn bush, and eventually to the deserts that are virtually devoid of vegetation other than such widely scattered xerophytic plants as the stipa grass, tamarisk, and date palm. In the Mediterranean climatic zone, stands of pine, juniper, cork, cedar, and olive are common.

Fauna. Animal life in Africa is remarkable for its great diversity, vast numbers, and the presence of both primitive and more advanced forms of life. This is due to the continent's general climatic stability and land connections with Asia. Animals such as the elephant evolved in Africa and spread to Asia across the Suez land bridge. Asia's elephants, monkeys, great apes, and certain bird groups such as the hornbills exhibit close relations with those in tropical Africa. Among the truly indigenous African animals are the aardvark, the secretary bird, and the whale-headed stork of the Nilotic marshes.

Africa's rain forests contain gorillas, chimpanzees, monkeys, wild pigs, and bongos. The tropical rivers, lakes, and swamps are populated by crocodiles, hippopotamuses, lizards, snakes, and an abundance of bird life including flamingos, pelicans, herons, storks, and kingfishers. The grasslands of the east and south contain some of the world's largest herds of elephant, rhinoceros, wildebeeste, giraffe, zebra, buffalo, and antelope as well as the carnivores that prey upon them, such as lions, leopards, cheetahs, hyenas, and jackals. The grasslands also support a great diversity of birds including the bustard, falcon, hornbill, and ostrich. Uncontrolled hunting and poaching have severely reduced the animal populations, especially the elephant and rhinoceros.

Africa's insects and other invertebrates are as varied

Children in Togo attend an outdoor primary school. In this West African nation, about 55% of children between the ages of 7 and 14 are enrolled in educational institutions, about half of which are operated by religious missions.

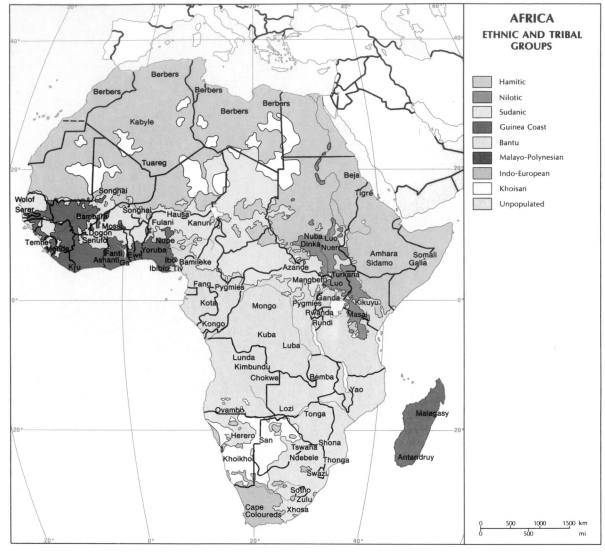

AFRICA
ETHNIC AND TRIBAL GROUPS

- Hamitic
- Nilotic
- Sudanic
- Guinea Coast
- Bantu
- Malayo-Polynesian
- Indo-European
- Khoisan
- Unpopulated

Berbers
Berbers
Berbers
Berbers
Berbers
Berbers
Kabyle
Tuareg
Songhai
Wolof
Serer
Songhai
Hausa
Bambara
Fulani
Kanuri
Mossi
Dogon
Senufo
Temne
Mende
Nupe
Yoruba
Kru
Fanti Ewe
Ashanti Ga
Ibo Bamileke
Ibibio Tiv
Fang Pygmies
Kota
Mongo
Kongo
Kuba
Luba
Lunda
Kimbundu
Chokwe
Bemba
Yao
Ovambo
Lozi
Tonga
Herero
San
Shona
Khoikhoi
Tswana
Ndebele Thonga
Swazi
Sotho
Zulu
Cape
Coloureds
Xhosa
Beja
Tigré
Nuba Luo
Dinka Nuer
Amhara
Sidamo
Somali
Galla
Azande
Mangbetu
Turkana
Luo
Ganda
Pygmies
Rwanda Masai
Rundi
Kikuyu
Malagasy
Antandruy

500   1000   1500 km
500   mi

The peoples of the African continent include (left to right) *the Berber, who inhabit Morocco and other North African countries; the Afrikaner, of European descent, who settled the Cape of Good Hope during the mid-17th century; and the San, or Bushman, whose ancestors are thought to have been the original inhabitants of southern Africa.*

Dar-es-Salaam, which means "haven of peace" in Arabic, is a seaport on the Indian Ocean. The modern city is Tanzania's capital and serves as headquarters of several pan-African organizations.

as the larger animals. The tsetse fly, which carries sleeping sickness (see TRYPANOSOMIASIS), and the malaria-bearing mosquito limit the amount of land that humans and livestock may occupy. Common snakes include the cobra, python, and mamba.

Water Resources. Africa has approximately 40% of the world's hydroelectric potential, about half of it in Zaire. Most countries have chosen to build a few large facilities rather than several small dams. Africa's largest hydroelectric facilities are Egypt's Aswan High Dam, Mozambique's Cabora Bassa, Zaire's Inga Dam, Ghana's Akosombo Dam, Nigeria's Kainji and Jos projects, and Cameroon's Edea project. A few projects, including the Aswan Dam, the Kariba Dam (shared by Zambia and Zimbabwe), and South Africa's Orange River Project, provide not only power but water for irrigation, fishing, and soil-conservation purposes.

Mineral Resources. African mineral resources are plentiful but only partially explored and exploited. Mining became an important and highly profitable activity during the colonial period, and today the bulk of prospecting and exploitation remains in the hands of multinational corporations. With few exceptions, Africa's minerals and fuels are exported and have not given rise to local industry and general economic prosperity. Minerals provide the bulk of foreign revenues in several states including Angola, Algeria, Libya, and Nigeria (petroleum); Liberia and Mauritania (iron ore); and Zambia (copper). South Africa has the greatest variety, total reserves, and current output of minerals in Africa.

The major oil and natural gas reserves are located in Algeria, Libya, Egypt, and in the coastal areas of Nigeria, Gabon, and Angola. Africa has limited coal reserves, especially coking coal for steel manufacture. The largest reserves are found in South Africa, Zimbabwe, Mozambique, and Nigeria. Uranium is widely distributed, but significant deposits occur in South Africa, Niger, Namibia, and Gabon. The largest iron ore deposits are found in South Africa, Liberia, Mauritania, Angola, and Algeria. The major copper producers are Zambia, Zaire, and South Africa. Africa has the largest known reserves of chromium, antimony, and manganese, as well as significant amounts of bauxite (Guinea), diamonds (South Africa, Botswana), cobalt, and zinc.

People

Africa contains many different peoples, languages, and cultures. Few of its states are ethnically homogeneous, and few have developed a strong sense of national unity. For centuries traditional values prevailed. Africans identified first and foremost with members of their own tribe or nation and avoided or competed with those who spoke a different language and were of a different culture. The imposition of colonial boundaries without regard for the indigenous cultural mosaic further divided the African people.

Population is unevenly distributed. Highest densities occur along the coast of the Gulf of Guinea, in the lower reaches of the Nile, in the highlands of East Africa and Madagascar, along the northern coast, and in the urban and mining areas of South Africa, Zimbabwe, and Zaire. Lowest densities are found in the deserts, high mountains, and thick forests.

In the Saharan states the dominant groups are ARABS, BERBERS, and TUAREG. Beyond the cities the Berbers are agriculturists, and the Tuareg are pastoral nomads. The Sahara forms an effective divide between these peoples and the predominantly Negroid peoples of the south. In the Sahelian zone sedentary farmers are interspersed with pastoralists, the major groups being the HAUSA, FULANI, Bambara, and Wolof. In the Horn of Africa (Somalia and eastern Ethiopia), the pastoral Somali and Galla are dominant, while the Dinka and Nuer prevail in the upper Nile. The densely settled coast of the Gulf of Guinea is home for literally hundreds of different ethnic groups, each with its own language, territory, culture, and values. Among the numerically strongest are the YORUBA and IBO of Nigeria, the ASHANTI and Ga of Ghana, and the Kru of Ivory Coast and Liberia. The sparsely populated forests of equatorial Africa are home to FANG, Bateke, PYGMY, and others. In the east African savannas, the pastoral people, including the MASAI, KIKUYU, and Kamba, have historically competed for grazing land and watering places. The Luo and Baganda occupy densely settled farms along the north shore of Lake Victoria.

Ethnic diversity and population density tend to be less south of Zaire, except in the urban areas of South Africa, Zambia, and Zimbabwe. South Africa has ten indigenous groups, the largest being the ZULU in Natal and the XHOSA of the eastern Cape; South Africa's AFRIKANERS are a people of Dutch and French descent. Swaziland, Lesotho, and Botswana are rare examples of ethnically homogeneous states and are populated by the Swazi, SOTHO, and TSWANA respectively. Arid Namibia's population includes the SAN (Bushmen), who are hunters and gatherers, and the HERERO, Damara, and OVAMBO. Other major groups in southern Africa are the Shona and Ndebele of Zimbabwe, the Bemba of Zambia, the Makonde and Makua of Mozambique, the YAO of Malawi, and the OVIMBUNDU of Angola. Madagascar is populated by the Betsimisaraka and by the Merina and Betsileo, whose ancestors came from Southeast Asia some 2,000 years ago.

The nonindigenous peoples of Africa include Europeans and South Asians in southern and eastern Africa, especially South Africa and Kenya; Europeans in most capital cities; and a few Syrians and Lebanese who live primarily as traders in the urban areas of the coast along the Gulf of Guinea.

Languages. The number of languages spoken in Africa has been variously estimated at between 800 and 1,700. Five major stocks are generally recognized. Afroasiatic languages, dominant in North Africa and the Horn, include Berber, Kushitic, Semitic, Chad, and Coptic languages. Click languages, so named because of their characteristic implosive "click" sounds, include Khoisan, which is spoken by the Khoikhoi of southern Africa. The Niger-Congo languages cover almost all of West Africa south of the Sahara and most of the Congo Basin and southern Africa and include Hausa, Peul, and Wolof in West Africa and SWAHILI, Tsonga, and Bemba east and south of Zaire. Sudanic languages include Kanuri, Songhai, Turkana, and Masai. The MALAYO-POLYNESIAN LANGUAGES of Madagascar were introduced from Southeast Asia about 2,000 years ago. (See AFRICAN LANGUAGES; AFROASIATIC LANGUAGES.)

Superimposed on this linguistic mosaic are English, French, Italian, Portuguese, German, and languages of the Indian subcontinent. English is the official language, or one of the two official languages, in all ex-British colonies, excluding Tanzania, where Swahili has been adopted. French is the official language of most former French possessions south of the Sahara. Arabic is the official language of seven Saharan states. Numerous lingua franca are used for commerce and in mixed-language areas. The multilinguistic nature of most states has hindered nationalism and perpetuates tribal and local identities.

Religion. The dominant religion of northern Africa is Islam, which replaced Christianity in the 7th century and spread west and south across the Sahara and into the equatorial zones. With an estimated 155 million believers, Islam is the fastest-growing faith in Africa.

The Christian churches claim a membership of some 140 million Africans of whom 55% are Protestants. Many denominations are present, including a number of indigenous churches. Christianity's earliest hold in Africa was in Egypt and Ethiopia, home of the COPTIC CHURCH. European missionaries introduced Christianity into sub-Saharan Africa during the 19th century. Approximately two-fifths of the African population follows traditional religions and animism.

Education. Educational standards, facilities, and programs vary considerably and reflect differences in class, ethnicity, sex, and location. In all countries literacy rates for women are lower than those for men and urban education is superior to rural. The richest countries invest more in education than the poorest, and in most states, secondary school enrollments are less than half the pri-

Conical, straw roofs and earthen walls are characteristic features of Mande dwellings and grain storage bins. The Mande, a group of agricultural tribes speaking related languages, live in the savanna region of West Africa.

(Left) *A crew of fellahin, or agricultural laborers, perform the arduous task of tilling by hand on a cooperative farm in southern Egypt. Because more than 90% of the nation's population are crowded into the Nile River valley, the government has instituted agrarian reforms and a land-reclamation project.*(Right) *Farm laborers plant potatoes on an experimental farm in Gabon, where food production has traditionally failed to meet the nation's demands. The establishment of modern agriculture in Africa's tropics is hindered by poor soils.*

mary school enrollments. Only a small fraction of Africa's young people attend universities. Because of the lack of prestigious universities in Africa, many qualified students receive their training in U.S. and European universities.

Health. There is an urgent need to improve general health and nutritional standards in Africa. A significant number of persons in every country suffers from chronic malnutrition due to poverty, ignorance, and poor agricultural practices. On a per capita basis, food production declined in the 1970s and 1980s, and malnutrition rates are the highest in the world. In several countries of the Sahel, Guinea Coast, and equatorial Africa, as much as 40% of the population are malnourished and suffer from such diseases as malaria, dysentery, schistosomiasis, and yaws. The Sahelian states from Senegal to Somalia recorded exceptionally high rates of death and malnutrition during the severe droughts of 1968–74, and again in the 1980s. Other common ailments include influenza, tuberculosis, river blindness, and a host of parasitic disorders associated with unsanitary living conditions.

Most of the doctors and general hospitals are situated in the capitals and towns, whereas the more populated rural areas have few health facilities and high incidences of disease, malnutrition, and infant mortality. Since World War II, national and international efforts to control mosquitoes, locusts, tsetse flies, and other pests have increased, but AIDS is a growing problem, especially in central Africa.

Demography. Africa's population numbered some 646 million in the late 1980s. The most populous states are Nigeria, Egypt, Ethiopia, Zaire, and South Africa. Improved diets and sanitary conditions and improved medical technologies and insecticides have lowered death rates considerably since 1960, but infant mortality rates remain the highest in the world. Life expectancy at birth is about 50 years, compared with more than 70 years in the United States. Birthrates will remain high unless the general desire for large families changes. Africa has the highest fertility rates in the world, and nearly half its population are under 15 years of age.

Africa is the most rural and least urbanized of the continents, but several countries, including South Africa, Egypt, Nigeria, and Morocco, have large urban-industrial areas. In most countries the largest city is the capital, which is often also the only city of significant size. Urban population growth rates exceed rural growth rates as more and more Africans migrate to the cities in search of jobs, education, and security. Slums are growing and urban living conditions are deteriorating in most countries.

In the 1970s, '80s, and '90s civil strife and political upheaval displaced millions of people in Ethiopia, Somalia, Sudan, Uganda, Angola, Liberia, and other areas. Few countries have been willing or able to accommodate the refugees despite United Nations assistance.

Economy

Despite Africa's great natural resources and energy potentials, industrialization is in its infancy. South Africa is the only modern industrial state, although manufacturing is becoming increasingly strong in Zimbabwe, Nigeria, Egypt, and Algeria. Handicaps to rapid industrialization are weak agricultural economies, inadequate and poorly integrated transport facilities, insufficient capital technology, political instability, a poorly trained work force, a small purchasing power, and economic policies and practices determined outside of Africa.

Since gaining independence, most African countries have promoted import substitution industries to reduce their dependence on European and American manufactured goods. Light industries, including textiles, clothing, pharmaceuticals, food processing, and beverages, are the most common. Heavy industry, including the manufacture of petrochemicals, iron and steel, rubber products, and cement, is concentrated in South Africa, which supplies a higher percentage of its industrial needs than any other African state. Industry tends to be concentrated in capital cities, is generally small scale, and is capital- rather than labor-intensive despite the cheap labor.

Agriculture. Agriculture accounts for about one-third of the continent's total economic output and more than half

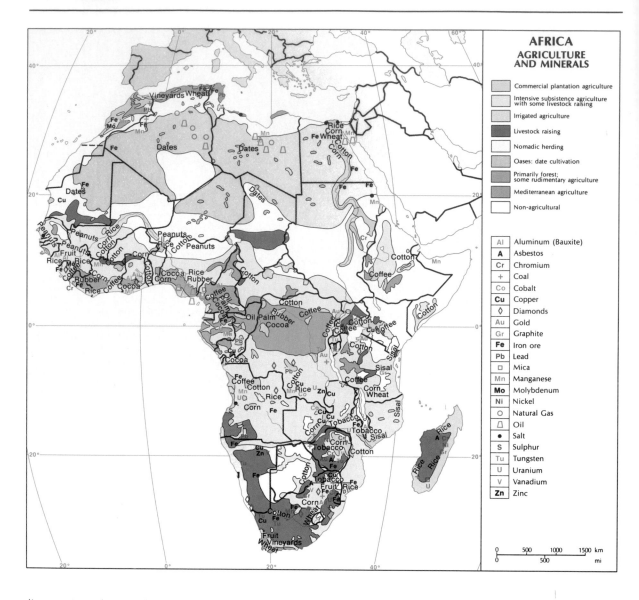

AFRICA
AGRICULTURE AND MINERALS

	Commercial plantation agriculture
	Intensive subsistence agriculture with some livestock raising
	Irrigated agriculture
	Livestock raising
	Nomadic herding
	Oases: date cultivation
	Primarily forest; some rudimentary agriculture
	Mediterranean agriculture
	Non-agricultural

Al	Aluminum (Bauxite)
A	Asbestos
Cr	Chromium
+	Coal
Co	Cobalt
Cu	Copper
◊	Diamonds
Au	Gold
Gr	Graphite
Fe	Iron ore
Pb	Lead
□	Mica
Mn	Manganese
Mo	Molybdenum
Ni	Nickel
O	Natural Gas
△	Oil
•	Salt
S	Sulphur
Tu	Tungsten
U	Uranium
V	Vanadium
Zn	Zinc

its export earnings; agriculture also employs 75% of the work force. Two distinct agricultural systems operate side by side: a traditional subsistence sector and a modern commercial sector. The traditional sector employs the majority of Africa's rural population and is characterized by small and frequently fragmented farms, little use of technology or fertilizer, high reliance on human labor, low yields, infrequent surpluses, and an emphasis on staple crops such as corn, millet, rice, cassava, sweet potatoes, peanuts, and other high-starch foods. Work on the farms is increasingly being left to women, children, and the aged as men migrate to the cities.

The modern commercial sector is the economic backbone of many countries and the principal source of their foreign-exchange earnings. Coffee, for example, is a ma-

jor export for Burundi, cocoa for Ghana, and peanuts for Gambia. Other major cash crops include cotton, sugar, bananas, tea, oil palm, tobacco, and citrus fruits. These are produced on large estates and plantations that are frequently owned by expatriates, urban elites, the state, and multinational corporations, and depend on cheap, abundant, and often seasonal labor. They tend to have much higher inputs of fertilizer, insecticides, and capital in the form of machinery, processing, and storage facilities than the traditional sector.

The raising of cattle, goats, and sheep is very important in much of the savanna and steppe lands. Africans are only gradually improving the quality of their herds, decreasing the traditional emphasis on herd size and the social importance attached to cattle ownership, and commercializing this activity. Commercial cattle farming is most advanced in areas of European settlement such as South Africa, Kenya, and Zimbabwe. Africa possesses about 14% of the world's cattle population.

In the 1970s food production for subsistence and local markets failed to keep pace with population growth and rising demands, especially in the urban areas. Famine conditions, which first appeared in the Sahel and Ethiopia during the droughts of 1972, later worsened and became more general. Low prices for farm products, rising costs of fertilizer, fuel, and seed, poor farm management, soil deterioration, and the common practice of using land for export crops rather than staple foods, have all contributed to the shortage of food. On a per-capita basis, less food is produced today than in 1970, and food imports are rising.

Forestry and Fishing. Although forests cover about 25% of Africa's land surface, the forest industry in general is not developed. High costs of clearing the forests, poor and costly transport, and a limited amount of usable forest have hindered profitable exploitation. Cameroon, Congo, Gabon, and Ivory Coast are the main producers; mahogany, ebony, and okoume are the major commercial woods.

Ocean commercial fishing is economically more important than freshwater fishing. The major fishing grounds are off South Africa, Namibia, and Angola; the West African coast from Morocco to Liberia; and in the Mediterranean Sea. Much of the catch from southern Africa is exported as fish oil, fish meal, and fertilizer. Fresh and dried fish are important as food in certain areas of Ghana, Sierra Leone, and Zaire, but in general fish plays a minor role in the diet, despite government promotion efforts. Tilapia is the most widely consumed fish.

Transportation and Communications. Africa's transportation systems were developed during the colonial era to move minerals and other raw materials to seaports for export. Roads and railroads were used by the Europeans mainly to facilitate control over their African possessions.

As a consequence, neighboring colonies were rarely linked, and even today the countries of Africa are poorly interconnected by road, rail, and air. Africa has the lowest railroad density in the world, and 13 countries (including landlocked Niger, Chad, and Burundi) have no railroads. South Africa has more than one-third of the continent's railroad tracks and the most modern railroad facilities.

Railroads continue to convey the bulk of Africa's minerals, although rail traffic has often been disrupted by war. The Great Uhuru (or Tan-Zam) Railway, built with help from China and completed in 1976, connects the copper mines of Zambia with Tanzania's Indian Ocean port of Dar es Salaam. The Benguela Railway carries copper from Zaire's Shaba province across Angola to the Atlantic port of Benguela. Zimbabwe's mineral areas are linked by rail with ports in Mozambique and South Africa.

Africa has the least developed road system in the world. The greatest densities of well-maintained roads occur in South Africa and the Mediterranean states. All countries need additional feeder roads to link the rural populations and agricultural projects with the towns, cities, and railroads. Isolation, particularly severe during the rainy season when unpaved roads may become impassable, is a major handicap to development.

River transport is handicapped by waterfalls and rapids and in many areas by irregular stream flow due to seasonal rainfall. Countries dependent on rivers to supplement their road and rail systems include Zaire, Congo, Nigeria, and Sudan. Lengthy unnavigable stretches of the Congo River are bypassed by railroads that carry copper and other exports to the coast.

Air transport is of growing importance in Africa. Since independence, many countries have established national airlines and extended their international routes. Few are profitable. In remote areas air travel is often the only practical means of transportation.

Africa's telecommunications systems are underdeveloped but expanding. Radio, television, and telephone systems are concentrated in the urban areas, however,

The copper mines of Shaba province, formerly known as Katanga, provide steady income and employment for the developing nation of Zaire. One of Africa's most mineral-rich regions, Shaba also contains the world's principal reserves of cobalt.

(Left) *Three Zulu warriors display the tribe's ornate battle regalia.* (Below) *Africans are driven toward the coast for sale to European traders in the west or Arab traders in the east. Most of the African slaves were shipped across the Atlantic to labor in mines and plantations in the New World colonies.*

and rural districts are poorly served.

Trade. Africa's principal trade is with Europe and North America. In most cases, an African country's leading trade partner is the colonial power with which it was formerly connected. Since independence, however, trade contacts have diversified and increased, especially with the United States and the Soviet Union. Under the Lomé Convention, first signed in 1975, 66 African, Caribbean, and Pacific (APC) countries have preferred-trade and economic-aid agreements with the European Economic Community (EEC). The African members of APC send about half their exports, mainly agricultural and mineral products, to the EEC and receive about half their imports, mainly manufactured goods, from the EEC.

Trade between African nations is very limited, but mechanisms exist to promote it. West Africa has two regional trade groups: the 16-nation Economic Community of West African States (ECOWAS) and the smaller, French-speaking *Communauté Economique de l'Afrique de l'Ouest* (CEAO), whose seven members also belong to ECOWAS. In southern Africa, Angola, Botswana, Lesotho, Malawi, Mozambique, Swaziland, Tanzania, Zambia, and Zimbabwe formed the Southern African Development Coordination Conference in 1979 to reduce their economic dependence on South Africa.

This engraving was based on Henry Morton Stanley's personal description of his rendezvous with Dr. Livingstone. David Livingstone, a British explorer who had discovered and named the Victoria Falls, set out in 1866 to discover the headwaters of the Nile. No word of his whereabouts had been heard for several years when Stanley, a journalist, embarked on an expedition to find the missing explorer. After an 8-month search, Stanley found Livingstone in 1871 at Ujiji, a village near Lake Tanganyika.

History

Although the oldest dated bones of human beings have been found in Africa, little else is known of the 3 or 4 million years from the days of these ancestors to the earliest substantial accounts of African peoples. For the prehistory of Africa and the ancient civilizations of North Africa, see: AFRICAN PREHISTORY; CARTHAGE; CYRENE; EGYPT, ANCIENT.

Early Africa. CUSH, with its Egyptian like civilization on the Nile, and the flourishing, irrigation-based culture of SHEBA together contributed in about the 2nd century AD to the rise of the kingdom of AKSUM (Axum) in the highlands above the Red Sea. To the south a profitable commerce had begun to develop between the peoples of the coastal towns and seafaring merchants from Arabia, Persia, and other Asian centers. Their descendants formed the nuclei for a series of impressive East African city-states that flourished until the arrival of the more powerful Portuguese in the 16th century.

During the centuries of the ascent of Aksum and the city-states, there were massive migrations of agriculturists moving from eastern Nigeria southeastward toward the border of Zaire and Zambia, then westward, southward, and northeastward until they met a southern- and western-moving flank of peoples involved in pastoral pursuits.

The main theme of early West African history was the rise and fall of imperial fortunes along the great rivers that thread through the sub-Saharan dry zones. Ghana, the earliest of the great empires, reached its imperial zenith in the 10th and 11th centuries, governing peoples living as far south and east as the middle reaches of the Senegal River and the great bend of the Niger River. It was conquered from the south in the middle of the 11th century by Islamic fundamentalists, the Almoravids, who swept out of what is now Senegal and across Ghana, into Morocco, and eventually subdued all of southern Spain. By the mid-13th century, the empire of Mali, which re-placed Ghana as the most important kingdom of the western Sudan, reigned supreme from the upper Senegal River to the great bend of the Niger River to the east, and from the Sahara in the north to the upper Volta rivers in the south. SONGHAI succeeded Mali as the major empire of the sub-Saharan region, while KANEM-BORNU, the growning empire to the east, dominated the Lake Chad region until the onset of colonialism.

Early Modern Africa. Seeking a sea route around Africa to the Orient, Portuguese sailors rounded the Cape of Good Hope in 1487 and established themselves on the coast of Mozambique in the 16th century. Portugal and Spain were the original merchants of the Atlantic slave trade. After about 1550 an increasing demand for slaves to open up America (see SLAVERY) attracted competition. England, France, and others established trading posts

Menelik II, emperor of Ethiopia, is considered the founder of modern Ethiopia. His use of European weapons and fighting methods enabled him to defeat an Italian army at the Battle of Adowa in 1896. Because of this victory, Ethiopia remained independent when Africa was partitioned by the European powers in the late 19th century.

(Left) *Sékou Touré was Guinea's leader from 1958, when the country gained its independence, until his death in 1984.* (Center) *Zimbabwe's prime minister Robert Mugabe is shown here following his party's victory at the polls in February 1980.* (Right) *Julius Nyerere was Tanzania's president from 1964, when Tanganyika and Zanzibar merged to form that nation, until 1985.*

and forts along the coast of West Africa with the cooperation and toleration of African entrepreneurs. European guns gave the forest kingdoms new power over their neighbors and assisted in the rise to power of Benin (see BENIN, KINGDOM OF) and Oyo in western Nigeria; Dahomey, Akwamu, and Ashanti along the Gold Coast; and smaller states to the west and north but little influenced the evolution of inner Africa, where rivalries between agriculturists and pastoralists for available arable lands continued, until about 1700.

As the slave trade increasingly affected inland as well as coastal regions, some peoples (such as the MASAI of East Africa and the kingdoms of RWANDA and Buganda) remained little affected. Other new states, such as the ZULU nation in the southeast, gained power as a result of the chain of reactions set off by the increasing activity and encroachment of Europeans. Much of the west was affected by the activities of Muslim fundamentalists such as the FULANI, who subdued the HAUSA city-states under the leadership of USMAN DAN FODIO.

The European conquest of Africa was fueled by the explorations of Mungo PARK, David LIVINGSTONE, Sir Henry Morton STANLEY, Sir Richard BURTON, and Joseph THOMSON. Also important were commercial interests, the activities of Roman Catholic and Protestant missionaries, and political rivalries in Europe. Between 1880 and 1914, European countries occupied Africa. They met little resistance, due in part to their superior weapons and in part to a lack of African unity. Many Africans welcomed white protection against powerful neighbors.

The National Period. In North Africa, Egypt regained independence in 1922, after World War I. Libya regained independence in 1951 and Morocco and Tunisia in 1956. In 1961, after a bloody struggle, Algeria became the last of the French holdings in North Africa to become independent. In Ethiopia, which had been only briefly colonized (by Italy, 1936–41), the monarchy was overthrown in 1974.

Elsewhere, the coerciveness and racism of colonial rule sparked an increasingly hostile response. Britain granted independence to the Sudan in 1956 and to the Gold Coast (as Ghana) in 1957. Only Guinea separated from France in 1958, when France's overseas territories voted on membership in the new French Community, but the other French colonies peacefully gained their independence in 1960, along with Togo and Cameroon (French-run trust territories of the United Nations). British Nigeria gained its independence that same year, as did Sierra Leone, followed by the Gambia in 1965. Also in 1960, Belgium

South African leader Nelson Mandela celebrates his release, on Feb. 20, 1990, from 26 years of imprisonment, with his wife Winnie, Archbishop Desmond Tutu (right) and ANC leader Walter Sisulu (left).

granted independence to the Congo (now Zaire) with a minimum of preparation; the ensuing Congo Crisis provoked United Nations intervention. East of the Congo, the British colonies of Uganda (1962) and Kenya (1963) also gained independence, as did Tanganyika (1961), which became Tanzania in 1964. Spain granted independence to Equatorial Guinea in 1968 and renounced its claims to WESTERN SAHARA in 1976. A revolution in Portugal in 1974 contributed to independence for Guinea-Bissau in 1974 and for Cape Verde, São Tomé and Príncipe, Mozambique, and Angola in 1975. The Comoros separated from France in 1975, leaving the island of Mayotte as a French colony. The Seychelles, also in the Indian Ocean, became independent from Britain in 1976.

In Southern Africa, Britain created the Federation of Rhodesia and Nyasaland in 1953, transferring power to white settlers. The ensuing nationalist struggle led to independence for Nyasaland (Malawi) and Northern Rhodesia (Zambia) in 1964. Southern Rhodesia, whose whites unilaterally declared its independence as Rhodesia in 1965, became the majority-ruled nation of Zimbabwe in 1980. The British-run monarchies of Lesotho and Swaziland were given independence in 1966 and 1968, respectively. In 1966, Botswana also gained independence. South Africa, which had the continent's sole remaining white minority government, illegally governed Namibia until 1990, when it became Africa's newest independent nation.

Recent Developments

Since independence Africa has faced a variety of obstacles to economic growth, many of which are beyond its ability to control. Nearly three-fourths of all African nations are dependent upon one or two exports for the bulk of all foreign exchange earnings. Drops in world prices for many of these commodities, coupled with rising prices for imports, have reduced the money available for development. In addition, many governments borrowed heavily to finance prestigious but often economically unviable large-scale projects; the cost of debt service has nearly bankrupted some countries.

Improvements in health care contributed to rapid population growth that, in most countries, exceeded gains in food production and resulted in an overall decline in the standard of living. In the 1980s and early 1990s, the spread of AIDS placed new burdens on health facilities in central Africa. Prolonged and recurrent drought and other natural disasters have aggravated food shortages and destructive pressures on marginal lands and increased the refugee population. (Africa has less than 12% of the world's people and more than one-third of its refugees.) The percentage of Africans living in urban areas more than doubled between 1960 and 1985. By keeping urban food prices low to discourage unrest, governments accelerated rural-to-urban migration and deprived farmers of incentives to grow more food. African food imports tripled between 1974 and 1984, heightening trade imbalances and forcing factories, most of which are final-stage assembly operations, to cut production and lay off workers due to shortages of imported raw materials and spare parts.

By 1990 the average per capita income in Africa was below what it had been in 1960, and more than half of all foreign aid was consumed by debt service. Tribal conflicts and civil wars diverted scarce resources and hampered efforts at nation-building in many nations, including Ethiopia, Sudan, Somalia, Liberia, Mozambique, and Angola. Other inter-African disputes hampered the work of the ORGANIZATION OF AFRICAN UNITY, founded in 1963 to foster pan-African cooperation. The 1991 war in the Persian Gulf caused further economic distress for the oil-importing nations of the region and for Egypt and other countries that had depended heavily on wages sent home by expatriate workers in the Gulf region.

Economic distress, the wave of change sweeping Eastern Europe, and popular dissatisfaction with corrupt and autocratic rulers spurred demands for political and economic reforms. In country after country, due in part to demands made by international lenders, governments made efforts to increase prices paid to farmers for their crops and to reduce the role of government in the economy. The early 1990s were marked by a variety of changes. Many countries introduced or announced plans to introduce multiparty political systems, while the South African government lifted a 30-year ban on the black nationalist AFRICAN NATIONAL CONGRESS in 1990 and pledged to dismantle APARTHEID, although a peaceful resolution of the nation's internal problems still seemed far away.

The Organization of African Unity, headquartered in Addis Ababa, Ethiopia, was founded in 1963 to promote unity among African states and to eradicate colonialism.

African-American literature African-American literature, as defined by many contemporary literary critics, is the literature produced in the United States (or in exile therefrom) by blacks about blacks and most often has a strong didactic flavor. As such, the term would exclude such black writers as the poet Phillis WHEATLEY and the contemporary novelist Frank YERBY.

African-American literature can be said to have begun with the slave narratives and folktales that were transmitted orally during the period of the "peculiar institution" and later dictated and written down. These narratives, chronicling the harsh treatment experienced by enslaved blacks, form part of the centuries-long, worldwide tradition of oral literature and today serve as an important source for American historians. In a more sophisticated vein, the escaped slave and prominent abolitionist Frederick DOUGLASS inaugurated the tradition of black autobiographical writing with the publication of his *Narrative of the Life of Frederick Douglass* (1845).

19th Century. The first published work of African-American fiction was William Wells Brown's abolitionist novel *Clotel; or, the President's Daughter* (1853). A generation later, Charles W. CHESNUTT's short story "The Goophered Grapevine" (1887) appeared in the prestigious *Atlantic Monthly.* This led to the publication of two volumes of short stories by Chesnutt, *The Conjure Woman and Other Tales* and *The Wife of His Youth,* (both 1899). Even though the three novels that followed struck themes that have persisted in African-American literature, Chesnutt is best remembered for the artistry and insight he brought in his short stories to the complexities of slavery. At the same time, Paul Laurence DUNBAR was experimenting with the use of black folk material in his lyric poetry.

Harlem Renaissance. The support of white patrons of the arts, the countrywide acceptance of JAZZ, the mass migration of Southern American, Caribbean, and African blacks to Harlem during and after World War I, and the mix of attitudes and cultures thereby produced all combined to bring about the literary flowering known as the HARLEM RENAISSANCE (1920–30). An additional driving force was the determination of the NAACP, especially under the leadership of W. E. B. Du BOIS, himself the author of *The Souls of Black Folks* (1903), to improve the lot of blacks in America. Alain LOCKE, a Harvard Ph.D., Rhodes scholar, and editor of a book of essays called *The New Negro* (1925), spoke for this movement when he articulated the responsibility of the black to become a "collaborator and participant in American civilization."

This injunction was echoed in the works of the outstanding Renaissance writers, among whom were the Jamaican poet and novelist Claude McKAY; the poet and short-story writer Langston HUGHES; Jean TOOMER, author of the fragile miscellany *Cane* (1923); and the lyric poet Countee CULLEN. What these different writers shared was a need to trace the injustices perpetrated against blacks and the desire to give expression to the character of black life.

The versatility of the Harlem group was matched in the decade of the Great Depression by Richard WRIGHT, whose violent, Chicago-set novel *Native Son* (1940) constituted a powerful and bitter indictment of the social and economic inequities that continued to dash black aspirations in the period between the two world wars. Wright's autobiography *Black Boy* (1945), the short stories in *Uncle Tom's Children* (1938), and his 1953 novel *The Outsider* cast a searching light on the racial and political conditions that led some blacks, at least for a time, to embrace the Communist party.

Postwar. The archetypal novel of the early 1950s was Ralph ELLISON's *Invisible Man* (1952), the odyssey of a Southern youth's search for self and acceptance. Incorporating the folk, the classical, and the mythic, the book is considered a landmark. In a more traditional mold, Gwendolyn BROOKS and Lorraine HANSBERRY reflected the black American's urban experience in highly regarded poetry and plays. Also in the 1950s and early 1960s, James BALDWIN began to pursue the themes of the son's search for acceptance by a father, of homosexuality, and of race relations in his novels *Go Tell It on the Mountain* (1953), *Giovanni's Room* (1956), and *Another Country* (1962), as well as in plays and essays. The search, with religious overtones, is the essence of much of this author's writing, whose 1963 nonfictional investigation into the status of U.S. blacks, *The Fire Next Time,* galvanized white America.

Baldwin's work served as a transition to the revolutionary sixties when both MALCOLM X and Martin Luther KING, Jr., before their assassinations, brought a new dimension to speechmaking and political writing through an electrifying blend of moral fervor and rhetorical richness. The new black nationalist awareness was reflected by LeRoi Jones (later Imamu Amiri BARAKA), who stressed the didactic mission of black writers in his intense, frightening plays and essays. A writer of myriad talents, Jones moved from the status of middle-class intellectual as a Howard University undergraduate to political activist. His literary reputation at this time was matched only by that of the BLACK PANTHER minister of information, Eldridge CLEAVER, whose autobiographical *Soul on Ice* (1968) and later poetry interpreted the radicalizing prison experience of blacks of a different class.

Contemporary. From the late 1970s through the 1980s the steady production of plays by blacks was an established fact of American theatrical life. The imaginative use of autobiographical material characterized the work of novelists Toni MORRISON, Maya ANGELOU, and Alice WALKER, and the popular poet Nikki GIOVANNI. Other well-regarded novelists include Ernest J. Gaines, Ishmael REED, Toni C. Bambara (*Salt Eaters,* 1980), and Gloria Naylor (*The Women of Brewster Place,* 1982). Nowhere, however, was the growing interest in the black historical experience, among both blacks and whites, better demonstrated than in the enormous audience won by the 1977 and 1979 televised dramatizations of *Roots,* Alex HALEY's fictional exploration of a black family's journey from enslavement in Africa to its eventual emancipation after generations of bondage in America.

African Americans African Americans are those persons in the United States who trace their ancestry to members of the Negroid race in Africa. They have at various times in U.S. history been referred to as African, colored, Negro, Afro-American, and black. The vast majority of African Americans are descendants of people forcibly removed to North America as slaves; the population also includes more recent immigrants from black Africa, the West Indies, and Latin America.

The black population of the United States has grown from three-quarters of a million in 1790 to more than 26 million in 1980. As a percentage of the total population, African Americans declined from 19.3 in 1790 to 9.7 in 1930. A modest percentage increase has occurred since that time.

Exactly what portion of the African American population is of solely African ancestry is not known. Historically, the predominant attitude toward racial group membership in the United States has been that persons having any black African ancestry are considered to be black. In some parts of the United States, especially in the ante-bellum South, laws were written to define racial group membership in this way, generally to the detriment of those who were not Caucasian.

Blacks under Slavery: 1600–1865

The first Africans in the New World arrived with Spanish and Portuguese explorers and settlers. By 1600 an estimated 275,000 Africans, both free and slave, were in Central and South America and the Caribbean area. Africans first arrived in the area that became the United States in 1619, when a handful of captives were sold by the captain of a Dutch man-of-war to settlers at JAMESTOWN. Others were brought in increasing numbers to fill the desire for labor in a country where land was plentiful and labor scarce. By the end of the 17th century, approximately 1,300,000 Africans had landed in the

Black families were often broken up when sold at auction to slave buyers. Slavery developed in America largely because the South's plantation-based agricultural system demanded inexpensive, manageable labor. (Chicago Historical Society.)

New World. From 1701 to 1810 the number reached 6,000,000 with another 1,800,000 arriving after 1810. Some Africans were brought directly to the English colonies in North America. Others landed as slaves in the West Indies and were later resold and shipped to the mainland.

Slavery in America. The earliest African arrivals were viewed in the same way as indentured servants from Europe, but by the latter half of the 17th century, clear differences existed in the treatment of black and white servants. A 1662 Virginia law assumed Africans would remain servants for life. By 1740 the SLAVERY system in colonial America was fully developed.

Prior to the American Revolution, slavery existed in all the colonies. The ideals of the Revolution and the limited profitability of slavery in the North resulted in its abandonment in Northern states during the last quarter of the 18th century. At the same time the strength of slavery increased in the South, with the continuing demand for cheap labor by the tobacco growers and cotton farmers of the Southern states. By 1850, 92 percent of all African Americans were concentrated in the South, and of this group approximately 95 percent were slaves.

Life on the plantations was hard, and no consideration was given to the cultural traditions of Africans. In the slave market men were separated from their wives and children were taken from their mothers; family and tribal links were thus almost immediately cut. Fifty percent of the slaves were owned by 10 percent of the 385,000 slave owners.

Under the plantation system gang labor was the typical form of employment. Overseers were harsh as a matter of general practice, and brutality was common. Punishment was meted out at the absolute discretion of the owner or the owner's agent. Slaves could own no property unless sanctioned by a slave master, and rape of a female slave was not considered a crime except as it represented trespassing on another's property. Slaves could not present evidence in court against whites. Housing, food, and clothing seldom exceeded what was considered minimally necessary to maintain the desired level of work. In most of the South it was illegal to teach a black to read or write.

Opposition by Blacks. All Southern states passed slave codes intended to control slaves and prevent any expression of opposition. Outbreaks of opposition did occur, however, including the Prosser and Bowler Revolt of 1800, the revolt led by Denmark VESEY in 1822, Nat TURNER's rebellion in 1831, and numbers of smaller uprisings. As a result, repressive laws against Africans became more severe. Blacks were forbidden to carry arms or to gather in numbers except in the presence of a white person.

Free Africans, whether living in the North or South, were confronted with attitudes and actions that differed little from those facing Southern slaves. Discrimination existed in most social and economic activities as well as in voting and education. In 1857 the DRED SCOTT V. SANDFORD case of the U.S. Supreme Court placed the authority of the Constitution behind decisions made by states

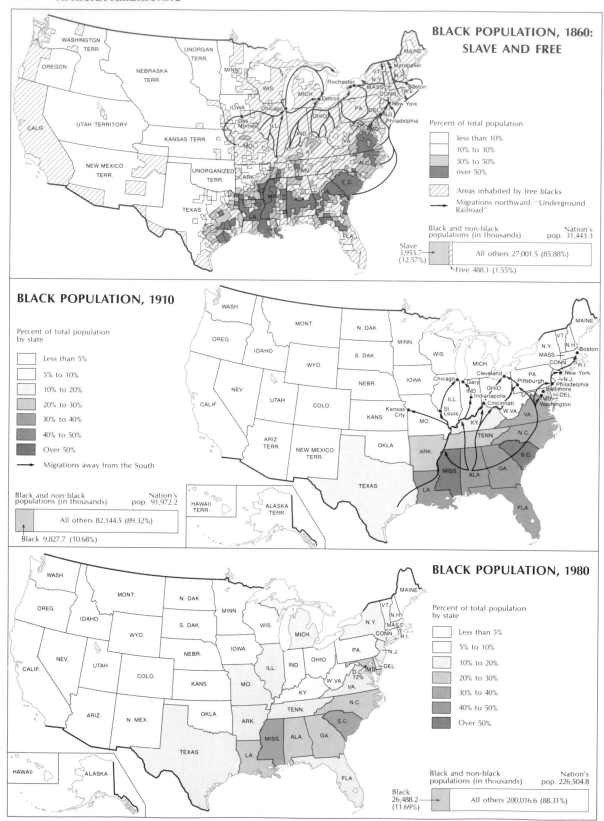

BLACK POPULATION, 1860: SLAVE AND FREE

Percent of total population

- less than 10%
- 10% to 30%
- 30% to 50%
- over 50%

Areas inhabited by free blacks

Migrations northward: "Underground Railroad"

Black and non-black populations (in thousands)   Nation's pop. 31,443.3

Slave 3,953.7 (12.57%)   All others 27,001.5 (85.88%)

Free 488.1 (1.55%)

BLACK POPULATION, 1910

Percent of total population by state

- Less than 5%
- 5% to 10%
- 10% to 20%
- 20% to 30%
- 30% to 40%
- 40% to 50%
- Over 50%

Migrations away from the South

Black and non-black populations (in thousands)   Nation's pop. 91,972.2

All others 82,144.5 (89.32%)

Black 9,827.7 (10.68%)

BLACK POPULATION, 1980

Percent of total population by state

- Less than 5%
- 5% to 10%
- 10% to 20%
- 20% to 30%
- 30% to 40%
- 40% to 50%
- Over 50%

Black and non-black populations (in thousands)   Nation's pop. 226,504.8

Black 26,488.2 (11.69%)   All others 200,016.6 (88.31%)

The 54th Massachusetts Colored Regiment, one of many black units serving in the Union army after the Emancipation Proclamation, led the charge against Confederate positions at Fort Wagner, S.C., in July 1863. (Library of Congress, Washington, D.C.)

in the treatment of blacks. The Dred Scott decision was that African Americans, even if free, were not intended to be included under the word *citizen* as defined in the Declaration of Independence and could, therefore, claim none of the rights and privileges provided for in that document.

In spite of the absence of legal status and the adverse effects of the domestic slave trade, the African family retained its traditional role in ordering the relations between adults and children. Much religious activity among slaves reflected the influences of African religious practices and served as a means by which slaves could return some sense of cultural heritage. Outside the South, Africans established separate churches and, eventually, denominations within Protestantism, including many black Baptist churches. The African Methodist Episcopal Church, initially called the Free African Society, was founded (1787) in Philadelphia by Richard ALLEN.

Civil War. The issue of slavery appeared in national politics from the start of the nation. In 1820 it was the subject of the MISSOURI COMPROMISE, a measure enacted by Congress to prohibit slavery north of the state of Missouri. In the 1850s the slavery issue further divided the nation along regional lines. For the most part, however, both proslavery and antislavery positions included antiblack attitudes.

When the South seceded (1860–61) because of the dangers to slavery it perceived in Lincoln's election, the North declared that it was not slavery but the act of secession that precipitated the CIVIL WAR. President Lincoln supported a Constitutional amendment that would have given federal protection to slavery in the Southern states. On his order slaves who escaped into the Union lines were returned to their owners by federal troops early in the war.

Later, as the cost of the war and national support for the ABOLITIONISTS grew, President Lincoln shifted his position. In 1862 his EMANCIPATION PROCLAMATION declared slaves to be free if the areas in which they were held were still in revolt against the Union on Jan. 1, 1863. Slaves within the Union and in areas of the Confederacy under Union control, however, were initially excluded from the provisions of the proclamation. Thus at its inception, the proclamation functioned principally as military propaganda: slaves were declared free only in those areas where no real authority existed to free them. In those areas under federal authority, no action was taken. Nevertheless, the Emancipation Proclamation represented a point of no return on the issue of slavery.

Beginning in 1862, provisions were made for enlisting blacks into the Union army. They were organized into all-black units referred to as the U.S. Colored Troops. Of the 209,000 African Americans who entered service, 93,000 came from the area of the Confederacy. Units composed of soldiers from this area included the 1st and 3d Louisiana Native Guard and the 1st South Carolina Volunteers. The Confederacy at first refused to recognize them as soldiers. Unlike other Union troops who were captured, black soldiers were at first not allowed to surrender. Many were shot. The most infamous of such occurrences was at Fort Pillow, which fell to Confederate troops under Gen. Nathan B. FORREST (later a founder of the KU KLUX KLAN).

Blacks took part in more than 200 battles and skirmishes. In all, 68,178 died in battle or as the result of wounds or disease during the war. Lower pay for blacks and other forms of discrimination were common, but desertion among blacks was more than 50 percent lower than for the Union army as a whole.

Reconstruction and Its Aftermath: 1865–1915

During the period of RECONSTRUCTION (1865–77), Union policy evolved to embrace the total abolition of slavery, as provided in the 13th Amendment to the Constitution, passed in 1865. Government policy also moved toward equality of rights for African Americans as reflected in the 14th Amendment (1868) and 15th Amendment (1870) and in related legislation. Opposition to equal rights for blacks was almost universal in the South and nearly so in the North, however. Passage of the 14th and 15th amendments had been primarily motivated by the desire of the Republican party to maintain political control in the former Confederacy.

Participation by Blacks. Blacks took an active part in all aspects of public life during Reconstruction. They voted in large numbers and were active in the conventions that formulated new state constitutions in the South. Many held political office at the local and state levels; 14 were elected to the U.S. House of Representatives, and 2 were elected to the U.S. Senate. Blacks pressed for and helped to establish systems of public education where none had previously existed. They established private schools and colleges with the assistance of the FREEDMEN'S BUREAU, a federal agency, and Northern church groups. Legislation backed by federal troops made access to public accommodations possible. Many former slaves hoped that confiscated land of Confederate officials or land owned by the federal government might be divided into family farms and distributed among them. This was not done, however, and only a small number of blacks were able to purchase land, leaving the vast majority of Southern blacks economically dependent on former slave owners.

Opposition by Whites. The major attack on the rights of African Americans came from Southern whites, many of whom insisted that federal policies under Reconstruction were oppressive and vindictive. High among their complaints was the erroneous claim that state governments were controlled by blacks. Many sought to remove blacks from participation in policies and to restore, as closely as possible, conditions that existed before the war. As the federal government restored suffrage to former Confederates, a variety of legal and extralegal means were used to accomplish these goals. The illegal activities of the Ku Klux Klan and similar organizations founded in the late 1860s, coupled with waning interest in the North in pro-

tecting the rights of black citizens, resulted in the gradual return of control of state governments into the hands of the Democratic party. This was effectively accomplished by 1877, when all federal troops were withdrawn from the South, and Reconstruction was officially ended. White rule of the Southern states was fully restored, and the rights of black citizens were once again in jeopardy.

The Southern Race System. As Reconstruction ended, an extremely difficult period began for African American citizens. The disfranchisement that had begun in the South with illegal harassment and violence soon after the war was almost completed by the early years of the 20th century. Many Southern states instituted POLL TAXES, literacy tests, and the so-called GRANDFATHER CLAUSE as a means of removing blacks from voting while allowing white suffrage to continue. The success of these efforts is attested to by the decline in registered black voters in Alabama from 181,471 in 1900 to 3,000 as a result of constitutional changes effected in 1901. Similar action in Louisiana reduced registered blacks from 130,334 in 1896 to 1,342 in 1904.

The radical curtailment of black voting rights in the South facilitated the institutionalized separation of blacks from whites in various aspects of everyday life. Blacks were excluded from participation on juries and were refused service in hotels, restaurants, and amusement parks. They were forced to occupy separate sections in vehicles of public transportation and in public gathering places, and separate educational systems were provided for each race. By the outbreak of World War I, so-called JIM CROW LAWS that legalized segregation existed throughout the South, and in other parts of the United States as well, either by law or by local practice.

The judicial stamp of approval for Jim Crow came in 1896 with the case of PLESSY V. FERGUSON, whereby the U.S. Supreme Court declared constitutional a Louisiana law requiring separation by race on railroad coaches. The court held that enforcing such separation was a legitimate

(Left) *W. E. B. Du Bois, a black sociologist and author, was one of the founders of the NAACP.* (Right) *George Washington Carver, an educator and botanist, instructs a class at Tuskegee Institute in Alabama. Carver's research led to the development of important new products derived from such crops as peanuts, sweet potatoes, and soybeans.*

use of the police power of the states so long as equal facilities were provided. Such facilities for blacks were invariably inferior to those for whites, however. This inequality was perhaps most devastating in the area of education.

The powerlessness of blacks during the post-Reconstruction period is exemplified in the high incidence of lynchings (3,402) that occurred between 1882 and 1938. The several attempts to secure passage of a federal antilynching bill during this period were all unsuccessful. Yet the efforts of blacks after Reconstruction to improve their economic condition and exercise their political rights met with some measure of success. In 1870, 80 percent of African Americans over 10 years of age were illiterate; by 1900 illiteracy among blacks was reduced by almost 50 percent. Farm ownership, although still low, increased significantly; by 1901 about 25 percent of black farmers in the South owned their own land. Seven blacks were elected to the U.S. House of Representatives for a cumulative total of 13 terms between 1877 and 1901, and Jim Crow legislation was challenged in the courts, albeit unsuccessfully.

A variety of organizations sought to advance the rights of blacks, notably the NATIONAL ASSOCIATION FOR THE ADVANCEMENT OF COLORED PEOPLE (NAACP), founded 1909. One of its founders, William E. B. DU BOIS, was the leading spokesperson for full and immediate rights for African Americans. The accommodation of some blacks to post-Reconstruction racism was symbolized in the activities of the black educator Booker T. WASHINGTON, who cautioned blacks to be patient and to work hard toward attaining economic equality before striving for civil rights.

Period of Transition: 1915–45

World War I was a turning point in African American history. The trickle of blacks moving out of the South after 1877 increased enormously as war industries and the decline of European immigration combined to produce demands for labor in Northern cities. The coming together of large numbers of blacks in urban areas, the exposure of many of them to European whites who did not hold the same racial attitude as American whites, and war propaganda to "make the world safe for democracy" combined to raise the hopes, dreams, and aspirations of African Americans. Segregationists countered this optimism with an upsurge of lynchings, riots, and other antiblack violence after World War I, however. The Ku Klux Klan was revived and gained impetus in Northern as well as Southern states during the 1920s. In the same period notable productions of African American literature, music, and art took place; increasing race consciousness is reflected in the writings of the influential black leader Marcus GARVEY, founder of the Universal Negro Improvement Association and an ardent proponent of BLACK NATIONALISM.

In the 1930s blacks initially were less affected by the Depression than whites because the economy of the African American community was already depressed. Before long, however, the worsening economic conditions hit blacks, as the group at the low end of the economic scale, the hardest. In New Deal efforts to aid the poor blacks

Marcus Garvey defended the cultural achievements of blacks and attracted a considerable following of black Americans between 1916 and 1922 by encouraging them to found a sovereign nation in Africa.

encountered the first assistance from government since Reconstruction. Franklin D. Roosevelt's sensitivity to the existence of racism, coupled with growing disaffection with the Republican party, caused more and more voting blacks to support the Democratic party, and since the New Deal period blacks have increasingly voted for Democrats.

With the outbreak of World War II, wholehearted black support was given to the war effort with the hope that the fight against Nazi racism would weaken racism in the United States. Of the 891,000 African Americans who joined the military, approximately half a million served overseas. Black combat units included the 92d and 93d divisions and a small group of air force pilots. As in World War I the majority of blacks were organized into service units, and many were never trained in the use of basic weapons. In an attempt to encourage and improve job training for minority group workers in war industries, President Roosevelt established a national Fair Employment Practices Committee. The war ended, however, with no major attack on discrimination in employment and in labor unions, and Jim Crow practices persisted in many parts of both the North and the South.

The Civil Rights Movement

Many things influenced the changes in U.S. race relations after World War II. The anti-Nazi propaganda generated during the war increased the awareness by many Americans of the conflict between ideals and the reality of racism in their own country. The concentration of large numbers of blacks in cities of the North and West increased their potential for political influence. It also projected the problems related to race as national rather than regional. The growth of a white minority willing to speak out against racism provided allies for blacks. Most important in altering race relations in the United States, however, were the actions of African Americans themselves.

Legal Action Against Racism. The first major attack by

Dr. Martin Luther King, Jr., the most prominent civil rights leader of the 20th century, addressed a vast crowd of supporters at a 1957 rally in Washington, D. C. In recognition of his leadership, his belief in nonviolence, and his personal courage, Dr. King was awarded the Nobel Peace Prize in 1964. Four years later, he was assassinated.

blacks on racism was through the courts. In a series of cases involving professional and graduate education, the Supreme Court required admission of blacks to formerly all-white institutions when separate facilities for blacks were clearly not equal. The major legal breakthrough came in 1954. In the case of BROWN V. BOARD OF EDUCATION OF TOPEKA, KANSAS, the Supreme Court held that separate facilities are, by their very nature, unequal. In spite of this decision, more than a decade passed before significant school integration took place in the South. In the North, where segregated schools resulted from segregated housing patterns and from manipulation of school attendance boundaries, separation of races in public schools increased after 1954. A second major breakthrough in the fight against segregation grew out of the Montgomery, Ala., bus boycott in 1955. The boycott began when Rosa Parks, a black woman, was arrested for refusing to give up her seat on the bus to a white person. The boycott of buses on which racial segregation was practiced lasted for more than a year and was almost 100 percent effective. Before the courts declared unconstitutional Montgomery's law requiring segregation on buses, Martin Luther KING, Jr., a Baptist minister, had risen to national prominence and had articulated a strategy of nonviolent direct action in the movement for CIVIL RIGHTS.

Nonviolent Direct Action. Nonviolent direct action, born in the boycott, was taken up by blacks and white supporters throughout the country. It was applied at sit-ins and freedom rides, aimed at ending segregation in public places, and also at protest demonstrations of all kinds. Among these activities were the march on Washington of Aug. 28, 1963, in which more than 200,000 blacks and whites protested continued segregation and discrimination, and large-scale demonstrations in Birmingham, Ala. (April 1963), and Selma, Ala. (March 1965). These civil rights activities were directed by long-established groups such as the NAACP and CORE (the CONGRESS OF RACIAL

EQUALITY, founded 1942), by newly formed national groups such as the SOUTHERN CHRISTIAN LEADERSHIP CONFERENCE and SNCC (the Student Nonviolent Coordinating Committee; see SNCC), and by such local groups as the Dallas County (Ala.) Voters League and the Princeton (N.J.) Association for Human Rights.

Violence against black and white civil rights activists was commonplace. Three civil rights workers were brutally murdered in Philadelphia, Miss., in 1964; four black children were murdered in the bombing of the 16th Street Baptist Church in Birmingham in 1963; and dozens of black churches throughout the South were burned or bombed. Two whites and one black were murdered during the 1965 demonstrations in Selma, Ala. In 1968, Martin Luther King, Jr., the recognized leader of the civil rights movement, was assassinated.

The federal response to the violent reaction of segregationists was the passage of several new laws, the most important of which were enacted in 1964 and 1965. The CIVIL RIGHTS ACT (1964) undermined the remaining structure of Jim Crow laws and provided federal protection in the exercise of civil rights. The Voting Rights Act (1965) provided for federal action to put an end to practices by local governments and individuals that interfered with the right of African Americans to register and vote. Both these laws were upheld in challenges before the U.S. Supreme Court. (See INTEGRATION, RACIAL.)

Urban Unrest and Militant Protest. When Martin Luther King, Jr., was assassinated in 1968, a new wave of riots spread across the country. A report by the National Advisory Commission on Civil Disorders, appointed by President Lyndon B. Johnson, identified more than 150 riots or major disorders between 1965 and 1968. In 1967 alone, 83 people were killed (most of them African Americans), 1,800 were injured, and property valued at more than $100 million was destroyed. (See RACE RIOTS.)

The growing black consciousness movement and the

aggressive civil rights activism of the late 1960s resulted in what some have termed the white backlash. White supporters of moderate black organizations and activities declined. Federal programs beneficial to poor ghetto youth were cut back, and the direction taken by the Supreme Court weakened the base for progress set under Chief Justice Earl WARREN. Evidence began to leak out that the FBI had sought to discredit and destroy Martin Luther King, Jr., as a leader and had participated in efforts to reduce the effectiveness of some black organizations.

Black Pride. The chief characteristic of the black experience in the 1970s and early 1980s was the development of black consciousness and black pride. These values found renewed vigor as increasing numbers of African Americans came to believe that the key to dealing with problems of race in the United States was the way they felt about themselves as individuals and as a group. The concept of black pride had been earlier articulated in such slogans as *black is beautiful* and *black power*. The latter term, introduced (1966) by Stokely Carmichael, the chairman at that time of SNCC, became the rallying cry for the more radical civil rights activists of the latter half of the 1960s. It found organizational expression in the BLACK PANTHER PARTY, the BLACK MUSLIMS, the Organization of Afro-American Unity, and other groups. Leading spokespersons of the concept of racial pride included MALCOLM X, Imamu Amiri BARAKA (formerly LeRoi Jones), Ron Karenga, and Huey Newton. This concept frightened some whites who claimed to see it as black racism.

Black Political Activity. Beginning in the 1960s, many African Americans focused on political activity as a means of obtaining justice, equality of opportunity, and full political participation. During this Second Reconstruction, as the period has been called, a rapid increase occurred in the number of black registered voters, particularly in the South, followed by a marked increase in the number of black elected officials.

In 1984 the Rev. Jesse JACKSON, a civil rights activist in the 1960s, first campaigned in the primaries for the Democratic-party presidential nomination. He won over 3 million primary votes (and about 75 percent of the black vote) but fell far short of winning enough convention delegates to gain the nomination. In 1988 he ran second in the primary season, winning 6.6 million votes—92 percent of the black vote and 12 percent of the white—and about 30 percent of the delegates, to become the first "serious" African American contender for the presidency. In 1988 there were 6,680 black elected officials at all levels, from school boards to Congress. Since the 1960s dozens of African Americans have been elected to the House of Representatives. In 1967, Edward W. BROOKE of Massachusetts became the first black member of the Senate since Reconstruction. In 1990 Douglas Wilder of Virginia became the first elected black governor. The same year black mayors of major cities included Tom BRADLEY in Los Angeles, David DINKINS in New York, Richard Arrington in Birmingham, Sidney Barthelemy in New Orleans, Sharon Pratt Dixon in Washington, D.C., Wilson Goode in Philadelphia, Maynard Jackson in Atlan-

ta, Kurt Schmoke in Baltimore, Michael White in Cleveland, and Coleman Young in Detroit. And the chairman of the Democratic National Committee, Ron Brown, was an African American.

In 1967, Thurgood MARSHALL became the first black Supreme Court Justice, and in recent administrations African Americans have been part of every presidential cabinet.

African American Culture Today

The distinctive features of African American culture are most noticeable in music, art and literature, and religion. They may also exist in speech, extended family arrangements, dress, and other features of life-style. Whether African ancestry or survival in the hostile environment of slavery and Jim Crow was more important in shaping cultural patterns of black American life is a question that requires further study.

Music and the Arts. African American traditions in music reflect the mingling of African roots with the American experience: BLUES and spirituals (see GOSPEL MUSIC) can be traced back to the African call-and-response chant. The writings of James Weldon JOHNSON and the American and European tours of the Fisk University Jubilee Singers brought black religious folk music to the nonblack community, and Bessie SMITH and W. C. HANDY developed it. JAZZ, a direct descendant of blues, developed among African Americans in New Orleans and spread with their migration. By 1920 it was played throughout the country. The enduring popularity of Louis ARMSTRONG and Duke ELLINGTON over several decades attests to its continuing attraction. For decades black musicians including Paul ROBESON, Marian ANDERSON and Leontyne PRICE sustained impressive careers on the concert stage while such legendary performers as Lena HORNE and Sammy DAVIS, Jr., opened the doors to show business. In 1984, Michael JACKSON dominated the popular music world, winning an unprecedented eight Grammy Awards.

AFRICAN AMERICAN LITERATURE and art were slower to develop. Early artists and writers who were black dealt with themes that, in selection and approach, were indistinguishable from the works of whites. By the 1920s centers of artistic activity had developed, the best known being in New York. The HARLEM RENAISSANCE produced the poets Langston HUGHES, Countee CULLEN, and James Weldon Johnson; writers Claude McKAY and Jean TOOMER; painters Aaron Douglas (1899–1979) and Laura Wheeler (1887–1948); sculptor Meta Warrick (1877–1967), and, in music, Paul Robeson, Ethel WATERS, Harry T. Burleigh (1866–1949), and Nathaniel Dett (1822–1943). The work of the Harlem Renaissance and writers such as Richard WRIGHT reflected the growing race consciousness among African Americans and their opposition to the segregation encountered in all forms of life. These themes continue to be important in the work of such writers as James BALDWIN, Amiri BARAKA, Gwendolyn BROOKS, Ralph ELLISON, Douglas Turner WARD, and John A. WILLIAMS.

Religion. Religion has traditionally been important to African American life. The first major denomination among blacks, the African Methodist Episcopal Church, grew from the church established by Richard Allen in Philadelphia in 1787. Others were created or derived from white denominational groups. Slave churches existed prior to the Civil War, often without denominational attachments; with Emancipation, most former slaves joined Baptist or Methodist churches. These remain today as the church groups with the largest black memberships. Among non-Christian religious groups that have attracted sizable followings are the Peace Mission of Father DIVINE and the Nation of Islam, often referred to as the Black Muslims. Both are urban in origin and date from the 1930s. The Peace Mission is strongly integrationist in its teachings; in recent years its leadership and membership have become increasingly white, while the Nation of Islam, particularly under the leadership of Lewis Farrakhan, has urged separatism. In 1985 the main Black Muslim group was unified with the Muslim community worldwide.

Black ministers prominent in politics during the post–World War II period include Adam Clayton POWELL, Jr., Martin Luther King, Jr., Jesse Jackson, and Andrew YOUNG.

Education. Until the post–World War II period, most African Americans seeking higher education attended private BLACK COLLEGES located mainly in the South that had been started after the Civil War as a joint effort of blacks, Northern church groups, and the Freedmen's Bureau. Among these were Fisk University, Atlanta University, Talladega College, Morehouse College, and Spelman College. Late in the 19th century Tuskegee Institute was founded by Booker T. Washington, and a number of colleges were established by black church groups. In the 1940s some improvement was made in publicly supported institutions of higher education for blacks, and for the first time black students began to appear in colleges that had previously been all white. In the 1970s the percentage of blacks attending college increased markedly, but in the 1980s it declined.

Although desegregation of the public schools in the South proceeded slowly for the first decade after the *Brown* v. *Board of Education* decision, by 1969 school districts in every state were at least in token compliance with the 1954 ruling. By that time all forms of de jure segregation had been struck down by the courts. One

Shirley Chisholm, the first black female member of the U.S. House of Representatives, unsuccessfully sought the Democratic nomination for president in 1972.

Jesse Jackson was hailed at the Democratic national convention in Atlanta in 1988 after he ran a strong second in the race for the presidential nomination. He had also campaigned for the nomination in 1984.

method adopted to overcome de facto segregation was to bus children across school district lines in order to achieve racial balance in the schools. This caused major controversy in the early 1970s and led to instances of violent opposition (see BUSING, SCHOOL). The majority of African American children now attend legally integrated schools; many of these institutions, however, are attended exclusively or overwhelmingly by minority students.

The Press and Sports. The black press is another of the institutions strongly influenced by urbanization. The major African American papers, magazines, and radio stations exist because racial concentration in urban areas makes them necessary and profitable. Among the oldest and most prominent black newspapers are the *Baltimore Afro-American* (founded 1892), the *Chicago Daily Defender* (1905), the *New York Amsterdam News* (1909), and the *Atlanta Daily World* (1928). During the past few decades a score or more new publications have appeared. Among the most successful are *Jet* and *Ebony*, both published by Johnson Publications of Chicago.

In recent years the one area in which blacks and whites have most successfully competed on a basis of equality is sports. Before the 1940s, competition seldom existed across racial lines except in boxing and track. It was not until Jackie ROBINSON was hired by the Brooklyn Dodgers baseball team in 1947 that major changes began to occur. Today African Americans appear in disproportionately large numbers in the college and professional team sports of basketball, baseball, and football, and in boxing and track. Outstanding sports players include boxing champions Joe LOUIS and Muhammad ALI; track stars Jesse OWENS and Carl LEWIS; Jim BROWN and O. J. SIMPSON in football; Wilt CHAMBERLAIN, Bill RUSSELL, Kareem ABDUL-JABBAR, Michael JORDAN, and Magic JOHNSON in basketball; and baseball players Willie MAYS, Henry AARON, Frank ROBINSON, and Reggie JACKSON. There have been fewer than a dozen African American coaches and managers of major professional teams and a relatively small number of coaches of major college sports programs other than at historically black colleges. In the professional ranks these have included Bill Russell and K. C. Jones of basketball, Frank Robinson of baseball, and Art Shell of football. In the college ranks, John Thompson coached Georgetown University to the 1984 NCAA basketball title and then coached the U.S. team at the 1988 Olympics in Seoul; Lawrence Ellis, of Princeton University, coached the U.S. track and field team at the 1984 Olympics in Los Angeles.

Other Contributions; Recent Concerns. African Americans have also made significant contributions in many other fields. Charles Drew's work in hematology leading to the establishment of the American Red Cross blood bank and Ralph BUNCHE's appointment as undersecretary of the United Nations in 1950 are examples. The first African American in space was Air Force Lt. Col. Guion S. Bluford, who took part in a 1983 Space Shuttle flight as a mission specialist. In 1990, Gen. Colin Powell became Chairman of the Joint Chiefs of Staff.

In the 1980s the median income of blacks still remained significantly below that of whites. Although modest economic gains have been made, large numbers of African Americans continue to live in poverty. Many blacks share concern that actions taken by the Reagan administration—withdrawing funds from programs to aid the poor and reducing support for affirmative action—and George Bush's veto of the 1990 Civil Rights Act will seriously harm their communities. These fears, coupled with growing interest in Third World affairs, have fueled the efforts of African Americans to have a voice in federal, state, and local government proportionate with their numbers.

African art The traditional art of Africa consists principally of masks and figures of magico-religious significance, decorative objects used for personal adornment, and implements and insignia of rank or prestige. Most of these objects are in some way related to ceremonial and other structured activities (such as singing, dancing, drumming, and storytelling). Sculpture is generally considered Africa's greatest achievement in the visual arts. The majority of sculptures are of wood, but objects are also made in metal, stone, terra-cotta, mud, beadwork, ivory, and other materials.

Ancient rock paintings in southern and eastern Africa are attributed to the SAN (Bushman) people. The only other major rock art tradition in Africa is found in Algeria, Libya, and Chad, the work of the prehistoric inhabitants of the Sahara (see PREHISTORIC ART). Islamic influence is seen throughout the west African savanna and the east African coast.

From the 16th century, European travelers acquired objects of African art, particularly bronzes and ivories from the Benin court. Collections of African art were being formed in Europe by the 19th century. Early in the 20th century, African sculpture had an impact on the work of such modern artists as Georges BRAQUE, Henri MATISSE, Amedeo MODIGLIANI, and Pablo PICASSO, who were attracted by the aesthetic values they perceived in African art forms.

General Characteristics

Three basic themes recur in traditional African art: (1) the distinction between bush and village, (2) the problematic relationships between the sexes, and (3) the struggle to control various forces, natural and supernatural.

The dualism of bush and village is pervasive in Africa. The underlying notion is that the world consists of two complementary spheres: one a wild, chaotic, uncontrolled, exuberant region (nature); the other an ordered, controlled, measured, predictable domain (culture, the human world of the village). Among the Yaka and other Congolese groups, masks used early in initiation rites are made of rough bush materials and have relatively abstract features; those worn at the conclusion of the rites—when the boys have been symbolically brought from nature into culture—are made of wood, are more naturalistic, and are used to make fun of human foibles. For the Dogon of Mali, the distinction is embodied in the contrast between spirals (nature) and rectangles (culture).

To deal with problems and issues surrounding relations between the sexes, various African societies employ art as a therapeutic device. The Baule of the Ivory Coast, for example, carve images supposed to represent one's spirit lover. It is believed that these beings, if jealous, can cause the living unending problems with their spouses.

The principal function of art in traditional African society has been to help manipulate the forces that affect people's lives. Natural or supernatural, these powers are perceived as subject to influence and manipulation. Deliberately hideous masks intended to expel witches, such as the Senufo "firespitter" of the Ivory Coast and many related savanna forms, constitute a violent counterattack on witchcraft that literally fights fire with fire. The same is true of FETISHES—magically constructed and empowered objects found throughout Africa. These assemblages are

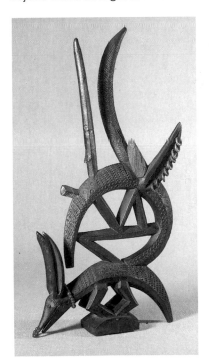

The wooden Bambara dance headdress from Mali is used in the agricultural rites of the Tyiwara society. (Nationalmuseet, Copenhagen.)

(Above) *The terra-cotta Nok sculptures from northern Nigeria, dating from about 600 BC to AD 200, are the oldest known sculptures of sub-Saharan Africa.*

(Right) *A bronze plaque from the court of Benin in Nigeria represents a king and his kneeling attendants. Dating from about 1550–1680, the plaque was produced by the lost-wax process. (Courtesy British Museum, London.)*

specific prescriptions aimed at bringing about a desired end, the breaking of a bad habit, the improvement of one's love life, the destruction of a human or supernatural enemy. In short, traditional African art is essentially functional and optimistic.

Regional Styles

Western Sudanic Region. This area includes Burkina Faso, western Mali, and northern Ivory Coast. Among its most famous art-producing peoples are the Dogon, Bambara, Bwa, and Senufo. The fertility of crops is of basic importance in this dry area, as is the placation of the ancestors and the indoctrination of the young in the ancient traditions of each society. To these ends, masks and figures representing legendary ancestors dance or receive sacrifices. Forms in the western Sudan tend to be relatively stylized, austere, and angular.

Central Sudanic Region. Centered in northern Nigeria, the central Sudan is dominated by the Muslim HAUSA and FULANI peoples. The art, mostly nonrepresentational, includes mud architecture, sometimes with molded, low-

relief decoration; embroidered textiles; metal and beadwork jewelry; and leatherwork decorated with geometric appliqué. Terra-cotta sculptures from *c.*500 BC to AD 200, associated with the so-called Nok culture, have been unearthed over a 480-km (300-mi) stretch of uplands. The Nok tradition represents the earliest known sculpture yet found in sub-Saharan Africa and seems to have paved the way for the tradition of superb portrait terra-cottas and bronzes at the holy city of IFE.

West Guinea Coast Region. In Guinea-Bissau, Sierra Leone, Liberia, and the densely forested coastal portion of Guinea and southwestern Ivory Coast, characteristic masks and figures are made by such peoples as the MENDE, Baga, Gola, and Dan. Forms are generally softer, shinier, and more rounded than in neighboring regions. Carved wood masks, the dominant art form, are worn to police ceremonies, punish wrongdoers, settle land disputes, and start and end wars.

Central Guinea Coast Region. The Central Guinea Coast extends from southeastern Ivory Coast, southern Ghana, Togo, Benin, and southern Nigeria to the lower Niger River, with an offshoot in the Cameroons grasslands. The art, from such well-known societies as the ASHANTI, YORUBA, and BENIN, is the richest and the most complex in Africa. These groups were courtly in character with divine kingship and other centralizing institutions; their art employs aristocratic materials including gold, silver, beadwork, silk, and ivory. Specialized guilds of artists attached to the courts produced intricately crafted stools, drums, terra-cotta figurines, combs, mirrors, pipes, and containers. The affluence and accompanying artistic wealth of the region were in part the result of lucrative trade with European ships.

East Guinea Coast Region. The lower Niger marks the approximate boundary between the aristocratic centralized societies of the central Guinea Coast and the more loosely organized peoples of southwestern Nigeria. There, in the absence of kings and paramount chiefs, elaborate-

ly developed masquerades and plays—sometimes staged by secret societies, sometimes by graded title societies—served to maintain law and order in groups that vested leadership in their elders. The IBO, Ibibio, Idoma, Ijo, Ejagham (Ekoi), and Ogoni produced a dazzling array of masks, puppets, headdresses, and other theatrical devices.

Equatorial Forest Region. Among the best-known peoples of the equatorial forest, which extends across Gabon and northern Zaire, are the FANG, Kota, Kwele, Ngbaka, Mbole, and Lega. The art-producing agricultural peoples arrived from southern Nigeria some 2,000 years ago, in what is frequently called the Bantu Expansion (see BANTU). Their art forms include masks, figures, beautifully designed weapons, divination objects and carved fetishes, wall paintings, musical instruments, and practical implements. One widespread visual motif is the so-called heart-shaped face, which is concave from the eye sockets

A Kota funerary figure from Gabon is made of wood covered with copper. Representing the spirit of the dead, it was used in ancestor-cult rituals. (Collection of Princess Gourielli, New York.)

This wooden fetish figure was fashioned by the Yaka tribe of Zaire. A fetish sculpture is believed to be endowed with magical properties that protect its owner. (Ethnographical Museum of Berlin.)

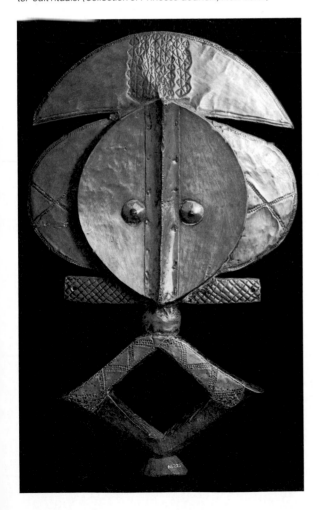

to the mouth. This motif may well have been brought by Bantu migrants from Nigeria, where it is also used.

Lower Congo Region. The styles developed in the vicinity of the mouth of the Congo River were influenced from *c.*1500 by the Portuguese, who converted the king (the *Mani-kongo*) and many of his courtiers to Christianity. After the Portuguese withdrawal, symbols borrowed from Christianity acquired pagan meanings; crucifixes, for example, became symbols of chiefly power. Christian origins have also been suggested for other Lower Congo art forms, mother-and-child figures and fetishes with nails driven into them.

Southern Savanna Region. In the broad upland belt of central Africa are numerous Bantu peoples such as the CHOKWE, LUBA, Songye, Yaka, Pende, and Kuba and related groups such as the MBUNDU and Makonde. Perhaps the prime generators of art in these groups are the initiation rites that mark the passage of boys from adolescence to manhood. Masks, figures, costumes, and spectacular theatrical effects function as didactic devices to instruct the boys in their culture and in proper manly behavior. The Kuba of central Zaire also have elaborate courtly art forms, including royal portrait statues and numerous regalia for persons of high rank.

Eastern Sudanic Region. The artistic production of most of the peoples in this area is restricted to decorative art, but a few groups in the southern Republic of the Sudan and southwest Ethiopia, including the Bongo, Konso, and Borana, carve wood figures to commemorate ancestors. This tradition probably relates more to the ancient pagan art still discernible in a broad arc across southern Asia than to the majority of African styles. Similarly distinct is Ethiopian art, which shows strong links with Egyptian Coptic art and Byzantine art.

East and Southern African Region and Madagascar. Apart from Bushman paintings and engravings, eastern and southern Africa have only a limited number of distinctive figural styles. The predominant arts are architecture and architectural decorations, including the boldly patterned wall paintings of the Ndebele in the Transvaal, and personal ornaments, especially beadwork. Madagascar, the only large island lying off Africa's coast, was first settled not from Africa but from Indonesia, perhaps early in the Christian era. Conspicuous there are the commemorative ancestor figure and *ikat* textiles typical of Indonesia.

African languages   More than 1,700 distinct languages are spoken on the African continent, and they constitute about 30 percent of all world languages. Groups of people who speak a distinct African language range in size from several million down to a thousand or even fewer. Apart from North Africa, only a few African countries—Somalia, Rwanda, and Burundi, for example—have a single or a dominant language.

History

The study of African languages began before 1600, by early Christian missionaries. Strictly scholarly interest in African languages dates back to about 1850 in South Af-

rica, the late 1920s in Europe, 1959 in the United States, and about 1960 in a number of other African countries. The survey of the classification of African languages in the last section of this article is, with a few minor refinements, that proposed by Joseph H. Greenberg in 1963. Recently, some revisions in the subclassification of the Niger-Congo languages have been suggested, Edgar Gregerson has recently theorized that the Nilo-Saharan and Niger-Kordofanian language families may have been related in the extremely distant past as members of an even older "Kongo-Saharan" superfamily.

Characteristics of African Languages

Because of the variety and number of African languages, they possess a number of phonetic and grammatical features, as well as marked similarities within families.

Phonetic Characteristics. Although the Khoisan languages, spoken by some hunting and gathering or cattle-raising peoples in southern Africa, make up only a fraction of the languages of Africa, they are of special interest because of their unique use of "click" consonants. This click is similar to the sound one makes when saying "tsk, tsk" or that one uses to spur on a horse. In most Khoisan languages, almost every noun, verb, and adjective begins with such a click. The use of clicks has spread into some neighboring Bantu languages, notably IsiXhosa; they are generally represented in the written language by the letters *c, x,* and *q,* which are not needed to represent other sounds.

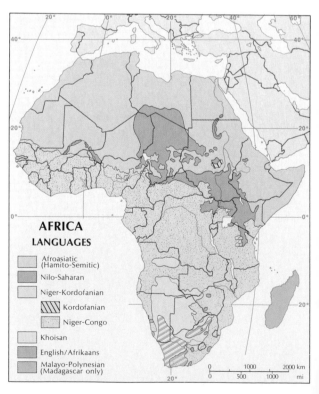

AFRICA

LANGUAGES

Afroasiatic (Hamito-Semitic)

Nilo-Saharan

Niger-Kordofanian

Kordofanian

Niger-Congo

Khoisan

English/Afrikaans

Malayo-Polynesian (Madagascar only)

0   1000   2000 km

0   500   1000   mi

Languages of the Niger-Kordofanian and Nilo-Saharan families, spoken by the majority of Saharan and sub-Saharan peoples, generally do not permit consonant sequences like those in such English words as *struts* or *prints*. Consonants followed by "glides," such as the *w* and *y* sounds, however, are common. Other common consonantal sequences are a nasal followed by an oral consonant: *mb, nd*, and *ng, mp, nt, nk,* and other combinations. These may function as unit consonants; some well-known names, for example, are properly syllabified as Ta-nza-ni-a, U-ga-nda, and Zi-mba-bwe. In some languages, however, nasals may be syllables in their own right; they are just hummed, without a preceding or following vowel.

Almost all languages of sub-Saharan Africa are tone languages; the northern West Atlantic languages, Swahili, and a few others are not. In a tone language, distinctions in pitch are as important as distinctions in consonants or vowels. In Igbo, for example, *ákwà* (high-low) means "cloth", *àkwà* (low-low) means "bed", and *àkwá* (low-high) means "egg." Tone may also signal grammatical differences. For example, in Kpelle, *è pìlì* (low-low-low) means "he jumped," but *é pílí* (high-high-high) means "he should jump." Some languages have two to four distinct tone levels; others have two, sometimes three levels, plus a slight lowering of nonlow tones, as much as six or seven times in a phrase or sentence.

Grammatical Characteristics. A striking grammatical feature of most African languages is that modifiers come after, rather than before, the noun. For example, the translation of the Swahili phrase *kisu kikubwa kimoja kile changu* ("that one big knife of mine") is literally "knife big one that my." In some languages, as in English, an object follows a verb. This is the rule in Igbo: *ó zuru mmà* ("he stole a knife"). However, in Kpelle the verb follows the object: *è kàli yà* (literally, "he a hoe bought").

At least some languages in every branch of the Niger-Kordofanian family, except Mande, have noun classes and agreement, or concord. Personal nouns in Swahili, for instance, have a singular prefix *m-* and a plural prefix *wa-*. Other singular-plural pairs are used as well as a "liquid mass" class with the prefix *ma-*, for example, *maji* ("water") and *mafuta* ("oil"). Each prefix determines an appropriate concord prefix for noun modifiers as well as for verbal subject and object markers. Such systems vary from language to language, including the use of class-marking suffixes rather than prefixes, but recognizable similarities pervade the Niger-Kordofanian languages.

Classification

Four main language families—groups of languages presumably descended from distinct ancestral languages—are recognized in Africa: Afroasiatic, Nilo-Saharan, Niger-Kordofanian, and Khoisan.

Afroasiatic. The various languages of the AFROASIATIC family are spoken primarily in northern Africa and in Ethiopia and Somalia, as well as outside Africa. The branch called Chadic is spoken in northern Nigeria and adjacent territories. Hausa is the most widely spoken of the Chadic languages and, after Swahili, the second most widely spoken language of sub-Saharan Africa. Between 10 and 15 million people are native Hausa speakers, and many others use it as a second language.

Nilo-Saharan. Languages in the Nilo-Saharan family are spoken in and just south of the Sahara, from Mali in the west to the Nile basin, and southward into Uganda, Kenya, and northern Tanzania. Consisting of Songhai, Dyerma, and Dendi, the Songhai branch of Nilo-Saharan is spoken along the great bend of the Niger from Mali to northwestern Nigeria. The Saharan branch, primarily Kanuri and Teda, is spoken from northeastern Nigeria north through Niger and Chad to the Libyan border. Maban, Fur, and Koman are three smaller branches.

The remaining branch of the Nilo-Saharan family is Chari-Nile. Several Chari-Nile languages, most spoken by only a small number of people, form the Central Sudanic group of languages, spoken by people scattered from the vicinity of Lake Chad to the Nile basin. An Eastern Sudanic group includes the Nilotic languages: Dinka, spoken by people of the savanna country around the Nile basin in southern Sudan; Nuer and Shilluk, also spoken in southern Sudan; Achooli and Lwo in Uganda; Nandi and Suk in Kenya; and Masai in northern Tanzania. Two small isolated languages, Berta and Kunama, complete the Chari-Nile branch.

Niger-Kordofanian. The Niger-Kordofanian languages are spoken in nearly all the areas from Senegal to Kenya and south to South Africa. Niger-Kordofanian is divided into two subfamilies: the smaller Kordofanian, which encompasses five branches—Koalib, Teqali, Talodi, Tumtum, and Katla—spoken in southern Sudan, and Niger-Congo, which includes a majority of all the languages of Africa.

The Niger-Congo subfamily comprises seven or eight branches. The Mande branch was apparently the first to diverge from the parent Niger-Congo stock, possibly 6,000 years ago. Mande languages are spoken in a large area of West Africa, from Senegal and Mali to Liberia and Ivory Coast (Côte d'Ivoire), but not along the Atlantic, except in Liberia, where a Vai-speaking population exists. Isolated Mande languages are spoken in eastern Ivory Coast and western Ghana, in Burkina Faso (formerly Upper Volta), and in Benin and Nigeria. Mandekan, the most widely spoken Mande language, is better known by the names of its major dialects—Bambara, Maninka or Malinke, and Dyula. Other important Mande languages are Mende in Sierra Leone and Kpelle in Liberia.

A second branch of Niger-Congo is West Atlantic, which may include two distinct branches of the subfamily—northern and southern; the latter is also called Mel. The major Mel language is Temne, spoken in Sierra Leone. The northern West Atlantic languages of Niger-Congo include Wolof, the major language of Senegal and its capital city, Dakar. Much more widely spoken, however, is Fula (also known as Fulani, Fulbe, or Peul). Major Fula concentrations are found in northern Guinea and about 2,400 km (1,500 mi) to the east, in northeastern Nigeria and Cameroon. Between these extremes are other permanent Fula settlements, and many more Fula speakers are seminomadic cattle herdsmen. Several West Atlantic languages are spoken by small groups of people along or near the Atlantic coast from Senegal to Liberia.

The Kru branch of Niger-Congo consists of about 30 languages spoken in southeastern Liberia and southwestern Ivory Coast. Probably the most widely used is the language known as Krahn in Liberia and as Guéré in Ivory Coast. Better known are Bassa, Kru, and Grebo in Liberia, and Bete in Ivory Coast. The Gur, or Voltaic, branch of Niger-Congo is spoken in interior parts of West Africa, from eastern Mali and northern Ivory Coast through northern Benin. The most widely used Gur language is Mooré, spoken by the Mossi people of Burkina; other languages of this group include Gurma, Dagomba, Kabre, Senufo, and Bariba.

Languages of the Kwa branch of Niger-Congo are spoken along the south-facing Atlantic coast from central Ivory Coast to Cameroon. Some major Kwa languages are Baule in Ivory Coast; Akan, including Fante, Twi, and Ashanti, in Ghana; Ewe in Ghana, and Togo along with Fon in Benin (the two perhaps constitute a single language); and Yoruba, Igbo (also known as Ibo), and Efik in Nigeria.

Languages of the Adamawa-Eastern branch are spoken from northeastern Nigeria east to Sudan, north almost to the Sahara, and south to extreme northern Zaire. Zande is spoken in northern Zaire and adjacent parts of Sudan and the Central African Republic. Sango, a derivative of Ngbandi in northern Zaire, has become a widespread language of trade and government in the Central African Republic and Chad.

The Benue-Congo branch of Niger-Congo includes a number of groups of languages in northern and eastern Nigeria, most not widely spoken, and almost all languages of the great southern projection of Africa from Nigeria to northern Kenya to Capetown. The latter are the well-known Bantu languages, long thought to be an independent language family because of the vast area in which they are spoken, the large number of languages that can be considered Bantu, and the large number of their speakers.

Most Bantu language names consist of a prefix and a stem. What is widely known as "Swahili," for example, is properly KiSwahili; in written references, the stem *-Swahili* is capitalized, because non-Africans commonly use the stem alone. According to this convention, the following Bantu languages, each spoken by a million or more people, may be distinguished: KiKongo and LiNgala (Zaire); Umbundu (Angola); IsiZulu and IsiXhosa, which are mutually intelligible (South Africa); SeSotho, SePedi, Setswana, which are mutually intelligible (Lesotho, Botswana, South Africa); ChiShona (Zimbabwe); ChiBemba (Zambia and Zaire); ChiNyanja (Malawi); ShiTswa (Mozambique); KinyaRwanda and KiRundi, which are mutually intelligible (Burundi and Rwanda); LuGanda (Uganda); GiKikuyu (Kenya); and KiSwahili (Tanzania, Kenya, and, to some extent, Uganda and Zaire).

Khoisan. The smallest language family of Africa is the Khoisan. Most Khoisan languages are spoken by the San Bushmen and Khoikhoi Hottentots of southern Africa. These peoples include a few cattle-raising groups such as the Nama, and hunting and gathering groups in the Kalahari Desert of Botswana and Namibia. Many of these are bands of fewer than a hundred speakers of distinct languages. Also included in the Khoisan family are two languages in northern Tanzania: Sandawe and Hatza. Many of the Pygmy groups found in Zaire and Cameroon are thought to be Khoisan peoples who have adopted their neighbors' Niger-Congo languages.

African literature   African literature comprises the oral and written works of the continent, composed in either African languages or foreign ones. Most formal African literature is still developing distinctive styles. The widespread African oral tradition, however, is rich in folktales, myths, riddles, and proverbs. Although some African poetry was written more than a thousand years ago, the majority of African literary works have been produced in the 20th century only, most of them after World War II. The earliest examples are Muslim-inspired religious writings from North Africa. Much of sub-Saharan Africa was illiterate until Christian missionaries arrived in the 19th century. Therefore, little African literature has existed for more than a hundred years; the major exceptions are an Arabic literature in the western Sudan, Swahili literature on the East African coast, and Ge'ez literature in Ethiopia.

African-language Literatures

Linguists estimate that more than a thousand languages are spoken in Africa. Written creative literature—novels, short stories, plays, and poetry—has been produced in about 50 of these. Because most early works were published by missionaries, they are heavily imbued with Christian didacticism. The first full-length narratives in Sesotho, Yoruba, and Ibo were modeled on John Bunyan's 17th-century allegory Pilgrim's Progress. The first written literature in several other African languages consisted of translated church hymns and retold biblical stories. Later, as more of the population became literate and government agencies began to publish books, newspapers, and magazines in local languages, a secular literature emerged, much of it focusing on problems of personal adjustment to Western ways or modern institutions.

The most important African literary languages are Sesotho, Xhosa, Zulu, and Northern Sotho in southern Africa; Nyanja, Bemba, and Shona in Central Africa; Swahili and Luganda in East Africa; and Yoruba, Asante-Twi, Akuampem-Twi, and Ewe in West Africa. The best-known works from these literatures are Thomas Mofolo's legendary romance *Chaka the Zulu* (1925; Eng. trans., 1931) and D. O. Fagunwa's folkloric *The Forest of a Thousand Daemons* (1938; Eng. trans., 1968).

African Literature in European Languages

African literature written in European languages—notably French (Francophone), English (Anglophone), and Portuguese (Lusophone)—is better known outside Africa than are translated works.

French. French-African writing first attracted international attention in the 1930s, when African and Caribbean students in Paris launched a literary and philosophical movement known as Negritude. By the late 1940s one of the founders of the movement, the Senegalese poet and statesman Léopold Sédar SENGHOR, had published his first volumes of verse, edited an influential anthology of Negritude poetry, and helped establish (1947) *Présence Africaine* as the most important literary journal in the black world. As a movement, Negritude was greatly influenced by such European political and artistic movements as Marxism and surrealism and by the Afro-American cultural awakening known as the Harlem Renaissance.

Negritude poetry fused anticolonial political ideas with romantic evocations of an idyllic African past expressed in vivid surrealist images. In the 1950s, as African nations prepared for independence, this highly charged poetry, emphasizing the humanity of black peoples, gave way to prose satirizing the colonizer and the colonized. Since independence, however, French-African writers have focused on current problems. Other influential French-African writers include Birago DIOP, Camara LAYE, Mongo Beti, David Diop, Ferdinand Oyono, Jean Joseph Rabearivelo, and Tchicaya U Tam'si.

English. The first major works in West Africa appeared in the 1950s at the end of the colonial era and were primarily concerned with reinterpreting African history from an indigenous point of view that stressed the dignity of the African past. Chinua ACHEBE's novel *Things Fall Apart* (1958) documents the disintegration of a rural community under the impact of Westernization; another classic is Amos TUTUOLA's *The Palm-Wine Drunkard* (1952). After independence, the literary emphasis changed from a preoccupation with the past to a confrontation with the present. Wole SOYINKA, Achebe, and Ayi Kwei Armah wrote bitter satires of contemporary evils in their societies, and Nigerian poets, novelists, and dramatists have described the horrors of the Nigerian-Biafran war.

Writers in Anglophone East Africa followed those of West Africa in first producing anticolonial fiction and then self-critical, satirical fiction and drama. The early works of Kenya's leading novelist, NGUGI WA THIONG'O, express nationalistic enthusiasm, but his later ones, postindependence disillusion. The East African literary scene is distinguished from that of West Africa by its poetry, particularly the comic singing introduced by Okot p'Bitek in *Song of Lawino* (1966).

In South Africa, creative writing in English by blacks and by Coloureds (racially mixed South Africans) has been impeded by racial oppression and censorship. The novelist Peter ABRAHAMS found conditions so repressive that he left South Africa in 1939 at age 20. The harsh Publications and Entertainments Act of 1963 severely limited publishing by nonwhites, and by the mid-1970s even black poetry was banned; many poets were imprisoned, and many others—including Dennis Brutus—fled. The literary works of white South Africans, even those critical of the regime, have generally been better received. Among the best-known white writers in English are Athol FUGARD, Nadine GORDIMER, Alan PATON, Olive SCHREINER, and Roy Campbell. (For a discussion of literature written in Afrikaans, see AFRIKANERS.)

Portuguese. Poetry has been the favorite literary form in Portuguese-speaking areas of Africa since the 19th century, but strong short-story movements emerged in Angola and Mozambique in the 1950s. Anticolonial political themes dominated until the mid-1970s, when Angola, Mozambique, and Guinea-Bissau achieved independence. Today, writers in Lusophone Africa are no longer concerned with white European models but base their work on indigenous African themes.

Recent Trends. Wole Soyinka won the Nobel Prize for literature in 1986—the first time a black African writer had been so honored and, in fact, the first international honor in literature ever won by a black African. Among the African authors now published in English, a number have been translated from the French. They include Sony Labou Tansi (*The Parentheses of Blood*, 1986), a Zairian whom some rank as the most talented contemporary black African writer, and North Africans such as the Moroccan, Driss Chraibi (*Flutes of Death*, 1985), Buchi Emecheta (*The Rape of Shavi*, 1985), a Nigerian woman, has written a number of novels in English. Many other black writers are published in Africa. Most continue to use French or English, although the influence of African languages is changing the feeling and meaning of these colonial tongues.

African music   The many music cultures of Africa may be broadly classified as North African and sub-Saharan. This article discusses only traditional music of the dominant population south of the Sahara, for North African culture is essentially Islamic or Arabic. The diversity of this population is reflected both in the number of languages spoken—about 800 to 1,000—and in the wide variety of music traditions cultivated. Fortunately, these traditions have many traits in common, permitting a discussion of them in general terms.

Musical Instruments

Africa probably has the largest variety of drums to be found in any continent, but virtually every other type of musical instrument is also represented throughout Africa.

Some distinctively African instruments, however, are unique to the continent. Of the drums, the most characteristically African are those known as "talking drums" because they can reproduce the tonal inflections and rhythms of African languages. Their musical potential is also fully realized. The western African hourglass drum is the most versatile talking drum. Squeezing the lacing between the two heads produces pitches that can vary more than an octave. The slit drum is made from a hollowed log on which two tones are produced by striking on either side of a longitudinal slot.

Of the myriad types of rattle, the western African net rattle, made of a handle gourd encased in a beaded net, is unique. The Yoruba *shekere* of Nigeria has a tight net, and the loose net on the Mende *shegbule* of Sierra Leone is held taut by the player. Because of the external beads, precise rhythms can be played on both these versions of the net rattle.

Xylophones, widespread in Africa, are of two basic types. The frame xylophone, such as those played by the

Mandé and Lobi of West Africa, the Fang of Cameroon, and the Chopi of Mozambique, has gourd resonators hung beneath each key. The loose-key xylophone, such as the Ganda *amadinda* of Uganda, is left unassembled when not in use; when played, the keys are laid across two banana stems.

As widespread as the xylophone, and unique to African and African-derived cultures, is the *mbira*, which consists of flat iron strips mounted on a board or box with one end of each strip left free to be plucked by the thumbs or thumbs and forefingers.

The simplest of the many stringed instruments found throughout Africa is the musical bow, resonated with a gourd or with the mouth of the player. Zithers and harps are common in eastern and central Africa, and the lyre, which has a hemispherical or rectangular body and two arms extending to a crossbar where the strings are attached, is played in Ethiopia and Uganda.

In western Africa the most common stringed instrument is the skin-covered lute, either boat-shaped with two to five plucked strings or hemispherical with one bowed string.

Three stringed instruments unique to Africa are the bridge harp (or harp lute), the harp zither, and the bow lute. The best-known form of the bridge harp is the 21-string Manding *kora* of western Africa. It is held facing the player, who plucks two planes of strings mounted in notches on either side of a high bridge. The harp zither, best known as the Fang *mvet* of Cameroon, also has a notched bridge that is mounted in the center of its long tubular body. The bow lute, such as the Bambara *ndang*, is plucked and has an individual curved neck for each string.

The flutes of Africa are of every type except the recorder. In eastern, central, and southern Africa, groups of musicians play sets of single-note vertical pipes, each person contributing a single note to create a complex polyphonic texture. Panpipes are also played in this area. Of the various reed instruments of Africa, the most notable is the Hausa *algaita* of Nigeria, a short conical-bore double reed. African trumpets include the *kakaki*, a straight herald trumpet of tin associated with Hausa aristocracy, but the most typical African trumpets are made of natural animal horns, ivory, or hollowed wood and are played in sets in the same manner as the single-note vertical pipes.

Musicians

Music is closely integrated into everyday activities in Africa. Vocal music, instrumental music, and dance are often inseparable, and the emphasis is on participation rather than on performance before an audience. Even in traditions where professionalism or virtuosity does result in a distinction between performer and audience, the audience often dances to show its appreciation.

Whether daily or festive, almost all African music plays a strong socializing role. Annoyances and jealousies are often vented in extemporized, obliquely stated song texts, which, if sung within hearing of the offender, can achieve the desired effect. Work-synchronizing songs promote efficiency and, together with those calendrical events in which everyone takes part, contribute to a feeling of group solidarity. Music and instruments associated with royalty or leadership command respect. In the past, some societies even regarded royal instruments as the seat of the king's power; if they were captured by enemies, it marked the downfall of the kingdom.

In those societies in which a high degree of political

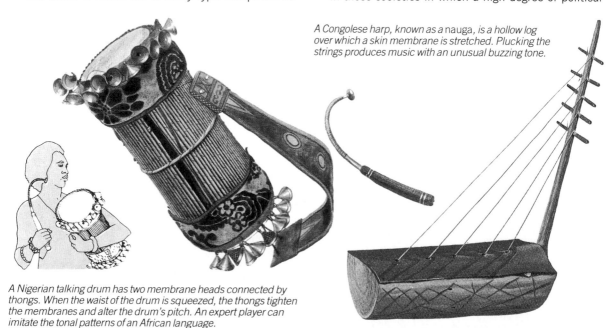

A Congolese harp, known as a nauga, *is a hollow log over which a skin membrane is stretched. Plucking the strings produces music with an unusual buzzing tone.*

A Nigerian talking drum has two membrane heads connected by thongs. When the waist of the drum is squeezed, the thongs tighten the membranes and alter the drum's pitch. An expert player can imitate the tonal patterns of an African language.

Members of a Hausa instrumental ensemble from northern Nigeria play the duma (1), the obodo (2), the gangi (3), the goge (4), the shantu (5), the sarewa (6), and the silver flute (7). The duma is a spherical drum made from a hollow gourd over which a skin is stretched. The musician beats the drum with one hand and a slightly bent stick. The obodo is a talking drum that has a wide tonal range. It is played with a narrow, curved stick. The gangi is a drum made from a calabash gourd. It is held against the musician's chest and beaten with two sticks. The goge is a lute-type instrument played with a bow. The soundboard is made of a calabash gourd and crocodile skin. The shantu, a horn instrument, is made from various sizes of gourds that are joined together with cow skin. When it is blown, a buzzing sound is produced. The sarewa is a flute made of bamboo and a cow's horn. A silver flute has a chain hanging from its bell, which affects the resonance.

organization exists, in which royal courts once flourished, and in which craft specialization has developed, the role of the musician is more clearly defined and distinct. For example, in the West African savanna, complex hierarchical societies grew hand in hand with the great empires of the 10th to 20th centuries, and musicianship and such related skills as oratory, historical narrative, genealogy, and stylized praise developed into a hereditary profession.

Today, descendants of these empires still largely regard music and related activities as the exclusive province of particular families. Although present-day musicians (known as *griots*) in these societies no longer perform at the courts of kings, they still direct much of their attention to the wealthy and influential, encouraging historical awareness through their commemorative songs. Their role is important, and their status is similar to that of professional experts anywhere. These musicians are highly respected for their knowledge and abilities and are valued for their role in ceremonies and festivities. At the same time, they are regarded with a degree of caution, because of the potential power of their words and actions. The privileges afforded members of the profession often include the right to criticize or make moral judgments.

As in all parts of the world today, the live performance of music in Africa is threatened by the ever-increasing popularity of transistor radios, cassette tape recorders, and other sources of recorded sound. Still, the participatory nature of most African music and its close association with dance assure the continuance of live performances for many occasions.

Stylistic Traits

In general, the sound of African music may be characterized as polyphonic (see POLYPHONY). Vocal-instrumental combinations are as common as purely instrumental music, and in all types of music a predilection for the combination of melodic and rhythmic sounds is apparent. Nearly all melodic instruments of Africa (including many drums) have a device that provides a percussive rhythmic accompaniment.

The stylistic trait for which African music is most famous is rhythmic organization. Although individual parts in some performances may be extremely complex rhythmically, in most instances rhythmic complexity is created by the manner in which the relatively simple rhythms of individual parts are combined. This combination is often effected in such a way that the accent patterns of each part run counter to each other, creating a composite rhythm or melody that no single part can play alone.

African melodies are built on scales of five, six, and

seven tones, and the intervals used are sufficiently close to Western scales to sound familiar and appealing. In addition, multipart music often employs the harmonic intervals of thirds, fourths, and fifths. The melodic style of instrumental music is based on a short repeated phrase (ostinato) that is subjected to minute but continuous variation with occasional breaks for longer improvised passages. Vocal lines may also be short but are often extremely long and complex. A descending melodic line is common, reflecting the tonal nature of many African languages.

The formal structure of most African music is based on the ostinato. In some performances several different ostinatos may be repeated in various sequences at the discretion of the performer. The ostinato form is used in vocal music as well, but it is usually modified by the addition of a solo part inserted between repetitions of the unchanging chorus part. The potentials for variation of this basic form are exploited to the fullest throughout the continent. An overriding stylistic trait of African music is its ability to generate an engaging mood and active involvement in the performance.

African National Congress   The African National Congress (ANC) is the foremost South African black nationalist movement. Formed in 1912, it originally stressed peaceful protest and dialogue with whites. The ANC became more militant in the 1940s, sponsoring strikes, marches, and protests against discriminatory legislation. In 1949 the ANC Youth League, led by Oliver Tambo, Nelson MANDELA, Walter Sisulu, and Anton Lembede, gained control of the organization. Membership soared in the early 1950s as the ANC, headed by Albert LUTHULI, promoted passive resistance campaigns. In 1955 the ANC issued its Freedom Charter, which calls for a nonracial democracy in South Africa. A period of increased militancy followed. The massacre of blacks protesting the pass laws at Sharpeville in 1960 led the ANC to call for nationwide work stoppages and civil disobedience. The government retaliated by declaring a state of emergency, banning the ANC, and detaining many of their leaders.

Nelson Mandela went underground and formed Umkhonto we Sizwe (Spear of the Nation), which began a campaign of sabotage against police stations and other symbols of APARTHEID. Mandela, who was sentenced to life imprisonment in 1964, became the symbolic leader of the nationalist movement. The ANC gained widespread support among black youths after the massacre of student protesters in Soweto in 1976. Many young militants left South Africa for ANC bases in neighboring countries. Despite South African raids on these bases in the 1980s, guerrilla and sabotage activities increased.

The 1989 Harare Declaration listed the ANC's conditions for negotiations with the government. Sisulu and others were released in October 1989, and the 30-year ban on the ANC was lifted in February 1990. Mandela was released that same month and named effective head of the ANC in March. In August the ANC suspended its armed struggle against white rule, although violence between followers of the ANC and of Zulu chief Gatsha Buthelezi's Inkatha movement intensified.

African prehistory   African prehistory encompasses the vast span of time before the practice of making written records began in Africa. The greater part of the continent's history lies within the realm of prehistory and can only be ascertained through archaeology, historical linguistics and related disciplines, and oral traditions (as far as they will reach back in time and only to the point where they are reliable).

The field of African prehistory is of special importance because more than 90 percent of the evidence concerning human origins has thus far come from Africa. Consequently, in the past several decades archaeological research in Africa has been part of a massive, investigative campaign that has involved many disciplines and research tools and a large, dedicated body of scientists.

Prehistoric Archaeology in Africa

Grounds now exist for the belief that it was in eastern Africa from Ethiopia to the Transvaal, where more early hominid fossils have been found than anywhere else in the world, that PREHISTORIC HUMANS evolved out of the common ancestry they shared with the apes. These ancestors occupied Africa at the time—about 20 million years ago—when CONTINENTAL DRIFT joined Africa to southern Asia. With the final shrinking of the sea then lying between the two continents, much of this tropical area became savanna or grassland.

About 14 million years ago an ape called *Ramapithecus* appeared that was better adapted to these new conditions; some archaeologists consider it the earliest known hominid, or ancestral human, although many do not. *Ramapithecus* probably did not walk upright, but between 8 million and 5 million years ago this ability did evolve in other ancestral forms. Important finds have been made of a number of bipedal hominids in the Afar and the Omo valleys in Ethiopia, on the shores of Lake Turkana (Rudolf) in Kenya, in OLDUVAI GORGE and Laetolil in Tanzania, and, in South Africa, at Makapansgat, Sterkfontein, Taung, Kromdraai, and Swartkrans. Among them were three AUSTRALOPITHECUS species, *A. africanus* and the later *A. robustus* and *A. boisei*. Many archaeologists consider *A. africanus* the first directly ancestral hominid, but this also remains a subject of unresolved debate. It is not clear whether these species were toolmakers and tool users; this ability more likely arose in another hominid, HOMO HABILIS, which evolved before the later species of *Australopithecus* had become extinct.

Old Stone Age in Africa. The earliest recognizable stone artifacts, dating from about 2 million years ago, have been found at East Turkana, in the Shungura Formation of the Lower Omo Valley, and at Olduvai Gorge. The Oldowan stone-tools tradition, primarily rough choppers, was succeeded, about 1 million years ago, by the so-called developed Oldowan, characterized by bifacial protohandaxes and scrapers. Acheulean tool industries (after

(Above) *Skull 1470, one of the oldest "complete" hominid skulls in existence, was discovered in 1972 by a fossil-hunting team near Lake Turkana, in Kenya. Its age has been put at 2.6 to 1.8 million years.*

(Left) *Famed British anthropologists Louis and Mary Leakey gaze out over Olduvai Gorge in northern Tanzania, site of their discovery of 1.8 million-year-old* Homo habilis, *or "tool-using man." The Leakeys' excavations have advanced the idea that the earliest ancestors of the human species evolved on the African continent.*

Saint Acheul in France, where they were first recognized) are characterized by many varieties of oval, pointed, and cleaver-edged handaxes. Acheulean tools are commonly associated with a more advanced type of hominid, HOMO ERECTUS. *Homo erectus* had a brain about twice the size of the australopithecines but only two-thirds the size of modern humans. This hominid species succeeded in "breaking out" of East Africa and spreading Acheulean tools over southern Eurasia, as well as other parts of Africa. In some areas, however, *Homo erectus* seems to have maintained the chopping-tool tradition.

Sites in Africa associated with *H. erectus* remains or early Acheulean tools include Sidi Abderrahman in Morocco; Ternifine in Algeria; Melka Kontoure in Ethiopia; Peninj in Kenya; and Swartkrans, Vereeniging, Sterkfontein, and Stellenbosch in South Africa. Later Acheulean sites have been investigated at AÏN HANECH in Algeria, Olorgesailie and Olduvai Gorge in Kenya, Kalambo Falls in Zambia, Kamoa in Zaire, and the Cave of Hearths in South Africa. (See PALEOLITHIC PERIOD.)

Middle Stone Age in Africa. The Acheulean tool industry persisted for a long time, until 100,000 to 50,000 years ago, but thereafter an increasing regionalized specialization occurred, first among the industries called Fauresmith in southern Africa and Sangoan in central and western Africa, and later among those of the African Middle Stone Age (see MESOLITHIC PERIOD). The human type in Africa was by then comparable to that of the NEANDERTHALERS of Europe and western Asia and includes the fossils of Broken Hill Man in Zambia and Saldanha man in South Africa.

Much greater regional diversity began to occur in Africa's Middle Stone Age. More and more specialized tool industries developed as different groups of the growing population adapted their way of life to a greater variety of ecological niches. Hunting, fishing, and gathering remained the basic way of life. The Acheuleans had a wooden thrusting spear, which later was made more lethal with a stone point, and many of the Middle Stone Age peoples had a light stone-tipped throwing spear. Modern humans, *Homo sapiens sapiens*, now ranged throughout Africa, and by the beginning of the Late Stone Age they used the bow and arrow and made composite tools of wood, stone, and bone.

Late Stone Age in Africa. In northwest Africa, the Aterian (c.40,000–25,000 BC), an advanced tool industry of the Middle Stone Age, was succeeded by the Oranian (c.14,000–8,000 BC) and Capsian (c.7,000–4,000 BC) tool cultures. South of the Sahara the Late Stone Age seems to have begun at dates ranging from 40,000 to 10,000 BC in different areas. Small shaped-stone artifacts, known as microliths—some of which were slotted into arrow shafts to make the points and barbs—indicate that in these communities hunting was an important economic activity. Gathering the products of the wild was also important, although it seems to have left less obvious traces in the archaeological record. (See NEOLITHIC PERIOD.)

As population increased, different communities ex-

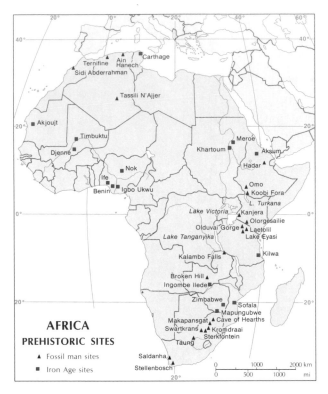

AFRICA
PREHISTORIC SITES

▲ Fossil man sites

■ Iron Age sites

that wild grain was extensively collected. Nubian cemeteries dating from 10,000 BC contain bodies pierced by stone arrow-points, which suggests intercommunity warfare.

From the 6th to the 4th millennium BC, the southern Sahara and the Sahel were considerably wetter than at present and supported communities that depended on fish from lakes and rivers for a considerable part of their diet, which would seem to imply at least a semisedentary type of existence.

Animal and Plant Domestication. The central Sahara was also wetter than at present, and the highlands in particular supported large numbers of cattle pastoralists. The cattle, widely portrayed in prehistoric rock art, may have been derived from an indigenous domestication of the wild North African ox or from cattle introduced via Tunisia or Egypt. The culture of these pastoralists and fishing peoples is sometimes referred to as the Saharan Neolithic.

By the 5th millennium BC, people in the lower Nile Valley adopted cereal agriculture, using the Nile floodwaters to irrigate their crops of wheat and barley. In sub-Saharan Africa, which lies in the summer rainfall area, it is impossible to grow wheat and barley by dry-farming methods. Therefore, local wild grasses had to be domesticated to form the African tropical cereals known today: the millets (Guinea corn, or sorghum; pearl, or bulrush; millet; finger millet); African rice; fonio; chindumba; and the tiny Ethiopian grain called teff. These cereals were domesticated in different areas of a broad zone stretching south of the Sahara from Senegal in the west to Ethiopia in the east and down into the northern Great Lakes.

From the beginning of the 3d millennium BC the Sahara began to dry up. The fishing populations must have found that the stands of wild grasses that they also depended on became thinner and harder to find, which probably stimulated the process of cereal domestication.

ploited an even greater range of environments and devised more specialized techniques for dealing with them. Seasonal movement was often involved, and in Nubia and in areas near the Nile Valley in Egypt, evidence indicates

Prehistoric rock paintings at Tassili n' Ajjer, in the Algerian Sahara, are believed to have been made about 3000 BC. Animals and agricultural activities portrayed in the artworks indicate that the region had a wetter climate before the Sahara Desert expanded.

A bronze head produced by the lost-wax method illustrates the quality of metalwork in 13th-century Ife, Nigeria.

from the Stone Age into the IRON AGE. Apparently only in Nubia and in the extreme west, in Mauritania, was there a period during which copper was exploited for tools and weapons before the advent of an iron technology. At Akjoujt, Mauritania, copper ores were exploited in the 5th century BC, and numerous copper arrowheads and other weapons and tools have been found in the surrounding area. It is not known whether the metallurgy practiced at Akjoujt gave rise to an iron technology or whether this knowledge was introduced to sub-Saharan West Africa from the area of North Africa influenced by CARTHAGE or from the Nubian kingdom of MEROË. Iron-smelting furnaces of about the 4th century BC in central Nigeria are associated with the Nok people, who produced the remarkable terra-cotta heads for which the Nok culture is famous. By the early 2d century AD, Meroë had been surpassed in importance by the newly emergent power of AKSUM. This kingdom was founded farther to the east in the highlands of present-day Ethiopia by Semitic-speakers who had earlier come from southern Arabia.

By this time there were long-established farming communities throughout the savanna lands. In the eastern forests of West Africa food production had also been established, presumably based on yams, tuberous crops, and oil-palm products. In the central parts of eastern Nigeria and in Cameroon, people speaking a language ancestral to the BANTU group of languages apparently began to move eastward through what is today the Central African Republic. In their migration they reached the northeast angle of the equatorial rain forest, where they turned southward. What generated this movement is not yet known; data are insufficient to demonstrate a population

Whatever the reason, domestication first occurred in the zone across Africa where they lived. Goats, sheep, and pigs must have been introduced into the rest of Africa from its northeast corner.

Bronze Age and Iron Age Africa

Most of sub-Saharan Africa missed out on a BRONZE AGE and passed directly, at different times in different areas,

The Zimbabwe Ruins, near Lake Kyle, consist of stone structures extending over an area of about 24 ha (60 acres). The site was first occupied by Iron Age farmers in the 4th century AD. From the 13th to the 15th centuries it was a center of the East African gold and copper trade.

explosion as the stimulus, although this is the most commonly offered explanation.

Another group from the same homeland area in southern Cameroon apparently reached the savanna lands south of the equatorial forest, either by traveling along the coast or along Zaire River tributaries, at a somewhat later date. These eastern and western streams of Bantu interacted and dispersed in complex ways over the rest of southern Africa as far as a line from Windhoek to Port Alfred. Much of this area had been inhabited by hunter-gatherer Khoisan-speaking peoples, among them the SAN (Bushmen). In some places the Khoisan-speakers survived and were able to maintain their way of life alongside the Bantu-speaking farmers; in others they were driven out or absorbed. In West Africa, a stone technology appears to have remained in use for more than a thousand years after iron was first used in other places.

Where a population of settled peasants remains over a long period, towns and other kinds of centralized institutions tend to become established. Two situations in sub-Saharan Africa combined to delay centralization. First, Africa's indigenous cereal grains had to be domesticated. Unlike Egypt and Europe, Africa could not, for climatic reasons, accommodate the grain grasses that were domesticated in southwest Asia. Second, just when the urban arts were being developed in Egypt, the great desiccation of the 3d millennium BC changed the region of the Sahara from a broad grassland corridor into a massive desert barrier. Nevertheless, towns did emerge in a number of widely separated places. With the Arab conquest of North Africa in the 7th century, long-distance trading was injected into localized exchange networks south of the Sahara. This development further stimulated both the growth of urbanized communities and the centralization of political power.

The ancient kingdom of GHANA prospered as middleman in the gold trade between the West African forests and the Islamic world and was succeeded by the kingdoms of MALI and SONGHAI. The state Bono Manso was based on the same trade, with Begho as the collecting point for gold on the way to the great market center of Djenné. The center of political power later moved into the forest itself when the ASHANTI established power. BENIN, IFE, and Igbo-Ukwu were other important West African centers of wealth and artistic achievement.

Another route by which the Islamic and Indian world obtained the tropical African products they desired, above all ivory, was by sea from the East African coast. Beginning about the 9th century, voyagers from the Persian Gulf, and later from northwest India, were able to take advantage of the monsoon winds in the Indian Ocean and establish a string of entrepôts from the Somali coast as far south as Sofala; the most important and the best investigated is Kilwa. The great fortified center of ZIMBABWE prospered in the 14th century as a result of its middleman position in this trade.

African violet   African violet is the common name for about 24 species of small evergreen plants, native to

The African violet, a plant originally from eastern Africa, has velvety, oval leaves crowned by long-lasting flowers. Many hybrids and varieties have been developed, offering a wide range of colors and of petal shapes and numbers.

Tanzania and Kenya, that make up the genus *Saintpaulia* in the family Gesneriaceae, which also contains the gloxinia. Since its discovery in the late 19th century, *S. ionantha* has become a popular house and greenhouse plant; other species are also cultivated. The wild *S. ionantha* has five-petaled, violet flowers and densely paired, dark green leaves that may be purplish below.

Afrikaners   The Afrikaners are a South African people of Dutch or French Huguenot descent. Formerly also known as Boers (from the Dutch word for farmer), Afrikaners make up about 65 percent of South Africa's white population of 4,820,000 (1984 est.). Their language is Afrikaans, a derivative of Dutch.

History. The first Afrikaners were Dutch pioneers who settled (1652) in what is now Cape Province. During the 18th and 19th centuries, Afrikaans-speaking settlers pushed into the interior, fighting both their Bantu neighbors and the British (see GREAT TREK). They established two independent states, the South African Republic (1852; later the Transvaal) and the Orange Free State (1854). After the Afrikaner defeat in the Second SOUTH AFRICAN WAR (1899–1902), these territories were annexed by the British, and in 1910 the Union of South Africa was formed. Politically, the Afrikaners played a secondary role to the English-speaking South Africans until 1948, when the electoral victory of the Afrikaner NATIONAL PARTY institutionalized the Afrikaners' political supremacy in South Africa. Right-wing Afrikaners opposed to any weakening of APARTHEID formed the Herstigte Nasionale (1969), the Conservative party (1980), and such activist organizations as the Afrikaner Resistance Movement, which claims more than 10,000 members and maintains a private army.

Originally a rural people for the most part, the Afrikaners began to migrate to the towns at the end of World War I. (Today more than 70 percent live in cities.) Until relatively recently they were the least prosperous of the white groups, employed mainly in farming or in laboring jobs. During the 1930s, South Africa's "poor whites"—mainly Afrikaners—accounted for nearly half the white population. Afrikaners began to rise rapidly in the socioeconom-

The South African Voortrekker Monument, near Pretoria, commemorates the Great Trek of the 1830s and '40s. Some 14,000 Afrikaner farmers and their families migrated from the Cape Colony into the interior, to escape British rule and to find more and better lands to farm.

ic scale after World War II. Today they hold key positions in the South African government and in industries that were formerly largely controlled by English-speaking whites.

Religion. The overwhelming majority of Afrikaners are Calvinists and belong to the three Dutch Reformed churches, which have been a powerful integrating force since the first years of settlement. Urbanization, however, has somewhat diminished the hold of the churches, as it has also weakened the power of the traditional Afrikaner family.

Language. Once a rural patois spoken mainly by poor people (Dutch was the language of the well educated), Afrikaans is the most widely spoken language in South Africa. It is the native tongue not only of the Afrikaners but also of the majority of South Africa's COLOUREDS, a people of mixed Euro-African background. Together with English, Afrikaans is the official language of the Republic of South Africa.

The efforts of the Gennootskap van Regte Afrikaners, an Afrikaner nationalist organization, led to the publication of the first Afrikaans grammar (1876), and to increasing commitment to Afrikaans as the Afrikaners' national tongue—concern with Afrikaans has always formed an essential component of Afrikaner nationalism. In 1925, Afrikaans officially superseded Dutch.

Literature. At the same time that Afrikaans was winning acceptance as their national language, the Afrikaners were developing a distinctive literature. In its 19th-century beginnings, its focus was essentially rural and religious. Eugene Marais (1871–1936) wrote what is considered the first important poem in Afrikaans, "Winternag" (1905). In the early part of this century several Afrikaner writers, notably C. J. Langenhoven (1873–1932), worked to teach their people to read in their own language. Two Coloured poets, P. J. Philander (1921–) and Adam Small (1936–), have published notable work in Afrikaans. The novelist Andre Brink (1935–), who writes in English as well as Afrikaans, produced the first Afrikaans work to confront the issue of apartheid (*Looking on Darkness*, 1973; Eng. trans., 1974), which was also the first work in that language to be banned by the South African authorities.

Afrikaner writers better known to the English-speaking world—either because they write both in English and in Afrikaans, or because their works have been translated and widely reviewed—include Breyten BREYTENBACH, poet and writer of memoirs; and J. M. COETZEE, whose novels have received wide attention in the West.

Afro-American literature see AFRICAN-AMERICAN LITERATURE

Afroasiatic languages Also known as Hamito-Semitic languages, Afroasiatic languages are spoken by 175 million people representing a wide range of cultures through most of the Middle East, the Horn of Africa, North Africa, and much of West Africa. The languages include Arabic and Hebrew. Afroasiatic is commonly divided into five main branches based on ancient roots: Egyptian, Semitic, Cushitic, Berber, and Chad. Omotic, formerly called West Cushitic, has recently been suggested as a sixth branch. These languages differ in their particulars, and the exact relationship among the branches has not been established. Scholars postulate, however, that all are derived from an unknown ancestor language probably spoken in northeast Africa or the Sahara about the 6th millennium BC.

Egyptian

Egyptian is the oldest attested language of the family and has the longest continuous history. As a written language it proceeded in five stages. The first three—Old Egyptian (c.3000 to c.2200 BC), Middle Egyptian (c.2200 to c.1200 BC), and Late, or Neo-Egyptian (c.1300 to c.700 BC)—were written in HIEROGLYPHICS. Demotic (c.700 BC to AD c.300) was written in a simplified cursive script based on hieroglyphics and was spoken by early Christians. Coptic (from AD 300), written in an alphabet based on Greek, was still widely spoken in the 16th century, and one dialect, Bohairic, is now the liturgical language of the Christian Monophysite Coptic Church.

Semitic

Semitic was originally confined to the Near East but gradually spread to the Horn of Africa and then throughout North Africa. It has two major groups, which in turn comprise many smaller ones. Semitic embraces the languages used by a number of cultures prominent in ancient times, including the people of the BIBLE, as well as modern Arabic and Hebrew.

East Semitic includes Akkadian, the language of the Assyro-Babylonians spoken in Mesopotamia from c.3000 to c.400 BC. It was written, usually from left to right, in a cuneiform script. West Semitic can be divided into central and southern branches and embraces Hebrew, Aramaic, Arabic, South Arabian, and Ethiopian. Most languages in this group were or still are written from right to left in a consonantal script without marked vowels. As Hebrew, Syriac, and Arabic developed, users added diacritical vowel symbols, or "points," which are now optional.

Aramaic. One of the branches of Central Semitic, Aramaic was once the colloquial language of the Near East after the decline of Akkadian. It was the native tongue of Jesus Christ and the language of the Jewish Talmud. Syriac, one of its eastern branches, was used to transmit early Christian culture up to the 13th century. Today eastern Aramaic is still spoken by about 100,000 people—many of whom are Jacobite and Nestorian Christians—in northeast Iran and neighboring areas of Iraq and the USSR, as well as by Jews from the same region who have immigrated to Israel. Mandaic, the language of a Gnostic sect, is also still spoken in the region.

Arabic. As a literary language, Arabic dates back to the 7th century AD. It is the language of the KORAN, the holy book of Islam, and thus assumed tremendous importance because it was adopted by most of the peoples conquered and converted by Muslim Arabs. Arabic has also been spoken by the Christian and Jewish minorities of the Islamic world. A North African branch, spoken by Christians and written in Roman characters, is the official language of Malta.

Canaanite. Canaanite comprises Hebrew and such ancient languages as Phoenician-Punic, Moabite, and Ugaritic. Hebrew, attested from the 10th century BC to the present, is the language of Judaism and the Old Testament. Its original domain included what is now Israel and

nearby areas. Biblical Hebrew is found in texts dating from c.1000 to 400 BC. Mishnaic (Rabbinic) Hebrew (AD c.200) is the language of the MISHNAH, the first great legal document of Judaism, and shows the influence of vernacular Aramaic.

Medieval Hebrew (6th to 13th century) was the written language of religious literature and poetry of Arabic-speaking Jews, notably in Spain. Early modern Hebrew developed in the 18th century and became the vehicle for a secular literature and for correspondence between Jews, mainly in Eastern Europe. The Zionist settlers of Palestine (Israel) also adopted it as a colloquial language, as a result of the systemization by Eliezer BEN-YEHUDAH early in this century.

Phoenician-Punic was spoken in what is today Lebanon from the 10th century BC to the beginning of the Christian era. Phoenicians brought their language to the colonies they established around the Mediterranean, the most famous being CARTHAGE. Moabite, related to biblical Hebrew, died out long ago, as did Ugaritic. Written in a cuneiform consonantal script, Ugaritic was the language of the city of UGARIT up to the 14th century BC. Its affiliations, as well as those of Amorite and of the language of EBLA, remain disputed.

South Semitic. South Semitic is represented by three branches whose exact relationship has not yet been discerned. The original language of the southern half of the Arabian peninsula was South Arabian, not Arabic. Epigraphic South Arabian is known only from short inscriptions dating from the 9th century BC to the 6th century AD. Modern South Arabian is not a descendant of the former. These languages are spoken by about 25,000 people in the Dhofar and on the island of Socotra (Soqotri).

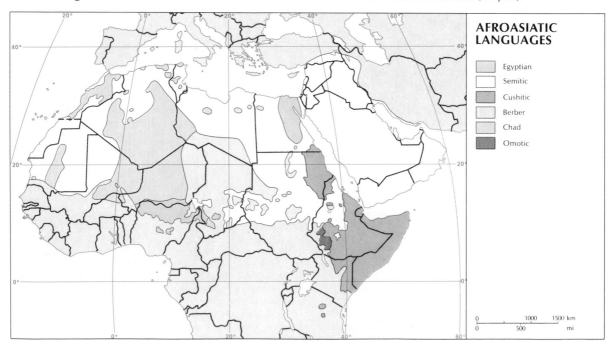

AFROASIATIC LANGUAGES

- Egyptian
- Semitic
- Cushitic
- Berber
- Chad
- Omotic

Ethiopian. Spoken in Ethiopia and Sudan in the Horn of Africa, Ethiopian languages were transplanted from South Arabia possibly around 2000 BC. The script, written from left to right, is a continuation of the South Arabian consonantal script. Here, however, a character stands for a consonant-vowel group, the vowel marked by a modification of the basic shape of the consonantal letter.

Ethiopian languages comprise northern and southern branches. In the North Ethiopic group—Ge'ez, Tigrinya, and Tigre—Ge'ez was the language of civilization centering on Aksum. First attested in inscriptions from the 4th century AD, it died out as a spoken language in the 9th century but continued to be used as a literary language and as the liturgical language of the Ethiopian Orthodox Church. Tigrinya has several million speakers in Eritrea and the region of Tigre. The Tigre language is spoken by fewer than a million people.

The South Ethiopic group has two branches: Transversal South Ethiopic and Outer South Ethiopic. The chief language of the former is Amharic, the official language of Ethiopia, with more than 8 million speakers. This branch also includes the almost extinct Argobba language, Harari—spoken in the Muslim city of Harar and East Gurage. Outer South Ethiopic includes the recently extinct Gafat and the rest of the so-called Gurage languages—Soddo, Chaha, and others.

Cushitic

Cushitic is the most heterogeneous of the Afroasiatic languages. It comprises about 40 different languages spoken by 15 million people in the Horn of Africa and surrounding areas. Beja, or Bedauye, spoken in eastern Sudan and northern Ethiopia by a small number of Muslims, has been classified as North Cushitic but may be an independent branch of Afroasiatic. Central Cushitic, comprising the Agau languages, is spoken within enclaves of predominantly Semitic Ethiopia. East Cushitic, the largest member of the group, with about 2 million speakers in South Central Ethiopia, comprises Highland East Cushitic (Burji, Sidamo, Hadiyya, and others) and Lowland East Cushitic. Its northern branch comprises the Afar-Saho or Dankali dialect cluster, with about 500,000 speakers in south Eritrea and the Republic of Jibuti.

The other branch contains the widest diversity. Somali, with about 4 million speakers, is the official language of Somalia and is also spoken in the Republic of Jibuti, the Ogaden area of Ethiopia, and the northwestern territory of Kenya. It is written in Roman script, Arabic and an indigenous script have also been used. Its closest relatives are Boni and Rendille in Kenya.

The most widely spoken Cushitic language is Oromo, or Galla, with about 8 million speakers. Spoken in the southern half of Ethiopia and in the adjacent areas of Kenya, it is written in the Ethiopian script. South Cushitic includes Dahalo, or Sanye, and Ma'a, or Mbugu (a mixture of Cushitic and Bantu), both of which are spoken in Kenya; Iraqw, Asax, and Quadza are spoken in Tanzania.

Omotic

About 30 Omotic languages are spoken in the Omo valley in southern Ethiopia by more than a million people. Once considered to constitute West Cushitic, the Omotic languages are so different from the other Afroasiatic languages that their inclusion in the family has been questioned. The most important of these languages is Walamo, followed by Gonga (Kafa) and Janjero.

Berber

The Berber languages (formerly Numidian and Libyan) once dominated the whole of North Africa west of Egypt. Today they are spoken by perhaps 10 million people. Tuareg is spoken in southern Algeria, Niger, and Mali. Morocco has the largest concentration of Berber speakers—with 6 million speakers of the Tamazight, Tashelhit, and Tarifit dialects—followed by Algeria, with 2.5 million. These dialects are written in Arabic script, although the consonantal writing of Libyan inscriptions still survives. (See BERBERS.)

Chad

The Chadic languages are spoken in west central Africa around Lake Chad. Hausa, with 15 million speakers, is the most widely spoken, mainly in northwestern Nigeria, Niger, Chad, and northern Ghana. It is written in Roman script, although Arabic script is also used. The other Chadic languages, between 100 and 200 with 7 million speakers, are spoken in areas east of the Hausa territory. Chadic languages comprise West Chadic (including Hausa, Bole, Kanakuru, Angas, Ron, Bade, Ngizim, Wanji), Biu-Mandara (including Tera, Margi, Higi, Mandara, Bata, Kotoko, Musgu), East Chadic (including Somrai, Dangla, Mubi, and Sokoro), and Masa as a separate branch.

Characteristics of Afroasiatic

Phonetically, all branches of Afroasiatic except Egyptian have a set of emphatic consonants in addition to voiced and voiceless ones. Lateral consonants (for example, *tl*, *dl*) are found in some languages. The Cushitic, Omotic, and Chadic languages also have tones.

All branches of the family have masculine and feminine gender distinction, usually characterized by the feminine marker *t* (Arabic: *kalb/kalbat,* "dog/bitch"); gender distinction in the plural, however, has disappeared in many of the languages. Ancient Egyptian and classical Semitic had not only singular and plural forms but a grammatical distinction for "two" or "double."

Egyptian, Semitic, Berber, and, in remnants only, Cushitic have a system in which a root made up of two, three, or four consonants is used to create different words; this is done by superimposing on it a pattern of vowels, and often of further consonants. Thus in Arabic, the root *k-t-b*, meaning "write," is used in various combinations to form allied words, such as "writer" (*ka:tib-*) or "written" (*maktu:b-*).

In Semitic, Berber, and, to a limited extent, Cushitic, basic verbal conjugations are characterized by the addition of prefixes and suffixes. Root vocalization marks tense. Egyptian, by contrast, has no prefix conjugation; its verbal system is of nominal origin—of the type "I am on/in/to doing," "is done by me," "I am a doer of" for various tenses and aspects of "I do." In Chadic, a typical conjugation comprises a preposition containing a subject marker and a tense-and-aspect marker, followed by one of the stem forms of the verb. A passive formation in *t* and a causative in *s* or its developments; a reduplication of the verb, of a syllable, or of a consonant for repeated actions; and other methods of word formation are attested everywhere. In many languages, the verb has special negative forms. Likewise, different verbal forms for main and subordinate clauses are found in several branches.

In the Cushitic and Omotic languages, the verb typically occupies the final position in the sentence, and subordinate clauses precede the main one. Ethiopian Semitic has adopted the same order of elements. In old Egyptian, Berber, and classical Semitic, the verb is at the beginning of a sentence. Akkadian, however, placed the verb at the end. Coptic, modern Arabic dialects, Aramaic, and Hebrew now use a subject-verb-object order, as do almost all the Chadic languages.

Linguistic Investigation

The formal study of Hebrew and Arabic has an extensive history. Motivated by the study of Judaism and Islam, it spread widely among scholars with the influence of the two religions. Ge'ez and Amharic were first studied in the 17th century. Investigation into most of the other Afroasiatic languages grew from contact between indigenous speakers and Europeans—first travelers, then missionaries and colonial administrators, and ultimately scholars whose motives were purely intellectual. The extinct languages—Egyptian, Libyan, and those of the Semitic group—were preserved in inscriptions that were copied and, with the help of bilingual inscriptions or of known related scripts, deciphered by scholars mainly during the past 100 years (see WRITING SYSTEMS, EVOLUTION OF).

___

Afternoon of a Faun, The   The orchestral music for the *Prelude to the Afternoon of a Faun* (*Prélude à l'Après-midi d'un faune*, 1894) by Claude DEBUSSY is one of the finest works of musical impressionism. Debussy's composition was inspired by the poem *L'Après-midi d'un faune* (1876) by his friend the French symbolist poet Stéphane MALLARMÉ.

The poem describes a faun who, while playing his flute on a hot afternoon, encounters two nymphs who are on their way to bathe. He becomes enamored of one of them, who escapes his advances, leaving him playing with her scarf.

Debussy, in musically illustrating the dreamy eroticism of the poem's text, used several devices: chromaticism, whole-tone scales and modes, dissonance, parallel chords, subdued dynamics, and subtle rhythm and meter changes. The woodwind solos, harp glissandi, and muted horns all suggest an idyllic dream. Composed in three continuous sections, the tone poem conveys constant, flowing motion.

The Afternoon of a Faun was first performed as a ballet in Paris in 1912 by the Ballet Russes de Serge Diaghilev and caused a scandal. Vaslav NIJINSKY, who choreographed the ballet and danced the part of the faun, eventually won acclaim for the work. In 1953 the American choreographer Jerome ROBBINS presented a contemporary interpretation of the work, which has since become a staple of the New York City Ballet's repertory.

___

Aga Khan [ah'-guh kahn]   The Aga Khan is the spiritual leader, or imam, of the ISMAILI sect of Shiite Muslims. The hereditary title was first granted by the Persian court to **Hasan Ali Shah**, 1800–81, a supposed descendant of Ali, son-in-law of the Prophet Muhammad. He revolted against the shah, however, and fled to India in 1840. His grandson **Aga Khan III** (Sultan Sir Mohammed Shah), b. Nov. 2, 1877, d. July 11, 1957, was a founder (1906) of the All-India Muslim League and took part in the London conferences on Indian constitutional reform in 1930–32. In 1937 he was president of the League of Nations Assembly. He was succeeded on his death by his grandson Karim al-Hussain Shah, **Aga Khan IV**, b. Dec. 13, 1936, who is known primarily for his business interests, including a horse-breeding enterprise. He has promoted development projects among the Ismailis and sponsored a major study of Islamic architecture.

___

Agadir [ah-guh-deer']   Agadir (1982 pop., 110,479) is a seaport in Agadir province of southwestern Morocco. It is located on the Atlantic coast, at the mouth of the Oued Sous, about 220 km (135 mi) southwest of Marrakech. Agadir is Morocco's main fishing port, noted for its sardine catch. Founded by the Portuguese in the 16th century, Agadir was the scene of confrontation between Germany and France in 1911 (see MOROCCAN CRISES). It was largely destroyed by earthquakes in 1960; a modern city was built around the port facilities.

___

Agam, Yaacov [ah-gahm', yah'-kawf]   Yaacov Agam, b. May 11, 1928, is a leading Israeli painter, sculptor, and kinetic artist. After studying in Jerusalem, Zurich, and Paris, Agam mounted his first one-man show in Paris in 1953. His painting and sculptural style is derived in part from the geometric severities of the Dutch modernist Piet MONDRIAN and the tradition of neoplasticism (the rules of abstract composition formulated by the movement called DE STIJL), into which Agam injects a characteristic liveliness and visual wit. His Holocaust memorial (1987) in Jerusalem consists of six glass pillars containing fire, set in water, and topped by stainless steel Stars of David.

___

agama [ag'-uh-muh]   Agamas are about 60 species of Old World lizards in the genus *Agama*, family Agamidae, order Squamata. These rough-scaled lizards have more or less flattened, robust bodies, well-developed limbs, and moderately long tails. They feed on insects and other small animals; some also consume vegetation. Most small species are ground-living. The large species often live on rocky cliffs or in trees. Agamas are found in southeastern Europe and in the jungles, steppes, savannas, and desert regions of Africa, Arabia, and Southwest and Central Asia.

See also: LIZARD; REPTILE.

Agamemnon [ag-uh-mem'-nahn] In Greek mythology, Agamemnon, a son of ATREUS, was the commander in chief of the Greeks in the TROJAN WAR. He was the king of Mycenae and a brother of MENELAUS, whose kidnapped wife, HELEN OF TROY, was the immediate cause of the conflict. On his way to Troy, Agamemnon agreed to sacrifice his daughter IPHIGENIA in order to ensure a fair wind for his ships. Upon Agamemnon's return from the war, his wife CLYTEMNESTRA, who had betrayed him with Aegisthus, resolved to avenge her daughter's sacrifice. When her husband was at ease in the bath, she and her lover murdered him. Agamemnon's death was later avenged by his son ORESTES. These tragic events are the subject of a trilogy, the ORESTEIA, written by the 5th-century BC dramatist AESCHYLUS.

Agana [ah-gahn'-ah] Agana (1980 pop., 896) is the capital of Guam, a U.S. unincorporated territory in the western Pacific. Situated on the west coast of the island, the town was destroyed in World War II and has been gradually rebuilt since then.

agar [ah'-gahr] Agar is a substance prepared from a mixture of red algae, such as *Gelidium*, for laboratory or industrial use. It is made mainly in the Far East—the name *agar*, or *agar-agar*, is a Malay word for a type of seaweed common in the area—and in California. The algae are washed and dried, and the agar, part of the cell wall, is extracted with boiling water, forming a gel as it cools. The gel is a complex mixture of sugar compounds.

Agar is the substance most commonly used in laboratories for making media in which to grow microorganisms. It is nontoxic, dissolves poorly in water, and is relatively unaffected by the salts and nutrients in the media or by the organisms themselves. Agar is used to stabilize and thicken emulsions such as ice creams, jellies, soups, and sauces. It is also used to size, or fill the pores of, textiles and paper and in treating some intestinal disorders.

Agassiz, Louis Rodolphe [ag'-uh-see] One of the most influential scientists of the 19th century, the Swiss-born American naturalist Jean Louis Rodolphe Agassiz, b. May 28, 1807, d. Dec. 14, 1873, did pioneering work on fossil fishes and originated the concept of ICE AGES.

A graduate in philosophy and medicine of the universities of Munich and Erlangen (1829, 1830), Agassiz worked in Paris with Georges CUVIER, the founder of the discipline of comparative anatomy, and in 1832 became professor of natural history at the College of Neuchâtel, Switzerland. There he undertook the research that resulted in his 5-volume work *Récherches sur les poissons fos-*

siles (Studies on Fossil Fish, 1833–44), which, using the principles of comparative anatomy, describes more than 1,700 species.

In the late 1830s Agassiz began his study of glaciers, charting their movement and asserting on the basis of geological evidence that ice had once covered much of the European continent. His view of this catastrophic event opposed the famous doctrine of the Scottish geologist Sir Charles LYELL that only uniform and gradual changes occur in the Earth's history. But geological formations, as well as the scratched surfaces of rocks in certain areas, supported Agassiz's theory.

In 1846, Agassiz went to the United States to deliver a series of lectures but remained for 25 years, teaching at Harvard and applying his theory of ice ages to North America. Renowned for his teaching abilities, Agassiz trained an entire generation of naturalists.

agate [ag'-uht] The common, widespread SILICA MINERAL (SiO_2) agate often occurs in bands of varying color and transparency. A semiprecious variety of CHALCEDONY, it has long been used as a GEM and as an ornamental material. Agate is identical with QUARTZ in composition and physical properties. The colored bands contain iron hydroxide impurities added during formation.

Agate forms when gas bubbles trapped in solidifying LAVA become filled with alkali and silica-bearing waters, which coagulate into a gel. The alkali attacks the iron in the surrounding lava, forming bands of iron hydroxide in the gel, which loses water and crystallizes, leaving the bands intact. Many agates, when cut in cross-section, reveal striking forms.

According to ancient superstition, wearing agate made one agreeable, persuasive, prudent, and bold. It brought God's favor and bestowed the power to vanquish enemies.

Idar-Oberstein, Germany, has been superseded as a source of the stones by the Rio Grande do Sul region of Brazil and Uruguay.

Agate is a semiprecious variety of transparent to translucent quartz arranged in curved or circular bands of different colors.

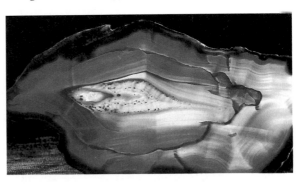

agave [uh-gah'-vay] Agave, genus *Agave*, is any of more than 300 species of plants with handsome foliage belonging to the agave family, Agavaceae. They form long, stiff evergreen leaves in clumps, or rosettes, from which tall, bare flower stems arise. Agave plants are native to warm arid and semiarid regions of North and South America. They are used as houseplants and, in the South, as landscape plants. The century plant, *A. americana*, erroneously received its name because it was believed to bloom only when 100 years old. It has leaves up to 1.8 m (6 ft) long and a flower stalk up to 12 m (40 ft) in height. It generally blooms after it is 10 years old; thereafter it dies back, but suckers sprout again from the base to form new plants. This is the most popular species for landscaping and potting.

Some common agaves have commercial value. Pulque agave, *A. atrovirens*, is used in Mexico to produce pulque, and tequila is fermented from other Mexican species. Fibers derived from henequen, *A. fourcroydes*, and sisal, *A. sisalana*, are used to make rope. The pulp of other species is used to produce soap and food.

age see AGING; LIFE SPAN

Agee, James [ay'-jee] An American writer, James Agee, b. Knoxville, Tenn., Nov. 27, 1909, d. May 16, 1955, won distinction in a variety of literary forms. His volume of poems *Permit Me Voyage* (1934) was included in the Yale Series of Younger Poets. His nonfictional *Let Us Now Praise Famous Men* (1941), illustrated with Walker EVANS's photographs of sharecroppers, is an evocative view of the Depression of the 1930s. As film reviewer for the magazines *Time* and the *Nation* in the 1930s and '40s, he brought unusual rigor and insight to film criticism; his reviews were later collected in two volumes, *Agee on Film* (1958, 1960). His autobiographical novel, *A Death in the Family* (1957; film, 1963), won the 1958 Pulitzer Prize for its poignant and honest treatment of the effect of a man's death on his 6-year-old son. Agee's credits as a screenwriter include *The Night of the Hunter* (1955) and the classic *The African Queen* (1951).

Agena (rocket) [uh-jee'-nuh] The Agena system was an upper rocket stage that employed a restartable rocket engine. It could operate as a satellite in its own right, or it could be used to launch satellites and space probes in conjunction with more powerful lower rocket stages. Typical first-stage boosters were THOR and ATLAS.

Agena B was used in early U.S. Air Force satellite projects, including DISCOVERER, SAMOS, Midas, and Vela, and a variety of NASA projects, including Echo, MARINER, NIMBUS, and RANGER. Agena stages also were used as docking targets in the GEMINI manned space program.

Agena D, the version of the vehicle in use after Agena B, carried more propellant than its predecessors. It could also accept a variety of payloads. It was launched atop TITAN 3B, Atlas SLV-3A, and Thor. The last Agena to be manufactured was launched in 1987.

Agency for International Development The Agency for International Development (AID) is an agency of the U.S. Department of State, established by the Foreign Assistance Act of 1961 to assist other countries in developing their economies and improving the quality of life for their inhabitants. AID makes loans and grants to less developed countries for economic improvement programs and for programs relating to population growth. It also administers famine and disaster relief assistance. In cooperation with the Department of Agriculture, it distributes farm commodities under the Food for Peace program.

Agent Orange see POLLUTANTS, CHEMICAL

ageratum [aj-ur-ay'-tuhm] *Ageratum*, a member of the aster family, Compositae, is a genus of about 29 species of herbs and shrubs native to central and tropical South America. Commonly called flossflowers, ageratums have clusters of small blue, white, or pink flowers with a pleasant odor. Because they flower for long periods, they are used as border plants in gardens and as summer bedding plants in temperate climates. One species, *A. conyzoides*, contains hydrocyanic acid, coumarin, and an alkaloid and is poisonous to animals.

The ageratum has clusters of tiny flowers and heart-shaped leaves. Wild ageratum grows in damp woodlands and along streams.

Agesilaus II, King of Sparta [uh-jes-i-lay'-uhs] Agesilaus II, c.444–360 BC, succeeded his half-brother Agis II as one of the two Spartan kings in 399. In Anatolia from 396, he defeated the Persian satrap TISSAPHERNES, and on his return to Greece he defeated (394) the Thebans and their allies at Coronea. When a Sparto-Persian alliance forced Athens and Thebes to abandon (386) the Greek cities in Anatolia to Persian domination, the Thebans and Athenians renewed war against Sparta. Following the breakdown of peace talks in 371, Agesilaus invaded Boeotia and was overwhelmingly defeated by the Thebans, led by EPAMINONDAS at Leuctra. Sparta never regained its military strength.

aggression Aggression is attacking behavior that may be either self-protective and self-assertive or hostile toward others or toward oneself. By far the most common forms of aggressive behavior among animals involve neither fighting, violence, injury, nor physical contact. Most animal aggression is ritualized, obviating the need for fighting.

Observers distinguish several kinds of aggression: (1) predatory aggression to a natural object of prey; (2) antipredatory aggression, elicited by the presence of a predator; (3) territorial aggression, elicited by an intruder; (4) dominance aggression, elicited by a challenge to the animal's rank; (5) maternal aggression, elicited by a threat to the young; (6) weaning aggression, when the parents will threaten or even (with restraint) attack their offspring; (7) parental disciplinary aggression to unwelcome suckling, rough or overextended play, wandering, and the like; (8) sex-related aggression, elicited by the same stimuli that produce sexual behavior; (9) intermale aggression, elicited by the presence of a male competitor of the same species; (10) fear-induced aggression, elicited by confinement or cornering or by the presence of some threatening agent; (11) irritable aggression, elicited by the presence of any object with characteristics (such as color or darting movement) that stimulate an attack response.

Clearly, then, aggressive behavior is not a single phenomenon, but something to be understood at many different levels. In most higher animals learning plays a role in the development of aggressive behavior, countering the theory that humans are basically aggressive.

Agincourt, Battle of [aj'-in-kort or ah-zhin-koor'] The English victory over the French at Agincourt in northwest France on Oct. 25, 1415, was one of the most significant battles in the HUNDRED YEARS' WAR. A triumph for the English bowmen, it is celebrated in Shakespeare's play *Henry V*.

aging Aging, or senescence, is a widespread biological phenomenon that occurs in all higher organisms and in many of the lower ones. Its signs usually are a decrease in such functional capacities as the metabolic rate, the ability to sense and respond to stimuli, and the ability to move and also to reproduce. Aging organisms also have an increased susceptibility to disease, injury, and predators. In contrast, protoplasm—the living substance that makes up both the cytoplasm and nuclei of cells—appears to be potentially immortal.

Chronological age refers to the passage of time; generally, when the question is asked how old a person or an animal is, the answer is given in units of time. Physiological age means the condition of the organism in relation to aging. A mouse of 3 years is a "very old" mouse, but a dog is not "very old" until about 15 years, nor a human being until 80 (see OLD AGE).

The Process of Aging

The decline of metabolic rate (see METABOLISM) is an important index of the progress of aging. This decline, however, is more complex than appears at first sight. The oxygen uptake in human beings, for example, does not decrease with advancing age; the mean resting heart rate, on the other hand, continues to decline throughout fetal and postnatal life.

The organism ages primarily because the cells of the body, especially those which cannot replace themselves, undergo changes that result in decreased function, degeneration, and death. The different kinds of cells vary markedly in their ability to replace themselves. Such surface layers of cells (epithelia) as those which form the outermost skin and the lining of the digestive and other tracts are able to replace themselves rapidly. Blood cells also are constantly generated. The nervous system, conversely, has generally irreplaceable cells known as neurons. As a consequence, with the loss of neurons the brain, the spinal cord, and the ganglia age. Cells of the heart, the voluntary muscles, and certain parts of the immune and endocrine systems also cannot be easily replaced.

Among mammals the size of the body is limited (determinate growth), and when growth ceases certain changes set in. With increasing age come changes in the genetic components of a certain number of somatic (body) cells. These changes may be marked aberrations in the size and shape of the cell nuclei and nucleoli, abnormalities of chromosomes, and the occurrence of irregular cell division. The nucleic acid DNA may incur permanent lesions, especially in the liver.

Immunological changes involve the defense mechanisms, especially those against bacteria, viruses, and other foreign substances. The cellular defenses consist of the white blood cells, including some phagocytes that devour bacteria and others that produce antibodies. During the aging process in certain mammals, marked changes—including decrease in size—occur in the lymph nodes, spleen, and bone marrow where these cells are produced. Macrophages—large phagocytic cells in the tissues—become clogged with pigment. Certain immune functions decrease with age, while the incidence of cancer, immune diseases, and infections increases.

The steps leading to the death of cells of the nervous system include a decrease or disappearance of the Nissl substance, which is a basophilic material rich in ribosomes that is located in the cytoplasm. Lipofuscin, a yellow green pigment, begins to accumulate in the cytoplasm, and cell nucleoli and nuclei degenerate. These changes are known to occur in such mammals as mice, rats, guinea pigs, dogs, and apes. Changes in human neurons, and the loss of these cells, occur in all parts of the human brain.

Hormonal changes (see HORMONES) profoundly affect the functioning of the body. The most apparent change in humans is the decreased production of sex hormones, producing the onset of MENOPAUSE in women and certain changes in men. Among other changes, lowered levels of insulin occur, causing increased risk of diabetes mellitus. In plants, certain hormones serve to delay senescence.

The stage in which changes occur in the functioning of the nervous system is termed SENILITY. It is difficult to differentiate senility from senescence. Changes in gait, for example, may be due to changes in the nervous system or to changes in joints, ligaments, or muscles. Senility is probably a distinct condition, not just an acceleration of normal aging. Personality changes are common in senility, as are the onset of paranoid tendencies and fits of irritability or depression.

Differences among Various Life Forms

Vast structural differences exist among classes and phyla of animals, making difficult any comparisons of change of structure with age. Some such comparisons have been detailed.

Plants. Because of the nature of the life processes in plants, their photosynthetic capacity, and their long-continued ability to grow, any statement about aging in plants is complicated. Plants nevertheless share with animals the general properties of life. As knowledge of the ultrastructural features of cells increases, more and more similarities of plant cells to those of animals have been discovered.

Even in natural conditions the life span of different kinds of plants varies from a few days or hours—as in single-celled plants that reproduce continuously by cell division—to plants that flower annually or perennially to such giant trees as the redwoods that live thousands of years.

As a higher plant passes from youth to old age, the areas of the leaf enclosed by the smallest branches of the fibrovascular bundles—areas known as islets—become smaller and smaller. Propagation by asexual means does not reverse or change this trend; offspring grown from seed, on the other hand, have larger islets. Leaves and fruits show signs of senescence and eventual death. Such functional traits as respiratory intensity in leaves decrease with aging.

Invertebrates. Within the phylum Protozoa—organisms that consist of a single cell—are numerous species that reproduce by fission and in which some investigators have observed a real or potential immortality. Other kinds of Protozoa produce offspring within the body of a mother. In such species the adult body shows definite changes of senescence. Clones of certain Protozoa begin to show age changes in their individual members after a certain number of generations.

In other invertebrate phyla, such as the Rotifera, a more typical relation to aging exists. In rotifers, the older the mother from which an egg is produced, the shorter the life and the more rapid the aging process of the individual derived from the egg. In higher phyla of the invertebrates, such as Mollusca, Annelida, and Arthropoda, a decrease in reproductivity capacity occurs with age, and senile changes occur in tissues and cells, especially in the nervous system.

Vertebrates. The five classes of vertebrates differ considerably in the length of the growth period, in the duration of reproductive processes, and in the aging process.

Many fishes exhibit such characteristics as indefinite growth, no evidence of declining vigor, and no definite life span. Conversely, accelerated aging occurs in migratory salmon; they pass from vigorous sexual maturity to death in a period of a few weeks, with extensive aging of tissues throughout the body.

Many species of Amphibia have a definite growth period and an absolute adult size, but some species of salamanders and frogs do not. Among vertebrates, reptiles show the greatest longevity. Individuals of at least five species of turtles have lived to more than 100 years of age in captivity. Evidence of a decline in reproductive capacity with age is scanty for snakes, but many species do grow to a specific size at a relatively early age. In birds, the small and fast-breeding species are shorter-lived than the larger and more slowly breeding ones.

In the mammals, determinate growth, definite adult size, and rather well-defined life span are the predominant traits. Changes during aging in tissues and organs occur at about the same time in individual species. The major changes with age in humans are graying of the hair; wrinkling of the skin; formation of the arcus senilis, a light-colored ring at the edge of the iris of the eye; bowing of the back; and atrophy of the muscles. The internal organs similarly display certain characteristics of aging.

Theories on Aging

Various theories of the aging process have been proposed. Among these are the environmental theory, the metabolic theory, the genetic theory, and the immunological theory.

The environmental theory of aging stresses the importance of the changes with age in the environment of the living cells. For instance, such deposits as collagen and calcium salts may accumulate, and in a number of organs—including the thyroid gland, the gonads, and the muscles—the number of fibers and the bulk of fibrous tissue may increase. As a result, the epithelial cells often are living in a different and less favorable environment in old than in young individuals.

The metabolic theory is a more scientific version of the old "wear and tear" theory, which says that a body—like many machines produced by humans—has a life span limited by the amount of daily use. According to this concept, a life of stress and overexertion, with inadequate rest and recuperation, is a deterrent to longevity. A recent extension of the metabolic theory suggests that the production of oxygen FREE RADICALS by damaged tissues, over time, causes further cell death.

Animal longevity is almost always species-specific, which indicates to some investigators that a genetic basis for life span exists. The genetic, or gene-mutation, theory of aging stresses that during the life of an animal spontaneous mutations lead to an accumulation of errors in the control of gene expression that result, finally, in senescence.

The immunological, or autoimmune, theory states that every cell in an individual organism is immunologically similar to every other cell in that organism. If cells undergo change from their genetic pattern, as occurs in mutation, the immunological character of those cells may change. Both nuclei and cytoplasm of such cells may produce substances known as autoantigens. Other cells react to autoantigens by rejecting and killing such cells or by walling them off by deposits.

Premature Aging

Premature aging (progeria) is a condition that has been observed only in humans. Two forms are distinguished by the age of onset. Infantile progeria occurs in childhood, usually after an apparently normal infancy. Retarded growth, dwarfism, and progressively increasing malformation of the head and face may be observed. The skin atrophies, and hypertension occurs. Cataract and other phenomena usually associated with old age often manifest themselves. Mental development is often precocious in individuals so afflicted, and they generally die of coronary disease before the age of 30.

Adult progeria, or Werner's syndrome, usually occurs after growth has been largely or wholly completed. Persons affected by Werner's syndrome often are short and exhibit characteristics similar to those observed in persons with infantile progeria. In the third or fourth decade the skin atrophies. Hypogonadism, calcification of the arteries, and, in about half of such patients, a tendency to diabetes also are evident.

See also: ALZHEIMER'S DISEASE; GERIATRICS.

Aglipay, Gregorio [ah-glee-py'] Gregorio Aglipay, 1860–1940, was the first bishop of the Philippine Independent Church. A Roman Catholic priest in Manila, he became chaplain to the forces of Emilio Aguinaldo in the revolution (1898) against Spanish rule. He was appointed vicar-general by Aguinaldo and was excommunicated as a result. Aglipay and his followers then formed (1902) the Philippine Independent Church, which, although divided into trinitarian and unitarian factions, continues in existence today. In 1935, Aglipay unsuccessfully sought election to the presidency of the Philippines as a militantly nationalist candidate.

Agnatha [ag'-nuh-thuh] The Agnatha (superclass Agnatha) are primitive vertebrate fishes that lack true jaws, vertebrae, and pelvic fins. Living species have long eel-like bodies. Two living groups, the HAGFISHES and the LAMPREYS, diverged almost 500 million years ago. The hagfishes, family Myxinidae, are marine scavengers with fingerlike whiskers around the mouth. The lampreys, family Petromyzontidae, inhabit both fresh and marine habitats. All lampreys breed in freshwater streams, where the young go through a larval stage. Some species are parasitic and grow into adults that prey on other fish. In nonparasitic species the adults live only long enough to breed.

Agnew, Spiro T. Spiro Theodore Agnew, b. Baltimore, Md., Nov. 9, 1918, is a former U.S. vice-president and governor of Maryland. Agnew studied law at the University of Baltimore and was admitted to the bar in 1949.

He served as Baltimore County executive from 1962 to 1966, when he was elected Republican governor.

As Richard Nixon's vice-president (1969–73), Agnew became known for his colorful speeches attacking dissidents and the news media. Charged with accepting bribes while governor and vice-president, he resigned on Oct. 10, 1973. He pleaded no contest to one count of income tax evasion and was sentenced to three years probation and fined $10,000. In 1983, as a result of a civil suit, he paid Maryland $270,000 as reimbursement for kickbacks he allegedly received. He has written a novel, *The Canfield Decision* (1976).

Agnon, S. Y. [ahg'-nohn] Shmuel Yosef Agnon, b. July 17, 1888, d. Feb. 17, 1970, earned his reputation as a master craftsman of the Hebrew novel and short story. The dean of Hebrew letters, he received international recognition when awarded the Nobel Prize for literature in 1966. Fully rooted in the traditions of his people, Agnon depicted the spiritual richness of East European Jewish life and its sad decline in the 1930s, as well as the struggles of the early Jewish settlers in Palestine. He wrote realistic, psychological fiction and highly symbolic tales. In expressionistic dreamlike stories he portrayed human helplessness in a manner reminiscent of Franz KAFKA.

Agnon, whose family name was originally Czaczkes, was born in Galicia (now in Poland). He emigrated to Palestine in 1908, and, except for 11 years in Germany, lived in Jerusalem for most of his adult life. His first major novel, *The Bridal Canopy* (1930; rev. Eng. trans., 1967), offered a panoramic view of Jewish life in late 18th and early 19th-century Galicia. *In the Heart of the Seas* (1933; rev. Eng. trans., 1967) is a folktale about the pilgrimage of pious 19th-century Jews to Palestine. In his autobiographical work *A Guest for the Night* (1939; Eng. trans., 1968), Agnon revisits his hometown and views its postwar decline. Many look upon *Temol Shilshom* (The Day before Yesterday, 1945), which concerns the problems of the westernized Jew, as his greatest novel.

agnosticism [ag-nahs'-tuh-sizm] Agnosticism is the philosophical position that it is impossible to know about the nature or existence of GOD. The term was coined in 1869 by Thomas H. HUXLEY from the Greek *agnōstos* ("unknowable") to refer to his own conviction that knowledge is impossible on many matters covered by religious doctrines. Agnosticism considers valid only knowledge that comes from ordinary and immediate experience. It is distinct from ATHEISM on the one hand and SKEPTICISM on the other. Atheists reject belief in the existence of God. Skeptics hold the strong suspicion or probabilistic estimate that God does not exist. Agnostics refuse to make such judgments.

The agnostic position can be traced to the skeptics of ancient Greece. In modern times, agnosticism became prevalent during the 18th and 19th centuries, mainly because of the growing mass of scientific data that seemed to contradict the biblical position and because of the disagreement of theologians and church authorities over the use of textual and historical criticism in the interpretation of the Bible. Many of the best-known philosophers have been agnostics. Among them are Auguste Comte, William James, Immanuel Kant, George Santayana, and Bertrand Russell.

agora [ag'-uh-ruh]   In ancient Greece, an agora was a public area or marketplace, usually located in the middle of the city or near a harbor. Generally square, it was always surrounded by a colonnade. In early Greek times public assemblies were held in the agora; later it functioned primarily as the commercial heart of the city, and eventually it became a religious center with temples, altars, commemorative statues, and sometimes tombs of important personages. The porticoes were often decorated with murals. The Roman FORUM was essentially an adaptation of the ancient Greek agora.

   See also: GREEK ARCHITECTURE; STOA.

agouti [uh-goo'-tee]   The agouti, genus *Dasyprocta*, is a rodent belonging to the family Dasyproctidae, order Rodentia. About 24 species exist. Agoutis are about 61 cm (24 in) long, have short tails (10–35 mm / ⅖–1⅖ in), and weigh up to 3 kg (7 lb). The coarse, glossy coat ranges from pale orange to shades of brown and near-black; the underparts are whitish. The body is slender with a high, muscular rump well adapted for running. The front paws have five claws and the hind have three much thicker claws. Agoutis live from southern Mexico to southern Brazil. They flourish in cool, damp lowland forests, grasslands, and brush, and feed on leaves, fruit, nuts, and roots. They dig burrows in which they raise litters of two to four.

The orange-rumped agouti tames easily and is sometimes kept as a pet. In the wild, the agouti burrows among boulders, under trees, and into riverbanks.

Agra [ah'-gruh]   Agra, a city in north central India on the right bank of the Yamuna River, is the administrative headquarters of the Agra district in Uttar Pradesh state. The population is 694,191 (1981). Although Agra has a rich Muslim heritage, the majority of its present population is Hindu. Agra was developed as a trading post and strategic capital site. Today light industry and tourism are significant. Agra University was founded in 1927.

   Babur, founder of the Mogul Empire (1526), informally established Agra as the administrative seat of his rule. In 1566, Akbar, grandson of Babur, formally made the city the imperial capital. Agra is famous for its fine examples of Mogul architecture. These include Agra Fort, a red-sandstone fortress complex, the mausoleum of Itimad-ud-daulah, and the world-renowned TAJ MAHAL, a white-marble tomb constructed by Shah Jahan for his wife Mumtaz Mahal.

agranulocytosis [ay-gran-yuh-loh-sy-toh'-suhs]   Agranulocytosis is a blood disorder in which the number of white cells is markedly reduced, usually resulting in the development of infected ulcers on the skin and in the throat, intestinal tract, and other mucous membranes. The condition is usually caused by interference with the production and release of white cells in the bone marrow. This may result from damage to the bone marrow by ionizing radiation or by drugs used to treat cancer and leukemia, as well as by certain antibiotics, tranquilizers, antidepressants, antithyroid agents, antiinflammatory drugs, insecticides, and solvents. The condition may also be caused by certain hereditary disorders affecting the bone marrow by a deficiency of folic acid and vitamin B_{12}. Acute cases are characterized by chills, fever, and prostration. Because white blood cells are an important defense against invading microorganisms, agranulocytosis may cause a bacterial infection to become life-threatening.

Agrarians   see FUGITIVES AND AGRARIANS

agribusiness   Agribusiness is the sector of the economy that buys and processes agricultural commodities—and often produces them—and fabricates and sells agricultural production materials and equipment. Agribusiness is much larger than the farming industry. Of each dollar spent by consumers on food, less than one-third goes to farms; the rest is absorbed by the transportation, processing, packaging, refrigerating, storage, marketing, and retailing of foods transformed from farm commodities. In addition, the agribusiness sector processes the fertilizers, insecticides, herbicides, veterinary supplies, feed, and feed additives for growing or raising food. It also supplies improved seed varieties, machinery and equipment, automotive vehicles, and many other needs of modern farming.

   The growth of agribusiness parallels the rapid rise in capital-intensive industry during the past half century and is largely responsible for the present-day U.S. food industry. Tractors, machines, and other equipment have replaced most farm labor. Chemical fertilizers, pesticides, and other materials have greatly increased farm yields (although their effects on such components as soil and water may be harmful in the long run). Sophisticated food technology, combined with massive advertising expenditures, has created consumer acceptance of highly processed packaged foods. The rapid growth of the fast-food industry is an extension of this trend.

   Another result of the growth of agribusiness has been the vertical integration of portions of the FOOD INDUSTRY. A case in point is broiler-chicken production. A firm will supply a farmer with baby chicks, feed, and the antibiotics necessary to keep the flocks alive. In specially constructed broiler sheds, the farmer raises the chickens to market weight, at which point they are purchased, processed, shipped, and marketed (see FACTORY FARMING).

Agricultural technology is another field requiring the financial inputs that only large firms can afford. Many of the biggest pharmaceutical producers are deeply involved in the search for genetically improved plants and animals and for genetically engineered vaccines, fertility and growth hormones, and other tools of biotechnology for agricultural use.

The accumulation of very large areas of productive land is another attribute of agribusiness. In the United States some 1,000 farms each sell more than $5 million annually, and about 28,000 gross more than $500,000. The nation's largest farming organization, specializing in the production of hogs and chickens, sells $1.5 billion annually. Most of these huge farms are family enterprises but are organized as corporations. Others are, in fact, corporation owned.

Agricola, Georgius [uh-grik'-oh-luh, jor'-jee-uhs]

The German educator, city official, and physician Georgius Agricola (Latinized form of Georg Bauer), b. Mar. 24, 1494, d. Nov. 21, 1555, is best known as the author of *De re metallica* (1556), a treatise on mining and metallurgy. Agricola studied medicine at Leipzig University. He became a devoted follower of Erasmus, who wrote a foreword to one of Agricola's books. While town physician of Joachimsthal (now Jáchymov, Czechoslovakia), he became interested in all aspects of the mining and metallurgy industry by which the town thrived and began a 25-year study of the subject, which culminated in his posthumously published masterpiece. The 12-chapter treatise included 292 woodcut illustrations by Blasius Weffring. Agricola also wrote on medicine, geology, mineralogy, politics, and economics.

Agricola, Gnaeus Julius [gnay'-uhs] Gnaeus Julius Agricola, b. June 13, AD 37, d. Aug. 23, 93, was a

Roman general who served ably as a conqueror and governor (78–84) of Britain. He subdued North Wales and expanded Roman rule north into Scotland, defeating the Caledonians at Mons Graupius (location unknown) in 83. Agricola Romanized Britain in a shrewd and gradual fashion, fostering urbanization and partial self-rule in the south. His son-in-law TACITUS left an account of his enlightened rule.

Agricultural Adjustment Administration The

Agricultural Adjustment Administration (AAA) was created by the U.S. Congress in 1933 to combat the effects of the DEPRESSION OF THE 1930S on the nation's farms. Under the administration's Domestic Allotment Plan, benefits were paid for lowered production of such staple crops as wheat, cotton, corn, and tobacco. This helped raise commodity prices. Land-owning farmers benefited most; tenant farmers and share-croppers often faced eviction when production was reduced.

In 1936 the U.S. Supreme Court declared the Domestic Allotment Plan unconstitutional on the grounds that subsidies imposed an unacceptable system of regulation. Congress responded by passing the Soil Conservation and Domestic Allotment Act (1936), which allowed the AAA to pay benefits to farmers who planted soil-enriching instead of staple crops, and the Agricultural Adjustment Act (1938), which allowed the AAA to fix acreages for staple export crops and grant loans on the basis of stored surplus crops. In 1945 the AAA was absorbed by the Production and Marketing Administration.

agricultural extension service Agricultural ex-

tension services worldwide provide education on farming techniques and management skills on a local or regional level (see AGRICULTURE AND THE FOOD SUPPLY). The Cooperative Extension Service of the U.S. Department of Agriculture was established in 1914 to apply the results of agricultural research done in U.S. land-grant colleges. Operating through state and county extension agents, it helps U.S. farmers to learn and use new agricultural techniques. Home-demonstration agents supply information and advice on food-preserving and cooking techniques and on farm economics and financing. The 4-H PROGRAMS train young people in agricultural, food-processing, and management techniques.

Many other developed countries operate extension services for their farming communities. In less developed countries, where farm populations are huge, extension services are often rare or nonexistent. Such countries as India, however, have educated enough agricultural specialists that they can now offer extension-service education at the village level.

agriculture, history of Agriculture involves raising

deliberately bred crops and livestock (see ANIMAL HUSBANDRY) for food, fiber, and other materials. Although thousands of plant and animal species exist, only 200 plant and about 50 animal species have been domesticated. About 12 or 13 plant crops are important staples, and almost all of these are GRAINS—especially wheat, rice, and maize (corn)—that were domesticated from wild GRASSES by deliberate cultivation of their seeds.

During the PALEOLITHIC PERIOD—from at least 2.5 million years ago to about 8000 BC—people hunted, fished, or gathered their food (see PREHISTORIC HUMANS). From about 11,000 to 8000 BC, flint-edged wooden sickles were used to gather wild grains, which were stored in caves; about 9000 BC, sheep were domesticated in the Near East. From approximately 8300 to 6500 BC, during the MESOLITHIC PERIOD, groups of people began to practice natural plant husbandry by simply broadcasting seeds and waiting for the harvest. The only crude tool needed was a haft of bone, wood, or antler fitted with a microlith—a small, sharp blade of stone—for reaping grain.

Dogs were the first animals to be tamed, usually to help in hunting. In the Near East such herd animals as goats, sheep, and cattle were domesticated.

The practice of cultivating plants became established in the Near East and Europe about 6500 to 3500 BC, in southeast Asia about 6800 to 4000 BC, and in Mesoamerica and Peru about 2500 BC. Most areas where cultivation began were located in river valleys having semiarid climates. The process of cultivation in the Old World (see NEOLITHIC PERIOD) involved preparing soil by harrowing—breaking down and smoothing with a tree branch—and sowing choice seeds with a stick plow. In Mesoamerica, where no species of draft animal existed and where the chief grain—maize—required individual planting, a plowless form of cultivation developed, whereby a digging stick was used to make holes for the seeds.

Early Agriculture in the Old World. The evolution from nomadic HUNTER-GATHERERS to cultivators allowed people to establish permanent villages because they had a reliable food supply close at hand. More people were freed from providing food and were able to develop technologies and services that led to the shift from farming communities to towns; eventually, agriculture-based civilizations were formed.

In MESOPOTAMIA, the region between the Tigris and Euphrates rivers in present-day Iraq (see FERTILE CRESCENT), cultivation began in the 9th millennium BC. The wheel was invented, pulleys were used to draw water from artificial canals, and complex IRRIGATION systems were constructed. Mesopotamians raised wheat and other cereal grains; were skilled in gardening; and domesticated the camel, donkey, and horse.

Relying on the water and fertile silt of the Nile, Egyptians (see EGYPT, ANCIENT) irrigated land to ensure large crops of wheat and barley, which, along with flax, provided the basis for their agriculture. Several types of palm trees were cultivated, and wild papyrus was harvested to make paper. In addition to oxen and horses, the Egyptians kept poultry, sheep, goats, and swine.

The INDUS CIVILIZATION of northern India, which existed from about 2300 to 1750 BC, raised wheat, barley, and rice. These people grew such plants as cotton, sesame, tea, and sugarcane. Chickens were domesticated from Indian jungle fowl, and the water buffalo and zebu cattle were used as draft animals. Farmers used plows, designed effective irrigation systems, and built large granaries. Among the river valleys of China, people learned how to cultivate soybeans, oranges, peaches, pears, hemp, and tea. They kept livestock, practiced intensive gardening, and excelled at flower horticulture.

Agriculture in Pre-Columbian America. In Mesoamerica—what is now Mexico and Central America—gourds, peppers, avocados, and a grain, amaranth, were domesticated from 7000 to 5000 BC. The people of Mesoamerica were nomadic hunters and semiagriculturists, however, until 2500 BC, when maize was domesticated. The Maya-Toltec-Aztec civilization flourished in Mexico and Central America from AD 250 to 1600 (see AZTEC; MAYA). These people hybridized corn to increase yields and also cultivated beans, squash, chili peppers, and avocados.

They grew tobacco and several species of cotton. They built irrigation canals and made artificial gardens that floated on water, such as those seen at XOCHIMILCO. Dry farming—cultivation of nonirrigated lands by moisture-retaining tillage—was practiced.

At about AD 1200 the INCA were carving out an empire in the Andes amid a harsh environment. They used stone hoes and digging sticks with a foot rest for pushing the end into the soil. Terraces, irrigation, and drainage systems were constructed; land was fertilized, and stone storehouses were built to preserve food. The Inca cultivated such foods as corn, white and sweet potatoes, and squash. They domesticated the llama as a beast of burden and kept alpacas for wool.

Early Greece and Rome. From 2000 BC on, the Greeks cultivated cereal grains (chiefly barley), raised olive and fig trees, and kept vineyards and livestock. The Greeks are credited with inventing a water wheel equipped with buckets to raise water to a higher level. Farmers used wooden implements primarily, including a threshing sledge with rocks for teeth.

The Romans advanced farm technology in the Mediterranean world by making tools, including the plow, reaper, hoe, and sickle, that had iron parts. They cultivated wheat, barley, and millet; kept vineyards; and raised livestock. Before 200 BC, Roman farmers were independent, each owning about 1.8 to 6.1 ha (4 to 15 acres). During the next 200 years the wealthy acquired publicly owned lands until they each controlled hundreds or thousands of hectares, which were worked by slaves.

Throughout this period a series of agrarian laws were enacted to divide land held by the wealthy and distribute it to small farmers. These attempts at land reform eventually failed, and by AD 200 many farmers were tenants on estates. By AD 400 the rights of these tenants were reduced until they became serfs, bound to the land.

Medieval Europe. Farmers who did own small holdings divided their land among their sons. These small holdings ensured poverty among independent farmers, and especially after the Roman Empire collapsed in AD 476, small farmers were forced to surrender their lands to powerful nobles in return for protection. This arrangement evolved during the High Middle Ages (AD 1000–1300) into MANORIALISM, especially in England, France, and Germany.

Under manorialism, serfs lived in villages near the lord's manor and farmed their own plots in open, commonly held fields as well as laboring on the lord's land, or demesne. Each serf farmed 5 to 12 ha (12 to 30 acres), which were divided into 0.4-ha (1-acre) strips and scattered throughout three fields among the holdings of other serfs. One field remained fallow for a year in order to rejuvenate its fertility. Such crops as wheat, barley, beans, oats, and rye were planted in the other fields. Similar manorial systems developed in China, Japan, and India.

Enclosure and the Agricultural Revolution. During the 15th century the owners of English landed estates began to enclose their lands with hedges (see ENCLOSURE). The first enclosure movement (1485–1603) converted arable land to pasture for sheep. Enclosure movements of the 1600s and especially from 1750 to 1831 permitted

A 15th-century Flemish miniature of farming activities includes (at top right) *the persuading of swarming bees into their hives—the four round structures sheltered by a thatched roof—by beating sticks on metal dishes. Oxen, sheep, horses, and a boar are herded* (center right) *to the music of a recorder. A field* (foreground) *is plowed and harrowed with ironwrought implements, and a laborer broadcasts seed. Five men* (center left) *with iron billhooks prune young trees in an orchard. To their rear, workers use axes to chop wood at the edge of a forest. By the Middle Ages in Europe, horses had replaced oxen as the principal draft animals. One of the greatest contributions to agriculture of this period was the invention of the horse collar, which remained unchanged in design for centuries.*

holders to cultivate large sections of land with the same crop. This procedure was more efficient than farming strips, eliminated the practice of letting land lie fallow, and allowed farmers to experiment with crop rotation and other agricultural technologies. Enclosure of lands, however, served to displace farmers, who either became tenants or landless farm laborers or migrated into the growing cities (see INDUSTRIAL REVOLUTION). Other European countries slowly began to enclose lands after 1800.

The invention of mechanical farm implements during the 17th and 18th centuries created an agricultural revolution in England. The inventions included Joseph Boyce's REAPER (1799) and Jethro TULL's horse-drawn drill (1701), a mechanical seed planter. Charles, 2d Viscount TOWNSHEND, of Norfolk introduced crop rotation of clover, wheat, turnips, and barley—an alternation of grain crops with nitrogen-fixing legumes and grasses that put nutrients back into the soil. Such FERTILIZERS as guano, lime, gypsum, and sandy clay, known as marl, were used to improve the soil. The first agricultural society (founded

1793) included Arthur Young (1741–1820), an educator who spread English agricultural innovations to the rest of Europe and the United States.

With the age of colonialism, the European powers established plantations in Asia, the islands of the Pacific and the Caribbean, and Latin America. On these new holdings such cash crops as tea, coffee, bananas, sugar, and rubber were introduced and cultivated on a large scale, either by indigenous laborers or—in the Americas—by slaves imported from Africa. The agricultural exploitation of Africa itself, however, began only in the 19th century.

Colonial North America. Throughout the coastal colonies settlers were taught by native Americans how to plant corn and other indigenous crops. In Canada during the 1700s mainly fur trappers and only a few farmers in Quebec occupied the land. Farmsteads along the St. Lawrence River were laid out in long strips, with one edge along the river and the farm building along a road; agriculture was on a subsistence level because the land was relatively infertile and the growing season short. New England farms were small subsistence farms, yielding rye, corn, barley, oats, and apples. Livestock was allowed to forage in woodlands. The larger farms of the middle colonies—New Jersey and Pennsylvania, for instance—originally grew New World crops because they were easier to plant and yielded more per hectare than Old World crops. These larger farms later introduced wheat, however, a crop that could be sold to the European market and that allowed farmers to become more commercial. Southern plantations—which used slave labor—covered hundreds of hectares and usually grew one crop intensively for commerce, particularly tobacco (introduced in 1614), rice (1696), indigo (mid-1700s), and cotton (1780s). Eli WHITNEY invented (1793) the cotton gin, which spurred Southern states to intensive cotton planting.

18th- and 19th-Century North America. After the American Revolution the U.S. government began to develop land policies that would promote settlement of the West quickly and at low cost. The Land Ordinance of 1785 stipulated that land be surveyed and sold in mile-square sections. The Northwest Ordinance encouraged settlement by providing for local self-government (see NORTHWEST TERRITORY). Federal expansion policies continued in the 1800s following the Louisiana Purchase (1803), the acquisition of Texas (1845), the Oregon settlement (1846), and the Mexican Cession (1848).

Such improved transportation as canals (see ERIE CANAL), steamboats, and railroads allowed commercial crops to be shipped more easily and quickly to market. Wars in Europe increased the demand for cotton, tobacco, and food. Such inventions as Cyrus McCORMICK's reaper (1831) and John DEERE's steel plow (1837) allowed the heavy, rich soils of the prairie to be tilled, opening new regions for the cultivation of wheat. The invention of barbed wire and the steel windmill made farming possible in what had been open range for Texas longhorn cattle. Food-processing techniques, such as canning, improved flour milling, and refrigeration, were developed during the 1840s. Refrigeration was especially important in making it possible for such distant countries as Argentina (beef) and New Zealand (mutton, milk, butter, and cheese) to export food to Europe.

In 1862, Abraham Lincoln signed the HOMESTEAD ACT, which allowed a settler 160 acres (64.7 ha) free after working it for 5 years. The U.S. Department of Agriculture

(Above) *A steel plow patented by John Deere in 1837 was the first implement capable of breaking sod in the U.S. prairies. Unlike cast-iron plows, the steel plow could cut through the deeply rooted prairie grass, and the heavy soil did not stick to the blade.*

(Right) *A combine harvester is pulled through an Oregon wheat field in this 1880s photo. Horse-drawn combines, which both cut and threshed wheat, used teams of 30 or more horses. In the late 1800s the wide, flat wheat fields of the western and midwestern United States easily accommodated these huge machines.*

(Above) *The Case steam engine, patented in 1886, replaced horses in pulling plows and combines. Modeled on early railway engines, this tractor was used for a short time until the invention of gasoline-powered engines.*

(Left) *A machine harvests wheat on a large farm in the state of Washington. Farming has been mechanized in the United States and other developed countries to such an extent that almost all work formerly performed by hand is now done by machine.*

was formed in 1862, a year that also saw the passage into law of the Morrill Act, which granted land to states for the establishment of agricultural colleges (see LAND-GRANT COLLEGES). In 1867 the National GRANGE, an organization for improving the economic and social condition of farmers, was created.

During the 1870s wheat farmers and cattle ranchers flourished in the prairies. A specific variety of wheat—Turkey Red—adapted particularly well to prairie soil, and wheat economy improved. Ranchers began to feed cattle grain, which resulted in better-quality beef sold to urban markets. The development of steam power resulted in mechanized COMBINES, TRACTORS, and threshers, which further improved wheat farming.

Although Canada's expansion policies did not open up prairie land until the 1870s, Thomas Douglas, 5th earl of SELKIRK, attempted to establish an experimental colony in Manitoba in 1812. He had received a land grant from the Hudson's Bay Company for the site where present-day Winnipeg exists and brought Scotch and Irish settlers to work the land. Despite crop failure, the agricultural inexperience of the farmers, and hostilities of the neighboring métis (people of mixed French and Indian ancestry), this RED RIVER SETTLEMENT eventually succeeded, especially after the introduction of an iron plow in 1824. Further colonization was minimal until legislation to section off land in squares and a homesteading act in 1870 encouraged immigration.

In 1887 the HATCH ACT, in the United States, ensured federal funding to land-grant colleges in order to set up agricultural experiment stations. During this time the agricultural scientist George Washington CARVER developed soybean flour, 118 products from sweet potatoes, and 300 products from peanuts at his research station at Tuskegee Institute, Alabama, in an effort to spur economic growth in the South by developing new crop potentials.

20th-Century United States. By the 1890s the gasoline tractor had been invented, providing power to do in minutes what took horses and farmers days. Gregor Johann MENDEL's theories of heredity came to light in the early 1900s, after which PLANT BREEDING became a science. By 1910 most of the arable land in the United States had been settled, and with the foresight of conservationists, methods for prevention of soil erosion began to be developed (see CONSERVATION). In 1914 the SMITH-LEVER ACT provided funding for extension work (see AGRICULTURAL EXTENSION SERVICE), which involves educators' traveling to instruct farmers and their families in farm management and home economics.

U.S. and Canadian farmers mobilized to provide food for Europe during World War I. As a result of European postwar poverty and U.S. overproduction, however, farmers experienced a depression lasting from 1922 to 1927. Nevertheless, Clarence BIRDSEYE perfected (1920s) a method for freezing foods, and supermarkets were springing up; both spurred farming of produce previously too perishable to be of commercial value. The Capper-Volstead Act (1922) allowed farmers to join COOPERATIVE organizations that controlled the marketing of their commodities, resulting in greater profits. Despite the progress, farmers' incomes were lower than the national level; therefore, legislative efforts to aid farmers began.

In the early 1930s droughts and dust storms caused by poor tillage practices devastated farms and ranches of the Great Plains (see DUST BOWL). Franklin D. Roosevelt's NEW DEAL sought to satisfy the demands of striking farmers by a series of acts that included the Agricultural Adjustment Act (1933; see AGRICULTURAL ADJUSTMENT ADMINISTRATION)—by which the secretary of agriculture could control crop production and maintain fair produce prices—and acts to improve rural roads, introduce electricity, and promote soil conservation. The Agricultural Marketing Act (1938) improved prices for producers of perishables and allowed the federal government to buy surpluses, which were donated to the poor and used in school-meal and food-stamp programs. During the 1930s more-powerful tractors were built, and harvesters for root and vegetable crops were invented. Hybrid corn was planted, and the Santa Gertrudis and American Brahman cattle, which could tolerate hot weather, were bred.

By the 1960s farmers required a huge outlay of capital and demanding marketing skills to deal with suppliers and food distributors in a network known as AGRIBUSINESS. High-powered machinery, feed, fertilizers, and pesticides began to be used, and poultry was raised in completely controlled environments (see FACTORY FARMING and EGG PRODUCTION). At the same time, lobbies of migrant laborers, environmental groups, and consumers began to affect agricultural policy. Some farmers initiated organic farming—using nonpolluting, nontoxic methods of cropping and animal breeding. The GREEN REVOLUTION of the 1960s, spearheaded by the plant geneticist Norman Ernest BORLAUG, was the result of crop improvement programs established to help small farmers of developing nations. These programs continue, with emphasis now on breeding new crop varieties that need little fertilizer or irrigation. Once-ignored plants such as soybeans, sunflowers, and sorghum have become major commercial crops, and research has encouraged the increasing cultivation of such arid-land plants as JOJOBA and guayule. Other exotic crops that are being grown as possible future commercial sources of food include AMARANTH and quinoa (cultivated for their nutritious seeds); triticale, a cross between wheat and rye that has a high yield and a rich protein content; and various tropical fruits, roots, and vegetables. In addition, GENETIC ENGINEERING offers the possibility of increasing crop yields by genetically implanting desired traits—disease resistance, for example—into agricultural plants, or by synthesizing hormones that can be used to increase growth rate or milk production in farm animals.

The enormous increase in the production of basic foods has paradoxically created problems of oversupply in Europe and the United States, whose governments buy and stockpile vast amounts of such staples as wheat, cheese, and butter in order to maintain prices that will keep farming profitable.

See also: AGRICULTURE AND THE FOOD SUPPLY; FARMS AND FARMING.

Agriculture, U.S. Department of

The U.S. Department of Agriculture administers programs and services concerned with farmers and consumers. These include farm price-supports, food stamps for low-income citizens, loans to farmers, soil conservation, biological research, the inspection of food products, and the promotion of agricultural exports.

Established in 1862, the department was given cabinet status in 1889. Among its agencies, the Forest Service manages national forests and grasslands. The Agricultural Stabilization and Conservation Service works to stabilize commodity prices by making loans and purchasing surplus crops. The Foreign Agricultural Service promotes export sales of farm products. The Food and Nutrition Service makes low-cost food available to needy people through such channels as the FOOD STAMP PROGRAM. The Science and Education Administration works to improve research and teaching in the food and agricultural sciences. It conducts research programs in animal and plant production and human nutrition and cooperates with state governments in the Cooperative Extension System, which assists in such areas as agricultural production, natural resources, food and nutrition, and 4-H development.

agriculture and the food supply

The supply of food depends on three factors: how much has been produced by agriculture and fishing (see FISHING INDUSTRY); how much has been consumed; and how much has been preserved by safe processing and storage. The most important agricultural products for the world's food supply are cereals (see GRAINS), pulses, and, to a lesser extent, livestock (see ANIMAL HUSBANDRY). Cereals, such as wheat, rice, maize (corn), millet, and sorghum, provide nearly all the food energy (calories) and up to 90% of all protein consumed by the world's people. Pigs are the chief meat animal worldwide, followed by poultry, beef cattle, and sheep. Pulses—the seed parts of such legumes as beans, soybeans, and peanuts (groundnuts)—are important sources of protein in the world food supply. Except for sugar and bananas, few of the other crops that are prominent in the world agriculture trade have nutritional significance in the food supply. Many fruits, grains, and vegetables that are often unfamiliar to Western agricultural scientists, however, serve as important local food supplies.

Supply and Population. About 90% of all grain produced is consumed in the countries where it is grown. The 10% that enters world trade comes from the few countries—the United States, Canada, Australia, and Argentina—where the grain produced far exceeds domestic needs. Most countries depend to some extent—and developing countries tend to depend heavily—on cereal imports to augment their own crops.

Some authorities predict that population growth will eventually surpass world food production and that massive famine will result. Other authorities, who point to a recent decrease of population growth rates as well as to dramatic gains in agricultural production, insist that such a tragedy can be prevented by a combination of appropriate governmental policies and appropriate research and technology.

Economic Issues. Both high population growth and the effects of a minority of the world's people having the money to consume more than they need can cause stresses in the food supply. Persistent poverty, however, is the underlying cause of the world's hunger problem because in many places the ability to obtain food is determined by income and purchasing power no matter how large the supply may be. People or governments without enough purchasing power lack what is called *effective demand* for food in the marketplace.

Sometimes the laws of effective demand hurt the poor in unexpected ways when traditional agriculture in developing countries is modernized and brought into the international market system. When India's farmers, for example, found wheat and rice production more profitable, they lost interest in traditional pulse production. As pulses became less plentiful in the local markets, their prices rose. Malnutrition increased because the poorest could no longer afford to balance their incomplete grain-protein diet with pulses.

Many governments find it necessary to protect the nutritional needs of their own low-income populations, and sometimes those of others, with special programs. The most extensive food-aid program undertaken is the Food for Peace program conducted since 1954 by the U.S. government. Through this program, U.S. surplus grain either can be sold to developing countries at normal market prices with the aid of low-interest loans or can be distributed at no charge by such organizations as Catholic Relief Services or Cooperative for American Relief Everywhere (see CARE) to developing countries faced with food emergencies.

Recipient countries do not want to become dependent on donor nations for food supplies, however: domestic grain prices too often fall when food aid arrives, discouraging local farmers and slowing development. Less-developed countries (LDCs) need international outlets for their surplus production at the same time that many of the richer countries—which have donated agricultural assistance—establish trade barriers to protect their own subsidized systems. Nations specializing in cash crops such as cocoa or coffee often find themselves at the mercy of markets they cannot control. Also, although some LDCs can grow commodity crops more cheaply than can Western agricultures, their governments cannot compete on international markets because they have no money to subsidize the export of surpluses.

Factors Affecting Food Supply

Basic farming practices (see FARMS AND FARMING)—planting, harvesting, and storage of crops—are generally similar everywhere, but various systems of farming exist. In many developing nations much of the cropland is currently devoted to subsistence agriculture, a food-production system characterized by minimal mechanization, high reliance on human labor, and mostly on-farm consumption of what is grown. About 60% of the world's cropland is estimated to be in subsistence agriculture. Another form of food production, particularly in North America, Europe, Central America, and Oceania, is commercial agriculture, which is large-scale, highly mechanized, and entirely market-oriented (see AGRIBUSINESS). A third important system is characteristic of centrally planned, or socialist, nations. This system includes state farms and collective farms, as in the USSR, and communes, as in China. In general, these are designed to provide food for the workers on the farms in return for their labor and also to provide food for the nation as a whole according to a national plan.

Arable Land. Agriculture depends ultimately on arable land—land that has the potential to produce a crop. Some 3.2 billion ha (7.9 billion acres) of arable land ex-

The Ifugao tribe of the Philippines cuts terraces into steep, fertile mountain slopes. The heavy rainfalls caught by these terraces supply the water necessary for rice cultivation. The construction of terraces is one of many ways that farmers of various regions in the world adapt land to meet agricultural needs.

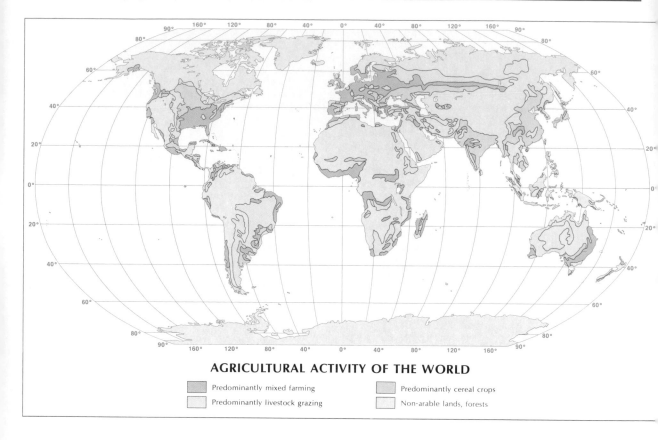

AGRICULTURAL ACTIVITY OF THE WORLD

Predominantly mixed farming

Predominantly livestock grazing

Predominantly cereal crops

Non-arable lands, forests

ist worldwide, which is about 24% of the total ice-free land. Currently, less than half of this land is actually under cultivation. The largest reserves are in Africa, where 72% of the arable land is not used for crops. Huge investments would be necessary to do the clearing, leveling, disease control, and irrigating required for much of this land to become fully productive.

As demand for food has increased, land and SOIL mismanagement has occurred with alarming frequency. In the past 100 years in parts of the American Midwest, more than 50% of the topsoil has been lost to wind and water erosion (see EROSION AND SEDIMENTATION) through improper cropping and tillage practices. About 1 million ha (2.5 million acres) of cropland are lost each year in the developing nations, due mostly to poor land management. Overgrazing and deforestation of land have occurred in such areas as Mexico, Malaysia, and the Sahel. Arable land may be turned to DESERT by the combined effects of destroyed vegetation and erosion.

Arable land worldwide has also been lost by conversion for housing and business purposes. Generally, this land can only be replaced by bringing less productive, or more erosion-prone, land under cultivation. Efforts are now being made by the United States and other wealthy nations to preserve their best remaining agricultural land.

Water Supply. Many experts believe that in the 1990s lack of water (see WATER RESOURCES) rather than lack of arable land will be the major obstacle to expanded worldwide food production.The amount of water available for agricultural use cannot easily be increased, but it can be better used. Research is being done in the areas of IRRIGATION and seawater DESALINATION to improve water availability and increase the amount of land that can be farmed.

Climate and Weather. Climate, the long-term atmospheric conditions of a region, determines the cropping possibilities in an area. Rice grows in a wet, tropical climate, for instance, and corn grows in a humid subtropical or temperate climate. Weather is the daily expression of climate and can change greatly from day to day or seasonally. Weather patterns may occasionally set limits on agricultural productivity, even in generally favorable climates. Famines in India and China can be traced to such erratic weather patterns as high (causing floods) and low (causing droughts) precipitation in climate zones that otherwise would be expected to produce successful crop yields. Climates, although relatively stable, also change. In the Northern Hemisphere, for example, climatic patterns appear to be becoming more extreme, which may cause serious agricultural disruption.

Fertilizer. Because soils often lack the right kind and amount of plant nutrients for the best crop results, the farmer must supply such missing nutrients. In many parts of the world, fertility needs are met by the use of inorganic chemical FERTILIZER. For developing nations, the cost of such fertilizer is often too high; instead, organic sources of plant nutrients are widely used to increase soil fertility.

Pests. Once a crop has been established, the farmer is immediately threatened with crop losses from a variety of pests. Annual losses due to pests amount to 20–40% of potential production. In developed nations, pests have been controlled by chemical HERBICIDES and pesticides (see PESTICIDES AND PEST CONTROL). Chemical pesticides, however, can cause ecological damage and present hazards to human health. Increasingly, chemical pesticides and their hazardous potential are being introduced into developing regions of the world. Appropriate pest-control strategies, however, can replace the exclusive use of chemicals; they include a combination of management practices that create environments unfavorable to pests.

Energy. Increased food productivity is related to increased use of energy. In the developing world the major source of power for agriculture continues to be human labor and animal power. In developed nations, power is supplied by agricultural machinery that is fueled largely by petroleum. Much energy is also consumed in irrigation, transportation, food processing, and the manufacture of agricultural chemicals and fertilizers. One effect of such modernization is that fewer people can produce greater quantities of food. A point of diminishing returns can be reached, however, where adding more energy to agricultural processes becomes an inefficient use of that energy. In mechanized agricultural systems, as much as 10 times more energy is used to produce food than is returned to society as food for consumption. In many developing nations, however, energy invested in agriculture generally returns up to 20 times more in food products than is expended during production. Nevertheless, developing nations, to most fully utilize their food potential, will have to apply much more energy than previously to agriculture, especially in the areas of improved tillage, more fertilizer, and timely harvesting.

Increasing Food Production

If standards of living in less developed countries (LDCs) are to be raised beyond subsistence level, increases in food production must exceed population growth in those countries.

Land Reform. In many parts of the world—particularly Latin America—the distribution of land is grossly inequitable, with small minorities of wealthy landowners controlling major portions of the best agricultural land. Often these landowners focus on the production of cash crops for the export market. Poor subsistence farmers are forced to farm small plots of marginally productive land to provide for their own needs. The need for reform is apparent, but land reform is a political issue; often those with the power to direct land-reform policies are the very people who stand to lose land. Consequently, land-tenure patterns tend to change slowly. Governments of several nations—notably China, Cuba, Egypt, Iran, Kenya, Mexico, and Taiwan—have experienced some success with land-reform programs. Generally, these programs provide poor farmers with secure access to agricultural land through such policies as rent control for tenant farmers or direct expropriation and redistribution of large land holdings.

Use of Machinery. In the more affluent nations, large-scale mechanization of agriculture has increased the amount of food that can be produced by each worker in agriculture and thus has reduced the need for labor and the number of on-the-farm jobs. In many LDCs, however, where labor is plentiful and incomes often desperately low, governments now seek technologies scaled to the small size of typical farms and designed to improve labor efficiency but not to replace it.

Where modern agricultural technologies—artificial fertilizers and pesticides, complex sophisticated machinery, large and expensive irrigation projects—have been applied in countries with "undeveloped" agricultures, the results often have been unsatisfactory. Large dams may prove to have negative environmental impacts. Heavy machinery breaks down, needs expensive fuel, and affects fragile soils. New seeds prove to be unsuited to the climate, soil, or growing conditions of the new countries where they are planted.

Crop-dusting planes spread pesticide over an Arizona cotton field. To prevent the pesticide from drifting into residential or business sites, dusting can be carried out only in windless weather.

Trying to impose advanced techniques in areas that practice traditional agriculture may often do more harm than good. Recent attempts to improve traditional technologies seek to provide small-scale devices that are inexpensive, are easy to produce, and meet the needs of a specific region. Stoves, for example, may not seem vital to a village's well-being, but traditional ways of cooking, such as using open fires, are inefficient, consume firewood out of proportion to the cooking heat they provide, and are the principal cause of deforestation in many undeveloped regions. Clay, stone, or scrap-iron stoves have been designed that are inexpensive to make and use less than half the fuel of open fires. Solar stoves capture the Sun's heat to provide fire for cooking. Solar vegetable dryers can preserve a season's crop of fruits and vegetables. These and many other devices could lighten the burden of work in villages and preserve resources as well.

Improving the productivity of farm animals is another neglected area. Using specially designed scoops, a team of oxen can dig out a pond to catch and hold rainwater. Although most animal-pulled plows require two draft animals, a plow has been designed for farmers who own only one animal.

Other areas of small but important technological advance include improving animal nutrition and soil fertility by growing nitrogenous food and fodder, such as cowpeas; using gasoline-powered plows and other machinery that can be managed and operated by one person; increasing the use of terraces in hilly regions to lower erosion; and building raised seedbeds to increase evaporation from waterlogged soils.

Genetic Technology. PLANT BREEDING is modification of a plant's genetic makeup in a purposeful way. The general goal of plant breeding is to assemble into single varieties the best possible combination of genes that control desirable traits. The traits of importance include yield, local environmental adaptation, uniformity, quality, disease or insect resistance, and early maturity. Numerous plant-breeding methodologies can be used worldwide, but actual testing of experimental varieties must be done in the regions in which they are planned for use in order to ensure suitability. Because the raw material for plant breeding is genetic diversity, gene banks—which have collections of seeds of wild relatives and unimproved and improved varieties of crops—have been organized to preserve genetic resources for future use by plant breeders.

Research efforts in the 1960s to find ways for farmers in developing countries to produce far more food on the same amount of land led to early successes popularly called the GREEN REVOLUTION. Research centers in Asia, Africa, and Latin America conduct applied research on subsistence food crops and livestock problems of regional importance. The International Rice Research Institute in the Philippines, for example, developed hardy, short-stemmed rice. By the mid-1970s, more than a quarter of all rice land was sown in the new rice. Enthusiasm for such early successes has been tempered by a growing realization that agricultural change is much more complex than had originally been anticipated, and that high production levels with the new seeds require a costly package that includes, for instance, chemical fertilizers and pesticides often unavailable to small farmers.

There are, however, many opportunities for countries to develop native plants into important food crops. Ethiopia, plagued by drought and famine in the 1980s, provides a case in point. The Ethiopians grow a grain called t'ef, which, it is believed, has barely developed from its original wild form. Unlike other staple grains, t'ef needs little rain and grows well in high, cold regions. Its straw makes excellent fodder, and its tiny grains are highly nutritious for humans. Breeding the right varieties of t'ef— that is, working with those seeds which currently grow on marginal land under arid, cold conditions—could result in a grain that might provide basic food needs for Ethiopia as well as for other mountainous African countries.

Ethiopia is one of the rare places in the world where many plant species that now grow in a host of different varieties around the world can still be found in their primitive, uncultivated forms. Some offer great potential: there are hundreds of wild pea varieties, for example. These, and many other plants that offer great genetic diversity, are collected and sent to gene banks, but their existence on their native soil is threatened by the introduction of new, high-yielding foreign plants developed by plant breeders outside Ethiopia.

Agricultural Education. New information and technology that can help farmers increase their production must be communicated effectively if it is to achieve its purpose. Physical constraints, such as a poor road system, can handicap the spread of information, but various cultural constraints—including verbal or scientific illiteracy among farmers or the communication gap between farmers and agricultural researchers and technicians created by such differences as economic class and cultural assumptions—may present an even greater challenge.

Effective communications with small farmers varies in approach according to circumstances. India, for example, has developed a highly successful national agricultural management program called the Training and Visit System. Village Extension Workers (VEWs) work in the fields as part of their training—unlike workers in other countries, who may be graduates of agricultural schools but know little about practical cultivation methods. VEWs make the same circuit of visits every two weeks, appearing regularly to teach new technologies and methods to farmers, and to listen to their problems. They carry legitimate complaints back to research agriculturists, who attempt to find appropriate answers. VEWs also work with village women, setting up nutrition programs and helping to create small cottage industries that will bring added cash into the village. The techniques employed in India are now being tried in some 40 different countries, with emphasis on Africa where small farms abound.

Cultivation of New Crops. The discovery of the New World resulted in an increase of available foods both in Europe and in the colonized territories. Such new crops as potatoes, tomatoes, corn, and green peppers gradually became staples in countries throughout the world.

The world is still rich in foods that might be adapted to cultivation in many countries, although these foods now grow only in a single area. South America, in particular, has many indigenous crops of interest. Among these are a wide range of potato varieties, each with different growth and keeping habits. Tarwi, an Andean legume, has nitrogen-fixing properties and thus enriches the soil, while its seed equals soybean in protein and oil content. AMARANTH, a protein-rich seed, flourishes throughout warmer areas of Latin America. Kiwicha is a grain that can be processed like corn or wheat. Oca, a bright yellow tuber, can serve as a potato substitute.

Ecological Concerns. There is increasing evidence and concern that current agricultural practices will not be sustainable as energy, water, and other natural resources become more scarce or more expensive. The adoption of more ecologically sensitive approaches could reduce the use of such resources, enhance soil fertility, and reduce pest infestations. For example, the use of integrated pest management—the cultivation of pest-resistant plant species; the maintenance of predator populations; reduced reliance on single-crop (monoculture) systems, which are particulary susceptible to pest outbreaks–may be less costly and more ecologically sound in controlling pest populations than the routine use of pesticides. Organic farming has demonstrated the validity of the ecological approach. Organic farmers may not grow as much corn or soybeans as their industrialized neighbors, but their costs are far lower, the soil generally richer, and their crops healthier.

World Organizations and Agricultural Aid

Agricultural assistance and adequate food supply have been issues of primary interest to the FOOD AND AGRICULTURE ORGANIZATION, the WORLD BANK, and the United Nations Development Program. The UNITED NATIONS CHILDREN'S FUND has among its programs one in which village women of developing nations are helped to produce and process food.

Until recently, relatively little consideration was given by governments to the politics or sociology of agriculture and economic development—how to redistribute national income or to increase the income of the poor so that they can participate fully in the market for food, or how to give small farmers more incentives to produce for the market through land ownership, credit on reasonable terms, or farming necessities at fair prices. A growing international consensus, however, is that food should be economically available to people having low income and that small farmers of developing nations need aid to produce more food in ways that fit their circumstances. The underlying problem, according to this view, is not a lack of food but rather the lack of political will to resolve food problems using available knowledge and resources.

Agrigento [ah-gree-jen'-toh]   Agrigento is the capital of Agrigento province in southwestern Sicily, Italy. It has a population of 51,931 (1981); the economy centers on agriculture, tourism, and sulfur and potash mining. Founded by Greeks c.580 BC as the colony of Akragas, it became one of the largest and richest Greek cities of the

classical world. In 480 BC an alliance between Akragas and SYRACUSE brought about a decisive victory over the Carthaginians and put most of Sicily under Greek control for 70 years. This period of economic expansion—reflected in a prolific output of silver coinage—saw the rapid construction of at least ten temples, including the huge (113 by 56 m/372 by 184 ft) temple of Zeus, and the organization of a grid of streets for a population of about 150,000 at its peak.

Destroyed by CARTHAGE in 406 BC it was refounded by Syracuse after 338, but it suffered badly during the PUNIC WARS, falling to Rome in 210 BC. Called Agrigentum by the Romans, the city was colonized by Saracens in 828 and was captured by the Norman rulers of Sicily in 1086. The ancient site, which has been partially excavated, includes a row of well-preserved temples from the 5th century BC. Agrigento is also the site of early Christian CATACOMBS and two medieval churches.

agrimony [ag'-ruh-moh-nee]   The common name *agrimony* is used for two different plants in two different families. One plant, the genus *Agrimonia* in the rose (Rosaceae) family, is a widely distributed genus of perennial herbs that includes agrimony, cocklebur, and harvest lice.

A. eupatoria, bearing slender clusters of yellow flowers in the fall, has long been used as a mild astringent and to treat diarrhea and liver ailments. The plant contains a compound that causes human skin to become light-sensitive, resulting in a sunburnlike rash after contact with the plant followed by exposure to sunlight. A yellow dye is produced from the leaves.

The other plant, a perennial herb known as hemp agrimony (*Eupatorium cannabinum* in the Compositae family), is found in wet areas throughout Europe, northern Africa, and west and central Asia.

Agrippa, Marcus Vipsanius [uh-grip'-uh, vip-say'-nee-uhs]   Marcus Vipsanius Agrippa, c.63–12 BC, was a Roman general and trusted friend of Octavius (later Emperor AUGUSTUS). As consul he organized (37 BC) a fleet for Octavius that won decisive victories over Sextus Pompeius at Mylae and Naulochus. Subsequently, his masterful deployment of the fleet in the Battle of ACTIUM (31 BC) was the principal cause of Mark ANTONY's defeat. During Augustus's rule, Agrippa consolidated Roman power in the east, in Gaul, and in Spain. He spent much of his personal fortune on public works for Rome, building the Pantheon and the first public baths. His third wife was Julia, Augustus's daughter.

Agrippina II [ag-ruh-pee'-nuh]   The Roman matron Julia Agrippina, b. AD 15, was the daughter of GERMANICUS CAESAR and Agrippina I, and mother (by her first husband Ahenobarbus) of NERO. She held power during the reign of her brother CALIGULA but was banished after plotting against him. Her uncle CLAUDIUS I recalled her to

Rome and married her in 49. He allowed her ambitions full scope and favored Nero over his own son, Britannicus. Agrippina is thought to have poisoned Claudius to make Nero emperor. Ruling with Nero for a time, she abused her power and quarreled with his supporters. In 59 he ordered her put to death.

agronomy   see AGRICULTURE AND THE FOOD SUPPLY; FARMS AND FARMING

Aguascalientes (city) [ah'-gwahs-kahl-yayn'-tays] Aguascalientes is the capital of Aguascalientes state in central Mexico. The population is 293,152 (1980). The city lies at an altitude of about 1,890 m (6,200 ft) in a mountainous area about 420 km (260 mi) northwest of Mexico City. Its mild climate and hot mineral springs have made Aguascalientes a popular health resort. The city is noted for its plazas, parks, and colonial architecture. It is also a textile center and is famous for breeding fighting bulls.

The city was founded in 1575 as a fortified Spanish outpost on the trail from silver mines to Mexico City. In 1914 the Convention of Aguascalientes—an unsuccessful meeting of the revolutionary leaders Emiliano Zapata, Pancho Villa, and Venustiano Carranza—was held there. Underneath the city are extensive tunnels, apparently built by an ancient Indian civilization of unknown identity.

Aguascalientes (state) Aguascalientes (1989 est. pop., 702,615) is a state in central Mexico on the Anahuac plateau, 900 to 3,050 m (3,000 to 10,000 ft) above sea level. The capital city is Aguascalientes. Climate is moderated by the high elevation; numerous thermal springs in the region give it its name, which is Spanish for "hot waters." Aguascalientes is a fertile agricultural region, much of which is irrigated. Crops include fruit, maize, and grapes (for wine). Livestock raising is important, and zinc, silver, and gold are mined. First explored by the Spanish in the 16th century, Aguascalientes was the scene of heavy fighting during the revolution of 1910–20.

Aguinaldo, Emilio [ah-gee-nahl'-doh] Emilio Aguinaldo, b. Mar. 29, 1869, d. Feb. 6, 1964, was a leader of the revolution to end Spanish rule of the Philippines. Becoming mayor (1895) of Kawit in his native province of Cavite, he subsequently directed attacks against the Spanish military presence in Cavite, making it a focal point in the nationalist revolt and earning himself the title of general from his followers.

In 1897 he was elected president of the revolutionary assembly at Tejeros, Cavite. Exiled to Hong Kong when the insurrection faltered, Aguinaldo was encouraged to return by the United States when the SPANISH-AMERICAN WAR that erupted in the Caribbean was extended to the Philippines. Declaring the independence of his country

from Spain on June 12, 1898, he became president of the first Philippine Republic on Jan. 23, 1899. The American defeat of Spain was followed in 1899 by war between the previously allied Filipinos and the United States. Aguinaldo was captured in 1901, and when war ended (1901), he swore allegiance to the United States, which annexed the Philippines, and retired from public life. After World War II, he was charged with cooperating with the Japanese but was never tried. The Philippines finally became independent in 1946.

Agulhas, Cape [uh-gul'-uhs] Cape Agulhas is the extreme southern point of the African continent. Located in the Cape Province of South Africa, it is on the dividing line between the Atlantic and Indian oceans. Early sailors erroneously believed the tip of Africa to be the Cape of GOOD HOPE, about 145 km (90 mi) to the northwest.

Ahab, King of Israel [ay'-hab] Ahab (r. c.870–850 BC), son of Omri, was a major ruler of the northern kingdom of ISRAEL. The Bible, which narrates his reign in detail (1 Kings 16–22), portrays him unfavorably because he married the Phoenician princess JEZEBEL and permitted the worship of her god BAAL, but also recounts his victories over the Syrian king Ben-hadad and tells of "all the cities that he built" (1 Kings 22:39). Extensive remains of Ahab's building projects have been excavated at SAMARIA, HAZOR, MEGIDDO, and other sites. Assyrian records mention him as a principal member of the coalition that fought SHALMANESER III at the battle of Karkar in 853 BC. Ahab died fighting the Syrians at Ramoth-gilead.

Ahad ha-Am   see ACHAD HA-AM

Ahaz, King of Judah [ay'-haz] Ahaz was king (r. c. 735–720 BC) of JUDAH, the southern kingdom of the Jews. He is described in 2 Kings 16 as worshiping BAAL and even sacrificing his own sons. When Judah was threatened by Aram (Syria) and the northern kingdom of ISRAEL, Ahaz appealed to the Assyrian king, over the objections of the prophet ISAIAH. The Assyrians conquered the entire area and exercised a decisive political and religious influence.

Ahmadabad [ah'-mah-dah-bahd'] Ahmadabad, a city in Gujarat state of western India, was founded in 1411 by a Gujarati king, Ahmad Shah. It is an industrial and cultural center lying 445 km (280 mi) north of Bombay and has a population of 2,548,047 (1981). Ahmadabad is India's most important center for cotton textile manufacture. The city is also known for its dyeing and printing industries, handicrafts, and brass articles.

The old city, situated on the left bank of the Sabarmati River, is crowded and interspersed with busy shopping districts. The area on the right bank of the river is better planned and more functional. Gandhi Ashram, located on a bluff of the river, is where Mahatma GANDHI spent a considerable part of his political career. Historic mosques and tombs represent a fusion of Islamic, Hindu, and Jain traditions.

Ahmose I, King of Egypt [ah'-mos]   Ahmose I, king of Egypt (r. *c.*1570–1546 BC), was the founder of the 18th dynasty, one of the most outstanding in the history of ancient Egypt. His principal achievement was to weaken the HYKSOS, who had dominated Egypt for some 300 years, by taking Avaris, their citadel in the north.

Ahmose II, King of Egypt   Ahmose II was king of Egypt from about 570 to 526 BC, in the 26th dynasty. He came to power by overthrowing King Apries, who had been blamed for the failure of an attack on Libya. According to the Greek historian Herodotus, Ahmose II's reign was prosperous: he left many architectural monuments, developed relations with Greece, and married Ladice of Cyrene, a Greek. He may also have conquered Cyprus. After his death, his son Psammetichus III was deposed when the Persians under Cambyses II invaded Egypt.

Ahura Mazda   see ZOROASTRIANISM

Aïda [ah-ee'-duh]   Giuseppe VERDI's (1813–1901) *Aïda* received its world premiere at Cairo, Egypt, on Dec. 24, 1871. Negotiations with the composer had begun in 1869, initiated by the Khedive of Egypt in connection with the opening of the Suez Canal and the building of a modern opera house in Cairo, the nation's capital. Verdi at first demurred, but he was spurred by receipt of a prose sketch based on an incident in Egypt's past, the work of a noted historian, Auguste Mariette. Verdi invited the French librettist Camille du Locle to expand this sketch and summoned the poet Antonio Ghislanzoni to supply the necessary Italian verses, a project in which Verdi himself shared.

The plot, set in ancient THEBES, concerns a young Egyptian warrior, Radames, chosen to lead his country's army against the enemy, Ethopia. Secretly, Radames loves Aïda, an Ethiopian slave, and is loved in turn by the jealous Princess Amneris, the pharaoh's daughter. Radames returns victorious but is tricked into betraying military secrets to Aïda's father, Amonasro, the defeated king of Ethiopia, who has been taken captive while in disguise. About to flee with Aïda, Radames is caught and sentenced to die in a sealed tomb beneath the Temple of Ptah. Somehow Aïda manages to join him there, and as both bid farewell to Earth, Amneris implores peace for their souls in the temple above.

AIDS   Acquired immune deficiency syndrome, or AIDS, is a recently recognized disease. It is caused by infection with the human immunodeficiency virus (HIV), which at-tacks selected cells in the immune system (see IMMUNITY) and produces defects in function. These defects may not be apparent for years. They lead in a relentless fashion, however, to a severe suppression of the immune system's ability to resist harmful organisms. This leaves the body open to invasion by various infections, which are therefore called opportunistic diseases, and to the development of unusual cancers. The virus also tends to reach certain brain cells. This leads to so-called neuropsychiatric abnormalities, or psychological disturbances caused by physical damage to nerve cells.

Since the first AIDS cases were reported in 1981, through 1990 about 160,000 AIDS cases and 100,000 deaths have been reported in the United States alone. This is only the tip of the iceberg of HIV infection, however. It is estimated that between 1 and 1.5 million Americans had been infected with the virus by the late 1980s but had not yet developed clinical symptoms. AIDS cases have also been reported in about 150 countries worldwide. Central Africa in particular appears to suffer a heavy burden of this illness.

No cure or preventive vaccine now exists for AIDS. Many of those infected with HIV may not even be aware that they carry and can spread the virus. Combating it is a major challenge to biomedical scientists and health-care providers. Over the years to come, HIV infection and AIDS will represent one of the most pressing public-policy and public-health problems worldwide.

Definition of AIDS. The U.S. CENTERS FOR DISEASE CONTROL has established criteria for defining cases of AIDS that are based on laboratory evidence, the presence of certain opportunistic diseases, and a range of other conditions. The opportunistic diseases are generally the most prominent and life-threatening clinical manifestations of AIDS. It is now recognized, however, that neuropsychiatric manifestations of HIV infection of the brain are also common. Other complications of HIV infection include fever, diarrhea, severe weight loss, and swollen lymph nodes (see LYMPHATIC SYSTEM).

When HIV-infected persons experience some of the above symptoms but do not meet full criteria for AIDS, they are given the diagnosis of AIDS-related complex, or ARC. The growing feeling is that ARC and HIV infection without symptoms should not be viewed as distinct entities but, rather, as stages of an irreversible progression toward AIDS.

Historical Background. In the late 1970s, certain rare types of cancer and a variety of serious infections were recognized to be occurring in increasing numbers of previously healthy persons. Strikingly, these were disorders that would hardly ever threaten persons with normally functioning immune systems. First formally described in 1981, AIDS was observed predominantly to be affecting homosexual and bisexual men. Soon thereafter, intravenous drug users, hemophiliacs, and recipients of blood transfusions were recognized as being at increased risk for the disease as well. It was also noted that sexual partners of persons displaying AIDS could contract the disease.

Further study of AIDS patients revealed marked de-

HUMAN IMMUNODEFICIENCY VIRUS (HIV)

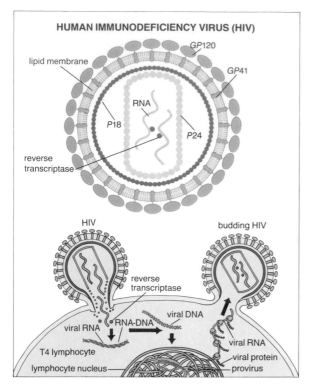

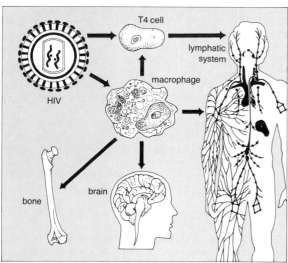

pletion of white BLOOD cells called T4 lymphocytes. These cells play a crucial role in coordinating the body's immune defenses against invading organisms. It was presumed that this defect in AIDS patients was acquired in a common manner. Then, in 1983, a virus that attacks T4 cells was separately discovered by Robert Gallo at the U.S. National Institutes of Health and Luc Montagnier at France's Pasteur Institute. The virus is now officially called human immunodeficiency virus (HIV); considerable evidence indicates that it is indeed the causative agent for AIDS. A second strain that has been identified, HIV-2, is thus far relatively rare outside of Africa.

Little is known about the biological and geographical origins of HIV. Apparently, however, this is the first time in modern history that the virus has spread widely among human beings. Related viruses have been observed in animal populations, such as certain African monkeys.

The Nature of the Virus. HIV is an RNA RETROVIRUS. It has a dense cylindrical core that encases two molecules of viral RNA genetic material. A spherical outer envelope surrounds the core. Like all retroviruses, HIV possesses a special enzyme, called reverse transcriptase, that is able to make a DNA copy of the viral RNA. This enables the virus to reverse the normal flow of genetic information (see GENETIC CODE) and to incorporate its viral genes into the genetic material of its host. The virus may then remain in a latent form for a variable and often lengthy period of time until it is reactivated.

A critical step in HIV infection is the binding of the virus to a so-called receptor on the cell it attacks, enabling it to gain entrance. Studies have shown that a molecule called CD4, which occurs predominantly on the surface of the T4 cell, serves as this receptor. Although the T4 cell is a major HIV target, virtually any cell having the CD4 surface molecule can become infected with HIV. Thus blood cells known as monocytes and macrophages also are important targets.

Modes of Transmission. Researchers have isolated HIV from a number of body fluids, including blood, semen, saliva, tears, urine, cerebrospinal fluid, breast milk, and cervical and vaginal secretions. Strong evidence indicates, however, that HIV is transmitted only through three primary routes: sexual intercourse, whether vaginal or anal, with an infected individual; exposure to infected blood or blood products; and from an infected mother to her child before or during birth.

At least 97% of all U.S. AIDS cases have occurred through one of these three routes, with transmission between homosexual men accounting for about 60% of these cases. Heterosexual transmission in the United States accounts for only about 5% of cases. About 21%

of AIDS cases are caused by intravenous drug abusers exposed to HIV-infected blood through the sharing of needles. The current practices of screening blood donors and testing all donated blood and plasma for HIV antibodies have reduced the number of cumulative cases due to transfusion to about 1%.

The number of new cases of AIDS in women of reproductive age is increasing at an alarming rate. From 1987 to 1988 the death rate due to AIDS in women 15 to 44 years of age increased by 40%. This trend forecasts the devastating impact AIDS will have on infant mortality, since more than 80% of HIV-infected children under age 13 acquired HIV from their infected mothers. Between 24% and 33% of children born to infected women will develop the disease.

No scientific evidence supports transmission of HIV through ordinary nonsexual contact. Careful studies demonstrate that despite prolonged household contact with infected individuals, family members have not become infected—except through the routes described above. Similarly, studies of nurses, physicians, and other health professionals caring for AIDS patients have revealed no instances in which HIV was transmitted through routine contact. In addition, claims of transmission by insects have been disproved.

Clinical Signs. Following infection with HIV, an individual may show no symptoms at all, or may develop an acute but transient mononucleosislike illness. The period between initial infection and the development of AIDS is currently observed to vary from about 6 months to 11 years. Various estimates indicate that somewhere between 26% and 46% of the infected individuals will go on to develop full-blown AIDS within a little more than 7 years following infection. Once a diagnosis of AIDS is certain, the clinical course generally follows a relentless decline, with death occurring within one to two years.

Opportunistic Infections and Cancers. Because the T4 cell is involved in almost all immune responses, its depletion renders the body highly susceptible to opportunistic infections and tumorous growths. The most predominant and threatening complication is *Pneumocystic carinii* PNEUMONIA, which is frequently the first infection to occur and is the most common cause of death. Other infections include the parasites *Toxoplasma gondii* (see TOXOPLASMOSIS) and *Cryptosporidiosis*; fungi such as *Candida* (see CANDIDIASIS) and *Cryptococcus* (see FUNGUS DISEASES); mycobacteria such as *Mycobacterium avium, intracellulare*, and *tuberculosis* (see TUBERCULOSIS); and viruses such as cytomegalovirus and herpes simplex and zoster (see HERPES). Increased susceptibility to bacterial infection is noted particularly among children with AIDS.

Many AIDS patients develop CANCERS, including Kaposi's sarcoma (KS), non-Hodgkin's lymphoma, and HODGKIN'S DISEASE. KS occurs in patients who manifest hardly any evidence of immunological impairment, indicating that other factors may also be at work in the development of such cancers. Among the non-Hodgkin's lymphomas are immunoblastic and Burkitt's-type lymphomas as well as primary brain lymphomas. These tumors tend to be unusually aggressive and poorly responsive to che-

motherapy, particularly in AIDS patients who have already experienced opportunistic infections.

Other HIV-Related Disorders and Cofactors. Neuropsychiatric manifestations occur in about 60% of HIV-infected persons. It is now well established that HIV can exist and proliferate within the brain, spinal cord, and peripheral nerves. This results in a broad range of symptoms, including meningoencephalitis (see ENCEPHALITIS) and DEMENTIA.

Blood-cell abnormalities of HIV patients include ANEMIA, reduced white-blood-cell counts, and platelet deficiencies. Other HIV-related syndromes include nephritis (see KIDNEY DISEASE), ARTHRITIS, and lung inflammation (pneumonitis).

Certain cofactors appear to play an important role in HIV infection and AIDS by increasing susceptibility to infection and by enhancing viral-disease activity. Other sexually transmitted diseases appear to be of particular significance. Damage to genital skin and mucous membranes may facilitate transmission of the virus. In addition, laboratory studies show that certain other microbes frequently found in AIDS patients, such as mycoplasmas, also probably act as cofactors.

Treatment of HIV. Two major avenues are being pursued by biomedical scientists in the fight against HIV infection and AIDS. One strategy is to develop a vaccine that can induce neutralizing antibodies against HIV and protect uninfected individuals if exposed to the virus itself. The second approach involves the discovery and development of therapeutic agents against HIV infection and AIDS.

At present no vaccine exists to protect against infection, although recent advances have led some experts to predict that a vaccine should be available within the next 10 years. The primary obstacles are due to the variability of the virus itself. Many different strains of HIV exist, and even within a given individual's body the virus can undergo mutations rapidly and easily. Nonetheless, by 1990 a number of candidate vaccines were in the early phases of testing in human volunteers.

Dramatic strides were also being made in the treatment of HIV infection and its complications. Efforts were being focused on two major areas: antiviral drugs with a direct effect against the causative agent; and immunomodulators, or substances that act to reconstitute or enhance immune-system function. Efforts to develop and improve treatments of specific opportunistic infections and tumors are also being made.

Because of the complex life cycle of HIV, however, the successful development of antiviral and immune-enhancement therapies represents an enormous scientific challenge. Unlike most known disease-producing microorganisms, HIV infects the very cells that are intended to lead the immune system's attack against invaders. This makes it technically very hard to kill the virus without destroying the already threatened immune system. Furthermore, there may be several important reservoirs in the body for HIV that will be difficult to deal with while not causing fundamental damage to the host cells involved. For example, macrophage cells can support HIV replication while harboring the virus from the body's immune surveillance. Circulating blood cells of the kind called macrophages appear to play an important role in the propagation of HIV throughout the body.

In the search for effective therapies, other important considerations are involved. Thus, since the brain is an important target of HIV infection, an effective anti-HIV agent should be able to cross the blood-brain barrier (see BRAIN). It would also be desirable if therapies could be taken orally, since it is likely that AIDS drugs would have to be taken for a long period and perhaps a lifetime. Dozens of agents have been tested in humans, but thus far the only one licensed by the U.S. Food and Drug Administration (FDA) for AIDS treatment itself is azidothymidine (AZT). AZT interferes with virus replication, can prolong life significantly in certain patients, and can delay onset of AIDS in HIV-infected persons with no symptoms, but its potentially toxic side effects may preclude use in many cases. Several drugs have shown therapeutic value against major opportunistic illnesses, and the FDA has approved such drugs as ganciclovir (against an opportunist infection of the eye) and aerosolized pentamidine (against *Pneumocystis carinii* pneumonia). Increasingly, experts believe the best hope to fight this complicated disease will be by combining drugs in a way that minimizes drawbacks while amplifying strengths.

The slow process of FDA approval of new AIDS drugs has developed into a political issue. AIDS activists are demanding that the government speed up authorization by postponing certain tests comparing efficacy and ability to prolong life until after the drug is on the market. While a faster approval rate may expose patients to unforeseen side effects, activists argue that patients with life-threatening diseases who have no alternative therapy should still be entitled to choose these drugs.

Efforts at Prevention. In the absence of an effective vaccine or therapy, education and risk reduction remain the most powerful tools in the fight against AIDS. Because of the limited number of transmission routes, the further spread of AIDS could virtually be stopped by avoiding behaviors that place persons at risk. Although behavior change is often very hard to achieve, studies of the groups most affected by AIDS in the United States have provided encouraging indications that such change is beginning to occur.

In 1983 the major U.S. blood-banking organizations instituted procedures to reduce the likelihood of HIV transmission by asking individuals at increased risk of AIDS to refrain from donating blood. In addition, they expanded screening procedures to exclude anyone with a history of risk behavior for AIDS or signs or symptoms suggestive of AIDS. In 1985 a test to screen blood directly for antibodies to HIV was developed. The presence of antibodies, which generally take weeks or months to develop, means only that an individual has been infected by the virus. It does not indicate whether that individual has or will develop AIDS, although this is almost certain.

All blood intended for use in transfusion or the manufacture of blood products is now tested for the antibody.

Blood that tests positive is eliminated from the blood-donation pool. Tissue and organ banks use a similar process. The act of donating blood does not itself pose any risk of HIV infection, because sterile equipment is always used.

Conclusion. The U.S. Public Health Service estimates that in the early 1990s an estimated 2 out of every 100 health-care dollars will be spent on persons with AIDS, and the annual cost of the epidemic will approach $17 billion. Thus AIDS is having a profound impact on many aspects of medicine and health care. Yearly AZT expenses, for example, can average approximately $6,000, although in 1989 the drug's maker did offer to distribute AZT freely to HIV-infected children.

The effects of AIDS on society at large are also increasingly evident. Mandatory screening for the disease has been proposed, and AIDS tests are required in the military services. Some nations have instituted stringent rules for testing long-term foreign visitors or potential immigrants. There also have been occasional reports of AIDS patients being kept in quarantine. In the United States efforts have sometimes been made to keep school-age children with AIDS isolated form their classmates, if not out of school altogether. However such social issues are resolved, the ultimate physical toll of the AIDS epidemic will be high, as will its economic costs.

——

Aiken, Conrad [ay'-ken]   Conrad Potter Aiken, b. Savannah, Ga., Aug. 5, 1889, d. Aug. 17, 1973, was an American poet, fiction writer, and critic best known for the musical quality of his poetry. He sought to divest verse of its intellectual content to achieve "absolute" poetry, in which the poet employs detached emotion. In some of Aiken's poetry, however, and much of his prose, he is concerned with metaphysical matters and psychoanalytic insights.

Aiken's early poetry, which shows the influence of T. S. Eliot (a classmate at Harvard), John Masefield, Edgar Lee Masters, Edgar Allan Poe, and the imagists, is largely narrative verse but foreshadows the mature Aiken as musician-poet. This musicality is evident in his best-known lyric, "Morning Song from Senlin," contained in *The Charnel Rose* (1918). His *Selected Poems* (1929), which won the Pulitzer Prize for poetry, reflects both Aiken's attempt to create musical structure with words and his exploration of the psyche. Similar emphases appear in *Collected Poems* (1953) and throughout his often moody and dreamlike short stories and novels.

As a critic, Aiken helped establish Emily Dickinson's reputation by editing and writing an introduction for her *Selected Poems* (1924). His reviews were published as *Collected Criticism* in 1958. *Ushant: An Essay* (1952; repr. 1971), Aiken's autobiography, is unique in obscuring chronology and the true identities of the characters.

——

Aiken, Howard Hathaway   Howard Hathaway Aiken, b. Hoboken, N.J., Mar. 8, 1900, d. Mar. 14, 1973, was an American engineer who invented the first large-scale automatic COMPUTER. He earned a B.S. degree in electrical engineering and a Ph.D. in physics. By 1937, Aiken had developed the basic plan for a programmable mechanical computer, the Mark I, which was built by International Business Machines (IBM) between 1939 and 1944. Aiken designed three increasingly advanced computers; the last, the Mark IV, was completed in 1952.

aikido   see MARTIAL ARTS

ailanthus [ay-lan'-thuhs]   The ailanthus is a deciduous tree of southeastern Asia and northern Australia. About 15 species exist, constituting the genus *Ailanthus* in the quassia family, Simaroubaceae. The most common species, *A. altissima*, has been naturalized in temperate climates, where it is valued as a shade tree for its high tolerance of air pollution. The ailanthus has spreading limbs and can grow as high as 20 m (65 ft) or more—hence its name, a Moluccan word meaning "tree of heaven." The leaves, up to 1 m (3 ft) long, are composed of from 11 to 35 oval, pointed leaflets. The small, greenish flowers grow in clusters on upper branches. In autumn the female flowers ripen into reddish orange samara (winged fruit).

The ailanthus is a tree that spreads quickly, even in smoggy cities. Its male flowers emit a lingering, unpleasant odor.

Ailey, Alvin [ay'-lee]   Alvin Ailey, b. Rogers, Tex., Jan. 5, 1931, d. Dec. 1, 1989, was America's foremost black choreographer and is generally considered the first modern dancer to have choreographed for a ballet company

Alvin Ailey performs Blues Suite *with Hope Clark. His important body of work includes* Revelations *(1960), to traditional black music;* Flowers *(1971), to music by Pink Floyd and Janis Joplin;* The Lark Ascending *(1972), to music by Ralph Vaughan Williams; and* For Bird—With Love *(1984), a tribute to jazz musician Charlie "Bird" Parker.*

(*Feast of Ashes*, for the Joffrey Ballet, 1962). His own troupe, the Alvin Ailey American Dance Theater, was formed in 1958. Ailey's highly theatrical and energetic dances were often drawn from the black heritage and experience. They effectively blended styles derived from African ethnic, American black vernacular, and modern dance idioms.

Ailey began dancing with the Horton Dance Theater in Los Angeles in 1950 and became its director in 1953. He also was a dancer on Broadway and in films. In addition to works for his own company, he choreographed for several important ballet companies. Also, the American Dance Theatre often mounted dances created by the troupe's members and other choreographers. In 1987, Ailey arranged for the reconstruction and performance of 14 of anthropologist/choreographer Katherine DUNHAM's works. Following Ailey's death, dancer-choreographer Judith JAMISON was named director of the American Dance Theater.

Ailly, Pierre d' [uy-ee']   The French philosopher and theologian Pierre d'Ailly, b. 1350, d. Aug. 9, 1420, was a vigorous promoter of church unity and reform. He dominated the early sessions of the Council of Constance (1414–18), which brought to an end the Great Schism. Educated at the University of Paris, he became its chancellor, bishop of Cambrai (1397), and cardinal (1411). He wrote the geographical treatise *Imago mundi,* which Christopher Columbus read.

AIM   see AMERICAN INDIAN MOVEMENT

Aïn Hanech [yn hah-nek']   Aïn Hanech is an important Lower Pleistocene site in Tunisia consisting of a series of streambeds of gravel and sand in which tools were found that are associated with distinctive extinct mammal forms. This helps assign the site to a period between 1.5 and 3 million years ago.

The Aïn Hanech artifacts consist of crudely flaked pebbles and rocks shaped into polyhedral artifacts and simple choppers. These artifacts bear some resemblance to early human artifacts of the Oldowan type found at Olduvai Gorge in Tanzania and elsewhere. The site expands the distribution of the earliest human culture into northern Africa.

—

Ainu   The Ainu are an aboriginal people of the northern Pacific, who live principally on Hokkaido, the northernmost island of Japan, and in the southern part of the Soviet island of Sakhalin. Until recently, they also occupied the Soviet Kuril Islands, where their population is now extinct. The Ainu population is rapidly dwindling as a result of intermarriage and cultural assimilation by the Japanese. Only a small percentage of the estimated 12,000 Ainu on Hokkaido and 600 on Sakhalin are of unmixed descent.

Unlike other East Asian peoples, Ainu possess wavy brunette hair, light-skinned complexions, and abundant body hair. They also lack the epicanthic fold of skin over the upper eyelids, a Mongoloid racial characteristic. Their language is unrelated to any known Asian linguistic family.

An Ainu chief and his wife wear traditional ceremonial costumes. The intricate embroidery is an art that is highly developed among the Ainu. The man wears a woven hat adorned with a wooden carving of a bear, and the woman has tattooed lips.

The Ainu, a hunting and gathering people, formerly lived throughout the Japanese archipelago but were gradually pushed north to their present location by the invading Japanese. The men used the bow and arrow to hunt bear, deer, fox, otter, and other land animals during the winter; in summer they fished the sea and rivers. The women gathered wild foods such as roots, berries, mushrooms, and nuts and also engaged in small-scale agriculture based on crop rotation.

Traditionally the Ainu traced their genealogical descent through both parents, and the family was the most important social and economic unit. The men were skilled woodcarvers; women were experts in embroidering and weaving. They had many songs, games, epic tales, and riddles, and their chief musical instruments were the drum and flute. Their highly animistic religious beliefs included many gods of the mountains, land, sky, and sea. Most important was the bear cult, which each year culminated in an elaborate ritual sacrifice of a captive bear raised from a cub in the Ainu community.

air   see ATMOSPHERE

—

air-conditioning   Air-conditioning is a method of providing clean air to an area at the proper temperature and humidity. The term usually describes a REFRIGERATION system designed to cool the air within a space. In the process of removing heat, the system also removes moisture, further increasing comfort levels. Auxiliary filters may be used to remove pollutants from the air. Air-conditioning for an entire building can be provided by a single, central air conditioner. Another common type is the self-contained room conditioner that fits into a window.

The key element of the air conditioner is a refrigerant, often a FLUOROCARBON, that flows through the system, becoming a liquid and giving off heat when compressed, and becoming a gas (evaporating) and absorbing heat when the pressure is reduced. The mechanisms that evaporate and compress the refrigerant are divided into two areas: an air filter, fan, and cooling coil on the room side and a compressor, condenser coil, and fan on the outside of the window.

Warm room air is drawn through the filter, blown over the cooling coil containing the refrigerant fluid so that it is

Air conditioners take in warm room air, then blow it over cooling coils and back into the room. The heat removed is discharged outdoors.

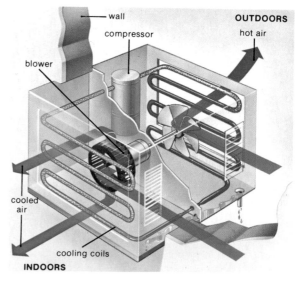

cooled, and then passed through a grille back into the room. In the compressor, the refrigerant gas from the cooling coil is further heated by compression. In the condenser coil it gives up heat and becomes a liquid, which is circulated back to the cooling coils. A THERMOSTAT controls the compressor motor to regulate the room temperature.

Houses can be centrally air-conditioned if they have forced-air HEATING SYSTEMS, which use a blower fan and ducts to distribute heated air in winter. During summer months, these ducts can be used to carry cooled air.

Large buildings may have cooling units in which a fresh-air intake mixes fresh outside air with inside air. This mixture is filtered and then cooled by passing it over the coils of a large cooling unit. In regions where the air is dry, moisture is added. Finally, the cooled air passes into the interior of the building.

Credit for the first practical conditioning system is generally given to American inventor Willis Carrier, who designed a mechanical air conditioner in 1911 and began manufacturing conditioners in 1915. It was not until the 1930s, however, that air-conditioning systems began to be installed in buildings, trains, and buses. By 1950, air-conditioning had also become an option in automobiles. To-

day, most large buildings in North America are constructed with computer-controlled central air-conditioning.

air-cushion vehicle The air-cushion vehicle (ACV), also known as a ground-effect machine and often popularly called a Hovercraft, is a conveyance that rides on a cushion of air at a pressure slightly above atmospheric. Air must be constantly pumped into the cushion, and this consumes at least as much power as is needed to propel the vehicle. A great advantage of the ACV, however, is its versatility; it can be routed over such surfaces as water, ice, mud, quicksand, and marsh.

The basic idea of an air-cushion vehicle is a century old, but the modern ACV stems from work done in the 1950s by the British electronics engineer Sir Christopher Cockerell. He constructed a model from two coffee tins and a hair dryer and measured its lift with kitchen scales. He obtained a patent in 1955, and in 1959 the first full-scale ACV, the SR.N1, was successfully tested in England.

The largest of today's ACVs is the SR.N4, a class of vehicle that is used for ferry service across the English Channel. When originally built, the N4 class carried 34 cars and

The British Hovercraft Corporation's SR.N4, one of the largest air-cushion vehicles (about 200 tons), carries about 10 percent of the English Channel passenger traffic. Some of its parts are: lift-fan air intakes (1); main bevel drive gearbox (2); 12-blade lift-fan (3); skirt fingers (4); flexible skirt (5); main passenger cabin (6); entrance to passenger cabins (7); extensible stairs (8); engine air intakes (9); gas turbine (10); pylon (11); fin (12); rear car ramp (13); car deck (14); propeller for drive and dynamics (15); propeller gearbox (16); radio antenna (17); radar scanner (18); control deck (19); and forward car ramp (20).

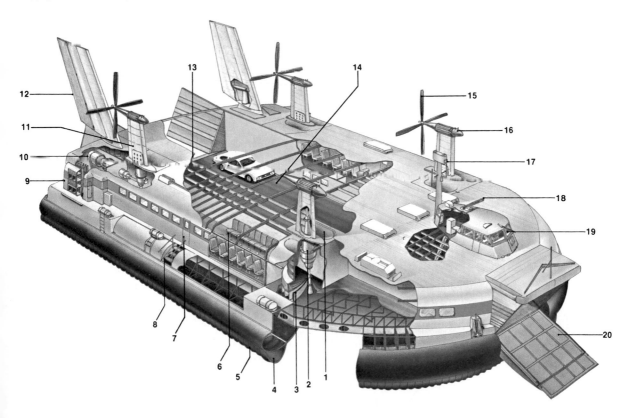

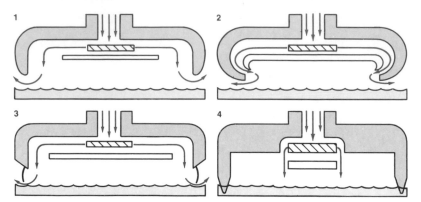

Several designs of air-cushion vehicles differ in how they direct and release the air (red arrow) that creates the cushion on which the crafts ride. In the simplest type (1), air pumped into the plenum chamber escapes beneath the chamber walls. A more complex design is the peripheral jet (2), which uses a high-speed jet of air directed toward the center of the chamber by the inward-sloping walls to supply more lift. The most important contribution to air-cushion vehicle design is the flexible skirt (3), which greatly increases the height of the vehicle over the surface, enabling it to travel over high waves or uneven terrain. The sidewall craft (4) is designed for traveling over water. Air escapes only at bow and stern.

174 passengers; the larger Super 4 type can transport 60 cars and 416 passengers. Powered by four 3,800-horsepower gas-turbine engines that drive four lift fans and four swiveling air propellers, these big craft cruise smoothly at up to 77 knots.

Some purely marine ACVs have rigid sidewalls extending down into the water along each side to help contain the air cushion. This reduces the power needed to keep the cushion inflated but increases drag (resistance to motion) because part of the vehicle is immersed in the water. Most ACVs have a flexible skirt of tough, rubberized fabric around the underside.

Many ACVs are used by the military. They can be armed with various weapons and equipment. In Vietnam, ACVs were used for patrolling rivers. Since they ride above the water, they are less vulnerable to torpedoes and undetectable by sonar. Small ACVs are used as customs enforcement vehicles, and as amphibious, sporting runabouts.

A special class of ACV is the tracked ACV, or hovertrain, which was pioneered in France. One experimental version, called the Aérotrain, set a railroad speed record of 375 km/h (233 mph) in 1967. Problems with the skirt materials remain to be solved, however.

—

air force An air force is the branch of a nation's armed forces that uses aircraft and missiles as its chief weapons. In peacetime, its primary mission is to deter or guard against an enemy attack. In wartime, it tries to destroy or neutralize hostile forces and to defend friendly forces or territories. It seeks to gain and maintain general and local air supremacy, to destroy enemy targets or interdict supply lines, to support friendly ground and sea forces in battle and provide them with supplies and transportation, and to carry out reconnaissance, rescue, and other aerial missions. In order to do these things, the air force organizes, trains, and equips combat and support units; develops, tests, and produces AIRCRAFT, missiles, and associated weapons and communications systems; and establishes, maintains, and defends air bases and installations.

The United States and the USSR maintain the world's largest air forces. They are the only nations capable of carrying out intercontinental air and space warfare with powerful, long-range bombers and missiles. They also have strong tactical and air-defense forces. Great Britain, France, and the People's Republic of China maintain shorter-range strategic forces as well as tactical air units. Countries such as Vietnam, Cuba, North and South Korea, the nations of Eastern Europe, Germany, Japan, Israel, and some other Middle Eastern nations have strong tactical air forces. The United States is the only country still possessing a strong naval air force.

Development of Air Forces

Modern military aviation began with the development of the BALLOON at the end of the 18th century. Successful balloon flights in France led to the establishment (1794) of what can be regarded as the world's first air force: the Aerostatic Corps, which briefly conducted aerial reconnaissance for the armies of revolutionary France. In the American Civil War, the Balloon Corps of the Army of the Potomac constituted, in effect, the first American air force, although it did not outlast the war. In the decades that followed, several European armies developed balloon corps, but not until 1892 was a balloon section established as part of the U.S. Army Signal Corps.

The introduction of powered flight by means of the dirigible, and more important, by the first primitive airplanes, gave impetus to the development of military air forces. In 1907, four years after the first flight of the Wright brothers, the U.S. Army established a small aeronautical division that in 1914 became the much larger aviation section, still within the Signal Corps. Military aviation was finally removed from the Signal Corps in 1918 with the creation of the Army Air Service.

First Air Fleets. Organized military aviation came into its own in Europe during WORLD WAR I (1914–18). All the major participants had small air forces when the war began, but these were used at first primarily for reconnaissance missions. As the war went on, opposing flyers began to shoot at each other with hand weapons and machine guns, and the development of a MACHINE GUN synchronized to fire through a plane's propeller opened the way for large-scale aerial combat. Large air fleets soon appeared over the battlefields. The air units not only fought each other in ambitious efforts to gain control of the skies but also bombed and strafed troops and installations on the ground.

Despite the relatively primitive state of World War I aircraft, the possibilities of air power were apparent to some military leaders. The emerging theories of airpower called for the establishment of separate air forces that by their own independent actions could bring about the defeat of an enemy. Freed of the necessity to support ground and sea forces, air units would first drive hostile aircraft from the skies and then penetrate deep into rear areas to bomb at will, until the enemy was forced to surrender. Americans such as William ("Billy") MITCHELL, Benjamin D. Foulois, and Henry ("Hap") ARNOLD were passionate supporters of these views.

Separate Air Forces. England established a separate Royal Air Force (RAF) in 1918, and Canada and Australia quickly followed suit. Italy created a separate air force in 1923, France in 1934, and Germany in 1935. By the eve of World War II, only three major powers—the United States, the USSR, and Japan—lacked separate air forces.

In the United States the interwar years had seen a good deal of progress toward an independent air force. In 1926, Congress had replaced the Air Service with the Army Air Corps. Creation of the General Headquarters Air Force in 1935 to provide centralized command of combat air units gave the Air Corps increased autonomy. At the same time, the development of a heavy bomber and of a strategic doctrine for its use lent additional weight to the arguments for a separate air force. Finally, on June 20, 1941, all army air elements were combined into the Army Air Forces (AAF). Nominally a part of the army, the AAF soon gained equal status with the ground forces.

The United States and Great Britain fought World War II with essentially separate air forces. The navies of both countries, however, maintained their own air arms, and U.S. naval aircraft carriers played a major role in the war in the Pacific. Other major air forces were closely tied to support of ground or naval forces. The German Luftwaffe failed in its effort to mount a strategic bombing campaign against England largely because of its prewar concentration on tactical operations, and only the United States and Great Britain had the means to carry out sustained long-range bombing attacks.

The dominant role of air power in World War II made postwar organizational changes almost inevitable. On Sept. 18, 1947, the U.S. Air Force became a fully independent military force. Although the U.S. Navy continued to maintain its own air arm, the Air Force quickly assumed responsibility for strategic bombing as well as tactical and logistical support of the ground forces. With the advent of long-range missiles, the Air Force also became responsible for the development and operation of land-based strategic missiles.

In Great Britain, the Royal Air Force retained its independent status, while the USSR, the only other nation to

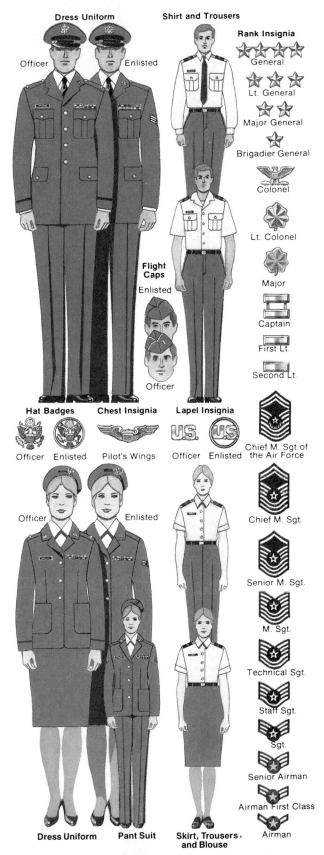

Dress Uniform — Officer / Enlisted

Shirt and Trousers

Flight Caps — Enlisted / Officer

Rank Insignia

General

Lt. General

Major General

Brigadier General

Colonel

Lt. Colonel

Major

Captain

First Lt.

Second Lt.

Chief M. Sgt. of the Air Force

Chief M. Sgt.

Senior M. Sgt.

M. Sgt.

Technical Sgt.

Staff Sgt.

Sgt.

Senior Airman

Airman First Class

Airman

Hat Badges — Officer / Enlisted

Chest Insignia — Pilot's Wings

Lapel Insignia — Officer / Enlisted

Dress Uniform — Officer / Enlisted

Pant Suit

Skirt, Trousers, and Blouse

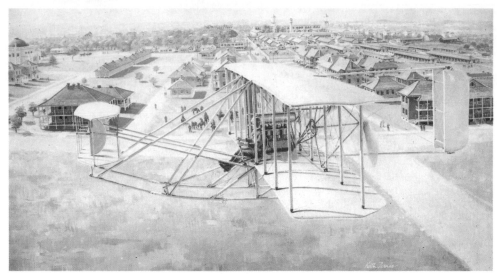

The three paintings on this and the next page by aviation artist Keith Ferris illustrate specific incidents in the history of the United States Air Force. (Left) Lt. Benjamin D. Foulois pilots his Wright Type A biplane to a height of 31 m (100 ft) over Fort Sam Houston in San Antonio, Tex. The flight, which took place on Mar. 2, 1910, was one of the first by a military aviator in a government-owned plane. (Courtesy National Bank of Fort Sam Houston.)

Fortresses Under Fire depicts a flight of B-17 Flying Fortresses under attack by German planes over Germany in 1944. The Flying Fortress, armed with 2,727 kg (6,000 lb) of bombs and 13 machine guns, was one of the principal U.S. strategic bombers of World War II. (Courtesy National Air and Space Museum, Smithsonian Institution).

An American F-105 Thunderchief pulls into a steep climb to evade surface-to-air missiles and antiaircraft shells after a strike on the Paul Doumer Bridge in Hanoi, the capital of North Vietnam. The F-105, a single-seat fighter-bomber, achieved speeds of more than twice the speed of sound in combat. (Courtesy U.S. Air Force Art Collection/Fairchild Republic Company.)

remain a major air power, maintained an air force that was autonomous in many respects. Most other nations followed the American example, although the independent status of many air forces remained somewhat weakened by their primary responsibility to support the ground forces.

The U.S. Air Force

The U.S. Air Force is one of three military departments, under civilian secretaries, within the Department of Defense. The Air Force is headed by a chief of staff, a four-star general who reports to the secretary of the Air Force. The Air Force chief of staff also serves as a member of the Joint Chiefs of Staff, together with the Army and Navy chiefs.

Under the chief of staff, the Air Force includes an Air Staff, 13 major commands, and 16 separate operating agencies. Among the major commands are the following: the Strategic Air Command, comprising the nation's long-

range striking force of bombers and missiles; the Military Airlift Command, furnishing worldwide aerial transportation and supply to the entire defense establishment; the Tactical Air Command, responsible for tactical air support of U.S. combat forces; the Air Force Systems Command, which manages scientific and technical resources; the Air Force Logistics Command, responsible for procurement, maintenance, and distribution of equipment and supplies; and the United States Air Forces in Europe, which make up the U.S. air forces of the North Atlantic Treaty Organization. Other major commands include the Air Force Space Command, Air Force Communications Command, Pacific Air Forces, and the Air University. Behind the Air Force stand both the Air Force Reserve and the Air National Guard.

The U.S. Air Force employs a wide variety of aircraft and missiles, such as the Minuteman and Peacekeeper (MX), as well as many air-to-air and air-to-surface mis-

siles. The strategic bomber force consists of some 315 B-52s and FB-111s, in addition to a fleet of 96 B-1 bombers. They are supported by KC-135 and KC-10 tankers, which also supply aerial refueling. By the mid-1990s, the Air Force also anticipates operating a fleet of 75 new B-2, or Stealth, bombers. Fighters and fighter-bombers in the Air Force inventory include such aircraft as the F-4, F-15, F-16, and F-111. Transports such as the C-5, C-130, and C-141 supply airlift; A-7s and A-10s fly close ground-support missions; and a variety of other aircraft carry out reconnaissance, communication, rescue, and other special tasks. The U.S. Air Force has about 6,900 aircraft, including helicopters. The Air National Guard and Air Force Reserve have approximately another 2,250 planes.

Air Force active and reserve forces are stationed at about 135 major Air Force bases and nearly 1,200 smaller installations throughout the United States and overseas. Approximately 560,000 personnel are in the active Air Force, about 265,000 in the reserve. The Air Force Academy, the Reserve Officers Training Corps, and Officer Training School are the primary sources for officers. Some 2,000 pilots and 850 navigators are trained each year. (See also DEFENSE, NATIONAL.)

air law Air law is the body of laws, regulations, and international agreements that apply to civil aviation. Each country has its own air laws and can choose to prevent foreign aircraft from entering, as the United States did in 1976 with the French and British CONCORDE. The basic principle of international air law—first affirmed in 1919 at the Paris Convention on the Regulation of Aerial Navigation—gives every nation sovereignty over the airspace above its territory. Subsequent international meetings— principally, the Chicago Convention on International Civil Aviation (1944)—considered such matters as liability for damage to passengers and cargo on international flights, AIRPLANE HIJACKING, and sabotage, and established the International Civil Aviation Organization (ICAO, 1947). The ICAO, affiliated with the United Nations, is concerned with problems of air law and with the improvement of navigation facilities. Membership in the ICAO includes every country whose planes fly internationally.

A national airspace is prohibited to another nation's military aircraft. Where civil aircraft are involved in unannounced intrusions, however, the issues become far less clear. In 1983 a Korean passenger plane was shot down over Siberia, provoking international denunciation.

air lock see CAISSON

air mass An air mass is a body of air with fairly uniform temperature and moisture over an area of at least 1,000 km² (400 mi²). The principal distinction in temperature is between tropical and polar air masses; the latter are formed mainly in central Canada and Siberia. The terms *maritime* and *continental* distinguish between high and low moisture. The four principal air masses are the continental polar, maritime polar, continental tropical, and maritime tropical. Polar and tropical air masses are also distinguished by temperature in the upper ATMOSPHERE.

air pollution   see POLLUTION, ENVIRONMENTAL

—

airborne troops   Airborne troops are soldiers trained and equipped to go into battle from the air, particularly by parachute. Units in which all members must be parachutists are generally considered airborne regardless of how they are deployed. Infantry units that conduct helicopter assaults are usually termed air-assault units or air cavalry; units intended to be carried into action by powered transport aircraft are normally termed air-landing or air-transportable units.

The main advantages of airborne operations are surprise, the ability to bypass ground defenses, and speed of movement from assembly areas to distant targets. Helicopter operations share all but the last of these advantages, being limited by relatively short range and slow speed. All airborne units, however, are handicapped by the fact that the equipment they use in an assault must be light and small enough to be dropped by parachute.

Germany perfected the first airborne striking force, which it employed with great effect during the invasion of the Low Countries in 1940. British and American airborne forces were successfully used later in the war, particularly in the Normandy invasion. During their involvement in Vietnam (1964–73), where they had numerous helicopters, the Americans avoided large airborne operations. In recent years airborne troops have increasingly become an elite force of shock infantry.

—

Airborne Warning and Control System   The Airborne Warning and Control System (AWACS) is a U.S. Air Force plane designed to monitor all air and sea activities over a large area. A modified Boeing outfitted with radars, sensors, and computers, the plane's distinguishing feature is a 9-m (30-ft) rotating radome that houses its special antennae. The AWACS is considered the ultimate battlefield management center. The U.S. Air Force completed acquisition of its fleet of 35 AWACS in 1984. Another 18 of the craft are operated by NATO. The USSR has 9 TU-126 planes, modified to carry AWACS equipment.

—

airbrush   The airbrush is a device for applying liquid as a fine spray. It is commonly used by commercial artists to facilitate drawing, shading, and retouching artwork. It can also be used to touch up photographs. An industrial type is used to apply various surface finishes, most commonly paint, but also ink, varnish, enamel, and lacquer. The liquid is fed into the nozzle of the airbrush by gravity or suction, or under pressure. A flow of compressed air atomizes the liquid (breaks up the particles into a fine mist), which is then carried along with the airstream coming out of the nozzle. A paint spray gun is essentially an airbrush. The principle is similar to that of the perfume atomizer and automobile carburetor.

The airbrush is designed so that normally only the supply of liquid is adjusted; the air supply and consequently the air flow from the nozzle remain constant. This design minimizes the spattering and dribbling of the pigment.

—

aircraft   The development of the airplane and other heavier-than-air craft has had the most far-reaching effects of any 20th-century invention. Although many scientific disciplines are involved in the rapid advances in aviation technology, none is as important as the aircraft itself. In this article the anatomy of an airplane is examined along with recent developments in such unconventional aircraft as helicopters. Basic principles of flight can be found in AERODYNAMICS; the history of airplane development and a description of contemporary air transportation are the subjects of AVIATION and AIRPORT. Lighter-than-air craft are discussed in AIRSHIP.

The first powered, controllable aircraft, Orville and Wilbur WRIGHT's flying machine, demonstrated in its structure the same basic principles of flight as do today's high-flying jets. The wings, or airfoils, of the original 1903 Wright *Flyer* resembled a box kite. A small pair of wings, called a canard, was located forward of the main wings and provided control about the pitch axis, allowing the aircraft to climb or descend. The canard performed the same function as the elevators that are attached to the horizontal stabilizers on most modern aircraft. Controlled, coordinated turns in the air were achieved through a method called "wing warping," which deflected the rear, or trailing, edges of the wing and rudder. With no cockpit, the pilot lay prone over the wing in a cradle arrangement and moved his body from side to side to produce wing warping, thus changing the plane's direction.

The Wright *Flyer* was an extremely difficult aircraft to fly because it was statically unstable: it could not "fly by itself" but had to be constantly controlled by the pilot. European inventors believed that an aircraft should be inherently stable, and they soon developed dynamically stable and controllable aircraft.

By the time World War II began, the aviation industry had accumulated enough experience in aerodynamics, materials, and structures to ensure uniformity in aircraft development. As a result, most modern aircraft exhibit many structural similarities. They are almost always monoplanes—single- rather than double-winged. They are made of metal, are powered by one to four jet or reciprocating engines, and are supported on the ground by retractable landing gear.

Anatomy of the Airplane

The main structural components of modern aircraft are the fuselage; wings; empennage, or tail surfaces; power plant; and landing gear, or undercarriage.

Fuselage. The fuselage is the main body structure to which the wings, tail, landing gear, and power plants are

The first controlled airplane flight, lasting 12 seconds, was made by the Wright brothers on Dec. 17, 1903, at Kitty Hawk, N.C. Orvill piloted the craft. Wilbur is seen at the right.

attached. It contains the cockpit or flight deck, passenger compartment, cargo compartment, and—in the case of fighter aircraft—the engines and fuel tanks.

Wings. The wing is the most important lift-producing element of an aircraft. Wing designs vary, depending on the type and purpose of the aircraft. Propeller-driven aircraft normally have an all-metal straight wing with a thick camber, or curvature. Jet transports have swept-back wings of medium camber that lower aerodynamic drag and improve performance at high airspeeds. Both straight- and swept-wing aircraft normally have ailerons attached to the outermost trailing edges of the wing. These ailerons raise and lower in opposition to one another, to increase or decrease lift on their respective wing in order to facilitate turning the aircraft. The wing also has flaps along the trailing edge, inboard of the ailerons. Flaps increase aerodynamic lift and drag and are used during takeoff and landing to increase lift at low speeds. Modern swept-wing transport aircraft have, additionally, high-lift devices called leading-edge slats, which extend in conjunction with the flaps to further increase the lifting capability of the wing.

An aircraft flies when the lift, or upward force generated by the wing, increases to a value larger than the aircraft's total weight. The most critical element in a wing's ability to produce lift is its cross-sectional shape. Early aerodynamic research on kites and gliders indicated that a flat plate would produce lift, but even more lift could be produced if the plate was inclined slightly into the wind. If the leading edge of the flat plate was rounded and the trailing edge tapered to streamline the wing, drag could be reduced. By increasing the camber of the top surface of the wing, while flattening the lower surface, lift could be dramatically improved.

Tail Surfaces. The tail, or empennage, provides stability and control for the aircraft and is mounted on the aft portion of the fuselage. It consists of two main parts: the vertical stabilizer, or fin, to which the rudder is attached; and the horizontal stabilizer, to which the elevator is connected. The rudder is used in conjunction with the ailerons to make coordinated turns, while the elevator is used to climb or descend.

Propulsion Systems. The many aircraft propulsion systems include those which drive a PROPELLER, primarily reciprocating and turbine (turboprop) engines; and propellerless systems that use the energy of rapidly expanding gases as a propulsive force (see JET PROPULSION). The turbojet and the turbofan—a turbojet modification—are the most widely used commercial jet engines, and the reciprocating engine is still used extensively in light general aviation aircraft.

With respect to performance, turbojet engines operate most efficiently at high altitudes; turbo-props at mid altitudes; and reciprocating engines at low altitudes.

Landing Gear. Fixed gear consists of a simple design of struts, wheels, and brakes that is not retractable into the wings or fuselage. It is usually found on light aircraft of simple design. Retractable gear is used on more complex aircraft. Since it reduces drag, it increases range significantly.

Flying Controls. The relatively simple controls on a light, general aviation airplane govern the speed of the craft and its direction, both on the ground and in the air. The control wheel at which the pilot sits may be pushed forward or pulled back to move the tail elevators. The control wheel also alters the position of the ailerons. The movements of the rudder are controlled from foot pedals. Wing-flap controls are usually powered. Engine thrust, and thus airplane speed, is controlled by a throttle.

The basic structure of an airplane comprises an airframe (fuselage, wing, tail assembly, and landing gear) and an engine. The ailerons, elevators, flaps, trim tabs, and rudder all serve to control the plane's flight. This light aircraft is a Piper Cherokee, 7 m (23 ft) long.

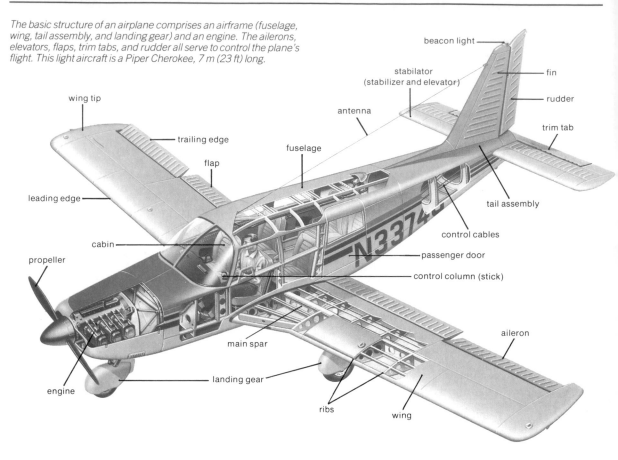

beacon light

stabilator (stabilizer and elevator)

fin

rudder

antenna

trim tab

wing tip

trailing edge

fuselage

flap

leading edge

tail assembly

cabin

control cables

propeller

passenger door

control column (stick)

aileron

main spar

engine

landing gear

ribs

wing

Unconventional Aircraft

Many of today's new craft are heralded as innovations, although some are old, reliable concepts wrapped in new packaging. Hang gliders, for example, operate on the same principles as the early gliders developed in the 19th century.

The GLIDER, or sailplane, has the same basic structure as other "heavier than air" machines but does not use a power plant. Instead, it is towed into the air by another aircraft and released at an altitude that permits it to soar along the "thermals," the columns of warm air that help keep it aloft.

STOL, VTOL, and V-STOL Aircraft. Modern short takeoff and landing aircraft (see STOL) utilize advanced lightweight structural materials, new improved engines, and high-lift devices.

Vertical takeoff and landing aircraft (see VTOL), which include HELICOPTERS, are still being developed for commercial and military use. Some aircraft combine vertical and short takeoff and landing (V/STOL) capabilities. The propellers, the craft's power plants, or the wings themselves can tilt upward for takeoff and landing, but reverse to a horizontal position for flight. The Harrier, a British fighter plane, achieves vertical takeoff by rotating the ex-

haust nozzles of its jet engines downward in what is called a deflected thrust.

Airships, or Blimps. The high price of aircraft fuel has inspired a new interest in lighter-than-air AIRSHIPS, which use relatively little fuel and promise great economy.

Supersonic and Hypersonic Planes. Supersonic transports, or SSTs, aircraft that can fly faster than the speed of sound, have been used by the military for many years. Commercial supersonic flight has been limited to the CONCORDE, built by the British and French in 1976, which has not proved as successful as anticipated. A hypersonic transport that would travel beyond the stratosphere at speeds in excess of 8,000 km/h (5,000 mph) is under consideration.

Ultralight Aircraft. Small aircraft made from ultralight, superstrong materials are increasing the range of present-day aeronautics. A hang glider was equipped with a small golf-cart engine and a propeller in 1976. World records achieved by ultralights include the 1986 triumph of the *Voyager,* whose hollow plastic body holds four tons of fuel. With two pilots, the *Voyager* flew around the world nonstop in nine days. Ultralight airplanes also figure in experiments with human-powered flight (see FLIGHT, HUMAN-POWERED), first successfully achieved in 1977 by the 35-kg (77-lb) *Gossamer Condor.*

Aircraft Navigation

Map reading and "dead reckoning"—manual speed and distance calculations—were the principal methods of navigation during the pioneer days of aviation, when a sudden change in weather combined with inadequate charts or maps could result in a forced landing or crash. One of the first reliable radio navigation aids was the Non-Directional Beacon, a radio signal that could be picked up by a cockpit device and used as a checkpoint to verify that the aircraft was on course. VOR (Very High Frequency Omni Directional Range) and TACAN (Tactical Air Navigation) were developed by the military and combined into the present-day VORTAC system that provides the majority of checkpoints that mark today's airway system.

Among the new navigation technologies that are or will soon be used by commercial aviation, Area-Navigation, or R-Nav, is an on-plane system using computers, dopplers, and inertial navigation to produce a self-contained navigational system that needs no ground-based signals as reference points. Omega, developed originally for ships, uses Very Low Frequency radio beams sent out by eight ground-based stations located across the globe. The signals can be picked up by any plane equipped with Omega receivers. The Global Positioning Satellite system uses a number of Earth-orbiting satellites to provide two- or three-dimensional fixes (including altitude). GPS will be operational for civilian use in the near future.

All of these new systems permit the pilot to do his or her own navigation. Fifty percent of all fatal air accidents occur during the approach and landing phase of flight, and it is imperative that the most precise navigational aids be utilized during this critical period. The ILS, or Instrument Landing System, is the best navigational aid available. An airport ILS transmits several electronic signals to the pilot of an approaching plane. These define the approach course and glide slope—the angle of descent that must be used. The MLS, or Microwave Landing System now being installed at many airports, is similar to the ILS but allows curved approaches to be flown to the runway, alleviating the noise and congestion problems that plague the modern jet airport.

RADAR is used by an airport's Air Traffic Control to separate aircraft and vector them to the airport for landing.

Aircraft Instrumentation

Power, performance, and navigational instruments are used by the pilot to evaluate the well-being of the aircraft and to check its course. The power instruments check engine performance, power output, and airspeed. The TACHOMETER is the basic power-indicating instrument. Jet aircraft use engine-pressure ratio gauges to determine thrust output. On piston-powered aircraft manifold pressure gauges measure the pressure under which the fuel-air mixture is supplied to the engine. Turboprop aircraft measure power output on a torque gauge that monitors the power available at the prop shaft. All aircraft have instruments that check oil temperature and pressure and fuel flow. The electrical and hydraulic systems are also monitored with gauges and caution lights.

Performance instruments show how well and at what altitude the aircraft is flying. They include the artificial horizon, a gyroscope-mounted device that shows the pilot the plane's relation to the real horizon; the altimeter and vertical velocity gauges, which indicate height above mean sea level and the rate of climb or descent; and the airspeed indicator. A turn-and-bank indicator and an accelerometer, or G meter, keep the pilot informed as to the direction of turn and the loading, or strain, on the aircraft.

The location of these instruments in the cockpit is vital to the pilot's ability to assess conditions quickly and accurately. Instrument design and location is a science in itself and is constantly undergoing study. The "electronic cockpit," or EFIS (Electronic Flight Information System),

Three rotational motions are possible for an airplane. Rolling, or rotating an aircraft about a longitudinal axis from nose to tail, is accomplished by turning the control column so that one aileron is pulled up and the other aileron is pulled down. Yawing, or rotation about a vertical axis, utilizes the vertical rudder on the tail, which is controlled by the rudder pedals. Pitching, or rotation about an axis from one wing tip to the other, depends on the elevators and is achieved by moving the control forward (to dive) or backward (to climb).

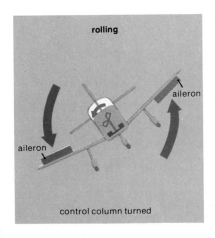

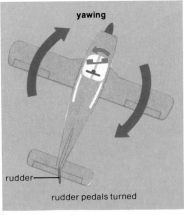

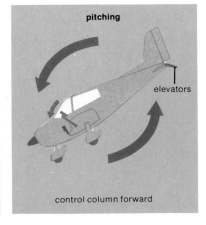

a computerized instrumentation array that includes the presentation of flight information via television screens, is revolutionizing the way flight instruments are used.

——

aircraft, military The importance of aircraft designed specifically for use by the military was recognized within a decade of the initial controlled, power-driven airplane flights achieved by Orville and Wilbur Wright on Dec. 17, 1903. Although zeppelins had been flown since 1900—and more than 100 were built by Germany for use in World War I (see AIRSHIP)—the smaller, faster, more maneuverable airplane quickly proved superior for warfare and today is the principal weapon of military attack and defense. (See AIRCRAFT and AVIATION for the technology and development of planes. For the development of independent military air units, see AIR FORCE.)

Types of Military Aircraft

The military aircraft's original function was large-scale reconnaissance. A scout plane equipped with bombs proved to be a weapon of unprecedented destructive potential; inevitably, the use of bomber aircraft led to the development of the fighter, an airplane capable of intercepting and destroying bombers. In addition to its use above the battlefield, the fighter was used extensively against enemy aircraft for home defense, as a protective escort for bombers, and as a strike plane against such objectives as enemy airports and railroads.

The introduction of the airplane provided a TORPEDO-launching device with several advantages over ships, particularly in speed of approach to a target. Torpedo-dropping experiments commenced early in the development of aircraft and were soon followed by the production of specialized torpedo-bombers.

Mine-laying aircraft were used to inhibit enemy ship movements, and during World War II the airplane was also adapted to counter the magnetic mine by exploding it electronically in the water after locating it.

Between the wars increasing attention was paid to the development of transport aircraft, in particular for the landing of troops and equipment and for the deployment of both soldiers and arms by PARACHUTE (see AIRBORNE TROOPS). For a short time during World War II, GLIDERS were also used extensively. They were towed to their destination and then released to land with their cargoes. Since 1945, development has been concentrated on the HELICOPTER as a transport vehicle, because it can take off and land vertically and can hover to provide support for ground troops. As early as 1942 the helicopter was also being tested as a combat craft, and it has been developed into a strike aircraft heavily armed with cannon, machine guns, rockets, torpedoes, and a variety of powerful missiles. It can be equipped to operate as an antisubmarine weapon as well.

During World War II the AIRCRAFT CARRIER demonstrated its worth in highly specialized actions in the war in the Pacific. Two aircraft-related innovations, however, transcended all others: The turbojet engine and the ATOMIC BOMB.

The outstanding success of the fighter in strike mis-

sions during World War II was responsible for the production after the war of an entirely new class of airplane, the attack aircraft, designed specifically for close support and strike functions but also able to intercept. Emphasis in an attack aircraft is on flexibility and bomb transport and targeting capacity, coupled with the ability to fly at low altitudes to evade RADAR detection, ground fire, and ground-to-air missiles.

The counterinsurgency (COIN) aircraft has emerged as a distinct class of warplane since World War II, serving as a comparatively lightweight, low-cost, and simple strike plane for close support of ground forces in relatively elementary tactical operations. In many cases obsolescent strike and trainer planes have been adapted to serve as COIN aircraft.

The serious threat to a nation's shipping posed by fleets of advanced nuclear submarines requires the maintenance of strong maritime patrol forces and antisubmarine aircraft. With long ranges and advanced equipment and weapons, these types of aircraft have assumed a role of the utmost significance since 1945.

The need for immediate warning of approaching hostile aircraft has led to the development of extremely sophisticated airplanes capable of extended patrol missions. A plane equipped with an AIRBORNE WARNING AND CONTROL SYSTEM (AWACS) is vastly more effective, and has much greater range, than a similar system based on the ground or at sea.

Training aircraft have also assumed a vital role, and specialized airplanes have been developed to train crews for all categories of operational aircraft. Many of these training planes can be converted quickly into warplanes.

New Technologies

The most significant recent advances in military aviation technology have been made in the area of flight guidance and control—both of the planes themselves and their weaponry. The pilotless plane, or drone, is a prime example. One of the first drones, the Firebee (originally produced in 1959), is launched and controlled from the ground or a plane; or, when fitted with a computer, it is capable of following a preset course and returning. The present-day Firebee can fly at altitudes of up to 18,250 m (60,000 ft) at speeds approaching 800 km/h (500 mph). It is usually equipped with radar and camera systems and functions as a reconnaissance craft.

The technologies used in advanced drones—sophisticated radar systems capable of ground mapping, laser inertial navigation, computers that can control and target weapons systems—are also used in piloted military aircraft, which supplement these systems with sophisticated electronic display panels.

The V/STOL (vertical short takeoff and landing) plane is capable of taking off and landing either vertically or on very short runways. Some new craft are hybrid mixtures of helicopters and conventional airplanes, whose wings carry large-bladed propellers that can be rotated parallel to the wing to lift the vehicle or moved forward to allow it to cruise like a plane. Important advances have also been made in the area of radar avoidance. The materials and

Fokker D.VII

P-51D Mustang

F-86 Sabre

MIG 21

F-15A Eagle

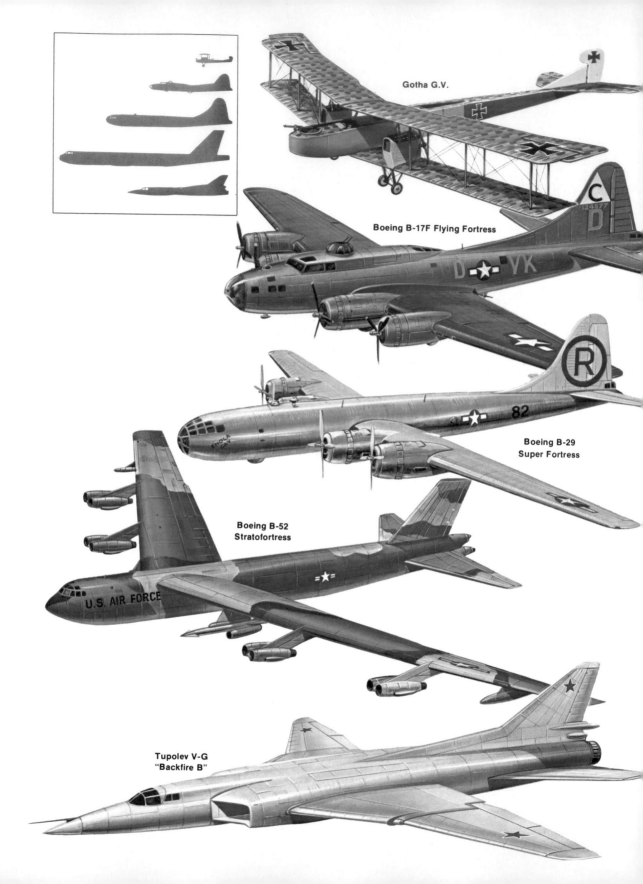

Gotha G.V.

Boeing B-17F Flying Fortress

Boeing B-29
Super Fortress

Boeing B-52
Stratofortress

U.S. AIR FORCE

Tupolev V-G
"Backfire B"

design used to construct the STEALTH BOMBER render it immune to detection by conventional radar.

See also: B-1 BOMBER; B-52 STRATOFORTRESS; CORSAIR; F-16 FIGHTING FALCON; MESSERSCHMITT BF-109; MIG; MIRAGE; MOSQUITO; MUSTANG; P-38 LIGHTNING; P-40; SOPWITH CAMEL; SPAD; SPITFIRE; STUKA; U-2; ZERO.

---

aircraft carrier   An aircraft carrier is a warship that contains a flight deck for launching and recovering AIRCRAFT and associated hangaring and support facilities. It is usually distinguished by a full-length flight deck and arresting gear to halt landing aircraft in the limited space available. Recent years, however, have seen the development of cruiser-carrier hybrids, notably the Soviet navy's *Kiev*, that carry a mixed complement of HELICOPTERS and VTOL (vertical takeoff and landing) fighters. Specialized amphibious assault ships, or commando carriers that carry only helicopters, are operated by several navies, but these are distinct from true aircraft carriers.

Shipboard air operations are complicated and difficult. Aircraft are catapulted off the deck and land over the stern, using the carrier's forward velocity to reduce the speed of approach to the carrier; the aircraft also use tailhooks to engage arresting cables stretched across the flight deck. Large elevators are set into the flight deck and along its sides to transfer aircraft to and from the hangar deck below. Because the amount of space on a carrier is limited, aircraft must have folding wings and tails, and helicopters are equipped with folding rotors.

The aircraft carrier is basically a British, American, and Japanese development. Eugene Ely, an American aviator, pioneered shipboard takeoffs and landings from improvised platforms in 1910–11. Britain converted the cruiser *Furious* into the first carrier in 1917; the *Argus*, which was the first carrier with a true flight deck, soon followed. The first American carrier, the converted collier (coal cargo ship) *Langley*, became operational in 1922, the year in which Japan's *Hosho*, the first ship specifically designed as a carrier, was launched.

By the onset of World War II, both Japan and the United States had powerful carrier forces. Following the Japanese attack on Pearl Harbor by carrier-based aircraft, carriers dominated fleet engagements in the Pacific. British carrier deployment was more limited but still had major impact.

After World War II, Britain pioneered the technical developments that made jet-carrier operations practical—the steam catapult, visual approach aids, and the angled deck. The last refers to a deck that has the landing section laid out at an angle to the takeoff section so that a plane approaching poorly can fly off the deck and make

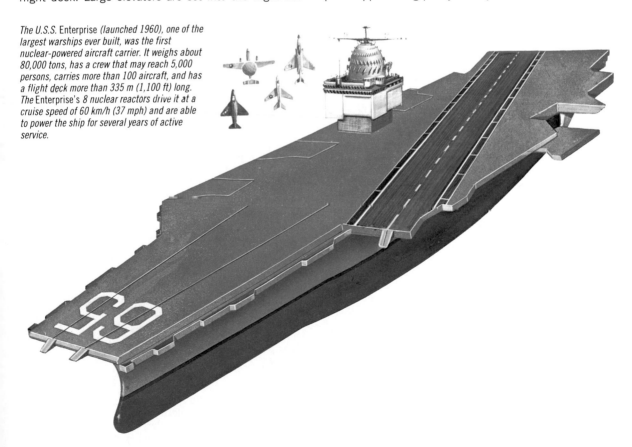

The U.S.S. Enterprise (launched 1960), one of the largest warships ever built, was the first nuclear-powered aircraft carrier. It weighs about 80,000 tons, has a crew that may reach 5,000 persons, carries more than 100 aircraft, and has a flight deck more than 335 m (1,100 ft) long. The Enterprise's 8 nuclear reactors drive it at a cruise speed of 60 km/h (37 mph) and are able to power the ship for several years of active service.

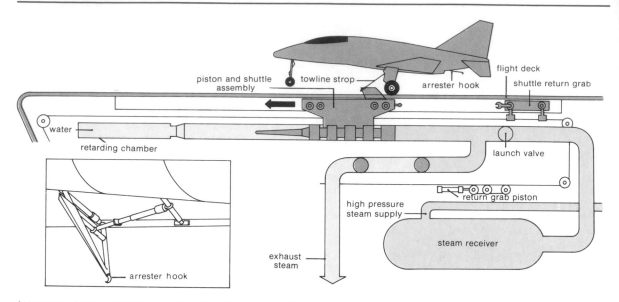

A steam catapult on the U.S.S. Enterprise *aids in launching aircraft from the carrier deck. Four such catapults are in operation aboard the vessel. Powered by high-pressure steam from the ship's eight nuclear reactors, each catapult can launch four aircraft a minute. A 36-ton aircraft can be accelerated to a speed of 260 km/h (161 mph) in a little more than 2 seconds with the use of only 76 m (250 ft) of flight deck. The arrester hook* (inset) *of a landing plane engages a wire strung across the ship's flight deck, stopping the craft within a few meters.*

another attempt without danger of running into other planes.

American carriers were used effectively in Korea and Vietnam, and the U.S. Navy, with 14 carriers, is the main exponent of carrier aviation today. The first nuclear carrier, the U.S.S. *Enterprise,* was launched in 1960. It was followed in 1972 by the *Nimitz,* the first in a class that has since become the U.S. standard for aircraft carriers. The U.S. Navy now operates four Nimitz-class carriers, which are ranked as the most powerful surface warships afloat. Two more Nimitz-class carriers have been built and are scheduled to be commissioned in the early 1990s.

Recent criticism of the aircraft carrier has been widespread, however, and has centered on its high cost and vulnerability to missile attack. The Nimitz-class *Theodore Roosevelt,* with its complement of aircraft and protective escort ships, cost an estimated $17 billion. Many strategists have now come to favor smaller, less expensive carriers, such as the fleet Britain built in the 1980s: each of its three carriers houses only 8 V/STOL (vertical short takeoff and landing) aircraft and 12 helicopters. France is planning to launch two midsize nuclear-powered carriers in the 1990s. The Soviet Union's new *Tbilisi*-class aircraft carriers are medium-sized and conventionally powered.

The Airedale terrier, the largest member of the terrier group, is an intelligent breed and a vigilant watchdog.

Airedale terrier [air'-dayl]   The Airedale terrier, the largest of the terriers, is a wiry-coated black-and-tan dog that has a muscular, compact body and a docked tail. It has a square muzzle, upright but folded ears, and keen, intelligent eyes. It is classified a long-legged terrier, mea-

sures 57–59 cm (22–24 in) high at the shoulder, and weighs 17–22 kg (38–50 lb). It is a good swimmer and runner.

Dog breeders of Aire Valley, northern England, developed the Airedale terrier in the mid-19th century from the otterhound and a now-extinct breed of English fox terrier. During World War II, Airedale terriers were trained to carry messages between troops; now they are used as guard dogs and for hunting big game in India and in Africa.

airglow   Airglow is a luminosity of the Earth's upper ATMOSPHERE that occurs globally day and night. Like the

AURORAS, airglow derives from interactions of the Earth's MAGNETOSPHERE with the SOLAR WIND. Night airglow, which is twice as bright as all starlight, originates at altitudes of 100–190 km (62–118 mi). The light is emitted by atoms and molecules excited by ultraviolet radiation and X rays and by collision with charged particles in the upper atmosphere. Airglow hampers ground-based astronomical observation of faint celestial objects. In itself, however, airglow is of interest to scientists because of the exotic chemical reactions taking place in the upper atmosphere, including reactions of excited atoms and molecules of oxygen and nitrogen that cannot be observed in ground-based laboratories. Such studies are important for understanding the processes affecting the atmosphere's OZONE LAYER, which protects the Earth's surface from excessive ultraviolet radiation, and for learning more about the ways in which solar radiation changes affect CLIMATE.

airmail   Airmail is the delivery of letters and other postal material by aircraft. Before World War I, experimental airmail flights were made in both England and the United States, but the world's first regularly scheduled airmail service began in the United States on May 15, 1918, when the War Department started routes between New York, Philadelphia, and Washington, D.C. The Post Office Department continued airmail service after the war and in 1920 developed a coast-to-coast route in conjunction with the railroads, which carried mail sacks during the nighttime segments. Four years later, a string of flashing beacons and emergency landing fields was established across the country to permit around-the-clock operations, providing a 32-hour coast-to-coast airmail delivery that was at the time three days faster than railroad service.

Under the terms of the Air Mail Act of 1925 (the Kelly Bill), the Post Office Department contracted for service with privately owned airlines. These early mail routes became the basis for major companies that currently serve the United States. Air express also began in the later 1920s, gradually developing into a significant aspect of modern air transport. By the late 1930s, transoceanic routes carried passengers, freight, and mail across the Caribbean, Pacific, and Atlantic, completing the pattern of today's global air network. Depending on the distance involved, almost all domestic first-class mail is currently delivered by air.

See also: POSTAL SERVICES.

airplane   see AIRCRAFT

airplane hijacking   Airplane hijacking is the forcible seizure of a commercial aircraft and the holding of its crew and passengers hostage against the acceptance of the hijackers' demands. Between 1948 and 1960 some 32 hijackings took place; almost all were attempts by Eastern Europeans to escape from Communist countries to the West. In 1959 several planes carrying escapees from the Cuban Revolution were forcibly diverted to the United States and were welcomed by U.S. authorities. The violence inherent in the act of hijacking became apparent to much of the world only in the early 1960s when U.S. jetliners were detoured at gunpoint to Cuba, by Cubans seeking to return or by people with ideological or criminal motives. Arab terrorists have used hijacking from the late 1960s on to attempt to enforce political demands.

To counter the threat of hijacking, X-ray and other machines have been used to screen passengers and baggage at airports. The Hague Convention of 1970 required its signers to prosecute or extradite hijackers who landed in their countries. Several of the nations that had offered a safe haven to hijackers did not sign the Convention agreement; but since 1980—during a period of resurgence in U.S. hijack attempts—many of them have ceased to offer sanctuary. Nevertheless, the crime has spread throughout most of the world.

airport   An airport is a facility for handling the arrival and departure of AIRCRAFT, passengers, and freight. Today's are shaped by certain exacting requirements: sufficient space to accommodate the long runways needed, as well as the hangars, terminals, parking lots, and cargo and accessory buildings necessary for efficient airport operation; sufficient highways and public transportation to allow passengers access; and sufficient distance from residential areas so that adjacent neighborhoods will not be subjected to aircraft noise. (See also AVIATION.)

History

Before World War I any spot large and level enough for a pilot to take off and land was considered an airport. The brothers Orville and Wilbur WRIGHT made do with a level pasture. Between 1909 and 1914 the airplane gained popularity. Well-publicized world records for speed, altitude, and distance of flights were continually surpassed, and a number of races, with cash prizes, were organized.

Europe. Shortly after World War II, a few former British military pilots acquired some surplus warplanes and refitted them for passengers. By 1919, London-to-Paris passenger services were inaugurated, and within the year scheduled passenger flights were offered to other cities on the Continent. By about 1928, most cities had adequate airports.

United States. In the years after World War I, manufacturers left with large inventories of airplane parts began to produce planes for peacetime use, but few people were willing to fly. Charles LINDBERGH's transatlantic flight of 1927, however, triggered an upsurge in public interest.

A string of small airports and emergency fields had been established from coast to coast to service AIRMAIL planes. During the early 1930s transcontinental operations were inaugurated. The first long-distance airline schedules were begun in conjunction with the existing railroad systems. Airports were sited adjacent to railroad stations, and passengers flew by day and traveled in railroad sleeping cars at night. Coast-to-coast travel time was

John F. Kennedy International Airport (JFK), in Queens, New York City, is among the world's busiest. The central terminal area shown here consists of ten airline terminals surrounding five large auto parking lots. Runways and taxiing and parking areas for aircraft form the spokes to the central hub of the terminal area. A major highway enters the terminal area from bottom right.

about 48 hours by combined rail and flight. By 1932, light beacons and radio communication had been installed along the airways, making night flights possible and reducing travel time to about 33 hours.

Overseas Flights. In the late 1930s commercial overseas services to South America and Europe were started. The plane most widely used over water was the flying boat (a large four-engine vehicle with a watertight body that acted as a hull), operating out of harbors (see SEAPLANE). By the end of World War II, however, development and plans for future use of flying boats were abandoned.

Types of Airports in the United States

Three types of airports are now in common use: government airports, general-aviation airports, and commercial airports. Federal regulations govern their operational methods and set safety standards.

Government Airports. Government airports serve the military, as well as NASA and various installations for research and development. They also support such special activities as the landing and recovery of space vehicles on 8-km (5-mi) desert runways.

General-Aviation Airports. General-aviation activities—including private flying for recreation, instruction, and business—account for 80 percent of the air-hours flown, and the number of privately owned planes is increasing rapidly. Of more than 12,000 airports listed in the U.S. directories, the majority are available for general use, subject to FEDERAL AVIATION ADMINISTRATION (FAA) rules and regulations. General-aviation airports are often privately owned and are usually near small towns that are

not along the routes of commercial airlines.

Commercial Airports. Commercial airports are usually publicly owned, and operated by municipal, county, or other government agencies. The location of many modern urban airports was originally determined largely on the basis of available real estate and local politics. Before World War II, airfields in such major cities as London and New York often occupied fewer than 202 ha (500 acres). (By contrast, the Dallas/Fort Worth Airport in Texas has an area of more than 7,080 ha/17,500 acres, and Montreal's Mirabel Airport has more than 35,600 ha/88,000 acres in reserve, although at present it uses only about one-fifth of its total area.) As airline traffic increased in the 1950s and '60s, airports enlarged to accommodate it; the most important single change in aviation, however, was the introduction (1958) of jet planes, which made unprecedented demands on the length of runways. As a result, cities with major airports enlarged them greatly or moved them into nearby rural areas.

Despite the enlarging of airport facilities, many hub airports—those in large cities which serve as major transfer points—find themselves increasingly short of space. Their problems are exacerbated by the growth of the neighboring suburban areas. Expanding an existing airport or building a new one is equally difficult because of population pressures, environmental issues, and the huge costs involved.

Airport Facilities

The modern airport consists of facilities for handling airplanes: runways and taxiing areas; hangars and machine shops for plane maintenance, repair, and fueling; and traffic-control towers, whose personnel track aircraft and guide them through landings and takeoffs. Passengers are received in the terminal buildings, which are connected to nearby highways and to parking facilities by access roads and which contain airline ticket counters and reception desks, baggage-handling facilities, plane-boarding gates, security-inspection devices, and such ancillary services as restaurants. In addition, airports provide special buildings and services for air freight.

Traffic Control. The most conspicuous and important structure at any airport is the TRAFFIC CONTROL tower. Located approximately in the center of the runway complex, it is high enough to permit a clear view of landing, takeoff, and loading areas. It contains a complex of communications and electronic surveillance gear by which the airport controllers monitor and direct all plane movements on or near the field.

All commercial airlines, the military, and most general-aviation flights operate according to flight plans. Prepared by pilots before their departure, flight plans are filed with the originating airport and transmitted to the airport of destination. Flights follow predetermined routes. Control towers are advised of the estimated time of arrival (ETA) for all aircraft in their approach areas. The pilots are then given detailed landing instructions, such as approach routes to be followed, rate of descent, and proximity of other aircraft. For departures, pilots are also given necessary information.

In 1981 the Professional Air Traffic Controllers Organization (PATCO), the union representing all nonmilitary air traffic controllers, called a strike over issues of pay and working conditions. President Reagan declared the strike illegal and fired 11,500 of the 16,500 controllers, replacing some of them with controllers borrowed from military airfields. At about the time of the strike, the FAA began working on plans for reducing air-traffic facilities in the future by relying more heavily on new computer capabilities, new plane-borne radar signaling devices, and new automated control systems. These plans should lead to a reduction in the number of major air-traffic control centers, as well as the smaller flight service stations.

In the meantime, however, concern about air safety has grown, along with statistics indicating a pattern of increasing overcrowding and delays on the ground and in the air at major airports, a rising number of near collisions, and a lowering of airplane maintenance standards.

Noise. Aircraft NOISE became a major issue in the early 1960s, when commercial jet aircraft first came into wide use. Although those who live and work near large airports have long complained of the extraordinary burden of noise they bear, the first widely publicized controversy developed over the landing of the CONCORDE, the Anglo-French supersonic transport, at Kennedy International Airport in New York City on Oct. 19, 1977. Strenuous protests led to court hearings, delays, and, for a time, restricted experimental service. Today Concorde landings are limited to a few airports, and the plane is not allowed to exceed the speed of sound when it flies over the continental United States.

In suits brought against airports by nearby towns or citizens' groups, the courts have generally found airport operators primarily responsible for controlling noise. Since 1976 the FAA has funded noise studies at most large airports and has issued guidelines for reducing airport noise. These guidelines recommend restrictions on airport acquisition of land and on the utilization of runways whose flight paths are over residential areas.

Security. AIRPLANE HIJACKING has been a problem since the 1950s, and several aircraft in flight have been destroyed by hidden bombs. The December 1988 explosion over Lockerbie, Scotland, of a Pan Am passenger jet en route from London to New York City was caused by a bomb hidden in an audiocassette player. This and other terrorist attacks in the late 1980s forced airports and airlines to increase security measures.

The demarcation of responsibility between airports and airlines is not precisely drawn. Airlines would seem to be responsible for their own passengers; airports for the security of the area and for passenger traffic in general. Israel's El Al and Air India are said to have the most rigorous airline security. Although their passenger interrogations and careful manual searches of luggage are carried out efficiently, they cause long delays and demonstrate that real security can be had only at great expense of money and time.

The X-ray machines used in airports can detect guns and other metal objects, but their screens cannot show plastic explosives. The new "thermal neutron analyzer" is capable of detecting many different explosives, including those made of plastic. Its cost, however, is about $1 million per machine.

The airport's air-traffic control center tracks airplane movements by radar within a radius of 20–50 km (12–30 mi). A computer digests the data from the radar and displays it on a screen. Air controllers use such screens to guide pilots to safe takeoffs and landings.

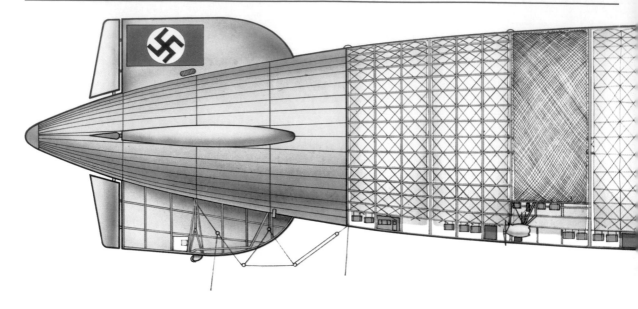

The airship, or dirigible, marked the climax of travel in lighter-than-air aircraft. The longest airship ever built was the German Hindenburg, (above) which was 245 m (804 ft) long. It carried 200,000 m³ (7 million ft³) of hydrogen in envelope bags, housed within an aluminum framework covered with cotton fabric. The airship had quarters for 70 passengers and 45 crew members. In 1937, the Hindenburg caught fire and burned while docking at Lakehurst, N.J., with the loss of 35 lives. The Hindenburg was a rigid airship.

The Effects of Airline Deregulation on Airports. The Airline Deregulation Act of 1978 removed route-regulating authority from the Civil Aeronautics Board (CAB), leaving each airline free to choose whatever routes seemed to promise the most success and to set its own fares. This led to great changes in the structure of the airline industry. The giant airlines that once dominated U.S. air travel have either diminished in size and market share or have disappeared, their routes and fleets taken over by several regional airlines. The airlines have overloaded major airports, while leaving many smaller airports, once on mandatory CAB routes, without regular airline service. Some small cities have sought and obtained scheduled commuter service, but many communities are now shut out of the air-route network. At present a large hub airport may be unable to provide "slots" (landing rights) for every airline wishing to use its facilities, which has led to some legal actions.

In the coming years, air traffic inevitably will increase, and the problems of noise and lack of runway and terminal space will grow more pressing. In addition to the more obvious solutions, such as increasing the size of airports or building new ones, operators have suggested improved Instrument Flight Rule (IFR) systems to permit reduced spacing between parallel runways and shorter distances between arriving or departing aircraft, and the construction of separate, shorter runways for commuter and business aircraft.

airship An airship is a type of lighter-than-air AIRCRAFT with propulsion and steering systems; it is used to carry

passengers and cargo. It obtains its buoyancy—as does a balloon—from the presence of a lighter-than-air gas such as hydrogen or helium.

Types of Airship

Two basic types of airship have been developed: the rigid airship, the shape of which is fixed by its internal structure; and the nonrigid "blimp," which depends on the pressure created by a series of air diaphragms inside its gas space to maintain the shape of its fabric hull. Today only the nonrigid airship is used.

Rigid Airship. The rigid airship's structure resembled a cage that enclosed a series of balloons called gas cells. These cells were tailored to fit the cylindrical space and were secured in place by a netting that transmitted the lifting force of their gas to the structure.

Also on board was a ballast system that used water as ballast. When part of it was released, the airship ascended to a cruising altitude where the engines supplied propulsion. As fuel was consumed, the airship became lighter and tended to climb. This was countered in hydrogen-inflated airships by simply releasing gas into the atmosphere.

The method was uneconomical, however, with helium-inflated airships, and they were therefore equipped with ballast generators, apparatuses that condensed moisture out of the engines' exhaust gases.

Nonrigid Airship. The nonrigid blimp has no internal structure to maintain the shape of its hull envelope, which is made of two or three plies of cotton, nylon, or Dacron impregnated with rubber for gas tightness. Inside the gas space of the hull are two or more air diaphragms called

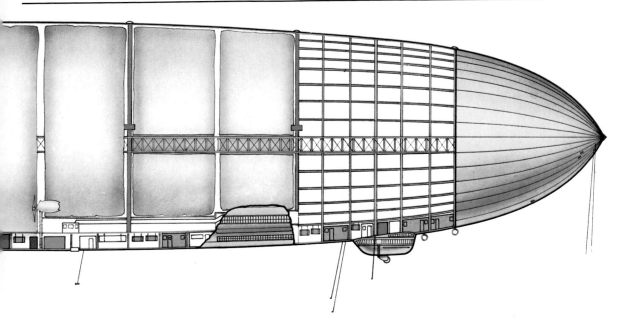

ballonets that are kept under slight pressure. The ballonets in turn exert pressure on the gas, which fills the envelope. Air can be bled from the ballonets or pumped back into them in order to compensate for varying conditions.

History of Rigid Airships

The German company Luftschiffbau Zeppelin had the most success in building rigid airships (see ZEPPELIN, FERDINAND, GRAF VON). The first Zeppelin was flown on July 2, 1900; it was 126 m (419 ft) long. Its range and payload were negligible. The last Zeppelin was the *Graf Zeppelin II*, which was first flown on Sept. 14, 1938; it was 245 m (803 ft) long. It was scrapped in May 1940.

A total of 119 Zeppelins were built, most of them during World War I. The most famous Zeppelin was the original Graf Zeppelin, which during 1928–37 made numerous flights all over the world, including one flight around the world. Another famous Zeppelin was the airliner HIN DENBURG, which was destroyed by fire at Lakehurst, N.J., on May 6, 1937.

The British made intermittent efforts to develop the rigid airship. The most noteworthy was the *R-34*, which in July 1919 made the first transatlantic round-trip flight. An effort to develop two airships of 141,000 m^3 (5,000,000 ft^3) for intercontinental air service came to grief in October 1930 when the *R-101* crashed and burned in France. In the United States, the development of rigid airships was undertaken by the navy, and only five were operated. The navy-built ZR-1 *Shenandoah* made its first flight on Sept. 4, 1923, and was torn to pieces by a thunderstorm over southern Ohio on Sept. 3, 1925. The ZRS4 *Akron* and ZRS5 *Macon* were built by the Goodyear-Zeppelin Co. of Akron, Ohio. These sister ships were 239 m (785 ft) long. The *Akron* first flew on Sept. 23, 1931, and was lost in a storm over the Atlantic on Apr. 4, 1933; the *Macon* first flew on Apr. 21, 1933, and crashed in the Pacific on Feb. 12, 1935.

History of Nonrigid Airships

The first successful nonrigid airships were built by the French. In 1852, Henri Giffard built an airship of 3,200 m^3 (113,000 ft^3) powered by a steam engine. At the turn of the century the Brazilian aeronaut Alberto SANTOS-DU-MONT built and flew a series of small airships in France, all of which used gasoline engines. Blimps were effectively used by the British and French in World War I in maritime reconnaissance against German submarines.

In World War II the United States was the only power to use airships. The navy used them for minesweeping and antisubmarine patrols. After 1945 the navy continued to use blimps in antisubmarine warfare and for early offshore warning of bomber attacks against the United States. On Aug. 31, 1962, the navy terminated its use of blimps.

The Goodyear Blimps

The most long-lasting use of airships has been by the Goodyear Tire and Rubber Company, which began building its fleet in 1919. During the 1930s, 12 Goodyear airships flew advertising banners, and during World War II the fleet was used by the U.S. Navy. Three airships still operate, including the new *Spirit of Akron* (62.6 m/205.5 ft, with a displacement of 7,023 m^3/248,000 ft^3), launched in 1989, the world's largest airship.

The Future of Airships

Many aerospace and transportation engineers have long been convinced of the value of airships in cargo and passenger transport, and their experiments with innovative designs and materials periodically make the news. Yet, with the exception of the Goodyear fleet, no commercial airships operate in the United States today. Several are aloft in other countries, however. Britain flies two "sky ships," each powered by two 6-cylinder Porsche automobile engines, which are used for sightseeing tours.

The U.S. Navy has revived its interest in airships, primarily to counter the threat of low-flying weapons such as the CRUISE MISSILE.

airsickness   see MOTION SICKNESS

Airy, Sir George Biddell [air'-ee]   The English astronomer George Airy, b. July 27, 1801, d. Jan. 2, 1892, is best known for modernizing the Royal Greenwich Observatory during his 45 years as astronomer royal. A graduate of and professor of astronomy at Cambridge, he exerted considerable influence on British astronomy and played a controversial role in the famous priority dispute over the discovery of Neptune by delaying action on the prediction of John Couch ADAMS.

Airy disk   The Airy disk, named for the British astronomer Sir George B. Airy, is a small, disklike image produced by the DIFFRACTION of light when it passes through a telescope. Airy first calculated the size of the disk and found that it depended both on the wavelength of the light and the diameter of the objective lens or mirror; the larger the aperture (diameter) of the objective, the smaller the Airy disk. A telescope with an aperture of 25 cm (10 in) produces an Airy disk that is 1 arc second in diameter for visible light.

Aisne River [ayn]   The Aisne River is in the northern part of France. It rises in the Meuse department and flows north past Vouziers and then west to Compiègne, where it joins the Oise River. It is about 265 km (165 mi) long, and its main tributaries are the Aire and Vesle rivers. The major city is Soissons. The Aisne marked part of the front lines during much of World War I.

Aix-en-Provence [eks-awn-proh-vawns']   Aix-en-Provence is a city in the Bouches-du-Rhône department of Provence in southeastern France. It lies on the principal routes to Italy and the Alps. Aix has a population of 124,550 (1982) and is an agricultural center, producing almonds, olives, and wine. Founded by the Romans in 123 BC near mineral springs, it is the site of Marius's defeat of the Teutons (102 BC). In succession, Visigoths, Franks, Lombards, and Moors invaded and plundered the town. In the Middle Ages it was a center for the arts and Provençal literature, fostered by rulers such as RENÉ OF ANJOU. After René's death (1480), Aix was annexed (1486) by France. The city has long been a favorite spot for artists, including Paul Cézanne, who was born here.

Aix-la-Chapelle   see AACHEN

Ajaccio [ah-yah'-choh]   Ajaccio (1982 pop., 54,089) is the capital city of the French island of Corsica. It is located on the western coast of the island at the Mediterranean Sea. The main industry is tourism. Napoleon Bonaparte's birthplace in the town is a museum. Ajaccio was the first Corsican town to revolt (1943) against Fascist occupation in World War II.

Ajanta [uh-jahn'-tuh]   Ajanta is a village in Aurangabad district of Maharashtra state in western India. It is the site of famous rock-cut Buddhist sanctuaries dating from the 2d century BC to the 7th century. The Ajanta caves contain extraordinary interior wall paintings. The 29 hollowed-out chambers pierce a crescent-shaped granite cliff north of the village. The caves, which served as a Buddhist monastery and a stopping place for pilgrims using the trade route through western India, are of two types: monasteries (viharas) and vaulted temple halls (caityas) for worship. Intricately carved pillars and niches decorate the facades and interiors of the caves. On the walls and ceilings are frescolike paintings, primarily depicting scenes from the life of the Buddha before his enlightenment. The exuberant paintings, although essentially religious in theme, convey much information about contemporary secular life. The finest date from the 4th to the 7th century, and the style of their sensuously modeled human forms influenced later Buddhist art throughout Asia. With Buddhism's decline in India, the Ajanta caves were abandoned and forgotten until British soldiers rediscovered them in 1819.

Ajax   In Greek mythology, Ajax (or Aias) was the name of two heroes, both of whom fought in the TROJAN WAR. Ajax of Salamis, sometimes called the Greater Ajax, was the son of King Telamon, an old comrade of HERCULES. Although characterized by HOMER as slow-witted, Ajax of Salamis was nevertheless one of the best fighters among the Greeks and was famed for his steadfast courage in the face of adversity. After the death of ACHILLES, whose armor had been claimed by both Ajax and ODYSSEUS and was finally awarded to Odysseus, Ajax's resentment drove him mad, and he eventually killed himself.

Ajax of Locris, or the Lesser Ajax, was also a good fighter, but his ill-mannered and violent behavior is frequently mentioned by Homer. Shipwrecked on his way home to Greece after the war, Ajax of Locris managed to swim ashore with the aid of the sea god POSEIDON. Later, however, he boasted that he had saved himself without divine assistance, and for this impertinence Poseidon caused him to fall into the sea and drown.

Akan [ay'-kuhn]   Akan is a group of AFRICAN LANGUAGES of the Kwa subfamily of the Niger-Congo stock, spoken by several peoples of Ghana and Ivory Coast. The word Akan also signifies speakers of these languages having other tribal names, such as the ASHANTI and FANTI.

The Akan are subsistence farmers who produce such cash crops as cacao. They live mostly in compact villages and towns, with well-developed systems of local trade. Descent is matrilineal, and marriage is polygynous. Most Akan societies were traditionally complex states with kings and a hierarchical organization of government, courts, slavery, and, in some tribes, human sacrifice. Akan peoples are also noted for their highly developed art forms, in gold, silver, bronze, wood, and clay.

Akbar, Mogul Emperor of India [ak'-bahr] Akbar (Akbar the Great), b. Oct. 15, 1542, d. Oct. 16, 1605, the third Mogul emperor of India, is considered one of the greatest Indian rulers. The son of Emperor HUMAYON and originally named Jalal ud-Din Muhammad, he ascended the throne of Delhi on Feb. 15, 1556, and ruled under a regency until 1560. His position was immediately confirmed by the defeat of the Afghan claimant to the throne at Panipat on Nov. 5, 1556, which firmly reestablished the Mogul dynasty on the throne of Delhi.

Akbar set out to unite all India under Mogul rule. Akbar first set up his court at Agra and then in 1569 built the royal city of Fatehpur-Sikri, which was his capital from 1570 to 1585. He began consolidating his power in northern India by annexing Malwa (1562), and by 1595 he had taken Gujarat, Bihar, part of Bengal, Kabul, Kashmir, Sind, and Baluchistan. He moved toward the south in 1596 with the occupation of Berar. He took Khandesh and Ahmadnagar in 1600, but further conquests were thwarted by a rebellion led by his son, Salim.

Akbar moved his court to Lahore in 1585 and returned it to Agra in 1599. In his attempt to unite India, he took Hindu chiefs (particularly the Rajputs) into his administration and otherwise sought to conciliate Hindu interests. He established a fair tax system and a uniform system of weights and measures, developed trade, and practiced religious tolerance. Although illiterate himself, he surrounded himself with scholars and promulgated a new religion, the *Din-i-ILahi* (Divine Faith), a blend of Islam, Hinduism, and other traditions. He also kept a Jesuit mission at his court.

akeake [ah-kee-ah'-kee] The akeake, *Dodonaea viscosa* in the family Sapindaceae, native to tropical and semitropical regions, is abundant in New Zealand and Australia and is found in the southwestern United States. It ranges in size from a small shrub to a slender tree up to 9 m (30 ft) tall. Leaves and young branches secrete a resinous substance. The wood is extremely tough and durable, and New Zealand's Maori have used akeake to fashion clubs and other weapons. (The Maori name *akeake* means "forever and ever.")

Akhenaten [ah-kuh-nah'-tuhn] The Egyptian pharaoh Akhenaten, or Ikhanaton, was one of the earliest monotheists, but his religious reforms did not survive. He succeeded his father, AMENHOTEP III, in 1379 BC and imme-

diately began building a new type of roofless temple to the Aten ("Sun disk"). He soon forbade the worship of other gods, especially of the state god Amen, or AMON-RE, of THEBES. In 1374 BC he changed his name from Amenhotep ("Amon is satisfied") to Akhenaten ("beneficial to Aten") and left Thebes for a new capital at Tell el-AMARNA. Living there with his queen NEFERTITI, six daughters, and possibly several sons, he fostered new styles in art and literature.

Akhenaten was a complex figure whose historical significance is still debated. His physical abnormalities were exaggerated in contemporary art, and no evidence supports the charge of mental instability that is often leveled against him. He lost Egyptian-held territory in Syria and Palestine but maintained Egypt's status as a great power. Within Egypt he combined religious reform and skillful tactics to strengthen absolute royal power over the bureaucracy and the army, but his monotheism was genuine and innovative. His religious reforms were detested, however, and after his death in 1362 his successors restored traditional religion. The Aten temples were demolished, and Akhenaten came to be called "the Enemy."

Akhetaten see AMARNA, TELL EL-

Akhmatova, Anna [ahk'-muh-toh'-vuh] Anna Akhmatova is the pseudonym of Anna Andreyevna Gorenko, b. June 23, 1889, d. Mar. 5, 1966. She is considered one of the foremost Russian poets of the 20th century. Together with her first husband, Nikolai GUMILEV, and Osip MANDELSTAM, she founded (1910) the ACMEISTS, a Russian literary movement that opposed the mystical vagueness of symbolism. For more than 50 years she wrote polished and elegant yet emotionally charged verse in the manner of PUSHKIN.

Akhmatova's poetry, as shown in her first volumes, *Vecher* (Evening, 1912) and *Chiotki* (The Rosary Beads, 1914), is intensely personal and frequently concerns her favorite themes—love, loneliness, and grief. Her work after the Russian Revolution, published in such volumes as *Belaya staya* (The White Flock, 1917) and *Anno Domini MCMXII* (1922), is more patriotic but retains the basic grace and simplicity of the early poems. Nevertheless, her refusal to write optimistic verse that glorified Soviet accomplishments led to frequent criticism of her work, and she was not allowed to publish again until 1940. In 1946 her poetry was branded as erotic and mystical, and she was expelled from the Soviet Writers' Union. *Requiem* (1935–40; Eng. trans., 1976), a cycle of poems inspired by her son's arrest and exile to a Soviet concentration camp, has appeared only in fragments in the USSR. After Stalin's death (1953), Akhmatova's verse began to appear again, and a collection of it, *The Course of Time*, was published in the USSR a year before her death.

Akiba ben Joseph [ah-kee'-bah] Akiba ben Joseph, AD 40–135, was a prominent Palestinian rabbi and master of the TALMUD. In his youth he was an untutored shepherd, but after a period of intensive study he became a man of deep knowledge. He was the first to collect the interpretations of the Hebrew laws, arranging them in what later became known as the MISHNAH. His favorite book of the Bible was the Song of Songs, which he understood to refer, allegorically, to the love between God and Israel. His maxim was "man is created in the image of God." He actively supported the anti-Roman rebellion of BAR KOCHBA and died a martyr.

Akihito, Emperor of Japan [ah-kee-hee'-toh] Akihito, b. Dec. 23, 1933, the oldest son of the Japanese emperor HIROHITO, succeeded to the throne on Jan. 7, 1989. In 1952 he was formally declared heir to the throne, the 125th in his dynasty. He was educated at the university for the nobility but studied English with an American, Elizabeth Gray Vining. He married Michiko Shoda, the daughter of a wealthy industrialist, in April 1959. She was the first commoner to marry an heir apparent to the Japanese throne. As crown prince, Akihito visited many countries in Asia and the Western Hemisphere, including the United States.

Crown Prince Akihito of Japan succeeded to the throne on the death of his long-reigning father, Hirohito, on Jan. 7, 1989. Akihito and his wife, Empress Michiko, have three children: Prince Naruhito Hironomiya, Prince Fumihito Ayanomiya, and Princess Nori.

Akkad [ak'-ahd] Akkad was an early name for northern BABYLONIA, derived from the capital city of SARGON of Akkad (fl. *c.*2350 BC). For almost a century and a half Sargon and his successors dominated all of MESOPOTAMIA and at times held tributary lands situated to the east and west. The principal ruler after Sargon was Naram Sin, possibly a grandson, who rivaled his ancestor as a conqueror; monuments and inscriptions of his reign have been found over a wide area. Although the Akkadian dynasty finally collapsed as a result of invasions from the north about 2200 BC, the name Akkad continued to be applied to the country, and from about 2000 BC rulers of Babylonia often styled themselves kings of SUMER and Akkad.

Sargon and his Akkadians were Semites. Their lan-

guage (Old Akkadian) is the earliest written Semitic dialect known, and their religious and social institutions clearly set them apart from the people of Sumer to the south. Nevertheless, the Akkadians borrowed and modified numerous cultural elements from the older and more complex civilization of the Sumerians. Among these were the cuneiform system of writing and some aspects of political organization.

The Akkadian period was remembered by later generations as a golden age of unity and imperial greatness, and the Akkadian language took its place with Sumerian as one of the classic languages of Mesopotamian culture. It was still being used as a literary language as late as the Neo-Assyrian period (8th–6th centuries BC).

Akko see ACRE (Israel)

Akmak [ahk'-mahk] Akmak is the name given to an early archaeological assemblage of stone artifacts from the northwest Alaskan site of Onion Portage, located on the Kobuk River about 200 km (125 mi) from its mouth. The site was discovered (1941) by the American archaeologist J. Louis Giddings. Excavations have brought to light one of the longest stratigraphic sequences of prehistoric tool industries yet found in the Americas; the oldest is the Akmak (from the Alaskan Eskimo word for "hard chert"), estimated to date from 13,000 to 6000 BC.

The Akmak assemblage is composed of large and small tools, including tiny chipped flakes, or microliths. Its closest parallel is found in Siberian tool types associated with sites near Lake Baikal. Although the artifacts are generally similar, clear differences in details suggest that Akmak culture developed independently after its isolation from Siberian influence. It further appears that certain developments initiated in the Akmak tradition gave rise to the ESKIMO culture.

Akron Akron is a city in Ohio and the seat of Summit County. Known as the rubber capital of the world, it is situated on the Little Cuyahoga River in the northeastern part of the state, 56 km (35 mi) southeast of Cleveland. The city has a population of 223,019 (1990), and the metropolitan area, 660,328 (1980).

Akron experienced its first growth surge shortly after being founded in 1825; with the completion (1827) of the Ohio and Erie Canal, it became a trading and transportation center. Benjamin F. GOODRICH opened Akron's first rubber factory in 1870, and the city's second period of growth began, accelerating sharply as automobile use grew in the early 20th century.

Today several hundred manufacturing plants are located in Akron, producing rubber, chemicals, plastics, aircraft equipment, heavy machinery, and trucks. The University of Akron was founded in 1913, and the city is also host to the Jonathan Hale Homestead, an authentic Western Reserve home, and the home where John Brown lived from 1844 to 1847.

Aksakov, Sergei Timofeyevich [ahk-sah'-kawf, sir-gay teem-oh-fay'-e-vich] Sergei Timofeyevich Aksakov, b. Oct. 1 (N.S.), 1791, d. May 12 (N.S.), 1859, was a prominent Russian writer and literary figure. His early books on fishing and hunting are masterpieces of observation and description. *A Family Chronicle* (1856; Eng. trans., 1917), a fictionalized account of his family and the founding of their estate, was followed by the more overtly autobiographical sequel *Childhood Years* (1858; Eng. trans., 1917). His memoirs (1890) of Nikolai Gogol are basic to the study of that writer.

Aksenov, Vasily Pavlovich [ahks-yawn'-awf, vuh-see'-lee pahv'-lo-vich] Vasily Pavlovich Aksenov (also transliterated Aksyonov), b. Aug. 20, 1932, is an expatriate Russian writer living in the United States. The son of parents who were exiled to Siberia, Aksenov grew up in an orphanage for "Children of Enemies of the State." His works of the 1960s, exemplified by his novel *A Ticket to the Stars* (1961; Eng. trans., 1962), did not overly offend the authorities, although they featured "materialistic" youth in rebellion against Soviet ideals. Censorship grew more stringent, however, and by the 1970s almost none of Aksenov's writing was being published. In 1979 he and about 20 other writers published *Metropol*—a collection of works banned in the USSR—in the United States. As a result, he lost his membership in the Soviet Writers' Union. He was allowed to emigrate in 1980. His greatest work, *The Burn* (written 1969–75, published in Russian and English in 1980 in the United States), is yet to be read in the USSR.

Aksum [ahk'-soom] Aksum (Axum) is a town in Tigre province of northern Ethiopia, about 135 km (84 mi) south of Asmara. It is an agricultural market center, with a population of 21,595 (1980 est.). As the ancient African commercial town of Axumis, it was the capital of the Axumite kingdom, which during the first two centuries of the Christian Era included much of modern Ethiopia and Sudan. For Coptic Christians, it is the traditional site of the ark of the covenant, brought from Jerusalem by the descendants of King Solomon and the Queen of Sheba.

Akutagawa Ryunosuke [ah'-koo-tah-gah-wah,ryoo'-noh-su-ke] Akutagawa Ryunosuke, b. Mar. 1, 1892, d. July 24, 1927, was one of Japan's greatest short-story writers. His mother's insanity and early death and his own poor physical and mental health cast a dark shadow, and he eventually committed suicide. "The Hell Screen" (1916; Eng. trans., 1948) and the novella *Kappa* (1926–27; Eng. trans., 1947) are among the best illustrations of his preoccupation with madness and social contradictions. Akira Kurosawa's film *Rashomon* (1951) is based on Akutagawa's story of the same title (1915; Eng. trans., 1930) and his "In a Grove" (1921; Eng. trans., 1952).

al-Bayda see Beida

al-Faiyum [ahl-fy-oom'] Al-Faiyum (also El Faiyum or El Fayum) is the capital of al-Faiyum governorate in northeastern Egypt. Located about 113 km (70 mi) south of Cairo, it lies below sea level in the Faiyum Depression, the bed of ancient Lake Moeris, between the Nile River and Lake Qarun. It has a population of 206,100 (1983 est.). An irrigated oasis with a hot, dry climate, it is linked to the Nile by canals built in the 17th century BC. The local economy is based on cotton, cereal, and sugarcane, which are processed in the city. Among the many nearby archaeological sites are Setje (later Crocodilopolis), the ancient seat of crocodile worship, founded about 2300 BC, and the 4,600-year-old pyramid at Meidum. During the Roman period the city was named Arsinoë for the wife-sister of Ptolemy II.

Alabama Alabama, one of the southern states of the United States, is largely rectangular in shape and is landlocked except for a short coastline along the Gulf of Mexico. It is bordered by Tennessee on the north, by Georgia on the east, by the Florida panhandle on the south, and by Mississippi on the west. The state was visited by Spaniards in the early 16th century, but the first permanent white settlement (present-day Mobile) was not established until 1711. Alabama became a state in 1819, and during the Civil War it was a member of the Confederacy. The state was profoundly affected by the civil rights movement of the 1950s and '60s. Long a primarily agricultural area, Alabama by the final decades of the century had a diversified economy, dominated by manufacturing. The state is named for the Alabama River, whose name was derived from the Alabama Indians, a small Muskogean-speaking group that formerly lived on its banks. The word *Alabama* probably means "I make a clearing."

Land and Resources

About two-thirds of Alabama is made up of a low-lying coastal plain, which merges, toward the northeast, into regions consisting of medium-altitude hills and mountains. The highest point in the state is Cheaha Mountain (733 m/2,405 ft), which is in the east, and the lowest elevation is sea level, along the Gulf of Mexico.

Physiographic Regions. Alabama may be divided into four physiographic regions. A vast coastal plain covers the southern half of the state and much of the northwest. The plain includes the famous Black Belt, an area of productive black-clay soils that forms a narrow east-west band across the middle of the state. The southeast also has good farmland, but the soils of the rest of the coastal plain are generally deeply weathered and are of limited agricultural value. A second region, separated from the coastal plain by the FALL LINE, is the PIEDMONT PLATEAU, located in the east central part of the state. It is rolling to hilly, with highly eroded red soils.

ALABAMA

Land: Area: 133,915 km² (51,705 mi²); rank: 29th.
Capital: Montgomery (1990 pop., 187,106). Largest
city: Birmingham (1990 pop., 265,968). Counties: 67.
Elevations: highest—733 m (2,405 ft), at Cheaha Mt.;
lowest—sea level, Gulf of Mexico.

People: Population (1990): 4,062,600; rank; 22d;
density: 30.3 persons per km² (78.6 per mi²). Distribution (1988): 67.5% metropolitan, 32.5% nonmetropolitan. Average annual change (1980-90): +0.2%.

Government (1991): Governor: Guy Hunt, Republican.
U.S. Congress: Senate—2 Democrats, House—5 Democrats, 2 Republicans. Electoral college votes: 9. State
legislature: 35 senators, 105 representatives.

Economy: State personal income (1988): $52.7 billion;
rank: 24th. Median family income (1979): $16,347;
rank: 46th. Agriculture: income (1988)—$2.4 billion.
Fishing: value (1988)—40 million. Forestry: sawtimber
volume (1987)—64.5 billion board feet. Mining: value
(1987)—$2.2 billion. Manufacturing: value added
(1987)—$18.6 billion. Services: value (1987)—$11.4
billion.

Miscellany: Statehood: Dec. 14, 1819; the 22d state.
Nickname: Heart of Dixie State; bird: yellowhammer;
flower: camellia; tree: Southern pine; motto: *Audemus
Jura Nostra Defendere* ("We dare defend our rights");
song: "Alabama."

Camellia

Yellowhammer

The Appalachian Region encompasses much of northeastern Alabama. The eastern portion of this region is an
area of sandstone ridges, separated by fertile limestone
valleys. The western portion, a continuation of the CUM-
BERLAND PLATEAU, is a hilly, forested area of poor soils. The
fourth region is the Highland Rim, a section of smooth,
rolling plains located in the north, astride the TENNESSEE
RIVER. Underlaid by limestone, the Highland Rim, as well
as the eastern Appalachian Region, has formed sinkholes
and caverns as a result of the solution of the limestone in
the humid climate.

Rivers and Lakes. Alabama has several major rivers.
The main rivers flowing north to south are the Alabama
River (507 km/315 mi long), formed by the confluence,
near Montgomery, of the Coosa and Tallapoosa rivers, and
the TOMBIGBEE RIVER, which rises in Mississippi. The Alabama and Tombigbee meet in the southwestern part of
the state and then form the Mobile and Tensaw rivers,
which continue south to Mobile Bay (an arm of the Gulf of
Mexico). Other important rivers are the CHATTAHOOCHEE,
which forms part of the eastern border of Alabama, and
the Tennessee, which flows west across nearly all of the
northern part of the state.

Alabama has no large natural lakes. Dams on rivers,
however, have created several extensive artificial lakes,
the largest being Guntersville Lake (272 km²/105 mi²),
on the Tennessee River.

Climate. Alabama has a humid, subtropical climate.
Summers are hot (average July temperature, 27° C/80° F)
and humid, with frequent heavy thunderstorms. Winters
are cool (average January temperature, 7° C/45° F), with
considerable precipitation, including some snow in the
north. The amount of annual precipitation generally increases from north to south, ranging from 1,321 mm (52
in) at HUNTSVILLE to 1,600 mm (63 in) at Mobile. Southern
Alabama is occasionally affected by hurricanes in the late
summer. Tornadoes, which are associated with cold fronts,
are most common in the months of March and April.

Vegetation and Animal Life. About two-thirds of Alabama is covered by forests, largely made up of southern
yellow pine, red cedar, and other conifers. The most common deciduous trees are hickory, sweet gum, and several
species of oak. Alabama has a varied wildlife population
with numerous deer, foxes, bobcats, game birds, and other animals. Large numbers of migratory ducks and geese
winter in the state.

Mineral Resources. Alabama has significant deposits of several important minerals. Coal, iron ore, and limestone—all used in the production of iron and steel—are found in the north central part of the state, notably around Birmingham. Major crude-petroleum fields are in the southwest, and bauxite deposits are in the southeast.

People

Alabama has a population of 4,062,608 (1990), giving the state an average population density of about 30.3 persons per km² (78.6 per mi²). In the two decades from 1970 to 1990, Alabama's rate of growth was below the national average. In 1980 about 75% of the population were white, 25% were black, and there were small numbers of Indians. After several decades of considerable net out-migration (mainly a result of blacks leaving Alabama for better opportunities elsewhere), the state had a net in-migration between 1970 and 1980. More recently there again has been an out-migration. About two-thirds of the people live in areas defined as urban; the largest cities are BIRMINGHAM, MOBILE, MONTGOMERY, HUNTSVILLE, and TUSCALOOSA. The great majority of all Alabamians were born in the United States of American parents. The majority of the people are Protestants.

Education. Alabama established a statewide public school system in 1854, but schools received inadequate financial support until the 20th century. Almost all black and white children attended separate public schools until the 1960s. By 1980, slightly more than 55% of Alabama's residents of 25 years of age or more were high-school graduates. Alabama's more important institutions of higher education include Auburn University (founded 1856), main campus at Auburn; Jacksonville State University (1883), at Jacksonville; Samford University (1841), at Birmingham; Troy State University (1887), main campus at Troy; Tuskegee Institute (1881), at Tuskegee Institute; the University of Alabama (1831), campuses at Tuscaloosa, Birmingham, and Huntsville; the University of North Alabama (1872), at Florence; the University of South Alabama (1963), at Mobile; Alabama Agricultural and Mechanical (1875), at Normal; and Alabama State (1874), at Montgomery.

Cultural Institutions. Among the museums of the state are the Alabama Museum of Natural History, at University; the Alabama Space and Rocket Center, at Huntsville; and the Birmingham Museum of Art. The decommissioned World War II battleship *Alabama*, now anchored in Mobile Bay, also contains a museum. Large libraries include the University of Alabama Library, at University, and the Birmingham Public and Jefferson County Free Library. Huntsville and Birmingham have professional symphony orchestras, and Birmingham supports a ballet company.

Historical Sites. Russell Cave National Monument (at Bridgeport) contains archaeological records of human habitation dating from at least 7000 BC. At Mound State Monument (near Moundville) are several large mounds of the Indian MOUND BUILDER culture, and Horseshoe Bend National Military Park (near Dadeville) was the site of a decisive defeat (1814) of the Creek Indian Confederacy

by Andrew JACKSON. At Tuskegee Institute National Historic Site (Tuskegee Institute) are early buildings of the noted college founded (1881) for blacks. The first capitol (the present state capitol) and the first White House of the Confederacy are both in Montgomery. Alabama has many historic homes, some built before the Civil War.

Communications. Alabama has plentiful radio stations and a number of television stations, some of which are operated by the state's Educational Television Commission. Cable television systems also are available. Among the more influential daily newspapers are the *Birmingham News*, the *Huntsville Times*, and the *Montgomery Advertiser*. The state's earliest newspaper was the short-lived *Mobile Centinel* [sic], which first appeared in 1811. The oldest newspaper still in existence is the *Mobile Register*, founded in 1813.

Economy

Until the late 19th century, when iron and steel mills were established at Birmingham, Alabama's economy was overwhelmingly agricultural, and cotton was the only important cash crop. By the 1930s industrialization was well under way, and manufacturing eventually became the dominant sector of the economy. By the 1980s that trend was altering, and manufacturing, although still dominant, was somewhat on the decline.

Agriculture. Among Alabama's primary crops are soybeans, peanuts, hay, and cotton. Large numbers of hogs, cattle, and broiler chickens are raised for market, and many productive dairy farms operate throughout the state.

Forestry and Fishing. Alabama's extensive forests are used to produce much pulpwood and lumber. A small fishing industry operates mainly in the Gulf of Mexico, and the catch includes shrimp, croakers, red snappers, and catfish.

Mining. Alabama's mineral output, valued at slightly more than $2.5 billion a year, consists mainly of bituminous coal, crude petroleum, natural gas, limestone, stone, sand and gravel, and bauxite. Until the 1960s considerable quantities of iron ore were produced in the state.

Manufacturing. Manufacturing firms in Alabama employ about one-fourth of the state's labor force, and the manufacturing sector accounts for about one-fourth of the gross state product. Principal manufactures include paper, chemical, rubber, and plastic products; clothing and textiles; food products; and iron and steel products, long of importance to Alabama's economy. Important manufacturing centers in the state are in GADSDEN, Birmingham, Anniston, Bessemer, Mobile, Montgomery, and Tuscaloosa.

Tourism. Alabama has a substantial tourist industry. Many vacationers stay at beach resorts along the Gulf of Mexico, notably on Dauphin Island, at the entrance to Mobile Bay. Hunters and anglers are attracted by the state's ample opportunities for such activity, and many tourists visit Alabama's historic sites, state parks, and national forests.

Transportation. Extensive transportation facilities exist in Alabama, with Birmingham the hub of the state's road

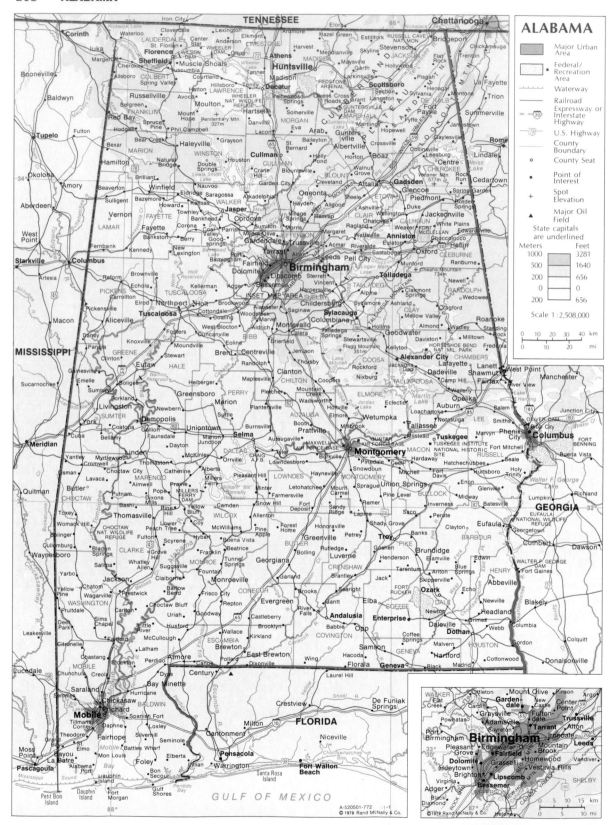

ALABAMA

	Major Urban Area
	Federal/ Recreation Area
	Waterway
	Railroad
	Expressway or Interstate Highway
	U.S. Highway
	County Boundary
○	County Seat
■	Point of Interest
+	Spot Elevation
▲	Major Oil Field

State capitals are underlined

Meters	Feet
1000	3281
500	1640
200	656
0	0
200	656

Scale 1 : 2,508,000

0 10 20 30 40 km
0 10 20 mi

A-520501-772 -1-1
© 1979 Rand McNally & Co.

© 1979 Rand McNally & Co.

and rail systems. Major interstate highways that intersect there include I-65, I-59, and I-20. The Tennessee-Tombigbee Waterway, which opened in 1985, provides a barge route partly through Alabama to Mobile, the state's only seaport, which also has easy access to the Gulf Intracoastal Waterway. The Alabama-Coosa and Black Warrior–Tombigbee river systems are also navigable through a system of locks and dams.

Energy. About half of Alabama's electrical capacity and production comes from private sources. The Alabama Power Company, a private utility, operates a number of hydroelectric projects on the Alabama, Black Warrior, Coosa, and Tallapoosa rivers. Much of the remaining electric power comes from the federally owned TENNESSEE VALLEY AUTHORITY through its Guntersville, Wheeler, and Wilson dams. Nuclear power plants and coal-burning or other fossil-fuel-burning plants also operate in the state.

Government and Politics

Alabama is governed under a 1901 constitution, as amended; previous constitutions had been adopted in 1819, 1861, 1865, 1868, and 1875. The chief executive of the state is a governor, popularly elected to a 4-year term; a governor may not serve more than two consecutive terms. The state has a bicameral legislature, consisting of a 35-member Senate and a 105-member House of Representatives; all legislators are elected to 4-year terms. The state's highest tribunal is the Supreme Court, made up of 9 judges elected to 6-year terms. The 67 counties of Alabama are each governed by a board of commissioners. The state is represented in the U.S. Congress by 2 senators and 7 representatives. It has 9 electoral votes in national presidential elections.

The Democratic party dominates Alabama politics at the state and local levels. In contests for U.S. president, however, the Democrats after World War II lost their traditional firm hold on the state's electoral vote. Since 1948 the state's presidential electoral votes have often gone either to the Republicans or to minor-party candidates, as in 1968, when Alabama governor George C. WALLACE carried the state as the American Independent party candidate.

History

Excavations of archaic Indian remains indicate that people lived in the region of Alabama at least as early as 7000 BC. During the Mound Builder, or Mississippian, cultural period (AD 700–1700), large temple mounds were built along the major rivers of the state, notably around Moundville. By the early 16th century this remarkable culture was in a state of decline. At that time, the principal Indian groups in the state were the CHICKASAW, in the northwest; the CHEROKEE, in the northeast; the CREEK, in the center and southeast; and the CHOCTAW, in the southwest.

European Exploration and Early Settlement. European contact with the Alabama area began when the Spanish navigator Alonso Álvarez de Piñeda explored Mobile Bay in 1519. In 1540 another Spaniard, Hernando DE SOTO, led an army of about 500 men through Alabama; on Oct.

A plantation home near Mobile, with its Spanish-moss-laden oaks and blooming azaleas, evokes memories of the Old South. The antebellum period produced some of America's most charming regional architecture.

Birmingham is Alabama's largest city. Although famous as the South's leading producer of iron and steel, Birmingham has become important as a center of commerce and education.

18, 1540, they crushed a large force of Choctaw under Chief Tuscaloosa. The Spanish failed to establish a firm foothold in Alabama, and the French founded (1711) the first permanent white settlement, at present-day Mobile. The French also established large farms, and in 1719 the first black Africans arrived to work as slaves on the farms.

In 1763 France ceded Alabama to Great Britain, and in 1783 most of it became part of the United States. The region around Mobile had been taken by the Spanish during the American Revolution, and it was captured by the United States in 1813, during the War of 1812. Also during that conflict, at the Battle of Horseshoe Bend (Mar. 27, 1814), the power of the Creek Indians was broken by U.S. troops under Andrew Jackson. In the following 25 years nearly all of Alabama's Indians were removed to the western United States.

Statehood. Alabama was organized as a separate territory in 1817, and on Dec. 14, 1819, it was admitted to the Union as the 22d state. Huntsville was the first capital; the capital was moved to Cahaba in 1820, to Tuscaloosa in 1826, and, finally, to Montgomery in 1847. The state's population grew from 127,000 in 1820 to 964,000 (435,000 of whom were slaves) in 1860. The economy was dominated by large plantations (mostly in the Black Belt) that produced cotton for export. The rivers were the prime means of transportation, although the state's first railroad began operations in 1832, and by 1860 about 1,100 km (683 mi) of railroad track had been laid. The state was overwhelmingly rural; Mobile, a growing seaport, was the only sizable city.

The Civil War and Reconstruction. Most white Alabamians viewed slavery as an integral part of their economic and social systems, and they opposed attempts to abolish it. Soon after the election of President Abraham LINCOLN, perceived by Alabamians as a particularly strong opponent of slavery, Alabama seceded (Jan. 11, 1861) from the Union, the fourth state to do so. In February 1861, the Confederate States of America was organized at Montgomery, and Jefferson DAVIS was inaugurated as its president at the Alabama state capitol. Montgomery re-

mained the Confederate capital until May 1861. Alabama contributed about 100,000 troops to the Confederacy, and perhaps 25% of them died during the Civil War. No major land battle was fought in the state, but the Union admiral David G. FARRAGUT won an important naval engagement at Mobile Bay in August 1864. Union armies captured the Tennessee Valley in 1862 and took Montgomery in early 1865.

Alabama's State Capitol, overlooking downtown Montgomery, is often called the "Cradle of the Confederacy." The building hosted the convention that founded the government of the Confederate States of America.

The Reconstruction period, which followed the Confederate surrender in April 1865, was one of confusion in Alabama. Because it refused to ratify the 14th Amendment to the U.S. Constitution, Alabama was placed under military rule in 1867. After the amendment was ratified, and blacks were assured citizenship, Alabama reentered (June 1868) the Union. During the next few years black and white Republicans exercised considerable power, but by 1874 white Democrats, including numerous former supporters of the Confederacy, had regained control of the state. In the following years racial segregation was written into many state and local laws.

Economic Recovery. Although Alabama began large-scale industrialization in the late 19th century, the economy continued to be dominated by cotton culture. Cotton was grown mainly by small farmers, largely tenants or sharecroppers, many of whom became debt-ridden because of the low prices paid for the crop. Alabama was fertile ground for agrarian reformers, and the POPULIST PARTY had numerous adherents in the state during 1890s.

In the early 20th century cotton declined in importance, partly because boll weevil infestations made farming more precarious; many rural Alabamians left the state, especially for cities of the northern United States. The state's economy was rejuvenated by the demands of the American effort during World War I; steelmaking boomed, and Mobile developed an important shipbuilding industry. The state was severely affected by the Depression of the 1930s; many banks failed and unemployment increased drastically. World War II marked the beginning of a long-term economic upswing.

Civil Rights. Race relations were a major issue in Alabama in the 1950s and '60s, as civil rights advocates worked to end racial segregation in the state. During 1955–56, Martin Luther KING, Jr., organized a black boycott that ended racially separate seating on municipal buses in Montgomery. In 1954 the U.S. Supreme Court had ruled racial segregation in public schools to be unconstitutional, but white officials in Alabama avoided implementing the decision until 1963, when, after tense confrontations between Gov. George C. Wallace and federal officials, integration was begun.

In 1963 four black children were killed when a bomb destroyed part of their Birmingham church. The incident, widely deplored in the nation, helped create the atmosphere for passage of the landmark federal Civil Rights Act of 1964. In 1965, King led a march from SELMA to Montgomery to protest discrimination in voter registration. The U.S. Congress responded with the VOTING RIGHTS ACT of 1965, which helped add many blacks to the voting rolls in Alabama and thereby encouraged white politicians in the state to moderate their views in order to attract black votes.

By the early 1970s most of Alabama's schools had been integrated. Progress continued for blacks through the 1970s and 1980s, with Alabama electing numerous black mayors. Governor Wallace, whose tenure had spanned the civil rights movement, retired in 1987 after four (nonconsecutive) terms in office. His successor, Guy Hunt, was the state's first Republican governor in 112 years.

Alabama (Indian tribe) The Alabama, a North American Indian tribe, lived near the junction of the Coosa and Tallapoosa rivers (in present-day Alabama) early in the 18th century. A Muskogean-speaking people, they were members of the CREEK confederacy and lived by hunting, fishing, and farming. They numbered 770 in 1715. From their base at Mobile, Ala., the French established relations with the Alabama early in the 18th century and erected (1714) Fort Toulouse in their midst. After 1763, when French territory in North America was ceded to Britain, the Alabama began to move west. They first settled (1764) at Bayou Manchac in Louisiana; by 1810 their settlements extended as far west as the Big Thicket region of East Texas. In 1854 the state of Texas granted the tribe 518 ha (1,280 acres) of land in Polk County. Today the Alabama and Coushatta Indians occupy a reservation there. Together they number about 925 (1989), with 475 on the reservation.

Alabama (ship) The *Alabama,* a cruiser built in Birkenhead, England, and equipped in the Azores with cannon from British vessels, served the Confederacy in the U.S. Civil War. From 1862 to 1864 it captured 65 to 70 Union merchant ships and destroyed most of them. On June 19, 1864, the U.S.S. *Kearsarge* engaged and sank the *Alabama* off Cherbourg, France. French researchers confirmed the location of the hull in 1987.

The ship lent its name to a controversy known as the Alabama Claims. The United States sought indemnity from Britain for damage to U.S. shipping inflicted during the war by the *Alabama* and several other less notorious British-built or equipped raiders. The United States contended that Britain aided the Confederacy in violation of NEUTRALITY laws. After a period of bitter dispute, the two countries agreed (1871), in the Treaty of Washington, to submit the question to international arbitration. A panel of American, British, Brazilian, Swiss, and Italian arbitrators met in Geneva and awarded (1872) the United States the sum of $15.5 million.

Alabama River The Alabama River is formed in south central Alabama by the junction of the Coosa and Tallapoosa rivers near Montgomery. It drains 58,534 km^2 (22,600 mi^2) of the state, flowing west to Selma and then south to join the Tombigbee River and create the Mobile and Tensaw rivers, which enter the Gulf of Mexico at Mobile. Navigable throughout its length (512 km/318 mi), the river has been an artery for traffic in cotton, lumber, and textiles.

alabaster   see GYPSUM

Alaca Huyuk [ahl'-ah-jah hoo-yook'] The archaeological site of Alaca Huyuk, located 160 km (100 mi) east of Ankara, Turkey, was first investigated in the late 19th and early 20th centuries by scholars who concentrated on

HITTITE remains. It is best known for its monumental stone gate with sphinx guardians and lateral reliefs depicting ritual scenes. Excavations begun in 1935 have revealed considerable local wealth and achievement before the time of the Hittites, with the earliest occupation dating from the 4th millennium BC. Tombs of the 3d millennium BC feature metal vessels, jewelry, weapons, and pole finials of bulls, stags, and abstract forms often interpreted as solar symbols. Major finds are displayed in the Ankara Archaeological Museum.

Aladdin   Aladdin is the idle, good-for-nothing boy hero of one of the most famous tales from *The Thousand and One Nights* (see ARABIAN NIGHTS). He obtains a magic lamp that, when rubbed, has the power to summon a genie who will do his bidding. With the lamp, after many narrow escapes, he gains wealth, power, and the hand of the sultan's daughter.

Alain-Fournier   [ah-lan-foorn-ee-ay']   The French poet, journalist, and novelist Alain-Fournier, b. Oct. 3, 1886, d. Sept. 22, 1914, is remembered primarily for his masterful *Le Grand Meaulnes* (1913; trans. as *The Wanderer*, c.1928), a novel about the innocence of childhood and the awe of first love. Blending memory, dream, and reality, Alain-Fournier creates an idyllic landscape for his adolescent heroes. The novel influenced many 20th-century writers dissatisfied with realism and naturalism. Alain-Fournier's verses and his correspondence with the critic Jacques Rivière are lyric and philosophic. The author was killed in World War I.

Alalakh   [ahl'-ah-lahk]   The ancient city of Alalakh, modern Tell Atchana, is a mound site on the Amuq plain of southeastern Turkey. Sir Leonard WOOLLEY and others excavated the site in 1937–39 and 1946–49; 17 building phases were discovered, including a monumental palace complex (level VII) dating from the first half of the 2d millennium BC. On the basis of cuneiform tablets found there, Alalakh has been identified as the center of the ancient kingdom of Yamkhad. Destroyed by the expanding Old Hittite Empire (see HITTITES), the site was later absorbed politically and culturally by the New Hittite Empire. Its final destruction (c.1200 BC) is attributed to the invaders referred to in Egyptian texts as the SEA PEOPLES. Artifacts reveal the influence of southwest Asian and early Aegean cultures.

Alameda   Alameda (1990 pop., 76,459) is a city in west central California, located on an island off the eastern shore of San Francisco Bay. First settled in the 1850s, it is now primarily a residential city, but its waterfront is dominated by ship-service industries and by the Alameda Naval Air Station.

Alamein, El   see WORLD WAR II

The Alamo, a mission in San Antonio, came to be a symbol of Texas's struggle for independence from Mexico. In 1836, fewer than 200 Texans resisted a Mexican siege for almost 2 weeks.

Alamo, The   The Alamo, site of a heroic battle of the TEXAS REVOLUTION, was founded in 1718 as a Spanish mission during the original settlement of San Antonio, Tex. Secularized in 1792, it fell into decay and was used variously as a hospital and troop garrison.

When the Mexican dictator Antonio López de SANTA ANNA invaded Texas during the Texas Revolution, the Texans withdrew into the crumbling walls of the mission's inner courtyard. There about 185–190 defenders were besieged by an army of 5,000–6,000, sustaining almost continuous cannonades for 12 days. On the 13th day—Mar. 6, 1836—the Mexicans broke through and massacred all the Texan men. A Mrs. Dickenson, her child, and possibly two servants were the only non-Mexican survivors. Although a convention had declared the independence of Texas four days earlier, this was unknown to the Alamo martyrs. Thus they died fighting under the Mexican flag and defending the Mexican constitution of 1824, which Santa Anna had abrogated.

Alamogordo   [al-uh-muh-gohr'-doh]   Alamogordo (1990 pop., 27,596), a city in south central New Mexico, is the seat of Otero County. A railroad shipping point for lumber from the Sacramento Mountains, which lie just to the west, Alamogordo was settled in 1898 as a railroad shop center for the Southern Pacific line. The first atomic bomb was exploded (July 16, 1945) 97 km (60 mi) northwest of Alamogordo on what is now the WHITE SANDS MISSILE RANGE. Also nearby are Holloman Air Force Base, Fort Bliss, White Sands National Monument, and Mescalero Indian Reservation.

Alarcón, Pedro Antonio de [ah-lahr-kohn',pay'droh ahn-toh'-nee-oh day]   Pedro Antonio de Alarcón, b. Mar. 10, 1833, d. July 19, 1891, a major Spanish novelist, is best known for *The Three-Cornered Hat* (1874; Eng. trans., 1891), a bedroom farce on which Manuel de Falla based his ballet music of the same name. Alarcón published his first novel, a romance in the manner of George Sand, at 18;years of age and then served in the Spanish campaign in Morocco, the setting for his incisive war memoirs published in 1859. In *Captain Venom* (1881; Eng. trans., 1914) and in a longer novel, *The Scandal* (1875; Eng. trans., 1945), he demonstrated his wit and skills as an observer. Alarcón was also a newspaper writer and politician.

Alaric I, King of the Visigoths [al'-uh-rik]   Alaric, c.370–410, was a Visigothic king whose capture of Rome in 410 signaled the final decline of the Roman Empire in the West. The leader of Visigothic mercenaries in the Roman army, he rebelled (395) and was proclaimed king by his troops. He led his army toward Constantinople and then into Greece, where he took increasing advantage of the divisions between the eastern and western halves of the empire. In 397 the emperor in the East, Arcadius, gave Alaric military command of Illyria, from which he invaded (401) Italy, and in 410 stormed and devastated the capital. He died while preparing to invade Africa.

Alaska   Alaska, the largest in area but among the least populated U.S. states, lies astride the Arctic Circle, apart from the "Lower 48" conterminous states. It is bordered on the north by the Arctic Ocean, on the east by the Yukon Territory, on the southeast by British Columbia, on the south by the Gulf of Alaska and the Pacific Ocean, and on the west by the Bering Sea, the Bering Strait, and the Chukchi Sea. Little Diomede Island, in the Bering Strait, is only 4 km (2.5 mi) from the USSR's Big Diomede Island.

Initially inhabited by Eskimos, Aleuts, Athabascans, Tlingit, and Haida, Alaska was first visited by Europeans in the early 18th century. In 1867 the United States purchased Alaska from Russia for only $7.2 million. Alaska's modern economic development was accelerated by World War II, when U.S. military bases were established there. Alaska became a state in 1959, and in 1968 great deposits of petroleum and natural gas were discovered in the Arctic coastal plain, or North Slope.

The name *Alaska* comes from an Aleut word thought to mean "mainland" or "land that is not an island"; the name originally was restricted to the Alaska Peninsula but by 1800 was used to denote all of present-day Alaska.

Land and Resources

Alaska has vast areas of unspoiled natural beauty, including rugged, snowcapped mountains; spectacular glaciers; and vast expanses of rolling tundra. The state's highest peak is Mount McKinley, or Denali (6,194 m/20,320 ft),

the loftiest point in North America. The state contains the northernmost land point of the United States—Point Barrow—as well as the country's westernmost point—on western Attu Island (one of the Aleutian Islands).

Physiographic Regions. Alaska may be divided into four geographic regions—the Pacific mountain system of the south, the central region of uplands and lowlands, the Brooks Range (the northernmost extension of the Rocky Mountains), and the Arctic coastal plain, or North Slope.

The Pacific mountain system is a complex region of high mountains, broad valleys, and many islands. The Coast Ranges dominate southeastern Alaska, a 644-km-long (400-mi) area known as the Alaska Panhandle. The ranges, many of which have large glaciers, rise to 5,489 m (18,008 ft) at Mount Saint Elias, in the Saint Elias Mountains, and to 4,996 m (16,391 ft) at Mount Blackburn, in the Wrangell Mountains. Just off the southeast coast is the Alexander Archipelago. The principal landform of south central Alaska is the Alaska Range, which contains such lofty peaks as Mount McKinley and Mount Foraker (5,304 m/17,400 ft). In extreme south central Alaska is an extensive area of lowlands. Southwestern Alaska is made up of the Alaska Peninsula, the Aleutian Islands, Kodiak Island, the Shumagin Islands, and several other islands. The Alaska Peninsula and the Aleutians are dominated by the volcanically active Aleutian Range.

Central Alaska, between the Alaska Range and the Brooks Range, contains modestly elevated mountains and large lowland regions. Higher elevations include West Point (1,788 m/5,865 ft). In the north is the rugged Brooks Range, as well as the De Long, Baird, Schwatka, and Endicott mountains. Lofty points in the Brooks Range include Mount Isto (2,761 m/9,058 ft), and Mount Chamberlin (2,749 m/9,019 ft). The Arctic coastal plain gradually slopes downward from the Brooks Range to the Arctic Ocean to the north. Permafrost lies under the surface of the plain, as do great deposits of petroleum and natural gas.

Rivers and Lakes. The chief river of Alaska is the Yukon, which flows westward across the central part of the state for 2,036 km (1,265 mi) before emptying into the Bering Sea. The Yukon's principal tributaries in Alaska are the Porcupine, Tanana, and Koyukuk rivers. Other major rivers in the state include the Kuskokwim, which flows westward to the Bering Sea; the Kobuk and Noatak, which empty into an arm of Kotzebue Sound; the Kokolik, Meade, and Colville, which flow into the Arctic Ocean; the Copper, which empties into the Gulf of Alaska; and the Susitna and Matanuska, which flow into Cook Inlet.

Alaska has many lakes, the largest of which is Iliamna Lake (2,675 km^2/1,033 mi^2) in the south. Several big lakes, such as Becharof Lake, Naknek Lake, and Kukaklek Lake, are on the Alaska Peninsula.

Climate. Southeastern Alaska and the flanks of the Coast Ranges in south central Alaska, as well as the Aleutians, are characterized by a maritime climate. Some areas have a mean annual precipitation of more than 5,080 mm (200 in), with 1,651 mm (65 in) being normal for low-lying places. Temperatures are relatively mild in winter and usually are cool in summer. Juneau has av-

AT A GLANCE

ALASKA

Land: Area: 1,530,693 km² (591,004 mi²); rank: 1st. Capital: Juneau (1990 pop., 26,751). Largest city: Anchorage (1990 pop., 226,338). County equivalents: 23. Elevations: highest—6,194 m (20,320 ft), Mount McKinley; lowest—sea level.

People: Population (1990): 551,947; rank; 49th; density: 0.36 persons per km² (0.94 per mi²). Distribution (1988 est.): 41.7% metropolitan, 58.3% nonmetropolitan. Average annual change (1980-80): +3.6%.

Government (1991): Governor: Walter J. Hickel, Independent. U.S. Congress: Senate— 2 Republicans; House—1 Republican. Electoral college votes: 3. State legislature: 20 senators, 40 representatives.

Economy: State personal income (1988): $10 billion; rank: 46th. Median family income (1979): $28,395; rank: 1st. Agriculture: income (1988)—$30 million. Fishing: value (1988)—$1.3 billion. Forestry: sawtimber volume (1987)—176.1 billion board feet. Mining: value (1987, nonfuels only)—$125 million. Manufacturing: value added (1987)—$827 million. Services: value (1987)—$2.2 billion.

Miscellany Statehood: Jan. 3, 1959; the 49th state. Nicknames: The Last Frontier and Land of Midnight Sun State; bird: willow ptarmigan; flower: forget-me-not; tree: Sitka spruce; motto: "North to the Future"; song: "Alaska's Flag."

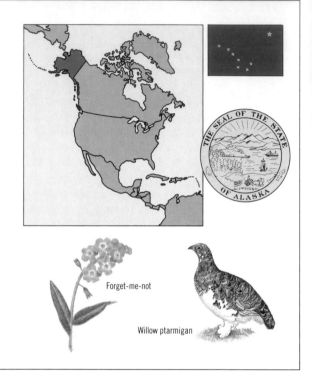

Forget-me-not

Willow ptarmigan

erage temperatures of -5° C (23° F) in January and 13° C (56° F) in July.

The lowlands along the lower Yukon and Kuskokwim rivers, the Cook Inlet area, the Copper River basin, and the southern Seward Peninsula have a transitional climate, with warm summers, cool winters, and precipitation ranging from 305 to 762 mm (12 to 30 in) a year. Summer temperatures are highest in the Copper River basin and decline to the west because of the moderating influence of the Bering Sea. Anchorage has a mean January temperature of -12° C (11° F) and an average July temperature of 14° C (58° F).

The interior of Alaska is shielded from marine influences by the Alaska and Brooks ranges. Thus it receives only 254–610 mm (10–24 in) of precipitation a year and has long winters, with typical temperatures of -40° C (-40° F) and occasional periods when temperatures drop to as low as -57° C (-70° F). Summers, however, usually are hot—temperatures reach 32° C (90° F), skies are clear, and sunlight lasts for twenty hours a day. Fairbanks has an average January temperature of -25° C (-13° F) and a mean July temperature of 16° C (61° F). Northern and northwestern Alaska has an arctic climate. This is the region of long, dark winters and short, cool summers, with 24 hr of darkness during part of the winter and 24 hr of daylight during part of the summer. Annual precipitation

is low, normally between 203 and 533 mm (8 and 21 in). Winter temperatures are not as low as in the interior, but high wind speeds frequently cause extreme chill factors.

Vegetation and Animal Life. About half of Alaska is covered with tundra vegetation, which mainly consists of small plants (such as lichens, mosses, flowering plants, and grasses) and some high brush. Tundra is found on higher mountain slopes and covers most of western Alaska and all of Arctic Alaska. Almost one-third of the state is covered by forest. Southeastern and south central Alaska have large forests composed mainly of hemlock and Sitka spruce, and the interior has extensive forests of black and white spruce, birch, aspen, and larch. About one-sixth of the forest land is within the Chugach National Forest and Tongass National Forest. Common flowering plants in the state include roses, lilacs, lilies, peonies, and delphiniums.

Alaskan wildlife includes numerous big animals. The southern part of the state has many bears (notably the Alaskan brown bear, or kodiak bear) and deer; large herds of fur seals are found on the PRIBILOF ISLANDS. Alaska has herds of moose, caribou, and reindeer, and mountain goats and sheep. Arctic Alaska has polar bears, caribou, and arctic foxes. The state's numerous streams are well stocked with trout, salmon, and other fish, and coastal marine waters contain abundant salmon, halibut, cod, her-

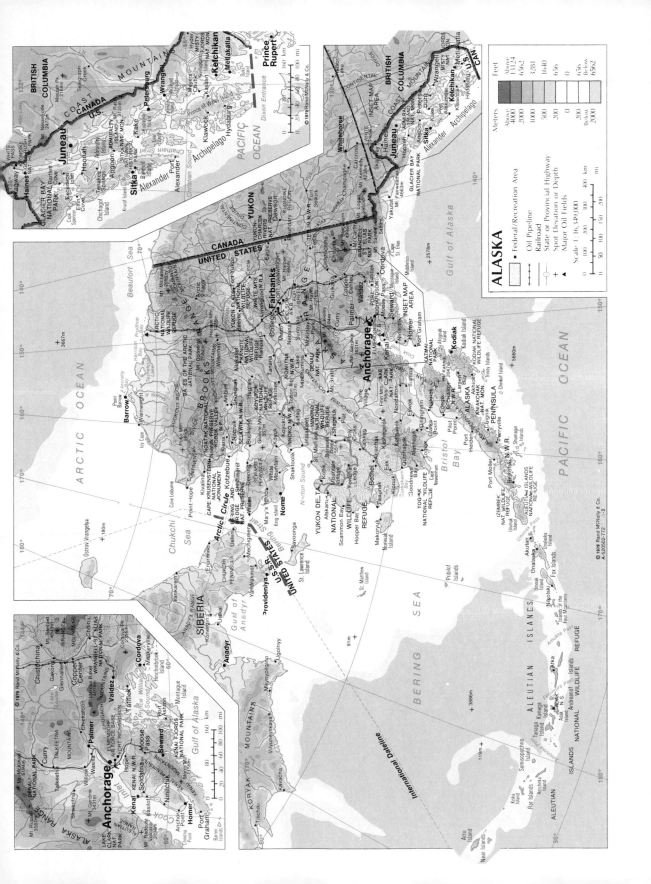

ring, pollack, shrimp, clams, and crabs as well as whales.

Mineral Resources. The most valuable mineral deposits in Alaska are petroleum and natural gas, found in great quantities in the Arctic coastal plain (especially around PRUDHOE BAY) and in lesser but significant amounts on the Kenai Peninsula and in Cook Inlet and the Gulf of Alaska. Gold is found in the central Yukon River basin, on the southern Seward Peninsula, and in the Alaska Panhandle. Alaska contains one of North America's largest bituminous coal reserves, located in Cook Inlet, the Nenana area, along the Yukon, and in northwest Alaska. Other minerals include iron ore, copper, molybdenum, antimony, silver, platinum, tin, and mercury.

People

Alaska is one of the least populous of the U.S. states, but its population grew more than 32% during the 1970s and 37% during the 1980s. Most of the increase resulted from a large net in-migration. Many persons entered the state in the 1970s to work in the petroleum industry or in jobs associated with oil production and transportation. This trend continued into the 1980s.

Only seven communities are of significant size—ANCHORAGE, FAIRBANKS, JUNEAU (the state capital), Kenai, Ketchikan, SITKA, and Kodiak. Most of these cities experienced a rapid pace of growth in the 1970s and '80s. Some smaller places, such as BARROW, NOME, VALDEZ, Bethel, Petersburg, Seward, and Wrangell (most with fewer than 3,000 inhabitants), are regional economic centers. The great majority of Alaska's inhabitants are white.

The combined population of American Indian, ESKIMO, and ALEUT is 64,047 (1980). The majority of this number are Eskimo (Inuit), most of whom live in the north and east. The principal American Indian groups are the Athabascan-speaking Indians of the interior and the HAIDA, TLINGIT, and TSIMSHIAN of the southeast. The Aleut, close-

ly related to the Eskimo, live on the Alaska Peninsula and on the Aleutian and Shumagin islands. Religious groups in Alaska include Roman Catholic, Orthodox, Presbyterian, Baptist, Episcopalian, and Methodist.

Education. The first schools in Alaska were established by Russians during the 1820s, but the school system did not expand significantly until the region was organized as a U.S. territory in 1912. Education in Alaska is largely state funded. About 10% of the children attend schools operated by the U.S. Bureau of Indian Affairs.

The University of Alaska (1917) has upper-level campuses at Anchorage, Fairbanks, and Juneau and a network of 10 community colleges. Sheldon Jackson College (1878) was Alaska's first institution of higher learning.

Cultural Institutions. Leading museums reflecting Alaska's native traditions and history are found in Fairbanks (University of Alaska), Juneau (Alaska State Museum), and Sitka (Sheldon Jackson). Anchorage has a museum of fine arts and native crafts. Major libraries include Rasmussen Library at the University of Alaska, Fairbanks; a growing library at the University of Alaska, Anchorage; and the Alaska Historical Library in Juneau. The state has several local drama and music groups.

Historic Sites. Places of historic interest in Alaska include Klondike Gold Rush National Historical Park, with buildings in Skagway associated with the Klondike gold rush of 1897–98; Sitka National Historical Park, encompassing the site of the 1804 battle in which Tlingit Indians were defeated by Russian colonizers; and several communities in the Aleutian Islands and southern part of the state having Russian Orthodox churches dating from the early 19th century.

Communications. Alaskan communities are served by radio and television as well as by newspapers. The most influential dailies include the *Anchorage Daily News*, the *Anchorage Times*, the *Fairbanks Daily News-Miner*, and

The Alaska Range, which separates the state's southern coastal region from the immense central plateau, includes Mounts McKinley (right), the highest in North America; Hunter (center), and Foraker (left). Mount McKinley National Park was established in 1917 and renamed Denali National Park in 1980.

Juneau, a center of the Alaskan fishing industry and the state capital, occupies a coastal strip bounded by the Gastineau Channel and the steep slopes of Mount Juneau. Through an extension of its municipal limits in 1970, Juneau became, in terms of the area, the largest city in the United States.

the *Juneau Southeast Alaska Empire*. The state's first commercial newspaper was the *Alaska Times*, initially published at Sitka in 1868.

Government

Alaska is governed under a constitution (as amended) that was adopted in 1956 and became effective in 1959. The capital of Alaska is Juneau. The state's chief executive is a governor, elected to a 4-year term; a governor may not serve more than two consecutive terms. Alaska has a bicameral legislature made up of a senate (whose 20 members are elected to 4-year terms) and a house of representatives (whose 40 members are elected to 2-year terms). The principal tribunals are the 5-member supreme court and the 29-member superior court; the justices of both are appointed by the governor to terms of 3 years, at the end of which they must be popularly elected to additional longer terms.

Alaska is divided into organized boroughs and the so-called unorganized borough. Organized boroughs are similar to counties, and each of the 11 such units is supervised by a small assembly. The unorganized borough includes about 80% of the state's area but less than 20% of its population. It is administered by the state government.

Jay Hammond, a Republican who was governor from 1974 to 1982, was succeeded by Bill Sheffield, a Democrat. Sheffield was defeated in the Democratic primary in 1986, and the victor, Steve Cowper, went on to win the November 1986 election. In 1990, Walter J. Hickel, who had been Alaska's second governor, ran as an independent, defeating the Republican and Democratic candidates to become the state's eighth governor.

Economy

Concerted economic growth in Alaska began only during World War II, when the federal government established several important military bases in the territory. The state now is the major employer in Alaska, and the state's income is based on taxes and royalties from petroleum production. The state suffered from the drop in world oil prices during the mid-1980s and later. Alaska continues nonetheless to produce a very significant percentage of U.S. oil, and the oil industry is crucial to the state's economy. Also important are such traditional industries as lumbering, fishing, and tourism.

Agriculture and Forestry. Alaska's annual cash income from farming is usually the lowest among U.S. states. The chief farm products are milk, eggs, greenhouse crops, hay, and potatoes. The principal cropland is in the lower Matanuska River valley, near Anchorage. Some sheep and cattle are raised, and Alaska has thousands of horses, many used as pack animals. Southeastern Alaska has an important logging and paper-pulp industry.

Fishing. Alaska has an important fishing industry, and the annual value of its catch generally surpasses all other states. Salmon account for the largest share of the annual fishing receipts; also valuable are king crabs, snow crabs, halibut, shrimp, cod, herring, scallops, and clams.

Wild-Animal Products. The Pribilof Islands yield valuable pelts from fur seals. Elsewhere, fur trapping on a small scale provides a significant source of income for some people. Harvesting of moose, caribou, seals, and whales is very important to the economy of native Alaskans.

Mining. Petroleum is the leading mineral produced in Alaska. The principal oil field is on the Arctic coastal plain, around Prudhoe Bay. Petroleum from this field is transported by the 1,287-km-long (800-mi) TRANS-ALASKA PIPELINE to Valdez, where it is transferred to oceangoing tankers. The field began producing in mid-1977, when the pipeline was completed; during its first decade of operation, the pipeline delivered 5.5 billion barrels of petroleum. Other major oil fields are on the Kenai Peninsula and in Cook Inlet.

Other minerals recovered in Alaska include stone, sand and gravel, gold, coal, gemstones, lead, platinum, silver, and barite.

Manufacturing. Alaska has a small manufacturing industry. The chief products are processed fish, paper, lumber, and refined petroleum. The main manufacturing centers are Anchorage, Fairbanks, Juneau, and Ketchikan.

Logs taken from the nearby Tongass National Forest are readied for processing at a pulp mill in Ketchikan. The preparation of lumber for export has become a profitable state industry.

Tourism. Alaska's splendid scenery, as well as its many opportunities for outdoor recreation, annually attract many thousands of tourists. National Parks include Denali (formerly Mount McKinley), Gates of the Arctic, Glacier Bay, Katmai, Kenai Fjords, Kobuk Valley, Lake Clark, and Wrangell–Saint Elias national parks; Bering Land Bridge, Noatak, and Yukon-Charley Rivers national preserves; Aniachak and Cape Krusenstern national monuments; and Klondike Gold Rush and Sitka national historical parks.

Transportation. Alaska has limited land transportation facilities. Perhaps the best-known road is the ALASKA HIGHWAY. Most of the several hundred miles of railroad track is part of the Alaska Railroad, running from Seward to Fairbanks via Anchorage. Another rail line runs from Skagway to Whitehorse, Yukon Territory. Small airplanes, operated by "bush pilots," carry freight and passengers to remote communities. Major airports are at Anchorage, Fairbanks, and Juneau.

An excellent system of ferries links the insular communities of southeast Alaska with nearby mainland communities and with Prince Rupert, British Columbia, and Seattle, Wash. Valdez, a terminus of the Trans-Alaska Pipeline, is a major port for shipping crude petroleum; other important ports include Anchorage, Ketchikan, Seward, Sitka, and Skagway.

Energy. In 1987, Alaska had an installed electricity-generating capacity of 1.7 million kW, and annual production totaled 4.1 billion kW h.

The state's rivers, notably the Yukon and Susitna, have great potential for producing hydroelectricity, but only a few waterpower facilities have been constructed.

History

The first settlers of present-day Alaska migrated in successive waves from Asia across the BERING LAND BRIDGE from about 30,000 to 10,000 years ago. When the region was first visited by Europeans, in the early 18th century, it was inhabited by Eskimo, Aleuts, Athabascans, Tlingit, and Tlairda.

During the first half of the 1700s the Danish navigator Vitus BERING, sailing for the Russian government, undertook two voyages to Alaska. Soon Russian adventurers were trapping in the Aleutian Islands, and in 1784, Grigory SHELEKHOV founded the first permanent white settlement in Alaska, on Kodiak Island. In 1799, Tsar Paul I chartered the RUSSIAN-AMERICAN COMPANY. Under Aleksandr BARANOV, who headed the company during 1800–17, the fur harvest was increased substantially, and several settlements were established, including New Archangel (later renamed Sitka), the capital of Russian America.

From 1820 onward, the Russian-American Company built iron foundries and schools and developed coal mining, trading routes, farming, and sheep raising. As a result of the Crimean War, however, the Russian government wished to sell Alaska to the United States. The Russians feared losing Alaska to the British in the event of another war.

After the Civil War, the U.S. secretary of state William H. SEWARD negotiated (1867) the purchase of Alaska. A treaty of cession was signed by Russia and the United States on Mar. 30, 1867; Alaska was formally transferred to the United States on Oct. 18, 1867. The United States paid $7.2 million for Russia's rights in Alaska. Americans moved quickly to exploit the profitable Pribilof fur seal trade.

During the early years of U.S. control Alaska was called "Seward's Folly" because it was believed to be useless. Although some economic development was undertaken, the region was generally neglected, and civil government was not established until 1884. Fishing grew in importance after 1867, and in 1878 the first salmon cannery was opened. During the late 19th century, large numbers of fur seals, whales, sea otters, and walruses were killed.

The modern economic development of Alaska began

in 1897–98 with the rush to the KLONDIKE gold fields in nearby Canada. In 1899 gold was found on the beach at Nome, and an Alaskan gold rush was quickly under way. By mid-1900 about 10,000 gold seekers were in Nome. In the next ten years important gold discoveries were made in other areas. Much copper ore was recovered in the Copper River basin near McCarthy from 1911 to 1938. The number of whites in Alaska increased from about 4,000 in 1890 to 36,400 in 1910.

Juneau was made the official capital of Alaska in 1900, but government offices were not moved there from Sitka until 1906, the same year that Alaskans elected their first delegate (nonvoting) to the U.S. House of Representatives. In 1912, Alaska was constituted as a U.S. territory, and Alaskans were able to elect a territorial legislature, whose decisions, however, were subject to veto by the federally appointed governor. In the 1920s and '30s the Alaskan economy grew slowly.

World War II brought great changes to Alaska. In 1942 the Japanese bombed Dutch Harbor (on Amaknak Island, near Unalaska Island) and briefly occupied Attu and Kiska islands, in the Aleutians. The United States countered by building a supply road, the Alaska Highway, and by establishing several military bases in the territory. The military buildup, which carried over to the postwar period, fostered economic development in Alaska and was largely responsible for the territory's population growth from 72,524 persons in 1939 to 128,643 persons in 1950.

During the 1950s and '60s, Alaska's economy continued to expand as the tourist trade grew. Fishing fleets and canning and timber-processing facilities were enlarged and modernized, and an important petroleum industry was established soon after the discovery, in 1957, of major oil fields in the Kenai Peninsula-Cook Inlet region. As the population increased, so did sentiment for statehood. In mid-1958 the U.S. Congress approved statehood for Alaska, and on Jan. 3, 1959, Alaska became the 49th state. Its first governor was William A. Egan, a Democrat, who served until 1966, when he was succeeded by Walter J. Hickel, a Republican. One of Alaska's initial U.S. senators was Ernest H. Gruening, a noted public official and an influential leader in the drive for statehood. In 1964 a powerful earthquake struck south central Alaska; Anchorage suffered extensive damage but was quickly rebuilt.

The crew of a commercial fishing vessel sorts and unloads a catch of Alaskan king crabs, one of many valuable species taken off the shores of Alaska.

A new era in Alaska began in 1968 with the discovery of great petroleum and natural-gas deposits in the Arctic coastal plain, or North Slope, around Prudhoe Bay. The decision to send the oil by pipeline from the north coast through the interior to the ice-free port of Valdez, where it would be transferred to oceangoing tankers, brought strong objections from environmentalists, but after considerable debate the U.S. Congress gave its approval in 1973. The Trans-Alaska Pipeline was completed in mid-1977. The government of Alaska gained large new revenues from taxes and other imposts levied on petroleum exploitation. Oil wealth spurred the state legislature to eliminate the state income tax and to begin distributing shares of Alaska's oil royalties to its citizens in 1982.

A major issue confronting Alaskans during the 1970s concerned the status of its vast area. At statehood the government of Alaska had been promised eventual control over about 28% of the state, and the U.S. government retained authority over the rest. Under national legislation passed in 1971, an additional 17.8 million ha (44 million acres) of federal holdings in the state were reserved for Alaska's Eskimo, Indians, and Aleuts. In 1980 Congress passed—against strong Alaskan opposition—the controversial Alaska Lands Bill, which restricts future de-

The Trans-Alaska pipeline, one of the most ambitious engineering projects in history, was completed in 1977. The 1,287-km-long (800-mi) pipeline carries petroleum from Prudhoe Bay, on the Arctic Ocean, to the ice-free port of Valdez, on the Gulf of Alaska.

velopment of more than 40 million ha (100 million acres).

In March 1989 the supertanker *Exxon Valdez* spilled 41.6 million l (11 million gal) of oil into Prince William Sound off Valdez. This catastrophe soiled several hundred kilometers of coastline and killed much wildlife.

Alaskan malamute [mal'-uh-myoot]   The Alaskan malamute, a working dog, originally pulled sleds for the Malamute (Mahlmut) Indians of northwestern Alaska. This dog is known for its endurance as a draft animal and for its affectionate nature: it is especially good with children.

The malamute has a compact, powerfully built body and a broad head. It stands 54–63.5 cm (21.5–25 in) high at the shoulder and weighs about 35 kg (80 lb). The coat is double-layered with woolly underhair and a coarse topcoat. The tail is bushy and loosely curled over the back. The paws are large and well padded with fur, enabling the dog to run over snow. The malamute's brown, almond-shaped eyes and its coat—gray or black and white—give it a wolflike appearance.

The Alaskan malamute traditionally has been used to pull heavily loaded sleds over great snow plains.

Alaskan Pipeline   see TRANS-ALASKA PIPELINE

Alba, Fernando Álvarez de Toledo y Pimentel, Duque de   The duque de Alba, or Alva, b. Oct. 29, 1507, d. Dec. 6, 1582, was a leading Spanish general and statesman under King PHILIP II. After serving Philip's father, Holy Roman Emperor CHARLES V, in many campaigns, he was named chief of household for Philip and became the leader of a major political faction at his court.

Alba helped negotiate the Treaty of Cateau-Cambrésis (1559), ending the long war with France, and in 1567 he was dispatched to the Low Countries to quell the DUTCH REVOLT. There, his persecution of the Protestants turned a rebellion into a war of independence. He was recalled in 1573. In 1580 Alba led the Spanish armies in the annexation of Portugal, where he died.

Alba Longa   Alba Longa was an ancient Latin city about 19 km (12 mi) southeast of Rome, set in the Alban Hills. According to legend, it was founded (*c.*1152 BC) by Aeneas's son, Ascanius, and was the birthplace of ROMULUS AND REMUS. The principal city of the LATINS, it retained its dominance until the 7th century BC, when it was probably destroyed by Rome. Excavations of its necropolis have revealed tombs dating from the 12th century BC. The site of Alba Longa is near Castel Gandolfo, summer residence of the popes.

albacore   see TUNA

Alban, Saint   Saint Alban, d. 304?, was the first British martyr. According to tradition, he was baptized by a fugitive priest whom he sheltered during DIOCLETIAN'S persecution. When the emperor's soldiers came to search his house, Alban, disguised in the priest's cloak, was arrested and then beheaded. Verulamium (present-day Saint Albans, England) was the site of the martyrdom. Feast day: June 17 (Church of England); June 22 (other Western).

Albanel, Charles   Charles Albanel, b. 1616, d. Jan. 11, 1696, was a Jesuit missionary and explorer in Canada. Having come to Quebec from France in 1649, he worked for many years among the Montagnais Indians at Tadoussac. In 1671–72 he traveled overland to Hudson Bay, probably the first European to do so. During a second journey (1673–74) to the bay, Albanel was seized by agents of the English Hudson's Bay Company and sent to England. He later returned (1676) to the Canadian missions, serving at Green Bay and Sault Ste. Marie.

Albanese, Licia [ahl-bah-nay'-zay, lee'-chah]   Licia Albanese, b. July 22, 1913, is an Italian-American singer who was for 25 years one of the leading sopranos of the Metropolitan Opera. She studied in Italy and made her debut in Milan in 1934 as Madame Butterfly. After 1940, except for the war years, she sang almost exclusively at the Metropolitan, giving more than 1,000 performances before her final appearance there in 1966. She was chosen by Arturo Toscanini to record *La Bohème* and *La Traviata* under his leadership. In 1985 she was a cast member of the concert revival of Stephen Sondheim's musical *Follies*, which was recorded.

Albania   Albania, one of Europe's smallest countries, lies in the western part of the Balkan Peninsula. It has a 360-km (225-mi) coastline on the Adriatic and Ionian

AT A GLANCE

PEOPLE'S SOCIALIST REPUBLIC OF ALBANIA

Land: Area: 28,748 km² (11,100 mi²). Capital and largest city: Tiranë (1987 est. pop., 225,700).

People: Population (1990 est.): 3,237,000. Density: 113.8 persons per km² (289.3 per mi²). Distribution (1989): 35% urban, 65% rural. Official language: Albanian. Major religions: Islam, Orthodoxy, Roman Catholicism.

Government: Type: Reform Communist state. Legislature: People's Assembly. Political subdivisions: 26 districts.

Economy: GNP (1989 est.): $3.8 billion; $1,200 per capita. Labor distribution (1987): agriculture—24.1%; manufacturing, mining, and public utilities—36.4%; construction—9.9%; transportation and communication—5%; trade—7.2%; public administration and defense—12.1%; other—5.3%. Foreign trade (1987): imports—$2255 million; exports—$378 million. Currency: 1 lek = 100 qintars.

Education and Health: Literacy (1989): 75%. Universities (1989): 1. Hospital beds (1987): 16,943. Physicians (1987): 6,308. Life expectancy (1990): women—78; men—72. Infant mortality (1990): 52 per 1,000 live births.

seas and borders Yugoslavia on the north and east and Greece on the southeast. The Albanians' name for their country, *Shqipëri*, means "eagles' land," aptly suggesting its isolation, ruggedness, and fierce independence. A rigidly Communist country since 1944, Albania tried to resist the currents of change that swept Eastern Europe in 1989, but student demonstrations and a flight of thousands of Albanians to foreign embassies during 1990 forced the government to embark on reforms.

Land

Albania is predominantly mountainous; approximately three-fourths of its territory are highlands with elevations greater than 300 m (1,000 ft). The highest peak, Korab (2,751 m/9,025 ft), lies on the eastern border with Yugoslavia. Most of the people live in the basins and plateaus of central Albania. The narrow coastal zone of fertile alluvial lowlands (with some marshes) extends inland along some rivers.

Most of the rivers in Albania flow eastward, descending rapidly to the coast, many in narrow gorges. The longest river is the Drin. The major lakes (all divided by Albania's borders) are Ohrid, Shkodër, and Prespa.

Climate. The coastal lowlands enjoy a typically Mediterranean climate: hot, dry summers and mild, wet winters. At Durrës, nearly 80% of the annual rainfall occurs between October and March, and the average daily minimum temperature in January is 6° C (42° F). The interior highlands have a continental climate, with cold winters and warm summers. Annual rainfall averages from 760 mm (30 in) in the southeastern highlands to 2,030 mm (80 in) in the northern coastal plain.

Resources. Albania is relatively rich in minerals and is the world's fourth leading producer of chrome. Other minerals include oil, natural gas, bitumen, copper, iron, nickel, and salt. The river systems, especially the Drin, provide hydroelectric power. Forests of oak, chestnut, beech, pine, and fir supply the needs of woodworking and paper industries.

People

Albanians, comprising 90% of the population, are believed to be descendants of the ancient Illyrians, who were among the earliest inhabitants of the Balkan Peninsula. Despite centuries of foreign domination, the Albanians have managed to preserve their national identity. Albanian is a separate branch of the Indo-European language family. Minorities include Greeks (8%), and Gypsies, Serbs, and Bulgarians (2%).

In 1967 the country was officially declared an atheist state and all religious institutions were closed. At that time, about 70% of the population were Muslims, 20% were Orthodox Christians, and 10% were Roman Catholics. In 1990, as a part of the reforms spurred by the

Eastern European upheavals, the government permitted Albanians to worship in their homes, and in January 1991 the first public Muslim service since 1967 took place.

Demography. Albania's birthrate, the highest in Europe, is closer to that of a Third World country. The urban population, although small by European standards, has more than doubled since 1940. Major cities include TIRANË, the capital, DURRËS (Durazzo), SHKODËR (Scutari), Elbasan, VLORË (Valona), and Korçë (Koritza), none of which, except Tiranë, has more than 100,000 inhabitants.

Education and Health. Eight years of primary education (from ages 6 to 14) are free and compulsory. Secondary education consists of four-year technical or professional courses, and higher education is offered by Enver Hoxha University in Tiranë (founded in 1957), three teacher training schools, and two agricultural colleges.

Albania has about 800 hospitals and more than 3,000 outpatient clinics. Medical care is free, and medication is free for children up to one year of age.

Cultural Activity. Albanian literature, which first appeared in the 15th and 16th centuries, was for a long time primarily religious. Ottoman political authorities and the Greek Orthodox patriarch discouraged the development of Albanian culture, but by the 19th century, a number of writers had established a secular literature with nationalistic themes.

Albanian literature and culture began to flourish after the achievement of independence in 1912. Since 1945, cultural activity has been rigidly controlled; consequently, with the exception of folk music, the folk arts, and a few literary works, Albanian culture has attracted little foreign interest.

Economic Activity

Before World War II, Albania was one of the least developed countries in the world, with the economy almost completely based on agriculture. After the war, a highly centralized socialist economic system was introduced, and although the Communist rulers have sought to transform the country into a modern industrial-agricultural state, Albania remains extremely backward. One of the causes of this backwardness was Albania's resolute isolationism, which even led to the prohibition of all foreign borrowing.

Less than one quarter of the labor force is engaged in agriculture, either in state farms or cooperatives. Throughout the Communist period, peasants have been permitted to cultivate small private plots. Industry in Albania, all of it owned by the state, includes the processing of mineral resources, textile manufacture, and food products.

In May 1990 the government announced an economic reform program, intended to decentralize the economy and encourage individual initiative. The ban on foreign credits was lifted, and peasants were permitted to sell produce from their small private plots at peasants' markets.

Government

Under the 1976 Constitution the unicameral People's Assembly is the country's highest political authority, but the actual power is held by the (Communist) Albanian Party of

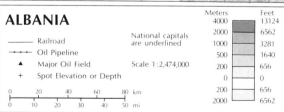

ALBANIA

——— Railroad
•━•━• Oil Pipeline
▲ Major Oil Field
+ Spot Elevation or Depth

National capitals are underlined

Scale 1:2,474,000

	Meters	Feet
	4000	13124
	2000	6562
	1000	3281
	500	1640
	200	656
	0	0
	200	656
	2000	6562

0   20   40   60   80 km
0 10   20   30   40 50 mi

Labor (APL). APL first secretary Enver HOXHA dominated the country from 1944 until his death in 1985.

Following the fall of Communist regimes in Eastern Europe, pro-democracy demonstrations took place in Albania throughout 1990, and the Communist leadership split into conservative and reformist groups. In late 1990, political parties were legalized, and the first multiparty elections ever in Albania were expected to take place in March 1991.

History

From the 7th century BC the Greeks colonized the coastal areas of what is now Albania. In about 350 BC an independent kingdom, ILLYRIA, emerged in the region near Shkodër. Illyria and EPIRUS to the south were conquered by Rome in 168 BC. In the 4th century AD, the area came under Byzantine rule, and in the succeeding centuries it was overrun by the Goths, Bulgars, Slavs, Serbs, and Normans (see BALKANS).

In the early 15th century the Turks began their conquest of the region. In 1443 Albanian resistance to the Turks was led by SKANDERBEG, the greatest national hero. He expelled the Turks and kept Albania independent for more than 20 years. After his death in 1468, however, the Turks came back and incorporated Albania into the OTTOMAN EMPIRE. During the nearly five centuries of Ottoman rule most Albanians converted to Islam.

Albanian nationalism revived in the early 19th century and spurred repeated revolts. In 1912, in the First Balkan War, the Turks were driven from much of the Balkan Peninsula, and Albania became independent (see BALKAN WARS).

During World War I, Albania was a battleground for other Balkan powers and Italy, but its sovereignty was upheld at the Paris Peace Conference (1919). In 1925 a conservative northern tribal chief, Ahmed Zogu, seized

The small town of Gjirokastër in southern Albania, is the birthplace of the nation's longtime leader Enver Hoxha. Despite the rugged terrain, the area is an important producer of olives, tobacco, and wheat.

power, and in 1928 proclaimed Albania a monarchy and became King ZOG. In 1939, Italy invaded Albania, forcing Zog into exile.

During World War II a power struggle developed between the Communist and the non-Communist liberation forces. After the Germans withdrew in 1944, a provisional Communist government was established. Between 1944 and 1948 Albania was a close ally of Yugoslavia.

In 1948, after the Yugoslav-Soviet rift, Albania allied itself with the USSR. Relations between the two countries worsened in the late 1950s after Nikita Khrushchev denounced Stalin. In 1961, Albania and the USSR severed diplomatic relations.

From 1961 to 1978, Albania found an ally in China; after that the country became completely isolated. In the late 1980s the new Communist party chief, Ramiz Alia, took cautious steps toward reestablishing diplomatic and trade contacts with other countries. At the same time, relations with Yugoslavia were troubled by the question of equal rights for the ethnic Albanian minority in that country. Albania resisted the wave of liberalization that swept across Communist Eastern Europe in 1989, but in 1990 the government responded to the pressure for change by ending the ban on religion, permitting its citizens to travel abroad, and initiating economic reform.

Albany (Georgia) Albany (1990 pop., 78,122) is a city on the Flint River in southwestern Georgia and is the seat of Dougherty County. Crops from the surrounding area, processed in the city, include Spanish peanuts, cotton, and pecans. Aircraft and farm tools are manufactured. Albany State College, Albany Junior College, and Albany Naval Air Station are located there. Founded in 1836, the city was named for Albany, N.Y.

Albany (New York) Albany, the capital of New York State, is located at the confluence of the HUDSON RIVER and the NEW YORK STATE BARGE CANAL system in the east central part of the state. It is a U.S. port of entry and also serves as the seat of Albany County. It has a population of 101,082 (1990).

Located at the eastern terminal of the Erie Canal, Albany serves as an important port connecting shipping between the Great Lakes and Canada and Atlantic ports. Since the opening (1932) of the Port of Albany, the city has been an important maritime center. Industrial development in the area is extensive and highly diversified, with the manufacture of automotive parts, textiles, chemicals, drugs, plastics, machine tools, felt, and paper. Operation of the state government also adds substantially to the economy.

Although the Dutch established a temporary post (Fort Nassau) there in 1614, the first permanent settlement was in 1624, when a group of Walloon families built Fort Orange. A Dutch colony until 1664 when the British assumed control, Albany was renamed in honor of the duke of York and Albany, later James II of England. Albany became the permanent state capital in 1797.

Albany Congress The Albany Congress was a meeting held at Albany, N.Y., in June–July 1754, attended by representatives of the colonies of New York, Pennsylvania, Maryland, Massachusetts, Connecticut, Rhode Island, and New Hampshire and of the five Iroquois nations. Although its purpose was to cement ties between the colonies and the Iroquois in preparation for war with the French, it is chiefly remembered as the occasion when Benjamin FRANKLIN presented his Albany Plan of Union. Franklin proposed that the colonies form a self-governing federation under the British crown. Even though the plan was not realized, in many respects it foreshadowed the later union of the American states.

Albategnius see BATTANI, AL-

albatross Albatross is the common name for large web-footed marine birds belonging to the family Diomedeidae, order Procellariiformes. Some of the 13 or 14 species of albatross also are known as mollymawks or gooney birds. Albatrosses are concentrated in southern oceans but are also seen in warmer northern waters and may migrate farther north in the summer. Their narrow, graceful wings—wingspan may exceed 3.7 m (12 ft), more than any other living bird—make them superb gliders. Albatrosses often travel great distances. Along with the related PETRELS and SHEARWATERS, albatrosses are the most marine of birds. They sleep on the ocean's surface,

The albatross is one of the largest of all birds. It may remain at sea for months. Some travel entirely around the globe between mating seasons. The black-browed albatross (top) has a 2.1-m (7-ft) wingspan. The head of the wandering albatross (bottom), shows the characteristic hooked beak and nostril tubes.

drink seawater, and subsist on squid and other small marine life. Some are scavengers, trailing ships for their refuse.

Albatrosses range in length from 50 to 125 cm (20 to 50 in). Plumage varies from white through dark gray or gray-brown, with combinations of all three being common. The large hooked bill, covered with horny plates, has prominent tubular nostrils. The three front toes are webbed, and the rear toe may be absent or vestigial. Albatrosses live on land only during the breeding season, usually nesting in colonies on remote oceanic islands. Courtship displays are highly elaborate. Incubation of a single egg lasts two to three months.

Because of the albatross theme in Samuel Taylor Coleridge's *Rime of the Ancient Mariner*, the bird's name has become a metaphor for a troublesome burden.

albedo [al-bee'-doh] Albedo is a measure of the reflecting power of an object or surface. It is mathematically defined as the ratio of the amount of light reflected from a surface to the amount that is incident upon it, often expressed as a percentage. A surface that reflects half the light it receives has an albedo of 0.5, or 50%. The average value of the Earth's albedo is 35%, largely because of the high reflecting power of clouds, snow cover, and deserts. Planets with cloudy atmospheres have a high value for the albedo (76% for Venus, for example). Rocky surfaces absorb most of the light they receive; hence, the Moon has an albedo of 7%.

Albee, Edward [al'-bee] Edward Franklin Albee, b. Washington, D.C., Mar. 12, 1928, is one of the most important American playwrights of the 1960s and the one most closely identified with the THEATER OF THE ABSURD. His plays are characterized by sharp dialogue, biting satire, often illogical confrontations between characters, and unconventional theatrical effects.

His first play, *The Zoo Story* (1958), produced in West Berlin in 1959 and in New York City the next year, is a short, ominous two-character play about how the failure of communication leads to violence. *The Sandbox* (1959) and *The American Dream* (1960), closely related one-act plays, absurdly parody family life and the American dream of success; *The Death of Bessie Smith* (1960) comments on racial prejudice and human cruelty. Albee attained popular and critical success with his first full-length Broadway play, WHO'S AFRAID OF VIRGINIA WOOLF? (1962; film, 1966), a painful verbal and psychological duel that presents in mature form the concerns of his early short plays. *Tiny Alice* (1964), a complex, puzzling work about sex, morality, and metaphysics, proved to be less successful than his earlier plays.

His other plays include two Pulitzer Prize winners, *A Delicate Balance* (1966) and *Seascape* (1975); the experimental *Box* and *Quotations from Chairman Mao Tse-tung* (*Box-Mao-Box*, 1968) and *All Over* (1971); and such adaptations as *Ballad of the Sad Café* (1963) from Carson McCullers's novella.

Albers, Josef   The German-born American painter Josef Albers, b. Mar. 19, 1888, d. Mar. 25, 1976, contributed much to modern art through his investigation of color and light perception in nonfigurative painting.

Albers taught design at the BAUHAUS School in Dessau and Berlin from 1923 to 1933; his association with the constructivist movement (see CONSTRUCTIVISM) is derived from this background, although he was not concerned merely with formal abstraction. Albers's experimentation related optics and the natural phenomena of color and light. His first creations at the Bauhaus were composed of glass shards that could not produce subtle gradations of tone, and his later painting demonstrated his proclivity for flat geometry and pure, unmixed color. He is considered the father of hard-edge painting.

Albers arrived in the United States in 1933 to teach at Black Mountain College in North Carolina, where he taught (and occasionally dismissed) many of today's avant-garde artists. He subsequently served as a visiting professor at various U.S. universities. From 1950 to 1960 he headed the Department of Design at Yale University. Yale published Albers's major theoretical writings, including his monumental *Interaction of Color* (1963; rev. ed., 1975). The culmination of Albers's development is his famous "Homage to the Square" series, on which he worked from 1949 until his death. Typified by *Homage to the Square: Insert* (1950; The National Collection of Fine Arts, Washington, D.C.), the corpus of his work is concerned not with emotional expression but with the physical fact and psychic effects of seeing.

Albert, Carl   Carl Bert Albert, b. McAlester, Okla., May 10, 1908, served as speaker of the U.S. House of Representatives from 1971 to 1977. A Democrat, he represented a rural district of his native Oklahoma in the House from 1947 to 1977, when he retired. He had been a Rhodes scholar and a lawyer before entering politics.

Albert, Lake   Lake Albert (Bantu: Albert Nyanza) is located in east central Africa on the border of Zaire and Uganda. Cradled in the western branch of the Great Rift Valley, the shallow, saline lake lies at an altitude of about 610 m (2,000 ft) and is bordered by tall, forested cliffs in the west and east. Lake Albert is 160 km (100 mi) long and 35 km (22 mi) wide. It is fed by the Victoria Nile and the Semliki River and is drained by the Albert Nile into the White Nile. Sir Samuel White Baker sighted the lake in 1864.

Albert I, King of the Belgians   Albert I, b. Apr. 8, 1875, d. Feb. 17, 1934, king of the Belgians (1909–34), is remembered especially for his strong leadership during World War I. In August 1914, when the German armies demanded right of passage through Belgium, Albert refused the ultimatum and assumed personal command of the Belgian armed forces in resisting the German advance. He remained in the small, unoccupied area of Belgium throughout the war, and in September 1918 led Belgian and French troops in the final Allied offensive.

After the war, Albert promoted the economic reconstruction of Belgium. His death in a mountain-climbing accident was deeply mourned. He was succeeded by his son, LEOPOLD III.

Albert I, Margrave of Brandenburg (Albert the Bear)   Albert I, or Albert the Bear, b. c.1100, d. Nov. 18, 1170, founder of the state of BRANDENBURG, was one of the leaders of the 12th-century German eastern expansion called the DRANG NACH OSTEN. He inherited the Saxon estates of his father and, after services to Holy Roman Emperor LOTHAIR II, received (1134) the Saxon Nordmark, lying east of the Elbe and Havel rivers. Albert campaigned successfully against the Slavic Wends. His family, the Ascanians, ruled until 1320.

Albert, Prince Consort of England   Albert, called the Prince Consort, was the husband of Queen VICTORIA of Britain. The son of the Duke of Saxe-Coburg-Gotha, he was born on Aug. 26, 1819, near Coburg, Bavaria. He married Victoria in 1840, and as her closest advisor exercised a restraining influence on her. Albert worked well with Sir Robert PEEL but quarreled frequently with Viscount PALMERSTON. In the TRENT AFFAIR of 1861 the prince moderated the hostility of Palmerston's government toward the United States.

A patron of the arts and sciences, Albert helped organize the Great Exhibition of 1851. His zeal for public improvements, and his industriousness and stern moralism set the tone of mid-Victorian England. After Albert's death on Dec. 14, 1861, Victoria went into seclusion for several years.

Albert, 1st Duke of Prussia   Albert, b. May 17, 1490, d. Mar. 20, 1568, was the first duke of PRUSSIA. A member of the HOHENZOLLERN family, he was chosen (1511) grand master of the TEUTONIC KNIGHTS. On becoming a Protestant, however, he secularized (1525) the lands of the knights, converting them into the hereditary duchy of Prussia.

Alberta   Alberta is the westernmost of the Prairie Provinces of Canada. It stretches about 1,215 km (755 mi) north from Montana to the Northwest Territories. Alberta is the fourth largest province of Canada and the fourth most populous, with one of the largest growth rates. Traditionally associated with wheat-growing and cattle ranching, Alberta is today especially important because of its fuel resources, the largest in Canada.

The first European explorer to penetrate the region is thought to have been Anthony Henday, in 1754, and the first European settlement was a fur-trading post established in 1778 in the northeastern part of today's province.

Land: Area: 661,190 km² (255,287 mi²); rank: 4th. Capital: Edmonton (1986 pop., 573,982). Largest city: Calgary (1986 pop., 636,104). Municipalities: 351. Elevations: highest— 3,747 m (12,293 ft), at Mount Columbia; lowest—176 m (577 ft).

People: Population (1989 est.): 2,423,200; rank: 4th. Density: 3.8 persons per km² (9.7 per mi²). Distribution (1986): 79.4% urban, 20.6% rural. Average annual change (1981–86): +1.2%.

Government (1991): Lieutenant Governor: Gordon Towers. Premier: Donald R. Getty, Progressive Conservative. Parliament: Senate—6 members; House of Commons— 25 Progressive Conservatives, 1 New Democrat. Provincial legislature: 79 members. Admitted to Confederation: Sept. 1, 1905, with Saskatchewan, the 8th and 9th provinces.

Economy (monetary figures in Canadian dollars): Total personal income (1987): $43.3 billion; rank: 4th. Median family income (1987): $39,956. Agriculture: net income (1986)—$720 million. Fishing: landed value (1984)—$1.25 million. Forestry: lumber production (1985)—1.1 billion board feet. Mining: value (1986)— $17.5 billion. Manufacturing: value added (1986)—$5 billion.

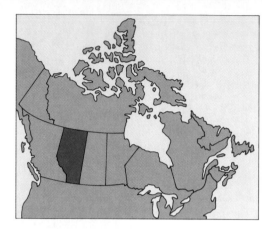

In 1882, Alberta was made a district of the former Northwest Territories and named for a daughter of Queen Victoria who was the wife of the then governor-general of Canada.

Land and Resources

The eastern three-fourths of Alberta's terrain is made up of plains, which rise from less than 300 m (1,000 ft) in the northeast to more than 1,220 m (4,000 ft) in the southwest. The plains vary locally from very flat and extensive old lake bottoms to rolling landscapes with many lakes and depressions. These landforms reflect the former presence of Pleistocene ice sheets, which, at maximum extent, covered all the province except for a few high pockets. In places, hilly or plateau areas (for example, Cypress Hills and Swan Hills) may rise to 600 m (2,000 ft) above the general surface of the plain.

To the west of the plains, an area of foothill ridges of higher elevation is bordered by the ROCKY MOUNTAINS. The Rockies, with several peaks over 3,660 m (12,000 ft), make up the other major physical region of the province.

Geologically the province includes almost a complete range in age, from the ancient Precambrian of the CANADIAN SHIELD in the extreme northeast corner through progressively younger formations in the southwest, including Tertiary deposits.

Soils. Soil types are arranged in concentric arcs from the southeastern part of Alberta and reflect the moisture and natural vegetation patterns. Brown prairie soils are succeeded by rich black soils with a deep humus layer in the central parts of the province. However, more than two-thirds of Alberta, in the northern and western sectors, is marked by podzols, or gray-wooded soils, which are less fertile.

Lakes and Rivers. Most of southern and central Alberta drains eastward into Hudson Bay via the NELSON River system, which in Alberta includes such major rivers as the North Saskatchewan and the South Saskatchewan. West central and northern Alberta is drained into the Arctic Ocean by the MACKENZIE RIVER system, which includes such important rivers as the PEACE, ATHABASCA, and Hay. A small sector of the extreme south drains into the Milk River, which is part of the Missouri-Mississippi system. Groundwater aids irrigation, as do diverted mountain-origin rivers in parts of southern Alberta.

Lakes are especially numerous in the central and northern parts of the province. Lake Claire and Lesser Slave Lake are the two largest lakes wholly within Alberta. The western third of Lake ATHABASCA also lies within the province. Lake LOUISE in the Rocky Mountains is known for its beautiful scenery.

Climate. Alberta has a continental climate with long, cold winters and short, cool summers, although summers are longer and warmer in the southeastern quarter. At EDMONTON the average January temperature is -20° C (-4°

F), and the July temperature is 23° C (74° F). Precipitation is moderate to light, with the southeast being particularly dry. The average annual precipitation for Edmonton is 440 mm (17 in), much of which falls as snow in the winter. The western foothills and mountains receive more abundant precipitation.

A distinctive local feature that often moderates the winter temperatures of southern Alberta in the foothills and western plains is the CHINOOK, a warm westerly wind that descends the eastern face of the Rockies.

Vegetation and Animal Life. Two-thirds of Alberta is forested. The grasslands of the southeast reflect that region's warmer summers and sparser precipitation. Most of Alberta's forest is a mixture of conifers (white spruce, jack pine) and deciduous trees (aspen, poplar, white birch). However, conifers become dominant in the northeast (the taiga, or boreal coniferous forest) and in the foothills and lower mountains (subalpine forest). In the mountains, TUNDRA occurs above the tree line.

Surviving grassland animals include pronghorn antelope, ground squirrels, and coyotes. Forested areas include a variety of fur-bearing animals (bear, otter, ermine, beaver) and big game animals (moose, caribou, elk, deer), as well as North America's largest surviving herd of wild buffalo.

Resources. Alberta's major natural resources are fuels, forests, and productive soils. The province's water resources, which include the source regions for parts of the continent's major river systems, are particularly important. Many of the mountain and foothill zones are included in national or provincial parks and are protected by the government.

Economic Activity

Since the early 1950s, when Alberta's economy was dominated by agriculture, mining and manufacturing have grown so rapidly that they now greatly overshadow agricultural activities. Petroleum production is a crucial income source.

Manufacturing and Mining. Alberta's manufacturing originally concentrated on processing food products. Food and beverage industries are still a very important manufacturing group. Since the discovery (1947) of the Leduc oil fields near Edmonton, however, both the value and diversity of manufacturing have increased greatly. Over 80% of all Canadian oil production and 90% of natural gas production occur in Alberta. Petroleum-product processing is now a dominant industrial activity, and it furnishes raw materials for a new petrochemical industry. Exploitation of major oil-sand deposits in northern Alberta has begun, but immense potential remains. Alberta contains approximately half of Canada's huge minable coal reserves.

Agriculture and Forestry. Cattle ranching, in the foothills and the drier south, is an important agricultural sector of the economy. Wheat and barley are the principal grain crops. Irrigation farming, which is centered in Lethbridge, produces vegetables, sugar beets, and livestock feed. Central Alberta concentrates on mixed farming and dairying, with cash crops and seed production in the

Peace River district to the northwest. Sawmills operate in the forested areas of the north and west.

Tourism. Of the five national parks, three in the Rocky Mountains—Waterton Lakes, Banff, and Jasper—draw visitors from all over the world. Local events, such as the many rodeos, Calgary Stampede, and Edmonton Klondike Days, as well as sport fishing and hunting, also attract tourists.

Transportation. The province is crossed by two transcontinental highway systems (the Trans-Canada Highway and the Yellowhead Highway) and by two transcontinental railroads (the Canadian Pacific Railway and the Canadian National Railways). Alberta is crisscrossed by a network of oil and gas pipelines, the major focus of which is Edmonton.

People

Alberta's population continued to increase during the recession years 1981–86, although the growth rate (6.1%) slowed markedly compared with the increase (21.7%) during the previous census period 1976–81. Alberta has received many immigrants from other provinces and from abroad. English is the native language of more than 80% of Alberta's population, followed by German, Ukrainian, French, and various Scandinavian languages. Native Indians are a small number of the total population and include the BLACKFOOT and the CREE.

Education and Cultural Activity. Alberta has four provincial universities. The oldest and largest is the University of Alberta (1906), in Edmonton. The University of Calgary was established after World War II as an affiliate of the University of Alberta but has been an independent institution since 1966.

Alberta enjoys a variety of cultural institutions. The major collections in the province are housed in the modern Provincial Museum and Archives in Edmonton and the Glenbow-Alberta Institute in CALGARY. Both Edmonton and Calgary have symphony orchestras and professional theater, ballet, and opera companies. The province is well served by communications networks.

Places of Interest. Wood Buffalo National Park in northernmost Alberta is, at 44,800 km^2 (17,300 mi^2), Canada's largest national park. Within its wilderness area, besides the buffalo, are the nesting grounds of the near-extinct whooping crane. Resorts are popular in the mountains and the lake areas of central Alberta. The oldest and best known resort is BANFF.

Government

Alberta is a parliamentary democracy, without a formal provincial constitution. It is governed by a Legislative Assembly comprising 83 members, with an Executive Council, or cabinet, made up of members drawn from the Assembly. The Executive Council is headed by the premier, who is the leader of the majority party in the Assembly. The SOCIAL CREDIT PARTY dominated Alberta's government from 1935 to 1971. The Conservatives then won control, led—until 1985—by Peter Lougheed. Donald Getty succeeded Lougheed as party leader and premier and won elections in 1986 and 1989.

Local government is provided by 30 counties and 18

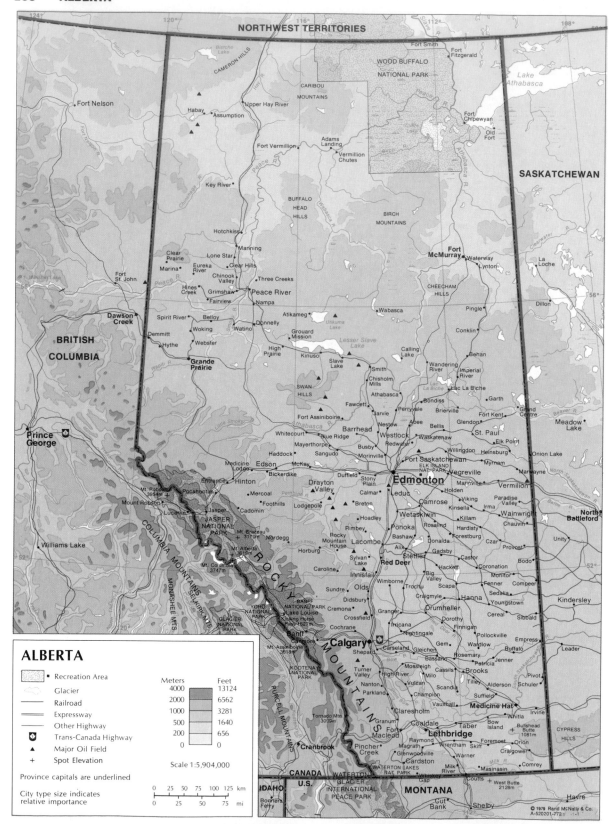

NORTHWEST TERRITORIES

SASKATCHEWAN

BRITISH
COLUMBIA

ALBERTA

- Recreation Area
- Glacier
- Railroad
- Expressway
- Other Highway
- Trans-Canada Highway
- ▲ Major Oil Field
- + Spot Elevation

Province capitals are underlined

City type size indicates
relative importance

Meters	Feet
4000	13124
2000	6562
1000	3281
500	1640
200	656
0	0

Scale 1:5,904,000

0 25 50 75 100 125 km

0   25   50   75 mi

© 1979 Rand McNally & Co.
A-520201-772-1 -1-1

MONTANA

Fort Nelson

Fort Smith   Fort
Fitzgerald

WOOD BUFFALO

NATIONAL PARK

Lake
Athabasca

Habay   Assumption
Upper Hay River

CAMERON HILLS

CARIBOU
MOUNTAINS

Adams
Landing
Fort Vermillion   Vermillion
Chutes

Fort
Chipewyan   Old
Fort

Key River

BUFFALO
HEAD
HILLS

BIRCH
MOUNTAINS

Hotchkiss

Manning
Lone Star
Clear
Prairie   Clear Hills
Marina   Eureka
River   Chinook
Valley
Three Creeks
Fort
St. John   Hines
Creek   Grimshaw   Peace River
Fairview   Nampa

Fort
McMurray   Waterway
Lynton

CHEECHAM
HILLS

La
Loche

Dillon

Dawson
Creek   Spirit River   Belloy
Demmitt   Woking   Watino
Hythe   Webster   High
Prairie   Kinuso   Slave
Lake

Atikameg   Wabasca
Grouard
Mission   Utikuma Lake
Lesser Slave
Lake

Pingle
Conklin

GRANDE
PRAIRIE   Donnelly

Calling
Lake   Behan

Smith
Chisholm
Mills
Athabasca

Wandering
River   Imperial
River

Garth

Lac
La Biche   Lac La Biche

Grand
Centre   Meadow
Lake

SWAN
HILLS

Fawcett   Bondiss   Brierville
Fort Assiniboine   Narvie   Perryvale   Abee   Fort Kent   Glendon
Nestow   Bellis   St. Paul
Whitecourt   Barrhead   Westlock   Waskatenau   Elk Point
Blue Ridge   Busby   Redwater   Willingdon   Heinsburg
Mayerthorpe   Sangudo   Morinville   Fort Saskatchewan   Myrnam   Onion Lake
Haddock   McKay   Vegreville   Marwayne
Medicine
Lodge   Edson   Bickerdike   Duffield   Stony   Mannville   Vermilion   North
Hinton   Mercoal   Drayton   Plain   EDMONTON   Holden   Battleford
Foothills   Valley   Leduc   Viking   Paradise
Entrance   Calmar   Camrose   Valley   Wainwright
Mt. Robson   Pocahontas   Cadomin   Lodgepole   Breton   Wetaskiwin   Kinsella   Irma   Chauvin
3954m   Lucerne   Hoadley   Ponoka   Rosalind   Hardisty   Unity
Mount Robson   JASPER   Rimbey   Killam
NATIONAL   Mt. Brazeau   Rocky   Forestburg
PARK   3170m   Nordegg   Mountain   Lacombe   Donalda   Czar   Provost
Williams Lake   Mt. Alberta   House   Horburg   Gadsby   Castor
3619m   Sylvan   Red Deer   Stettler   Bodo
Lake   Hackett   Coronation
Mt. Columbia   Caroline   Innisfail   Big   Monitor   Compeer
3747m   Valley   Fenner
Wimborne   Sedalia   Kindersley
Sundre   Olds   Trochu   Scapa   Youngstown
Didsbury   Craigmyle   Hanna   Cereal   Sibbald
BANFF   Cremona   Granger   Drumheller
NATIONAL PARK   Crossfield   Dorothy   Pollockville
Lake Louise   Iricana   Nightingale   Finnigan   Empress
Kicking Horse   Cochrane   Gem   Wardlow   Buffalo
Pass 1627m   Wardlow   Leader
Canmore   Shepard   Carseland   Gleichen   Bassano   Jenner
Mt. Assiniboine   CALGARY   Turner   Rosemary
3618m   Valley   Milo   Patricia
High River   Cassils   Brooks   Pivot
Nanton   Vulcan   Tilley   Alderson   Schuler
Parkland   Scandia   Suffield
Champion   Vauxhall   Medicine Hat   Irvine
Claresholm   Whitla
Tornado Mtn.   Milk   Bullshead   CYPRESS
3099m   Granum   Coaldale   River   Butte   HILLS
KOOTENAY   Fort   Taber   Island   1081m
NATIONAL   Macleod   Bow
PARK   Lethbridge
Raymond   Foremost   Orion   Craigower
Cranbrook   Pincher   Magrath   Skiff
Creek   Glenwoodville   Wrentham   Warner   Comrey
PURCELL   Cardston   Milk R.   Masinasin
MOUNTAINS   Whiskey   West Butte
CANADA   WATERTON   Gap   Coutts   2128m
U.S.   LAKES
IDAHO   GLACIER   MONTANA
Bonners   INTERNATIONAL   Cut   Shelby   Havre
Ferry   PEACE PARK   Bank

Prince
George

COLUMBIA MOUNTAINS

MONASHEE MTS   SELKIRK MTS

GLACIER
NATIONAL
PARK

YOHO
NATIONAL
PARK

ROCKY   MOUNTAINS

Edmonton, Alberta's capital, expanded rapidly following the discovery of oil nearby. It is the site of the world's largest shopping mall, which opened in the mid-1980s.

municipal districts. The sparsely settled areas are included in 22 improvement districts, administered by the provincial department of municipal affairs.

History

Before European settlement two distinctive Indian groups lived in Alberta. In the grasslands of the southeast were the Plains Indians, who depended mainly on buffalo hunting. They included the Blackfoot Confederacy—which comprised the Blood, Peigan, and North Blackfoot—and the Sarcee, Stoney, and Plains Cree. In the forested regions, with their more varied hunting patterns, were the Woodland Cree, Beaver, and Chipewyan tribes.

For about 125 years after the visit (1754) of the first European, Alberta was mainly of interest as a fur-producing region. The few European inhabitants were based in trading posts that were established on rivers in forested areas. The Hudson's Bay Company administered the region during this period. For a few years after 1870, when western Canada was sold by the Hudson's Bay Company to the Canadian government, whiskey traders from the United States moved into southern Alberta and began selling illegal liquor to the Indians. To stop this practice and establish Canadian authority in the area, the North-West Mounted Police (now the Royal Canadian Mounted Police) was formed and marched west to build small forts. Fort Macleod (1874) was the first such fort in Alberta, and Calgary had its origin (1875) in a similar fort. Soon large ranches were established in the southern grasslands and foothills region.

The arrival of the transcontinental Canadian Pacific Railway at Calgary in 1883 launched the large-scale settlement of Alberta. The settlement process was generally peaceful and orderly. An interruption occurred in 1885 when unrest among Indians and métis (people of Indian and European ancestry) over land ownership flared briefly

into the Riel Rebellion (see RIEL, Louis). On Sept. 1, 1905, the district of Alberta, with some adjacent territory, was made a province of Canada. It remained a predominantly agricultural province until the development of the petroleum and natural-gas resources in the post-World War II period.

During the early 1980s strains between Alberta and the federal government developed over control of the

Rodeo events highlight the Calgary Exhibition and Stampede, an annual celebration of international fame that also features livestock shows and a festive parade.

province's energy resources. In 1980 the federal government announced a new National Energy Program designed to make Canada self-sufficient in energy and to increase the federal share of revenues from exploitation. In protest, Alberta reduced its oil production in 1981. An accord was reached on oil prices in September 1981, but the oil and gas industries then experienced recession because of low world prices. Effects of the recession lingered, although Albertans were cheered by playing host to the 1988 Winter Olympics at Calgary.

Alberti, Leon Battista   Leon Battista Alberti, b. Genoa, Feb. 14, 1404, d. Apr. 25, 1472, was an Italian humanist, architect, painter, sculptor, and musician who contributed greatly to Renaissance art theory. He is called the father of modern architectural theory, and is probably the first person to whom the term *Renaissance man* can be applied.

Between 1428 and 1443 Alberti wrote, in Latin and Italian, love poems and dialogues, a Latin comedy, fables, and treatises on virtue, sculpture, agriculture, the care of horses, law, and marriage. One of the finest of these is *Della tranquilità dell' animo* (On Peace of Mind, 1442). A member of the inner circle of humanists in Tuscany, among them the sculptor Donatello, Alberti was recognized as an authority on art and classical literature. He became especially interested in the work of the sculptor-architect Filippo Brunelleschi, to whom he dedicated the Italian edition of *Della pittura* (1436; *On Painting*, 1956), a treatise on the theory and technique of painting.

Alberti's involvement in architecture encompassed both theory and practice. Among his most accomplished reconstructions are the Malatesta Temple (Rimini, 1450) and the churches of Santa Maria Novella (Florence, 1456) and San Sebastian (Mantua, 1460). His original designs include the Palazzo Rucellai (Florence, 1446–51) and the Church of Sant' Andrea (Mantua, designed 1470). He went to Rome in 1452 as a recorder of pagan monuments and papal consultant in remodeling medieval churches, including Old ST. PETER'S BASILICA.

Alberti's primary literary work is *De re aedificatoria*, a 10-book Latin treatise on architecture, completed about 1452 and published posthumously in 1485. The work is considered a major modern contribution to architecture and influenced the development of architectural style in the Renaissance.

Alberti, Rafael   Rafael Alberti, b. Dec. 16, 1902, is a Spanish poet who abandoned his first career as a painter to write poetry. His first volume, *Marinero en tierra* (Sailor Ashore, 1925), won Spain's National Prize for literature for 1924–25. Alberti became a Communist about 1930, and since then his poetry has reflected his strong social and political concerns. He participated in the Spanish Civil War on the loyalist side and after the fall of the Republic in 1939 became an exile. He lived for a while in France and Argentina and since 1964 has lived in Italy. Alberti has published several other volumes of

poetry and an autobiography, *The Lost Grove: Autobiography of a Spanish Poet in Exile* (1959; Eng. trans., 1976).

Albertus Magnus, Saint   Albert, b. *c.*1200, d. Nov. 15, 1280, was a medieval German (Swabian) theologian, scholastic philosopher, scientist, and the teacher of Thomas AQUINAS. In his own day, Albertus was accepted as an authority equal to Aristotle in philosophy and was known as "the universal doctor" for his work in natural science.

St. Albertus Magnus, the medieval philosopher and theologian, was acclaimed for his commentaries on Aristotle.

He was received (1223) into the Dominican Order at Padua and spent the next 18 years studying and teaching theology in the Rhineland. He received his doctorate at the University of Paris in 1245 and taught there for three years. In 1248 he was assigned to open the first great center of learning in Germany, which eventually became the University of Cologne. Although Albert was provincial of the Dominicans (1254–57), bishop of Regensburg (1260–62), and preacher of the Crusades (1263–64), his main work was paraphrasing and commenting on Aristotle's philosophy. He staunchly advocated the autonomy of human reason and natural experience in defense of the Christian faith.

Albert was beatified by Gregory XV in 1622. On Dec. 16, 1931, Pope Pius XI declared him a saint and a doctor of the church. Feast day: Nov. 15.

Albigenses   [al-buh-jen'-seez]   The Albigenses were the members of a religious sect in southern France during the 12th and 13th centuries. Their name is derived from the French town of Albi, where they were centered. Similar groups in other parts of Europe were called Cathari, meaning the pure ones.

Like the ancient Manichaeans (see MANICHAEISM), the Albigenses adhered to a strict dualism. They considered the material world as evil; redemption meant the liberation of the soul from flesh. This led them to condemn marriage and sex. Meat, milk, eggs, and other animal products were forbidden. They also rejected the traditional teachings on hell, purgatory, and the sacraments because of the material elements involved. Their own sacrament, the *consolamentum*, or baptism of the soul, was administered by laying on of hands. Only the "perfect" (*perfecti*) received it, and they were expected to live by a rigorous ethical code. The majority remained in the state of "believers" (*credentes*) and lived less rigorously. The sect's efficient organization, with bishops and clergy supported by the local nobility, helped it to survive even when most of its congregations had been destroyed.

Official countermeasures, such as preaching efforts and conciliar decrees of the church (Combers, 1165; Verona, 1184; Fourth Lateran Council, 1215), were only partly effective. When a papal legate was assassinated in the territory of Count Raymond of Toulouse, Pope INNOCENT III called for a crusade that developed into the infamous Albigensian wars (1209-29). Asked how to separate Christians from heretics, one leader is said to have replied: "Slay them all. Good knows his own." Throughout the 13th century the remnants of the Albigenses, with other Catharist groups and the WALDENSES, were the main target of the INQUISITION throughout Europe.

albinism [al'-buh-nizm] Albinism is a group of genetic disorders affecting one out of every several thousand humans and other animals. It involves a deficiency of melanin, the dark brown pigment responsible for coloration. Eyes, skin and hair, and other body parts may be affected. A totally albino animal has milky-white skin and white hair or feathers. The iris of the eyes is pink, and reflected light in the retina is red, because no color masks the blood vessels. The eyes are light-sensitive and often astigmatic. Occasionally albinism is associated with mental or physical retardation.

Total albinism is rare in wild animals because few survive to reproductive age. They may lack protective coloration against predators, be driven away by their fellow creatures, or be unable to bear exposure to needed sunlight. Partial albinism is less disabling and is characterized by the appearance of white spots on the skin or white patches in the hair. Vitiligo is the absence of pigment in some body areas only.

Several independent defects can cause albinism: a complete lack of melanocytes, or pigment cells; interference in the migration of the cells to their proper location during embryo development; failure of the cells to produce melanin because of lack of tyrosinase, the stimulating enzyme; or abnormalities within the cells. The gene involved in albinism is recessive and may appear in the offspring of normally pigmented parents who are carriers of the trait. At present, no method for curing albinism is known.

Albinoni, Tommaso [ahl-bee-noh'-nee] Tommaso Albinoni, b. June 8, 1671, d. Jan. 17, 1750, was an Italian composer and violin virtuoso. He is now known mostly because Johann Sebastian Bach used his themes in three popular compositions. A member of a wealthy family, Albinoni had no need to support himself, and his only appointment was as chamber musician to the duke of Mantua. Stylistically, his string music is a transition between that of Arcangelo Corelli and Antonio Vivaldi and the new courtly style of the classic era. His many operas tend toward the developing opera buffa. The popular "Adagio for Strings" is actually a posthumous concoction based on one of Albinoni's unfinished themes.

Albizu Campos, Pedro [ahl-bee'-sookahm'-pohs] Pedro Albizu Campos, b. 1891, d. Apr. 21, 1965, was a leader of the Puerto Rican independence movement. Heading the radical Nationalist party from the early 1930s, he was imprisoned (1937–43) in Atlanta, Ga., for his revolutionary activities. In 1950, when Nationalists tried to assassinate President Harry S. Truman, Albizu Campos was charged with inciting the would-be assassins and jailed once again. In 1954 several party members fired shots in the U.S. House of Representatives, wounding five congressmen, and Albizu Campos, who had been pardoned, was sentenced to life imprisonment. He was pardoned a second time in 1964.

Ålborg [awl'-bawr] Ålborg is the seat of Nordjylands County, in Jutland, Denmark, on the Lim Fjord. It is an important port and commercial center. The population is 113,650 (1986 est.). Industry is diversified and includes shipbuilding, cement, tobacco, and liquor. The city's historical landmarks include St. Botolph's Cathedral (c.1500), Ålborghus Castle (1539), and the Jens Bang Stonehouse (1624); museums with Viking artifacts attract many tourists. Settled about 1000, Ålborg was chartered in 1342. Steady growth followed, and the city was a prosperous commercial center by the 17th century. The Danish surrender during the Thirty Years' War occurred there in 1627.

Albright, Ivan Le Lorraine Ivan Le Lorraine Albright, b. North Harvey, Ill., Feb. 20, 1897, d. Nov. 18, 1983, was a painter famous for his greatly detailed works reflecting the theme of life's decay. He painted very slowly and produced relatively few works. His paintings include *That Which I Should Have Done I Did Not Do* (1941; Art Institute of Chicago) and the final horrifying portrait for the film *The Picture of Dorian Gray* (1943–1944).

Albright, Jacob Jacob Albright, b. May 1, 1759, d. May 18, 1808, an American itinerant preacher, became the first bishop of the Evangelical Association. A Pennsylvania German brickmaker, he had no formal education. After converting from Lutheranism to Methodism, he was licensed in 1796 to preach among the German-speaking people of the Shenandoah Valley. His followers, known at first as the Newly Formed Methodist Conference and after his death as the Evangelical Association, gradually formed independent units. They declared Albright their ordained pastor in 1803 and a bishop in 1807. The association came to be known as the Evangelical Church in 1922. In 1946 the Evangelical Church joined with the United Brethren in Christ to form the EVANGELICAL UNITED BRETHREN CHURCH.

albumen print   see PHOTOGRAPHY

---

albumin   An albumin is a protein that is soluble in water and in half-saturated salt solutions, in contrast to a globulin, which is soluble only in dilute salt solutions. Albumins include ovalbumin from egg white, lactalbumin from milk, and serum albumin from BLOOD serum. They make up about half of the protein in human serum, where their main functions are to maintain normal water balance between blood and tissues by osmotic mechanisms and to serve as transport proteins for less soluble substances that can bind to them, such as amino acids. The detection of albumins in the urine is an indication of some types of KIDNEY dysfunction.

Albuquerque   [al'-buh-kur-kee]   Albuquerque, the largest city in New Mexico, has a population of 384,736 (1990) in the city proper and 480,577 in the metropolitan area. It is located on the Rio Grande in the central part of the state and is the seat of Bernalillo County. Low rainfall and mild temperatures make the city a health resort. The economy is based on the manufacture of truck trailers, lumber, clothing, gypsum products, and aerospace components, and the city also serves as a center for mining, timber, and ranching operations. Numerous federal agencies have been established in Albuquerque since the 1930s. After World War II the development of nuclear and aerospace technology stimulated large population growth.

Founded in 1706 by the Spanish, the city was named for the duque of Alburquerque, then viceroy of New Spain. As the SANTA FE TRAIL achieved importance in the 1800s, more settlers arrived. In 1846 the U.S. Army built a fort there. The city was captured and held briefly by Confederate forces in 1862. The arrival of the railroad in 1880 spurred growth. The University of New Mexico (1889) is located in the city.

Albuquerque, Afonso de [ahl-boo-kair'-kuh]   Afonso de Albuquerque, b. 1453, d. Dec. 16, 1515, founded the Portuguese empire in the Indian Ocean, which lasted for more than a century. In 1506 he explored the coast of East Africa with Tristão da Cunha, and in 1508 he arrived in India to replace Francisco de ALMEIDA as viceroy. Albuquerque seized Goa (1510), and then Malacca (1511) on the Malay Peninsula. In 1515 he completed the capture of HORMUZ, while other Portuguese established relations with Macao in China. Portugal thus gained access to the SPICE TRADE of the East Indies.

Alcaeus [al-see'-uhs]   Alcaeus of Lesbos, Greek poet, b. *c.*620 BC, is, along with SAPPHO, the principal writer of archaic Aeolic lyrics. Of more than ten books that he wrote, only fragments survive. War, wine, travel, and the turbulent politics of Lesbos were his main subjects. Intensely personal, rich in detail, energetic, yet reflective, his poems depict the life-style and social and political prejudices of a Levantine nobleman in the 7th century BC. He also wrote drinking songs, hymns, and mythological poems. A colloquial stylist, he experimented with various meters; one, the Alcaic stanza, bears his name.

Alcatraz   Alcatraz is an island in San Francisco Bay, the site of the famous prison of the same name. The island was discovered by the Spanish in 1545, and named in 1775 for its pelicans (in Spanish, *alcatraces*). Owned by the U.S. government since 1850, it was fortified and used as a military prison until 1933, when it became a federal prison. The prison was considered escape-proof because of its fortresslike structure and the strong, cold currents in the surrounding waters. Closed in 1963, the structure stood empty until it was seized by a group of Indians in November 1969. They held it until June 1971 in an unsuccessful attempt to gain government recognition of their claim to the island. The island was opened (1972) to the public as a part of the Golden Gate National Recreation Area.

---

alchemy   Alchemy is an ancient pseudoscience concerned with the transmutation of base metals, the more reactive metals, into gold and with the discovery of both a single cure for all diseases and a way to prolong life indefinitely.

Alchemy emerged as a pseudoscience in China and in Egypt during the early centuries of this era. In Egypt, the methods of transmutation of metals became widely known (2d century) at the academy in Alexandria. Alchemy had its basis in the skills of Egyptian artisans, Eastern mysticism, and Aristotelian theory of composition of matter. Aristotle taught that all matter was composed of four elements: water, earth, fire, and air. According to his theory, different materials found in nature had different ratios of these four elements. Therefore, by proper treatment a base metal could be changed into gold. These ideas were further supported by astrological speculations from Mesopotamia.

Astrology

Astrologers believed that celestial bodies—the Sun, the Moon, and the stars—had a profound influence on the activities of humans. Thus, for alchemists to transmute metals effectively, the heavenly bodies had to be in a favorable configuration. Astrological influence led to ascribing each metal to a heavenly body: for example, gold to the Sun, silver to the Moon, copper to Venus, and iron to Mars. Each metal was represented by the astrological sign of the appropriate celestial body.

As in China and later in Western Europe, the alchemical writing in Alexandria became allegorical and confusing. At the end of the 4th century, the destruction of the academy and its library scattered the alchemists from Alexandria to Byzantium, Syria, and countries of the Near East. There they were persecuted by governments and the church as practitioners of black magic. Their activity thus became limited to writing commentaries on the works of ancient alchemists.

The Arab Influence

The Arab alchemists modified the Aristotelian concept of four elements by postulating that all metals were composed of two immediate components: sulfur and mercury. They also adopted the Chinese alchemists' concept of a "philosopher's stone"—a medicine that could turn a "sick" (base) metal into gold and also act as an elixir of life. A number of alchemical treatises were attributed to Jabir ibn Hayyan, or GEBER (fl. 8th century), the most notable Arab alchemist. Although their thinking was clouded with mysticism, Arabian alchemists discovered new chemicals such as the alkalies and such processes as distillation.

Medieval Period

Close contact with Arabs in Spain and Sicily in the 11th and 12th centuries brought to Europe a new interest in Arabic philosophers, physicians, and scientists. Alchemical explanation of the nature of matter was included in

(Left) *A painting of a 16th-century alchemical laboratory is the work of the Flemish artist Jan van der Straet. The alchemist (pointing, lower right) oversees the work of his many assistants. The retort to which he points was called the Philosopher's Egg, in which magical gold-making liquid known as the Philosopher's Stone was supposed to be formed.* (Below) *A 16th-century engraving of the green lion devouring the Sun is an allegorical alchemical schema for a real chemical process in which aqua regia (nitric and hydrochloric acids) dissolved gold (the Sun). Because gold often carried copper impurities, the resulting liquid had a bluish green tint—the lion's color.*

the treatises of such scholars as Arnold of Villanova (1240–1313), Roger Bacon (1214–94), and Albertus Magnus (1193–1280).

The works of another Jabir, or Geber, a practicing Spanish alchemist of the 14th century, became the textbooks of alchemy. They contained not only mystical theory but also important practical recipes. Arnold of Villanova described distillation of wine; Roger BACON gave a recipe for gunpowder and directions for constructing a telescope; ALBERTUS MAGNUS defined a flame as ignited smoke and postulated that "like seeks like." The alchemist became a recognizable figure on the European scene, and kings and nobles often supported alchemists in the hope of increasing their resources. Frequently, however, alchemists who failed in their attempt to produce the promised gold lost their lives.

In time, alchemy fell into disrepute because of the nefarious character of its practitioners. It is said that Frederick of Wurzburg maintained special gallows for hanging alchemists. From the 15th to the 17th century, alchemical symbolism and allegory became increasingly complex. Practical alchemists turned from attempting to make gold toward preparing medicinals. A leader in this movement was Phillippus Aureolus PARACELSUS (1493–1531). He was the first in Europe to mention zinc and to use the word *alcohol* to refer to the spirit of wine.

Classical scholarship in the 16th century shifted attention away from Aristotelian theory and toward Greek atomism. Interest in transmutation was limited to astrologers and numerologists. The chemical facts that had been accumulated by alchemists as a by-product of their search for gold became the basis for modern chemistry.

See also: CHEMISTRY, HISTORY OF.

Alcibiades [al-suh-by'-uh-deez] Alcibiades, c.450–404 BC, the nephew of PERICLES, was a charismatic Athenian political leader possessed of high intelligence, remarkable physical beauty, and great capacity for leadership. Yet his career ended in disaster.

In 415, during the PELOPONNESIAN WAR, he urged the conquest of SYRACUSE (Sicily), and along with NICIAS and Lamachus was placed in command of a mighty Athenian expedition. Shortly after it reached Sicily, however, Alcibiades was recalled to stand trial on a charge of impiety. He fled to SPARTA, and while the Syracusan expedition, deprived of his leadership, was ending disastrously, Alcibiades advised the Spartans on how best to wage war against Athens. He changed sides again in 411. After considerable service to Athens, however, he fell under suspicion in 406 and was murdered in Anatolia at his enemies' instigation.

---

alcid see AUK

---

alcohol The class of substances known as alcohols comprises hundreds of organic compounds. Most familiar among them is grain alcohol, or ethanol, which is found in alcoholic beverages. Other well-known types are wood alcohol (methanol) and rubbing alcohol (isopropanol). Alcohols are characterized by a hydroxyl group (OH) bonded to a carbon atom. They may contain more than one hydroxyl group per molecule provided each hydroxyl group is attached to a different carbon atom. Such alcohols are called polyhydric alcohols, or polyols.

Alcohols that are derived from a simple hydrocarbon are named by adding either *ol* or *yl* plus the word *alcohol* to the name of the parent hydrocarbon. For example, the monohydric alcohol—an alcohol with one hydroxyl group per molecule—derived from the simplest hydrocarbon, methane (CH_4) may be called either methyl alcohol or methanol (CH_3OH). The monohydric alcohol derived form ethane (CH_3CH_3) may be called either ethyl alcohol or ethanol (CH_3CH_2OH). The three-, four-, and five-carbon alcohols derived from straight-chain hydrocarbons are propyl alcohol or propanol ($CH_3CH_2CH_2OH$), which is used as a solvent and an antiseptic; butyl alcohol or butanol ($CH_3CH_2CH_2CH_2OH$), which is used in making esters and plastics resins; and pentyl alcohol or pentanol, also known as amyl alcohol ($CH_3CH_2CH_2CH_2CH_2OH$), which is used as a solvent and in making pharmaceuticals.

Dihydric alcohols—those with two hydroxyl groups per molecule—may be named as GLYCOLS. Ethylene glycol (CH_2OHCH_2OH), for example, is the major component of automotive antifreeze solutions. More complex alcohols, such as CHOLESTEROL, are not named so systematically.

Every alcohol with three or more carbon atoms can have ISOMERS (different structures). The three-carbon alcohol has the two isomers propanol and isopropanol.

$$CH_3CH_2CH_2OH \qquad CH_3CHCH_3$$
$$\qquad\qquad\qquad\qquad\qquad\qquad |$$
$$\qquad\qquad\qquad\qquad\qquad\qquad OH$$

Propanol   Isopropanol

The number of isomers increases markedly with the number of carbon atoms. Alcohols may be classified according to the number of hydrogen atoms attached to the carbon with the hydroxyl group. If the carbon has two hydrogens attached (as in propanol), the alcohol is primary; if it has one (as in isopropanol), the alcohol is secondary; if it has none, the alcohol is tertiary.

Simple, low-molecular-weight alcohols are colorless, volatile, flammable liquids that are soluble in water. As the molecular weight increases, the boiling point, melting point, and viscosity increase, while solubility in water decreases. Physical properties may be altered by the presence of other functional groups. Adding hydroxyl groups increases the boiling point and solubility in water and often produces sweetness. Branching the carbon chain increases solubility in water and decreases the boiling point.

The important reactions of alcohols are chiefly those of the hydroxyl group. The hydrogen atom of the OH can be replaced by an active metal; dehydration causes the production of unsaturated compounds or ethers; reaction with carboxylic acids forms esters, and the OH may be replaced by other functional groups. The product of oxidation depends on the class of the alcohol. Primary alcohols oxidize to aldehydes, and secondary alcohols oxidize to ketones. Tertiary alcohols do not oxidize readily, and they give products containing fewer carbon atoms than the original compound. It is difficult to reduce alcohols to hydrocarbons.

When ingested in moderate amounts, lower-molecular-weight alcohols act on the central nervous system and higher centers of the brain, lowering inhibitions and affecting judgment. Larger amounts may produce a loss of muscular control, unconsciousness, and even death. METHYL ALCOHOL (methanol) is extremely toxic, affecting the optic nerve and causing blindness, and as little as 30 ml (1 oz) has caused death. Ethyl alcohol (ethanol) is the least toxic. Thereafter toxicity increases with molecular weight until the compound is insoluble in water. Most of the lower-molecular-weight alcohols have commercial importance. They are used as solvents, in the preparation of dyes, pharmaceuticals, antifreeze, esters, and other compounds, and mixed with gasoline and used as motor fuels (see GASOHOL).

alcohol consumption

Of the numerous types of alcohol, ethyl alcohol is the type consumed in drinking. In its pure form it is a clear substance with little odor. People drink alcohol in three main kinds of beverages: BEERS, which are made from grain and contain from 3% to 8% alcohol; WINES, which are fermented from fruits such as grapes and contain from 8% to 12% alcohol naturally, and up to 21% when fortified by the addition of alcohol; and distilled beverages (spirits) such as WHISKEY, GIN, and VODKA, which on the average contain from 40% to 50% alcohol. Drinkers may become addicted to any of these beverages.

Physical Effects of Alcohol. The effects of alcohol on the human body depend on the amount of alcohol in the blood (blood-alcohol concentration). This varies with the rate of consumption and with the rate at which the drinker's physical system absorbs and metabolizes alcohol. The higher the alcohol content of the beverage, the more alcohol will enter the bloodstream. The amount and type of food in the stomach also affect the absorption rate; drinking when the stomach is filled is less intoxicating, because foods delay alcohol absorption. Another factor is body weight; the heavier the person, the slower the absorption rate. Studies indicate that sex is a further factor. That is, the stomachs of women contain relatively lesser amounts of an enzyme that breaks down alcohol than do the stomachs of men, so relatively larger amounts of alcohol enter the bloodstreams of women when drinking.

Alcohol is absorbed through the walls of the intestines into the bloodstream and carried to the various organ systems of the body. Most of the alcohol is metabolized by the liver. The body metabolizes alcohol at about the rate of three-fourths of an ounce to one ounce of whiskey an hour.

Alcohol begins to impair the brain's ability to function when the blood-alcohol concentration (BAC) reaches 0.05%, that is, 0.05 grams of alcohol per 100 cubic centimeters of blood. Most U.S. state traffic laws presume that a driver with a BAC of 0.10% is intoxicated. With a concentration of 0.20% (a level obtained from drinking about 10 ounces of whiskey), a person has difficulty controlling the emotions and in walking. When the blood-alcohol content reaches about 0.30%, as when a person rapidly drinks about a pint of whiskey, the drinker will have trouble comprehending and may become unconscious. At levels from 0.35% to 0.50%, the brain centers that control breathing and heart action are affected; concentrations above 0.50% may cause death.

Moderate or temperate use of alcohol is not harmful, but excessive or heavy drinking is associated with alcoholism and numerous other health problems. The effects of excessive drinking on major organ systems of the human body are cumulative and become evident after heavy, continuous drinking or after intermittent drinking over a period of time that may range from 5 to 30 years. The parts of the body most affected by heavy drinking are the digestive and nervous systems. Digestive-system disorders that may be related to heavy drinking include cancer of the mouth, throat, and esophagus; gastritis; ulcers; cirrhosis of the liver; and inflammation of the pancreas. Disorders of the nervous system can include neuritis; lapse of memory (blackouts); hallucinations; and extreme tremor, or delirium tremens ("the DTs"), which may occur when a person stops drinking after a period of heavy imbibing. Permanent damage to the brain and central nervous system may also result, including Korsakoff psychosis and Wernicke's disease. Pregnant women who drink may give birth to infants with FETAL ALCOHOL SYNDROME.

The combination of alcohol and drugs, such as commonly used sedatives and tranquilizers, can be fatal even when the doses, taken separately, would not have a lethal effect. Drugs to counter the effects or aftereffects of alcohol on the body have also been investigated.

Drinking Patterns. Every culture has its own general ethos or sense of decorum about the use and role of alcoholic beverages within its social structure. In some cultures drinking is either forbidden or frowned upon. The Koran contains prohibitions against drinking, and Muslims are forbidden to sell or serve alcoholic beverages. Hindus take a negative view of the use of alcohol; this is reflected in the constitution of India, which requires every state to work toward the prohibition of alcohol except for medicinal purposes. Abstinence from alcohol has also been the goal of temperance movements in Europe and the United States. Some Christian religious groups enjoin abstinence.

In some ambivalent cultures, such as the United States and Ireland, the values of those who believe in abstinence conflict with the values of those who regard moderate drinking as a way of being hospitable and sociable. Other cultures have a permissive attitude toward drinking, including those of Spain, Portugal, Italy, Japan, and Israel. The proportion of alcohol users in these cultures is high, but the rates of alcoholism are lower than in Irish and Scandinavian groups.

Subgroups within a society do not all have the same attitudes toward alcoholic beverages or the same drinking patterns. Drinking behavior differs significantly among groups of different age, sex, social class, racial status, ethnic background, occupational status, religious affiliation, and regional location.

alcoholism   Alcoholism refers to the drinking of alcoholic beverages to such a degree that major aspects of an individual's life—such as work, school, family relationships, or personal safety and health—are seriously and repeatedly interfered with. Alcoholism is considered a disease, meaning that it follows a characteristic course with known physical, psychological, and social symptoms. The alcoholic continues to consume alcohol despite the destructive consequences. Alcoholism is serious, progressive, and irreversible. If not treated, it can be fatal. It is generally thought that once the disease has developed, the alcoholic will not drink normally again. An alcoholic who abstains from drinking, however, can regain control over the aspects of life with which alcohol interfered. The alcoholic is then said to be "recovering," not "cured" of the disease. It is important to note that the particular symptoms and pattern of drinking problems may vary with the individual. Alcoholism is, therefore, a very complex disorder, and this complexity has led some researchers to question the accuracy of the disease concept of alcoholism.

A person does not have to drink every day to be an alcoholic. Moreover, someone who drinks frequently or sometimes gets drunk is not necessarily an alcoholic. It is possible to abuse alcohol for a short or contained period of time without developing alcoholism. For example, some people may drink abusively during a personal crisis and then resume normal drinking. It is often difficult to distinguish such heavy and abusive drinking from the early stages of alcoholism.

More than 10 million Americans are estimated to be alcoholics. Alcoholism is found among all age, sociocultural, and economic groups. An estimated 75 percent of alcoholics are male, 25 percent female. Alcoholism is a worldwide phenomenon, but it is most widespread in France, Ireland, Poland, Scandinavia, the United States, and the USSR.

Symptoms and Causes.   Some common signs of alcoholism in the early stages are constant drinking for relief of personal problems, an increase in a person's tolerance for alcohol, onset of memory lapses while drinking ("blackouts"), surreptitious drinking, and an urgent need for the first drink ("craving"). In the middle and late phases, dependence on drinking increases and memory blackouts become more frequent. A physical dependence on alcohol first appears with early morning tremors and agitation that require a drink for relief. In the late stage, drinking bouts are usually very frequent. There is an acute withdrawal syndrome (delirium tremens, or DTs) when drinking ceases. This includes agitation, tremor, hallucination, and possibly seizures.

Most likely, a combination of biological, psychological, and cultural factors contribute to the development of alcoholism in any individual. Alcoholism often seems to run in families. Although there is no conclusive indication of how the alcoholism of family members is associated, studies show that 50 to 80 percent of all alcoholics have had a close alcoholic relative. Some researchers therefore suggest that some alcoholics have an inherited physical predisposition to alcohol addiction. Studies of animals and of human twins lend support to the theory. A 1990 research report also indicated that susceptibility to at least one form of alcoholism may be linked to the presence of a particular gene on chromosome 11. The gene is apparently involved with the production of receptor sites, on BRAIN cells, of the NEUROTRANSMITTER dopamine.

Alcoholism can also be related to underlying emotional problems. For example, alcoholism is sometimes associated with a family history of manic-depressive illness, and some alcoholics have been known to use alcohol unwittingly to "medicate" a biological depressive order. In addition, like so many other drug abusers, alcoholics often tend to drown depressed or anxious feelings by drinking. Conversely, some drink to reduce strong inhibitions or guilt about expressing negative feelings. Psychologists variously suggest that alcoholics have conflicts about dependency, sex roles, and family roles. While many alcoholics share experiences of loneliness, frustration, or anxiety, however, no one has identified a single personality type who later becomes an alcoholic.

Social and cultural factors may play a role in establishing drinking patterns and alcoholism. Among some cultures there is conflict between values of abstinence and the acceptance of alcohol as a usual way to change moods or to be sociable. These conflicts within the culture may make it difficult for some people to develop their own stable attitudes and moderate patterns of drinking.

Social Effects of Alcoholism.   The effects of alcoholism range from the direct physiological impact on the individual (see ALCOHOL CONSUMPTION) to a widespread effect on society. In the United States, one family in three is estimated to be affected in some way by a drinking problem.

Children may be affected by a parent's alcoholism in several ways. Having a parent who is a problem drinker increases the risk of becoming a problem drinker oneself. This may happen because of identification with or imitation of the alcoholic parent, but also because the social and family conditions associated with alcoholism are among those believed to contribute to the development of alcoholism. These include family conflict, divorce, job insecurity, and social stigma. Children of alcoholic parents may also suffer from speech disorders, hyperactivity, psychosomatic complaints, school problems, antisocial behavior, and drug use.

Alcoholism and alcohol abuse in the United States cost society an estimated $40 to $60 billion annually, due to lost production, health and medical care, motor vehicle accidents, violent crime, and social programs that respond to alcohol problems. One-half of all traffic fatalities and one-third of all traffic injuries are related to the abuse of alcohol. Also, one-third of all suicides and one-third of all mental health disorders are estimated to be associated with serious alcohol abuse. Accidents and suicides associated with alcohol problems are especially prominent among teenagers.

Treatment. Alcoholism is a complex disorder for which a combination of treatments may be necessary for recovery. If the alcoholic is in the acute phase of alcoholism and is suffering from complications such as delirium tremens or serious health problems, hospitalization may be necessary. Because alcoholism is a chronic condition, however, hospitalization is only a first step toward recovery. Many alcoholics go through several hospitalizations before they commit themselves to a program of recovery. A comprehensive treatment plan can incorporate various types of facilities, including hospitals, out-patient clinics, halfway houses, psychotherapists, social centers, religious organizations, foster homes, and self-help groups. An assessment of the patient's medical, emotional, and social needs is important in making the proper referral.

The best-known and most experienced recovery program is Alcoholics Anonymous (AA). AA was founded in 1935 as a fellowship organization for those with the common problem of alcoholism. AA defines alcoholism as a disease as well as a spiritual problem. There are no dues, and members may attend AA meetings as often as and wherever they wish. By the late 1980s about 44,000 AA groups, with an estimated membership of 850,000, existed in the United States and Canada. About 32,000 AA chapters functioned in 118 other countries.

Although alcoholism, according to the AA philosophy, can never be cured—that is, the alcoholic can never safely drink again—the alcoholic can "recover" to lead a productive and normal life as long as he or she remains sober. Since its inception, AA has provided invaluable social and psychological support to many alcoholics. The organization has also reduced popular misconceptions of alcoholics by educating both professionals and the public about the nature of alcoholism. The related organizations Al-Anon and Al-Ateen provide similar support to the families and children of alcoholics.

No one can make an alcoholic commit him- or herself to recovery. Some therapists suggest, however, that family members may influence the alcoholic by not supporting drinking activities, by seeking therapy for themselves, and by not joining in the alcoholic's denial of the problem. Because alcoholism is sometimes thought of as a family disease, the involvement of family members can aid the progress of the alcoholic's recovery.

Perhaps a minute percentage of alcoholics can return to moderate drinking. But no one knows how to identify these few individuals. For the overwhelming majority, abstinence is the one real hope of returning to a normal life.

Alcott, Amy   The professional golfer Amy Strum Alcott, b. Kansas City, Mo., Feb. 22, 1956, is one of the few Ladies' Professional Golf Association members to have won more than $2 million in her career (1975–). In 1980, Alcott won the U.S. Women's Open and was awarded the annual Vare Trophy (for best average score per round). In all, she has won about 30 LPGA tournaments.

Alcott, Bronson [awl'-kuht]   Amos Bronson Alcott, b. Wolcott, Conn., Nov. 29, 1799, d. Mar. 4, 1888, was a transcendentalist philosopher and educator. Because his teaching methods were radically egalitarian, the schools he established failed. He and his family were poor until his daughter Louisa May became a literary success. He was a reforming superintendent of the Concord, Mass., public schools from 1859 to 1865 and conducted the Concord School of Philosophy from 1879 until his death. He was a vegetarian, an abolitionist, and a women's-rights advocate.

Alcott, Louisa May   The American children's novelist Louisa May Alcott is best known for *Little Women*, the story of the development of four sisters into young women. She also wrote approximately 270 other works.

Alcott was born Nov. 29, 1832, in Germantown, Pa., the second of four daughters of Bronson and Abigail Alcott. Because of her father's involvement in a number of financially disastrous utopian schemes, the family was continually in desperate need of money. The experiences of the March girls in *Little Women*—Jo, Meg, Beth, and Amy—recall those of the young Alcott sisters. When the family moved to Concord, Mass., their neighbors and friends included Thoreau, Hawthorne, Fuller, and Emerson. To help her family, Alcott worked as a seamstress, servant, and schoolteacher, finally turning to writing. She sold her first story in 1852, and other salable fiction rapidly followed. By 1860 she had published a book of fairy tales, *Flower Fables* (1854), and was a regular contributor to the *Atlantic Monthly*.

Alcott became a respected and financially successful novelist with her largely autobiographical *Little Women* (1868). Sequels soon followed: *Little Men* (1871) and her next-to-last book, *Jo's Boys* (1886). Also successful were *Aunt Jo's Scrap Bag* (6 vols., 1872–82), *Eight Cousins* (1875), and *A Garland for Girls* (1888). Her adult novels *Work* (1873) and *A Modern Mephistopheles* (1877) were less popular.

Louisa May Alcott, a 19th-century American novelist, achieved her life's ambition, financial security, with the publication in 1868 of Little Women, *an autobiographical story about growing up in New England.*

Alcuin [al'-kwin] The English scholar Alcuin, b. c.735, d. May 19, 804, was the leading figure in the Carolingian Renaissance. While head (from 778) of the cathedral school of York, he was invited by CHARLEMAGNE to establish a palace school at Aachen. He taught there from 782 to 796 and was rewarded with the abbacy of St. Martin of Tours.

Alcuin introduced English scholastic methods to the Franks. He established the curriculum of the seven liberal arts—grammar, rhetoric, dialectic, arithmetic, geometry, astronomy, and music—that became basic to medieval education, and he initiated the transcription and preservation of ancient texts. Alcuin also wrote letters, school manuals, and theological treatises, and revised the liturgy of the Frankish church.

aldehyde [al'-duh-hyd] An aldehyde is an organic compound that contains a carbonyl group (an oxygen atom doubly bonded to a carbon atom) and possesses at least one hydrogen atom covalently bonded to the carbonyl carbon. The structure of aldehydes may be represented as

$$\begin{matrix} & \text{O} \\ & \| \\ \text{R}-&\text{C}-\text{H} \end{matrix}$$

but is often written as RCHO. R may be hydrogen or any organic group. Aldehydes are close relatives of KETONES, which are carbonyl compounds that possess two carbon groupings linked covalently to the carbonyl carbon.

The common names for specific aldehydes are derived from the CARBOXYLIC ACIDS to which they can be oxidized. Formaldehyde, HCHO, is readily oxidized to formic acid, HCOOH; acetaldehyde, CH_3CHO, is readily oxidized to acetic acid, CH_3COOH. The systematic names for aldehydes are derived from the name of the ALKANE having the same number of carbon atoms by appending the suffix *al* in place of the last letter of the hydrocarbon suffix *ane*. Thus HCHO is methanal (from methane), CH_3CHO is ethanal (from ethane), and CH_3CH_2CHO is propanal (from propane).

Aldehydes are prepared in the laboratory by oxidizing primary alcohols with expensive reagents such as potassium permanganate ($KMnO_4$) or potassium dichromate ($K_2Cr_2O_7$). Commercially, aldehydes are made by catalytically removing two hydrogen atoms from a primary alcohol, usually over a copper catalyst at 250° C (520° F) or by air oxidation. FORMALDEHYDE and acetaldehyde are the two most widely used and industrially important aldehydes.

Aldehydes are more reactive than ketones because their carbonyl carbon-to-hydrogen bond is easily oxidized. In addition to being readily oxidized to form organic acids and reduced to form alcohols, aldehydes can also undergo polymerization. The first commercially successful synthetic resin, Bakelite, for example, is a polymerization product of formaldehyde and phenol, and Formica derives from formaldehyde and urea. Aldehydes are used as intermediates in the production of resins, dyes, pharmaceuticals, and other products, and are employed as solvents and perfume ingredients. Biologically, various sugars and hormones found in the body contain the aldehyde structure.

Alden, John John Alden, b. 1599?, d. Sept. 12, 1687, was one of the Pilgrim Fathers who came to America in the MAYFLOWER, signed the Mayflower Compact, and founded Plymouth Colony in 1620. Thereafter he held various public offices, including that of deputy governor of Massachusetts (1664–65, 1667). The unfounded details of his wooing of fellow Pilgrim Priscilla Mullens (or Molines)—whom he did marry—were the subject of the Longfellow poem "The Courtship of Miles Standish."

Alders grow rapidly in a cool, wet climate to a height of more than 20 m (66 ft). The spread of the North American white alder (top) is half its height, as compared to the thinner European, or black, alder (bottom). Male and female alder flowers are called catkins.

alder The alders, genus *Alnus*, are deciduous hardwood trees and shrubs that belong to the birch family, Betulaceae. About 30 species of alders are found in north temperate zones. Alders have smooth to scaly, usually gray bark. The alternate leaves are short-stalked, ovate, usually doubly saw-toothed, and often wavy on the edges. The fruits are small, hard, blackish cones, which in summer mature and release minute nutlets.

European alders, *A. glutinosa*, were originally introduced into the United States for charcoal manufacture. They now have become naturalized and are planted as landscaping trees. The common stream-bank alder of the eastern United States and Canada is the speckled alder, *A. incana*.

The red alder, *A. rubra*, is the largest species of the genus and is the most important hardwood of the Pacific Northwest and coastal Alaska. Red alders are sometimes used as a "nurse crop" to precede more valuable conifer species.

Alder, Kurt The German chemist Kurt Alder, b. July 10, 1902, d. June 20, 1958, was coreceipient with Otto DIELS of the Nobel Prize for chemistry in 1950 for his studies of DIENE reactions and synthesis. The key reaction, first published in 1928 and now called the Diels-Alder reaction, involves the synthesis of complex organic molecules from simpler ones. Specifically, a conjugated diene (a compound with two sets of double bonds separated by a single bond) reacts with an ALKENE, a hydrocarbon such as ethylene, of the form C_nH_{2n}. The product always contains a six membered carbon ring with a double bond. The Diels-Alder reaction has wide application in the synthesis of substances, including STEROIDS and TERPENES.

alderman An alderman, in the United States, is an elected public official who represents a specific ward or district in the city legislature. In most U.S. cities, aldermen serve 2 year terms.

In England and Ireland, aldermen are officers or magistrates chosen by a city council or municipal corporation. They serve for 6 years. An alderman is called a bailie in Scotland.

Aldington, Richard see DOOLITTLE, HILDA

Aldiss, Brian W. Brian W. Aldiss, b. Aug. 18, 1925, is an English writer and critic best known for his apocalyptic and sometimes humorous science fiction. He wrote about the elevation of psychology to a form of religion in *Non-Stop* (1958), the postatomic holocaust world in *Greybeard* (1964), and the worship of science in *Frankenstein Unbound* (1973). The planet Helliconia, whose seasons each last hundreds of years, is the subject of a trilogy of novels (1982–85). *The Billion Year Spree*

(1973), a critical history of science fiction, is also highly regarded.

aldosterone see HORMONE

Aldrich, Nelson Wilmarth Nelson Wilmarth Aldrich, b. Foster, R.I., Nov. 5, 1841, d. Apr. 16, 1915, was an American businessman and politician. Starting in the wholesale grocery business in Providence, R.I., he further invested in sugar, rubber, street railways, and utilities and became a multimillionaire. In the political arena, he served on the Providence city council (1869–74) and in the Rhode Island legislature (1875–76), the U.S. House of Representatives (1879–81), and the U.S. Senate (1881–1911).

In the Senate, Aldrich wielded enormous power—especially after 1897—on behalf of the Republican majority. For a time he was the nemesis of President Theodore Roosevelt, with whom he clashed on foreign policy and railroad legislation. Aldrich advocated a conservative social philosophy on such issues as currency and banking, the tariff, and business regulations. He became chairman of the National Monetary Commission in 1908. Its report, the so-called Aldrich Plan (1911), was the basis of the Federal Reserve Act of 1913 establishing a central bank in the United States.

Aldrich, Thomas Bailey The American writer Thomas Bailey Aldrich, b. Portsmouth, N.H., Nov. 11, 1836, d. Mar. 19, 1907, had an illustrious career as an editor of the *Atlantic Monthly*, where he succeeded William Dean Howells, and as a poet and novelist. He is best remembered for his semiautobiographical novel, *The Story of a Bad Boy* (1870), a work that resembles but predates by six years Mark Twain's *Tom Sawyer*.

Aldridge, Ira Ira Frederick Aldridge, b. New York City, July 24, 1804, d. Aug. 7, 1867, was the first great black American actor. His father was an ex-slave who became a lay preacher. Ira followed an acting company to London, where he made his debut in 1825 as the African prince Oroonoko in *The Revolt of Surinam, or a Slave's Revenge*. Hailed as the "African Roscius," he was considered outstanding as Othello, Macbeth, Lear, and Aaron the Moor and was especially popular in Germany. He became a British citizen in 1863.

Aldrin, Edwin E. The American astronaut Edwin E. "Buzz" Aldrin, b. Glen Ridge, N.J., Jan. 20, 1930, was the second man to walk on the Moon. In addition to his achievements as an astronaut, Aldrin's doctoral thesis on orbital mechanics and rendezvous laid the foundation for flight techniques that made the lunar landing possible. Aldrin graduated third in his class from the U.S. Military Academy in 1951 and received his Air Force pilot's wings

Edwin Aldrin, the second man to walk on the surface of the Moon, was photographed by the Apollo II mission commander, Neil Armstrong.

in 1952. During the Korean War he flew 66 combat missions. He earned a doctorate of science in astronautics from the Massachusetts Institute of Technology in 1963 and later that year was selected as an astronaut.

On his first flight in space (1966), Aldrin piloted *Gemini 12* with commander James Lovell. He was lunar-module pilot for the first lunar-landing mission (APOLLO *11*) in July 1969. His reponsibilities included monitoring the lunar-module systems while commander Neil Armstrong concentrated on landing.

Two years after the Moon landing, Aldrin left NASA to become commander of the Air Force Aerospace Research Pilots School. In 1972 he resigned from the Air Force with the rank of colonel and entered private business. His autobiography, *Return to Earth* (1973), relates the pressures on the *Apollo 11* crew and his subsequent nervous breakdown and recovery.

Aldus Manutius   see MANUTIUS, ALDUS

ale   Ale is brewed from the same basic ingredients as lager BEER; the difference in flavor is caused in part by a different strain of yeast. Ale yeast ferments at higher temperatures than lager and imparts a distinctive tang and a somewhat higher alcohol content. Ale is also generally brewed with more hops than is beer. Until lager beer was introduced to the United States in the mid-19th century, ale was the predominant beverage. Today, it is low in popularity in America. English "bitter" refers to a highly hopped pale ale, which is aromatic, rather than bitter, to the taste.

aleatory music   [ay'-lee-uh-tor-ee]   Aleatory music is any music that results from the application of chance processes. The term is derived from the Latin word *alea*

("dice"). An aleatory score may include a set of verbal instructions for applying these processes to musical materials. Some typical aleatory devices are the following: dice throwing; random splattering of ink on music paper; drawing of cards; improvising music suggested by a graphic design.

Contemporary composers who have used aleatory devices include Pierre BOULEZ, John CAGE, Karlheinz STOCKHAUSEN, Christian Wolff, Sylvano Bussotti, and Barney Childs. As early as the 18th century, "musical dice games" were a common amusement.

Alechinsky, Pierre   The French abstractionist Pierre Alechinsky, b. Brussels, Oct. 19, 1927, was one of the founders (1949) of the artists' group CoBrA, for Copenhagen–Brussels–Amsterdam, which helped pioneer abstract expressionism in Paris. His own painting was influenced by oriental and cartoon styles and took on the appearance of visual commentary and abstract calligraphy. Line is paramount in his work, which often acquires the dripped casualness of Jackson POLLOCK's work. In 1977, Alechinsky won the newly activated Andrew W. Mellon Prize for excellence in contemporary art.

Aleichem, Sholem   [ah-lay'-kem]   Sholem Aleichem (Hebrew, "Peace be with you") was the pen name of the supreme Yiddish humorist, Solomon Rabinowitz. Along with Mendele Mokher Sefarim and Y. L. PERETZ, he is a member of Yiddish literature's classical triumvirate.

Sholem Aleichem is best known for his fictional recreations of the world of the Eastern European *shtetl,* or small Jewish town, and for his ragged, quaint characters who remain invincibly optimistic in the face of poverty, persecution, and spiritual anguish. Among the characters exemplifying his "laughter through tears" philosophy are the impetuous, impractical Menachem Mendel; the quintessentially honest dairyman Tevye, and the cheerful orphan boy, Mottel.

Born Mar. 3 (N.S.), 1859, in the Ukraine, Sholem Aleichem received a religious education and served for a time as a rabbi. He began publishing Yiddish sketches and short stories in 1883. Two novels, *Stempenyu* (1889) and *Yosele Solovey* (1890), appeared in *Di Yidische Folksbibliotek,* a literary annual he founded. Years of struggle and ill health after 1890 were capped in 1905 by a pogrom in Kiev, which led him to leave Russia. From 1914 until his death on May 13, 1916, he lived in New York City.

Sholem Aleichem wrote a prodigious number of short stories, novels, and plays. English-language collections of his stories include *Adventures of Mottel, the Cantor's Son* (1953); the autobiographical *Great Fair, Scenes from My Childhood* (1955); *Selected Stories* (1956); *Tevye Stories* (1966; retrans., 1988); and *Adventures of Menachem-Mendel* (1979). Two novels, *In the Storm* and *Marienbad,* appeared in English translation in 1984. The hit musical *Fiddler on the Roof* (1964; film, 1971) was based on the Tevye stories.

Aleijadinho [al-lay-zhah-deen'-yoh] Antonio Francisco Lisboa, 1738–1814, known as "O Aleijadinho" ("Little Cripple"), was the most renowned sculptor and architect of the Brazilian rococo period. After disease crippled his hands, he worked with a hammer and chisel strapped to his arms. As an architect he is most noted for the design of the church of São Francisco de Assis in Ouro Preto; his sculptural masterpiece is the series of 12 stone prophets and 6 polychromed wood scenes of the Passion of Christ (1800–05) at the church of Bom Jesus de Matozinhos in Congonhas do Campo (Minas Gerais).

Aleixandre, Vicente [ah-layks-ahn'-dray] The Spanish poet Vicente Aleixandre, b. Apr. 28, 1898, d. Dec. 13, 1984, won the Nobel Prize for literature in 1977. Born in Seville, he spent his early childhood in Málaga and moved to Madrid in 1909. He first suffered kidney tuberculosis in 1925, which left him an invalid. Sickness left its mark on his poetry—desperate songs of his journey from evasion and darkness to an affirmation of life and love. A member of the group Generation of 1927, Aleixandre won Spain's National Prize for literature in 1933 with *La destrucción del amor* (Destruction of Love), picturing a visionary world of dangerous erotic love. In later collections Aleixandre portrays man as a being who suffers and dies but nevertheless remains part of a vast cosmic reality. In *Diálogos del conocimiento* (Dialogues of Knowledge, 1974), he sought to reconcile existential awareness with transcendental intuition.

Alemán, Mateo [ah-lay-mahn', mah-tay'-oh] Mateo Alemán, 1547–c.1614, was a Spanish novelist whose fame rests on his picaresque novel, *The Rogue; or, The Life of Guzmán de Alfarache* (1599; part 2, 1604; Eng. trans., 1622). The work, a narrative interspersed with moralizing digressions, presents a valuable picture of 16th-century Spain. Alemán viewed humankind as universally corrupt but able to achieve salvation through divine grace. After a troubled life—he was twice jailed as a debtor—Alemán migrated (1608) to Mexico, where he spent his last years.

Alembert, Jean Le Rond d' [dah-lahm-bair'] Jean Le Rond d'Alembert, b. Nov. 17, 1717, d. Oct. 29, 1783, was a French mathematician and physicist who developed the early stages of CALCULUS, formalized mechanics, and was the science editor of Diderot's *Encyclopédie*. He was a leading figure of the ENLIGHTENMENT in France.

In 1741 d'Alembert was admitted to the Paris Academy of Science, where he worked for the rest of his life. He was one of the first to understand the importance of functions and the concept of limits to the calculus, and he pioneered the use of DIFFERENTIAL EQUATIONS in physics. By improving Newton's definition of force, he helped to resolve the controversy in physics over the conservation of kinetic energy. He also studied hydrodynamics, the mechanics of rigid bodies, and the three-body problem in astronomy.

Aleppo [uh-lep'-oh] Aleppo is a city of northwestern Syria, the country's second largest, with a population of 1,308,100 (1989 est.). An oasis town on the ancient trade route between Europe and Asia, modern Aleppo is Syria's leading industrial center and the site of a major university. Manufactures include textiles and garments, cement, vegetable oils, flour, processed foods, leather goods, and articles of gold and silver.

The old city is enclosed by a wall first built during Hellenistic times and reconstructed in the Middle Ages. Among the most important buildings are the noted citadel and the Great Mosque (AD 715), said to contain the tomb of Zacharias, the father of John the Baptist.

In its 4,000-year history Aleppo has witnessed much conflict and has been repeatedly captured by Egyptians, Turks, Arabs, and Mongols. Known as Halab by its earliest inhabitants, the city was renamed Beroea by the Persians, who conquered it in the 6th century BC. It was absorbed into the Roman province of Syria in the 1st century BC and later flourished under Byzantine rule. When it was conquered by the Arabs in AD 637, the city reverted to the Semitic name of Halab. Aleppo rose to great prominence in the 10th century under the Arab Hamdanid dynasty. Although never captured, it saw much action during the Crusades, and under Ottoman rule (1516–1920) it functioned as a provincial seat.

Alessandria Alessandria is the capital city of Alessandria province in the Piedmont region of northwest Italy and is located southeast of Turin. It has a population of 100,523 (1987 est.) and is an important agricultural and wine market and a railroad center. The city was founded in 1168 by the Lombard League as a part of its defense of Lombardy against Emperor Frederick Barbarossa. First called Civitas Nova, it was renamed for Pope Alexander III. The Visconti dukes of Milan took the free commune in 1348. Remains of the city's fortifications, the cathedral, and the Romanesque-Gothic Church of Sta. Maria di Castello date from the Middle Ages. The city was taken in 1707 by Prince Eugene and ceded to Savoy in 1713. In 1833, as a center of Piedmont's freedom movement, it was the scene of a pro-Giuseppe Mazzini conspiracy.

Alessi, Galeazzo [ah-les'-see, gah-lay-ahts'-soh] Galeazzo Alessi, 1512–72, was an important High Renaissance architect, best known for his work in Genoa and Milan. After receiving (c.1536–1542) his training in Rome, probably as a pupil of Michelangelo, Alessi settled (c.1548) in Genoa. His most significant works include the domed church of Santa Maria di Carignano (begun c.1549; Genoa), with a centralized plan based on Donato Bramante's designs for St. Peter's Basilica in Rome, and the Palazzo Marino (1553–58; Milan). Alessi's designs are distinguished by his combination of architectural simplicity with rich decorative detail.

Aletsch Glacier [ah'-lech]   Aletsch Glacier is in the Bernese Alps in Valais canton of south central Switzerland. With an area of 171 km^2 (66 mi^2), it is thought to be the largest alpine glacier. It is composed of three parts: Great Aletsch (the main body) and Upper and Middle Aletsch (branches). Great Aletsch, 16 km (10 mi) long, is fed by streams of ice from the Aletschhorn and other mountains; it flows to the southwest toward the Rhône Valley.

Aleut [uh-loot' or al'-ee-oot]   The people known as the Aleuts are the native inhabitants of the islands stretching for about 1,800 km (1,100 mi) southwestward from the Alaskan mainland and now called the Aleutian Islands. They also inhabit part of western Alaska. The Russians called them "Aleuts," the meaning of which is unknown; their name for themselves is *unangan* ("the people").

Although racially and ethnically related to the ESKIMO, the Aleuts have their own language and culture. Before contact with outsiders in the 18th century, they lived in scattered villages of semisubterranean houses, practiced a form of bilateral descent, and had a class system that included nobles and slaves. Their hunting skills were exploited by Russian fur traders who came to the islands after about 1750 in search of sea otter, fur seals, and foxes. Over the next 100 years the Aleut population severely declined because of sickness and harsh treatment. Today about 1,000 Aleuts remain; before contact with foreigners they had a population estimated at 12,000 to 25,000.

Aleutian Islands   The Aleutian Islands are a chain of islands stretching west 1,800 km (1,100 mi) from the tip of the Alaska Peninsula and separating the Bering Sea on the north from the Pacific Ocean on the south. Part of the state of Alaska, they include about 70 islands and

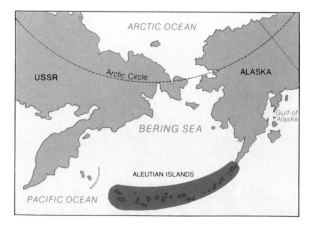

scores of islets and have an area of 17,666 km^2 (6,821 mi^2). The population is 7,768 (1980). Five major island groups stretch from east to west: the Fox, Islands of the Four Mountains, Andreanof, Rat, and Near. Partially submerged peaks of the volcanic Aleutian range, they rise sharply from the sea. The highest summit is Mount Shishaldin (2,856 m/9,387 ft) on Unimak Island. Virtually no trees grow on the islands, and vegetation includes grasses, sedges, and low flowering plants. Cold air and currents of the Bering Sea meet the warmer influences of the Pacific and cause a year-round mixture of fog, rain, high winds, and relatively uniform temperatures (annual average about 3° C/38° F). Discovered in 1741 by Vitus Jonassen BERING and Aleksei Chirikov, the islands were claimed by Russia. The Russians exploited the fur resources (blue foxes, seals) and nearly eliminated the native Aleut population. The islands were purchased along with Alaska from Russia by the United States in 1867. Unalaska (1760–75) is the oldest settlement.

Alexander, Grover Cleveland   The right-handed American baseball pitcher Grover Cleveland "Pete" Alexander, b. Elba, Nebr., Feb. 26, 1887, d. Nov. 4, 1950, was, with Christy Mathewson, one of the two 20th-century major leaguers to win 30 or more games in 3 consecutive years (1915–17). In his 20 big-league seasons (1911–30), all in the National League, "Alexander the Great" won 373 games, tied for 3d on the all-time list, while losing only 208. He led the National League in earned run average 5 times (2d all time) and was inducted into the Hall of Fame in 1938.

Alexander, Harold George, 1st Earl Alexander of Tunis   Field Marshal Earl Alexander of Tunis, b. Dec. 10, 1891, d. June 16, 1969, was one of Britain's most successful generals in World War II. Commissioned into the Irish Guards, he was decorated for his service in World War I. In World War II he withdrew (1942) British and Indian forces from Burma and then directed the great Allied offensive to Tunis in North Africa, followed by the invasion of Sicily and Italy. Alexander served as governor-general of Canada (1946–52) and as minister of defense (1952–54) in Sir Winston Churchill's cabinet. He was made a viscount in 1946 and an earl in 1952.

Alexander, Lloyd   Lloyd Alexander, b. Philadelphia, Jan. 30, 1924, American writer and translator, wrote the contemporary children's classic *Prydain Chronicles*, comprising *The Book of Three* (1964), *The Black Cauldron* (1965), *The Castle of Llyr* (1966), *Taran Wanderer* (1967), and *The High King* (1968). Inspired by Arthurian legend and the collection of Welsh myths, the *Mabinogion*, they create a world of both humor and the struggle between good and evil. Other works include *The Marvelous Misadventures of Sebastian* (1970), *The Beggar Queen* (1984), and *The El Dorado Adventure* (1987).

Alexander Archipelago

Alexander Archipelago   The Alexander Archipelago is a group of about 1,100 islands stretching some 485 km (300 mi) along the southeastern coast of Alaska. Actually the tops of a submerged mountain range, the islands have irregular, steep coasts and dense evergreen forests. The main industry is lumbering; fishing and canning are also important. The largest island is Prince of Wales (225 by 64 km/140 by 40 mi), and the largest towns are Ketchikan (1980 pop., 7,198) on Revillagigedo Island and Sitka (1980 pop., 7,803) on Baranof Island. The islands were discovered by the Russians in 1741.

Alexander the Great, King of Macedonia

Alexander III, the world's first great military genius and the first king to be called "the Great," conquered the Persian empire and annexed it to Macedonia. The son of PHILIP II and OLYMPIAS, he was born in 356 BC and brought up as crown prince. Taught for a time by Aristotle, he acquired a love for Homer and an infatuation with the heroic age. When Philip divorced Olympias to marry a younger princess, Alexander fled. Although allowed to return, he remained isolated and insecure until Philip's assassination in 336.

Winning the army's support, Alexander eliminated all potential rivals, gained the allegiance of the Macedonian nobles and of the Greeks (after a rebellion, in which he destroyed THEBES), and defeated the neighboring barbarians. Then he took up Philip's war of aggression against Persia, adopting his slogan of a Hellenic Crusade against the barbarian. He defeated the small force defending Anatolia, proclaimed freedom for the Greek cities there while keeping them under tight control, and, after a campaign through the Anatolian highlands, met and defeated the Persian army under DARIUS III at Issus (near modern İskenderun, Turkey). He occupied Syria and—after a long siege of Tyre—Phoenicia, then entered Egypt, where he was accepted as pharaoh. From there he visited the famous Libyan oracle of Amon (identified by the Greeks with Zeus) and was hailed as Amon's son.

After organizing Egypt and founding Alexandria, Alexander crossed the Eastern Desert and the Euphrates and Tigris rivers, and in the autumn of 331 defeated Darius's grand army at Gaugamela (near modern Irbil, Iraq). Darius fled to his mountain residence of Ecbatana, while Alexander occupied Babylon, the imperial capital Susa, and Persepolis. Henceforth, Alexander acted as legitimate king of Persia, and to win the support of the Iranian aristocracy he appointed mainly Iranians as provincial governors. A major uprising in Greece worried him so deeply that he lingered at Persepolis until May 330 and then, before leaving, destroyed the great palace complex as a gesture to the Greeks. At Ecbatana, after hearing that the rebellion had failed, he proclaimed the end of the Hellenic Crusade and discharged the Greek forces. He then pursued Darius, who had turned eastward. Darius was at

The territory conquered by Alexander the Great reached from Greece to India and included Egypt and the Persian Empire. The arrows on the map indicate the route of conquest, beginning in Macedonia in 336 BC and ending with Alexander's death in Babylon in 323 BC.

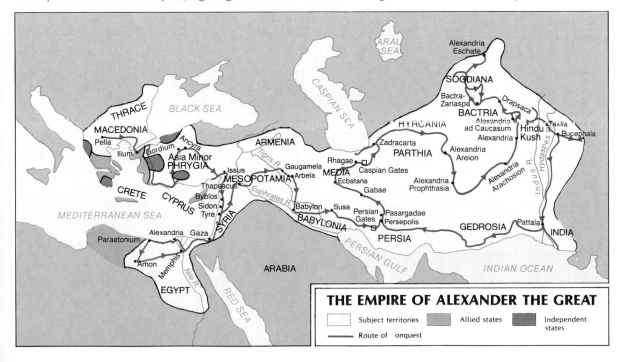

THE EMPIRE OF ALEXANDER THE GREAT

□ Subject territories   Allied states   Independent states

—— Route of conquest

Alexander the Great of Macedonia, one of history's foremost military leaders, established an empire that extended from Greece to India. This detail from a mosaic shows Alexander in the Battle of Issus (333 BC), where he defeated King Darius III of Persia.

once assassinated by Bessus, the satrap of Bactria, who distrusted Darius's will to keep fighting and proclaimed himself king. As a result, Alexander now faced years of guerrilla war in northeastern Iran and central Asia, which ended only when he married (327) ROXANA, the daughter of a local chieftain. The whole area was fortified by a network of military settlements, some of which later developed into major cities.

During these years, Alexander's increasingly Oriental behavior led to trouble with the Macedonian nobles and some Greeks. Late in 330, Philotas, commander of the cavalry and chief opponent of the king's new policies, was eliminated in a carefully staged coup d'état, and his father Parmenion was assassinated. Another old-fashioned noble, Cleitus, was killed by Alexander himself in a drunken brawl. Alexander next demanded that Europeans follow the Oriental custom of prostrating themselves before the king, but resistance by Macedonian officers and by the Greek Callisthenes defeated the attempt. Callisthenes was soon executed on a charge of conspiracy.

With discipline restored, Alexander invaded (327) the Punjab. After conquering most of it, he was stopped from pressing on to the distant Ganges by a mutiny of his soldiers. Turning south, he marched down to the mouth of the Indus, engaging in some of the heaviest fighting and bloodiest massacres of the war. On reaching the Indian Ocean, he sent the Greek officer Nearchus with a fleet to explore the coastal route to Mesopotamia. Part of the army returned by a land route, while Alexander, with the rest, marched back through the desert of southern Iran.

He emerged safely in the winter of 325–24, after the worst sufferings and losses of the entire campaign, to find his personal control over the heart of the empire weakened by years of absence and rumors of his death. On his return, he executed several of his governors and senior officers, replaced others, and also ordered the governors to dismiss their mercenary armies, composed mostly of exiled Greeks. A number of Greek cities at this time offered him deification in order to obtain concessions.

In the spring of 324, Alexander held a great victory celebration at Susa. He and 80 close associates married Iranian noblewomen. In addition, he legitimized previous so-called marriages between soldiers and native women and gave them rich wedding gifts, no doubt to encourage such unions. When he discharged the disabled Macedonian veterans a little later, after defeating a mutiny by the estranged and exasperated Macedonian army, Alexander forced them to leave their wives and children with him. Because national prejudices had prevented the unification of his empire, his aim was apparently to prepare a long-term solution by breeding a new body of high nobles of mixed blood and by creating the core of a royal army attached only to himself.

In the autumn of 324, at Ecbatana, Alexander lost his boyhood friend Hephaestion, by then his grand vizier—probably the only person he had ever genuinely loved. He next embarked on a winter campaign in the mountains, then returned to Babylon, where he prepared an expedition for the conquest of Arabia. He died in June 323 without designating a successor. His death opened the anarchic age of the DIADOCHI.

Alexander at once became a legend to the peoples that had seen him pass like a hurricane, and by way of the *Alexander Romance* made his way into the literature of the Middle Ages. His historical legacy was the spread of a veneer of Greek culture far into central Asia; the acceptance of the idea of a universal kingdom, which prepared the way for the Roman Empire; and the opening up of the Greek world to new Oriental influences, which prepared the way for Christianity.

Alexander Nevsky   Alexander Nevsky, b. *c.*1220, d. Nov. 14, 1263, was an outstanding Russian prince and military leader who earned his surname by defeating the Swedes at the mouth of the Neva River on July 15, 1240. He also won a famous victory over the German order of Livonian Knights on the ice of Lake Peipus in 1242. Alexander was the son of Yaroslav Vsevolodovich, prince of Novgorod. When his father became prince at Kiev in 1236, Alexander succeeded him as prince of Novgorod. Alexander became grand prince of Vladimir in 1252. He pursued a policy of cooperation with the Mongol suzerains of Russia, who reciprocated by abandoning demands for Russian troops and by withdrawing tax collectors. Alexander was canonized locally in Vladimir in 1380 and generally by the Russian Orthodox church in 1547.

Alexander I, Emperor of Russia   Alexander I, b. Dec. 12, 1777, d. Nov. 19, 1825, became emperor of Russia on Mar. 12, 1801, following the murder of his father, PAUL I, by members of a conspiracy in which Alexander was indirectly involved. Intelligent and well-educated, Alexander was also vain, suspicious, and pedantic. He wanted to make Russia into a modern state, but his irresolution barred the way to comprehensive reform. Nevertheless, he toyed with numerous reform schemes and in 1815 was instrumental in the introduction of constitutions into Poland and the Grand Duchy of Finland.

Alexander relied on favorites to formulate his reform

Alexander I, emperor of Russia (1801–25), played a leading role in the defeat of Napoleon I of France and emerged as one of the most powerful rulers in Europe. He was the architect of the Holy Alliance (1815), intended to affirm the Christian principles of the European nations but became instead the symbol of repressive policies in Russia, Austria, and Prussia.

he then closed himself off to all except a few favorites. Their influence gave a reactionary temper to the latter half of his reign. A member of the People's Will, an extremist offshoot of the NARODNIKI (populist movement) assassinated Alexander the same day he signed a manifesto creating a national consultative assembly. The tragedy of Alexander's death was compounded by the failure of his successor, Alexander III, to implement this progressive act.

Alexander III, Emperor of Russia

Alexander III, b. Feb. 26, 1845, d. Oct. 20, 1894, emperor of Russia, was an ardent adherent of unfettered autocracy. Coming to the throne on Mar. 1, 1881, following the assassination of his father, Alexander II, he immediately repudiated the limited constitution his father had signed the day he died and dismissed the more progressive ministers.

Alexander spent much of his reign evading or undoing the reforms of his father. A state of emergency, declared in August 1881 but lasting through the reign, circumvented the courts and gave imperial administrators arbitrary powers. Acts promulgated in 1889, 1890, and 1892 sharply circumscribed autonomy at the provincial and municipal levels, and censorship prior to publication was reasserted in 1882. His vigorous program of Russification included considerable anti-Semitic legislation. Alexander's reign muted the voices of change, but the fundamental problems of Russian society remained unresolved.

Alexander III, King of Scotland

Alexander III, b. Sept. 4, 1241, d. Mar. 18–19, 1286, king of Scotland, succeeded his father, Alexander II, in 1249 while still a young boy. HENRY III of England took advantage of the situation by trying to establish suzerainty (political control) over Scotland, but the bishop of St. Andrews, with help from the papacy, prevented it. In 1263 the Scottish king confronted Haakon IV of Norway concerning the possession of the Hebrides and defeated the Norwegians in the Battle of Largs. Alexander established a united and economically prosperous Scotland. His sudden death, however—followed by that of his heir, Margaret, maid of Norway—opened the way for EDWARD I of England to intervene drastically in Scottish affairs.

projects. The earliest example was his Unofficial Committee, composed of four of his youthful companions. Subsequently, he turned to Mikhail Mikhailovich SPERANSKY and, following the defeat of NAPOLEON I, to Aleksei Andreyevich Arakcheyev (1769–1834). The results were few, and Alexander in his frustration embraced religious mysticism, which strongly colored his policies during the decade after 1812. The most notable example was his proposed HOLY ALLIANCE in 1815.

Alexander had some success, however. Although defeated by Napoleon at Austerlitz (1805) and Friedland and forced to submit to the humiliating Treaty of Tilsit (1807), he withstood Napoleon's invasion of 1812 and then played a leading role in the final defeat of the French. Europe's adulation of Alexander as its liberator secured for him a place in history. The failure of his domestic policies, however, precipitated the Decembrist revolt (see DECEMBRISTS) of 1825.

Alexander II, Emperor of Russia

Alexander II, b. Apr. 17, 1818, d. Mar. 1, 1881, emperor of Russia, emancipated the serfs on Feb. 19, 1861, and ushered in an era of reform. The changes included an overhaul of the courts, a tempering of censorship, autonomy for the universities, elected local and provincial assemblies, and universal military conscription. Alexander succeeded his father, NICHOLAS I, on Feb. 19, 1855, during the CRIMEAN WAR. The humiliating loss of that war and the national weaknesses it revealed played a role in Alexander's subsequent reform efforts, but a personal conviction that Russia had to modernize may have been as important.

Alexander II somewhat resembled his uncle, Alexander I. Handsome, charming, and sentimental, he was also irresolute. Attempts on his life began in 1866, and

Alexander, King of Yugoslavia

Alexander, b. Dec. 16, 1888, first king of Yugoslavia, was the son of King PETER I of Serbia. In June 1914, Peter, being of poor health, appointed Alexander regent of Serbia. During World War I, Alexander was the nominal commander in chief of the Serbian army. On his father's death (Aug. 16, 1921) he became king of the new kingdom of Serbs, Croats, and Slovenes. Faced with governmental instability caused mainly by discord between the Serbs and Croats, Alexander abolished (Jan. 6, 1929) the constitution and instituted absolute rule, calling himself king of Yugoslavia. On Oct. 9, 1934, he was assassinated in

Marseilles by a terrorist in the pay of Croatian separatists. He was succeeded by his son PETER II.

Alexander III, Pope   Alexander III, b. *c.*1105, d. Aug. 30, 1181, was pope from Sept. 7, 1159, until his death. His name was Orlando Bandinelli. One of a continuing line of papal reformers in conflict with the German monarchy, he inherited a war with FREDERICK I. Although he obtained the support of HENRY II of England and Louis VII of France, he was forced into exile in France (1163–1165). He finally achieved a reconciliation with Frederick in 1177 owing to Frederick's defeats at the hands of the Italian communes. He also had to moderate the quarrel between Thomas BECKET and Henry II of England.

Earlier in his life, Alexander III had been a professor at Bologna, where he achieved a reputation for his knowledge of theology and canon law. One of the great medieval popes, he fostered the scholastic revival of the 12th century.

Alexander VI, Pope   Alexander VI, b. *c.*1431, d. Aug. 18, 1503, was pope from 1492 to 1503. A Spaniard, he was named Rodrigo de Borja (Borgia), a member of the famous BORGIA family. He was the nephew of Pope CALLISTUS III, who created him a cardinal in 1456; his election to the papacy was accomplished largely through bribery. Alexander was denounced during his pontificate by the Florentine reformer Girolamo SAVONAROLA, who declared his election to the papacy invalid as a result of simony. This led to Savonarola's excommunication (1497) and to his execution as a heretic (1498).

Of the Renaissance popes, Alexander is the most notorious for political involvement in favor of his children and for the immorality of his personal life. He contributed comparatively little as a patron of art and letters.

Alexandra Fyodorovna, Empress of Russia
[fyaw'-duh-rawv-nuh]   Alexandra Fyodorovna, b. June 6 (N.S.), 1872, d. July 16–17, 1918, was the consort of NICHOLAS II, the last tsar of Russia. The daughter of the grand duke of Hesse-Darmstadt and a granddaughter of Queen Victoria of Britain, she married Nicholas on Nov. 26, 1894. Alexandra was a determined, narrow-minded reactionary, with pretensions to mysticism, and she dominated her irresolute husband. During World War I she became the virtual ruler of Russia, and the debauched monk Grigory Yefimovich RASPUTIN—who claimed healing power over the hemophiliac heir to the throne, Aleksei—was her chief advisor. After the Bolshevik Revolution (1917), Alexandra and Nicholas and all their children were shot during the night in Ekaterinburg (now Sverdlovsk).

Alexandria (Egypt) Alexandria (Arabic: al-Iskandariya) is the chief port and second largest city of Egypt. The population is 2,917,327 (1986 est.). Alexandria is located on the west side of the Nile Delta on a strip of land between Lake Maryut and the Mediterranean Sea. An isthmus about 1.5 km (1 mi) wide connects the former island of Pharos with the mainland, separating the East and West harbors. The West Harbor serves as the city's port.

Contemporary City. Isthmian Alexandria is characteristically Egyptian. The European quarter stands on the mainland south of the East Harbor. The city has numerous mosques, palaces, monuments, parks, and gardens. A suburb, al-Raml, with its fine beaches, is known as the Egyptian Riviera. The West Harbor is the commercial center. Industries in the city include oil refining, motor-vehicle assembly, food processing, and textile weaving. The bulk of Egypt's foreign trade passes through the port of Alexandria. Excellent railroads and highways connect it with Cairo and other cities.

History. For more than 2,000 years Alexandria was the largest city of Egypt. It was founded in 332 BC by Alexander the Great and was well planned. A lighthouse, one of the SEVEN WONDERS OF THE WORLD, was built on the island of Pharos in 280 BC.

Famous buildings in the early city included the Temple of Serapis, the Temple of Poseidon, the Soma (mausoleum of Alexander the Great and the Ptolemies), a museum, a theater, an emporium, and the Alexandrian Library, founded by PTOLEMY I. Under the Ptolemies, the city was the literary and scientific center of the Hellenistic world. Later, under the Romans, its location made it the center of world commerce. Many artifacts from the ancient city are displayed in the Greco-Roman Museum.

Alexandria was captured by the Arabs in AD 642 and nearly destroyed by them. The lighthouse was devastated by an earthquake in 1324. The new lighthouse that took its place stands at Ras el-Tin, overlooking the West Harbor. Napoléon Bonaparte held the city from 1798 to 1801. In 1882, Alexandria was bombarded and occupied by the British, and during World Wars I and II it served as a British naval base.

Alexandria (Louisiana) Alexandria (1990 pop., 49,188), a city in central Louisiana, is the seat of Rapides Parish. Settled in the 1760s, surveyed and named in 1805, and incorporated in 1819, the city became a cotton, sugarcane, and cattle center. It was burned (1864) by Union forces during the Civil War. Recovery came with the arrival of the railroad and the reestablishment of forestry. Today, farm products and livestock complement the forestry industry.

Alexandria (Virginia) Alexandria is a city in northern Virginia, on the west bank of the Potomac River, 10 km (6 mi) south of Washington, D.C. It has a population of 111,183 (1990). A residential community and commercial center, the city has many old buildings that make it a tourist attraction. The site was first settled in 1695; in 1732 Scottish merchants founded a village, which they named Belhaven. In 1749, by act of the Virginia House of Burgesses, the town was established and renamed Alexandria. Although Alexandria was included in the boundaries of the District of Columbia in 1791, it was returned to Virginia in 1846 as an independent city, free of county affiliations (which it remains). The city was occupied by Union troops throughout the Civil War. The estate of George Washington (who helped lay out Alexandria's streets) is 15 km (9 mi) south.

alexandrine [al-ig-zan'-drin]   The alexandrine is a 12-syllable line of verse composed of 6 iambic feet. The term is probably derived from the late-12th-century poem *Roman d'Alexandre* and other elevated verse celebrating Alexander the Great. The alexandrine has been a standard meter in French poetry since the 16th century, used in such classical works as the tragedies of Jean Racine. It is also an important feature of Dutch and German poetry. A celebrated example of the alexandrine in English literature, where it is called iambic hexameter, is in Edmund Spenser's The Faerie Queene (1590–96), where it concludes each stanza.

See also: VERSIFICATION.

Alexeyev, Vasily [ah-lek-syay'-ef]   Vasily Alexeyev, b. Jan. 7, 1942, an extraordinary Soviet weight lifter, won the Olympic Games superheavyweight class in 1972 and again in 1976. He also won 8 consecutive world championships (1970–77) and set 80 world records. At the time of his Olympic victory in Montreal (1976), Alexeyev, an engineer, weighed 156 kg (345 lb). He had a 162-cm (60-in) chest, 53-cm (21-in) biceps, and 86-cm (34-in) thighs. He set an Olympic record that year by lifting a combined 440 kg (970 lb)—185.1 kg (408 lb) for the snatch and 254.9 kg (562 lb) for the clean-and-jerk. After a poor performance at the 1980 Moscow Olympics, he virtually retired.

Alexis, Tsar of Russia   Alexis, b. Mar. 10, 1629, d. Jan. 29, 1676, tsar of Russia (1645–76), was a religious and humane but authoritarian ruler. He was the son of Tsar Michael, the first of the ROMANOV dynasty to rule Russia. Alexis's reign was beset by popular revolts, the most serious being that of the DON COSSACKS under Stenka RAZIN. Alexis harshly suppressed this (1671) and other uprisings. Russian expansion continued under Alexis with the acquisition (1667) from Poland of much territory, part of the later Ukraine. The religious reforms enacted by the patriarch NIKON, which led to the great schism within the Russian church, also occurred during Alexis's reign. Alexis was succeeded by his son Fyodor III, who was in turn succeeded (1682) by his brothers Ivan V and Peter I under the regency of Sophia.

Alexius I Comnenus, Byzantine Emperor [kuhm-nee'-nus]   Alexius I Comnenus, b. *c.*1048, d.

Aug. 15, 1118, ruled the Byzantine Empire from 1081 to 1118. With the support of the army and his relatives, he usurped the throne from Nicephorus III. The empire was beset by foes: Seljuks occupied the Asian provinces, Pechenegs ravaged the Danubian regions, and Normans from southern Italy attacked Epirus. During 1081–92, Alexius fought the Normans and Pechenegs and then utilized (1097–98) the victories of the First Crusade over the Seljuk Turks at Nicaea and Dorylaeum to regain the coastal regions of Anatolia. From 1099 to 1104 he contended with Bohemond I for Antioch and in 1107–08 he overcame Bohemond's army in Epirus. Alexius reformed the monetary and taxation systems. Well-educated himself, he vigorously repressed the unorthodox philosopher John Italus and the BOGOMIL heretics. He was succeeded by his son, John II.

alfalfa   Alfalfa, *Medicago sativa*, a legume forage plant belonging to the pea family Leguminosae, has been an animal feed longer than any other forage crop. Alfalfa was planted in hot, dry regions of Mesopotamia before recorded history. It now is grown throughout the world under extremely varied climatic conditions. The United States produces between 73,000 and 82,000 metric tons (80,000 and 90,000 U.S. tons) annually.

Alfalfa is a perennial plant and will under normal conditions live for 6 or more years. Its shoots may grow to stems of more than 1 m (3 ft). The plant produces compound leaves and yellow to purplish blue flowers, and kidney-shaped seeds develop inside the curled pods. The roots are extraordinarily long, often extending more than 7 m (25 ft) deep, which makes alfalfa an ideal crop for dry climates. It also enriches soil with nitrogen.

Alfalfa will grow in a wide variety of conditions, but it does best in deep, loamy, well-drained soils. It responds well to irrigation and to fertilizers. Seed is generally sown in the spring in cooler climates or in the fall if winter

Alfalfa is the most important cattle-fodder crop. The flowers (detail, right) *grow in dense, short, terminal clusters.*

temperatures are moderate. It can be sown with other grains, such as oats, to reduce weed growth. When sown for pasture, it is sometimes mixed with rye, bromegrass, bluegrass, timothy, or fescue.

Procedures used to harvest alfalfa depend on the yield, nutritional quality, and physical condition desired. The maximum yield occurs when the plant is cut at full bloom, but other considerations such as stem size, moisture, and vitamin content may alter cutting time. Cuttings range from two to seven or eight a year, depending on the environment.

Alfalfa is valuable for feeding all kinds of livestock. It is used for pasture, for soil building, for dehydration, as meal, or as silage. Dehydrated alfalfa is a common ingredient of feedstuffs and supplies vitamins, protein, lipids, and minerals.

Alfieri, Vittorio [ahl-feeay'-ree]   Vittorio Alfieri, b. Jan. 16, 1749, d. Oct. 8, 1803, a tragic poet, became the prophet of Italian political and cultural resurgence, or RISORGIMENTO. A member of an aristocratic family in Asti, he achieved early success with a play, *Cleopatra* (1775). In 1777 he fell in love with Louise Stolberg, countess of Albany, with whom he lived after her separation from her husband, Charles Edward Stuart (Bonnie Prince Charlie), the pretender to the English throne. Alfieri's works include classical dramas (*Filippo*, 1783; *Saul*, 1787), prose political works (*Della tirannide*, 1777 [*On Tyranny*, 1961]), and poetic political works (*America libera*, 1782–83; *Parigi sbastigliata*, 1789). In *Il Misogallo* (The French Hater, 1790–99), he inveighed against the French and voiced pro-Italian feelings. His themes primarily concern the struggle of heroic individuals for freedom against tyranny and oppression.

Alfonsín, Raúl [al-fohn-seen']   Raúl Ricardo Alfonsín Foulkes, b. Mar. 12, 1927, took office as president of Argentina on Dec. 10, 1983, ending nearly 8 years of military rule. A lawyer, former congressman, and Radical party leader, he successfully moved to prosecute high military officers responsible for the disappearance of at least 9,000 persons in the 1970s. Military pressure in 1987, however, forced him to back an amnesty law for most officers. Although Alfonsín took measures to improve Argentina's economy, economic problems persisted and eventually became severe. He was succeeded as president in 1989 by Carlos MENEM, a Peronista.

Alfonso V, King of Aragon (Alfonso the Magnanimous)   Alfonso V, b. 1396, d. June 27, 1458, king of Aragon and Sicily (1416–58), also acquired the kingdom of Naples. Queen Joan II of Naples (r. 1414–35) adopted him as her heir but later changed her mind and offered Naples to Louis of Anjou. By 1442, Alfonso V had overcome all opposition and entered Naples in triumph. His nickname was bestowed because he was a notable patron of Renaissance humanists. He left Aragon and Sicily to

his brother John II and Naples to his illegitimate son FERDINAND I.

Alfonso I, King of Portugal   Alfonso I, b. *c*.1109, d. 1185, was the first king of Portugal. The son of Henry of Burgundy (d. 1112), count of Portugal, and of Teresa, illegitimate daughter of Alfonso VI of Castile, Alfonso seized control of Portugal from his mother in 1128. He resisted the domination of the neighboring Spanish kingdoms and attacked the Muslim lands south of Coimbra with the help of foreign crusaders. He conquered Santarém and Lisbon in 1147 and Évora in 1165. Though Alfonso had claimed the title of king for 40 years, the papacy did not officially recognize him until 1179.

Alfonso II, King of Portugal   Alfonso II, b. *c*.1185, d. Mar. 25, 1223, was king of Portugal from 1211. He helped Castile defeat the Moors at Las Navas de Tolosa (1212) and later (1217) captured Alcácer do Sal from the Moors. Alfonso promoted the compilation of Portuguese law regarding personal and property rights and clashed with the church by investigating the legal titles of church properties and attacking abuses by clergy. As a result he was excommunicated in 1220.

Alfonso III, King of Portugal   Alfonso III, b. May 5, 1210, d. Feb. 16, 1279, king of Portugal, completed the reconquest of Portugal by winning the Algarve from the Moors. The younger son of Alfonso II, he became king in 1248. Embroiled in conflict with the church over seizures of church lands, Alfonso broadened support for himself by summoning (1254) representatives of the towns to the Cortes for the first time. He introduced administrative reforms and promoted commercial and cultural development. He was succeeded by his son, DINIS.

Alfonso VI, King of León and Castile   Alfonso VI, d. 1109, Spanish king of León (1065–1109) and Castile (1072–1109), is best known for his capture of TOLEDO, the ancient Visigothic capital, from the Moors in 1085. The marriage of his two daughters to French nobles established the Burgundian dynasties in León, Castile, and Portugal.

Alfonso X, King of Castile (Alfonso the Wise)   Alfonso X, b. Nov. 23, 1221, d. Apr. 4, 1284, Spanish king of Castile and León (1252–84), won distinction as a scholar but failed as a statesman. Known as Alfonso the Wise, he set scholars to work compiling a law code, the *Siete Partidas*, and a *General History of Spain*, as well as translating scientific texts from Arabic to Castilian. He also wrote poems, chiefly in honor of the Virgin Mary. In 1257, Alfonso was elected Holy Roman emperor. His attempts to impose legal uniformity and his increasing taxation, coupled with a succession dispute, caused his son

Sancho to rebel against him in 1282. At his death his son succeeded him as Sancho IV.

Alfonso XII, King of Spain

King Alfonso XII, b. Nov. 28, 1857, d. Nov. 25, 1885, is remembered for bringing peace to Spain after years of civil war. Exiled with his mother, Isabella II, in 1868, he returned as king in January 1875. His second wife, María Cristina of Austria, bore him two daughters and a son (later ALFONSO XIII). Alfonso, a weak monarch, left politics to his premiers, especially Antonio Cánovas del Castillo (1828–97). During his reign the constitution of 1876 was enacted, the CARLISTS were defeated, and the TEN YEARS' WAR in Cuba ended (1878) in a truce.

Alfonso XIII, King of Spain

Alfonso XIII was king of Spain from 1886 to 1931. Born on May 17, 1886, a few months after his father, Alfonso XII, had died, he was proclaimed king at birth, with his mother, María Cristina of Austria, as regent. In 1906 he married Victoria Eugenia of Battenberg, a granddaughter of Queen Victoria of Britain.

At age 16, Alfonso began to impose his views on his ministers. Because Spanish political life was unstable and corrupt, his influence was often decisive. During World War I he kept Spain neutral. He supported the 1923 coup d'état of Gen. Miguel PRIMO DE RIVERA and the ensuing dictatorship. After Primo de Rivera left Spain in 1930, Alfonso tried to remain king, but his popularity was damaged by his association with the dictator. A republican landslide in municipal elections in 1931 convinced him to leave Spain. Alfonso died on Feb. 28, 1941, having abdicated his rights to his third son, Juan, whose son JUAN CARLOS was restored to the throne in 1975.

Alfred, King of England

Alfred, b. 849, d. Oct. 26, 899, succeeded his brother Æthelred as king of WESSEX in April 871. Both he and his brother were sons of King Æthelwulf. The only English king called "the Great," Alfred is renowned both for his ability as a war leader and for his love of learning. With CHARLEMAGNE, he was one of the two most outstanding rulers of the 9th century.

Alfred was almost constantly at war with the Danes from 876 until the end of his life and he became a symbol and focus of national unity. Although effective ruler only of Wessex and English MERCIA, he was regarded as the protector of all the English living under Danish rule. His capture of London in 886, which marked the farthest extent of his territorial expansion, led to general English recognition of his leadership.

A learned layman, Alfred urged the bishops of the Anglo-Saxon church both to teach and to seek out students. He himself translated into Anglo-Saxon the *Pastoral Care* of Pope Gregory I, Orosius's *Seven Books of History against the Pagans,* Boethius's *Consolation of Philosophy,* (possibly) the *Ecclesiastical History* of the Venerable Bede, and part of Saint Augustine of Hippo's *Soliloquies.* Alfred's military victories saved English culture and national identity from destruction, and his intellectual activities began the education of his people in the Latin heritage.

Alfvén, Hannes

[ahl-vayn', hah'-nes] The Swedish astrophysicist Hannes Olof Alfvén, b. May 30, 1908, shared the 1970 Nobel Prize in physics for his investigation of the properties of diffuse ionized gas, or PLASMA, in interstellar space, and in particular for his discovery of fixed electromagnetic field lines within plasmas. He correctly predicted that a perfectly conducting fluid moving transverse to these field lines would produce a shear wave that he called a magnetohydrodynamic wave; such waves are now called Alfvén waves. Alfvén received his Ph.D. from Uppsala University in 1934, and from 1940 to 1973 was a professor at the Royal Institute of Technology in Stockholm. His theories are now widely applied in astronomy, nuclear reactors, and MAGNETOHYDRODYNAMICS.

algae

Algae are a diverse group of primarily aquatic, mostly plantlike organisms that occur in such dissimilar forms as microscopic single cells; loose, filmy conglomerations; matted or branched colonies; or giant seaweeds with rootlike holdfasts and structures resembling stems and leaves.

Most of the algae have characteristics in common with plants, in that they have cell walls, contain the green pigment CHLOROPHYLL, and manufacture their own food through the process of PHOTOSYNTHESIS. The chlorophyll may be masked by other pigments, giving the various types of algae predominantly different colors. Some types, more animallike, are motile (capable of moving about) and ingest organic food, although they may also contain chlorophyll and conduct photosynthesis. Soft, even gelatinous cell surfaces are usual, but some types form shells or scales, and others produce stony, corallike, or calcareous deposits.

Algae are worldwide in distribution, thriving in all bodies of water, rocky coastlines, and terrestrial environments with ample moisture. Some species are adapted to hot springs or arctic snows. Others survive in deserts. The various marine and coastal algae are found in the ocean and on beaches and cliffs, living in distinct zones that vary according to degree of wave action, height of tides, and light intensity.

Reproduction

Methods of reproduction in algae may be vegetative by division of a single cell or fragmentation of a colony, asexual by production of motile spores (zoospores) or thick-walled nonmotile spores, or sexual by union of gametes (sex cells). The gametes may be identical (isogametes); differentiated into male and female (anisogametes); or markedly differentiated (heterogametes) into small, motile male cells and large, nonmotile female cells. Many species of algae reproduce by an ALTERNATION OF GENERATIONS, requiring separate asexual and sexual organisms to complete a life cycle.

Classification

Algae are differentiated mainly by cell structure; composition of pigment; nature of the food reserve; and the presence, quantity, and structure of flagella. The following phyla, or divisions, are recognized: blue-green algae (Cyanophyta); euglenids (Euglenophyta); yellow-green and golden-brown algae (Chrysophyta); dinoflagellates and similar types (Pyrrophyta); red algae (Rhodophyta); green algae (Chlorophyta); and brown algae (Phaeophyta). A rare class of Pyrrophyta, Cryptophyceae, are sometimes placed in a separate phylum, Cryptophyta.

In systems that divide life into plant and animal kingdoms, algae have been traditionally classified as plants and placed, along with bacteria and fungi, in the subkingdom Thallophyta. A thallophyte is negatively defined by the plant features that the cell or thallus (plant body) lacks: roots, stems, leaves, and embryo formation within a parent plant. Some motile algae that ingest food, such as euglenids, have been placed in the animal kingdom by zoologists. In systems that divide life into several kingdoms, algae are divided among the kingdoms MONERA, PROTISTA, and Plantae according to their complexity of organization and their evolutionary relationships. Blue-green algae are placed with bacteria in the most primitive kingdom, Monera, comprising single-celled organisms that have no cell nucleus. Single-celled free-living and colonial algae (euglenids, yellow-green and golden-brown,

dinoflagellates) are placed in the kingdom Protista. Multicellular or multinucleatic algae with characteristics more closely resembling higher plants (red, green, brown, and stoneworts) are placed in the kingdom Plantae in some schemes but are considered protists in others.

Cyanophyta. The BLUE-GREEN ALGAE, Cyanophyta, are somewhat larger than most bacteria but resemble them in structure and most functions. Unlike true algae they are procaryotes, or one-celled organisms, lacking organelles such as a nucleus (although DNA is present in the cytoplasm) and chloroplasts (although photosynthetic pigments are present in some forms). Unlike bacteria, no Cyanophyta exhibit sexual reproduction; nor do any have flagella, although a few forms are motile by unknown means. Cyanophyta also have chlorophyll *a*, which no photosynthetic bacterium possesses, and they produce gaseous oxygen as a waste product just as do all other algae but no bacterium. Some Cyanophyta are able to fix atmospheric nitrogen, which is of great ecological importance. Others are thermophiles ("heat-lovers") that represent much of the life found in hot or boiling springs or pools.

Euglenophyta. The Euglenophyta are free-swimming one-celled organisms of a wormlike shape; they lack cell walls and usually have one or two flagella and a red, light-sensitive eyespot. Most species are green but contain other pigments besides chlorophyll. Some subsist both by photosynthesis and by ingesting other organisms. Because of their ambiguous form, euglenids have been

(Below) *A colony of* Volvox *(magnified 336 ×) separates from its parent.* Volvox, *a genus of green algae, are organized into a hollow, spherical shape.*

(Above) *A stagnant, freshwater pond in the New York Catskill Mountains is covered with a "bloom" of green algae. Like plants, green algae contain chlorophyll, for photosynthesis; some green algae can freely propel themselves through water.*

Algae differ widely in size, shape, and color. Rockweed (left) *is brown algae that clings to rocks of temperate coasts of the Northern Hemisphere. Red algae* (right) *include beautiful forms of tropical and subtropical seaweed. Many genera of red algae, such as dulse and Irish moss, are important food sources.*

classified as animals by some zoologists and as plants by some botanists. The best known and the most representative of the Euglenophyta phylum is EUGLENA, which are found in ponds and are frequently studied in classrooms and laboratories.

Yellow-Green and Golden-Brown Algae. The phylum Chrysophyta contains diverse marine and freshwater algae that are free-living, one-celled, or occasionally filamentous. Many form shells composed of silica or lime. Most have one or two flagella. Chrysophyta are grouped mainly by color, ranging from yellowish-green through golden to golden-brown, depending on the proportion of chlorophyll to carotene and xanthophyll, yellow and brownish pigments. Chlorophylls a and e have been reported, and many forms store oil rather than starch. The best known are the biflagellate DIATOMS, the most abundant of the marine plankton. Sometimes called the "grass of the sea," they produce more oxygen than all green land plants combined. Some common lake-dwelling species of the genera *Dinobryon* and *Uroglena* have been found to obtain much of their energy from consuming bacteria when low light levels reduce photosynthesis.

Pyrrophyta. The Pyrrophyta, commonly called dinoflagellates, are one-celled free-swimming biflagellates abundant in tropical waters. They contain chlorophyll, carotene, and a large proportion of a golden-brown xanthophyll. One flagellum surrounds the organism and the other trails. Many dinoflagellates have a cellulose wall arranged in two interlocking plates; a few resemble AMOEBA and ingest organic food. Dinoflagellates are second in importance to diatoms as providers of oxygen and as a base in the food chain. Many generate light when disturbed (see BIOLUMINESCENCE) and glow at night in tropical seas.

Rhodophyta. The red algae are multicellular branching filamentous seaweeds, abundant in warm coastal waters. Their color is derived primarily from the pigment phycoerythrin, which enables them to utilize light for photosyn-

thesis at much deeper ocean levels than any other marine algae. Most have gelatinous cell walls. Some species concentrate lime from seawater; they contribute to the formation of coral reefs. The red algae are the only algae that produce no motile cells.

Chlorophyta. The green algae variously occur as single cells, as scum or film, as filamentous branching or matted colonies, or as multicellular marine forms with leaf-like fronds. They are diverse in habitat and are the most conspicuous algal type, forming in ponds and streams, on rocks and trees, and on almost any damp surfaces, including the hair and claws of certain animals. They are also common in soils. Their resemblance to higher plants in pigment content (the same proportions of chlorophylls a and e and carotene), in food storage (starch), and in cell walls (true cellulose) suggests to scientists that the higher plants are descended from the Chlorophyta.

The most common algae found as a mat on rocks and tree trunks are of the genus *Protococcus*, which multiplies by cell division and may also combine with fungi as various lichens. The STONEWORTS, often covered with lime, differ from all other algae in having a multicellular reproductive structure and are sometimes placed in a separate division, Charophyta.

Phaeophyta. The brown algae, Phaeophyta, possess the brown pigment fucoxanthin that masks the green color of chlorophyll. All brown algae are multicellular seaweeds with differentiated parts that may superficially resemble true plants. Familiar types are the giant kelps and members of the genus *Sargassum*, which form dense mats in the Sargasso Sea.

Economic Importance

It has been estimated that the marine algae account for more than 90 percent of the world's photosynthetic activity, making them the most important source of oxygen. Algae are also the main source of food for other aquatic life. Seaweeds are used as food by many coastal peoples and are ground into livestock meal. The gelatinous substances carrageenan (from Irish moss, a red alga) and algin (found in kelp and other brown seaweed) are used widely to impart a smooth consistency to ice cream, puddings, processed cheeses, jams, light beers, and other food products. They are also used for finishing leathers. Algin is an ingredient in cosmetics, car polishes, paints, and insecticides. Agar, extracted from red seaweed, is widespread in the Orient as a delicacy and is a familiar laboratory medium for culturing microorganisms. Fertilizers, detergents, polishes, and insulating and soundproofing materials often contain diatomaceous earth, composed primarily of sedimentary shells of diatoms. Now being investigated is the use of unicellular green algae as food for humans and livestock. When grown under suitable conditions, certain types, such as *Chlorella*, provide a good source of protein, fats, and carbohydrates. In sewage treatment, green and blue-green algae are a source of oxygen for bacteria that decompose wastes.

Harmful Effects

Algae can be harmful to both plants and animals. Parasitic algae are a cause of plant rust. A recurrent RED TIDE of certain dinoflagellates produces a potent nerve toxin that may kill millions of fish in temperate and subtropical waters. In lakes and ponds overrich in nutrients, blanketing growths of green and blue-green algae may smother fish and plant life (see NUTRIENT CYCLES). Shellfish feeding on the dinoflagellate *Gonyaulax* absorb large quantities of an alkaloid toxin and may become poisonous. *Lyngbya*, a Cyanophyta, produces severe skin rashes in some human beings when it is handled.

See also: PLANKTON; PROTOZOA; SEAWEED.

---

algebra   The word *algebra* relates to procedures for solving EQUATIONS, and the original scope of algebra was confined to this topic. Gradually, however, the subject of algebra has been enlarged to include many more topics. It is an indispensable tool in other branches of mathematics, such as CALCULUS, and in almost every part of applied mathematics.

As long ago as 2000 BC, the Babylonians and the Egyptians posed problems like those found in today's elementary algebra texts. For example, in the Rhind papyrus, dating from about 1650 BC, problem 24 asks for the value of "heap" if heap and a seventh of heap is 19. In modern terminology and notation this problem could be formulated as "What number plus a seventh of that number is 19?" A letter such as x could be used to represent the unknown number, and the equation could be written

$$x + \frac{1}{7}x = 19 \qquad (1)$$

In algebra, $\frac{1}{7}x$ means $\frac{1}{7}$ times x, and a fraction such as $\frac{1}{7}$ is usually written in text in the form 1/7 or $\frac{1}{7}$.

Finding a number x such that $x + \frac{1}{7}x = 19$ is called solving the equation. Learning how to use letters to write equations that describe problems in arithmetic, biology,

chemistry, economics, engineering, geometry, and physics, and learning how to solve such equations, are the primary concerns of elementary algebra.

Here is an example of a problem that might occur in a chemistry laboratory: How many liters of water must be added to 2 liters of a 30% solution of acid to obtain a 20% solution? The reasoning in solving this problem might be as follows: First, the beginning amount of acid equals the final amount of acid, because only water is to be added. Next, the number of liters of acid at the beginning is 30% of 2 liters, which is $0.30 \times 2 = 0.60$. Now if x is the number of liters of water that need to be added, the total amount of liquid obtained after the water is added will be $x + 2$ liters, and, of this, only 20% is supposed to be acid. Therefore, the number of liters of acid at the end equals 20% of $(x + 2)$, which equals $0.20(x + 2)$. So the equation that needs to be solved is

$$0.60 = 0.20(x + 2) \qquad (2)$$

Equations 1 and 2 are examples of LINEAR EQUATIONS in one variable.

Properties of Numbers

The procedures for solving equations or systems of equations can become very complicated. All the procedures, however, are based on a fundamental set of properties of numbers called field properties (see ARITHMETIC). The following properties are needed to solve Equation 1.
(1) For any number x:

$$1 \cdot x = x \text{ (the multiplicative property of 1)}$$

It is customary in algebra to use a centered dot ($\cdot$) rather than a multiplication sign ($\times$) to indicate multiplication so as not to have $\times$ confused with x.
(2) For all numbers x, y, and z:

$$xz + yz = (x + y)z \text{ (the DISTRIBUTIVE LAW)}$$

In algebra xz means x times z, yz means y times z, and $(x + y)z$ means $(x + y)$ times z.
(3) If $x = y$:

$$\text{then } zx = zy \text{ (a property of equality)}$$

(4) For all numbers x, y, and z:

$$x(yz) = (xy)z \text{ (the associative law of multiplication)}$$

Kinds of Numbers

In addition to the numbers of ordinary arithmetic (whole numbers and fractions), algebra deals with negative numbers, IRRATIONAL NUMBERS, and COMPLEX NUMBERS. Negative numbers were first systematically developed by the Hindu mathematician Aryabhata in the 6th century and were used to solve such equations as $x + 3 = 2$, with its solution the negative number -1. Irrational numbers are numbers such as $\sqrt{2}$ and π that are not expressible as fractions. Complex numbers were developed in the 16th century but were not generally accepted until late in the 18th century.

Whatever the kind of numbers or the notation used, algebra, until fairly recently, was done rather mechanically. It was not until the early 19th century that such mathematicians as George Peacock (1791–1858) and George BOOLE began to investigate the basic properties of numbers.

Algebraic Theorems

Algebraic thought has grown through the slow development of famous theorems. An example is the BINOMIAL THEOREM, usually attributed to the 17th-century French mathematician Blaise PASCAL but known prior to him. The binomial theorem indicated how binomial expressions could be expanded. Consideration of the theorem helped lead to work on mathematical SERIES and the calculus.

Equations and Graphing

In algebraic expressions, constants and coefficients are unchanging numbers, whereas variables can be substituted by a set of values. When strung together, discrete algebraic terms (monomials) make up what are called POLYNOMIALS. Equations are characterized by the types of polynomials involved, and especially by the numbers of variables and the exponents on the variables. When solutions to equations are graphed, the relation between algebra and GEOMETRY becomes apparent (see GRAPH). The solutions of linear equations, when graphed by Cartesian COORDINATE SYSTEMS, produce points, lines, or planes, depending on whether the equations contain one, two, or three variables, respectively. Equations with variables of power 2 (and no higher) are called equations of the second degree, or quadratics.

Algebraic equations and systems of equations are sometimes used to construct, or define, geometric structures (see ANALYTIC GEOMETRY). On the other hand, graphical methods can sometimes be used to solve algebraic problems.

Matrices

In the early 19th century mathematicians began to investigate algebraic systems in which the elements under consideration were no longer numbers and whose properties were somewhat different. For example, Arthur Cayley developed (mid-1800s) the algebra of matrices (the singular is MATRIX). An example of this algebra is the set of 2×2 ("two by two") matrices

$$\begin{pmatrix} a & b \\ c & d \end{pmatrix}$$

where a, b, c, and d are numbers. Addition of matrices is defined by

$$\begin{pmatrix} a & b \\ c & d \end{pmatrix} + \begin{pmatrix} e & f \\ g & h \end{pmatrix} = \begin{pmatrix} a+e & b+f \\ c+g & d+h \end{pmatrix}$$

The operation of addition for these matrices has properties similar to the properties of addition of numbers. For example, if A and B are any 2×2 matrices, then $A + B = B + A$ (COMMUTATIVE LAW of addition for matrices); this corresponds to the equation $a + b = b + a$ when a and b are numbers. If A, B, and C are any 2×2 matrices, $A + (B + C) = (A + B) + C$ (associative property of addition for matrices).

Multiplication of 2×2 matrices is defined as follows:

$$\begin{pmatrix} a & b \\ c & d \end{pmatrix} \times \begin{pmatrix} e & f \\ g & h \end{pmatrix} = \begin{pmatrix} ae+bg & af+bh \\ ce+dg & cf+dh \end{pmatrix}$$

Matrix multiplication is not commutative. In other words, if A and B are 2×2 matrices, then it is not necessarily true that $A \times B = B \times A$; on the other hand, for all numbers a and b, it is true that $a \times b = b \times a$. However, just as it is true that $a \times (b \times c) = (a \times b) \times c$, for all numbers a, b, and c, it is also true that $A \times (B \times C) = (A \times B) \times C$ for all matrices A, B, and C—the associative property of multiplication for matrices. Matrices were first developed in connection with an abstract concept in mathematics (the theory of linear TRANSFORMATIONS).

Groups

Studying a set on which just one operation is defined led to the concept of a group. Groups, like matrices, were first developed in connection with abstract concepts in mathematics, but GROUP THEORY soon found uses in other parts of pure and applied mathematics.

As an example of a group, consider the five ways in which three letters written in a given order can be rewritten in a different order. There are a total of six permutations (see PERMUTATION AND COMBINATION), including the original order. The five ways of changing the order can be denoted P_1, P_2, P_3, P_4, and P_5, described as follows:

P_1
$abc \rightarrow acb$ (the second and third letters are interchanged)

P_2
$abc \rightarrow bac$ (the first and second letters are interchanged)

P_3
$abc \rightarrow bca$ (the first letter becomes the third; the second letter becomes the first; and the third letter becomes the second)

P_4
$abc \rightarrow cab$ (the first letter becomes the second; the second letter becomes the third; and the third letter becomes the first)

P_5
$abc \rightarrow cba$ (the first and third letters are interchanged).

In addition to the interchanges (permutations) of letters denoted by P_1, P_2, P_3, P_4, and P_5, the identity permutation, P_0, can be defined by $abc \rightarrow abc$ (no letters are interchanged).

Furthermore, P_0 acts as 1 does in multiplication of numbers. That is, just as $1 \times a = a \times 1 = a$ for all numbers a, so $P_0 \times P_0 = P_0$, $P_0 \times P_1 = P_1 \times P_0 = P_1$, $P_0 \times P_2 = P_2 \times P_0 = P_2$, ..., $P_0 \times P_5 = P_5 \times P_0 = P_5$. Finally, for every P, another of the same P exists such that their product is P_0. For example, $P_0 \times P_0 = P_0$, $P_1 \times P_1 = P_0$, $P_2 \times P_2 = P_0$, $P_3 \times P_4 = P_4 \times P_3 = P_0$, and $P_5 \times P_5 = P_0$.

This system is an example of a group. A group is a set on which there is an operation, $\times$, such that

1. if a is in G and b is in G, then $a \times b$ is in G (closure property);
2. if a, b, and c are in G, then $a \times (b \times c) = (a \times b) \times c$ (associative property);
3. there is an element e in G, such that $e \times a = a \times e = a$ for all a in G (existence of an identity; this is the element P_0 in the above example);
4. for every element a in G, there is an element b in G, such that $a \times b = b \times a = e$ (existence of inverses).

Other Systems

The trend toward rigorous classification of algebraic systems characterized by strict definitions of elements and operations has also produced theories dealing with fields and rings. A field is a system for which the properties of addition and multiplication are defined. Rings are systems that satisfy fewer postulates; for example, a ring may or may not be commutative.

Algeciras [ahl-hay-thee'-rahs]   Algeciras, a port city in Cádiz province, Andalusia, is located in southern Spain on the Bay of Algeciras opposite Gibraltar. The port, with a population of 86,042 (1981), handles transatlantic shipping and passengers bound by ferry to and from North Africa. Mild winters and nearby mineral springs combine to make it a resort. Fishing and tourism are the main industries. The town, taken by the Moors in 711, is probably built on the site of the Roman colony of Portus Albus. Although the port was captured in 1344 by Alfonso XI of Castile, it was retaken in 1368 by the Moors, who then razed it. Charles III rebuilt the city in 1760. The Algeciras Conference of 1906 ended the so-called first Moroccan crisis (see MOROCCAN CRISES).

Alger, Horatio   Although an ordained Unitarian minister, Horatio Alger, b. Jan. 13, 1834, d. July 19, 1899, is best known for such juvenile novels as *Ragged Dick* (1867), *Luck and Pluck; or, John Oakley's Inheritance* (1869), and *Tattered Tom* (1871). The Alger formula is always the same: a brave but poor youth performs a daring rescue that wins the gratitude and patronage of a wealthy benefactor. *Mabel Parker,* written in 1878 but not published until 1986, is one of Alger's few novels for adults; it shares with his other works a clumsy plot and multitude of stereotypes. Despite their mediocrity, however, more than 20 million of Alger's books were sold during his lifetime.

Algeria   Algeria, in northwest Africa, is part of the region known as the MAGHRIB. The continent's second largest nation, after Sudan, Algeria borders Tunisia, Libya, Niger, Mali, Mauritania, Morocco, and Western Sahara and stretches from its nothern coastline on the Mediterranean Sea south through a varied topography to the vast SAHARA. Algiers, the capital and leading port, is one of the largest cities in Africa.

Given its geographic location, Algeria has long interacted with African, Asian, and European cultures. The bitter Algerian War (1954–62) that ended French colonial rule has significantly influenced Algeria's national identity. Its prominent position among Third World nations has enabled it to play a major role in international diplomacy.

Land and Resources

Algeria consists of a series of contrasting, approximately parallel east-west topographic zones. The narrow, discontinuous alluvial plains along the coast, which contain the most fertile land, are separated from the SAHARA by the ranges and plateaus of the ATLAS MOUNTAINS. Separating the Tell Atlas from the Saharan Atlas is a semiarid plateau with an average elevation of 1,100 m (3,610 ft). In the east the plateau merges with the Aurès Mountains, which include Mount Chélia (2,331 m/7,648 ft), the highest peak in northern Algeria. South of the Saharan Atlas is the immense Sahara, with its gravel expanses, occasional plateaus, sand dunes (*ergs*), and the fantastic, lunarlike Ahaggar massif, where Mount Tahat, the nation's highest peak, rises to 3,003 m (9,852 ft). Northern Algeria has a history of seismic disturbances.

Climate and Drainage. Northern Algeria, in the temperate Mediterranean zone, has seasonal average temperatures ranging from 11° C (52° F) to 25° C (77° F). In the ranges and plateaus of the Atlas Mountains, mean temperatures range from 4° C (39° F) to 28° C (82° F). Temperatures in the Sahara often reach 50° C (122° F) in summer but can drop to -10° C (14° F). Extreme daily temperature variations are common when the scorching sirocco winds blow in from the desert.

Rainfall is abundant in the coastal region, although less rain falls in the west (38 cm/15 in annually in Oran) than in the east (66 cm/26 in annually in Algiers). The Tell Atlas is also much drier in the west than it is in Kabylia, which receives about 102 cm (40 in) of rainfall a year. The interior plateau receives about 30 cm (12 in) of rainfall annually, the Saharan Atlas about 25 cm (10 in), and the practically rainless Sahara less than 13 cm (5 in).

The Chéliff River in the coastal plain, the only significant stream, is unnavigable, but it provides water for irrigation. In the interior there are seasonal streams called *wadis* and many shallow salt lakes called *shatts* (or *chotts*).

Vegetation and Animal Life. Grapevines, fig trees, and indigenous olive and cork oak trees flourish along the coast, and there are forests of pine, juniper, and cedar in the Tell Atlas. Vegetation in semiarid areas includes drinn

AT A GLANCE

DEMOCRATIC AND POPULAR REPUBLIC OF ALGERIA

Land: Area: 2,381,741 km² (919,595 mi²). Capital and largest city: Algiers (1987 pop., 1,483,000).

People: Population (1990 est.): 25,556,507. Density 10.7 persons per km² (27.8 per mi²). Distribution (1987 est.): 50% urban, 50% rural. Official language: Arabic. Major religion: Islam.

Government: Type: republic. Legislature: National Assembly. Political subdivisions: 48 *wilayat* (deparments).

Education and Health: Literacy (1989): 52% of adult population. Universities (1990): 13. Hospital beds (1987): 63,000. Physicians (1987): 17,760. Life expectancy (1990): women—64; men—61. Infant mortality (1990): 87 per 1,000 live births.

Economy: GNP (1988): $58.3 billion; $2,450 per capita. Labor distribution (1985): serivces—29%; agriculture—26%; mining, manufacturing, and public utilities—15%; construction—17%; trade—8%; transportation and communications—5%. Foreign trade (1989 est.): imports—$7.8 billion; exports—$9.7 billion. Currency: 1 Algerian dinar = 100 centimes.

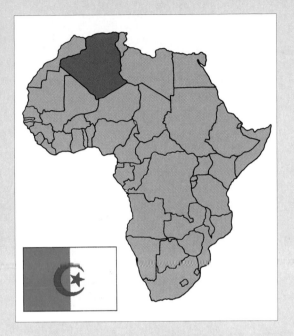

and esparto grass, while acacia trees and date palms are found on Saharan oases. Since 1975 the government has been erecting a "green wall" of vegetation across the northern edge of the Sahara to stem the desertification process. The harsh environment limits the wildlife population.

Resources. Less than 20% of Algeria's land, mostly along the coast, is arable. The country has petroleum deposits and the fourth largest natural gas reserves in the world. There are also deposits of iron ore, phosphates, mercury, and zinc.

People

Algerians are primarily of ARAB and BERBER descent. More than 1,000,000 Algerians live abroad, chiefly in France. Arabic, the national language, is spoken by about 82% of the population. Berber dialects are also spoken, especially in Kabylia. The Shawia of the Aurès, the Mozabites centered in the city of Ghardaïa, and the nomadic TUAREG speak their own dialects. Although French is now regarded as a foreign language, it is still spoken. Almost all Algerians are Sunni Muslims (see SUNNITES).

Demography. More than 90% of the population live in the north, and the large cities are located there. The most populous cities in addition to Algiers are ORAN, CONSTANTINE, and Annaba. Algeria's birthrate is extremely high; 70% of the population are under the age of 24. The government is hard-pressed to provide services and employment for the rapidly growing population.

Education and Health. The government has placed a high priority on education to produce technically trained managers and workers for its industries and to reduce illiteracy (90% at independence). Nearly 30% of the budget is allocated to education. Arabic is the language of instruction in primary schools, attended by 84% of all Algerian children. French is often used in institutions of higher education.

Algerians have been guaranteed free medical care since 1974, although the medical system is still handicapped by a lack of doctors and facilities. Particular emphasis is placed on preventive medicine.

Economic Activity

During the colonial period Algeria's major exports were wines and citrus fruits. The discovery of Saharan petroleum and natural gas in the mid-1950s accelerated French investment and initiated the ongoing transformation of the Algerian economy. Almost all foreign enterprises were nationalized after independence, including (in 1971) French oil and natural-gas interests. The economy remains largely under state control, despite the return of some land and businesses to private hands in the 1980s; Algeria is dependent on oil and gas exports to finance internal development. Because state planning has generally been capital rather than labor intensive, there is severe under- and unemployment in some areas. Since 1980, however, increased attention has been paid to ag-

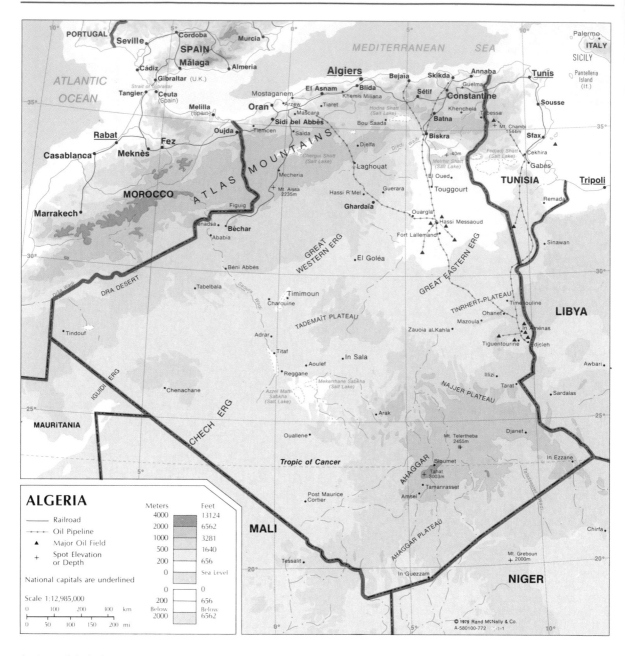

ALGERIA

— Railroad
·+·+· Oil Pipeline
▲ Major Oil Field
+ Spot Elevation
  or Depth

National capitals are underlined

Scale 1:12,985,000

Meters	Feet
4000	13124
2000	6562
1000	3281
500	1640
200	656
0	Sea Level
0	0
200	656
Below 2000	Below 6562

© 1979 Rand McNally & Co.
A-580100-772   -1-1

riculture, light industry, and the provision of human services.

Mining and Industry. Petroleum and natural gas provide 98% of Algeria's export earnings. Initial development plans concentrated on the development of heavy industry, particularly the building of ultramodern petrochemical and gas liquefaction complexes to complement Algeria's oil and natural-gas fields. There is a large steel works at Annaba, and trucks, textiles, cement, and paper are major manufactures.

Agriculture. Despite the proclaimed 1971 "Agrarian Revolution," agricultural production increased only 0.2% between 1970 and 1979, and Algeria must still import 60% of its food. To boost food production and reduce unemployment, development plans since 1980 have invested heavily in agriculture and many state controls have been relaxed.

Wine remains an important export. The government, however, has uprooted many vineyards (a cultural contradiction under Islam, which prohibits the consumption of alcohol) and replaced them with plantings of cereal crops. Other commercial crops are citrus fruits, vegetables, olives, figs, and dates. Livestock raising (mainly sheep and goats) provides a livelihood for nomads in sparsely settled semiarid areas.

Transportation and Trade. The French left an impressive infrastructure, which the Algerians have maintained and expanded. The excellent road system now includes a Trans-Saharan highway connecting northern Algeria with the far south, and there are plans to increase the rail network. Air Algérie, the national airline, operates internationally. Algeria also has a fleet of tankers and ferry service to France.

Although France remains the primary trading partner, Algeria has successfully diversified its markets. A trans-Mediterranean pipeline, completed in 1983, transports natural gas to Italy and other European markets. Petroleum and natural gas are exported to the United States and other nations.

Government

The National Liberation Front (FLN from its French name) led Algeria to independence and was the country's only legal political party until 1989. A 1976 constitution provided for a unicameral National Assembly and a powerful president. A new National Charter, approved in 1986, increased the role of the private sector and declared socialism and Islam the twin pillars of the state. In November 1988 voters overwhelmingly approved increasing the power of the prime minister, who was made responsible to the legislature, and in February 1989 they approved a new constitution that paved the way for the July 1989 legalization of a multiparty system. Local government is based on *wilayat* (department); each has a governor and an elected legislature.

History

Until the 1500s, Algeria's history was closely linked to that of neighboring Tunisia and Morocco. The region's earliest inhabitants were the Berbers. Phoenician traders arrived on the Algerian coast in the 12th century BC. The Phoenician city of CARTHAGE, in present-day Tunisia, eventually dominated the entire western Mediterranean, including the coast of what is now Algeria, which had become known as NUMIDIA. Northern Algeria was united under the Numidian tribal leader MASINISSA after he supported Rome in the Second Punic War (218–201 BC). Carthage's destruction in 146 BC and the defeat of Numidia's King JUGURTHA in 105 BC left Rome in control of the Maghrib, although Berber tribes continued to dominate the interior.

The prosperity of northern Algeria under Roman rule is evident from the ruins of thriving agricultural communities such as TIMGAD. Christianity flourished; Algerian-born Saint AUGUSTINE (AD 354–430), one of the most influential of all Christian thinkers, was bishop of Hippo (now Annaba). Invasions by VANDALS ended Roman rule in the 5th century, although most of the area remained under Berber control. In the early 6th century the BYZANTINES extended their influence as far west as present-day Algiers.

The Arabs forced the Byzantines from North Africa in the 7th and 8th centuries, and the Maghrib became part of the UMAYYAD caliphate. The Berbers converted to Islam but resisted Arab dominance. From the 10th to the 13th centuries, Algeria was ruled by a series of Muslim dynasties that originated in the Maghrib, including the FATIMIDS, the Almoravids, and the Almohads. The particularly prosperous Almohad period united North Africa and Spain under Muslim rule.

In the late 15th century Christian Spain, having expelled the Muslims from the Iberian peninsula, captured several Algerian ports. They were forced off the coast with Turkish assistance, and Algeria became nominally part of the OTTOMAN EMPIRE in 1518. The local rulers of the North African BARBARY STATES had a high degree of autonomy. Piracy against European shipping led to British and American intervention in the early 19th century. This was followed in 1830 by a French invasion and the deposition of the dey (regent) of Algiers.

The French campaign to conquer northern Algeria ended in 1847 with the defeat of Algerian leader Abd al-Qadir (c.1807–83). The French gradually extended their influence southward, despite fierce local resistance, until Algeria's current boundaries were drawn in 1902.

France had encouraged European colonization of Algeria from about 1834; the area was declared an integral part of France in 1848. The European settlers confiscated Muslim land and created a flourishing colonial society removed from the Muslim majority. Muslims had almost no political rights and did not share in colonial prosperity. Organized Algerian nationalist movements arose after World War I under the leadership of Messali Hadj, who desired complete independence, and the moderate Ferhat Abbas, who wanted France to live up to its assimilationist ideals. European settlers, however, bitterly resisted any efforts to grant political and economic equality to the Muslims.

Algeria was under Vichy administration during the early years of World War II. After 1942, it served as a major base for the Allied North Africa campaign; Algiers was the capital of free France until the liberation of Paris. The nationalist hopes aroused during the war were not met, and thousands of Muslims perished in bloody reprisals after 88 Frenchmen were massacred during a disorderly 1945 nationalist demonstration at Sétif. Although the French government granted Muslims the vote on a separate electoral roll in 1947, demands for full political equality and further reform were opposed by the European colonists. The nationalist movement gained support and became increasingly radicalized.

In 1954 the FLN proclaimed a war of liberation, launching terrorist attacks against the French in both Algeria and France. The long Algerian War led to the fall of the Fourth Republic and the return to power of Charles DE GAULLE in 1958. On July 3, 1962, de Gaulle finally proclaimed Algeria's independence. After a power struggle within the FLN, Ahmed BEN BELLA became Algeria's first president in 1963.

Confronting a society devastated by war and the subsequent flight of European capital and skilled workers, ben Bella nationalized abandoned colonial holdings and announced his support of national liberation movements in other colonial lands. Conflict with Morocco, economic problems, and ben Bella's dictatorial personality provoked a bloodless coup (1965) led by Houari BOUMEDIENNE. Boumedienne maintained Algeria's image as an avant-garde Third World state and began its support of Polisario demands for an independent WESTERN SAHARA. His nationalization of French oil and natural gas concessions in 1971 symbolized Algeria's economic liberation, although his government still accepted French aid.

CHADLI BENJEDID, who became president in 1979 after the death of Boumedienne and was reelected in 1984 and 1988, maintained Algeria's prominence as a speaker for the Third World. He also pursued a "Greater," or unified, Maghrib: Algeria, Tunisia, Libya, Mauritania, and Morocco established the Arab Maghrib Union in 1989. In 1988, Algeria restored diplomatic ties with Egypt and Morocco and sought international mediation of the war in Western Sahara. Benjedid liberalized economic policies somewhat, but high unemployment, inflation, and corruption sparked massive unrest in October 1988. Constitutional referenda in November 1988 and February 1989 ended the commitment to socialism and the FLN's monopoly of power. In June 1990 local elections—the first multiparty elections since 1962—the fundamentalist Islamic Salvation Front won almost 65% of the popular vote to the FLN's 30%.

Algiers   Algiers (French: Alger; Arabic: al-Jazair) is the capital, largest city, and chief port of Algeria. The city has 29 km (18 mi) of waterfront on the Bay of Algiers, an inlet of the Mediterranean, and, backed by hills, it has the appearance of a huge amphitheater facing the bay. The population is 1,483,000 (1987). In colonial times Algiers was essentially a French city, but today less than 2% of the population is non-Arab. Despite new suburbs, the construction of public housing, and an international effort to restore the crumbling Casbah (the precolonial heart of the city), Algiers has a serious housing shortage.

Port activities are the mainstay of the economy. Products from the surrounding agricultural region are exported along with iron ore, and the harbor serves as a refueling depot for large vessels. Oil and natural gas deposits in the Sahara are an important source of revenue. Cement, chemicals, and paper products are manufactured in the city. Algiers is the site of the University of Algiers (1879).

Algiers was known to the Romans as Icosium. After being destroyed several times by invaders, the present site was settled in the 10th century by the Berbers. Until the 18th century Algiers was a home base for Barbary pirates, who terrorized ships on the Mediterranean. In 1516, Algiers came under the control of the Turks. The French captured the city in 1830, and it became the colonial headquarters of France until Algeria's independence in 1962. During World War II, Algiers served as a major headquarters for the Allies and for a brief period was the provisional capital of free France.

ALGOL [al'-gahl]   ALGOL, which stands for algorithmic language, is a COMPUTER LANGUAGE widely used for COMPUTER PROGRAMMING. It was developed in Europe in the early 1960s and had a profound influence on subsequent programming languages, including PL/1, Pascal, and Simula 67. ALGOL introduced important control structures, such as the 'if' statement, 'begin' and 'end' blocks for grouping statements into a unit, and more flexible rules for declaring variables. Because of its simplicity, it is often used for communicating or publishing programs.

Algonquin [al-gahn'-kwin]   The Algonquin (or Algonkin), a North American Indian tribe, inhabited in the 17th century the upper St. Lawrence and the lower Ottawa River areas of present-day Quebec, Canada. Early French settlers applied the name to a number of independent bands of hunting peoples whom they encountered in that region. These small foraging bands spoke closely related languages of the Algonquian (Algonkian) family and were similar in culture and social organization.

Algonquian-speaking bands allied themselves with the French in their efforts to settle Canada and to block Five Nations IROQUOIS attempts to dominate the fur trade in the eastern interior of North America. Hard-pressed by Iroquois raids, however, the Algonquins were eventually forced to abandon their villages and hunting grounds. Some moved west to the Lake Huron region and may be ancestors of the peoples known as the OTTAWA and the Nipissing. Others moved north and east out of range of Iroquois war parties. Some who later returned to the French colony aided the French in the FRENCH AND INDIAN WARS until the British conquest (1763) of New France. About 2,000 Indians regarded as descendants of the original St. Lawrence–Ottawa River Algonquins today live on small reservations in Canada mainly in Ontario and Quebec.

algorithm   An algorithm is a procedure for solving a usually complicated problem by carrying out a precisely determined sequence of simpler, unambiguous steps. Such procedures were originally used in mathematical calculations (the name is a variant of *algorism*, which originally meant the Arabic numerals and then "arithmetic") but are now widely used in computer programs and in PROGRAMMED LEARNING. FLOWCHARTS are frequently used to facilitate understanding of the sequence of steps.

See also: COMPUTER PROGRAMMING.

Algren, Nelson   The American writer Nelson Algren, b. Detroit, Mar. 28, 1909, d. May 9, 1981, became famous as the mythographer of the big-city slum, particularly the Chicago slum where he grew up. The work that brought Algren the widest acclaim was his novel *The Man* *with the Golden Arm* (1949; film, 1955), which won a 1950 National Book Award. Equally impressive, however, was *A Walk on the Wild Side* (1956), a republication of Algren's first novel, *Somebody in Boots* (1935). *The Neon Wilderness* (1947) and *The Last Carousel* (1973) are collections of short stories. Just before his death, Algren was elected to the American Academy and Institute of Arts and Letters.

Alhambra   see GRANADA; MOORISH ART AND ARCHITECTURE

▬

Ali   Ali (Ali ibn Abi Talib), b. *c*.600, d. Jan. 24, 661, fourth caliph of the Muslim community, is regarded by SHIITE Muslims as the only legitimate successor of the Prophet Muhammad. The first cousin of Muhammad and husband of the Prophet's daughter FATIMA, Ali was passed over in the caliphal succession until 656. He was immediately challenged by a faction led by the prophet's widow, AISHA, whom he defeated. Ali then became involved in a civil war with Muawiyah, governor of Syria. When Ali was murdered by a schismatic group of his own followers, the Kharijites ("seceders"), Muawiyah seized the caliphate and founded the first Muslim dynasty, the UMAYYADS. Ali's partisans, the Shiites, claimed that only Ali's sons could rightfully have succeeded him.

▬

Ali, Muhammad   The American boxer Muhammad Ali, b. Louisville, Ky., Jan. 17, 1942, was perhaps the most celebrated sports figure in the world during most of the 1960s and '70s. He was originally named Cassius Marcellus Clay, Jr., and fought under that name until after he won his first world heavyweight championship. His rise to prominence may be attributed to a combination of circumstances—his role as a spokesman for, and idol of, blacks; his vivacious personality; his dramatic conversion to the Black Muslim religion; and most important, his

Muhammad Ali, the flamboyant, three-time heavyweight boxing champion, was known for his precise punching and great speed. His most memorable fights were against such hard punchers as Sonny Liston, Joe Frazier, and George Foreman.

staying power as an athlete. Ali first came to world attention in 1960, when he won the Olympic light-heavyweight championship. In 1964, he took the world heavyweight title with a surprising victory over then champion Sonny Liston.

Ali proved to be a "fighting champion," accepting the challenges of every heavyweight with ranking credentials. He was stripped of his title in 1967 for refusing military service on religious grounds during the Vietnam War but was allowed to resume fighting in 1970 and had his appeal of conviction upheld by the U.S. Supreme Court in 1971. Ali regained the championship in a 1974 bout with George Foreman. He lost the crown again in 1978 to Leon Spinks but regained it the same year, thus becoming the first man to win the title three times. In 1980, Larry Holmes foiled Ali's try for a fourth heavyweight championship. Ali retired in 1981 with a 55-5 record.

▬

Ali Baba   Ali Baba, a woodcutter, is the protagonist of "Ali Baba and the Forty Thieves," one of the most popular tales from the collection known as the ARABIAN NIGHTS. When thieves stash their stolen treasures in a secret cave, Ali Baba accidentally witnesses the act and learns their magic password, "Open Sesame," which he then uses to enter the cave and make off with the gold himself. The robbers' attempts to kill Ali Baba are subsequently foiled by his slave, Morgana, when she finds the band hiding in giant jars.

▬

Alicante   [ah-lee-kahn'-tay]   Alicante, the capital of Alicante province, is a port city in southeastern Spain. Located on the Mediterranean Sea, 124 km (77 mi) south of Valencia, the city has a population of 251,387 (1981). Industries include textiles, wine, cigars, and tourism. Settled during the 4th century BC, it later became the Roman port of Lucentum (201 BC). The city was captured by Moors in 713 and by James I of Aragon in 1265.

▬

Alice Springs   Alice Springs, with a population of 22,000 (1984 est.), is the chief town of the interior of Northern Territory, Australia. It is the commercial center of the surrounding cattle-raising and mining region. Tourism is important because of the long, warm winter (May to September). The northern terminus of the Central Australia Railway, Alice Springs is also accessible by air and the Stuart Highway. It was settled in 1871.

▬

Alice's Adventures in Wonderland   The publication of *Alice's Adventures in Wonderland* in 1865 marks the beginning of what is often called the Golden Age of CHILDREN'S LITERATURE, a period when, for the first time, children's works were written for purposes other than moral uplift. Author Lewis CARROLL invented a dream world where Alice, a naive but wise child, encounters a series of adult eccentrics (among them, the Mad Hatter,

"The Mad Hatter's Tea Party," from Alice's Adventures in Wonderland, was drawn in 1865 by Sir John Tenniel, an English political cartoonist. Tenniel's illustrations were specified by the book's author, Lewis Carroll.

the Ugly Dutchess, the Mock Turtle) who utter parodies of well-known, platitudinous poems of the period and otherwise indulge in bizarre illogic and imperious but ineffectual command. For many years the most widely read English-language work for children, the book has had many famous illustrators, including Sir John TENNIEL, who worked on the original edition, Arthur RACKHAM in 1907, and Salvador Dalí in 1969. The book's almost-as-famous sequel is THROUGH THE LOOKING-GLASS (1872).

alicyclic compounds [al-ih-sik'-lik]   Alicyclic compounds are members of a class of organic CYCLIC COMPOUNDS, which contain three or more atoms joined to form a closed ring. The ring in alicyclic compounds is composed of only carbon atoms; HETEROCYCLIC COMPOUNDS contain other elements besides carbon in the ring, the most common being oxygen, nitrogen, and sulfur. The more stable alicyclic compounds possess C_5 (5-carbon) and C_6 rings and are called naphthenes. The alicyclic compounds containing only single bonds are named using the prefix *cyclo-* followed by the name of the corresponding open-chain hydrocarbon, for example, CYCLO-HEXANE, which can be formed from the 6-carbon open-chain compound, hexane. More complex molecules are usually given nonsystematic names.

alien   An alien is a foreign-born person who is not a citizen of the country in which he or she resides. Aliens are not entitled to all the rights of citizens, but in most countries aliens who enter legally are guaranteed the basic protections of the laws. In the United States most legally admitted aliens have temporary status, such as visitors or students. Resident aliens are admitted permanently; they have the same rights under the law as

U.S. citizens except that they cannot vote or run for most public offices. Another category of aliens comprises political refugees. Large numbers of resident illegal aliens prompted Congress to pass the Immigration Reform and Control Act of 1986. This law established penalties for employers of illegal aliens, but it also provided legal status for illegal aliens living in the United States since Jan. 1, 1982.

See also: CITIZENSHIP; IMMIGRATION; NATURALIZATION.

Alien and Sedition Acts   Four acts passed by the U.S. Congress in 1798 came to be known collectively as the Alien and Sedition Acts. By this legislation the dominant Federalist party hoped to cripple its political enemies, the Democratic-Republicans. The latter had attracted the support of many radical immigrants, especially from Ireland, and were critical of Federalist foreign policy. The Quasi-War with France, which followed the XYZ AFFAIR, convinced many Federalists that this criticism was disloyal, and thus the legislation was pushed through Congress, despite the mixed feelings of the president, John Adams.

The Naturalization Act (June 18, 1798) raised the residence requirement for aliens seeking citizenship from 5 to 14 years. The Alien Act (June 25, 1798), limited to two years' duration, empowered the president to deport any foreigner he regarded as dangerous "to the peace and safety of the United States." The Alien Enemies Act (July 6, 1798), passed with some Republican support, gave the president broad powers to deal with enemy aliens during time of war. The Sedition Act (July 14, 1798), also of two years' duration, made it a crime to publish anything false or scandalous against the government. The last act violated the spirit of the 1st Amendment, although it is notable for revising the concept of seditious libel to accept truth as a defense and to allow juries to rule on questions of law as well as fact—both departures from common law.

As a result of the Republican victory of 1800, the Naturalization Act was repealed in 1802. The others were allowed to expire. With the steady growth of democratic practice in the 19th century, few lingering Federalists publicly defended their wisdom or validity.

alienation   Alienation is a term widely used to describe and explain a state of estrangement of the individual from the natural environment, social life, or the self. Alienation was a major perspective of 19th-century thought, but its antecedents date from the early Christian Era.

Christian Concept. Saint Paul taught that man, by his innately sinful nature, alienates himself from a loving father (God). Saint AUGUSTINE worried about man's reconciliation with God and disputed with the Pelagians (see PELAGIANISM), who denied that man's nature is essentially evil. From the time of Thomas AQUINAS until the present century, God was no longer conceived of as a personal being but as all-powerful and requiring the intercession of others; alienation and reconciliation therefore declined as central theological concerns.

The romantic movement in Western philosophy and literature (see ROMANTICISM) viewed civilization as corrupting and alienating man from nature. Certain schools of contemporary psychology still hold this view and maintain that an integrated person could be discovered if the problems of role and authority did not interfere.

Philosophical Views. Alienation occupies a central place in Georg HEGEL's *Phenomenology* (1807), in which he asserts that when people try to realize their protentials, this realization is mediated by physical objects, institutions, and mores. According to Hegel, these impede people's full realization, that is, they are an alienation from self. One of Hegel's disciples, Bruno Bauer, popularized the term *self-alienation* when he proposed that religious beliefs cause a separation in human consciousness between a received idea of the world and the world as it is experienced.

Ludwig FEUERBACH, another disciple of Hegel, taught that religion is a projection of inner human nature and desire and is therefore alienating because it makes people locate their humanity in an external idea and subject themselves to the forces and superstitions of traditional organized religion. Feuerbach's concept, like Hegel's, influenced Karl MARX, who was developing a secular view of alienation.

In Marx's early writings (1846), alienation was discussed as a social phenomenon. He used the term to refer to the ways in which human powers of perception, orientation, and creation become stunted and crippled by the very nature of the industrial organization and by the capitalist economic system. People are alienated from their work because they play no role in deciding what to do or how to do it, alienated from the product of their work because they have no control over what they make or what is done with it, and alienated from other people by economic competition and class hostility. Marx felt that humans suffer from alienation to the extent that they do not realize the full potential of their being.

Alienation has been viewed as inherent in human nature by the theologians Martin BUBER and Paul TILLICH and by the existentialists (see EXISTENTIALISM) Jean Paul SARTRE and Albert CAMUS; they have argued that some degree of dissociation of the self in thought and life is inescapable, for humans are strangers in the world.

Modern Concept. Alienation as a consequence of social organization and culture is a key generative concept of modern sociology; it underlies the analyses of Emile DURKHEIM, Max WEBER, and Georg SIMMEL. Durkheim used the term *anomie* to describe the rootlessness (often resulting in suicide) that resulted from the breakdown of traditional community and religious mores. For Weber, the increasing rationalization of bureaucratic life caused personal relationships to become more specialized and situational. Simmel used the concept to denote the tension within a person seeking to "preserve his autonomy and individuality in the face of overwhelming social forces, of historical heritage, of external culture, and of the techniques of life." The term *alienation* is used to explain, among other things, voter passivity in political elections and the mobilization of people in social movements.

alimentary canal   see DIGESTION, HUMAN; DIGESTIVE SYSTEM

alimony   Alimony is the money allowance that a court awards to a marriage partner after legal separation or divorce. Temporary alimony may be allowed during litigation. Traditionally, alimony has been paid by the husband to the wife. However, an independently wealthy wife or one whose job gives her a comfortable living may not be awarded alimony. In some cases, well-to-do wives may be ordered to support husbands who are unable to maintain themselves.

Alimony payments may stop if the spouse receiving them remarries. Child-support payments, however, are covered by a separate agreement and usually remain in effect while the children are minors; these payments may include school or college expenses or medical bills. Often a spouse who plans to remarry will accept a low alimony settlement in exchange for a generous child-support agreement.

aliphatic compounds   [al-i-fat'-ik]   An aliphatic compound is any of a major group of organic, or carbon compounds, characterized by a continuous or branched open-chain arrangement of the carbon atoms. Other major groups are the ALICYCLIC COMPOUNDS (carbon atoms arranged in a ring), AROMATIC COMPOUNDS (involving the benzene-ring structure), and HETEROCYCLIC COMPOUNDS (rings incorporating other atoms as well as carbon).

Most organic compounds can be considered as hydrogen–carbon compounds (hydrocarbons), or as compounds in which other elements have substituted for the hydrogen. Aliphatic hydrocarbons comprise three subgroups: ALKANES (paraffin series), characterized by the existence of only single bonds connecting the carbon atoms; ALKENES (olefins), which have at least one double bond; and ALKYNES (acetylenes), which have one or more triple bonds.

Alkanes are relatively unreactive. They will burn, producing heat, carbon dioxide, and water; long chains can be pyrolyzed (heated without air), producing either shorter chains or alkenes; and other atoms can substitute for hydrogen, primarily chlorine and bromine atoms. Alkenes and alkynes are much more reactive. They readily add other molecules or form long chains of repeating molecular units (see POLYMERIZATION).

When a hydrogen atom of an aliphatic compound is removed, an alkyl RADICAL (R) is formed. Radicals often occur as intermediates in reactions but do not exist independently except for short periods of time. The number of radicals that can form generally increases with the complexity of the compound. For example, the gas propane, $CH_3CH_2CH_3$, can have a branched-chain radical form by removing a hydrogen from the central carbon, or a straight-chain radical form by removing a hydrogen from the end carbon.

Functional groups added to the radicals produce the entire spectrum of aliphatic compounds. When the hydrogen atom of an aliphatic compound is replaced by one or more hydroxyl groups (OH), ALCOHOLS (ROH) are formed. Substitution by a halogen (fluorine, chlorine, bromine, or iodine) produces an alkyl halide (RX); such industrially important compounds do not occur in nature. Two molecules of an alcohol may combine, with the loss of a molecule of water, to form an ETHER (ROR). Alcohols can be oxidized to form the carbonyl compounds, ALDEHYDES and KETONES.

An amino group (NH_2), containing nitrogen (N), can be attached to the radical, forming an AMINE (RNH_2). Substituted amines can also be formed if the hydrogen atoms on the nitrogen atom are replaced by one or two alkyl groups. The amines are unique in that they are the only common type of basic, or alkaline, organic compounds. They are all reactive and have a distinctive property—a disagreeable odor.

Controlled oxidation of aliphatic compounds, except the saturated hydrocarbons, in which all possible positions are filled by hydrogen atoms, will produce a CARBOXYLIC ACID. ESTERS are produced by the reaction of a carboxylic acid with an alcohol. They are characterized by a pleasant odor; many of these compounds occur in nature.

Other aliphatic compounds are the sulfur-containing mercaptans (RSH) and the nitrogen-containing nitriles (RCN) and nitro (RNO_2) compounds. In addition, many aliphatic compounds contain two or more functional groups in the same molecule.

alizarin   see DYE

alkali [al'-kuh-ly]

In chemistry, alkali refers generally to any strongly basic compound (see ACIDS AND BASES). Alkalies are usually SALTS or hydroxides of sodium, potassium, lithium, or ammonia. Mineral deposits containing large quantities of such compounds are also called alkali.

In a more specific sense, alkali is either potassium hydroxide (KOH) or sodium hydroxide (lye, NaOH). These two strong bases have such similar properties that chemists often specify alkali when either compound may be used.

alkali metals

The alkali metals are the elements CESIUM, FRANCIUM, LITHIUM, POTASSIUM, RUBIDIUM, and SODIUM. These elements form Group IA of the periodic table. The alkali metals react violently with water to form strong bases, called alkalies. The alkali metals are monovalent, the outer electron shell consisting of a single electron. This electron is easily shed to form a stable cation—a positively charged ion—that has the electron configuration of an inert gas. The alkali metals readily donate electrons to HALOGEN atoms to form stable salts. Because of their high reactivity, alkali metals are never found in nature as free elements; instead they occur in compounds such as silicates or chlorides. The alkali metals have low density, low melting point, and high ductility.

alkaline earth metals [al'-kuh-lyn]

The alkaline earth metals are BARIUM, CALCIUM, and STRONTIUM, all of which are members of Group IIA of the periodic table. They form strong bases, or alkaline solutions, and are called earths because of the incombustibility and insolubility of their oxides. Sometimes the other members of Group IIA—BERYLLIUM, MAGNESIUM, and RADIUM—are included in the class.

alkaloid [al'-kuh-loyd]

An alkaloid is any of a class of nitrogen-containing natural products of plant origin that have an alkaline, or basic, chemical nature (see ACIDS AND BASES). Some alkaloids are simple, monocyclic (one-ring) AMINES (see CYCLIC COMPOUNDS), but many are very complex, polycyclic amines.

Occurrence. More than 200 alkaloids are known. They are present in only about 10 to 15 percent of all vascular plants. Often found in the dicotyledon group of the angiosperms, or flowering plants, they seldom occur in monocotyledons or in other plant groups, such as gymnosperms. The most actively growing parts of such plants usually contain the highest percentage of the compounds. Among the more familiar alkaloids are aconitine (from monkshood), atropine (from belladonna), CODEINE, MORPHINE, and papaverine (from opium poppy), NICOTINE (from tobacco), QUINIDINE and QUININE (from cinchona bark), solanine (from potato and tomato), ricinine (from castor bean); and STRYCHNINE and brucine (from *Nux vomica*).

Function. Why certain plants contain alkaloids remains a mystery, although a number of theories have been formulated: that alkaloids are by-products of plant metabolism; that alkaloids are means of defense for plants against animal and insect attacks; or that they are reservoirs for protein synthesis, regulators of growth and reproduction, or detoxifying agents.

Uses. Alkaloids are most widely employed for their physiological effects, which range from poisonous to sedative to hallucinogenic. Socrates was killed by the alkaloid coniine, from POISON HEMLOCK. The poisons aconitine and strychnine were once used medically but are now generally considered too hazardous. Morphine and codeine are analgesics, atropine is a pupil dilator, and SCOPOLAMINE (from henbane) is a sedative. Lysergic acid, an ERGOT alkaloid, is a starting material in synthesizing lysergic acid diethylamide (see LSD), a powerful hallucinogen. Another hallucinogenic alkaloid is mescaline (from PEYOTE).

Alkan

Alkan was the name adopted as a performer by the French pianist Charles Henri Valentin Morhange, b. Nov. 30, 1813, d. Mar. 19, 1888. A child prodigy, he became a recluse in his 20s and devoted his life to composing. The 24 piano studies in op. 35 and 39, representing all the major and minor keys, are among his best works. Influenced by Chopin, Alkan was melodically weaker; his music incorporates classical structures but is often bold in its harmonies.

alkane [al'-kayn]   Alkanes are a class of ALIPHATIC hydrocarbons characterized by open chains of carbon atoms with only single bonds between adjacent carbon atoms. All members of this series have the general chemical formula C_nH_{2n+2} where n is an integer.

The carbon atoms may form continuous or branched chains; branching increases the number of possible ISOMERS, or different structures with the same formula. There is only one CH_4 (methane) compound but there are five compounds with the formula C_6H_{14} (hexane), 75 $C_{10}H_{22}$ (decane) compounds, and 366,319 $C_{20}H_{42}$ (eicosane) compounds.

Except for the first four (methane, ethane, propane, and butane), alkanes are named using the Greek or Latin prefix for the number of carbon atoms in the chain combined with the characteristic ending *ane*.

All alkanes are insoluble in water; other physical properties vary with molecular weight. Thus C_1 through C_4 are gases at room temperature; C_5 through C_{17} are liquids. Higher members are solids and are often called the paraffin hydrocarbons. The average increase in boiling point is 20° per CH_2 group.

The primary sources of alkanes are natural gas and crude petroleum. The major uses of alkanes include energy production from the combustion of natural gas and gasoline, lubrication by oil and grease, and the manufacture of chemicals such as alkenes and polymers.

alkene   An alkene is any of a group of organic compounds that contain a carbon–carbon double bond. The molecules of alkenes are composed only of carbon and hydrogen atoms but contain less hydrogen per carbon atom than the ALKANES, or paraffins, to which they can be converted by the addition of hydrogen. The alkenes (often called olefins) are unsaturated hydrocarbons; they have the general formula C_nH_{2n}. Ethene or ethylene, C_2H_4, is the simplest member of the series. Systematic names for alkenes are derived by appending the suffix *ene* to the root name for the alkane with the same carbon content. Thus C_3H_6, commonly called propylene, has the systematic name *propene,* and C_4H_8 is either 1-butene (CH_2═ CHCH$_2$CH$_3$), or 2-butene (CH_3CH═$CHCH_3$), depending on the position of the double bond. Whereas carbon–carbon single bonds permit rotation of the atoms or groups of atoms linked to the carbons, double bonds between two atoms completely restrict rotation about the double bond. As a result 2-butene can exist in two different configurations of its atoms, called geometric ISOMERS:

cis-2-butene   *trans*-2-butene

Alkene hydrocarbons are much more chemically reactive than the alkanes because the double bond is more susceptible to attack by other reagents. The double bond can readily be oxidized or reduced, and a wide variety of reagents can be added to the alkene molecule at the double-bond site.

Ethylene, propylene, and related compounds are leading organic raw materials in the CHEMICAL INDUSTRY; they are used in the production of many other compounds, including various polymers.

See also: DIENE; ETHYLENE.

Alkmaar [ahlk'-mahr]   Alkmaar is a town in the North Holland province of the western Netherlands. Located about 32 km (20 mi) northwest of Amsterdam, it lies on the North Holland Canal, some 10 km (6 mi) inland from the North Sea. Dating from the 12th century, the town has a population of 83,892 (1984 est.); some 120,000 live in the metropolitan area. Alkmaar is famous for a cheese market, now a major tourist attraction, which operates much as it has since it opened in 1571. Alkmaar was the first Dutch town to resist a Spanish siege led by the duque de Alba in 1573, thus paving the way to Dutch independence. Notable buildings include the Gothic-style Town Hall, housing the Municipal Museum; the late 15th century St. Lawrence's Church; and the 16th-century Weigh House.

alkyne [al'-kyn]   An alkyne is any of a class of organic compounds similar to the ALKENES but characterized by a triple bond between two carbon atoms. The general formula for alkynes is C_nH_{2n-2}. They are sometimes called the acetylene series because the simplest member of the alkyne family is the colorless gas ACETYLENE, C_2H_2. Names for the other alkynes are derived by adding the suffix *yne* to the root name for the ALKANE of the same carbon content.

Alkynes, like alkenes, undergo addition reactions; that is, substances such as hydrogen, bromine, and water can add to the molecule at the triple bond. Whereas a simple alkene can absorb only one MOLE of H_2 during reduction to an alkane, an alkyne such as propyne can consume two moles of H_2 during its stepwise conversion to propene and then to propane:

$$CH_3C\equiv CH + H_2 \xrightarrow{Pd\text{-}C} CH_3CH\equiv CH_2 + H_2 \xrightarrow{Pd\text{-}C} CH_3CH_2CH_3$$
propyne   propene   propane

Acetylene is the only member of the alkyne series produced commercially in large amounts. It is made from coal and limestone by the reaction of coke and lime (CaO), in an electric furnace to produce calcium carbide, which then reacts with water at room temperature to give acetylene.

In recent years acetylene has been made from natural gas, which is mostly methane. When methane is heated to a high temperature (1,400–1,600° C) and passed over a catalyst, acetylene is one of the products obtained in fairly high yield.

Pure acetylene (bp −83° C) in liquid form decomposes explosively when compressed to several hundred grams per square centimeter. Consequently, when acetylene is used for fuel in oxyacetylene torches, it is dissolved in acetone under pressure in a cylinder packed with an inert porous material.

Almost half of the acetylene produced is used for the synthesis of other organic chemicals. The catalytic addition of water to acetylene produces acetaldehyde. Addition of hydrogen cyanide to acetylene produces acrylonitrile, which is used for the production of synthetic fibers and rubber. Acetylene adds to itself to give vinylacetylene, which serves as a precursor to chloroprene and thence to neoprene, a solvent-resistant synthetic rubber.

All Quiet on the Western Front   *All Quiet on the Western Front*, first published in Germany under the title *Im Westen Nichts Neues* in 1929 and translated into English the same year, was not only the finest novel of Erich Maria REMARQUE but also one of the most influential pieces of fiction to appear in the period between the two world wars. Based on Remarque's firsthand experience of trench warfare in World War I, it realistically and compassionately chronicles the hardships and embittering experiences endured by a group of young German soldiers, the most sensitive of whom is killed shortly before the armistice. By exposing the horror, cruelty, and uselessness of war, the novel quickly won worldwide acclaim and served as a symbol to the post–World War I LOST GENERATION. Banned by the Nazi regime for its antimilitaristic sentiments, the novel remained a focus for the pacifism that played a powerful political role in the Western democracies until the outbreak of World War II. An effective motion-picture version (directed by Lewis Milestone, 1930) became a film classic.

All Saints' Day   In the Christian church, All Saints' Day is the feast of all known and unknown SAINTS. It is observed on November 1 in the West. During the Middle Ages, the feast was called All Hallows' Day, giving its name to HALLOWEEN (All Hallows' Eve), the preceding day.

All Souls' Day   In Roman Catholicism, All Souls' Day is the feast that commemorates all the dead; special prayers and masses are offered for souls in PURGATORY. It is celebrated on November 2, the day following ALL SAINTS' DAY. In Buddhism, a similar observance is held as an expression of filial piety for deceased family members.

Allah   Allah is the proper name of God in ISLAM. He is one, unique and incomparable, and his unlimited sovereignty implies absolute freedom. But there is also a firm relationship between him, the Lord of Mercy, and all human beings, based on his being the creator and sustainer and on his providing in nature and history abundant signs of his goodness, reflected specifically in his sending of messengers and prophets. The interrelated emphases on

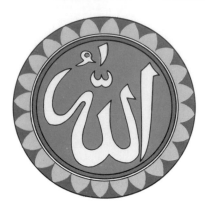

The Muslim name for God, Allah, in Arabic script and surrounded by an ornamental design, is used as a decorative emblem of Islam. Belief in Allah is the basis of the Muslim faith.

Allah's uniqueness and on the significance of his revelatory act are expressed in the Islamic witness: "There is no God but Allah, and MUHAMMAD is his messenger."

Allahabad   [a-lah-huh-bahd']   Allahabad is a north central city of India, situated at the confluence of the Ganges and the Yamuna, two of the most sacred Hindu rivers. Located in Uttar Pradesh state, it is the seat of the Uttar Pradesh High Court. Allahabad, whose population is 616,051 (1981), is a center of light industry and food processing. Allahabad University was established in 1887.

The Mogul emperor Akbar erected a fort there in 1583 and designated it Al-Ilahabad ("city of God"). The ancient name of the city was Prayag. The city was ceded to Britain in 1801 and was the scene of extensive violence during the Indian Mutiny (1857). Before 1947 the city was a center for India's nationalist movement and was the headquarters of the All-India Congress Committee until 1948. On Feb. 12, 1948, the ashes of Mahatma Gandhi were placed in the holy waters at Allahabad. Two important religious fairs—the annual Magh Mela and the Kumbha Mela, occurring every 12th year—are held in Allahabad.

Allegheny Mountains   The Allegheny Mountains, extending more than 800 km (500 mi) from central Pennsylvania to central West Virginia and southwestern Virginia, mark the eastern edge of the high Allegheny Plateau, which is the western part of the Appalachian mountain system. The highest peak is Spruce Knob in West Virginia (1,481 m/4,860 ft). The ridges are covered with forests of conifers and hardwoods, including oak, maple, and hickory. Huge deposits of coal are mined in West Virginia and Pennsylvania. The barrier of the Alleghenies delayed westward expansion of the early North American coastal settlements, and the region was not occupied until late in the 18th century.

Allegheny River   The Allegheny River rises in north central Pennsylvania, flows north into New York, and then turns south and southwest through Pennsylvania to Pittsburgh. At Pittsburgh it joins the Monongahela River to form the Ohio River.

The Allegheny is 523 km (325 mi) long, and it drains an area of 29,530 km² (11,400 mi²). It traverses a region once rich in petroleum and natural gas reserves that are now largely depleted. Industrial cities on its banks, in addition to Pittsburgh, are Olean, N.Y., and Warren and Oil City, Pa. Before railroads were built, the river was a busy commercial artery. A system of dams on the river and on its main tributaries—the Kiskiminetas, Clarion, and Conemaugh rivers—is important in flood control.

allegiance   Allegiance is the obligation to support and obey a leader or government in return for protection. In medieval times the vassals owed allegiance to their feudal lord, but now citizens owe allegiance to their government.

Traditionally, a national of one country could not change allegiance without that government's consent, but in 1868 the U.S. Congress declared that any U.S. citizen had the right to change allegiance at will. Britain has allowed free choice of allegiance since 1870. Countries in the Soviet bloc require official approval before a citizen can change allegiance.

allegory   An allegory, in poetry or prose, is a narrative in which the characters, events, and setting represent deeper truths—religious, moral, political, or personal—than those suggested by the surface story.

John Bunyan's *Pilgrim's Progress* (1678) is probably the best example of allegory in all literature. In the surface story a hero named Christian travels toward the Celestial City through a landscape marked by the Slough of Despond, the Valley of the Shadow of Death, and Vanity Fair, and he meets characters such as Faithful and Mr. Worldly Wisdom. The deeper story deals with individual salvation.

Like other symbolic literary forms, such as the BESTIARY, FABLE, and PARABLE, an allegory is an extended met aphor. It is distinguished from those simpler types chiefly by its greater length and complexity. Many classical myths may be considered allegorical, and Plato's myth of the cave in the *Republic* is explicitly so. The great age of allegory, however, was the medieval period. Interpretation of Scripture in terms of its allegorical content flourished, explaining the sensuous Song of Solomon as showing the love of God for his people. Allegory was also central to the popular morality play, which featured personages representing abstract concepts such as Everyman or Beauty.

Among the more famous allegories are the 13th-century ROMAN DE LA ROSE, parts of Dante's DIVINE COMEDY (1310–14), Langland's PIERS PLOWMAN (1377), Spenser's FAERIE QUEENE (1590, 1596), Dryden's *Absalom and Achitophel* (1681), Jonathan Swift's GULLIVER'S TRAVELS (1726), Samuel Butler's *Erewhon* (1872), and George Orwell's *Animal Farm* (1945).

Allen, Ethan   Ethan Allen, American Revolutionary soldier and frontiersman, was born in Litchfield, Conn., on Jan. 10, 1738, and moved in 1769 to Vermont—a territory then claimed by both New Hampshire and New York. He became leader of the Green Mountain Boys, a military force of Vermonters who fought against New York to protect their landholdings. When the American Revolution broke out, Allen's Green Mountain Boys helped to capture (May 10, 1775) Fort TICONDEROGA from the British. On Sept. 25, 1775, during the invasion of Canada, he was taken prisoner. After his release (May 6, 1778) Allen received the brevet rank of colonel in the Continental Army, but he did not serve. Upon returning to Vermont, he was given command of the militia with the rank of major general.

Vermont, although not recognized as independent by the Continental Congress, had declared itself a separate republic in 1777. Allen, along with his brother Ira (1751–1814), entered into negotiations with the British from 1779 on to obtain a guarantee of Vermont's independence. After the Treaty of Paris (1783), which ended the war, he continued to resist New York's claims. He did not live to see Vermont become a state. He died on Feb. 12, 1789.

Allen, Fred   Fred Allen was the stage name of John F. Sullivan, b. May 31, 1894, d. Mar. 17, 1956, known as the "king of the quick quip." Allen, a native of Cambridge, Mass., was an American comedian famous for his topical wit delivered in a dry, sad, singsong drawl. He first appeared as an inept juggler and then performed in Broadway musicals and in movies before achieving fame in the 1930s with the radio show "Town Hall Tonight." Allen wrote two autobiographies, *Treadmill to Oblivion* (1954) and *Much Ado about Me* (1956).

Allen, Frederick Lewis   Frederick Lewis Allen, b. Boston, July 5, 1890, d. Feb. 13, 1954, was a contemporary historian and editor. His best-sellers *Only Yesterday* (1931) and *Since Yesterday* (1940) were informal histories of the 1920s and '30s. As associate editor (1931–41) and editor (1941–53) of *Harper's Magazine*, he wrote and edited articles explaining contemporary social, political, and economic problems. Allen also wrote *The Lords of Creation* (1935), an economic history of the United States in the 20th century, and a 1949 biography of J. Pierpont Morgan.

Allen, Gracie   see BURNS AND ALLEN

Allen, Richard   Richard Allen, b. Philadelphia, Feb. 14, 1760, d. Mar. 26, 1831, the son of slave parents, was the founder and first bishop of the African Methodist Episcopal Church. Allen was asked to preach occasionally at St. George's Methodist Church (see METHODISM) in Philadelphia, and his sermons soon attracted large numbers of black people. One Sunday in 1787, some of the black worshipers were pulled from their knees during prayer by white members and asked to leave. They withdrew peacefully and under Allen's leadership organized the Free African Society. In 1793 this society became Bethel Church, an independent Methodist church. In 1799, Allen was ordained a deacon, the first black man regularly ordained to the ministry of the Methodist Church. In 1816 representatives of a number of black Methodist churches met in Philadelphia and organized the African Methodist Episcopal Church as the first national black denomination and chose Allen as their bishop. During his ministry he involved the church in various social issues.

Allen, Steve   Stephen Valentine Patrick Allen, b. New York City, Dec. 26, 1921, is an American humorist who specializes in low-key, informal comedy. He began as a disc jockey and songwriter and gained national fame as the creator and first host of NBC's "Tonight Show" (1954–56). His other television shows include the award-winning "Meeting of the Minds" (1977–78). Allen starred in the screen biography *The Benny Goodman Story* (1955) and has written hundreds of songs and film scores and more than 25 books.

Allen, Woody   Woody Allen is the stage name of Allen Stewart Konigsberg, b. Brooklyn, N.Y., Dec. 1, 1935. He is considered America's best living film comedian and one of its finest film directors. Allen's highly personal work focuses on contemporary fears and insecurities. Having written for such celebrities as Sid Caesar and Garry Moore, he became a successful stand-up comedian in the early 1960s. He made his screen debut as an actor-screenwriter in *What's New, Pussycat?* (1965).

Allen's first film project as director-writer-star was *Take the Money and Run* (1969). His other movies include *Bananas* (1971), *Sleeper* (1973), *The Front* (1976), *Annie Hall* (1977; four Academy Awards), *Interiors* (1978), *Manhattan* (1979), *Zelig* (1983), *Hannah and Her Sisters* (1986), *Radio Days* and *September* (both 1987), *Crimes and Misdemeanors* (1989), and *Alice* (1990). Allen's writings include comic and satirical collections and several Broadway plays, including *Play It Again, Sam* (1969; film, 1972).

Allenby, Edmund Henry Hynman, 1st Viscount Allenby of Megiddo   Edmund Henry Hynman Allenby, b. Apr. 23, 1861, d. May 14, 1936, was a British general who commanded the British forces in the Middle East during World War I. He went to France as commander of British cavalry and subsequently led (1915–17) the Third Army. Sent to Egypt, he began a systematic campaign to expel the Turks from Palestine, capturing Jerusalem in December 1917. His victory at Megiddo (Sept. 18–21, 1918) began the offensive that pushed the Turks back through Syria. Created (1919) a viscount, Allenby was high commissioner for Egypt (1919–25).

Allende, Salvador [ahl-yen'-day]   Salvador Allende Gossens, president of Chile from 1970 to 1973, was the second Marxian socialist (after Cheddi Jagan in British Guiana) elected to lead a country of the Western Hemisphere. Born July 26, 1908, into an upper-middle-class family, he became involved in radical politics while attending medical school at the University of Chile. In 1933 he helped organize Chile's Socialist party.
   After three unsuccessful campaigns for the presidency (1952, 1958, 1964), Allende was elected president in

Woody Allen appears here with Mia Farrow in a still from his black-and-white film Broadway Danny Rose *(1984). Allen's sense of humor and of humanity have become part and parcel of the American cinema—and therefore of the consciousness of the American moviegoing public. Allen's seriocomic movies—despite their New York City orientation—continue to zero in on widespread foibles in contemporary American life.*

Salvador Allende (left), the Marxist president of Chile, appears at the entrance of Moneda Palace on Sept. 11, 1973, during the coup that overthrew his government. He either was killed or committed suicide a few hours after the photograph was taken.

1970. His administration nationalized many industries (including the copper mines, in which U.S. business had a major investment) and accelerated land reform. This antagonized right-wing elements, and severe economic problems, aggravated by strikes, resulted in widespread disaffection, which was encouraged by the U.S. Central Intelligence Agency. Allende died on Sept. 11, 1973, during a military coup led by Augusto PINOCHET. His successors declared that he had committed suicide; his supporters claimed that he was murdered.

Allentown   Located on the Lehigh River in the Pennsylvania Dutch country in eastern Pennsylvania, Allentown is a busy industrial city with a great variety of manufactures. It has a population of 105,090 (1990) and is the seat of Lehigh County. It serves as the marketing, processing, and shipping center for the agricultural products of the fertile Lehigh Valley. Allentown is also an educational center, with Muhlenberg College, Lehigh Community College, and several other colleges located there.

The area was settled in the 1600s by Germans seeking religious freedom. The city, originally called Northhamptontown, was founded in 1762 by Pennsylvania Chief Justice William Allen. Allentown's reconstructed Zion Reformed Church contains a replica of the Liberty Bell.

allergy   Allergy is an abnormal reaction of the body to substances normally harmless, such as pollen, dust, certain foods, drugs, and insect stings. The term *allergy* is of Greek origin and means "abnormal response." An estimated 35 million people in the United States suffer from various allergies, some of which are mistaken for the common cold.

Allergy symptoms vary with the causative agent, which is called an allergen (or ANTIGEN), and with the part of the body affected. The symptoms, or allergic reactions, may include sneezing, watery eyes, and nasal congestion, as in hay fever and allergic rhinitis; a rash, stomach upset, and itchy swellings on the skin (HIVES), as in some food or drug allergies; spasms within the lungs that interfere with breathing, as in ASTHMA; and, in rare cases, anaphylactic shock (see ANAPHYLAXIS), which may lead to asphyxiation and death. Anaphylactic shock occasionally follows injections of penicillin or other drugs and may follow the sting of a bee or a wasp.

Common allergens, in addition to those mentioned above, include animal fur, feathers, cosmetics, textile dyes, smoke, bacteria, poison ivy and other plants, molds, chemical pollutants in the atmosphere, animal excretions, and blood serum received by transfusion, which may cause serum sickness. Even heat, cold, and light may cause allergy in susceptible people. Allergens may act following inhalation, injection, ingestion, or contact with the skin.

The Allergic Reaction

An allergic reaction occurs when the immune system, which is the body's normal defense against dangerous foreign substances, "mistakes" a normally harmless substance for an invader, such as a virus. No one knows why this abnormal reaction occurs in some people and not others. People who have this type of unusual immune system are said to be hypersensitive, and medical scientists often use the term *hypersensitivity* instead of *allergy*.

The body's immune system reacts to an allergen in many different ways to cause the discomforting symptoms of an allergy. In many allergies, the process begins when the allergen stimulates the immune system to manufacture ANTIBODY molecules called immunoglobulin E (IgE). The antibody molecules then combine with the allergen molecules and bind to cells called mast cells and basophils, causing the release of histamine (see ANTIHISTAMINE) and other active compounds. The histamine in turn affects the blood vessels and mucous membranes, leading to swelling, congestion, and leakage. Typically, these physiological changes lead to a runny nose if the allergen is airborne and inhaled. Other cells and other constituents of the blood serum can cause other types of allergies, such as POISON IVY dermatitis and serum sickness.

Types of Allergy

Allergies characteristically are not symptomatic with the first exposure to the allergen, and the symptoms occur only upon reexposure to the same agent. A person is said to have been sensitized by the first contact. That is, the immune system somehow "learns" to respond to the agent with an allergic reaction, but it reacts only at contacts that occur later. Sensitization of this type occurs in a variety of infectious diseases, such as brucellosis, glanders, SYPHILIS, and coccidioidomycosis, in which allergy develops to the infecting bacteria, fungi, or viruses.

In many persons, heredity is responsible for the tendency to be allergic to a variety of substances. Those persons with such inherited tendencies are called atopic. The common atopies include hay fever; asthma; infantile ECZEMA, which is an itchy skin lesion; contact DERMATITIS, which is a skin inflammation caused by poison ivy or a variety of chemicals that may contact the skin; and perhaps some food or drug allergies. Persons who have one disease in this group are more likely to have other diseases of the group than is the general population. Many people so afflicted have a family history of allergic diseases, usually of the same group.

Diagnosis

Allergic disease is diagnosed from the patient's medical history; symptoms; and so-called skin, or patch, tests, which help to identify the allergen. Small doses of many of the most common allergens are injected just below the skin in separate patches, and substances to which the patient is allergic usually cause redness and swelling at the injection site. Skin tests are often "false positive," however; they may indicate a sensitivity when in fact none exists.

Treatment

If the allergens can be identified, treatment of allergy may be merely the avoidance of the offending agents. If they cannot be avoided, as with house dust, pollen, insect stings, and perhaps animal fur, treatment may consist of so-called hyposensitization, or desensitization. In desensitization, small amounts of the substance that causes the allergy are injected under the skin during repeated visits to a physician. After many such injections, the body may "learn" not to react to the substance. With the determination in 1988 of the structure of the IgE receptors on mast cells, researchers hope to develop more direct means of blocking allergic reactions.

The discomforting symptoms of allergy are sometimes relieved by three types of medication: antihistamines, which block release of the histamines that cause swelling and congestion of mucous membranes; anti-inflammatory agents, such as corticosteroids; and decongestants, of short-term help but then counterproductive.

See also: IMMUNITY; RHINITIS.

alligator   Alligators are large temperate-zone amphibious reptiles. Members of the family Crocodylidae, order Crocodylia, they are related to CROCODILES but have a broad snout and lack the side notch that exposes the long fourth tooth of the lower jaw in crocodiles. In alligators the teeth of the upper jaw overlap those of the lower, hiding them from view.

The smaller of the two alligator species, the Chinese alligator (*Alligator sinensis*), is now found only in the lower Yangtze River valley of eastern China. It seldom attains a length of more than 1.5 m (5 ft). The American alligator (*A. mississippiensis*) is much larger; an individual specimen 5.8 m (19 ft 2 in) long is on record. Most such alligators have been killed by hunters, however, and a 3.6-m

In addition to consuming such small animals as fish, adult alligators can prey on much larger creatures, sometimes seizing, drowning, and consuming piecemeal full-grown cattle and deer.

(12 ft) animal is now considered large. American alligators are found in lakes, swamps, and slow-moving streams of the eastern U.S. coastal plain from North Carolina to Texas. For both species, individuals have been known to live more than 50 years.

Alligators eat a wide variety of animals. Small ones feed on insects, crayfish, minnows, and frogs. Adults eat larger fish, water birds, turtles, and various small mammals and occasionally consume larger mammals and such domestic animals as dogs and hogs. They rarely attack humans.

The American alligator's life history is better known than that of any other crocodilian. After mating in the spring, the female prepares, on the bank of a pond, a nest of water plants and mud that may be 1.8 m (6 ft) in diameter and 0.9 m (3 ft) high. The female then digs a hole in the top of the nest, lays 30 to 80 eggs in it, and covers them with wet vegetation and mud. The eggs are incubated by the heat of the Sun and hatch in about 60 days. The young call when hatched, and the mother alligator, who has been nearby during the incubation period, then carries them in her mouth or leads them to the pond, where they remain with her during their first year.

Because the belly skin of alligators lacks the bony plates typical of crocodile and CAIMAN skin, it can be made into an excellent leather for shoes, handbags, and other items. Alligators have therefore been prime targets for hide hunters, who greatly reduced populations in the past. The American alligator was placed under federal protection in 1969, and its numbers have since increased. In 1987 the U.S. Fish and Wildlife Service declared the species to be out of danger.

Allingham, Margery   Margery Allingham, b. May 20, 1904, d. June 30, 1966, an English writer, produced classics in two detective-novel genres—the thriller and the problem story. Both feature her series hero, Albert

Campion. The earlier stories, notably *Mystery Mile* (1930), abound in hair-raising adventures and criminal conspiracies. Beginning with *Death of a Ghost* (1934), the problem to be solved turns on the interaction of the characters, usually sophisticated Londoners.

alliteration SEE FIGURES OF SPEECH

Allosaurus [al'-oh-sohr-uhs] *Allosaurus* (Greek: *allos* ["other"]; *saurus* ["lizard"]), a large, carnivorous DINOSAUR of the Jurassic and Cretaceous periods, ranged in length from 5 to 12 m (16 to 40 ft) and probably weighed 4 metric tons (about 8,800 lb). Like all other theropods, *Allosaurus* walked on only two legs, using its long, heavy tail for balance. The short forelimbs bore three sharp, curved claws adapted for grasping prey. The hindlimbs were powerful, with birdlike feet. The head was large, nearly 1 m (3 ft) long, with long jaws and serrated, blade-like teeth.

See also: FOSSIL RECORD; GEOLOGIC TIME.

The Allosaurus *was a typical, meat-eating dinosaur of the Late Jurassic Period, about 150 million years ago. It used the huge claws on its forelimbs and powerful jaws to attack its prey.*

allotrope [al'-oh-trohp] Allotropes are the individual forms of an element that occur when atoms of the element can combine in more than one way. Elements that have allotropes include oxygen, carbon, sulfur, phosphorus, iron, and tin, among others. Usually one allotrope is most abundant and indefinitely stable at ordinary temperature and pressure, and the others can be formed only in unusual conditions. No general explanation can be given for the existence of more than one form; each case must be considered individually.

Allouez, Claude Jean [ahl-way'] Claude Jean Allouez, b. June 6, 1622, d. Aug. 27, 1689, a French Jesuit missionary in North America, baptized more than 10,000 Indians in the Great Lakes region. Arriving in Canada in 1658, he was appointed vicar general of the Northwest in 1663. He traveled in the territory west and south of the Great Lakes, working among the Potawatomi, the Miami, the Illinois, and other tribes. His reports, published in *The Jesuit Relations* (the Jesuits' record of their activities in North America, 1632–73), attracted attention to the Great Lakes area.

alloy An alloy is a mixture or solution of metals that may also include other chemical elements. Well-known alloys are BRASS, BRONZE, and STAINLESS STEEL (see IRON AND STEEL INDUSTRY). Alloys consisting of metals alloyed with semimetals, such as arsenic or antimony, or with nonmetals, such as carbon or silicon, are widely used. Alloys are divided into two basic groups: ferrous alloys, containing iron as the elemental metal, and nonferrous alloys, containing a metal other than iron, such as copper or titanium.

Structure of Alloys

Most components of alloys are partially miscible (capable of being mixed) or even completely miscible in the liquid state. Different types of alloys can be distinguished, depending on the degree of homogenization in the solid state.

Solid Solutions. These are relatively hard alloys in which the atoms of the components are randomly mixed throughout the crystals.

Intermetallic Compounds. In these alloys the atoms of the different compounds alternate regularly in the crystal lattice.

Multiphase Alloys. A multiphase alloy consists of a mechanical mixture or mixed phase of two or more kinds of crystals with different composition. Its structure and properties depend markedly on the cooling rate of the molten mass.

Ion-Implantation Alloys. Metal surfaces can be hardened and made more corrosion resistant by treating them with beams of selected ions, producing a surface alloy without changing the properties of the underlying material.

Properties of Alloys

A wide range of metal properties can be controlled by alloying, such as mechanical strength, corrosion-resistance, and electrical characteristics. An example of the change achievable in mechanical properties by alloying is the AMALGAM used for dental work. Alloys were first used to improve the mechanical strengths of metals, for example, bronze and brass. The tensile strength of iron can be nearly quadrupled by adding only a small amount of carbon.

For aircraft and aerospace applications, titanium alloys have been developed with tensile strengths up to

$1,400 \times 10^6$ N/m² (200,000 lb/in²), and with a density of only 60 percent that of steel. The development of jet engines, with their high internal temperatures, was made possible by the availability of superalloys based on nickel and cobalt, which are used for turbine blades.

Alloys with low melting temperatures can be made by using lead, cadmium, bismuth, and other low-melting-temperature metals. Various metal and ceramic alloys are also used as superconductors (see SUPERCONDUCTIVITY).

See also: METALLURGY.

Allport, Gordon W.

Gordon Willard Allport, b. Nov. 11, 1897, d. Oct. 9, 1967, was an American psychologist whose theory of PERSONALITY emphasized the uniqueness of the individual. Allport taught at Harvard (1924–26, 1930–67) and also edited the *Journal of Abnormal and Social Psychology* from 1937 to 1949. He maintained that motives were "functionally autonomous" and could not be said to be merely the search for pleasure and the avoidance of pain or derived from an individual's past history. Among his works are *Personality: A Psychological Interpretation* (1937) and *The Nature of Prejudice* (1954).

allspice

Allspice is the dried, nearly ripe berry of the allspice tree, *Pimenta dioica*, of the MYRTLE family. The name is derived from its flavor, which suggests a mixture of cloves, cinnamon, and nutmeg. Allspice is native to the West Indies and Central America but today is primarily cultivated in Jamaica. It is used whole or ground in pickling spices, mincemeat, roast meats, and baked goods. Its ESSENTIAL OIL is used in meat sauces, catsup, spice blends for pickles, and sausages, as well as for reproducing certain fruit flavors.

The allspice tree, a tropical tree with large, simple leaves and tiny flowers, yields fruit that turns a dark purple when it is dried. The unripe berry, used as a seasoning, is named for its flavor.

Allston, Washington

Washington Allston, b. Georgetown, S.C., Nov. 5, 1779, d. July 9, 1843, was a pioneer in American landscape painting and the first important American romantic painter. He studied (1801–03) with Benjamin WEST at the Royal Academy in London and at the Louvre and in Italy, where he absorbed the color techniques of the 16th-century Venetian school and the serene classicism of Nicolas POUSSIN. In Italy (1804–08) he befriended Samuel Taylor COLERIDGE, whose ideas strongly influenced him.

A subjective artist, Allston had greater success with lyric landscapes and seascapes, such as the introspective *Moonlit Landscape* (1819; Museum of Fine Arts, Boston), than with figure paintings. The monumental allegory, *Belshazzar's Feast* (begun 1817; Detroit Institute of Arts), was incomplete at the time of his death. Allston's use of color and light to create luminous, atmospheric effects had a great influence on the HUDSON RIVER SCHOOL.

allusion   SEE NARRATIVE AND DRAMATIC DEVICES

alluvial fans

An alluvial fan is a huge, flat cone of detritus deposited by a stream at the mouth of a channel, typically at the edge of a mountain-ringed desert basin.

A stream confined to a mountain canyon flows rapidly because the channel is deep and narrow. Upon leaving the mountains and reaching the flat floor of a basin, the stream spreads out. Flow decelerates, and the stream's ability to carry rock debris is reduced. The stream adjusts to this by depositing debris along its length.

Alluvial fans are common landforms that are produced when water-transported debris is swept out of canyons and deposited in valleys as low cones, resembling open Japanese fans.

The size of the debris diminishes as the stream spreads out and its flow slackens. Boulders are dumped at fan heads; silt and clay are carried beyond the fan margins. The shape of a fan depends on the processes that formed it. MUDFLOWS create the steepest fans, and streams with high rates of discharge form flatter fans than streams with low rates.

See also: DESERT; EROSION AND SEDIMENTATION; RIVER AND STREAM.

Alma-Ata [ahl-mah-ah-tah']   Alma-Ata is the capital of the Kazakh republic of the Soviet Union and the administrative center of Alma-Ata oblast, in southeast Kazakhstan. The city has a population of 1,128,000 (1989 est.). It is located at the foot of the Trans-Ili Mountains, a range of the Tian Shan system. Situated in an area of apple orchards, the city takes its name from the Kazakh *Almaty*, meaning "apple place."

Alma-Ata has a population that is 70% Russian and only 12% Kazakh. It is a diversified manufacturing center (apparel, food products, machinery) and is the site of a university. Founded by the Russians in 1854 as a strongpoint in their advance into Central Asia, it was known as Verny (meaning "loyal") until the present Kazakh name was adopted in 1921.

Alma-Tadema, Sir Lawrence [al-muh-tad'-uh-mah]   Sir Lawrence Alma-Tadema, b. Jan. 8, 1836, d. June 25, 1912, a Dutch-born British artist, achieved enormous success in his lifetime as a historical painter, specializing in elegant scenes of everyday life in ancient Greece and Rome, as he imagined it. Carefully correct in their archaeological detail, Alma-Tadema's anecdotal canvases exhibit faultless, almost photographic technique and finish. Such paintings as *A Reading from Homer* (c.1880–1885; Philadelphia Museum of Art) and *Spring* (1894; Getty Museum, Malibu) are regarded as exemplars of their period and tradition. An esteemed member of the Royal Academy, Alma-Tadema was knighted in 1899.

Almagest   see PTOLEMY.

Almagro, Diego de [ahl-mah'-groh]   Diego de Almagro, b. 1475, was a leader, with Francisco PIZARRO, in the Spanish conquest of Peru. He went to Panama in 1514 and joined Pizarro in the abortive 1524–25 expedition along the west coast of South America. Almagro was also Pizarro's partner in the second expedition of 1526–28 and in the conquest of Peru (1533).

In 1534 the king of Spain named Almagro leader of the expedition into what is now northern Argentina and Chile. In 1537 Almagro returned to Peru, where he put down an Indian insurrection and fought against Pizarro's brothers, who had taken control of Cuzco. He was ultimately defeated and executed on July 8, 1538, in Cuzco. His son continued the war with the Pizarros until 1542.

almanac   An almanac is a book or table comprising a calendar of the year. Today, almanacs also catalog miscellaneous events that occurred during the previous year and publish selected statistical data. Besides showing the days, weeks, and months, early almanacs registered feast days and saints' days, recorded astronomical phenomena, and sometimes contained meteorologic and agricultural forecasts and miscellaneous advice.

The term *almanac* may be derived from the Spanish-Arabic *almanakh* (*manakh*, "calendar", *manah*, "sundial"). Among the earlier almanacs were the "clog" almanacs of the Danes and Normans. These were blocks of wood on which days of the year were notched. The first printed almanac dates from 1457. Most English almanacs were published by the Stationers Company, the best known being the *Vox stellarum* of Francis Moore, first issued about 1699. The first American almanacs were printed in Cambridge, Mass., under the supervision of Harvard University, the earliest being *An Almanac for New England for the Year 1639*. Many followed in the 18th century, including Benjamin Franklin's POOR RICHARD'S ALMANACK (1733). The 18th-century almanac is considered the forerunner of the modern magazine. Between 1700 and 1900 more than 2,000 almanacs were issued in the United States. Many, such as Robert Thomas Baily's *The Old Farmer's Almanac*, founded in 1793, are still published.

almandine   see GARNET

Almeida, Francisco de [ahl-may'-thah]   Francisco de Almeida, b. c.1450, was the first viceroy of Portuguese India. He was appointed to that office in 1505 by King MANUEL I. On his way to India, Almeida captured Kilwa and Sofala and destroyed Mombasa on the East African coast. He then established himself at Cochin in India. In 1508 Almeida's son was killed in a naval battle against the Arabs, but the following year Almeida destroyed the Arab fleets at Diu. Replaced as viceroy by Afonso de ALBUQUERQUE, Almeida refused to accept his dismissal until 1509. On his way back to Europe, he was killed in an encounter with the Khoikhoin in South Africa on Mar. 1, 1510.

Almería [al-mair-ee'-uh]   Almería is the capital of Almería province in the Andalusian region of southeastern Spain. The city has a population of 154,911 (1987 est.). An important Mediterranean seaport at the head of the Gulf of Almería, it is an export point for white grapes, oranges, and other fruits. Almería's Costa del Sol beaches and its pleasant climate make it a tourist center. Landmarks include the cathedral (completed 1543) and the Moorish fort Alcazaba.

Almería was settled by Phoenicians about 238 BC. Subsequently it was the Roman city of Portus Magnus and then a Moorish seaport. The city was captured in 1147 by Alfonso VII of Castile but was retaken by the

Moors, who held it until 1489 when it reverted to Spain. It was seriously damaged during the Spanish Civil War (1937).

almond [ah'-muhnd]   The almond tree, *Prunus amygdalus*—known alternatively as *Prunus dulcis*—produces the oldest and most widely grown of all of the world's NUT crops. The almond tree is indigenous to western Asia and North Africa. Today it is grown in most temperate regions. A member of the rose family and similar in appearance to the peach tree, the almond tree reaches a height of 3–7 m (9–22 ft) and has pink or white flowers that bloom in early spring. The dry, leathery almond fruit surrounds a seed or kernel—the almond nut—which is harvested when the fruit dries and splits open.

Of the two major types of almonds grown, the sweet almond, *P. dulcis,* is cultivated for its edible nut. The bitter almond, *P. amara,* is inedible but contains an oil—also present in the sweet almond and in the ripe kernels of the apricot and peach—which, when combined with water, yields hydrocyanic (prussic) acid and benzaldehyde, the ESSENTIAL OIL of bitter almonds. The oil is used in making flavoring extracts and in some sedative medicines.

Almond trees are propagated primarily by budding, with bitter almond, almond, or peach seedlings used as rootstocks. Harvests begin the fourth year after planting, and full production is reached by the seventh.

The sweet almond tree is grown in temperate areas for its fragrant blossoms as well as for its nuts. A leathery hull surrounds the woody shell of a nut and splits open when the kernel is ripe. The milky white kernel is consumed raw or processed as almond oil and almond meal.

aloe [al'-oh]   Aloe is any of about 200 species and hybrids of perennial succulent plants that belong to the lily family, Liliaceae. They are used as landscape plants in dry,

The ox-tongue gasteria, or warty aloe, is an easy-to-grow, attractive aloe that has white raised spots covering its leaves.

frost-free areas and are sometimes grown as houseplants. Their leaves are fleshy, stiff, and spiny along the edges and are often crowded together into a rosette. The flowers, which are mostly reddish, are produced on showy spikes that may extend 6 m (20 ft) above the ground; some species produce yellow, orange, or whitish-green flowers. Water-aloe is sometimes designated *Stratiotes aloides*, or the water soldier. Juice from the leaves is used to treat burns. The plant is also a source of a purgative drug.

Alonso, Alicia   Alicia Alonso, born Martinez, in Havana, Cuba, on Dec. 21, 1921, is considered one of the outstanding international ballerinas. Alonso danced with the American Ballet Theatre intermittently from 1941 to 1960. Her rise was plagued by recurring eye problems, involving several operations and lengthy periods of immobile recuperation. Alonso emerged to become one of the great interpreters of Adolphe Adam's *Giselle*, as well as the first to dance the demanding ballerina role in George Balanchine's *Theme and Variations*. With her husband, Fernando Alonso, she founded the Ballet Alicia Alonso (1948), renamed Ballet de Cuba (1955), which became in 1961 the National Ballet of Cuba.

Alorese [al'-uh-reez]   The Alorese are an Indonesian people who inhabit the mountainous forest interior of Alor, an island located 32 km (20 mi) north of Timor, and the nearby island of Pantar. The present population of Alorese is estimated at more than 100,000. They speak a language associated with the Malayo-Polynesian linguistic family (see MALAYO-POLYNESIAN LANGUAGES).

The Alorese live in settled villages and raise rice, corn, and various root crops. Their religion is animistic and mainly concerned with honoring or appeasing environmental and guardian spirits.

Alouette [al-oo-et']   *Alouette* (French, "lark"), launched on Sept. 28, 1962, was Canada's first artificial space SATELLITE. Developed to measure variations in the density of electrons in the ionosphere as a function of time of day and latitude, it was a cooperative scientific effort in NASA's Topside Sounder program.

See also: SPACE PROGRAMS, NATIONAL.

Alp-Arslan Alp-Arslan, b. *c.*1030, d. 1073, the second sultan and real builder of the Turkish Great SELJUK empire, began his reign in 1063. Successfully fighting off the challenge of the Ghaznavids of Afghanistan and other dynasties that had arisen after the decline of the Abbasid empire of Baghdad, Alp-Arslan restored unity to Iran and Iraq. He then undertook a series of expeditions into Anatolia, where he defeated (1071) the Byzantines at the Battle of Manzikert, and ravaged the Armenian and Georgian territories in the Caucasus. His victorious campaigns opened the way to the subsequent occupation of Anatolia by the Turks. Aided by his minister Nizam al-Mulk, Alp-Arslan also defended Sunnite Islam against the influence of the Shiite Fatimid dynasty of Egypt.

---

alpaca [al-pak'-uh] The alpaca is a domesticated LLAMA, *Lama pacos*, bred in South America principally for its wool. Because its fleece is longer and more silky than that of other llama species, it was prized by the Inca, who wove its hair into robes reserved for royalty. Today, alpaca is used to make soft, lustrous, pile-weave fabrics for coats. The alpaca requires about two years, spent high in the Andes, to produce a full growth of wool.

The alpaca grows a lightweight coat of wool that insulates the animal against cold weather of the high Andes plains. The wool is spun and woven into a fine cloth, valued for its softness and warmth.

Alpha Centauri see STAR

alpha particle see RADIOACTIVITY

alphabet see WRITING SYSTEMS, EVOLUTION OF

Alphonsus Liguori, Saint [lee-gwaw'-ree] Saint Alphonsus Liguori, b. Sept. 27, 1696, d. Aug. 1, 1787, an Italian churchman, founded the Congregation of the Most Holy Redeemer (the Redemptorists) in 1732. His original name was Alfonso Maria de Liguori. He was or-

dained a priest in 1726 and served as bishop of Sant' Agata dei Goti from 1762 to 1775. In his writings on moral theology he developed a system of casuistry tending toward a stricter interpretation of the law in the application of ethical principles. Canonized May 26, 1839, he was made a Doctor of the Church in 1871 and patron of confessors and moralists in 1950. Feast day: Aug. 1 (formerly Aug. 2).

---

alphorn The alphorn is a wooden, tubular instrument best known in its Swiss form, although it is commonly found in many parts of the world. It may be straight or curved and 1.5 to 4 m (3 to 10 ft) in length. The alphorn does not have valves or finger holes and so can play only the pitches in the natural harmonic series. Swiss mountain herdsmen still use the instrument to summon their cows. Numerous composers have used the characteristic alphorn melodies in orchestral pieces but have given them to traditional orchestral instruments. The German name is *Alpenhorn.*

The alphorn, or alpenhorn, is a wooden horn made without finger holes or valves. Although the alphorn is still used by Swiss herders to call their cattle, the instrument is primarily of interest to tourists.

Alps The Alps constitute Europe's most extensive mountain system, encompassing parts of France, Italy, Switzerland, Germany, Austria, Yugoslavia, and most of Liechtenstein. Beginning along the Mediterranean, at the French-Italian border, as a relatively narrow chain, the mountains gradually widen into a broad arc west of Vienna. More than 965 km (600 mi) long and 200 km (125 mi) wide, they cover an area of more than 207,200 km² (80,000 mi²).

Peaks average 1,800-2,400 m (5,940-7,920 ft), and many rise above 3,050 m (10,000 ft). About 1,200 mountain glaciers cover an area of 3,900 km² (1,500 mi²).

Regional Cultures. Throughout history, this extensive mountain system has acted as a barrier between Mediterranean and northern cultures. However, communication between civilizations has been continuous, aided in part by a series of mountain passes and longitudinal valleys. The term *alps* refers to a specific landscape feature, the high mountain pastures. The idea of an alpine way of life is based on the economy and life-style developed within this region.

The cultural diversity of the region is apparent from the variety of languages: French, German, Italian, Slovene, and Romansh. Population density varies with altitude. The Alpine forelands and broader longitudinal valleys are more densely populated than the narrower, more isolated valleys and summit areas.

Topography. Europe's newest folded mountain range, the Alps have not yet been worn down to old mountain stumps. Three zones are recognized: a central zone of crystalline mountain rocks, surrounded by two zones of limestone, one to the north and one to the south. The parallel chains of mountains are separated by longitudinal valleys in many places. Where major rivers have turned and broken through the limestone ranges, transverse valleys have formed. Alpine glaciers of the ICE AGES filled these valleys and portions of the surrounding plains as well. When the glaciers retreated, they left dams of MO-RAINE, creating finger lakes such as Como, Maggiore, and Geneva.

The famed Matterhorn, one of the Pennine Alps, juts into the skies near the Italo-Swiss border. The alpine village of Zermatt (foreground) is an internationally known ski resort.

The Alps can be divided into the western and eastern sections along a line from Lake Como north to the Italo-Swiss border, through Splügen Pass, and down the Rhine

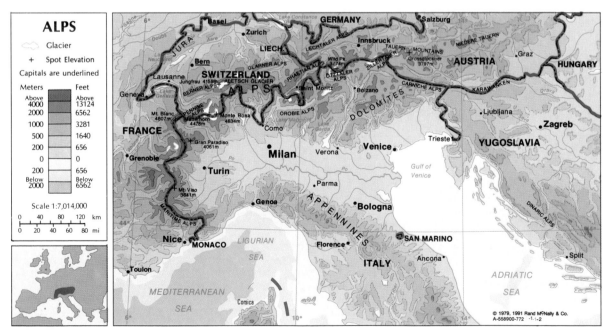

ALPS

Glacier
+ Spot Elevation
Capitals are underlined

Meters	Feet
Above 4000	Above 13124
2000	6562
1000	3281
500	1640
200	656
0	0
200	656
Below 2000	Below 6562

Scale 1:7,014,000

0 40 80 120 km
0 20 40 60 80 mi

© 1979, 1991 Rand McNally & Co.
A-558900-772 -1-1-2

Valley to Lake Constance. The western Alps are higher and narrower, with more extensive glaciers and deeply incised valleys. The longitudinal valleys of the eastern Alps are wider, and a number of important cities are located in them. Mont BLANC (4,807 m/15,771 ft) is the highest peak in the western Alps; Piz Bernina (4,048 m/13,281 ft) is the highest in the eastern Alps.

Climate and Drainage. Topographic influences give rise to a complex mosaic of microclimates. Precipitation and average temperatures and extremes in temperature decrease with altitude. The Rhine and Rhône rise in the central Alps, as do tributaries of the Po, such as the Ticino and the Oglio, and major Danube tributaries, such as the Inn, the Salzach, and the Enns. The Alps thus form a divide between Atlantic, Mediterranean, and Black Sea drainage.

Vegetation and Animal Life. The montaine, or lower level, has deciduous trees extending up to about 1,370 m (4,500 ft). Next is a zone of coniferous forests up to about 1,675 m (5,500 ft), then a zone of bare rocks and grass slopes (alps), followed by the snow line, ranging from 2,440 m (8,000 ft) to 3,050 m (10,000 ft) depending on location.

Alsace-Lorraine [al-sas'-lohr-rayn']   Alsace and Lorraine (German: Elsass and Lothringen) are two historic provinces in eastern France. Part of the Holy Roman Empire until 1648, Alsace was added to France by the Treaty of Ryswick in 1697. Lorraine was part of the kingdom of LOTHARINGIA, which was divided (959) into the duchies of Lower and Upper Lorraine. The latter, which became modern Lorraine, was an independent but much-fought-over duchy until 1766. Between 1871 and 1918, Alsace (the departments of Bas-Rhin and Haut-Rhin) and the eastern part of Lorraine (now the department of Moselle) were annexed to Germany as a result of France's defeat in the Franco-Prussian War. From 1919 to 1940 the area belonged to France; from 1940 to 1945, to Germany. It was returned to France in 1945. The three departments of Meuse, Meurthe-et-Moselle, and Vosges remained French.

Geologically western Lorraine is composed of clay vales separated by the north-south trending limestone ridges of the Côtes de Meuse and Côtes de Moselle. The heavy soils of the vales support mixed farming—dairying, oats, and wheat. The ridges are barriers to communication and invasion. METZ, NANCY, VERDUN, Thionville, and Toul are route centers and fortress cities defending gaps in the ridges. The battle for Verdun was one of the bloodiest of World War I.

The Lorraine iron ore fields, the second-highest-producing fields in Western Europe, run from Nancy northward to the primary iron and steel district around Longwy, Thionville, and Metz. The French part of the Saar coalfield, containing half the French reserves, lies 64 km (40 mi) to the east.

Southeastward, Lorraine rises gradually to the summits of the Vosges. The political and linguistic divide be-

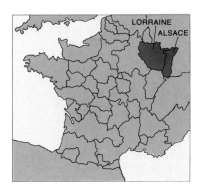

The historic French provinces of Alsace and Lorraine lie along the border between the French- and German-speaking areas of Europe. From 1871 to 1918 and from 1940 to 1945, Alsace and part of Lorraine belonged to Germany.

tween French-speaking Lorraine and German-speaking Alsace runs along its crest. At the foot of the steep eastern slope of the Vosges is a famous vineyard region. An adjoining belt of fertile loess soils produces cereals, fruit, tobacco, and vegetables. It also produces hops for Alsatian and German breweries.

STRASBOURG, a major port on the Rhine famous for its university and its pâté, is the traditional capital of Alsace. Nancy is the region's traditional capital and university center. Mulhouse, with a chemical industry based on substantial local potash deposits, and Colmar are centers of the textile industry of Alsace and eastern Lorraine.

Alsop, Joseph and Stewart   Joseph and Stewart Alsop, in collaboration and separately, became two of the best-known reporter-columnists in American journalism. In the *Reporter's Trade* (1958) they conveyed their belief that the columnist is primarily a reporter. **Joseph**, b. Avon, Conn., Oct. 11, 1910, d. Aug. 28, 1989, was educated at Harvard University; his brother **Stewart**, b. Avon, Conn., May 17, 1914, d. May 26, 1974, at Yale. Joseph was cowriter with Robert Kintner of the column "The Capital Parade" from 1937 to 1940. The Alsop brothers later collaborated (1945–58) on the widely syndicated column "Matter of Fact." In tones of approaching doom, they wrote many exclusive stories about ballistic-missile developments in the 1950s.

Alston, Walter   Walter Emmons Alston, b. Butler County, Ohio, Dec. 1, 1911, d. Oct. 1, 1984, was a surprise choice when named to manage the Brooklyn Dodgers starting in 1954, but he stayed 23 years to lead the baseball team (which moved to Los Angeles in 1958) to its greatest successes. "Smokey" Alston made the majors as a player for the St. Louis Cardinals in 1936 but went to bat only one time. As a manager for the Dodgers' minor-league chain in the 1940s, he helped prepare some of the first black players for their historic integration of major-league baseball. As a big-league manager, he won the World Series in 1955 and again in 1959, 1963, and 1965. He led the team to three other National League pennants, was manager of the year three times, and was inducted (1983) into the Hall of Fame.

Altai Mountains [al'-ty]   The Altai Mountains (Mongolian: Altain-ula, "mountains of gold") are an extensive mountain system of Central Asia located at the juncture of the USSR, China, and Mongolia. They cover about 1,600 km (1,000 mi). The range rises to a maximum elevation of 4,653 m (15,266 ft) in the Taban Bogdo Knot. The Altai comprises the Sayan, the Katun, the Sailyugem, and the Tannu-Ola. The 1,450-km-long (900-mi) Mongolian Altai is the longest range in the system. About 70% of the mountain territory is under dense forest. The range's mean elevation is about 1,500 m (5,000 ft), and steep, deeply eroded mountainsides are typical.

Formed by geological uplift 300 million years ago, the Altai ranges have slowly been worn down to smooth contours. Glaciers, which still cover an area of almost 1,554 km² (600 mi²), deepened their valleys and fed many lakes and rivers. The Altai contain the source of the Ob, the Irtysh, and the tributaries of the Yenisei. The region has a continental climate. Silver, copper, lead, zinc, and mercury are mined in eastern Kazakh republic where much of the range lies.

Tribal Altaic herders (Kazakhs, Mongolikhalks, and Oyrat) were the original inhabitants, but the region's resources are drawing immigrants, especially in the USSR.

Altaic languages   see Ural-Altaic languages

Altamira [ahl-tah-mee'-rah]   Altamira is the site of a cave near Santillana del Mar in the province of Santander, northeast Spain. Paleolithic cave paintings discovered there in 1879 by Don Marcelino de Sautuola are acknowledged as one of the summits of prehistoric art. The painted ceiling near the entrance depicts, in color, large animals, mainly bison. Their vivid impact is enhanced by the artists' apparent incorporation of the natural protru-

A reclining bison appears in a painting from the Altamira cave in Spain. The work is one of a number of naturalistic animal paintings on the walls and ceiling of the cave.

sions and hollows of the surface into the painted and engraved representations. In the rear of the cave are paintings of animals and symbols, outlined in black and red pigment, and many engravings, the finest being that of a group of hinds. The cave art is dated from the late Solutrean to the middle Magdalenian periods.

altar   An altar is a table or elevated platform intended for the offering of a religious sacrifice. Ancient altars sometimes were composed of the ashes of previous offerings compacted by time, more often of earth or stone. The size was determined by its specific use: small altars were used for the burning of incense, larger altars were required for the offering of animals. Altars were commonly built outdoors, usually in a sacred enclosure in front of a temple.

In the Christian church, the altar is a tablelike structure that serves as the focal point of worship and on which the Eucharist is celebrated. Although the table, or mensa, is the only essential part of an altar, other features were added through the centuries: a platform (predella), a canopy, a shelf (retable), a screen (reredos), and a tabernacle (receptacle) for storing the consecrated elements of the Eucharist.

Traditionally, the altar stood at the east end of the church in the center of the sanctuary, and the position of the altar determined the orientation of the building. The altar was frequently built over a crypt containing the remains of a saint or martyr. Later, additional altars were sometimes installed along the side walls of a church or in chapels dedicated to saints.

During the Middle Ages, altars were lavished with rich decorations by artists and sculptors. For example, the altar of the Capella della Nunziata at the cathedral of Pisa is famous for a cover worked in chased silver. The antique altar in Saint Mark's Basilica in Venice is ornamented with carved anchors and dolphins. The high altar of Saint Peter's Basilica in the Vatican is highlighted by Bernini's baldachino, one of the most magnificent altar decorations in Christendom. Many of the best-known examples of Italian and Flemish painting originally formed parts of altarpieces.

Altdorfer, Albrecht [ahlt'-dorf-ur, ahl'-brekt]   Albrecht Altdorfer, b. 1480, d. Feb. 12, 1538, a German Renaissance painter, draftsman, printmaker, and architect, is best known as the developer of pure landscape painting. He is generally considered the greatest artist in the Danube School, which also included Lucas Cranach the Elder, Wolfgang Huber, Jörg Breu, and Jörg Kölderer.

Altdorfer may have learned his precision in draftsmanship and landscape painting in Regensburg from his father, who was an illuminator, and from his study of Albrecht Dürer's and Cranach's paintings and Michael Pacher's *St. Wolfgang* altarpiece.

The Emperor Maximilian I employed him along with such rivals as Dürer and others to make numerous woodcuts, engravings, and illuminations. Altdorfer's style re-

Albrecht Altdorfer, the foremost artist of the Danube School, was the father of modern landscape painting. His Danube Landscape near Regensburg *(c. 1520–25) depicts the region surrounding his home town. (Alte Pinakothek, Munich.)*

mained independent and personal. His constant concern with natural growth, his faultless depiction of foliage and trees, and his ability to integrate human moods and action with landscape are evidenced in his St. Florian altarpiece (1509–18), since broken up and dispersed to museums in Nuremberg, Prague, and Florence. Altdorfer's interest in magic, ruins, fantastic landscape, and mysterious light are exemplified in his masterpiece of large spatial organization, *The Battle of Alexander* (1529; Alte Pinakothek, Munich).

alteration, mineral Alteration is the geologic process whereby natural chemical solutions react with rocks to form new MINERALS. The most common alteration minerals, precipitated from hot aqueous (water-based) solutions reacting with GRANITE and other IGNEOUS ROCKS, are quartz, mica, clay, feldspar, and pyrite. They are usually distributed in regular patterns around ORE DEPOSITS. Prospectors use alteration minerals as clues in searching for ore. OXIDE MINERALS formed by the WEATHERING of ore minerals on or near the earth's surface serve as guides to subsurface ore.

Alteration reactions may cause a mineral-forming so-

lution to precipitate ore minerals, or make a rock permeable enough to permit ore-forming solutions to enter it.

alternating current A direct current (DC) always flows through a conductor in one direction, but an alternating current (AC) constantly reverses itself as a result of reversing electromotive force. One complete reversal is a cycle, and the number of cycles per second is the frequency of the alternating current. The standard frequency of alternating current in the United States and the rest of North America is 60 Hz (1 Hz, or hertz, equals 1 cycle per second); in Europe it is 50 Hz. Originally, only direct current was generated for public use. The enormous advantages of alternating current were not realized until George Westinghouse developed the TRANSFORMER in the late 19th century. Buffalo, N.Y., was the first U.S. city to be lighted using alternating current.

The transformer made it possible to change the voltage (and therefore the current) of AC by a simple, static device; this was not possible with DC. When electricity is transmitted, power loss is minimized by stepping up the voltage from the generator, thus transmitting a high voltage, and stepping down the voltage at the user's end. When required, DC is easily obtained from an AC current with a RECTIFIER. Converting DC to AC requires an inverter, which is a more complex device. AC motors and alternators (AC generators) have greater reliability than their DC counterparts, because they do not require commutators (metal slip rings for picking up current). In most countries power is supplied at 240 V; exceptions are the United States and Canada, which supply 110 V of electricity. Numerous simple electrical devices, such as the light bulb, work equally well on AC or DC, although their rates of power consumption may differ slightly.

See also: CIRCUIT, ELECTRIC; ELECTRICITY; POWER, GENERATION AND TRANSMISSION OF.

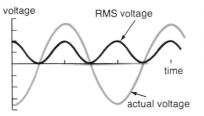

voltage | RMS voltage | time | actual voltage

Alternating currents exhibit a definite relation between rms and peak voltages.

alternation of generations *Alternation of generations* is a biological term referring to the reproductive cycle in which a sexual stage alternates with an asexual stage. This is common in most plant groups, including some algae, ferns, mosses, and seed plants. It is rare in the animal kingdom, coelenterates (jellyfish, sea anemones, hydra) being one notable exception (see REPRODUCTION).

The life cycle comprises two structurally distinct organisms, the gametophyte (sexual form) and the sporophyte (asexual form). The gametophyte produces male and female gametes, or sex cells, that fuse to form a zygote, which develops into the embryo of the sporophyte, or asexual generation. The sporophyte gives rise to the gametophyte through spore or somatic-cell production.

The evolutionary trend in vascular plants (those having stems, roots, and leaves) has been toward the reduction in size of the gametophyte stage. Extreme reduction has occurred in flowering plants in which the sexual stage is represented by only a few cells retained in the flower. Thus the sporophyte has become the dominant generation, and the gametophyte is actually dependent on the sporophyte. In mosses, the gametophyte is dominant, and the sporophyte is dependent during its entire existence.

Altgeld, John Peter   John Peter Altgeld, b. Germany, Dec. 30, 1847, d. Mar. 12, 1902, was a controversial governor (1892–96) of Illinois. Raised on an Ohio farm, Altgeld was a Union soldier in the Civil War, became a teacher, then a lawyer, and first held political office as a Democratic county attorney in Missouri.

Moving to Chicago, he found law unremunerative and became a wealthy builder. He was elected county judge (1886) and then governor of Illinois.

In 1893, Altgeld caused a furor when he pardoned the anarchists convicted as a result of the HAYMARKET RIOT, citing an unfair trial. The next year he protested vehemently when President Grover Cleveland sent troops into Chicago during the PULLMAN STRIKE, because the local authorities felt competent to handle the situation. Convinced that Cleveland represented corporate interests, Altgeld led the FREE SILVER forces in the Democratic party, wrested control of the 1896 national convention from Cleveland, and wrote a platform that reshaped the party. He was defeated in his bid for reelection and, his wealth gone, practiced law until his death.

altimeter   An altimeter is an instrument that measures the height above a reference surface, such as sea level or the ground surface. This MEASUREMENT can be based on the variation of atmospheric pressure with changing height above the Earth's surface. In essence, such an altimeter is an aneroid BAROMETER graduated in feet or meters instead of millibars. This is the type used by mountaineers to ascertain their height above sea level. An altimeter is a necessary part of an aircraft's equipment. A sophisticated radio altimeter, in which a pulse of radio energy is beamed downward and the echo received on the aircraft, enables a pilot to judge the altitude. Signals from a radio altimeter are sometimes incorporated into a control system used for automatic landing.

altitude   In astronomy, navigation, and surveying, the altitude of a celestial object is its angular distance above or below the celestial horizon. The angular distance is measured along the vertical circle—the circle passing through both the celestial object and the zenith, an imaginary point directly above the observer. A celestial ob-

ject's altitude and azimuth—the angular distance of its vertical circle from the north (or south) vertical circle, measuring eastward from that circle—are used to give its position on the CELESTIAL SPHERE, as observed at a specific moment of time from a specific location.

See also: COORDINATE SYSTEMS (ASTRONOMY).

Altman, Robert B.   Robert B. Altman, b. Kansas City, Mo., Feb. 20, 1925, was recognized as a trend-setting directorial stylist in American films in the 1970s. He first won acclaim for *M*A*S*H* (1970). *McCabe & Mrs. Miller* (1971), *The Long Goodbye* (1973), and *California Split* (1974) drew increasing attention for their textural richness, multilayered soundtracks, and improvisatory flow. With *Nashville* (1975) Altman had his second commercial success. Critics saw less quality in such films as *Buffalo Bill and the Indians* (1976), *3 Women* (1977), *Quintet* (1979), and *Beyond Therapy* (1987) but praised *Thieves Like Us* (1974) and *Health* (1979). Other credits include *Come Back to the 5 and Dime Jimmy Dean, Jimmy Dean* (stage and film, 1982), the films *Streamers* (1983), *Fool for Love* (1985), and *Vincent and Theo* (1990), and television projects including *The Dumb Waiter* (1987), *The Caine Mutiny Court-Martial* (1988), and *Tanner '88: The Dark Horse*, a collaboration with Garry Trudeau.

alto   see CONTRALTO

Altoona   Surrounded by the rugged Allegheny Mountains in a coal-mining area of south central Pennsylvania, Altoona is an industrial city with a population of 57,078 (1980). It was founded in 1849 by the Pennsylvania Railroad Company, which chose that site to begin the difficult span across the Alleghenies. Altoona is still an important railroad center, with extensive trackage and enormous construction and repair shops. It also has many new diversified manufactures. To the northwest, Wopsononock Mountain, with a height of more than 780 m (2,580 ft), offers a view of six counties. The famous Horseshoe (railroad) Curve, which moves through a central angle of 220 degrees, is 8 km (5 mi) to the west.

altruism   [al'-troo-izm]   Altruism is behavior that benefits others at some cost to the individual. As a philosophical concept, altruism was originally devised by Auguste Comte as an ethical antithesis to EGOISM. In recent years social scientists and biologists have been especially interested in altruism, although the two groups approach the subject differently.

To most social scientists, altruism occurs when one individual consciously comes to the aid of another, without expecting anything in return. Several things are believed to influence this behavior: empathy, an emotional response that results from being aware of another's emotions; group norms, society's expectation of how people "should" behave toward others; social learning, the personal experiences one has with others; and immediate context, the actual situation at the time an altruistic act is called for (being in a good mood, considering oneself helpful, being with others rather than being alone).

Social scientists emphasize the importance of social experiences in producing altruistic behavior. By contrast, biologists, especially sociobiologists, take a different position. They view altruism as any behavior that reduces the Darwinian fitness (reproductive success) of the altruist while increasing the fitness of another. Accordingly, the occurrence of altruism in nature is a biological puzzle, since genes whose effect is to make themselves more rare in future generations should soon disappear altogether. Many examples of animal altruism, however, are known: worker bees, ants, and wasps are themselves sterile while assisting the queen to reproduce. It is common for animals to share food, help provide for another's young, defend others against predators, and give alarm calls when a predator appears. All these acts enhance the fitness of others while often reducing that of the altruist (see SOCIO-BIOLOGY).

Sociobiologists have several explanations for the evolution of altruism. First, a behavior may only seem altruistic. It might actually contribute to one's reproductive success and thus be a selfish act after all. Second, apparent altruism could arise by natural selection if the giver eventually receives comparable benefits from the getter. This reciprocity is actually selfish behavior, although both parties ultimately benefit.

Two mechanisms for the evolution of behavior that actually reduce the personal fitness of the altruist are recognized by sociobiologists: kin selection and group selection. Kin selection is actually genetic selfishness. Altruistic genes can prosper as long as they succeed in making enough copies of themselves in relatives who are fitter because of the altruistic act.

The notion of group selection is that altruism could theoretically be selected if altruists benefited others within the group so that the group as a whole did better than other groups that lacked altruists. Individual altruists, however, would be at a disadvantage within each group. Therefore, group selection is considered less likely than kin selection as a mechanism for evolving altruism, although it is theoretically possible.

alum An alum is any of a group of compounds that contain the sulfates of two different metals—aluminum is often one of the metals—and water of hydration. Commercially, the most important alums are aluminum potassium alum, also known as potassium alum, or potash alum; and aluminum ammonium alum. Other double sulfates known as alum include ferric ammonium sulfate (ferric alum), sodium aluminum sulfate (soda alum), and potassium chromium sulfate (chrome alum). The alums have many uses, particularly in paper manufacture, in textile dyeing, in fireproofing, in water purification, and in medicine as astringents, styptics, and emetics.

alumina Alumina, or aluminum oxide, Al_2O_3, is the compound from which commercial aluminum is produced. It occurs in nature as both CORUNDUM and as an important constituent of BAUXITE, which is mined and refined to produce a purified, calcined alumina in the form of a fine white powder.

Alumina is also used to make abrasives and high-temperature refractories, ceramics, and glass. Heated alumina has a porous structure that easily absorbs moisture and vapors; it is therefore used to dehydrate liquids and gases. Aluminum sulfate, or activated alumina—the product of alumina, or clay, or bauxite, treated with sulfuric acid—is important in paper manufacture as a color binder and a filler. Other alumina compounds produce alums and are used for waterproofing fabrics and as the antiperspirant in commercial deodorants.

aluminum Aluminum is the third most abundant element (8%) in the Earth's crust, exceeded by oxygen (47%) and silicon (28%). Because of its strong affinity to oxygen, aluminum never occurs as a metal in nature but is found only in the form of its compounds, such as alumina (Al_2O_3).

The metal's name is derived from *alumen*, the Latin name for alum. In 1807, Sir Humphry DAVY assigned the name *alumium* to the metal and later agreed to change it to *aluminum*. Shortly thereafter, the name *aluminium* was adopted to conform with the *-ium* ending of most elements, and this spelling is now in general use throughout the world, except in the United States and Italy (where *alluminio* is used).

Physical Properties

Aluminum, symbol Al, is a silvery white metal in Group IIIA of the periodic table. Its atomic number is 13, its atomic weight 26.9815. It is ductile, nonmagnetic, and an excellent conductor of heat and electricity. The density of aluminum at 20° C is 2.699 g/cm³ (0.1 lb/in³); it melts at 660.24° C and boils at 2,450° C.

The role aluminum plays in human physiology is not known. Although the metal is ingested through food and water, most of it is believed to be excreted. Aluminum has been detected in the brain cells of ALZHEIMER'S patients, but it is not known whether the metal's presence is a cause or an effect of the disease.

Lightness and Strength. Perhaps the best-known quality of aluminum is its light weight; it is only about one-third as dense as iron, copper, or zinc. Despite its light weight, it can easily be made strong enough to replace heavier and more costly metals in thousands of applications. Aluminum ALLOYS have the highest strength-to-weight characteristics of any commercial metal.

Resistance to Corrosion. Aluminum and its various alloys are highly resistant to corrosion. When exposed to air, the metal develops a thin film of Al_2O_3 almost immediately. The reaction then slows, however, because the film seals off oxygen, preventing further oxidation or chemical reaction. The film is colorless, tough, and nonflaking. Few chemicals can dissolve it.

Electrical and Thermal Conductivity. Aluminum's electrical alloy has the highest conductivity per pound of any commercially sold conductor. Because aluminum is only one-third as dense as copper, it supplies about twice the conductivity per pound. For this reason more than 90% of the transmission and distribution lines in the United States are made from aluminum. Aluminum is an excellent conductor of heat as well. Because of this it is widely used in automobile radiators; cooling coils and fins; heat exchangers in the chemical, petroleum, and other industries; and heater fins in baseboard and other types of heaters.

Reflectivity and Emissivity. Aluminum is an excellent reflector of all forms of radiated energy. This characteristic is commonly put to work in building insulation, including roofing materials. Because it reflects about 90% of radiated heat, aluminum is effective at keeping heat out or in. Aluminum foil can also be used to jam radar by reflecting it.

The Aluminum Industry

The aluminum industry, founded in 1854, is the newest of the nonferrous metal industries.

Bauxite, the Source of Aluminum. Most aluminum produced today is made from BAUXITE. First discovered in 1821 near Les Baux, France (from which its name is derived), bauxite is an ore rich in hydrated aluminum oxides, formed by the weathering of such siliceous aluminous rocks as feldspars, nepheline, and clays.

Most of the large bauxite deposits are found in tropical and subtropical climates, where heavy rainfall, warm temperatures, and good drainage combine to encourage the weathering process. Because bauxite is always found at or near the surface, it is mined by open-pit methods.

Early History of Extraction Processes. Credit for first separating aluminum metal from its oxide, in 1825, goes to the Danish physicist Hans Christian OERSTED. His product was so impure, however, that he did not succeed in determining its physical properties beyond observing a metallic luster.

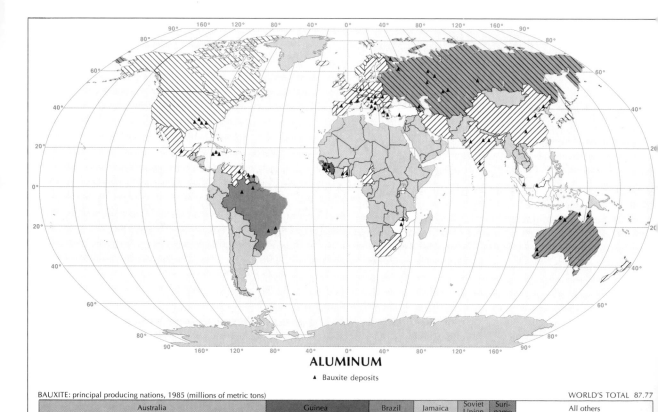

ALUMINUM

▲ Bauxite deposits

BAUXITE: principal producing nations, 1985 (millions of metric tons)   WORLD'S TOTAL 87.77

Australia 32.40	Guinea 14.74	Brazil 6.43	Jamaica 6.22	Soviet Union 4.60	Suriname 3.74	All others 19.64

ALUMINUM: principal producing nations, 1985 (millions of metric tons)   WORLD'S TOTAL 19.35

U.S.A. 5.26	Soviet Union 2.41	Canada 1.34	Japan 1.10	Australia 0.93	Norway 0.75	All others 7.56

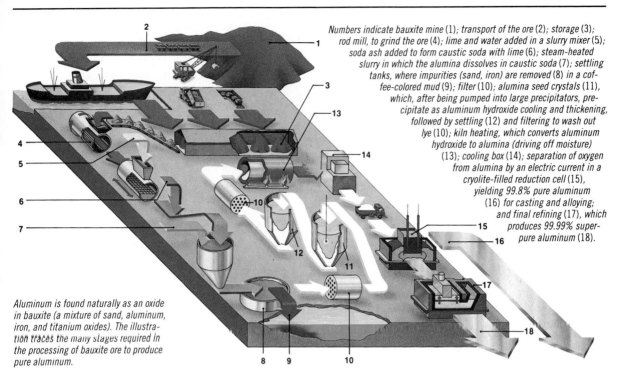

Numbers indicate bauxite mine (1); transport of the ore (2); storage (3); rod mill, to grind the ore (4); lime and water added in a slurry mixer (5); soda ash added to form caustic soda with lime (6); steam-heated slurry in which the alumina dissolves in caustic soda (7); settling tanks, where impurities (sand, iron) are removed (8) in a coffee-colored mud (9); filter (10); alumina seed crystals (11), which, after being pumped into large precipitators, precipitate as aluminum hydroxide cooling and thickening, followed by settling (12) and filtering to wash out lye (10); kiln heating, which converts aluminum hydroxide to alumina (driving off moisture) (13); cooling box (14); separation of oxygen from alumina by an electric current in a cryolite-filled reduction cell (15), yielding 99.8% pure aluminum (16) for casting and alloying; and final refining (17), which produces 99.99% super-pure aluminum (18).

Aluminum is found naturally as an oxide in bauxite (a mixture of sand, aluminum, iron, and titanium oxides). The illustration traces the many stages required in the processing of bauxite ore to produce pure aluminum.

In 1854, Henri Sainte-Claire Deville produced the first commercial quantities of aluminum in a small plant near Paris. Bars and various objects made of this metal were shown at the Paris Exposition in 1855, and the ensuing publicity was in large measure responsible for launching the industry.

In 1886, Charles Martin Hall of Oberlin, Ohio, and Paul L. T. Héroult of France, both 22 years old at the time, discovered and patented almost simultaneously the process by which alumina is dissolved in molten cryolite and decomposed electrolytically. This reduction process, generally known as the Hall-Héroult process, has survived many attempts to supplant it; it remains the only method by which aluminum is produced in commercial quantities today.

Two years after Hall and Héroult made their discovery, Karl Joseph Bayer, a German chemist, developed a process that improved the method for making alumina from bauxite ores low in silica content, a step necessary before the Hall-Héroult process could be applied. This achievement completed the foundation for a commercially feasible aluminum industry.

Bayer Process: Bauxite to Alumina. The Bayer process for separating alumina from bauxite ore was patented in 1888 and is still used today. Bauxite is first pulverized, and water and lime (CaO) added to produce a slurry. Next, the slurry is treated with soda ash (Na_2CO_3) and heated with steam, causing the alumina to dissolve and making possible its separation from sand, iron, and other insoluble impurities. Then, in precipitators up to six sto-

ries high, solid aluminum hydroxide ($Al(OH)_3$) is separated from the solution. Finally, purified alumina is produced by washing the aluminum hydroxide to remove soluble impurities and heating it to more than 1,000° C (1,830° F) to drive off water.

Hall-Héroult Process: Alumina to Aluminum. Aluminum production is carried out in large reduction cells made of steel with a carbon lining that serves as the cathode. The cells, 1,000 or more in a modern plant, are filled with molten cryolite maintained at about 980° C (1,800° F).

Alumina (about 6%) is dissolved in the hot cryolite and converted to molten aluminum by the energy of direct electrical current, which enters the cells through carbon anodes suspended from busbars over the cells. During operation, the molten aluminum, which is more dense than the cryolite, flows to the bottom of the cells where it is drawn off, and oxygen freed from the alumina combines with carbon from the anodes (which must be replaced regularly) to produce carbon dioxide. A crust of solid cryolite forms at the cooler upper surface of liquid in the cell, and the concentration of alumina dissolved in the cryolite is maintained by periodically placing alumina on top of this crust and then breaking the crust and stirring in the alumina. Molten alumina from the reduction cells is either transported to a holding furnace, from which it is poured to form ingots of 99.5% pure aluminum, or it may be alloyed before being poured into ingots.

Alloys: Aluminum to Aluminum Products. Aluminum alloys are generally divided into two basic types, casting alloys and wrought alloys. Aluminum casting alloys most

(Left) *Aluminum is used extensively in aircraft, such as this Boeing 747, because of its good mechanical properties, high corrosion resistance, and light weight.* (Below) *Pots and pans are among the most useful aluminum products for the household because of the metal's nontoxic nature, compatibility with food, and excellent conductance of heat.*

frequently contain silicon, magnesium, copper, zinc, or nickel, alone or in various combinations. Silicon improves the fluidity and castability of molten aluminum; copper and zinc harden the alloy and increase its strength; magnesium improves corrosion resistance, strength, and machinability; and nickel improves dimensional stability and high-temperature strength.

Wrought alloys are alloys that have been mechanically worked after casting. Working operations include FORGING, rolling, drawing, and extruding. Alloying elements (magnesium, silicon, copper, and others) usually make pure aluminum stronger and harder but also render it less ductile and more difficult to fabricate. Working and heat treatments change these alloys' structure, which in turn determines their corrosion resistance and mechanical properties.

Uses for Aluminum. Aluminum is increasingly used to conserve energy both in home heating and cooling and in the transportation industry. Aluminum storm doors and windows, insulation backed with aluminum foil, and aluminum siding are excellent insulators. Because substituting aluminum for heavier metals in cars saves fuel, aluminum is used in engine parts, drive shafts, suspension parts, and wheels.

The container and packaging industry is by far the largest user of aluminum, consuming about 30% of total U.S. production. Most of the aluminum used by the industry has gone into the production of aluminum cans. Several new packaging concepts, however, have recently shown potential for replacing the standard can and other container forms. Milk and other beverages can now be packaged in "aseptic" containers that are made of a paper-plastic film-aluminum foil lamination. Liquids in aseptic containers need not be refrigerated and can be kept for a considerable time without spoiling.

Production. The United States is the world's largest aluminum producer, followed by the USSR, Canada, and Australia. Together, these four nations manufacture half

the total world production. The United States is also the world's largest aluminum consumer, using over 6.5 million metric tons (7 million U.S. tons) annually.

The U.S. aluminum industry consumes 1% of the nation's energy, largely in the form of electricity. The amount of electricity used per pound of metal in smelting, which accounts for about two-thirds of the industry's total energy consumption, has decreased steadily, and today the average is about 7 kWh. Aluminum can be recycled for less than 5% of the energy required for producing virgin metal. U.S. aluminum-can recycling provides over half the aluminum used in making new cans, and recycling of aluminum scrap equals almost half of total aluminum production.

Alvarado, Juan Bautista   Juan Bautista Alvarado, b. Feb. 14, 1809, d. July 13, 1882, was an important figure in California government and politics during the period of Mexican rule. A participant in governmental affairs from the age of 18, he led a revolt against Mexico in 1836 and served as governor, even after he had made his peace with Mexico, until 1842. He was also a major backer of the revolution in 1844–45 that made Pio Pico governor and reduced Mexico's effective control of California. While Alvarado was governor, the earliest American merchants and settlers, including John A. SUTTER, arrived there.

Alvarado, Pedro de   The Spanish explorer Pedro de Alvarado, b. *c.*1485, d. July 4, 1541, was one of the key figures in the Spanish conquest of Central America. Reaching the New World with an expedition to the Yucatán in 1518, Alvarado joined Hernán CORTÉS in the conquest of Mexico (1519–21). His harsh rule in TENOCHTITLÁN (Mexico City) led to the Aztec revolt of 1520, which forced the Spanish to evacuate the city temporarily. In 1523, Alvarado was sent to conquer El Salvador and Guatemala, an area that then covered much of Central America. After successfully completing this mission in 1524, he became governor of Guatemala.

In 1534, Alvarado led a force over the Andes to Quito, Ecuador, then held by Francisco PIZARRO. The latter, however, bought him off for a reputed 100,000 gold pesos, and Alvarado returned to Guatemala. He then joined the search for the legendary Seven Golden Cities of CIBOLA in northern Mexico, participated in the Mixtón War against the Indians of Jalisco, and was killed in a fall from his horse.

Alvarez, Luis Walter The physicist Luis Walter Alvarez, b. San Francisco, June 13, 1911, d. Sept. 1, 1988, is known for his work in high-energy physics, especially his improvements of Donald Glaser's BUBBLE CHAMBER and his discovery of atomic particles with this device, for which he received the 1968 Nobel Prize for physics. A graduate of the University of Chicago, Alvarez became professor of physics at the University of California, Berkeley, in 1945. His memoirs, *Alvarez: Adventures of a Physicist,* were published in 1987. In 1980, Alvarez and his son Walter aroused controversy when they and two other physicists published a theory suggesting that the EXTINCTION of the dinosaurs had been caused by a meteor collision with the Earth. The theory was based on geochemical studies of rock strata.

alyssum [uh-lis'-uhm] *Alyssum* is a genus of annual, biennial, and perennial herbs or subshrubs in the mustard family, Cruciferae. Some species of the Cruciferae genera *Lobularia* and *Aurinia* are also called alyssum. All are native to the Mediterranean region. Their foliage is generally grayish. Some dwarf forms attain a height of less than 8 cm (about 3 in), but others grow up to 23 cm (9 in) tall. The best-known species, *Aurinia saxatilis,* is called goldentuft alyssum, gold dust, or rock madwort.

Alzheimer's disease Alzheimer's disease (AD) is an incurable degenerative disease of the brain first described in 1906 by the German neuropathologist Alois Alzheimer. AD is a progressive dementing illness in which the core symptom is memory loss. Other associated symptoms include impairments in language, abstract reasoning, and visual spatial abilities. Personality changes are common and range from apathy to restless agitation. Psychiatric symptoms, including depression, delusions, and hallucinations, may also occur during the course of AD. AD is the most common cause of dementia in adults, and is estimated to affect more than 2 million men and women over the age of 65 in the United States. Symptoms worsen every year, and death usually occurs within 10 years of initial onset.

The clinical manifestations of AD stem from dysfunction and death of neurons in the brain. The hallmarks of AD are fibrous structures, called neurofibrillary tangles, found in dying neurons, and senile plaques composed of degenerating nerve-cell elements surrounding a core of amyloid protein. The parts of the brain that direct cognition are especially affected, whereas regions that primarily detect sensations and control muscular movement are generally spared. Biochemical abnormalities associated with neuron failure include accumulation of aluminum in senile plaques and tangled neurons; deposition of amyloid protein in cerebral blood vessels and senile plaques; disrupted nerve-cell-membrane phospholipid metabolism; and decreases in NEUROTRANSMITTER substances such as acetylcholine, serotonin, norepinephrine, and somatostatin. Definitive diagnosis of AD is only possible through autopsy, although positron emission tomography has proven helpful as a diagnostic tool.

Although the cause of AD is not known, two risk factors have been identified: advanced age and genetic predisposition. The risk of developing AD is less than 1% before the age of 50 years old but increases steeply in each successive decade of life to reach 30% by the age of 90. In patients with familial AD, immediate-family relatives have a 50% chance of developing AD because the tendency is transmitted as an autosomal dominant trait. In some familial AD cases, an abnormal gene site has been located on chromosome 21. Other genetic or environmental factors are likely to be discovered in the future.

Until the cause of AD is determined, a cure will remain elusive. There are no treatments that reverse the primary cognitive impairments in AD, or that retard the course of illness. Most current experimental drug trials have sought to correct the defect in acetylcholine neurotransmission. To date, such medicines have proven ineffective, but developing drugs to correct other biochemical abnormalities detected in the brain of patients with AD may yet lead to useful treatments.

AM see AMPLITUDE MODULATION

AMA see AMERICAN MEDICAL ASSOCIATION

Amadi, Elechi [ah-mah'-dee] Elechi Amadi, b. May 12, 1934, is a Nigerian novelist with a remarkable talent for re-creating the atmosphere of traditional African life. An Ibo, Amadi was commissioned in the Nigerian army but resigned to take a teaching position. *The Great Ponds* (1969), generally regarded as his best work, examines the conflict between two villages in precolonial Nigeria. He has also published *The Concubine* (1966), *Sunset in Biafra* (1973), a civil-war diary, *The Slave* (1979), *Ethics in Nigerian Culture* (1982), and *Estrangement* (1985).

Amado, Jorge [ah-mah'-due, zhor'-zhee] Brazilian novelist Jorge Amado, b. Aug. 10, 1912, was elected to the Brazilian Academy of Letters in 1961. Amado depicts life in his native state of Bahia in the early 1900s when cacao planters dominated the land, as in *The Violent Land* (1942; Eng. trans., 1945) and *Gabriela, Clove and Cinnamon* (1958; Eng. trans., 1962). In *Dona Flor and*

Her Two Husbands (1966; Eng. trans., 1969) his characters gain greater individuality. Amado's lyricism, imagination, and humor have given him a worldwide reputation. Two early novels, *Jubiabá* (1935) and *Sea of Death* (1936), were published in English translation in 1984, and several other works from the same period appeared in English translation in 1988.

Amalfi [ah-mahl'-fee] Amalfi is a town in Salerno province of southern Italy, southeast of Naples, with a population of 6,052 (1981). Built on the Gulf of Salerno and enjoying a mild climate and picturesque scenery, the town is a fishing port and one of Italy's most famous tourist areas. Its origins are unclear, but in the 9th-century Amalfi became one of the early Italian maritime republics and rivaled the power of Pisa, Genoa, and Venice. Although Amalfi rapidly declined from the 11th century on, its maritime code, the *Tavola Amalfitana*, remained influential in the Mediterranean area until the late 16th century. The town's most impressive monument is the cathedral of Sant' Andrea, begun in the 9th century and subsequently much rebuilt.

Amalgamated Clothing and Textile Workers Union The Amalgamated Clothing and Textile Workers Union (ACTWU) is a LABOR UNION affiliated with the American Federation of Labor and Congress of Industrial Organizations. The union represents workers in the clothing and textile, shoe and hat, dry cleaning and laundry industries, as well as some retail clerks. The union was formed in 1976 by the merger of the Amalgamated Clothing Workers of America (founded in 1914 with Sidney HILLMAN as president) and the Textile Workers Union (founded 1939). In 1979 the United Shoe Workers Union was absorbed.

Amalienburg Pavilion   see NYMPHENBURG PALACE

Amana Society [uh-man'-uh]   The Amana Society is a religious group in east central Iowa that is conservative in theology and pacifistic; it has a strong communal tradition. Its origins are to be found in German PIETISM of the early 1700s. Some 800 members of the group migrated to the United States in 1842, settling first in Ebenezer, N.Y., but moving later to Iowa. Initially, the members held all property in common, but in 1932 they discarded many communal practices and formed a business corporation to take over the group's farmland and other productive properties. The Amana Society continues as a religious organization; the corporation engages in farming and makes kitchen appliances.

amaranth [am'-uh-ranth]   Amaranth is the common name for members of a family (Amaranthaceae) of warm-region herbs, trees, and vines, especially those of the genus *Amaranthus*, often characterized by reddish pigment

Love-lies-bleeding is a species of amaranth that adds an old-fashioned air to gardens. Many other amaranth species are grown as ornamental plants, and a few are cultivated as food. The amaranth family also includes a number of weeds, such as the tumbleweed of the western American prairies.

in the stems and leaves. Many species, including tumbleweed, *A. alba*, are troublesome weeds. Others are flowering perennials and garden ornamentals, such as love-lies-bleeding, or tasselflower, *A. caudatus*, which has crimson, chenille-textured flower spikes, and *A. tricolor*, with its green, yellow, scarlet, or multicolored leaves.

A. caudatus is thought to be the species that was cultivated in Mexico as a food plant until it was almost extirpated by the Spanish conquistadors, who associated its use with Aztec blood rituals. In the Far East and India several amaranth species are cultivated today as green vegetables, or for their edible seeds, which contain more high-quality protein than wheat. Research holds out great promise for the development of amaranth species that will be heavy grain producers, with cultivation potential in harsh climates and difficult soils.

Amarillo   Amarillo (1990 pop., 157,615) is the major metropolis of the windswept Texas Panhandle. Situated both in Randall and Potter counties (the seat of the latter), it is the center of a three-state area where beef and wheat are raised; it is also rich in oil and natural gas. Amarillo is an important producer of helium gas, and although studded with oil refineries, zinc smelters, and heavy manufactures, it is modern and attractive—a glass and concrete oasis rising from desolate plains. Its giant grain elevators and famous cattle auctions give it a Western character. The city was founded when two railroads crossed at that site in 1887. Its name, which is Spanish for "yellow," refers to the color of clay in the area.

Amarna, Tell el- Tell el-Amarna, on the east bank of the Nile about 306 km (190 mi) south of Cairo, was the capital of Egypt under the heretic king AKHENATEN (Amenhotep IV, r. *c*.1379–1362 BC). This 18th-dynasty ruler founded the city as the center of his monotheistic religion dedicated to the worship of the sun-god Aten. Tell el-Amarna is a misnomer, combining the name of the village Et-Tell with that of a tribe, the Beni Amran, who settled nearby approximately two centuries ago. Its ancient name was Akhetaten, meaning "horizon of Aten."

Akhenaten chose the site for the city and planned its layout, a record of which was carved on 14 stelae marking its boundaries, 3 of them west of the Nile. The administrative offices, the chief palace, and the great temple of Aten stood in the center of the city, flanking the main road. In this region most of the so-called Amarna tablets—diplomatic correspondence in CUNEIFORM script with rulers and vassals in western Asia—were found by chance in 1887. The site was extensively excavated (1891–92) by Sir Flinders PETRIE and by later British and German expeditions. In the crescent-shaped rocks east of the city, the Egyptians constructed tombs of the courtiers, mostly unfinished, and the tomb of the king. The tombs are famous for their lively wall reliefs, the scenes being executed in the so-called Amarna style, which radically departs from the expressive restraint of most Egyptian art. Early in his reign Tutankhamen (*c*.1361–1351 BC) abandoned Tell el-Amarna and restored the capital to Thebes.

Amaryllis *Amaryllis* is a genus of South African bulbous plants that bear large, lilylike flowers and belong to the Amaryllidaceae family. The only true species is the belladonna lily, *A. belladonna*, which is native to South Africa. Plant breeders have produced varieties with white to red flowers, which are grown outdoors in some warm regions of the United States.

The more common amaryllises of horticulture, however,

The Amaryllis H. vittatum *blooms in winter and in spring, displaying trumpet-shaped clusters of flowers. Colors range from white to various shades of pink, orange, and red.*

are species of *Hippeastrum*. Most are hybrids of the Peruvian *H. vittatum*. Single large flowers borne on 60-cm (2-ft) stems bloom in a wide variety of colors.

Amateur Athletic Union of the United States The Amateur Athletic Union (AAU) was founded in 1888 to correct widespread problems of amateur athletes in the United States. Since 1889, it has been composed of district associations of clubs and schools, which numbered 58 in 1991. Those associations encompass 300,000 volunteer workers, 372,000 registered athletes, and millions of participants. A Junior Olympics program for athletes of ages 8 through 18 is one of the AAU's most successful programs, but it also sponsors senior divisions in many sports. Its headquarters are in Indianapolis, Ind.

The AAU was once the U.S. governing body for many of the Olympic sports, and it conducted developmental programs and national and international competitions in those and other sports as well. The power of the AAU was somewhat reduced in the 1960s when federations backed by the National Collegiate Athletic Association (NCAA) disputed the AAU's authority over several individual sports. By 1978 all Olympic sports had become autonomous. Each now has its own governing body, although the AAU remains the supervisor for millions of American amateur athletes.

Since 1930 the AAU has conducted the annual poll for the Sullivan Award, which is presented to an outstanding amateur athlete. The award is given in memory of James E. Sullivan, a founder of the organization and later its secretary (1889–1906) and president (1906–14). Another prominent figure was Dan Ferris, who was an official for more than 70 years until his death in 1977.

Amati (family) [ah-mah'-tee] Amati is the name of a family of violin makers in Cremona, Italy, in the 16th, 17th, and 18th centuries. Together with the STRADIVARI and GUARNERI families, they brought violin making to its highest levels. The Amatis were minor nobility and had long been famous for lutes, viols, and other instruments when they began to make VIOLINS. All members of the Amati family were born and died in Cremona.

Andrea, *c*.1520–*c*.1611, began making violins about 1564; a few of his violins and some of his violas and cellos survive. Andrea's sons **Antonio**, 1550–1638, and **Girolamo** (Geronimo), 1551–1635, usually called the "Amati brothers," were partners in the business. **Nicolò**, b. Dec. 3, 1596, d. Apr. 12, 1684, the son of Girolamo, is considered the greatest craftsman of the family. His son **Girolamo**, b. Feb. 26, 1649, d. Feb. 27, 1740, carried on the family tradition, but his violins are not equal to those of Guarneri and Stradivari, who were his contemporaries and fellow apprentices in the Amati workshop.

Virtually all surviving Amati instruments are known and catalogued. Thousands of violins by lesser makers bear Amati labels.

See also: STRINGED INSTRUMENTS.

Amazon River   The Amazon, approximately 6,450 km (4,000 mi) in length, is, after the Nile, the second longest river in the world. Flowing eastward across Brazil in the broad equatorial part of South America, it has the world's largest drainage basin, more than 7 million km^2 (2.7 million mi^2) or nearly 5% of the world's total land area. It carries nearly 20% of the Earth's total water discharge to the ocean—more than the six next-largest rivers combined. The flow is so powerful that it perceptibly dilutes the ocean water of the Atlantic 160 km (100 mi) beyond the coastline.

The River's Course and Environment. The Amazon's headstreams form in the Peruvian Andes little more than 160 km (100 mi) from the Pacific Ocean. In 1541 the Spanish explorer Francisco de ORELLANA began European exploration there, descending the river to the Atlantic and giving the river its name, which refers to the AMAZONS of Greek mythology. Most of the river's generally low-lying drainage basin lies east of the Andes.

The Amazon's mouth is an estuary, 240 km (150 mi) wide at the coast and studded with low muddy islands. These represent the beginnings of a delta formed 5,000 years ago when melting glaciers created an ocean level higher than it is today. A submerged delta built during periods of glacial maximum and low ocean level stands on the continental shelf.

The estuary's tidal range reaches 5.7 m (18.7 ft), and a tidal bore, or wave, occurs from time to time. Ocean tides are felt as far as Obidos, 960 km (600 mi) inland, where the river's discharge is an average 180,000 m^3/sec

Road building in the Amazon Basin has opened vast areas to large-scale exploitation. Millions of hectares have been cut by loggers or burned to clear land for agriculture. Because decaying jungle vegetation no longer replaces the nutrients leached from the soil by heavy rains, however, many ranches and farms become wastelands.

(6,350,000 ft^3/sec) and 283,000 m^3/sec (about 10 million ft^3/sec) at bank-full stage. The mean annual temperature in the basin is 26° C (79° F); precipitation, 2,000 mm (79 in). The climate sustains the world's largest rain forest and promotes intensive land weathering. The suspended load of silt and clay is 350 million metric tons per year (385 million U.S. tons per year). Oceangoing

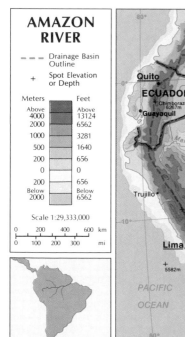

AMAZON RIVER

- - - Drainage Basin Outline

+   Spot Elevation or Depth

Meters		Feet
Above 4000		Above 13124
2000		6562
1000		3281
500		1640
200		656
0		0
200		656
Below 2000		Below 6562

Scale 1:29,333,000

0   200   400   600 km
0   100   200   300   mi

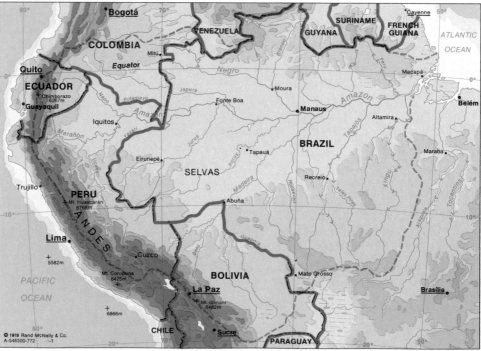

The river port of Manaus, at the Amazon's confluence with the Rio Negro, is the capital and commerical hub of the Brazilian state of Amazonas.

ships can travel as far as MANAUS; vessels drawing 6 m (18 ft) can reach Iquitos in Peru, 3,700 km (2,300 mi) inland. Of the chief tributaries, the NEGRO, Japurá, Putumayo, Napo, Ucayli, Juruá, and Purus are also navigable for long distances. Rivers remain the chief means of transport, but airstrips and highways arc opening the basin to development.

Resources and Development. The Amazon Basin is home to more than 2 million insect species, 100,000 plants, 2,000 species of fish, and 600 mammals, many of which are found nowhere else in the world. The basin also has huge reserves of bauxite, gold, manganese, nickel, copper, tin, and timber and vast hydroelectric potential. In 1978 the eight Amazon Basin nations signed the Treaty of Amazon Cooperation (Amazon Pact), agreeing to share in the region's resources.

In recent years thousands of landless Brazilian peasants have flocked to the sparsely populated region to build homesteads, leading to clashes between farmers and ranchers, settlers and large-scale developers, and newcomers and indigenous aboriginal groups. Many scientists fear that unregulated exploitation of the Amazon Basin will have devastating effects on its fragile ecosystem.

Amazons　In Greek mythology, the Amazons were a race of women warriors who lived in Anatolia and fought with the Trojans against the Greeks in the TROJAN WAR. At that time, their queen was Penthesileia, who was eventually killed by the Greek hero ACHILLES. Legend had it that the Amazons dealt with men for only two reasons, procreation and battle, and that they reared only their female young. A number of Greek heroes fought against the Amazons: HERCULES had to obtain the girdle of Queen HIPPOLYTE as one of his Twelve Labors; THESEUS abducted Queen Hippolyte, who bore him a son, HIPPOLYTUS, and who led her tribe in an invasion of Attica; BELLEROPHON had to fight them and escaped with his life, presumably riding PEGASUS; DIONYSUS conquered them as part of his exploits. The Amazons were frequently depicted by artists as being in battle with men.

Ambartsumian, Viktor Amazaspovich　[ahm-bart-soo-myahn', ah-mah-zahs'-poh-vich]　The Armenian astronomer Viktor Amazaspovich Ambartsumian, b. Sept. 18, 1908, is noted for his work on galactic and STELLAR EVOLUTION and his discovery of stellar associations. A graduate (1928) of the University of Leningrad, Ambartsumian taught there until 1944, when he left to become professor of astrophysics at Yerevan University. The following year he founded the Byurakan Astrophysical Observatory in Yerevan, Armenia, and became director of it. He advanced a widely accepted theory that the radio waves emitted by certain galaxies are caused by enormous explosions within the galaxies. Ambartsumian also made important contributions to scientific discussions of the possibility of communicating with extraterrestrial life.

ambassador　see FOREIGN SERVICE

amber　Amber is fossilized tree resin that has lost its volatile components after millions of years of burial. One of the first substances used for decoration, it was an object of trade and barter for ancient Baltic peoples.

Amber is an organic substance produced by a now-extinct species of coniferous tree. Its warm, golden color and soft, waxy luster obtained after polishing have resulted in its extensive use for thousands of years in elaborate carvings and jewelry.

Amber occurs as irregular masses, nodules, or drops that are a transparent to translucent yellow, sometimes tinted red, orange, or brown. It may be clouded by innumerable minuscule air bubbles or contain fossilized insects or plants. Amber softens at about 150° C and melts at 250°–350° C. It was called *electrum* or *elektron* by the Greeks, who were aware of its ability to produce a static electrical charge. Of widespread occurrence, amber is particularly abundant along the shores of the Baltic Sea, where it is mined extensively, Amber is still popular in jewelry and as a decorative material.

ambergris [am'-bur-gris]   Ambergris is formed in the intestines of sperm whales. When fresh, it is black, greasy, and malodorous, but after exposure to the air it hardens, turns gray, and develops a pleasant aroma. Ambergris was used in ancient times as a perfume and for its purported medicinal properties. Today it is blended with other fragrances to make perfume.

Ambler, Eric   The prolific English novelist Eric Ambler, b. June 28, 1909, an acknowledged master of the thriller, popularized the spy story featuring the disenchanted secret agent. The well-known *A Coffin for Dimitrios* (1939) features the typical Ambler hero: a man with no heroic ambitions whose basic motive is survival in a sordid, dangerous world. Ambler has twice won (1964, 1975) the Edgar Allan Poe Award and is a talented writer of screenplays (including that for *Topkapi,* 1964, based on his own *The Light of Day,* 1962). Several of his other novels have been filmed, most notably *Journey into Fear* (1940; film, 1942). Ambler's autobiography, *Here Lies,* was published in 1986.

Ambonese [am'-buh-neez]   The Ambonese (Amboinese), also known as South Moluccans, live on the island of Ambon in the Moluccas (Maluku), an island group east of Sulawesi (Celebes) and north of Timor in Indonesia. An ethnic mixture of Southeast Asians and Melanesian peoples of New Guinea, they speak a Malayo-Polynesian (Austronesian) language. A typical Ambonese village consists of about 1,500 people who live in houses of woven sago leaves or plastered bamboo on stone foundations; they cultivate surrounding hillsides. The Ambonese have been heavily influenced by Islam and Christianity, and indigenous customs have largely disappeared.

Ambrose, Saint   Saint Ambrose, b. *c.*340, d. Apr. 4, 397, bishop of Milan, was one of the Fathers of the Christian church. The son of a high Roman official, he was appointed Roman governor of Liguria and Aemelia (*c.*370). When Auxentius, bishop of Milan, died in 374, a dispute arose over who should succeed him. While Ambrose, as governor, was trying to calm the people, a cry went up, "Ambrose for bishop!" Although he had not yet been baptized, he reluctantly accepted the office.

Ambrose became a strong opponent of ARIANISM and paganism and vigorously asserted the independence of the church against the Roman state. His greatest gift was his power as a preacher. Among his writings were *De officiis,* a treatise on the duties of the clergy; commentaries on various books of the Bible; and possibly the Athanasian CREED. He also is regarded as one of the founders of Western church music. Feast day: Dec. 7.

ambulance   SEE PARAMEDIC

amebiasis [am-i-by'-uh-suhs]   Amebiasis is a general name for human infections caused by the amoeba *Entamoeba histolytica.* Intestinal infections alone are called amoebic DYSENTERY. Amebiasis occurs worldwide—nearly 3,000 cases were reported in the United States in a recent year—but is most prevalent in tropical regions. In some areas more than half of the population is likely to develop amebiasis at some time. The parasite is usually ingested in encysted form in contaminated food or water. Dysentery symptoms may take a week to a year or more to develop and may recur after long remissions; some people remain symptomless but act as carriers. Untreated amebiasis can lead to stomach ulcers and peritonitis, and the amoeba may be carried in the blood to the liver and cause amoebic hepatitis or ulcers. Abscesses may also develop in other organs or, rarely, the brain. Several drugs are effective against amebiasis, but liver and other complications may require surgery.

Ameling, Elly [am'-uh-ling]   Elly Ameling, b. Feb. 8, 1938, a Dutch soprano, is world renowned for her recitals of German and French songs and for her superlative interpretive gifts. She is equally at home in chamber music, orchestral music, operas, and oratorios. She made her U.S. recital debut at New York's Lincoln Center in 1968 and her opera debut in 1974 as Ilia in Mozart's *Idomeneo* in Washington, D.C. Contemporary works, particularly by her countrymen Bertus van Lier and Robert Heppener, are also part of her large repertoire. Ameling has won many coveted recording prizes. For her services to music, the Dutch government made her Ridder in de Orde van Oranje Nassau (Knight in the Order of Orange-Nassau).

Amenhotep I, King of Egypt [ah-men-hoh'-tep]   Amenhotep I, king of Egypt from 1546 to 1526 BC, was the son of AHMOSE I, founder of the 18th dynasty. Amenhotep undertook military campaigns in Libya and Nubia (now Sudan), extending the boundaries of his empire. The name also appears as Amenophis.

Amenhotep III, King of Egypt   The 18th-dynasty king Amenhotep III ruled (1417–1379 BC) Egypt at the height of its power. His extensive diplomatic contacts with other Near Eastern states, especially Mitanni and Babylonia, are revealed in the AMARNA tablets. Of the great temple he built near Thebes, only two statues, the so-called colossi of MEMNON, remain. Amenhotep's wife Tiye, a woman of humble birth, was prominently associated with him during his long and peaceful reign.

Amenhotep IV   see AKHENATEN

amenorrhea   see MENSTRUATION

America   The name *America* applies to either continent of the Western Hemisphere (North America or South America) or to all the land masses in that hemisphere. America is also used as an abbreviated form of the United States of America. The name, derived from that of Italian navigator Amerigo VESPUCCI, was first used on a map in 1507 by Martin Waldseemüller.

American Academy of Arts and Letters   The American Academy of Arts and Letters, located in New York City, was created in 1904 as a subdivision of the National Institute of Arts and Letters to further the progress of American literature, music, and the arts. Its membership, limited to 50 persons at any one time, has included such notables as Aaron Copland, Ralph Ellison, Lillian Hellman, and Georgia O'Keeffe. In 1976 the academy, which granted numerous awards and scholarships, merged with its parent organization to become the American Academy and Institute of Arts and Letters.

American Academy of Arts and Sciences
After John ADAMS's suggestion in 1779 that a Boston-based society be formed for the "cultivation and promotion of Arts and Sciences" similar to Philadelphia's AMERICAN PHILOSOPHICAL SOCIETY, the Massachusetts legislature passed an act in 1780 incorporating the American Academy of Arts and Sciences. Today, more than 2,000 elected fellows grouped in four specialty classes pursue the same broad purposes as their Revolutionary-era predecessors. The academy also conducts interdisciplinary studies of current social and intellectual issues, which are reported in the quarterly journal *Daedalus*.

American art and architecture   Two opposite forces have coexisted in American art since the establishment of the first colonies. Although American artists have been aware of their European cultural heritage and of continuing innovation in Europe, they have had to adapt European forms to the exigencies of their native situation. This interaction between rival forces is hardly unique to American art—all art grows within a tradition—but what distinguishes the American experience is the ambivalent attitudes brought to that tradition. To many of the early settlers, the ambivalence was clear, since so many of them were religious and political exiles. Yet despite the pressures of conscience and conviction, the European traditions persisted in memory, so that the first American

art and architecture were adaptations of European styles and modes, modified to suit the colonists' urgent needs in a new and often hostile world. The conflict, aroused by traditions at once alienating and indispensable, has served as the underlying dynamic for the rise and progress of art and architecture in the United States.

American Architecture

In a virgin land the art form that developed most rapidly was the one for which the need was most pressing—ARCHITECTURE. The earliest extant buildings are the dwellings, meeting houses, and churches that made up the nuclei of the first colonial settlements in Virginia and Massachusetts. The dwellings, simple in plan and elevation, like the Adam Thoroughgood House, Princess Anne County, Va. (1936–40), resembled English houses of the late medieval or TUDOR STYLE. The most innovative in design were New England meeting houses, because the separatists sought to avoid any associations with the established church in England. These handsome buildings, such as the Old Ship Meeting House, Hingham, Mass. (1681), were either square or rectangular in plan and served as the focal center for northern towns.

Colonial Buildings. As the colonies flourished, more and more elaborate structures were required. By the end of the 17th century, most American public buildings were derived from Sir Christopher WREN's designs for the rebuilding of London after the Great Fire in 1666. The best were the so-called Wren Building (1695–1702) of the College of William and Mary and the Governor's Palace (1706–20), both at WILLIAMSBURG, Va. To stay the random growth of cities, the concept of URBAN PLANNING was introduced, beginning with Thomas Holme's grid plan of 1682 for Philadelphia, then second in population to London within the English-speaking world. By the middle of the 18th century, architects were designing churches,

The Capitol at Williamsburg, Va., originally built in 1701–05, is an example of the colonial American style derived from Sir Christopher Wren. This building is a reconstruction.

(Above) *The State Capitol (1785–96) at Richmond, Va., was designed by Thomas Jefferson and Charles Louis Clérisseau. It is derived from the Roman temple.* (Left) *Richard Upjohn's Trinity Church (1839–46), New York, was America's first Gothic Revival public building.*

mansions, and public buildings in the current English GEORGIAN STYLE, named for King George I.

Post-Revolutionary Architecture. After the Revolutionary War, the first attempt to create a style expressive of the new republic was made by Thomas JEFFERSON. He based the design of the new capitol building at Richmond, Va., on that of a Roman temple, the Maison Carrée at Nîmes, France. In so doing he laid down an American precedent of modifying an ancient building style for modern use. The Virginia State Capitol (1785–96), both building and symbol, was meant to house the kind of government envisioned by Jefferson, and the Maison Carrée became a paradigm for American public structures.

Jefferson was influential in setting forth the style of monumental NEOCLASSICISM that supplanted Georgian ar-

The Wainwright Building (1890–91) was built in St. Louis by the Chicago architects Louis Sullivan and Dankmar Adler. It established the basic style for American skyscraper design through the first decade of the 20th century.

chitecture with its taint of monarchy and colonialism. Monumental neoclassicism came to represent the new political and social entity that was the United States of America. Architects committed to neoclassicism designed not only the new CAPITOL OF THE UNITED STATES in Washington, first designed (1792) by William Thornton and Stephen Hallet, and other government buildings, but also factories, schools, banks, railroad stations, and hospitals, modernized by the frequent use of materials such as iron, concrete, and glass. The English-born Benjamin LATROBE, who began his American employment working with Jefferson on the Richmond Capitol, brought American neoclassicism to maturity. Latrobe invented new formal configurations for buildings as varied in function as the Bank of Pennsylvania (1798–1800) and the Centre Square Pump House (1800; both in Philadelphia and both destroyed) and Baltimore's Roman Catholic Cathedral (1806–21). Chosen in 1815 to supervise the rebuilding of the Washington Capitol, gutted by fire during the War of 1812, Latrobe set about producing a truly monumental American architecture. In 1817 he procured the assistance of Charles BULFINCH, who had just completed Boston's Massachusetts General Hospital. Together the two men completed plans for the first major building phase of the Capitol.

Revival Styles. Latrobe and Bulfinch were the preeminent architects in the neoclassical mode. The generation following preferred Greek over Roman forms and produced the GREEK REVIVAL. A principal contribution of this style was a modification of the Greek prostyle temple for domestic and public buildings; the style's sphere of influence was rapidly extended north, south, and west. Major surviving examples are William STRICKLAND's Philadelphia Merchants' Exchange (1832–34) and Alexander Jackson DAVIS's La Grange (Lafayette) Terrace (1832–36) in New York. Up to the 1850s classical revival styles led to a homogeneity in American architecture that was never to prevail again. Yet even before 1810, American architects, following the lead of their English contemporaries, had begun to introduce a rival style of the American scene—the GOTHIC REVIVAL. It is appropriate that this movement, which originated with the rise of ROMANTICISM in England, should have been taken over in a country where romanticism constituted the first intellectual flowering after the nation's founding. Not surprisingly, the style lent itself most naturally to church architecture. Richard UPJOHN a prolific ecclesiastical architect, made his Trinity Church (1839–46) in New York the prototype for Gothic Revival churches. The style was also widely applied to college buildings, thus identifying those institutions with the prestigious English universities of Oxford and Cambridge.

Before the Civil War other revival styles such as the Romanesque, the Egyptian, and the Italian villa style were introduced, but with less applicability. More widespread was the cottage architecture for the middle class advocated by Andrew Jackson DOWNING. Moderate in price and well constructed, these Downing designs exploited the possibilities of wood both as construction material and as decoration.

Cast-Iron Architecture. An important development was the proliferation of industrial and commercial structures requiring extensive use of iron. At first engineers rather than architects were responsible for buildings that demanded advanced technical planning. Because cast- and wrought-iron columns replaced heavier masonry construction, it became possible to construct a lighter skeleton, use prefabricated modules, and introduce more glass into the facade. James Bogardus, an inventor and manufacturer of machinery, is generally credited with the development of CAST-IRON ARCHITECTURE, as demonstrated in his "Cast Iron Building" (Laing Stores; 1848) in New York. In his proposed plan for the Industrial Palace of the New York World's Fair (1853), also called the New York Crystal Palace, and his Wanamaker Department Store in New York (c.1859; destroyed), he pushed this type of engineered building to the limits then possible.

After the financial crash of 1857 and the Civil War, both of which had temporarily halted building construction, Americans gravitated to a style that demonstrably symbolized the nation's rapidly increasing wealth. Mansions and government and civic buildings were designed in the Second Empire style, promoted in France by Napoleon III to bolster his imperial ambitions and exemplified by John McArthur's massive Philadelphia City Hall (1874–1901). Also of great importance was the extension of the Gothic Revival into its Victorian phase. This movement, inspired by the writings of John RUSKIN, emphasized craft and permitted the manipulation of architectural detail to create bold new effects. Two great architects, Frank Furness and Henry Hobson RICHARDSON, emerged from Victorian Gothic; Furness created works of idiosyncratic originality, while Richardson created a new vision within a revival style.

Richardson, the most independent and imaginative architect since Latrobe, attained prominence when he gave a new Romanesque form to Boston's Trinity Church

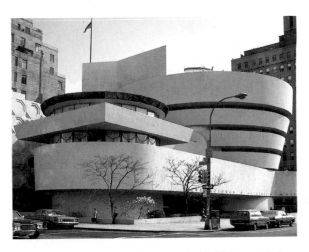

The Solomon R. Guggenheim Museum (1956–59) in New York City is one of Frank Lloyd Wright's most original buildings, employing a spiral ramp to display the museum's collection.

(1872–77). Besides churches, Richardson designed numerous residences, libraries, railroad stations, civic and commercial buildings, and even a prison, creating models of their kind for each type. He favored the Romanesque because he believed it expressed the pervasive energy and dynamism of the American scene. But it was his Marshall Field Wholesale Store (1885–87) in Chicago that was to prove seminal. Its rusticated masonry and multistoried arrangement of arches, reminiscent of Romanesque and expressive of Richardson's sense of ordering masses on a large scale, would be applied by his successors in Chicago to problems of skyscraper design.

Skyscraper Architecture. The skyscraper, defined here as a tall commercial structure, is America's original contribution to the history of architecture. Commercial buildings of several stories, constructed during the 1850s in Philadelphia, anticipated the skyscraper. But before it could become a reality, architects had to incorporate the elevator into the structure. This was done, beginning in the '50s in New York. Chicago, however, was the city where skyscraper design soon attained a kind of canonical perfection.

Since many of the city's commercial buildings needed to be replaced after the great fire of 1871, Chicago served as an excellent testing ground for architects. Preeminent among them was Louis SULLIVAN. He and others working in teams evolved the glass cage that became the hallmark of the Chicago school of architecture. William Holabird and Martin Roche's Tacoma Building, Daniel H. BURNHAM and John Wellborn ROOT's Reliance Building, and Sullivan's Gage Building are outstanding examples of the progressive stages in the skyscraper's development.

Yet just at the time that an architecture of originality and daring was emerging in Chicago, the New York firm of McKIM, MEAD, AND WHITE successfully introduced a monumental Beaux-Arts style for impressive public buildings such as the Boston Public Library (1887–98). This pref-

(Above) *Frank Lloyd Wright's Robie House (1909) in Chicago is a prime example of his "prairie house" style. With its horizontal emphasis, simplicity of materials, and relationship to its setting, the dwelling typifies Wright's early domestic architecture.*

(Right) *The Seagram Building (1956–59), New York City, was designed by Ludwig Mies van der Rohe and Philip Johnson. An example of the glass curtain-wall design for skyscrapers, it displays the clear lines that characterize the International Style of the Bauhaus.*

erence for revival styles continued well into the 20th century, with interesting variations. When, for instance, New York began its campaign to raise the world's tallest buildings, their decorative systems were adapted to revival styles, culminating in the best-known Gothic skyscraper, Cass GILBERT's Woolworth Building (1913) in New York.

Modern Architecture. Far more significant than revival styles to MODERN ARCHITECTURE was, on the one hand, the unfolding of the brilliant indigenous talent of Frank Lloyd WRIGHT and, on the other, the infusion of European modernism through the work of the BAUHAUS architects Walter GROPIUS, Marcel BREUER, and Ludwig MIES VAN DER ROHE, and the independent work of Eric MENDELSOHN and Eliel SAARINEN. Wright, who early in his career worked for Sullivan in Chicago, believed that the West and Midwest embodied the "real American spirit." Acting on this belief, he designed the houses that were to win him international renown. His "prairie houses" were horizontal, often of one story, with rooms merging in a continuous open space. Wright was a man of fertile imagination; before his long career ended, he designed buildings as various as the Imperial Hotel (1916–22; destroyed) in Tokyo; the Johnson Wax Company Building (1936–39) in Racine, Wis.; and New York's GUGGENHEIM MUSEUM (1956–59).

Wright branded as "un-American" the plans and models of the European INTERNATIONAL STYLE of architecture exhibited at New York's MUSEUM OF MODERN ART in 1932, although European modernists had admired and borrowed from Wright's work. Furthermore, they had studied such American technical achievements as John A. ROEBLING's BROOKLYN BRIDGE, Ernest Ransome's ferroconcrete cage construction for modern factories, and the midwestern multistory cylindrical grain elevators. Despite some native resistance, from the 1930s on the presence of European modernists was felt in America's urban and in-

dustrial culture. After Gropius was appointed chairman of architecture at Harvard University's Graduate School of Design in 1938, many young Americans were trained in the ideas of the German Bauhaus. After the hiatus in building produced by World War II, the influences of Wright and European modernists were balanced.

Postwar Architecture. In architecture the stark, boxy forms of European modernism by way of the Bauhaus dominated American cityscapes in the building boom following World War II. Of special importance was the use of glass curtain-wall construction for the design of large skyscrapers and other buildings, as in the United Nations complex, erected in 1947–53 under the supervision of LE CORBUSIER and Wallace K. HARRISON, and the SEAGRAM BUILDING (1956–59) of Ludwig Mies van der Rohe and Philip JOHNSON. It was the skyscrapers of the Chicago school, however, that made possible the later use of glass curtain-wall construction. Thus in architecture as in painting, what has come to represent and even symbolize the dynamism of American life—whether it be a sky-scraper or an abstract expressionist painting—is born out of both the Old World and the New.

American Sculpture

Of the three arts, sculpture was the least appreciated in the United States until the 19th century. Expensive to produce because of the materials involved, sculpture seemed a form of conspicuous display and therefore wasteful for a democracy. Also, in attempting the nude in order to follow the outstanding European exemplars, American sculptors tended to run afoul of native Puritan attitudes. Sculptors also employed allegorical symbolism inherited from European humanist tradition, so that their work at first was little understood.

19th-Century Sculptors. The first sculptor of note was the Philadelphian William RUSH. He started as a carver of ship figureheads, and his freestanding statues, character-ized by an archaic vigor, were also executed in wood. For-eign sculptors, however, made a more favorable impres-sion at the time. Foremost among them was Jean Antoine HOUDON, who traveled to the United States in 1785 to ex-ecute portrait busts of famous Americans, in particular George Washington. Other sculptors, such as the Italians Giuseppe and Carlo Franzoni, Giovanni Andrei, and Luigi Persico, seized the opportunity to provide the marble statues required for the Capitol Building, under construc-tion in Washington in the early 19th century.

Aspiring young Americans, wishing to work in marble and finding no one to train them at home, soon began traveling to Italy. Horatio GREENOUGH was first in a flood tide that, between 1825 and 1875, included Hiram POWERS, Thomas Crawford, William Wetmore Story, and Harriet Hosmer, the group Henry James dubbed the

Horatio Greenough's white marble George Washington *(1840) is based on the statue of the* Olympian Zeus *by Phidias. (Smithsonian Institution, Washington, D.C.)*

The bronze Trooper of the Plains *is by the American frontier sculp-tor Frederic Remington. Remington also completed a large num-ber of illustrations and paintings that dramatized frontier life. (Gilcrease Institute, Tulsa, Okla.)*

"white marmorean flock." Some never returned from Ita-ly; they worked primarily in the neoclassical style and de-pended on Italian stonecutters to translate their clay models into marble. It was the American-based John Rogers, however—the modeler of statuettes, called Rog-ers Groups, in realistic, sentimental genre scenes—who first made sculpture appeal to a wide public, primarily through his large mail-order operation.

After 1855 the center of study shifted to Paris, where American sculptors observed that the French, under the Second Empire, received extensive government support. Wishing to create the same situation at home, they trained at the ÉCOLE DES BEAUX-ARTS, then joined forces with those American architects executing the grandiose commissions, both private and governmental, of the day. Augustus SAINT-GAUDENS and Daniel Chester FRENCH were the major practitioners, working in a style infused with the academic eclecticism of the Beaux-Arts tradition. The sculpture and architecture of the WORLD'S COLUMBIAN EX-POSITION OF 1893 in Chicago epitomized the Beaux-Arts phase in the United States and set the style for public monuments for almost 40 years.

Four sculptors forged visions independent of academ-ic eclecticism. Frederic REMINGTON managed to express the raw energy of the American West in his bronze figures of cavalry charges, cowboys, and barroom brawls. Gutzon BORGLUM, realizing a failed dream of Michaelangelo's, took on a mountain when he cut the giant heads of four

Alexander Calder's mobile Red Petals *(1942) is made of painted organic shapes, connected by wires. It is kept in constant motion by air currents in the room. (Arts Club, Chicago.)*

presidents into Mount Rushmore. To George Gray Barnard, Americans owe a special debt, not only for his sculpture but also for his assembly of a superb collection of medieval sculpture now housed at The Cloisters in New York. Finally, William Rimmer, isolated and unappreciated, nevertheless worked with authority and daring to produce sculpture more like Auguste Rodin's than any American contemporary.

20th-Century Sculptors. The Armory Show, exhibiting sculptures by Constantin Brancusi, Henri Matisse, and Pablo Picasso, brought American sculpture into the 20th century. From the 1920s on, the presence in the United States of such renowned European artists as Elie Nadelman, Max Ernst, Naum Gabo, and Jacques Lipschitz, and the activities of the MUSEUM OF MODERN ART, further altered the course of American sculpture.

Taking a variety of approaches to both representational and nonrepresentational forms, American sculptors invented new ways to integrate form with space: John Flan-

nagan invested animal and human shapes with a primal, dynamic energy; Joseph CORNELL created miniature fantasies by arranging subtly related small objects in boxes; Alexander CALDER gave the world a new sculptural form, the mobile; Louise NEVELSON's large, freestanding forms restructured the experience of space; and David SMITH conceived large metal sculpture for landscape and architectural sites. The visions of these sculptors, although different from one another, combined to create a significant and influential body of works. After World War II, with the emergence of younger sculptors such as Isamu NOGUCHI, Louise BOURGEOIS, and Tony SMITH, sculpture in the United States became equal to the other arts.

American Painting

As architecture flourished first because it was needed, so PORTRAITURE, which was also early in demand, emerged as the first American art of PAINTING. Religious painting was unpopular in a land settled by Protestant sects, and LANDSCAPE, STILL LIFE, and GENRE PAINTING seemed too frivolous to the colonists. But images of the living, ancestor portraits to the next generation, testified to humankind's presence as a civilizing force on a wild continent. The first portraitists, working in a primitive version of the English Tudor style, were called LIMNERS (from the Old French word *euminer*, "to illuminate"). Limners, largely self-taught, borrowed heavily from English engravings. By 1729, however, when the Scotsman John Smibert brought over his casts, copies, and engravings to establish himself as a portraitist and teacher in Boston, American artists were becoming aware that their provincialism required correction.

18th-Century American Painters. The next generation produced the first major native talent in Boston's John Singleton COPLEY. His portraits, stressing surface detail and the solidity of forms, are a vivid record of such important Revolutionary figures as Paul Revere and other prominent Boston citizens. In 1774 Copley traveled to London for further academic training. His fellow American Benjamin WEST, who had made the pilgrimage 14 years earlier, took Copley into his studio. West and Copley represent American painting coming of age; they also established a precedent for later generations of artists by emmigrating to Europe.

West became painter to King George III, president of England's Royal Academy, and host to American artists seeking training and sympathetic support in a foreign city. West's portraits and his historical and religious paintings do not rank with the best of his English contemporaries, but as a catalyst among personalities West was outstanding, and his success enhanced the role of the artist in the eyes of Americans.

The third artist to achieve distinction before the 19th century was Charles Willson Peale (see PEALE family). A moving force among artists, he helped launch America's first official painting exhibition in 1795 and was one of the founders of the nation's oldest museum, the PENN-SYLVANIA ACADEMY OF THE FINE ARTS (1805) in Philadelphia. In addition, he influenced a dynasty of artists, both men and women, named for artists of the past; two of

John Singleton Copley's portrait of Paul Revere *(1768) illustrates the direct style of one of America's earliest and most distinguished portrait painters. (Courtesy Museum of Fine Arts, Boston. Gift of Joseph W., William B., and Edward H. R. Revere.)*

Raphaelle Peale's charming work After the Bath *was painted in 1823. The oldest son of the portraitist Charles Willson Peale, Raphaelle Peale is known best for his still-life paintings. (Nelson Gallery-Atkins Museum of Fine Arts, Kansas City, Mo.)*

these outstanding artists were Raphaelle and Rubens Peale.

American Romantic Painters. After the turn of the century, a greater range of painting types was produced. Copley's and West's success with history paintings executed in England encouraged John TRUMBULL and John VANDERLYN to essay history paintings for an American audience. Neither succeeded in capturing the public's favor, but theirs was an ambitious failure, for they opened the field for other kinds of paintings besides portraiture. Raphaelle Peale, although unrecognized in his lifetime, persisted in the face of economic hardship as a sensitive painter of still life. Back from Europe, Washington ALLSTON executed highly original landscape and figure compositions that revealed a genuinely romantic imagination.

Portraits, however, continued to be the artist's mainstay. Artists of lesser ability fanned out to the edges of the frontier, accepting commissions wherever they could find them. Gilbert STUART and Thomas SULLY returned from England, where they had learned to paint with a lighter, unblended stroke, to become the fashionable portraitists of their day. But the most frequently painted face was that of the *pater patriae*, George Washington. The demand for his image continued long after his death, with Gilbert Stuart duplicating his Atheneum version (1796; Museum of Fine Arts, Boston) some 70 times and Rembrandt Peale turning out 79 "porthole" portraits of Wash-

ington (the head framed by a painted stone "porthole" or oval window).

Not long after the turn of the century the artist-actor-entrepreneur William DUNLAP was sufficiently impressed with the whole artistic enterprise to calculate that the public would welcome a book on the subject. Like Giorgio Vasari in the Renaissance, he collected anecdotes about dead artists, solicited biographies of the living, added his own critical comments, and in 1834 published America's first art history, the *History of the Rise and Progress of the Arts of Design in the United States.*

American Landscape and Genre Paintings. Two significant trends were just beginning when Dunlap's opus appeared, one in landscape painting, the other in genre painting. Landscape emerged as the subject for expressing themes of symbolic importance in a culture where the land itself was equated with the life of the people. Thomas COLE conceived great multicanvas cycles, *The Course of Empire* (1836; New York Historical Society) and *The Voyage of Life* (1840; Munson-Williams-Proctor Institute, Utica, N.Y.), which served as sermons in paint. By the 1820s a generation of painters was forming whose vision of grandiose scenes untouched by the incursions of civilization remains as a record of a lost past. Asher B. DURAND, Thomas DOUGHTY, Frederick CHURCH, John KENSETT, Sanford Gifford, and Cole all painted in the eastern mountainous regions of the Catskills and along the Hud-

Kindred Spirits *(1849) is often considered Asher Durand's master-piece. Durand, a member of the Hudson River school of landscape painting, portrays is founder, Thomas Cole, and the poet William Cullen Bryant in a Catskill mountain glen. (New York Public Library.)*

son River valley—hence their designation as the HUDSON RIVER SCHOOL. Martin Heade and Fitz Hugh LANE, in works now called Luminist, depicted haunting seascapes and scenes along the coastal waters and marshes. Other artists, notably Karl Dodmer and George CATLIN, set out for the West to paint the terrain and the rapidly vanishing world of the Indian.

Genre painting began to grow in popularity and importance by the 1830s. Scenes of Long Island and New England life were portrayed by William Sidney MOUNT and Eastman JOHNSON. The folkways of the Midwest river towns, to which Mark Twain would later give literary form, were charmingly preserved in the paintings of George Caleb BINGHAM.

By the 1940s genre artists such as Johnson and Bingham, as well as those aspiring to history painting, such as Emanuel LEUTZE, were traveling to Düsseldorf for further training. That small Prussian town was the home of the Düsseldorf Akademie, where artists received a thorough grounding in figure drawing and composition. It was in Düsseldorf, after the Revolution of 1848, that Leutze posed German friends for what was to become an American national icon, *Washington Crossing the Delaware* (1851; Metropolitan Museum of Art, New York). There too, in 1848, the promising young genre painter Richard Caton Woodville painted *War News from Mexico* (National

Academy of Design, New York), a scene concerning America's recent victory over the Mexicans.

Painting at midcentury reflected the life of the people and received broad-based support. Genre and landscape paintings captured the rural, optimistic, and essentially innocent spirit of the times. Still lifes gave evidence of nature's bounty. Portrait commissions continued to abound, although artists had to compete with a new form of portraiture in the DAGUERREOTYPE, the first form of PHOTOGRAPHY, introduced into America in 1839–40. Well-to-do businessmen felt it their patriotic duty to patronize the arts, and the American Art Union distributed paintings by lottery to a wide public.

American Art After the Civil War. The Civil War, in art as in so many other areas of American life, constituted a watershed. At war's end the earlier vision of America as the new Eden had faded. Life in the teeming cities, the struggle to survive in the business world, and the accumulation of wealth in the hands of a few were the overriding realities. From the vulgarity of post–Civil War America, artists chose different avenues of escape. Some determined upon a period of expatriation. Others, principally Thomas EAKINS, Winslow HOMER, and Albert Pinkham RYDER, withdrew from the urban environment. Homer, who had provided illustrations of the Civil War for *Harper's Weekly Magazine*, in the 1870s favored genre scenes of a rural life that was becoming anachronistic, as depicted in *The Country School* (1871; Art Museum, St. Louis, Mo.). In the 1880s he turned to painting scenes of the sea, and until the end of his life he took as his leitmotiv the survival of humans against the elements, as in *The Wreck* (1896; Carnegie Institute, Pittsburg, Pa.). Ryder, an introverted recluse, delved into his imagination to give expression to human isolation when he painted *Moonlight Marine* (1890–99; Metropolitan Museum of Art, New York) and *The Race Track (Death on a Pale Horse)* (1890–1910; Museum of Art, Cleveland, Ohio). He also found inspiration in Norse mythology. Eakins, following three years of training at the École des Beaux-Arts, re-

Winslow Homer's Northeaster *(1895) captures the power of the sea. One of the most prolific 19th-century American artists, Homer favored marine painting in his later career. (Metropolitan Museum of Art, New York.)*

turned full of hope to his native Philadelphia. But the work he intended as his masterpiece, *The Gross Clinic* (1875; Jefferson Medical College, Philadelphia, Pa.), shocked Philadelphians; his use of a stripped male model for teaching life drawing to young ladies outraged them and led to his dismissal from the Pennsylvania Academy of the Fine Arts. Following a nervous breakdown, he resumed painting, mostly introspective portraits of friends, usually gratis. Although Homer had the support of collectors, particularly successful businessmen, Eakins and Ryder became typical of the alienated American artist who worked beyond the pale of public sympathy and private patronage.

From the time of Benjamin West, artists had traveled to Europe, but by the 1870s they interacted to a greater extent with the main line of European innovation. The centers of study shifted from London and Düsseldorf to Paris and Munich. In Paris, Americans became aware, after a time lag, of *réalisme*, Gustave COURBET's revolutionary departure from the idealizing styles then in vogue. Courbet's REALISM was an attempt to get on canvas a truthful rendition of the commonly observable facts of contemporary life. Courbet and Édouard MANET were the pioneers of realism; of the artists of the past, Diego VELÁZQUEZ was the most admired. William Merritt CHASE and Frank DUVENECK, studying in Munich with the German realists, learned to paint with a loaded brush and a dark palette. John Singer SARGENT, a student of the Parisian society portraitist Émile Auguste Carolus-Durand, achieved his own facile version of realism, sometimes with remarkable success, as in his *Daughters of Edward Darley Boit* (1882; Museum of Fine Arts, Boston). Even

The Daughters of Edward Darley Boit, *painted in 1882 by John Singer Sargent, is one of the portraits for which the artist is most admired. (Courtesy Museum of Fine Arts, Boston. Gift of the Boit Daughters in memory of their father.)*

James Abbott McNeill Whistler's Arrangement in Gray and Black, No. 1, The Artist's Mother *(1872) is also known as Whistler's Mother. (Louvre, Paris.)*

so independent a temperament as William HARNETT, the *trompe l'oeil* (illusionist) painter of the oddments of American life, spent four years in Munich, where he refined his realist technique.

American Impressionism. IMPRESSIONISM, which can be understood as the logical end result of realism, also was taken up, after a time lag, by Americans. In 1866, Mary CASSATT arrived in Paris and was invited by Edgar Degas to exhibit with the impressionist circle in 1877. She formed a close friendship with Degas, and although she never became his equal as an artist, in her chosen subjects—the mother and child, or women together—she managed subtle observations. Other Americans, in Cassatt's wake, learned to master the new impressionism. Childe HASSAM, John TWACHTMAN, Julian Alden Weir, and Sargent created works that are distinguished by a lighter palette and unblended strokes. American Impressionists differ from the French in their unwillingness to dissolve objects in light so radically.

Of the artists who chose a period of expatriation, James A. McNeil WHISTLER is the most significant. Whistler was the one American cognizant of French avant-garde developments as they were occurring. Courbet befriended the younger artist and introduced him to his creed of realism. Whistler's *The White Girl* (1862; National Gallery of Art, Washington, D.C.) was rejected by the same Paris salon that rejected Manet's *Déjeuner sur l'herbe* (1863; Louvre, Paris) for similiar reasons. In time Whistler regretted the realist influence on his art and, like Sargent, Cassatt, and the French impressionists, turned to the Japanese print as a source of inspiration. By the end of his career Whistler himself constituted an avant-garde, when he publicly propounded a theory of art for art's sake. The importance of Whistler was not recognized by Americans. Whistler created that American national icon, *Arrangement in Gray and Black No. 1, The Artist's Mother* (*Whistler's Mother*; 1872; Louvre, Paris); the French understood the work's significance and bought it for the Louvre. As a consequence of its neglect, Whistler repudiated his native culture. Asked why he never visited the United States, he explained "It has been suggested many times, but you see I find art so absolutely irritating to the people that really, I hesitate before exasperating another nation."

Whistler's stance toward the public was, of course, exceptional. Most artists painted to please and never more so than when they eschewed innovation to conform to the conservative tastes of the wealthy. Landscape painting continued in popularity, and two artists, Albert BIERSTADT and George INNESS, arrived at highly successful landscape formulas. Bierstadt's preferred subject was the West, which he portrayed on huge canvases concentrating on dramatic effects rendered with careful attention to detail, typified by *Mount Corcoran* (1875–77; Corcoran Gallery of Art, Washington, D.C.). Inness's canvases were smaller and intimate in conception, with romantic, often tree-shrouded scenes painted as though perceived through a veil, as in his *Peace and Plenty* (1865; Metropolitan Museum of Art, New York). William Morris HUNT and John LA FARGE, both members of the upper middle class, achieved styles that romanticized a modified realism. Hunt, who studied with Jean François MILLET, introduced the BARBIZON SCHOOL of painting to Americans; La Farge, after he was commissioned by Richardson to decorate the interior of Boston's Trinity Church, became the premier interior designer of his time, receiving numerous commissions for church interiors, private houses, murals, and stained glass windows.

Development of 20th-Century Painting. By the end of the 19th century, American collectors and a limited segment of the population were catching up with the understand-

John Sloan's Sixth Avenue and Thirtieth Street *was painted in 1907 and is in a private collection. A prominent member of the Ashcan school, Sloan painted realistic scenes of life in New York City.*

ing by some American artists of advanced trends in European painting. Mary Cassatt served the Havemeyer family with prescience when she advised them to buy impressionist works. A few Americans became early and enthusiastic patrons of artists then unappreciated by the French; thus American museums later were bequeathed important holdings of impressionist paintings. This was also the period, however, when Americans looked nostalgically to the past. Magnates amassed collections of old-master paintings; the moneyed class and the general public were one in admiring the works of French academicians and their American counterparts.

In reaction to an art of and for the middle and upper-middle classes, a group of Philadelphia artists arose who chronicled the activities of the masses. Robert HENRI, George LUKS, John SLOAN, and William GLACKENS began as artists trained to provide illustrations for newspapers and magazines. Henri was their leader, and his loosely brushed, dark realist style, as in *Laughing Child* (1907; Whitney Museum of American Art, New York), was emulated by the others. These artists, who became known as the ASHCAN SCHOOL, were the first group in America to make trenchant social comments in their work. But their adherence to a realist style placed them, by the second decade of the 20th century, in the aesthetic rear guard.

The Armory Show. Innovation continued to be a European preserve. In 1913 examples of Europe's most advanced painting and sculpture were introduced to the public by the painter Arthur B. DAVIES, who organized a large exhibition of avant-garde European and American art at the 69th Regiment Armory. This, the epochal ARMORY SHOW, brought the public and the artists abreast of European modernism on native ground. Not suprisingly, some resisted the show. One critic spoke for many when he said at a press dinner, "It was a good show, but don't do it again." Nevertheless, American artists, among them

Young Woman Sewing in the Garden *(1886) by Mary Cassatt shows the influence of Edgar Degas. Cassatt, who lived and studied in Europe, is one of America's few impressionist painters. (Louvre, Paris).*

Arthur Dove, Marsden Hartley, John Marin, Alfred Maurer, Georgia O'Keeffe, and Max Weber incorporated modernist innovations in their art. Even before the Armory Show, Alfred Stieglitz had exhibited these artists, together with the European modernists, at his Photo-Secession Gallery in New York. Gertrude Stein and her circle in Paris served as another conduit for the latest European art. Finally, five important European modernist collections, those of Albert Barnes, John Quinn, the sisters Claribel and Etta Cone, Walter Arensberg, and Lillie P. Bliss, were formed. In the 1920s and 1930s the dual currents of Social Realism and European modernism continued to flow through American cultural life. After the onset of the Depression, private patronage for artists declined alarmingly, and the federal government assumed that role under the aegis of the Works Progress Administration (WPA). Artists frequently depicted subjects of social concern, often in the form of murals for public buildings, for which work of the Mexican muralists José Orozco and Diego Rivera often provided inspiration. Another infusion of European culture came about with the appearance of works by the eminent European surrealists André Breton, Marcel Duchamp, and Max Ernst. Finally, European modernism became institutionalized with the

(Right) *Jasper John's* Flag on an Orange Field *(1957) is an example of pop art, which emerged in reaction to abstract expressionism. (Wallraf-Richartz Museum, Cologne.)* (Below) *Jackson Pollock's* Reflection of the Great Bear *(1947) is a work of the "gestural" wing of abstract expressionism. (Stedelijk Museum, Amsterdam.)*

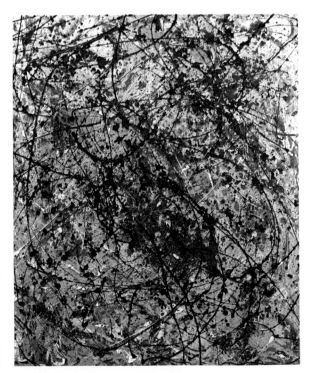

founding of the Museum of Modern Art (1929) and the Guggenheim Museum (1937), both in New York.

Abstract Expressionism. The fall of Paris in 1940, the late critic Harold Rosenberg wrote, shut down the laboratory of the 20th century. When experimentation started up again it was in New York and among a group of artists whose work has come to be known collectively as Abstract Expressionism: the painters Willem de Kooning, Adolf Gottlieb, Franz Kline, Robert Motherwell, Jackson Pollock, Mark Rothko, and Clyfford Still and the sculptor David Smith. During the Depression many of those artists had been employed by the WPA to paint in the social realist mode. But coming to maturity in the Depression, they had a sense that their survival as artists was always in doubt. Having nothing to lose, they felt free to make radical departures from previous art. "The situation was so bad that I know I felt free to try anything no matter how absurd it seemed," Gottlieb remembered. The abstract expressionists painted for each other. Some experimented with pure color, and others needed the promptings of their subconscious. Some of their nonobjective, abstract paintings were large enough to become actual environments.

Elements of abstract expressionism had appeared in earlier paintings, and Surrealism had made the content of the subconscious the content of its art. What made abstract expressionism distinctly American was the emphasis on the energetic large gesture essential to the creative process, and the disdain for conventional notions of beauty. By the 1950s the abstract expressionists had forged a distinctive style; for the first time since Whistler, American artists had international impact. More significantly, they achieved a new order of creation that was neither imitation nor assimilation of European art—it was a new synthesis.

Since World War II, intense interest has been shown in American art, and art historians and critics have made numerous attempts to isolate the American factor. The answer has been sought in the culture, in the lives of the artists, in the topography of the land, in the folkways of the people, in their politics, and in their particular dynamism and energy. It is too early to tell whether the generalizations born of this search will stand. But it is certain that American artists and architects have attempted to achieve a synthesis of their culture and that of Europe.

See also: ART COLLECTORS AND PATRONS; COLONIAL STYLES IN NORTH AMERICA; FOLK ART; MODERN ART; PAINTING; SCULPTURE.

American Association for the Advancement of Science
The largest scientific organization representing all fields of science, the American Association for the Advancement of Science was founded in 1848 to further the work of scientists and to foster scientific freedom and responsibility. Its headquarters is in Washington, D.C. The association holds annual conventions, conducts seminars, establishes awards for young students, produces radio programs, and publishes the weekly *Science* and many books.

American Association of Retired Persons
Founded in 1958, with headquarters in Washington, D.C., the American Association of Retired Persons (AARP) strives to improve all aspects of living for older persons. Eligible for membership is anyone 50 years of age or older, retired or not. The AARP lobbies for political goals and sponsors community-service programs such as crime prevention. It provides pharmacy services and a health-, auto-, and household-insurance program, and offers discounts on various other services.

American Association of University Professors
The American Association of University Professors (AAUP), founded in 1915, is the professional organization of college teachers. Its headquarters is in Washington, D.C. The AAUP Statement on Academic Freedom and Tenure has served in the United States as the established definition of what is meant by ACADEMIC FREEDOM. The organization investigates claims of violations of freedom and maintains a list of censured institutions. It has promoted job security, economic welfare, and intellectual freedom for professors.

American Association of University Women
Established in 1882 in Boston, the American Association of University Women (AAUW) is a national organization of women graduates of regionally accredited colleges. The AAUW has worked for women's suffrage, equality in pay, the election and appointment of women to public office, and equality and justice for women in all areas. Fellowships are granted for undergraduate and graduate work as well as for dissertations and postdoctoral research.

American Automobile Association
The American Automobile Association (AAA) was founded in 1902 to coordinate the activities of various local organizations of motorists. It has become a federation of local automobile clubs, with all states represented and a combined membership of about 29 million. Its headquarters is in Falls Church, Va. The AAA promotes highway improvement and supplies travel information and assistance, legal aid, insurance, and emergency road service for its members.

American Ballet Theatre
American Ballet Theatre (ABT) is one of the two classical ballet companies in the United States to have achieved worldwide renown, the other being the New York City Ballet. ABT, which first performed in 1940—as Ballet Theatre, its present name dating from 1957—was founded by Richard Pleasant and Lucia CHASE. Chase was the company's chief financial support and codirector, with scenic designer Oliver Smith, until 1980. She and Smith were replaced by Mikhail BARYSHNIKOV, who resigned in 1989. Jane Hermann and Oliver Smith became codirectors of the company in 1990. From the beginning, ABT has been a showcase for visiting artists—distinguished choreographers as well as star dancers. Consequently, the character of the company has remained both eclectic and unstable. Many of the outstanding original ballets in ABT's repertoire were created early: Anthony Tudor's *Pillar of Fire* (1942) and *Romeo and Juliet* (1943), Jerome Robbins's *Fancy Free* (1944), and George Balanchine's *Theme and Variations* (1947). Beginning in the mid-1960s the company focused on evening-length classics. Exceptions to this trend were *Push Comes to Shove* (1976) by Twyla THARP, who became a resident choreographer at ABT in 1988, and ABT premieres by Clark Tippet and Mark Morris. Among notable dancers who have appeared with ABT are Alicia Alonso, Erik Bruhn, Fernando Bujones, Anton Dolin, Carla Fracci, Cynthia Gregory, Gelsey Kirkland, Natalia Makarova, and Rudolf Nureyev.

American Bankers Association
The American Bankers Association, founded in 1875, endeavors to promote "the general welfare and usefulness of banks." Through its divisions, corresponding to the division of banks into national, state, mortgage, and savings institutions, the association disseminates to bankers the latest information on activities in their field. It publishes several journals and bulletins, conducts educational and training programs for bankers and bank employees

through such schools as the Stonier Graduate School of Banking and the American Institute of Banking, and sponsors symposia and conferences. Its membership includes about 95 percent of U.S. commercial banks.

American Bar Association   The American Bar Association (ABA), founded in 1878, is the largest professional association of U.S. lawyers, with members from all states. Along with promoting social and professional activities, the ABA helps to maintain high standards within the legal profession. The ABA also seeks to improve the practice of law and the administration of justice.

The association has been influential in securing uniform laws and judicial decisions throughout the 50 states, and in approving candidates for judicial posts. Much of its work is accomplished by its numerous committees on the legal aspects of a broad range of subjects such as legal education and maritime activity. The ABA has its headquarters in Chicago, where it publishes the *American Bar Association Journal*.

American Book Awards   see NATIONAL BOOK AWARDS

American Broadcasting Company   see RADIO AND TELEVISION BROADCASTING

American Civil Liberties Union   The American Civil Liberties Union (ACLU) is an organization dedicated to the protection of constitutional rights and liberties in the United States. It was founded in 1920 by a group of civil libertarians including Jane Addams, Helen Keller, Norman Thomas, Morris Hillquit, and Roger Baldwin, who served as its executive director for 30 years.

The ACLU operates by providing legal counsel in cases involving civil liberties. It has been active in cases relating to academic freedom, separation of church and state, the right to privacy, due process of law, freedom of speech, other freedoms guaranteed in the Bill of Rights, electoral reapportionment, and desegregation. It has opposed capital punishment, censorship, and loyalty oaths. Many important civil rights or liberties cases arising in the United States since 1920 have involved the ACLU, either directly or through the filing of an amicus curiae brief. In addition to engaging in litigation, the ACLU issues public statements, presents testimony before legislative committees, conducts educational programs, and publishes pamphlets and a monthly newspaper.

In its mission, the ACLU has stirred controversy—supporting unpopular causes (the right of American Nazis to demonstrate) or assailing widely accepted practices (municipally financed nativity scenes).

American Colonization Society   The American Colonization Society, organized on Dec. 28, 1816, sought to settle free American blacks in Africa. In 1822 it established the colony of Liberia, to which 2,638 blacks migrated during the next decade. The society won support from many clergy as well as from some leading free blacks who believed that blacks would never receive just treatment in America. Most free blacks, however, opposed the scheme because they believed that its promoters were primarily interested in removing the threat posed to the institution of slavery by the presence of free blacks. They were also repelled by the society's racist arguments, which characterized them as an inferior, degraded class that should be removed from the United States. The society continued its efforts into the 20th century, although it was never successful in convincing large numbers of blacks to emigrate to Africa.

American Farm Bureau Federation   The American Farm Bureau Federation is a federation of county farm organizations founded in 1919 to "promote, protect and represent the business, economic, social, and educational interests of the farmers of the nation." The federation developed from local farm bureaus formed in conjunction with the county agricultural agent plan. Farm Bureau agents, many of whom were employed by the Agricultural Extension Service, had the task of demonstrating improved farming methods to farmers. In 1920 the new national organization opened an office in Washington, D.C., to lobby for the passage of legislation favorable to the federation.

The federation's policies have tended to be conservative. Leaders have favored a minimum of government interference and control and have promoted soil and water conservation and rural education. Membership is on a family basis.

American Federation of Labor and Congress of Industrial Organizations   The American Federation of Labor and Congress of Industrial Organizations (AFL-CIO) is a national federation of LABOR UNIONS in the United States. It was formed in 1955 by the merger of the AFL, an organization composed primarily of craft unions founded in 1886, and the CIO, a federation of industrial unions founded in 1938. (Craft unions organize workers by trades—bricklayers may form one union, carpenters another. Industrial unions enroll members from an entire industry regardless of trade or level of skill.)

The CIO was first formed within the AFL as the Committee for Industrial Organization in 1935; its mission was to organize workers in mass-production industries, which had few unions at that time. In 1938 the CIO was expelled from the AFL and became the Congress of Industrial Organizations. The conflict between the two federations was largely over whether the mass-production industries were to be organized along industrial or along craft lines. The leadership of the CIO included John L. LEWIS of the UNITED MINE WORKERS, David DUBINSKY of the INTERNATIONAL LADIES' GARMENT WORKERS' UNION, Sidney HILLMAN of the AMALGAMATED CLOTHING AND TEXTILE WORKERS UNION, and Charles Howard of the INTERNATIONAL TYPOGRAPHICAL UNION.

By 1955, when the two federations merged into the

AFL-CIO, the original divisive issue had lost much of its force. A need was felt for unity in the face of antiunion legislation and a slowdown in union growth.

The AFL-CIO acts as the political and legislative voice of the trade union movement. It seeks to influence legislation in Congress and state legislatures. It maintains a staff of researchers, social-insurance experts, lawyers, public-relations officers, and specialists in fields ranging from civil rights to veterans' affairs. The AFL-CIO's chief governing body is the executive council, composed of the president, the secretary-treasurer, and a varying number of vice-presidents. Questions of general policy may be referred to a general board made up of the executive council, one principal official from each of the national and international unions, and one official from each of the trade and industrial union departments, which represent interests in a particular industry.

The TEAMSTERS were expelled from the AFL-CIO in 1957 on grounds of corruption; in 1987 the 1.6 million Teamsters were readmitted to the AFL-CIO. The United Mine Workers withdrew voluntarily from the AFL-CIO but voted in 1989 to reaffiliate; the UNITED AUTO WORKERS also withdrew, reaffiliating in 1981. Other unions have never affiliated. George MEANY, who had served as president of the AFL-CIO since its merger in 1955, stepped down in November 1979. He was succeeded by Lane KIRKLAND, previously the secretary-treasurer.

American Federation of Musicians   The American Federation of Musicians (AFM) is a LABOR UNION of performing and recording musicians, affiliated with the American Federation of Labor and Congress of Industrial Organizations. It was founded in 1896. Through much of its history the AFM has been faced with competition from other media that threatened its members' livelihood: amateur musicians, radio broadcasts, and military bands were threats. Under James C. Petrillo, its president from 1940 to 1958, the union tried unsuccessfully to force radio stations to hire standby musicians when playing recorded music. Major strikes in 1944 and 1948 resulted in contracts with the film and record industries that allowed the union to collect royalties on recordings made by its members.

American Federation of State, County, and Municipal Employees   The American Federation of State, County, and Municipal Employees (AFSCME) is a LABOR UNION representing local and state government workers, as well as clerical workers in some private institutions. Founded in 1936, it is affiliated with the AFL-CIO. Public-employee associations were formed in several states in the early 20th century. The Wisconsin State Administrative Employees Association was a forerunner of the present union. It faced jurisdictional competition, however, from the American Federation of Government Employees. When the AFL granted the AFSCME its charter in 1936, the rivalry ended. The union experienced rapid growth after World War II. It has worked to repeal state laws that restrict collective bargaining and prohibit strikes by government employees.

American Federation of Teachers   The American Federation of Teachers (AFT) is a teachers' union within the AFL-CIO (see LABOR UNION). Founded in 1916 with the aid of John Dewey, its headquarters is in Washington, D.C. Growth of the AFT accelerated in 1961 after an affiliate became the bargaining agent for New York City public school teachers. The AFT integrated its southern locals in 1956 and in the late 1960s began organizing among college professors.

American Film Institute   Founded in June 1967 with combined federal and private support, the American Film Institute, located in Washington, D.C., attempts to collect and document, in collaboration with the Library of Congress, every film made in America since 1893. It also supports young filmmakers. The institute's annual Life Achievement Award, established in 1973, has honored such film greats as Bette DAVIS, John FORD, and Orson WELLES.

American foxhound   The American foxhound is a medium-sized, short-coated breed of hound that stands 55–63 cm (21–25 in) at the shoulder and weighs 27–32 kg (60–70 lb). Its coat is usually black and tan on a white body, but any color is permitted in breed contests. The breed is one of the rarest in the United States; only a few dozen are registered annually with the American Kennel Club. It is believed, however, that large numbers of unregistered dogs are maintained in fox-hunting packs.

The American breed has a distinguished history and can be traced to packs imported from England, France, and Ireland. The earliest known pack was brought to Maryland in 1650. These early imports were used to hunt the gray fox, but to cope with the faster English red fox—

The American foxhound was developed from English foxhounds imported during the 17th century. The breed is used for the sport of fox hunting.

introduced to the colonies in the early 1700s—American foxhounds were interbred with other hound strains imported from France and Ireland.

American Friends Service Committee   The American Friends Service Committee, a Quaker organization for social service, was formed in 1917 principally to carry out relief programs in war-ravaged areas of Europe and to arrange for its members and other conscientious objectors to replace their required military service with alternative contributions. Since World War I, the committee has participated in national and international humanitarian programs of all kinds and was particularly active during the Korean and Vietnam wars. In 1947 it shared the Nobel Peace Prize with the Service Council of the British Society of Friends.

American Fur Company   At the peak of its influence in the early 19th century, the American Fur Company was the wealthiest fur-trading firm in the United States. It contributed to the economic development of the West, and the MOUNTAIN MEN it employed made important contributions to western exploration. Formed in 1808 by the German immigrant John Jacob Astor (see ASTOR family), the company founded the trading post of Astoria at the mouth of the Columbia River in 1811, and Astor's employees developed an overland route to the Pacific.

Astor was forced to sell Astoria to the NORTH WEST COMPANY of Canada during the War of 1812. He then concentrated on the upper Mississippi River valley until the 1820s when he bought out competitors, allied himself with the Columbia Fur Company, and directed his immense resources farther west.

Soon after founding Fort McKenzie among the feared Blackfoot Indians on the upper Missouri River, the company dominated the region and then began a bitter competition with the Rocky Mountain Fur Company farther south. Astor sold out his interest in 1834. Within a few years much of the region's furs had been depleted. His successors operated mainly from trading posts on the Great Plains until the American Fur Company sold out to the North Western Fur Company in 1864.

American history   see UNITED STATES, HISTORY OF THE

American Independent party   The American Independent party nominated George WALLACE as a third major candidate for president of the United States in 1968. Wallace, nationally known for his racist positions and anti-integration activities as governor of Alabama, ran a campaign that stressed states' rights, increased defense spending, Americanism, support for law enforcement agencies, and decreased federal expenditures for many domestic programs. With retired air force general Curtis E. LeMay as his vice-presidential running-mate, Wallace had widespread support from white lower-middle-class voters. The party polled 9.9 million votes, or about 13.5 percent of the popular vote, and won 45 electoral votes from five Southern states–not enough to force a deadlock in the electoral college and gain the party some political concessions.

In 1969, Wallace supporters reorganized as the American party. In 1972, John G. Schmitz ran for president, winning one percent of the popular vote. The party split in 1976.

American Indian Movement   The American Indian Movement (AIM), an activist Indian group concerned with the civil rights of American Indians, was formed in 1968 in Minneapolis, Minn., to deal with discriminatory practices of the police in the arrest of Indians in Minneapolis and Saint Paul. The appeal of the social movement quickly spread. In November 1972, AIM was instrumental in the week-long occupation by Indians of the Bureau of Indian Affairs building in Washington, D.C., and early in 1973 the group's 10-week takeover of WOUNDED KNEE, on the Pine Ridge Sioux Reservation (S.Dak.), attracted world attention.

Although largely an urban phenomenon that arose in response to racist attitudes in urban ghettos, AIM has also become involved in tribal affairs on Indian reservations, pressing for restitution of lands or reparations. Many tribal peoples disclaim affiliation with the movement, which has been accused of provoking confrontation.

AIM has established "survival schools" in urban areas. It has also sponsored international treaty conferences on several Lakota Sioux reservations, resulting in the 1977 International Treaty Conference with the UN in Geneva, Switzerland.

In addition to being a social activist movement, the group claims to be oriented toward native religion. Members are not considered bona fide until they have participated in the SUN DANCE ritual on the Pine Ridge reservation. AIM reported a membership of about 5,000 in the late 1980s.

American Indians   see INDIANS, AMERICAN

American Kennel Club   The American Kennel Club (AKC), founded in 1884, is a nonprofit organization established to aid in developing and maintaining purebred DOG bloodlines. As the principal agency in the United States for the registration of individual, purebred dogs, the AKC maintains records—some dating from 1878—on the breeding of more than 21 million dogs. It registers more than 1 million dogs annually. In addition, the AKC has established, and enforces, the standards and rules governing dog shows and obedience and field trials. The organization publishes (monthly) *Pure-Bred Dogs* and *Stud Book Register*.

American Legion   The American Legion is the largest U.S. veterans' organization; its members are drawn from the veterans of the two world wars and the wars in

Korea and Vietnam. The legion was founded in 1919. It has about 2.6 million members organized in about 15,000 local posts.

The legion's headquarters is in Indianapolis, Ind., and it has an office in Washington, D.C. Basically concerned with the social and political interests of veterans, the Legion is also dedicated to community affairs and sponsors patriotic and charitable programs. It has four major fields of activity: rehabilitation of veterans through medical and educational benefits; child welfare; national security; and Americanism. The Legion sponsors junior baseball leagues and Boy Scout troops, high school oratorical contests, and the study of government through its Boys' State and Nation groups. On the national level it has been a powerful lobby for military preparedness and veterans' benefits.

American Library Association

American Library Association The American Library Association (ALA), founded in 1876, is devoted to the advancement of library science and the improvement of library services. Its annual conference is well attended by librarians from around the world.

ALA activities cover such issues as library education, library publications, and the establishment of library standards. The association encourages the use of open stacks; the increase of special services, such as those for children and the blind; the enrichment of rural libraries; and the establishment of interlibrary loan facilities. The organization also is involved in the accreditation of library schools and the publication of the monthly *American Libraries* and the book review journals *Booklist* and *Choice*. The many annual ALA awards include the two most prestigious awards for children's books, the Caldecott and the Newbery medals.

The ALA is headquartered in Chicago. It has a membership of 40,000 and a staff of 250, with an additional voluntary staff.

American literature

American literature From its origins in colonial America to its present status internationally, American literature has stressed the diversity and uniqueness of the American character and experience. The Puritans attempted to demonstrate that God had ordained their emigration and had intended that their communities stand as examples of holiness and right for the rest of the world. In Revolutionary times this idea of specialness came to include unique American types, such as the Yankee, and a belief that the country was destined to produce a new literature. As it matured, American literature followed the major movements of Western literature in the 19th century—romanticism, realism, and naturalism. American writers, however, concentrated on the American scene and sought to affirm a distinct national identity.

Colonial Literature

The colonial period extends from the 17th-century Virginia and Massachusetts settlements through the Great Awakening, a religious revival in the 1740s, and its aftermath. Although dominated by Puritan-Calvinistic doc-

trine, early American literature was not confined to religion. The religious writings, as well as the more secular, chronicle the lives of exceptional individuals who rose above the physically difficult and spiritually demanding environment of the New World. These early writers set the tone and the rhetoric and foreshadowed the major concerns of later American writing.

The first generation of settlers wrote sermons, religious tracts, diaries, and histories of their undertakings. The leading religious controversialists were John COTTON, Anne HUTCHINSON, Roger WILLIAMS, and John Winthrop (see WINTHROP family). Winthrop's *Journal*, originally printed as a *History of New England from 1630 to 1649*, remains a major historical source. It was followed by William BRADFORD's *History of Plimouth Plantation* (pub. 1856), Edward Johnson's *History of New England* (1654), and Thomas MORTON's *New English Canaan* (1637), which stands out for its irreverence and hints of bawdiness. Histories of the South with enduring literary qualities were Capt. John SMITH's *The Generall Historie of Virginia* (1624) and, much later, William BYRD's *History of the Dividing Line* (composed and reworked from 1728 but not published until 1841).

Puritan writers stressed religious and didactic themes. The first book published in America was the *Bay Psalm Book: The Whole Book of Psalmes Faithfully Translated into English Metre* (1640). Michael WIGGLESWORTH continued in the Puritan vein, exhorting against sin in his popular poem, *Day of Doom* (1662). Meanwhile, poetry of genuine accomplishment and a less stern, Puritan emphasis was written by Anne BRADSTREET in *The Tenth Muse Lately Sprung Up in America* (1650) and by Edward TAYLOR, whose poems were not discovered until 1939. More in accord with the Puritan temperament are the spiritual autobiographies, which describe the Puritan experience of conversion. Thomas Shepard's *The Sincere Convert* (1640) is one of the first; Jonathan Edwards's "Personal Narrative," originally published in 1765 in the *Life of the Rev. J. Edwards* by the theologian Samuel Hopkins, is one of the last.

The memorable works of the colonial period depicted the conditions of life in the New World. The first and best-known narrative of captivity by Indians was Mary

Cotton Mather, Boston's leading theologian in the late 17th and early 18th centuries, wrote more than 450 works of literature, many defending the established Puritan religion of the Massachusetts colony.

Rowlandson's *Captivity and Restauration* (1682). Among diarists, Sarah Kemble Knight's account of her journey (1704) from Boston to New York on horseback and Samuel SEWALL's diaries (spanning 1673 to 1729) describe life in the colonies.

The Puritan literary ideal is best summed up in the gargantuan ecclesiastical history by Cotton Mather, the *Magnalia Christi Americana, or the Ecclesiastical History of New England from its First Planting in the New Year 1620, unto the Year of our Lord 1698* (1702). This compendium celebrates America and its religious Puritan leaders in a rhetoric of magnificent extravagance. An equally intense piety pervades the writings of Jonathan EDWARDS early in the 18th century. Besides his spiritual autobiography, Edwards is known for *A Treatise Concerning Religious Affections* (1746) and *Freedom of the Will* (1754), both of which try to incorporate the philosophy of John Locke, and for what is probably the most famous sermon of hellfire and brimstone ever preached, "Sinners in the Hands of an Angry God" (1741). The young Benjamin FRANKLIN wrote during the same period as Edwards. Although his *Poor Richard's Almanack* (1732) anticipated a more rational moralism, it contained much of the proverbial wisdom that Franklin had learned from works such as Cotton Mather's *Bonifacius, or Essays To Do Good* (1710). Similarly, Franklin's *Autobiography* reflected a concern for one's actions that was typical of the Puritan spiritual autobiographers.

Revolutionary Literature

The American Revolutionary period extends from the first agitations by patriots in the early 1760s through the adoption of the Constitution in 1787. The ardor and disputatiousness characteristic of the Puritans were felt early in this period in the sermons of Jonathan Mayhew and the political tracts of the patriots. Prominent among the so-called pamphleteers were James OTIS, who wrote five controversial and often intemperate pamphlets; John DICKINSON, the author of a series of letters widely printed in newspapers during 1767 and 1768 and signed "A Farmer in Pennsylvania"; and John ADAMS, the author of *A Dissertation on Canon and Feudal Law* (1765), the first of a long series of works more properly considered philosophical literature than political pamphlets. It was, however, Thomas PAINE's pamphlet *Common Sense,* advocating American independence, that had the greatest revolutionary impact in the colonies and that received the most attention abroad.

The Revolution itself fostered an outpouring of patriotic verse, much of it consisting of satirical attacks on the Loyalists. The most popular of the satires was John Trumbull's *M'Fingal*, a burlesque of Tory politics written in 1775 and expanded in 1782. Trumbull was a leading figure among the Connecticut Wits, who wrote satires similar to his own. A common poetic subject of the Revolutionary period, the coming greatness of America, was expressed in the title of the Princeton college commencement poem of 1771, *On the Rising Glory of America* (1772), written by Philip FRENEAU in collaboration with Hugh Henry Brackenridge.

American literature during this period continued to be expressed largely in histories, journals, personal diaries, letters, and political writing conceived in the revolutionary spirit. An exception was the accomplishment of Phillis WHEATLEY, an African slave, now considered America's first important black writer. Her derivative but finely wrought *Poems on Various Subjects, Religious and Moral* was published in London in 1773. The diverse prose of the time included the *Journal* (1774) of John WOOLMAN, a Quaker; the *Letters of an American Farmer* (1782) by the French-born Jean de CRÈVECOEUR; the *Travels* (1791) in the Floridas, Georgia, and the Carolinas of William Bartram; and the Revolutionary-period letters of Abigail ADAMS, the wife of John Adams. Probably the best-remembered works of the period are the state papers, beginning with Thomas JEFFERSON's *Declaration of Independence*. In 1787 and 1788 Alexander HAMILTON, John JAY, and James MADISON collaborated in writing 85 essays defending the new Constitution and collected as *The Federalist*.

The first American play, William Godfrey's *The Prince of Parthia* (1765), appeared during this period despite the moral censure accorded to theater in the colonies. A heroic tragedy in blank verse, it was first performed in 1767. It was followed by the first stage comedy to be produced in the United States, Royall Tyler's *The Contrast* (1787), which introduced Jonathan, the first stage Yankee.

Early National Literature

The years from the adoption of the Constitution (1787) to the period of Jacksonian nationalism (1828–36) mark the emergence of a self-consciously national literature. The poet Joel BARLOW, who was, like John Trumbull, one of the Connecticut Wits, greeted the new United States with his epic *The Columbiad* (1807), a reworking of his earlier *The Vision of Columbus* (1787). Philip Freneau wrote lyric poetry that fused the native scene and native expression. Other writers strove to develop an American literature but did not concentrate on strictly American subjects, using instead the universal themes of romance, virtue, vice, and seduction that pervaded popular novels in England and on the Continent. William Hill Brown's *The Power of Sympathy* (1789), an imitation of Goethe's *Sorrows of Young Werther*, is regarded by some as the first American novel. Susanna Rowson's sentimental and didactic tale of seduction, *Charlotte Temple*, published (1791) in London as *Charlotte: A Tale of Truth*, was extremely popular. In contrast to the prevailing sentimental novel was Hugh Henry Brackenridge's massive *Modern Chivalry* (1792–1815), a picaresque novel with an underlying satire on bad government. The first professional novelist was Charles Brockden Brown, whose gothic and philosophical romances, beginning with *Wieland* (1798), anticipated Edgar Allan Poe.

Early in the 19th century, Washington IRVING gained European recognition as America's first genuine man of letters. *A History of New York* (1809) is a whimsical satire of pedantic historians and literary classics. His best-known tales, "Rip Van Winkle" and "The Legend of Sleepy Hollow," appeared in *The Sketch Book of Geoffrey*

Herman Melville (1819–91)

Edgar Allan Poe (1809–49)

Emily Dickinson (1830–86)

Crayon, Gent, which was published serially in 1819–20. William Cullen BRYANT emerged in the 1820s as a poet of international stature. His "Thanatopsis" (1817), influenced by the English Graveyard Poets, linked American literature to the emerging English ROMANTICISM. Still, despite European influences, American writers attempted to create a distinctive literature during a time of rising literary nationalism. Noah WEBSTER contributed *An American Dictionary of the English Language* (1828), in which he insisted that the country possessed its own language. The nationalist theme was echoed by William Ellery CHANNING, Edward EVERETT, and most memorably by Ralph Waldo EMERSON in his Phi Beta Kappa address at Harvard, "The American Scholar" (1837), which Oliver Wendell HOLMES called "our intellectual Declaration of Independence."

James Fenimore COOPER was the first important American novelist to succeed with subjects and settings that are largely American. Cooper achieved international prominence with his second novel, *The Spy* (1821), a tale of the Revolution. His many novels blending history and romance resulted in his being called "the American [Sir Walter] Scott," a title that put him in the company of one of the period's most popular and respected authors. Cooper became best known for his Leatherstocking Tales, five novels that run from *The Pioneers* (1823) to *The Deerslayer* (1841). Cooper's settings capture the American idea of nature, and his hero, Natty Bumppo, expresses the self-reliant, pioneering spirit of America.

Much of Cooper's sense of America was caught by the Fireside Poets, who celebrated American history and a benign American nature. Henry Wadsworth LONGFELLOW displayed his skill at telling a story in verse in *Hiawatha* (1855), *The Courtship of Miles Standish* (1858), and *Evangeline* (1847). But Longfellow and his contemporaries succeeded best in public poetry intended for recitation. Still powerful are Longfellow's *The Midnight Ride of Paul Revere* (1863), John Greenleaf WHITTIER's "Barbara Freitchie" (1863), and Oliver Wendell Holmes's "Old Ironsides" (1830).

Edgar Allan POE stood apart from literary nationalism and represented a gloomier side of romanticism. As a reviewer, he was a harsh critic of second-rate American writing, but he dabbled in many popular sensationalistic forms. His often technically complex poetry uses commonplace romantic themes but gives them a philosophical and mystical application. Many of his short stories remain internationally famous, and he may be said to have invented the detective story. In "The Fall of the House of Usher" and "The Tell-Tale Heart," Poe perfected the tale of gothic horror.

American Renaissance

The American renaissance, also known as the American romantic movement, began with the maturing of American literature in the 1830s and '40s and ended with its flowering in the 1850s. During the 1830s Ralph Waldo Emerson established himself as the spokesman for TRANSCENDENTALISM, first set forth in his essay *Nature* (1836). The group known as the transcendentalists that gathered around him in Concord, Mass., included Bronson ALCOTT, Margaret FULLER, Theodore PARKER, and William Ellery Channing, who joined with Emerson in the publication of *Dial* magazine (1840–44). They subscribed to Emerson's faith that all people are united in their communion with the oversoul, a postreligious equivalent of God. Each individual, Emerson said, finds his or her own way to transcendence through self-knowledge, self-reliance, and the contemplation of nature.

Henry David THOREAU came closest to putting Emerson's ideas into practice. After two intermittent years at Walden Pond in Concord, Mass., he wrote *Walden or Life in the Woods* (1854). In this book, Thoreau observes nature from the viewpoint of a naturalist-philosopher reflecting on the quiet desperation of humanity and the transcendental solace of the natural world. No less consciously indebted to Emerson was Walt WHITMAN, who dedicated the first edition of his poetry, *Leaves of Grass* (1855), to him. Whitman celebrated an untrammeled communion with nature with overtones of sensuality that appeared shocking even though his poetry expressed

Walt Whitman (1819–92)

Mark Twain (1835–1910)

Henry James (1843–1916)

sound transcendental doctrine. Whitman also took seriously Emerson's appeal for American originality; he devised a loose, "natural" form of versification that seemed unpoetic and jarring to his contemporaries. After the Civil War, Whitman gained wider acceptance with his elegy on the death of Lincoln, "When Lilacs Last in the Dooryard Bloomed" (1865). Whitman's prose works include *Democratic Vistas* (1871), containing his philosophy of American democracy along with prophecies of its future greatness and the coming greatness of its literature, and *Specimen Days* (1882), an autobiographical account of his Civil War experiences as a volunteer nurse.

Unknown to the public, another American innovative poet, Emily DICKINSON, was writing in Amherst, Mass. Her poems, written mostly from the late 1850s through the 1860s, were unconventional and deceptively simple lyrics concerned with death, eternity, and the inner life. Few were published in her lifetime, but when they were rediscovered in the 1920s, Dickinson took her place as a major American poet.

Nathaniel HAWTHORNE represents American romanticism with its roots firmly planted in the Puritan past. His stories were collected in *Twice-Told Tales* (1837), which established his importance as an American writer. Some were tales of the Puritans and of early American history; others used a mixture of symbolism and allegory that, together with certain recurrent themes, was carried over into Hawthorne's novels. His masterpiece, the *Scarlet Letter* (1850), is a symbolic romance set in Puritan New England. Hawthorne had been attracted to Emerson's thought but rejected its optimism both here and in *The Blithedale Romance* (1852), a novel based on the transcendentalists' utopian experiment, BROOK FARM. Herman MELVILLE also rejected Emerson's philosophy. His first novel, *Typee: A Peep at Polynesian Life* (1846), based on his own adventures after deserting his ship while on a whaling voyage, challenged the spiritual substance of Christianity. Melville continued to write of the sea and adventure, but now with increasing philosophical complexity and a mixture of allegory and symbolism comparable to Hawthorne's. The culmination of his growth came in *Moby Dick* (1851). This philosophical adventure satisfied the age's aspiration for an epic of nature and America, yet its greatness was not recognized at the time. Certainly it came nowhere near the success of Harriet Beecher STOWE's best-seller *Uncle Tom's Cabin* (1852). After the failure of Melville's next novel, *Pierre* (1852), Melville continued to write, but he became increasingly discouraged with his inability to reach an audience. At his death in 1891 he was virtually unknown. He left behind poetry on Civil War themes, notably *Battle Pieces and Aspects of the War* (1866), and the short, unfinished novel *Billy Budd*. These and other late manuscripts, neglected for many years, were rediscovered in the 1920s by critics and scholars, whose assessments established Melville as a superior American writer.

Post–Civil War Literature

The post–Civil War period extends roughly from the rise of realism to the advent of naturalism, up to World War I. The Civil War itself affected literature less than did the industrial expansion that came in its aftermath. Yet the war was the basis for poetry by Melville, Emerson, Lowell, and Whitman, and of significant autobiographical accounts by Thomas Wentworth HIGGINSON, Charles Francis ADAMS, Jr., and Ulysses S. GRANT.

Mark TWAIN led the movement away from the romanticism typical of the American renaissance to a worldly realism that dealt with actual places and situations. In his dialogue he produced equivalents of American speech never before attempted. Twain drew extensively from his personal experiences: on his own travels for *The Innocents Abroad* (1869) and *Roughing It* (1872), on his days as a riverboat pilot for *Life on the Mississippi* (1883), and on his youth for his boyhood stories *Tom Sawyer* (1876) and the *Adventures of Huckleberry Finn* (1884). *Huckleberry Finn* is considered by many critics to be the first modern American novel; it is more than likely the best known and is undoubtedly one of the great American literary achievements.

Booker T. Washington (1856–1915)   *Stephen Crane (1871–1900)*   *T. S. Eliot (1888–1965)*

The choice of the pen name Mark Twain by Samuel Clemens followed a practice common among American humorists who wrote during the 19th century. James Russell Lowell wrote as Hosea Bigelow, Joel Chandler HARRIS as Uncle Remus, David Ross Locke as Petroleum V. Nasby, Charles Farrar Browne as Artemus WARD, and Finley Peter DUNNE as Mr. Dooley.

As novelists and critics, William Dean HOWELLS and Henry JAMES contributed to the shift from romance to realism. Howells's *The Rise of Silas Lapham* (1885) concerns a farmer who becomes wealthy and moves to Boston but whose spiritual rise comes only when he loses his wealth. Despite a prolific output, Howells's significance rests mostly on his literary criticism and opposition to provincialism in American literature. James departed even further from the provincial scene. He portrayed expatriate Americans in a European setting in *Daisy Miller* (1879) and in his triumph of psychological realism, *The Portrait of a Lady* (1881). Conversely, James presented the reactions of Europeans to a New England background in *The Europeans* (1878). In *The Bostonians* (1886) he satirized New England reformers and philanthropists. As prolific as Howells, James was also a self-conscious critic and an advocate of realism. In his last novels, notably *The Golden Bowl* (1904), James created a new, complex language and symbolism that heralded the age of modernism.

Regionalism, the literature of particular sections of the country, flourished, however. Many authors who used this form of realistic local color were women, among them Willa CATHER, Kate CHOPIN, Mary E. Wilkins FREEMAN, Ellen GLASGOW, Sarah Orne JEWETT, and Edith WHARTON. Other writers of the period who are thought of as regionalists are Ambrose BIERCE, Hamlin GARLAND, and Bret HARTE. Much of the literature of black Americans was regional in setting, by force of circumstance. Charles CHESNUTT and William Wells Brown were early black novelists. In *Lyrics of Lowly Life* (1896), the poet and novelist Paul Laurence DUNBAR used dialect and humble settings in a blend of pathos and humor. Some of the most powerful writing by African Americans has been autobiographical; in the post–Civil War period, works depicting the experiences of black Americans include *The Narrative of the Life of Frederick Douglass, an American Slave* (1845), *Up from Slavery* (1901) by Booker T. WASHINGTON, *The Souls of Black Folk* (1903) by W. E. B. DU BOIS, and the *Autobiography of an Ex-Colored Man* (1912) by James Weldon JOHNSON.

In the 1890s novels emphasizing a harsher view of reality began to appear, marking the beginnings of American naturalism. Stephen CRANE's *Maggie, A Girl of the Streets* (1893) was little noticed, but his *Red Badge of Courage* (1895) was immediately recognized as a classic. Frank NORRIS more nearly exhibited the features of naturalism than did Crane, especially in *McTeague* (1899), *The Octopus* (1901), and *The Pit* (1903). Norris's works, often concerned with the Darwinian struggle for survival, focus on human greed, depravity, and suffering. Theodore DREISER created the most striking naturalistic works, beginning with *Sister Carrie* (1900) and culminating in *An American Tragedy* (1925). Dreiser's works reflect compassion and an understanding of human motivations. They analyze with dramatic insight the dilemma of the individual in contemporary society.

Social protest and utopianism went hand in hand with naturalism. Upton SINCLAIR exposed the deplorable conditions in the meat industry in *The Jungle* (1906), Jack LONDON rejected society in his autobiographical novel *Martin Eden* (1909), and Jacob RIIS depicted the lives of poor immigrants in photographs and words in *How the Other Half Lives* (1890). Henry Adams, in *The Education of Henry Adams* (1918), critically and ironically explored the quest for meaning in the face of social, historical, and economic change.

American poets in the early part of the 20th century led in developing literary modernism. Vachel LINDSAY and Carl SANDBURG followed in the Whitman tradition of loose versification and the celebration of America, as, to some extent, did Edgar Lee MASTERS in his *Spoon River Anthology* (1915). More traditional in form yet more penetrating in psychology were the works of Edwin Arlington ROBINSON

Robert Frost (1874–1963)

F. Scott Fitzgerald (1896–1940)

Eugene O'Neill (1888–1953)

and, particularly, Robert FROST. By the 1930s Frost had become America's best-known and most-beloved native poet. Two American expatriates in London, Ezra POUND and T. S. ELIOT, became leading poets of the century. Eliot's *The Waste Land* (1922) represents the extreme of complexity and profundity in modern poetry. Two of Eliot's contemporaries, Wallace STEVENS and William Carlos WILLIAMS, were possibly as influential as Eliot on the rising young poets. Williams, in particular, extended into IMAGISM Whitman's exploration of American themes and rhythms.

Post–World War I Literature

American literature of the 1920s was characterized by disillusionment with ideals and even with civilization itself. The writers of the so-called lost generation reacted with disillusionment to the war and adopted the despairing tone of *The Waste Land*. The young poet E. E. CUMMINGS used his wartime experience as the basis for a novel, *The Enormous Room* (1922), as did John DOS PASSOS and William FAULKNER. Ernest HEMINGWAY, however, captured the experience of war and the sense of loss most lucidly in his first novel, *The Sun Also Rises* (1926), which probes the experience of a group of disillusioned expatriates in Paris, and in *A Farewell to Arms* (1929). American writers gathered in Paris during the 1920s, partly to escape what they regarded as the small-town morality and shallowness of American culture. Among them, F. Scott FITZGERALD had the greatest success in the United States. His masterpiece, *The Great Gatsby* (1925), helped create the image of the Roaring Twenties, the age of the flapper, and the jazz age.

In the United States, a group of writers chronicled their escape from small-town America and exposed its hypocrisies. Sherwood ANDERSON inspired the rest with *Winesburg, Ohio* (1919), based on Anderson's hometown of Clyde, Ohio. Sinclair Lewis attacked provincialism in *Main Street* (1920) and added a word meaning "unthinking conformist" to the language with *Babbitt* (1922). H. L. MENCKEN took up the attack on the "booboisie" in his essays, as did Ring LARDNER in his sports stories and, at the end of the decade, Thomas WOLFE in the autobiographical novel, *Look Homeward, Angel* (1929).

The influence of European modernism reached the United States during this period. Gertrude STEIN's experiments with the sounds and speech patterns of the American language, developed earlier in Paris, influenced Hemingway and many others. Marianne MOORE edited the *Dial* magazine and for several decades influenced American poetry with her disciplined, often unconventional verse. Hart CRANE attempted an alternative to Eliot's less vernacular modernism with his American epic, *The Bridge* (1930). William Faulkner assimilated the technique of the STREAM OF CONSCIOUSNESS novel from James Joyce's *Ulysses* and put it to use in *The Sound and the Fury* (1929). The doctrines of modernism were championed in little magazines such as the *Criterion, Dial*, and *Hound and Horn*. Meanwhile, American literature began to be studied critically. D. H. LAWRENCE's *Studies in Classic American Literature* (1923) was followed by William Carlos Williams's *In the American Grain* (1925) and V. L. Parrington's *Main Currents in American Thought* (1927–30).

During this period the American drama flowered, primarily because of Eugene O'NEILL's plays. With such brooding, symbolic, and intensely psychological works as *The Emperor Jones* (1920), *Mourning Becomes Electra* (1931), and his later, poetically autobiographical masterpiece *Long Day's Journey into Night* (1956), O'Neill set a new standard for American playwrights. He was joined by a host of talented dramatists, including Maxwell ANDERSON, Lillian HELLMAN, Elmer RICE, Thornton WILDER, Philip Barry, and later by Edward ALBEE, Arthur MILLER, and Tennessee WILLIAMS.

The 1930s

The depression and the rise of fascism in Europe dominated American literature during the 1930s. Proletarian literature consciously aimed at stimulating protest—and, in some cases, revolution—by the working class. John Dos Passos chronicled the age in his trilogy, *U.S.A.* (1930; 1932; 1936). James T. FARRELL supplied natu-

William Faulkner (1897–1962)   *Ernest Hemingway (1899–1961)*   *Robert Lowell (1917–77)*

Photo Jill Krementz © 1975

ralistic detail in *Studs Lonigan* (1935), as did Meyer Levin in *The Old Bunch* (1937). The plays of Clifford ODETS and Sidney Kingsley and John STEINBECK's immensely successful *The Grapes of Wrath* (1939) are better remembered today than are the more overtly political works of the time.

Concurrent with socially conscious literature, a detached school of literary criticism emerged. The NEW CRITICISM, represented by Yvor WINTERS and Richard P. Blackmur, was dominated by the Southern critics Cleanth BROOKS, John Crowe RANSOM, Allen TATE, and Robert Penn WARREN. Relatively untouched by the literary or political developments of the period, however, were such innovators as Henry MILLER and Nathanael WEST.

From the 1930s a great many American writers have used the short story as their principal means of expression. Notable exponents of this form were John O'HARA and Katherine Anne PORTER, who were followed in the 1940s and '50s by Carson McCULLERS, Eudora WELTY, and Flannery O'CONNOR. Such writers as Donald BARTHELME and John UPDIKE continue to devote much of their energy to short fiction, as did John CHEEVER. The detective short story and novel were also perfected in the 1930s by James M. CAIN, Raymond T. CHANDLER, and Dashiell HAMMETT.

Literature Since World War II

Many of the new writers of the 1940s and '50s were affected by World War II but did not always express their concern explicitly. James JONES, with *From Here to Eternity* (1951), and Norman MAILER, with *The Naked and the Dead* (1948), made their reputations as war novelists. The poets Randall JARRELL, Robert LOWELL, Jr., and Karl SHAPIRO wrote of the war but later, like Theodore ROETHKE and Delmore SCHWARTZ, turned their attention to private events.

American drama began to flourish once again in the years after the war. Tennessee Williams explored the themes of innocence and experience in *The Glass Menagerie* (1944) and *A Streetcar Named Desire* (1947). Arthur Miller's *Death of a Salesman* (1949) is a classic

modern tragedy. Edward Albee introduced the tradition of the THEATER OF THE ABSURD in *The Zoo Story* (1958) and *Who's Afraid of Virginia Woolf?* (1962).

The appearance of Saul BELLOW's *The Victim* (1947) and Bernard MALAMUD's *The Assistant* (1957) seem, in retrospect, the first signs of what is loosely described as a "Jewish movement." During the 1950s and '60s many Jewish writers emerged, including Philip ROTH, J. D. SALINGER, AND Herbert Gold.

The social movements of the 1960s—youth, counterculture, antiwar protest—profoundly affected literature. The Vietnam War gave rise to journalism by Mary McCARTHY, Susan SONTAG, and Frances Fitzgerald; the memoir *Dispatches* (1977), by Michael Herr; and novels by Robert Stone (*Dog Soldiers,* 1974) and Tim O'Brien (*Going after Cacciato,* 1978).

The protest writing of the 1960s and '70s was influenced by earlier experiments in which fictional techniques were used for nonfiction writing. Truman CAPOTE's *In Cold Blood* (1965), an account of a murder, and Norman Mailer's *Armies of the Night* (1968) and *The Executioner's Song* (1980) are examples of this mode. Tom WOLFE's exuberant, rhetorical prose in *The Kandy-Kolored Tangerine-Flake Streamline Baby* (1965) helped establish the "new journalism" (see JOURNALISM).

From the 1960s many American writers aligned themselves with ethnic and feminist causes. Ralph ELLISON's *Invisible Man* (1952) kept within the literary mainstream. The poet Gwendolyn BROOKS and the playwright Lorraine HANSBERRY (*A Raisin in the Sun,* 1959) also worked within established conventions, and James BALDWIN began as a writer of traditional prose. With *The Fire Next Time* (1963), however, Baldwin's work grew increasingly committed to the black protest movement of the 1960s and '70s. He was followed by the angry writings of Imamu Amiri BARAKA (LeRoi Jones), Eldridge CLEAVER, and Ishmael REED, and by the less strident work of Nikki GIOVANNI, Toni MORRISON, and Alice WALKER.

Women writers, partly inspired by the example of Betty FRIEDAN's *The Feminine Mystique* (1963), also developed a distinct genre of writing that deals almost exclusively with feminine experience. Sylvia PLATH assumed great importance for reasons that concerned her life as much as her poetry. Tillie OLSEN (*Tell Me a Riddle,* 1961) and Grace PALEY (*The Little Disturbances of Man,* 1959) produced humorous accounts of domestic life. The poets Denise LEVERTOV, Adrienne RICH, and Anne SEXTON also took up feminist concerns in the 1960s. Joan DIDION (*Play It as It Lays,* 1970) described the contemporary situation of women in novels and essays. Joyce Carol OATES, writing in both traditional and experimental forms, was the most prolific novelist of the period, whose women writers also include Kate MILLETT and Elizabeth Janeway.

Styles of contemporary American literature are as diverse as its subject matter, and whereas several novelists, such as John HAWKES, have experimented radically with technique, others have worked within traditional narrative forms to produce work that draws on several modes of writing. Kurt VONNEGUT has used fantasy and science fiction; Bellow mingled philosophy with the epistolary novel in *Herzog*; Gore VIDAL has exploited the historical novel; and John BARTH, Joseph HELLER, and Thomas PYNCHON have written arcane, fantastic, but basically traditional narratives. Wright MORRIS, Walker PERCY, and Peter TAYLOR have maintained the strong tradition of regional writing, and the novel of manners, exemplified by Edith Wharton's works, is continued by Louis AUCHINCLOSS.

Among the most influential innovators of this period was the Russian-born Vladimir NABOKOV, who, after the publication of *Lolita* (1958) and *Pale Fire* (1962), became a best-selling U.S. novelist. The experiments of William S. BURROUGHS and William GADDIS are celebrated but less widely read. John GARDNER, who began his career with ambitious attempts to create ironic, allegorical versions of myths, argued (in *On Moral Fiction,* 1979) in favor of what he called "moral," or socially responsible, fiction.

Among poets a diversity of style and subject matter prohibits easy summary. The publication of Robert Lowell's *Life Studies* (1959) is often thought to have inaugurated a "confessional" mode in the work of such poets as Plath, Sexton, Levertov, and W. D. SNODGRASS. The work of Charles OLSON and the BLACK MOUNTAIN SCHOOL OF POETRY retained its importance to John ASHBERY, Robert BLY, James MERRILL, and James Wright. The highly respected poet W. S. MERWIN has developed his own distinctive manner from acquaintance with the styles of W. H. Auden, Robert Graves, and Ezra Pound. Allen GINSBERG, developing out of the BEAT GENERATION movement of the late 1950s, and Gary SNYDER emphasized Oriental and American Indian spirituality. Two of the most notable poets of the 1960s and '70s, Elizabeth BISHOP and Richard WILBUR, seemed independent of influence or fashion, and they developed distinct personal modes of utterance. The number of "little magazines" and small presses increased during the 1970s and '80s, creating unprecedented opportunities for the publication of poetry.

Although American literature in the 1980s stood divided among special-interest groups and opposed aesthetics, its oldest traditions remained recognizable. The major practitioners continued to think of themselves as social critics and harbored a utopian, hopeful attitude even when pessimistic.

See also: AFRICAN-AMERICAN LITERATURE; such genres as the NOVEL, SHORT STORY, SCIENCE FICTION, and WESTERNS.

—

American Medical Association   The American Medical Association (AMA) is a national federation of 54 state and territorial medical groups. It was founded in 1847 and is today the largest medical organization in the world. Activities of the AMA include the publication of medical research and review articles in its widely read weekly *Journal of the American Medical Association* and in other medical journals; the supervision of standards at medical schools and other institutions in the field of health education; and the sponsorship of scientific councils and committees and more than 1,000 yearly meetings.

For the past three decades the AMA has funded a powerful lobby in Washington. Through this group it has attempted to influence the direction of medical legislation. It fought unsuccessfully against paid health care for the aged (Medicare) and against the creation of peer review systems to oversee the quality of publicly funded medical-care programs. Its longest struggle has been against any program of nationalized health care; it has proposed instead legislation for private health insurance to be partly funded by the federal government.

—

American music   The history of American music may be roughly divided into three periods: (1) the colonial period (the 17th and 18th centuries), dominated by British influence; (2) the period from about 1800 to about 1930, when the United States depended heavily for its musical culture on the importation of music and professional musicians from continental Europe; and (3) the period since about 1930, during which American music has attained an international importance equal to that of European music.

Colonial Period

Music had an important place in the life of the Puritan settlers in New England. They used metrical psalms (see HYMN) in their worship, a practice that emphasized text more than music, but they also must have brought with them folk songs that remained unwritten and are therefore unknown today. The first generations to settle in the New World were not skilled in music, and the psalms were perpetuated by "lining out," in which a leader recited or sang each line ahead of the congregation. During the 18th century, itinerant singing masters taught the rudiments of music and created a market for the many collections of psalm tunes that reprinted English pieces but also contained the music of American composers, including James Lyon's (1735–94) *Urania* in 1761. Except for William BILLINGS, whose ANTHEMS and fuging tunes expressed a rugged individual style, most music of American composers mirrored the styles that were in vogue in England.

Religious vocal music touched all walks of life in the American colonies, but a taste for concerts and more sophisticated music developed early in the cities. Evidence indicates concerts in Boston in 1731, in Charleston in 1732, in New York in 1736, and in Philadelphia in 1757.

The market for concert music attracted foreign musicians, many of them English, who were readily accepted after the Revolutionary War. As business prospered and cities grew, the large number of immigrant urbanites demanded a semblance of the musical life they had known in their homelands.

Even so, the newly arrived musicians found it useful to have another means of livelihood, and from their numbers came the early music-store owners and music publishers. They also taught music, repaired instruments, and organized performing groups. Alexander Reinagle (1756–1809), Benjamin Carr (1768–1831), James Hewitt (1770–1827), and Gottlieb Graupner (1767–1836) were among the early composer-performer-teachers who established a cultured level of musical taste alongside the vernacular idiom.

A high level of musical creativity was reached in the 18th century by the Moravians in Pennsylvania, Ohio, and North Carolina. They composed and performed CHORAL and instrumental music that can be compared to North German works of the late BAROQUE period. The Moravians kept apart from the life outside their communities, and their music failed to influence the development of an American idiom.

The 19th Century

Lowell Mason (see MASON family), an important figure in the early years of the Boston Handel and Haydn Society, and a founder of the Boston Academy of Music (1832), influenced 19th-century musical life in a number of ways. He introduced much European choral music to the United States, pioneered in public-school music education, and sired a musical dynasty that included publish-ers, organ and piano builders, teachers, and the composer Daniel Gregory Mason (1873–1953). He and his contemporaries, Thomas Hastings (1784–1872), William Bradbury (1816–68), and Isaac B. Woodbury (1819–58), wrote many hymns that continued to be used in the 20th century.

Following the European REVOLUTION OF 1848 many German musicians immigrated to the United States. Among them was the Germania Musical Society, an orchestra of about 25 players that toured the country. Concert artists arrived on tour to play in communities of all sizes. The Austrian pianist Henri Herz, the Norwegian violinist Ole Bull, the Swedish soprano Jenny LIND, and the French conductor Louis Jullien attracted large audiences, only some of whom had any experience with musical performances. Performers became show-business properties: P. T. BARNUM promoted the concerts of Jenny Lind; Jullien, engaged by Barnum, beguiled his audiences with stunts and showmanship that often overshadowed his music. The American-born pianist Louis Moreau GOTTSCHALK returned from his European studies in 1853 and undertook concert tours rivaling those of the great European virtuosos.

Vocal music had the most direct appeal to the majority, and singing families, probably patterned after European folk-singing groups, became popular. The best known was the Hutchinson family, who associated their singing with social causes, especially temperance and abolition.

The minstrel shows that arose in the 1820s combined song with the theater. These song, dance, and comedy-skit shows, performed in blackface, remained popular for a century. At first they were entirely the domain of white performers in costume, but by the mid-1850s blacks also performed in them. The minstrel show was probably begun by T. D. "Daddy" Rice (1808–60) and was popularized by Daniel Decatur Emmett (1815–1904), composer

(Below) *Lowell Mason, a 19th-century composer and educator, wrote about 1,200 Protestant hymns. He introduced music education into the Boston public school system.*

(Above) *Jenny Lind, known as "the Swedish nightingale," captivated American audiences during her triumphal tour in 1850–51. This contemporary cartoon took a satirical view of her admirers.*

of "Dixie," and E. P. Christy (1815–62). It brought the music of Stephen Collins FOSTER, composer of "Jeanie with the Light Brown Hair" and "Camptown Races," to public attention. His contemporaries included the English-born Joseph P. Knight (1812–87) ("Rocked in the Cradle of the Deep") and Henry Russell (1812–1900) ("Woodman, Spare That Tree"), and the Americans Septimus Winner (1827–1902) ("Whispering Hope" and "Listen to the Mocking Bird") and John H. Hewitt (1801–90) ("All Quiet Along the Potomac"). The last, along with "Dixie" and "Tenting on the Old Camp Ground," was one of the popular songs spawned by the Civil War.

In New York City, the emerging center for the arts, the cry for American music by American composers was first raised. William Henry Fry's (1813–64) opera *Leonora*, performed in Philadelphia in 1845, was the first by an American composer; George F. Bristow's (1825–98) *Rip Van Winkle*, performed in New York in 1855, was the first on an American subject.

Music spread westward before the middle of the 19th century, mainly to cities that had a large European-born population. St. Louis, Milwaukee, Cincinnati, and Chicago were early in establishing orchestras, opera companies, and choral groups. The NEW YORK PHILHARMONIC was formed in 1842. The BOSTON SYMPHONY ORCHESTRA came into existence in 1881; the CHICAGO SYMPHONY ORCHESTRA was formed a decade later. New Orleans had an established opera house in 1810.

The rise of performing groups brought the need for competent conductors, and a number of people came forward to guide the course of those organizations. Theodore Thomas (1835–1905), who had played violin in Jullien's orchestra, organized his own group in 1864, and after 1869 toured the entire country with his musicians. He later conducted various established orchestras, including the New York Philharmonic, before organizing the Chicago Symphony in 1891.

BANDS were popular on the American scene; one of the earliest known band concerts was given in Boston in 1771 by Josiah Flagg's (1737–95) 64th Regiment Band. Many 18th-century bands were attached to military units and were little more than small fife and drum corps, but they were heard in public concert, and the enthusiasm for wind music was widespread. By the outbreak of the Civil War, there were more than 3,000 bands in the country; their place in concert life after the war was assured by Patrick Sarsfield Gilmore (1829–92), composer of "When Johnny Comes Marching Home," and by John Philip SOUSA, composer of "The Stars and Stripes Forever," "El Capitan," and "The Washington Post" marches. Gilmore was bandmaster of the Union forces in Louisiana. At the close of the war he remained in New Orleans and gave a concert that featured more than 500 band members and 5,000 voices. Later, he organized his own band and toured widely. Sousa's impact was even stronger. He directed the U.S. Marine Band from 1880 to 1892, then formed his own group, hiring some of Gilmore's best musicians after the latter's death, and toured America and Europe to great acclaim.

Before the Civil War, a serious student of music had to

Stephen Foster was the best-known composer of American popular music during the 19th century. Many of his simple tunes and lyrical ballads, such as "Old Folks at Home," are familiar songs even in the present day.

study with European masters, preferably German, since American conservatories were still in the planning stage. The emergence of native musicians and the rise of music schools went hand in hand: the former needed the latter as places to study in their youth and to teach in their maturity. The United States now has a system of private and college-supported music schools, but it has been little more than a century since the teaching of music was first organized. The first conservatory of music was at OBERLIN COLLEGE (1865), followed by the NEW ENGLAND CONSERVATORY OF MUSIC in Boston two years later. Schools were opened in Cincinnati and Chicago in that same year, and the first professor of music at Harvard was appointed in 1875. The country today has hardly an educational institution without a program of music study.

Nevertheless, during the 19th century, music schools and conservatories in the United States served more as preparatory institutions than as finishing ones. Whenever possible, hopeful performers and composers went to Europe to study with the masters at the famous conservatories of Berlin, Leipzig, and Munich. John Knowles PAINE prepared himself in that traditional manner. Arthur Foote (1853–1937), one of the few who studied only in the

Edward A. Macdowell was an American composer and pianist who won the patronage of Franz Liszt and gained recognition in Europe.

(Left) *Louis Armstrong* (center) *gained worldwide recognition as the symbol of American jazz. Here he appears with King Oliver's Jazz Band, popular in the 1920s.* (Below) *George Gershwin, a 20th-century composer, wrote scores for musical plays, symphonic jazz such as* Rhapsody in Blue *and the opera* Porgy and Bess.

United States, was Paine's student at Harvard. He, George Chadwick (1854–1931), and Horatio Parker (1863–1919), the so-called Boston Group, taught many composers and teachers of the next generation, including Daniel Gregory Mason, Charles IVES, and Douglas MOORE.

A contemporary of the Boston Group, Edward MAC-DOWELL went directly to the conservatories of France and Germany after private instruction in New York. His work marked one of two mainstreams in future American composition—imitation of the European practice in the larger forms. The other, the development of an American idiom employing Negro tunes and rhythms, was developed by his pupil, Henry F. Gilbert (1869–1928).

The 20th Century

The dependence on German training continued unabated until World War I, during and after which fascination with the German models for music diminished sharply. The postwar center for music study was Paris, where Nadia BOULANGER was teaching a new generation of American composers. Those who remained at home found the American schools prepared to teach them at a high level of competence. Seeking a distinctive American idiom, a number of composers turned to folk sources and the country's unique musical utterance, JAZZ.

Rooted in the RAGTIME of Scott JOPLIN's generation and developing through the addition of the BLUES style, jazz emerged at the close of World War I, spreading northward from the brothels of New Orleans to achieve respectability and wide acceptance in nightclubs and cafés. A host of specialized jazz artists, highly skilled in improvisation, developed, and jazz influenced European composers as well as Americans. Jazzmen of the stature of Louis "Satchmo" ARMSTRONG and Edward "Duke" ELLINGTON were world figures. George GERSHWIN brought the jazz idiom to the attention of the concert world with his *Rhapso-*

dy in Blue (1924) and *An American in Paris* (1928). His opera *Porgy and Bess* (1935) combines the Broadway musical and grand opera.

Some 20th-century American composers set out along unique paths; Charles IVES was the first to combine popular American melodies with DISSONANCE, polytonality, and other advanced techniques. Others were deeply indebted to the wave of Europeans who came to the United States during the 1930s, among them Arnold SCHOENBERG and Igor STRAVINSKY. Thus, contemporary American music is characterized by its use of a wide variety of forms and sounds. Composers who have sought a musical Americanism include Walter PISTON, Virgil THOMSON, Roger SESSIONS, Roy HARRIS, Aaron COPLAND, Elliott CARTER, Samuel BARBER, and William SCHUMAN, among the older generation of 20th-century composers. The list of important experimental composers must include Carl RUGGLES, Edgar VARÈSE, John J. Becker, Henry COWELL, John CAGE, Milton BABBITT, George Crumb, and Charles WUORINEN.

Others particularly involved in the making of ELECTRONIC MUSIC include John Harbison, Jacob Druckman, Otto Luening, Gordon Mumma, Morton Subotnick, and Vladimir Ussachevsky.

In 1948 the city of Louisville, Ky., founded the Louisville Orchestra Commissioning Project, providing money for the commissioning of new works by contemporary American composers, to be premiered at concerts given by the Louisville Orchestra. Over a period of 12 years the project commissioned some 120 orchestral works as well as several operas, both from established composers and from younger artists such as Ned ROREM and Lukas FOSS.

Another important funding source has been the National Endowment for the Arts, which, since its inception in 1965, has provided grants of assistance to music groups of all kinds. As a result, many small professional groups—chamber orchestras, for example—have been

Aaron Copland is best known for ballet and symphonic scores incorporating folk melodies and jazz. Among his ballet works are Billy the Kid *(1938) and* Appalachian Spring *(1944).*

formed at universities or under the sponsorship of musical organizations or municipalities. Such composers as Gunther SCHULLER, John Corigliano, Andrew Imbrie, Leon Kirchner, and George Rochberg have reached wider audiences through their commissions and their performances of new works.

The field of opera once belonged exclusively to the Europeans; successful American opera seemed to be confined to Gershwin's *Porgy and Bess* (which was not ranked as a true opera until the 1980s), the left-protest operas of Mark BLITZSTEIN, and, more recently, Gian Carlo MENOTTI's popular, Italianate works. More recent decades, however, have witnessed a gratifying growth in successful operatic works by Americans, as well as the establishment of new opera companies and small opera groups. Numbered among American opera composers today are Dominick Argento, Mario Davidovsky, Norman DELLO JOIO, and Douglas Stuart MOORE. The group of notable opera composers who are women includes Libby Larsen, Joan Tower, Vivian Fine, and Pulitzer Prize winner Ellen Taaffe Zwilich. All of them, as well as John Adams and Philip GLASS, work equally successfully in opera and other forms.

Of all forms of contemporary American music, musical comedy has proven the most successful. Beginning with Victor HERBERT and George M. COHAN, the musical theater has nurtured a host of famous names: Jerome KERN, Cole PORTER, Irving BERLIN, George GERSHWIN, Richard RODGERS, Alan Jay LERNER, Stephen SONDHEIM, and Leonard BERNSTEIN, who was also famous as a conductor and a composer of "serious" music.

Even as American orchestras, opera companies, and other musical organizations flourish, the enthusiasm of U.S. audiences for American music remains lukewarm, at best. American listeners, for the most part, prefer the European "classics." The few American composers who have succeeded with American listeners—Ives, Gershwin, Thomson, Copland—have largely drawn on popular traditions.

Thus, in the United States, only popular music can support itself by means of the box office. Since the advent of ROCK MUSIC, American popular music has become a major industry, capable of employing thousands of tal-

ented young musicians and exercising a significant musical influence around the world. The easy accessibility of recordings, radio, and television has made music a constant companion in American life and has exposed listeners to musical styles that have been drawn from around the world. This willingness to incorporate the musical languages of cultures as diverse as African Zulu and Irish Gaelic—or to explore obscure American idioms of the past—energizes and renews popular music.

A group of composers, among whom Philip Glass, Steve REICH, and John Adams are the most widely known, have discovered attractive new languages for "serious" music. Their work may awaken American enthusiasm for contemporary composition.

See also: BARBERSHOP QUARTET; BLUES; COUNTRY AND WESTERN MUSIC; GOSPEL MUSIC.

American National Theater and Academy

The American National Theater and Academy (ANTA) is an organization established in 1935 by an Act of Congress to raise the standards of drama performance in the United States. It has sent American productions, notably *Porgy and Bess*, on foreign tours. ANTA leaders have included Helen Hayes, Peggy Wood, Robert Breen, and Alfred de Liagre. The American National Theater Company, an ANTA-created repertory group, was active at the Kennedy Center in Washington, D.C., from 1983 to 1986.

American Philosophical Society

The American Philosophical Society for Promoting Useful Knowledge is the oldest learned society in the United States. Derived from an earlier group dating from 1743, the society was founded in Philadelphia in 1769. Benjamin FRANKLIN was its first president. Its early fame declined after the American Revolution. A chartered but private association, the society depended largely on members' dues until a bequest in 1931 revived its fortunes. The society, which is still located in Philadelphia, is governed by committee and has a large and distinguished membership. It publishes *Transactions* and *Proceedings*, meets semiannually, and maintains a library and a wide program of grants.

American Psychiatric Association

Founded in 1844, the American Psychiatric Association (APA) is the oldest national medical association in the United States. By 1990 its membership had reached 36,000. At its inception the APA was an organization geared toward the needs of medical superintendents of insane asylums. However, it gradually expanded its scope to include improving patient treatment, promoting research and professional education, advancing psychiatric standards, and promoting the dissemination of psychiatric knowledge to other fields. The APA publishes the *American Psychiatric Journal* and the *Diagnostic and Statistical Manual of Mental Disorders*.

American quarter horse   see HORSE

American Revolution The American Revolution, the conflict by which the American colonists won their independence from Great Britain and created the United States of America, was an upheaval of profound significance in world history. It occurred in the second half of the 18th century, in an "Age of Democratic Revolution," when philosophers and political theorists in Europe were critically examining the institutions of their own societies and the notions that lay behind them. Yet the American Revolution first put to the test ideas and theories that had seldom if ever been worked out in practice in the Old World—separation of church and state, sovereignty of the people, written constitutions, and effective checks and balances in government.

A struggle to preserve and later to expand the dimensions of human freedom, the American Revolution was also an anticolonial movement, the first in modern history. Before then, countries had usually come into existence through evolutionary processes, the result of tradition and history, geography and circumstance. The United States, on the other hand, had a birth date, 1776; it was "the first new nation," a republic born in revolution and war, a pattern followed by scores of fledgling states since that time, especially in the so-called Third World areas of the globe since 1945.

The Colonies in 1763

No revolution, of course, can be fully exported. A vast array of factors that include the political and social backgrounds of a people will shape the precise course of any and all revolutions. So it was in America, where the colonists were not an alien people with a culture very different from that of the motherland. They were for the most part British in origin, English-speaking, Protestant, rural, and agrarian in their principal characteristics. They were proud of their Anglo-Saxon heritage and of the empire of which they were a part. At that time the colonists gave little thought to cutting loose from their imperial moorings. They considered the British political system the best in Europe, noted for its equilibrium between King, Lords, and Commons assembled in Parliament. They imported British books, furniture, and clothing; wealthy planters and merchants imitated the manners of the English aristocracy. Even with the restrictions imposed on their external trade by the NAVIGATION ACTS—or perhaps because of them—they had prospered in their direct economic intercourse with Britain, the most industrialized country in Europe. Nor was their trade rigidly confined; they were also permitted to sell an assortment of valuable products such as grain, flour, and rice on non-British markets in the West Indies and in southern Europe.

In 1763 the colonists were an expanding and maturing people; their numbers had reached a million and a half, and they were doubling every quarter of a century. If most provincials were sons of the soil, Americans could nonetheless boast of five urban centers, "cities in the wilderness"—Philadelphia, Boston, New York, Charleston, and Newport. The cities served as filters through which new ideas of the European Enlightenment entered the colonies, helping to generate an inquisitive spirit about humankind and the total environment. Newspapers and colleges in the cities and towns served as disseminators of the thought and culture of what was truly an Atlantic civilization. A new mobility, together with a receptivity to new ideas, was a hallmark of American society. It came about because of high wages, cheap land, and an absence of legal privilege. Americans were—except for their African slaves—one of the freest people in the world. Another sign of that freedom was their almost complete control over their internal political and domestic affairs, exercised largely through their popularly elected lower houses of assembly, which in turn served as nurturing ground for such future Revolutionary leaders as John ADAMS, John DICKINSON, Thomas JEFFERSON, and George WASHINGTON.

Although the colonists had reached a high level of maturity, there was not at mid-century a meaningful American nationalism. The word *American* appeared infrequently; people were more likely to describe themselves as English or British, or as Virginians or Pennsylvanians. Nor did the provincials display a marked degree of intercolonial cooperation; their own rivalries and jealousies over boundaries and western land claims tended to retard American national feeling. Nothing, however, unites a people like a commonly perceived threat to their way of life; and after 1763 the colonists felt endangered within the empire. There is a real irony in the way the American Revolution began, for the very elements that had wedded the colonists to the mother country—especially their political and economic freedoms—were viewed in London as signs that the colonists were fast heading down the road to full autonomy or absolute independence. Those sentiments, growing steadily in the 18th century, crystallized during the FRENCH AND INDIAN WAR (1754–63) when British officials complained that Americans cooperated poorly in raising men and supplies and in providing quarters for British troops, to say nothing of trading illegally with the enemy and generating friction with western Indians over land and trade goods.

Whatever the truth of these charges—and they were partly true, if exaggerated—it was not unreasonable after 1763 for Britain to ask more of its prosperous dependencies. Britain's heavy national debt and concurrent tax burdens stemmed partly at least from a series of 18th-century wars that were fought to some extent for the defense of the colonies. Nor was it wrong to argue that a measure of reorganization in American administration would lead to greater economy and efficiency in imperial management. But Britain embarked upon this course with a lack of sensitivity, ignoring the concerns of its maturing subjects, who were scarcely the children they had once been.

Britain's was a mentality unable to appreciate the aims and aspirations of its colonial people. When Britain adopted a new imperial program, the colonists were never meaningfully consulted. Furthermore, Britain's tactics could hardly avoid arousing the Americans. Having left

affix the STAMP.

This is the Place to

(Above) *A satirical cartoon from a colonial publication suggests this design for the tax stamp intended for use on legal documents, newspapers, and other paper goods, according to the terms of the Stamp Act of 1765. The act enraged the American colonists and stirred up revolutionary sentiments.*

(Right) *The Boston Massacre of Mar. 5, 1770, was provoked by a group of colonists taunting British soldiers. As Paul Revere's engraving depicts, the panic-stricken troops fired into the crowd, killing three colonists and mortally wounding two others. The incident aroused resentment against British rule. (Courtesy the Metropolitan Museum of Art. Gift of Mrs. Russell Sage, 1910.)*

the colonies virtually alone for decades with a de facto attitude of "salutary neglect," the London government now attempted too much too quickly.

The Growing Ferment

Even before the termination of the French and Indian War, visible indications had appeared of a new direction in colonial affairs. Beginning in 1759, small-scale disputes broke out between Britain and the colonies over disallowance of measures passed by the popular assemblies, over writs of assistance empowering the royal customs officials to break into homes and stores, and over judicial tenure in the colonial courts. Subsequent decisions made in London forbade "for the time being" western settlement beyond the Appalachian divide (the Proclamation of 1763), eliminated provincial paper currency as legal tender, bolstered the customs department, and enlarged the authority of the vice-admiralty courts in relation to enforcement of the Navigation Acts.

Taxation without Representation. When these unpopular measures were followed almost immediately by Parliament's placing taxes on Americans for the first time in their history, the result was an explosion that shook the empire to its foundations. George GRENVILLE, chief minister from 1763 to 1765, pushed the controversial bills through Parliament in 1764 and 1765. The Sugar Act of 1764 cut the duty on imported foreign molasses from sixpence to threepence a gallon; but it was to be vigorously enforced, and it was now called a revenue measure rather than a law designed merely to regulate trade. The next year Grenville secured passage of the so-called STAMP ACT, placing taxes on all legal documents and on newspapers, almanacs, and other items. Soon afterward came a third law, the Quartering Act, a form of indirect taxation that required American assemblies to provide British troops with temporary housing and an assortment of provisions.

"Taxation without representation" was the central is-

British troops and local colonial militia, the famous "Minutemen," clashed for the first time on Apr. 19, 1775, at Lexington, Mass. The skirmish, which cost the lives of eight colonists, marked the opening of hostilities in the American Revolution.

sue in the imperial rupture. It raised a fundamental question concerning the limits of parliamentary power that was debated throughout the dozen or so years before the declaration of American independence. Although Americans complained about the stream of British acts and regulations after 1759, they now agreed that the constitutional issue of taxation posed the gravest threat of all to their freedom as individuals. Americans believed thay they could be taxed only by their own directly elected representatives.

When Parliament retreated in 1766, reducing the Sugar Act to the level of a trade duty and repealing the Stamp Act, it was responding to retaliatory colonial boycotts on British trade goods, not to the justness of American constitutional pronouncements. In 1767, Chancellor of the Exchequer Charles Townshend persuaded a Parliament already antagonistic toward the colonies to pass the TOWNSHEND ACTS. These levied new and different taxes on the American colonists: duties to be collected at the ports on incoming lead, paper, tea, paint, and glass. Besides meeting other imperial expenses such as the upkeep of the army in America, these Townshend duties might go to pay the salaries of royal governors and other crown officials who previously had been paid by the colonial assemblies, which had used this power of the purse to make the king's appointees somewhat responsive to their wishes. A final Townshend scheme reorganized the customs service in America, establishing its headquarters in Boston, where mounting friction between collectors and townspeople led to the dispatch of regular troops to the city to keep order in 1768.

Resistance and Retaliation. The new tensions subsided into a three-year period of calm beginning in 1770, but only because a second round of American reprisals

against English trade prompted the removal of all the Townshend duties save the one on tea, which was retained to show symbolically that Parliament had not renounced its right to tax America. Additionally, the British troops, popularly known as "redcoats," had been withdrawn from Boston following the embarrassing and unplanned BOSTON MASSACRE (1770). Unfortunately for the empire, those years were not used to bring about permanent agreements between Americans and Britons on such subjects as the constitutional relationship between the colonies and the mother country and what might be a reasonable way for the provinces to share the costs of imperial administration. An atmosphere of suspicion and distrust prevailed. Instead of rescinding the remaining Townshend tax and exploring inoffensive methods of aiding the financially troubled British East India Company, Parliament enacted the Tea Act of 1773, designed to allow the company to bypass middlemen and sell directly to American retailers. It was hardly a plot to persuade Americans to drink taxed tea at a low price, but the colonists interpreted it in that fashion. Everywhere there was opposition to landing the dutied commodity, and in the Massachusetts capital the famous BOSTON TEA PARTY resulted in the destruction by patriots of 340 tea chests on ships in the harbor.

Parliament's retaliation against Massachusetts was swift and severe: the so-called INTOLERABLE ACTS closed the port of Boston, altered town and provincial government, permitted royal officials and functionaries to go to Britain for trial for any alleged crimes, and provided for the quartering of troops once again in Boston. The other colonies rallied to the defense of Massachusetts in a CONTINENTAL CONGRESS that met in Philadelphia in September 1774 and denounced the acts.

Lexington and Concord. War clouds were gathering rapidly. The sending of more than 3,000 British army regulars under Maj. Gen. Thomas GAGE to Boston further exacerbated the imperial rift. When a column of these troops under Lt. Col. Francis Smith moved into the countryside to collect arms and munitions gathered by the patriot militia, hostilities erupted at Lexington and Concord on Apr. 19, 1775. Soon afterward militia contingents from places throughout New England took up positions outside Boston, putting the city under siege. Forts TICONDEROGA and Crown Point in upstate New York fell to other rebel parties. The misnamed Battle of Bunker Hill was fought on Breed's Hill across from Boston (June 17, 1775). Although Gage's units dislodged the rebels from their advanced positions threatening the city, the British casualties came to 42 percent of the 2,500 redcoats engaged, their heaviest losses of the war. The Second Continental Congress, then meeting at Philadelphia, took control of the New England forces opposing Gage. The lawmakers chose as commander of this "Continental Army" George Washington, a 43-year-old delegate from Virginia, a planter and a ranking militia officer in the French and Indian Wars.

Resources of the Opponents

Britain seemingly had enormous advantages in a war against its colonies. It possessed a well-established government, a sizable treasury, a competent army, the most powerful navy in the world, and a large LOYALIST population in the colonies. By contrast, the American rebels had no chief executive such as the king, nor a cabinet whose members had assigned responsibilities. In fact, the Americans had no separate or independent departments of government such as war, treasury, and foreign affairs until near the end of the conflict. The Continental Congress itself had as its rivals the 13 state legislatures, which often chose not to cooperate with their delegates in Philadelphia. Indeed, Congress was an extralegal body, existing at the pleasure of the states before the ARTICLES OF CONFEDERATION were ratified in 1781.

Yet fortified by the arguments in the highly influential pamphlet *Common Sense* by Thomas PAINE, the Continental Congress felt strong enough to separate the American colonies from Britain, adopting the immortal words of Thomas Jefferson in the DECLARATION OF INDEPENDENCE on July 4, 1776.

American Advantages. The Americans, however, were not without their own advantages. A vast reservoir of manpower could be drawn upon. For the most part, men preferred short-term enlistments—and many who served came out for a few weeks or months—but they did serve: the best estimates are that over 200,000 participated on the patriot side. General Washington was often short of shoes and powder, but rarely were he and other commanders without men when they needed them most. Moreover, Americans owned guns, and they knew how to use them. If the Continental Army won few fixed battles, it normally fought reasonably well; it extracted a heavy toll on the enemy, who usually could not easily obtain reinforcements. Although only Washington and Maj. Gen. Nathanael GREENE were outstanding commanders, many others were steady and reliable, including Henry KNOX, Benjamin LINCOLN, Anthony WAYNE, Daniel MORGAN, Baron von STEUBEN, the Marquis de LAFAYETTE, and Benedict ARNOLD, before he defected to the enemy in 1780.

The Americans also were fighting on their own soil and consequently could be more flexible in their military operations than their opponents. Washington and other Continental Army commanders usually followed the principle of concentration, that is, meeting the enemy in force wherever British armies appeared. In the interior, however, against bands of Loyalists and isolated British outposts and supply trains, the American militia not infrequently employed guerrilla or partisan tactics with striking successes. The major contribution of the militia was to control the home front against the Revolution's internal enemies—whether Indians or Loyalists—while the Continental Army contended with British armies in the eastern or coastal regions in more formalized warfare.

British Disadvantages. British advantages were steadily negated by the vastness of the struggle, by waging war 3,000 miles from Europe against an armed population

The American naval officer John Paul Jones's Bonhomme Richard (center left) *battered the larger* Serapis *into submission during a battle in the North Sea on Sept. 23, 1779. This battle, depicted in the painting by Robert Dodd, was the most famous of the naval duels during the Revolution.*

Three examples of military dress from the American Revolution:
(Left) The infantryman from Washington's Continental Army; (cen-
ter) The camouflaging dress of a colonial rifleman; and (right) The
grenadier of the 2d Foot Guard, an elite force within Britain's
colonial army.

spread over hundreds of miles, from the Atlantic to the Mississippi, from Maine to Georgia. The land was forested, ravined, swampy, and interlaced by myriad streams and rivers. It was discouraging to win battle after battle and see Britain's armies bled of men and supplies in the process, while the beaten rebels always bounced back.

To the British it seemed to take forever—6 to 12 weeks—for word of campaign strategies to pass from London to commanders in the field, for provisions to arrive, and for naval squadrons to appear in time for cooperation with land forces. The scope of the contest also reduced the Royal Navy's effectiveness in blockading the long American coastline. Stores could be landed at too many rivers, bays, and inlets. Nor could the British employ their fast frigates and formidable ships of the line (battleships of the 18th century) against an American fleet. The patriots took to the sea in single ships, either privateers or vessels commissioned by Congress. Consequently, the British-American naval war can be told largely as a story of individual ship duels. The triumph of John Paul JONES in the *Bonhomme Richard* over H.M.S. *Serapis* in the North Sea in 1779 was the most famous of these encounters.

Britain faced a further problem with the nature of its leadership, both civilian and military. King GEORGE III was a conscientious but supremely obstinate monarch whose reluctance to countenance the loss of the colonies probably resulted in a prolongation of the war. However, responsibility for the conduct of the war was not in his hands but in those of his compliant chief minister, Lord NORTH. North, a dull, unimaginative politician, headed a

ministry of undistinguished men. Into the leadership vacuum left by North's weakness stepped Lord George GERMAIN, who increasingly assumed the direction of military operations in the colonies.

Unfortunately for Britain, its generals in the field were much like the political leaders at home, possessed of average talents at best. John BURGOYNE, Guy CARLETON, Sir Henry CLINTON, Charles CORNWALLIS, William HOWE, and Thomas Gage were probably reasonably endowed to fight conventional wars on the plains of western Europe, where orthodox linear formations were in order. Eighteenth-century European generals, however, were scarcely professionals in a modern sense. Officers lacked a body of strategic doctrine from which to choose between alternatives for practical application. The British generals revealed themselves grossly inept at improvisation in a unique struggle in America that demanded rapid movement, original tactics, winter campaigning, and—most important—contending with a people in arms. Moreover, some British commanders were deliberately slow in prosecuting the war because they favored a political reconciliation with the rebels.

For all these reasons American generals, even with amateurish militia backgrounds, were not at so serious a disadvantage as they might have been. Washington and his comrades lacked experience in directing massive formations and planning campaigns; but, then, so did British generals—and admirals too.

Course of the War

Britain was slow to take the offensive in the opening rounds of the war, since most of its troops in America were at Boston, which continued under siege. Unable to break out of their entrenchments, and threatened by Washington's artillery on Dorchester Heights, British troops evacuated the city by sea in March 1776 and established themselves temporarily at Halifax, Nova Scotia.

Clinton's Southern Expedition. That same spring a small British expedition under Sir Henry Clinton sailed along the coast of the southern colonies in the hope of arousing the Loyalists against the newly established American governments in the Carolinas and Georgia. Reaching the Cape Fear River in North Carolina, Clinton learned that a Loyalist uprising had been smashed by the patriots at the Battle of Moore's Creek Bridge near Wilmington (Feb. 27, 1776). Then, continuing southward, Clinton's fleet bombarded the harbor fortifications at Charleston, S.C., perhaps seeking to establish a coastal base for local Loyalists. In any case, the expedition was beaten off (June 28, 1776), terminating important British activity in the South for over two years.

Invasion of Canada. At best, both sides might consider the first year of conflict a draw. Although the king's regiments had withdrawn from New England, the colonists in turn had failed to capture the former French province of Quebec. The Americans had hoped to persuade the French inhabitants to join their cause, since they feared that Canada might become a staging area for an invasion of the thirteen colonies. An American army under Brig. Gen. Richard MONTGOMERY advanced from upper New

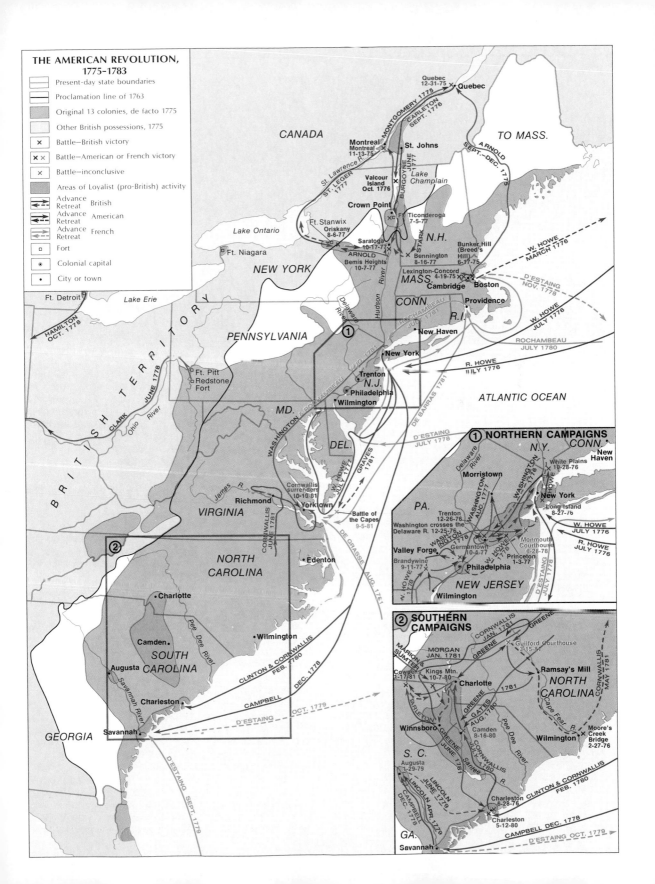

THE AMERICAN REVOLUTION, 1775–1783

- Present-day state boundaries
- Proclamation line of 1763
- Original 13 colonies, de facto 1775
- Other British possessions, 1775
- × Battle—British victory
- ×× Battle—American or French victory
- × Battle—inconclusive
- Areas of Loyalist (pro-British) activity
- Advance Retreat British
- Advance Retreat American
- Advance Retreat French
- □ Fort
- ⊙ Colonial capital
- • City or town

CANADA

Quebec 12-31-75 ×
Quebec

TO MASS.

Montreal
Montreal 11-13-75
St. Johns

MONTGOMERY JUNE 1775

ARNOLD SEPT.–DEC. 1775

St. Lawrence R.

ST. LEGER 1777

Valcour Island Oct. 1776

Lake Champlain

BURGOYNE JUNE 1777

CARLETON SEPT. 1776

Crown Point

× Ft. Ticonderoga 7-5-77

STARK

Ft. Stanwix Oriskany 8-6-77

Lake Ontario

Ft. Niagara

NEW YORK

Saratoga 10-17-77

ARNOLD Bemis Heights 10-7-77

N.H.

× Bennington 8-16-77

Bunker Hill (Breed's Hill) 6-17-75

Lexington-Concord 4-19-75 ××

MASS.
Cambridge Boston

W. HOWE MARCH 1776

D'ESTAING NOV. 1778

Ft. Detroit

Lake Erie

HAMILTON OCT. 1778

BRITISH TERRITORY

CLARK

Ohio River

PENNSYLVANIA

Ft. Pitt
Redstone Fort

Delaware River

Hudson River

CONN

R.I.
Providence

① New Haven

ROCHAMBEAU JULY 1780

W. HOWE JULY 1776

R. HOWE JULY 1776

New York

Trenton
N.J.

⊙ Philadelphia

Wilmington

MD.

DEL.

ATLANTIC OCEAN

D'ESTAING JULY 1778

WASHINGTON ROCHAMBEAU AUG. 1781

DE BARRAS 1781

Richmond

James R.

VIRGINIA

Cornwallis surrenders 10-19-01

Yorktown

W. HOWE JULY 1776

GRAVES 1781

Battle of the Capes 9-5-81

DE GRASSE AUG. 1781

CORNWALLIS JUNE 1781

②
NORTH CAROLINA

• Charlotte

• Edenton

• Wilmington

Pee Dee River

SOUTH CAROLINA

Camden

Augusta

CLINTON & CORNWALLIS FEB. 1780

CAMPBELL DEC. 1778

Savannah River

Charleston

GEORGIA

Savannah

D'ESTAING SEPT. 1779

① NORTHERN CAMPAIGNS

N.Y. CONN.

White Plains 10-28-76

New Haven

Delaware River

Morristown

WASHINGTON AUG. 1777

W. HOWE 1776

New York

Long Island 8-27-76

PA.

Trenton 12-26-76
Washington crosses the Delaware R. 12-25-76

WASHINGTON 1778

W. HOWE 1776

W. HOWE OCT. 1777

Germantown 10-4-77

Monmouth Courthouse 6-28-78

W. HOWE JULY 1776

R. HOWE JULY 1776

Valley Forge

Brandywine 9-11-77

Princeton 1-3-77

⊙ Philadelphia

D'ESTAING JULY 1778

W. HOWE 1776

NEW JERSEY

Wilmington

② SOUTHERN CAMPAIGNS

MARION SUMTER

MORGAN JAN. 1781

CORNWALLIS JAN. 1781

GREENE

Guilford Courthouse 3-15-81

GREENE 1781

CORNWALLIS MAY 1781

Cowpens 1-17-81

Kings Mtn. 10-7-80

• Charlotte

Ramsay's Mill

NORTH CAROLINA

TARLETON

GREENE 1781

GATES AUG. 1780

CORNWALLIS JULY 1780

Cape Fear R.

Moore's Creek Bridge 2-27-76

Winnsboro

S.C.

Camden 8-16-80

Pee Dee River

• Wilmington

Augusta 1-29-79

LINCOLN JUNE 1781

GREENE JUNE 1781

Santee R.

Charleston 6-28-76

LINCOLN APR. 1779

Charleston 5-12-80

CLINTON & CORNWALLIS FEB. 1780

LINCOLN DEC. 1778

CAMPBELL DEC. 1778

GA.

Savannah

CAMPBELL DEC. 1778

D'ESTAING OCT. 1779

This colored engraving portrays a great fire that swept through New York as the city was being occupied by the British in September 1776. Despite orders from the Continental Congress to hold New York at any cost, an outflanked General Washington ordered that the city be abandoned.

York and seized Montreal (Nov. 10, 1775), while Col. Benedict Arnold led a second force northward through the Maine wilderness. Uniting before the city of Quebec, they attacked the walled capital but were beaten back, and Montgomery was killed (December 30). Although the Americans continued to blockade the city until May 1776, the only serious American threat to Canada in the war had been ended.

Britain's Northern Offensive of 1776. From the summer of 1776 the strategic initiative was taken by the British, who believed that the real core of the insurrection was in the northern tier of colonies, especially in New England. To bring the war to an end in 1776, British planners sent reinforcements to Maj. Gen. Guy Carleton, governor of Quebec, who had already defeated Arnold and Montgomery. Carleton should push the Americans from their remaining toeholds in Canada and pursue them down the Lake Champlain-Hudson River trough, which might be a means of cutting the colonies in half. Simultaneously, a much larger army headed by Maj. Gen. William Howe, who had replaced Gage as supreme commander, should capture New York City and its splendid harbor, a strategic base from which it could advance up the Hudson, unite with Carleton, and overrun New England. But Carleton, after driving his opponents back, was delayed by problems of supply and the difficulties of wilderness campaigning. Then, near Valcour Island on Lake Champlain, his naval complement was checkmated by a tiny American fleet hastily assembled by Benedict Arnold. Time was always of the essence in fall campaigning, and the lateness of the season now prompted Carleton to return to Canada for the winter.

Howe's chances of completing his part of the two-pronged offensive seemed more promising than Carleton's. Howe launched his campaign with the largest force he or any other British general had at his disposal during

the war: 32,000 soldiers, together with 400 transports and 73 warships under his brother, Vice Admiral Richard, Earl Howe, with whom he shared the American supreme command. From a military viewpoint, Washington should not have attempted to retain New York City, with its hard-to-defend islands, rivers, bays, and inlets, although Congress saw strong psychological reasons for holding a major city whose loss might dispirit patriots everywhere. As it was, Washington suffered a defeat on Long Island (Aug. 27, 1776). Fortunately for him, Howe did not attempt to follow up his victory quickly. Washington fought a series of rearguard actions with Howe on Manhattan Island, forcing the sluggish Howe to take from August to November to clear his opponents from New York City and the surrounding area. Howe, like Carleton, never made his move along the Hudson, but contented himself with pursuing the retreating Washington across New Jersey until the Americans managed to escape over the Delaware River into Pennsylvania (Dec. 7, 1776).

Battles of Trenton and Princeton. With the Revolution seemingly at its nadir and desperately in need of a lift, Washington unexpectedly struck back, showing a determination and a persistence that were to be his hallmarks during a war that lasted eight and a half years, the longest in American history before Vietnam. Washington noted that Howe, in characteristic European fashion, preferred to avoid winter campaigning and had divided his army between New York City and various New Jersey towns. Collecting scattered regulars and militiamen, the Virginian returned to New Jersey and in a little more than a week of dazzling maneuvers captured the garrison of German mercenaries at Trenton (Dec. 26, 1776) and routed another enemy contingent at Princeton (Jan. 3, 1777).

Saratoga Campaign. Once again in 1777, British campaign planning focused on the northern states. Once again, too, the Canadian-based army and Howe's forces were to mount offensives. This time the Canadian troops, now commanded by Maj. Gen. John Burgoyne, were numerically much stronger, but they had no promise of cooperation from General Howe as they proceeded down the Lake Champlain–Hudson River course. For his part, Howe appeared uncertain for several months about his own course of action. Finally, he resolved not to march north in support of Burgoyne but rather to leave a garrison under Sir Henry Clinton in New York City and to transport his army by sea for a strike against Philadelphia. Incredibly, neither Howe nor Burgoyne had corresponded with each other about the campaign—each would handle his own affairs. Even so, the greatest fault lay with Lord George Germain, who had approved the campaign but failed to give it a unifying concept.

Burgoyne's operation began well, as was true of most British campaigning during the Revolution. The American Northern army, plagued by shortages and internal divisions, initially offered slight opposition. Events were soon to show, though, that Burgoyne suffered from overconfidence, which actually increased when he recaptured Fort Ticonderoga (July 5, 1777) at the juncture of Lakes Champlain and George. He set a leisurely pace that allowed the Americans precious time to regroup and to make an ally of the dense wilderness of upper New York. They destroyed his only road south, felling trees to block his progress, and sent out guerrilla bands to harass his flanks and lines of communication.

In mid-August Burgoyne learned that one of his units commanded by Lt. Col. Barry ST. LEGER had been mauled by American militia under Nicholas HERKIMER while laying siege to Fort Stanwix in the Mohawk Valley, and that St. Leger had returned to Canada. More bad news came from Bennington, Vt., where a contingent of his German troops in search of packhorses and provisions had been routed by the militia of Brig. Gen. John STARK. At length, Burgoyne reached the rugged Bemis Heights on the west bank of the Hudson, where he collided with a well-entrenched and much-revitalized Northern army under Gen. Horatio GATES, ably supported by Maj. Gen. Benedict Arnold and Col. Daniel Morgan Twice—on September 19 and October 7—Burgoyne lunged at the American lines, and both times was driven back with heavy losses. With his southward progress blocked and no help forthcoming from Clinton in New York, he surrendered at Saratoga (Oct. 17, 1777).

British Capture of Philadelphia. Howe, meanwhile, was winning victories in Pennsylvania, although their long-term value was more illusory than real. Washington, amazed at Howe's desertion of Burgoyne, hurried south from Morristown, N.J., and positioned his army astride Brandywine Creek to parry his opponent's obvious thrust at Philadelphia. But on September 11, in several hours of furious fighting, Washington's right flank collapsed, and he hastily withdrew.

Soon after the British commander entered the patriot capital, causing Congress to flee, Washington made a night assault on the enemy's advance base at Germantown, Pa., but his plan was probably too complicated for his troops, who nonetheless fought well until they were forced to retire (October 4).

The year 1777 had seen another British failure to

The British general Burgoyne offers his sword to Horatio Gates, American commander at Saratoga, in John Trumbull's painting. The surrender (Oct. 17, 1777), which prompted France's entry into the war, is regarded as the turning point of the Revolution.

crush the rebellion. While one army had been lost, another had occupied Philadelphia. However, the city itself was hardly a staggering loss for the Americans, whose armies were still intact. Howe, too, had paid a heavy price in casualties, whereas the patriots were able to replenish their own depleted ranks.

The French Alliance

The new year, 1778, was a time of transition in the Revolutionary War because of Britain's inability to win in the northern colonies and because of the increasing part played by France. The French foreign minister, the Comte de Vergennes, eager to settle an old score with Britain, convinced his royal master Louis XVI to permit France to funnel secret aid to the patriots in 1776 and 1777. That

aid took the form of the government's handing over munitions, arms, and clothing to the playwright Caron de BEAUMARCHAIS and his fake "Hortalez and Company," which in turn arranged with Benjamin FRANKLIN and other patriot commissioners in Paris to have them shipped across the Atlantic.

Vergennes, however, was not willing to risk war with Britain until he was sure that the Americans had the ability to continue the fight and the commitment to eschew reconciliation with George III. Gates's victory at Saratoga, combined with rumors that Britain would offer America major concessions in return for peace, finally pushed France over the brink. Formal treaties of commerce and alliance were signed by American and French diplomats on Feb. 6, 1778. France became the first nation to rec-

(Above) *General Washington reviews the dispirited men of the Continental Army at his winter headquarters in Valley Forge. Washington devoted the harsh winter of 1777 to reorganizing his army.* (Right) *General Washington rallies his troops at the Battle of Monmouth Courthouse, N.J., in June 1778. When an American attack on a British column turned into a disorderly retreat, Washington rode into battle and inspired his men to stand and fight.*

ognize the infant country; it renounced all claims to North America east of the Mississippi River and agreed with the United States that neither would lay down its arms until American independence was won.

Valley Forge and the Battle of Monmouth. The winter of the signing of the French alliance was also the Continental Army's time of cruel suffering at VALLEY FORGE. Spring brought Washington not only new recruits, but also an army better trained than ever before, due in considerable part to the labors of the Prussian general Baron von Steuben in drilling the troops at Valley Forge.

Spring meant, furthermore, additional pressure on British forces in the New World now that France was entering the struggle. Accordingly, Sir Henry Clinton, who became the new commander in chief when the Howes resigned (May 1778) and returned to England, now received important orders: evacuate his army from Philadelphia, concentrate his forces at New York City, and send men to guard against French threats against British islands in the Caribbean.

Washington, his confidence up, pursued Clinton on his cross-country march through New Jersey, and at Monmouth Courthouse the two armies clashed (June 28, 1778). For the Continentals, who traded volley for volley with the finest soldiers in Europe, it was a moral victory, although the outcome itself was indecisive. In three years of fighting, Britain had little to show for its exertions to regain America, and so it would remain in the northern states, where the heavy campaigning was at an end. Washington, who followed Clinton northward after Monmouth, spent the next three years observing the British from lines outside New York City.

War in the West. In one sense, the struggle on the western frontier paralleled the fighting to the east, in that neither side managed to get the upper hand. To be sure, most Indian tribes that involved themselves in the fray did so in the cause of the "great white father," George III. They had long nourished grievances against the colonists, who had cheated them in land transactions and trade. But it is not clear that the aid of the tribesmen was a positive influence for Britain; their ferocious tactics may well have alienated many colonists who had been neutral or apathetic. Furthermore, because they demanded food in winter and a great variety of other goods and supplies, the Indians were a great financial and administrative burden for British frontier leaders.

Although Kentucky settlers were threatened periodically, in 1778 the young George Rogers CLARK weakened Britain's hold on the interior by overrunning enemy-controlled villages in present-day Illinois and Indiana. Less significant was the role of the Kentuckian Daniel BOONE, a steady if unspectacular leader.

Elsewhere in the West the contest seesawed back and forth. In the lower South the Cherokee proved to be the most formidable of Britain's warrior allies; although the patriot militia handed them a series of stinging defeats in 1776, the Cherokee continued to be troublesome, if not a serious threat. To check the devastating raids of the Iroquois on the New York–Pennsylvania frontier, Washington sent a striking force headed by Maj. Gen. John SULLIVAN into western New York, where the Americans laid waste to many tribal towns.

Even so, American commanders could not eliminate all the anchor points of British power in the interior. Loyalist and Indian parties based in Detroit and Niagara continued to harass frontier communities even after the conclusion of the war, thus contributing to the renewal of war between Britain and the United States in 1812.

General Washington (center right) presides over the surrender of Charles Cornwallis at Yorktown, Va., on Oct. 19, 1781. The surrender of the British army marked the end of major fighting in the Revolution. Cornwallis does not appear in this painting by John Trumbull. He refused to meet his American conqueror, sending a surrogate with his sword of surrender.

General Washington receives a hero's welcome from grateful citizens of New York as he leads a column of troops into that city. As his triumphal procession marched in on Nov. 25, 1783, British troops were abandoning New York, their last stronghold on the Atlantic seaboard.

War in the South. In the South, a region long neglected by Britain, the war reached its conclusion. Because of the British inability to prevail in the North, London's strategists gradually shifted their attention to the South, beginning in late 1778. They felt that section contained a higher percentage of Loyalists than any other part of America. Then, too, if choices had to be made after France's entry into the war had stretched British resources tissue thin, England preferred to save the South above all other areas. Its raw materials were the most valuable of all American commodities in the mother country's mercantile scheme.

Britain, as usual, opened a new theater of campaigning with a string of triumphs. In December 1778 small British expeditions from New York and Florida subdued Georgia. Fighting in 1779 was inconclusive along the Georgia–South Carolina border, and a combined Franco-American assault on British-held Savannah was beaten off. In February 1780 Britain greatly expanded its southern beachhead when Sir Henry Clinton arrived in South Carolina from New York with 8,700 additional troops. He soon laid siege to Charleston, where on May 12 American Maj. Gen. Benjamin Lincoln surrendered the city and its more than 5,000 defenders. A second, hastily assembled American Southern army under Horatio Gates was crushed at Camden in upper South Carolina (Aug. 16, 1780) by Lord Cornwallis, whom Clinton had left in command when he returned to New York.

These English victories did not extinguish the flames of rebellion. Britain found pacification of the back country difficult. Rebel small-unit operations continued under such local, legendary guerrilla leaders as Francis MARION and Thomas SUMTER. And a body of patriot frontiersmen, mainly from the Watauga settlements in present-day eastern Tennessee, wiped out a 1,000-man contingent of Loyalist troops at King's Mountain on the border of the Carolinas (Oct. 7, 1780).

As the guerrillas tied down Cornwallis, still a third American army formed in the South under Maj. Gen. Nathanael Greene, who then launched the most effective military campaign of the war. Greene's basic plan was to keep his numerically superior antagonist, Cornwallis, off balance by a series of rapid movements and by cooperating with the South Carolina guerrilla leaders. Greene audaciously divided his small army, sending Brig. Gen. Daniel Morgan into western South Carolina, where he destroyed Lt. Col. Banastre Tarleton's Tory Legion at Cowpens (Jan. 17, 1781). When Cornwallis pursued Morgan, Greene united his army, led Cornwallis on an exhausting chase into North Carolina, and finally fought him to a draw at Guilford Courthouse (Mar. 15, 1781). While the British general limped eastward and then northward to the Virginia coast, the resourceful Greene returned to South Carolina, and between April and July picked off, one by one, every British post save Charleston and Savannah, where the enemy remained isolated and impotent until peace came.

Cornwallis, meanwhile, was sealing his own fate in Virginia, where he united with a raiding expedition under Benedict Arnold (now in British service), already in that state, and erected a base at the port of Yorktown. Both his superior, Clinton, in New York and General Washington recognized that Cornwallis was vulnerable to a land-and-sea blockade on a Virginia peninsula. But Cornwallis refused to leave, arguing the doubtful proposition that Britain would have to capture Virginia in order to have lasting success in the lower South.

At this point, Franco-American army and naval operations, hitherto disappointing in their results, now determined the fate of Cornwallis. Adding to his forces the French troops of the Comte de ROCHAMBEAU in Rhode Island, Washington raced southward and opened siege operations before Yorktown on October 6, while a French fleet under the Comte de GRASSE sealed off a sea escape. Clinton hastened a naval squadron from New York to the Chesapeake, but it was repulsed by de Grasse. After suffering through an intensive artillery bombardment, Cornwallis, on Oct. 19, 1781, surrendered his nearly 8,000 troops to the 17,000-man allied force. The British failed in the South for several reasons, including an exaggerated estimate of Loyalist support, an inadequate program of pacification, and a failure to recognize the significance of sea power.

Conclusion. The war in America rapidly ground to a halt after Yorktown, a war in which neither side had seemingly the energy or the resources to obtain a total victory. Certainly British leaders had lost all enthusiasm for subduing America. As for the Americans, they scored a decisive triumph at the peace conference in Paris. Taking advantage of suspicions between the European rivals and sensing England's desire to be generous in order to pry America out of the French orbit, John JAY and Benjamin Franklin secured not only British recognition of American independence but also the entire region from the Appalachians to the Mississippi River as part of the United States. The final Treaty of Paris was signed on Sept. 3, 1783, and ratified by the Continental Congress on Jan. 14, 1784.

American saddle horse   see HORSE

American Samoa
American Samoa is an island group in the south central Pacific Ocean about 2,576 km (1,600 mi) northeast of New Zealand. An unincorporated territory of the United States, it consists of seven islands: Aunu'u, Ofu, Olosega, Rose, Swain's, Tau (or Ta'u), and Tutuila. The last is the main island. The total area is 199 km² (77 mi²). The population is 37,300 (1986 est.), and the capital and major city is Pago Pago. American Samoa was created by an 1899 treaty among Great Britain, Germany, and the United States.

The islands are eroded remnants of volcanic landmasses. The climate is tropical, with temperatures ranging from about 20° C (70° F) to about 30° C (90° F). The rainy season extends from November to April, and hurricanes are prevalent from May to November. Natural resources are limited. The majority of the population is of Polynesian descent, and both Samoan and English are spoken. Village life is communal, based on a complicated social system headed by the matais, or chiefs. Education is compulsory for children 6 to 18 years of age, and the islands have a community college. The main industry is tuna canning. Executive power is held by a governor, elected by popular vote since 1977. The legislature—the Fono—was established by the constitution of 1960. The Samoa Islands were first visited by Europeans in the 18th century but were not settled until 1830. The Samoan

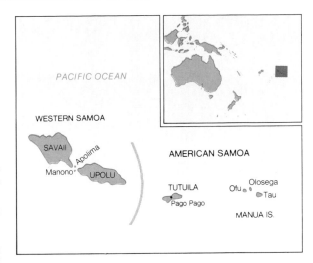

kingdom, established in 1889, was dissolved by the 1899 treaty. From 1900 to 1951 the territory was administered by the Department of the Navy and since then by the Department of the Interior, under which the islands have received significant aid. A new airport was built, and industry and tourism were stimulated.

See also: SAMOA; WESTERN SAMOA.

American shorthair cat
The American shorthair cat, also called the domestic shorthair, was brought to North America from England in early colonial times. An excellent rodent killer and an intelligent, affectionate pet, it has been selectively bred to take top awards at cat shows. It has a large head, well-developed shoulders and chest, and powerful, rippling muscles. The tail is medium long, the coat thick and even. Popular colors include silver tabby, brown tabby, and red tabby.

The American shorthair cat, popularly known as the tabby, was developed as a show breed.

(Left) The American Staffordshire terrier is a cross between the bulldog and the terrier. Powerfully built with strong paws, it was once used in dogfighting.

(Right) The American water spaniel was bred in the 19th century for the hunting and retrieving of waterfowl.

American Staffordshire terrier   The American Staffordshire terrier is a strongly built breed of dog, with a broad head, large cheek muscles, powerful jaws, thick neck, and forelegs set fairly wide apart. It is 43–48 cm (17–19 in) at the shoulder and weighs 15.9–22.7 kg (35–50 lb). The short, stiff coat may be any of the usual dog colors. Uncropped ears are preferable and are held erect; the short tail is carried low. The Staffordshire has been bred in the United States since the mid-19th century but was not recognized by the American Kennel Club until 1935, under the name of Staffordshire terrier. The breed's name was officially changed to American Staffordshire terrier on Jan. 1, 1972, in part to distinguish the breed from the smaller STAFFORDSHIRE BULL TERRIER of England. The two breeds are closely related, having a common background of cross between bulldog and terrier. They were bred as pit, or fighting, dogs, but today's Staffordshires have stable temperaments and make good household pets.

American water spaniel   The American water spaniel is a sporting breed of dog that stands 38–46 cm (15–18 in) at the shoulder and weighs 11.3–20.4 kg (25–45 lb). The dense, tightly curled coat is dark liver or chocolate, and a little white on the chest or toes is accepted in the show ring. The long, drooping ears are wide, and the slightly curved tail is carried a bit below the level of the back. The dog is one of only a few breeds developed in the United States. Its origins are unknown, but its appearance suggests crosses among the Irish water spaniel, curly coated retriever, and early spaniel types. The breed was recognized by the American Kennel Club in 1940. Although mainly popular as a hunting dog, it makes a good household companion.

Americans for Democratic Action   Americans for Democratic Action (ADA), based in Washington, D.C., is a political action organization dedicated to the advancement of liberal causes. It was created in 1947 by such prominent Americans as Marquis CHILDS, David DUBINSKY, Hubert H. HUMPHREY, Jr., Walter REUTHER, Eleanor ROOSEVELT, and Arthur M. SCHLESINGER, Jr. Its stated objective is to "map a campaign for restoring the influence of liberalism in the national and international policies of the United States." The ADA is formally nonpartisan, but in practice it has mainly endorsed Democratic party candidates, and it is closely identified with the liberal wing of the Democratic party. Besides endorsing candidates, the ADA publishes a yearly appraisal of the performance of members of Congress on important issues. It also formulates liberal positions on national issues and proposes legislation.

America's Cup   The America's Cup is competitive yachting's most prestigious prize. From 1851 to 1980 the best yachtsmen in the world tried unsuccessfully to wrest the trophy from American sailors. In 1983 the Australians succeeded, but a U.S. yacht regained the cup in 1987. The competition originated when the New York Yacht Club sent the schooner *America* to England in 1851 to challenge for the Royal Yacht Squadron's Hundred Guinea Cup. The *America* defeated 17 British opponents in a 93-km (58-mi) race around the Isle of Wight and won the cup. In 1857 the *America*'s owners presented the cup to the New York Yacht Club, which renamed it America's Cup and began to sponsor challenges for possession. The competition was expanded in 1876 to the best of 3 races, in 1893 to the best of 5, and in 1930 to the best of 7. From 1930 to 1983 the races were held off Newport, R.I.; in 1987 they were held off Perth, Australia, and in 1988 off San Diego, Calif. From 1958 to 1987 the contest was between vessels of the 12-Meter Class. In 1988, New Zealand sued successfully in court for the right to challenge in a different vessel, overturning several other conventions as well. The *New Zealand*, a 40.5-m (133-ft) monohull, was handily beaten, however, by a U.S. catamaran skippered by Dennis Connor. Connor was also the U.S. captain in 1980, 1983, and 1987.

AMERICA'S CUP WINNERS[*]

1851	*America* defeated *Aurora*, England (1-0)
1870	*Magic* defeated *Cambria*, England (1-0)
1871	*Columbia* (first three races) and *Sappho* (last two races) defeated *Livonia*, England (4-1)
1876	*Madeline* defeated *Countess of Dufferin*, Canada (2-0)
1881	*Mischief* defeated *Atalanta*, Canada (2-0)
1885	*Purifan* defeated *Genesta*, England (2-0)
1886	*Mayflower* defeated *Galatea*, England (2-0)
1887	*Volunteer* defeated *Thistle*, Scotland (2-0)
1893	*Vigilant* defeated *Valkyrie II*, England (3-0)
1895	*Defender* defeated *Valkyrie III*, England (3-0)
1899	*Columbia* defeated *Shamrock*, Ireland (3-0)
1901	*Columbia* defeated *Shamrock II*, Ireland (3-0)
1903	*Reliance* defeated *Shamrock III*, Ireland (3-0)
1920	*Resolute* defeated *Shamrock IV*, Ireland (3-2)
1930	*Enterprise* defeated *Shamrock V*, Ireland (4-0)
1934	*Rainbow* defeated *Endeavor*, England (4-2)
1937	*Ranger* defeated *Endeavor II*, England (4-0)
1958	*Columbia* defeated *Sceptre*, England (4-0)
1962	*Weatherly* defeated *Gretel*, Australia (4-1)
1964	*Constellation* defeated *Sovereign*, England (4-0)
1967	*Intrepid* defeated *Dame Pattie*, Australia (4-0)
1970	*Intrepid* defeated *Gretel II*, Australia (4-1)
1974	*Courageous* defeated *Southern Cross*, Australia (4-0)
1977	*Courageous* defeated *Australia*, (4-0)
1980	*Freedom* defeated *Australia*, (4-1)
1983	*Australia II* defeated *Liberty*, U.S.A. (4-3)
1987	*Stars & Stripes* defeated *Kookaburra III*, Australia (4-0)
1988	*Stars & Stripes* defeated *New Zealand* (2-0)
1992	*America[3]* defeated *Il Moro di Venezia*, Italy (4-1)

[*]All winners, except in 1983, have been from the United States.

Hexagonal (6-sided) amethyst crystals often are found lining the interior of a geode, or rock cavity. Colors of amethyst vary from shades of lilac to rich, dark purple, and some stones may be heated slightly to distribute the colors more evenly. Amethysts ranked among the most precious of gems until the 18th century and the discovery of large deposits in South America.

americium [am-uh-ris'-ee-uhm] Americium is a transuranium element, a radioactive metal of the ACTINIDE SERIES. Its symbol is Am, its atomic number is 95, and the atomic weight of its stablest isotope is 243. Americium does not occur naturally. It was synthesized for the first time in 1944, when scientists bombarded plutonium-239 with helium ions and obtained the isotope ^{241}Am. The known isotopes of americium, whose mass numbers range from 237 to 246, are radioactive. The stablest isotope, ^{243}Am, has a half-life of 7,370 years. Usable amounts of ^{241}Am are obtained by bombardment of plutonium-241 in nuclear reactors. Because it emits strong gamma radiation, ^{241}Am is used in various types of measuring devices and in radiography.

amethyst [am'-uh-thist] Amethyst, a violet, crystalline variety of QUARTZ, is the birthstone for February. When transparent and of good color, it is valued as a semiprecious GEM and is usually step-cut or intaglio-carved. The color, thought to be caused by impurities of iron, manganese, or hydrocarbons, is changed to citrine yellow by heat; most commercial citrine is heat-treated amethyst. The mineral occurs in cavities in volcanic rock and is found in the Ural Mountains, Brazil, Sri Lanka, and the United States. The ancients probably applied the name to purple corundum and garnet as well as to true amethyst.

Amhara [am-hahr'-uh] The Amhara are a people of the central highlands of Ethiopia. Numbering about 10 million in the early 1980s, they are descended from mixed Hamitlo-Semitic groups that entered the highlands from southern Arabia between the 6th century BC and the 1st century AD. Since their establishment of the Solomonid dynasty in the 13th century, they have dominated the history of Ethiopia.

The Amharic language, originally a court language, is the official tongue of Ethiopia. It is a Semitic language closely related to Ge'ez, the sacred literary language of the Ethiopian Orthodox church. Together with the Tigré to the north of them, the Amhara consider themselves the only true Christians. They are identified closely with their church—formerly headed by the Ethiopian emperors—and adhere to MONOPHYSITISM.

The Amhara, whose economy is chiefly agricultural, lay great emphasis on land ownership. Although descent, which is traced through the male line, is important among them, their society is organized primarily around a system of patron-client relationships based on landholding. Their traditional dress resembles a toga under which men wear tight-fitting trousers and women wear a gown.

Amherst (Massachusetts) Amherst (1990 pop., 35,228) is a town in the Connecticut River valley of west central Massachusetts. Settled in the 1730s, it developed an economy based on farming. Today, Amherst is a college town, the site of the University of Massachusetts, Amherst College, and Hampshire College.

Amherst (Nova Scotia)   Amherst (1986 pop., 9,671) is located in northern Nova Scotia, near the Cumberland Basin. It overlooks the Tantramar Marshes. Its economic activities include dairy farming, tourism, and some light industry. Settled by the French, it was renamed in 1759 for Jeffrey Amherst.

Amherst, Jeffrey, Baron Amherst   Lord Amherst, b. Jan. 29, 1717, d. Aug. 3, 1797, was an able British general who conquered Canada during the FRENCH AND INDIAN WAR (1754–63). After serving in Europe in the War of the Austrian Succession (1740–48), he was ordered to America to command the expedition against the seemingly impregnable French fortress at LOUISBOURG. As a result of his careful planning, the fortress fell on July 26, 1758.

Appointed commander in chief in British North America in 1759, Amherst captured the forts at TICONDEROGA and Crown Point. With his forces converging on Montreal from three directions, he captured that city on Sept. 8, 1760, and thus won control of Canada. Amherst was appointed governor-general of British North America and governor of Virginia. Returning to England, he was created a baron in 1776 and made a field marshal in 1796.

Amherst College   Established in 1821, Amherst College is a private 4-year liberal arts college in Amherst, Mass. Cooperative programs with Hampshire, Mount Holyoke, and Smith colleges and the University of Massachusetts make libraries and certain courses mutually available. Amherst administers the Folger Shakespeare Library in Washington, D.C.

Amichai, Yehuda [ah-mee-ky']   Yehuda Amichai, b. Germany, May 3, 1924, is perhaps the best-known contemporary Israeli poet. An adolescent emigrant (1936) to Israel, Amichai has long struggled with the issues of identity and of reconciling the present with the horrendous Jewish past—issues most directly addressed in his novel *Not of This Time, Not of This Place* (1963; Eng. trans., 1968). His poetry has been praised for the intense lyricism he creates using an idiom that is colloquial and concrete. It includes, in English translation, *Amen* (1977), *Great Tranquility* (1983), *The World Is a Room and Other Short Stories* (1984), and *Selected Poetry* and *Travels* (both 1986).

amide [am'-yd]   Amides are a class of organic compounds related to ammonia and commonly found in nature. Amides have the general structural formula $RCONH_2$ or $RCONHR$, in which R is a hydrocarbon group, and are derivatives of carboxylic acids ($RCOOH$). Amides in solution are essentially neutral. In general, amides have higher melting points and boiling points and are less soluble in water than are their component acids and AMINES (RNH_2).

Molecules that have two amide groups are diamides; molecular chains formed from amide repeating linkages (-CONH-) are called polyamides. The simplest naturally occurring amide is UREA, H_2NCONH_2, a diamide that is excreted in the urine of many mammals as a product of protein metabolism. Urea is of some commercial importance as starting material in the manufacture of certain polymers. Proteins are a class of high-molecular-weight polyamides formed by the combination of AMINO ACIDS with each other. Important nonprotenoid amides include penicillin G; niacinamide; piperine, found in black pepper; and many other compounds with physiological activity. NYLON is a synthetic polyamide made from a dicarboxylic acid and a diamine to form a long-chain polymer. Cyclic amides include riboflavin (vitamin B_2) and some other B vitamins, DNA, RNA, caffeine, uric acid, and barbiturates.

Amiens [ah-mee-en']   Amiens (1982 pop., 131,332), the capital of Somme department in Picardy in northern France, is located on the Somme River. An important rail junction and a trade center for the surrounding agricultural region, its manufactures include textiles, chemicals, machinery, and tires. Amiens Cathedral is the largest and one of the most famous (with Chartres and Reims) High Gothic cathedrals. Much of its construction was overseen by Robert de Luzarches and Thomas de Cormont and his son Renaud between 1220 and 1269, although the towers flanking the west end were added in the 14th and 15th centuries and the spire over the crossing in the 16th. Amiens is the site of the University of Picardy (1965).

Amiens was originally the capital of the Ambiani tribe and was under Roman rule when Christianity was introduced in the 4th century. Under French rule from 1185, the city passed to the Burgundians in 1435. It came under French rule again in 1477. The city was the site of the Peace of Amiens (1802) during the Napoleonic Wars. It fell to the Prussians in 1870 and was occupied by the Germans in both world wars, during which it suffered much damage. It has been largely rebuilt.

Amin Dada, Idi [ah-meen' dah-dah, ee'-dee]   Idi Amin Dada, b. Koboko, Uganda, c.1925, was president of Uganda from 1971 to 1979. During his years of brutal and erratic rule, some 300,000 Ugandans are said to have died, and the nation's economic and social structure was shattered. A Muslim and a member of the Kakwa tribe, Amin served in the British army and later helped Prime Minister Milton OBOTE overthrow (1966) Kabaka Mutesa II, president of the federation of Uganda. In 1971 Amin ousted Obote, proclaiming himself field marshal in 1975 and president-for-life in 1976. The excesses of his dictatorship led to his overthrow by Tanzanian regular troops and Ugandan exiles in April 1979. He went into exile, first in Libya and later in Saudi Arabia.

amine [uh-meen']   Amines are a class of organic compounds that are important in the formation of proteins and are present in great numbers in living organisms. Many have pronounced physiological effects. Among the physiologically active amines are spermine, many ENZYMES, serotonin, ephedrine, dopamine, amphetamine, and adrenaline.

In amines, one, two, or three of the hydrogen atoms of AMMONIA, NH_3, are replaced by hydrocarbon groups, symbolized by R. Thus RNH_2 is called a primary amine, RR'NH or R_2NH a secondary amine, and RR'R"N or R_3N a tertiary amine (R' and R" may represent different groups). Like ammonia, amines are bases and easily react with an acid to form a SALT, so that NH_3 yields NH_4Cl and RNH_2 yields RNH_3Cl, when they react with hydrochloric acid, HCl. If R has a low molecular weight, the corresponding amines are gaseous (like ammonia) or are low-boiling liquids and are soluble in water. As the molecular weight of R increases, water solubility declines.

amino acid   Amino acids are organic compounds that are the building blocks of PROTEIN. In most animal metabolisms, a number of amino acids play a crucial role. The GENETIC CODE determines the assembly of amino acids into body proteins.

Each amino acid has at least one carboxyl (COOH) group and one amino (NH_2) group. In protein synthesis, amino acids join together in long chains, in which the carboxyl group of one amino acid links with the amino group of another by a peptide bond. A chain of amino acids is known as a polypeptide, and proteins are large, naturally occurring polypeptides containing perhaps 250 amino acids. In some proteins a change in just one amino acid in the chain, or even a change in its position, can cause the protein to become nonfunctional or to perform its function differently.

The 20 major amino acids are: alanine, arginine, asparagine, aspartic acid, cysteine, glycine, glutamic acid, glutamine, histidine, isoleucine, leucine, lysine, methionine, phenylalanine, proline, serine, threonine, tryptophan, tyrosine, and valine.

Amis, Kingsley [ay'-mis]   An English novelist, poet, critic, and teacher, Kingsley Amis, b. Apr. 16, 1922, came to prominence as one of England's Angry Young Men with the publication of his first novel, *Lucky Jim* (1954; film, 1957), a sharp satire on education and the establishment. His other novels include *That Uncertain Feeling* (1955; film, 1962), *I Like It Here* (1958), *Take a Girl Like You* (1960; film, 1970), *The Anti-Death League* (1966), *The Green Man* (1969), and *Jake's Thing* (1978). *The Old Devils* (1986) won the Booker Prize. Amis has also written volumes of poetry and volumes of political and literary criticism.

Amish   see MENNONITES

Amman [ahm-mahn']   Amman, the capital and largest city of Jordan, is located about 40 km (25 mi) northeast of the Dead Sea. A small town until it became the capital of Transjordan in 1921, it now has a population of 900,000 (1988 est.). A commercial as well as administrative center, Amman exports phosphates mined nearby at El Hasa. Manufactures include textiles and leather goods. Amman is the site of the Jordan Archaeological Museum and the University of Jordan (1962).

Amman may have been settled as early as the 17th century BC; it was the biblical city Rabbah (Ammon) and the main city and capital of the Ammonites. As the ancient Greek city Philadelphia, southernmost of the ten cities of the Decapolis, it prospered under the leadership of Ptolemy II Philadelphus (r. 285–246 BC) and later under the Roman Empire. The city assumed its current name in the 7th century.

Ruins of Ammonite tombs, a Roman theater seating 6,000, a citadel, and an acropolis remain, although many ancient buildings have been destroyed by earthquakes. Amman was further damaged by fighting between Palestinian guerrillas and the Jordanian Army in 1970 and 1971.

Ammanati, Bartolommeo [ah-mah-nah'-tee, bahr-toh-loh-may'-oh]   Bartolommeo Ammanati, b. June 18, 1511, d. Apr. 13, 1592, was a leading Florentine sculptor and architect of the Italian Renaissance. In Padua he designed, under the influence of Jacopo SANSOVINO, the monumental arch (1544) of the Benavides Palace and the Benavides Tomb (1546) in the Church of the Eremitani. He married the poetess Laura Battiferri in 1550. In Rome he collaborated with Giacomo Barozzi da Vignola and Giorgio VASARI on the Villa Giulia (1552–55) and executed the Del Monte family tombs (1550–53) in the church of San Pietro in Montorio.

After 1555, Ammanati resided in Florence and was responsible for some of the most important projects of the day: the Santa Trinitá Bridge (1567–70; destroyed 1944, rebuilt 1957); the grandiose courtyard (1558–70) of the PITTI PALACE; and the Neptune Fountain (1563–75) in the Piazza della Signoria.

Ammann, Othmar Hermann [ahm'-mahn]   The Swiss-born engineer Othmar Hermann Ammann, b. Mar. 26, 1879, d. Sept. 22, 1965, designed many of the most famous bridges in the United States, the Lincoln Tunnel under the Hudson River, Dulles International Airport in Washington, D.C., and other major projects. He was also involved in the design and construction of New York City's Lincoln Center for the Performing Arts. After studying in Zurich, Ammann immigrated to the United States in 1904. Ammann was named chief engineer for the Port of New York Authority in 1927, and in the succeeding years he designed three of the world's longest suspension bridges: the George Washington Bridge in New York

(1,067 m/3,500 ft), completed in 1931; San Francisco's Golden Gate Bridge (1,280 m/4,200 ft), completed in 1937; and the Verrazano-Narrows Bridge (1,298 m/4,260 ft), connecting Brooklyn and Staten Island, completed in 1964.

ammeter [am'-meet-ur]   An ammeter measures the flow of current by converting electrical energy to mechanical energy. Most ammeters measure direct current (DC) and make use of D'Arsonval's classic GALVANOMETER principle, in which the magnetic field of a current-bearing coil opposes that of a fixed magnet. Because a very small current will cause full-scale deflection of the coil, the ammeter must be modified to measure larger currents. This may be done by using a low-resistant path, or shunt. The introduction of more sophisticated digital measuring devices in recent years has somewhat decreased the use of ammeters.

ammonia   Ammonia (NH_3), one of the most important nitrogen compounds, is a colorless, poisonous gas that can be distinguished by its characteristic irritating odor. It is extremely soluble in water. The ammonia commonly sold as a household cleanser and disinfectant is a dilute solution of ammonium hydroxide, an alkaline compound that can exist only in aqueous solution.

Ammonia is manufactured directly from its elements, hydrogen and nitrogen, by the Haber-Bosch process (see HABER, Fritz). The ammonia is then stored either in pressurized cylinders or as an aqueous solution. In the laboratory, ammonia may be prepared by heating an ammonium salt with sodium hydroxide (lye, NaOH). Large quantities of ammonia are used in manufacturing nitric acid and ammonium salts, and ammonia and its compounds are the principal nitrogen sources for fertilizers, synthetic fibers, and explosives. The Solvay process uses ammonia to manufacture sodium carbonate from common salt.

Ammonia is easily liquefied and thus is widely used as a refrigerant (see REFRIGERATION). It is especially useful for this purpose because it has low density, high stability, low corrosiveness, and a high heat of vaporization. Ammonia salts are commonly used as SMELLING SALTS to relieve faintness.

ammonoid [am'-uh-noyd]   Ammonoids are an extinct subclass, Ammonoidea, of cephalopod MOLLUSKS, related to the OCTOPUS, SQUID, and cuttlefish. Their fossils, prized as ornaments for hundreds of years, are now highly sought after by geologists, who use them for correlating sedimentary rock strata from one area to another (see STRATIGRAPHY). The univalve (one-piece) shells underwent many changes in size and shape during the ammonoids' 325-million-year history. An order with highly ornamented shells, the ammonite evolved during the last stages of that history.

Ammonoids were, at least in part, coiled and also chambered. Thin plates, or septa, walled off the part of the shell no longer occupied, as in the modern NAUTILUS. A thin cord of tissue, called the siphuncle, extended from the living animal through the vacated chambers of the shell. The edges of the septa made a wavy, often intricate pattern on the outer shell surface, distinguishing ammonoid shells from NAUTILOID shells, which display much simpler patterns. Shell diameters range from 5 to 15 cm (2 to 6 in) in some species, up to as much as 2.7 m (9 ft) in others.

Ammonoids appear to have lived in open ocean, or at least in saline waters. Many were nektic (free-swimming), with some species benthonic (bottom-dwelling) during adulthood; others were planktic (drifting or floating). Ammonoids came close to extinction several times. They first appeared in the Devonian Period of the Paleozoic Era and diversified rapidly. They declined markedly in the Devonian Period, recovered later in the Paleozoic, then came close to extinction by the end of the era (see GEOLOGIC TIME). Widespread and diverse in the Jurassic and Cretaceous periods, ammonoids died out as the Mesozoic Era ended (see EXTINCTION).

Ammons, A. R. [am'-uhnz]   American poet Archie Randolph Ammons, b. Whiteville, N.C., Feb. 18, 1926, moved from short lyric forms to complex poetic speculations about perception and language. *Ommateum*, his first book, was published in 1955. *Collected Poems 1951–71* received a National Book Award (1973), and Ammons himself won the Bollingen Prize in 1975. An expanded edition of *Selected Poems* was published in 1987.

ammunition   Ammunition includes a variety of devices used to deliver an explosive, chemical, or pyrotechnic charge to a target. Military ammunition includes aerial BOMBS, MINES, TORPEDOES, ROCKETS AND MISSILES, and a broad spectrum of EXPLOSIVE and nonexplosive projectiles. Common usage limits the term to devices designed to be ejected from a FIREARM, CANNON, or MORTAR.

Ammunition consists of three basic elements: the primer (detonator), the propellant, and the projectile. Most ammunition also has a casing, or cartridge, that encapsulates the primer and propellant and often grips some portion of the projectile.

Primer. Early ammunition was assembled as needed. A fine black powder served as the primer charge to detonate the propellant charge, a coarser powder. Matchlocks, wheel locks, and flintlocks were used to ignite the primer charge. A new method of ignition, the percussion cap, was introduced in the early 19th century. This was a soft copper cup filled with a sensitive explosive and placed over a nipple with a small hole leading to the propellant. A hammer struck the cap and fired the weapon. Percussion caps survive in the form of primers located in the center or the rim of the base of the cartridge.

Propellant. From the late 13th century to the late 19th century, the sole propellant was black powder, or GUNPOWDER. Its composition has varied little in seven centu-

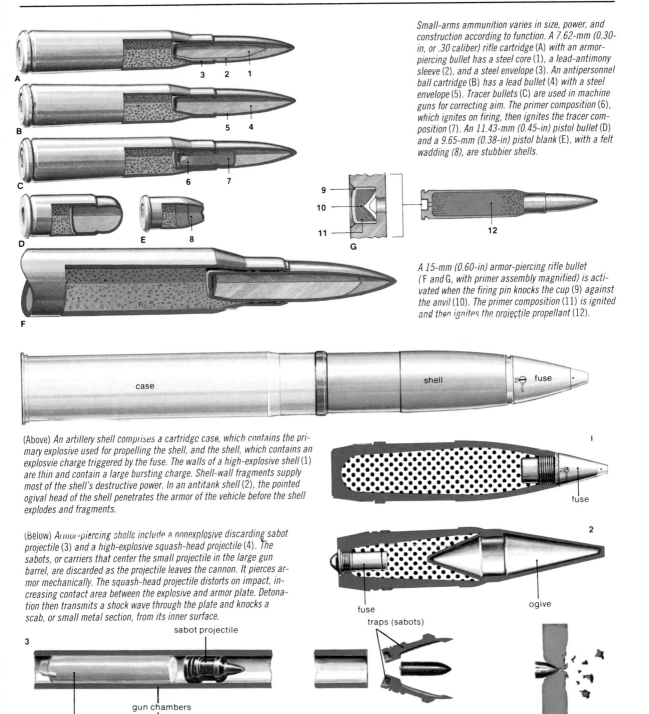

Small-arms ammunition varies in size, power, and construction according to function. A 7.62-mm (0.30-in, or .30 caliber) rifle cartridge (A) with an armor-piercing bullet has a steel core (1), a lead-antimony sleeve (2), and a steel envelope (3). An antipersonnel ball cartridge (B) has a lead bullet (4) with a steel envelope (5). Tracer bullets (C) are used in machine guns for correcting aim. The primer composition (6), which ignites on firing, then ignites the tracer composition (7). An 11.43-mm (0.45-in) pistol bullet (D) and a 9.65-mm (0.38-in) pistol blank (E), with a felt wadding (8), are stubbier shells.

A 15-mm (0.60-in) armor-piercing rifle bullet (F and G, with primer assembly magnified) is activated when the firing pin knocks the cup (9) against the anvil (10). The primer composition (11) is ignited and then ignites the projectile propellant (12).

(Above) An artillery shell comprises a cartridge case, which contains the primary explosive used for propelling the shell, and the shell, which contains an explosive charge triggered by the fuse. The walls of a high-explosive shell (1) are thin and contain a large bursting charge. Shell-wall fragments supply most of the shell's destructive power. In an antitank shell (2), the pointed ogival head of the shell penetrates the armor of the vehicle before the shell explodes and fragments.

(Below) Armor-piercing shells include a nonexplosive discarding sabot projectile (3) and a high-explosive squash-head projectile (4). The sabots, or carriers that center the small projectile in the large gun barrel, are discarded as the projectile leaves the cannon. It pierces armor mechanically. The squash-head projectile distorts on impact, increasing contact area between the explosive and armor plate. Detonation then transmits a shock wave through the plate and knocks a scab, or small metal section, from its inner surface.

ries, the traditional recipe being 10% sulfur, 15% charcoal, and 75% saltpeter (potassium nitrate). Although it was unchanged for centuries, black powder has its drawbacks. It produces a large cloud of smoke and fouls the bores of firearms after relatively few shots. Black powder also readily attracts moisture, hence the admonition "keep your powder dry."

Nitrocellulose-base smokeless powders, of which GUNCOTTON was the first, began to replace black powder in the late 1880s; within 20 years, they were being used almost exclusively. The new propellants overcame black powder's deficiencies and were much more powerful.

Small-Arms Projectiles and Cartridge Assemblies. Until the early-19th century, small-arms projectiles consisted of round lead-alloy or iron balls of fractionally smaller diameter than the weapon's smooth-bore. Later, spiral-grooved (rifled) bores, designed to make the projectile spin, became prevalent, although smooth-bore shotguns of limited range still exist. Modern projectiles generally have pointed or rounded noses and are clad with copper or brass. The diameter, or caliber, of a projectile is expressed in fractions of an inch or millimeters. With the advent of the more powerful smokeless powders, the caliber of military shoulder weapons has undergone a drastic reduction. The last U.S. military black-powder rifle round was .45 caliber (0.45 in); a .30 caliber round replaced it; today the caliber is .223, or 5.66 mm.

Paper cartridges, incorporating the powder and projectile into a paper casing, were introduced in Europe during the 16th century. The entire assembly was rammed down the bore. The first successful metallic cartridge to incorporate projectile, propellant, and primer was invented in 1836. Experimentation during the next 50 years resulted in small-arms ammunition as we know it today.

Modern ammunition can be categorized by its degree of preassembly. In fixed ammunition, all the components are held together by a cartridge case. Semifixed ammunition features a projectile that is not firmly held by the cartridge case and is inserted just before firing, allowing adjustments to be made to the propellant. Separated ammunition is similar to semifixed, but the cartridge case comes sealed and is loaded after the projectile. Small-arms ammunition is typically fixed, whereas larger types of ammunition are usually separate-loading.

Modern ARTILLERY projectiles are highly specialized to defeat a number of diverse targets. Fuses are available that detonate the projectile when it is a certain selected distance from its target (proximity fuse), at a predetermined point in its trajectory (variable time fuse), upon impact (quick and superquick fuse), and after impact (delay fuse). The ultimate artillery projectile, the nuclear round, was developed in the early 1950s. It is currently available in the United States for weapons as small as the 155-mm howitzer.

Latest innovations in artillery ammunition include rocket-assisted projectiles and a laser-guided projectile that homes in on a target that is illuminated, or "painted," by a laser beam.

amnesia Amnesia is the inability to remember past experiences. It occurs normally during infancy because the brain has not yet developed the myelin needed to wrap and insulate neurons; thus the ability to retain messages in sequence is impaired. Amnesia also may occur as the result of severe head injury, shock, or certain drugs. Retrograde amnesia involves impaired memory of events that occurred before the trauma that caused the condition, whereas anterograde amnesia affects events that follow. Broca's amnesia, or APHASIA, is a loss of the ability to use either written or spoken language; verbal amnesia is loss of memory for words; visual amnesia is the inability to recall objects that have been seen; and lacunar amnesia is the inability to remember isolated events rather than a total loss of memory.

amnesty An amnesty is an exemption from prosecution for criminal acts, usually issued by a government after a time of crisis such as a war or a revolution. The amnesty may be for acts such as rebellion or treason. It is usually granted to groups of citizens on condition that they abide by the law in the future.

Many amnesties are partial. President Andrew Johnson, after the Civil War, excluded the leaders of the Confederacy when he extended amnesty to former rebels who would support the federal government. The end of the Vietnam conflict in 1973 produced the most controversial amnesty question in U.S. history. Presidents Nixon, Ford, and Carter denied amnesty to deserters and draft evaders of that period, but Ford offered clemency to those who were willing to do public service work, and Carter pardoned most draft evaders. Also controversial was the 1986 immigration act amnestying illegal aliens who were U.S. residents since before Jan. 1, 1982.

Amnesty International Amnesty International, based in London, is an organization devoted to helping people imprisoned for their political or religious beliefs, provided that they have not used or advocated violence. It was awarded the Nobel Peace Prize for 1977 for its contribution to "securing the ground for freedom, for justice, and thereby also for peace in the world." It has national sections in 44 countries, local groups in 60 countries, and a membership of more than 500,000 individuals.

The organization grew out of an appeal launched in 1961 by Peter Benenson, a British lawyer, on behalf of prisoners of conscience. Amnesty International opposes the use of torture and the death penalty, and it issues reports on human rights conditions throughout the world. It calls for observance of the United Nations Universal Declaration of Human Rights and other international human rights agreements.

amniocentesis [am-nee-oh-sen-tee'-sis] A diagnostic procedure in medical genetics, amniocentesis is a technique in which a sample of the amniotic fluid that bathes the human fetus is removed from the pregnant uterus by suction with a very fine needle. Fetal cells suspended in the fluid can then be grown in the laboratory and studied to detect various genetic disorders in the unborn child.

Amniocentesis is usually performed during the 15th week of pregnancy, thus giving ample time to complete the appropriate studies, and, if necessary, permit therapeutic ABORTION by the 20th week of pregnancy, when it is still relatively safe.

Amniocentesis may be advisable for women who are over age 35 or who previously had been found to have chromosomal abnormalities, thus increasing the risk of giving birth to a child with DOWN'S SYNDROME or other chromosomal disorders. When parents are known to have, or to carry genes for, an inherited biochemical disorder or a sex-linked disorder, such as HEMOPHILIA, amniocentesis can be performed to determine whether the fetus is normal. Also, some congenital malformations of the brain and spinal cord are associated with increased levels of alpha-fetoprotein, a substance in the amniotic fluid. Since the risk of recurrent congenital malformations is higher in some families than in the general population, a woman who has given birth to an affected child might seek amniocentesis during future pregnancies.

See also: PREGNANCY AND BIRTH.

amniotic sac   see DEVELOPMENT; PREGNANCY AND BIRTH

---

amoeba [uh-mee'-buh]   An amoeba is any of several microscopic, one-celled Protozoan organisms commonly found in fresh and salt water, in soil, and as animal parasites; some specialized forms are found in plants. The term *amoeba* usually refers to members of the order Amoebida in the class Rhizopoda. Amoebas move in a creeping or gliding fashion by extending their protoplasm; the projections are called pseudopodia (false feet). The pseudopod is also extended to surround other organisms

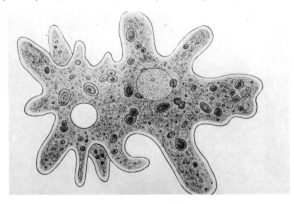

A common freshwater amoeba moves and engulfs food by using pseudopods, or false feet, formed by stretching its body.

or food particles and draw them into the body. The characteristic movement by extension is called amoeboid movement and is a common form of locomotion in other cells.

Despite constantly varying shapes, amoebas are identified by basic form and their distinct type of locomotion. Amoebas vary in size from 0.01 mm (0.0004 in) to 1 mm (0.04 in). They have a contractile vacuole that empties any excess water that has been drawn into the cell. Some amoebas resist unfavorable conditions such as drying or lack of food by secreting a resistant body covering in a process called encystment. Others have permanent shells into which they can withdraw.

The amoeba commonly used in classrooms and as a research tool is *Amoeba proteus*, which reproduces by nuclear division followed by binary fission, or splitting into two. Of the six or seven types of amoebas found in humans, only one, *Entamoeba histolytica*, is harmful. It causes amoebic DYSENTERY, an inflammation of the intestine that if unchecked can lead to abscesses of the liver and brain and to eventual death.

Amon-Re [ah'-muhn ray']   Amon-Re was the supreme god of the Egyptian religion during the New Kingdom period (1570–1085 BC). Amon and Re were originally two separate deities. Re (or Ra) was a Sun god whose cult at Heliopolis (On) in Lower Egypt was promoted by the Egyptian kings beginning with the 5th dynasty (c.2494–2345 BC). Represented in art with a man's body and a falcon's head surmounted by a solar disk, Re was believed to sail across the sky in a boat each day and under the world at night. At Heliopolis he was associated with the god Horakhty, but during the Middle Kingdom (c.2040–1786 BC) he became identified with Amon (or Amun), a god worshiped at Thebes in Upper Egypt. The Amon-Re of the New Kingdom took on the characteristics of a national deity, served by a wealthy and powerful priesthood. His temple at KARNAK is one of the chief architectural monuments of ancient Egypt.

Amorites [am'-uh-ryts]   The Amorites were a Semitic people of the ancient Near East, mentioned in the Bible as inhabitants of Canaan at the time the Hebrews settled there. Apparently dominant in Syria and Palestine c.2000–1600 BC, they are also known from Babylonian records as the founders of the Amorite, or Old Babylonian, dynasty of Mesopotamia (c.1900–c.1550 BC). Ezek. 16:3 suggests that they were closely related to the Hebrews.

---

amortization   Amortization, in finance, is the gradual reduction of a debt over a period of time. A familiar amortization plan is a home mortgage, payable in monthly installments, usually of equal amount, that cover both principal and interest. As the interest on the unpaid balance decreases each month, the payment on the principal increases by a like amount. The longer the amortization period, the larger the total interest on the debt, but the amount of each installment is smaller.

Amortization, in accounting, is the gradual reduction of an amount by periodic accounting entries. When applied to fixed assets such as plant and equipment, it is called depreciation. For example, a $10,000 machine with an expected useful life of 10 years may be depreciated at $1,000 a year.

Amos, Book of   Amos, a book of the Old Testament, is the third book of the Minor Prophets. It takes its name from the prophet Amos who lived c.750 BC as a shepherd at Tekoa in the southern kingdom of Judah. It was to the northern kingdom of Israel, however, that his prophetic message was addressed. Writing during a time of prosperity, when a sharp contrast existed between the luxurious life of the nation's leaders and the oppression of the poor, Amos preached the urgency of social justice and the threat of impending divine judgment. The structure of the book falls into nine parts, each dominated by a negative message containing threats of darkness, famine, and destruction. Amos is the oldest of the prophetic books of the Bible.

Amos 'n' Andy   "Amos 'n' Andy" was the name of a radio program (1928–60) that caricatured the lives of African Americans, and of a television show (1951–53) inspired by it. Created by two white men, Freeman Gosden (1899–1982) and Charles Correll (1890–1972)—who also portrayed the characters on radio—the program featured comic situations involving Amos Jones and Andy Brown, joint owners of the Fresh-Air Taxi Company. In later years, Amos was largely replaced by George "Kingfish" Stevens, head of the Mystic Knights of the Sea lodge, also played by Gosden. Other characters included Amos's wife, Ruby, the Kingfish's wife, Sapphire, and Andy's girlfriend, Madame Queen. The television program starred two black actors, Spencer Williams, Jr., as Andy, and Tim Moore as the Kingfish. Its demise was hastened by the protests of civil rights groups, which considered it insulting to blacks.

Amoy   see XIAMEN.

Ampère, André Marie [ahm-pair']   André Ampère, b. Jan. 10, 1775, d. June 10, 1836, was a French physicist who laid the foundations for the science of electrodynamics through his demonstration that electric currents produce magnetic fields, and through his subsequent investigation into the relationship between these two phenomena. Ampère's most notable achievements were his independent determination (1814) of Avogadro's law and his work from 1820 to 1827 based on Oersted's discovery, announced in 1820, that a magnetic needle moves in the vicinity of an electric current. Ampère succeeded in explaining the latter phenomenon by assuming

that an electric current is capable of exciting a magnetic field. He further demonstrated that the direction of the magnetic field is determined by the direction of the current. He developed a quantitative relationship for the strength of a magnetic field in relation to an electric current (Ampère's theorem) and propounded a theory as to how iron becomes magnetized. Ampère also devised a rule governing the mutual interaction of current-carrying wires (Ampère's law) and produced a definition of the unit of measurement of current flow, now known as the AMPERE.

ampere [am'-pir]   The ampere, symbol A, is the unit for measuring electric current. It is defined in terms of two straight parallel conductors of infinite length and negligible cross section, placed one meter apart in a vacuum. If a constant current is maintained, one A is the amount of current that would produce a force between them equal to 2×10^{-7} newtons of length. (One newton is the force that gives a mass of one kilogram an acceleration of one meter per second per second.)

See also: CIRCUIT, ELECTRIC; ELECTRICITY; UNITS, PHYSICAL.

amphetamine [am-fet'-uh-meen]   Amphetamines are a group of synthetic DRUGS that are strong STIMULANTS of the central nervous system, increasing the heart rate and raising blood pressure. Administered in capsule or tablet form, they increase alertness and reduce hunger. They are used for these purposes and for treating some forms of DEPRESSION and the SLEEP disorder called narcolepsy. They have also been prescribed for HYPERACTIVITY, but this use has caused controversy. Derivatives of chemicals related to the hormone adrenaline, they act by increasing the effects of noradrenaline, a NEUROTRANSMITTER. The three kinds—methamphetamines, dextroamphetamines, and certain salts—differ somewhat in potency and side effects. They are sold under such trade names as Benzedrine, Dexedrine, and Methedrine, among others.

The first amphetamine was made in 1887, but medical uses were discovered only in the 1920s. Amphetamines came to be widely prescribed in following decades. At the same time, they found increasing nonmedical use as "pep pills" or "uppers" for staying awake. They also gained popularity as recreational drugs (see DRUG ABUSE).

Abuse became an increasingly serious problem after the early 1950s, as the drugs began to be injected intravenously. Amphetamine-heroin mixtures, called "speedballs" after earlier cocaine-heroin mixtures, gave rise to the name "speed" for injections of amphetamine alone. Prolonged abuse leads to states of extreme irritability, paranoid delusions, and hallucinations, during which an individual is prone to violence. The abuser is also likely to experience profound depression and thoughts of suicide during periods of withdrawal. Drug overdoses can be fatal for persons with high blood pressure or cardiac problems, and for athletes overtaxing their hearts, because the drug masks their fatigue.

Later manifestations of amphetamine abuse include "ecstasy," a combination of methamphetamine with a synthetic psychedelic drug (see MDMA), and a smokable form of crystalline methamphetamine called "ice."

The American bullfrog is the largest frog of North America. Although adapted to breathing air, it prefers to remain underwater. The male bullfrog has a distinctive, loud call, which is heard mostly at night.

amphibians   Amphibians are members of the class Amphibia, subphylum Vertebrata, phylum Chordata. The class Amphibia includes frogs, toads, salamanders, newts, and caecilians. Amphibians are characterized by a glandular skin without external scales, by gills during development (and in adulthood in some), and by eggs that may have jelly coats but develop without formation of extraembryonic membranes such as the amnion. Most amphibians also have four limbs. Limbs and lungs are adaptations for life on land; the limbs evolved from the ancestral fishes' lobed fins. The scales and amniote egg evolved by reptiles, which distinguish them from amphibians, are adaptations for greater terrestriality than amphibians possess.

The class Amphibia comprises three living orders and several extinct ones. The living members of the class include those forms which have been mentioned above. Amphibians are thought to have arisen from lobe-finned crossopterygian fishes. These fishes had fins supported by bones, a well-ossified skeleton, lungs, and, in some species, internal openings to nasal passages. Considerable conjecture exists, however, as to whether amphibians actually arose from several lineages. Some scientists favor separate lineage for each of the modern orders; other scientists support the idea of two lineages, one giving rise to frogs, the other to salamanders and caecilians. The characteristics of vertebrae, teeth, and skull bones form the basis for these hypotheses.

Two major subclasses of extinct amphibians are found in the fossil record: the Labyrinthodontia and the Lepospondyli. Labyrinthodontia, which lived during the late Devonian through Triassic periods (346 to 190 million years ago), include the most primitive amphibians represented by the genus *Ichthyostega*. They were fresh-water carnivorous animals, with tail fins, small scales, and a fishlike vertebral column. Their skulls had many bones, as did those of their presumed crossopterygian ancestor. The Labyrinthodontia include three extinct orders: the Ichthyostegalia, the Temnospondyli, and the Anthracosauria. The Anthracosauria are thought to be the ancestors of reptiles and hence of modern birds and mammals. The Temnospondyli are thought by some scientists to be the ancestors of modern frogs.

The amphibians of the subclass Lepospondyli, which lived during the Mississippian through lower Permian periods (340 to 270 million years ago), include the extinct orders Nectridea, Aistopoda, and Microsauria. Members of the latter two orders were elongate. Some had limbs, some had reduced limbs, and some had no limbs. Many scientists suggest that the ancestors of modern salamanders and caecilians are among the lepospondyls.

The red-backed salamander is found throughout the eastern half of North America. Salamanders can be identified by grooves that run down their sides.

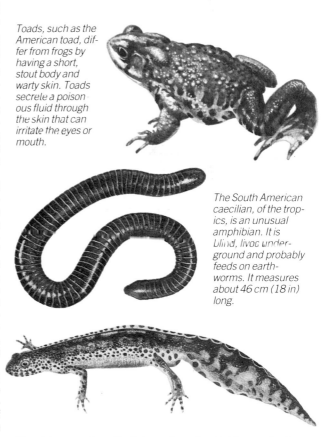

Toads, such as the American toad, differ from frogs by having a short, stout body and warty skin. Toads secrete a poisonous fluid through the skin that can irritate the eyes or mouth.

The South American caecilian, of the tropics, is an unusual amphibian. It is blind, lives underground and probably feeds on earthworms. It measures about 46 cm (18 in) long.

The alpine newt, found in alpine regions of central Europe, feeds on small insects and worms. The male, about 7.5 cm (3 in) long, develops bright colors during the breeding season.

The modern, extant orders of the Amphibia are placed in the subclass Lissamphibia. The superorder Salientia includes extinct froglike forms, and the extant order Anura consists of the frogs and toads. The order Caudata includes the salamanders. The order Gymnophiona includes the limbless caecilians. These three groups are allied in the Lissamphibia by characteristics of tooth, skin, and fat body structure. Vertebral and skull structure, as well as other characteristics, differ markedly among the three groups. This suggests to many scientists separate origins for each of the three modern orders.

Habitat and Distribution

The distribution of amphibians is worldwide, except in Antarctica and Greenland. They are found on landmasses and in fresh water. Frogs are the most widespread of the three groups, occurring on all major landmasses inhabited by amphibians. They live in a great variety of habitats, ranging from deserts to rain forests, permanent ponds to high mountain meadows. With only a few exceptions, an aquatic situation is required for breeding and tadpole development.

Salamanders are primarily a north temperate group, occurring in North America, Europe, and Asia. Some species are found in Africa north of the Sahara, and one group of some 200 species has had an extensive adaptive radiation in the tropics of Central and South America. Salamanders occupy a variety of terrestrial and aquatic habitats; those found in dry environments, such as the Mexican plateau, usually live in ponds. When on land, they are often found in moist leaf litter and under rocks and logs. In northern areas several species are found in ponds, streams, or rivers. Many species require water for breeding and development, but many other species breed on land and forgo the larval stage.

The caecilians are tropical in distribution. They occur in the New World from southern Mexico to northern Argentina, in tropical Africa, and in Southeast Asia. These limbless animals are usually burrowers. They are found in stream banks, under debris, and along root channels from sea level to 3,000 m (9,840 ft). One family of South America is aquatic and lives in streams, especially in the drainage basin of the Amazon River. The larvae of certain species also inhabit streams.

Classification

The order Anura or Salientia, the frogs and toads, includes 12 to 18 families, according to the characteristics that are stressed in classification. Familiar species are the leopard frog and the grass frog (genus *Rana*), which is used in many biology laboratory exercises; the brown, warty-skinned, drier-adapted toads (genus *Bufo*); and the aquatic, tongueless African clawed frog (genus *Xenopus*). The latter was once used in pregnancy tests and is now used in research on genetics and development. Several species are found in the eastern United States. Breeding choruses after the spring rains may include the following: two species of toads; leopard frogs, green frogs, pig frogs, and gopher frogs (*Rana*); woods tree frogs, green tree frogs, squirrel tree frogs, barking tree frogs, and little

grass frogs (*Hyla*); cricket frogs (*Acris*); and eastern narrow-mouthed toads (*Microhyla*). Among the more bizarre frogs are the following: the giant frog of Africa (*Conraua* or *Giganturana goliath*), which may reach 1 m (39 in) in body length; *Smithillus*, the smallest frog, at 12 mm (0.5 in) in body length, which lays one egg a year; *Centrolene* of Central America, whose skin is translucent and whose bones are green; and *Pseudis paradoxicus*, whose tadpoles are larger than the adult frogs.

Experts usually list from 7 to 10 families in the order Caudata or Urodela, the salamanders and newts. Among the best known genera are the Eastern North American red eft (*Notophthalmus*); the European newts (*Triturus*); and the Spanish *Pleurodeles*, used in developmental studies. Many species are found in the Appalachian Mountains of the southeastern United States. The largest is the Japanese giant salamander (*Andrias*), which extends up to 135 cm (53 in) in length; the smallest is the tropical genus *Thorius*, at 16 mm (0.6 in).

The order Gymnophiona or Apoda includes the little-known caecilians—the limbless, elongate, tropical amphibians that burrow or swim. These are considered to look wormlike because of their body shape and the presence of many rings, which resemble the segments of worms. The smallest caecilians (*Idiocranium*) are mature at 90 mm (3.6 in); the largest (*Caecilia*) are more than 1,300 mm (52 in).

Structure and Function

The three orders of amphibians are allied by structure of their TEETH and their SKINS particularly. Their teeth have two parts—an upper crown and a pedicel (a thin extension) that is attached to the jaws. The skin is smooth and contains numerous mucous and toxic glands, giving the animals a moist feeling. The outer layer of the skin is keratinized but does not form the epidermal scales seen in reptile skin. In fact, amphibians lack scales except for some species of caecilians that have fishlike scales embedded in the skin. The organ systems of amphibians modify the typical vertebrate plan. Amphibians have a relatively straight digestive system with a short intestine, and they have a three-chambered heart; they respire by lungs and sometimes skin as adults and by gills as larvae. Their digestive, excretory, and reproductive systems empty into a common terminal chamber, the cloaca. Their nervous systems are complex and have attributes to facilitate both aquatic and terrestrial life. Larvae and some aquatic adults have multidirectional sensory systems. All amphibians hear. Frogs and salamanders (except those which live in permanently dark locations) have good vision. Vision is nearly lost in caecilians, whose eyes are covered by skin and sometimes bone. They perceive by chemical cues, using their unique tentacles to conduct stimuli to olfactory centers.

Voice production is largely an attribute of frogs. Salamanders and caecilians produce noises, coughs, and grunts, but apparently not for communication. Frogs have complex sound production and perception systems, with species-specific warning, defensive, and breeding communications.

The life cycle of the leopard frog (perhaps the most commonly known amphibian in North America) imitates in a few weeks the evolutionary sequence from fish to land animal. Adult frogs live in grassy meadows near marshes and ponds (top). Breeding begins in April when the male and female (right) return to the water. The female lays the eggs while the male clings to her back and fertilizes them. Tadpoles, (lower right), hatch in about 9 days. Breathing is done through three pairs of external gills. Within a few weeks a fold of skin (operculum) covers the external gills, and four pairs of internal gills take over the respiratory function (similar to that of a fish). Eight weeks after hatching, rear legs are present (lower left); part of the ventral surface is cut away to show internal gills. All the limbs have been developed three months after hatching (upper left), and the lungs have become functional. The frog leaves the water to live in the wet meadow grass.

Amphibians are poikilotherms, or cold-blooded organisms; their body temperature is slightly higher than that of the environment. They are active at optimal temperatures and withdraw from extreme heat or cold.

Mode of locomotion varies greatly. Limbless caecilians burrow, using their heads like shovels and gaining thrust through contraction of muscles to force the body against the soil. The caecilians that swim, and most swimming salamanders, are like eels, using body muscle contraction to propel themselves through the water. Salamanders use their limbs very little in swimming. On land, the limbs give considerable propulsion to the body. The limbs are sprawled out from the body, and the middle of the trunk usually rests on the ground—in contrast to the faster lizards, whose legs are under the body and raise it above the ground. Frogs make use of their long hind-limbs to effect several kinds of locomotion—jumping, hopping, swimming, burrowing, and climbing.

Life Cycle and Behavior

Breeding in most amphibians is seasonal, usually correlated with temperature and moisture optima. Frogs court by using sounds or actions as attractants; salamanders depend primarily on visual and tactile cues. It is not known how male and female caecilians find each other. The modes of FERTILIZATION vary. Almost all frogs practice external fertilization, the females laying eggs in water and the males spraying sperm over them. Primitive salamanders have external fertilization, but most other salamanders have internal fertilization, with the female taking up the male's spermatophore. All caecilians have internal fertilization, with the male depositing sperm in the female's cloaca.

Other trends in amphibian reproductive biology include the following: (1) Many frogs lay large numbers of eggs. Few salamanders and fewer caecilians do. (2) Most frog species have tadpoles, a free-living larval stage; few have direct development or retain developing young in the body of the female. (3) Many salamander species have larvae; several have direct development. Only a few retain the young. (4) Few caecilians have larvae; some have direct development. Several have a mode of VIVIPARITY in which the female nourishes her developing young by oviductal secretions, and they are born after metamorphosis. (5) A number of species of salamanders and caecilians brood their egg clutches. Few frogs do, but some carry eggs on their backs, legs, or vocal sacs until hatching or metamorphosis. (6) The species that have direct development, brooding, or maternal retention have reduced litter sizes compared to those which lay eggs and abandon them. The larvae of the three orders are morphologically very different, although all are free-living, foraging animals.

Protective behaviors of amphibians include hiding or staying still in the presence of danger and having coloration matching the environment so that the animal is not obvious. Frogs have warning calls that alert other members of the population. Some salamanders and frogs, when disturbed, arch their backs, stiffen, and rock on their bellies. Other salamanders and frogs have flash colors that warn predators away. Several species of each kind of amphibian have toxic skins; predators learn to avoid them. Some nontoxic species mimic the coloration of toxic species so that they too are not consumed. Some species of salamanders have tails that break off when they are attacked. As the predator pursues the twitching tail, the salamander quietly escapes.

The importance of amphibians is evident throughout the world. They are major components of their ecosystem, both predator and prey. They are food for several human cultures. Interest in them ranges from their aesthetic appeal to their use as a source of arrow poison. They are of considerable importance to science, furnishing material for study of cell function, genetics, and development. As laboratory specimens they are used to study anatomy, behavior, ecology, and evolution.

See also: ANIMAL COURTSHIP AND MATING; AXOLOTL; CLASSIFICATION, BIOLOGICAL; COLORATION, BIOLOGICAL; DEVELOPMENT; FOSSIL RECORD; FROG; MIMICRY; SALAMANDER AND NEWT; TOAD.

▬

amphibious warfare   Amphibious warfare is a military operation that is launched from the sea by naval and landing forces and involves a landing on a hostile shore. An amphibious assault, the primary form of a combined sea-and-land operation, is conducted to establish a force

ashore, usually to capture a beachhead as a necessary preliminary to further assaults ashore. The Normandy landings in World War II and the Inchon landing in the Korean War are examples of successful amphibious assaults. In both instances, troops and matériel were ferried from warships to beaches by small, motorized landing craft.

Raids and withdrawals are other types of amphibious operations. In an amphibious raid the objective area is occupied only briefly, followed by a planned withdrawal. Such raids are conducted to damage the enemy, gain information, or carry out rescues. An amphibious withdrawal is essentially an amphibious assault conducted in reverse. The removal of Allied troops from DUNKERQUE, France, in World War II and the evacuation of U.S.–South Korean forces from Hungnam in 1950, are examples of successful amphibious withdrawals.

Amphibious warfare must be fast and flexible. It uses all forms of troop transport, from helicopters to troop-carrying aircraft and landing craft (see ARMORED VEHICLE). Several types of ships are used in amphibious assaults, including command ships that serve as the control centers of combined land-sea-air operations; assault ships specialized in launching attack planes and helicopters; and transport docking ships (see also NAVAL VESSELS).

▬

amphibole   [am'-fuh-bohl]   The amphiboles are an important group of rock-forming SILICATE MINERALS characterized by a particular arrangement of atoms and by similar optical, physical, and chemical properties. Their composition can vary widely, however, hence their name, from the Greek word for "ambiguous". They occur as both minor and major constituents of a wide variety of igneous and metamorphic rocks. Hornblende is the most common amphibole. Anthophyllite and riebeckite (crocidolite) are fibrous amphiboles from which ASBESTOS is produced, and actinolite and tremolite are the chief constituents of nephrite, a hard, dense variety of JADE.

The basic building block of silicate minerals, the SiO_4

Hornblende, the most common amphibole, has a variable composition, and it may be black, brown, or dark green in color. It is generally opaque to translucent and has a vitreous luster.

tetrahedron, is linked in amphiboles to form double chains of Si_4O_{11} composition. The complex chemistry of the group results from the great flexibility of the crystal structure, which will accomodate a wide range of cations (positively charged ions). All the major cations—aluminum, boron. calcium, iron, magnesium, and sodium—fall within the range of the average composition of the Earth's crust, which explains the widespread occurrence of the amphibole minerals. The same group of elements that occur in the amphiboles also occur in the PYROXENES, but the amphiboles all contain, in addition, a HYDROXYL GROUP (OH).

amphioxus [am-fee-ahk'-suhs] An amphioxus, or lancelet, is any of about 30 species of primitive chordates classified in the genus *Branchiostoma* (formerly *Amphioxus*), which constitutes the subphylum Cephalochordata. The genus is conjectured to have descended from the kind of primitive chordate from which all vertebrates evolved. The lancelet has a lance-shaped tail on a semi-transparent, streamlined body that is usually 4–7 cm (1.5–3 in) long. It is eyeless and earless and has no distinct head. The animals live in coastal waters of temperate and tropical oceans.

amphipod [am'-fuh-pahd] Amphipods are tiny animals, usually no more than 12 mm (0.47 in) long, that belong to the order Amphipoda of crustaceans. The order encompasses about 3,800 species of mostly marine, shrimplike creatures, including the common sand or beach flea family, Talitridae; a sand flea can hurl itself many times its own length with its taillike telson. Amphipods usually are flattened laterally, they lack a carapace, and their long legs are unsuited for walking. Numerous species that scavenge in the Antarctic are a primary source of food for many fish. The largest and most important group of amphipods is the suborder Gammaridea, which includes about 300 species in Siberia's Lake Baikal alone, the blind "well shrimps" (*Niphargus*) that live in caves and in wells, and about 600 species that live in fresh-water or moist land environments. All members of the family Cyamidae are parasites of whales and dolphins, clinging to the skin of their hosts and eating the surface layers. Members of the suborder Caprellidea are known as skeleton shrimp because of their extremely slender bodies.

Amphitryon [am-fi'-tree-ahn] In Greek mythology, Amphitryon was the son of Alcaeus, king of Tiryns. His wife, Alcmene, asked him to avenge the death of her eight brothers. While Amphitryon was away on this mission, ZEUS, disguised as Amphitryon, visited Alcmene and made her pregnant. When Amphitryon returned, he also made Alcmene pregnant. She gave birth to twin sons—Iphicles, the son of Amphitryon, and HERCULES, the son of Zeus. PLAUTUS based the comedy *Amphitruo* on this theme.

amplifier Any device or circuit that makes a signal stronger, ideally without changing the signal in any other way, may be called an amplifier. The term usually refers to devices that amplify electronic signals within electronic equipment. In most high-fidelity sound systems, the amplifier is combined with a preamplifier. In many cases a radio tuner is also included (see SOUND RECORDING AND REPRODUCTION).

Electronic amplifiers can be based on ELECTRON TUBES or SEMICONDUCTOR devices. However, in most modern devices, electron tubes have been replaced by semiconducting circuit elements, such as the TRANSISTOR.

Operation of Amplifiers. In a basic transistor amplifier, the transistors act as sources of current or voltage whose output value is larger than but controlled by a current or voltage related to the signal. When the smaller current flows, so does the larger one, in proportion to the power of the smaller current. As the input modulates, so does the output. The ratio of the output voltage to the input voltage is called the voltage gain of the amplifier, which is generally made greater than unity. The current gain is the ratio of output current to input current, and the power gain is the ratio of power output to power input.

In order to increase the amplification, amplifiers often connect several stages in cascade, with the output of one stage supplying the input signal to the next stage. The overall gain of such a multistage amplifier is the product of the gains of the individual stages. In modern equipment, such amplifiers are usually manufactured on tiny square silicon wafers.

Transistors have three internal elements. Since external input and output circuits have two pairs of connections, it is necessary to choose one internal element to be connected in common to an input and output terminal. The choice of the common element determines the performance of the amplifier.

To obtain the required gain and to improve the matching of the input and output impedances, two circuits may be combined in cascade. It is also possible to use three-stage connections.

Kinds of Amplifiers. Amplifiers can be classified according to the frequency range that they are designed to handle. For example, an audio amplifier is for the range from zero to about 100,000 cycles per second, or hertz; an intermediate-frequency (IF) amplifier is for 400 kilohertz (kHz) to 5 megahertz (MHz); a radio-frequency (RF) amplifier handles signal frequencies up to several hundred MHz; and an ultrahigh-frequency (UHF) amplifier can operate above 100 MHz.

The response or gain of an amplifier varies with the signal frequency. The gain may be held constant down to zero frequency or that of a steady input, but inevitably, at some high frequency, the gain will start to drop. It is possible to design circuitry so that uniform, or flat, response is obtained over most of the frequency range of the signal.

Amplifiers can also be distinguished by the fraction of the cycle during which there is an output current. Some amplifiers are designed to handle large power outputs;

they can be provided with means of cooling—such as cooling fins, forced air, and liquid cooling—to remove the heat that is generated. Another approach, however, is to reduce such heat losses by reducing the time of current conduction per signal cycle. Amplifiers classified on this basis are designated as Class A, B, C, or D, depending on whether the current conduction is continuous (Class A); there is an output current for about half the input cycle (Class B); current conduction is in pulses that last for less than half the input cycle (Class C); or constant-amplitude current pulses are employed, where it is the duration of the pulse that varies with the modulating signal (Class D).

A special, monolithic form of amplifier has positive and negative inputs, giving an output controlled by the difference of the input signals, and is called a differential amplifier. This amplifier discriminates against noise and other inputs common to the two terminals. It is often used with various feedback circuits and is then called an operational amplifier (op-amp), because it was originally used for mathematical operations on signals, such as summation, differentiation, and integration.

amplitude modulation   Amplitude modulation is a technique for varying the height, or amplitude, of a wave in order to transmit information. Much of radio broadcasting uses amplitude modulation (AM), although other types of MODULATION are possible. A convenient and efficient means of transmitting information is by the propagation of waves of ELECTROMAGNETIC RADIATION (see WAVES AND WAVE MOTION). Sound waves in the audible range, such as speech and music, have a frequency that is too low for efficient transmission through the air for significant distances. By the process of modulation, however, this low-frequency audio information—the signal—can be impressed on a carrier wave that has a much higher frequency and can propagate through space for great distances. The transmitter at a radio station generates a carrier wave having constant characteristics, such as amplitude and frequency. The signal containing the desired information is then used to modulate the carrier; that is, the signal produces a variation in the form of a certain characteristic of the carrier wave. This new wave, called the modulated wave, will contain the information of the signal.

In AM, it is the amplitude of the carrier wave that is made to vary so that it will contain the information of the signal. When the modulated wave reaches a radio receiver tuned to the proper frequency, it is demodulated, "revealing" the wave that was carried. (Demodulation is the process of reconstructing the original signal from the modulated wave; it is essentially the opposite of modulation.) The signal can then reproduce the desired sound by using a loudspeaker. AM radio is still a popular form of radio broadcasting, but it does have a number of shortcomings. The quality of reproduction is relatively poor because of inherent limitations in the technique and because of interference from other stations and other elec-

trical signals, such as those produced by lightning or by electronic devices. When the frequency, rather than the amplitude, of the carrier wave is modulated, the process is called FREQUENCY MODULATION or FM.

Amritsar [um-rit'-sur]   Amritsar, district headquarters for Punjab state, is a city in northwestern India with a population of 589,229 (1981). It is located about 48 km (30 mi) from the Pakistan border and is an important regional agricultural market and the center for border security in the northwest. Manufactures include textiles, particularly carpets, silks, and brocades.

Amritsar, the most important SIKH religious center, was founded in 1577 by Ram Das, the fourth Sikh guru. Ram Das also began construction of the *Amrita Saras* ("Pool of Immortality"), an artificial lake from which the city takes its name. On an island in the lake is the most important Sikh shrine, the Golden Temple. In its present form the temple, which contains the most sacred text of the Sikhs, the Granth Sahib, dates from the reign (1792–1839) of the Sikh ruler Ranjit Singh.

In the Amritsar Massacre (Apr. 13, 1919) troops commanded by the British general Reginald Dyer fired on an Indian crowd peacefully demonstrating against the Rowlatt Acts, by which the British administration had recently given itself emergency powers. Casualties were officially estimated at 379 deaths and some 1,200 wounded. The site of the massacre, an open area called the Jallianwallah Bagh, is now a national shrine.

In 1982, Sikh extremists launched a terrorist campaign to force the Indian government to grant Sikhs greater autonomy. They have used the Golden Temple as a sanctuary, turning it into a fortified base. As a result the temple has been attacked several times by Indian troops.

Amsterdam   Amsterdam is the chief city and nominal capital of the Kingdom of the Netherlands (The Hague is the seat of government). It lies where the little IJ River flows into the IJSSELMEER (formerly the Zuiderzee). Its name is derived from a dam once built on the Amstel, which flows into the IJ at this point. Amsterdam has 691,738 (1988 est.) inhabitants, making it the largest city in the country. Its urban agglomeration population is 936,410 (1983 est.).

The city lies below sea level and is built on piles into the soft alluvial clay. By the late 16th century Amsterdam had become the chief Dutch port; for a century it was Europe's most important port and commercial center. Much of the building in the inner city dates from this period. The docks along the IJ River were formerly approached from the Zuiderzee, but in 1876 the North Sea Canal was opened from the city westward to the coast at IJmuiden.

The Contemporary City.   Amsterdam is primarily a commercial and financial center. Its industries have developed from its role as a port trading with the East. The processing of oil seeds, tobacco, coffee, tea, and other imported goods is important, as are engineering and

Amsterdam's extensive system of canals, totaling more than 80 km (50 mi), has earned the city its reputation as the "Venice of the North." Although The Hague, to the southwest, serves as the Netherlands' administrative center, Amsterdam is the official capital and the nation's largest city in population.

shipbuilding. Diamond cutting and polishing is a major industry, and there is a large trade in timber. The port of Amsterdam tends to concentrate on light cargoes, leaving the handling of bulk cargoes to its neighbor to the south, Rotterdam. A network of canals links the city with the rest of the Netherlands and with the Rhine River. Amsterdam has excellent railroad service and is served by Schiphol Airport, to the southwest.

Amsterdam is the chief educational and cultural center in the Netherlands. It has two universities and is noted for its museums, including the RIJKSMUSEUM, which contains a large collection of paintings by the Dutch masters. The Concert Hall is the home of the famous CONCERTGEBOUW ORCHESTRA. The architecture of the Old City has made Amsterdam a center of tourism. Near the city center are the Royal Palace (1648–65), the Oude Kerk ("Old Church"; early 14th century), and fragments of the city's medieval defenses.

History. Amsterdam developed in the Middle Ages as a small fishing port and commercial center. It was greatly expanded during the 14th century by the counts of Holland; joining the HANSEATIC LEAGUE in 1369, its merchants opened up trade with the Baltic. In the late 16th century, with the decline of Antwerp, Amsterdam became the chief port of northwestern Europe. During its golden age, the city welcomed political and religious refugees, including Flemings from the Spanish Netherlands, Jews from the Iberian Peninsula, and Huguenots from France. In the 18th century, because of a gradual silting of the

Zuiderzee, much of the Rhineland trade passed to Rotterdam. The city was revitalized by the opening of the North Sea Canal in 1876, and in the late 19th century it again became the chief domestic port for the Netherlands. During World War II Amsterdam's port was destroyed by the occupying Germans. It has since been rebuilt.

Amtrak Amtrak is the semipublic corporation, created by the Rail Passenger Service Act of 1970, that has provided most of the intercity rail passenger service in the United States since May 1, 1971. The legislation instructed the secretary of transportation to establish a reduced but basic rail passenger service for the United States, financed by payments made by the participating RAILROADS and by federal grants and guaranteed loans.

Postwar Decline in Rail Service. The establishment of Amtrak followed several years of public concern over the continuing decrease in the number of passenger trains and a long period of ever-increasing deficits for passenger service that began after World War II. Railroad companies, which had been losing as much as $600 million yearly on passenger service, dropped so many routes that passenger trains used only about one-quarter of the national rail network. By 1970 only 7 percent of all intercity passenger travel was accomplished by rail.

Amtrak Service. When Amtrak went into operation in 1971, 18 of the 22 large passenger railroads joined the corporation immediately; Amtrak reduced routes and service by roughly half, to a total of 21 routes serving 340 U.S. cities on about 32,000 km (20,000 mi) of track. Amtrak now supplies all intercity passenger rail service—involving about 500 stations—with the exception of city-suburb commuter lines, although in recent years Amtrak itself has become a major commuter contract operator, managing such large-scale networks as Boston's MBTA commuter trains. Federal funds spent on rehabilitating stations and maintenance facilities, purchasing new rolling stock, improving the computerized communications system, and rebuilding the heavily used Boston-Washington corridor have led to greater efficiencies and a significant rise in passenger use.

Amu Darya [ah-moo dahr'-yah]   The Amu Darya is the longest river in the Central Asian region of the USSR. Formed by the joining of the Pyandzh and Vakhsh rivers, which originate in the Pamirs, the Amu Darya flows for 2,540 km (1,578 mi) to the Aral Sea, where it forms a marshy delta. The river carries little traffic but supplies much of the area's hydroelectric power. Its drainage basin extends about 965 km (600 mi) from north to south, and more than 1,450 km (900 mi) from east to west. Much of the Amu's water is drawn off for desert irrigation (Kara Kum Canal system) or is lost to drainage or evaporation before reaching the sea.

amulet   An amulet is an object used as a charm, either to protect against harm or to promote good fortune. It is usually worn or carried on the person but may be attached to animals, houses, automobiles, or other property. Examples include the scarab of ancient Egypt, the horseshoe and other iron objects used against WITCHCRAFT in early European tradition, the blue beads used in some Islamic countries to guard against the EVIL EYE, and charms for good luck, such as the rabbit's foot. Stones, horns, bones, figurines, coins and medallions, and many other objects are used as amulets in a great range of cultures. Persons especially vulnerable, such as children or the sick, are often thought to need amulets. Some amulets bear religious images or texts; others have astrological significance.

Amundsen, Roald (ah'-mun-suhn, roh'-ahl]   The Norwegian Roald Engelbregt Grauning Amundsen, b. July 16, 1872, d. June 18, 1928, explored the Arctic ice cap and Antarctica and led the expedition that first reached the SOUTH POLE. Between 1903 and 1906 he passed from east to west across the Arctic Ocean above North America, the so-called Northwest Passage. He was mounting an expedition to the North Pole when he learned that an American, Robert PEARY, had already reached the pole (1909).

In June 1910 he sailed from Norway, intending to be the first to reach the South Pole. A similar expedition was launched by the British under the direction of Robert Fal-

con SCOTT. Their race captured the imagination of Europe. Amundsen, who used dogs to pull the sleds and provide food for the return journey, arrived at the pole with four men on Dec. 14, 1911, one month ahead of the British. Amundsen left a sympathetic note to Scott at the pole. It was found with the frozen bodies of Scott and his men, who died on the way back to their base camp. Amundsen died when his plane went down over the Arctic Ocean on an expedition to rescue the stranded Italian explorer Umberto Nobile.

Amur River [uh-moor']   The Amur River (Chinese: Heilong Jiang) is located in eastern Asia and forms part of the Soviet-Chinese border. It flows 2,825 km (1,755 mi) from the confluence of the Shilka and Argun rivers, north of Inner Mongolia, eastward to its mouth at the Tatar Strait, which separates Siberia from the Sakhalin Islands. The longest river in the eastern Soviet Union, it is an important trade route when navigable (May to November). It also supplies water for irrigation and supports many fish.

The Amur River arises in the mountains, passes through the Zeya-Bureya Depression and plains, and then flows through marshes, where it is joined by numerous other streams. The principal city along the river is Khabarovsk. The population of the surrounding region is composed of Russians as well as the original tribal population (including the Yakut and the Buryat) in the north and Chinese, Mongolians, and Manchurians in the south. The Amur is rain-fed, and its basin has a monsoon climate. As a result, flooding is common along much of its course from May to October.

amusement park   SEE CARNIVALS AND FAIRS

amyl nitrite [am'-ul ny'-tryt]   Amyl nitrite is a volatile drug used to relax spasms of arteries, control convulsions, and relieve asthmatic paroxysms. Administered by inhalation, it acts within 30 seconds by briefly widening constricted blood vessels. It relieves the pain of angina attacks but should not be used in cases of cerebral hemorrhage or heart attack. Amyl and other alkyl nitrites are also employed illicitly as "poppers" for the intense light-headedness and the muscle relaxation that they induce.

amyotrophic lateral sclerosis   Amyotrophic lateral sclerosis (ALS) is a degenerative disease of the nervous system, affecting the motor neurons that carry impulses from the brain and spinal cord to the muscles. Degeneration of these neurons causes muscle weakness, spasticity, and atrophy, usually starting in the hands and arms and then spreading to other parts of the body. Difficulty with speaking, swallowing, and breathing ensues, and death usually follows within 3 to 10 years. Onset commonly occurs between the ages of 50 and 60, slightly more frequently in men than in women. ALS is also called Lou Gehrig's disease, named for the baseball star who died of it. Research thus far has failed to establish any definite cause, although slow-acting viruses have been suspected, and, in a small percentage of cases, a genetic link might be involved. No specific treatment yet exists, and patients can be aided only by supportive therapy.

An-shan see ANSHAN

Anabaptists

Anabaptists, or rebaptizers, were members of a variety of 16th-century religious groups that rejected infant BAPTISM. Since they believed that only after an adult had come to faith in Christ should he or she be baptized, they taught that converts who had been baptized in infancy must be rebaptized.

Anabaptists held the church to be the congregation of true saints who should separate themselves from the sinful world. Their theology was highly eschatological (see ESCHATOLOGY), and they claimed direct inspiration by the Holy Spirit. The Anabaptists refused to take oaths, opposed capital punishment, and rejected military service. Their beliefs made them appear subversive and provoked persecution. Many of the Reformers disclaimed them, regarding them as fundamentally opposed to the ideas of the REFORMATION.

In Zurich, Conrad Grebel performed the first adult baptism on Jan. 21, 1525, when he rebaptized Georg Blaurock in the house of Felix Manz. Anabaptism spread to southwest Germany, Austria, Moravia, along the Danube, and down the Rhine to the Netherlands. Numbering less than 1 percent of the population, the Anabaptists were for the most part of humble social origin. Among their leaders were Balthasar Hubmaier, Hans Denck, Jacob Hütter, and Hans Hut.

In 1534 militant Anabaptists, inspired by radical Melchior Hofmann, seized control of the city of Münster. Led by Bernt Knipperdollinck, Jan Mathijs, and Jan Beuckelson, better known as John of Leiden (c.1509–36), they drove out all Protestants and Roman Catholics. John set up a theocracy, became king, and established polygamy and communal property. After a 16-month siege, the bishop of Münster recaptured the city and executed the rebels. Menno Simons, a Dutchman, restored the reputation of the Anabaptists through his moderate and inspired leadership. His followers have survived and are known as MENNONITES. The HUTTERIAN BRETHREN are descendants of the group led by Hütter.

Anaconda

Anaconda (1990 pop., 10,278) is a city in southwestern Montana. Formerly the county seat of Deer Lodge County, in 1977 it was consolidated with that county to form a single administrative unit. The city was founded in 1883 by Marcus DALY as a smelting center for ores from his copper mine. Originally named Copperopolis, it was incorporated in 1888 and renamed Anaconda for Daly's mine. Its smelter, which had been one of the world's largest, was closed in 1980.

The giant anaconda, or water boa, kills a collared peccary before swallowing it whole. The largest constrictor in the Western Hemisphere, the giant anaconda may live 50 years.

anaconda

The anaconda, *Eunectes murinus*, a semiaquatic snake of the BOA family, Boidae, is found in Central America and tropical South America. The largest boa in the Western Hemisphere, it can reach a length of 7.6 m (25 ft). Both the young, which are born alive in large broods, and the adults are dark green with round black markings. A smaller species, *E. notaeus*, the yellow anaconda, is found in rivers of southern South America. It is yellowish green in color with irregular dark blotches. Although not venomous, anacondas can defend themselves by biting. They feed on birds and small animals.

Anacreon

[uh-nak'-ree-ahn] Anacreon, c.570–478 BC, was a Greek lyric poet. He composed imaginative verses about love, friendship, and wine. Although a number of serious epigrams and hymns are also attributed to him, he gained fame for the graceful style of his verse. The *Anacreontea*, a collection of poems written in imitation of his style, influenced writers for centuries.

anaerobe

[an'-uh-rohb] Anaerobes are organisms that can obtain energy from nutrients (see METABOLISM) without the use of oxygen. Some of them, such as methanogens, may be related to the earliest life forms. Most anaerobes obtain energy from oxygen-lacking organic compounds by means of FERMENTATION. The anaerobic BACTERIA found near vents on the ocean floor, however, thrive on inorganic chemicals such as sulfur, manganese, and iron by a process called chemosynthesis (see HYDROTHERMAL VENT). Anaerobes that cannot use oxygen and are in fact poisoned by it are called obligate anaerobes. Other anaerobes, including many bacteria and YEAST, can survive in the presence of oxygen and are called facultative anaerobes. With the exception of some internal parasites, higher life forms require oxygen and are called obligate aerobes.

anagram   A word or phrase formed by rearranging the letters of another word or phrase is an anagram (*shape: phase; revolution: love to ruin*). The making of anagrams as a game dates back to ancient times, and such letter rearrangements have also been used to disguise names or messages and to coin pseudonyms. *Erewhon,* for example, the title of Samuel Butler's utopian novel, is an anagram of *nowhere.*

Anaheim [an'-uh-hym]   Anaheim, a suburban city in the Santa Ana River valley in southern California, lies 40 km (25 mi) southeast of Los Angeles. Its growth has been extremely rapid as industries and housing replaced the citrus groves and vineyards planted by the early settlers. Since 1950, when the population was less than 15,000, Anaheim has grown to a city of 266,406 (1990); metropolitan Orange County, which also includes Santa Ana and Garden Grove, has a population of 1,931,570 (1980).

Anaheim is the site of DISNEYLAND amusement park, Anaheim Stadium (home of the California Angels baseball team), and the Anaheim Convention Center. Industries produce aerospace systems, electronic equipment, paper converters, greeting cards, and processed foods. The city was founded by German immigrants in 1857 as an experiment in communal living. Its name means "home on the Ana."

analgesic [an-ul-jee'-zik]   Analgesic drugs and techniques diminish the perception of painful stimuli while causing minimal loss of sensibility to other stimuli. Analgesic drugs include aspirin, acetaminophen, ibuprofen, MORPHINE and other narcotics, general anesthetics in low doses, and local anesthetics (see ANESTHETICS). Analgesic techniques include ACUPUNCTURE, BIOFEEDBACK, HYPNOSIS, electrical stimulation, and surgical separation of nerve fibers.

Treatment of acute PAIN is necessary after surgery, dental procedures, muscular strains and sprains, or trauma. Chronic pain requiring therapy may arise following infection, with malignancies, or with nerve irritation or compression—for example, a pinched nerve. Pain may be a symptom of an underlying problem that needs further treatment.

Some of the drugs most often used as analgesics are acetylsalicylic acid (aspirin), the drug most commonly taken for the relief of mild pain; phenacetin and acetaminophen (Tylenol), which are comparable to aspirin in reducing pain and fever but are much less effective in alleviating inflammation; and ibuprofen (Advil), which is less irritating to the stomach than aspirin and also acts to reduce inflammation. All of the above drugs achieve their analgesic effect through inhibition of the synthesis of prostaglandins in the body. Propoxyphene (DARVON), which is effective in relieving mild pain, has been used in the treatment of narcotic addiction. Narcotic analgesics are used only for the treatment of severe pain. OPIUM, derived from the juice of the poppyseed capsule, has

been in use for centuries; CODEINE, HEROIN, and morphine are derivatives.

Small amounts of general anesthetics can be used for pain relief without producing unconsciousness. Topical local anesthetics, such as benzocaine (ethylaminobenzoate), are widely used for blocking the transmission of pain signals to the brain from the affected area. A local anesthetic can be injected near nerve fibers to block pain sensation in an entire area of the body. This procedure is useful for analgesia in treatment of chronic pain and during localized surgery.

Electrical stimulation of large fibers by the placement of electrodes on the skin, in specific nerves, or within the spinal cord has produced analgesia. Hypnosis is a proven method for achieving pain relief in both acute and chronic disorders in some susceptible patients, but the effectiveness of this technique cannot be predicted. Acupuncture, a technique derived from Chinese medicine and involving the insertion of needles into the skin at certain points on the body, is also sometimes successful in producing adequate analgesia for some surgical procedures and for the relief of chronic pain. Biofeedback control has been useful in relieving some forms of chronic pain; the patient learns to modify his or her response to stress through concentration and relaxation.

The PLACEBO effect—by which patients given a sugar pill experience the same lessening in pain as when given an analgesic—must be considered whenever analgesics are compared. Studies have shown that up to 30 percent of a group of patients will experience some relief of pain when only a dummy pill has been administered.

In the early 1970s it was discovered that opiates bind to specific receptors in the brain. Subsequently, naturally occurring compounds called encephalins and endorphins, which bind to the OPIATE RECEPTORS, were isolated from animal brain tissue. As more is learned about these compounds, artificial regulation of their levels may produce effective analgesia.

analog devices   An analog device is an apparatus that uses a continuously variable physical phenomenon to describe, imitate, or reproduce another dynamic phenomenon. An example is a mercury thermometer, in which a rising or falling (expanding or contracting) column of mercury represents a rising or falling temperature. Phenomena are properly analogous when mathematical analysis reveals similar underlying formulas. Analog devices can be contrasted with digital devices (see DIGITAL TECHNOLOGY), which employ a limited number of discrete bits of information to approximate continuous phenomena.

Many early measurement instruments were analog devices. In the sundial, the movement of a shadow represented the passage of time (actually the rotation of the Earth).

Analog Computers

An analog computer is an apparatus that employs continuously variable physical phenomena, such as mechanical motions, flows of fluids, or currents of electricity, to make computations. It may be contrasted with the digital computer (see COMPUTER), which makes use of digital, or discrete, elements to make computations. A primitive example of an analog computer is the immersion of an object of irregular shape in water contained in a graduated vessel to determine the volume of the irregular object. The displaced volume of water is equal to the volume of the object. This example uses continuously variable magnitudes as input data, as well as throughout the computational process and even to convey the outcome.

Addition and subtraction of continuously variable magnitudes may easily be done using sliding mechanical displacements. The logarithmic SLIDE RULE adds or subtracts two input lengths by straight-line sliding of one part relative to another so that the output length equals their sum or difference.

The two basic operations of calculus (differentiation and integration) can be viewed as finding the tangent to a curve at each point and as finding the area under a curve. Integration can be performed by a simple and elegant mechanism, known since about 1800, called a disc-and-wheel integrator, which acts like a transmission having a continuously variable ratio. The independent variable x turns a shaft carrying a disc much like a phonograph turntable. A small follower wheel is maintained at disc radius equal to the variable y and is turned by friction contact with the disc at that radius. A wheel of unit radius turns y times as much as the x shaft and thus turns in proportion to the area.

Many varieties of the disc-and-wheel integrator have been developed. Mechanisms designed to solve differential equations automatically were called DIFFERENTIAL ANALYZERS. The most widely used analog computer, the domestic electric watt-hour meter, computes the energy consumed.

Analog versus Digital

Today many analog devices have been replaced by digital devices, mainly because digital instruments can better deal with the problem of unwanted information, or noise. This is illustrated by the technologies employed in recording sound on disc and reproducing it. On a phonograph record, sounds are encoded in a groove that varies continuously in width and shape. In the digital technology of the COMPACT DISC, sounds are translated into binary code and recorded on the disc as discrete pits.

In the field of computer processing, electronic analog computers continue to be used in certain applications, although the major data-processing tasks of modern technologies are met by electronic digital computers. Computer designers are now exploring and employing the techniques of PARALLEL PROCESSING, in which numerous processors operate in tandem.

See also: HYBRID COMPUTER; SOUND RECORDING AND REPRODUCTION.

analog-to-digital converter The analog-to-digital, or A/D, converter is a device that converts analog signals to numerically equivalent form for input to a digital

COMPUTER. The analog signals are electrical voltage levels derived from transducers that measure such continually varying physical properties as temperature and pressure.

A typical A/D converter is made from a register that can hold a digital value, an operational amplifier, and a voltage comparator. The register outputs are electrically summed to produce an electric current proportional to the digital value of the register. This current causes a proportional voltage gain at the amplifier output. The amplified voltage is compared with the unknown input analog signal. As long as there is a discernible difference, the comparator allows the register value to change one step at a time until there is no difference.

Analog-to-digital converters are common computer INPUT-OUTPUT DEVICES for control applications. Computer-produced control signals may require the complementary conversion to analog form by using DIGITAL-TO-ANALOG CONVERTERS.

analytic geometry Analytic geometry, also known as coordinate geometry, is a branch of mathematics in which geometric investigations are carried out by algebraic procedures. Although originally designed to investigate problems in plane geometry (geometry in a two-dimensional plane), analytic geometry can also be used to explore spaces of higher dimensions. Plane analytic geometry includes the systematic study of CONIC SECTIONS.

In analytic geometry, positions of points are specified by means of suitable sets of numbers (coordinates) so that geometrical relationships between the points are equivalent to algebraic relationships between their coordinates. Because of this correspondence between algebra and geometry, it is often possible to prove propositions concerning geometric relationships by means of algebraic calculations.

History

The invention of analytic geometry is generally credited to the 17th-century French philosopher and mathematician René DESCARTES in 1637. Pierre de FERMAT had also worked out the methods of analytic geometry at the same time, but his treatise on the subject was not published until 1679. The subject in its present form was developed later by Leonhard EULER (see MATHEMATICS, HISTORY OF).

Plane Analytic Geometry

Two perpendicular lines—the coordinate axes—are needed to fix the position of a point in a plane. The point of intersection of these axes is called the origin and is denoted by O. Usually the x-axis is a horizontal line, and the y-axis is the vertical line at the origin. The positive x-axis is the part to the right of the origin, and the positive y-axis is the part above the origin.

The x-coordinate of any point P on the plane is the perpendicular distance of P from the y-axis; it is taken to be positive if P is to the right of the y-axis (in the first or fourth quadrant), zero if P is on the y-axis, and negative if P is to the left of the y-axis. Similarly, the y-coordinate of P is the perpendicular distance of P from the x-axis and can also be positive, zero, or negative. If the x-coordinate of P is x and the y-coordinate of P is y, then the ordered pair *(x,y)* represents the Cartesian coordinates (named in honor of Descartes) of P with respect to the fixed coordinate axes. Every ordered pair *(x,y)* of real numbers represents a unique point on the plane, and vice versa. The origin is the point (0,0). The point P with coordinates *(x,y)* is symbolically represented as *P(x,y)* (see COORDINATE SYSTEMS).

A polar coordinate system is determined by a fixed point O, called the origin, or pole, and a fixed axis through the point, called the polar axis or polar line. A point P on the plane can be located by specifying two quantities: (1) the angle θ through which the polar axis must be rotated counterclockwise so that it will pass through P, and (2) the positive distance r of the point P from the origin. The angle determines a line by specifying its rotation about the fixed axis, and the distance r indicates how far along the line to proceed from the origin to reach P. The point P in polar coordinates is represented as *P (r,θ)*.

The path traced by a moving point *P(x,y)* in the plane is a CURVE. An EQUATION in two variables x and y that is satisfied by those points on the curve and by no other points is called the equation of the curve. Any first-degree equation of the form $ax + by + c = 0$ (where a, b, and c are constants) is the equation of a straight LINE, or a LINEAR EQUATION.

The equation of a CIRCLE with its center at the origin and radius r is $x^2 + y^2 = r^2$. A conic section can be represented by a second-degree equation in x and y; the general equation is $ax^2 + bxy + cy^2 + dx + ey + f = 0$, where a, b, c, d, e, and f are constants. Basic conics are the ELLIPSE, HYPERBOLA, PARABOLA, and circle.

Solid Analytic Geometry

The concepts outlined above can be easily generalized to a space of three dimensions. Through an arbitrary point O (the origin), three mutually perpendicular coordinate axes are drawn (the x-axis, the y-axis, and the z-axis), dividing the space into eight parts, or octants. The plane determined by the x-axis and the y-axis is known as the xy-plane; the xz-plane and yz-plane are similarly defined. These three planes are called the coordinate planes. The x-coordinate of a point P is the perpendicular distance from P to the yz-plane. The other two coordinates are defined similarly.

---

analytic and linguistic philosophy   The analytic and linguistic philosophical movements focus on the logical clarification of language.

The analytic movement began about the turn of the century with Bertrand RUSSELL and G. E. MOORE. Both Russell and Moore reacted against the neo-Hegelian idealism of F. H. BRADLEY, which held that the world one experiences is only appearance, not reality. But whereas Russell rejected idealist metaphysics in favor of a metaphysics of his own, "logical atomism," Moore abandoned metaphysical speculation altogether. Moore embodied the respect for common sense that became characteristic

of much subsequent analytic and linguistic philosophy, a respect that Russell never shared.

In "On Denoting (1905)," Russell first put forward his theory of descriptions, suggesting that the underlying logical forms of propositions might be quite different from their surface grammatical forms. For example, the theory of descriptions shows that making a meaningful statement about "the greatest prime number" does not by itself commit one to belief in the existence of such a number. Since knowledge is more secure when one is committed to the existence of fewer different kinds of things, analysis seemed to promise a new, more scientific approach to metaphysical and epistemological questions: what things ultimately exist, and how secure is knowledge of them?

Russell's greatest analytic achievement was his reduction of mathematics to logic by the development of a new system of symbolic LOGIC, far more powerful than the traditional Aristotelian theory of the syllogism. Russell and Alfred North WHITEHEAD's monumental *Principia Mathematica* came out in three volumes from 1910 to 1913. By accounting for the distinctive character of mathematical truths without recourse to problematic metaphysical assumptions, Russell opened the way for a new, logically sophisticated version of EMPIRICISM, for which he was a leading spokesperson.

Russell thought of the new logic as the bare bones of an ideal language, a language in which the wording of all propositions would reveal their true logical forms. One of Russell's pupils, the Austrian Ludwig WITTGENSTEIN, argued that language's capacity to represent the world depended on their sharing a common structure, the structure of logic. Thus what Russell saw as an ideal, Wittgenstein saw as already hidden in language, waiting to be uncovered by analysis. According to Wittgenstein, any meaningful statement not belonging to logic or pure mathematics was a statement of fact. Moreover, all statements of fact had to be analyzable into "elementary propositions," which were, in a technical sense, "logical pictures" of possible facts.

The adherents of LOGICAL POSITIVISM, who were strongly influenced by Wittgenstein's ideas, held that any significant proposition that was not a tautology had to be observationally verifiable. They argued that propositions that did not meet this condition—for example, those belonging to ethics, religion, and, above all, traditional metaphysics—might have a certain emotional significance, but were literal nonsense. For the logical positivists, philosophical analysis became the clarification of statements belonging to science: in particular, making clear the relation between various kinds of theoretical claims and the observational evidence by which they could be verified or refuted.

Beginning in the 1930s and coming to fruition in the 1940s and '50s, however, there was a reaction against the Russellian and positivist conceptions of analysis. The leading figures in this movement were Wittgenstein and John WISDOM at Cambridge and Gilbert RYLE and J. L. Austin at Oxford.

Unlike earlier analytic philosophers, these ordinary-language philosophers saw no need for a general program of analysis. Rather, propositions needed to be clarified only if they were already a source of philosophical perplexity. Moreover, clarification came to be seen, most notably in the work of Austin and the later Wittgenstein, as showing how statements that have generated philosophical puzzles function in ordinary concrete contexts. Philosophy came to be seen as descriptive more than theoretical, its aim being the elimination or "dissolving" of problems by diagnosing the misuses of language that generate them. This "linguistic philosophy" should not be confused with philosophy of language—a branch of philosophic inquiry dealing with problems about language itself.

Russell's heir in analytic philosophy is the American philosopher Willard Van Orman QUINE. Like Russell, Quine attempts to clarify and reduce the ontological commitments of language. And although he sees himself as an empiricist of sorts, he is a critic of the kind of empiricism espoused by Russell and the logical positivists. His claim that beliefs are tested against experience as a body, not one at a time, resembles the idealist views Russell reacted against when the analytic movement began.

Although the philosophy taught and practiced in major British and American universities today is by and large the outgrowth of the analytic and linguistic movements, many of these philosophers question or reject most of the theoretical presuppositions of analytic and linguistic philosophy as it was originally formulated. In calling themselves analytic philosophers, they indicate their interest in the problems that the analytic tradition addressed and their respect for the standards of clarity and rigor in argument that are its legacy.

analytical chemistry Analytical CHEMISTRY is a branch of chemistry principally concerned with determining the chemical composition of materials. Chemical analysis of these materials can also determine their molecular structures and measure such physical properties as pH, color, and solubility. QUALITATIVE CHEMICAL ANALYSIS is used to detect and identify one or more constituents of a sample, and QUANTITATIVE CHEMICAL ANALYSIS is used to determine the amounts of those constituents.

anapest see VERSIFICATION

anaphylaxis [an-uh-fuh-lak'-sis] Anaphylaxis is an extreme allergic reaction to a foreign substance (see ALLERGY). Subsequent exposure can produce an overwhelming body reaction called anaphylactic shock. Symptoms of an anaphylactic reaction include severe itching, muscle spasms, facial swelling, obstruction of respiration from swelling in the larynx, and a drastic fall in blood pressure caused by widespread dilation of blood capillaries. The drop in pressure can lead to circulatory collapse and death.

In some individuals hypersensitive to bee or wasp venom, death from anaphylaxis can occur within an hour of a sting. Anaphylaxis can also occur in patients receiving serum therapy, which is still administered for such diseases as botulism and tetanus and for the prevention of rabies after exposure to infection. Such serums are prepared by injecting animals with a specific antigen to produce antibodies in the serum. The animal serum is then injected into a patient to neutralize the same antigen. Because the injected serum is foreign, however, patients can produce antibodies against it. Repeated injections may then cause an allergic reaction called serum sickness, which can range from a mild reaction to anaphylaxis. Serum therapy has been discontinued for most infectious diseases since the development of antimicrobial drugs, but these drugs can also produce anaphylaxis in some individuals.

Anaphylaxis is treated by injecting powerful stimulants to restore blood circulation and using ANTIHISTAMINES to combat the allergic reaction.

anarchism Anarchism is an ideology that regards abolition of government as the necessary precondition for a free and just society. The term itself comes from the Greek words meaning "without a ruler." Anarchism rejects all forms of hierarchical authority, social and economic as well as political. To anarchists, the state is a wholly artificial and illegitimate institution, the bastion of privilege and exploitation.

Anarchist Thought. Although the roots of anarchist thought can be traced at least as far back as the 18th-century English writer William GODWIN, anarchism as a revolutionary movement arose in the late 19th and early 20th centuries. Its immediate objective was annihilation of the state and of all authority imposed "from above downward." Once liberated from political oppression, society would spontaneously rebuild itself "from below upward." A multitude of grass-roots organizations would spring up to produce and distribute economic goods and to satisfy other social needs.

While battling the established order, anarchists also battled the alternatives proposed by liberalism and socialism. Like Marxism, anarchism was anticapitalist and scorned liberalism's dedication to political liberty on the grounds that only the propertied classes could afford to enjoy it. Anarchists rejected with equal vehemence, however, the Marxist "dictatorship of the proletariat."

Anarchism in Practice. Anarchism attracted a following mainly in the countries of eastern and southern Europe, where the state's repressiveness was especially pronounced and communal traditions remained strong. It had its greatest impact in Russia, where anarchist groups participated in the revolutionary movement both before and during 1917. The two outstanding anarchist theorists also were Russians: Michael BAKUNIN, whose advocacy of popular revolution had considerable influence, and Prince Peter KROPOTKIN, whose writings spelled out some of the constructive sides of the anarchist social vision. In only two instances did anarchists have a real opportunity to put their social ideals into practice. During the Russian civil war of 1917–21 (see RUSSIAN REVOLUTIONS OF 1917), a peasant partisan movement in the Ukraine tried to implement anarchist principles, and in the SPANISH CIVIL WAR of 1936–39 anarchism was a significant force in the regions of Catalonia and Andalusia. The results of these experiments were limited and inconclusive. In the United States the leading proponent of anarchism was Emma GOLDMAN.

Because anarchism regarded doctrinal and organizational discipline as contradictions of its principles, it gave rise to a wide variety of interpretations. Anarchist-communists shared many of the collectivist principles of socialism but sought to realize them in autonomous local communities. Anarcho-SYNDICALISM, an adaptation of anarchist ideas to modern industrial conditions, advocated the running of factories by the workers themselves rather than by owners or managers. And the novelist Leo Tolstoi formulated a kind of Christian anarchism that rejected the state on religious grounds.

Contrary to widespread belief, terrorism was never an integral part of anarchist theory or practice. Some anarchists, however, did engage in acts of terror and assassination against state officials and property owners.

See also: NIHILISM.

Anasazi [ahn-uh-sah'-zee] Anasazi (from a NAVAJO word meaning "the ancient ones") is the term archaeologists use to denote the cultures of the prehistoric Basket Makers and the PUEBLO Indians of North America. Anasazi culture has been divided into eight periods: (1) Archaic (5500–100 BC), (2) Basket Maker II (100 BC to AD 400), (3) Basket Maker III (400–700), (4) Pueblo I (700–900), (5) Pueblo II (900–1100), (6) Pueblo III (1100–1300), (7) Pueblo IV (1300–1600), and (8) Pueblo V (1600 to present).

The Anasazi built the numerous communal dwellings, or pueblos, on the high plateau of the southwestern United States. The oldest remains are in the Four Corners region, where Arizona, Colorado, New Mexico, and Utah adjoin. At the time of its greatest extent, the Anasazi culture was spread over most of New Mexico, northern Arizona, southwestern Colorado, and much of Utah—a region comparable in size to modern France—but great uninhabited stretches lay between the villages, which were located where water was available.

Origins. The Anasazi culture is believed to have evolved gradually from the ancient Desert culture once widespread in western North America. It may have been

The Cliff Palace of Mesa Verde, in Colorado, was an Anasazi center of trade and religion, reconstructed here in an artist's rendering. The pueblo, built in the sheltered recess of a cliff, contains more than 200 rooms and 23 kivas, or ceremonial chambers. To maintain a reliable food supply, the Anasazi cultivated maize and are thought to have domesticated the wild turkey.

in part derived from the Mogollon culture, an older tradition of settled agriculturalists and ceramics producers who flourished from *c.*100 BC to AD 1400 in the mountain areas of east central Arizona and west central New Mexico. There are many evidences of trade and cultural interchange between the Mogollon and the Anasazi.

The Basket Makers. Archaeologists have postulated an initial phase of Anasazi culture, formerly designated Basket Maker I but now called Archaic. This would have been a preagricultural, nonceramic stage during which the Basket Makers were nomadic hunter-gatherers.

Although Basket Maker I remains hypothetical, Basket Maker II is fairly well known. The Basket Makers were given their name because of the profusion of skillfully woven baskets discovered in sites associated with their culture. Many have been well preserved by the exceedingly dry conditions in the shallow caves where the Basket Makers stored their belongings. Perishable bags, sandals, and nets of yucca fiber have also survived. Clothing was scanty, consisting of woven G-strings for the men and short skirts of fiber for the women.

The seminomadic Basket Makers of this period hunted deer and small game with light spears and darts propelled by spear-throwers, and used a variety of nets and snares. They had also begun to cultivate squash and a type of maize. They lived in simple shelters of perishable materials or in shallow caves or rock shelters; some of them made more substantial houses of logs and mud over saucer-shaped depressions. To supplement their meager harvests of farm crops, they roamed over the country periodically on hunting and gathering expeditions, caching treasured articles and reserve supplies in storage pits or cists they excavated in the dry floors of caves. The cists were used also as sepulchers, in which the dead were buried with accompanying mortuary offerings.

Basket Maker III (AD 400–700) witnessed the expansion of Basket Maker territory and the introduction of several new cultural items, including pit houses, erected over shallow excavations, and pottery. With the addition of beans and new varieties of maize, agriculture became more important; greater reliance on farming made it possible for the Basket Makers to begin a sedentary mode of life in villages. Toward the end of the period, the spear was replaced by the bow and arrow.

The Pueblo People. Pueblo culture developed directly out of that of the Basket Makers and continued the same basic mode of life, elaborated with inventions and innovations and enriched by diffusion from alien cultures. The Pueblo I and II periods (700–1100) represented a time of territorial expansion and transition; among the important developments were the introduction of cotton cloth, the building of above-ground houses of stone and adobe masonry, and the improvement of pottery. The Pueblo people were experimenting at this time in the building of houses, but the trend was toward single-story, multiroom pueblos of stone and adobe masonry. The old pit houses persisted in some districts, and in other places they survived as ceremonial chambers called KIVAS. Villages were usually located on the tops of mesas or at the edges of canyons. Pottery was of two general types: culinary wares

ANASAZI RUINS IN NATIONAL PARKS AND MONUMENTS

Aztec Ruins National Monument. In northwest New Mexico, near the town of Aztec. Established 1923; 11 ha (27 acres). An excavated pueblo, built in AD 1100–25 (Pueblo III period), and a completely restored kiva.

Bandelier National Monument. In northern New Mexico, near Los Alamos. Established 1916; 11,864 ha (29,661 acres). Cliff dwellings and open sites of the Pueblo III and IV periods (1100–1600), located in Frijoles Canyon.

Canyon de Chelly National Monument. In northeast Arizona on the Navajo Indian Reservation, near the town of Chinle. Established 1931; 33,140 ha (83,849 acres). Several Anasazi ruins, ranging from Basket Maker II (1st century AD–450) to the Pueblo III period (1100–1300), including the White House cliff dwelling.

Chaco Culture National Historic Park. In northwest New Mexico, 101 km (64 mi) north of Thoreau and 101 km (64 mi) south of Aztec. Established in 1907; 8,604 ha (21,509 acres). A major center of Anasazi culture, ranging from Basket Maker sites through huge communal buildings of the Pueblo III period (1100–1300).

Gila Cliff Dwellings National Monument. In western New Mexico, north of Silver City. Established 1907; 215 ha (533 acres). Cliff dwellings of mixed Anasazi-Mogollon derivation.

Kinishba National Historic Landmark. In east central Arizona on the Fort Apache Indian Reservation. An excavated and partially restored pueblo of the period 1000–1400.

Mesa Verde National Park. In southwest Colorado, near Cortez. Established 1906; 20,830 ha (52,074 acres). Numerous, massive cliff dwellings and open pueblos of the Pueblo III period (1100–1300).

Navajo National Monument. In northeastern Arizona, 217 km (135 mi) north of Flagstaff. Established 1909; 146 ha (360 acres). Large cliff dwellings of the 13th century (Pueblo III).

Pecos National Monument. In northern New Mexico, 16 km (25 mi) southeast of Santa Fe. Established 1965; 138 ha (341 acres). Ruins of a great pueblo of the Pueblo IV period (1300–1600) and of a Spanish mission.

Salinas National Monument. In central New Mexico, 40 km (25 mi) south of Mountainair. Established 1909; 247 ha (611 acres). Ruins of a pueblo of Pueblo IV period (1300–1600) and a Spanish mission.

Walnut Canyon National Monument. In northern Arizona, near Flagstaff. Established 1915; 761 ha (1,879 acres). Anasazi and Sinagua ruins, including pit houses and pueblos of the period 1100–1300.

Baskets woven of coiled fabrics (left) *and pottery decorated with geometric designs* (right) *are artistic hallmarks of Anasazi civilization. Prior to the importation of pottery-making techniques in the 8th century, baskets were daubed with mud to create watertight containers.*

in which the coils were pinched to produce a corrugated effect, and decorated wares with black designs in elaborate patterns on a white background.

The climax of Pueblo development was reached during the Pueblo III period (1100–1300). Anasazi achievements in art and architecture were then at their height. The finest styles of black-on-white and corrugated pottery date from Pueblo III, and polychrome wares appeared with black-and-white designs on orange or red backgrounds. The spectacular cliff dwellings at Mesa Verde in southwest Colorado were constructed during this time.

Toward the end of Pueblo III and continuing into Pueblo IV (1300–1600), there was marked contraction of Pueblo territory, with a gradual abandonment of the outlying areas. This may have been due in part to raids by marauding nomads, in part to factional quarrels among the Pueblo, and in part to a prolonged drought between 1276 and 1299 that caused famine. The people were obliged to migrate to places with a better water supply to the south and east, particularly to the drainage area of the Rio Grande in New Mexico, to the HOPI country in northeastern Arizona, and to the ZUÑI country of western New Mexico. Pueblo V (c.1600 on) marks the start of the historic period, which dates from the time of the arrival of the first Spanish colonists in the Southwest. The Hopi, Zuñi, and Rio Grande Pueblo peoples of today are the direct descendants of the prehistoric Anasazi, although the Zuñi have merged with the Mogollon descendants.

See also: CLIFF DWELLERS; HOHOKAM CULTURE; INDIANS, AMERICAN; NORTH AMERICAN ARCHAEOLOGY.

▬

Anatolia, ancient [an-uh-toh'-lee-uh]   Anatolia is the Asiatic portion of contemporary Turkey, extending from the Bosporus and Aegean coast eastward to the borders of the Soviet Union, Iran, and Iraq. The Greeks and Romans called western Anatolia "Asia." Later the name "Asia Minor" was used to distinguish Anatolia from the land mass of the greater Asian continent.

Already in late prehistoric times, occupation by cave dwellers set the stage for Anatolia's emergence as a center of the agricultural revolution identified with the Neolithic Period. Villages and towns of this era appear at Siirt, Diyerbakir, and Urfa (southeastern Anatolia); Tarsus and Mersin in the Cilician Plain; the Amuq Plain; ÇATAL HÜYÜK (southeast of Konya); Hacilar (southwestern Anatolia); and Suberde (southwest of Konya). Individual city-states abounded during the Chalcolithic and Early Bronze ages (3d to early 2d millennium BC). Between 1940 and 1780 BC, Old Assyrian merchants from Mesopotamia established a score of trading colonies in central and eastern Anatolian cities, thereby drawing the region into wider focus.

The Hittites. Enduring political unification of Anatolia was achieved by the HITTITES, who subdued the kingdoms of the central plateau about 1750 BC. They established the Old Hittite Kingdom, eventually ruling from BOGAZKÖY (Hattusa). Their confederation, whose chief members were Luwians, Palaites, and Neshites, entered Anatolia from Europe well before 2000 BC. Under Hattusilis I (fl. c.1650 BC) the Hittite kingdom began to expand into northwest Syria. His adopted son, Mursilis I (fl. c.1620 BC), raided down the Euphrates Valley and defeated Babylon (c.1600 BC). Thereafter the kingdom suffered internal strife until stability was reestablished by Telepinus I (c.1525 BC).

The chief architect of the Hittite Empire period was Suppiluliumas I (r. c.1380–1346 BC), who reconquered much of central Anatolia and dominated Syria and the state of Mitanni in eastern Anatolia. Hittite successes made them major players in the international intrigues of the day and brought them into deadly rivalry with the Egyptian empire to the south for control of Syria and Palestine. A major battle between the Hittites under Muwattalis (r. c.1315–1296 BC) and the Egyptian king RAMSES II, fought at Kadesh on the Orontes River c.1300 BC, gave victory to the Hittites. A peace treaty between the two powers was concluded between Ramses II and Hattusilis III (r. c.1289–1265). Thereafter, serious disruptions occurred in Anatolia, and the Hittites' vassals and allies in the west attempted to gain independence. Finally, inva-

ANATOLIA IN GRECO-ROMAN TIMES

The map shows the provinces of Anatolia, or Asia Minor (now Turkey), under Roman rule at the beginning of the Christian era.

sions of SEA PEOPLES from the Aegean and attacks by mountainous Gashga peoples destroyed Hittite power in Anatolia c.1200 BC.

Political Fragmentation. After the Hittite state's collapse, Anatolia had no political centrality or cohesion for nearly half a millennium. About 1160 BC, Assyrian armies moved into southeastern Anatolia, and thereafter beyond the Euphrates, where they encountered the Neo-Hittite (Syro-Hittite) kingdoms, some 16 of which occupied the region between the Taurus Mountains and the Euphrates. Incursions of Aramaean nomads into Syria, and Assyrian reaction to these, spelled the demise of the Syro-Hittite kingdoms as independent states by the 8th century BC.

In mountainous eastern Anatolia the state of URARTU, in its turn, was defeated by the Assyrians in 743 BC. In western Anatolia, Phrygians had arrived from southeastern Europe perhaps earlier than the Trojan War (c.1190 BC). By the 8th century BC they had created a state (PHRYGIA) with its capital at GORDION, southwest of modern Ankara. On Anatolia's western coast, Lycians, Carians, and Mysians inhabited defined areas. By the 6th century BC, LYDIA had emerged as the region's dominant state. The fall of Assyria in 612 BC, and of Babylon in 539 BC, left the field open to the Persians, who, after Cyrus the Great's victory over CROESUS of Lydia in 546 BC, incorporated Anatolia, including the Ionian Greek cities, into their empire.

During the 5th and 4th centuries BC, Persia meddled in Greek affairs from its bases in Anatolia. The rise of Philip II of Macedonia and his son, ALEXANDER THE GREAT (mid-4th century BC), initiated a victorious Pan-Hellenic crusade that destroyed the Persian Empire. After Alexander's death a number of independent states emerged in Anatolia—among them BITHYNIA, CAPPADOCIA, PERGAMUM, and PONTUS—all eventually absorbed by the Roman Empire in the 1st century BC. Out of Pergamum, the Romans formed the province of Asia, which included Lycia, Caria, Mysia, and Phrygia. For the later history of the area, see BYZANTINE EMPIRE, OTTOMAN EMPIRE, and TURKEY.

anatomy   Anatomy is the branch of biology involving the structure of plants, animals, and other biological organisms. A related discipline, comparative anatomy, is concerned with the difference in structure of animal forms.

Anatomy is divided into several subdisciplines. Gross anatomy involves studies on structures that can be seen with the naked eye. HISTOLOGY is the study of tissue structure and CYTOLOGY that of cell structure. When the word *functional* is placed before any of these words, as in "functional anatomy," reference is being made to the subject of PHYSIOLOGY, the study of the function of organisms.

EMBRYOLOGY is commonly called developmental anatomy because it is concerned with the genesis and development of a fully differentiated tissue organ, or organism. Paleoanatomy is the study of the structure of extinct organisms.

Early History of Anatomy

The first recorded attempts to study anatomy were made by ARISTOTLE (384–322 BC), the founder of biological science. He dissected plants and animals but not the human body. Soon after Aristotle's death, the Ptolemies (kings of Egypt) encouraged human dissections. Herophilus (335–280 BC) and Erasistratus (310–250 BC) were perhaps the most active practitioners. Herophilus proved that the brain is the center of the nervous system and the seat of intelligence. Erasistratus observed lymph carrying fat toward the heart, described the function of the epiglottis, and distinguished sensory from motor nerves. He studied the CIRCULATORY SYSTEM intensively but held that the arteries contain air.

Despite many incorrect observations by the ancients,

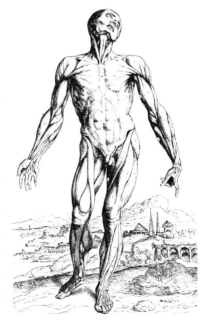

Andreas Vesalius, a 16th-century anatomist, changed the concepts of internal human anatomy with his accurate, detailed illustrations of muscles, blood vessels, and organs.

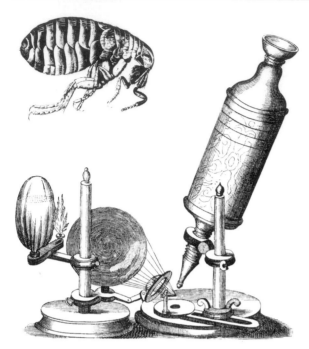

A detailed drawing of a flea is one of many illustrations in Robert Hooke's book Micrographia *(1665). He used the microscope* (bottom) *to study plants and animals and coined the word* cell *after observing the structure of cork.*

imental approach. He compared the anatomy of various animals with that of humans and noted the fallacy of extrapolating from one to the other. His *On the Structure of the Human Body* (1543) was the first work to contain accurate depictions of the inner structure of the human body. In less than a century, other anatomists completed much of the basic studies on gross anatomy. This culminated in the accomplishments of William HARVEY (1578–1657), who was the first to postulate that blood moves in a circle from the left heart to arteries to veins to the right heart. He also postulated the existence of thousands of kilometers of microscopic blood capillaries, a theory that was proved correct after microscopes became available.

History of Microscopic Anatomy

Rapid strides were made as microscopic anatomy began to be established and, together with gross anatomy, merged with comparative and developmental anatomy. Marcello Malpighi (1628–94) demonstrated that blood went through capillaries in the lungs before reaching the left heart. He also described many other histological features.

Based on microscopic observations of cork, Robert HOOKE (1635–1703) coined the word *cell*. His observations helped later investigators advance the concept that cells are the unit structures of tissues. Robert Brown (1773–1858) discovered the cell nucleus. M. J. Schleiden (1804–81) and Theodor SCHWANN (1810–82) advanced the theory that all tissues, including bone, are composed of cells. Their work brought cytology into existence as a separate, although interrelated, field of inquiry.

Antoni van LEEUWENHOEK (1632–1723) was the first to observe and describe bacteria, protozoa, and other microorganisms, as well as sperm and the cross striations of skeletal and cardiac MUSCLE. In addition, he provided visual proof that William Harvey's theory on blood circulation was indeed correct. Another notable microanatomist, Jan Swammerdam (1637–80), is famous for his remarkable work on the developmental anatomy of various insects and is considered the first person to observe and describe (1658) red blood cells.

Near the end of the 17th century, histology emerged as a distinct discipline of study. Its development went hand in hand with advances in the microscope, the invention of instruments (microtomes) for cutting thin sections of plant and animal tissues, and the introduction of staining procedures. The major advances in each of these technological fields were especially prominent in the 19th century.

History of Comparative Anatomy

Comparative anatomy studies evolutionary advances in animal structure and the anatomical and physiological adaptations animals have made in response to environmental demands. Researchers beginning with Aristotle involved themselves in comparative anatomy, but Georges Buffon (1707–88) was the first to attempt a major compilation of data.

Buffon's accomplishments paved the way for Georges, Baron CUVIER (1769–1832), the first to try to place com-

perhaps as many principles were known by the end of Cleopatra's reign (*c.*30 BC) as were to be discovered during the next 1,000 years. Most notable among those who strove to advance anatomical understanding in the following centuries was Claudius GALEN (AD 131–200). He showed that urine is formed in the kidneys and that sectioning of the spinal cord results in paralysis to that part of the body below the cut. His monumental work, *On the Use of the Parts of the Human Body*, served as the standard medical text for 1,400 years.

Unfortunately, religious views prohibited Galen from dissecting human bodies; many of his conclusions were based on studies of oxen, dogs, swine, and apes. Also, he perpetuated false beliefs developed by others, namely, that cosmic life is taken into the body with each breath and that three spirits live in the body: a "natural" spirit in the liver, a "vital" spirit in the heart, and an "animal" spirit in the brain.

Because of religious antipathy, anatomical studies were virtually abandoned, except for work done by Arab scholars such as AVICENNA (AD 980–1037). Unfortunately, their studies were based on Aristotle's and Galen's work.

As the Renaissance became established, Andreas Vesalius (1514–64) ushered in the modern era of anatomy. Rather than accept many of the observations of Galen and pursue the study of the topic through metaphysical dialectic, Vesalius took a straightforward scientific exper-

parative anatomy into a framework of principles. Instead of trying to fit fact to preconceived theory, Cuvier attempted to establish new theories based on available facts. Many anatomists followed Cuvier's lead, but none contributed as much as Richard Owen (1804–92), who originated the concept of homology. This concept concerns anatomical structures in terms of their embryology and evolutionary origin.

History of Developmental Anatomy

In the 17th century, embryological studies were conducted by Swammerdam (on invertebrates) and Malpighi (on chicks), but it was not until the 19th century that this science gained considerable momentum. Among the most famous embryologists are E. R. Lankester (1847–1929); Oscar HERTWIG (1849–1922); Richard Hertwig (1850–1937); F. M. Balfour (1851–82); and Ernest Haeckel (1834–1919), who advanced the useful concept that in the development of an advanced organism, such as a mammal, the embryo proceeds progressively through the stages of its forebears, including fishes and amphibians.

Modern Work

Anatomical studies today are characterized by their interdisciplinary nature and their emphasis on function, or physiology. At the whole-body level, anatomists with training in physics are attempting to learn the anatomical

Marcello Malpighi, known as the founder of embryology, made detailed observations in 1672 of the development of a chick embryo. In addition to his anatomical studies, he completed the work on blood circulation begun by William Harvey

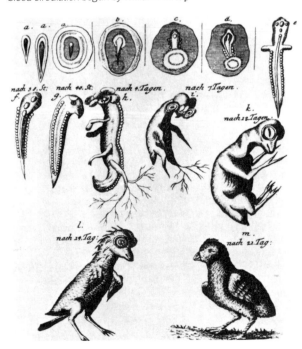

bases of animal movements and capabilities. In the study of specific organs, neurobiologists are attempting to map out brains in order to correlate complex functions, such as behavior, with networks of neuronal circuitry. Histologists are exploring problems relating to the origin of hormones, the occurrence of enzymes, and the storage depots of trace elements. Cytologists use a wide variety of approaches, including electron microscopy, ultracentrifugal separation of subcellular organs (organelles), cytochemistry, and biochemistry.

See also: HUMAN BODY; MEDICINE.

Anaxagoras [an-ak-sag'-uh-ruhs] Anaxagoras of Clazomenae, *c.*500–428 BC, was a pre-Socratic Greek philosopher. A native of Ionia, he spent much of his life in Athens, where he was associated with the leader Pericles. Only fragments of his writings survive.

Anaxagoras was influenced by Parmenides, who argued that all change is impossible. Anaxagoras tried to find a way to allow for change and a plurality of existing things. He posited a world composed entirely of an indefinite number of unchanging everlasting substances. No matter how finely divided, these substances do not change into something else. Change is possible because each everlasting substance contains smaller portions of all other substances. Thus, in Anaxagoras's view, when a child drinks milk, portions of bone in the milk aggregate to the child's bones and increase their size.

Complex organisms, he believed, are not everlasting. They come about by the mingling of everlasting substances through the activity of Mind (*Noûs*), a force he described as unlimited and independent. This concept, which probably originated with Anaxagoras, was of major significance in later Greek philosophy.

Anaximander [an-ak'-suh-man-dur] Anaximander of Miletus, *c.*610–545 BC, is the earliest Greek thinker about whom much is known. Called a pupil of THALES, he wrote a comprehensive history of the universe. His bold use of nonmythological explanatory hypotheses radically distinguishes his work from earlier literary cosmologies.

Anaximander challenged Thales' view that a single element can be the origin of all. He argued that known elements are constantly opposing and changing into one another, and that therefore something different from these elements must underlie and cause changes.

Anaximander believed that the universe is symmetrical, the Earth remaining stable at the center because it has no reason to move one way rather than another. This was apparently the first argument from sufficient reason. He also drew the first Greek world map and boldly speculated about the marine origins of animal life. He is sometimes called the founder of astronomy.

Anaximenes [an-ak-sim'-uh-neez] The Greek philosopher Anaximenes flourished in Miletus *c.*545 BC and was the last of the Milesian school founded by Thales. Anaximenes' primary concern was the origin and structure of the universe. He maintained that the primary substance is air (Greek, *aer*); everything else in the world, including the gods, is no more than rarefied or condensed air. He believed that by rarefaction air grew hot and became fire; this formed the Sun and heavenly bodies. By condensation air grew cold and became wind, water, and earth. Anaximenes' writings, except for a few fragments, are lost.

ancestor worship   Ancestor worship refers to the rites conducted in honor of deceased relatives by their descendants. Related to animism, such worship is based on the idea that the dead continue to influence the world of the living. Ancestor worship has been the most popular ritual in China and is also widespread in Korea, Japan, India, and sub-Saharan Africa. In China it began as a practice of a fertility cult, which used the phallus as an ancestral symbol. In the Shang dynasty (1558–1027 BC) and the Zhou dynasty (1027–256 BC), only royal ancestors were worshiped. But beginning with the Han dynasty (206 BC–AD 220), the preceding four generations of ancestors of all classes were honored. Chinese villages and towns had ancestral halls where ancestors of the same paternal lineages were worshiped.

See also: PHALLIC WORSHIP.

Anchisaurus [ang'-ki-sohr'-uhs]   *Anchisaurus* (Greek for "near lizard"), a dinosaur of early Jurassic time, was among the first of the dinosaurs recognized (1885) in North America. Most of what is known about it comes from skeletons found in Connecticut and South Africa. Of modest proportions (length about 270 cm/106 in) and relatively slender build, the body was intermediate in form between the distantly related carnivorous saurischian dinosaurs, such as Tyrannosaurus and *Antrodemus*, and the huge Jurassic and Cretaceous sauropod dinosaurs, such as Diplodocus and *Camarasaurus*—descendants of the prosauropods. The animal was herbivorous, and although basically quadrupedal, it could also stand on its hind feet.

See also: FOSSIL RECORD; GEOLOGIC TIME.

Anchises [an-ky'-seez]   In Greek mythology, Anchises was the father of Aeneas, whose descendants founded Rome. A handsome young man, Anchises was seduced by Aphrodite who, disguised as a shepherdess, bore his son Aeneas. During the Trojan War, Aeneas carried the aged Anchises to safety; they were refugees first in Carthage, then in Italy. Their adventures are described in Virgil's Aeneid.

anchor   An anchor is a device designed to hold a buoy, boat, or ship in a stationary position by digging into the seabed or by its own weight. It is attached with a heavy cable or chain and is usually in the shape of a double or triple hook.

Early anchors were relatively simple in design. They were sometimes simply baskets of rocks or lead-weighted logs, or they were made of three or four long poles lashed together with wooden hooks secured at the bottom end. The poles formed the shank, and the hooks were called the crown. At the top of the shank was a fixed crosspiece, the stock, which served to tilt the anchor against the sea bottom so that one of the hooks would catch and hold.

Later iron anchors had U-shaped hooks, or flukes, and removable stocks. Modern anchors for large ships are generally stockless so that they may be drawn up into the opening for the anchor cable, called a hawsehole.

Grapnels—light anchors with four or five flukes—are used to anchor small boats. A sea anchor, a floating metal and cloth device, is used when the ship is under way in order to slow it or to keep it pointing into the waves.

A stockless anchor (left) *has heavy, pronglike flukes for digging into the sea bottom and is generally used on large ships. An admiralty* (right), *used on small boats, has a crosspiece stock, which has been eliminated in most other types.*

Anchorage   Anchorage is the most populous city in Alaska, with a population of 226,338 (1990), and one of the country's largest in terms of area. Located at the head of Cook Inlet, a bay of the Pacific Ocean, it was founded in 1914 as a construction base for the Alaska Railroad. It developed as a railroad town, vital to the coal, gold, and fishing industries. Construction of the immense Fort Richardson and Elmendorf Air Force Base during World War II made the city an important transportation and defense center. The international airport services domestic, European, and Far Eastern flights. Discoveries of oil nearby made Anchorage a focus of the state's rapidly expanding oil, coal, and natural-gas industries. The seaport is equipped to handle oil shipments year round. In 1964 a severe earthquake damaged much of the city, necessitating a major urban-renewal program. Alaska Pacific University and the University of Alaska at Anchorage are there.

anchovy [an'-choh-vee]   The anchovy is a herringlike member of the fish family Engraulidae. Many of the 20 genera and more than 100 species are found throughout the temperate and tropical seas of the world. A few species of anchovy are confined to fresh waters. The common anchovy, *Anchoa mitchilli*, is a small, almost translucent fish, with a silvery stripe on the side of its body and a large mouth. It grows to a maximum length of about 10 cm (4 in) and runs in extensive schools in inshore waters from Cape Cod to Yucatán. Its principal food is small, shrimplike animals. The fish themselves are the prey of seabirds.

A Mediterranean species of anchovy is used as human food. Others are processed into fish meal, fertilizer, or oil.

The European anchovy is valuable to the European fishing industry, which catches tons of anchovies for canning, salting, or conversion into fish pastes.

Ancient Mariner   see RIME OF THE ANCIENT MARINER

Ancona [ang-koh'-nah]   Ancona, situated on a promontory in the Adriatic Sea in central Italy, is the capital of Ancona province and Marche administrative region. Its population is 104,409 (1987 est.). A rail and sea transportation hub and market center, Ancona is active in trade with Yugoslavia across the Adriatic. The city has a petroleum refinery, and its industries manufacture chemicals, ships, foodstuffs, furniture, and musical instruments. Fishing is also important to the local economy. Ancona has been the seat of an archbishopric since the Middle Ages.

Settled about 390 BC by Greeks from Syracuse, Ancona was taken by Rome during the 2d century BC and became a flourishing port after the harbor was enlarged under Emperor Trajan. Ancona was under papal rule from 1532 until 1860, except for a relatively brief period of French control (1797–1816). In 1860 it became part of Italy. The city was severely damaged by Allied bombing during World War II. Notable landmarks that have been restored are the marble Arch of Trajan (AD 115) and the 12th-century Cathedral of St. Ciriaco.

Andalusia [an-duh-loo'-zhuh]   Andalusia (Spanish: Andalucía) is a historic region of Spain lying in the extreme south of the country. It is generally considered the area south of the Sierra Morena, which roughly coincides with Spain's eight southernmost provinces. Andalusia covers approximately 87,000 km² (33,500 mi²) and has

a population of 6,152,600 (1982 est.). Its name is derived from al-Andalus, the Moorish name for the Iberian Peninsula.

Andalusia has both an Atlantic and a Mediterranean coast. Its chief topographical feature is the wide, fertile plain of the GUADALQUIVIR RIVER, which flows west across the region. In the extreme south is the SIERRA NEVADA, the highest mountain range in Spain.

Andalusia is primarily an agricultural region. Grapes, tomatoes, and other fruits, olives, wheat, and barley are grown. The region is famous for its horses, bulls (for bullfighting), and sheep; sherry, textiles, leather, and cork are leading manufactures. Fishing is important along the coast. SEVILLE, the chief city of Andalusia, has a busy inland port; ALGECIRAS, CADIZ, and MALAGA are ocean ports.

Andalusia was settled in turn by Phoenicians, Greeks, Carthaginians, Romans, and Visigoths. It was conquered by the Moors in 711. The independent Moorish caliphate of Andalusia, with its capital at CÓRDOBA, was the center of culture and learning in Europe. Three successive dynasties, the UMAYYADS, Almoravids, and Almohads, ruled until the Christians finished conquering Andalusia in 1492.

andalusite [an-duh-loo'-syt]   Andalusite is an aluminum SILICATE MINERAL (Al_2SiO_5) used in the manufacture of spark-plug porcelain and other refractories. Polished specimens of the variety chiastolite show a cross of black, carbonaceous impurities against a grayish ground. Andalusite forms reddish brown prismatic crystals. Hardness is 7½, luster vitreous, and specific gravity 3.2. Small amounts occur in many contact METAMORPHIC ROCKS, and pebbles of the mineral are found in some gem gravels.

Andaman Islands [an'-duh-muhn]   The Andaman Islands are a group of more than 200 islands in the eastern Bay of Bengal, about 480 km (300 mi) southwest of Rangoon; together with the Nicobar Islands, the Andamans form one of the territories of India. The area of the Andamans is 6,408 km² (2,474 mi²), and the population is 158,287 (1981). Most of the islands are hilly and forested. The Andamans are separated from the Nicobars to the south by the Ten Degree Channel. Port Blair, the territorial capital, is the only sizable town (1981 pop., 49,632). The first British settlement was in 1789. From 1858 to 1945 the Andamans served as a British penal colony, and many Indian and Burmese inhabitants are descended from guards or convicts. Indigenous Andamanese, originally of a Stone Age culture, number in the hundreds. Rice, coconuts, and especially timber are economic staples.

Andersen, Hans Christian   The Danish writer Hans Christian Andersen, b. Apr. 2, 1805, d. Aug. 4,

Hans Christian Andersen, a 19th-century Danish novelist, dramatist, and poet, is remembered chiefly as a creator of fairy tales. Andersen's 168 stories, the first of which were published in 1835, have been translated into more than 100 languages.

1875, is renowned for his fairy tales that combine child-like fantasy with a penetrating wisdom. Between 1835 and 1872 he wrote 168 such tales, as well as poetry, novels, plays, travel sketches, and memoirs.

Andersen was the son of a poor cobbler and a superstitious, illiterate mother. At the age of 14 he left his home in Odense for Copenhagen, where he worked as an actor with the Royal Theater. Largely through the help of Jonas Collin, a director of the theater, Andersen entered grammar school at Slagelse, and then attended Copenhagen University in 1827–28. His poetry and prose, which began to appear soon afterward, exhibited the romantic influence of Sir Walter SCOTT and of such German writers of fantasy as Ernst Theodor Amadeu HOFFMANN. During the 1830s Andersen traveled throughout Europe and the Mediterranean, briefly settling in Italy. He described these travels in *A Poet's Bazaar* (1842; Eng. trans., 1846) and other books.

In 1835, Andersen published *The Improvisatore* (Eng. trans., 1845), the first and most successful of his six autobiographical novels. During that year he also published *Tales Told for Children*, which contained his first four fairy tales: "The Tinderbox," "Little Claus and Big Claus," "The Princess and the Pea," and "Little Ida's Flowers." Most of Andersen's subsequent tales appeared in sets of four. They include the classics "The Emperor's New Clothes," "The Ugly Duckling," "The Snow Queen," "The Nightingale," "The Red Shoes," "The Little Fir Tree," "The Little Match Girl," and "The Constant Tin Soldier." Now translated into more than 100 languages, his tales rely heavily on elements of fantasy and folklore yet also reveal a deep, often pessimistic insight into human nature. Andersen used his own difficult life as the basis for many of them. In 1855 he published the autobiographical *Fairy Tale of My Life* (Eng. trans., 1954).

Andersen Nexø, Martin see NEXØ, MARTIN ANDERSEN

Anderson, Carl David   The American physicist Carl David Anderson, b. New York City, Sept. 3, 1905, d. Jan. 11, 1991, won the 1936 Nobel Prize for physics for his work on COSMIC RAYS. In his CLOUD CHAMBER studies, Anderson found decisive proof of the existence of the POSITRON, a positively charged electron. In 1938 he and Seth H. Neddermeyer announced the discovery of the MESON, a type of subatomic particle whose existence had earlier been predicted by Hideki YUKAWA. In 1948, Cecil Powell found that in reality another meson, called the pi-meson, or pion, had the properties of Yukawa's model and decayed to the known meson discovered by Anderson.

Anderson, Dame Judith   Judith Anderson, b. Adelaide, Australia, Feb. 10, 1898, d. Jan. 3, 1992, was an actress noted for her powerful portrayals of tragic characters. She made her debut in Sydney in 1915 and went to the United States three years later. Her first major New York success was in *Cobra* (1924), but she is equally remembered for her parts in Luigi Pirandello's *As You Desire Me* (1930–31) and Eugene O'Neill's *Mourning Becomes Electra* (1932). In 1936, Anderson appeared in *Hamlet* opposite John Gielgud and in 1937 as Lady Macbeth opposite Laurence Olivier. Her riveting portrayal of Medea in 1947 is often considered her best performance. She also appeared in films, notably as the formidable Mrs. Danvers in *Rebecca* (1940).

Anderson, John   John Bayard Anderson, b. Rockford, Ill., Feb. 15, 1922, represented Illinois in the U.S. House of Representatives from 1961 to 1981 and ran unsuccessfully for U.S. president in 1980. Trained in law, Anderson entered the foreign service in 1952. Elected to Congress in 1960, he served as chairman of the House Republican Conference from 1969 until 1979, when he declared his presidential candidacy. Defeated by Ronald Reagan for the Republican nomination, Anderson campaigned as an independent, winning about 7 percent of the popular vote.

Anderson, Margaret   The American publisher Margaret Anderson, b. Indianapolis, Ind., c.1890, d. Oct. 18, 1973, introduced works by such important literary figures as T. S. Eliot, Ernest Hemingway, and James Joyce in *The Little Review*, which she founded in Chicago in 1914 and edited with Jane Heap. Anderson, with the encouragement of Ezra Pound, foreign editor from 1917 to 1919, supported all modernist literary movements. She became involved in a celebrated obscenity case when she published Joyce's novel *Ulysses* in installments beginning in 1918. In a 3-volume autobiography—*My Thirty Years' War* (1930), *The Fiery Fountains* (1951), and *The*

Strange Necessity (1969)—she described her life and literary acquaintances.

Anderson, Marian   Marian Anderson, b. Philadelphia, Feb. 17, 1902, was the first black singer to perform at the Metropolitan Opera House in New York City. Anderson, who was a contralto, made her debut (1955) as Ulrica in Giuseppe Verdi's *Un Ballo in Maschera.* She was, however, primarily a concert artist and was particularly acclaimed for her singing of spirituals. Anderson first sang in church choirs. Because of her race she had to overcome great difficulties to obtain the training necessary for a career. In 1935 she sang for Arturo Toscanini, who said she had "a voice that comes once in a hundred years." In 1939 the Daughters of the American Revolution denied her access to Washington's Constitution Hall for a concert; Eleanor Roosevelt then arranged her concert outdoors on the steps of the Lincoln Memorial before an audience of 75,000 people. Anderson was named by the government as an alternate delegate to the United Nations in 1958. She sang at the inaugural balls of Presidents Eisenhower (1957) and Kennedy (1961). Anderson made many recordings and was noted for the warm, deep timbre and for the style of her oratorio singing. She retired after a successful concert tour in 1965. In 1978 she was one of five recipients of the first Kennedy Center Honors.

The contralto Marian Anderson, known for her rich voice and wide range, was the first black to sing at the Metropolitan Opera. She was named to the National Arts Hall of Fame in 1972, and she was cited for her contribution to the American performing arts at the first annual Kennedy Center Honors in 1978.

Anderson, Maxwell   James Maxwell Anderson, b. Atlantic, Pa., Dec. 15, 1888, d. Feb. 28, 1959, was one of the most admired American playwrights of his time. His colorful historical verse plays—*Elizabeth the Queen* (1930), *Mary of Scotland* (1933), *Valley Forge* (1934), and others—are now criticized for their unrealistic plots and clumsy poetry. His most durable work is the prose play *What Price Glory?* (1924), a collaboration with Laurence Stallings (1895–1968), about American soldiers in France during World War I. The comedy *Both Your Houses* (1933), a satire on congressional corruption, won Anderson the Pulitzer Prize. Other works include *Key Largo* (1939) and the musicals on which he collaborated with composer Kurt Weill, *Knickerbocker Holiday* (1938) and *Lost in the Stars* (1949), which was based on Alan Paton's novel *Cry, the Beloved Country.*

Anderson, Sherwood   The prolific American novelist, short-story writer, and critic Sherwood Anderson, b. Sept. 13, 1876, d. Mar. 8, 1941, is best known for his sensitive portrayals of the lives of small-town midwesterners. Born in Camden, Ohio, and raised in nearby Clyde, Anderson served in the Spanish-American War, became a copywriter in Chicago, then managed a paint plant in Elyria, Ohio, before taking up writing as a career in 1913.

Anderson's first novel, *Windy McPherson's Son* (1916), set in a small town in Iowa, was followed by *Marching Men* (1917). He achieved fame with WINESBURG, OHIO (1919), a group of interconnected stories about smalltown people whose frustrations and shattered dreams turn them into what he called "grotesques." This remained a primary focus, the means by which Anderson illustrated the effects of industrialization on individual lives. The theme found further expression in the novels *Poor White* (1920), *Many Marriages* (1923), and *Dark Laughter* (1925).

Anderson permanently influenced the short story, concentrating on mood and psychological insight rather than plot. Three collections, *The Triumph of the Egg* (1921), *Horses and Men* (1923), and *Death in the Woods* (1933), show his mastery of the genre. Some of his finest writing appears in his autobiographical works: *A Story Teller's Story* (1924), *Tar: A Midwest Childhood* (1926), and *Sherwood Anderson's Memoirs* (1942).

Andersonville Prison   Andersonville Prison, near Americus, Ga., was a Confederate stockade for Union prisoners during the Civil War. The inmates suffered from overcrowding, starvation, and the cruelty of the superintendent; about 13,000 died. The prison is now a historic site that includes Andersonville National Cemetery.

Andersson, Johan Gunnar   Johan Gunnar Andersson, b. July 3, 1874, d. Oct. 29, 1960, was a Swedish geologist and archaeologist who laid the foundations of Chinese prehistoric studies in the 1920s. In 1921, his discovery of an occupation site at Yang-shao T'sun in Honan demonstrated the existence of Chinese Neolithic culture. This site gave its name to the Yang-shao culture. He was also responsible for the first excavations at Chou-k'ou-tien, where skeletal evidence of PEKING MAN, was subsequently found. He published an account of his own career in *Children of the Yellow Earth: Studies in Prehistoric China* (1934).

ANDES

	Glacier
+	Spot Elevation or Depth

National capitals are underlined

Meters	Feet
Above 4000	Above 13124
2000	6562
1000	3281
500	1640
200	656
0	0
200	656
Below 2000	Below 6562

Scale 1:34,412,000

0   200   400   600   800 km

0   100   200   300   400   500 mi

Andes   The Andes (Spanish: Los Andes, or Cordillera de los Andes, the latter for "Andes Mountain Range"), one of the world's major mountain systems, form the backbone of South America. Paralleling the Pacific coast of the continent, they extend north about 7,250 km (4,500 mi) from Cape Horn at the tip of Tierra del Fuego to the Caribbean coast of Colombia and Venezuela. Although the Andes have a relatively narrow width—generally less than 325 km (200 mi), except in Bolivia—they form one of the longest uninterrupted high barriers of the world. More than 40 peaks exceed 6,100 m (20,000 ft). The Andes are not a single high range, but a complex series of ranges (cordilleras) separated by plateaus and elevated basins.

The geological evolution of the Andes began with the folding and uplift that took place in the Cretaceous Period (140 to 65 million years ago). The modern Andes, however, are the result of mountain-building activity that began in the Pliocene Epoch (6 million to 2 million years ago).

Topography

From Tierra del Fuego north to 40° south latitude, the Andes form a single dominant range, with a mean elevation less than 2,000 m (6,600 ft) but with occasional higher peaks. Extensive glaciation has left many glacier-fed lakes on the eastern flanks, and many islands and fjords on the west. North to 27° south latitude, the single range, with a mean elevation of 3,960 m (13,000 ft), contains Aconcagua (6,960 m/22,840 ft), the highest peak in the Western Hemisphere. It then splits into three ranges. Two of these continue north into Bolivia as the Cordilleras Occidental (western) and Oriental (eastern). Between them is the Altiplano, a string of high intermontane basins. Lake TITICACA, the largest South American lake and the highest large lake in the world, occupies the northernmost basin. The Cordillera Oriental veers northwest, as the Cordillera Real, at 17° south latitude, the point at which the Andes is the widest.

In Peru the Andes extend northwest to Ecuador as a high plateau with a mean elevation that declines from 4,575 to 3,050 m (15,000 to 10,000 ft). Above this surface rise mountains to heights exceeding 6,400 m (21,000 ft), including HUASCARÁN (6,775 m/22,200 ft). Tributaries of the Amazon have cut deep gorges into this surface. In Ecuador, where the Andes narrow to less than 115 km (70 mi), the Cordilleras Oriental and Occidental overlook an intercordilleran depression divided into 15 distinct basins. This two-cordillera pattern continues northward into Colombia, where the Andes fan out into three major northeast-trending ranges: the Occidental, Central, and Oriental, separated by the Cauca and Magdalena river valleys. The Cordillera Oriental forks north of Bogotá. One branch continues north as the Sierra de Perijá to form the west edge of the Maracaibo Basin. The other extends northeast to Barquisimeto as the Sierra de Mérida. It continues east as the Central Highlands, a double row of lower ranges, the Sierra de Cumana and the Paria Peninsula.

primarily on supplying basic manufactures for local consumption. The heavily mineralized Andes, long mined for gold and silver, are now more valued for copper and tin, along with smaller amounts of lead, zinc, and antimony. Colombia and Peru produce small amounts of coal for local use. Snowcapped peaks are an additional source of irrigation water and are scenic attractions for a growing tourist industry.

andesite [an'-duh-zyt] Andesite is a fine-grained, gray-to-black, volcanic IGNEOUS ROCK. Andesite PORPHYRY contains phenocrysts of plagioclase FELDSPAR and dark SILICATE MINERALS. Although it tends to resemble BASALT, andesite is chemically distinct, containing a higher percentage of silica, sodium, and potassium than basalt and less iron, magnesium, and calcium.

Andesite commonly occurs as lava flows and DIKES in zones where continental plates converge: the RING OF FIRE, including volcanoes of the Andes—from where *andesite* is derived; the Caribbean; and the north edge of the Mediterranean (see PLATE TECTONICS).

Andorra [an-dohr'-uh] Andorra is a tiny state of 453 km² (175 mi²), located on the border of France and Spain and surrounded by them.

Land and People

Set in the eastern PYRENEES, Andorra is a contrast of high mountains and deep valleys. Summer temperatures in the valleys can reach 32° C (90° F), but winters are cold (average January temperature is about 0° C/32° F), with a lot of snow. A highway and other roads connect Andorra with France and Spain, but there is no railroad.

About 60% of Andorra's citizens are Spanish; 6% are French. One-third are descendants of an ancient tribe of Andosians, from whom the country got its name. The main language is Catalan, and Spanish and French are spoken widely. Roman Catholicism is the official religion.

Economy

The country imports food from France and Spain, but tobacco, potatoes, rye, and buckwheat are grown in the valleys. Large flocks of sheep are brought from France and Spain each summer to graze on the mountain pastures. Small quantities of iron, lead, silver, and alum are mined. Three hydroelectric plants enable Andorra to export electricity to Spain.

For centuries Andorra's most profitable, although unofficial, industry was smuggling. It still remains a profitable sideline, but since the 1960s, when Andorra became a duty-free area, tourism has been the largest industry. Excellent skiing in the winter, hunting, fishing, and folk festivals in the summer, as well as the spa at Escaldes, have attracted more than 6 million visitors a year. Andorra has no sales tax, and both French and Spanish currency are used (the country has no currency of its own). Its postal system is free, being supported by the sale of Andorran stamps to collectors worldwide.

Bowler-type hats and woven blankets insulate the Indian women of Copacabana, Bolivia, against the crisp Andean climate. Despite hardships associated with the area's high altitude, the Andes have been a center of Indian cultures since ancient times.

Climate, Vegetation, and Fauna

The wide latitudinal range of the Andes results in a series of climates resembling those along the western edge of North America from Panama to southern Alaska. About two-thirds of the Andes lie within the tropics. More significant, however, is the vertical zonation of climates caused by changes in elevation. The *tierra caliente* ("hot land"), extending from sea level to 900 m (3,000 ft), has a mean temperature of 26° C (79° F), abundant rainfall, and tropical rain forest vegetation. The *tierra templada* ("temperate land"), extending to 1,800 m (6,000 ft), is cooler and humid, with a mean temperature of 21° C (70° F) and subtropical forest vegetation. The *tierra fría* ("cold land"), extending to 3,000 m (10,000 ft), has a mean temperature of 15° C (59° F). Above the *tierra fría*, the humid and cloudy *páramo* extends to the snow line, which is at about 4,500 m (15,000 ft) near the equator.

At low and intermediate elevations, Andean bird life is rich, and mammals include the cougar, ocelot, opossum, and coatimundi. The llama, alpaca, guanaco, and vicuña are found in the Altiplano. The now rare condor inhabits higher elevations.

People and Economy

Spanish invaders settled the intermontane basins within the *tierra templada* and *tierra fría*, which had long been occupied by Indians, including the INCA in Peru and the CHIBCHA in Colombia. About 60% of the Andean inhabitants reside in these basins.

Subsistence agriculture based on corn, wheat, potatoes, and grazing predominates in the *tierra fría*, and subtropical crops—sugar, rice, and, in Colombia especially, coffee—in the *tierra templada*. Industry focuses

AT A GLANCE

PRINCIPALITY OF ANDORRA

Land: Area: 453 km² (175 mi²). Capital and largest city: Andorra-la-Vella (1983 est. pop., 15,698).

People: Population (1990 est.): 51,895. Density (1990): 114 persons per km² (296 per mi²). Distribution (1983): 66.2% urban, 33.8% rural. Official language: Catalan. Major religion: Roman Catholicism.

Government: Type: limited rule by co-princes. Legislature: General Council of the Valleys of Andorra. Political subdivisions: 7 parishes.

Economy: Foreign trade (1986, with France and Spain only): imports—$531 million; exports—$17 million. Currency: 1 Spanish peseta = 100 céntimos; 1 French franc = 100 centimes.

Education and Health: Literacy (1986): 100% of adult population. Universities (1985): none. Infant mortality (1990): 7 per 1,000 live births.

Government and History

In 1278 the feudal state of Andorra was placed under the joint rule of the Spanish bishop of Urgel and the French count of Foix. The system remains the same today, though the count has been replaced by France's presi-

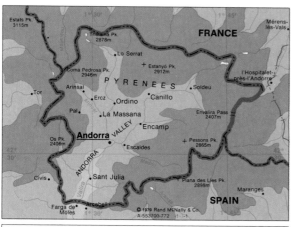

ANDORRA

	City type size indicates relative importance	Meters	Feet
—— Railroad		4000	13124
		2000	6562
+ Spot Elevation	Scale 1:500,000	1000	3281
National capitals are underlined	0 5 10 km	500	1640
	0 1 2 3 4 5 mi		

dent. Governed by a council of 24 elected representatives, Andorra is in actual practice independent and pays token homage to Spain and France. Women obtained the right to vote in 1970, but only men can hold public office. Andorra, like Switzerland, is strictly neutral in international affairs.

Andrada e Silva, José Bonifácio de [ahn-drah'-thah ay sil'-vah, hoh-say' boh-nee-fah'-see-oh day]   José Bonifácio de Andrada e Silva, b. June 13, 1763, d. Apr. 6, 1838, was a Brazilian political leader and an internationally known geologist. He led the movement that persuaded PEDRO I to declare Brazil an empire independent of Portugal in 1822. Bonifácio served as prime minister until Pedro dismissed him in 1823 for seeking a liberal constitution. Vindicated by the adoption of the 1824 constitution, which incorporated many of his ideas, he later tutored PEDRO II.

Andrade, Mário de [ahn-drah'-day]   A novelist, poet, literary and art critic, musicologist, and teacher, Mário Raul de Morais Andrade, b. Sept. 9, 1893, d. Feb. 25, 1945, was a leading figure in Brazil's modernist movement. His book of poetry, *Hallucinated City* (1922; Eng. trans., 1968), can be considered a manifesto toward popularizing art. Andrade's dynamic leadership and enormous influence led to his being called the "Pope of Modernism." Several of his short stories and *Macunaíma* (1928), his most famous prose work, are considered masterpieces.

Andrássy, Gyula, Count [awn'-drah-shee, dyu'-luh]

The Hungarian statesman Count Andrássy, b. Mar. 3, 1823, d. Feb. 18, 1890, played a key role in European diplomacy in the late 19th century. He took part in the unsuccessful Revolution of 1848 and then lived in exile until 1857. Andrássy worked with Ferenc DEÁK to arrange the Compromise of 1867, which created the Dual Monarchy of AUSTRIA-HUNGARY. He served (1867–71) as prime minister of Hungary before becoming foreign minister (1871–79) of the Dual Monarchy.

As foreign minister, Andrássy sought closer alignment with Germany. He first agreed (1872) to an alliance with both Russia and Germany, the so-called Three Emperors' League; but distrusting Russia's ambitions in the Balkans, he concluded (1879) the Dual Alliance with Germany. This was expanded into the TRIPLE ALLIANCE when Italy joined in 1882. In 1878, Andrássy represented his country at the Congress of Berlin (see BERLIN, CONGRESS OF), where he secured for Austria-Hungary the right to occupy BOSNIA AND HERCEGOVINA.

His son, also named **Count Gyula Andrássy**, b. June 30, 1860, d. June 11, 1929, was foreign minister of the Dual Monarchy at the end of World War I (1918).

André, John

John André, b. May 2, 1750, was a British officer involved in the treason of the American revolutionary general Benedict ARNOLD. In the summer of 1780, Arnold, commander of West Point, contacted Major André in New York City and offered to surrender his post to the British. André met Arnold secretly near West Point on September 21 but was captured by the Americans while on his way back to New York. Because he was in civilian clothes and was carrying incriminating papers, he was condemned to death as a spy and hanged on Oct. 2, 1780, at Tappan, N.Y.

Andrea del Castagno [ahn-dray'-ah del kahstahn'-yoh]

Andrea del Castagno, b. c.1421, d. Aug. 19, 1457, one of the most forceful painters of the Early Renaissance, was recognized even in his own time as a master of DRAWING and PERSPECTIVE. The jealousy of lesser talents spawned the rumor that he had murdered his fellow artist DOMENICO VENEZIANO. Giorgio VASARI, in his biographies of artists, perpetuated these slanders, and it remained for 20th-century scholars to restore Castagno's good name.

He achieved recognition in Florence for a representation on the facade of the Palazzo del Podestà (Bargello) of hanged men who had been traitors to Florence during the Battle of Anghiari in 1440. For this work he earned the sobriquet *Andreino degli Impicatti* ("Little Andrew of the Hanged Men"). Castagno worked at the Florence Duomo (cathedral), where he supplied the cartoon for the stained glass window depicting the deposition of Christ. The full scope of his technique is best seen in his mural paintings. Many of his frescoes were detached from their original locations, revealing Castagno's superb *sinopia*, or preparatory drawings, on the plaster beneath them. The frescoes and their *sinopia* are displayed in the refectory of the Monastery of Sant'Apollonia, Florence. This refectory, now the Castagno Museum, is the site of one of Castagno's largest and most important frescoes, *Last Supper* (1447).

Castagno frequently manipulated perspective to underscore the expression and content of a painting, as in the extreme foreshortening of the image of the Holy Trinity in the fresco *Trinity with St. Jerome and Two Holy Women* (c.1453; Santissima Annunziata, Florence). In his later works the elements of movement and vigorous action are increasingly accentuated.

Castagno's paintings and drawings exerted a powerful influence on such artists as the young Michelangelo, Antonio and Piero Pollaiuolo, and Andrea del Verrocchio. His early Venetian works were important models for the development of 15th-century Venetian painting.

Andrea del Sarto [ahn-dray'-ah del sahr'-toh]

Andrea del Sarto, b. July 14, 1486, was a major painter in the classical tradition during the Florentine High Renaissance and Mannerist periods. Even so, he was overshadowed by LEONARDO DA VINCI, MICHELANGELO, and RAPHAEL before they left Florence in 1508–09.

Giorgio VASARI, who studied in Sarto's studio, characterized Sarto's paintings as "faultless" but called his per-

Andrea del Sarto's Madonna of the Harpies *(1517), one of his most famous works, depicts the Virgin and Child with St. Francis and St. John the Evangelist. (Uffizi Gallery, Florence.)*

sonality "weak," since he usually deferred to his domineering wife, Lucrezia del Fede. Essays, operas, a poem by Robert Browning, and a psychoanalytic discussion by Ernest Jones have suggested that the lack of excitement in Sarto's personal life led him to depict figures lacking emotional depth, but recent studies have purged these romantic biographical theories from assessment's of Sarto's career.

Sarto's early (1510) S. Filippo Benizzi fresco series in the atrium of Santissima Annunziata in Florence owe their fantastic landscapes to the conservative style of PIERO DI COSIMO, to whom he had been apprenticed (1498–1508). After 1511 Sarto developed new classical interests, made greater use of *sfumato* (extremely subtle shading), and painted psychologically animated portraits such as the *Annunciation* (1512; Pitti Palace), his *grisaille* (monochromatic) frescoes in the Chiostro dello Scalzo (1511–26), and his fresco cycle for the cloisters of Santissima Annunziata, as in *Birth of the Virgin* (1514).

Sarto established this mature style through contact with Leonardo, Fra BARTOLOMMEO, Raphael's paintings, contemporary sculpture (especially that of Jacopo SANSOVINO, with whom he collaborated), and the prints of DÜRER. The *Madonna of the Harpies* altarpiece (1517; Uffizi, Florence) is the most famous of his popular dark-eyed madonnas. It does not evoke the Mannerist forebodings of contemporary Raphael altarpieces but displays instead classical formal harmony, deep colors, and noble sweetness, which characterized all Sarto's subsequent works.

The crucial influences on his last 12 years were Raphael and the Roman High Renaissance. Sarto's late style became more heroic and controlled, as in the *Last Supper* (1522–27; San Salvi refectory). Some of his late compositions, such as *The Sacrifice of Isaac* (1529; Dresden), either seem protobaroque or else suggest the Mannerist experiments that his famous pupils—PONTORMO, ROSSO FIORENTINO, and Vasari—were then undertaking. He died on Sept. 28 or 29, 1530, during one of the frequent Florentine plagues.

Andretti, Mario

Mario Andretti, b. Montona, Trieste, Italy, Feb. 28, 1940, is an American auto racer known for a hard-driving style that enabled him to win the championship on the international Formula One Grand Prix circuit in 1978. He was only the second American, and the first since 1961, to win racing's most prestigious title. He went to the United States with his family at the age of 15. One of the most versatile drivers ever, Andretti won with stock, Indy, and Grand Prix cars. He was U.S. Auto Club champion three times (1965, 1966, 1969). He won the Daytona 500 stock-car title in 1967, the Indianapolis 500 title in 1969, and the Grand Prix in 1978, becoming the only driver ever to win all three events. Andretti also was the Championship Auto Racing Teams (CART) champion in 1984.

Andrew, Saint

St. Andrew was a fisherman whom Jesus called to be an APOSTLE (Matt. 4:19). He was also the brother of Simon Peter. According to a popular but mistaken tradition, Andrew was crucified on an X-shaped cross. The crossed bars of the Scottish flag are derived from this belief. St. Andrew is the patron saint of Scotland and Russia. Feast day: Nov. 30.

Andrew II, King of Hungary

Andrew II, b. 1176?, d. Sept. 21, 1235, was one of the better-known, although not highly regarded, kings of Hungary (1205–35). The son of Béla III (r. 1173–96) and brother of Imre (r. 1196–1204), he deposed Imre's son, Ladislas III (1205). Andrew's reign was characterized by foreign misadventures (including a costly crusade to the Holy Land in 1217) and by a growing conflict between the king and the powerful magnates, as well as by a struggle between the latter and the emerging lower nobility. To protect their social and economic position, the lower nobility forced the king to issue a Golden Bull (1222)—the Hungarian Magna Carta—which became the foundation of Hungarian constitutionalism.

Andrewes, Lancelot

Lancelot Andrewes, b. 1555, d. Sept. 26, 1626, was the leading theologian of the High Church party in the Church of England during the 17th century. Educated at Cambridge, he had a command of biblical languages and early church history. He was bishop successively of Chichester, Ely, and Winchester.

As a result of his participation in the Hampton Court Conference of 1604, convened to consider English church reforms requested by the Puritans, Andrewes helped prepare the King James Version of the Bible. Andrewes's *Private Devotions* (1648) became known as a spiritual classic. He was firmly in the Anglican tradition of the church, midway between Catholicism and Puritanism.

Andrews, Roy Chapman

Roy Chapman Andrews, b. Beloit, Wis., Jan. 26, 1884, d. Mar. 11, 1960, was an American explorer and naturalist who made many important contributions to paleontology and zoology. Andrews joined the staff of the American Museum of Natural History in 1906 and later, from 1935 to 1942, served as its director. Traveling on whaling expeditions, he helped build the museum's collection of aquatic mammals into one of the world's foremost. From 1921 to 1930, Andrews led expeditions to Central Asia, where he discovered the first dinosaur eggs known to science; found the first traces of dinosaurs north of the Himalayas; made important finds about now-extinct mammals, including the largest known land mammal, *Baluchitherium*; and found evidence of early Stone Age humans in Central Asia.

Andreyev, Leonid Nikolayevich

[ahn-dray'-yef, lee-uh-neet' nik-uh-ly'-uh-vich] The Russian writer Leonid Andreyev, b. June 18 (N.S.), 1871, d. Sept. 12, 1919, became famous for his short stories and novels, many of which dealt in an exaggerated fashion with sex, crime, and death. He consciously imitated Leo TOLSTOI, especially Tolstoi's moralistic tales, and was also influenced by Fyodor DOSTOYEVSKY and Arthur SCHOPENHAUER.

Andreyev is best remembered for his stories *The Red Laughter* (1904), *King Hunger* (1908), and *The Seven That Were Hanged* (1908) and for his plays *Life of a Man* (1906) and *He Who Gets Slapped* (1916). An agnostic and pessimist, Andreyev saw death and sex as the only realities of life and denounced everything else as idealistic illusion. His nihilistic attitude was taken by many as the best expression of the mood of intellectuals after Russia's defeat in the Russo-Japanese War of 1905 and the failure of the revolution that followed. His close friendship with Maksim Gorky ended when Andreyev refused to accept the Bolshevik Revolution. In 1919 he appealed to the Western powers to intervene in the Russian Civil War. He emigrated to Finland, where he died.

Andrić, Ivo [ahn'-drich, ee'-voh]   Ivo Andrić, b. Oct. 10, 1892, d. Mar. 13, 1975, was a Yugoslavian writer who won the 1961 Nobel Prize for literature. His novels, short stories, poems, and essays portray the various nationalities and creeds of his native Bosnia, using local color while dealing with universal concerns. His major novel, *The Bridge on the Drina* (1945; Eng. trans., 1959), is set at the crossroads of the East and West, symbolically connected by a stone bridge; in it he depicts the centuries-old struggle of his people against various invaders. *Bosnian Story* (1945; Eng. trans., 1959) concerns the Turkish occupation, and *The Devil's Yard* (1954; Eng. trans., 1962) extols the victory of human dignity over the lust for power.

Androcles [an'-droh-kleez]   Androcles was a 1st-century AD Roman slave who, according to a story by Aulus Gellius, once helped a lion by removing a thorn from its paw. Later, when he was thrown to the wild beasts in the arena, the lion recognized him and refused to harm him. The story was the subject of George Bernard Shaw's play *Androcles and the Lion* (publ. 1916).

androgen   see SEX HORMONES

Andromache [an-drahm'-uh-kee]   In Greek legend, Andromache was the wife of HECTOR, the Trojan hero killed during the TROJAN WAR. When Andromache learned that Hector was dead, she tried to throw herself down from the city walls in grief. She was taken captive, however, and made the concubine of NEOPTOLEMUS, one of the victorious Greek warriors. Andromache is one of the great tragic figures of literature and art. She is the subject of plays by EURIPIDES and Jean RACINE; the farewell scene between Andromache and Hector in the *Iliad* has been frequently depicted in paintings.

Andromeda (astronomy) [an-drahm'-uh-duh]   Andromeda, named for a princess in Greek mythology, is a constellation most prominent during autumn in the Northern Hemisphere. Situated between the constella-tions Cassiopeia and Pegasus, Andromeda's brightest star, Alpheratz, forms one corner of the square of Pegasus. Andromeda contains the Andromeda Galaxy, M 31, located more than 2.2 million light-years from Earth, and the planetary nebula NGC 7662, located within our galaxy about 5,000 light-years distant.

Andromeda (mythology) [an-drahm'-uh-duh]   In Greek mythology, Andromeda was an Ethiopian princess, daughter of King Cepheus and Queen Cassiopeia. When Cassiopeia boasted that Andromeda was more beautiful than the sea-goddesses called Nereids, POSEIDON, god of the sea and father of the Nereids, sent a sea monster to ravage Ethiopia. Only the sacrifice of Andromeda could persuade Poseidon to call off the monster, so Andromeda was chained naked to a sea cliff. The hero PERSEUS saw her plight, rescued her, and killed the monster. Thereupon, Poseidon turned the dead monster into the sea's first coral. Perseus married Andromeda, and they eventually became king and queen of the Greek city of Tiryns.

Andromeda galaxy   The Andromeda galaxy is the nearest spiral galaxy beyond the Milky Way, but, at a distance of 2.2 million light years, it is also the most distant celestial object visible to the naked eye. It is listed in astronomical catalogs as M 31 or NGC 224. The Andromeda galaxy has an estimated mass of 300 billion solar masses and a diameter of 130,000 light-years, about 1.3 times that of our galaxy. Like our galaxy, it has globular CLUSTERS, open clusters, and NEBULAE of gas and dust. It is sometimes erroneously referred to as the Andromeda Nebula because it was believed to be a nebula when discovered.

The Andromeda spiral galaxy and its dwarf elliptical companions M 32 (bottom) and NGC 205 (upper right) are members of our local group of galaxies. The points of light are all stars in our Milky Way system.

Andropov, Yuri V. [an-draw'-pawf]   Yuri Vladimirovich Andropov, b. June 15 (N.S.), 1914, d. Feb. 9, 1984, was general secretary of the Soviet Communist party and thus leader of the USSR from November 1982 until his death. A native of the Stavropol region of the northern Caucasus, Andropov became active in the Communist Youth League (Komsomol), rising in 1938 to be first secretary of the Yaroslavl region group. He soon became a full-time party activist.

Andropov organized guerrilla activity against the Germans during World War II. Intelligent and hardworking, he advanced rapidly. In 1947 he became second secretary of the regional party committee in the Karelo-Finnish SSR, and in 1951 he was transferred to the central committee apparatus in Moscow. Appointed ambassador to Hungary in 1953, he impressed his superiors with his handling of the Hungarian Revolution of 1956 and was brought back to Moscow to help coordinate diplomatic affairs for the central committee. He became a member of that body in 1961 and a secretary in 1962.

In May 1967, Andropov was named head of the KGB, the political police and intelligence agency. Tough, shrewd, and a skillful administrator, he made serious efforts to understand the nature of Soviet dissidence, even while overseeing its repression. In 1973 he became a full member of the politburo, the party's chief executive organ.

Assuming power on the death of Leonid Brezhnev, Andropov made it his principal task to revitalize the Soviet economy. In foreign affairs, he generally continued the policies of his predecessor.

During his brief tenure as leader of the Soviet Communist party and president of the USSR, Yuri Andropov began an effort to improve efficiency and productivity in the Soviet system.

Andros, Sir Edmund   Sir Edmund Andros, b. Dec. 6, 1637, d. Feb. 27, 1714, was a colonial governor in the expanding British empire in America. As deputy of the duke of York (later King James II), Andros accepted the final Dutch surrender of New York (1674) and became governor of the province. He had frequent disputes with the colonists and with neighboring colonies and was recalled (1681) when charged with profiteering.

When James became king, he appointed (1686) Andros governor of the Dominion of New England, which consolidated the New England colonies and, subsequently, New York and New Jersey into one viceroyalty. Andros was given enormous powers, and his unpopular measures convinced the New England Puritans that his regime subverted their institutions and way of life. Following James II's overthrow (the GLORIOUS REVOLUTION), they rebelled, in April 1689. The Dominion government collapsed, and Andros was sent back to England. Andros later served as governor of Virginia, where his administration (1692–97) was regarded as more successful and popular.

anemia [uh-nee'-mee-uh]   Anemia is the loss of the oxygen-carrying capacity of the blood resulting from a deficiency in quantity or quality of red blood cells or the hemoglobin in the blood. Symptoms include pale skin, weakness, fatigue, and dizziness. Severe anemia may cause difficulty in breathing and heart abnormalities.

The most common type of anemia is iron deficiency anemia, which most often results from chronic blood loss and also from lack of iron in the diet, impaired absorption of iron from the intestine, or increased need for iron, as in pregnancy. Iron is an essential component of the hemoglobin, which carries oxygen to the tissues in chemical combination with its iron atoms. Pernicious anemia is a chronic inherited disease of middle-aged and older people in which the stomach fails to produce a factor needed for the absorption of vitamin B_{12}, which is essential for mature red blood cells. The disease can be treated by lifelong injections of the vitamin. Aplastic anemia is the result of the failure of bone marrow cells to manufacture mature red cells. It is usually caused by toxic chemicals (for example, benzene) or by radiation. Treatment includes preventing further exposure to the causative agent, eliminating any remaining toxic substance from the body, stimulating the proliferation of remaining bone-marrow cells, and preventing infection, while keeping the patient alive with blood transfusions. Erythropoietin (EPO), a kidney hormone that promotes formation of red blood cells, is now being produced by biotechnology and is proving useful in the treatment of anemia induced by dialysis. It may eventually also be used for treating other anemia-related ailments.

See also: COOLEY'S ANEMIA; SICKLE-CELL DISEASE.

anemometer [an-uh-mah'-muh-tur]   The anemometer is an instrument designed to measure wind speed. The earliest wind-speed indicator was the pressure anemometer, in which the displacement of a hanging plate indicated wind speed. The rotation anemometer may consist of a windmill or propeller or, more often, three or more semiconical cups rotating on a pivot attached to an electric generator. The hot-wire anemometer measures the amount of electric current required to keep a hot wire at a constant temperature as the wind blows past.

Pressure anemometers are no longer widely used, with the exception of the Pitot tube. Rotation anemometers are standard in most weather stations, and the hot-wire and acoustic types are used mainly for research.

___

anemone [uh-nem'-uh-nee]   Anemone, or windflower, is any of the perennial flowering herbaceous plants belonging to the genus *Anemone* in the buttercup family. They produce cup-shaped yellowish, white, purple, violet, or red flowers that make attractive additions to perennial flower gardens. Among the most popular are the autumn-flowering Japanese anemone, *A. hupehensis*; and the spring-flowering, tuberous-rooted poppy anemone, *A. coronaria*, with its red, white, and blue range of color.

The Japanese anemone, like other species of anemone, has large, colorful sepals instead of petals. Sepals in other plants are generally small, green leaves that surround the petals of a flower.

___

anesthetics [an-es-thet'-iks]   An anesthetic is a substance or procedure that produces a state of insensibility to pain, usually administered for performance of SURGERY. Anesthesia, the state of being insensible to pain, may or may not be associated with loss of consciousness. Anesthesiology is the medical specialty concerning anesthesia and anesthetics. Anesthetics may be administered by anesthesiologists—physicians specializing in anesthesiology—or by anesthetists—certified registered nurses—working under the supervision of a physician. Although postanesthetic problems and side effects can occur, modern anesthetic techniques generally permit complex surgical procedures to be performed without pain and with minimal complications.

History

Prior to the availability of anesthetics, surgery was infrequent. Operations were completed in minutes because of the pain and shock accompanying operation on unanesthetized body parts. For centuries physicians sought agents that would permit painless surgery. Alcohol and opium compounds were used. The Chinese used hashish, while the Inca used the coca extract, cocaine, on the skin. Direct pressure and cold on nerve trunks were occasionally used. Each of these was only partially effective. A dramatic breakthrough became known in 1846 at the Massachusetts General Hospital in Boston, when William Morton, a dentist, administered diethyl ETHER to a patient, and Dr. John C. Warren painlessly removed a tumor from the patient's jaw. (A Georgia physician, Crawford W. Long, had actually been using ether as an anesthetic since 1842 but did not publish his results until 1849.) The news of the Boston operation spread rapidly, and within two years general anesthesia was being widely used throughout the United States and Europe.

General Anesthesia

During general anesthesia, DRUGS primarily affecting the brain render the patient unconscious and insensible to pain and surgical stimulation. The patient awakens only when the administration of the drug is discontinued. A patient has no memory of events that occur during anesthesia.

Inhalants. Some general anesthetics are inhaled by the patient. They are known as inhalational agents and can be either gases or volatile liquids. The anesthetic gases are mixed with oxygen in measured concentrations just before delivery to the patient. The anesthetic liquids are placed in vaporizers. Of all the known inhalational agents, only three—nitrous oxide, halothane, and enflurane—are in widespread use. In most patients, nitrous oxide—sometimes termed laughing gas—will not produce anesthesia when used alone, but it makes it possible for decreased amounts of other drugs to be used. The side effects are minimal and include asphyxia and diffusion anoxia (lack of oxygen). Halothane (Fluothane) is more potent and can be used alone, but it is more likely to produce the side effects typical of general anesthesia. Halothane has been associated with liver toxicity (halothane hepatitis), which can be fatal. Enflurane (Ethrane) is similar to halothane in its properties and side effects, although liver toxicity has not been established. With enflurane, however, increased electrical activity occurs in the brain at deep levels of anesthesia, and recordings of the electroencephalogram have revealed seizure activity in some patients. Isoflurane (Forane) has properties similar to those of halothane and enflurane.

Drugs. Some general anesthetics are administered intravenously. Thiopental (Pentothal), thiamylal (Surital), and methohexital (Brevital) are intravenous anesthetics belonging to the BARBITURATE group of drugs. They are characterized by rapid onset of anesthesia (30–90 seconds); the duration of action is short (5–10 minutes). Although consciousness is lost quickly, patients tend to respond to surgical stimulation unless high doses are used. The barbiturates are particularly useful in beginning an anesthetic. Anesthesia is then maintained with such agents as halothane or enflurane. Barbiturates used with nitrous oxide, narcotics, and muscle relaxants can often produce anesthesia sufficient for many types of surgery.

Diazepam (VALIUM), a TRANQUILIZER, can produce anesthesia when given intravenously. It has less effect on the heart and respiration than the barbiturates, and the dose of diazepam needed to produce loss of consciousness is variable. Ketamine, while not a general anesthetic, is an intravenous drug with many anesthetic properties and is useful for short procedures. A drawback is that 10 to 15 percent of adult patients have vivid, often unpleasant dreams during emergence.

Two other groups of drugs are important in modern anesthetic practice. The first is such narcotics as morphine, meperidine (DEMEROL), and fentanyl. These drugs are ANALGESICS (pain relievers), not anesthetics. Their properties, however, add to the effects of anesthetic agents. The second group comprises such muscle relaxants as succinylcholine, d-tubocurarine, gallamine, and pancuronium, which interfere with the transmission of impulses from nerve to muscle.

Anesthetic Action. The exact mode of action of general anesthetics is difficult to explain because of the many effects of anesthetic drugs and the complexity of the central NERVOUS SYSTEM. Consequently, many theories of anesthetic action exist. The site of action is the brain, the basic unit of which is the neuron, or nerve cell. Proponents of neurophysiological theories hold that anesthetics work by decreasing transmission across the neural synapse, the gap between nerve cells. Recent research has also suggested that specific binding sites may exist in the brain. Biochemical theories hypothesize that anesthetics decrease energy production within the nerve cell, thus decreasing the ability to produce nerve impulses. A recent combination of these two theories states that the decrease in energy production shifts metabolic pathways and allows an increase in the production of certain compounds, such as gamma-amino butyric acid, that decrease synaptic transmission. Several theories have been proposed to explain the effect of anesthetic molecules on the nerve-cell membrane. Anesthetic molecules dissolved in the cell membrane are believed to alter the arrangement of membrane lipids or proteins. This will disrupt the flow of ions across the membrane and interfere with nerve impulse conduction.

Because general anesthetics interfere with the brain's chemical messages, cold conditions in the operating room may cause a shivering reflex that the brain cannot signal the muscles to stop. If unchecked, such postoperative shivering is sometimes severe enough to become serious.

Local Anesthesia

In contrast to general anesthesia, regional anesthesia affects only the part of the body on which surgery is to be performed. In general, the patient is awake and remembers the operating room, but no pain occurs during surgery. The anesthetic drugs used to produce regional anesthesia are called local anesthetics. Commonly used local anesthetics such as procaine (including Novocain) and tetracaine are metabolized in the blood, and their duration of action is therefore shorter than that of other local anesthetics, such as lidocaine, bupivacaine, and etidocaine, which are metabolized in the liver. Some anesthetics, such as lidocaine, are absorbed through mucous membranes and can be used to anesthetize the inner surface of the mouth, pharynx, nose, or other mucous membranes. (See also COCAINE.)

Four major types of local anesthesia are in use. In infiltration anesthesia, the anesthetic is injected into the area upon which surgery is to be performed. In nerve-block anesthesia, the local anesthetic is injected near specific nerves that innervate the area of operation. In general, the local anesthetic is applied at some distance from the actual site of operation. In spinal anesthesia, a small amount of local anesthetic is introduced into the subarachnoid space of the vertebral canal, spreading into the cerebrospinal fluid and anesthetizing the nerve roots coming out of the spinal cord. This technique can be used for surgery on the entire lower half of the body. Epidural and caudal anesthesia involve depositing anesthetic into the epidural space of the vertebral canal. These techniques are popular for labor and delivery.

Complications can occur with the use of local anesthetics. By blocking normal regulation of blood vessels, spinal and epidural anesthesia can decrease the blood pressure. High blood levels of local anesthetic, obtained by inadvertent intravenous injection or excessive drug dosage, produce distinct effects on the brain. At first, lightheadedness and dizziness occur, and this can be followed by disorientation or drowsiness. With still higher blood levels, seizures can occur.

Other Techniques

Anesthesia can also be produced by some nonchemical means. HYPNOSIS is used, but very few patients can achieve a trance profound enough for major surgery. It can be useful, however, for minor procedures and in the preoperative preparation of patients for surgery. The traditional Chinese medical art called ACUPUNCTURE may be used, selectively, but its success as the sole anesthetic agent is unpredictable.

—

aneurysm [an'-yur-izm]   An aneurysm is a widening or dilation of a blood vessel caused by thinning of the vessel wall. A potentially lethal complication is the rupture of the vessel with resultant massive hemorrhage. Aneurysms usually occur in arteries but may also be seen in the heart after local damage, or in veins.

Arterial aneurysms occur most often in elderly, diabetic, or hypertensive persons. They may be caused by congenital thinning of the muscular portions of the artery; during atherosclerotic degeneration of the aorta or of the carotid or basilar arteries; by trauma to a vessel wall; by infectious injury; or by degeneration. The likelihood of rupture is increased by high blood pressure. Defects in eye arteries may result in miliary (small, multiple) aneurysms of the retina.

Treatment of a person with a ruptured aneurysm may include reduction of blood pressure, bed rest, replacement of the weakened vessel by a graft or by encasement in plastic, or mechanical stoppage of blood flow to or through the aneurysm.

angel An angel (Greek: *angelos*, "messenger") is a celestial being believed to function as a messenger or agent of God in CHRISTIANITY, ISLAM, JUDAISM, and ZOROASTRIANISM. In the Near Eastern antecedents to Judaism, angels were often understood to be gods or lesser divinities. Their existence was taken for granted by the biblical authors. The use of the word *angel* may have been a way of describing what was believed to be an appearance of God in human form.

In the Old Testament, angels are called "messengers," "men," "powers," "princes," "sons of God," and the "heavenly host." They have either no body or one that is only apparent. They come as God's messengers to aid or punish, are assigned to individual persons or nations, and often have a name (Michael, Gabriel, Raphael, Uriel). New Testament statements about angels reflect Jewish views of these beings. Angels, for example, announced Christ's birth (Luke 2) and resurrection (Matt. 28).

Ancient and medieval peoples widely accepted the influence of good spirits, or angels, and evil spirits, or fallen angels (see DEMON; SATAN). During the Middle Ages, theologians developed a hierarchy of angels. They were classified in the following nine ranks (beginning with the lowest): angels, archangels, principalities, powers, virtues, dominations, thrones, cherubim, and seraphim. Angels are a popular subject in folklore, literature, and art.

Angel Falls Angel Falls (Spanish: Salto Angel) is the highest waterfall in the world. It is located within Canaima National Park, in Bolívar state in southeastern Venezuela, about 258 km (160 mi) southeast of Ciudad Bolívar, where the Rio Churún falls from the flat mountain plateau of Auyán-Tepuí in the Guiana Highlands. The greatest uninterrupted drop is 800 m (2,640 ft). James Angel, a U.S. explorer and aviator, discovered the falls in 1935.

angelfish The angelfish, in the family Chaetodontidae, are among the showiest denizens of the sea. Most species exhibit brilliant colors, some with irregular patterns that serve as camouflage. Often the young are differently colored than the adults. At night when these diurnal fish enter a state of torpor, their colors may change. The angelfish inhabit warm seas and are abundant in coral reefs. They usually swim singly or in pairs.

Angelfish have thinly compressed bodies and a strong, backwardly directed spine on the lower part of each cheekbone. The mouth is small and protractile with narrow bands of fine bristlelike teeth. Angelfish feed primarily on sponges, tunicates, zoantherians, and algae. Some

Angelfish are among the most colorful of all fish. Their exotic coloration facilitates territoriality by warning off intruders. (Clockwise, starting at upper left): *emperor angelfish; French angelfish; blue-faced angelfish; blue angelfish; and majestic angelfish.*

Lamentation over the Dead Christ *is one of a series of frescoes executed about 1437–45 by Fra Angelico and his assistants for the convent of San Marco in Florence. Highly spiritual in expression, the work reflects Angelico's purity of form and spatial clarity.*

species act as cleaners, picking external parasites and necrotic tissue from the surface of other fish. Most individuals are less than 43 cm (17 in) long. Fish of the genus *Pterophyllum*, family Cichlidae, also called angelfish, are popular in home aquariums.

Angelico, Fra   Fra Angelico was one of the most prolific and beloved painters of the Italian Renaissance. In a letter written in 1438, DOMENICO VENEZIANO called Fra Angelico and Fra Filippo LIPPI the two most important Italian painters of the day. Each continued, in parallel directions, the heritage of MASACCIO, generally considered the father of Florentine Renaissance painting. Together with Veneziano, ANDREA DEL CASTAGNO, PIERO DELLA FRANCESCA, and Paolo UCCELLO, they developed a second Florentine painting style that flourished from the 1430s through the 1450s.

It has been determined recently that Fra Angelico was born about 1400 (not 1387, as Giorgio VASARI records) and given the name Guido di Pietro. He was known to his contemporaries as Fra Giovanni da Fiesole. His nickname *Angelico* first appeared in 1469, 14 years after his death,

and he is also known in Italian as *Beato* ("Blessed One"). Apparently a member of the Dominican order, Angelico became the artistic spokesman for the Dominicans, as Masaccio was for the Carmelites. Among his influential early works are the Cortona *Annunciation* panel (1432–38; Diocesan Museum) and the *Linaiuoli Triptych* (Museum of San Marco, Florence).

In 1436, Cosimo de' Medici and Pope Eugene IV requisitioned the decaying convent of San Marco and invited the Dominicans to build and decorate a new monastery. In collaboration with the architect MICHELOZZO, Angelico and his assistants frescoed various scenes from the life of Christ in the 44 monks' dormitory cells and connecting corridors. Angelico's San Marco altarpiece, *Madonna and Saints in a Sacred Conversation* (1438–39; Museum of San Marco)—he created the form called *Sacra Conversazione*—although now overcleaned, is a masterpiece remarkable for its rendering of the human figure and its use of natural light and systematic perspective.

About 1445, Angelico was called to Rome. All the buildings he worked on there have been destroyed, except for the private chapel of Pope Nicholas V in the Vatican, which contains Angelico's frescoes of scenes from the lives of St. Stephen and St. Lawrence. When he died in

Rome on Feb. 18, 1455, Angelico was considered the most influential of all contemporary Florentine painters. Although his art was sentimentalized by the 19th-century Nazarenes and Pre-Raphaelites, it has always been admired, imitated, and widely reproduced.

Angelou, Maya [an'-juh-loh, mah'-yah]

Maya Angelou, b. St. Louis, Mo., Apr. 4, 1928, is a black American writer, stage performer, and composer. Her widely acclaimed autobiography, *I Know Why the Caged Bird Sings* (1970), is a moving and often humorous account of her childhood in segregated Arkansas. In addition to several autobiographical sequels, including *The Heart of a Woman* (1981) and *All God's Children Need Traveling Shoes* (1986), she has written plays, books of poetry, and screenplays.

anger   see EMOTION

Angers [ahn-zhay']

Angers, the capital of Maine-et-Loire department in western France, is situated on the Maine River about 560 km (160 mi) southwest of Paris. The population is 136,038 (1982). The city is known for its black slate quarries. Other industries include electronics, textiles, and paper products. Tourists are attracted by the 12th-century Cathedral of Saint-Maurice and the Museum of Tapestry housed in the walled chateau, built 1230–40. The University of Angers dates from 1875. First a Gallic settlement and then the Roman city of Juliomagus, Angers became the seat of the counts of Anjou in 870. It suffered extensive damage during World War II.

Angevins (dynasties) [an'-juh-vinz]

The two Angevin dynasties in medieval Europe originated from the French countship of Anjou. In 1131, Fulk V, count of Anjou, became king of the Latin Kingdom of Jerusalem, which his descendants ruled until 1186. Fulk's eldest son, Geoffrey Plantagenet, married (1128) Matilda, queen of England, and their son Henry II became (1154) the first Angevin, or Plantagenet, king of England. This house ruled England until Richard II was overthrown (1399) by Henry IV of Lancaster.

A second Angevin dynasty came into being after King Louis IX of France gave (1246) Anjou to his brother, who became (1266) Charles I of Naples. The latter's son, Charles II of Naples, had seven children. They, with their descendants, created a tangled dynastic situation for Naples, involving the royal houses of both France and Aragon. One grandson became (1308) king of Hungary as Charles I, but the Angevin line in eastern Europe ended on the death (1382) of his son, Louis I, king of Hungary and Poland.

See also: Jerusalem, Latin Kingdom of; Naples, Kingdom of.

angina   see HEART DISEASES

angioplasty

The medical technique known as percutaneous transluminal angioplasty, or PTA, is used in the treatment of coronary HEART DISEASES. PTA involves the widening of coronary arteries that have been dangerously narrowed by the buildup of deposits called plaque on their interior walls (see ATHEROSCLEROSIS). A flexible tube, or catheter, is first inserted percutaneously (through a skin incision) into an artery. The catheter is manipulated transluminally (through the arterial system) until it reaches the constriction site. A small balloon at the end of the catheter is then inflated, compressing the plaque and widening the passage. Since its introduction in the late 1970s, PTA has come to rival the much more traumatic surgical technique called coronary bypass, and angioplasty of peripheral vessels is now fairly common. Clogged arteries remain hard to clear by PTA alone, however, and in about 30 percent of cases new and often equally severe obstructions arise. Various complementary techniques are being developed, such as the use of atherectomy devices—rotary scrapers that are worked through blood vessels to reach the clogged site—and the similar use of lasers.

angiosperm [an'-jee-oh-spurm]

Angiosperms are the most highly evolved PLANTS, constituting diverse flowering species, from garden-variety flowers and such grains as corn and wheat to flowering trees, shrubs, and vines. They inhabit almost all regions except the open ocean.

Angiosperms constitute the class Angiospermae in the plant phylum Tracheophyta (vascular plants; see TRACHEOPHYTE). The SEEDS of these plants are developed and retained within an ovary, which, after seed formation, expands into a fruit (see FRUITS AND FRUIT CULTIVATION). The two distinct subclasses of Angiospermae are Dicotyledonae, or dicots, and Monocotyledonae, or monocots (see COTYLEDON). The FLOWER, and the fruit that develops from it, most readily distinguish angiosperms from other vascular plants. Four types of floral whorls exist: calyx, consisting of sepals; corolla, the petals; androecium, composed of stamens; and gynoecium, or pistil, consisting of stigma, style, and ovary. Of most biological importance to the plant are the stamens and pistil. One or both of these structures constitute a flower.

Angkor [ang'-kor]

Angkor, north of Tonlé Sap in northwest Cambodia, was the great capital city of the Khmer Empire from the city's founding c.880 until about 1225. Lost in the jungle for centuries, it was discovered by French missionaries in the 1860s. Its immense temple complexes, larger in scale than the Egyptian pyramids, rank among the masterpieces of world architecture.

Temple City. Angkor was both a sacred temple city and the center of a huge irrigation system. Its Hindu temple architecture, inspired perhaps by the monuments at Borobudur, was built by successive kings on an increasingly vast scale.

The early temples were built of brick; the later, beginning with the Ta Keo (*c.*1020), of stone. All these so-called temple mountains were elaborately ornamented and filled with stonecut images. The central icon represented the monarch in the guise of his patron deity. The two earliest surviving structures, built during the reign of Yasovarman I (889–900), are the Bakong (881) and the Bakheng (893), which had 108 tower-shrines around its central sanctuary. The Pre Rup (961) was the first temple intended as a dwelling for the deified spirit of a dead king.

Angkor Wat. The greatest temple designed for this purpose is the huge Angkor Wat ("Angkor Temple") of the early 12th century. Built under Suryavarman II (r. 1113–50), the complex of terraces and cloisters covers an area of 1,500 by 1,300 m (4,920 by 4,265 ft) and is surrounded by a vast moat 180 m (590 ft) wide. Throughout the compound elaborate carved reliefs illustrate scenes relating to the Hindu god VISHNU, to whom the temple was dedicated.

Angkor Thom. Following the sack of Angkor by the Chams in 1177, Angkor Wat was abandoned. In the early 13th century Jayavarman VII (1181-*c.*1281) established a new capital and sacred precinct, Angkor Thom ("Great Angkor"). The four gateways into the city bear huge masks of its new patron, the Buddhist deity Lokesvara, Lord of the Universe. After the destruction of Angkor by Thai forces in 1431, the Khmer capital was moved to Phnom Penh, and the site fell into ruin.

See also: SOUTHEAST ASIAN ART AND ARCHITECTURE.

angle   A plane angle is the measure of the amount of rotation when a line segment rotates in a plane about a fixed point. By convention, a counterclockwise rotation is positive, and a clockwise rotation is negative. The Babylonians divided a complete rotation using units of 60 (a sexagesimal system):

$$1 \text{ revolution} = 360 \text{ degrees } (360°)$$
$$1 \text{ degree} = 60 \text{ minutes } (60')$$
$$1 \text{ minute} = 60 \text{ seconds } (60'')$$

An angle equal to the angle between the horizontal (horizon) and vertical (upright) directions is equal to 90° and is called a right angle. In advanced mathematics the usual unit is the radian (1 revolution = 2π radians).

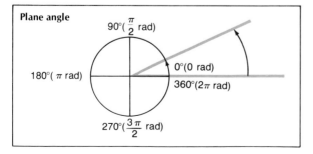

Plane angle

A solid angle is generated by an infinite set of line segments having a common vertex and passing through a simple closed curve. In the accompanying diagram, the solid angle subtended at P by the surface S is measured by the area U, which is the portion of the spherical surface with center P, and radius 1, lying within the solid angle. The unit solid angle is the steradian, the largest solid angle being 4π steradians. If the steradian is defined by the solid angle at the vertex of a right circular cone, opposite generating lines of the cone will make an angle of about 65° 32′.

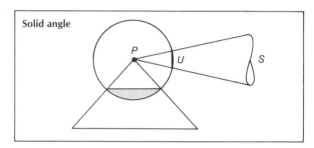

Solid angle

anglerfish   Anglerfish is the common name for more than 200 species of marine fishes in the order Lophiiformes, including goosefish, frogfish, batfish, and several families of deep-sea anglers. Anglerfish are named for their method of catching prey, using a specialized spiny ray above the snout that serves as a fishing rod with a lure; the ray, a modified portion of the dorsal fin, is tipped with a baitlike piece of flesh.

Goosefish range in length from 1 m (3 ft) to 1.5 m (5 ft) and weigh about 23 kg (51 lb). The short-bodied *Lophius piscatorius* of the eastern Atlantic has a large flattened head, an enormous mouth, dorsally situated jaws, and eyes on the top of its head. Its mouth and expandable stomach allow it to swallow fish as big as itself.

Frogfish rely on camouflage to catch their prey. When lying motionless among rocks or seaweed, the fish dangles its lure until prey is attracted. When the lure is touched, the enormous mouth gapes, creating a vacuum that sucks the prey within range of the fish's back-pointing teeth. The best-known frogfish is the sargassum fish, *Histrio histrio*, which is common along the Florida coast and in the Caribbean. It lives in floating seaweed, climbing about with its pectoral fins.

Named for their large, winglike pectoral fins, batfish are best known for the manner in which they "walk" along the sea bottom using their stout fins. The most modified of all anglerfish, batfish are flat-bodied, scaleless fish that swim poorly. Batfish can draw their fishing rods into tubes when they are not using them to gather food.

Most deep-sea anglerfish are found at ocean depths ranging from 300 m (984 ft) to 4,000 m (13,210 ft). These jet black or dark brown fish cruise slowly in dark waters, guided by fishing rods with lighted lures. The light in the lure is supplied by luminous bacteria shining

A particularly ugly species of anglerfish, a goosefish is shown catching its meal. It lies in wait, camouflaged against the ocean floor, and attracts a fish by dangling a fleshy appendage that looks like a fishing bait and line. As the victim touches the lure, the anglerfish opens its huge jaws and gulps down its prey.

through skin that has lost its pigment. In four families of deep-sea anglers, the males are parasitic on the females. At an early age the male attaches itself to the female permanently and obtains nutrients through vascular connections between the two individuals.

Anglesey   see GWYNEDD

Anglican Communion

The Anglican Communion is a worldwide fellowship of independent churches derived from the Church of England. Although independent, the member churches acknowledge a common heritage including the BOOK OF COMMON PRAYER, the THIRTY-NINE ARTICLES, and the threefold ministry of bishops, priests, and deacons. The bishops meet every ten years, at the invitation of the archbishop of Canterbury, in the Lambeth Conference. Cooperation between the member churches is facilitated by the Anglican Consultative Council, with its secretary general and with the archbishop of Canterbury as president. Regional councils link provinces within specific geographical regions.

In 1888 the Lambeth Conference adopted as its basis the reunion of all Christian churches. It also defined those things essential to any church: (1) "The Holy Scriptures of the Old and New Testaments, as 'containing all things necessary to salvation'"; (2) "The Apostles' Creed, as the Baptismal Symbol; and the Nicene Creed, as the sufficient statement of the Christian faith"; (3) "The two Sacraments ordained by Christ Himself—Baptism and the Supper of the Lord—ministered with unfailing use of Christ's words of Institution, and of the elements ordained by Him"; (4) "The Historic Episcopate, locally adapted in the methods of its administration to the varying needs of the nations and peoples called of God into the Unity of His Church."

See also: ENGLAND, CHURCH OF; EPISCOPAL CHURCH.

Anglo-Dutch Wars

England and the Dutch Republic fought four wars (called the Dutch Wars by the English and the English Wars by the Dutch) between 1652 and 1784. The principal issue was the maritime and commercial rivalry between the two countries, sharpened by conflicts over the ties between the House of ORANGE and the British ruling family.

The **First Anglo-Dutch War** (1652–54) pitted England under Oliver CROMWELL against the Dutch Republic during its first period of government. At first, success in the war swung between the two sides, but by 1653 the English were winning, and in 1654 the Dutch had to accept the humiliating first Peace of Westminster. The **Second Anglo-Dutch War** (1665–67) reflected English merchants' resentment of Dutch mercantile success and the hatred of the English king CHARLES II for the Dutch republicans. The Dutch navy, rebuilt by the grand pensionary Johan de WITT, defeated the English fleet in battle (June 1666) and then destroyed it at anchor in the Medway (1667). The war ended in the Peace of Breda (1667). Charles sought his revenge in the **Third Anglo-Dutch War** (1672–74), which he waged in alliance with LOUIS XIV of France. Dutch naval victories and English popular opposition compelled Charles to make a separate peace at Westminster (1674). The **Fourth Anglo-Dutch War** (1780–84) resulted from a desperate Dutch attempt to break English interference with their trade during the American Revolution. The Dutch were defeated and had to accept English conditions in the Peace of Paris (1784).

Anglo-Saxon Chronicle, The The Anglo-Saxon Chronicle, a compilation of writings begun in the 9th century, still serves as the principal contemporary source for the history of Britain before the Norman Conquest. Although the chronicle was kept erratically by monks before his reign, King Alfred the Great (r. 871–99) is generally credited with establishing it as a continuous register of national events. The work is especially valuable as a record of his times. Seven manuscript versions of the text are extant, the latest of which extends to the accession of Henry II in 1154. As a literary work, the chronicle is often considered the first great book of English prose.

Anglo-Saxon literature see ENGLISH LITERATURE

Anglo-Saxons When the Angles, Saxons, and Jutes—coming from areas in and around what is now Denmark—invaded Britain in the second half of the 5th century, they were taking part in a great series of incursions by mostly GERMANIC PEOPLES into a steadily weakening Roman Empire. By 600 they were well established in Britain, having driven the Romanized Celtic Britons west-

During the 8th century, Mercia was the dominant Anglo-Saxon kingdom. England was finally unified by the kings of Wessex.

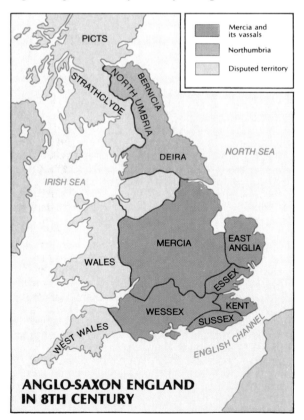

	Mercia and its vassals
	Northumbria
	Disputed territory

ANGLO-SAXON ENGLAND IN 8TH CENTURY

ward into Wales and Cornwall. By the end of the 7th century these tall, blond, blue-eyed pagans had been converted to Christianity by St. AUGUSTINE OF CANTERBURY and other missionaries from the continent.

First called Saxons, the German invaders were later referred to as Angles, and in 601 the pope called Æthelbert of Kent *rex Anglorum* ("king of the Angles"). The West Germanic language of the invaders, on the other hand, was apparently always referred to as English, whether spoken by Angles, Saxons, or Jutes (and perhaps some Frisians). About AD 890 the name *Engla lande* ("the land of the Angles") was used. The term *Anglo-Saxon* was also used before the Norman Conquest (1066); it was revived in the 16th century.

Early Anglo-Saxon society was organized around families and clans, or tribes, and centered on the warrior and a system of reciprocity called *comitatus*. The lord (*ealdormann* or *eorl*) expected martial service and loyalty from his *thegns*, or thanes (similar to the later KNIGHTS), who on their part expected protection and rewards from the lord. From the 7th to the 11th century a rich Anglo-Saxon culture flourished, and the tribal system gradually gave way to larger kingdoms, most importantly MERCIA, NORTHUMBRIA, and WESSEX. Eventually (by 959), all England was rather loosely united under the kings of Wessex, the greatest of whom was the scholar-king ALFRED (r. 871–99). The Wessex line of kings was interrupted (1016) by the conquest of the Danish king CANUTE, culminating a centuries-long series of Danish, or VIKING, raids on England. Anglo-Saxon kings (St. EDWARD THE CONFESSOR and HAROLD II) ruled again briefly (1042–66) before the so-called Anglo-Saxon period of English history ended in conquest by the NORMANS under WILLIAM I.

Angola [an-goh'-luh] Angola, the second largest country in Africa south of the Sahara, is situated on the Atlantic Ocean. It is bordered to the north by Congo and Zaire, to the east by Zambia, and to the south by Namibia (South West Africa) and includes the mineral-rich enclave of Cabinda. Angola gained its independence from Portugal in November 1975 after a 14-year guerrilla war and a brutal civil war. Intervention by the United States, the USSR, Cuba, and South Africa prolonged the civil war, draining the country of its resources and preventing development of a basic infrastructure.

Land and Resources

Two-thirds of Angola is a north-south running plateau with altitudes ranging from 1,300 to 2,000 m (4,265 to 6,560 ft). The highest point in the country is Mount Moko (2,620 m/8,596 ft). The terrain varies from heavily wooded hills and jungle-covered mountains in the north to flat, dry bush and barren desert in the south. The plateau is separated from the coast by lowlands ranging in width from 50 to 160 km (30 to 100 mi).

Most of the country's major rivers originate in the central plateau and empty into the Atlantic Ocean. The Zambezi, Cuando, and Cubango rivers, however, rise in the highlands and run eastward to the Indian Ocean.

PEOPLE'S REPUBLIC OF ANGOLA

Land: Area: 1,246,700 km² (481,353 mi²). Capital and largest city: Luanda (1988 est. pop., 1,134,000).

People: Population (1990 est.): 8,534,483. Density: 6.8 persons per km² (17.7 per mi²). Distribution (1987): 30% urban, 70% rural. Official language: Portuguese. Major religions: traditional religions, Roman Catholicism, Protestantism.

Government: Type: one-party state. Legislature: People's Assembly. Political subdivisions: 18 provinces.

Economy: GNP (1988 est.): $5.0 billion; $600 per capita. Labor distribution (1985): agriculture—85%; industry and other—15%. Foreign trade (1989 est.): imports—$2.5 billion; exports—$2.9 billion. Currency 1 kwanza = 100 lwei.

Education and Health: Literacy (1984): 39% of adult population. Universities (1990): 1. Hospital beds (1986): 13,145. Physicians (1986) 655. Life expectancy (1990): women 46, men 42. Infant mortality (1990): 158 per 1,000 live births.

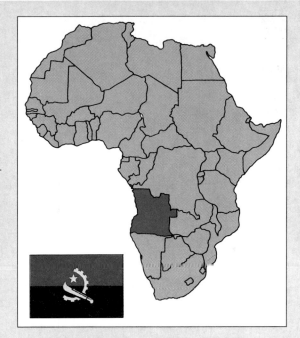

Located between the equator and the tropic of Capricorn, Angola has a tropical climate, moderated by the Benguela Current. The dry season extends from May to August, and the rainy season is from September to April.

Angola is a rich country, endowed with water, fertile agricultural lands, and minerals, but it lacks the economic resources and political stability to exploit its wealth.

People

Angola has three major ethnic groups: The OVIMBUNDU, who constitute about 35% of the population and live in the central highlands and the southern part of the country; the MBUNDU (25%), who live in the Luanda area and eastward; and the Kongo (15%), who live in the north. Before independence Portuguese numbered about 400,000; today they are fewer than 80,000. *Mestiços*, people of mixed ancestry, number about 160,000. Portuguese is the administrative language. Almost 60% of the population describe themselves as Christian; the remainder practice traditional religions.

Traditionally, 80% of the population lived in rural areas, but civil war caused hundreds of thousands to flee to the cities. Half the urban population is thought to be destitute. In addition to LUANDA, the capital, major cities include Huambo, Lobito, and Benguela.

Health facilities, never well developed, today are almost nonexistent. The infant mortality rate is now among the highest in the world. Educational facilities receive only 10% of the budget, and literacy is low.

Economic Activity

The civil war, the mass exodus of skilled people, and the government's nationalization plans crippled the economy. Military spending consumed nearly 45% of export earnings in 1986, and the purchase of military equipment has contributed to a substantial foreign debt.

The descent from the plateau to the coastal plain in Angola is often precipitous, offering great potential for hydroelectric power generation. These magnificent waterfalls are located on the Malange Plateau, west of Luanda.

(Right) *The population of Luanda, the capital of Angola, swelled from 300,000 in 1975 to nearly two million in 1988 due to an influx of war refugees from the countryside. Thousands of refugees in this and other cities live in squalid, overcrowded conditions.*

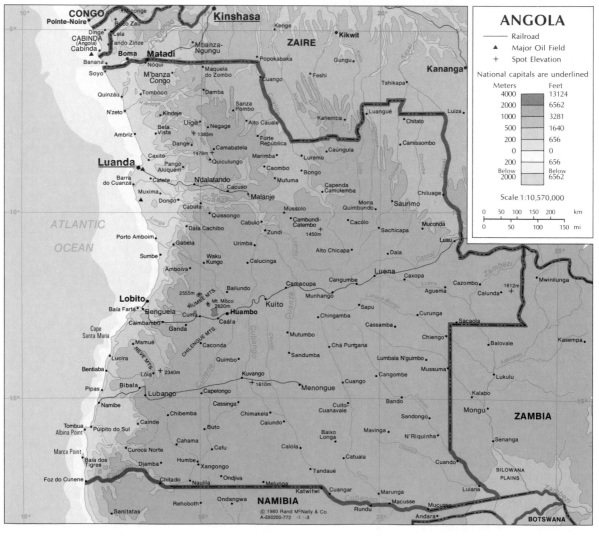

ANGOLA

— Railroad

▲ Major Oil Field

+ Spot Elevation

National capitals are underlined

Meters	Feet
4000	13124
2000	6562
1000	3281
500	1640
200	656
0	0
200	656
Below 2000	Below 6562

Scale 1:10,570,000

0 50 100 150 200 km
0   50   100   150 mi

© 1980 Rand McNally & Co.
A-580200-772 -1- -3

Angola once exported coffee, cotton, sugarcane, bananas, citrus fruits, and corn, but agricultural production was severely disrupted by the war. Bié and Huambo provinces, once the breadbasket of the nation, now produce less than half of the country's food needs, and food must be imported. The creation of state farms and centralized marketing systems also discouraged production. In 1988 the government announced a three-year plan to liberalize marketing practices and break up the collective farms.

Angola is rich in mineral resources: oil, diamonds, and iron ore. All mining except oil production (in Cabinda) was nearly halted by the war and the destruction of the infrastructure. The rail network, especially the important Benguela railway that connects mines in Zaire and Zambia with Atlantic ports, was periodically shut down, and roads in the central highlands became impassable because of land mines.

Electric power is not dependable; Luanda often suffers blackouts. In many areas, the water is not potable.

History and Government

Present-day Angola was originally inhabited by Khoisan hunters and gatherers. In the 13th century, Bantus migrating from West Africa pushed the Khoisan to the less productive areas. Several powerful Bantu kingships evolved, including the Kongo (see KONGO, KINGDOM OF), Loango, and Mbundu in western Angola. Lunda traders settled in the northeast, and to the south were the Ovimbundu and other small kingdoms.

Portuguese explorers first reached Angola in 1583. The colonial economy revolved around the slave trade until the late 1840s. The Portuguese lived in coastal cities, only gradually gaining enough control of the interior to claim Angola as a "sphere of influence."

After World War II, two African resistance groups were formed in Angola: the Popular Movement for the Liberation of Angola (MPLA), centered in Luanda and consisting mainly of Mbundu, and the Union of North Angolan Peoples, later the Union of Angolan Peoples (UPA). In 1961, Portugal dispatched thousands of troops to quell an African insurrection, killing nearly 50,000 Angolans and forcing the nationalists into exile. The exiled UPA merged with another group and became known as the National Front for the Liberation of Angola (FNLA). The FNLA, led by Holden Roberto, was recognized by the Organization of African Unity and received covert funding from the U.S. Central Intelligence Agency. Jonas SAVIMBI, the FNLA foreign minister, split with Roberto in 1964 and two years later formed the Union for the Total Independence of Angola (UNITA). In Brazzaville, Congo, Agostinho NETO revived the MPLA.

The three nationalist groups carried out low-level guerrilla activities, but internecine rivalries often inflicted more casualties than the Portuguese forces did. Suddenly, after a coup at home by the Portuguese military, Portugal decided in 1974 to liberate its colonies. Angola's liberation groups could not put aside their differences, however, and involvement by outside countries also increased. China and the United States supported the FNLA; the USSR and Cuba backed the MPLA; and South

Africa aided UNITA. In 1975 the war intensified as the MPLA pushed southward and South African troops crossed the Angola-Namibia border and marched toward Luanda. Cuba sent in thousands of combat troops to support the MPLA. Despite the absence of elections, the MPLA became the nominal governing party when Portugal withdrew in November 1975. Neto, the first president, died in 1979 and was succeeded by José Eduardo dos SANTOS.

As the MPLA extended its control, the FNLA faded and the contest for control fell to the MPLA and UNITA. In 1986 the United States began funding and supplying UNITA. In late 1987, South African troops moved into southern Angola in support of UNITA. Cuba responded by sending an additional 10,000 troops and, with its superior air power, forced South Africa to withdraw. In December 1988, Angola, Cuba, and South Africa signed accords setting forth timetables for the withdrawal of Cuban troops from Angola (by June 1991), an end to South African involvement there, and independence for neighboring Namibia (achieved 1990). In November 1990 the MPLA accepted the idea of multiparty democracy; in January 1991 it accepted in principle an international peace plan calling for a cease-fire and elections.

---

angora [ang-gohr'-uh]   Angora is the long, silky hair from either the Angora goat or the Angora rabbit; the goat is bred and raised commercially in the United States, South Africa, and Turkey and is named for the Turkish province of Angora, the historic name for Ankara. Angora goat hair, alone or blended with other fibers, is used to make mohair, a soft, luxurious, and expensive fabric. Mohair yarn is also blended with wool or synthetic fibers in a pile for coatings, draperies, and upholstery, or combined with cotton, wool, or rayon and woven into a shiny, stiff clothing material.

Angora cat   The term *Angora cat* once referred to a particular breed of long-haired cat thought to have originated in Turkey. By the 19th century, however, specific

The Turkish Angora, a new breed in the United States, has a regal appearance accentuated by its long body, plumelike tail, and long, fine hair. Its eyes are blue or amber. Occasionally, it has one eye of each color.

Angora characteristics had disappeared as Angoras were interbred with Persian cats. *Persian* then was used as the nomenclature for all long-haired cats. The Turkish Angora, a relatively new breed in the West, has been imported from Turkey and bred since 1953. It has a wedge-shaped head, silky white hair, and blue or amber eyes.

Angoulême [ahn-goo-lem']   Angoulême is the capital of Charente department in western France. Situated on the Charente River, it is about 100 km (60 mi) northeast of Bordeaux. Its population is 45,495 (1982). Angoulême manufactures a wide variety of goods, such as machinery, carpets and textiles, and paper products. It is also a center for the wine trade. The city has many Romanesque buildings, including the Cathedral of Saint Pierre (built 1105–28). Angoulême was taken by Clovis, king of the Franks, in AD 507 and became the seat of the counts of Angoulême in the 9th century. The city was much fought over and damaged during the Wars of Religion of the 16th century.

angstrom [ang'-struhm]   The angstrom is a unit of length used principally for expressing the wavelengths of radiation in the optical range. It is also used for smaller distances, such as those involving atoms and molecules. The unit was named for Anders Jonas Ångström of Sweden, who in 1868 first attempted to measure the wavelengths of light in metric units. One angstrom unit (abbreviated Å) is equal to 10^{-10} (one ten-billionth) meter, approximately the diameter of a hydrogen atom. Visible light is radiation that has wavelengths within the range of about 4000 to 7000 angstroms. Current terminology favors the use of the nanometer (nm) instead of the angstrom. One nanometer equals 10^{-9} meter, or 10 angstroms.

Ångström, Anders Jonas [awng'-strurm]   The Swedish physicist Anders Jonas Ångström, b. Aug. 13, 1814, d. June 21, 1874, was one of the founders of spectroscopy. He was appointed (1843) assistant professor of astronomy at Uppsala Observatory and was (1858–74) professor of physics at the University of Uppsala. In 1861, Ångström discovered hydrogen lines in the solar spectrum and subsequently confirmed the likely existence of other elements in the Sun. In 1867 he initiated spectral studies of auroras and, a year later, published an authoritative chart of the Sun's spectral lines, whose wavelengths he expressed in ångström (or angstrom) units.

Anguilla [ang-gwil'-uh]   Anguilla is a small British dependency located at the northern end of the Leeward Islands in the Caribbean Sea. It is a low-lying, semiarid coral island with an area of 91 km^2 (35 mi^2) and a maximum elevation of 61 m (200 ft). Its dry climate and thin soil hamper commercial agricultural development. An-guilla has a number of scenic beaches, and tourism and British aid are important to the economy. Most residents are involved in fishing and subsistence farming, raising such crops as pigeon peas, sweet potatoes, Indian corn, and beans. Anguilla has a population of 6,883 (1990 est.), which is predominantly black.

Discovered by Columbus in 1493, Anguilla was made a British colony in 1650. It was governed as part of Saint Kitts-Nevis-Anguilla from the early 18th century. Rebellion and secession occurred in 1967; following British intervention in 1969, Anguilla became a separate dependency with internal self-government, which was formalized by the Anguilla Act of 1980.

Anguissola, Sofonisba [ahng-gwee-soh'-lah, sohfawn-eez'-bah]   Sofonisba Anguissola, b. 1532?, d. Nov. 16, 1625, was one of the first prominent Italian women artists. The daughter of a Piedmontese nobleman, she left numerous self-portraits in which she emphasized her high social standing and education. Among Anguissola's best-known works is a family group portrait depicting her sisters playing chess (Muzeum Narodowe, Poznań, Poland).

angular momentum   Angular momentum is a measure of the energy of a rotating object or system of objects. The amount of angular momentum depends on the speed of rotation, mass, and mass distribution of the object or system. Mass distribution is known as the MOMENT OF INERTIA.

The significance of angular momentum is that it is a conserved quantity, as are matter and energy (see CONSERVATION, LAWS OF). Not only the magnitude, but also the direction of angular momentum of an isolated system, is conserved. Spinning skaters, for example, can control their rotation speed by raising or lowering their arms. Lowering outstretched arms decreases the moment of inertia, which causes an increase in the rate of rotation. Thus the angular momentum of the skaters remains constant.

The Earth and Moon serve as a good example of how angular momentum is conserved in a system. They revolve about a common center of gravity, and each turns on its own axis. The Earth's spin is gradually slowing down as a result of the influence of the tides. The loss of angular momentum from the Earth's rotation is transferred to the Moon's orbit and causes the Moon to slowly recede from the Earth.

Spinning tops and GYROSCOPES remain upright because the direction of angular momentum is conserved. Thus they resist the outside forces, such as gravity, that tend to topple them (see PRECESSION).

See also: CORIOLIS EFFECT; MOTION, CIRCULAR; TORQUE.

Angus   Angus, previously called Forfarshire, was a county in eastern Scotland until 1975, when it was incorporated into the Tayside administrative region. Angus was bounded by the North Sea on the east and the Firth of Tay on the south. Forfar was the county town. DUNDEE is the largest city and major port in the area. Cattle and sheep are raised in the glens and upland areas, and the fertile lowlands produce cereal grains, sugar beets, and seed potatoes. Industries include linen and jute mills, fishing, shipbuilding, and engineering. Occupied by the Picts during the Roman period, Angus began to prosper during the 12th century when Flemish immigrants introduced the wool and linen industries.

Angus cattle   see CATTLE AND CATTLE RAISING

Anhui (Anhwei) [ahn'-hway]   Anhui is a province in east central China along the Chang Jiang (Yangtze) River. Covering 140,000 km^2 (54,000 mi^2), it is bounded by the provinces of Jiangsu on the north and east, Zhejiang on the south, and Henan on the west. Its capital is HEFEI, and its population is 52,726,000 (1987 est.). In the drier and cooler northern half of Anhui, wheat, millet, soybeans, and cotton are cultivated. In the hilly sections of southern Anhui, tea, rice, and silkworms are grown. Iron ore, coal, lead, and zinc are mined, and refined near the cities of Ma'anshan, Hefei, and Anqing. Textiles, chemicals, paper, and machinery are manufactured in those cities. Anhui was ruled by the Ming dynasty from the 14th to the 17th century as part of the province of Jiangnan. It was made a separate province under the Qing (1644–1911) dynasty.

anhydride [an-hy'-dryd]   In chemistry, an anhydride is a compound produced by removing water or the elements of water from an acid or a base. Acid anhydrides are usually oxides of the nonmetallic elements. For example, phosphorous pentoxide, P_2O_5, is the anhydride of phosphoric acid, H_3PO_4. Basic anhydrides are usually oxides of the metallic elements. For example, calcium oxide, CaO, or lime, is the anhydride of calcium hydroxide, $Ca(OH)_2$, or slaked lime. Organic acid anhydrides are an important class of compounds with the following general formula:

$$R-\overset{\overset{\textstyle O}{\|}}{C}-O-\overset{\overset{\textstyle O}{\|}}{C}-R'$$

in which R and R′ denote hydrocarbon groups. The addition of water to an organic anhydride generates the two carboxylic acid molecules RCOOH and R′COOH.

anhydrite [an-hy'-dryt]   Anhydrite, $CaSO_4$, is a calcium SULFATE MINERAL resembling GYPSUM but without any water in its chemical makeup. It forms pearly white masses showing cubic cleavage and has a hardness of 3–3½ and a specific gravity of 2.9–3.0. It is found with halite, gypsum, and other EVAPORITES and is used as a soil conditioner and as an additive to cement.

ani [ah-nee']   Ani is the common name for three species of tropical American birds that make up the genus *Crotophaga* in the cuckoo family, Cuculidae. Dull to iridescent black, anis resemble grackles but have longer, heavier tails and somewhat parrotlike bills. Anis prefer farm country and feed on a wide variety of seeds, fruits, and insects. They have short wings and a weak, flapping flight, and they habitually flip their loosely hinged tails in all directions.

The smooth-billed ani and the groove-billed ani (bottom), are found in the southern United States. Anis, also called tickbirds, often pick ticks off cattle.

aniline [an'-uh-lin]   Aniline is an oily, toxic liquid that is colorless when pure and has a peculiar aroma. Its formula is $C_6H_5NH_2$; it boils at 184°–186° C and solidifies at -6° C. Aniline is the simplest member of the class of aromatic AMINES, which are related to both benzene and ammonia. Aniline is manufactured on a large scale. It is used to make a wide variety of other organic chemical compounds, particularly substances that accelerate the vulcanization of rubber and that protect rubber from attack by oxygen. Aniline also is converted into pharmaceuticals, photographic chemicals, and DYE intermediates.

animal   Animals are members of the kingdom Animalia, which comprises all multicellular organisms whose cells are bound only by a plasma membrane and not by a cell wall of cellulose, as in plants. Animals obtain energy by acquiring and ingesting their food, unlike plants, which use photosynthesis to manufacture their nutrients. Both animals and plants are eucaryotes; that is, their cells contain organelles. In animals, the cells are organized into tissues and specialized tissue systems that permit the animals to move freely in search of food or that allow nonmotile, or fixed, animals to draw food toward themselves. A developed nervous system enables animals to receive environmental stimuli and to respond with specialized movements. In contrast with plants, most animals have a limited growth pattern and mature to reach a well-defined shape and size.

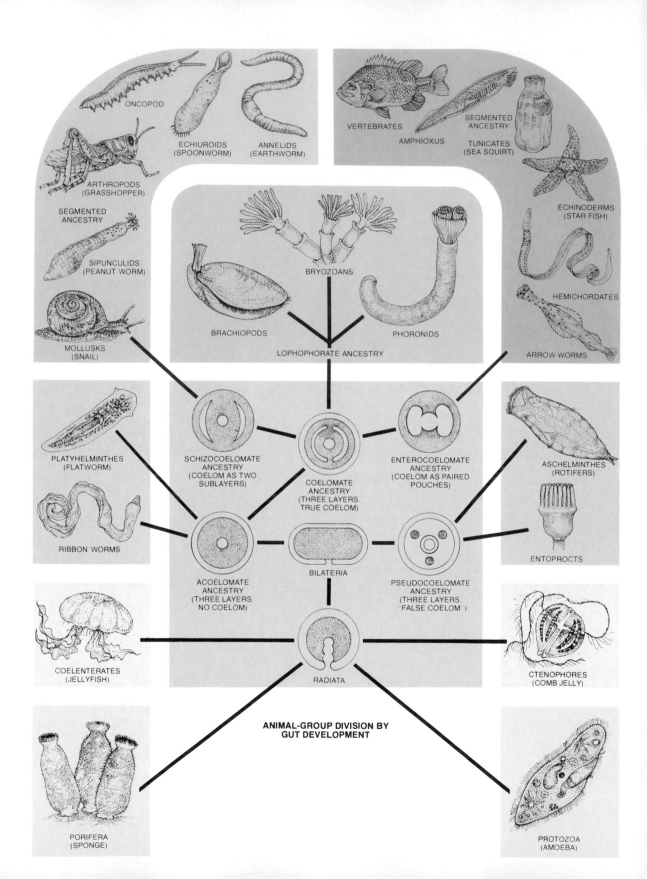

ONCOPOD

ECHIUROIDS
(SPOONWORM)

ANNELIDS
(EARTHWORM)

ARTHROPODS
(GRASSHOPPER)

SEGMENTED
ANCESTRY

SIPUNCULIDS
(PEANUT WORM)

MOLLUSKS
(SNAIL)

VERTEBRATES

AMPHIOXUS

SEGMENTED
ANCESTRY

TUNICATES
(SEA SQUIRT)

ECHINODERMS
(STAR FISH)

HEMICHORDATES

ARROW WORMS

BRYOZOANS

BRACHIOPODS

PHORONIDS

LOPHOPHORATE ANCESTRY

PLATYHELMINTHES
(FLATWORM)

RIBBON WORMS

SCHIZOCOELOMATE
ANCESTRY
(COELOM AS TWO
SUBLAYERS)

COELOMATE
ANCESTRY
(THREE LAYERS,
TRUE COELOM)

ENTEROCOELOMATE
ANCESTRY
(COELOM AS PAIRED
POUCHES)

ASCHELMINTHES
(ROTIFERS)

ENTOPROCTS

ACOELOMATE
ANCESTRY
(THREE LAYERS,
NO COELOM)

BILATERIA

PSEUDOCOELOMATE
ANCESTRY
(THREE LAYERS,
"FALSE COELOM")

COELENTERATES
(JELLYFISH)

RADIATA

CTENOPHORES
(COMB JELLY)

**ANIMAL-GROUP DIVISION BY
GUT DEVELOPMENT**

PORIFERA
(SPONGE)

PROTOZOA
(AMOEBA)

The differences between plants and animals led to a division of all life into the two kingdoms Plantae and Animalia. On investigation of microorganisms, however, it was found that some were clearly plantlike while others, PROTOZOA, resembled animals in that they had locomotion and digested food. Initially protozoans were placed in a subkingdom of Animalia. This classification still presented problems: some forms showed mixed characteristics, and some groups had photosynthetic members that were plantlike with close relatives that were animallike. Eventually a five-kingdom system came into general use, in which Plantae and Animalia are more restricted in definition and protozoan groups are assigned to the kingdom PROTISTA (see CLASSIFICATION, BIOLOGICAL).

The kingdom Animalia can be subdivided into two subkingdoms. The subkingdom Parazoa comprises SPONGES, phylum Porifera. Their nutritional needs are met through ingestion by individual cells located along internal water canals that open to the outside of the body. They are nonmotile organisms, but certain cells are flagellated. The tissue is the highest organizational level. The larger subkingdom is Eumetazoa, which means "advanced multicellular animals." These animals can be classified into two groups, Radiata and Bilateria, according to the type of body symmetry of the animal, whose organizational level goes beyond that of tissue.

Radiata. The Radiata comprise two phyla, Coelenterata and Ctenophora, with radial symmetry. The COELENTERATES include CORALS, HYDRAS, JELLYFISHES, and SEA ANEMONES. Their mouths are encircled by tentacles. Within the tentacles and elsewhere in the body are nematocysts—harpoonlike structures that are discharged from specialized cells in which they are cocked when not in use. The nematocytes stun prey, then the tentacles bring the prey into the mouth. Coelenterates have a "two-layered" body. The ectoderm is the outer layer, and the endoderm is the inner layer. The two layers surround the digestive cavity, the coelenteron, which has only one opening. Thus the highest level of complexity in Radiata is the organ. The Ctenophora, or COMB JELLIES, are similar to the Coelenterata, but they have two tentacles and eight rows of hairlike structures (cilia), each row resembling a comb (cteno).

Bilateria. The Bilateria are bilaterally symmetrical. The body plan is organized along a longitudinal axis, and one half is a mirror image of the other. The organ system is the highest level of complexity reached. Bilateria can be divided into three groups—Acoelomata, Pseudocoelomata, and Coelomata.

The Acoelomata lack a true body cavity, the COELOM. They have a "three-layered" body. The space between the ectoderm and endoderm is occupied entirely by the mesoderm. The FLATWORMS, phylum Platyhelminthes, and RIBBON WORMS, phylum Nemertia, are members of Acoelomata. The best known of the flatworms is the PLANARIAN, whose muscle cells and principal organ systems are of mesodermal origin, as in higher animals. Although like coelenterates they have a digestive cavity, or gut, with only one opening, an excretory system is present.

The Pseudocoelomata differ from the Acoelomata in that the mesodermal layer does not completely occupy the region between the ectoderm and endoderm. The free space is a body cavity, in this case a "pseudo," or false, body cavity. The cavity is present only because the germinal tissue (meso), which ordinarily gives rise to a coelom, does not develop as extensively as in acoelomates. Thus this cavity is not formed within tissues that appear in this region in the course of embryonic development. The most familiar animals in this group are roundworms, or nematodes. The tubular gut has openings to a mouth and an anus.

The Coelomata constitute the remaining Bilateria. The mesoderm comes to form two sublayers, one along the ectoderm and the other along the endoderm. The space between is the coelom, a true body cavity, enclosed entirely with mesoderm with a membrane lining, the peritoneum.

The development of a true body cavity is of great evolutionary significance. Space in the mesoderm means that organ systems have the flexibility to bend or twist, and functional space can be increased by increasing the surface area; an example is the 6 m (20 ft) or more of coiled human small intestine. Also, organs in the body can more easily fill and empty.

The Coelomata are subdivided depending on where the mouth is formed during embryonic development. The two subdivisions are protostomes and deuterostomes. In protostomes, the mouth develops where the blastopore is present. When an egg cell has been fertilized by a sperm cell, a hollow sphere of cells, or blastula, forms. The blastopore is an opening on the outer space of the blastula and leads directly into the gut. Commonly known protostomes are ANNELIDS, such as EARTHWORMS; ARTHROPODS, such as INSECTS and LOBSTERS; and MOLLUSKS, such as CLAMS and SNAILS. BRACHIOPODS, BRYOZOANS, phoronids, sipunculids, and echiuroids are lesser-known members of this group. The Acoelomata and Pseudocoelomata are also protostomes.

In deuterostomes, the mouth develops in a region diametrically opposite to where the blastopore is present. In a sense it is a second mouth. The first mouth—the blastopore—seals off at the hind region of the embryo after the primitive gut has formed. SEA URCHINS, STARFISH, and all vertebrates are commonly known deuterostomes. Acorn worms, HEMICHORDATES, and ARROWWORMS, Chaetognatha, are lesser-known members.

The relationships between certain animal groups are shown (opposite page) *in terms of the evolution of the coelom, the body cavity in which the principal internal organs are located. As unicellular organisms developed into multicellular animals, such as jellyfish, cells were grouped into two layers—the external ectoderm and the internal endoderm—separated by the mesoderm, a middle layer derived from one or both of the other layers. While the mesoderm became organized into tissues and organs in acoelomates, such as flatworms, it completely filled the interior region of the body. In pseudocoelomates such as rotifers, the mesoderm and its derived organs were restricted to particular sections of the body, leaving a fluid-filled cavity between the ectoderm and endoderm. Higher animals, however, developed a true coelom, a cavity completely lined by a mesodermal membrane, which forms the central core of the body.*

The Coelomata are also subdivided into three super-phyla, depending on the method by which the coelom arises in the embryo. In lophophorates the coeloms form in several unique ways. In schizocoelomates, the coelom arises when the original mesoderm layer splits into outer and inner layers. This group, as well as the lophophorates, includes the protostome Coelomata. The enterocoelo-mates are the remaining Coelomata and are deuteros-tomes. Their coeloms form as paired pouches growing out of the endoderm. Later the pouches lose their connection with the endoderm and become independent mesoderm sacs enclosing coelomic spaces. Included in the group is the phylum Chordata.

Chordate Animals

To be classified as a CHORDATE, an animal must have, at some time in its development, a notochord, a hollow dorsal nerve cord (spinal cord), and a slitted pharyngeal cavity (gill slits). Urochordates (TUNICATES), a subgroup of Chordata, have these features in the larval stage. In metamorphosing into adults they retain the pharynx but lose the notochord and nerve cord. A second subgroup, the CEPHALOCHORDATA (AMPHIOXUS), retains all three chordate features throughout life. Members of the third subgroup, the Vertebrata, are distinguished by a vertebral column, which surrounds the dorsal notochord. This structure is formed from cartilage or bony tissue, or both. In some vertebrates, especially the HAGFISH and LAMPREYS, it appears only in an incipient form, which is scarcely discernible. The notochord is a stiff, rodlike structure that appears in the embryo along the median line of the back. It is retained throughout life in only a few chordates, such as in the amphioxus, a group of wormlike marine species. In these animals, as well as in all other chordates, the notochord induces the formation of the hollow dorsal nerve cord.

Invertebrate Animals

Before the evolutionary relationship between urochordates and cephalochordates to vertebrate chordates was understood, the word INVERTEBRATE was coined for animals that lack a vertebral column. Today it is customary to think of nonchordate animals as invertebrates; although it is not incorrect to think of urochordates and cephalochordates as being invertebrates, in practice it is the vertebrate biologist who is most concerned with these two groups of chordates because of their direct evolutionary link to vertebrates.

See also: ZOOLOGY.

──

animal behavior   Behavior is a fundamental characteristic of animal life. All species, whether single-celled protozoans or the largest of mammals, possess the capacity to respond to stimuli in their environment. An understanding of how and why animals behave the way they do has come from the disciplines of psychology and biology. Psychologists have focused on the learned components of behavior and the experimental dissection of the bases of learning. John B. WATSON's *Behaviorism* (1925)

led to the development of the behaviorist school, whose main modern exponent has been B. F. SKINNER.

Biologists, however, have devoted their efforts primarily to the analysis of the innate components of behavior with an emphasis on nonexperimental studies of animals under natural conditions. The biological study of animal behavior was developed between 1930 and 1950 by Konrad LORENZ and Nikolaas TINBERGEN, the founders of ETHOLOGY. These European biologists used as a guiding principle of their research the idea that behavioral traits were likely to be adaptive, that is, they were likely to help individuals reproduce successfully. This argument is a direct outgrowth of the theory of evolution presented by Charles DARWIN in 1859. Darwin's theory of evolution by NATURAL SELECTION serves as a conceptual framework for modern biology. Darwin realized that evolution occurs when members of a species differ in the number of surviving offspring they produce. Traits that produce individual reproductive success tend to survive in populations, and traits associated with reproductive failure tend to disappear.

The European ethologists assumed that the behavior of animal species had evolved by natural selection. They recognized that each species of bird, fish, or insect possesses a well-defined and unique repertoire of behavioral patterns. The key question that energized the ethologists was: how might the particular behavioral abilities of a given species help individuals leave as many surviving descendants as possible? To explain why species differ behaviorally, the ethologists developed two different approaches. Their first goal was to determine the adaptive, or reproductive, significance of each species' behavior pattern. A kittiwake gull builds an elaborate nest with a deep cup on a narrow cliff ledge; a black-headed gull constructs a casual, shallow nest of grass stems on the ground. This difference appears to have adaptive significance, since the cup-shaped nest prevents the kittiwake's eggs from rolling off the cliff and thus enhances its reproductive success, whereas the ground-nesting gull has no adaptive gain from the extra effort of carefully building a nest.

The second avenue of research was to understand how the genetic-physiological mechanisms within an individual produce its behavior patterns. The ethologists found evidence that the nervous systems of many species have components designed to detect and respond to simple cues, or sign stimuli. A European robin will violently attack a tuft of red feathers tied to a limb in its territory, just as if the tuft were a male intruder. The red feathers act as a sign stimulus that activates a brain mechanism and triggers a programmed response, or fixed action pattern, to the releasing cue.

These two kinds of research—one focusing on adaptive or evolutionary properties of behavior and the other on underlying mechanisms of behavior—continue to be the major concerns of ethology. Because ethology is linked to genetics, physiology, ecology, and evolutionary biology, it has improved the understanding of these diverse subjects. It has also raised the hope that knowledge gained from a study of other animals may lead to a better understanding of human behavior.

Categories of Behavior

Partly as a result of work on the genetic and physiological bases of behavior, many scientists are no longer willing to accept a division of behavior patterns into just two categories—instincts and learning. Behavior geneticists have shown that no behavior is purely "genetically determined" or purely "environmentally determined." Instead, they claim that all behavioral traits have both a genetic and an environmental foundation. This does not mean that all behavioral patterns are fundamentally the same. Physiological work has demonstrated that many different kinds of neural and hormonal mechanisms are responsible for the different abilities of animals.

Closed Instincts. One of the many possible categories of behavior could be called closed instincts—behavior patterns that are produced in complete and functional form the first time they are given and that cannot be altered by experiences associated with their performance. Many animal courtship displays and signals may belong in this category. For example, in one species of grasshopper the male courts the female with a complex sequence of leg-rubbing movements, head rocking, antenna waving, and intense stridulation; the activities and the sequence in which they are performed never vary. The animal appears to have a "motor tape" that is resistant to modification and that can be played back over and over.

Open Instincts. Some innate responses are open to change. Open instincts may be altered as a result of the consequences of these behaviors. Presumably, the underlying neural circuitry can store information about the effects of the behavior and modify it so that the animal achieves rewards more often and punishments less often. A jackdaw has an innate tendency to collect materials when building its nest for the first time, but it may return

Konrad Lorenz, an Austrian ethologist, is followed by greylag goslings, imprinted to consider him their mother. Lorenz's clarification of the concept that simple cues or sign stimuli trigger certain behaviors complemented his work on imprinting.

to its nest site with ice cubes or light bulbs. When the bird attempts to shove unsuitable objects into the mound of nest material, it cannot do so, but when it brings back twigs, it can. Jackdaws store information gained by trying to fit different things into a nest mound; this modifies their original response. Eventually, the bird will collect only those twigs which result in the construction of a strong, stable platform.

Closely related to open instincts are behavior patterns that develop fully only if the individual is exposed to a special learning experience. A classic example is IMPRINT-ING. Soon after hatching, ducklings follow their mother from the nest and form an attachment that endures during their dependent period. As they follow the mother, they learn the visual traits that characterize all females of their species. The males use this acquired information

(Right) *Nikolaas Tinbergen, a Dutch-born founder of ethology, is shown painting chicken eggs to look like herring-gull eggs as part of a field experiment to test the adaptive value of gull behavior. (Below) The Austrian Karl von Frisch won the Nobel Prize (with Lorenz and Tinbergen) for his work on honey-bee behavior and for the discovery of a complex communication system used by worker bees to convey information about food sources.*

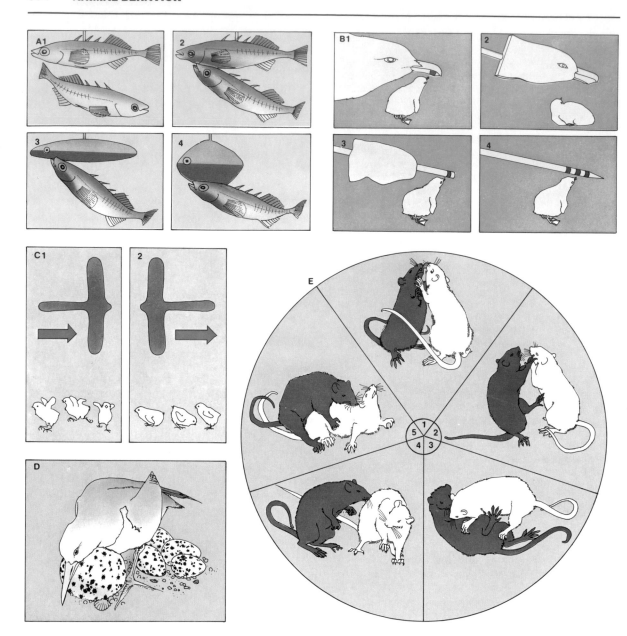

Five well-known animal behavior studies demonstrate instinctive and learned interactions among animals. (A) The male stickleback (1) ignores other males except during mating season, when the bellies of all males turn red. Then, a male (2) attacks another male as well as differently shaped objects (3,4) that have red markings, indicating that the red belly stimulates aggression. (B) A herring gull chick pecks at a red spot on its parent's beak (1), the parent in response feeding its offspring. The chick ignores a gull-like model (2) that has no red spot; oddly shaped objects (3,4) with red spots, however, stimulate a feeding response from the chick. (C) Turkey chicks run from a hawk-shaped silhouette (1) but not from the shadow of a long-necked bird (2). Newly hatched chicks run from all shadows but later learn to distinguish familiar shadows, such as commonly seen geese, from unfamiliar ones, such as a hawk. Chicks of many species crouch when an unfamiliar shadow passes by. (D) A herring gull tries to brood a large model egg in preference to its own eggs, revealing a magnified response to stimuli. (E) A female rat (white) rejects a male's sexual overtures for three days of her hormonal cycle and goes into heat the 4th and 5th days.

many months later to recognize females for courtship and mating. If very young male ducks or geese are experimentally removed from their mother and permitted to follow a chicken or even a human being, they will attempt to court and copulate with members of these species when they are mature.

Another highly specialized form of learning that occurs during a relatively short but critical period of a bird's ear-

.ly life is song learning. Experiments with white-crowned sparrows have shown that the young male can learn only the territorial song that is peculiar to his species and that the song can be learned only during the first eight weeks of his life. Isolated white-crowned sparrows that hear another bird species' song, but not a white-crown song, will never sing their species' typical song. This also holds true if they are not exposed to their species' song until late in the first year of life or if they are held in complete auditory isolation.

Young humans are also remarkably adept at imitating human language sounds and extracting the grammatical rules that organize a language. For example, English-speaking children learn at a young age that adding *ed* to a verb indicates that the action took place in the past. They use this rule to create novel words, such as *teached*. Therefore, human language learning may also depend on a selective neural mechanism for information storage and speech development.

Other kinds of learning are even more open than language learning. For example, a wide variety of animals have the ability to store information about visual landmarks and other cues that are associated with their home range. In addition to exploratory learning, conditioning (or trial-and-error learning) falls into the category of flexible learning. Many animals can be conditioned through reward or punishment to associate certain cues with any of a broad variety of actions. Thus, laboratory rats can quickly learn to vacate a room when a light comes on if a shock regularly follows the light. Conditioning procedures can also be used to train humans to lower their heart rate or to alter their brain waves.

Researchers interested in the adaptive significance of behavior have suggested that the variety of behavior types (and the variety of underlying neural and hormonal mechanisms associated with the behaviors) have evolved because different behaviors solve different kinds of problems. For example, if females copulate only with males that give clear and unambiguous signals that they belong to the same species, closed instincts for male courtship-display may be superior to any learned behavior. Many escape responses fall into this category because the avoidance of enemies is usually best accomplished by a single, innate reaction.

Genetics of Behavior

All behavioral abilities depend on underlying genetic mechanisms. Animal behavior is the product of nerve cells and muscles. The development of these tissues is dependent on the genetic information in the cells of the developing animal. Genes contain information that is used to make key protein molecules (enzymes) that regulate the biochemical reactions within cells and thereby control their developmental destiny. A greylag goose can roll a displaced egg back into her nest because her neural networks enable her to detect the egg and maneuver it into the nest with her bill. These networks could not have developed without specific enzymes, and these in turn required genetic information for their manufacture.

The degree to which specific genes or batteries of

This sequence shows that even so-called lower animals, such as the digger wasp, are capable of learning.

A female digger wasp, also called a "bee wolf," carries its paralyzed honeybee prey back to its offspring, contained within a nest burrow in the ground (1). She learns the nest's location by memorizing nearby landmarks. (2) In a famous demonstration of landmark learning, pine cones were placed around the nest while the wasp was inside. (3) The wasp emerged and made a brief orientation flight around the nest before flying off to hunt. (4) The experimenter moved the circle of pine cones, and later, when the wasp returned with prey, it flew to the ring's center, instead of the actual nest entrance.

genes are responsible for the control of individual behavior patterns is an unresolved issue being explored in the discipline of BEHAVIORAL GENETICS. Already, behavioral geneticists have demonstrated that a manipulation of genetic factors influences the development of specific behavioral abilities. They have discovered that behavioral differences among some individuals may be a result of a single genetic difference. Examples are mice that have abnormal patterns of locomotion and honeybees that fail to uncap a brood cell to remove a diseased pupa from the hive. In each case these behavioral variants occur because of the alteration of a single gene. This does not show that only one gene exists for each behavior pattern or ability but rather that the molecular product of one gene can be so important to muscle or nervous-system development that if it is altered the development of the foundation for a behavioral ability will be changed.

Scientists interested in the role of the environment in behavioral development have also shown that certain kinds of experience may be influential. For example, social interactions in young monkeys and apes have a strong effect on their capacity to exhibit normal social behavior later in life. An integrated interaction of genetic and environmental factors is required for the development of functional nervous and endocrine systems in an animal. These systems in turn are responsible for the behavior patterns of the individual.

The Physiology of Behavior

Behavioral geneticists are just beginning to explore the relationship between specific genes and the development of the physiological mechanisms for behavior. In the past, physiologists have shown how some neural and hormonal mechanisms control certain behavior patterns. They have

Lions are classic examples of animals that cooperate primarily in order to increase their chance to survive and reproduce. The members of a pride may cooperate to kill a prey, such as the Thomson's gazelle shown here. But after the kill, individuals compete fiercely for possession of the prey. As a result, cubs must fend for themselves and often starve

found specialized sensory neurons in a variety of animals that react preferentially to biologically important stimuli. Thus, in the retina of the leopard frog's eye are cells that produce many impulses when a small, dark, rounded object passes erratically through the visual field of the frog. Since bugs have such properties, these cells have been labeled bug detectors. They make a major contribution to the leopard frog's ability to detect and capture flying insects, which are a prime component of the frog's diet. The male silk moth's antennae have many sensory cells that send impulses ("fire") only when air containing the chemical sex attractant, or sex PHEROMONE, of female silk moths passes over the antennae. Only males that detect the pheromone are able to find a mate and reproduce.

Animals not only perceive biologically significant objects in their environment, they react appropriately to their perceptions. The frog's bug detectors are linked to neural components that activate orientation, mouth opening, and tongue flipping. When a male silk moth's pheromone detectors fire, they send messages to regions of the brain; this causes the moth to fly upward toward the source of the pheromone.

A special neural foundation is the basis for the fixed action patterns of lower animals and also for the learned behavior of humans and other species. Neurophysiologists have found well-defined regions of the human cerebral cortex that contribute to language learning. One region is involved in storing information about the sounds associated with words; this source contributes to the recognition of word meaning. Another portion of the brain plays a key role in extracting the right words from the language memory bank and putting them together in a grammatical order so that they will make sense to a listener. Damage to the first region results in the loss of the ability to produce meaningful sentences, and the person can no longer understand spoken or written language. Damage to the second region of the cortex leads to the loss of the ability to speak fluently and grammatically, although the person can still read and understand spoken language.

The brains of animals appear to have special batteries of nerve cells responsible for detecting certain stimuli and performing biologically correct responses to them. Moreover, animals are able to decide which of their behavior patterns to employ at a given moment, even though they may be receiving sensory information from various objects that could trigger contradictory activities, such as flying to

Musk-oxen of the arctic tundra of Greenland and northern Canada cooperate to ward off an attack by wolves. The oxen mass in close formation, in which the bulls, with their hooves and sharp horns, face outward, and cows and calves huddle in the center. This behavior furnishes protection against wolves but has made the oxen easy prey to humans, who shoot them from a distance.

a mate and avoiding an onrushing enemy. The neural networks responsible for different behavior patterns are organized according to a schedule of priorities. For example, escape behavior usually takes precedence over attempts to find a mate.

The hierarchy of priorities need not be constant. A frog that has just eaten a great deal no longer responds to stimuli that would have activated a response when it was hungry. Feeding may or may not have priority over other activities, depending on the internal condition of the animal. Individuals have sensors to detect changing conditions and to alter their behavioral tendencies accordingly. Of special interest are annual cycles of behavior. These are often regulated by changing patterns of hormonal releases. For example, increasing day-length in spring is usually an important cue for migratory birds. This environmental change triggers multiple hormonal effects, leading to fat deposition and migratory restlessness. After the birds migrate, new patterns of hormone release cause development of the gonads, territoriality in males, courtship, and then incubation of the eggs and feeding of the young. If any element of behavior were to occur out of phase, the result would be reproductive failure.

The Adaptive Significance of Behavior

A key technique for determining the function of a behavioral trait is to compare animal species. If unrelated animals exhibit behavioral similarities and if they also share a similar ecological pressure, the behavior may have evolved because it solved the shared ecological problem. For example, in langurs, females and their offspring form groups that live and forage together. A male that can join a band will have many more progeny than a male that cannot. As a result, male langurs compete fiercely. If an outsider succeeds in ousting a resident male, he tries to kill the infant members of the band, despite the attempts of the females to protect their offspring. Although this was once thought to be pathological behavior, the infanticidal male is behaving in a way that probably maximizes his reproductive success. By killing his competitor's progeny he is lowering the reproductive output of another individual and thereby raising his own success relative to that male. In addition, the females that lose their infants become receptive again, ovulate, and are fertilized by the new male. If they had not lost their offspring, they would not have become receptive for several years. Thus, the in-

A male gelada monkey from an all-male troop raids a harem protected by one adult male. The two males display a threat yawn by rolling back their upper lips and baring their teeth. Threat gestures permit individuals to assess their chances of winning in a "real" fight. Males that determine they would lose in all-out combat retreat to fight another day.

fant-killer gains more opportunities to pass on his genes. This behavior can plausibly be interpreted as the product of natural selection. Selection, it should be noted, favors traits that help one individual to have more offspring than another, whether or not this is in the best interests of the species as a whole.

This process also occurs in totally unrelated species that are subject to similar ecological conditions. Female lions form groups (prides) that are the object of aggressive competition among males. Single male lions or small groups of males that claim a pride exclude other males from it, sometimes assaulting and even killing competitors. If intruders succeed in driving out the former leaders of the pride, they often systematically search out and kill the infants sired by the deposed males.

Although the imprint of natural selection is evident most strongly in reproductive behavior itself, the evolved function of other categories of behavior also enhances the reproductive success of individuals. Many behavior patterns associated with selecting a place to live, avoiding predators, and finding food have a positive effect on individual reproductive output. For example, habitat selection by the desert woodrat is tied to the presence of cholla

cactus in its environment. This cactus produces sausage-like limbs that easily break off and fall to the ground or attach themselves tenaciously to a passing animal. A woodrat will gingerly use pieces of cactus for construction of a home nest. The cacti help make the rat's home safe against its many predators.

Researchers feel that the importance of safe and productive living space is seen in the number of species that will defend a home area against intruders. Territoriality evolves in species living in an area that is small enough to be economically defensible and that contains valuable resources that are in limited supply and are important for reproductive success. Individuals are often territorial when a relatively small area contains a nest site or a high concentration of food items; males will often defend such a territory if it is inhabited by females of the species. In a number of nectar-feeding birds, measurements have been made on the calories expended to defend a territory containing the flowers. Results have shown that sunbirds and hummingbirds are territorial only when the calories gained exceed the calories expended in defense. The social system of these species is flexible, with individuals establishing and abandoning territories as nectar production and the number of intruders vary. This flexibility enables birds to maximize energy gained from feeding and so, presumably, to maximize the number of offspring they produce.

The importance of feeding behavior has resulted in the evolution of many unusual adaptations. For example, certain predatory fireflies wait in the vegetation for a light-flashing male of another species to pass by. When the passing male gives his species-specific courtship signals, the predator responds with the "come hither" light flash that is normally given by a female of his species. Males that alight and hurry to the calling predator are killed.

Prey species have evolved many effective antipredator adaptations. Social species often take advantage of group cooperation for mutual defense, as in the defensive circle formed by attacked musk-oxen. Group defense reaches extreme complexity in the insect societies. In ant and termite colonies, members of a soldier caste may employ elaborate communication systems for alerting each other when danger threatens. Groups of defenders converge on the intruders and dispatch them with crushing jaws or chemical sprays, or, in one case, by hurling themselves at the enemy while bursting open their bodies and spilling entangling glue from a ruptured abdominal gland on their foe. Cases in which individuals commit suicide pose a special problem for evolutionary theorists because such behavior would appear to eliminate the very genes that contribute to the development of the behavior. But suicidal ant workers are, in the first place, sterile; their AL-TRUISM, or self-sacrificing behavior, indirectly helps propagate their own genes by protecting reproducing relatives that share the same genes.

The Evolution of Human Behavior

Ever since Darwin's time, applying evolutionary theory to human beings has been controversial. Edward O. Wilson's *Sociobiology* touched off an academic firestorm in 1975 because of a chapter that claimed that human behavior has been designed by natural selection to promote the genetic success of individuals (see SOCIOBIOLOGY). In part this controversy stemmed from fears by some that evolutionary analyses are easily misunderstood and easy to misuse. Thus, although evolutionary biologists such as Wilson have not concluded that human behavior is a collection of closed instincts nor that it is morally correct to try to have as many offspring as possible, critics of human sociobiology fear that the evolutionary approach may foster the belief that all human behaviors, including AGGRESSION and sexism, cannot be changed and should not be changed because they are supposedly adaptive.

Proponents of human sociobiology claim that their goal is simply to test evolutionary hypotheses for human attributes. For example, it is well known that humans generally find bitter substances repellent and sweet-tasting foods pleasing. This preference is controlled by neural networks in the brain that could not have developed without special genetic information possessed by humans. Evolutionary biologists have asked why current human taste perceptions might have increased an individual's chances of producing surviving offspring in the past. One hypothesis is that the human brain "encourages" the consumption of foods that contain valuable calories, while discouraging ingestion of life-threatening substances. This hypothesis leads to the prediction that sweet-tasting foods are edible and nutritious whereas extremely bitter-tasting materials are toxic, which is generally the case.

Attempts to test ideas about the reproductive significance of human behavior have now been made on a wide spectrum of human activities. For example, it is clear that parental behavior is a costly exercise in the sense of requiring much energetic effort and exposing parents to risks that might shorten their adult lives. The evolutionary return may be an increased chance of survival of the children that the parents help. This increase can advance the genetic interests of the parent only if the children are the genetic offspring of the parent. Therefore, evolutionary biologists have hypothesized that all parental species, humans included, should have evolved psychological mechanisms that engender discriminating child care only for their own offspring.

This hypothesis leads to the prediction that males will be highly concerned about the paternity of their wives' offspring and will often react with rage and withdrawal of parental support if they discover or suspect that their wives have committed adultery; this is apparently the case in most societies. Another prediction that flows from the evolutionary analysis of parental care is that child abuse will occur more often in households with step-parents than in households with two biological parents. Various studies have supported this prediction. Evolutionary biologists do not claim that excessive sexual jealousy or child abuse is adaptive behavior per se. Instead their point is that if our psychological mechanisms have evolved as a result of past differences in individual reproductive success, the mechanisms can be expected to bias human behavior in predictable ways that would usually, but not always, raise individual reproductive success.

Much remains to be learned about both the mechanisms and the adaptive significance of the behavior of humans and other animals. Future research will surely focus on the links between genetic information, physiological design, and behavioral traits. Improved knowledge of these relationships will aid in understanding how natural selection can shape the evolution of behavior by affecting the transmission of genes from one generation to the next.

See also: ADAPTIVE RADIATION; ANIMAL COMMUNICATION; ANIMAL MIGRATION; BIOLOGICAL CLOCK; ECHOLOCATION; EVOLUTION.

animal communication Communication in animals has been defined most broadly as any behavior on the part of one organism that affects the behavior of another and, more specifically, as the exchange of information between individuals. In practice, the term is usually restricted to the exchange of species-typical signals that perform a communicative function. Because communication is an interaction, the signals are specialized on the part of both the sender and the receiver. Verifying the communicative signal is sometimes difficult, however, because the responsive behavior may be internal or delayed, or may take the form of not carrying out an intended act.

All social interactions, from a one-celled animal finding a mate to a baboon leading other troop members to food, are based on the ability of two or more individuals to coordinate their activities. Communication is the means by which such coordination is accomplished.

Functions of Signals

The function of a signal and the fact of its being a signal at all must be inferred from the circumstances under which it is given and the way other animals respond to it. The function of a signal may be different in different contexts, and the recipients' responses may vary according to their situations. For example, the territorial song of a male bird may attract females but repel other males.

One way to try to understand the "meanings" of the signals is to analyze the kind of information they make available—what can be learned or predicted on the basis of the signal. This can range from information about the age, sex, location, or breeding condition of the sender to information about the presence of food or predators, or the conditions of the external environment. One must also study the behavior of the recipient, since there is no guarantee that the recipient can extract all the information made available by the signal; even more important, it is only by looking at the response that the function of the signal can be understood.

Signal Channels

Signals can be sent through any of the available sensory channels: chemical (taste, smell), photic (vision), mechanical (touch, hearing), and even electrical (as in certain fish).

The use of chemical signals, called pheromones, is probably the most primitive means of communication and is employed by species at all levels of complexity. The most important attribute of chemical signals is their long

(Above) *The Atlantic puffin communicates its desire to mate in breeding season, during which time its beak and the feathers around its eyes change color.* (Below) *A caterpillar of the Malayan butterfly raises itself and displays large eyespots on its body, which may scare away predatory birds.*

duration. Thus, chemical signals are ideally suited for marking territories and trails and for long-term influence of behavior. Protozoans such as paramecia, for instance, influence one another's behavior through chemical exudates. Higher invertebrates produce more specific and specialized substances—for example, the trail-marking odors produced by ants. Ant trails are composed of a series of scent spots produced when the abdomen of the worker ant touches the ground. An attacked ant secretes a pheromone from an anal gland to warn or alert other members of the colony. Some fish secrete chemicals that attract mates and stimulate courtship behavior, and odors involved in social and sexual behavior are well known among many species of mammals. Territory-marking behavior in male dogs is a form of chemical communication.

Visual communication, indicating the presence of food, predators, or suitable mates, may consist of such bodily gestures as the courtship flights of butterflies, the stylized dancing of bees, the aggressive movements of Siamese fighting fish, and the brilliant colors of the genital areas in certain apes and monkeys. The male stickleback fish is normally grayish brown, but at mating time its eyes turn blue and its belly bright red, signals that attract the female. One limitation to visual signals is the line-of-sight requirement.

Sounds, like visual signals, are also complex and may convey a variety of messages. They are more suitable for communication over distances or in dense vegetation, since these become lesser obstacles to identifying the source and receiving the stimuli. In the common house cricket, rhythmic patterns of the chirps differentiate sig-

A worker ant, family Formicadae, secretes a chemical substance known as a pheromone, which acts as a trail (yellow lines) for other ants to follow. An ant detects this trail by using its antennae. If it lacks an antenna (bottom), it has greater difficulty tracking the chemical trail, and it swerves from the path to a greater degree than an ant (center) with two antennae.

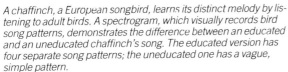

"educated" song

"uneducated" song

A chaffinch, a European songbird, learns its distinct melody by listening to adult birds. A spectrogram, which visually records bird song patterns, demonstrates the difference between an educated and an uneducated chaffinch's song. The educated version has four separate song patterns; the uneducated one has a vague, simple pattern.

Cichlids are freshwater fishes that may change skin color and pattern according to their emotional state. Three such states, shown in a male, are (from top to bottom) neutral, neither aggressive nor frightened; frightened with no shelter in which to hide; and highly aggressive, in preparation to fight.

nals for courtship, aggression, or territorial defense. Each tern has an individual "fish call" when returning to its young with a meal of fish. The young are unresponsive to the fish calls of other members of the colony; they respond only to the returning parent. Songbirds, with their complex musical sounds, appear to have attained some higher forms of communication, but the various complexities still serve primarily for species, sex, and individual recognition; the songs indicate such things as readiness to breed, aggression, alarm, and the presence of food.

Language is believed to be a communication system unique to the human species. Present knowledge indicates that only humans are capable of using distinct sounds as symbols to express abstract concepts. Humans are also able to convey information about the communication system itself.

Development

The development of communication in individuals of different species exhibits different kinds and degrees of dependence on previous experience. The production of pheromones in social insects and the sound signals of crickets and cicadas, for example, do not depend directly on contacts the young animals have with other members of the species. In many songbirds, on the other hand, exposure of the young to the sounds of their own species is essential for developing a normal species-typical song pattern. In many mammals, social and psychological conditions play a large role in communication development. A monkey raised apart from other monkeys usually

does not develop any social behavior or communication skill, yet chimpanzees reared by humans can learn forms of communication so complex that some consider it language.

Current Research

Project Washoe (1966–70) was the first successful attempt to teach a nonhuman primate to use symbols in communicating. Researchers taught a young chimpanzee more than 130 hand-signs of the American language of the deaf. Since then studies of language use among a variety of primates indicate that they are capable of using sounds as symbols to exchange information about objects in their environment.

Advances are being made in studying communications among many other kinds of animals as well. In 1985, for example, scientists discovered that some elephant vocalizations, like those of some WHALES, lie below the range of human hearing. More generally, the behavior of social animals—invertebrates as well as vertebrates—has led many scientists to believe that all such animals may be using sophisticated systems of communication that are not yet recognized for what they are. Besides their pheromone communications already mentioned, for example, honeybees have been receiving the attention of scientists for a number of years because of their so-called "dance language." Researchers in the late 1980s managed to develop a computerized robot bee that was accepted by members of the hive and could communicate messages to them, opening up new vistas of research in this field.

See also: ANT; BEE; DOLPHIN.

animal courtship and mating

Courtship in animals is any behavior whereby sexually mature individuals of a species become mating pairs. Precise descriptions of the processes in all animals are impossible because courtship habits vary widely. Some behaviors, however, are common to many species. For example, two animals may be brought together at the proper moment for mating by PHEROMONES, the secretion of odorous chemicals; by mating calls such as the special croaking of the male frog; by such elaborate displays as the mating dances of the scorpion or of certain fishes; or by the male peacock flaunting its brilliant plumage. Most animal courtship patterns appear to be inherited or instinctive and to have evolved to promote the survival of the species through efficient reproductive behavior. Among humans, however, courtship consists more of learned behavior than of instinctive acts. Thus, no justifiable inferences about human behavior can be drawn solely from animal behavior.

Visual Cues, Odors, and Sounds. Visual cues identify and attract members of the opposite sex. The male spider, for example, may wave its legs to distinguish itself from animals on which the female normally preys. In monkeys a swelling and change in coloration in the genital area of the female occurs during estrus. The sound of a male pigeon's cooing may stimulate ovulation in a female.

The female cockroach secretes pheromones that attract males from considerable distances. Among mammals, many males have scent glands that secrete odorous substances that attract females. For example, deer rub their hind legs, which contain scent glands, against trees. Other animals, including female dogs, have sexual attractants in their urine.

Role of Territory. Many animals form territories or social relationships that reduce competition and serve as mating or nesting sites. The male bowerbirds of Australia build elaborate houses, or bowers, which attract females. The male stickleback fish builds a nest on its territory and

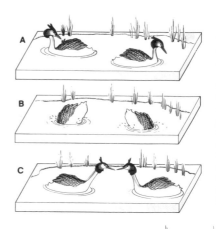

(Left and below) *The courtship ritual of the great crested grebe takes place on water, unlike mating, which occurs at the nesting site.* (A) *Initially, both preen and fish, occasionally shaking their heads.* (B) *The pair then dive and* (C) *swim toward each other with outstretched necks, again shaking their heads.*

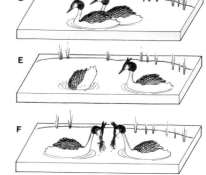

(D) *The two swim parallel to each other until* (E) *the female dives, followed by the male.* (F) *They meet again, holding weeds pulled from the lake bottom.*

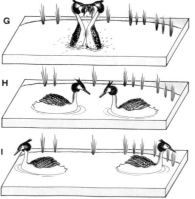

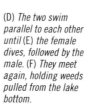

(G) *The ritual culminates when the grebes meet and rise breast to breast. They remain for a few seconds in this position, rocking back and forth.* (H) *After settling back into the water, they continue shaking their heads for a while until* (I) *they drift apart to feed. The ceremony begins again after the grebes have fed and rested.*

(Below) *During the courtship of grayling butterflies, the female settles on the ground, and the male displays his boldly patterned wings to her. He traps the female's antennae between his forewings, which contain scent glands that function to stimulate the female to mate with him.*

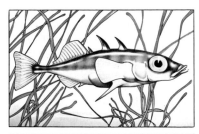

(Top) *A male three-spined stickleback normally has a gray-green coloration that helps the fish to blend into its environment. Sticklebacks live in schools until breeding season, during which time the males choose individual territories.* (Center) *The male's belly turns red as a warning sign to other males that enter his territory. He attacks any other males that have red bellies, and his territorial defense posture involves hovering in water head down. The stickleback spends most of his time building a nest of waterweeds that is glued together by a secretion from his kidneys.* (Bottom) *When the nest is completed, his back turns blue as a courtship signal to females. He displays his colors to attract a female and performs a zigzag dance to lead her to his nest. The female is directed to the entrance by the male, and she swims in. The male prods the female's tail to stimulate her to lay eggs. Afterwards, the female leaves; the male takes care of the eggs and later guards the hatched fish.*

then lures the female to the nest with a zigzag dance pattern. Some male mammals, including the sea lion, reduce competition by establishing a harem of females on their territory. This ensures mating with the strongest and most-fit males. Strictly monogamous pair-bonds are not common, but they do occur in many birds and animals that have altricial offspring—born helpless, like humans.

Mating. After a mate has been found, courtship may arouse sexual interest and synchronize the behavior of each individual so that actual mating, or copulation, can take place. In many animals, postural adjustments are required. In the rat, for example, the female must remain motionless and raise her hindquarters for the male to successfully mount her.

Mating habits have also evolved to aid animals in adapting to their modes of life and habitats. Mating in such herbivores as antelope and deer occurs very quickly,

with minimal physical contact, because these animals live on the open plains in sight of predators. These species tend to move quickly at all times, and the young develop rapidly. Such carnivores as bears, dogs, and cats often require extended periods of copulation. These animals tend to be comparatively slow in other behaviors, and the young take longer to develop.

See also: ANIMAL BEHAVIOR; ANIMAL COMMUNICATION.

animal experimentation   Animal experimentation is the scientific study of life processes in animals to advance biological knowledge. It is used primarily in research and teaching in such areas as product safety and effectiveness, disease states and possible cures, and anatomy and physiology. The animals commonly used in testing are mice, rats, hamsters, guinea pigs, rabbits, cats, dogs, frogs, and turtles, but many other species are also used.

In the health-care field, extensive animal experimentation is done annually to meet the strict requirements of the U.S. Food and Drug Administration (FDA) for new products. In addition, tests are performed to find new uses for established products. Products tested on animals include drugs, cosmetics, chemicals, and medical devices. Cosmetics are tested for toxicity, irritation, and eye damage. Animals are used in vitamin studies to test symptoms of deficiency. They are also used to test life-support systems in spacecraft. Nonhuman primates are valuable for studies on the eye, blood, and atherosclerosis; the rhesus monkey is extensively used for experimental surgical techniques.

Studies are also conducted using animals to test the effects of long-term exposure to toxic agents (including pesticides), smoking, marijuana, and drugs. Rabbits are widely used in toxicology and are also used to help develop oral contraceptives. Through many years of use in controlled situations, animals have furnished extensive data on which researchers can confidently rely. For example, the rate of human metabolism for a new drug can be determined, within limits, by experimentation with a given species, the metabolic rate of which has been established over a long period of time. It is advantageous if several generations of offspring can be observed. In mice, five generations can be obtained within a year.

Sometimes animals are selected because of their unique susceptibility to disease organisms. Certain animals are also more susceptible to metabolic diseases (chickens and gout); skin diseases (primates and balding); respiratory diseases (horses and emphysema); and eye diseases (cocker spaniels and glaucoma). The first use of hamsters was to study kala-azar, or leishmaniasis, a disease of children in the Mediterranean area and in Asia. Only the Syrian hamster proved to be satisfactory for this experiment.

The number of animals used each year in experiments is not known with any certainty—records of rats and mice used, for example, are often not kept—but it probably exceeds 100 million. The term *vivisection* has come to be applied to any experimentation using live animals, and for several years various groups have conducted antivivisection campaigns to obtain more humane treatment for laboratory animals, if not to do away with such experimentation altogether. In reaction to these efforts, such U.S. legislation as the Animal Welfare Act of 1966 (amended in 1970, 1976, and 1985) has been passed, and researchers are seeking such alternatives to animal experimentation as cell and tissue culture and computer modeling. In order to obtain government funding, proposed research projects must adhere to strict guidelines. Groups such as the American Association for Laboratory Animal Care and the Institute for Laboratory Animal Resources are also helping to improve laboratory standards.

See also: ANIMAL RIGHTS.

Animal Farm   see ORWELL, GEORGE

---

animal husbandry   Animal husbandry is the art and science of the care, management, and improvement of domestic animals and their products. The manipulation of animals for the benefit of human beings is an integral part of the story of civilization. Animal production in different areas and cultures of the world reflects the importance of domestic animals as sources of food, power, fiber, hides, and skins.

A large proportion of the world's land area is unsuitable for crop production because of topography, climate, and deficiencies in soil fertility or rainfall. In many such areas the use of grazing animals is the only feasible way economically to convert the natural materials of plant growth into products of use to people. Even where grains or food crops are cultivated intensively, only selected parts of the plants can be eaten, because the human ability to digest fibrous materials is limited. With the use of animals, however, such crop residues positively contribute to the human food supply.

Of the total edible protein produced in the world, it is estimated that 30% comes from animal products. Half of the remaining 70% is derived from cereals. The relative contribution of animal protein to total protein intake varies from about 23% in the Middle East to about 70% in North America.

Domestication of Animals

Domestication involves producing, from the wild animal, a tame variety that can breed in captivity and that is incapable of living in a wild state. The process had been largely accomplished before the era of recorded history. Domestication of many farm animals may have occurred independently, at different times, and in several regions. The original motives for domestication may not necessarily have been utilitarian; some animals may first have been bred as pets, for sport, or for ritual purposes. Nevertheless, early in the process it was discovered that some species could be selectively mated to achieve certain desirable physical and temperamental characteristics.

The DOG was apparently the first animal to be domesticated, perhaps 10,000 to 12,000 years ago. GOATS and SHEEP were bred from wild species in the Middle East and Central Asia, possibly as early as 7000 BC. Archaeological evidence puts the first domesticated cattle (see CATTLE AND CATTLE RAISING) in South Asia, the Middle East, and Europe by the 4th millennium BC. The humped ZEBU, thought to have originated in India, eventually spread into the Middle East and Africa. PIGS, domesticated about the same time as cattle, probably originated from only two wild species. CAMELS, REINDEER, donkeys, and HORSES were among the last animals to be domesticated in Europe and Asia.

New World domestication was restricted to the few native animals that were suitable: the ALPACA, DUCK, LLAMA, TURKEY, and dog. Since human settlement occurred there long after it had taken place in the Old World, ani-

African cattlemen tending their herd are illustrated in a rock painting found at Tassili in the central Sahara (c.3000 BC). Cattle were domesticated in northern Africa somewhat later than in Europe and Asia.

(Above) *Carefully bred hogs, such as these on an Iowa farm, are fed high-energy rations and reach a market weight of 90 to 100 kg (198 to 220 lbs) in about 6 months.* (Right) *A camel caravan hauls salt through the Ténéré desert of Niger.*

mal domestication was also a later development.

During the more or less 10,000 years since the beginnings of animal domestication, the basic characteristics of the tamed species have changed. Changes in appearance—size, shape, and coloration—are the most obvious, but even more striking are the alterations in characteristics for which the animals were bred: a modern milk cow yields a volume of milk thousands of times greater than its wild ancestor; the egg production of hens (see POULTRY) has increased by a factor of perhaps 100 over that of the first domesticated fowl; sheep's wool is heavier, finer, and more uniform than that of the original wild sheep. A fundamental change involves the reproductive cycle. The ancestors of domesticated animals could reproduce only during a limited season, whereas many types of domesticated livestock can be bred during most of the year.

Modern Livestock

The most important domesticated livestock worldwide include horses, pigs, llamas, camels, sheep, and goats, among others.

Horses. The two important domesticated species of the genus *Equus* are horses and ponies (*E. caballus*) and asses (*E. asinus*). They and their cross, the mule, have been an intimate part of human history. The horse was apparently domesticated in Central Asia and North Africa. The Arabian breed, dating back to about 500 BC, has contributed to most of the improved breeds of horses subsequently developed.

China is the world's leading horse-producing country. Others include the United States, Mexico, Brazil, and the USSR. From the standpoint of size and use, the major subdivisions are draft horses, which are large and heavily muscled; light, or riding, horses; and ponies. The use of the horse or mule as a source of power has declined in developed countries since tractors and mechanical power sources were introduced.

Pigs. The pig, *Sus scrofa*, is the only domesticated species of the genus *Sus*. Pigs are raised worldwide; they find a place in the economy of developing countries because they can be fed on scraps and gleanings and because they can convert high-energy feeds efficiently. The leading countries in pig production are China, the USSR, the United States, Brazil, Poland, and Germany.

Llamas and Camels. The *Lama* genus of the Camelidae, or camel family, includes the GUANACO, alpaca, and llama. The first remains wild; the latter two are domesticated. All are native to the high elevations of the Andes. They serve as beasts of burden and contribute to the economy of the area through the production of fiber used in making wool textiles.

The *Camelus* genus includes the single-humped dromedary, native to North Africa, and the double-

Because water buffalo can withstand hot, humid climates such as Indonesia's, they are the preferred draft animal. They also provide the people of these areas with milk, meat, and hides.

(Above) *At a modern feed lot in California, a truck is used to funnel feed to cattle. Controls for automatically weighing and distributing the feed are located inside the truck's cab.* (Right) *A rancher on horseback herds sheep in Australia, a major sheep-raising country.*

humped Bactrian camel of Asia. Both serve as beasts of burden and as a source of meat, milk, hides, and wool. Somalia, the Sudan, India, Ethiopia, and Pakistan possess the largest herds.

Yaks and Water Buffalo. Both the YAK and the water BUFFALO belong to the family Bovidae. Yaks and yak-cattle crosses are found only in the higher elevations of the Himalayas. In an area where perhaps less than 5% of the land can be cultivated, yaks are a source of food, power, fuel, and fiber.

Domestic buffalo constitute only one genus, *Bubalus,* the Asiatic water buffalo. More than 90% are found in the Far East, with large populations also in South Asia. Domestic buffalo have traditionally been kept as triple-purpose animals—for work, milk, and meat.

Goats. Goats belong to the genus *Capra.* They are found in all countries of the world and have long been an important domestic animal. Large numbers are raised in Central and North Africa, the Middle East, South Asia, and China. Only a few of the 60 or more recognized breeds in the world are important in the United States, although U.S. herds of ANGORA goats—raised primarily for their hair—account for about 50% of the world's mohair production. The goat's small size, efficiency of milk production, and fertility are advantages in converting scarce plant resources into food.

Sheep. Sheep belong to the genus *Ovis.* Raised throughout the world, they are the main source of wool and in many areas are major providers of meat, milk, and cheese. The principal sheep-producing countries are Australia, the USSR, China, New Zealand, India, and Turkey. About 3 million metric tons (3.3 million U.S. tons) of wool are produced annually, with Australia and New Zealand accounting for most of the wool moving in world trade.

Cattle. Two species make up the population of beef-

and milk-producing cattle: *Bos taurus* is predominant in temperate climates, although it may be found in countries from the fringes of the tropics to the Arctic; *B. indicus,* or zebu cattle, originating in India, are now native in the tropics around the globe. Variations of these species and their crosses have served people in many ways. Cattle supply milk and meat; oxen (castrated cattle) make useful draft animals; cattle are a primary source of some 300 biological materials, including their hides, which are used for clothing, shelter, and equipment, and their dung, which is used for fuel and fertilizer.

India is by far the largest cattle-raising country, followed by Brazil, the USSR, the United States, China, and Argentina.

Reindeer. Reindeer, domesticated caribou, are general-purpose animals of the Arctic, furnishing meat, skins, and milk, as well as pulling loads and carrying packs. They have long been important in the economics of Lapland and Siberia.

Other Types of Livestock. Many indigenous species thrive under domestication in various parts of the world. In South America, two rodent species are successfully bred and reared: the giant capybara in Venezuela and the guinea pig in Peru. In Africa south of the Sahara, native herbivores have only recently been reared or ranched. They include antelope such as the eland, oryx, and impala; the grasscutter (or cane rat), a large rodent; and the ostrich. Other newly domesticated animals include deer and, in the United States, the bison and alligator.

Increasing Livestock Numbers

In regions where nomadic herding is still practiced or where the use of modern husbandry science is not possible, livestock producers are subject to a host of natural conditions—weather, the prevalence of livestock diseases, the availability of water or forage—that have a telling effect on livestock numbers. In developed areas, however, the factors influencing the efficiency of livestock production are almost all within the control of the producer. They include intensive rearing (see FACTORY FARMING); feeding programs to ensure rapid weight gain or increased milk production; and breeding programs using the newest techniques in biotechnology and GENETIC ENGINEERING. Since World War II these methods have nearly doubled the amount of milk produced per dairy cow in the United States and have increased the rate and quality of livestock growth. Future gains, however, will probably depend on the use of sophisticated breeding techniques.

In addition to ARTIFICIAL INSEMINATION, which has been used effectively since the 1930s, basic breeding techniques include various manipulations of egg and embryo. Typically, a prize dairy cow will be injected with a hormone that causes it to produce as many as 20 mature eggs during ovulation, rather than the usual one or two. The eggs are fertilized via artificial insemination, and the embryos flushed out within a week. Transferred into a surrogate-mother cow, an embryo will develop into a calf with the desirable characteristics of its genetic parents and its surrogate dam as well. Other techniques involve the cloning of embryos and the freezing of both eggs and embryos for storage or shipment.

The use of gene manipulation to produce more commercially useful animals may prove to be the most important breeding technique. An animal and its offspring can be programmed for a specific trait by adding a foreign gene to its embryo. Perhaps the first practical success in the field has been the development of the cow hormone, bovine somatotropin, which can be produced in quantity by genetically modified bacteria and which increases milk production when given to cows.

animal migration

animal migration Migrations are periodic movements of animals from one place to another. In a general sense these movements follow similar routes and return the animals to the same locality each time they occur; if the animals that return are a new generation of that species, the term *remigration* is also used. Movements from one locality to another are also called *emigrations*.

Migrations occur because some animals need to exploit a variety of environments in order to reproduce successfully. Migrational periodicity is usually the result of the Earth's seasonal changes, which are associated with climatic changes and resulting alterations in the growth and production of plants. These variations in climate and food availability cause animals to move from areas less suitable for feeding or for raising young, or both, to more suitable regions. Thus the extent to which animals are migratory depends, in large part, on the foods that they eat, their requirements for reproduction, and the degree of seasonal climatic change in their environments. Migrations are sometimes the result of the animal reaching a particular stage in life. Some species of salmon, for example, spend most of their lives in salt water, although

they are born, reproduce, and die in the freshwater streams of the continents. After hatching, pink salmon journey from the rivers of Canada and Alaska into the Pacific and may spend most of their lives along the coasts of North Korea, 5,600 km (3,500 mi) away. Upon reaching sexual maturity, however, they return to the exact stream of their birth.

The timing as well as the routing of migratory movements may be quite predictable. Many animals key their migrations to seasonal changes in the position of celestial bodies as well as to more immediate climatic changes. Some species arrive and depart on their migration with great regularity.

Examples of Migration

Migration occurs in a variety of forms of animal life, ranging from invertebrates to humans. Most of these organisms share the capacity for long-distance movement as well as the need to exploit different environments in their life cycles.

Insects. The locusts of North Africa and the Middle East are well known for their large-scale movements that may cover 2,200–3,200 km (1,400–2,000 mi). The migrations seem to be a dispersal of young adult locusts from areas where their extremely dense populations sometimes cause severe damage to crops and grazing lands. Locusts generally move from dry areas toward regions of somewhat greater rainfall.

The migrations of the monarch butterfly of North America are similar to those of birds. The monarch exploits a single food source, milkweed, which occurs throughout North America from Mexico to southern Canada. During the temperate summer, monarchs are spread across California, the Great Basin, and western plains and, in the East, are found north of the Great Lakes and in New England and Ontario. When temperatures drop in autumn, however, monarchs migrate to concentration areas, where hundreds of thousands of them settle in specific tree groves to spend the winter. They remain in these groves in a semitorpid state until the following spring, when at least some of them return to their warm-season feeding areas. In the course of these flights they may cover 130 km (80 mi) or more a day.

Reptiles. In the life cycle of the green sea turtle, only egg laying, incubation, and hatching are strictly terrestrial processes; all other important life-events take place in the seas of the world. Upon hatching, young turtles immediately head for the water and apparently return to their hatching site only when they themselves engage in reproduction. These hatching sites are frequently small, and sometimes isolated, islands, such as Ascension Island in the Atlantic or the Galápagos in the Pacific. Long-distance migratory movements to and from these mating and nesting sites take place every 2 or 3 years in the life of the adult turtle.

Birds. Terrestrial birds that fly over oceans must frequently cover vast distances without rest or food. For example, Pacific golden plovers fly from northern Alaska, Canada, or Siberia to Hawaii in the autumn—more than

Some animals migrate over great distances to and from their breeding grounds. Others migrate in an endless search for food. A few are driven to mass emigration by overcrowded conditions. The logarithmic scale (bottom) measures each tenfold increase in distance of migration with one scale unit. Birds are able to travel farthest because they can fly over mountains and oceans. The arctic tern travels from its summer nesting site in the Arctic circle to winter quarters in Antarctia, a distance of more than 19,000 km (12,000 mi). Other long-distance fliers are the European swallow and an American songbird, the bobolink. The salmon is known for its migration from the ocean to its spawning ground in a freshwater stream. In contrast, a European eel travels from rivers to the ocean to spawn. The blue whale frequently is sighted off North American shores when it migrates from the ice-packed Arctic ocean to the tropics. The green turtle, the bonito, and the fur seal are also well-documented migratory swimmers. Both the migratory locust and the Norwegian lemming undertake one-way migrations when their populations exceed a certain density. The red bat, during its migration from the northern to the southern United States, rests by day, hanging upside down on trees. The caribou and bison are migratory animals that travel great distances across land.

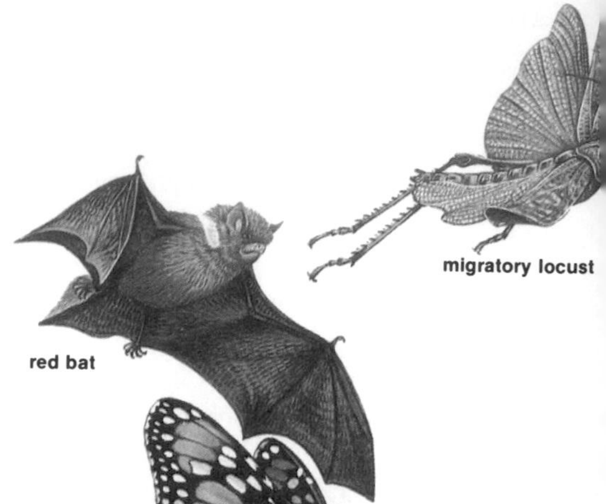

migratory locust

red bat

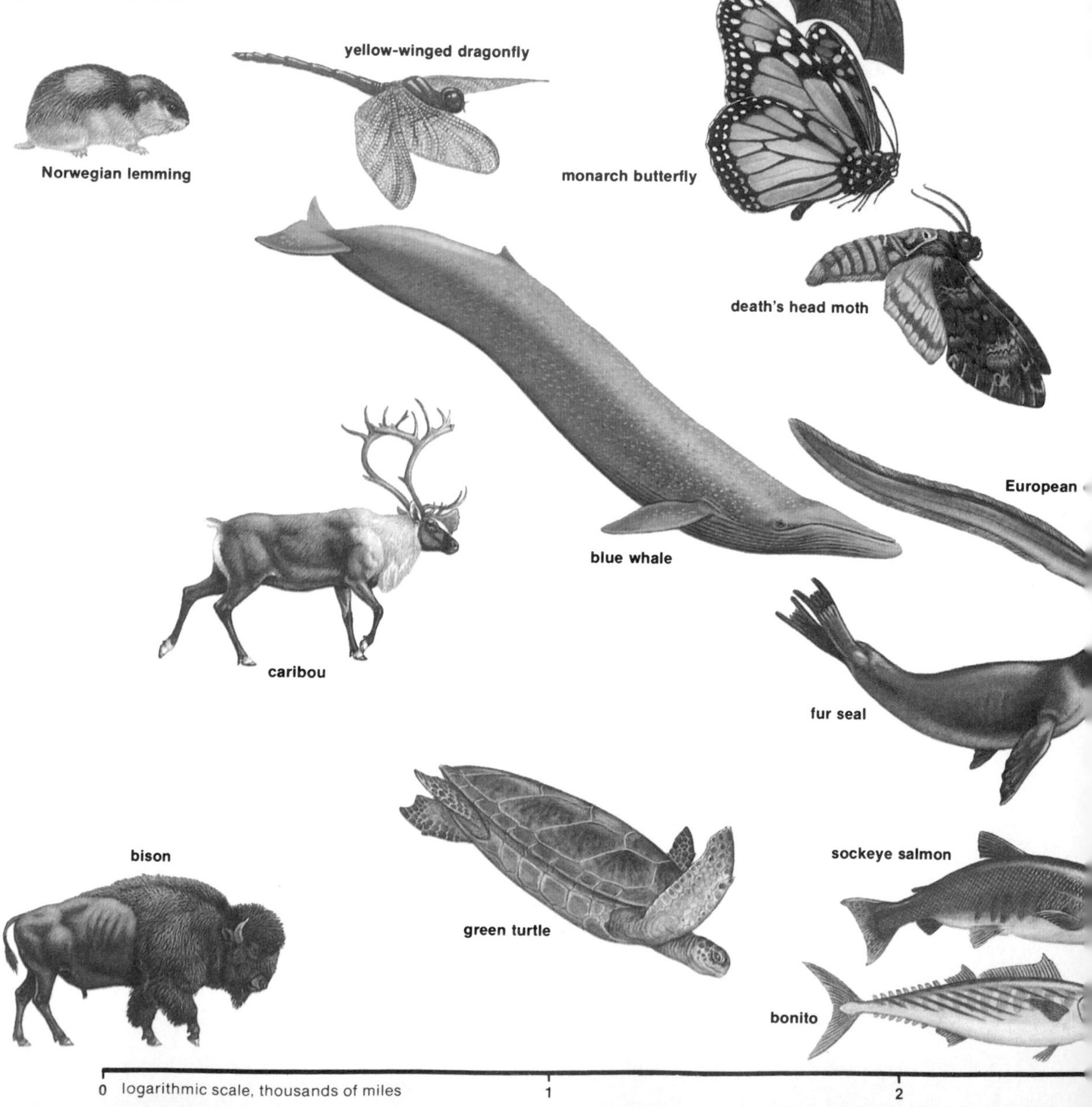

yellow-winged dragonfly

monarch butterfly

Norwegian lemming

death's head moth

blue whale

European

caribou

fur seal

bison

sockeye salmon

green turtle

bonito

0   logarithmic scale, thousands of miles   1   2

3,200 km (2,000 mi)—without a landfall. The Arctic tern is the long-distance migratory champion of the animal world, although its migratory flights are partially along coastlines. It nests in the far north of Europe, Asia, and North America and spends the northern winter along the shores of Antarctica. To make this journey of as much as 19,000 km (12,000 mi) twice a year requires the bird to spend about 8 months on migration.

Fish. Many fishes migrate between fresh water and salt water at various times in their lives, especially species in the genus *Salmo*, which includes some salmon and trout. Many other types of fishes never inhabit fresh water but undertake long migrations at sea. These include tuna and bonito, among others.

In contrast to the salmon, which lives at sea and breeds in fresh water, the European eel spends most of its life in fresh water but breeds, spawns, and hatches in the mid-Atlantic, in the region of the Sargasso Sea. The eel's migratory journey, like that of the salmon, requires a physiological shift in kidney function to accomplish the move to salt water.

Marine Mammals. Marine mammals also undertake long migratory journeys. For example, northern fur seals migrate annually. For a period of about 6 months, from May to October, the North Pacific island breeding grounds are occupied at progressive intervals by adult males, adult females and young, and recently matured young. Bad weather sends the fur seals to Asiatic waters off the coasts of Japan and as far south as Mexico on the American side of the Pacific.

The migratory movements of whales seem keyed both to reproductive behavior and to the location of food resources such as krill or plankton. The availability of plankton is much greater near the poles, so baleen whales such as the blue and humpback whales spend the tem-

perate summers in polar oceans. In winter they retreat to tropical waters. In some whales this is the period when the young are born.

Land Mammals. On the Serengeti Plain in East Africa the entire population of 300,000 wildebeests makes a concerted annual migration between the short-grassed Masai Steppe and the savanna woodland region near Lake Victoria. The wildebeests, along with less numerous zebras and gazelles, make these migrations in direct response to food availability. As the Serengeti dry season progresses, they withdraw to the woodlands until the rains begin again—or, if the rains are delayed too long, die of starvation.

Another ungulate, the caribou of Alaska and Canada, spends the brief Arctic summer on the tundra, where continuous daylight causes rapid plant growth and supplies the animal with food. Cold weather and deep winter snow drive the caribou south into the borders of the boreal forest. Through the long polar winter the caribou depend on lichens as their only reliable food source. As with the wildebeest, a fine balance exists between survival and starvation for the caribou. An unusually short summer or long winter will almost certainly result in death to some and, possibly, many individuals.

Mechanisms of Migration

At least two prerequisites must be met for successful migration: the strength and stamina to make the journey and the ability to find the way to the goal.

Energy Needs. Long-distance movements may demand a tremendous expenditure of energy. Among some long-distance migrants, special physiological adaptations help prepare the animals. For instance, the energy expended in flight by passerine birds may be 12 times as great as the standard metabolic rate. This means that the birds must continuously replenish their energy resources while migrating or else have large prior reserves of energy. In some passerines the physiological system alters metabolism in a way that causes the birds to eat large amounts of food and accumulate heavy fat deposits before migration; the bodies of some songbirds may be 40 percent fat prior to their migratory flight. During migration these fat stores are metabolized to supply energy.

Modes of Navigation. Navigation, the means by which animals locate themselves in space and determine their heading and progress, has been studied most extensively for birds. The studies have identified a diversity of senses that may be used by different birds or by the same bird under different circumstances. Many birds seem capable of sensing location and heading by the position of the Sun. Celestial navigation, using the stars, also appears quite common. On partially clouded nights the ability to navigate with only partial glimpses of the stars is probably crucial, and sophisticated planetarium experiments have demonstrated that, indeed, large blocks of the sky may be obscured and navigation can still be effective. In addition, experiments have indicated an ability on the part of some birds to sense magnetic fields and use these in navigation. Some species appear to use visual landmarks in addition to other means of navigation, and a current

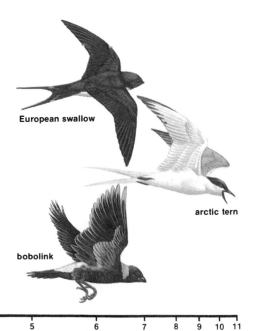

European swallow

arctic tern

bobolink

5   6   7   8   9   10 11

hypothesis is that many birds have redundant sets of navigational senses that may function together or alone, depending on prevailing environmental conditions.

Although fishes, like birds, may use a variety of senses in navigation, their olfactory sense is critically important. It has been shown that salmon can detect minuscule levels of molecules dissolved in water through their olfactory senses. Thus they may be able to identify their home river, or a small branch thereof, merely by its odor.

See also: BIOLOGICAL CLOCK.

animal rights   The concept of animal rights has come to play an important role in several areas of concern over human treatment of other animals. These areas range from the hunting and trapping of animals, to obvious cases of mistreatment of work or sport animals or pets, to less apparent cases such as the widely accepted practices of ANIMAL EXPERIMENTATION for scientific purposes and FACTORY FARMING. Concern further extends to broad ecological issues of human responsibility for the Earth's environment and the threat of extinction to ENDANGERED SPECIES.

The question of whether or not animals have any inherent rights has often been raised in religion and philosophy. The cultural history of the relationship between humans and animals is complex, but a basic contrast might be made between cultural attitudes that have emphasized the unity of being and those which have placed humanity at the center of creation. In a religion such as JAINISM, for example, all forms of life are considered to have souls and are therefore not to be injured. Judeo-Christian thought, on the other hand, has specifically limited the concept of the soul to humans, and the predominant trend of thought in the Western world has been to consider other forms of life as subservient to human needs and desires. With the advent of modern technology and the explosive growth of human populations, this attitude has come under serious attack by a number of persons active in the area of animal rights, for practical as well as ethical reasons.

Animal-rights activists have sought, with some success, to obtain better control over the use of animals in laboratories for scientific research and the testing of products. A number of activists would eventually ban such use altogether and would also promote the practice of VEGETARIANISM.

animation   Film animation applies techniques of cinematography to the graphic and plastic arts in order to give the illusion of life and movement to cartoons, drawings, paintings, puppets, and three-dimensional objects. Beginning with crude and simple methods, animation has become a highly sophisticated form of filmmaking, involving the use of automation, computer, and even laser technology to achieve its effects. Some animation techniques overlap with those used to produce special effects in live-action cinematography. In watching such films as

Skeleton Dance *(1929), the first in the Disney cartoon series "Silly Symphonies," achieved a comic choreography by matching the movements of the figures to a prerecorded sound track.*

2001—A Space Odyssey (1968) and *Star Wars* (1977), a person often finds it difficult to tell whether a certain result has been achieved through animation or through special effects.

Animation Techniques

Basic graphic animation is produced by a technique called stop-frame cinematography. The camera records, frame by frame, a sequence or succession of drawings or paintings that differ only fractionally from one another. The illusion of progressive movement is created by projecting the series of frames through a camera at the normal rate for sound film (24 frames a second). The same method is used in puppet or object animation; the position of the figures or objects is changed very slightly prior to each exposure. In graphic animation, the drawings may vary from the simplest outlines, as in such traditional animated films as *Felix the Cat*, to elaborately modeled and colored paintings, such as those produced in Walt DISNEY's studios during the 1930s.

The first animated cartoons were produced before 1910 by pioneers such as Émile Cohl of France and Winsor McCay of the United States, whose *Sinking of the Lusitania* (1918) has been called the first animated feature film. In these early productions, a simple drawing of a mobile figure was photographed against an equally simple background, and a new drawing was required for each exposure. Relief from the labor of drawing hundreds of pictures for each minute of action came only when the figures could be made momentarily static. The evolution of cel (for celluloid) animation after 1913 enabled animators to use a single, more elaborate background for each shot or scene in the action. The mobile figures in the foreground were inked in black silhouette on transparent celluloid sheets and then superimposed in series on the background. With the introduction of color filming early in the 1930s, animators began to use opaque paints in place of black ink. Greater efficiency was achieved when artists began to specialize in particular figures or other mobile elements of cartoons. Such teams of animators collectively created drawings for feature-length films, for example, Walt Disney's *Snow White and the Seven Dwarfs* (1937) and *Fantasia* (1940).

Most animated films are recorded by an automated rostrum camera. The many improvements made in this camera since the 1950s have contributed to the increased technical capabilities of the medium. The adjustable camera is suspended above the horizontal table on which the combination of cels, one upon the other, have been superimposed on the background and locked or pegged into position. The cels are then successively photographed to produce a precision image offering a faultless illusion of movement. Such cinematic effects as tracking, panning, and zooming may also be achieved.

(Right) *A pencil drawing of the characters in an animated cartoon sketches in action, expression, and placement of the picture elements. A finished drawing (below) is traced with black ink on a transparent sheet of celluloid, or cel, and opaque colors are applied.*

(Below) *The colored cel is superimposed on a background prepared earlier, and the combined images are photographed as one frame of cartoon film by a stop-motion camera.*

History of Animation

Since the early, popular shorts involving such animals as Felix the Cat and Mickey Mouse, the international history of animation has been characterized by the introduction of ever more complex forms. Many advances were made in Europe: Lotte Reiniger employed mobile silhouettes; Oskar Fischinger and Len Lye experimented with abstract designs choreographed to music; and George Pal of Holland created techniques of puppet animation. From the 1940s until the early 1980s, Norman McLAREN, one of the most versatile of all animators, experimented with three-dimensional animation and with such other innovations as drawing images directly on film.

Since the 1960s, computer animation has achieved the ability to create moving images and backgrounds of great complexity. The basic tool, usually called a PAINT-BOX, is an electronic surface on which the artist draws figures and backgrounds and selects colors. Other devices manipulate the figures and change the backgrounds. The work is reproduced on a TV monitor and stored on a computer disc. Computerized animation is widely used in television commercials and titles, and in making music videos (see VIDEO, MUSIC), and provides many of the special effects in the films of directors like George Lucas (see COMPUTER GRAPHICS; VIDEO ART).

Old-style cel animation continues to be the sole technique by which quality animators, such as The Walt Disney Company, create characters. Backgrounds, and the movement of objects within a scene, however, are often computer-generated.

Television, with its insatiable need for new material, introduced a type of semianimation in its cartoon programs for children. Compared with traditional animation, the movement of characters is primitive, colors are limited, and detail is minimal. Costs of TV animation are a minute fraction of the costs for quality movie animation. For the cartoon-and-live-character film *Who Framed Roger Rabbit?* (1988), the Disney Studio spent $250,000 per minute to make one hour of animation.

---

animism [an'-uh-mizm]   Animism is the belief that a spirit or divinity resides within every object, controlling its existence and influencing human life and events in the natural world. Animistic religious beliefs are widespread among PRIMITIVE SOCIETIES, particularly among those in which spiritual beings are believed to control different aspects of the natural and social environment.

See also: FETISH; PRIMITIVE RELIGION; SHAMAN; TOTEM.

anion   see ION AND IONIZATION

---

anise [an'-is]   Anise, *Pimpinella anisum*, is an annual herb of the CARROT family, cultivated for aniseed, its small, fragrant fruits. Aniseed is used as a flavoring in baked goods. Its ESSENTIAL OIL is used to flavor licorice candies, cough drops, liqueurs such as absinthe and anisette, and some tobacco blends. Anise is native to the eastern Mediterranean but is cultivated today in southern Europe, the USSR, and North and South America.

Chinese star anise is the dried fruit of *Illicium verum* (family Illiciaceae). It is native to southeastern Asia and is also used as a flavoring.

The licorice-flavored fruits of the herb anise are used throughout the Mediterranean region to make certain alcoholic beverages. In France, they are known generically as pastis; in Greece, as ouzo; in Turkey, as arrack or raki.

Anjou [ahn-zhoo'] Anjou is a former province of western France. Straddling the Loire Valley, it is bordered on the west by Brittany and on the east by Touraine. Its name is derived from the Andes or Andecavi, a Celtic tribe conquered by the Romans. The ANGEVIN or Plantagenet line of English kings originated in 1154, when the count of Anjou ascended the English throne as HENRY II. English kings ruled Anjou for the next 50 years. The county of Anjou was finally added to the French crown in 1480. In 1790 Anjou was divided into Maine-et-Loire and parts of adjacent departments with its administrative center at Angers, the former provincial capital.

The characteristic Breton landscape of hedgerows and small fields prevails in northern Anjou, where wheat, fodder crops, and beef are grown. Vegetables, flowers, fruit, and vineyards are important in the sheltered Loire Valley.

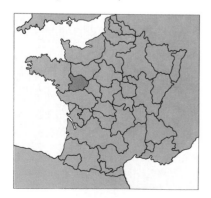

The Anjou region is indicated (red area) on the locator map of France, which also shows the boundaries of all former provinces.

The vineyards extend southward over the rolling sedimentary plateau of southern Anjou. High-quality rosé wines and the sparkling wines of Saumur have the widest reputations of the wines produced in the region. Angers on the Maine and Saumur on the Loire in the east of Anjou are market centers.

Ankara [ang'-kuh-ruh] Ankara (formerly Angora) is the capital and second largest city of Turkey. It has a population of 3,462,880 (1985). Located in north central Anatolia, about 360 km (225 mi) east-southeast of Istanbul, Ankara lies on the Ankara River.

Ankara is the governmental and commercial center of Anatolia and an important market for agricultural products and consumer goods. The Angora goat is raised nearby, and cement, tiles, beer, leather goods, and chemicals are manufactured in the city. Ankara is linked with other cities of Turkey and with neighboring countries by road, rail, and air.

A modern, planned city, European in appearance, Ankara is the only large urban center in interior Turkey. The mausoleum of Kemal ATATÜRK, founder of the Republic of Turkey, occupies one of the highest hills in the city. Nearby are the ruins of a temple erected in the 1st or 2d century BC, an ancient citadel, and the University of Ankara (1946).

Ankara has been an important commercial city since early times. The HITTITES occupied the site about 2000 BC, and the Phrygians took over about a thousand years later. It was captured by ALEXANDER THE GREAT in 333 BC. As Angora, the city was the capital of the Celtic kingdom

Ankara, the capital of Turkey since the nation's independence in 1923, traces its history over 4,000 years. Home of the State Opera and Ballet, the National Library, and the Atatürk Museum, the growing metropolis has become a center of Turkish culture.

of GALATIA in the 3d century BC and of the Roman province of the same name after 25 BC. It was subsequently conquered by Persians, Arabs, Seljuk Turks, European Crusaders, Mongols, and Ottoman Turks and became part of the Ottoman Empire in 1431. Turkish nationalists established a provisional government in the city in 1920, and when the Republic of Turkey was proclaimed in 1923, it became the capital. The name was changed from Angora to Ankara in 1930.

ankh   see CROSS

ankylosaur   Ankylosaurs were a widespread group of heavily armored plant-eating DINOSAURS, suborder Ankylosauria, order Ornithischia, that lived throughout the Cretaceous period until the great dinosaur EXTINCTION 65 million years ago (see GEOLOGIC TIME). They replaced the less successful stegosaurs (see STEGOSAURUS), with whom they may have shared an ancestor. Ankylosaurs had weak, tiny teeth and broad bodies and heads covered by a mosaic of bony plates. Many species also bore large spikes on the sides and tail or had a clublike, bony mass on the tail. The hips stood higher than the front legs, and all four feet were short and broad. The animals ranged up to about 4.5 m (15 feet) in length.

Ann Arbor   Ann Arbor (1990 pop., 109,592), the seat of Washtenaw County in southeastern Michigan, was founded in 1824. A railroad connection to Detroit in 1839 spurred its growth as a leading agricultural center, and the University of Michigan was established there in 1837. Ann Arbor is Michigan's leading medical center and an aeronautical, space, nuclear, chemical, and metallurgical research center.

Anna, Empress of Russia   Anna Ivanovna, b. Jan. 28, 1693, d. Oct. 17, 1740, was empress of Russia during 1730–40. The niece of Emperor Peter I (Peter the Great), she was married (1710) to the duke of Courland, whose Baltic principality she controlled after his death (1711). In 1730, bureaucrats seeking a weak ruler invited Anna to become empress under agreements limiting her authority. She accepted and then overthrew the limitations.

Anna's reign was marked by strong German influences, growing aristocratic control over the peasantry, and by the extension of Russia's influence in Poland (by the War of the POLISH SUCCESSION) and against Turkey (by the RUSSO-TURKISH WAR of 1736–39). Anna was succeeded by her cousin Elizabeth.

Anna Karenina [kah-ray'-nee-nah]   One of the great works of European fiction, Leo TOLSTOI's novel *Anna Karenina* (first published serially, 1875–77) centers on the adulterous love of an unhappily married woman for a dashing young officer, Count Vronsky. She leaves her husband for the sake of Vronsky but cannot choose between son and lover. After increasingly self-destructive behavior, Anna is led finally to suicide. Her love, dominated by sexual passion, is contrasted throughout with the calm, family-centered love between two other characters, Konstantin Levin and Kitty. Through Levin, the liberal Russian landowner, Tolstoi expresses his own humanistic views and attachment to the land.

Annam   see VIETNAM

Annapolis [an-ap'-oh-lis]   Annapolis is the capital of Maryland and the county seat of Anne Arundel County. It has a population of 33,187 (1990). First settled as the town of Providence in 1649, Annapolis is located 3 km (2 mi) from the Chesapeake Bay on the Severn River. It is the site of the UNITED STATES NAVAL ACADEMY and of ST. JOHN'S COLLEGE. There is some commercial fishing and shellfishing (crabs and oysters), and numerous small boatyards service the pleasure and commercial vessels that use the city's protected harbor. The downtown area is not radically different from its colonial plan. Narrow streets radiate from Church Circle and from State Circle, site of the historic statehouse where George Washington resigned (1783) as commander of the Continental Army and where, a few weeks later, Congress ratified the Paris Peace Treaty. In 1786 the city hosted the Annapolis Convention, which led to the Constitutional Convention in 1787. The city was named in honor of Princess (later to become Queen) Anne in 1694 when the colonial capital of Maryland was moved to Annapolis from St. Mary's City.

Annapolis, the capital of Maryland, was one of early America's most important settlements. The historical district features more that 80 pre-Revolutionary buildings. The most significant of these is the state capitol (lower left), the oldest state capitol still in use. The present structure dates from 1772.

Annapolis Convention The Annapolis Convention, a meeting of delegates from New York, New Jersey, Delaware, Pennsylvania, and Virginia in Annapolis, Md., on Sept. 11–14, 1786, was a precursor of the CONSTITUTIONAL CONVENTION. Too few states were represented to carry out the original purpose of the meeting—to discuss the regulation of interstate commerce—but informal debate yielded agreement that there was a larger question at issue, namely, the inadequacy of the ARTICLES OF CONFEDERATION. Alexander Hamilton successfully proposed that the states be invited to send delegates to Philadelphia to "render the constitution of the Federal Government adequate to the exigencies of the Union." As a result, the Constitutional Convention was convened in May 1787.

Annapolis Royal Annapolis Royal, a Canadian town (1986 pop., 631) in southwestern Nova Scotia, is located at the mouth of the Annapolis River on the Bay of Fundy. Samuel de Champlain and Pierre du Gua de Monts constructed Port Royal Habitation there in 1605, making it one of the oldest colonies in North America and Canada's oldest settlement. Port Royal was the seat of the French government in ACADIA until it was captured by the British in 1710, when it took its present name in honor of Queen Anne. It was the provincial capital from 1710 to 1749.

Annapurna [an-uh-poor'-nuh] Annapurna is a 48-km-long (30-mi) massif in the Himalayas of north central Nepal. Its highest peak (Annapurna I) is at the western end and rises to 8,078 m (26,504 ft). Annapurna II, at the eastern end, is 7,937 m (26,041 ft) high. Annapurna III (7,577 m/24,858 ft) and Annapurna IV (7,525 m/24,688 ft) lie between them. Called the Goddess of the Harvests by the Nepalese, Annapurna I was first climbed in 1950 by Maurice Herzog and his party; it was the first mountain peak above 7,925 m (26,000 ft) to be scaled.

Anne, Saint Saint Anne is the name traditionally given to the mother of the Virgin Mary. She is not mentioned in the Bible, but her name and the legend of her life are given in the 2d-century nonbiblical *Gospel of James*, one of the writings of the Apocryphal New Testament. Artistic representations of Anne with Mary and the infant Jesus were popular during the Middle Ages and the Renaissance. She is the patron saint of Brittany and of Quebec province. Feast day: July 26 (Western); July 25 (Eastern).

Anne, Queen of England, Scotland, and Ireland Queen Anne, b. Feb. 6, 1665, d. Aug. 1, 1714 was the last English monarch to preside over cabinets and veto parliamentary legislation. The daughter of JAMES II, she remained devoted to the Church of England despite her father's conversion to Roman Catholicism. To uphold the Anglican church, she joined her brother-in-law, WILLIAM III, when he invaded (1688) England and forced her father

into exile. During William's reign, Anne became great friends with Sarah Churchill, later duchess of MARLBOROUGH. When Anne came to the throne in 1702, she gave Sarah the highest court appointments and made Sarah's husband, John, the duke of Marlborough, commander in chief in the War of the SPANISH SUCCESSION.

After seven years of the war against France, Anne realized that her subjects were tiring of it. In 1710 she helped overthrow the Whig government, which was committed to an uncompromising peace treaty, and instituted a Tory government, which favored an immediate peace. Anne broke with the Churchills, turning to her chief minister, Robert HARLEY, who concluded the Peace of Utrecht.

Despite frequent pregnancies by her husband, Prince George of Denmark, none of Anne's children survived childhood. Patriotic and conscious of her rights, Anne aimed at improving her people's welfare, and they loved her. She was succeeded by the Hanoverian GEORGE I.

Anne of Austria Anne of Austria, b. Sept. 22, 1601, d. Jan. 20, 1666, was the wife of LOUIS XIII of France and, after his death (1643), regent for their son LOUIS XIV. The daughter of Philip III of Spain, she went to France upon her marriage in 1615. In 1637 she was found by the principal minister, Cardinal RICHELIEU, to be secretly corresponding with the rulers of Spain, with whom France was at war. As regent, however, she continued Richelieu's anti-Spanish policy, relying upon his successor, Cardinal MAZARIN. Her support for Mazarin enabled him to survive the revolts of the FRONDE (1648–53), and they governed France together until his death in 1661.

Anne of Brittany Anne of Brittany, b. Jan. 25, 1477, d. Jan. 9, 1514, inherited the French duchy of Brittany in 1488 and took care to preserve its autonomy in her marriages to two kings of France: Charles VIII (1491) and Louis XII (1499). An earlier proxy marriage (1490) to Maximilian of Austria (later Holy Roman Emperor Maximilian I) was broken off when Charles VIII attacked Brittany. Anne's daughter by Louis, Claude, married the future Francis I of France in 1514, and Brittany was finally incorporated into the French kingdom in 1532.

Anne of Cleves Anne of Cleves, b. Sept. 22, 1515, d. July 16, 1557, was the fourth wife of HENRY VIII of England. The marriage was arranged to secure an alliance between Henry and Anne's brother, the duke of Cleves, a powerful German Protestant prince. Henry tired of Anne, and the marriage was annulled after only six months—January to July 1540.

annealing [uh-nee'-ling] Annealing is a method of heating and cooling a metal, alloy, or glass under precise controls to remove internal stresses and make the material more ductile and less brittle. The method is applied after a metal has been shaped by forging, extruding, rolling, or drawing, at temperatures where softening does not occur (cold-working). At this point the metal tends to resist further working, and a condition known as work-hardening occurs. Annealing returns the metal to its original state so that it can be worked further.

The process of annealing can be best explained by reference to the microscopic structure of metallic crystals. The atoms in a crystal normally form a regular pattern; a metal, in turn, is made up of many crystals whose tops are all aligned in planes, called slip planes. As force is applied to a single grain of metal, the grain distorts along the slip planes and expands, making the metal ductile. As cold-work is applied to the metal, however, the original grain slips, distorts, and reorients so that instead of having a single grain with all the slip planes parallel, the structure is now composed of grain fragments, which increase the hardness of the metal.

Heating affects cold-worked metal in two stages, recovery and recrystallization. Recovery occurs as the temperature of the cold-worked metal is gradually raised. Internal stresses are relieved as the atoms in the metal rearrange themselves into the positions that they occupied in the preworked state. Recrystallization occurs as the temperature of the metal is raised further and nuclei for the growth of new, stress-free crystals begin to form, restoring most of the original physical properties of the metal.

The degree of softening resulting from an annealing treatment depends on the temperature to which a metal is heated as well as the length of time for which it is heated.

See also: EXTRUSION; METALLURGY.

---

annelid [an'-uh-lid]   Annelids, including the familiar EARTHWORM and LEECH, are a phylum, Annelida, of about 8,700 or more species of segmented worms found in almost every variety of moist habitat. Diverse in appearance, habitat, and mode of living, all are divided into externally visible segments. Such segmentation is thought to have evolved as an adaptation for burrowing, but aquatic species may also swim freely or wander on the bottom, and some leeches live entirely as parasites. Annelids are important because they aerate the soil; they also serve as food and bait, and leeches have been used medicinally.

The segments reflect the annelid's internal structure. In general, each segment contains a similar arrangement of connected nerves and blood vessels and pairs of excretory organs. The body cavity, or COELOM, between the gut and the muscular body wall is also segmented into membranous partitions (septa) and is filled with an incompressible fluid that functions as a skeleton when the body wall muscles contract, allowing rapid movement. In more specialized annelids, some segments may be greatly modified for different functions; for example, they may bear gills. Annelids have eyespots (light-sensitive cells) or eyes; a few marine worms have eyes similar in complexity of structure to the human eye. Reproduction ranges from asexual budding to hermaphrodism to true sexual differentiation.

Annelids probably evolved from the FLATWORMS and are thought to have given rise to the ARTHROPODS. The three classes of annelids are the POLYCHAETES (marine worms, usually bearing bristles, or setae, and lateral appendages called parapodia); Oligochaeta (earthworms and many freshwater worms, usually without setae); and Hirudinea (the leeches). Sometimes marine worms are split into two further classes: Archiannelida (primitive forms without parapodia) and Myzostomaria (parasitic forms with sucker mouths).

---

annexation   In international law annexation is the act by which a state unilaterally declares its sovereignty over territory outside its borders. Annexation effected by the threat or use of military force is not recognized as legitimate in international law, and the Charter of the United Nations holds that self-determination by the inhabitants of a territory is the only legitimate means of transferring territory. Forcible annexations have often been made to appear acceptable to the inhabitants of the annexed territory, as in the German annexation of Austria (the Anschluss) in 1938 or the Indian annexation of Sikkim in 1974–75.

Within a state, the term *annexation* refers to the act by which municipal governments assert jurisdiction over adjacent unincorporated areas. This generally, but not always, requires formal approval by the voters of the annexed area.

---

annihilation   In physics, annihilation is a process in which a particle and an antiparticle combine and release their rest energy. This released energy can appear in the form of MESONS and PHOTONS. The annihilation of particles was first observed when a positron, e^+, and an electron, e^-, collided and "disappeared," releasing energy in the form of gamma rays. Conversely, the production of a particle-antiparticle pair by gamma rays of sufficient energy is called creation. Annihilation can occur when particles and antiparticles are moving with respect to each other at a significant velocity (annihilation "in flight"), or when the two particles—with opposite electric charges—form a temporary atomlike liaison (annihilation "at rest").

See also: ANTIMATTER; FUNDAMENTAL PARTICLES.

---

annuity   An annuity is, in its strict sense, a payment made every year; but it has come to mean payments made at other regular intervals. An annuity is a contract, usually made with an insurance company, that pays the annuity purchaser a regular income. Most often, payments end only with the death of the annuity owner. Unlike LIFE INSURANCE buyers, who in effect bet against insurers that their lives will end before actuarial predictions, annuity owners buy protection against living beyond the statistical probabilities. Women, who are generally longer lived, often pay higher purchase prices than men for annuities that provide the same income.

Annunciation   see MARY

Annunzio, Gabriele D'   see D'ANNUNZIO, GABRIELE

ILLUSTRATION CREDITS

The following list credits or acknowledges, by page, the source of illustrations used in this volume. When two or more illustrations appear on one page, they are credited individually left to right, top to bottom; their credits are separated by semicolons. When both the photographer or artist and an agency or other source are given for an illustration, they are usually separated by a slash. Those illustrations not cited below are credited on the page on which they appear, either in the caption or alongside the illustration itself.